HANDBOOK OF
LATIN AMERICAN STUDIES:
No. 45

A Selective and Annotated Guide to Recent Publications
in Anthropology, Economics, Education, Geography,
Government and Politics, International Relations, and Sociology

VOLUME 46 WILL BE DEVOTED TO THE HUMANITIES:
ART, FOLKLORE, HISTORY, LANGUAGE, LITERATURE, MUSIC, AND PHILOSOPHY

EDITORIAL NOTE: Comments concerning the *Handbook of Latin American Studies*
should be sent directly to the Editor, *Handbook of Latin American Studies*,
Hispanic Division, Library of Congress, Washington, D.C. 20540.

HANDBOOK OF LATIN AMERICAN STUDIES. NO. 45

SOCIAL SCIENCES

Prepared by a Number of Scholars
for the Hispanic Division of The Library of Congress

Edited by DOLORES MOYANO MARTIN

1983

UNIVERSITY OF TEXAS PRESS   *Austin*

International Standard Book Number 0-292-73033-0
International Standard Serial Number 0072-9833
Library of Congress Catalog Card Number 36-32633

Requests for permission to reproduce material
from this work should be sent to
Permissions, University of Texas Press,
Box 7819, Austin, Texas 78713.

First Edition, 1985

IN MEMORIAM

WILLIAM E. CARTER (April 29, 1927–August 14, 1983)

Chief of the Hispanic Division of the Library of Congress since January 1979 and friend and supporter of the *Handbook of Latin American Studies* even before that, William E. Carter died on August 14, 1983. He was only 56 at the time of death. The loss suffered by his family, his many friends, the Library of Congress, and Latin Americanists everywhere is incalculable. He had given and achieved so much already that we were selfishly looking forward to still more years of the same caliber of service.

Readers of the *Handbook* do not need to be told again what publications Bill authored—they are duly listed and annotated in past volumes—or what positions he held as he moved by stages from Methodist missionary to professor of anthropology to head of the world's greatest repository of published (and some unpublished) sources of Hispanic culture. Because of my affiliation with the University of Florida, I remember above all his work as Director of our Center for Latin American Studies, 1968–79. I also remember, with special admiration, how this scholar whose outward appearance and conscientiously methodical approach to all he did were so quintessentially North American, felt an empathy for things Hispanic that all too many of his compatriots, even when specializing in related fields, do not seem to have. He did not just study Latin America, he loved it—and that sympathetic understanding was not limited to the strictly "Latin" component, as his Aymara friends made clear in an unusual statement of personal tribute shortly before his death. His wife Bertha, herself Bolivian, naturally had something to do with this, as a quiet yet strong-willed collaborator over the years.

At least what Bill Carter accomplished will not be easily forgotten. As the Spanish scholar Julián Marías observed, his life was governed by "the conviction that what one does is *forever*—and therefore one must do it well." He did indeed.

David Bushnell
University of Florida

CONTRIBUTING EDITORS

SOCIAL SCIENCES

Michael B. Anderson, *Inter-American Development Bank*, ECONOMICS
Patrick J. Brennan, *International Business Consulting, Kansas City*, SOCIOLOGY
Roderic A. Camp, *Central College, Pella, Iowa*, GOVERNMENT AND POLITICS
Lyle Campbell, *State University of New York at Albany*, ANTHROPOLOGY
William L. Canak, *Brown University*, SOCIOLOGY
William E. Carter, *Library of Congress*, ANTHROPOLOGY
Manuel J. Carvajal, *Florida International University*, ECONOMICS
Donald V. Coes, *University of Illinois, Urbana*, ECONOMICS
Lambros Comitas, *Columbia University*, ANTHROPOLOGY
David W. Dent, *Towson State College*, GOVERNMENT AND POLITICS
Clinton R. Edwards, *University of Wisconsin, Milwaukee*, GEOGRAPHY
Everett Egginton, *University of Louisville*, EDUCATION
Robert C. Eidt, *University of Wisconsin, Milwaukee*, GEOGRAPHY
Gary S. Elbow, *Texas Tech University*, GEOGRAPHY
Yale H. Ferguson, *Rutgers University, Newark*, INTERNATIONAL RELATIONS
Michael J. Francis, *University of Notre Dame*, INTERNATIONAL RELATIONS
William R. Garner, *Southern Illinois University*, GOVERNMENT AND POLITICS
George W. Grayson, *College of William and Mary*, INTERNATIONAL RELATIONS
Norman Hammond, *Rutgers University, Newark*, ANTHROPOLOGY
Kevin J. Healy, *Inter-American Foundation*, SOCIOLOGY
John R. Hébert, *Library of Congress*, BIBLIOGRAPHY AND GENERAL WORKS
Mario Hiraoka, *Millersville University of Pennsylvania*, GEOGRAPHY
John M. Hunter, *Michigan State University*, ECONOMICS
Thomas B. Hutcheson, *World Bank*, ECONOMICS
John M. Ingham, *University of Minnesota*, ANTHROPOLOGY
W. Jerald Kennedy, *Florida Atlantic University*, ANTHROPOLOGY
Waud H. Kracke, *University of Illinois at Chicago Circle*, ANTHROPOLOGY
Thomas J. LaBelle, *University of California, Los Angeles*, EDUCATION
Robert M. Malina, *University of Texas at Austin*, ANTHROPOLOGY
Markos Mamalakis, *University of Wisconsin, Milwaukee*, ECONOMICS
Tom L. Martinson, *Ball State University*, GEOGRAPHY
Betty J. Meggers, *Smithsonian Institution*, ANTHROPOLOGY
Ernesto C. Migliazza, *Washington, D.C.*, ANTHROPOLOGY
Andrew M. Modelski, *Library of Congress*, GEOGRAPHY
Lisandro Pérez, *Louisiana State University*, SOCIOLOGY
Jorge F. Pérez-López, *U.S. Department of Labor*, ECONOMICS
Sergio Roca, *Adelphi University*, ECONOMICS
Jorge Salazar-Carrillo, *Florida International University*, ECONOMICS
Margaret J. Sarles, *University of Maryland, College Park*, GOVERNMENT AND POLITICS
John V.D. Saunders, *Mississippi State College*, SOCIOLOGY
Stephen M. Smith, *University of Idaho*, SOCIOLOGY
Barbara L. Stark, *Arizona State University*, ANTHROPOLOGY

Andrés Suárez, *University of Florida*, GOVERNMENT AND POLITICS
Francisco E. Thoumi, *Inter-American Development Bank*, ECONOMICS
Antonio Ugalde, *University of Texas at Austin*, SOCIOLOGY
Nelson P. Valdés, *University of New Mexico, Albuquerque*, SOCIOLOGY
Robert E. Verhine, *Universidade Federal da Bahia, Salvador, Brazil*, EDUCATION
Carlos H. Waisman, *University of California, San Diego*, SOCIOLOGY
Gary W. Wynia, *University of Minnesota*, GOVERNMENT AND POLITICS

HUMANITIES

Earl M. Aldrich, Jr., *University of Wisconsin, Madison*, LITERATURE
Joyce W. Bailey, *Handbook of Latin American Art, New Haven, Conn.*, ART
Jean A. Barman, *University of British Columbia*, HISTORY
Roderick J. Barman, *University of British Columbia*, HISTORY
Judith Bissett, *Miami University, Oxford, Ohio*, LITERATURE
David Bushnell, *University of Florida*, HISTORY
D. Lincoln Canfield, *Southern Illinois University at Carbondale*, LANGUAGES
Donald E. Chipman, *North Texas State University, Denton*, HISTORY
Sue L. Cline, *Harvard University*, HISTORY
Don M. Coerver, *Texas Christian University*, HISTORY
Michael L. Conniff, *University of New Mexico, Albuquerque*, HISTORY
René de Costa, *University of Chicago*, LITERATURE
Edith B. Couturier, *National Endowment for the Humanities*, HISTORY
Ethel O. Davie, *West Virginia State College*, LITERATURE
Lisa E. Davis, *York College*, LITERATURE
Ralph E. Dimmick, *Organization of American States*, LITERATURE
Roberto Etchepareborda, *Organization of American States*, HISTORY
Leonard Folgarait, *Vanderbilt University*, ART
Fernando García Núñez, *University of Texas at El Paso*, LITERATURE
Magdalena García Pinto, *University of Missouri, Columbia*, LITERATURE
Naomi M. Garrett, *West Virginia State College*, LITERATURE
Jaime Giordano, *State University of New York at Stony Brook*, LITERATURE
Cedomil Goić, *University of Michigan, Ann Arbor*, LITERATURE
Roberto González Echevarría, *Yale University*, LITERATURE
Richard E. Greenleaf, *Tulane University*, HISTORY
Oscar Hahn, *University of Iowa*, LITERATURE
Michael T. Hamerly, *Dumbarton Oaks Collection, Washington*, HISTORY
John R. Hébert, *Library of Congress*, BIBLIOGRAPHY AND GENERAL WORKS
Carlos R. Hortas, *Yale University*, LITERATURE
Regina Igel, *University of Maryland, College Park*, LITERATURE
Djelal Kadir, II, *Purdue University*, LITERATURE
Norma Klahn, *Columbia University*, LITERATURE
Franklin W. Knight, *Johns Hopkins University*, HISTORY
Pedro Lastra, *State University of New York at Stony Brook*, LITERATURE
Asunción Lavrin, *Howard University*, HISTORY
Maria Angélica Guimarães Lopes, *University of Pittsburgh*, LITERATURE
William Luis, *Dartmouth College*, LITERATURE
Murdo J. MacLeod, *University of Arizona*, HISTORY
Wilson Martins, *New York University*, LITERATURE
Robert J. Mullen, *University of Texas at San Antonio*, ART
José M. Neistein, *Brazilian American Cultural Institute, Washington*, ART
Julio Ortega, *University of Texas at Austin*, LITERATURE
José Miguel Oviedo, *University of California, Los Angeles*, LITERATURE

CONTENTS

EDITOR'S NOTE

I. GENERAL AND REGIONAL TRENDS

The growing sophistication of Latin American scholarship that we noted in *HLAS* 43 (p. xiii) is once more the outstanding feature of this volume. It is especially true in economics, a field in which the enrichment of the literature coincides with the decline of its subject: the Latin American economies, now in the grip of an unprecedented crisis affecting most of the hemisphere, from Cuba's socialist experiment to Chile's free market economy. Explanations for the underlying causes are manifold but some common themes can be detected. Chief among them are studies of the causes and implications of the massive foreign debt (items **3020** and **3044**). In Argentina, where a large body of theoretical writings has been produced by the nation's economists, the collapse of the liberal experiment is attributed to the military government's failure to address crucial issues such as the impact of transnational corporations, new technologies and their effects on international relations, and the hegemony in international commerce of the OECD (Organization for Economic Cooperation and Development) (p. 329). In Brazil—where new critical standards applied by economists to themselves and their peers are evident in the demand for the specification of hypotheses in empirically testable forms—the new *abertura* or climate of free discussion has resulted in "a few sacred cows" being "sacrificed or at least seriously gored" (p. 335). Indeed, as Brazil moves onto a more open and democratic discussion of its basic and largely economic problems, the economists' direct role as "technocrats" may decline, but "their indirect role in clarifying the nation's economic choices may prove more valuable in the long run" (p. 336). In the Caribbean, the economic literature attests to the existence of an indigenous strain of social and economic thought that is both eclectic and original. Most publications concern poverty and the disparate distribution of wealth, causes of their persistence as well as remedies for their alleviation (p. 270). Among the causes are the Caribbean's history of economic dependency, the extent of both past and present US influence and the effect of transnational corporations who, by extracting the natural wealth in order to maximize profits, are regarded as the chief obstacle to development (p. 269).

Although Colombian economists have generated some notable works, there are few theoretical writings, the majority being empirical studies of narrow topics that are easy to fund. Colombia's lack of the type of government-funded institutions exemplified by Brazil's Fundação Getúlio Vargas and El Colegio de México—organizations which grant researchers the security of permanent commitment—is one reason for the small influence of Colombian economists on Latin American economic thought (p. 295).

A critical lesson drawn from the Peruvian experiment with agrarian reform is that although the latter could not eradicate rural misery nor guarantee overall rural prosperity, it could "eliminate absolute poverty." Only a comprehensive rural reform, that is to say, the transformation and modernization of *all* rural activities (e.g., agricultural, industrial, mineral, service ones) can usher in lasting prosperity (p. 311). In fact, progress in only one area of the rural sector can result in "high social and national cost" (p. 645) as in, for example, the detrimental effect on Paraguayan society of rapid agricultural growth built upon the mechanization and proliferation of agro-industries, multinational transfers and colonization. Many studies document processes of economic development that, by intensifying capital accumulation and aggravating the disparate distribution of wealth (p. 270), exacerbate social and economic inequalities between and within social classes (p. 645).

The growing proficiency in methodology and the consistency of output of the economic literature on Venezuela is evident, among other things, in the sophistication of Marxist studies of the nation's economy, studies which in the past have been more prone to rhetoric than to rigor (p. 304). In the past and in fields such as Mexican ethnography, for example, applications of Marxist or neo-classical theory have confounded more than clarified understanding. Now, however, worthwhile syntheses of theory and ethnography such as a study of relations of production in eastern Morelos (item **1033**) succeeds precisely because the author's Marxist sensibilities "inform rather than constrain the narrative" (p. 94).

In Colombia, where the effect of *La Violencia* on Colombian culture and the concern with understanding that impact is reflected in the number of works on the subject, sociologists are generating "research of interest and relevance well beyond the borders of their country" (p. 637). The unprecedented high quality of publications by Bolivian and Paraguayan social scientists can be largely attributed to the emergence of national and private social science research centers in which more empirical national sociology attuned to the problems faced by these societies is underway (p. 645). For example, Bolivian urban sociology has made notable progress in recent years through the contributions of Albó and Calderón (items **8281** and **8284**).

The coming of age of the social sciences in Latin America is most evident in Mexico where the development of particular disciplines is now subject to scrutiny. In this volume, a Mexican scholar traces the evolution of international relations, as taught and studied in Mexico, following its trajectory from the traditional discursive writings of the past into the rigorous discipline of today (item **7202**). Our contributor for Brazilian sociology points out that in *HLAS 43* about half of the titles were written by foreigners whereas in this volume, three fourths are by Brazilians (p. 659). In some fields, however, foreign scholars continue to dominate as in Peruvian and Mesoamerican archaeology (pp. 16 and 63), and to an extent, in South American geography in which French writings "have taken such precedence over Germany that of the total publications annotated, one third were French and one fifth German" (p. 415). The notable increase in the number of Soviet studies of Latin America is apparent throughout this volume and especially evident in the International Relations section. Its contributor remarks on the improvement in library facilities available to Soviet authors judging from their bibliographies but notes that although the "most interesting items . . . concern the role of the Catholic Church in supporting social and political change" (items **7027, 7059, 7078, 7092,** and **7095**) the overall quality of Soviet writings is still poor with "little evidence of variety and sophistication," its "overwhelming characteristic" being "dreary predictability" (p. 540).

Despite the deepening economic crisis, democratic institutions have been restored throughout much of the hemisphere, a development that is reflected in the literature. In Brazil, for example, the *abertura* or relaxation of censorship has stimulated "highly critical analyses" (p. 383) of past governments and the publication of prison memoirs, a new genre, which is serving as a primary source of data in the now "fullblown debate" on human rights abuses (p. 538). Among the more significant contributions on the topic are studies sponsored by Chile's Catholic Church addressing the military government's human rights policy (items **6289**, **6291**, and **6295**).

Interest in the role of the military which we noted in *HLAS 43* (p. xiv) continues with some outstanding works such as the one by a French social scientist who advances a controversial thesis as to the political role of the Argentine military (item **6408**). The Peruvian and Bolivian military governments are also subject to scrutiny (items **6341**, **6361**, **6380**, and **6383**). However, little has appeared that is either "theoretical or empirical" on "the breakdown" of these "authoritarian regimes in Latin America" (p. 488). An unusual work singled out as one of "the best political histories" of a Latin American country is a "sociopolitical analysis of power within Ecuadorian society" written by the country's current President (item **6281**).

One of the most notable increases in the last two years has been the volume of works on Central America. As recently as 1979, *HLAS 41* had only two entries each on the government and politics of El Salvador and Nicaragua (p. 468). The problem is no longer the quantity of materials published on these countries which is considerable but the quality which is still poor. Nevertheless, a sociologist is optimistic about research underway in Nicaragua. He notes that it has remained more open than Cuba to US social scientists becoming a veritable "laboratory for the study of development constraints after capitalism" with many researchers following the social process that unfolds in a revolutionary setting (p. 611). On the other hand, the "ideological and polemical tendency of the literature" (p. 468) issued by the governments of both Nicaragua and El Salvador is deplored by several contributors, one of whom observes that the former's consists of "a large volume of propaganda with little if any objective content" (p. 269) while the latter's appears "altogether oblivious to the fighting" underway in the country (p. 270).

The most notable event in the international relations of Latin America during the biennium was the Falklands/Malvinas War, a graphic demonstration of the potential for conflict in the hemisphere, underestimated by some writers in the past. One analyst who specializes in inter-American relations predicts a higher probability of conflicts as the US "security shadow" diminishes (item **7055**). So far, the literature on the war is less concerned with its long range implications than with Argentina's role which is subject to more scrutiny than England's (p. 547).

The environment continues as a major theme of this volume. Almost all "environmental concerns recognized in North America and Europe can now be identified in the geographical and related literature of Latin America" (p. 399). The enthusiasm for development so prevalent a few decades ago is now tempered by the realization that environmental costs may be too high. The number of symposia, conferences, and publications on this issue attest to such concerns in the questions that are asked: Will the substitution of meat production for the harvesting of forest products prove beneficial in the long run? The ecological disaster caused by the expansion of cattle ranching in eastern Ecuador (p. 156) provides one answer. Other questions such as the need "to relate overpopulation to resource utilization" (p. 399) are being raised in the literature on urban population growth, a dominant theme of the last four social science volumes of *HLAS*. Concern with the deterioration of the environment and ecological problems is especially noticeable in the literature on Panama, Costa Rica, the Dominican Republic, and the Brazilian Amazon which has taken the lead from the Northeast as the favored area for Brazilian economic and environmental studies (p. 426).

In *HLAS 43*, we regretted that sophisticated understanding of tropical forests cultures was emerging just as these indigenous groups were succumbing to so-called progress, their members shunted aside as "ignorant savages" and their environment rapidly converted into grasslands (p. xv). The worsening economic crisis in South America will aggravate the already grim prospects of these indigenous cultures whose hard won reservation lands are threatened with inundation by dams while financial assistance for their resettlement is dwindling (p. 127). The urgent need to protect the rain forest peoples has prompted new research interests as well as organized action on the part of both the people themselves and anthropologists. This volume, for example, lists 15 organizations, many of them new ones that provide regular information on the situation of these cultures (p. 132). Their possible extinction has stimulated much research in three fields: ethnic identity, interethnic relations, and ethnohistory (p. 129).

Concurrent with the study of threatened indigenous groups is research into population movements, a topic which has dominated the social science literature of the last 10 years. For example, in Brazil most demographic titles are concerned with migration (p. 659) while in the US scholars are paying more attention to immigration, an "extraordinarily sensitive" subject "that lends itself to passionate rather than dispassionate treatment." One sociologist emphasizes the "increasing policy concerns within the US with a wave of illegal migration that has been characterized as uncontrollable" (p. 611). One indication of such concern is the number of items on Mexican sociology that deal with Mexican migration to the US (p. 611). In the Southern Cone, the study of migratory currents and the assimilation of Europeans to the New World has long been a traditional area of research and in Uruguay, emigration leads as a research topic.

In *HLAS 43* (p. xiv) we noted that "the fastest growing field in anthropology" was medical or epidemiological anthropology, a trend that continues in this volume in the section entitled Human Biology. A dominant theme of the latter (also referred to as physical anthropology or biological anthropology) is the "understanding of human biological variation, its nature, distribution, and significance within the context of evolutionary theory and culture" (p. 192). The biological framework of human biology is especially evident in the nutritional and medical problems of Latin American populations. And since a significant agent in the adaptive process of these populations has been infectious disease, the disease history of the hemisphere is of interest to many disciplines covered in *HLAS*. A notable development, for example, has been the emergence of *ethnomedicine* or the study of the interplay between native Latin American healing traditions and modern medical practice (p. 195). The study of human adaptability is another leading topic as in, for example, the biological response to altitude stress (see items **1745–1746**, **1760**, and **1780**). Adaptability and growth studies also illustrate the impact of socioeconomic differentials in Latin America (items **1743**, and **1747–1748**). This impact is evident in the nutritional literature that is expanding at an accelerated rate, ranging from biochemical studies of lesser-known edible plants (items **1833–1834**) to the "protein hypothesis" for tribal warfare (item **1798**).

II. CHANGES IN VOLUME 45

Anthropology

Barbara L. Stark, Arizona State University at Tempe, collaborated with Norman Hammond, Rutgers University, in preparing the section on Mesoamerican archaeology. The section on linguistics, renamed *Anthrolinguistics*, has been subdivided into two areas of responsibility: a) the Indian languages of Mexico and Central

America which are the responsibility of Lyle Campbell, State University of New York, Albany; and b) the Indian languages of South America covered by Ernesto Migliazza, Consultant in Anthrolinguistics, Washington, D.C. Robert Malina, University of Texas, annotated the literature on biological anthropology in the section renamed *Human Biology*.

Economics

The literature on Mexico was reviewed by Sergio Roca, Adelphi University. Materials on Colombia were annotated by Francisco Thoumi, Inter-American Development Bank, in collaboration with Thomas Hutcheson, The World Bank, who reviewed works on Ecuador. Stephen M. Smith, University of Idaho, covered the literature on Bolivia, Uruguay and Paraguay. Donald V. Coes, University of Illinois, Urbana, was responsible for materials on Brazil.

Education

Robert E. Verhine, Universidade de Bahia, Brazil, and Thomas J. LaBelle, University of California, Los Angeles, collaborated in preparing the section on Brazilian education.

Government and Politics

Roderic A. Camp, Central College, Pella, Iowa, was responsible for reviewing materials on Mexico and Central America. Margaret J. Sarles, University of Maryland, annotated the literature on Brazil.

International Relations

Because of the extraordinary increase in the volume of materials published on the above subject, this section has been subdivided into three areas of responsibility: a) Yale Ferguson, Rutgers University, prepared the General subsection; b) George Grayson, College of William and Mary, covered Mexico, Central America, and the Caribbean; and c) Michael J. Francis, Notre Dame University, was responsible for South America.

Sociology

Lisandro Pérez, Louisiana State University, collaborated with Nelson Valdés, University of New Mexico, Albuquerque, in preparing the section on the Caribbean and the Guianas. William L. Canak, Brown University, reviewed materials on Colombia and Venezuela. Patrick J. Brennan, International Business Consultants, St. Louis, Missouri, covered works on Peru and Ecuador. Kevin J. Healy, Inter-American Foundation, Rosslyn, Virginia, was in charge of the literature for Bolivia and Paraguay. John V.D. Saunders, Mississippi State University, annotated materials for Brazil.

Subject Index

As noted in *HLAS 44* (p. xv), the policy of the *HLAS* subject index is to use the Library of Congress subject headings as much as possible but when necessary to adapt them to terms that predominate in the literature as familiar and useful ones to Latin Americanists.

Other Changes

Changes in the editorial staff of the *Handbook*, the administrative officers of the Library of Congress, and membership in the Advisory Board are reflected in the title page of the present volume.

Dolores Moyano Martin

Washington D.C., December 1983

HANDBOOK OF
LATIN AMERICAN STUDIES:
No. 45

BIBLIOGRAPHY AND GENERAL WORKS

JOHN R. HÉBERT, *Hispanic Division, The Library of Congress*

THE AMOUNT AND QUALITY OF BIBLIOGRAPHICAL compilations and general works related to Latin American themes have not diminished in this past year. The reduced number of entries in this section, compared with previous years, is due in part to the change in the production schedule of the *Handbook*. Subsequent compilations of this section will equal previous submissions.

A number of useful general bibliographies and national bibliographies have appeared. Two works on countries that rarely produce general bibliographies are Elena Richer de González Petit and Rubén Morel Solaeche's *Bibliografía de obras paraguayas* (1982, item **1**), which lists 19th and 20th century items in the national university's library, and Miguel Laguerre's *The complete Haitiana* (1982, item **2**) which contains nearly 10,000 unique entries on Haiti published in the 20th century. The latter work complements Max Bissainthe's excellent *Dictionnaire de bibliographie haitienne* (1951 and 1973).

As usual, fine compilations of national bibliographies from the Caribbean appeared in 1982. Among the works are the *Guyanese National Bibliography* (item **6**) and the *Jamaican National Bibliography* (item **7**). Complementary works, such as *The Caricom Bibliography* (1981, item **5**) and Mario Argueta's *Anuario bibliográfico hondureño 1980* (1982, item **4**), serve as additional useful tools.

A broad range of themes are subjects of bibliographies or general works. In the area of social thought are Mario Argueta's article "Tendencias e Investigaciones Recientes de la Sociología Hondureña" (1983, item **9**) and Patrick Bellegarde-Smith's "Haitian Social Thought: A Bibliographical Survey" (1982, item **10**), both valuable additions to the literature.

The normal number of excellent bibliographies and reference works related to literature have appeared. David William Foster's bibliographies of secondary works, *Peruvian literature* (1981, item **14**) and *Puerto Rican literature* (1982, item **15**), are recent installments in his attempt to provide information on national literatures. The Columbus Library of the Organization of American States compiled *Catálogo de la colección de la literatura chilena en la Biblioteca Colón* (1983, item **34**), and Augusto Guzmán produced *Biografías de la literatura boliviana* (1982, item **43**), which covers selected authors for the period 1520–1925.

For contemporary politics and problems there are bibliographic works or guides to research. In this volume the problems in Central America and the issue of human rights are considered in David Samuel Krusé and Richard Swedberg's *El Salvador bibliography and research guide* (1982, item **17**) and the Library of Congress' Hispanic Division publication *Human rights in Latin America, 1964–1980* (1983, item **18**). Both works attempt to identify resources available for the study of these current themes.

At times the number of publications dealing with one geographic area produces a workable corpus of data. In this compilation this is true of both Mexico and Argentina. In the case of Mexico, both colonial and 20th century themes are covered.

Víctor Urruchua Hernández, in *Archivos microfilmados en la Biblioteca Nacional de Antropología e Historia* (1982, item **35**), lists the various collections in the Library of INAH; Julieta Avila's study *Acolman* (1981, item **36**) provides a detailed account of the Acolman Archives in the Biblioteca Nacional de Antropología e Historia; and, finally, Shirley Weathers *et al.* produced the *Bibliographic guide to the Guatemalan collection* (1981, item **30**), which describes the holdings of the Archivo General de Centro-América in Guatemala City filmed by the Genealogical Society of Utah. For 20th century Mexico, two outstanding works have appeared. W. Dirk Raat's *The Mexican Revolution: an annotated guide to recent scholarship* (1982, item **22**), and Roderic Ai Camp's revised *Mexican political biographies 1935–1981* (1982, item **38**) are essential reference guides for the serious scholar.

In the case of Argentina, numerous books and articles providing bibliographic information on 20th century politics and history appeared. Worthy of note among these works is Alberto Ciria's "La Década del Treinta en la Historiografía Argentina" (1982, item **12**); Roberto Etchepareborda's "Elementos Bibliográficos para una Historia Argentina: 1943–1982" (1982, item **13**); a special issue of *Informaciones* (item **16**) was produced to commemorate the centenary (1882–1982) of the city of La Plata (1983); and Sara de Mundo Lo's *The Falkland/Malvinas Islands; a bibliography of books 1619–1982* (1983, item **20**). With the changes now occurring in Argentina, it is probable that bibliographies on contemporary Argentine politics will increase.

Major works providing access to periodical articles are always welcome, although, of course, the *Handbook* is intended to provide selected coverage of the field. Unique items include the recent four volume publication by the Felipe Herrera Library of the Inter-American Development Bank, *Index of periodical articles on the economics of Latin America* (1983, item **46**), which provides access to periodical articles appearing between 1950 and 1977; and Paula Covington's *Indexed journals: a guide to Latin American serials* (1983, item **45**), which describes and evaluates indexes and abstracts of current journals related to Latin America and was compiled with the cooperation of the Seminar on the Acquisition of Latin American Materials' Committee on Bibliography.

Worldwide interest in Latin American studies continues. Carmelo Mesa Lago's *Latin American Studies in Asia* (1983, item **52**) describes Latin American area studies programs in Japan, China, and India; this work complements his previous work (1979) *Latin American Studies in Europe* (see *HLAS* 42 : 153). The interest of Latin American studies in Asia is further noted in Satoru Ueda's "A Roster of Mesoamerican Studies in Japan" (1982, item **59**). Finally, J.C.M. Ogelsby has produced the interesting article, "Latin American Studies in Canada, 1966–1981" (1982, item **65**).

As this brief overview demonstrates, the variety of publications providing bibliographic and research access to materials on Latin America is as rich this year as in previous years.

GENERAL BIBLIOGRAPHIES

1   Bibliografía de obras paraguayas: homenaje de la Biblioteca Central en el cincuentenario de la defensa del Chaco. Elena Richer de González Petit and Rubén E. Morel Solaeche, compiladores. Asunción: Biblioteca Central, 1982. 76 p.

Contains a listing, by subject, of materials on Paraguay in the university library. Lists mainly 20th-century titles, although some 19th-century pieces appear. Includes separate author, title, and subject indexes.

2   Laguerre, Michel S. The complete Haitiana: a bibliographic guide to the scholarly literature, 1900–1980. Millwood,

N.Y.: Kraus International Publications, 1982.
2 v.: bibl., index.

Contains nearly 10,000 unique entries on Haiti published in the 20th century. Materials are arranged in 65 different subject groupings. Includes author index. Complements Max Bissainthe's *Dictionnaire de bibliographie haïtienne* (1951 and *supplément* 1973). For anthropologist's comment, see item **1096**.

3   **Manigat, Max.** Haitiana 1971–1975: bibliographie haïtienne. LaSalle, Canada: Collectif Paroles, 1980. 83 p.: bibl., index.

Covers works on Haiti, the Dominican Republic, and Hispaniola by Haitian and foreign authors. Entries in alphabetical order by author and in single year sections. Appendixes list works from the 60s, index specific journal issues (e.g., *Europe, Culture et dévèloppement en Haiti*, and a separate author/subject index).

NATIONAL BIBLIOGRAPHIES

4   **Argueta, Mario.** Anuario bibliográfico hondureño 1980. Ciudad Universitaria: Universidad Nacional Autónoma de Honduras, 1982. 33 p.

Lists separately by author and subject, books and government publications produced in Honduras in 1980. Gives list of national periodicals. This publication represents the only comprehensive listing of national publications.

5   *The Caricom Bibliography.* Caribbean Community Secretariat, Information and Documentation Section. Vol. 5, No. 1, 1981– . Georgetown, Guyana.

This bibliography (358 p.) provides cumulated subject list of current national imprints of Caribbean community member countries, arranged according to Dewey Decimal Classification. Compiled from national bibliographies of Barbados, Guyana, Jamaica, and Trinidad and Tobago along with entries from territories which do not yet produce national bibliographies. Includes author-title-series index, section on non-book material, and list of publishers and their addresses. Includes 1979 and 1980 imprints.

Centro de Documentación e Información Pedagógicas, *Cuba.* Bibliografía nacional de educación, 1959–1969. See item **4409**.

6   *Guyanese National Bibliography.* National Library of Guyana. Jan./Dec. 1982– . Georgetown.

Subject list of new books printed in Guyana, based on books and non-book material deposited at National Library. Lists items in separate classified and alphabetical order, and provides lists of publishers' and non-book material. Appendix includes list of single bills, acts, subsidiary legislation and parliamentary debates for 1982.

7   *Jamaican National Bibliography.* National Library of Jamaica, Institute of Jamaica. Jan./Dec. 1981– . Kingston.

This annual cumulation (139 p.) contains a subject listing of Jamaican materials received in the National Library arranged according to Dewey Decimal Classification. Includes author/title/series index and list of Jamaican publishers. Lists articles from Jamaica's *Social and Economic Studies* and *Jamaica Journal* as well as ministry papers for 1981.

8   *Jamaican National Library.* National Library of Jamaica. Vol. 6, Nos. 1/4, 1982– . Kingston.

Subject list of Jamaican materials received in the National Library arranged according to Dewey Decimal Classification. Includes author/title/series index and list of Jamaican publishers.

Rossi Etchelouz, Nelly Yvis; María Teresa Recardininde León; María del Carmen D'Angelo; and Daniel Mernes Orbe. Bibliografía analítica. See item **4346**.

UNESCO. Regional Office for Education in Latin America and the Caribbean. Bibliografía sobre construcciones escolares y equipamiento educativo. See item **4353**.

Vólov, Boris. Centro de la latinoamericanística soviética. See item **4355**.

SUBJECT BIBLIOGRAPHIES

9   **Argueta, Mario R.** Tendencias e investigaciones recientes de la sociología hondureña: un ensayo bibliográfico (Boletín del Sistema Bibliotecario de la UNAH

[Universidad Nacional Autónoma de Honduras, Tegucigalpa] 12 : 2, abril/junio 1983, p. 2–19)

Bibliographical essay attempts to document development of sociology in Honduras with heavy concentration on current research. For period since 1970 separate sections provide information on rural and urban sociology, housing, women, unemployment, begging, and underdevelopment.

10 Bellegarde-Smith, Patrick. Haitian social thought: a bibliographical survey (RIB, 32 : 3/4, 1982, p. 330–337)

Author believes that Latin America and Africa are linked in Haitian social thought. Haitians were pioneers in fields such as social development, national integration, race relations, and small state foreign relations. Bibliography covers 200 years of history with systematic review of key works.

11 *Boletín Bibliográfico.* Consejo Nacional de Población, Centro de Documentación. No. 1, 1982–   . Lima.

First issue of serial contains 145 annotated citations on general theme of population in Peru that have appeared since 1975. Provides author and subject indexes.

12 Ciria, Alberto. La década del treinta en la historiografía Argentina: una introducción (RIB, 32 : 3/4, 1982, p. 322–324)

Provides brief review of existing scholarship on Argentina in 1930s decade. Points out gaps in the literature that merit more serious research.

13 Etchepareborda, Roberto. Elementos bibliográficos para una historia argentina: 1943–1982 (CRIT, 55 : 1894/1895, dic. 1982, p. 22–34)

Selected, annotated bibliography of works concerning the past 40 years of Argentine political and labor history organized as follows: 1) general history; 2) peronism and the peronist regimes (1946–55 and 1973–76); 3) periods of restoration following the overthrow of peronism (1955–58 and 1976–82); 4) civilian governments (1958–63 and 1963–66); and 5) military rule (1966–73). Provides useful collection of materials for an introduction of the subject. Works on Perón and peronism are especially helpful.

14 Foster, David William. Peruvian literature: a bibliography of secondary

sources. Westport, Conn.: Greenwood Press, 1981. 324 p.: index.

Consists of critical works on general themes of Peruvian literature and covers 38 specific authors, including Concolorcorvo, Manuel González Prada, Ciro Alegría, Mario Vargas Llosa, and César Vallejo. Also provides author index to secondary sources.

15 ———. Puerto Rican literature: a bibliography of secondary sources. Westport, Conn.: Greenwood Press, 1982. 232 p.: index.

Follows format of author's previous listings of Peruvian and Chilean literature. Includes references to critical works on general themes and 80 specific authors of Puerto Rican literature. Also provides index to authors of critical works.

16 *Informaciones.* Número especial en conmemoración del centenario de la Ciudad de La Plata, 1882–1982. Universidad Nacional de La Plata, Biblioteca Pública. marzo 1983–   . La Plata, Argentina.

Lists publications, books, pamphlets, journals, and newspapers that contain information on La Plata and are in the library's collections. Consists of 1200 citations in alphabetical order by author or title. Includes subject index.

17 Krusé, David Samuel and **Richard Swedberg.** El Salvador bibliography and research guide. Cambridge, Mass.: Central American Information Office, 1982. 233 p.: ill., index.

Provides selected but extensive listing of publications affecting current political and economic activities in El Salvador and Central America. Listings of materials, preceded by informative introductory essays, appear for various subjects (e.g., US policy toward El Salvador agrarian reform, right-wing policy advocates in the US, opposition to US policy, media coverage, Salvadoran economy and social structure, Salvadoran politics, military, opposition forces in El Salvador, women, the Church, and resources for further study and action).

18 Library of Congress. Hispanic Division. Human rights in Latin America, 1964–1980: a selective, annotated bibliography. Compiled and edited by the Hispanic Division. Washington: Library of Congress, 1983. 257 p.

Citations are organized according to country or special groups (e.g., churches, Amnesty International, International Commission of Jurists, and international organizations such as OAS, UN). Includes listing of newsletters, bibliographies, directories, and human rights organizations as well as author index.

19   Lima, Maria Regina Soares de and **Gerson Moura.** Brasil-Argentina: fontes bibliográficas (RIB, 32 : 3/4, 1982, p. 295–321)

Provides annotated entries for selected items related to the study of the subject and concerning general works, specific events, and contemporary questions. Article was compiled in an attempt to fill the void of bibliographic materials on bilateral relations between Latin American countries.

20   Mundo Lo, Sara de. The Falkland/ Malvinas Islands: a bibliography of books (1619–1982). Urbana, Ill.: Albatross, 1983. 65 p.

Lists 480 publications that contain information on the topic, including 23 titles related to the 1982 war. Includes subject index.

21   Pollak-Eltz, Angelina. Nuevos aportes a la bibliografía afro-venezolana. Caracas: Universidad Católica Andrés Bello, Centro de Religiones Comparadas, 1983. 17 p. (mimeo)

Lists 208 citations collected on a variety of themes, including Afro-American studies, black folklore, magic and cults, Afro-Venezuelan music, art, popular medicine, and popular fiestas and dances. Items, articles and monographs, appear in alphabetical order by author. Includes general subject index.

22   Raat, W. Dirk. The Mexican Revolution: an annotated guide to the recent scholarship. Boston: G.K. Hall, 1982. 275 p.: indexes (Reference publications in Latin American studies)

Serves as guide to books, monographs, and journal articles published 1960-July 1980 on history of the Mexican Revolution (1900–40). Includes selected, annotated listing, and historiographical essay. Separate chapters deal with: general works; regional and state history; documentary sources; contemporary history; biographies; the Por-

firiato; the Revolution (1910–20); northern dynasty (1920–34); and Cárdenas (1934–40). Provides subject and name indexes.

23   Russell, Roberto. Elementos bibliográficos para una historia latino-americana: 1930–1982 (CRIT, 55 : 1894/1895, dic. 1982, p. 13–21)

Selective, annotated listing of key works published on Latin America. Items appear in alphabetical order by author in separate sections on general history, economy, politics and society, and international relations.

24   Sabino, Robin. A selected bibliography of materials on language varieties spoken in the Virgin Islands. Charlotte Amalie, St. Thomas: Bureau of Libraries, Museums and Archaeological Services, Department of Conservation and Cultural Affairs, Government of Virgin Islands, 1980. 8 p. (Occasional paper; 6)

Listing of works available in the Virgin Islands on varieties of Dutch, English, and French spoken therein. Items appear in alphabetical order by author.

25   Universidad de Chile. Facultad de Filosofía, Humanidades y Educación. Instituto Profesional de Santiago. Departamento de Bibliotecología. Bio-bibliografía de la filosofía en Chile desde el siglo XVI hasta 1980. Edited by Fernando Astorquiza Pizarro. Santiago: 1982. 295 p.

Collection of articles and bio-bibliographies on Chile includes Walter Hanisch Espíndola's "La Filosofía en Chile desde el Siglo XVI hasta 1818;" Santiago Vidal Muñoz's "Introducción a la Historia de las Ideas Filosóficas en Chile, en el Siglo XIX;" Joaquín Barceló Larraín's "La Actividad Filosófica en Chile en la Segunda Mitad del Siglo XX," and three separate bio-bibliographies for the periods 1500–1818, 1818–1900, and 1900–80. Includes citations for 3355 items, and separate indexes for authors, theses mentors, and periodicals.

LIBRARY SCIENCE AND SERVICES

26   Brahm, Luis and **Gonzalo Gutiérrez.** REDUC: an educational documentation network serving development in Latin America (UNESCO/JIS, 5 : 2, April/June 1983, p. 89–94)

Describes the experience of the Latin American Educational Documentation Network (REDUC) which has been functioning in various countries of the region since 1972.

27 Conference of the Association of Caribbean University and Research Libraries (ACURIL), 6th, *Charlotte Amalie, Virgin Islands, 1974.* La centralización de los servicios en las bibliotecas académicas y de investigación: documentos oficiales = Centralization of academic and research library service: official documents. Caracas: ACURIL, 1982. 188 p.: ill.

Provides a record of the six major working papers of the conference, a list of delegates, the program, resolutions, and other administrative reporting, e.g., committee reports, president's report, for the 6th ACURIL conference held in 1974, in the Virgin Islands.

28 Lorenzo López, Carmen. The role of information in the Major Project on Education (UNESCO/JIS, 5:2, April/June 1983, p. 104–112)

Overview of efforts to plan an international cooperative project on education in Latin America and the Caribbean. A joint project for international cooperation, with the participation of UNESCO and the OAS, could foster the final establishment of a regional system of educational information.

ACQUISITIONS, COLLECTIONS, AND CATALOGUES

29 Biblioteca de Martín Ferreyra. Sección Historia, Genealogía, y Heráldica, *Córdoba, Argentina.* Catálogo. Presentación de Carlos A. Luque Colombres. Advertencias de Aída M. Paradelo de Parodi. Córdoba: La Biblioteca, 1982. 253 p.: indexes.

Catalogue of Martín Ferreyra's personal library (Malagueño, Córdoba, Argentina) consisting of 2,000 volumes including many limited editions and manuscripts, mostly on the history of Spain, Portugal, and the Viceroyalties of Peru and the River Plate. Detailed catalogue includes many annotated entries and several indexes (e.g., author, subject, family name, century). [Ed.]

30 Church of Jesus Christ of Latter-Day Saints. Genealogical Department. Bibliographic guide to the Guatemalan collec-

tion. Shirley A. Weathers with Patricia Hart Molen, Jackie Perry, and Tom Graman, compilers. Salt Lake City: University of Utah Press, 1981. 533 p. (Finding aids to the microfilmed manuscript collection of the Genealogical Society of Utah; 7)

Concerns holdings of Genealogical Society of Utah as filmed at Archivo General de Centroamérica in Guatemala City. Describes impressive quantities of civil, governmental, and judicial documentation of the colonial government of Guatemala as well as major documents for 19th and early 20th centuries. Sections of the guide provide references to *bienes de difuntos,* governmental, judicial, matrimonial documents, personal information, population and tribute statistics, protocolos, land records and miscellaneous documents. Includes records for other Central American entities as well as Mexico.

31 Henderson, Donald C. and **Grace R. Pérez.** Literature and politics in Latin America: an annotated calendar of the Luis Alberto Sánchez correspondence, 1919–1980. University Park: Pennsylvania State University Libraries, 1982. 498 p.: index.

Nearly 2,000 citations to correspondence and other materials with English abstracts appear in alphabetical order by correspondent with an internal chronological arrangement. Includes general index. Sánchez, whose collection is in the Pennsylvania State University Library, is a Peruvian polygraph, literary critic, politician, and polemist identified with the APRA.

32 Mexico. Archivo General de la Nación. Lista de fichas hemerográficas. Elaborado por Gerald L. McGowan. México: El Archivo, 1981. 150 leaves (Serie Guías y catálogos; 63)

Lists 1,018 Mexican periodical titles of the 19th and 20th centuries in Archivo General de la Nación. Provides information on Mexico City periodicals, governmental publications, provincial publications by province, and foreign periodicals; does not indicate holdings of individual titles.

33 Naylor, Robert A. Documentos sobre Centroamérica en los archivos de Gran Bretaña (Mesoamérica [Centro de Investigaciones Regionales de Mesoamérica, Antigua, Guatemala] 3:4, dic. 1982, p. 443–455)

Provides brief assessment of documents related to Central America. In addition to voluminous records in the British Library, Public Record Office, and at Oxford, references to other sources, e.g., Scottish Record Office, appear.

34   Organization of American States. General Secretariat. Columbus Library. Catálogo de la colección de la literatura chilena en la Biblioteca Colón. Washington: 1983. 154 p. (Documentation and information series; 7. OEZ/SG/O.1/IV/III.7)

Listing of library's Chilean literature works in alphabetical order by author. Also includes separate author and title indexes.

35   Urruchua Hernández, Víctor. Archivos microfilmados en la Biblioteca Nacional de Antropología e Historia. México: Instituto Nacional de Antropología e Historia, 1982. 28 leaves (Notas; 10)

A listing of 86 microfilm collections in the library of INAH. Highlights include 44 reels of codices and manuscripts, 52 reels on the 20th-century religious conflict in Mexico, and extensive collections on Guatemala, Hacienda San Antonio Tochatlaco, the archives of León, materials related to Maximillian, the Casa de Morelos, and the Unión Nacional Sinarquista. Some collections have guides/keys available.

REFERENCE WORKS AND RESEARCH

36   Avila H., Julieta; Beatriz Cano S.; and María Eugenia Fuentes B. Acolman: fuentes para su historia. México: Biblioteca Nacional de Antropología e Historia, 1981. 216 p., 19 leaves of plates: facsims., indexes, map (Cuadernos de la Biblioteca. Serie Sección de manuscritos; no. 6)

Detailed guide to the collections of Acolman Archive in Mexico's Biblioteca Nacional de Antropología e Historia includes references to original and facsimile materials. Provides onomastic and toponomic indexes.

37   Barberena Blásquez, Elsa. Indice de la revista *Arte de México*: 1a. época, números 1–60, 1953–1965. México: Universidad Nacional Autónoma de México, 1982. 301 p.

Provides separate author-subject

and illustration indexes to major Mexican journal.

38   Camp, Roderic Ai. Mexican political biographies, 1935–1981. 2. ed., revised and expanded. Tucson: The University of Arizona Press, 1982. 447 p.: bibl.

Useful listing of political figures chosen from heads of the revolutionary family, presidents of Mexico, factional leaders of the Revolution, cabinet members including governors and military chiefs, Supreme Court justices, senators, labor leaders, directors of large state industries, academic administrators, and opposition party officials. Appendixes include lists of Supreme Court justices, 1935–80; senators, 1934–82; deputies, 1937–82; directors of federal departments, agencies, and banks, 1935–80; ambassadors to major countries and international organizations, 1935–80; governors by state, 1935–80; rectors of the national universities, 1935–80; National Executive Committees of PNR, PRM, and PRI, 1935–80; and presidents of PAN, the Popular Socialist Party, and the Authentic Party of the Mexican Revolution, 1939–80.

39   *Caravelle*. Cahiers du monde hispanique et luso-brésilien. Deuxièmes tables décennales: 1973–1983. Université de Toulouse, Institut d'Etudes Hispaniques, Hispano-Américaines et Luso-Brésiliennes. 1983- . Toulouse, France.

Provides access to the outstanding French journal through separate author and subject indexes. A listing of the table of contents for each issue over the past 10 years also appears.

40   Durón, Jorge Fidel. El libro hondureño en 1982 (Boletín del Sistema Bibliotecario de la UNAH [Universidad Nacional Autónoma de Honduras, Tegucigalpa] 12:1, enero/marzo 1983, p. 2–17)

Author provides useful bibliographical essay of books published in Honduras during 1982.

41   Ethnic studies in North America: a catalog of current doctoral dissertation research. Ann Arbor, Mich.: University Microfilms International, 1983. 65 p.

Contains citations of 3,045 doctoral dissertations and masters theses completed between 1978–83. Individual dissertations and theses are arranged under broad ethnic categories (e.g., Africans, Asians, Europeans). Works related to Latin Americans, especially Mexican-Americans, appear on p. 47–58.

42   A Guide to reviews of books from and about Hispanic America 1981/Guía a las reseñas de libros de y sobre Hispano-américa 1981. Edited by Antonio Matos. Detroit: Blaine Ethridge-Books, 1983. 285 p.

Provides reviews of books on Hispanic America which appeared in over 685 of the principal periodicals which include such reviews. Citations are presented in alphabetical order by author. Includes indexes to title, subject, and author of review. Annotations appear in Spanish or English. Titles brought to author's attention are included as of 1972.

43   Guzmán, Augusto. Biografías de la literatura boliviana: biografía, evaluación, bibliografía. Ilustraciones de Carlos Rimassa. Cochabamba, Bolivia: Editorial Los Amigos del Libro, 1982. 307 p.: ill. (Enciclopedia boliviana)

Includes biographies for Bolivian authors born between 1520 and 1925, covering generations from colonial period to first centennial of the republic. Authors appear in chronological order from earliest (Luis de Rivera, 1520–70) to latest Julio de la Vega (b. 1924). Includes brief biographical sketches and listing of works for each author.

44   Hernández Montemayor, Laura. Catálogo de fuentes para el estudio de la historia de Tamaulipas: introducción, ordenamiento, selección y traducción de datos y notas de documentos y manuscritos en lo concerniente a la historia de Tamaulipas, en los catálogos de los Archivos de Juan E. Hernández y Dávalos *et al.* Cd. Victoria, México: Universidad Autónoma de Tamaulipas, Instituto de Investigaciones Históricas, 1979. 284 leaves: bibl., indexes.

Study based on a review of three principal archives of the history of Mexico which are at the library of the University of Texas (i.e., the calendar of the Juan E. Hernández y Dávalos Collection, the Mariano Riva Palacio Archives, and the catalog of manuscripts of the Archive of Valentín Gómez Farías). Pertinent contents of each collection are listed separately and not integrated. Includes separate onomastic indexes to the Hernández y Dávalos and the Gómez Farías Collections.

45   Indexed journals: a guide to Latin American serials. Compiled by Paula Hattox Covington. Madison, Wis.: Seminar on the Acquisition of Latin American Library Materials, 1983. 458 p. (Bibliography series; 8)

Consists of description and evaluation, by discipline, of principal indexes and abstracts which cover journals published in or relating to Latin America, and a list of these journals with an indication of indexes in which each is covered. Compiled with the cooperation of the SALALM Committee on Bibliography with the collaboration of Walter Brem, Russ Davidson, Paul Figueroa, Fred Fischer, Mary Gormly, John Hébert, Celia Leyte-Vidal, Barbara Robinson, Carole Travis, Barbara Valk, and Gayle Williams. Guide covers approximately 1,500 periodicals, indexed in over 100 abstracting and indexing services.

46   Inter-American Development Bank. Felipe Herrera Library. Index of periodical articles on the economics of Latin America. v. 1, Author index. v. 2, Title index. v. 3, Subject index. v. 4, Geographical index. Boston: G.K. Hall, 1983. 4 v. (580, 592, 448, 465 p.)

Four-volume index covers periodical articles on Latin American economics that appeared between 1950–77. Includes separate author, title, and subject index; a geographical index provides access by country and lists articles for each one in alphabetical order by author.

47   International inventory of current Mexico-related research. La Jolla: University of California, San Diego, Center for U.S.-Mexican Studies, 1983. 1 v. (Research report series; 3. Working papers in U.S.-Mexican studies)

Annual publication, edited by Ricardo Anzaldúa Montoya and Wayne A. Cornelius, provides a comprehensive, interdisciplinary, and international compendium on advanced research in progress relating to Mexico. The volume contains descriptions of 451 research projects being conducted by 578 researchers. These projects include work in the areas of Mexico and the world; border, Chicano, health, and marine studies; agricultural, biological, and physical sciences. The area of Mexican studies is divided into agriculture and agrarianism, anthropology and archaeology, education, history, literature and the arts, politics and political economy, sociology and demography, and urban studies. Each entry contains pertinent information on the researchers and their projects. Author, subject, and institutional indexes are provided.

48   Investigaciones en curso (RIB, 32:3/4, 1982, p. 383–404)
Lists research in progress and completed by investigators throughout the world. Presented by author in alphabetical order.

49   Latin America: a catalog of current doctoral dissertation research. Ann Arbor, Mich.: University Microfilms International, 1983. 28 p.
Lists 1,348 doctoral dissertations and masters theses completed between 1980–83. Items are arranged by country within 26 subjects or disciplines (e.g., anthropology, biological sciences, earth sciences, economics, history, language and linguistics, and sociology).

50   Lombardi, Cathryn L.; John V. Lombardi; and K. Lynn Stoner. Latin American history: a teaching atlas. Madison: University of Wisconsin Press *for the* Conference on Latin American History, 1983. 104 p.: index.
Maps in the atlas are designed to provide students and teachers of Latin American subjects with a set of useful cartographic materials that emphasize themes and topics appropriate for undergraduate courses in Latin American affairs. Atlas includes introductory section that displays basic physical features of the Latin American landscape and 12 parts covering the colonial period into the last quarter of the 20th century. Includes index of names and topics on the maps.

51   Martínez G., Eric Jorge. Indices de archivos parroquiales: Tegucigalpa y Yuscarán (YAXKIN, 3:3, junio 1980, p. 189–198)
Lists existing indexes from the 18th to 20th century for sacramentales, and other Church related records for the Cathedral and Parishes of Tegucigalpa and Yuscarán. Documents indexed are located in the *Secretariado* of the Cathedral in Tegucigalpa and the Rectory of Yuscarán Parish.

52   Mesa-Lago, Carmelo. Latin American studies in Asia. With the collaboration of Shirley A. Kregar. Pittsburgh, Pa.: Univer-

sity of Pittsburgh, Center for Latin American Studies, 1983. 65 p. (Latin American monograph & documents series; 7)
Deals with fairly comprehensive scholarly, multidisciplinary area study programs established at university and research institutions in Japan, the People's Republic of China, and India. Describes in full 24 major programs and briefly 14 smaller ones. Publication complements Mesa-Lago's 1979 *Latin American Studies in Europe* (see *HLAS 42:153*).

53   Nicaragua. Instituto Nacional de Estadísticas y Censos. Anuario estadístico de Nicaragua, 1982. Managua: 1983. 259 p.
Contains statistical data from 1978–82, although the 1982 data is preliminary. Includes chapters on climate and population, economy, economic sectors, and social data. Major categories include exports, agriculture, industry, internal commerce, education, employment and salaries, and population.

54   Quién es quién en América del Sur, diccionario biográfico argentino, 1982–1983. Edited by Pablo Raúl Vitaver. Buenos Aires: Publicaciones Referenciales Latinoamericanos, 1982. 799 p., 118 p.
Lists approximately 6,000 professionals and businessmen in Argentina. Includes separate section devoted to 56 business enterprises that supported the publication.

55   Recent articles (RIB, 32:3/4, 1982, p. 418–455)
Provides articles published 1981–82 by subject culled from issues of several journals.

56   *Resúmenes sobre Población en América Latina.* United Nations, Comisión Económica para América Latina, Centro Latinoamericano de Demografía. Vol. 6, No. 1, junio 1982- . Santiago, Chile.
Consists of abstracts of publications on population organized according to eight categories: 1) general population; 2) mortality; 3) fertility; 4) migration; 5) geographic distribution; 6) economically active population; 7) nuptiality and family; and 8) population characteristics and needs. Includes separate subject and author indexes. Publications are in the CELADE (Latin American Demographic Center) Library in Santiago.

57 *Revista Interamericana de Bibliografía:* catalog of articles, review articles, and book reviews in vols. 1–32, 1951–82, with author indexes. Washington: Organization of American States, 1983. 199 p.

Includes articles, review articles, and book reviews published in 32 volumes of *Review,* a total of 122 issues. References appear in alphabetical order within subject arrangements; book reviews are listed by book author in alphabetical order. Also includes separate indexes to authors of indexes and book reviews.

58 *Statistical Abstract of Latin America.* University of California, Latin American Center. Vol. 22, 1983- . Los Angeles.

This issue (668 p.), edited by James W. Wilkie and Stephen Haber, provides a wealth of socioeconomic data with cumulative indexes to vols. 18–22. Contains articles on the following topics by these authors: Manuel Moreno Ibáñez on problems of measuring housing and shelter in Latin America, 1940–80; T.D. Proffitt on Protestant church growth in 20th-century Central America and the Caribbean; Roy L. Prosterman on the demographics of land reform in El Salvador since 1980; James W. Wilkie on US foreign policy and economic assistance in Bolivia, 1948–76; Samuel Schmidt on the many aspects of Mexico's public debt, 1970–76; Stephen Haber on modernization and change in Mexican communities, 1930–70; and James W. Wilkie on management and mismanagement of national and international statistical resources in the Americas. An invaluable reference tool.

59 **Ueda, Satoru.** A roster of Mesoamerican studies in Japan (Mexicon [Berlin] 4:5/6, Nov. 1982, p. 84–86)

List of publications in English by Japanese scholars, since 1964, and list of periodicals on Latin America published by Japanese academic societies. [H. von Winning]

60 **Zapata Cuéncar, Heriberto.** Antioquia, periódicos de provincia. Medellín?, Colombia: Editorial Lealor, 1981. 135 p.: ill.

Provides description of 800 local 19th and 20th-century newspapers appearing in towns and cities of Antioquia. Useful documentation on establishment of paper, owners and editors, and frequency of issuance.

GENERAL WORKS

61 **Augsburger, Alberto E.** El mercado del libro en América Latina: situación actual y perspectivas. Paris: UNESCO, 1981. 122 p.

Evaluates current state and future orientation of book development in Latin America, indicating means that can be used to improve the local book industry. Discusses problems of paper production, lack of book laws (i.e., production and deposit) and difficulties in the circulation of book materials within the region.

62 **Fernández-Caballero, Carlos.** Educational documentation and information for Latin America and the Caribbean: the Documentation and Information Centre for the Regional Office for Education in Latin America and the Caribbean, OREALC (UNESCO/JIS, 5:2, April/June 1983, p. 86–88)

Describes the OREALC Documentation and Information Center in Santiago de Chile whose functions and activities include study and research, documentation and dissemination of information, training of personnel for educational services, and technical cooperation and support for ongoing national and regional projects.

63 **Lateinamerika: Gesellschaft, Kirche, Theologie.** Bd. 1, Aufbruch und Auseinandersetzung. Bd. 2, Der Streit um die Theologie der Befreiung. Edited by Hans-Jürgen Prien. Göttingen: Vandenhoeck und Ruprecht, 1981. 2 v.: bibl., indexes.

Collection of essays on liberation theology in Latin America, with specific articles on the Latin American Church between Medellín and Puebla by Enrique Dussel; the Church in Argentina and Brazil by Hans-Jürgen Prien, the Church in Chile and Cuba by Othmar Noggler; a summary of the Puebla conference by Hans-Jürgen Prien; and essays on the success of Protestant sects in Latin America.

64 **Márquez, Natacha.** A cooperative network for information on higher education in Latin America and the Caribbean (UNESCO/JIS, 5:2, April/June 1983, p. 95–99, bibl.)

Provides summary of proceedings of regional meeting of experts of information in higher education in Latin America and the Caribbean, held in Caracas, Oct. 1982.

65   Oglesby, J. C. M. Latin American studies in Canada: 1966–1981 (RIB, 32:3/4, 1982, p. 347–355)

Traces development of Latin American studies in Canada since 1966. Concludes that, in spite of a funding reduction, these studies are established in Canada, primarily because of increased academic and governmental interest in the region. Lists major research conducted by Canadians.

66   Orígen, desarrollo y proyección de la imprenta en México. Catálogo, textos: María Teresa Bosque Lastra *et al.* México: Palacio de Minería, 1981. 186 p.: ill.

Provides brief overview of the history of printing in Mexico. Prepared to coincide with opening of the International Book Fair held in Mexico in 1980. Contains many illustrations.

67   Valle, Rafael Heliodoro. Historia de la cultura hondureña. Tegucigalpa: Editorial Universitaria, 1981. 235 p.

Collection of five historic essays, on *periodismo,* folklore, the book, literature, and scholarship in Honduras, by Rafael Heliodoro Valle (d. 1959) in honor of the 90th anniversary of his birth.

NEW SERIAL TITLES

68   *Historia y Geografía.* Revista del Museo Nacional de Historia y Geografía. No. 1, 1982- . Santo Domingo.

New journal (109 p.) edited by Roberto Marte, dealing with the Dominican Republic and Hispaniola, and produced by the newly inaugurated (1982) Museo Nacional de Historia y Geografía. Its frequency is not given. For further information about the publication write to: Depto. de Investigaciones, Museo Nacional de Historia y Geografía, Plaza de la Cultura, Santo Domingo, República Dominicana.

69   *Obra Citada.* Revista de investigación y análisis. Obra Citada Editores. Año 2, No. 1, enero/marzo 1983- . México.

Quarterly publication produced by Obra Citada Editores, Miravalle 809-A, Col.

Miravalle, Deleg. Benito Juárez, 03580, México, D.F., México. Contains items of interest on Mexican politics and culture, in addition to worldwide events.

70   *Pensamiento Iberoamericano.* Revista de economía política. Instituto de Cooperación Iberoamericana, Dirección de Cooperación Económica. No. 1, enero/ junio 1982- . Madrid.

First issue of a new biannual journal, supported by the ECLA and the Spanish Instituto de Cooperación Iberoamericana. It intends to stimulate intellectual exchange among the countries of Spain, Portugal, and Latin America concerning the theme of Latin American economic policy. Includes articles, discussion, brief notes, and book reviews; a final section provides the tables of content of major Iberoamerican economic and development journals. The editor is Aníbal Pinto; copies are available from: Instituto de Cooperación Iberoamèricana, Dirección de Cooperación Económica, Avda. de Reyes Católicos, 4, Madrid 3, Spain. Annual subscription is $50.00 (US).

71   *Pie de Página.* Revista de bibliografía. Pie de Página Editores. Año 1, No. 1, sept./oct. 1982- . México.

Lists and reviews new titles of Mexican and other publications. Appears six times a year and costs $12.00 a year. For a subscription, write to: Pie de Página Editores, Martillo 14, Col. Aarón Saenz, 15870 México, D.F., México.

**JOURNAL ABBREVIATIONS
BIBLIOGRAPHY AND
GENERAL WORKS**

CRIT   Criterio. Editorial Criterio. Buenos Aires.

RIB   Revista Interamericana de Bibliografía (Inter-American Review of Bibliography). Organization of American States. Washington.

UNESCO/JIS   Unesco Journal of Information Science, Librarianship and Archives Administration. United Nations Education, Scientific and Cultural Organization. Paris.

YAXKIN   YaxKin. Instituto Hondureño de Antropología e Historia. Tegucigalpa.

ANTHROPOLOGY

GENERAL

251 Aldunate del Solar, Carlos. Museo Chileno de Arte Precolombino. Santiago: s.n., 1983. 85 p.: ill.

This museum opened in late 1981 as a collaboration between the Municipality of Santiago and private collector who assembled objects over many decades. Several specimens are illustrated in color, but principal importance of publication is the illustrated catalog. Each piece is represented by b/w photograph accompanied by cultural identification, chronological position, and measurements. Collection includes excellent examples from ceramic complexes throughout region from Mesoamerica to Chile. [B.J. Meggers]

252 ———. La música en el arte precolombino. Santiago: Museo Chileno de Arte Precolombino, 1982. 1 v. (Unpaged): bibl., ill.

Some 107 artifacts capable of producing sound were assembled from 24 institutions and private collections. Geographical representation extends from southern Mesoamerica to central Chile. Data on each specimen include cultural affiliation, description with illustration, and identification of the sound produced. [B.J. Meggers]

253 Carter, George F. On precolumbian discoveries of America (AAC/AJ, 19:2, 1981, p. 10–17, ill.)

Deplores recent efforts to deny all diffusionist explanations as "cultist," the consequences of unbalanced minds, and the consequent stifling of discussion of the evidence. [B.J. Meggers]

254 Echeverría, José. Glosario arqueológico. Otavalo, Ecuador: Instituto Otavaleño de Antropología, 1981. 343 p.: ill. (Colección Pendoneros; 1)

Defines terms applicable to archaeological sites, artifacts, concepts, features, excavations, materials, etc. in effort to encourage consistency among archaeologists writing in Spanish. Provides English equivalents; illustrations supplement text. [B.J. Meggers]

255 Falsifications and misreconstructions of precolumbian art: a conference at Dumbarton Oaks, Oct. 14–15, 1978. Edited by Elizabeth H. Boone. Washington: Dumbarton Oaks, 1982. 142 p.: bibl., ill.

Eight authorities discuss aspects of identifying and interpreting falsified objects from Mesoamerican and Peruvian contexts. In addition to intentional frauds, examples are provided of restorations in which valuable information has been destroyed. Variety of materials and means of detection discussed make this an important source for anyone concerned with problems of authentication. [B.J. Meggers]

256 Mythen der Neuen Welt, zur Entdeckungsgeschichte Lateinamerikas. Karl-Heinz Kohl, editor. Berlin: Frölich & Kaufmann, 1982. 358 p.: bibl., ill., plates (Ausstellung des 2. Festivals der Weltkulturen)

Profusely illustrated exhibition catalog of artifacts, books, and pictorial materials concerning the discovery of the New World, with 23 essays on Latin American anthropology and art history (see item **307**). [H. von Winning]

257 Las Representaciones de arquitectura en la arqueología de América. v. 1, Mesoamérica. Daniel Schávelzon, coordinator. México: Universidad Nacional Autónoma de México, 1982. 445 p.: bibl., ill.

Descriptive and interpretative compilation (37 articles by various authors) of architectural models in clay or stone, and of pictorial representations of temple designs in codices. Profusely illustrated. [H. von Winning]

258 Schobinger, Juan. ¿Vikingos o extraterrestres?: sobre el origen de las culturas precolombinas. Buenos Aires: Editorial CREA, 1982. 222 p.: ill. (Colección Temas básicos)

Archaeologist exposes misuse of data, fallacious logic, and other weaknesses in "evidence" drawn from visits to the New World by precolumbian travelers from the Old World. Excellent, readable discussion. [B.J. Meggers]

259   Stoll, David. The Summer Institute of Linguistics and indigenous movements (LAP, 9:2[33], Spring 1982, p. 84–99)

Beginning with an observation on the ambiguous social implications of millenary religiosity, article perceptively discusses contradictory role of the Wycliffe translators as brokers between states and native peoples in contexts of internal colonialism in Mexico, Guatemala, and Brazil. [J.M. Ingham]

260   Tichy, Franz. Geographische Ausdrucksformen des Weltbildes in Al-

tamerika: Mexico und Peru im Vergleich (*in* Festschrift für Felix Monheim. Aachen, FRG: Geographisches Institut, 1981, p. 15–37, bibl., ill.)

Similarities of space-time concepts in Mexico and Peru. Independently from their astronomical-calendrical connotations, both areas had developed a geometry based on vigesimal/decimal divisions of the right angle in a cardinal-oriented grid system for ceremonial centers and settlements. [H. von Winning]

261   Vreeland, James and **Jorge C. Muelle.** Breve glosario de terminología textil andina (PUCIRA/BSA, 17:18, p. 1975/1976, p. 7–21, bibl.)

Spanish-English glossary of technical terms used in describing tools, techniques, structures, and all other aspects of textiles. [B.J. Meggers]

ARCHAEOLOGY: Mesoamerica

NORMAN HAMMOND, *Associate Professor of Archaeology, Douglass College, Rutgers University*
BARBARA L. STARK, *Associate Professor of Anthropology, Arizona State University*

MESOAMERICAN STUDIES HAVE BENEFITTED from new syntheses that place the enormously increased data of the past decade in perspective. A supplement volume to the *Handbook of Middle American Indians* is divided into two parts, one with reviews of a number of major research projects (items **276, 298, 326, 346, 346, 370, 376, 402, 413,** and **452**), and another that addresses general themes concerning prehistoric change—sedentarism (item **356**), urbanism (item **275**), and social complexity (item **301**). Some substantive papers of this supplement are more than reviews; they present research results not yet available elsewhere in the same detail and comprehensive treatment (items **296** and **482**).

Two new books designed as texts make available reading for specialists as well because their individual "stamps" reflect the authors' differing conceptions of what recent research means. Weaver (item **366**) emphasizes culture history, while Blanton and others (item **277**) place greater emphasis on a theoretical framework to explain processes of social change.

Many regional settlement pattern projects in Mexico reached the publication stage (items **278, 309–310, 327, 337,** and **347**). These survey programs have been a leading aspect of highland research in recent years. In particular, survey and excavations in Morelos, Puebla, and the Tula Valley (item **412**) have revealed more amply and accurately the nature of Teotihuacán's effect on areas outside the Valley of Mexico.

New discussions about the reasons for development of a complex society in Mesoamerica are noteworthy. Most take as their starting point the developmental patterns in particular highland valleys (items **278, 341, 343, 347,** and **355**). The exception is Coe and Diehl's (item **403**) final report on San Lorenzo Tenochtitlán. The pros and cons of particular ecological and demographic arguments, especially those based on highland surveys, continue to receive close examination (items **317, 325, 348,** and **362**). Ideological factors are attracting increasing attention, although a coherent theoretical position about the role of ideology has not emerged. Overall, in recent years Mesoamerican literature has been one of the most prolific and provocative in the world on the origins and changing character of prehistoric complex societies.

Amidst the wide variety of new substantive reports, one region has attracted an unusually large share of interest. Oaxacan publications have been prolific, ranging from the survey projects mentioned above to site reports and specialized works (items **276–277, 300, 472, 489, 534, 536–538,** and **590**). Studies in the central highlands, apart from the survey projects, continue, as usual, to be numerous. Many represent research by INAH and UNAM. Particularly welcome are a growing series of publications concerning the recent excavation and restoration of the Aztec Templo Mayor (items **473** and **476**), and other investigations of Tenochtitlan-Tlatelolco (items **395, 433,** and **528**). These help to counterbalance the tendency toward over-reliance on documents for Aztec studies.

Several reports based on salvage archaeology in the Middle Balsas have appeared (items **430, 471,** and **486**). In addition, scattered publications in western and northern Mexico have added to the spotty information from these parts of greater Mesoamerica (items **381, 383, 405, 455, 483,** and **491**), but the topics are so diverse that the western and northern Mexican records remain poorly understood in an integrated regional fashion.

Olmec studies continue to attract attention, although recent publications generally deal with prior information and many focus exclusively or strongly on iconography (items **331** and **358**). The main contributions of new field data concern San Lorenzo (item **403**), Chalcatzingo (items **437, 446, 464,** and **510**), and an Olmec hinterland center in Chiapas.

Some special topics have received illuminating treatments. The so-called Mixtec-Puebla horizon style in the postclassic has been reanalyzed (items **351,** and **353**). Consequently, the poorly understood terminal classic and early postclassic relations among regions are emerging as one of the more exciting, if perplexing, topics of research. Data from Cacaxtla, Tlaxcala (items **421, 460,** and **468**) and Xochicalco, Morelos (items **438, 450,** and **514**) have contributed information about the complexity of developments in this time period.

Ethnohistoric research of this area, which has been plentiful (items **283, 550, 567, 578,** and **583**) will be examined in detail by S.L. Cline in the Ethnohistory section of the humanities volume, *HLAS 46*, scheduled for publication in 1985.

For the Maya area two syntheses have appeared, designed as both texts and general accounts (items **302** and **308**), and the attention devoted to Maya civilization in each of the general Mesoamerican volumes noted above (item **277**) is less than the area deserves.

Field research continues to yield valuable data on periods preceding the classic, including the first, which constitutes indubitable proof of Paleo-Indian occupation in the Maya lowlands (item **408**). MacNeish's search for preceramic sites (item **469**) continues to yield further ambiguous results. Studies of lowland formative sites indicate the presence of massive public architecture from 400 BC onwards (item **493**) and the presence of the stela cult by AD 100 (item **442**). Final publication of the 1960s Seibal and Dzibilchaltun projects demonstrates the presence of large formative period communities underlying the classic sites (items **375** and **418**). The long formative ceramic sequence from northern Belize has been further clarified (items **458** and **496**), while in the highland zone the origins of Usulutan ceramic decoration in the middle formative and its complex late formative development have been documented (item **410**). An important site in this respect is Santa Leticia, El Salvador, where the "pot-bellied" sculptural style has been firmly dated to the late formative (item **411**). The role warfare played in the emergence of classic civilization at the end of the late formative is perhaps further illuminated by the discovery of an impressive, possibly 'protoclassic' fortification at Murralla de León in El Petén, Guatemala.

Monographs on classic period ceremonial centers include those on Seibal and Dzibilchaltun noted above, and vol. 2 of the Altun Ha report (item **492**). The nature of classic period macro-settlement patterns and site relationships is dealt with in a paper proposing ranking criteria (item **263**), and the microstructure of centers as astronomically determined layouts in another paper (item **320**). The subsistence economy of the formative was investigated by flotation of plant remains and studies by both radar survey (item **264**) and excavation (item **365**) examined the widespread presence of raised- and channeled-field networks reflecting ancient intensive agriculture. The continuing controversy over the possible subsistence contribution of *ramon* nuts (items **462** and **574**) is apparently resolved, with an edaphic reason for the presence of *ramon* around Maya sites and its recovered food remains both of which indicate that the contribution was nugatory.

Studies of exchange concentrated on the Caribbean coast, with three papers devoted to aspects of material from Moho Cay, Belize (items **303, 382,** and **394**), a fourth to the potential of Belize's offshore cays (item **417**), and to reporting the presence of mercury at Lamanai (item **493**).

The classic collapse is treated in two mathematical papers (items **279** and **323**), and the intrusive presence of Yucatecans in the central area at Nohmul in this period is further documented (items **286** and **399**). Postclassic sites have been investigated in the lowlands (items **398, 447,** and **493**) and highlands (see *HLAS 44 : 1506*), with extensive use of ethnohistoric records. An initial synthesis of post-postclassic archaeology in Yucatan has appeared (item **374**).

Technical studies include the characterization of Guatemalan obsidians using bulk elements (item **329**) and dating of the same sources using hydration (item **451**), the use of neutron activation analysis for the study of Fine Paste pottery in the lowlands (item **370**), and a plausible explanation for the manufacture of Maya Blue pigment (item **321**).

Scholarship based on looted, and in some cases doubtfully authentic, material continues to appear (item **505**), and the impact of looting on Maya sites has been reemphasized (item **494**).

To assess current research not yet in the publication stage for Mesoamerica, consult Stark (item **356**) and Kowaleski (item **317**).

The following annotation of literature contains contributions by Suzanne Lewenstein, who assisted Stark, and by Hasso von Winning, a prior contributor to this section. The authors thank the many colleagues and publishers who generously assisted us by providing references, reprints, and publications. Of course, in some cases items were not available for examination and could not be included. Regrettably, limitations of space have required us to list several volumes below without separately covering each individual paper contained therein.

GENERAL

262 **Adams, R.E.W.** Ancient Maya canals: grids and lattices in the Maya jungle (AIA/A, 35:6, Nov./Dec. 1982, p. 28–35)
Illustrated account of recent discoveries using airborne radar. [NH]

263 ———— and **Richard C. Jones.** Spatial patterns and regional growth among classic Maya cities (SAA/AA, 46, 1981, p. 301–322)
Uses courtyard counts to rank centers, and then suggests regional development trajectories based on rank-size distributions. Concludes overall that the "periphery" sites such as the Rio Bec-Chenes region developed first, but entered period of stasis during the florescence of the "core" regions around Tikal and Calakmul and continued to grow only after the collapse of the Peten centers. [NH]

264 ————; **W.E. Brown, Jr.;** and **T.P. Culbert.** Radar mapping, archaeology, ancient Maya land use (AAAS/A, 213, 1981, p. 1457–1463)
Synthetic-aperture sidelooking airborne radar has been used to detect linear and reticulate patterns in the Maya lowland landscape, of which ca. 25 percent are estimated to be canal systems and other features of prehispanic cultural origin. [NH]

265 **Alden, John R.** A reconstruction of Toltec period political units in the Valley of Mexico (in Transformations: mathematical approaches to culture change. Colin Renfrew and Kenneth L. Cooke, editors. New York: Academic Press, 1979, p. 169–200, bibl., ill., maps, tables)
Political units are estimated using an algorithm incorporating site distances and population sizes to determine interaction. Aztec and Toltec cases are analyzed, with the Aztecs serving as a control. [BLS]

268 **The Art and iconography of late postclassic central Mexico:** a conference at Dumbarton Oaks, October 22nd and 23rd, 1977. Elizabeth P. Benson, organizer. Elizabeth Hill Boone, editor. Washington: Dumbarton Oaks, Trustees for Harvard University, 1982. 1 v.: bibl.
Essays cover Aztec sculpture (especially deities), dress, symbolism at Malinalco, legal process, Aztec and Mixtec pictorial representations, and the Mixteca-Puebla concept. [BLS]

269 **Aveni, Anthony F.** Skywatchers of ancient Mexico. Austin: University of Texas Press, 1980. 355 p.: bibl., ill., index (The Texas Pan American series)
Comprehensive treatment of archaeoastronomy, providing coverage of documentary and archaeological evidence. Includes astronomical background and comparisons with other New World areas. [BLS]

270 **Bailey, Alison Kennedy.** Ecce Bufo: the toad in nature and in Olmec iconography (UC/CA, 23:3, June 1982, p. 273–290, ill.)
Speculation, with use of cross-cultural parallels, on function of toads as bio-mediators and members of a general class of toxic consumed fauna. Suggests that the San Lorenzo lagunas and drains were toad/duck breeding installations. [NH]

271 **Barrera Rubio, Alfredo.** La obra fotográfica de Teobert Maler en la Península de Yucatán (IAI/I, 6:1, 1980, p. 107–124, ill.)
Reports on Maler's invaluable photographs and related documents on Maya ruins, in Mérida archives. [HvW]

272 **Barthel, Thomas.** Planetary series in ancient India and prehispanic Mexico: an analysis of their relations with each other (MLV/T, 30, Nov. 1981, p. 203–230, bibl.)
Restates the case for relationship between Indian and Mesoamerican astronomical-calendric structures. [NH]

273 **Becker, Marshall Joseph.** Theories of ancient Maya social structure: priests, peasants, and ceremonial centers in historical perspective. Greeley, Colo.: George E. Fay, 1979. 89 leaves: bibl. (Katunob, occasional publications in Mesoamerican anthropology; no. 12)
Historiographical examination of Thompson's priest-peasant model of Maya society and modifications enforced by later evidence. Revised from 1971 dissertation. [NH]

274 **Blanton, Richard E.** Cultural ecology reconsidered (SAA/AA, 45:1, Jan. 1980, p. 145–151, bibl.)

Argues for Monte Alban as a political capital, not an outgrowth of local agricultural and exchange conditions. [BLS]

275 ———. The rise of cities (in Archaeology. Edited by Jeremy A. Sabloff and Patricia A. Andrews. Austin: University of Texas Press, 1981, p. 392–400, bibl. [Supplement to the Handbook of Middle American Indians; v. 1])

Focuses on rise of Teotihuacan and Monte Alban in a regional perspective; contains critical analysis of ecological approach to urbanism. [BLS]

276 ——— and **Stephen A. Kowalewski.** Monte Alban and after in the Valley of Oaxaca (in Archaeology. Edited by Jeremy A. Sabloff and Patricia A. Andrews. Austin: University of Texas Press, 1981, p. 94–116, bibl., maps [Supplement to the Handbook of Middle American Indians; v. 1])

Period by period synthesis of Oaxaca prehistory following the founding of Monte Alban, emphasizing settlement pattern results from survey and mapping of part of the valley. [BLS]

277 ———; ———; **Gary Feinman;** and **Jill Appel.** Ancient Mesoamerica: a comparison of change in three regions. Cambridge: Cambridge University Press, 1981. 300 p.: bibl., ill., index, maps, tables (New studies in archaeology series)

Compares the course of social change in the Valley of Oaxaca, Basin of Mexico, and Maya lowlands. Scale, integration, and complexity are pivotal comparative concepts. Focus is on the theoretical implications of culture change and social organization, not on culture history. Useful as text and scholarly work. [BLS]

278 ——— et al. Regional evolution in the Valley of Oaxaca, Mexico (Journal of Field Archaeology [The Association for Field Archaeology, Boston University] 6:4, Winter 1979, p. 369–390, ill., maps)

Brief report, period by period, of settlement patterns in the central and southern parts of the valley. Population pressure does not seem to have influenced the early growth of social and complexity, according to their analysis. [BLS]

279 **Bové, Frederick J.** Trend surface analysis and the lowland classic Maya collapse (SAA/AA, 46, 1981, p. 93–112)

Statistical processing does not reveal either diffusionary or invasionary trends in the collapse as documented by monument cessation. Suggests five regional spheres, whose increased competition may bear on the collapse process. Complex but unconvincing. [NH]

280 **Bricker, Victoria R.** The origin of the Maya solar calendar (UC/CA, 23:1, Feb. 1982, p. 101–103, ill., tables)

Suggests that the calendar began, using the winter solstice as a point of origin, ca. 550 BC (i.e. the middle formative). [NH]

281 **Brumfiel, Elizabeth M.** Specialization, market exchange, and the Aztec state: a view from Huexotla (UC/CA, 21:4, Aug. 1980, p. 459–478, bibl., maps, tables)

Regional exchange is said to intensify after formation of the Aztec state, with Huexotla specializing more in foods. Political expansion and urbanization at Tenochtitlan are posited as the stimuli for commercialization—non-food tribute was exchanged in urban markets for foods. [BLS]

282 **Calnek, Edward E.** Tenochtitlan in the early colonial period (in International Congress of Americanists, 42d, Paris, 1976. Actes [see HLAS 43:255] v. 8, p. 35–40)

Describes decline of Aztec elite and reduction of natives to urban proletariat prompted by Spanish appropriation of urban properties and by repeated subdivision of Aztec estates among increasing numbers of male heirs. Notes corresponding decline in artisanship and long-distance luxury trade. [SL]

Carmack, Robert M. The Quiché Mayas of Utatlán: the evolution of a highland Guatemala kingdom. See HLAS 44:1506.

283 **Carrasco, David.** Quetzalcoatl and the irony of empire: myths and prophecies in the Aztec tradition. Chicago: University of Chicago Press, 1982. 233 p.: bibl., ill., index.

Cognitivist discussion of urban centers in Central Mexico and their symbolic, sacred links to Quetzalcoatl. Considers Teotihuacan, Xochicalco, Tula, Cholula, and Tenochtitlan. [BLS]

284 **Charlton, Thomas H. III.** Historical archaeology in the Valley of Mexico (in International Congress of Americanists, 42nd, Paris, 1976. Actes [see HLAS 43:255] v. 8, p. 21–33, bibl., ill.)

Archaeological data for three postconquest phases in the rural Teotihuacan Valley indicate no regular, gradual, or continuous fusion of Spanish and Indian cultures, but instead a delayed cultural impact on the Aztecs, except for religion. [SL]

285 Charlton, Thomas H. and **Roberta Reiff Katz.** Tonalá Bruñida ware: past and present (AIA/A, 32:1, Jan./Feb. 1979, p. 45–53, ill., map)

Survey of post-conquest occupation in the Teotihuacan Valley encountered earlier sherds (1650–1810) related to modern Tonalá pottery. Traces history, distribution, and marketing of the ware. [BLS]

286 Chase, Diane Z. and **Arlen F. Chase.** Yucatec influence in terminal classic northern Belize (SAA/AA, 47:3, July 1982, p. 596–614, ill., map, tables)

Reiterates observation that terminal classic buildings at Nohmul exhibit Yucatec traits, and compares two buildings with examples at Chichen Itza. [NH]

287 Christenson, Andrew L. Change in the human food niche in response to population growth (*in* Modeling change in prehistoric subsistence economics. Timothy K. Earle and Andrew L. Christenson, editors. New York: Academic Press, 1980, p. 31–7, bibl., ill., tables)

Dietary components based on least-cost resource selection are held to be responsive to population size. In prehistoric subsistence data from the Tehuacan Valley, food diversity (niche width) changes in accordance with general predictions. [BLS]

288 Clark, John E. Manufacture of Mesoamerican prismatic blades: an alternative technique (SAA/AA, 47:2, April 1982, p. 355–376, bibl., ill.)

Replication experiments confirm it is possible to detach prismatic blades by using techniques which match 16th-centry written descriptions of native practices. [BLS]

289 Coggins, Clemency. The shape of time: some political implications of a four-part figure (SAA/AA, 45:4, Oct. 1980, p. 727–739, bibl., ill., maps)

Suggests that Maya quadripartite spatial symbolism relates to a vertical-circle model (east-above-west-below) with a dominant east-west trajectory following the sun's

path. If correct, this has serious implications for models assuming a horizontal-circle (east-south-west-north) symbolism (see *HLAS* 39:555). [NH]

290 Cohodas, Marvin. The Great Ball Court of Chichen Itza, Yucatan, Mexico. New York: Garland Pub., 1978. 302 p., 53 leaves of plates (2 fold.): bibl., ill. (Outstanding dissertations in the fine arts)

Updated version of Ph.D. dissertation, which proposes an AD 630–690 date for the Great Ball Court and some other buildings at Chichen Itza, with an AD 690–720 date proposed for most others. The scheme is far earlier than other reassessments of the chronology, which would place all these structures 150–250 years after. [NH]

291 ———. Radial pyramids and radial-associated assemblages of the Central Maya area (SAH/J, 39:3, Oct. 1980, p. 208–223, ill., maps, plates, tables)

Suggests that four-stairwayed pyramids were for public rituals, involving celebration of the passage of time. The pyramid was part of a cosmic model and could function secondarily as an observatory, marking the passage of the sun. [NH]

292 Deal, Michael. Functional variation of Maya spiked vessels: a practical guide (SAA/AA, 47;3, July 1982, p. 614–633, ill., plates, tables)

Uses ethnographic comparisons to suggest that a range of ritual functions was served by spiked vessels, including incense burning, brewing, offering of produce on altars. [NH]

293 Di Peso, Charles C. Culture change in northern Mexico: the bureaucratic conquest of the Gran Chichimeca, AD 1540-AD 1600 (*in* International Congress of Americanists, 42nd, Paris, 1976. Actes [see *HLAS 43:255*] v. 8, p. 10–20, bibl.)

Finding no 16th-century native bureaucratic elite that could be usurped in the Gran Chichimeca, Spanish conquerors treated the area as a source of labor. Basque colonists brought sheep to northern Mexico, resulting in environmental deterioration. [SL]

294 Dillon, Brian D. Estudio sobre la fabricación de sal por los mayas en las Salinas de los Nueve Cerros, Guatemala (IAHG/AHG, 2:3, 1981, p. 25–30)

Brief description of 1976 project at a salt-making center on the Maya highland/lowland border. [NH]

295 Dütting, Dieter. Aspects of classic Maya religion and world view (MLV/T, 29, Sept. 1980, p. 107–167, ill.)

Discussion of squint and spiral eyes in Palenque art, with postulated readings for numerous texts at that site and elsewhere, and consideration of social organization, with proposed matrilineal descent in late classic times. [NH]

296 Flannery, Kent V.; Joyce Marcus; and Stephen A. Kowalewski. The preceramic and formative of the Valley of Oaxaca (in Archaeology. Edited by Jeremy A. Sabloff and Patricia A. Andrews. Austin: University of Texas Press, 1981, p. 48–93, bibl., ill., maps, tables [Supplement to the *Handbook of Middle American Indians*; v. 1])

Overview of long-term survey and excavation project. Most complete presentation yet of Archaic data there. Best single synthesis currently available of Archaic and preclassic Oaxacan prehistory. [BLS]

297 Fox, John W. Chinautla Viejo, Mixco: un sitio estratégico en la frontera Pokomam-Cakchiquel (SGHG/A, 51:51, enero/dic. 1978, p. 13–25, ill., maps)

Brief description of a postclassic center in highland Guatemala. [NH]

298 García Cook, Angel. The historical importance of Tlaxcala in the cultural development of the central highlands (in Archaeology. Edited by Jeremy A. Sabloff and Patricia A. Andrews. Austin: University of Texas Press, 1981, p. 244–276, bibl., ill., maps [Supplement to the *Handbook of Middle American Indians*; v. 1])

Much new data on this previously under-studied region is presented period by period. Helps counteract scholarly overemphasis on highland Basin of Mexico and Oaxaca. [BLS]

299 Garza T. de González, Silvia and Edward B. Kurjack. El medio ambiente y los asentamientos mayas en época prehispánica (in Instituto Nacional de Antropología e Historia, México. Centro Nacional del Sureste. Congreso Interno, 1979, Mérida, Yucatán. Memoria. México, INAH, 1981, p. 17–28, bibl., table)

Defines 11 environmental zones in the Yucatan Peninsula and tabulates number and density of sites in each. Average "territory" of a site is 17 km² ranging from 4.5 km² on the coast to 460 km² in the *akalche* zone. [NH]

300 Gaxiola G., Margarita and **Marcus C. Winter.** La sociedad mixteca de la época prehispánica (Revista Mexicana de Estudios Antropológicos [México] 26, 1980, p. 81–93, bibl., map)

Archaeological and linguistic evidence indicate the emergence of the Mixtecs as a distinct ethnic group by 500 BC. Synthesizes archaeological evidence regarding the evolution of social stratificaton in the Mixteca Alta from early villages to the conquest. [SL]

301 Grove, David C. The formative period and the evolution of complex culture (in Archaeology. Edited by Jeremy A. Sabloff and Patricia A. Andrews. Austin: University of Texas Press, 1981, p. 373–391, bibl., map [Supplement to the *Handbook of Middle American Indians*; v. 1])

Concentrates on recent research in Gulf coast, Oaxaca, central highlands, and Pacific coast. Suggests differentials in maize and agricultural productivity partly account for differences among regions in the rate of development of complex society. [BLS]

302 Hammond, Norman. Ancient Maya civilization. New Brunswick, N.J.: Rutgers University Press, 1982. 337p.: bibl., ill., index.

General book, with an archaeological emphasis, concentrates on settlement, economic and social data with some consideration of architecture, art, and iconography. [NH]

303 ———. Classic Maya canoes (International Journal of Nautical Archaeology [Seminar Press, London] 10, 1981, p. 173–185)

Survey of models and depictions, used to reconstruct three classes of canoe of differing lengths. [NH]

304 Hartung, Horst. La arquitectura en Oaxaca de sus inicios hasta el postclásico: pts. 1/2 (Historia del Arte Mexicano [Salvat Mexicana de Ediciones, México] 4, 1982, p. 65–80; 5, 1982, p. 81–93, bibl., ill.)

Up-to-date and well illustrated (in color) synthesis of habitational and ceremonial architecture in the greater Valley of Oaxaca, from 1400 BC to conquest. [HvW]

305 ——— and **Anthony F. Aveni.** El Palacio del Gobernador en Uxmal: su trazo, orientación y referencia astronómica (Boletín de la Escuela de Ciencias Antropológicas de la Universidad de Yucatán [Mérida, México] 52, 1982, p. 3–11)

Discusses factors governing position and alignment of this structure. [NH]

306 **Hatch, Marion Popenoe.** The identification of rulers at Quirigua (Journal of New World Archaeology [Institute of Archaeology, University of California, Los Angeles] 5:1, 1982, p. 1–9)

Suggests new names for several Quirigua rulers, and that marriage rather than war was the basis of the strong relationship with Copan. [NH]

307 **Heikamp, Detlef.** Mexico und die Medici-Herzöge (in Mythen der Neuen Welt. Karl-Heinz Kohl, editor [see item **256**] p. 126–146, bibl., ill., plates)

Account of prehispanic and early colonial art from Mexico collected by the Medici family in the 16th century, and of other contemporary collections in Europe. [HvW]

308 **Henderson, John S.** The world of the ancient Maya. Ithaca, N.Y.: Cornell University Press, 1981. 271 p., 8 leaves of plates: bibl., ill. (some col.), index.

General book, with an up-to-date perspective and intelligent use of comparative Mesoamerican data. [NH]

309 **Hirth, Kenneth.** Eastern Morelos and Teotihuacan: a settlement survey. Nashville: Vanderbilt University, 1980. 193 p.: appendixes, bibl., ill., maps, tables (Publications in anthropology; 25)

Survey and surface collection of the Rio Amatzinac area documents settlement patterns before and after Teotihuacan takeover. The drainage is defined as a sustaining area in which Teotihuacan control increased the proportion of population in rural areas. [BLS]

310 ——— and **Jorge Angulo Villaseñor.** Early state expansion in central Mexico: Teotihuacan in Morelos (Journal of Field Archaeology [Boston University, Association for Field Archaeology] 8:2, Summer 1981, p. 135–150, maps, tables)

Compares Rio Amatzinac and Coatlan regions in Morelos concerning artifactual and settlement pattern changes associated with the Teotihuacan horizon. Suggests centralization of authority and intensification of agriculture for former region, decentralization and dispersion of population for latter. [BLS]

311 **Interacción cultural en México central.** Evelyn Childs Rattray, Jaime Litvak King, and Clara Díaz Oyárzabal, compilers. México: Universidad Nacional Autónoma de México, Instituto de Investigaciones Antropológicas, Arqueología, 1981. 221 p.: bibl., ill., maps, plates (Serie Antropológica; 41)

Fifteen papers cover: 1) general issues in ceramic analysis; 2) ceramic chronologies at Chalcatzingo, Tetelpan, and Loma Torremonte in the preclassic, and 3) at Los Teteles de Ocotitla, Xochicalco, and Ojo de Agua in the classic period. Other topics related to classic Teotihuacan are fine orange as a trade ware and the Teotihuacan presence in Morelos, around Tepeapulco, and the Tula area (including the Teotihuacan-Oaxacan populations there). Commerce in Veracruz and the Cacaxtla and Tula chronologies are also treated. [BLS]

312 **International Congress of Americanists,** *43rd, Vancouver, Canada, 1979.* Proceedings of the Symposium Space and Time in the Cosmovision of Mesoamerica. Edited by Franz Tichy. München, FRG: Wilhelm Fink Verlag, 1982. 196 p.: bibl., ill. (Universität Erlangen-Nürnberg. Lateinamerikanische Studien; 10)

Contains 11 articles including one on archaeology by Anthony F. Aveni and Horst Hartung "New Observations of the Pecked Cross Petroglyph" (p. 25–41). Their preliminary conclusion is that these petroglyphs may have served "to define another set of Teotihuacan axes: the true cardinal directions." [HvW]

313 **Jones, Christopher** and **Robert J. Sharer.** Archaeological investigations in the site core of Quirigua: epigraphic and archaeological data now provide evidence of an occupation history spanning half a millennium (UMUP/E, 23:1, Fall 1980, p. 11–19, ill., photos)

Discussion of architectural and monumental correlations. [NH]

315 King, Mary Elizabeth. The prehistoric textile industry of Mesoamerica (*in* The Junius B. Bird Pre-Columbian Textile Conference, Washington, D.C. May 19th and 20th, 1973. Edited by Ann Pollard Rowe, Elizabeth P. Benson, and Anne-Louise Schaffer. Washington: The Textile Museum and Dumbarton Oaks, Trustees for Harvard University, 1979, p. 265–278, bibl., ill., table)

Compares textiles from Oaxaca and other areas in Mesoamerica with Andean textiles. Most Mesoamerican samples are from preceramic caves or from postclassic contexts. Good descriptions and illustrations of basketry, net, and cloth remains. [SL]

316 Köhler, Ulrich. Räumliche und zeitliche Bezugspunkte in mesoamerikanischen Konzepten vom Mondzyklus (IAI/I, 7:2, 1982, p. 23–42, bibl., table)

Following compilation of data on Mesoamerican lunar cycle, author presents new data from three Tzotzil communities in Chiapas that substantially supplement ethnohistorical sources concerning subdivision of lunar phases and their relation to other celestial bodies. [HvW]

317 Kowalewski, Stephen A. Population-resource balances in Period I of Oaxaca, Mexico (SAA/AA, 45:1, Jan. 1980, p. 151–165, bibl., ill., maps, tables)

Period I population levels in Oaxaca were insufficient to constitute population pressure. Population is not distributed closely in accordance with land productivity. Variable rainfall and agricultural risk may have fostered exchange. [BLS]

318 Laporte Molina, Juan Pedro. Bibliografía de la arqueología guatemalteca. Guatemala: Ediciones de la Dirección General de Antropología e Historia, 1981. 1 v.: bibl. (Publicación extraordinaria. Dirección General de Antropología e Historia. Colección Arqueología)

Useful listing of publications by authors with names beginning A-I, up to 1979, generally inclusive but with curious omissions. [NH]

319 Lewenstein, Suzanne. Mesoamerican obsidian blades: an experimental approach to function (Journal of Field Archae-ology [Associaton for Field Archaeology, Boston University] 8:2, Summer 1981, p. 175–188, bibl., ill., tables)

Discusses results of experimental utilization of obsidian blades to perform tasks basic to lowland Mesoamerican subsistence. Use-damage is described, and serves as a basis for inferring functions of classic period tools from Patarata 52, coastal Veracruz, Mexico. Includes discussion of low vs. high magnification in lithic analysis. [SL]

320 Lish, Lawrence R. Distribution of southern lowland Maya ceremonial centers (UNC/K, 11:2, June 1979, p. 52–70, tables)

Suggests use of cardinal and intercardinal axes for layout of lowland centers; assumes that distribution is on a "preconceived, long-ranged planning program which permeated the Maya culture from the smallest to the largest ceremonial center." Speculative and unconvincing. [NH]

321 Littmann, Edwin R. Maya blue: further perspectives and the possible use of indigo as the colorant (SAA/AA, 47, 1982, p. 404–408)

Elegant experiments provide overwhelming proof that indigo fixed in attapulgite clay by heating is the source of Maya blue pigment. [NH]

322 Lorenzo, José L. Archaeology south of the Rio Grande (World Archaeology [Routledge & Kegan Paul, London] 13:2, Oct. 1981, p. 190–208, bibl.)

Contrasts differences in archaeology in North America, Europe, and Mexico. The goal of Mexican archaeology is to instill national identity and pride in the past. [SL]

323 Lowe, John W.G. On mathematical models of the classic Maya collapse: the class conflict hypothesis reexamined (SAA/AA, 47:3, July 1982, p. 643–652, tables)

Criticizes the mathematical base for Hamblin and Pitcher's model of the collapse (see *HLAS 43:280*), while not dismissing their peasant-revolt explanation. [NH]

324 Luckenbach, Alvin H. and **Richard S. Levy.** The implications of Nahua, Aztecan, lexical diversity for Mesoamerica culture-history (SAA/AA, 45:3, July 1980, p. 455–461, bibl., ill., maps, table)

Glottochronological analysis of 25 communilects in the Nahua branch of Uto-Aztecan establishes seven modes of separation for which the dates seem to correspond to plausible historical circumstances. [BLS]

325   McClung de Tapia, Emily. Ecología y cultura en Mesoamérica. México: Universidad Nacional Autónoma de México, 1979. 110 p., 2 leaves of plates: bibl., ill. (Serie Antropológica; 30. Cuadernos—Instituto de Investigaciones Antropológicas)

Concise historical introduction to issues in Mesoamerican ecological studies emphasizes those pertinent to agricultural populations. Focuses on environmental and agricultural characteristics of Teotihuacan, Monte Alban, and Tikal in relation to urbanism and political growth and decline. Concludes social factors may play a greater role than ecological ones. [BLS]

326   MacNeish, Richard S. Tehuacan's accomplishments (*in* Archaeology. Edited by Jeremy A. Sabloff and Patricia A. Andrews. Austin: University of Texas Press, 1981, p. 41–37, bibl., ill., map, table [Supplement to the *Handbook of Middle American Indians*; v. 1])

Recapitulates the results of Tehuacan research in substantive discoveries, theoretical ideas, and interdisciplinary methods. [BLS]

327   Markman, Charles W. Prehispanic settlement dynamics in Central Oaxaca, Mexico: a view from the Miahuatlan Valley. Nashville: Vanderbilt University, 1981. 184 p.: bibl., ill., maps, tables (Publications in anthropology; no. 26)

Survey provided settlement pattern data which is analyzed in comparison to the then-available Valley of Oaxaca patterns. This subsidiary valley was near but marginal to political developments in the Valley of Oaxaca. [BLS]

328   Maya subsistence: studies in memory of Dennis E. Puleston. Edited by Kent V. Flannery. New York: Academic Press, 1982. 368 p.: bibl., ill., index (Studies in archaeology)

Consists of 14 papers, mainly on aspects of ancient Maya agriculture, in memory of a talented and much-missed colleague who stimulated this aspect of Maya studies enormously in the 1960s and 1970s. [NH]

329   Michels, Joseph W. Bulk element composition versus trace element composition in the reconstruction of an obsidian source system (Journal of Archaeological Science [Academic Press, London] 9, 1982, p. 113–123)

Using El Chayal, Guatemala, as example, argues for use of cheaper bulk-element analyses where possible. [NH]

330   Monte Alban's hinterland. Richard E. Blanton *et al*. With contributions by Laura Finsten and Eva Fisch. Ann Arbor: Regents of the University of Michigan, Museum of Anthropology, 1982- . 506 p.: appendixes, bibl., ill., maps, tables (Prehistory and human ecology of the Valley of Oaxaca; v. 7. Memoirs of the Museum of Anthropology, University of Michigan; no. 15)

Survey of the central and southern portions of the valley reveals changing regional settlement patterns, demography, land use, and economy spanning rise and demise of Monte Alban as capital. Theoretical approach to interpretation emphasizes complex interactions among geographic, economic, demographic, and political factors. [BLS]

331   Murdy, Carson N. Congenital deformities and the Olmec were-jaguar motif (SAA/AA, 46:4, Oct. 1981, p. 861–871, bibl., ill.)

Olmec iconography is viewed as, in part, a representation of multifactorial neural tube defects. [BLS]

332   Nava Rodríguez, Luis. Tlaxcala prehispánica: de 800 años antes de Cristo hasta 1518 de la era cristiana. Tlaxcala, México: s.n., 1976. 372 p.: bibl., ill.

Joint Mexican-German Puebla-Tlaxcala Project deals with Tlaxcala from Olmec times up to Spanish conquest. Also recounts discovery of fluted Clovis point in central Tlaxcala. [SL]

333   O'Brien, Michael J. *et al*. A late formative irrigation settlement below Monte Albán: survey and excavation on the Xoxocotlán Piedmont, Oaxaca, Mexico. Austin: University of Texas, Institute of Latin American Studies, 1982. 240 p.: maps, plates, tables.

Reports on survey, surface collections, and a few test excavations of irrigation features and occupation in the Xoxocotlán area near Monte Alban. Occupation was primarily

Period I. Contains useful commentary on surface collection methods and biases (see item **489**). [BLS]

334 Offner, Jerome A. On the inapplicability of "oriental despotism" and the "Asiatic mode of production" to the Aztecs of Mexico (SAA/AA, 46:1, Jan. 1981, p. 43–61, bibl., tables)

Argues the Texcocan state was not formed on the basis of irrigation control, that there were private landholdings, and that the state did not dominate the economy (marketing was the principal economic mechanism). Hence Marx's and Wittfogel's typologies are inapplicable. [BLS]

335 The Olmec & their neighbors: essays in memory of Matthew W. Stirling. Michael D. Coe and David Grove, organizers. Elizabeth P. Benson, editor. Washington: Dumbarton Oaks Research Library and Collections, Trustees for Harvard University, 1981. 346 p.: bibl., ill.

Consists of 20 papers on Olmec ecology that compare Olmec centers, describe sites affected by Olmecs, and analyze iconography, style and distributions of Olmec goods. [BLS]

336 Ortiz de Montellano, Bernardo R. El canibalismo azteca: ¿una necesidad ecológica? (UNAM/AA, 16, 1979, p. 155–182, bibl., table)

Disputes Harner's argument that cannibalism was necessary for protein consumption. Estimates amount of food Aztecs received as tribute and yields of intensive agriculture. Sees no correlation between scheduling of mass human sacrifices and periods of food scarcity, according to ethnohistoric accounts. [SL]

337 Parsons, Jeffrey R.; Elizabeth Brumfiel; Mary H. Parsons; and David J. Wilson. Prehispanic settlement patterns in the southern Valley of Mexico: the Chalco-Xochimilco Region. Ann Arbor: University of Michigan, 1982. 504 p.: appendixes, bibl., ill., maps, plates, tables (Memoirs of the Museum of Anthropology; 14)

Reports on prehistoric survey results period by period. Also provides extremely useful analysis of post-conquest settlement and demography plus review of ethnohistoric data. Discusses survey methodology more

amply than in prior monographs. Detailed site descriptions and coverage of ceramic markers provide main data. [BLS]

338 Pendergast, David M. Ancient Maya mercury (AAAS/S, 217, 1982, p. 533–535)

Reports on cache with liquid mercury at Lamanai and examines sources and comparative material. [NH]

339 Perera, Victor and **Roberto D. Bruce S.** The last lords of Palenque: the Lacandon Mayas of the Mexican rain forest. Boston: Little, Brown, 1982. 311 p.: ill.

Chatty popular book with useful details and photos. [NH]

340 Peterson, David A. and **Thomas B. Mac Dougall.** Guiengola: a fortified site in the Isthmus of Tehuantepec. Nashville: Vanderbilt University, 1974. 69 p.: bibl., ill., maps, plates (Publications in anthropology; 10)

Short monograph on an important postclassic site, with processual explanation couched in terms of a trade-control model. Notable Central Mexican features in site planning. [NH]

341 Pollard, Helen Perlstein. Central places and cities: a consideration of the protohistoric Tarascan state (SAA/AA, 45:4, 1980, p. 677–696, bibl., maps, tables)

Tarascan centers in the Patzcuaro Basin are compared diachronically. Functionally complex urban capital at Tzintzuntzan is late, associated with establishment of unified Tarascan state, perhaps in response to outside political and military pressure. Outside Tzintzuntzan the regional settlement has non-congruent civic-ceremonial and economic settlement lattices. [BLS]

342 ———. Ecological variation and economic exchange in the Tarascan state (AAA/AE, 9:2, May 1982, p. 250–268, bibl., maps, tables)

Analyzes role of commoner market exchange and state controlled asymmetrical exchange in late postclassic Tarascan state. Demographic, dietary, and land use calculations indicate nutritional deficits in central area. Rising lake level is proposed as earlier environmental trigger of elite-motivated warfare and ensuing political centralization. [BLS]

343 —— and **Shirley Gorenstein.** Agrarian potential, population, and the Tarascan state (AAAS/S, 209:4453, 11 July 1980, p. 274–277, bibl., map, tables)

Modern land classes and other estimators provide a basis to estimate the productive potential of the Lake Patzcuaro Basin. Maize importation through tribute and markets is implied by the figures. [BLS]

344 **Robicsek, Francis.** *The Maya Book of the Dead, The Ceramic Codex:* the corpus of codex style ceramics of the late classic period. Comments on the hieroglyphic text by Donald M. Hales. Charlottesville: University of Virginia Art Museum, 1981. 257 p.: bibl., ill., map, tables.

Publication of numerous pottery vessels painted in "Maya" style, but of uncertain authenticity. [NH]

345 **Rutas de intercambio en Mesoamérica y norte de México** (*in* Mesa Redonda de la Sociedad Mexicana de Antropología, 16th, Saltillo, Coahuila, 9–14 de septiembre 1979. Mesa Redonda. Saltillo, México: Sociedad Mexicana de Antropología, 1980, p. 460, bibl., ill., maps, tables)

Includes several dozen short articles pertaining to archaeology. Topics include colonial history, exchange of metal, 16th-century tribute records, migrations in the Basin of Mexico, archaeology of Toluca, Morelos, north and west Mexico. [SL]

346 **Sanders, William T.** Ecological adaptation in the Basin of Mexico: 23,000 B.C. to the present (*in* Archaeology. Edited by Jeremy A. Sabloff and Patricia A. Andrews. Austin: University of Texas Press, 1981, p. 147–197, bibl., ill., maps, tables [Supplement to the *Handbook of Latin American Indians;* v. 1])

Highlights of an earlier book; has period by period analyses primarily of settlement patterns, with useful clear reductions of the original maps. [BLS]

347 ——; **Jeffrey R. Parsons;** and **Robert S. Santley.** The Basin of Mexico: ecological processes in the evolution of a civilization. New York: Academic Press, 1979. 561 p.: bibl., ill., maps, plates (Studies in archaeology)

Culmination of 15-year Basin of Mexico project. Traces development of increasingly complex socioeconomic systems from cultural materialist perspective. Emphasizes importance of population growth and irrigation agriculture. Includes set of large-scale maps showing resources and phase-by-phase settlement distributions. [SL]

348 **Santley, Robert S.** Disembedded capitals reconsidered (SAA/AA, 45:1, Jan. 1980, p. 132–145, bibl., table)

Disputes idea that Monte Alban was a "disembedded capital." Argues that population growth, agricultural intensification and other materialist factors favor an ecological explanation for the city's founding and growth. [BLS]

349 ——. Pricing policies, obsidian exchange, and the decline of Teotihuacan civilization (Mexicon [K.-F. von Flemming, Berlin] 2, 1980, p. 77–81, bibl., map)

Attributes discriminatory pricing of obsidian to Teotihuacan, although no evidence for this is presented. City's decline is attributed to successful competition by other polities and loss of control over obsidian markets. [BLS]

350 —— and **Eric K. Rose.** Diet, nutrition and population dynamics in the Basin of Mexico (World Archaeology [Routledge & Kegan Paul, London] 11:2, Oct. 1979, p. 185–207, map, tables)

Speculative attempt to calculate supplies of dietary elements and their effects on population growth during ceramic sequence of the Valley of Mexico. Reviews links between nutrition, fertility, and disease. [BLS]

351 **Schávelzon, Daniel.** El complejo arqueológico Mixteca-Puebla: notas para una redefinición cultural. México: Universidad Nacional Autónoma de México, 1980. 65 p.: bibl.

Historical overview of Mixteca-Puebla complex. Concludes with evaluation of broad generalization about the complex (see item **353**). [BLS]

352 **Sheets, Payson D.** Volcanoes and the Maya (AMNH/NH, 90:8, Aug. 1981, p. 32–41, ill., map)

Popular article concentrates on important discoveries at Cerén, El Salvador, and impact of the Ilopango and Laguna Caldera eruptions. [NH]

353 **Smith, Michael E.** and **Cynthia M. Heath-Smith.** Waves of influence in postclassic Mesoamerica?: a critique of the Mixteca-Puebla concept (Anthropology [State University of New York, Stonybrook] 4:2, Dec. 1980, p. 15–50, bibl., ill.)

Argues that the "Mixteca-Puebla horizon" confounds: 1) postclassic religious style; 2) Mixtec codex style; and 3) Mixteca-Puebla regional ceramic sphere. However, 1) does not emanate from the "nuclear" Mixteca-Puebla area, 2) does. No. 1 illustrates importance of sea trade and interaction among Mesoamerican polities peripheral to central highlands, especially in early postclassic. (see item **351**). [BLS]

354 **Spence, Michael W.** The social context of production and exchange (*in* Contexts for prehistoric exchange. Edited by Jonathon E. Ericson and Timothy K. Earle. New York: Academic Press, 1982, p. 173–197, bibl., ill., tables [Studies in archaeology])

Comparison of Late Archaic and Early Woodland data in the northeastern US and preclassic and classic Mesoamerican data concerning exchange in exotics. New items in limited supply are seen as catalysts that changed some egalitarian exchange networks into hierarchically controlled ones. [BLS]

355 **Spencer, Charles S.** The Cuicatlán Cañada and Monte Alban: a study of primary state formation. New York: Academic Press, 1982. 326 p.: bibl., ill., index (Studies in archaeology)

Using preclassic record from excavations at La Coyotera and survey in Cañada, tests model for state origins at Monte Alban. Analyzes Monte Alban's conquest of the Cañada as a facet of that change, and emphasizes inter-regional prestige exchange. [BLS]

356 **Stark, Barbara L.** The rise of sedentary life (*in* Archaeology. Edited by Jeremy A. Sabloff and Patricia A. Andrews. Austin: University of Texas Press, 191, p. 345–372, bibl. [Supplement to the *Handbook of Middle American Indians*; v. 1])

Discussion of the Mesoamerican Paleoindian and Archaic records, with consideration of processes of change and explanatory frameworks. [BLS]

357 **Steponaitis, Vincas P.** Settlement hierarchies and political complexity in nonmarket societies: the formative period of the Valley of Mexico (AAA/AA, 83:2, June 1981, p. 320–363, bibl., ill., map, tables)

Analyzes possible tributary relations among settlements on the basis of settlement size and catchment productivity. Example case is Valley of Mexico in preclassic. [BLS]

358 **Stocker, Terry; Sarah Meltzoff;** and **Steve Armsey.** Crocodilians and Olmecs: further interpretations in formative period iconography (SAA/AA, 45:4, Oct. 1980, p. 740–758, bibl., ill.)

Suggests that frequent crocodilian depictions represent food, fertility, and abundance as well as indicating a resource exported by the Olmecs. [BLS]

359 **Taladoire, Eric.** Routes d'échanges entre la Mesoamérique et le sudouest des Etats-Unis (Bulletin [Mission archéologique et ethnologique française au Méxique] 3, 1981, p. 55–70, ill., map)

Indicates northward diffusion of ball courts and ball game along a coastal and an interior route during classic and postclassic periods. [HvW]

360 ———. Les terrain de jeu de balle: Mésoamérique et sud-ouest des Etats-Unis. Mexico: Mission archéologique et ethnologique française au Méxique, 1981. 733 p., 87 p. of plates (1 fold.): bibl., ill. (Etudes mésoaméricaines = Etudios mesoamericanos, 0378–5726; série II, 4)

Comprehensive coverage of different types of ball courts by regions and discussion of function, evolution, and symbolism of the ball game, from archaeological and ethnohistoric data. [HvW]

361 **Thomas, Prentice M.** Prehistoric Maya settlement: patterns at Becan, Campeche, Mexico. New Orleans, La.: Middle American Research Institute, Tulane University, 1981. 116 p.: bibl., ill., 23 fold maps (Publication / Middle American Research Institute, Tulane University; 45)

Excellent report, with good maps, on dense settlement around center prominent in late preclassic and late classic periods. Concludes that an "urban" level of population nucleation, size and differentiation existed in the late classic. Admirable addition to small corpus of Maya area settlement studies. [NH]

362 Tolstoy, Paul. Advances in the Basin of Mexico: pts. 1/4 (Quarterly Review of Archaeology [Williamstown, Mass.] 2:2, June 1981, p. 3–4, 6, bibl; 2:3, Sept. 1981, p. 3–4, bibl.; 2:4, Dec. 1981, p. 3–4, bibl.; 3:1, March 1982, p. 8–9, bibl.)

Four-part, detailed critique of three quantitative studies concerning Valley of Mexico settlement patterns. Discusses results of nearest neighbor analysis, catchment analysis, and political interaction unit definition. [BLS]

363 ———. Advances in the Valley of Oaxaca: pts. 1/2 (Quarterly Review of Archaeology [Williamstown, Mass.] 3:3, Sept. 1982, p. 1, 8–11, bibl.; 3:4, Dec. 1982, p. 13–16, bibl.)

Detailed critique of three studies which draw on results of Oaxaca survey. Concentrates on demography in relation to land use and agricultural productivity. [BLS]

364 The Transition to statehood in the New World. Edited by Grant D. Jones and Robert R. Kautz. New York: Cambridge University Press, 1981. 254 p.: bibl., ill., index (New directions in archaeology)

Conference volume of mixed quality, with seven papers and introduction that synthesizes and disputes many points raised by authors of papers. Introduction and Carneiro's discussion of the chiefdom as precursor of the state are the most cogent contributions, MacNeish's the most ambitious. [NH]

365 Turner, B.L. II and **Peter D. Harrison.** Prehistoric raised-field agriculture in the Maya lowlands (AAAS/S, 213, 1981, p. 399–405)

Channelized and raised fields in Pulltrouser Swamp, northern Belize, were constructed and used in the late formative through late classic periods. Similar ground patterns in other wetlands suggest widespread occurrence of similar fields. [NH]

366 Weaver, Muriel Porter. The Aztecs, Maya, and their predecessors: archaeology of Mesoamerica. 2. ed. New York: Academic Press, 1981. 597 p.: bibl., ill., indexes, map and chart on lining papers (Studies in archaeology)

Text emphasizes updated, comprehensive culture-history of diverse regions and pays less attention to explanation and processes of change. Pre-ceramic coverage is more substantial in this edition. Overall, most detailed and recent overview of Mesoamerican data. [BLS]

367 Wilhelmy, Herbert. Welt and Umwelt der Maya; Aufstieg und Untergang einer Hochkultur. Munich, FRG: Piper Verlag, 1981. 541 p.: bibl., ill., index, maps, plates, tables.

Assessment of rise and fall of Lowland Maya in terms of their adaptation to natural environment. From vantage point of geographer-ecologist, author discusses farming methods, settlement patterns, ceremonial centers, population estimates, and trade, drawing parallels from worldwide cultures. Includes critical evaluations of current concepts. [HvW]

368 Wilkerson, S. Jeffrey K. Eastern Mesoamerica from prehispanic to colonial times: a model of cultural continuance (in International Congress of Americanists, 42nd, Paris, 1976. Actes [see *HLAS 43:255*] v. 8, p. 41–55, bibl., ill., maps)

Archaeological and ethnohistorical data indicate ethnic boundaries, Huastecan depopulation during the 16th century, and long-term Totonac migration to fill coastal fishing and salt-trading niches. [SL]

369 Willey, Gordon R. The concept of the "disembedded capital" in comparative perspective (UNM/JAR, 35:2, Summer 1979, p. 123–137, bibl.)

Asks whether Blanton's concept of a disembedded capital in early state formation at Monte Alban is applicable to other areas during state origins. Doubts it applies to Maya area, Peru, Mesopotamia, or China. Treatment of evidence from these regions is cursory. [BLS]

370 ———. Recent researches and perspectives in Mesoamerican archaeology: an introductory commentary (in Archaeology. Edited by Jeremy A. Sabloff and Patricia A. Andrews. Austin: University of Texas Press, 1981, p. 3–27, bibl. [Supplement to the *Handbook of Middle American Indians*; v. 1])

Summarizes and provides contextual remarks for other Mesoamerican essays in the volume. [BLS]

371 **Zeitlin, Robert N.** Toward a more comprehensive model of interregional commodity distribution: political variables and prehistoric obsidian procurement in Mesoamerica (SAA/AA, 47:2, April 1982, p. 260–275, bibl., ill., map)

As seen diachronically in the southern Isthmus of Tehuantepec, long-distance obsidian distribution reveals that simple distance-decay models have little utility when marked shifts in social and political factors affected inter-regional relations. [BLS]

EXCAVATIONS AND ARTIFACTS

372 **Adams, R.E.W.** and **Norman Hammond.** Maya archaeology, 1976–1980: a review of major publications (Journal of Field Archaeology [Association for Field Archaeology, Boston University] 9:4, Winter 1982, p. 487–512)

Evaluation of monographs and books by region, and of further publications including significant journal articles, by topic. [NH]

373 **Alcina Franch, José.** Agua Tibia: un poblado clásico tardío en Totonicapan (IAHG/AHG, 2:2, 1980, p. 231–244, bibl., ill.)

Fourth season excavation, near Quetzaltenango, of three masonry peasant dwellings, an unusual sweat bath, open kiln, with abundant bichrome lacquer ware, San Juan plumbate ware, and obsidian artifacts. [HvW]

374 **Andrews, Anthony P.** Historical archaeology in Yucatan: a preliminary framework (Historical Archaeology [Society for Historical Archaeology, Bethlehem, Pa.] 15, 1981, p. 1–18)

New approach to a neglected period in the archaeology of the Maya area. [NH]

375 **Andrews, E. Wyllys IV** and **E. Wyllys Andrews V.** Excavations at Dzibil-chaltun, Yucatan, Mexico. With an appendix on vertebrate faunal remains by Elizabeth S. Wing and David Steadman. Jennifer S.H. Brown, editor. New Orleans: Middle American Research Institute, Tulane University, 1980. 339 p., 2 fold. leaves of plates; appendixes, bibl., ill. (Publication / Middle American Research Institute, Tulane University; 48)

Fine completion by E. Wyllys Andrews V of the work by EWA IV, at major preclassic and late classic site in arid zone of northeast Yucatan. Complements Kurjack's settlement pattern study (*HLAS 37:643*) and Stuart *et al*'s maps (*HLAS 43:392*). [NH]

376 **Andrews, E. Wyllys V.** Dzibilchaltun (*in* Archaeology. Edited by Jeremy A. Sabloff and Patricia A. Andrews. Austin: University of Texas Press, 1981, p. 313–341, bibl., ill., map [Supplement to the *Handbook of Middle American Indians*; v. 1])

Period-by-period summary of history of this center with remarks about its place in larger configuration of Maya events. [BLS]

377 **Arnauld, Marie Charlotte.** Arqueología de la Alta Verapaz occidental: sociedad y patrones de asentamiento (IAHG/AHG, 2:2, 1980, p. 21–53, bibl., maps, tables)

Brief summary of settlement pattern study of region south of Coban, Alta Verapaz, from preclassic to postclassic periods, and incorporating colonial documentary evidence. Full study is a University of Paris dissertation, in French. [NH]

378 **Ashmore, Wendy.** The classic Maya settlement at Quirigua: recent agricultural activities have helped reveal the extent of the buried settlement (UMUP/E, 23:1, Fall 1980, p. 20–27, map, photos)

Describes use of fortuitously-cut drainage ditches to sample classic period settlement buried by the Motagua silts. [NH]

379 ———. Discovering early classic Quirigua: a unique opportunity to examine an important sector of the early center (UMUP/E, 23:1, Fall 1980, p. 35–44, ill., photos)

Description of important early evidence on the Quirigua settlement revealed in regularly spaced drainage ditches (see also item **378**, on the late classic settlement). [NH]

380 **Aveni, Anthony F.** and **Horst Hartung.** The cross petroglyph: an ancient Mesoamerican astronomical and calendrical symbol (IAI/I, 6, 1980, p. 37–54, bibl., ill.)

Quartered circle designs (or pecked crosses) near Teotihuacan and at Alta Vista, just south of the Tropic of Cancer, suggest 5th century attempts by Teotihuacanos "to practice scientific astronomy and develop a calendar." [HvW]

381 ———; ———; and **J. Charles Kelley.** Alta Vista, Chalchihuites: astronomical implications of a Mesoamerican ceremonial outpost at the Tropic of Cancer (SAA/AA, 47:2, April 1982, p. 316–335, bibl., ill., map, tables)

Argues that alignments of buildings at center and nearby pecked circles indicate an astronomical function. Tenuous argument for Teotihuacan intrusion affecting the center. [BLS]

382 **Ball, Joseph W.** A note on the ceramic history of Moho Cay, Belize, Central America (TU/CCM, 12, 1982, p. 49–55)

Ceramics from a small islet off the mouth of the Belize River demonstrate a major occupation in the middle classic, AD 400–750, with preceding late formative and succeeding early postclassic use at a lower level of organization. Site is important maritime trade locus (see item **394**). [NH]

383 **Barrera Rubio, Alfredo.** Patrón de asentamiento en al área de Uxmal, Yucatán, México (*in* Instituto Nacional de Antropología e Historia, México. Centro Regional del Sureste. Congreso Interno, Mérida, Yucatán, 1979. Memoria. México: INAH, 1981, p. 83–98, bibl., ill.)

Brief report on the environment and structure types. Test pits show occupation in the late formative and terminal classic periods. [NH]

384 **Baus Reed Czitrom, Carolyn.** Figurillas sólidas de estilo Colima: una tipología. México: Instituto Nacional de Antropología e Historia, Departamento de Investigaciones Históricas, 1978. 110 p.: bibl., ill. (Colección científica / SEP INAH, Instituto Nacional de Antropología e Historia; 66. Arqueología)

Examines sample of 400 west Mexican figurines of unknown provenience for anatomical and costume variations as well as for technological and stylistic differences. Typology, which orders artifacts spatially and temporally from 500 BC until conquest, agrees with placement of other dateable figurines. [SL]

385 **Beadle, George W.** The ancestry of corn (SA, 242:1, Jan. 1980, p. 112–119, bibl., ill., map)

Readable summary of botanical and genetic arguments in favor of teosinte as the ancestor of corn. [BLS]

386 ———. Origin of corn: pollen evidence (AAAS/S, 213:451, 21 Aug. 1981, p. 890–892, bibl., tables)

Teosinte, still disputed as possible ancestor of corn, can develop tetraploidy under some environmental conditions. Pollen grains from such plants are twice the size of the regular wild state and may account for very early (25,000–80,000 BP), large "corn" pollen in Mexico City cores. [BLS]

387 **Becquelin, Pierre** and **Claude F. Baudez.** Tonina, una cité maya du Chiapas, Mexique. Avec la collaboration de Marie Charlotte Arnauld *et al.* México: Mission archéologique et ethnologique française au Mexique, 1979–1982. 3 v. (1456 p.): bibl., ill., 1 fold. map in pocket (Etudes mésoaméricaines; v. 6)

Vol. 2 of extensive site report includes: 1) unique sculpture, midway between Palenque and Pacific coast in style, and donor of some Pacific and Highland traits to Palenque; 2) discussion of regional environment and settlement pattern; and 3) description and analysis of stone and pottery artifacts and other objects, including a fine series of late classic figurines. Vol. 3 contains illustrations for previous two parts (for vol. 1, see *HLAS 43:318*). [NH]

388 **Benavides Castillo, Antonio.** La distribución del asentamiento prehispánico en Coba, Quintana Roo: observaciones generales (*in* Instituto Nacional de Antropología e Historia, México. Centro Regional del Sureste. Congreso Interno, Mérida, Yucatán, 1979. Memoria. México: INAH, 1981, p. 83–98, bibl., ill.)

Description of environment and some residence types, together with a postulated concentric-zone model for the settlement structure of Coba. [NH]

389 ———. La gruta de Xcan, Yucatán, sitio de enterramientos prehispánicos (Mexicon [K.-F. von Flemming, Berlin] 5:2, March 1983, p. 32–36, bibl., ill.)

Cave was used as secondary burial sites, associated with early classic pottery. Same issue includes Alain Ichon's "Die Grabungskampagne 1981/82 am Rio Chixoy in Guatemala" (p. 36–37, ill.), French Mission's report on final season. Results of entire project will be published by Mission in *Archeologie de sauvetage . . .* [HvW]

390 Benson, Elizabeth P. Symbolic objects in Maya art (Mexicon [K.-F. von Flemming, Berlin] 4:3, July 1982, p. 45–47, bibl., ill.)

An encased cluster of quetzal feathers on Piedras Negras sculptures probably symbolizes transference of royal power. [HvW]

391 Boksenbaum, Martin W. Basic Meso-american stone-working: nodule smashing? (Lithic Technology [Center for Archaeological Research, University of Texas, San Antonio] 9:1, Aug. 1980, p. 12–26, bibl., ill.)

Crude tool-making tradition prevailed in Basin of Mexico during early and middle preclassic times. Includes descriptive typology and tabulation of artifacts. Hypothesizes that early farming communities made most tools by simple nodule smashing, while few prismatic blades were imported. [SL]

392 Brüggemann, Jürgen K. Estudios estratigráficos en Tlapacoya, Estado de México: una visión dinámica de la cerámica arqueológica. México: SEP, Instituto Nacional de Antropología e Historia, Departamento de Monumentos Prehispánicos, 1978. 80 p.: bibl., ill., map, tables (Colección científica; 59. Arqueología)

Describes ceramics from test excavations. Includes ceramic counts, analysis, and comparisons with known preclassic pottery from Valley of Mexico. Brief reference to middle and late preclassic agricultural terraces. [SL]

393 Bruhns, Karen Olsen. Two early postclassic caches from El Salvador (TU/CCM, 12, 1982, p. 1–10)

Discusses offerings from Cihuatan. [NH]

394 ——— and Norman Hammond. A Maya metal-worker's tool from Belize (AT/A, 56, 1982, p. 175–180)

Discussion of albite object from Moho Cay concludes that it is a hammer for working sheet metal, probably of early postclassic date (see item 382). [NH]

395 Cabrero G., María Teresa. Un área rural en la perifería de Tenochtitlan:

estudio arqueológico (UNAM/AA, 16, 1979, p. 21–33, bibl., ill., maps)

Consists of preliminary results of archaeological survey in area of Topilejo. Describes distribution of settlements during postclassic period. [SL]

396 Cedillo Alvarez, Luciano and Gabriela García Lascurain. La conservación de los mascarones de estuco en la zona arqueológica de Kohunlich, Quintana Roo (in Instituto Nacional de Antropología e Historia, México. Centro Regional del Sureste. Congreso Interno, Mérida, Yucatán, 1979. Memoria. México: INAH, 1981, p. 245–253, bibl., plates)

Silica-based, water-repellent compound was used to repair damage to stucco masks caused by salt efflorescence. [NH]

397 Charlton, Thomas H. The Aztec-early colonial transition in the Teotihuacan Valley (in International Congress of Americanists, 42nd, Paris, 1976. Actes [see *HLAS 43:255*] v. 8, p. 199–208, bibl., tables)

Discusses trends in ceramics (1500–1810) in eastern Teotihuacan Valley. Conquest had differential impact on precolumbian trade, cooking technique and religion. [SL]

398 Chase, Diane Z. The Maya postclassic at Santa Rita Corozal (AIA/A, 34:1, Jan./Feb. 1981, p. 34–43)

Popular illustrated account of field work. [NH]

399 ——— and Norman Hammond. Excavation of Nohmul Structure 20 (Mexicon [K.-F. von Flemming, Berlin] 4:1, March 1982, p. 7–12)

Reports on excavation of Yucatec-style building in northern Belize, carried out in 1978, with additional comparison to similar structures excavated at Nohmul in 1973–74. [NH]

400 Clark, John E. Guatemalan obsidian sources and quarries: additional notes (Journal of New World Archaeology [Institute of Archaeology, University of California, Los Angeles] 4:3, 1981, p. 1–15)

Discusses reduction sequence seen in quarry débris at several sources. [NH]

401 ———. A specialized obsidian quarry at Otumba, Mexico: implications for the study of Mesoamerican obsidian technology and trade (Lithic Technology [Center for Archaeological Research, University of Texas, San Antonio] 8 : 3, Dec. 1979, p. 46–49, bibl.)

Contrasts evidence of biface production at Otumba (near Teotihuacan) with prismatic blade manufacture at Pachuca and other Mesoamerican obsidian quarries. Emphasizes technological attributes combined with source analysis for reconstructing prehistoric exchange and political hegemony. [SL]

402 Coe, Michael D. San Lorenzo Tenochtitlan (*in* Archaeology. Edited by Jeremy A. Sabloff and Patricia A. Andrews. Austin: University of Texas Press, 1981, p. 117–146, bibl., ill., maps, table [Supplement to the *Handbook of Middle American Indians*; v. 1])

Provides overview of dating, pottery, monuments, site pattern, and ecology during the Olmec sequence. [BLS]

403 ———— and Richard A. Diehl. In the land of the Olmec. v. 1, The archaeology of San Lorenzo Tenochtitlan. v. 2, The people of the river. Austin: University of Texas Press, 1980. 2 v. (416, 198 p.): appendixes, bibl., ill., index, maps, tables (The Dan Danciger publication series)

Comprehensive report of archaeological investigation at Olmec site, San Lorenzo Tenochtitlan and of modern ecological and pottery studies in surrounding area. Archaeology volume describes excavations, pottery, lithics, other artifacts, carved monuments, and fauna and then reconstructs Olmec lifeways. Ethnographic volume uses photogrammetry to study soils and vegetation. The modern agriculture, hunting, and gathering patterns have riverine focus and provide model for prehistoric Olmec. [BLS]

404 Coe, William R. and William A. Haviland. Introduction to the archaeology of Tikal, Guatemala. Philadelphia: University Museum, University of Pennsylvania, 1982. 1 v.: bibl. (University Museum monograph; 46. Tikal report; no. 12)

Provides background and bibliography to introduce long-delayed final report on major Maya project of 1950s and 1960s. Stylis-

tically elliptical, but necessary guide to extant and forthcoming literature on Tikal. [NH]

405 Crespo Oviedo, Ana María. Villa de Reyes, SLP: un núcleo agrícola en la frontera norte de Mesoamérica. México: SEP, Instituto Nacional de Antropología e Historia, Departamento de Monumentos Prehispánicos, 1976. 125 p.: bibl., ill. (Colección científica—Instituto Nacional de Antropología e Historia; 42. Arqueología)

Hypothesizes migrations from Mesoamerica into this northern frontier zone as explanation for shifts in subsistence practices through time (hunting-gathering to agriculture and vice-versa). Includes good description of ceramic, lithic, and historic artifacts and their distributions. Also discusses external influences. [SL]

406 Daneels, Annick. La estela de Rincón del Copite, Municipio de Medellín, Ver. (Cuadernos de los Centros Regionales [Centro Regional de Veracruz, INAH, México] 2, 1982, p. 27–36, bibl., ill.)

Description of a postclassic monument with two carved calendar signs and dot numerals. [HvW]

407 Dávila C., Patricio. Las escaleras jeroglíficas de Resbalón: Quintana Roo (*in* Instituto Nacional de Antropología e Historia, México. Centro Regional del Sureste. Congreso Interno, Mérida, Yucatán, 1979. Memoria. México: INAH, 1981, p. 199–202)

Brief summary of the discovery of three hieroglyphic stairways at a site near Bacalar. Occupation begins in late formative and persists into late classic. [NH]

408 Davies, Nigel. Tula revisited (Mexicon [K.-F. von Flemming, Berlin] 3 : 6, Jan. 1982, p. 104–108, bibl.)

Recent archaeological work redefined Tula chronology but post-Tollan phase remains vague. Nor is it clarified by Topiltzin myth—here examined—because it refers to cyclical time concept not datable period. [HvW]

409 Davis, Keith F. Désiré Charnay, expeditionary photographer. Albuquerque: University of New Mexico Press, 1981. 212 p.: bibl., index.

Biography with fine original photos of

colorful figure in Maya archaeology, first person to employ photography to record sites. [NH]

410 Demarest, Arthur A. and **Robert J. Sharer.** The origins and evolution of Usulutan ceramics (SAA/AA, 47:4, Oct. 1982, p. 810–822)

Describes technical evolution of Usulutan pottery in western Salvador and adjacent regions from mid-first millennium BC through third century AD. [NH]

411 ———; **Roy Switsur;** and **Rainer Berger.** The dating and cultural associations of the "potbellied" sculptural style: new evidence from Western El Salvador (SAA/AA, 47:1, Jan. 1982, p. 557–571)

Dates "potbellied" figures, Santa Leticia site, El Salvador, to late formative, 500 BC-AD 100, on basis of ceramics and radiocarbon dates from two laboratories. Provides probable date for Monte Alto "potbellies" and similar figures in highland Guatemala. [NH]

412 Díaz Oyarzábal, Clara Luz. Chingú, un sitio clásico del área de Tula, Hgo. México: SEP, Instituto Nacional de Antropología e Historia, Departamento de Monumentos Prehispánicos, 1980 [i.e. 1981]. 100 p.: bibl., ill. (some col.), maps (5 fold.) (Colección científica; 90. Arqueología)

Mapping and surface collections indicate an urban community during Tlamimilolpa times, with civic architecture, Teotihuacan-style residential compounds, obsidian workshops, figurine manufacture, and a Oaxacan presence. Good data tables, distribution maps, and interpretations. [SL]

413 Diehl, Richard A. Tula (in Archaeology. Edited by Jeremy A. Sabloff and Patricia A. Andrews. Austin: University of Texas Press, 1981, p. 277–295, bibl., ill., maps, tables [Supplement to the *Handbook of Middle American Indians*; v. 1])

Survey, mapping, and testing program provides information on city's history and economy. Clarifies that Tula was not a factor in Teotihuacan's downfall. [BLS]

414 Dillon, Brian D. Bound prisoners in Maya art (Journal of New World Archaeology [Institute of Archaeology, University of California, Los Angeles] 5:1, 1982, p. 24–50)

Useful summary of evidence for the prisoner motif, concentrated in east Peten, Usumacinta valley and with outliers in Campeche and Yucatan. [NH]

415 ———. Camelá Lagoon: preliminary investigations at a lowland Maya site in El Quiché, Guatemala (Journal of New World Archaeology [Institute of Archaeology, University of California, Los Angeles] 4:3, 1981, p. 55–87)

Reports on small site, probably satellite of Nueve Cerros, on Río Chixoy. Location on an ox-bow suggests possible function as fish-farming center. [NH]

416 Drennan, Robert D. Prehistoric social, political, and economic development in the area of the Tehuacan Valley: some results of the Palo Blanco project. With contributions by John R. Alden, Elsa M. Redmond, Judith E. Smith, and Charles S. Spencer. Ann Arbor: University of Michigan, Museum of Anthropology, 1979. 259 p.: bibl., ill., maps, tables (Technical reports; 11. Research reports in archaeology; contribution 6)

Examines role of irrigation in prehistory of one locality and analyzes terminal preclassic ceramic workshop, surface survey at Quachilco, excavations at Cuayucatepec, survey in Cuicatlán Cañada, and valley's excavated botanical remains. [BLS]

417 Ester, Michael. The Cayes of Belize: an archaeological resource (BISRA/BS, 9:5/6, 1981, p. 10–17)

Summarizes previous work and discusses potential of offshore islands and barrier reef of Belize. [NH]

418 Excavations at Seibal, Department of Peten, Guatemala. Gordon R. Willey, general editor and project director. Cambridge, Mass.: Peabody Museum of Archaeology and Ethnology, Harvard University, 1982. 343 p.: bibl., ill., map, plates, tables (Memoirs of the Peabody Museum of Archaeology and Ethnology, Harvard University; v. 15, nos. 1–2)

Meticulously detailed report on major excavations in ceremonial center, which had late formative and terminal classic florescences, the latter associated with intrusive styles in architecture and sculpture. Second section analyzes Fine Paste pottery, and discerns Pasion Valley as well as lower Usumacinata manufacturing loci. [NH]

419 Fahmel Beyer, Bernd. El linaje de la vajilla Azteca I (UNAM/AA, 19, 1982, p. 21–44, bibl., ill.)

Compares form and decoration of Azteca I pottery in a broad context of southern Mesoamerican ceramic traditions (Maya, Gulf Coast). Suggests that Azteca I (which was not made by Aztecs) was already well developed in mid-9th century, or two to three centuries earlier than generally assumed. [HvW]

420 Feuchtwanger, Franz. Tlatilco-Terrakotten von Akrobaten, Ballspielern, Musikaten und Tanzenden (MV/BA, 28, 1980, p. 131–153, bibl., ill.)

Describes 21 preclassic figurines from central highland Mexico that represent acrobats, ball players, musicians and dancers. [HvW]

421 Foncerrada de Molina, Marta. Mural painting in Cacaxtla and Teotihuacan cosmopolitanism (*in* Palenque Round Table, 3rd, 1978. Third Palenque Round Table, 1978—part 2: proceedings of the Tercera Mesa Redonda de Palenque, June 11–18, 1978. Edited by Merle Green Robertson. Austin: University of Texas Press, 1980, p. 183–198, bibl., ill. [The Palenque Round Table series; v. 5. The Texas Pan American series])

Art historical attempt to link Cacaxtla murals to antecedent Teotihuacan, Gulf coast, and Maya stylistic canons. [BLS]

423 Ford, Anabel. Los mayas en El Petén: distribución de las poblaciones en el período clásico (Mesoamérica [Centro de Investigaciones Regionales de Mesoamérica, Guatemala] 3:3, junio 1982, p. 124–144, map, tables)

Presents demographic-pressure model relating early classic use of preferred econiches to late classic exploitation of all possible resources. [NH]

424 ———. Patrones de asentamiento maya durante el periódo clásico tardío y el problema de la complejidad económica y política (IAHG/AHG, 2:3, 1981, p. 7–23, bibl., graphs, maps)

Spanish summary of work reported in *HLAS 43:313*, on Tikal-Yaxha intersite transect survey. [NH]

425 Forsyth, Donald W. Archaeological investigations at Xcalumkin, Campeche, Mexico: the ceramics (TU/CCM, 12, 1982, p. 11–25)

Description of ceramic sequence, including formative and classic types. [NH]

426 Freidel, David; Robin Robertson; and **Maynard B. Cliff.** The Maya city of Cerros (AIA/A, 35:4, 1982, p. 12–21)

Illustrated account of work at an important late formative center. [NH]

427 Fuente, Beatriz de la. Temas principales en la escultura huasteca (IIE/A, 8:50/1, 1982, p. 9–18, bibl., ill.)

Classifies sculptures in round and low relief according to formal and iconographic aspects (see also author's catalog on Huastec sculpture, *HLAS 43:334*). [BLS]

428 García Moll, Roberto. Análisis de los materiales arqueológicos de la Cueva del Texcal, Puebla. México: INAH, Departamento de Prehistoria, 1977. 94 p.: bibl., ill., maps, tables (Colección Científica; 56)

Well-illustrated report breaks down distributions of artifact types into preceramic and one ceramic periods. Lithic materials sorted with hierarchical classification based on morphology. [SL]

429 Garduño Argueta, Jaime. Introducción al patrón de asentamiento del sitio de Cobá, Quintana Roo: tesis. México: Escuela Nacional de Antropología e Historia, 1979. 128 p.: ill.

Useful data on settlement pattern marred by jejeune Marxist theorizing. [NH]

430 González Crespo, Norberto. Patrón de asentamientos prehispánicos en la parte central del bajo Balsas: un ensayo metodológico. México: INAH, 1979. 109 p.: bibl., ill., maps (Colección Científica; 73. Arqueología)

Classifies 19 Río Balsas sites by numerical taxonomy according to similarities in location and architecture. Offers theoretical review of archaeological settlement patterns in general, but no interpretation of resultant typology. Emphasizes analytic method. Appendix volume contains 18 site maps. [SL]

431 González de la Mata, María Rocío and **Elía del Carmen Trejo Alvarado.** Playa del Carmen: excavaciones en la costa oriental de Quintana Roo, Temporada 1978 (*in* Instituto Nacional de Antropología e Historia, México. Centro Regional del Sureste. Congreso Interno, Mérida, Yucatán, 1979. Memoria. México: INAH, 1981, p. 123–138, bibl., map, plates)

Several groups of buildings along the coast are late postclassic in date, with colonial occupation following. There was a preceding late classic period in the vicinity. [NH]

432 González Fernández, Baltazar. Depósitos subterráneos en Uxmal, Yucatán (*in* Instituto Nacional de Antropología e Historia, México. Centro Regional del Sureste. Congreso Interno, Mérida, Yucatán, 1979. Memoria. México: INAH, 1981, p. 203–210, bibl., ill.)

Reports on several of 115 known *chultunob* at Uxmal, including examples with modeled stucco decoration on walls, and one with black-line painting of human figure with hieroglyphic inscription. [NH]

433 González Rul, Francisco. La lítica en Tlatelolco. México: INAH, Departamento de Salvamento Arqueológico, 1979. 35 p., 2 fold. leaves of plates: bibl., ill. (Colección Científica. INAH; 74. Arqueología)

Discusses "formal" chert and obsidian tools excavated from postclassic and colonial contexts at Tlaltelolco, Valley of Mexico. Hypothesizes on presence of obsidian knapping areas based on differential distribution of green (Pachuca) and grey (Otumba) obsidian in 30 test pits. [SL]

434 Graham, John and Mark Johnson. The Great Mound of La Venta (*in* Studies in ancient Mesoamerica, IV. Edited by John A. Graham. Berkeley: University of California, Department of Anthropology, 1979, p. 1–5, bibl., ill. [Berkeley contributions of the University of California Archaeological Research Facility; no. 4]

Brief topographic analysis of structure C-1. Series of vertical ridges and ravines that distinguish this great mound are not attributed to erosion. Structure may represent volcanic cone. [SL]

435 Graulich, Michel. Einige Anmerkungen zu den mesoamerikanischen Skulpturen mit der Bezeichnung Chac Mool (Mexicon [K.-F. von Flemming, Berlin] 3 : 5, Nov. 1981, p. 81–87, bibl., ill.)

Author's interpretation of Chac Mool sculptures as sacrificial altars for human offerings is challenged in discussions (p. 84–86) by Ursula Dyckerhoff and Sandra Taladoire. They confirm Acosta's (1956) conclusion that these sculptures, like atlanteans and standard-bearers, served as temple furnishings. [HvW]

436 Guevara Sánchez, Arturo. Los talleres líticos de Aguacatenango, Chis. México: INAH, Departamento de Prehistoria, 1981. 80 p.: bibl., ill., maps, tables (Colección Científica; no. 95)

Study of eight preceramic sites located near a fossil lake and close to area containing bones of extinct megafauna. Assemblage includes possible Lerma point and some patinated chert artifacts. Tools are not finely finished, they lack pressure retouch. C14 dates not available yet. [SL]

437 Guillén, Ann Cyphers. The implications of dated monumental art from Chalcatzingo, Morelos, Mexico (World Archaeology [Routledge & Kegan Paul, London] 13 : 3, Feb. 1982, p. 382–393, bibl., ill., map, plates)

Some carved monuments at Chalcatzingo have been dated via associated materials and radiocarbon dates to 700–500 BC. Believes stylistically epi-Olmec and Izapan sculptural traits indicate interaction with Late Olmec centers (e.g., La Venta) not Pacific coast centers (e.g., Izapa). [BLS]

438 ———. Una secuencia preliminar para el Valle de Xochicalco (UNAM/AA, 17 : 1, 1980, p. 33–52, bibl., ill.)

Ceramic sequence in Xochicalco region indicates affinities with Valley of Mexico during late preclassic. A local development in classic with few ties to Teotihuacan, sequence represents apogee in epiclassic, followed by impoverishment marking beginning of Tlahuica occupation. [HvW]

439 Gussinyer, Jordi. Les pintures rupestres de l'abric de "Los Monos" de Chiapas (UB/BA, 22 : 30, 1980, p. 125–180, bibl., maps, plates)

Describes (in Catalan) simple rock paintings in rock shelter on the Grijalva. [NH]

440 Gutiérrez Solana, Nelly. Estudio sobre un relieve identificado recientemente como huasteco (IIE/A, 8 : 50/1, 1982, p. 19–

Identifies relief fragment similar to Huilocintla reliefs in both Brooklyn and Berlin Völkerkunde Museums, as works of regional Tamuin art school. [HvW]

441 Hammond, Norman. The exploration of the Maya world (American Scientist [Burlington, Vt.] 70, 1982, p. 482–495)

General survey of current knowledge and ideas on Maya archaeology. [NH]

442 ———. A late formative period stela in the Maya Lowlands (SAA/AA, 47:2, April 1982, p. 397–403)

Cuello Stela 1, a small plain monument, is dated ca. AD 100 by stratigraphy and ceramics. [NH]

443 ———. *Pom* for the ancestors: a re-examination of Piedras Negras Stela 40 (Mexicon [K.-F von Flemming, Berlin] 3:5, Nov. 1981, p. 77–79)

Argues that Piedras Negras Stela 40 shows ruler venerating deified ancestor in vault by scattering copal incense. Extends identification of copal-scattering to monuments from Nim li punit (Belize) and Seibal (Peten). [NH]

444 ———. The prehistory of Belize (Journal of Field Archaeology [Association for Field Archaeology, Boston University] 9, 1982, p. 349–362)

History of research and synthesis of present state of knowledge of Belizean archaeology. [NH]

445 ——— and **Charles H. Miksicek.** Ecology and economy of a formative Maya site at Cuello, Belize (Journal of Field Archaeology [Association of Field Archaeology, Boston University] 8, 1981, p. 259–269)

Reconstructs environmental and dietary patterns based on macroscopic remains from sieving and flotation of excavated deposits, covering time span 2000 BC to AD 300 (radiocarbon years). [NH]

446 Harlan, Mark E. An inquiry into the development of complex society at Chalcatzingo, Morelos, Mexico: methods and results (SAA/AA, 44:3, July 1979, p. 471–493, appendixes, bibl., ill.)

Statistical analysis of iconic attributes of figurines over three periods at preclassic Chalcatzingo. Figurine attributes cluster spatially over time reflecting elite social differentiation. Suggested timing argues against

this being direct effect of Olmec interaction. [BLS]

447 Henderson, John S.; Ilene Sterns; Anthony Wonderley; and **Patricia A. Urban.** Investigaciones arqueológicas en el valle de Naco, Honduras occidental: un informe preliminar (YAXKIN, 3:2, dic. 1979, bibl., ill., maps)

Describes reconnaissance and excavations at mainly postclassic sites in NW Honduras (see *HLAS 43:350*). [NH]

448 Hester, T.R.; H.J. Shafer; T.C. Kelly; and **G. Ligabue.** Observations on the patination process and the context of antiquity: a fluted projectile point from Belize, Central America (Lithic Technology [University of Texas, Center for Archaeological Research, San Antonio] 11:2, p. 29–35)

Description and discussion of the Ladyville point of generalized Clovis type (more precisely, of Turrialba type), the first unequivocal evidence for Terminal Pleistocene or early Holocene human occupation of the Maya lowlands. [NH]

449 Hill, Robert M. Ancient Maya houses: at Cauinal and Pueblo Viejo Chixoy, el Quiché, Guatemala: pts. 1/2 (UMUP/E, 24:2, Winter 1982, p. 40–48, bibl., map, plates; 24:3, Spring 1982, p. 30–34, ill., map)

Description of settlement at small postclassic highland sites with line illustrations. [NH]

450 Hirth, Kenneth G. Transportation architecture at Xochicalco, Morelos, Mexico (SAA/AA, 23:3, June 1982, p. 322–324, bibl., map)

Paved ways link architectural units at Xochicalco. Two pavements extend at least three km into countryside. Suggests function is facilitation of regional transportation. [BLS]

451 Hurtado de Mendoza, Luis. Estimating a hydration rate for Chimaltenango obsidian (SAA/AA, 46, 1981, p. 159–162)

Chimaltenango source (a.k.a. Aldea Chatalun, San Martín Jilotepeque and Río Pixcaya) obsidians were identified by neutron activation analysis, and compared with hydration-dated El Chayal obsidians to obtain chronological control: this was extrapolated to give a hydration rate of 6.16 microns² per 1000 years. [NH]

452 Jones, Christopher; William R. Coe; and William A. Haviland. Tikal: an outline of its field study, 1956–1970, and a project bibliography (*in* Archaeology. Edited by Jeremy A. Sabloff and Patricia A. Andrews. Austin: University of Texas Press, 1981, p. 296–312, bibl., ill., maps [Supplement to the *Handbook of Middle American Indians*; v. 1])

Notes topics addressed by Tikal project, forecasts publication of long-developed reports, and gives bibliography of studies that have appeared. [BLS]

453 Jones, David M. The archaeology of nineteenth-century haciendas and ranchos of Otumba and Apan, Basin of Mexico. Iowa City: University of Iowa, Department of Anthropology, 1980. 186 p.: bibl., ill., maps, tables (Research report; no. 2. Mesoamerican Research Colloquium)

Microhistory of rural northeast Valley of Mexico, focuses on transition from cattle ranching to pulque production. Looks at artifact distributions from 12 surface collections as supplement to historic records and as reflective to time-lags in usage of artifacts. [SL]

454 Kelly, Isabel Truesdell. Ceramic sequence in Colima: Capacha, an early phase. Tucson: University of Arizona Press, 1980. 110 p.: bibl., ill. (Anthropological papers of the University of Arizona; no. 37)

Describes "Capacha" phase pottery from West Mexico, dated around 1800 BC. Discusses possible external ceramic relationships, including South American influence. Also treats burials and lithic artifacts. [SL]

455 Kelly, Joyce. The complete visitor's guide to Mesoamerican ruins. Norman: University of Oklahoma Press, 1982. 527 p.: bibl., ill. (some col.), index.

Very useful descriptive guide with directions for access and general travel, for most officially open sites in Mexico and Maya area. [NH]

456 Kolb, Charles C. The classic Teotihuacan period chronology: some reflections (UNC/K, 11:2, June 1979, p. 1–51, bibl., tables)

Discusses recent proliferation of Basin of Mexico chronological terminology. Evaluates obsidian hydration and C14 data from Teotihuacan, including contextual information on 22 C14 samples. [SL]

457 Konieczna, Barbara. La industria de piedra tallada en el área de Río Bec, Becan, Chicanna, Xpuhil: síntesis (*in* Instituto Nacional de Antropología e Historia, México. Centro Regional del Sureste. Congreso Interno, Mérida, Yucatán, 1978. Memoria. México: INAH, 1981, p. 181–198, bibl., tables)

Description of mainly classic period chert industry at three sites: most raw material is local, with allochthonous chert increasing in proportion in terminal classic/early postclassic and probably emanating from Belize. [NH]

458 Kosakowsky, Laura J. A preliminary summary of formative ceramic variability at Cuello, Belize (TU/CCM, 12, 1982, p. 26–42)

Development of refinement of Pring's Northern Belize sequence, based on 1978–80 excavations at Cuello, and embracing a sequence from early formative through terminal formative/protoclassic. [NH]

459 Krotser, Paula and Evelyn Rattray. Manufactura y distribución de tres grupos cerámicos de Teotihuacan (UNAM/AA, 17:1, 1980, p. 91–104, bibl., ill.)

Identifies ceramic workshops and distribution of wares (Thin Orange, "Copa Ware," and San Martín Orange) between AD 500–750. [HvW]

460 Kubler, George. Eclectism at Cacaxtla (*in* Palenque Round Table, 3rd, 1978. Third Palenque Round Table, 1978—part 2: proceedings of the Tercera Mesa Redonda de Palenque, June 11–18, 1978. Edited by Merle Greene Robertson. Austin: University of Texas Press, 1980, p. 163–172, bibl., ill., map [The Palenque Round Table series; v. 5. The Texas Pan American series])

Describes murals with very good line drawings. Explores stylistic relationships and argues that they reflect terminal classic synchronic eclectism, perhaps syncretic in nature. [BLS]

461 Lackey, Louana M. The pottery of Acatlán: a changing Mexican tradition. Norman: University of Oklahoma Press, 1982. 164 p.: bibl., ill., maps, plates.

Ethnographic study of pottery making includes discussion of Acatlan area as possible source for prehistoric thin orange and early Aztec ware. [BLS]

462   Lambert, J.D.H. and **J.T. Arnason.** *Ramón* and Maya ruins: an ecological, not an economic, relation (AAAS/S, 216, 1982, p. 298–299)

Ecological argument for natural concentration of *ramón* (*Brosimum alicastrum*) on the disturbed lime-rich habitat afforded by Maya ruins. Accords with paucity of archaeological evidence for *ramón* use. [NH]

463   Lee, Thomas A., Jr. New World Archaeological Foundation: obra, 1952–1980. Provo, Utah: N.W.A.F.: Brigham Young University, College of Family, Home, and Social Sciences, 1981. 142 p.: ill., map, plan, port.

Bibliography of New World Archaeological Foundation work in Chiapas. [NH]

464   Limón B., Ammie Ellen. Descripción de los animales y vegetales en los bajorelieves de Chalcatzingo, Morelos (UNAM/AA, 17, 1980, p. 15–32, bibl., ill.)

Identifies some animals and plants on reliefs, including one not published so far. Notes analogy among representations of tiger shark, tiger flower, and jaguar. [HvW]

465   Lister, Florence C. and **Robert H. Lister.** Sixteenth century maiolica pottery in the Valley of Mexico. Tucson: University of Arizona Press, 1982. 110 p.: bibl., ill., tables.

Categorizes post-conquest pottery from downtown Mexico City excavations in typology. Provides brief historical background concerning European influence on native industries. [BLS]

467   López de Molina, Diana. Rescate arqueológico en Cholula, Puebla (Cuadernos de los Centros Regionales [INAH, Centro Regional de Veracruz, México] 1, 1982, p. 5–23, bibl., ill.)

Salvage excavations near Franciscan convent, with pottery description. Issue contains three other articles on salvage operations in state of Puebla. [HvW]

468   —— and **Daniel Molina F.** Cacaxtla: guía oficial. Mexico: INAH, 1980. 55 p.: ill., map.

Provides brief descriptions of central layout, chronology, excavated and restored structures, and wall murals of predominantly terminal classic center in Tlaxcala. [BLS]

469   MacNeish, Richard S. Third annual report of the Belize Archaic Archaeological Reconnaissance. Andover, Mass.: Robert S. Peabody Foundation, 1982. 91 p.: bibl., ill.

Chatty report on search for preceramic sites in northern and central coastal Belize. [NH]

470   Maldonado Cárdenas, Rubén. Intervención de restauración en el juego de pelota de Uxmal, Yuc. (*in* Instituto Nacional de Antropología e Historia, México. Centro Regional del Sureste. Congreso Interno, Mérida, Yucatán, 1979. Memoria. México: INAH, 1981, p. 233–243, bibl., plates)

Reports on restoration of Uxmal ball court. Cehpech complex pottery from structure is dated as AD 800-1000. [NH]

471   ——. Ofrendas asociadas a entierros del Infiernillo en El Balsas: estudio y experimentación con tres métodos de taxonomía numérica. México: INAH, 1980. 233 p.: bibl., ill., maps (Colección científica. Arqueología)

Multivariate statistical treatment of burial attributes at 18 Río Balsas sites tested prior to construction of the Infiernillo dam. Sites are classified by funeral customs, which are discussed in terms of temporal phase, cultural tradition, and technological complex. [SL]

472   Marcus, Joyce. Zapotec writing (SA, 242:2, Feb. 1980, p. 50–64, bibl., ill., maps)

Particularly well-illustrated summary of changing complexity and functions of Zapotec writing through precolumbian sequence in Oaxaca. Content shifts from conquest themes, to diplomacy, to elite genealogies, but secular content dominates throughout. [BLS]

473   Matos Moctezuma, Eduardo. Les fouilles de Templo Mayor (ARCHEO, 162, jan. 1982, p. 10–21, ill., plan)

Describes successive construction phases and recent discoveries of offerings (see also in this issue Mireille Simoni Abbat's "Le Templo Mayor: une fabuleuse exposition au Petit Palais"). [HvW]

474   ——. Informe de la revisión de los trabajos arqueológicos realizados en Ichcateopán, Guerrero. México: Universidad Nacional Autónoma de México, 1980. 47 p., 35 p. of plates: bibl., ill. (Dictámenes Ichcateopan; 6)

Recent investigations in Guerrero indicate lack of scientific basis for claiming that skeletal remains found at Ichcateopán in 1949 were those of the Aztec leader Cuauhtemoc. Original excavations were poorly executed and inadequately recorded. Skeletal remains belong to at least eight individuals, and derive from more than one period. [SL]

476 ———. El Templo Mayor: excavaciones y estudios. México: INAH, 1982. 376 p.: bibl., ill., with separate volume containing 44 large-scale plans.

Comprehensive report with month-by-month accounts of excavations and restaurations (1978–81) of twin temples in ceremonial precinct, Mexico City. Describes offerings of stone figures and masks (including Olmec mask); bones of reptiles, fish, birds; shells; and pottery (see also *HLAS 43:362–363*). [HvW]

477 ———. Teotihuacan: excavaciones en la Calle de los Muertos, 1964 (UNAM/ AA, 17, 1980, p. 69–90, bibl., ill.)

Excavation and consolidation of ceremonial structures in the Street of the Dead. Report fills gap in paucity of reports on "Proyecto Teotihuacan, 1962–64." [HvW]

479 **Mayer, Karl Herbert.** Die Skulpturen von Santa Barbara in Yucatan, Mexiko (Das Altertum [Akademie der Wissenschafpen, Berlin] 28:4, Okt. 1982, p. 215–226, bibl., ill.)

Describes Puuc-style relief columns and glyphic inscriptions now incorporated in church of nearby Paraíso. [HvW]

480 **Michelet, Dominique.** La région de Río Verde, San Luis Potosí, et ses relations archéologiques avec la Huasteca: étude préliminaire (*in* International Congress of Americanists, 42nd, Paris, 1976. Actes [see *HLAS 43:255*] v. 9-B, p. 49–55, bibl., map)

Preliminary synthesis of 1970s work by French Archaeological Mission. Divides area's sedentary human occupation into three phases, based on ceramic and figurine morphology. Outlines demographic trends from late preclassic to postclassic, and notes Central Mexican, Veracruz, and Huastec stylistic influence. [SL]

481 **Miller, Arthur G.** On the edge of the sea: mural painting at Tancah-Tulum, Quintana Roo, Mexico. With appendixes by Joseph W. Ball, Frank P. Saul, and Anthony P.

Andrews. Washington: Dumbarton Oaks, 1982. 133 p., 16 p. of plates: appendixes, bibl., ill. (some col.), index.

Reports on field work at Tancah and discusses terminal classic-postclassic murals there and at Tulum, and extensive use of ethnohistoric records. [NH]

482 **Millon, René.** Teotihuacan: city, state, and civilization (*in* Archaeology. Edited by Jeremy A. Sabloff and Patricia A. Andrews. Austin: University of Texas Press, 1981, p. 198–243, bibl., ill., map [Supplement to the *Handbook of Middle American Indians*; v. 1])

Comprehensive synthesis of recent research concerning Teotihuacan. Best single essay on the subject. [BLS]

483 **Mountjoy, Joseph B.** An interpretation of the pictographs at La Peña Pintada, Jalisco, Mexico (SAA/AA, 47:1, Jan. 1982, p. 110–126, bibl., ill., maps)

Interprets postclassic West Mexican cave paintings by analogy to modern Huichol symbolism. Pictographs imply calendrical calculations based on movements of the sun, Venus, and possibly Orion. [SL]

484 **Müller, Florencia.** La alfarería de Cholula. México: INAH, 1978. 238 p.: bibl., ill. (Serie Arqueología)

Typological analysis of Cholula pottery and figurines. Describes changes over site sequence. [BLS]

486 ———. Estudio tipológico provisional de la cerámica del Balsas Medio. México: INAH, 1979. 65 p.: ill. (Colección Científica; 78. Arqueología)

Type-variety descriptions of ceramics from 22 sites. Discusses relative influence of south Pacific coast, central Mexican highlands, Maya area, and west Mexico from 1600 BC to AD 1500, based on ceramic affinities. [SL]

487 **Neff, Héctor.** Informe sobre el período clásico tardío de la zona litoral del suroccidente de Guatemala (IAHG/AHG, 2:3, 1981, p. 259–285, bibl., ill., graphs, map)

Background study of environment and resources of coastal SW Guatemala, as part of investigation of Plumbate pottery manufacturing areas. [NH]

488 **Nichols, Deborah L.** A middle formative irrigation system near Santa

Clara Coatitlan in the Basin of Mexico (SAA/AA, 47:1, Jan. 1982, p. 133–144, bibl., ill., maps)

This middle preclassic irrigation system is earliest found in Valley of Mexico. Stratigraphy indicates substantial preclassic erosion possibly linked to deforestation. Irrigation may have reduced agricultural risk as well as shifting fields from eroded areas. [BLS]

489 O'Brien, Michael J.; Dennis E. Lewarch; Roger D. Mason; and James A. Neely. Functional analysis of water control features at Monte Alban, Oaxaca, Mexico (World Archaeology [Routledge & Kegan Paul, London] 11:3, Feb. 1980, p. 342–355, bibl., ill., maps)

Central planning at Monte Alban is indicated by drainage, impoundment, collection/settling structures, dams and other civic water control technology, perhaps as early as Late Monte Alban I Period. Agricultural water control system therein is less elaborate than these other aspects of water technology (see item 333). [BLS]

490 Orrego Corzo, Miguel. Informes sobre la delimitación de los parques arqueológicos de Aguateca y Dos Pilas, El Petén, Guatemala (IAHG/AHG, 2:3, 1981, p. 243–257, bibl., ill.)

Describes and defines areas delimited as archaeological parks around important classic sites on Laguna Petexbatun. [NH]

491 Ortiz de Zárate, Gonzalo. Petroglifos de Sinaloa. Presentación de Pedro Bosch-Gimpera. México: Fomento Cultural Banamex, 1976. 216 p.: bibl., ill., maps.

Well-illustrated document of all known petroglyph sites in the state of Sinaloa. Includes precise locations, classification of motifs, and background on previous studies of non-moveable art in this area. [SL]

492 Pendergast, David M. Excavations at Altun Ha, Belize, 1964–1970. With architectural drawings by H. Stanley Loten. v. 2. Toronto, Canada: Royal Ontario Museum, 1982. 305 p.: bibl., ill., loose plans (in box), tables.

Second of five volumes forming the final report on the first site in Belize to be excavated in detail. Deals with architecture and stratigraphy, including burials and their furniture, in Groups B and C of the cere-

monial precinct and adjacent settlement. Superbly illustrated, factual account. All theorizing and synthesis are deferred until volume 5. [NH]

493 ———. Lamanai, Belize: summary of excavation results, 1974–1980 (Journal of Field Archaeology [Association of Field Archaeology, Boston University] 8, 1981, p. 29–53, ill., map)

Description, with map and illustrations, of work at important late formative, classic and postclassic site on New River Lagoon in north-central Belize. Of special importance are discovery of massive late formative architecture and of postclassic occupation persisting through 17th century with little detectable change in material culture. [NH]

494 ——— and Elizabeth Graham. Fighting a looting battle: Xunantunich, Belize (AIA/A, 34:4, July/Aug. 1981, p. 12–19)

Describes salvage of looted structure in Group B, and emphasizes damage done by looters to Maya sites. [NH]

495 Pope, Kevin O. and Malcom B. Sibberensen. In search of Tzultacaj: cave explorations in the Maya Lowlands of Alta Verapaz, Guatemala (Journal of New World Archaeology [Institute of Archaeology, University of California, Los Angeles] 4:3, 1981, p. 16–54)

Suggests change from early classic ceremonial visitation to late classic refuge residence. [NH]

496 Pring, Duncan and Norman Hammond. The stratigraphic priority of Swasey ceramics at Cuello, Belize (TU/CCM, 12, 1982, p. 43–48)

Tabulation of ceramic lots from one 5m² excavation unit at Cuello, documenting the Swasey-Mamom-Chicanel succession. [NH]

497 Proskouriakoff, Tatiana Avenirovna. A study of classic Maya sculpture. New York: AMS Press, 1980. 209 p., 37 leaves of plates (1 fold.): bibl., ill.

Reprinting of classic work. [NH]

499 Rattray, Evelyn Childs and María Elena Ruiz A. Interpretaciones culturales de La Ventilla, Teotihuacan (UNAM/AA, 17, 1980, p. 105–114, bibl., ill.)

Concerns significance of burial offerings as indicators of craft specialization, social class, age, and sex. Presence of Gulf Coast ceramics indicates intensive trade in Xolalpan phase (AD 400–600). [HvW]

500 Rice, Don S. and Prudence M. Rice.
Muralla de León: a lowland Maya fortification (Journal of Field Archaeology [Association for Field Archaeology, Boston University] 9, 1981, p. 349–362)

Reports dry-walled *enceinte* on plateau by Laguna Macanche, Petén, with maximum height of 4m and perimeter of 1.4 km. Enclosed structures are terminal formative through postclassic. Most pottery from wall fill is terminal formative ("protoclassic"), but some is postclassic. Authors prefer earlier date for wall construction, and relate it to coeval evidence of conflict and its role in the emergence of classic Maya civilization. [NH]

501 ——— and ———. La utilización de las sabanas Petén Central por los mayas clásicos (IAHG/AHG, 2:2, 1980, p. 69–81, maps)

Spanish summary of work already reported in *HLAS* 43:375–376. [NH]

502 Rivera Dorado, Miguel. Excavaciones arqueológicas en Salcajá, Guatemala (IAI/I, 6:1, 1980, p. 161–182, bibl., ill.)

Preliminary report by Misión Científica Española on explorations in Quetzaltenango region with vestiges of late formative/early classic household clusters, underground storage chambers, and drainage systems. [HvW]

503 Robertson, Robin. Classification of the ceramics from Cerros: a late preclassic site in Northern Belize (TU/CCM, 12, 1982, p. 66–69)

Divides late formative into three ceramic complexes. [NH]

504 Robicsek, Francis. Of Olmec babies and were-jaguars (Mexicon [K.-F. von Flemming, Berlin] 5:1, Jan. 1983, p. 7–19, bibl., ill.)

Dismisses various conjectural interpretations of obese, sexless baby figures as were-jaguar babies, were-toads, or victims of Down's syndrome. They portray well-fed infants with probably over-emphasized racial characteristics. [HvW]

505 ——— and Donald M. Hales. Maya ceramic vases from the classic period:

the November collection of Maya ceramics. Charlottesville: University of Virginia Museum, 1982. 1 v.

Catalog of collection of "Maya" vases of uncertain authenticity, from, if genuine, looted sites. [NH]

506 Robles Castellanos, José Fernando.
Xelha: un proyecto de investigación (*in* Instituto Nacional de Antropología e Historia, México. Centro Regional del Sureste. Congreso Interno, Mérida, Yucatán, 1979. Memoria. México: INAH, 1981, p. 101–121, bibl., ill., map)

Presents description and research design for small site, with *sacbe*, that may have functioned as a "port of trade" in classic period. [NH]

507 ———. La secuencia cerámica preliminar de El Meco, Quintana Roo (*in* Instituto Nacional de Antropología e Historia, México. Centro Regional del Sureste. Congreso Interno, Mérida, Yucatán, 1979. Memoria. México: INAH, 1981, p. 153–178, bibl., maps, plate)

Describes early classic and early/late postclassic ceramic sequence for small coastal site north of Cancun. [NH]

508 Ruiz Gordillo, P.A.J. Omar. Coyoxquihui, una zona arqueológica en la región de Papantla, Ver. (Cuadernos de los Centros Regionales [INAH, Centro Regional de Veracruz, México] 2, 1982, p. 13–26, bibl., ill.)

Exploration and consolidation of a late classic/early postclassic site with pyramid and ballcourt. [HvW]

509 ———. Nueva cabeza colosal en San Lorenzo, Tenochtitlan, Ver. (Cuadernos de los Centros Regionales [INAH, Centro Regional de Veracruz, México] 2, 1982, p. 5–12, bibl., ill.)

Gradual erosion partially exposed the face of a 160 x 150 cm basalt head which has been reburied for its protection. [HvW]

510 Schoeninger, Margaret J. Dietary reconstruction at Chalcatzingo, a formative period site in Morelos, Mexico. Ann Arbor: Museum of Anthropology, University of Michigan, 1979. 97 p.: appendixes, bibl., ill., map, tables (Technical reports; 9. Contributions in human biology; 2)

Atomic absorption spectrometry, microprobe, and neutron activation analysis of

Chalcatzingo burial bone samples for strontium, when compared with grave goods, suggests that higher ranking individuals had greater access to dietary meat. [BLS]

511 Schortman, Edward M. Archaeological investigations in the lower Motagua Valley (UMUP/E, 23:1, Fall 1980, p. 28–34, ill., map, photos)

Discusses settlement study undertaken as part of Quirigua project but beyond immediate area of dense settlement, downstream to the northeast. [NH]

512 Scott, John F. The monuments of Los Idolos, Veracruz (Journal of New World Archaeology [Institute of Archaeology, University of California, Los Angeles] 5:1, 1982, p. 10–50, bibl., ill.)

Illustrations and piece-by-piece discussions of dating and stylistic comparisons of Los Idolos sculpture. Emphasizes probable non-Olmec characteristics and Cotzumalhuapan, El Tajin, and Aztec relations. [BLS]

513 ———. Post-Olmec art in Veracruz (in La Antropología americanista en la actualidad: homenaje a Rafael Girard. México: Editores Mexicanos Unidos, 1980, v. 1, p. 235–251, bibl., ill.)

Focus on style of post-Olmec sculptures in the Tuxtla mountains of Veracruz, with comparisons to central Veracruz sites and the Pacific coast of Guatemala. [BLS]

514 Senter, Donovan Cowgill. Un estudio de la distribución de los tipos cerámicos del sitio Cerro Zacatepechi, Morelos (UNAM/AA, 16, 1979, p. 105–122, bibl., ill., maps, tables)

Presents distribution of non-utilitarian ceramics at small walled center near Xochicalco. Tables give sherd counts by square and level, from early to middle postclassic. [SL]

515 Serra Puche, Mari [sic] Carmen. La unidad habitacional en Terremote-Tlaltenco, D.F.: un análisis de distribución espacial para definir áreas de actividad: pts. 1/2 (UNAM/AA, 17, 1980, p. 167–185; 19, 1982, p. 9–20, bibl., ill.)

Two-part critical review of "cluster analysis" with reference to excavation of late preclassic habitational unit in Basin of Mexico. Conducted to determine distribution of material culture remains in order to infer areas of specialization. [HvW]

516 ——— and Yoko Sugiura Yamamoto. Terremote-Tlaltenco, D.F.: un asentamiento formativo en el sur de la cuenca de México, primera temporada (UNAM/AA, 16, 1979, p. 35–49, bibl., maps, ill.)

Preliminary results of ceramic analysis of local center in southern Basin of Mexico during preclassic. Offers tentative hypotheses about colonization therein. [SL]

517 Sharer, Robert J. The Quirigua Project, 1974–1979: a brief outline of the development and structure of the research (UMUP/E, 23:1, Fall 1980, p. 5–10, maps, photos)

Overview of six seasons' work, introducing a special issue of *Expedition* (see items **313, 378–379,** and **511**), that details results of work in ceremonial center and settlement of this southeastern classic Maya site. [NH]

518 Sharp, Rosemary. Chacs and chiefs: the iconology of mosaic stone sculpture in pre-conquest Yucatán, Mexico. Washington: Dumbarton Oaks, Trustees for Harvard University, 1981. 48 p.: bibl., ill. (Studies in pre-Columbian art and archaeology; no. 24)

Suggests that step-fret, T and mask elements in mosaic sculpture "used old symbols with new inter-regional political implications." [NH]

519 Solís, Felipe. Escultura del Castillo de Teayo, Veracruz, México. México: INAH, 1981. 122 p.: bibl., plates (Cuadernos de historia del arte; 16)

Descriptive catalog of 52 illustrated monuments without interpretative commentaries. [HvW]

520 Spence, Michael W. Obsidian production and the state in Teotihuacan (SAA/AA, 46:4, Oct. 1981, p. 769–788, bibl., ill., map, tables)

Compares local, regional, and public precinct obsidian workshops at Teotihuacan with regard to location, raw materials, and products. Argues against total state control of obsidian production and for a mixture of state-dominated procurement of green obsidian and a degree of workshop independence in procurement and manufacture. [BLS]

521 Stark, Barbara L. Habitation sites in the Papaloapan estuarine delta: locational characteristics (Historical Archaeology [Society for Historical Archaeology, Washington] 15:1, 1981, p. 49–65, bibl., ill., maps, tables)

Compares modern, historical, and prehistoric settlement patterns for habitation sites in the Lower Papaloapan Basin, Veracruz. Main topic is analysis of distribution of historic artifacts, predominantly pottery, on Patarata 52, Veracruz, Mexico, and the implications of the distribution for house location. [BLS]

522 —— and **Dennis Young.** Linear nearest neighbor analysis (SAA/AA, 46:2, April 1981, p. 284–300, bibl., ill., map)

Introduces improved treatment of linear nearest neighbor statistic, which can determine clustered, random, or regularly dispersed patterns. Case study of sites in Lower Papaloapan Basin, Veracruz, probably postclassic. These probable house mounds tend to be regularly dispersed. [BLS]

523 —— *et al.* Informe preliminar sobre investigaciones arqueológicas de zonas habitacionales en el Bálsamo, Escuintla, Guatemala (IAHG/AHG, 2:3, 1981, p. 287–323, bibl., graphs, ill., tables)

Brief report of 1977 excavations in the settlement of this important middle preclassic site on the Pacific slope of Guatemala. [NH]

524 **Stone, Andrea.** Recent discoveries from Naj Tunich (Mexicon [K.-F. von Flemming, Berlin] 4:5/6, 1982, p. 93–99)

Illustrated description of important cave site in eastern Peten, Guatemala (see item **526**). [NH]

525 **Strecker, Matthias.** Rock art of east Mexico and Central America: an annotated bibliography. With an introduction to the study of Central American rock art by C. William Clewlow, Jr. Los Angeles: University of California, Institute of Archaeology, 1979. 81 p. (Monograph—Institute of Archaeology, University of California, Los Angeles; 10)

Useful resource for the Maya area and lower Central America. [NH]

526 **Stuart, George E.** Maya art treasure is discovered in cave (NGS/NGM, 160:2, Aug. 1981, p. 220–235, plates)

Popular but authoritative up-to-date (first English-language illustration publica-

tion) account of wall paintings, including inscriptions, in the Naj Tunich cave near Belize-Guatemala border. Documents looting attempts after discovery. Paintings are late classic (8th century AD, see item **524**). [NH]

527 **Vargas Pacheco, Ernesto.** Consideraciones sobre Teotenango y Ojo de Agua, Estado de México (UNAM/AA, 17, 1980, p. 53–67, bibl., ill.)

Postulates fusion of local traits in Toluca Valley with Teotihuacan traits during and after its Metepec phase. See also Wanda Tommasi Magrelli's "Procesos de Cambio en los Valles de Toluca" in *Revista Mexicana de Estudios Antropológicos* (25, 1979, p. 173–181). Indicates strong Teotihuacan influence in Calixtlahuaca and Teotenango. [HvW]

528 **Vega Sosa, Constanza.** El recinto sagrado de México-Tenochtitlan: excavaciones 1968–69 y 1975–76. México: INAH, 1979. 106 p.: appendixes, bibl., ill., maps.

Set of papers about metro excavations and consolidation of cathedral supports which uncovered structures and artifacts at the central ceremonial precinct of Tenochtitlan. Well illustrated. [BLS]

529 **Velázquez Valadez, Ricardo.** Etapas de funcionalidad de las Grutas de Loltun (*in* Instituto Nacional de Antropología e Historia, México. Centro Regional del Sureste. Congreso Interno, Mérida, Yucatán, 1979. Memoria. México: INAH, 1981, p. 139–144, bibl., map)

Reports early formative through postclassic use of caves, following preceramic occupation reported in 1980. Early formative pottery is related to Olmec Gulf Coast, more abundant middle and late formative to the lowland Maya tradition. Only in late classic are all parts of cave complex penetrated. [NH]

530 **von Schuler-Schömig, Immina.** Altmexikanische Gefässfuss-Model (MV/BA, 28, 1980, p. 331–345, bibl., ill.)

Experiments with ceramic molds from Culhuacan reveal ancient manufacturing methods for casting vessel supports. [HvW]

531 **von Winning, Hasso.** Los decapitados en la cerámica moldeada de Veracruz (IAI/I, 6:1, 1980, p. 23–35, bibl., ill.)

Ballgame rituals on four bowls indicate that human sacrifice was practiced by decapitation and by heart excision in Central Veracruz, AD 500–700. [HvW]

532   Walters, Gary Rex. Proyecto Arqueológico San Agustín Acasaguastlán (IAHG/AHG, 2:3, 1981, p. 325–369, bibl., ill.)

Describes excavations in 1979–80 at Guaytán, with sequence from late preclassic to late classic. Separate areas of the site have discrete abundances of jade, obsidian and polychrome pottery. [NH]

533   Weaver, David S. An osteological test of changes in subsistence and settlement patterns at Casas Grandes, Chihuahua, Mexico (SAA/AA, 46:2, April 1981, p. 361–364, bibl., tables)

Skeletal porotic hyperostosis and periosteal reactions in 93 infants and children are used to test whether between the Viejo and Medio periods more maize was consumed (no) and whether infectious disease increased (yes), the latter perhaps related to greater settlement nucleation. [BLS]

534   Whalen, Michael E. Excavations at Santo Domingo Tomaltepec: evolution of a formative community in the Valley of Oaxaca, Mexico. Ann Arbor: University of Michigan, Museum of Anthropology, 1981. 225 p.: bibl., ill. (Prehistory and human ecology of the Valley of Oaxaca; v. 6. Memoirs of the Museum of Anthropology, University of Michigan; no. 12)

Excellent, well-organized site report details excavated data from preclassic sequence at this small community. Traces growing social complexity. Includes several valuable appendixes such as spatial and depositional analyses. [BLS]

535   Wilkerson, S. Jeffrey K. Huastec presence and cultural chronology in north-central Veracruz, Mexico (*in* International Congress of Americanists, 42nd, Paris, 1976. Actes [see *HLAS 43:255*] v. 9-B, p. 31–47, bibl., map, tables)

Brief summary of archaeological sequence from Archaic to modern times at small coastal site of Santa Luisa, 30 km downriver from El Tajín. Concludes that growth of Tajín state was related to control of adjacent riverine areas. [SL]

536   Wilkinson, Richard G. and **Richard J. Norelli.** A biocultural analysis of so-

cial organization at Monte Alban (SAA/AA, 46:4, Oct. 1981, p. 743–758, bibl., ill., tables)

Examines 321 Monte Alban burials in order to compare tomb and non-tomb interments biologically. Statistical analyses indicate no biological differences, including ones related to nutrition, but tombs tended to contain more adults, suggesting a degree of achieved status. Strong class endogamy is not apparent. [BLS]

537   Winter, Marcus C. and **Christopher G. Neill.** Santa Teresa: un sitio preclásico en la Mixteca Baja de Oaxaca. Oaxaca, México: INAH, Centro Regional de Oaxaca, 1982. 18 p.: bibl., ill., maps (Estudios de antropología e historia; 36)

Discovery of first known preclassic site in the Oaxacan Mixteca Baja. Includes site map and descriptions of middle and late preclassic ceramics. Hypothesizes that the site has an even earlier, Olmec period, occupation. [SL]

538   ——— and **Valerie Nardin.** Rescate arqueológico en Loma del Trapiche, Guadalupe Hidalgo, Etla, Oaxaca. Oaxaca, México: INAH, Centro Regional de Oaxaca, 1982. 14 p.: bibl., ill., map (Estudios de antropología e historia; 30)

Two kilns dating to Monte Alban IIIB-IV were exposed by construction and salvaged. [BLS]

539   Yamamoto, Yoko Sugiura. El material cerámico formativo del Sitio 193, Metepec, Edo. de México: algunas consideraciones (UNAM/AA, 17, 1980, p. 129–148, bibl., ill.)

Discusses relationships between central Valley of Toluca and Basin of Mexico in early and middle preclassic. [HvW]

540   Zaragoza de Dávila, Diana. Informe de los trabajos realizados sobre el material cerámico de Kohunlich, Quintana Roo, 1978/1979 (*in* Instituto Nacional de Antropología e Historia, México. Centro Regional del Sureste. Congreso Interno, Mérida, Yucatán, 1979. Memoria. México: INAH, 1981, p. 211–222, bibl., ill.)

Reports mainly late and terminal classic pottery, organized by paste color classes; no type variety analysis has yet been done. [NH]

NATIVE SOURCES AND
EPIGRAPHY

541 Aguilera, Carmen. Algunos datos sobre el chapopote en las fuentes documentales del siglo XVI (UNAM/ECN, 14, 1980, p. 335–343, bibl.)

Compilation of early mentions of native uses of bitumen: ritual, medicinal, aromatic, adhesive, and caulking. [BLS]

542 Anawalt, Patricia Rieff. Costume analysis and the provenience of the Borgia group codices (SAA/AA, 46:4, Oct. 1981, p. 837–852, bibl., ill., table)

Clothing differences between the Mixtec and Borgia group codices argue for cultural/geographic differences in origin. Three Borgia codices are suggested to derive from the Puebla-Tlaxcala area, two, from the central of southern Gulf Coast. [BLS]

543 ———. Indian clothing before Cortés: Mesoamerican costumes from the codices. Norman: University of Oklahoma Press, 1981. 232 p.: bibl., ill., maps, plates, table.

Native codices, murals, and postconquest documents are sources for a classification of Aztec, Tlaxcalan, Tarascan, Mixtec, Borgia group, and lowland Maya clothing and costume. Brief discussion of sociological, symbolic, historical, and functional implications of clothing patterns. [BLS]

544 Barrera Vázquez, Alfredo. Manik [Manik'], el séptimo dia del calendario maya (IAI/I, 6:1, 1980, p. 125–135, bibl., ill.)

The Maya day sign *manik* (hand) and its Nahua equivalent *mazatl* (deer) are analyzed in terms of their pictorial form and semantic significance. [HvW]

545 Barthel, Thomas S. Methods and results of Indo-Mexican studies; a preliminary report (IAI/I, 6:1, 1980, p. 13–21, bibl.)

Outlines methodology of Indo-Mexican studies and discusses syncretistic concepts in Borgia group that correspond to southeastern Asiatic religious systems. "Indo-Mexican studies systematically strive towards more historical precision by trying to show that Old World patterns participated in shaping New World configurations." [HvW]

546 ———. Ein siderisches Chronogramm im *Codex Vaticanus* 3773 (DGV/ZE, 106:1/2, 1981, p. 177–184, bibl.)

Systematic distribution of sets of attributes attached to the four serpents (fol. 73) is interpreted as being a sophisticated mechanism by which the priest-astronomers conveyed their knowledge of the revolution of Sun, Moon, and Pleiades. [HvW]

547 Berdan, Frances F. Aztec merchants and markets: local-level economic activity in a non-industrial empire (Mexicon [K.-F. von Flemming, Berlin] 2:1, 1980, p. 37–41, bibl., map)

Focuses on market patterns outside the Aztec capital, especially in provinces. Argues tribute requirements stimulated provincial marketing. Collects observations on the usual size of a market service area (up to 58 km) and on distances locals traveled to obtain goods of special interest (up to about 200 km). [BLS]

548 ———. Distributive mechanisms in the Aztec economy (*in* Peasant livelihood: studies in economic anthropology and cultural ecology. Edited by Rhoda Halperin and James Dow. New York: St. Martins Press, 1977, p. 91–101, bibl.)

Analyzes nature of and articulations among tribute, foreign exchange, and local marketing in the Aztec economy. [BLS]

549 ———. The Aztecs of central Mexico: an imperial society. New York: Holt, Rinehart and Winston, 1982. 195 p.: bibl., ill., maps, tables (Case studies in cultural anthropology)

Concise description of Aztecs including history, settlement pattern, economy, social structure, daily life, politics, religion, cultural achievements, and aftermath of the conquest (for ethnohistorian's comment, see *HLAS 44:1503*). [BLS]

550 Calnek, Edward E. Patterns of empire formation in the valley of Mexico, late postclassic period, 1200–1521 (*in* The Inca and Aztec states, 1400-1800: anthropology and history. Edited by George A. Collier, Renato I. Rosaldo, and John D. Wirth. New York: Academic Press, 1982, p. 43–62, bibl. [Studies in anthropology])

Late postclassic plethora of city-states in the Valley of Mexico developed as a consequence of migration into unoccupied lands.

City-states shared Toltec legitimization of rulers, and, after increased competition led to imperial unification, dynastic intermarriages contributed to Aztec tolerance of considerable city-state independence. [BLS]

551 Carmack, Robert M. and John M. Weeks. The archaeology and ethnohistory of Utatlan: a conjunctive approach (SAA/AA, 46:2, 1981, p. 323–341, bibl., ill.)

Use of archaeological settlement plan and ethnohistoric social data to reconstruct an internal social system (for ethnohistorian's comment, see *HLAS 44:1508*). [NH]

552 Carrasco, Pedro. The chiefly houses— *teccalli*—of ancient Mexico (*in* International Congress of Americanists, 42nd, Paris, 1976. Actes [see *HLAS 43:255*] v. 9-B, p. 177–185, bibl.)

Uses historical documents from the central highlands to outline relationship between Aztec chiefly houses and *calpulli* (barrios). Discusses *teccalli* in terms of social, economic, and political organization. [SL]

553 ———. The political economy of the Aztec and Inca states (*in* The Inca and Aztec states, 1400–1800: anthropology and history. Edited by George A. Collier, Renato I. Rosaldo, and John D. Wirth. New York: Academic Press, 1982, p. 23–40, bibl. [Studies in anthropology])

Emphasizes basic similarities in Inca and Aztec states, commenting on economy, social stratification, corporate groups, production units, distribution, and politics. Inca were more centralized, but the apparently greater importance of Mexican markets is downplayed, and both societies are viewed as variations in socially stratified systems. [BLS]

554 Closs, Michael P. On a Classic Maya accession phrase and a glyph for "rulership" (Mexicon [K.-F. von Flemming, Berlin] July 1982, p. 47–50, bibl., ill.)

Expanding on cited 1980 paper by Dütting (in press 1983), discusses usages of rulership glyphs and anniversary phrases in greater Usumacinta region with reference to early Maya-Chontal manuscript. [HvW]

555 The *Codex Pérez* and the *Book of Chilam Balam* of Maní. Translated and edited by Eugene R. Craine and Reginald C. Reindorp. Norman: University of Oklahoma Press, 1979. 209 p.: bibl., ill., index (The Civilization of the American Indian series)

First complete publication of a valuable ethnohistoric source on the Maya calendar and medical matters; portions have been published before, from Stephens in 1843 onwards. [NH]

556 Collier, George A. In the shadow of empire: new directions in Mesoamerican and Andean ethnohistory (*in* The Inca and Aztec states, 1400–1800: anthropology and history. Edited by George A. Collier, Renato I. Rosaldo, and John D. Wirth. New York: Academic Press, 1982, p. 1–20, bibl. [Studies in anthropology])

Overview of recent trends in ethnohistoric research. Case studies of particular (sub-imperial) areas are noteworthy, along with new recognition of continuity through colonial times of sub-imperial polities and traditions. Notes Aztec and Inca developmental cycles from coercive, to remunerative, to normative power relations. [BLS]

557 Dahlgren-Jordan, Barbara. Cambios socioeconómicos registrados a mediados del siglo XVI en un pueblo de la Mixteca Alta, Oaxaca, México (*in* International Congress of Americanists, 42nd, Paris, 1976. Actes [see *HLAS 43:255*] v. 8, p. 103–119, bibl., ill., tables)

Selections from *Codex Sierra* and accounting records from 16th-century native Mixtecan community. Demonstrates richness of ethnographic detail and potential for clarifying colonial period economic transactions, particularly in civil and religious sectors. [SL]

558 Doporto Uncilla, Serveriano. Tabasco en la época precolombiana. Villahermosa, México: Consejo Editorial del Gobierno del Estado de Tabasco, 1979. 54 p. (Serie Año del centenario Instituto Juárez. Colección de archivo; 4)

Excerpts from 1902 thesis which culled geographical, ethnohistoric, demographic, and commercial information on precolumbian Tabasco from 16th-century accounts and later historic documents. [SL]

559 Dütting, Dieter. Life and death in Mayan hieroglyphic inscriptions (DGV/ZE, 106:1/2, 1981, p. 185–228, bibl., ill.)

Detailed discussion of: a) hand grapheme T670 and its relation to birth, lineage rituals, and divination; b) descent and lineage themes at Piedras Negras; c) "birth trees" and the "tree birth" tradition in Mesoamerica; d) main sign T606; and e) war and death in central Peten inscriptions. [HvW]

560 ———. The 2 Cib 14 Mol event in the inscriptions of Palenque, Chiapas, Mexico (DGV/ZE, 107:2, 1982, p. 233–258, bibl., ill.)

This date (July 19/20, 690), recorded on Temples of the Cross, Foliated Cross, and Sun, is intimately associated with gods GI, GII, and GIII, to whom temples were dedicated. "Celestial events reveal a close encounter of the three outer planets (Mars, Jupiter, Saturn) with the Moon in the constellation Scorpio near the bright star Antares, which for the Maya probably meant the mythical birth of GI (Saturn?), GII (Jupiter?), and GIII (Mars?)." [HvW]

561 ———. Zum Charakter der Maya-Schrift und den Schwierigkeiten ihrer Entzifferung (Mexicon [K.-F. von Flemming, Berlin] 3:3, July 1981, p. 45–48, bibl., ill.)

Review of characteristics of Maya hieroglyphic writing and difficulties of decipherment. Present state of knowledge is exemplified by complete preliminary translation of text of Lintel I, Kuná-Lacanhá. Commentaries by Michel Davoust, J.F. Hochleitner, Berthold Riese in *Mexicon* (3:4, Sept. 1981, p. 58–61) and Thomas Forster and Thomas Barthel in *Mexicon* (3:5, Nov. 1981, p. 79–81). [HvW]

562 Durand-Forest, Jacqueline de. Les neuf Seigneurs de la nuit (IAI/I, 7:2, 1982, p. 103–129, bibl., ill., tables)

Characteristics of the nine lords of the night, based on written sources and pictorial manuscripts, with emphasis on their interrelationship and functions as a group. [HvW]

563 Foncerrada de Molina, Marta. Signos glíficos relacionados con Tláloc en los murales de la batalla en Cacaxtla (IIE/A, 50:1, 1982, p. 23–33, bibl., ill.)

Battle scenes (AD 750–800) of the murals include Teotihuacan features, among others, evident in Tlaloc imagery (the warlike Jaguar-Tlaloc), expressed by signs for heart/blood, and year sign as insignia of victorious warriors. [HvW]

564 Harvey, H.R. and B.J. Williams. Aztec arithmetic: positional notation and area calculation (AAAS/S, 210:4469, 31 Oct. 1980, p. 499–505, bibl., ill., tables)

Two census/cadastral documents from near Texcoco use place notation and a symbol representing some functions of zero; they suggest algorithms for computation of field areas. The usage is inferred to be native, not Spanish, and not a late Maya borrowing. [BLS]

565 Hassig, Ross. The famine of One Rabbit: ecological causes and social consequences of a precolumbian calamity (UNM/JAR, 37:2, Spring 1981, p. 172–182, bibl., maps)

Culminating in AD 1454, a series of poor harvests produced famine in central highlands, especially in Valley of Mexico. This ultimately contributed to investment in agricultural intensification because maize could not be profitably imported from lowland areas. [BLS]

566 ———. Periodic markets in precolumbian Mexico (SAA/AA, 47:2, April 1982, p. 346–355, bibl., ill.)

Analyzes variations in periodicity of native markets, arguing that daily markets in major centers and periodic five-day markets had primary importance. [BLS]

567 Hicks, Frederic. Tetzcoco in the early 16th century: the state, the city, and the *calpulli* (AES/AE, 9:2, May 1982, p. 230–249, bibl., map, table)

Social classes, labor service, dispersed urbanism, territorial and settlement units, craftsmen, and landholding are analyzed for late postclassic Texcoco, primarily from documents. [BLS]

568 Jones, Christopher and Linton Satterthwaite. The monuments and inscriptions of Tikal: the carved monuments. Illustrations by William R. Coe. Philadelphia: Univeristy Museum, University of Pennsylvania, 1982- . 1 v.: bibl., ill. (Tikal report; no. 33. University Museum monograph; 44)

Description of superb illustrations of stelae, alters, and lintels, with decipherments and discussion of dynastic succession. [NH]

569 Jones, Grant D.; Don S. Rice; and Prudence M. Rice. The location of

Tayasal: a reconsideration in light of Peten Maya ethnohistory and archaeology (SAA/AA, 46:3, 1981, p. 530–547, bibl., ill.)

Reaffirms traditional location of postclassic Tayasal, on Lake Petén Itza (see *HLAS 38:1975*. For ethnohistorian's comment, see *HLAS 44:1530*). [NH]

570 Kubler, George. The Mazapan maps of Teotihuacan in 1560 (IAI/I, 7, 1982, p. 43–55, bibl., ill.)

Important study of three related maps which, among other features, contain much detailed information on archaeological and mythological significance. [HvW]

571 Manuscrito de Chan Cah. Edited by Héctor M. Calderón. México: Grupo Dzibil A.C., 1982. 128 p.

First facsimile reproduction of this *Chilam Balam* with transcriptions and Spanish translation. It is related to the Tekax and Nah manuscripts (see item **572** and *Handbook of Middle American Indians*, Austin: University of Texas Press, 1975, v. 15, p. 379–382). [HvW]

572 Manuscritos de Tekax y Nah. Edited by Héctor M. Calderón. México: Grupo Dzibil, A.C., 1981. 1 v. (Unpaged)

First complete facsimile reproduction of 28 fol. of the *Chilam Balam* of Tekax and facsimile (60 fol.), transcription, and Spanish translation of the related Nah manuscript. For contents and bibliographical comments see *Handbook of Middle American Indians* (Austin: University of Texas Press, 1975, v. 15, p. 384 [item **1150**] and p. 386 [item **1154**]). [HvW]

573 Mayer, Karl Hebert. Eine Maya-Inschrift aus Xupá, Chiapas, Mexiko (MVW/AV, 35, 1981, p. 1–13, bibl., ill.)

Commentary on an incised stone fragment with glyphs and human figure, from vicinity of Palenque, after unpublished notes by Teobert Maler (1901). [HvW]

574 Miksicek, Charles H. *et al.* Rethinking *ramón*: a comment on Reina and Hill's *Lowland Maya subsistence* (SAA/AA, 46, 1981, p. 916–919)

Suggested identification of ramón (see *HLAS 43:407*) is more likely to be *achiote*. Evidence for prehispanic use of *ramón* is reviewed and found wanting. [NH]

575 Nicholson, H.B. Correlating Mesoamerican historical traditions with archeological sequence: some methodological considerations (*in* International Congress of Americanists, 42nd, Paris, 1976. Actes [see *HLAS 43:255*] v. 9-B, p. 187-198, bibl., tables)

A guide for postclassic archaeologists. Includes tables of principal classes of information on Mesoamerican native records and possible archaeological correlates. [SL]

576 Offner, Jerome A. Archival reports of poor crop yields in the early postconquest Texcocan heartland and their implications for studies of Aztec period population (SAA/AA, 45:4, Oct. 1980, p. 848–856, bibl., map, tables)

Crop yields in five post-conquest towns in the eastern and northern Valley of Mexico suggest low and variable productivity and favor lower published population estimates. Questions prior assumptions that modern and prehispanic maize productivity were equivalent (for ethnohistorian's comment, see *HLAS 44:1543*). [BLS]

577 ———. Aztec political numerology and human sacrifice: the ideological ramifications of the number six (UCLA/JLAL, 6:2, Winter 1980, p. 204–215, bibl., ill.)

Human sacrifice, the "flowery wars," taking captives, and Texcocan empire and city divisions used groups or divisions of six (or its multiples). This represents an ideological theme applied to the organization of human action (for ethnohistorian's comment, see *HLAS 44:1544*). [BLS]

578 ———. A reassessment of the extent and structuring of the empire of Techotlalatzin, fourteenth century ruler of Texcoco (ASE/E, 26:3, Summer 1979, p. 231–241, bibl., ill., table)

This ruler established a small empire during his reign, but it may not have outlasted him. His realm accepted many ethnic groups, but may not have interferred greatly in their affairs. Councils he established likely were for internal Texcocan affairs (for ethnohistorian's comment, see *HLAS 44:1547*). [BLS]

579 Pahl, Gary W. Notas sobre epigrafía maya: estudio de un altar del sitio de Polol, el Petén, Guatemala (IAHG/AHG, 2:3, 1981, p. 31–39, bibl., tables)

Suggests that Polol Altar 1 is a Cycle 7

monument. Plausible on stylistic grounds.
[NH]

580   **Pohl, Mary.** Ritual continuity and
       transformation in Mesoamerica: re-
constructing the ancient Maya *cuch* ritual
(SAA/AA, 46, 1981, p. 513–529)
       Uses ethnohistoric data allied to pre-
hispanic art to suggest continuity in the
cuch ritual, possibly of fertility significance.
Suggests the role of the stag as an agricultural supernatural in classic Maya religion
(for ethnohistorian's comment, see *HLAS
44:1552*). [NH]

581   **Riese, Berthold.** Katun-Altersangaben
       in klassischen Maya-Inschriften (MV/
BA, 28, 1980, p. 155–180, bibl., ill.)
       Examination of Proskouriakoff's
(1960–63) assumption that isolated *katun*
glyphs indicate a ruler's approximate age.
Testing inscriptions at Copan, Quirigua,
Tikal, Yaxchilan, and Palenque, this elaborated hypothesis appears to be valid and implies that the Maya calculated time not only
by precise days but also by approximate 20-
year units. [HvW]

582   ———. Die Popol Vuh Peten Platte:
       Naranjo Altar I (IAI/I, 7:2, 1982,
p. 143–157, bibl., ill., tables)
       Glyphic interpretation of the oldest
text from Naranjo, dealing with the genealogy of its first ruler. The monument is now
in the Popol Vuh Museum, Guatemala. [HvW]

583   **Rounds, J.** Dynastic succession and
       the centralization of power in Ten-
ochtitlan (*in* The Inca and Aztec states,
1400–1800: anthropology and history. Edited
by George A. Collier, Renato I. Rosaldo,
and John D. Wirth. New York: Academic
Press, 1982, p. 63–89, bibl., ill. [Studies in
anthropology])
       Provides detailed exegesis of changes
in Aztec dynastic succession and access to
high status. Changes were designed to increase cadre of elite persons and more clearly
demarcate them while controlling factionalism by narrowing pool of rivals for high
office. [BLS]

584   **Schele, Linda.** Maya glyphs, the verbs.
       Austin: University of Texas Press,
1982. 427 p.: bibl., ill.
       Study of verb morphology and syntax
in classic Maya hieroglyphic writing. Highly

important study of a writing system's structure and function, with very good general introduction, massive data base, and innovative
layout and design by author. Probably destined to become a classic. [NH]

585   **Spores, Ronald.** New World ethnohis-
       tory and archaeology, 1970–1980
(Annual Review of Anthropology [Annual
Reviews Inc., Palo Alto, Calif.] 9, 1980,
p. 575–603, bibl.)
       Inventories New World ethnohistoric
research under several topical headings. Reflective discussion of the history of ethnohistory, its relations with archaeology, and
research directions that should be pursued
balances the substantive review. [BLS]

587   **Tichy, Franz.** Jahresanfänge meso-
       amerikanischer Kalender mit 20-Tage-
Perioden; Typiesierung und Korrelation mit
dem Sonnenjahr (IAI/I, 6, 1980, p. 55–70,
bibl., ill., tables)
       Comparisons of various ancient and
surviving indigenous solar calendars and
analyses of their beginning dates, residual
nemomtemi days, and other characteristics.
[HvW]

588   ***El Tonalamatl* de la Colección de
       Aubin:** antiguo manuscrito en la Biblio-
teca Nacional de Paris, Ms. Mex. No. 18–19.
Tlaxcala, Mexico: Government of Tlaxcala,
1981. 1 v. (portfolio): col. facs., ill.
       Screenfold color reproduction based on
Seler's 1900–01 color lithograph facsimile,
with his annotated diagrams. Introductory
study by Carmen Aguilera. Possibly a preconquest divinatory almanac from Tlaxcala (?).
Each page depicts patron deities, 13 birds, 13
gods and Nine Lords of the Night associated
with each 13-day period of the 260-day cycle.
[HvW]

589   **Trautmann, Wolfgang.** Catálogo his-
       tórico-crítico de los nombres de lugar
relativos a Tlaxcala. Puebla, México: Fundación Alemana para la Investigación Científica, 1980. 74 p.: bibl. (Comunicaciones,
Proyecto Puebla-Tlaxcala. Suplemento; 8)
       Documentary study tabulates Tlax-
calan settlement place names, their political
location, and relevant source materials. [BLS]

590   **Whittaker, Gordon.** Los jeroglíficos
       preclásicos de Monte Albán. Oaxaca,
México: INAH, Centro Regional de Oaxaca,

1981. 16 p.: bibl., ill. (Estudios de antropología e historia; 27)

Examines preclassic glyphs, pointing out calendric as well as secular "readings." [BLS]

591 Williams, Barbara J. Aztec soil classification and land tenure (*in* National Congress of Americanists, 42nd, Paris, 1976. Actes [see *HLAS 43:255*] v. 9-B, p. 165–175, bibl., tables)

Soil glyphs from Aztec codices are used to examine relation between soil types and land tenure in 19 Indian villages. Land quality does not appear to correlate with size of holdings. There is some evidence for a negative correlation between household size and size of landholdings. [SL]

592 Zavala, José F. Einige Aspekte der Synchronizität anhand des mexikanischen, divinatorischen Kalenders *Tonalamatl* (SSA/B, 45, 1981, p. 61–69, ill.)

Applies Jung's concept of synchronicity (simultaneous effect of two unrelated events, one psychological, other physical, on the human mind) to divinatory sections of Mesoamerican calendars. Notes similarities between Sahagún's *Tonalamatl* texts and those of the Chinese *I'ching* augural method, based on archetypal *unus mundus* concepts. [HvW]

ARCHAEOLOGY: Caribbean Area

W. JERALD KENNEDY, *Associate Professor of Anthropology, Florida Atlantic University*

OVER THE PAST TWO YEARS there has been a change in the nature of the literature on Lower Central America and the Caribbean region. Although a wide variety of topics continues to be published, fewer publications deal with historical archaeology as in the preceding volume, *HLAS 43*.

CARIBBEAN ISLANDS

Articles deal with the following islands: the Bahamas, Cuba, Hispaniola, the Virgin Islands, Antigua, Barbados, Martinique, Puerto Rico, Jamaica, and Montserrat. The latter two were not covered in *HLAS 43*. Topics were varied and ranged from (seven) traditional site reports in the Dominican Republic (items **598, 607, 617,** and **622**); Martinique (item **595**); Virgin Islands (item **602**); Barbados (item **612**), to descriptions of specific artifacts.

Taino religion and associated artifacts of magico-religious paraphenalia continue to be of interest to some scholars as exemplified by the works of Veloz (item **631**), Pagan (item **620**), and Morban (item **616**).

Two themes which mark an important trend for future Caribbean studies concern precolumbian subsistence and diet and are treated by Rimoli (item **622**), Fraser (item **604**), and Lee (item **613**). Noteworthy also are articles about shell modification and food procurement techniques such as those by Jones (item **609**) and Keegan (item **610**).

Three articles that cover the colonial period in the Dominican Republic are by Brown (item **597**), Gartley (item **605**), in St. Croix, Virgin Islands, and Ortega (item **617**). Cruxent's use of Thermoluminescence (TL) to trace the origins and distribution of majolicas is important (item **599**).

Significant publications of a more general and theoretical nature also reviewed in this section are those by Alegría (item **594**), Veloz (item **631**), and Tabio (item **627**). For ongoing field research being conducted on many of the islands, the reader should consult Charles Hoffman's "Current Research Section" in *American Antiquity*

(47:4, 1982, p. 883–885). Vic Carbone (Interagency Archaeological Survey) and his colleagues are excavating a Spanish colonial site in Puerto Rico; John Winter (Malloy College) is conducting excavations on San Salvador; and Shaun Sullivan continued his work on the Middle Turks and Caicos during the summer of 1982.

Archaeological field schools were held on San Salvador in the Bahamas (Charles Hoffman, Northern Arizona University); the island of St. Eustatius, Netherland Antilles, led by Norman Barka (College of William and Mary); and Montserrat, West Indies (Linda Pulsipher and Conrad Goodwin, University of Tennessee).

Two important scientific congresses were held. The Ninth International Congress for the Study of Pre-Columbian Cultures of the Lesser Antilles convened in Santo Domingo, Dominican Republic, Aug. 1981, and over 150 persons representing 15 countries presented papers. The Third Bahamas Conference was held on San Salvador Island, March 18–22, 1982.

CENTRAL AMERICA

Publications concerning Costa Rica (21) and Nicaragua (19) predominate. For Costa Rica this is due, in large part, to the inclusion of a dozen articles from *Vínculos* (6:1/2, 1980) which focused on the prehistory of Culebra Bay in the nation's northwest. Overall, the gamut of topics on Central America is wide and ranges from reports on archaeological excavations in Costa Rica (11), Nicaragua (four), and Panama (two) to artifact analysis of monumental stone sculpture in Nicaragua (four) and celts in Costa Rica (item **645**). The number of articles on Costa Rica that focus on the analysis of skeletal populations and mortuary practices (items **660, 673–674,** and **676**) are symptomatic of a new trend, the attempt to reconstruct with greater accuracy the life style of the region's precolumbian people.

The Panama City excavation led by Richard Cooke and B. Rovira (item **649**) was the sole entry which concerned the colonial period.

Among all publications reviewed over the past two years, two stand out as exceptional, but, in many respects, still reflect the unevenness of our knowledge of the prehistory of Lower Central America. The long-awaited book by Paul Healy (item **652**) is certainly useful. Primarily, he establishes a base line, a cultural chronology in Southwestern Nicaragua where so little scientific archaeology has been done. The other, a book edited by Olga Linares of the Smithsonian Institution, sets a standard of excellence to which we might all aspire. Contributions to this work reveal that both Linares and her colleagues possess a commanding grasp of the complex interplay between man and land in Panama. This ecologically oriented study, reflecting many years of work by its contributors, supplants a rather well-established chronological framework and many preceding excavations within this region.

For ongoing field research, which appears extremely active in a variety of archaeological sub-areas both in Costa Rica and Panama, see Richard Cooke's "Current Research" in *American Antiquity* (47:1, 1982, p. 202–207 and 48:1, 1983, p. 176–178).

It remains to be seen whether the archaeological investigations initiated by Richard Magnus and Paul Healy (items **653** and **662**) will be followed up in Nicaragua.

A symposium "El Sureste de Costa Rica Como Región de Desarrollo" was held at San Isidro de El General, Costa Rica, 1981.

OBITUARIES

We shall all miss two colleagues who have worked so long in this area: Carlos Enrique Herra, Museo Nacional, Costa Rica, who died in Sept. 1981, and Reina Torres de Arauz, Director of the Patrimonio Histórico, Instituto Nacional de Cultura, Panama, who died in Feb. 1982.

RECENT DOCTORAL DISSERTATIONS

Fowler, William R., Jr. The Pipil-Nicaro of Central America. Univ. of Calgary, 1982.

Skirboll, Esther R. The transitional period in the central highlands of Costa Rica: an analysis of pottery from the Curridabat and Concepcion sites. Univ. of Pittsburgh, 1981.

Sullivan, Shaun. Prehistoric patterns of exploitation and colonization in the Turks and Caicos Islands. Univ. of Illinois, Urbana, 1981.

ANTILLES

593   Alcina Franch, José. Religiosidad, alucinógenos y patrones artísticos taínos (MHD/B, 10:17, 1982, p. 103–118)

Author presents thesis that Taino art was heavily influenced by vision-producing hallucinogens used in religious rituals called *Cohoba*.

594   Alegría, Ricardo E. El uso de la terminología etnohistórica para designar las culturas aborígenes de las Antillas (Cuaderno Prehispánicos [Seminario Americanista de la Universidad Casa de Colón, Valladolid, Spain] 9, 1981, p. 5–32, facs., ill.)

Author discusses various ethnohistoric terms used by the early chroniclers. Denotes indigenous groups that inhabited the Antilles at time of discovery and the three great cultures that emerge: Archaic (pre-agricultural Guanojatabeyes); Arawak (Arawakan Igneri, Tainos, sub-Tainos, Ciboneys, Lucayos); and Carib.

595   Allaire, Louis. Macabou excavations: Martinique, 1972–1979 (MHD/B, 10:16, 1981, p. 41–48)

Brief discussion of work conducted 1977–79 at important Macabou site on southeast coast of Martinique. Seven areas (A-F) were excavated and findings are summarized. Author notes that three Suazoid phases were found in Martinique, ca. AD 1100-AD 1400, and concludes that there is no reason to associate Island Caribs with Suazoid prehistoric people nor Suazoid components with historic period.

596   Arrom, José J. Taino mythology: notes on the Supreme Being (LALR, 8:16, Spring/Summer 1980, p. 21–37, ill.)

Excellent article in which author uses linguistic, ethnohistoric, and archaeological data to shed light on Tainos' Supreme Being: Yucahu Bagua Maorocoti, a sustaining being who ruled the creative forces of land and sea. Tripointed Zemis are considered to be representations of this sacred personage.

597   Brown, Robert S. The vernacular architecture of Fredriksted (Journal of the Virgin Islands Archaeological Society [St. Thomas] 8, 1979, p. 3–43, bibl., ill., maps)

Excellent article describes in detail three types of early Fredriksted's typical house architecture. Authors' intent is to alert island residents to preserve additional examples of this unique residential style. Well illustrated.

598   Castellanos, Reynaldo. La Plaza de Chacuey: un instrumento astronómico megalítico (MHD/B, 10:16, 1981, p. 31–40)

Presents data to suggest that many features of Plaza de Chacuey, a megalithic structure in Dominican Republic, had astronomical significance.

599   Cruxent, José and **José Eduardo Vaz.** Provenience studies of majolica pottery: type Ichtucknee Blue on Blue (*in* Archaeological essays in honor of Irving B.

Rouse. R. Dunnell and E. Hall, editors. The Hague: Mouton Publishers, 1978, p. unavailable [Studies in anthropology; 2])

Article is part of planned series treating authors' ongoing research in thermoluminescence (TL) to determine place of majolica pottery manufacture. Utilizing the TL method on 14 samples, Ichtucknee Blue on Blue, authors conclude majolica specimens were manufactured in Seville, Spain (10) and Albisola, Italy (four). Former were exported to Hispaniola and Venezuela, latter to Panama and Azua, Dominican Republic.

600 Dacal Moure, Ramón. De los ciboneyes del Padre Las Casas a los ciboneyes de 1966 (Universidad de La Habana [Departamento de Actividades Culturales] 211, abril 1979/dic. 1980, p. 6–41, ill.)

Author discusses problems associated with various groups called Ciboney. Notes confusion surrounding use of this term in both ethnohistoric and contemporary writings. Lists characteristic features and provenience of 42 Ciboney sites. Suggests that additional archaeological work will be needed for final classification.

601 Febles Dueñas, Jorge. Estudio tipológico y tecnológico del material de piedra tallada del sitio arqueológico canimar 1, Matanzas, Cuba (Academia de Ciencias de Cuba [La Habana] 1982, 51 p., ill.)

Basing his studies on lithic materials from Canimar I site, Matanzas, Cuba, author analyzes both technical and typological characteristics. Notes some similarities with several microlithic industries such as Momil I (Colombia); Machallia, Valdivia (Ecuador); and Jaketown (USA).

602 Figueredo, Alfredo E. A chert point from Krum Bay, St. Thomas (Journal of the Virgin Islands Archaeological Society [St. Thomas] 9, 1980, p. 41–42, bibl., ill.)

Brief comments on a unique chert point (or perforator) from Archaic period at Krum Bay in Virgin Islands.

603 ———. Pottery from Gun Creek, Virgin Gorda (Journal of the Virgin Islands Archaeological Society [St. Thomas] 9, 1980, p. 27–30, ill.)

Preliminary summary of excavations conducted in 1973 by author at Gun Creek Site, Virgin Gorda, British Virgin Islands. Middens appear to represent a single household. Ceramics suggest distinctive terminal insular Saladoid style called "Gun Creek." Dating has been placed between AD 500-AD 600.

604 Fraser, Linda J. The analysis of the vertebrate fauna from the Macabou site, Area F, Martinique (MHD/B, 10:16, 1981, p. 49–60)

Brief but informative summary of vertebrate faunal materials excavated by Allaire in 1977. Calculation of relative frequencies between two different areas within the site, as well as intrasite comparison with Barbados, Grenada, and St. Lucia is of interest.

605 Gartley, Richard T. Afro-Cruzan pottery: a new style of colonial earthenware from St. Croix (Journal of the Virgin Islands Archaeological Society [St. Thomas] 8, 1979, p. 47–61, ill., plates)

Description of unglazed ceramics manufactured in St. Croix after 1750 and widely used on island into 19th century. Suggests it was made originally by African slaves, and additional research will show it resembles pottery from West Africa at that time.

606 Gómez Acevedo, Labor and **Manuel Ballesteros Gaibrois.** Vida y cultura precolombinas de Puerto Rico. Río Piedras: Editorial Cultural, 1980. 132 p.: bibl., ill.

Authors present concise overview of aboriginal life and culture in Puerto Rico. Unfortunately most recent citations encompass works no later than 1974.

607 Guerrero, José G. Dos plazas indígenas y el poblado de Cotubanama, Parque Nacional del Este (MHD/B, 10:16, 1981, p. 13–30)

Discussion of National Park of the East, Dominican Republic in which author conducted visual archaeological reconnaissance. Suggests park's potential importance for archaeological sites. Ethnohistoric documents point to likelihood that one site, Cuadro de Piedras, may have been Cacique Cotubanama's residence.

608 Helms, Mary W. Succession to high office in precolumbian Circum-Caribbean chiefdoms (RAI/M, 15:4, Dec. 1980, p. 718–731)

Utilizing early 16th-century ethnohistoric records, author analyzes and compares rules of succession to high office in precolumbian chiefdoms in Circum-

Caribbean area. Presents evidence from Panama, Colombia's Muisca and Cauca Valley, and Taino of Greater Antilles. Suggests that determinate succession modes are preferred in these cases. Concludes tentatively that prime sociopolitical solidarity of ruling groups in 16th-century Circum-Caribbean chiefdoms was based on the lord's close female relatives, providing genealogical legitimacy and fulfiling roles as regents. Same determinate succession modes were seen as appropriate to other political and symbolic aspects of these Circum-Caribbean societies.

609 Jones, Alick R. A report on two types of modification to gastropod mollusc shells from Indian Creek, Antigua (Journal of the Virgin Islands Archaeological Society [St. Thomas] 9, 1980, p. 31–40, appendix, bibl., ill., table)

Discussion of whorl removal in whelk and columella and inner whorl removal in small gastropod shells found at Indian Creek site, Antigua. Former type of modification appears to be related to food preparation while latter remains unexplained.

610 Keegan, William F. A biological introduction to the prehistoric procurement of the *Strombus Gigas* (Florida Anthropologist [Florida Anthropological Society, Gainesville] 35:2, June 1982, p. 76–88)

Brief but useful article dealing with life history, spatial distribution and meat removal techniques associated with this widespread food source, the queen conch.

611 ———. Lucayan cave burials from the Bahamas (Journal of New World Archaeology [University of California, Institute of Archaeology, Los Angeles] 5:2, April 1982, p. 57–65)

Discussion of the archaeological remains of 10 individuals from Freeport, Grand Bahamas, and 22 individuals from six other islands in Central Bahamas. Using available data, author attempts to reconstruct mortuary practices and patterns of Lucayan social organization.

612 Lange, Frederick W. and Jerome S. Handler. The archaeology of Mapps Cave: a contribution to the prehistory of Barbados (Journal of the Virgin Islands Archaeological Society [St. Thomas] 9, 1980, p. 3–17, bibl., ill., maps, tables)

Brief description of excavations at the

Mapps Cave, Barbados. Data represents multicomponent site occupied relatively late in protohistoric period. Chronological placement is suggested by presence of Swazey Series (Caribe) and the absence of Caliviny ceramics (Arawakan).

613 Lee, James W. Arawak burens (Archaeology [Kingston, Jamaica] 80:2, 1980, p. 1–15, ill.)

Discussion of Arawakan burens (griddles), especially those found in Jamaica.

614 Martínez Arango, Felipe. Registro de todos los sitios arqueológicos investigados por la Sección Arqueológica Aborigen de la Universidad de Oriente. México: Litográfica Machado, 1982. 41 p., 1 folded leaf of plates: ill.

Brief description and complete listing of 134 aboriginal archaeological sites in Oriente Province, Cuba, investigated by Universidad de Oriente's Archaeological Section up to Nov. 1980.

615 Meggers, Betty and Clifford Evans. Un método cerámico para el reconocimiento de comunidades prehistóricas (MHD/B, 9:14, 1980, p. 57–74)

Authors remind us of and spell out Ford's ceramic seriation technique to assist in identifying prehistoric communities which share a common cultural tradition.

616 Morbán Laucer, Fernando A. Ritos funerarios: acción del fuego y medio ambiente en las osamentas precolombinas. Santo Domingo: Editora Taller, 1979. 157 p.: bibl., ill. (Academia de Ciencias de la República Dominicana, Comisión de Arqueología; v. 1)

Using historical sources and archaeological data, author focuses on use of fire as part of religious mortuary rite emphasized among various cultures on Santo Domingo Island. Discusses secondary burials and other practices associated with inhumation. Includes brief but interesting section on skeletal paleopathology and local environmental factors that contribute to preservation problems.

617 Ortega, Elpidio. Introducción a la loza común o alfarería en el período colonial de Santo Domingo. Santo Domingo: Fundación Ortega Alvarez, 1980. 166 p.: bibl., ill. (Serie científica; 3)

Detailed analysis of colonial ceramics found at Plaza de Los Curas, Dominican Republic, excavated in 1968. Focus is on simple nondecorated utilitarian wares, the most popular form of pottery used by the Spanish up to 19th century. Change in manufacturing techiques between AD 1600-AD 1700 points to change in way of life of the people at this time. Well illustrated.

618 —— and **José Guerrero.** Estudio de 4 nuevos sitios paleoarcaicos de la Isla de Santo Domingo. Dibujos, Dionisio Blanco. Santo Domingo: Museo del Hombre Dominicano, 1981. 226 p.: bibl., ill. (Serie Investigaciones antropológicas; no. 17)

Using nomenclatural scheme adopted by Pina, Veloz and García (1974), author provides excellent description and analysis of lithic artifacts excavated from four paleoarchaic preceramic sites in Dominican Republic (El Curro, Las Salinas, Los Toros, and Canade de Palma). Final chapter deals with Mordan culture's origin and dispersal.

619 —— and ——. El fecado del sitio Mellacoide Bois de Charrite, Haiti (MHD/B, 10:17, 1982, p. 29–54)

Description of preliminary site excavations by author at Bois de Charrite, Haiti, near Cape Haitian. Site is Mellacoid and C14 dates on shell place its occupation between AD 1180-AD 1440. Summary conclusions deal with distribution and distinctive features among Mellacoid cultures in Haiti and Dominican Republic.

620 **Pagán Perdomo, Dato.** Aspectos ergológicos e ideología en el arte rupestre de la Isla de Santo Domingo (MHD/B, 10:17, 1982, p. 55–94, ill.)

List of selected cultural elements depicted in petroglyphs and pictographs found in Dominican Republic. Illustrations.

621 —— and **Manuel García Arévalo.**

Notas sobre pictografías y petroglifos de las Guacaras de Comedero Arriba y El Hoyo de Sanabe, República Dominicana (MHD/B, 9:14, 1980, p. 13–56, ill.)

Brief discussion of pictographs and petroglyphs from two cave sites discovered 1978. Designs, principally anthropomorphic and zoomorphic figures, are similar to those associated with Taino mythology and rituals. Authors conclude that pictographs in the Dominican Republic comprise various "pic-

tographic styles:" in south central Dominican Republic the Borbon style, and Las Maravillas in the eastern region. Appended sections give details of other materials found in caves. Single C14 date of 825 BC is given for Guacaras de Comedero site. Illustrations.

622 **Rimoli, Renato O.** Estudio comparativo de la dieta en sitios precolombinos de La Española (MHD/B, 10:17, 1982, p. 141–148)

Brief article in which author compares various aspects of precolumbian diet inferred from ecological and archaeological data. Examples are taken from two Chicoid sites, El Soso and the Sitio Dumet, in the Dominican Republic.

623 —— and **Joaquín Nadal.** Cerámica temprana de Honduras del Oeste (MHD/B, 9:15, 1980, p. 17–82)

Site description of Honduras de Oeste, southwest of Santo Domingo in Dominican Republic. Lithic and ceramic artifacts are analyzed from this site, dated between 360 BC-AD 185.

624 **Rivero de la Calle, Manuel.** Pendientes aborígenes cubanos (BNJM/R, 72[23]:1, 3. época, enero/abril 1981, p. 49–59, ill.)

Author reports finding necklace composed of shell and two carved sea lion pendants in Ciboney burial at Cueva de la Pluma, Cubre Alta, Matanzas. This marks first report of the tropical sea lion (*Monachus tropicalis*) in Cuba.

625 **Robotham, Don.** Anthropology and archaeology in Jamaica (III/AI, 40:2, abril/junio 1980, p. 355–366)

Summary of the beginnings of anthropology and archaeology in Jamaica.

626 **Sued Badillo, Jalil.** Los caribes, realidad o fábula: ensayo de rectificación histórica. Río Piedras: Editorial Antillana, 1978. 187 p., 1 leaf of plates: bibl., ill.

Utilizing ethnohistoric, linguistic and archaeological data, author argues that aboriginal Caribbean precolumbian cultures were fundamentally homogeneous and all varieties should be seen as regional adaptations to varied ecological circumstances.

627 **Tabío, Ernesto E.** and **Estrella Rey.** Prehistoria de Cuba. 2. ed. corr. y aum. La Habana: Editorial de Ciencias Sociales, 1979. 234 p., 31 p. of plates: bibl., ill. (Historia)

Second up-dated edition of 1966 original. Excellent summary presentation of archaeological excavations and material culture of Ciboney (Guyabo Blanco and Cayo Redondo), the Mayari, Subtaino and Taino. Includes illustrations, bibliography, C14 dates.

628   Tilden, Bruce E. Cotton garden red-on-brown ware: some preliminary observations (Journal of the Virgin Islands Archaeological Society [St. Thomas] 9, 1980, p. 22–26, ill.)

Description of distinctive Cotton garden red-on-brown ware. This ware and its variations have been found at three sites on St. Croix, Virgin Islands (Fair Pain site/late prehistoric; Cramer Park site/late prehistoric-historic; Salt River Point site/multicomponent-prehistoric-historic). Author believes wares indicate continuation of local earlier traditions within new Chicoid context in Virgin Islands.

629   Vega, Bernardo. Los metales y los aborígenes de La Hispaniola. Santo Domingo: Ediciones Museo del Hombre Dominicano, 1979. 63 p.: bibl., ill. (Serie Investigaciones antropológicas; no. 12)

Detailed analysis of metal work (gold, copper, silver, brass, and copper-silver alloys) found in Dominican Republic. Author traces distribution of these metal artifacts and draws several possible conclusions regarding their origin.

630   ———. Un objeto enigmático de la Colección Hodges (MHD/B, 10:17, 1982, p. 21–28)

Reports on unique hollow tubular ceramic object from private collection in Cape Haitian, Haiti. Artifact comes from zone where Meillac, and occasionally Chicoid, cultures are found. Concludes this was pipe for smoking tobacco rather than inhaling cohoba; first tubular pipe reported for the Antilles.

631   Veloz Maggiolo, Marcio. Vida y cultura en la prehistoria de Santo Domingo. San Pedro de Macorís, República Dominicana: Universidad Central del Este, 1980. 169 p.: bibl., ill. (Serie científica. Universidad Central del Este; 10)

Excellent book by well-known Dominican scholar and archaeologist. Divided into three parts: 1) Hispaniola's precolumbian population, diversity of its cultures, economic organization, art and agriculture; 2) consists of two articles with similar titles, "Archaeology as Social Science;" and 3) covers three disparate themes: historical reconstruction of sweet potato in Antilles, development of Antillean archaeology, and use of archaeological materials as sources for historical research.

632   ——— and Carlos Angulo Valdes. La aparición de un ídolo de tres puntas en la tradición Malambo, Colombia (MHD/B, 10:17, 1982, p. 15–20)

Authors report presence of three-pointed idol (Cemi) excavated at Malambo in Northern Colombia. Archaeological context in which it was found has been dated between 400 BC-200 BC, thus making it earlier than its Caribbean counterparts.

633   ——— and Mao Ramos Ramírez. Informe sobre una nueva maraca monoxilla indígena hallada en Puerto Rico (MHD/B, 9:15, 1980, p. 11–16)

Brief description of wooden maraca fragment found in Puerto Rico at Los Chorros site. Authors note distribution of similar artifacts in Dominican Republic and Cuba. They conclude this represents widespread Taino influence serving dual function both as maracas and spatulas used in Cohoba ritual.

634   Watters, David R. A problematic artifact from Trant's Montserrat (Journal of the Virgin Islands Archaeological Society [St. Thomas] 9, 1980, p. 18–21, ill.)

Brief discussion dealing with unique slate or shale artifact found at Trant site in Montserrat. Several functions are considered but prove inconclusive.

CENTRAL AMERICA

635   Abel-Vidor, Suzanne. Dos hornos precolombinos en el sitio Vidor Bahía Culebra, Guanacaste (MNCR/V, 6:1/2, 1980, p. 43–50)

Discusses two ovens recently excavated at Vidor site in Northwestern Costa Rica. C14 dates place one in early Loma B Phase (800 BC-300 BC), the other, most likely a ceramic kiln, in initial part of Culebra Phase (AD 500-AD 800).

636   ———. The historical sources for the Greater Nicoya sub-area (MNCR/V, 6:1/2, 1980, p. 155–176, bibl.)

Commentary on potential of historical documents of contact period in Lower Central America and especially Greater Nicoya for anthropological and archaeological research. Bibliography included.

637 Accola, Richard M. Sitio Nacascolo: arqueología en un sitio saqueado (*in* Centenario de Gonzalo Fernández de Oviedo, 5th, Nicoya, Costa Rica, 1978. Memoria del Congreso sobre el Mundo Centroamericano de su Tiempo, 24–25–26 y 27 de agosto 1978. Nicoya?, Costa Rica: Comisión Nacional Organizadora, 1978, p. 167–174, bibl., ill.)

Describes excavation and preliminary findings from Nacascolo site on north side of Culebra Bay, Costa Rica. Salvage excavations of this badly disturbed site began in 1978 in conjunction with Costa Rica's National Museum. Well-preserved, sheltered materials are present. Associated funerary retainers point to Middle Polychrome (AD 1000-AD 1200) period occupation. Notes Mexican influences suggest that such similarities may reflect arrival of Nicarao in this area. Good description of excavation techniques employed on disturbed sites.

638 ——— and Peter R. Ryder. Excavaciones en el sitio Monte del Barco, Bahía Culebra (MNCR/V, 6 : 1/2, p. 67–80)

Discussion of results from recent excavations (1978) at Monte del Barco site. This single component site has been temporally placed in Panama Phase of the Middle Polychrome period (AD 800-AD 1000). Author, noting differences in shell remains from other sites in region, suggests this site was likely a collecting station which exploited specific gastropods and bivalves in the ecosystem.

639 Adaptive radiations in prehistoric Panama. Edited by Olga F. Linares and Anthony J. Ranere. Cambridge, Mass.: Peabody Museum of Archaeology and Ethnology, Harvard University, 1980. 530 p.: bibl., ill. (Peabody Museum monographs; no. 5)

This ecologically oriented look at Panamanian prehistory is, in author's own words, "An attempt to reconstruct a prehistoric example of adaptive radiation among human populations in the New World tropics and to evaluate divergent settlement and subsistence systems resulting from different eco-

logical and social conditions" (p. 3). Superb book of chapters contributed by specialists realizes goals of author-editor. Divided into six parts, topics range from preceramic shelters to large villages and centers of coastal settlements on Atlantic and Pacific sides, cultural inferences from artifactual remains, cultural inferences from organic remains, contemporary Indian societies in Western Panama, and conclusions. Twenty individual reports, covering a wide range of topics, round out this indispensible work. Well illustrated, bibliography.

640 Arellano, Jorge Eduardo. La Colección Squier-Zapatera: estudio de estatuaria prehispánica. Managua: s.n., 1979 or 1980. 184 p.: bibl., ill.

Discussion of Nicaraguan precolumbian stone statuary principally from Squier-Zapatero Patio Collection at Colegio Centroamericano in Grenada, Nicaragua. Includes review of earlier works and description and interpretation of statuary. Illustrations.

641 ———. El padre Andrés Rongier y sus exploraciones arqueológicas (BNBD, 35/36, mayo/agosto 1980, p. 15–16, ill.)

Brief commentary on Fray Andrés Roniger, S.J. (1879–1940) who conducted early archaeological studies on islands of Ometepe, Zapatera, La Ceiba, and three Tinajas in Nicaragua.

642 ———. El paleolítico en Nicaragua (BNBD, 35/36, mayo/agosto 1980, p. 116–119)

Study suggests potential for Paleo-Indian studies in Nicaragua. Notes abundance of sites, over a dozen, with fossil mammoth and extinct bison specimens, and briefly discusses distribution. Three sites are covered: 1) El Bosque, estimated to be 32,000 years old; 2) shell-middens at Monkey Point (Punta Mica), maritime site along Caribbean coast, approximately 7600 years; and 3) Acahualinca footprints on Pacific Coast (C14 5945 ± 145 BP).

643 ———. La situación antropológica y arqueológica en Nicaragua (III/AI, 40 : 2, abril/junio 1980, p. 399–403)

Highly encapsulated commentary of direction of anthropology and archaeology in Nicaragua since the Sandinista Revolution.

644   Benson, Elizabeth. Ancient arts of Costa Ria (OAS/AM, 34:4, July/Aug. 1982, p. 25–33, ill.)

Brief article on selected artifacts from three major archaeological zones in Costa Rica. Illustrations.

645   Bernstein, David. Artefactos de piedra pulida de Guanacaste, Costa Rica: una perspectiva funcional (MNCR/V, 6:1/2, 1980, p. 141–154)

Analyzes six celts from 11 archaeological sites in Guanacaste province, Costa Rica. When examined for macro- and micro-morphological attributes, the morphologically similar artifacts were categorized into five separate (functional) groups: axes, adzes, intermediate tools, percussors, and grinders. Use of celts for agricultural purposes is seriously questioned.

646   ———. El valor del análisis lítico en la reconstrucción de las actividades prehistóricas: un ejemplo de Guanacaste, Costa Rica (*in* Centenario de Gonzalo Fernández de Oviedo, 5th, Nicoya, Costa Rica, 1978. Memoria del Congreso sobre el Mundo Centroamericano de su Tiempo, 24–25–26 y 27 de agosto 978. Nicoya?, Costa Rica: Comisión Nacional Organizadora, 1978, p. 185–191, bibl., ill.)

This article deals with the term *celt*, its past usage and present lack of precision in usage. Author conducts microwear analyses of celts from Bahía de Culebra and Río Sapoa region in Costa Rica and tentatively delineates four categories based on different uses: 1) hachas, 2) azuelas, 3) cuñas, and 4) machacadores.

647   Blanco Vargas, Aída M. and **Silvia Salgado González.** Rescate arqueológico del sitio 26-CN-Barrial de Heredia (*in* Centenario de Gonzalo Fernández de Oviedo, 5th, Nicoya, Costa Rica, 1978. Memoria del Congreso sobre el Mundo Centroamericano de su Tiempo, 24–25–26 y 27 de agosto 1978. Nicoya?, Costa Rica: Comisión Nacional Organizadora, 1978, p. 133–139, bibl., photos)

Discusses recent excavations at Cenada en Barrial de Herredia site, west of Central Valley, Costa Rica. Preliminary work on this significant site revealed house foundations of rectangular configuration, in marked contrast to circular house mounds typical of Central Valley. Authors tentatively conclude features of this Cartago phase (AD 900-AD 1400) site are further indicative of Mesoamerican influences in this region.

648   Chávez, Crisanta. Sarcófagos y urnas del Museo Nacional de Nicaragua (BNBD, 35/36, mayo/agosto 80, p. 42–43)

Reprint of 1944 article briefly describes 20 burial urns and sarcophagi in Nicaraguan National Museum.

649   Cooke, Richard G. and **Beatriz Elena Rovira.** Historical archaeology in Panama City (Archaeology [New York] 36:2, March/April 1983, p. 51–57)

General article describes development of historical archaeology in Panama City with considerable attention given to excavations and artifacts recovered from Convent of St. Dominic, built 1673.

650   Demarest, Arthur; Roy Switsur; and **Rainer Berger.** The dating and cultural associations of the "potbellied" sculptural style: new evidence from western El Salvador (SAA/AA, 47:3, July 1982, p. 557–571, ill., maps, plates, tables)

Based on recent archaeological findings, including C14 dates at the Santa Leticia site, author assigns controversial potbellied sculpture to late preclassic period and concludes they are post-Olmec in their appearance.

651   Guerrero Miranda, Juan Vicente. Problemática de la investigación en la arqueología de rescate (*in* Centenario de Gonzalo Fernández de Oviedo, 5th, Nicoya, Costa Rica, 1978. Memoria del Congreso sobre el Mundo Centroamericano de su Tiempo, 24–25–26 y 27 de agosto 1978. Nicoya?, Costa Rica: Comisión Nacional Organizadora, 1978, p. 129–132, bibl.)

Using La Fábrica site as example, authors report that many archaeological sites with valuable data are being lost, largely because of budgetary problems. Proposes several suggestions for effectively dealing with this problem and preserving Costa Rica's cultural patrimony.

652   Healy, Paul F. Archaeology: the Rivas Region, Nicaragua. Waterloo, Canada: Wilfred Laurier University Press, 1980. 382 p.: bibl., ill., maps.

Major work on the archaeology of southwestern Nicaragua, primarily Rivas Region. Published originally as author's Ph.D.

dissertation, book's goal is to describe, classify and ultimately place area's prehistory in a chronological frame. Divided into four chapters: a) biogeographical and historical introduction; 2) archaeology of Rivas Region; 3) cultural remains of Rivas and their interpretation; and 4) Rivas culture history. While book is somewhat limited in its scope, author develops a ceramic typology and temporal framework which provides a more complex history of Nicaraguan culture than previously available. Painstaking detail along with clarity of presentation will make this work a basic reference for anyone studying Lower Central America.

653 ——. Los Chorotega y Nicarao: evidencia arqueológica de Rivas (BNBD, 43, sept./oct. 1981, p. 1–8, ill.)

Article focuses on last two periods of Nicaraguan prehistory: Middle Polychrome (AD 800-1200) and Terminal Polychrome (AD 1200-1523). Considers evidence and discusses impact of Mesoamerican cultures on Southwestern Nicaragua including Northwestern Costa Rica. Archaeological evidence suggests Mayan (Chorotegan) migration from Southern Mexico beginning about AD 800. Terminal Polychrome Period is a time of contact with Nahua-speaking peoples from Central Mexico. The Nicarao, leaving Mexico perhaps due to political instability in Central Mexico, begin displacing the Chorotega after AD 1200.

654 Jenkins, Jorge. Notas arqueológicas del Noroeste de Nicaragua (BNBD, 35/36, mayo/agosto 1980, p. 62–67, bibl.)

Short description of 1972 trip along Nicaragua's Atlantic Coast, Río Coco's vicinity. Comments on two unreported petroglyphs and artifacts observed near San Esquipulas and Santa Fe.

655 Kerbis, Julian. The analysis of faunal remains from the Vidor Site (MNCR/V, 6:1/2, 1980, p. 125–140)

Reports on abundant faunal remains recovered from shell-middens a Vidor site. Notes two volcanic ash layers dividing Middle Polychrome Period (AD 800-1000 and AD 1000–1200). Significant changes in frequences of aquatic and land animals occur during this time. Considers both cultural and natural explanations.

656 Lange, W. Frederick. The Formative Zoned Bichrome Period in North-western Costa Rica, 800 BC-AD 500: based on excavations at the Vidor Site, Bay of Culebra (MNCR/V, 6:1/2, 1980, p. 33–50)

Research recently conducted by the author at the Vidor site on the Bay of Culebra suggests a division of the formative period in Northwestern Costa Rica into three phases: Loma B Phase, 800 BC-300 BC; Orso Phase, 300 BC-AD 200; and Mata de Uva Phase, AD 300–500. Changes in social organization and subsistence practices are used but much additional work will be required for a more comprehensive understanding of cultural development in this region.

657 ——. Una ocupación del Policromo Tardío en Sitio Ruiz, cerca de Bahía Culebra (MNCR/V, 6:1/2, 1980, p. 81–96)

Excellent article in which author discusses his findings from Ruiz site near Culebra Bay. Site is primarily of Late Polychrome Period occupation which is now placed between AD 1350–1500 in this region. Presents comparison of Ruiz/Bay of Culebra with Greater Nicoya.

658 ——. La presencia de metales precolombinos en Guanacaste (*in* Centenario de Gonzalo Fernández de Oviedo, 5th, Nicoya, Costa Rica, 1978. Memoria del Congreso sobre el Mundo Centroamericano de su Tiempo, 24–25–26 y 27 de agosto 1978. Nicoya?, Costa Rica: Comisión Nacional Organizadora, 1978, p. 149–156, bibl., ill.)

Brief but significant article discusses recent find (1977) at Ruiz site, Guanacaste, Costa Rica. Ceramics point to Late Polychrome Period occupation (AD 1200–1500). Discoveries of fragmentary mold, used in the "lost wax" metallurgical technique, and gold frog are significant. They suggest localized manufacture with local resources. Includes commentary on other authors who have published on Costa Rican metallurgy.

659 ——; **Richard Accola;** and **Peter Ryder.** La administración de los recursos culturales en Bahía Culebra: un informe sobre la prospección realizada dentro de la Zona de Impacto del Desarrollo Turístico Bahía Culebra (MNCR/V, 6:1/2, 1980, p. 9–32)

On the basis of 60 archaeological sites located in Bay of Culebra, Costa Rica, authors spell out rationale, recommendations, and CRM strategies that emerged.

660 Laurencich-Minelli, Laura. Un sacro cenol nella penisola di Nicoya: un cimitero isolito (Archivo pel'Antropologia e l'Ethnologia [Firenze, Italy] 109, 1981, p. 247–256)

Article notes apparently unique precolumbian cemetery in Nicon Cave, Gran Nicoya, Northwestern Costa Rica. Burials were found in a cenote. Chronologically, burials range from Zoned Bichrome through latter part of Middle Polychrome periods. Author believes cenote burials are evidence of connection with rain, fertility, and ultimately Mesoamerican deity Tlaloc.

661 Magnus, Richard W. La Costa Atlántica de Nicaragua (BNBD, 35/36, mayo/agosto 1980, p. 68–73, ill.)

Brief summary statement covers author's 1971–77 field work along Nicaragua's Atlantic Coast, from Pearl Lagoon to Blue Fields Bay. Notes two major ceramic traditions (Siteioide and Smalloide) and four archaeological complexes (Siteia, Smalla, Jarkin, Cukra Point). They comprise a cultural sequence from 400 BC to AD 1600. Includes illustrations.

662 ——. La secuencia cerámica de la Costa Atlántica y la zona central de Nicaragua (BNBD, 35/36, mayo/agosto 1980, p. 52–61, ill.)

Based on his 1974 archaeological excavations, author presents summary analysis of ceramic sequence along Nicaragua's Atlantic Coast and central zone. Defines two main ceramic traditions for Atlantic Coast: Siteioid with one complex (400 BC-AD 200), and Smalloid with three ceramic complexes: Smalla, Jarkin, and Cukra Point. Cukra Point has a C14 date (AD 1185). Central zone sequence is very tentative but ceramic complexes, Copelito and Cerna, have been defined. Discusses future work plans. Includes description of ceramic types within each Atlantic Coast complex.

663 Matilló Vila, Joaquín. Collares precolombinos de Nicaragua (BNBD, 40, marzo/abril 1981, p. 57–62)

General description of precolumbian necklaces found in Nicaragua classifies them by material (gold, silver, bone, fish bone, teeth, clay and stone—precious, semiprecious, and common lithic materials). Inventory demonstrates variety and versatility of aboriginal craftsmen.

664 Miranda, Mariano. Las estatuas líticas de Chontales (BNBD, 34, marzo/ abril 1980, p. 49–56, ill., photos)

Description of 14 monumental stone sculptures from Nicaragua's Chontales region. Author attempts to show their distinctive characteristics to illustrate variety found within this style. Includes illustrations.

665 Montealegre, Silvia. Excavaciones de rescate en Chinandega: un estudio sistemático (BNBD, 35/36, mayo/agosto 1980, p. 74–115, bibl., ill.)

Describes salvage archaeological excavation at El Progresso, stratified site near city of Chinandegas, department of Chinandega, Northwestern Nicaragua. Article is significant because few systematic excavations have been conducted in this sector. These excavations by the author under the direction of Richard Magnus consisted of two test pits. Describes number of ceramic types in detail and draws several conclusions. Similarities found among ceramics strongly suggest a Mesoamerican tradition, especially from Honduras and El Salvador. Concludes that artifacts most likely correspond to the latter part of early classic period and early part of late classic period.

666 Moreau, Jean-François. A report on the Hunter-Robinson and Sardinai Sites (MNCR/V, 6:1/2, 1980, p. 104–124)

Report on data analyzed from two Late Polychrome inland shell-middens in Bay of Culebra region. Analysis of shell populations in midden deposits argues for two microphases in continuous occupations of Hunter-Robinson site. Similar conclusions are drawn from Sardinal site.

667 Nutting, Charles C. Antigüedades de Ometepe, Nicaragua (BNBD, 35/36, mayo/agosto 1980, p. 4–14, facsim., ill.)

Description of seven stone sculptures and a number of other artifacts, primarily ceramic, from Ometepe Island, Nicaragua, which are presently in museum collections.

668 Pardinas, Felipe. Hallazgos arqueológicos en Nicaragua: hasta 1938 (BNBD, 35/36, mayo/agosto 1980, p. 17–51, facsim., ill., maps, plate)

Presents historical review of archaeology in Nicaragua prior to 1938. Describes artifacts and investigations from various departments of Nicaragua (Granada, Rivas,

Chontales, Masaya, Carazo, Managua, León, and Segovia).

669   Reyes Mazzoni, Roberto. Petrograbados de serpientes y su asociación con el agua, sitios del centro y sur de Honduras: una interpretación iconográfica arqueológica (AHL/B, 3:25, dic. 1980, p. 71–80, bibl., ill., map)

Ethnohistoric documentation and archaeology converge as author attempts to demonstrate that precolumbian deity Quetzalcoatl is closely associated with water. Examines 19 sites and 28 representations of serpent motif in central and southern Honduras. Finds that 25 (85.7 percent) of serpent representations are located in sites less than 50 m from rivers or other sources of water.

670   Ryder, Peter. Informe de las investigaciones arqueológicas preliminares de la región de Guayabo de Bagaces, Guanacaste (*in* Centenario de Gonzalo Fernández de Oviedo, 5th, Nicoya, Costa Rica, 1978. Memoria del Congreso sobre el Mundo Centroamericano de su Tiempo, 24–25–26 y 27 de agosto 1978. Nicoya?, Costa Rica: Comisión Nacional Organizadora, 1978, p. 157–165, bibl., ill., maps)

Brief report of a two-phase project in the Guayabo de Bagaces region, Guanacaste, Costa Rica. This work was conducted jointly by the National Museum of Costa Rica and ICE in 1978. Region was surveyed and 20 sites (disturbed) were located, 18 of them burial mounds. One site, Murillo, was partially excavated. Tentatively concludes that both zoned Bichrome (AD 1-300) and Middle Polychrome Periods (AD 800-1200) are occupations present in this region. Burial mound at Murillo was constructed between AD 300–700 and may have up to 100 individual tombs. Data suggests a well-defined mortuary complex and stratified society.

671   Smutco, Gregorio. Arqueología de la Costa Atlántica de Nicaragua (BNBD, 35/36, mayo/agosto 1980, p. 120–126, ill.)

Summary of archaeology along Nicaragua's Atlantic Coast is basically a capsulized account of Richard Magnus' pioneering efforts (1971–76).

672   Snarskis, Michael J. and **Carlos Enrique Herra.** La Cabaña: arquitectura mesoamericana en el bosque tropical (*in* Centenario de Gonzalo Fernández de Oviedo,

5th, Nicoya, Costa Rica, 1978. Memoria del Congreso sobre el Mundo Centroamericano de su Tiempo, 24–25–26 y 27 de agosto 1978. Nicoya?, Costa Rica: Comisión Nacional Organizadora, 1978, p. 139–147, bibl., photos, plans)

Describes series of house mounds and other features excavated (1976–77) at La Cabaña site near Guacimo, in Atlantic Watershed region of Costa Rica. There are similarities with features for other sites dating between AD 1000–1500. Author estimates a household population of 20–30 people for large circular house foundation and 12–15 for smaller ones. Additionally, a combination of features suggest architectural similarities with Mesoamerica (quadrangular plazas) and the Intermediate area.

673   Vásquez Leiva, Ricardo. Consideraciones generales sobre un población de huesos humanos encontrados de Bahía Culebra, Guanacaste (*in* Centenario de Gonzalo Fernández de Oviedo, 5th, Nicoya, Costa Rica, 1978. Memoria del Congreso sobre el Mundo Centroamericano de su Tiempo, 24–25–26 y 27 de agosto 1978. Nicoya?, Costa Rica: Comisión Nacional Organizadora, 1978, p. 175–184, ill., map, tables)

Article is significant because few studies of precolumbian skeletal populations from Costa Rica have been published to date. Vásquez discusses and analyzes 135 specimens in Bahía Culebra, Guanacaste, Costa Rica. Findings point to high percentage of infants and juveniles. Author suggests a mortuary practice which utilizes specific burial areas for specific age groups. Also discusses osteoporosis, osteomelitis, and other paleopathological diseases.

674   ——— and David S. Weaver. Un análisis osteológico para el reconocimiento de las condiciones de vida en Sitio Vidor (MNCR/V, 6:1/2, 1980, p. 97–105)

Article treats various biocultural aspects of skeletal population recovered from multicomponent Vidor site in the Vicinity of Playa Panama in Northwestern Costa Rica. Of a total 1982 specimens 173 (90.1 percent) were analyzed. Only 12 (6.25 percent) were adults which suggests the likelihood of burial locations by age groups. Osteological pathologies and anomalies indicated an agrarian life style.

675 *Vínculos*. Museo Nacional de Costa Rica. Vol. 6, Nos. 1/2, 1980- . San Jóse. Entire issue (12 articles, 1973−79) devoted to archaeological studies of Bahía Culebra zone, Northwestern Costa Rica.

676 **Wallace, Henry** and **Richard M. Accola.** Investigaciones arqueológicas preliminares de Nacascolo, Bahía Culebra, Costa Rica (MNCR/V, 6:1/2, 1980, p. 51−65)
Findings from four test excavations (1978) at Nacascolo site, Bay of Culebra, Costa Rica. Badly disturbed site yielded significant information on two Monte del Barco phase (AD 800-1200) burials. Includes discussion of associated artifacts and paleopathology of skeletal material.

677 **Zelaya Hidalgo, Guillermo R.** El arte monumental de Chontales (BNBD, 35/36, mayo/agosto 1980,p. 47−51)
Brief but excellent description of stone sculpture from Chontales region in Southwestern Nicaragua, Cordillera de Amerrisque. Author examines photographs of 85 stone sculptures and analyzes various styles. Unfortunately, no plates or illustrations accompany this excellent description.

ARCHAEOLOGY: South America

BETTY J. MEGGERS, *Research Associate, Department of Anthropology, Smithsonian Institution*

THE NUMBER OF ENTRIES in this section is 40 percent less than in the preceding volume and is the lowest since *HLAS 27*, published in 1965. Use of the same procedures for identifying appropriate publications implies that output during the past two years has dropped substantially. Argentina shows the sharpest decline, with only 21 percent as many entries as two years ago. Guyana has none, as opposed to 11 in *HLAS 43*. The number of entries for Venezuela, Colombia, and Ecuador constitute 46, 57, and 57 percent of the totals reported two years ago. Peru and Chile fare somewhat better at 68 and 63 percent. The best record was achieved by Brazil and Bolivia, both of which show increases.

Examination of the entries suggests that the declines reflect several kinds of factors. The Argentine situation is attributable to economic conditions that have reduced funding for publication. The decline in number of entries for Colombia is compensated by the higher proportion of monographs. The Fundación de Investigaciones Arqueológicas Nacionales, a subsidiary of the Banco de la República, is supporting fieldwork and publication of high quality that is adding substantially to knowledge of the prehistory of this little-known part of South America. The relatively good showing by Peru is attributable to the high proportion of foreign authors, who produced two-thirds of the entries. Chile, which has an equally good record, owes it in good part to the initiative of the Universidad de Tarapacá, which produced three volumes of Chungara along with other reports by Chilean investigators. Brazil also has maintained a steady stream of publications of high quality by Brazilian authors.

A few contributions deserve special mention. The successful program of archaeological salvage in the Brazilian portion of the reservoir created by the Itaipú dam between western Paraná and Argentina is marked by vol. 5 of results (item **723**). The Japanese Expedition to Nuclear America issued another of their impressive monographs, this one on the archaeological sequence in the Cajamarca region of the north Peruvian highlands (item **892**). Two volumes describe results of intensive multidisciplinary studies by a US team in the Ayacucho Basin of the south Peruvian highlands (items **876−877**). Two interpretative books elaborate continent-wide themes. Schobinger provides an excellent critical evaluation of evidence for extra-continental influences on precolumbian cultures (item **258**); Sanoja presents a dynamic reconstruction of alternative pathways from wild to domesticated food economies (item **685**).

GENERAL

678 Allison, Marvin J. *et al.* La práctica de la deformación craneana entre los pueblos andinos precolombinos (Chungara [Universidad del Norte, Departamento de Antropología, Arica, Chile] 7, junio 1981, p. 238–260, bibl., ill.)

Describes and illustrates 11 kinds of devices for producing deformation of the skull, representing 14 distinct cultural groups. They were employed in the region between Huacho, Peru and Arica, Chile, chronologically, they extend from 5000 BP to Spanish contact.

679 ———; **Lawrence Lindberg; Calogero Santoro;** and **Guillermo Focaddi.** Tatuajes y pintura corporal de los indígenas precolombinos de Perú y Chile (Chungara [Universidad del Norte, Departamento de Antropología, Arica, Chile] 7, junio 1981, p. 218–236, bibl., ill.)

Skins of 343 mummies showed tatoo or painted decoration. They represented 11 cultural groups from the coast of south Peru and north Chile. Facial painting was observed among five; tatoo was restricted to Ica and Chimú-Casma. Sex, age, culture, and location of tatoo are provided in a table.

680 Ancient South Americans. Edited by Jesse D. Jennings. San Francisco: Freeman, 1983. 414 p.: bibl., ill., index.

General overview of South American precolumbian cultural development contains chapters on northern Andes (Ecuador and Colombia) by Robert Feldman and Michael Moseley; central Andean civilization by Moseley; south Andes (Bolivia, northern Chile and Argentina) by Alan Kolata; lowland South America and Antilles by Betty Meggers and Clifford Evans. Broad perspectives on local developments are provided by chapters on transoceanic contacts by Stephen Jett and the Paleo-Indians by Thomas Lynch (see item **684**). In spite of inconsistencies stemming from differences among authors in assessing evidence, volume offers students, teachers, and general readers most up-to-date introduction to this complex region.

681 Baumann, Peter. Wo die berge götter sind (WM, 10, Juli 1982, p. 78–89, ill., map, plates)

The existence of offerings at elevations up to 6740 in the southern Andes raises question of whether they were intended for celestial deities or if mountains themselves were worshipped.

682 Chávez, Sergio Jorge and **David Bruce Jorgenson.** Further inquiries into the case of the Arapa-Thunderbolt stela (IAS/NP, 18, 1980, p. 73–80, bibl., ill.)

Finding the base of this stela at Tiahuanaco and the upper part at Arapa, on opposite ends of Lake Titicaca, raised question of origin. Transport from Arapa area to Tiahuanaco, postulated from stylistic evidence, appears substantiated by petrographic analysis indicating source of the rock to be the Mumu quarry near Arapa.

683 Lumbreras, Luis Guillermo. Arqueología de la América Andina. Editor, Carlos Milla Batres. Lima: Editorial Milla Batres, 1981. 278 p.: bibl., ill., maps, plans.

Prepared as working document for UNESCO-sponsored conference (Peru, 1979) and revised to incorporate participants' concepts, volume summarizes general themes and problems. Pt. 1 reviews disagreements and inconsistencies in terminology, periodization, geographical divisions, and other conceptual aspects. Pt. 2 presents a framework of six geographical divisions and a brief description of cultural development in each. Pt. 3 discusses general themes, such as the peopling of the region, origin and diffusion of agriculture, origin and diffusion of pottery, origin of the state and urbanism. Useful as general overview, and as expression of views of leading Peruvian archaeologist.

684 Lynch, Thomas F. The Paleo-Indians (*in* Ancient South Americans. Edited by Jesse D. Jennings [see item **680**] p. 87–137, bibl., ill.)

Review of South American sites assigned to Paleo-Indian period, including assessment of validity of dating. Discusses lithic remains, faunal associations, environmental contexts, and possible wild plant foods. Earliest accepted dating is about 12,000 BC. Useful introduction to little-known period of South American prehistory.

685 Sanoja, Mario. De la recolección a la agricultura. Caracas: Academia Nacional de la Historia de Venezuela, 1982. 295 p.: ill. (some col.) (Historia general de América. Período indígena; 3)

Subtitled *Síntesis de la historia prehispánica de Brasil, Colombia, Venezuela, las Guayanas, las Antillas y Centro América*, this volume launches an international project supported by the OAS, the Instituto Panamericano de Geografía y Historia, and the Universidad Simón Bolívar to produce a general history of America in a series of volumes representing the indigenous (nine), colonial (11), and national (13) periods under the general direction of Guillermo Morón. The text (completed 1977, revised 1981) begins with aspects of the environment relevant to understanding cultural development. Chap. 2 reviews evidence for hunter-gatherers and chap. 3 discusses economic and social bases of village society, especially domesticated plants. Six chapters present highlights of precolumbian cultures in six political units specified in the subtitle. Final chapter summarizes effects of European contact. Liberally illustrated with plates in b/w and color, and providing chronological charts and maps, this volume fulfills its goal to provide the general reader with reconstruction of the manner in which diffusion, independent invention, convergence, and adaptation of varying environments molded precolumbian cultural development.

686 ———. Los hombres de la yuca y el maíz: un ensayo sobre el origen y desarrollo de los sistemas agrarios en el Nuevo Mundo. Caracas: Monte Avila Editores, 1981. 241 p.: bibl., maps.

Departing from the proposition that the transition from wild foods to agriculture depends not only on environmental factors but equally on social and ideological conditions, Sanoja provides a dynamic reconstruction of the paths to adoption of cereals and tubers as the primary domesticated staples. Introduction of the social organizational factor helps to explain the resistance of some groups to abandoning dependence on wild foods. Dependence on vegeculture is seen as inhibiting cultural development to the levels achievable with dependence on seed plants. A readable, comprehensive, and stimulating contribution by a leading Latin American archaeologist, essential for anyone concerned with the origins of agriculture.

687 Simposio de Correlaciones Antropológicas Andino-Mesoamericano, *1st, Salinas, Ecuador, 1971.* Primer Simposio Correlaciones Antropológicas Andino-Mesoamericano, 25–31 de julio de 1981. Jorge G. Marcos and Presley Norton, editors. Guayaquil: Escuela Superior Politécnica del Litoral, 1982. 495 p.: bibl., ill.

Consists of 25 papers delivered a decade ago but finally published, making available data and interpretations privately circulated since the symposium. Topics include: Ecuadorian Formative complexes; Mesoamerican-Ecuadorian correlations (two focusing on Olmec); northwest Argentina and the northern Andes; and, north Peruvian Formative complexes. Most authors interpret cultural similarities as evidence of long-term communication by sea between the coast of Ecuador and western Mesoamerica. Articles vary in quality; about one-third are in English, remainder in Spanish.

688 La Tecnología en el mundo andino. t. 1, Subsistencia y mensuración. Heather Lechtman and Ana María Soldi, editors. México: Universidad Nacional Autónoma de México, Instituto de Investigaciones Antropológicas, 1981. 496 p.: bibl., ill. (Serie antropológica; 36)

Compilation of articles representing theoretical and descriptive contributions, some previously published in Spanish or English and some original, to provide overview of indigenous practices. Pt. 1 discusses agriculture and pastoralism; pt. 2, preparation of food; and pt. 3, measurement, enumeration, and astronomical orientation. Important reference, designed to arouse interest in potential application of indigenous practices to modern life.

ARGENTINA

689 Bustos Dávila, Nicolás. Antigüedad de las ruinas de Malal-Hue (JEHM/R, 1:9, 1979, p. 75–102, bibl., photos)

Documentary evidence indicates that the stone corrals in the Department of Malahue, Mendoza, Argentina are no earlier than the 19th century.

690   Cione, Alberto L.; Ana Maria Lorandi; and Eduardo P. Tonni. Patrón de subsistencia y adaptación ecológica en El Veinte, Santiago del Estero (SAA/R, 13, 1979, p. 103–116, bibl., ill.)

Analysis of plant and animal remains from excavations at a site of Las Lomas Phase, dated between about AD 800 and AD 1260, indicates environment was wetter than today, supporting more abundant fauna and favoring more intensive agriculture. Maize is represented by carbonized cobs 1.5 to 4.0 cm long.

691   Crivelli Montero, Eduardo Adrián. La industria casapedrense: Colección Menghin (UBAIA/R, 13:1/2, 1976/1980, p. 35–57, bibl., ill.)

Lithic artifacts excavated by Menghin in Los Toldos Cave 3 during 1951–52 are classified, described, and illustrated. Tables give frequencies by levels. This industry is distinct from earlier Los Toldos; closest affiliations are with El Inga of Ecuador. A C14 date places its inception at the site about 5310 BC.

692   Fernández Distel, Alicia A. El arte rupestre del área de Huachichocana (UBAIA/R, 13:1/2, 1976/1980, p. 69–77, bibl., ill.)

Pictographs from eight locations are grouped into six styles, which appear to have chronological significance. The earliest is assigned a date of about AD 530; the latest is Indo-Hispanic.

693   Graiver, Bernardo. Argentina bíblica y biblónica: historia de la humanidad en la Argentina bíblica y biblónica. Buenos Aires: Editorial Albatros, 1980. 544 p.: bibl., ill.

Hodge-podge of "evidence" for influence from the eastern Mediterranean on New World precolumbian peoples, particularly those of northwestern Argentina. Useful as a compilation of pseudo-scientific comparisons which hinder the serious study of transoceanic communication.

694   Lagiglia, Humberto A. La técnica prehistórica del mosaico en cuero (Revista del Museo de Historia Natural de San Rafael [Mendoza, Argentina] 8:2, 1980, p. 43–66, bibl., ill.)

A bag from Atuel, dating about the beginning of the Christian era, is constructed using small angular pieces of skin to create an angular pattern. Similar designs are characteristic of rock art. Discusses origin and significance of patterns and technique after a detailed description of the bag's manufacturing technique.

695   Lorandi, Ana María; Jorge V. Crisci; María E. Gonaldi; and Silvia R. Caramazana. El cambio cultural en Santiago del Estero (SAA/R, 8, 1979, p. 85–101, bibl.)

Some 122 rim fragments and 55 complete vessels of plain pottery of known provenience from Santiago del Estero were classified using 33 characters, producing 83 Operational Taxonomic Units. A matrix was prepared and analyzed using three procedures employed by numerical taxonomy. Although a single tradition is represented, several changes in relative frequence and chronological occurrence were revealed.

696   Nacuzzi, Lidia R. and Alfredo Fisher. Análisis tipológico y técnico-morfológico de una colección de materiales de la "industria Jacobaccense" (MEMDA/E, 27/28, 1978, p. 12–37, bibl., ill.)

Although the Jacobaccense "industry" has been reported from sites in Río Negro and Chubut provinces, the artifacts have never been adequately studied. Classifies and describes surface collection from the type site, made in 1953–54 by Menghin. Author concludes the "industry" consists of unfinished specimens from workshop or quarry locations, possibly associated with Toldense industry.

697   Ortiz-Troncoso, Omar R. Inventory of radiocarbon dates from southern Patagonia and Tierra del Fuego (SA/J, 67, 1980/1981, p. 185–211, bibl.)

All dates obtained prior to June 1979 (160 samples) are listed with full information under four categories: archaeological samples, glaciological samples, samples related to volcanism, and samples related to sea level. Chart compares the dates from 13 sites, extending over the past 11,500 years.

698   Prehistoria de la cuenca del Río Limay. Dirección y coordinación, Amalia Sanguinetti de Bórmida. Buenos Aires: Universidad de Buenos Aires, Facultad de Filosofía y Letras, Instituto de Ciencias Antropológicas, 1981- . 1 v.: ill. (Trabajos de prehistoria; no. 1)

Three rock shelters in northern Patagonia provide information on cultural development between 2500 BC and AD 1500. Special reports discuss faunal remains, lithics, basketry, and coprolites from each shelter. Chronological chart aligns these sites with those previously known from the Chocón region.

699 Raffino, Rodolfo. Los inkas del Kollasuyu: origen, naturaleza y transfiguraciones de la ocupación inka en los Andes meridionales. Buenos Aires: Ramos Americana Editora, 1981. 301 p.: bibl., ill., plates.

Survey of Inca sites in northeastern Argentina reveals their predominance in regions providing noble metals (gold, silver) and copper, galena, lead, tin, semiprecious stones, and salt. Less than five percent are associated with subsistence resources. Author suggests that rapid, late Inca expansion into this region was motivated by these mineral deposits.

700 Sapiens. Museo Arqueológico Dr. Osvaldo F.A. Menghin. No. 4, Ed. Especial, 1980 . Chivilcoy, Argentina.

Papers delivered during the Symposium Dr. Osvaldo F.A. Menghin, 21–23 Sept. 1979, summarize the latter's contributions to Old World archaeology and theory and to the archaeology of northwestern Argentina. Most papers focus on a particular region or complex, reviewing his work in the light of subsequent investigations.

701 Ventura, Beatriz N. Aportes para la arqueología de San Andrés (MEMDA/E, 29/30, enero/dic. 1979, p. 11–19, bibl., ill., maps)

Three petroglyphs representing stylized faces suggest contacts with the Quebrada de Humahuaca to the west.

BOLIVIA

702 Arellano López, Jorge. Algunos aportes al conocimiento de la metalurgia prehispánica en Bolivia (IFEA/B, 11:3/4, 1982, p. 79–90, bibl., ill., map)

Analyzes 20 objects (15 copper, three gold, one silver, and one turquoise) representing Tiahuanaco, Mollo, Chiripa, Inca, and Mallku cultures, using emission spectrography, atomic absorption, and X-ray diffraction.

Map shows principal prehispanic mines in Bolivian highlands.

703 ——. Cultura Mollo: ensayo de síntesis arqueológica (Pumapunku [Instituto de Cultura Aymara, La Paz] 12, enero/marzo 1978, p. 87–113, bibl.)

Summary of geographical dispersal, environmental context, settlement pattern, architecture, burial practices, economy, social organization, and ceramics of the terminal culture of highland Bolivia, dated between AD 1100-AD 1485.

704 ——. Las indústrias lítica y ósea de Iskanwaya (IFEA/B, 11:3/4, 1982, p. 51–77, bibl., ill., map)

Description of bone and stone artifacts excavated from the site of Iskanwaya, northwest of La Paz. Grinding stones and bola stones are the principal lithic objects; weaving tools, flutes, needles, and ornaments were made of bone.

705 —— and **Eduardo E. Berberián.** Mallku: el Señorío Post-Tiwanaku del altiplano sur de Bolivia: provincias Nor y Sur López, Depto. de Potosí (IFEA/B, 10:1/2, 1981, p. 51–84, bibl., ill.)

Combines data from fieldwork and documents to reconstruct economy, settlement pattern, fortifications, and burial practices of a protohistoric chiefdom. Textiles, basketry, metallurgy, pottery, and rock art are described.

706 Boero Rojo, Hugo. Descubriendo Tiwanaku. La Paz: Editorial Los Amigos del Libro, 1980. 338 p., 12 leaves of plates: ill. (some col.) (Colección Bolivia mágica)

General popular introduction to Tiahuanaco, consisting principally of b/w and color illustrations of architectural details and artifacts, which aims to accord to the site "the cultural value it merits."

707 Browman, David L. New light on Andean Tiwanaku (American Scientist [Burlington, Vt.] 69, 1981, p. 408–419, bibl., ill.)

Recent excavations at Chiripá on southeastern margin of Lake Titicaca furnish new information relevant to reconstructing cultural development from 1500 BC to European contact. Plant remains establish the exploitation of numerous seed (quinoa, amaranth) and tuber (potato, oca) foods, as well as legumes by 1000 BC. Most of these have toxic properties that were minimized by freezing, leaching, and sun-drying, which also enhanced storage abilities. Changes in settlement pattern, evidence for trade, development of social and political integrations, and economic factors are summarized, leading to the emergence of the Wari and Tiahuanaco empires.

708 Bustos Santelices, Víctor. Una hipótesis de relaciones culturales entre el altiplano y la vertiente oriental de los Andes (Pumapunku [Instituto de Cultura Aymara, La Paz] 12, enero/marzo 1978, p. 115–126, bibl.)

Postulates that climatic deterioration in the eastern lowlands accounts for influence from this region on the highland cultures of Tiawanaku I, Chiripa, and Wankarani between 1500 BC and the Christian era.

709 Ponce Sanguinés, Carlos. Descripción sumaria del templete semisubterráneo de Tiwanaku. 5. ed. rev. La Paz: Librería y Editorial Juventud, 1981. 229 p., 11 folded leaves of plates: bibl., ill. (some col.), maps, plans.

This reprint of the 1969 edition is prefaced by a review of 100 years of investigation at Tiahuanaco. Description of the excavations at the temple, completed in 1964, is supplemented by numerous photographs and detailed plans. C14 dates available in 1965 are listed.

710 ———. Panorama de la arqueología boliviana. La Paz: Libreria y Editorial Juventud, 1980. 171 p.: bibl., ill. (some col.).

Pt. 1 describes pottery-making complexes defined in Bolivian highlands; pt. 2 reviews research on Tiahuanaco and offers "new perspective" on its origin and character; pt. 3 argues importance of prehistoric developments for achieving a national identity. Ponce defines village, urban, and imperial stages in Tiahuanaco culture, which he considers to reflect local, autonomous evolution over two and a half millennia.

711 Riester, Jürgen. Arqueología y arte rupestre en el oriente boliviano, Depto. Santa Cruz. Cochabamba, Bolivia; La Paz: Editorial Los Amigos del Libro, 1981. 232 p.: bibl., ill. (some col.) (Bolivia mágica)

During ethnographic research in the Santa Cruz Department, author was taken to various habitation sites and petroglyph locations. Describes and illustrates surface collections and specimens in museum or private collections by site or by region. Pottery styles are distinct from those known from the Mojos region to the west; one features patterns composed of bands of closely spaced parallel incisions.

712 Tapia Pineda, Félix. Investigaciones arqueológicas en Kacsili (Pumapunku [Instituto de Cultura Aymara, La Paz] 12, enero/marzo 1978, p. 7–37, bibl., ill.)

Description of architectural remains at six locations above 4000 m elevation assignable to a local post-Tiahuanaco, pre-Inca complex in the Department of Puno.

BRAZIL

713 Albano, Rosangela. Bibliografía sobre arte rupestre brasileira (Arquivos do Museu de História Natural [Belo Horizonte, Brazil] 4/5, 1979/1980 [i.e. 1982] p. 185–187)

Items relating to rock art are listed by state, using the numerical code employed in the general bibliography. A map shows locations by technique (painting vs. engraving) and subject (figurative vs. non-figurative).

714 Alves, José Jerónimo de Alencar and **José Seixas Lourenço.** Métodos geofísicos aplicados à arqueologia no Estado do Pará. Belém, Brazil: Museu Paraense Emílio Goeldi, 1981. 52 p.: bibl., ill. (Nova série. Geologia; 26)

Electro-resistivity methods applied to two archaeological sites revealed significant differences from the results obtained from natural formations, suggesting this method may provide useful data on subsurface features of cultural origin.

715 Anthonioz-Russell, Sydney. Une description des oeuvres rupestres de la "Lapa do Ballet," Minas Gerais, Brésil (SA/J, 67, 1980/1981, p. 31–48, bibl., ill.)

Discussion of anthropomorphic and zoomorphic pictographs in a cave in the Lagoa Santa region; the human figures are distinct from previously described ones from the region, whereas the zoomorphic ones are similar.

716 Arcaico do interior. Pedro Ignacio Schmitz, Altair Sales Barbosa, and Maira Barberi Ribeiro, editors. Goiânia, Brazil: Universidade Católica de Goiás, Instituto Goiano do Pré-história e Antropologia, 1978/1980. 127 p.: bibl. (*Anuário de Divulgação Científica*; 6. Temas de arqueologia brasileira; 2)

Summarizes archaic complexes of coastal Brazil with emphasis on ecological aspects. Contributions by Schmitz and Barbosa on Goiás, Dias and Prous on Minas Gerais, Guidón on Piauí, Tassone and T. Miller on Rio Grande do Norte, Schmitz on southern Brazil, and T. Miller and Caldarelli on São Paulo are followed by extended discussion among participants in a roundtable during the III Seminário Goiano de Arqueologia. Useful summary of the current status of knowledge.

717   Arcaico do Litoral. Pedro Ignacio Schmitz, Altair Sales Barbosa, and Maira Barberi Ribeiro, editors. Goiânia, Brazil: Universidade Católica de Goiás, Instituto Goiano de Pré-historia e Antropologia, 1978/1980. 74 p.: bibl. (*Anúario de Divulgação Científica*; 7. Temas de arqueologia brasileira; 3)

Summary of "archaic" sites on São Paulo's coast by Dorath Pinto Uchôa is presented in the form of a table listing 133 sites and their locations, grouped into four regions. C14 dates are available for 55; they extend from 5970 to 545 BP. Second half of text reports comments by participants of 3rd Seminário Goiano de Arqueologia on all aspects of research on Brazilian shell-middens.

718   Arqueologia do centro-sul de Goiás: uma fronteira de horticultores indígenas no Centro do Brasil. Pedro Ignacio Schmitz *et al.* (IAP/P, 33, 1982, p. 1–280)

Reports results of fieldwork (1975–80) in southern Goiás by phase and tradition. Describes, illustrates, and tabulates sites, excavations, pottery types, and lithics; seriates sequences for each phase using temper differences. Seven phases represent three traditions. Aratu and related Sapucaí traditions also occur over large areas to the east; Uru tradition has Amazonian elements and is known only in the study region. Seven C14 dates indicate the Mossâmedes phase (Aratu tradition) has minimal antiquity of 1100 years (AD 810). Earliest date for Uru tradition is AD 1190. First detailed synthesis of ceramic cultures of this part of Brazil.

719   Arte rupestre. Pedro Ignacio Schmitz, Altair Sales Barbosa, and Maira Barberi Ribeiro, editors. Goiânia, Brazil: Universidade Católica de Goiás, Instituto Goiano de Pré-história e Antropologia, 1978/1980. 79 p.: bibl. (*Anuário do Divulgação Científica*; 8. Temas de arqueologia brasileira; 4)

Niède Guidón proposes a classification of Brazilian rock art into two general categories: painted and carved. For each she defines three geographical subdivisions. André Prous offers an independent classification of traditions and styles in Minas Gerais. Map correlates both classifications and shows distributions of types. Brief contributions discuss rock art in Goiás, Paraíba, and São Paulo. Important as an initial effort toward coordination of methodology.

720   Barbosa, Altair Sales; Pedro Ignacio Schmitz; Angélica Stobäus; and Avelino Fernandes Miranda. Projeto Médio-Tocantins: Monte de Carmo, GO; fase cerâmica Pindorama (IAP/P, 34, 1982, p. 49–92, bibl., ill.)

Four sites produced undecorated pottery, faunal remains, and burials. Region is on frontier between Coastal Strip and Amazonia, and the ceramics reflect its transitional location. Earliest levels provide predominantly pottery with mineral temper, related to widespread coastal Aratu tradition. Later levels have increasing amounts of pottery tempered with cariapé, an Amazonian trait. C14 dates extend from 2000 BC to AD 1000. Date of 2360 ± 70 (SI-4068) or 410 BC is judged acceptable for the initiation of pottery-making.

721   Brochado, José Proenza. Tradição cerâmica tupiguarani na América do Sul (Clio [Revista do Curso de Mestrado em História, Universidade Federal de Pernambuco, Recife, Brazil] 3, 1980, p. 47–60)

Data from more than 1000 sites on the Brazilian coast are synthesized to characterize the pottery, stone artifacts, environmental context, and other traits of the Tupiguarani tradition. Comparison of data extracted from ethnohistorical accounts with archaeological evidence verifies association of archaeological tradition with speakers of Tupi-Guarani.

722   Carvalho, Eliana and **Paulo Seda.** Os sítios com sinalações pesquisados pelo

IAB: um guia para cadastramento (Boletim do Instituto de Arqueologia Brasileira [Rio de Janeiro] 9, 1982, p. 23–67, bibl.)

Proposes standardized format for describing rock art containing 20 categories of information and applies it to 64 examples from eastern Minas Gerais.

723 Chmyz, Igor. Projeto Arqueológico Itaipú: quinto relatório das pesquisas realizadas na área de Itaipú, 1979/1980. Curitiba, Brazil: Projeto Arqueológico Itaipú, 1980. 102 p.: bibl., charts, ill., maps.

Fifth report on results of archaeological salvage in region inundated by construction of Itaipú dam on Rio Paraná covers tributary Rio São Francisco Verdadeiro and left bank of Paraná upstream from its mouth. Among 36 sites encountered, 16 were preceramic and 20 ceramic. All of the latter represent phases of Tupiguarani tradition. Concluding chapter summarizes results of five years of fieldwork, which provide time-space framework extending from about 8000 BP to colonial period. Accompanying maps show distributions and phase affiliations of 187 sites.

724 ——. Relatório das pesquisas arqueológicas realizadas na área da usina hidroeléctrica de Salto Santiago: 1979–80. Florianópolis, Brazil: Eletrosul, 1980. 101 p.: bibl., ill.

Salvage investigations on middle Rio Iguaçu, prior to inundation, produced 41 sites. Nine represent two preceramic phases and remainder the Candói, Xagu, and Açungui phases of the Itararé ceramic tradition. Only a few sherds of Tupiguarani tradition affiliation were encountered in southern part of the survey area. Sites, pottery types, and non-ceramic artifacts are described in detail, tabulated, and illustrated by phase. Final chapter discusses chronology, distributions, and affiliations.

725 Os Cultivadores do planalto e do litoral. Pedro Ignacio Schmitz, Altair Sales Barbosa, and Maira Barberi Ribeiro, editors. Goiânia, Brazil: Universidade Católica de Goiás, Instituto Goiano de Pre-história e Antropologia, 1978/1980. 77 p.: bibl. (*Anuário de Divulgação Científica;* 9. Temas de arqueologia brasileira; 5)

Roundtable discussion among participants of 3rd Seminário Goiano de Arqueologia (March 1980) of diagnostic criteria of ceramic traditions defined for the Brazilian Coastal Strip, particularly differentiation between Aratú and Sapucai traditions in the northeast and Itararé and Casa de Pedra traditions in the south. Assesses relative importance of temper, surface treatment, and vessel shape, and reviews stone and pottery artifacts, settlement size, burial practices, and other features distinguishing traditions. Two maps show distribution of regional traditions and Tupiguarani tradition and its subtraditions. Phases included in each tradition and subtradition are listed, along with C14 dates where available.

726 Dias, Ondemar. Mapa arqueológico do Estado de Minas Gerais (Arquivos do Museu de História Natural [Belo Horizonte, Brazil] 4/5, 1979/1980 [i.e. 1982] p. 297–309, map)

Explanation of the system of site numeration proposed for Minas Gerais, compatible with a national system developed during the PRONAPA, and based on hydrographic divisions. Description of boundaries of regions and their identifying letters is accompanied by map showing divisions, and locations of principal ceramic phases.

727 —— and **Eliana Carvalho.** Notícias preliminares das escavações na Lapa da Foice II—MG-RP-8 (Boletim do Instituto de Arqueologia Brasileira [Rio de Janeiro] 9, 1982, p. 69–91)

Stratigraphic excavations in a rock shelter in eastern Minas Gerais produced a sequence of occupation estimated to extend from prior to 5000 BP to about 900 BP. Eight burials were encountered, two containing two individuals; half were primary, the remainder secondary with evidence of burning. Calcined human bones associated with animal bones in hearths raises possibility of cannibalism. Lithics occurred throughout the deposit; pottery of the Unaí Phase occurred near the surface. Fragments of basketry were encountered.

728 —— and ——. Pesquisas arqueológicas nos altos cursos dos rios Purus e Juruá (Aspectos da Arqueologia Amazônica [Instituto de Arqueologia Brasileira, Rio de Janeiro] Série: catalogos, 2, 1981/1982, p. 21–25)

Survey on upper Juruá and Purus Rivers in Brazilian state of Acre allows recognition of two ceramic traditions, one on each river. Neither is related closely to known Amazonian traditions.

729 Garcia, Caio del Rio and **Dorath Pinto Uchôa.** Piaçaguera: um sambaqui do litoral do Estado de São Paulo, Brasil (Revista de Pré-história [Universidade de São Paulo, Instituto de Pré-história, São Paulo] 2, 1980, p. 11–81, bibl., ill.)

Reports results of excavations from 1965–69 in a shell-midden, C14 dated about 4900 BP. Describes, tabulates, and illustrates artifacts of stone, bone, shell, and animal teeth. Provides metric, morphological, and pathological data on 87 human skeletons. Faunal remains imply primary dependence on estuary resources (fish, shellfish), supplemented by terrestrial hunting and gathering.

730 Guidon, Niède and **Margarida D. Andreatta.** O sítio arqueológico Toca do Sítio do Meio: Piauí (Clio [Revista do Curso de Mestrado em História, Universidade Federal de Pernambuco, Recife, Brazil] 3, 1980, p. 7–29, ill., tables)

Description and tabulation of lithic objects from excavations in rock shelter in southern Piauí. C14 dates of 12,200 ± 600 BP and 13,900 ± 300 BP were obtained from levels V and VI. The 39 stones showing use or intentional flaking were classified into 16 categories; no illustrations are provided.

731 Laroche, Armand François Gaston and **Adjelma Soares e Silva Laroche.** O sítio arqueológico de Mangueiros: Macaíba, RN. Recife, Brazil: Fundação Joaquim Nabuco: Editora Massangana, 1982. 57 p.: ill. (Série Monografias. Fundação Joaquim Nabuco; 24)

Site 61 km southwest of Natal, consisting of five patches of darker soil corresponding to house locations, produced pottery decorated principally with painting on a white slip. Two stratigraphic tests showed pottery concentrated in the upper 20 cm. Five C14 dates from four successive 20-cm levels were: 504, 738 and 811, 1796, and 3339 BP (the latter level produced no artifacts). Discusses affiliations with the Tupiguarani and Papeba traditions.

732 Martin, Gabriela; Alice Aguiar; Paulo Tadeu; and **Plínio Victor.** A "Pedra da Figura" em Taquaritinga do Norte, PE (Clio [Revista do Curso de Mestrado em História, Universidade Federal de Pernambuco, Recife, Brazil] 3, 1980, p. 31–46, ill.)

Pictographs executed in red include birds, lizards, human hands, a stylized human, and geometric figures. Site is 150 km northwest of Recife.

733 Meggers, Betty J. Archaeological and ethnographic evidence compatible with the model of forest fragmentation in the tropics (*in* Biological diversification in the tropics. Ghillean T. Prance, editor. New York: Columbia University Press, 1982, p. 483–496, bibl., maps)

Patterns of distribution of languages, archaeological traditions, and ethnographic cultural elements do not correlate with existing geographical routes and barriers in tropical lowland South America. Following analogy of distributions of components of flora and fauna, which are believed to reflect the impact of oscillations in climate during and since the Pleistocene, it is suggested that human biogeography may reflect the same environmental stress. Reviews evidence compatible with this interpretation.

734 Monzon, Susana. Des rapports entre les signes et les représentations anthropomorphes dans les peintures rupestres du Brésil (SA/J, 67, 1980/1981, p. 125–140, bibl., ill.)

Comparison of anthropomorphic figures from Minas Gerais and Piauí suggests that certain abstract renditions, previously classified as geometric, are stylized humans.

735 ———. Préhistoire du sud-est du Piauí: Brésil (MH/OM, 20:4, 1980, p. 153–160, ill., map, plates)

General summary of archaeological sequence reconstructed by Franco-Brazilian Mission from 1978–80. Principal evidence is paintings, which show a variety of activities among humans and animals, recorded in some 180 rock shelters.

736 ———. A representação humana na arte rupestre do Piauí: comparações com outras áreas (MP/R, 28, 1981/1982, p. 401–422, bibl., ill.)

The Varzea Grande pictograph style of southeastern Piauí is characterized by scenes incorporating one or several human figures in varying postures and activities, often with animals associated. The arrangements are far more complex than depictions reported from regions to the south.

737 Moraes, Agueda Vilhena de. Estudo da indústria lítica proveniente da primeira companha de escavações (1971), no sítio Almeida, Município de Tejupá, Estado de São Paulo. São Paulo: Fundo de Pesquisas do Museu Paulista da Universidade de São Paulo, 1977. 145 p.: bibl., ill. (Série de arqueologia; v. 4. Coleção Museu Paulista)

A site near the São Paulo-Paraná border consists of three successive preceramic occupations and a ceramic (Tupiguarani tradition) occupation. Efforts to identify significant differences in technology, raw material, and function among the three preceramic complexes were inconclusive, although dates imply separations of about a millennium (3600, 2400, and 1500 BP).

738 Morais, José Luiz de. Os artefatos em sílex de Santa Bárbara d'Oeste, SP (MP/R, 28, 1981/1982, p. 101–114, bibl., ill.)

The 405 worked stone pieces collected from a site in east-central São Paulo consist predominantly of flakes and cores; a projectile point with a contracting stem is illustrated. A C14 date of 5350 ± 120 BP was obtained. No information is provided on the site.

739 Paleo-indio. Pedro Ignacio Schmitz, Altair Sales Barbosa, and Maira Barberi Ribeiro, editors. Goiânia, Brazil: Universidade Católica de Goiás, Instituto Goiano de Pré-história e Antropologia, 1978/1980. 99 p.: bibl. (*Anuário de Divulgação Científica*; 5. Temas de arqueologia brasileira; 1)

Symposium during the 3rd Seminário Goiano de Arqueologia (March 1980) with contributions by Schmitz on Goiás, Dias and Prous on Minas Gerais, Guidón on Piauí, Tassone on Rio Grande do Norte, and Ab'Sáber on paleoclimate and paleoecology. Papers are followed by discussion. Useful summary of recent Paleo-Indian discoveries in northeastern Brazil.

740 Pallestrini, Luciana. Cerâmica há 1.500 anos, Moji-guaçu, Estado de São Paulo (MP/R, 28, 1981/1982, p. 115–129, bibl., ill.)

Brief résumé of excavations at a site of the Tupiguarani tradition in east central São Paulo, C14 dated at 1500 BP.

741 ———; Philomena Chiara; and José Luiz de Morais. Evidenciação de novas estruturas arqueológicas no sítio pré-

histórico Camargo, Piraju, SP (MP/R, 28, 1981/1982, p. 131–158, bibl., ill.)

Description of excavations at a preceramic site on the Rio Paranapanema that produced C14 dates extending from 4650 to 1030 BP.

742 Paula, Fabiano Lopes de and Paulo Roberto Seda. Catálogo de sítios (Arquivos do Museu de História Natural [Belo Horizonte, Brazil] 4/5, 1979/1980 [i.e. 1982] p. 201–295)

The 585 sites recorded from Minas Gerais are listed with the following information: municipality, site name and number, kind (open, rock shelter, cave), investigator, bibliographic reference, C14 dates, conservation, location of field notes, and cultural affiliation.

743 Pesquisas arqueológicas no litoral de Itaipú, Niterói, RJ. Lina Maria Kneip, Luciana Pallestrini, and Fausto L. de Souza Cunha, coordinators. Rio de Janeiro: Diretoria da Itaipú, Cia. de Desenvolvimento Territorial, 1981. 174 p.: bibl., graphs, ill., tables.

Salvage excavations were conducted in a shell-midden and a dune site. Chapters discuss geology, vegetation, history of archaeology, excavation, lithics, and bone artifacts from each site. Five C14 dates from the shell-midden extend from 7958 to 1410 BP.

744 Prous, André. Considerações gerais sobre a arqueologia de Minas (Arquivos do Museu de História Natural [Belo Horizonte, Brazil] 4/5, 1979/1980 [i.e. 1982] p. 191–199)

Review of status of archaeological investigation in the state of Minas Gerais, principal agents of destruction of sites, and suggestions for conservation. Relevant titles in the general bibliography on Minas Gerais are listed by their identifying number.

745 ———. Fouilles du grand abri de Santana de Riacho, Minas Gerais, Brésil (SA/J, 67, 1980/1981, p. 163–183, bibl., ill.)

Preliminary description of excavations in rock shelter north of Lagoa Santa. C14 dates range from 11,960 to 3990 BP. Paintings extend 100 m long the rear wall. Primary and secondary burials, lithic artifacts, and plant remains were encountered. Latter include maize in contexts dating ca. 4000 BP.

746 ———. História da pesquisa e da bibliografia arqueológica no Brasil (Arquivos do Museu de História Natural [Belo Horizonte, Brazil] 4/5, 1979/1980 [i.e. 1982] p. 11–24)

Review of highlights of Brazilian archaeology (1800–1980).

747 ——— and **Fabiano Lopes de Paula.** L'art rupestre dans les régions explorées par Lund, Centre of Minas Gerais, Brésil (Arquivos do Museu de História Natural [Belo Horizonte, Brazil] 4/5, 1979/1980 [i.e. 1982] p. 311–335, bibl., ill.)

Two rock art traditions have been differentiated in the portion of Minas Gerais investigated by Lund in the 19th century. These have been designated Planalto and Sumidouro. Six regional and/or chronological varieties have been recognized in the former. A third tradition occurs in the São Francisco valley.

748 **Ribeiro, Pedro Augusto Mentz.** O Tupiguarani no Vale do Rio Pardo e a redução jesuítico de Jesus Maria (Revista do CEPA [Centro de Ensino e Pesquisa Arqueológicas, Associação Pró-ensino, Santa Cruz do Sul, Brazil] 10, 1981, p. 1–225, bibl., ill.)

Reconstructs history of Tupiguarani occupation of lower Rios Pardo and Pardinho in central Rio Grande do Sul from seriated ceramic sequences and data on settlement pattern and artifacts. Distinguishes four archaeological phases, two pre-European and two post-European. Changes in settlement size and location occured in pre-contact phases; sites became increasingly dispersed during contact period. Most recent phase exhibits evidence of strong European influence on pottery manufacture. Describes pottery, stone, bone, and shell artifacts of indigenous manufacture, and china, glass, and metal of European origin. Estimated dating extends from AD 1550-AD 1900.

749 ———; **Antônio da Silva Martins; Catharina Torrano Ribeiro; and Itela da Silveira.** A ocupação de locais cobertos pelo Tupiguarani no vale do Rio Pardo, RS (Revista do CEPA [Centro de Ensino e Pesquisa Arqueológicas, Faculdades Integradas de Santa Cruz do Sul, Brazil] 11, abril 1982, p. 7–31, bibl., ill.)

Cave and a rockshelter on tributary of Rio Pardo produced pottery, bone points,

stone flakes showing use, and food remains. They define a new phase of Tupiguarani tradition, designated Canhadão phase, and reflect disintegration of indigenous society during 17th century.

750 **Rodrigues, Calasans.** São Tomé das Letras: a lenda e a arqueología (Boletim do Instituto de Arqueologia Brasileira [Rio de Janeiro] 9, 1982, p. 9–15, bibl., ill.)

Description of three locations with biomorphic pictographs in southern Minas Gerais.

751 **Rohr, João Alfredo.** O sítio arqueológico do Pântano do Sul, SC-F-10. Florianópolis, Brazil: Governo do Estado de Santa Catarina, 1977. 114 p., l leaf of plates: bibl., ill. (Coleção Cultura catarinense. Série Ciência)

Preceramic site extending 400 m along southeast coast of island of Santa Catarina was examined by excavations at each end and in center. Refuse and burials were encountered on sand hills at western end, as well as level land. Two C14 dates are 4460 and 4515 BP. Describes six "zooliths," two from excavations and the remainder encountered by local residents as well as stone and bone implements and human skeletons.

752 **Rubinger, Marcos Magalhães.** Pintura rupestre: algo mais do que arte pré-histórica. Belo Horizonte, Brazil: Interlivros, 1979. 79 p.: ill.

Departing from investigations in rockshelters in central Minas Gerais, author argues that prehistoric rock art is a mode of communication within the social group and a means of relating group to its environment.

753 **Schmitz, Pedro Ignacio.** Contribuciones a la préhistoria de Brasil (IAP/P, 32, 1981, p. 1–243, bibl.)

Spanish version of papers delivered at scientific meetings (1972–80) on aspects of archaeology, especially in Rio Grande do Sul and Goiás, ranging from Paleo-Indian to post-European periods. A reasonably up-to-date synthesis of results of investigations still largely unpublished.

754 ———. A formação da cultura indígena brasileira (IFCH/R, 8, 1979/1980, p. 249–260, bibl., maps)

Succinct review of origins, diffusion, and differentiation of precolumbian cultures in Brazil incorporating recent unpublished data from investigations both on the coast and in Amazônia.

755 ——— and **José Proenza Brochado.**
Petroglifos do estilo pisadas no centro de Rio Grande do Sul: Abrigos de Canhemborá, Lajeado dos Dourados, Linha Sétima e Pedro Grande (IAP/P, 34, 1982, p. 3–47, bibl., ill., map)

Records five locations with petroglyphs, including copying the markings and excavating floor of rockshelters. Lines and dots were produced by pecking and polishing; traces of black, green, or white pigment remain in some. Three chronological styles are recognized by differences in technique and principal motifs. Several C14 dates extend from about 1100 BC to AD 1600. In content and chronology, these petroglyphs correspond to the "animal track style" widely distributed in lowland Argentina.

756 ——— *et al.* Arqueologia de Goiás em 1976: Projeto Paranaíba (Estudos Goianienses [Universidade Católica de Goiás, Goiânia, Brazil] 4:5, 1. semestre, 1977, p. 19–77, bibl., graphs, ill.)

Investigations in 13 rock shelters in southwestern Goiás, including stratigraphic excavations in nine, permit reconstructing a relative chronology. C14 dates extend from 10,400 to 915 BP. Two general phases were defined: preceramic Paranaíba Phase and ceramic Jutaí Phase. Describes lithic industry, faunal remains, and pictographs and presents relative frequencies of categories by stratigraphic levels. Mammal remains predominate in lower levels; terrestrial mollusks in upper ones.

757 **Silva, Laura.** O Sítio D. Laura—RJ-LP-43: uma pesquisa de salvamento num sítio tupiguarani (Boletim do Instituto de Arqueologia Brasileira [Rio de Janeiro] 9, 1982, p. 17–22)

Large burial urn with spatulated corrugated decoration, covered with a painted bowl, was excavated intact. Above the lid was a layer of dirt, upon which was another bowl with a corrugated surface, and four rectangular bowls.

758 **Universidade Federal de Minas Gerais. Setor de Arqueologia.** Bibliografia geral (Arquivos do Museu de História Natural [Belo Horizonte, Brazil] 4/5, 1979/1980 [i.e. 1982] 25–183)

Lists 2017 titles relevant to the archaeology of Brazil in alphabetical order by author. Designed as an aid to researchers rather than an exhaustive compilation.

CHILE

759 **Aspectos del desarrollo cultural altiplánico y la incidencia del Tiwanaku en Chile y areas aledañas.** Mario A. Rivera, editor. Sede Antofagasta, Chile: Universidad de Chile, 1980. 144 p.: bibl. (Estudios arqueológicos, 5)

Papers delivered during a symposium of the 7th Congreso de Arqueología Chilena, 1977, deal with: analysis of coprolites from Alto Ramírez Phase; analysis of Caserones plain pottery using x-ray excitation; early agricultural settlements in northern Calchaquí Valley; pipes from preceramic sites on the Puna of northwest Argentina and associated use of hallucinogens; aspects of Tiahuanaco influence on the economy; settlement pattern; and other aspects of indigenous north Chilean culture.

760 **Biskupovic M., Marcos.** Excavación arqueológico en el área de Las Chilcas, V Región, Zona Central, Chile (CMALS/B, 17, 1979/1981, p. 222–232, bibl., ill.)

Description of stone artifacts, pottery, and fauna obtained during excavation in a rock shelter, interpreted as a single occupation dated by C14 about AD 1210.

761 **Bittmann, Bente.** Revisión del problema Chinchorro (Chungara [Universidad del Norte, Departamento de Antropologiá, Arica, Chile] 9, 1982, p. 46–79, bibl.)

Review of evidence for natural and artificial mummification on the north coast of Chile, conservatively dated between 3000 and 2000 BC, its social and religious implications, and problems needing investigation.

762 **Castillo Gómez, Gastón.** Pictografías en el Valle de Copiapó: área de Los Loros (Documentos de Trabajo [Instituto de Investigaciones Arqueológicas y de Restauración Monumental, Universidad de Antofagasta, Chile] 1981, p. 4–15, bibl., ill., map)

Geometric, zoomorphic, and anthropomorphic figures executed principally using red pigment occur on boulders in isolated locations. They are believed to date from the late agricultural period in the valley.

763 ———— and **Ivo Kuzmanic P.** Registro de colecciones inéditas del complejo cultural El Molle: trabajo descriptivo (CMALS/B, 17, 1979/1981, p. 122–221, bibl., ill.)

Description of 33 sites and associated artifacts deposited in the Museo de La Serena by Jorge Iribarren. Lithic, ceramic, shell, metal, and wooden objects are described in detail: location, environment, and other appropriate data are provided.

764 **Cea Egaña, Alfredo.** Embarcaciones de la antigua Isla de Pascua, con especial referencia a las canoas con flotador lateral, Vaka Ama (CMALS/B, 17, 1979/1981, p. 68–91, bibl., ill.)

From ethnohistoric accounts, pictographs, and information provided by local population, author recreates process of construction of boats by lacing together pieces of wood. Numerous sketches show details. Similar vessels were constructed in Tuamotú, where wood suitable for boat-building is also scarce.

765 **Clément, Georges.** Typologie d'une collection de bolas provenant de Ponsonby: Chili Austral (SA/J, 67, 1980/1981, p. 49–68, bibl., ill., tables)

Bolas from the three lowest levels of a midden in Tierra del Fuego were classified into six types using metric and morphological criteria. Correlations between criteria were tested statistically and are presented in dendrograms and tables.

766 **Dillehay, Tom D.** *et al.* Monte Verde: radiocarbon dates from an early-man site in south-central Chile (Journal of Field Archaeology [Boston University *for the* Association of Field Archaeology] 9, 1982, p. 547–550, ill.)

Wood and stone artifacts associated with mastodon bones in an ancient streambed deposit have been dated using wood and charcoal samples. Seven dates extend between 8207 and 13,965 BP (using the 5730 half-life). In general, they agree with the natural stratigraphy and imply the site was occupied no less than 12,000 and no more than 14,000 years ago.

767 **Focacci Aste, Guillermo.** Excavaciones en el cementerio Playa Miller 9 (Docu-

mentos de Trabajo [Departamento de Antropología, Universidad de Tarapacá, Arica, Chile] 2, sept. 1982, p. 126–213, bibl., ill.)

Describes 38 burials individually and classifies them into two cultural phases: Maytas Chiribaya and San Miguel. Offerings of pottery, basketry, textiles, and various kinds of artifacts are tabulated, showing grave lots. Among interesting items are miniature rafts, pyroengraved gourds, hafted arrows, wooden spoons and vessels, and other categories of perishable materials.

768 ————. Nuevos fechados para la época del Tiahuanaco en la arqueología del Norte de Chile (Chungara [Universidad del Norte, Departamento de Antropología, Arica, Chile] 8, dic. 1981, p. 63–77, bibl.)

Ten C14 dates establish contemporaneity of Cabuza-Sobraya, Maytas-Chiribaya, and Loreto Viejo phases. Coexistence of burials representing these three groups, with no evidence of acculturation or exchange, appears to affirm the existence of ethnic diversity among the lowland populations in the Arica valley. Dates extend from AD 380 to 1255. Tiahuanacan influence was insignificant.

769 **Hidalgo Lehuede, Jorge; Juan Chacama Rodríguez;** and **Guillermo Focacci Aste.** Elementos estructurales en la cerámica del estadio aldeano (Chungara [Universidad del Norte, Departamento de Antropología, Arica, Chile] 8, dic. 1981, p. 79–95, bibl., ill.)

Painted vessels from Arica region, dating between AD 320 and 1350, were classified into seven categories defined by subdivision of decorated surface into two, three or four areas or fields. Distinct categories characterize the five chronological phases within this period. Suggests divisions employed in decoration correlated with divisions in social organization among the populations.

770 **Moragas Wachtenforff, Cora.** Túmulos funerarios en la costa sur de Tocopilla, Cobija, II Región (Chungara [Universidad del Norte, Departamento de Antropología, Arica, Chile] 9, 1982, p. 152–173, bibl.)

Cobija-10, a cemetery containing about 90 burials dating between 300 BC and AD 300, represents southernmost extent of Alto Ramírez phase on Chilean north coast. Burials are extended, the bodies resting on a layer of cactus logs, reeds, and matting: associated cultural materials include stone tools, textiles, and other utilitarian objects.

771 Muñoz Ovalle, Iván. La aldea de Cerro Sombrero en el período del Desarrollo Regional de Arica (Chungara [Universidad del Norte, Departamento de Antropología, Arica, Chile] 7, junio 1981, p. 105–142, bibl., ill.)

Site has three sectors: habitation, corrals, and petroglyphs. Analysis of residential structures, subsistence remains, artifacts, and other sources of information indicates the site was an important center of exchange and redistribution of highland and coastal products between about AD 1200 and 1350.

772 ———. La Capilla 4: un asentamiento poblacional tardío en la costa de Arica (Documentos de Trabajo [Departamento de Antropología, Universidad de Tarapacá, Arica, Chile] 2, sept. 1982, p. 98–124, bibl., ill.)

Excavations at a site dating by C14 between AD 700-1200 provide details on habitation and cultural inventory, as well as subsistence, during this late ceramic period on the north Chilean coast.

773 ———. Dinámica de las estructuras habitacionales del extremo Norte de Chile: valle-costa (Chungara [Universidad del Norte, Departamento de Antropología, Arica, Chile] 8, dic. 1981, p. 3–32, bibl., map, tables)

Settlement pattern reflected in sites in Arica region suggests several stages of evolution, beginning with simple band camps during preceramic period, becoming increasingly sedentary with adoption of agriculture, and culminating in planned towns under Inca domination.

774 ———. Las sociedades costeras en el litoral de Arica durante el período arcaico tardío y sus vinculaciones con la costa peruana (Chungara [Universidad del Norte, Departamento de Antropología, Arica, Chile] 9, 1982, p. 124–151, bibl., ill.)

Unlike other investigators who have interpreted cultural development in north coastal Chile as the result of a unique set of factors, author considers it to have followed a course similar to that on Peru's coast, where inception was earlier and complexity greater. These differences reflect local ecological and social variables, and the marginal location of North Chile in the context of plant and animal domestication.

775 ——— and Juan Chacama Rodríguez. Investigaciones arqueológicas en las poblaciones precerámicas de la costa de Arica (Documentos de Trabajo [Departamento de Antropología, Universidad de Tarapacá, Arica, Chile] 2, sept. 1982, p. 3–96, bibl., charts, ill., tables)

Three sites were selected for intensive investigation with the aim of defining the chronology more precisely and expanding information on patterns of adaptation and exploitation of resources. The sites are La Capilla 1, a preceramic rockshelter with pictographs; Quiani 9, an early campsite; and Acha 2, a late preceramic camp. Provides details on environment, settlement pattern, plant and animal remains; stone, wood, textile, and other cultural remains. Incorporates data from previous work into overview of life from about 4500 BC to beginnings of dependence on agriculture about 2000 BC.

776 Niemeyer F., Hans. Dos tipos de crisoles prehispánicos del Norte Chico, Chile (CMALS/B, 17, 1979/1981, p. 92–109, bibl., ill.)

Description of two pottery crucibles from late prehispanic contexts, believed to have been used to transfer molten metal to molds.

777 ——— and Virgilio Schiappacasse. Aportes al conocimiento del período tardío del extremo Norte de Chile: análisis del sector Huancarane del Valle de Camarones (Chungara [Universidad del Norte, Departamento de Antropología, Arica, Chile] 7, junio 1981, p. 3–103, bibl., ill.)

Two contemporary villages were investigated, one representing Arica culture and another associated with black-on-red pottery. A third site appears to have been a way station between highlands and valley. Petroglyphs from valley exhibit motifs distinct from those at higher elevation. Archaeological evidence affirms increased intensity of contacts between lowlands and altiplano during Late Period, and suggests interaction was not always peaceful.

778 Núñez A., Lautaro. Asentamiento de cazadores-recolectores tardíos de la Puna de Atacama: hacia el sedentarismo (Chungara [Universidad del Norte, Departamento de Antropología, Arica, Chile] 8, dic. 1981, p. 137–168, bibl., ill.)

Artifacts and faunal remains from two preceramic sites, Tulán-52 and Puripica-1, are interpreted as reflecting independent transition from subsistence based on trans-humant hunting and gathering to one based on domesticated animals between 3000 and 2000 BC in Puna de Atacama region, following the process reported from the Central Andes between 5000 and 4000 BC. Similar local adaptive factors led to adoption of agriculture about 1500 BC.

779 ———. Cazadores tempranos en Andes meridionales: evaluación cronológica de las industrias líticas del Norte de Chile (Boletín de Antropología Americana [Instituto Panamericano de Geografía e Historia, México] 2, dic. 1980, p. 87–120, bibl., ill., tables)

Data from 54 preceramic sites from diverse environments provide a basis for recognizing three periods: 1) Early (8870–7810 BC); 2) Intermediate (7810–5470 BC); and 3) Late (5470–2000 BC). Each is represented by three to five complexes in different habitats and possessing different combinations of artifacts. Tables and charts give details of location, elevation, dating, and original source for each site.

780 ———. Paleo-Indian and Archaic cultural periods in the Arid and Semiarid regions of Northern Chile (*in* Advances in world archaeology. Fred Wendorf and Angela Close, editors. New York: Academic Press, 1983, v. 2, p. 161–203, bibl., ill.)

Review of sites, artifacts, subsistence remains, and other evidence for regional variations in cultural adaptation and transition from dependence on wild foods to domesticated plants and animals is based on most recent fieldwork and C14 dating. Includes author's unpublished data on period between 12,000 and 3000 BP.

781 ———. Temprana emergencia de sedentarismo en el desierto chileno: Proyecto Caserones (Chungara [Universidad del Norte, Departamento de Antropología, Arica, Chile] 9, 1982, p. 80–122, bibl.)

Discussion of subsistence resources, costs of procurement, nutritional yield, and other factors relevant to explaining emergence of semi-urban center of Caserones about beginning of Christian era.

782 ——— and **Henri J. Hall.** Análisis de dieta y movilidad en un campamento arcaico del Norte de Chile (IFEA/B, 11:3/4, 1982, p. 91–113)

Analysis of coprolites and organic remains from Tiliviche, C14 dated between 7810 and 4110 BC, indicates exploitation of marine and interior resources and permits reconstructing a pattern of seasonal movement that appears to have maximized the region's subsistence potential.

783 ———; **Juan Varela;** and **Rodolfo Casamiquela.** Ocupación paleoindia en Quereo, IV región: reconstrucción multidisciplinaria en el territorio semiárido de Chile (CMALS/B, 17, 1979/1981, p. 32–67, bibl., charts, ill.)

Résumé of results of excavations at Paleo-Indian site on Chile's central coast includes discussion of cultural, faunal, and geological evidence. Fauna include mastodon, horse, paleolama, and swamp deer. Human activity is implied principally by unnatural modifications of bone (fracture, polish, cut marks). Quereo I dates prior to 12,000 BP; Quereo II prior to 11,000 BP. Charts give details of cultural and natural stratigraphy and their implications. Important for Paleo-Indian specialists.

784 **Oyarzún Navarro, Aureliano.** Estudios antropológicos y arqueológicos. Compilación, introducción, notas y bibliografía de Mario Orellana Rodríguez. Santiago de Chile: Editorial Universitaria, 1979. 277 p.: bibl., ill.

Collected works of physician who became interested in anthropology and was co-founder of Museo Histórico Nacional de Chile. Of most value are chapters describing artifacts from shell-middens, workshop sites, and pictographs explored prior to 1920.

785 **Piazza K., Flavio.** Análisis descriptivo de una aldea incaica en el sector de Pampa Alto Ramírez (Chungara [Universidad del Norte, Departamento de Antropología, Arica, Chile] 7, junio 1981, p. 172–210, ill.)

Analysis with numerous diagrams of structural details represented in the dwellings and their arrangement at a late Inca site in lower Azapa valley, north coastal Chile.

786 **Prehistoric trails of Atacama: archaeology of Northern Chile.** Edited by Clement W. Meighan and D.L. True. Los Angeles: Institute of Archaeology, University of California, 1980. 228 p., lxi, 1 p. of plates: bibl., ill. (Monumenta archaeológica, 0363–7565; 7)

Submitted for publication in 1976, volume reports on research conducted by the University of California (Davis and Los Angeles) in collaboration with Chilean institutions on archaeology of North Chile. Chapters present a revised chronology based on C14 dates and the results of excavations at Tarapacá 18, Tarapacá 2A, Caserones, and Guatacondo. Specialized reports deal with preceramic bifacial artifacts, cultivated plant remains, fish remains, guanaco remains, and coprolites. Most detailed publication in English on north coastal archaeology.

787 Sanhueza Tapia, Julio A. Antecedentes preliminares y dos fechados radio-carbónicos del sitio "Pukar Qollu" o "Pukara de Isluga," (ILG-2). Altiplano de Iquique, Primera Región, Norte de Chile (Documentos de Trabajo [Instituto de Investigaciones Arqueológicas y de Restauración Monumental, Universidad de Antofagasta] 8, 1981, p. 32–41, bibl., ill.)

Description of pottery, lithic, and faunal remains obtained during test excavations at site composed of rooms, corrals, and walls. Two C14 dates were obtained: 1440 ± 50 and 1770 ± 50 BP or AD 510 and 180.

788 ——— and Olaf G. Olmos Figueroa. Usamaya I: cementerio indígena en Isluga, altiplano de Iquique, 1 Región, Chile (Chungara [Universidad del Norte, Departamento de Antropología, Arica, Chile] 8, dic. 1981, p. 169–187, bibl., ill.)

Describes nine cist tombs excavated at site 1300 m elevation as well as pottery and other artifacts from the tombs and surface. Blue glass beads establish its use at time of European contact.

789 Santoro Vargas, Calogero. Formativo temprano en el extremo Norte de Chile (Chungara [Universidad del Norte, Departamento de Antropología, Arica, Chile] 8, dic. 1981, p. 33–62, bibl., tables)

Discussion of characteristics of the Azapa phase, represented by habitation and burial remains, dated between 1300 and 560 BC, during which the transition from wild to domesticated plants was made. Although influences can be recognized from south-central coast of Peru, local development predominates.

790 ——— and Iván Muñoz Ovalle. Patrón habitacional incaico en el área de Pampa Alto Ramírez, Arica, Chile (Chungara [Universidad del Norte, Departamento de Antropología, Arica, Chile] 7, junio 1981, p. 144–171, bibl., ill.)

Inca site 8 km from the coast contains four zones with distinct functions. From north to south they are: 1) cultivation and storage; 2) habitation (houses, corrals, and refuse); 3) cemetery; and 4) geoglyphs. Site represents a brief intrusion from highlands just prior to European colonization.

791 ——— and Juan Chacama Rodríguez. Secuencia cultural de las tierras altas del área centro sur andina (Chungara [Universidad del Norte, Departamento de Antropología, Arica, Chile] 9, 1982, p. 22–45, bibl., ill.)

Nine periods are represented in sequence extending from 13,000 to 500 BP. Settled villages appear during Period 6 (3000–2000 BP). Suggests changes in climate as factors in gradually increasing specialization in hunting. Proposes evolutionary changes in stone projectile point forms. Favors adaptation to local resources over more popular hypothesis of transhumance.

792 Stehberg Landsberger, Rubén. Diccionario de sitios arqueológicos de Araucanía. Santiago: Museo Nacional de Historia Natural, 1980. 209 p.: bibl. (Publicación ocasional / Museo Nacional de Historia Natural; no. 31)

Alphabetical listing of 610 archaeological sites reported between Río Maule and Chiloé Island. Provides information where available on kind of site, latitude and longitude, geographic location, artifacts, excavations, C14 dates, etc., as well as bibliographic sources.

793 Ulloa Torres, Liliana. Estilos decorativos y formas textiles de poblaciones agromarítimas en el extremo Norte de Chile (Chungara [Universidad del Norte, Departamento de Antropología, Arica, Chile] 8, dic. 1981, p. 109–136, bibl., ill.)

Textiles from the cemetery of Playa Miller-9 were sorted by function, and then by technique, material, quality, color, decoration, and other traits. Three styles could be distinguished, each associated with a ceramic complex and corresponding to three chronological phases: Cabuza, Maitas-Chiribaya, and Regional Developmental.

794 ———. Evolución de la industria textil prehispánica en la zona de Arica (Chungara [Universidad del Norte, Departamento de Antropología, Arica, Chile] 8, dic. 1981, p. 97–108, bibl., tables)

Textiles obtained during archaeological excavations and deposited in the Museo Arqueológico San Miguel de Azapa were classified by technique of manufacture and ornamentation, function, and cultural affiliation. Two charts show temporal duration of these features from 2000 BC to AD 1500.

795 **Wassen, S. Henry** and **Wolmar E. Bondeson.** Archaeological notes and botanical research on endocarps from Quebrada Las Conchas: Antofagasta, Chile (EM/A, 1979/1980, p. 59–71, bibl., ill., map)

Presents circumstantial evidence to indicate that the plant remains from upper levels of Quebrada Las Conchas shell-midden date about 1380 BP rather 9680–7000 BP as has been asserted.

COLOMBIA

796 **Angulo Valdés, Carlos.** La tradición Malambo. Bogotá: Banco de la República, Fundación de Investigaciones Arqueológicos Nacionales, 1981. 206 p.: bibl., ill. (Publicación; 12)

Monograph gives detailed information on Malambo culture on Colombia's Caribbean coast, previously known only from brief preliminary description. Describes excavations at two sites, Malambo and Los Mangos, as well as pottery types, stone, pottery, and bone artifacts. Illustrates vessel shapes, appendages, and decoration and reviews evidence for subsistence. Similarities to pottery of the Barrancas tradition of the lower Orinoco suggest a relationship.

797 **Bray, Warwick; Leonor Herrera;** and **Marianne Schrimpff.** Introduction [untitled] (Pro Calima [Archäologisch-ethnologisches Projekt im westlichen Kolombien, Südamerika. Periodische Publikation der Vereinigung Pro Calima, Gassman AG, Solothurn] 2, Dez. 1981, p. 1–22, ill.)

Preliminary results of 1980 field season in Calima region of west-central Colombia indicate sequence of three periods:

1) "Early Calima" period is little known;
2) Yotoco dates between about the beginning of the Christian era and AD 1200; and
3) Sonso dates between AD 1200 and European contact. Reviews in English difficulties of conducting fieldwork, field procedures, and results, and includes informative maps and illustrations. House platforms, drainage canals, and "roads" are the principal surface features.

798 **Cardale de Schrimpff, Marianne.** Ocupaciones humanas en el altiplano cundiboyacense: la etapa cerámica vista desde Zipaquirá (MOBR/B, 4, sept./dic. 191, p. 1–20, bibl., ill.)

Search for salt deposits explains several deep sites with pottery and charcoal representing a premuisca occupation, C14 dated between about 400 BC and AD 100. Zoned incision on a plain or red-slipped surface, and fingernail marking are typical decorative techniques.

799 ——— Las Salinas de Zipaquirá: su explotación indígena. Bogotá: Banco de la República, Fundación de Investigaciones Arqueológicas Nacionales, 1981. 290 p.: bibl., graphs, ill., maps, tables (Publicación; 8)

A settlement in vicinity of Zipaquirá, central Colombia, was tested stratigraphically to obtain information on precolumbian salt production. Abundant fragments of large vessels used to evaporate briny water were encountered, as well as post holes, animal bones, and lithics. C14 dates place the occupation about the beginning of Christian era. Data from early documentary sources are summarized, as well as archaeological procedures and results.

800 ——— and **Ana María Falchetti de Sáenz.** Objetos prehispánicos de madera procedentes del altiplano nariñense, Colombia (MOBR/B, 3, sept./dic. 1980, p. 1–15, bibl., ill.)

Description of 28 wooden objects from a tomb of the Piartal-Tuza tradition dating from the eighth century, including spindle whorls, parts of a loom, lances, batons with carved heads, neck rests, a bench, and a spoon.

801 **Chaves Mendoza, Alvaro.** Los animales mágicos en las urnas de Tierradentro. Bogotá: Museo de Artes y Tradiciones Populares, 1981. 109 p.: bibl., ill.

Review of archaeological investigations at Tierradentro precedes discussion of symbolic significance of three animals most frequently depicted on pottery found in tombs: snake, lizard, and centipede. Data culled from ethnohistoric and ethnographic sources for Colombia, Mesoamerica, and Peru attributed sexual, fertility, and transformational significance to all three. Text in Spanish and English.

802 —— and **Mauricio Puerta Restrepo.** Entierros y vivienda prehispánica en Monserrate, Huila (PUJ/UH, 10:16, dic. 1981, p. 28–89, bibl., ill.)

This report on first archaeological investigations in Monserrate region describes five burials, seven petroglyphs, and contents of 11 stratigraphic pits. Pottery was sparse; detailed descriptions are provided by types. Although a few features seem distinctive, the culture forms part of general Tierradentro complex.

803 **Correal Urrego, Gonzalo.** Evidencias culturales y megafauna pleistocénica en Colombia. Bogotá: Banco de la República, Fundación de Investigaciones Arqueológicas Nacionales, 1981. 148 p.: bibl., ill. (Publicación; 14)

Remains of horse, mastodon, and other animals encountered at site north of Bogotá, in association with percussion-made flakes showing use, cores, and rare pressure-flaked tools, were C14 dated at 11,740 BP. Describes and illustrates excavations, stratigraphy, palinology, artifacts, and faunal remains. Complex resembles that from El Abra.

804 **Cubillos, Julio César.** Arqueología de San Agustín: El Estrecho, El Parador, y Mesita C. Bogotá: Fundación de Investigaciones Arqueológicas Nacionales, Banco de la República, 1980. 174 p., 28 leaves of plates (1 folded): bibl., ill. (some col.).

Three sites on land selected by the Corporación Nacional de Turismo for tourist development were investigated. Numerous burials were encountered at El Parador and Mesita C; excellent plans supplement detailed descriptions. El Estrecho, a habitation site, provided basis for a relative ceramic chronology. Provides characteristics of pottery types and vessel shapes along with tabulations of frequencies by levels. Several C14 dates, extending from 10 BC to AD 690, im-

ply region experienced relatively high cultural stability during this period.

805 **Duque Gómez, Luis** and **Julio César Cubillos.** Arqueología de San Agustín: Alto de los Idolos, montículos y tumbas. Bogotá: Banco de la República, Fundación de Investigaciones Arqueológicas Nacionales, 1979. 225 p.: bibl., ill.

Detailed description, well illustrated with photographs and diagrams, of tombs excavated in 1970–71 in cemetery 30 km from San Agustín. Tombs, walled and roofed with stone columns and slabs and containing monolithic sarcophagi and anthropomorphic sculptures, were erected and covered with earth, creating circular or ovoid mounds. C14 dates extend from the first to sixth century AD.

806 **Legast, Anne.** La fauna en la orfebrería Sinu. Bogotá: Banco de la República, Fundación de Investigaciones Arqueológicas Nacionales, 1980. 119 p.: bibl., ill., maps, plates, tables.

Five kinds of animals are represented among 1300 gold objects. Almost 90 percent are birds; the remainder are mammals, reptiles, amphibians, and fish. Classifications and tabulations show frequencies of various kinds of fauna on specific forms of ornaments; maps show geographical occurrences. Species, families, or orders are identifiable on most specimens. Comprehensive and well illustrated synthesis.

807 **Llanos Vargas, Héctor.** Los cacicazgos de Popayán a la llegada de los conquistadores. Bogotá: Banco de la República, Fundación de Investigaciones Arqueológicas Nacionales, 1981. 98 p.: bibl., maps (Publicación; 10)

Archivo General de Indias (Sevilla), Archivo Central del Cauca (Popayán), and other documentary sources were culled for information to reconstruct demography, economy, social and political structure, languages, and customs of the indigenous population of Popayán in the 16th century.

808 **Madersbacher, Fred.** San Agustín: un étrange civilisation en Colombie (ARCHEO, 170, sept. 1982, p. 34–40, maps, plates)

Résumé of lithic remains, chronology of investigation, and speculations about origin and significance of San Agustín, accompanied by several impressive photographs of ceremonial structures and stone sculptures.

809 Plazas, Clemencia and **Ana María Falchetti de Sáenz.** Asentamientos prehispánicos en el bajo Río San Jorge. Bogotá: Banco de la República, Fundación de Investigaciones Arqueológicas Nacionales, 1981. 136 p.: bibl., ill., maps (Publicación; 11)

Lower Río San Jorge flows across low flat land subject annually to inundation. Aerial photography revealed dense patchworks of ridges and intervening ditches, presumably constructed to permit year-round agriculture. Archaeological investigations defined settlement pattern and ceramic complex associated with ridged fields, and produced C14 dates placing their use between about 0-AD 600. Subsequently, the population dispersed to higher elevations along middle San Jorge and a group associated with different ceramic tradition, characteristic of lower Río Magdalena, moved into the lower San Jorge. Numerous maps, colored and black-and-white photographs showing ridge extent and patterns, as well as archaeological information, make this report important.

810 Schuler-Schömig, Immina von. A grave-lot of the Sonso period (Pro Calima [Archäologisch-ethnologisches Projekt im westlichen Kolombien/Südamerika. Periodische Publikation der Vereinigung Pro Calima, Gassmann AG, Solothurn] 2, Dez. 1981, p. 25–27, ill.)

Describes and illustrates contents of chamber and shaft tomb, including wooden coffin, spear-thrower, three darts, and crude pottery vessel.

811 Scott, David A. Cuentas de collar elaboradas en aleación de cobre procedentes de Nariño, Colombia (MOBR/B, 3, sept./dic. 1980, p. 18–29, bibl., ill.)

Cleaning an amorphous mass of corroded copper revealed it to consist of beads strung on vegetal fiber. Describes methods of cleaning and technological analysis. Ten beads were copper-arsenic and one copper-tin. The latter, the first example of prehispanic bronze from Colombia, is probably of Inca origin.

812 ———. Metallurgical studies of Calima ornaments (Pro Calima [Archäologisch-ethnologisches Projekt im westlichen Kolombien, Südamerika. Peri-

odische Publikation der Vereinigung Pro Calima, Gassman AG, Solothurn] 2, Dez. 1981, p. 22–24, ill.)

Electron microprobe analysis of six metal objects from excavations in the Calima region.

813 Silva Celis, Eliécar. Investigaciones arqueológicas en Villa de Leiva (MOBR/ B, 4, enero/abril 1981, p. 1–18, ill.)

Evaluates possible astronomical significance of rectangular enclosures bounded by a row of vertical monolithic columns, attributed to Chibcha. One location produced C14 dates extending between 2880 and 2180 BP.

814 Tello Cifuentes, Hernán. Geología de algunos sitios arqueológicos. Bogotá: Banco de la República, Fundación de Investigaciones Arqueológicas Nacionales, 1981. 112 p.: bibl., ill. (Publicación; 13)

Geological and petrographic studies were conducted in Departments of Cauca and Huila to establish origin of stone sculptures at San Agustín, Tierradentro, Quinchana, and Aguabonita. All stone used at San Agustín was local. Formation of columnar basalt in Quinchana region provides a natural source for columns found in archaeological sites.

815 Uribe, María Victoria. Reconocimiento arqueológico del Valle Medio del Río Guamués, Putumayo (ICA/RCA, 23, 1980/1981 [i.e. 1982] p. 253–276, bibl., ill., map)

Survey on the drainage of the Río Guamués, a tributary of the right bank of the Putumayo near the Ecuadorian border, produced three habitation sites. Surface collections of pottery are characterized by sand temper; necks of jars have plain or finger-pressed corrugation. There is no similarity to pottery from the Nariño highlands.

ECUADOR

816 Bedoya Maruri, Angel Nicanor. Las ruinas arqueológicas de Caranqui (IGME/RG, 15, dic. 1981, p. 79–91, maps)

Observations concerning the ruins of Caranqui near Ibarra in highland Ecuador culled from the writings of Cieza de León, Padre Juan Domingo Goleti, Antonio de

Alcedo, Juan de Velasco, and Edward Whymper.

817 Cochasqui: estudios arqueológicos.
Udo Oberem, compiler. Otavalo, Ecuador: Instituto Otavaleño de Antropología, 1981. 282 p.: bibl. (Colección Pendoneros; 4)

Reports on two aspects of the German Mission's excavations: lithic artifacts by Carlos Zalles Flossbach, and fine pottery and minor finds by Uwe Schonfelder. The 27 C14 dates from seven contexts extend from AD 930-1765. Of the 503 lithic artifacts analyzed, 320 were obsidian, 100 basalt, and the remainder other materials.

818 Cruz, Felipe and Olaf Holm. Un informe muy preliminar, San Lorenzo del Mate, Provincia de Guayas. Guayaquil: Banco Central del Ecuador, Museo Antropológico, 1981. 1 v.: bibl., ill.

Mound near Progreso was trenched, producing evidence of a perishable oval structure, a hearth, and fragments of pottery and stone artifacts. Pottery is reminiscent of Late Valdivia and early Machalilla, but includes compotera vessels not previously associated with these periods.

819 Ferdon, Edwin N., Jr. Holocene mangrove formations on the Santa Elena Peninsula, Ecuador: pluvial indicators or ecological response to physiographic changes (SAA/AA, 46, 1981, p. 619–626, bibl.)

Disputes thesis that periods of abandonment of Santa Elena Peninsula between 6500 BC and AD 1000 reflect arid climatic intervals; rather, coastal uplift seems likely to underlie changes in the abundance of mangrove, on which prehistoric populations depended for subsistence.

820 Hartmann, Roswith and Olaf Holm. La "romana" en tiempos prehispánicos y su uso actual en la costa del Ecuador (Miscelánea Antropológica Ecuatoriana [Boletín de los Museos del Banco Central del Ecuador, Cuenca] 1:1, 1981, p. 155–173, bibl., ill.)

Evidence from early chronicles is supplemented by surviving examples of balances used for weighing produce in rural parts of coastal Ecuador.

821 Holm, Olaf. Cultura manteña-huancavilca. Guayaquil: Banco Central del Ecuador, Museo Antropológico y Pinacoteca, 1982. 48 p.: bibl., ill.

Summary of characteristics of culture occupying coast of Ecuador between about AD 700 and Spanish contact, based on ethnohistoric and archaeological sources. Aspects treated include subsistence, social organization, navigation, urbanism, burial practices, arts and crafts.

822 Lynch, Thomas F. and Susan Pollock. Chobshi Cave and its place in Andean and Ecuadorian archaeology (in Anthropological papers in memory of Earl H. Swanson, Jr. Edited by Lucille B. Harten, Claude N. Warren, and Donald H. Tuohy. Pocatello: Idaho Museum of Natural History, 1980, p. 19–40, bibl., ill.)

Excavations in rock shelter in Azuay Province, elevation about 2400 m, produced unifacial and bifacial tools, including stemmed and ovoid projectile points, associated with deer and remains of other modern fauna. Four C14 dates extend from 8060 to 5585 BC. Site represents early stage of diversification following Paleo-Indian Horizon, and relates to El Inga in northern Ecuador and Ayampatín in northwest Argentina.

823 Marcos, Jorge G. and Presley Norton. Interpretación sobre la arqueología de la Isla de La Plata (Miscelánea Antropológica Ecuatoriana [Boletín de los Museos del Banco Central del Ecuador, Cuenca] 1:1, 1981, p. 136–173, bibl., ill.)

Recent excavations on La Plata produced concentrations of objects suggesting island was major ceremonial and commercial center linking Mesoamerican and Andean area from 2000 BC to European contact.

824 Mayer-Oakes, William J. Early man in the northern Andes: problems and possibilities (in Peopling of the New World. Edited by Jonathon E. Ericson, R.E. Taylor, and Rainer Berger. Los Altos, Calif.: Ballena Press, 1982, p. 269–283, ill., map, plates, tables [Ballena Press anthropological papers; 23])

Review of conflicting evidence from C14 and obsidian hydration measurements for antiquity of Ecuadorian highland sites of El Inga and San José. Inclines toward acceptance of younger dates, beginning about 4000 BC. All dates are presented: obsidian dates concentrate between 16,000 and 6000 BC.

825 Parducci Z., Resfa. Instrumentos musicales de viento del litoral ecuatoriano prehispánico. Guayaquil, Ecuador: Imprenta de la Universidad de Guayaquil, 1983. 39 p.: 22 figures, musical notation.

Wind instruments (flutes, whistles, ocarinas, trumpets) are classified according to number of tones they produce (1, 2, 3, etc.). Except for a shell trumpet, all are made from pottery. Most melodious ocarinas were played and sounds recorded in musical notation, although the melody is improvised.

826 Porras Garcés, Pedro I. Arqueología de Quito I: Fase Cotocollao. Quito: Pontificia Universidad Católica del Ecuador, Centro de Investigaciones Arqueológicas, 1982. 273 p.: bibl., ill., maps.

Cotocollao, northern suburb of Quito, is first Formative period site described from the Ecuadorian highlands. Pottery obtained from stratigraphic excavations was classified into types, which are described and illustrated. Comparisons are made with coastal Formative Valdivia, Machalilla, and Chorrera complexes. Three C14 dates, 2010, 1370, and 930 BC, are accepted as dating early, middle, and late portions of sequence.

827 ———. Don Jacinto Jijón y Caamaño y la arqueología de la sierra ecuatoriana: estudio crítico (Scripta Ethnológica [Buenos Aires] 7, 1981, p. 131–136)

After reviewing cultural chronology established by Jijón y Caamaño and summarized in *Antropología prehispánica del Ecuador* written in 1945, Porras commends Jijón for his pioneering efforts but suggests that sentiment should not prevent adopting more accurate reconstructions based on improved techniques of excavation and dating methods.

828 ———. Sitio Sangay A: informe preliminar de la primera etapa (Revista de la Universidad Católica [Quito] 9:29, marzo 1981, p. 105–145, bibl., ill.)

Sangay A consists of numerous elongated, L-shaped, and circular earth mounds systematically arranged on a plateau on left side of Río Upano at elevation of about 1300 m in southeastern Ecuador. This report describes site, excavations, and general characteristics. Five C14 dates extend from 180 BC to AD 270. Function, origin, and cultural affiliations of complex remain to be established.

829 ——— and Luis Zúñiga P. Arqueología del sitio La Ponga (*in* Arqueología de Palenque y La Ponga. Quito: Pontificia

Universidad Católica del Ecuador, Centro de Investigaciones Arqueológicas, 1983, p. 141–240, bibl., ill.)

Ceramics obtained from excavations at habitation site of La Ponga in Valdivia Valley of coastal Ecuador represent Machalilla Tradition of Formative period. Pottery was classified into types; detailed descriptions and illustrations are provided. Comparing the decorative techniques and vessel shapes with previously published data indicates site represents local variation of late Machalilla Phase. Two C14 dates are: 2950 ± 140 and 2840 ± 155 BP or 1000 and 890 BC.

830 ——— and Patricio Moncayo E. Arqueología del sitio Palenque (*in* Arqueología de Palenque y La Ponga. Quito: Pontificia Universidad Católica del Ecuador, Centro de Investigaciones Arqueológicas, 1983, p. 5–139, bibl., ill.)

Survey along right bank of Río Palenque located site with six artificial mounds 1.25 to 4.60 m high. Numerous stratigraphic pits in two mounds, and excavations in nearby habitation site are reported. Describes in detail pottery types and lithic artifacts, constructs seriated ceramic sequence. Decorative techniques and vessel shapes strongly resemble those of the Guayaquil Phase to the south, and C14 dates are contemporary. Two dates were obtained: 2220 ± 75 and 2170 ± 65 BP. Mounds are judged more similar in function and morphology to those of north highlands than to those of Milagro-Quevedo culture of the coast.

831 Rivera Dorado, Miguel. Arqueología y etnohistoria de la costa norte del Ecuador (IGFO/RI, 38:153/154, julio/dic. 1978, p. 547–562, bibl., map)

Summary of information from 16th-century observers of indigenous population on Esmeraldas coast. Cultural homogeneity they imply is attributed to adaptation to similar environments and continuous interaction.

832 Sánchez Montañés, Emma. Las figurillas de Esmeraldas: tipología y función. Madrid: Misión Arqueológica Española en el Ecuador, 1981. 120 p., 37 plates: bibl., figures (Memorias; 7)

Some 2000 examples of anthropomorphic figurines from public and private collections in Ecuador and from excavations on coast of Esmeraldas conducted by Spanish

Archaeological Mission provide basis for defining four styles, each composed of two to five types. Describes in detail and illustrates each style, and types and other variations included. One chapter discusses general aspects, such as evidence for cranial deformation, technology, economy, dress and ornament, society, beliefs, and aspects of life cycle that can be inferred from figurines' characteristics. Another reviews theories of possible function (as idols, ancestral figures, fertility symbols, religious offerings, burial offerings). Finding previous explanations incompatible with archaeological context and variety of representation, author proposes figurines were instruments of socialization, recalling and commemorating successive stages of individual life cycle. Chronologically, types extend from Formative through Integration periods.

833 Schávelzon, Daniel. Arqueología y arquitectura del Ecuador prehispánico. México: Universidad Nacional Autónoma de México, 1981. 435 p., 5 folded leaves of plates: bibl., ill.

Compilation of evidence from archaeological sites and representations in pottery of types of prehistoric architecture, principally from Ecuadorian coast during Regional Developmental and Integration periods. Models in pottery described and illustrated constitute most complete inventory of this source of information available.

834 Stothert, Karen E. Review of the early preceramic complexes of the Santa Elena Peninsula, Ecuador (SAA/AA, 48, 1983, p. 122–127, bibl.)

Presents evidence that Exacto, Manantial, and Carolina lithic complexes established by Lanning, are not of ancient origin. First two represent modern breakage; the third is undetectable. Fourth complex, Achallan, is also of dubious validity. Only the Vegas complex has survived as a legitimate preceramic culture.

835 Ubelaker, Douglas E. The Ayalán cemetery: a late Integration period burial site on the south coast of Ecuador. Washington: Smithsonian Institution Press, 1981. 175 p.: bibl., ill. (Smithsonian contributions to anthropology; no. 29)

Excavation of 54 large urns and 27 direct interments provides detailed information on population and burial practices of

Milagro culture. Urns contained up to 25 individuals, along with pottery, metal, stone, and shell artifacts, and faunal remains. Analysis of human remains permitted reconstructing life expectancy, infant mortality, pathologies, and cultural modifications, providing clues to diet, disease, and other aspects of precolumbian life. Significant contribution, both for results and for comprehensive presentation of data.

PERU

836 Agurto Calvo, Santiago. Cusco: la traza urbana de la ciudad inca. Cuzco, Perú: Offsett Color, 1980. 157 p.: bibl., ill.

Summary of methods and results of inventory of surface expressions of Inca construction in Cuzco, co-sponsored by UNESCO and Peruvian Government. Archaeological plan of city, reconstructed at scale of 1/2000, consists of central administrative sector, ring of residential units, and suburban zone. Population is estimated at 125,000. Numerous plans and maps make this volume significant for understanding the organization of Inca Cuzco.

837 Alcina Franch, José. Juegos y ritual funerario en Chincheros: Cuzco (in Congreso Peruano: El Hombre y la Cultura Andina, 3rd, Lima, 1977. El hombre y la cultura andina [see *HLAS 43:253*] v. 4, 1980, p. 441–456, bibl.)

Draws upon descriptions of precolumbian games to account for designs on stones encountered at Chincheros, and suggests "games" had ceremonial and specifically funerary purposes.

838 Angles Vargas, Víctor. Machupijchu y el camino inka. Cuzco, Peru: V. Angles Vargas, 1980. 103 p.: ill. (some col.).

Useful guide to archaeological park of Machu Picchu, with addition of plans and descriptions of sites along the last 40 km of Inca highway from Cuzco.

839 Antúnez de Mayolo R., Santiago E. La nutrición en el antiguo Perú. Lima: Banco Central de Reserva del Perú, Oficina Numismática, 1981. 189 p.: bibl., tables.

Archival information and surviving knowledge of traditional practices are combined to provide detailed reconstruction of diet under the Inca. Among numerous tables supplementing text, most impressive shows precolumbian diet to provide more calories, protein, carbohydrates, minerals, and vitamins than recommended modern national and international standards. Author argues for restoration of foods and methods of preparation now neglected as a solution to Peru's growing food crisis. Important compilation.

840 ———. La predicción del clima en el Perú precolombino (AI/I, 6:4, 1981, p. 206–209, bibl.)

Precolumbian Peruvians employed seven groups of variables to predict climate, giving results more accurate than are obtained using modern methods.

841 Ascher, Marcia and **Robert Ascher.** Code of the quipu: a study in media, mathematics, and culture. Ann Arbor: University of Michigan Press, 1981. 166 p.: bibl., ill.

Minute examination of 191 quipus permitted recognizing patterns in construction, which reveal their flexibility and utility for recording a greater variety and specificity of information than has been assumed. Instructions are given how to make a quipu. Each state of explanation is followed by exercises employing familiar information (such as converting a grocery cash-register receipt to a quipu record). Mathematical theory is drawn upon to infer meaning and assess the Inca intellectual achievement, revealing unique ways of combining concepts of number, geometric configuration, and logic. The definitive work on quipus and Inca mathematics.

842 Berezkin, Yuri E. An identification of anthropomorphic mythological personages in Moche representations (IAS/NP, 18, 1980, p. 1–26, bibl., ill.)

Analyzing representations on about 3000 vessels of Moche III-V, author differentiates three deities, designated A, B, and C, plus a Rayed God and a Goddess. An Iguana God is occasionally associated with God A, suggesting they may be twins. Also discusses possible relationships among other deities.

843 Bonavia, Duccio. Consideraciones sobre el complejo Chivateros (in Arqueología peruana. Ramiro Matos Mendieta, compilador. Lima: Seminario Investigaciones Arqueológicas en el Perú, 1979, p. 65–74)

Provides evidence that Chivateros is not a preceramic complex, but a quarry site. Similar "artifacts" characterize El Volcán, a quarry in the Department of Ancash.

844 Brennan, Curtiss T. Cerro Arena: origins of the urban tradition on the Peruvian north coast (UC/CA, 23:3, June 1982, p. 247–254, bibl., ill.)

Investigations at Cerro Arena reveal previous assessments of simplicity of Salinar culture are erroneous. During this period, centralized political administration, differentiated social organization, urbanism, warfare, commerce, and other aspects of the later North Coastal cultural configuration can be inferred from the archaeological evidence, along with the beginning of multivalley integration.

845 Burger, Richard L. The radiocarbon evidence for the temporal priority of Chavín de Huantar (SAA/AA, 46, 1981, p. 592–602, bibl.)

When C14 dates from Chavín de Huantar and from coastal sites with related styles (Haldas, Caballo Muerto, Garagay, and Ancón) are compared, the latter are earlier. Increasing importance of Chavín appears to reflect declining importance of coastal centers.

846 Buse de la Guerra, Hermann. Actividad pesquera. s.l.: Documenta, 1981. 141 p.: ill.

After reviewing role of the sea in the subsistence of precolumbian coastal Peruvian groups, before and after the adoption of agriculture, author devotes chapters to methods of fishing, nets and hooks, and evidence depicted on pottery. Ethnohistoric sources and contemporary tradition supplement archaeological data.

847 Cárdenas Martín, Mercedes. Obtención de una cronología del uso de los recursos marinos en el Antiguo Perú (PUCIRA/BSA, 19/20, 1977/1978, p. 3–26, ill.)

Departing from hypothesis that coastal Peruvian cultural adaptation was characterized by increasing institutionalization of planning for conservation and increase of resources, archaeological survey was conducted from 1975 to 1977 in the valleys of Piura, Chao, Santa, Huaura, Rímac, and Lurín. Some 1043 sites were recorded, more than 50 percent previously unknown. Hypothesis was confirmed and much data on ecology, social organization, and systematic application of astronomical knowledge were collected.

848 ———. Restos vegetales arqueológicos del período precerámico de la costa del Perú (Cuadernos Prehispánicos [Seminario Americanista de la Universidad Casa de Colón, Valladolid, Spain] 9, 1981, p. 91–96, bibl., ill.)

Lists sites representing the preceramic or incipient agricultural period from which remains of edible plants have been recovered.

849 **Chan Chan: Andean desert city.** Edited by Michael E. Moseley and Kent C. Day. Albuquerque: University of New Mexico Press, 1981. 373 p.: bibl., ill. (School of American Research advanced seminar series)

Participants in the Chan Chan-Moche project from 1969–74 met in 1976 to compare results. Chapters review the agrarian base, ciudadelas, settlement growth, burial platforms, elite compounds, lower-class social and economic organization, subsistence, antecedents, and management. Chimu state is viewed as major focus of development of Andean civilization that must be explained in its own terms.

850 **Conklin, William J.** The information system of Middle Horizon quipus (in Ethnoastronomy and archaeoastronomy in the American tropics. Edited by Anthony F. Aveni and Gary Urton. New York: New York Academy of Sciences, 1982, p. 261–281, bibl., ill. [Annals of the New York Academy of Sciences; v. 385])

Several quipus of Middle Horizon age indicate that the quipu was not an Inca invention, although it was refined greatly during Inca times. Earlier quipus have pendant cords wrapped with colored thread. Provides detailed description of largest, composed of 101 cords. There is no evidence the information encoded is concerned with astronomy.

851 **Dearborn, D.S.** and **R.E. White.** Archaeoastronomy at Machu Picchu (in Ethnoastronomy and archaeoastronomy in the American tropics. Edited by Anthony F. Aveni and Gary Urton. New York: New York Academy of Sciences, 1982, p. 249–259, bibl., ill. [Annals of the New York Academy of Sciences; v. 385])

Experiments at two structures, known as "Torreon" and "Intihuatana Stone," indi-

cate that the former is appropriate for observing the June solstice, the solar zenith passage, and possibly some constellations. The Intihuatana Stone alone appears not to have astronomical significance, but may form part of a complex that does.

852 **Donnan, Christopher B.** A Moche V bottle with complex fineline drawing (in The Shape of the past: studies in honor of Franklin D. Murphy. Edited by Giorgio Buccellati and Charles Speroni. Los Angeles: University of California, Institute of Archaeology, 1981, p. 56–64, bibl., ill.)

Detailed examination of procession depicted on painted Moche vessel indicates it represents significant ceremonial event, which occurred during last phase of Moche culture and which continued to be depicted on vessels of succeeding Chimu culture.

853 ———. The identification of a Moche fake through iconographic analysis (in Falsifications and misreconstructions of precolumbian art. Edited by Elizabeth H. Boone. [see item 255] p. 37–50, 142, bibl., ill.)

Minute examination of complicated features of dress and ornament, as well as arrangement of elements, reveals errors that exposed a Moche pottery vessel as a fake. Describes significant details and identifies and illustrates for comparison authentic examples drawn upon by the falsifier. In all other respects, the vessel is consistent with authentic pieces, and would be impossible to differentiate from legitimate examples.

854 **Fung Pineda, Rosa.** Notas y comentarios sobre el sitio de Valencia en el Río Corrientes (Amazonia Peruana [Centro Amazónico de Antropología y Aplicación Práctica, Lima] 4:7, 1982, p. 99–137)

Construction of headquarters of Petróleos del Perú on left bank of middle Río Corrientes, a tributary of Huallaga in northeastern Peru, unearthed large burial urns. Fung made brief visit, permitting description of site and collecting a pottery sample. Decoration includes fingernail marking, incision, zoned impressed rings, and white-on-red painting. Possible affiliations and ethnohistorical data are summarized.

855 **Grieder, Terence** and **Alberto Bueno Mendoza.** La Galgada: Peru before pottery (AIA/A, 34, March/April 1981, p. 44–51, ill.)

Preceramic site extending for a km along both sides of principal tributary of Río Santa in northern Peru has produced remains of architecture, both domestic and ceremonial, reminiscent of contemporary remains at Kotosh. Settlement was initiated about 3000 BC; inhabitants adopted crude pottery about 2000 BC. Shaft tombs from the initial ceramic period are the most ancient known. Other tombs may be prototypes for the galleries of the temple at Chavín de Huantar. Well preserved cotton textiles exhibit a variety of techniques. This site adds to the evidence for large permanent settlements and advanced social and religious organization during preceramic times in Peru.

856 Guffroy, Jean. Les pétroglyphes de Checta: éléments interprétatifs (SA/J, 67, 1980/1981, p. 69–96, bibl., ill.)

Description of petroglyphs on some 450 rocks at 1000 m elevation in the Chillón Valley, coastal Peru, dated in the Early Intermediate period. Distributions of several motifs are mapped; discusses possible mythological significance and proposes hypothesis of a correlation with coca cultivation in the area.

857 Hocquenghem, Anne-Marie. L'iconographie mochica et les rites andins: les scènes en relations avec l'océan (CDAL, 20, 2. semestre, 1979, p. 115–129, plates)

Departing from assumption that parallels among scenes of Mochica vessels and Inca or traditional Andean ceremonial behavior imply equivalent significance, author examines more than 4000 vessels in European and Peruvian museums. Results suggest several Inca customs began during Mochica times.

858 ———— and Patricia J. Lyon. A class of anthropomorphic supernatural females in Moche iconography (IAS/NP, 18, 1980, p. 27–48, ill.)

Interprets 43 representations on Phase V vessels (and rarely on other materials) as a class of anthropomorphic supernatural females. They are depicted in four contexts, labeled Presentation, Animated Objects, Moon/Boat, and Burial.

859 Huapaya Manco, Cirilo. Vegetales como elemento antisísmico en estructuras prehispánicas (PUCIRA/BSA, 19/20, 1977/1978, p. 27–38, bibl., ill.)

Two methods of incorporating plant materials into construction were observed in structures from Chao to Lurín. One, termed *Shicra*, resembles coarse netting, and surrounds stones in walls. The other, "layers of plant materials," is laid between successive courses of stone or rubble. It is hypothesized that these procedures were employed to improve resistance to earthquake damage.

860 Knapp, Gregory. Prehistoric flood management on the Peruvian coast: reinterpreting the "sunken fields" of Chilca (SAA/AA, 47, 1982, p. 144–154, bibl., ill.)

Excavated depressions considered to have been constructed to make water-table moisture accessible to growing crops are reinterpreted as efforts to manage flood waters.

861 Lausent, I. Hypotheses sur le peuplement pré-hispanique des Quebradas Yungas: Acos, Vallée du Chancay (IFEA/B, 7:3/4, 1978, p. 61–93, bibl., charts, maps)

Documents, place names, and archaeological remains permit reconstructing land use during late precolumbian period. Modifications introduced during Spanish occupation inadvertently encouraged emergence of small private properties at bottom of the valley, on land previously dedicated to support of religious sector.

862 Lavallée, Daniéle and Michèle Julien. Un aspect de la préhistoire andine: l'exploitation des camélidés et des cervidés au formatif dans l'abri de Telarmachay: Junin, Pérou (SA/J, 67, 1980/1981, p. 97–124, bibl., ill.)

Data presented on camelid and deer bones from Levels II and III, representing the Formative period in a rock shelter at 4420 m elevation, include adult-juvenile ratios, butchering and culinary evidence, spatial distribution of particular bones, and differential concentration. Short-term occupation is inferred for Level III (early Formative); possibly permanent occupation by a smaller population for Level II (late Formative).

863 Lechtman, Heather. Copper-arsenic bronzes from the north coast of Peru (NYAS/A, 376, 1981, p. 77–122, bibl., ill.)

Objects of copper-arsenic alloy, 17 worked and 33 cast, were analyzed to establish arsenic content and method of manufacture. Variation in arsenic content favors interpretation that natural ores rather than artificial alloys were used.

864 ————; **Antonieta Erlij;** and **Edward J. Barry, Jr.** New perspectives on Moche metallurgy: techniques of gilding copper at Loma Negra, Northern Peru (SAA/AA, 47:1, Jan. 1982, p. 3–30, bibl., ill., maps)

Loma Negra, a cemetery near Vicus on Peruvian coast, is the source of large number of metal artifacts. Although acquired by looting, they provide largest extant sample of Moche metal craft. A group of gilded and silvered copper objects subjected to analysis to establish the techniques employed, appears to have been produced using depletion gilding and electrochemical replacement plating. The methods used to create other color effects remain unknown.

865 **Linares Málaga, Eloy.** Principales centros arqueológicos conétimos quechuas, aymaras y puquinas en Arequipa. Arequipa, Perú: Universidad Nacional de San Agustin de Arequipa, 181. 57 leaves.

Compilation of 333 names of archaeological sites of Quechua, Aymara, or Puquina derivation, with correct spelling and meaning, arranged by provinces within Arequipa Department.

866 **Lynch, Thomas F.** Chronology and stratigraphy at Guitarrero cave, Perú (*in* Peopling of the New World. Edited by Jonathon E. Ericson, R.E. Taylor, and Rainer Berger. Los Altos, Calif.: Ballena Press, 1982, p. 263–268, tables [Ballena Press anthropological papers, 23])

Attempt to evaluate reasons for inconsistent C14 dates and to identify most probable ages of three stratigraphic complexes.

866a **MacNeish, Richard S.** *et al.* Prehistory of the Ayacucho Basin, Peru. v. 2, Excavations and chronology. Ann Arbor: University of Michigan Press, 1981. 292 p.: bibl., ill.

Excavation of 11 rock shelters and six open sites provided detailed chronology from peopling of Ayacucho basin to European contact. Relative sequence was divided into 17 periods, whose absolute durations were established using 16 C14 dates. Assumptions, procedures, and results described in detail, followed by résumé of settlement types and locations for each period in the form of a map and a table. As first well documented regional chronology from Peruvian highlands, this is an essential reference for all

archaeologists concerned with cultural development in the Americas.

866b ————; **Robert K. Vierra; Antoinette Nelken-Terner;** and **Carl J. Phagan.** Prehistory of the Ayacucho Basin Peru. v. 3, Nonceramic artifacts. Ann Arbor: University of Michigan Press, 1980. 358 p.: bibl., ill., tables.

As the principal category of material culture represented throughout history of human occupation of Ayacucho Basin, lithic remains afford primary evidence for chronological, spatial, functional, and technological variations. Describes process of achieving a uniform typology and classificatory system, specifies methods of recording and attributes recorded and discusses statistical manipulations. Chapters are devoted to type descriptions of haftable pointed bifaces, nonhaftable bifaces, terminally worked unifaces, and laterally worked unifaces. Chap. 6 discusses analysis of flakes. Remainder describes ground and pecked stone tools, bone tools, and other nonceramic artifacts. Typology allowed all components from stratified sites and surface collections to be placed in chronological order and to be assigned durations of a century or less. Phases are defined by introduction or loss of types. This sequence provides basis for reconstructing the culture of each phase. As demonstration of analytical procedures and artifact types potentially widely applicable in Andean region, this volume should be consulted by specialists in lithic technology as well as Andean archaeology.

867 **Málaga Alba, Aurelio.** El perro como expresión cultural del hombre primitivo en el Perú (*in* Congreso Peruano: el Hombre y la Cultura Andina, 3rd, 1977. El hombre y la cultura andina [see *HLAS 43:253*] v. 5, p. 829–842, bibl., tables)

Describes varieties of precolumbian dogs reported from Peru and provides metric data on skulls. Earliest specimen dates about 5500 BC.

868 **Mejía Xesspe, Toribio.** El calzado en el antiguo Perú (PUCIRA/BSA, 17:18, 1975/1976, p. 23–41, bibl., ill.)

Classification and description of varieties of footwear depicted on pottery and represented by specimens in archaeological sites from coast. Discusses indigenous nomenclature, regional variations in material and construction, and differences in status of wearer.

869 Niles, Susan Allee. Pumamarca: a Late Intermediate period site near Ollantaytambo (IAS/NP, 18, 1980, p. 49–62, bibl., ill.)

Pumamarca, four hours travel on foot from Ollantaytambo, is assigned to the Late Intermediate period on the basis of architectural features, and interpreted as used by higher social strata of local population.

870 Olivera de Bueno, Gloria. Algunos tejidos de Inca: tejidos de la donación Soldi (PUCIRA/BSA, 17:18, 1975/1976, p. 51–68, ill.)

Describes in detail 12 textiles from Hacienda Ocucaje, representing Paracas through Inca period.

871 Onuki, Yoshio. Una perspectiva prehistórica de la utilización ambiental en la sierra nor-central de los Andes Centrales (Senri Ethnological Studies [National Museum of Ethnology, Osaka, Japan] 10, 1982, p. 211–228, bibl.)

Résumé of manner in which interaction between natural environment and human groups channeled cultural development during eight millennia. Climatic oscillations are considered significant catalysts of changes in subsistence and settlement pattern. Exploitation of a wide variety of niches preadapted the populations for survival when changes in the environment altered the subsistence potential of major productive zones.

872 Ortloff, Charles R.; Michael E. Moseley; and Robert A. Feldman. Hydraulic engineering aspects of the Chimu Chicama-Moche intervalley canal (SAA/AA, 47:3, July 1982, p. 572–595, maps, tables)

Applying modern engineering principles for maximizing efficiency of irrigation canals reveals that designers of Moche-Chicama intervalley canal understood complex interrelationships of parameters controlling velocity not known in Europe and US until late 19th century. Existence of this sophisticated knowledge implies advanced technology-based government and helps explain why Chimu were able to dominate north coast of Peru.

873 La Pesca en el Perú prehispánico. Texto, Hermann Buse de la Guerra *et al.* Lima?: Empresa Pública de Producción

de Harina y Aceite de Pescado, 197-. 253 p.: col. ill.

Sponsored by the Empresa Pesca Perú, this volume provides 150 p. of color illustrations of pottery, textiles, and metal objects grouped into four categories: 1) implements and techniques; 2) representations of fish and mollusks; 3) artistic and religious connotations; and 4) dietary aspects. Specimens are from 25 museums and private collections. Introductory texts discusses role of fishing in precolumbian cultures.

874 Pozorski, Thomas. The Caballo Muerto complex and its place in the Andean chronological sequence (Annals of Carnegie Museum [Carnegie Institute, Pittsburgh, Pa.] 52:1, March 1983, p. unavailable, bibl., ill., tables)

Analysis of architecture, pottery, and C14 dates from Caballo Muerto complex in Moche Valley, dating between 1500 and 400 BC, highlights lack of consistency in definition of "Chavín" and "pre-Chavín" ceramics, and supports the view that Chavín was not a widespread unifying force throughout the central Andes.

875 Prehistoric Andean ecology: man, settlement, and environment in the Andes. Frédéric-André Engel, editor. v. 1, Paloma. v. 2, The deep south. Atlantic Highlands, N.J.: Distributed by Humanities Press *for the* Department of Anthropology, Hunter College, City University of New York, 1980. 2 v.: bibl., ill. (Papers of the Department of Anthropology, Hunter College of the City University of New York)

Vol. 1 reports results of Engel's archaeological fieldwork on Peruvian coast during past 25 years showing locations of sites. Symbols on the map, comprising half the text, identify time period, constructions, agricultural features, and other aspects of archaeology and environment. La Paloma, a large and early village is only site described. Vol. 2 lists all sites encountered during intensive survey of coastal strip between 0 and 1000 m elevation, from Chilean border to southern margin of Paracas Peninsula and includes catalog number (for reference to maps in vol. 1), common name, elevation, period of occupation, kind of site, C14 dates, and other relevant data. Five chapters provide general data on environment, adaptive limitations, and more extended information on sites of major interest. Important contribution to the archaeology of the Peruvian south coast.

878 Ravines, Rogger. Chanchán: metrópoli chimú. Colaboradores, Anthony Andrews *et al.* Lima: Instituto de Estudios Peruanos: Instituto de Investigación Tecnológica Industrial y de Normas Técnicas, 1980. 390 p.: bibl., ill., index (Fuentes e investigaciones para la historia del Perú; 5)

Chapters by US archaeologists discuss city's development, economy and agriculture, religion and the cult of the dead, architecture and social classes. Ravines provides synthesis of previous investigations, ethnohistorical data on Chimu civilization, and significance of Chanchán in Peruvian cultural development.

879 Raymond, J. Scott. The maritime foundations of Andean civilization: a reconsideration of the evidence (SAA/AA, 46, 1981, p. 806–821, bibl.)

Moseley's hypothesis that large sedentary populations were supported mainly by seafood prior to adoption of agriculture is rejected after calculating calories represented by marine fauna in representative sites. Evidence is presented to support thesis that expanding population supported by cultivation of tubers led to intensification of seafood acquisition.

880 Ríos, Marcela and **Enrique Retamozo.** Vasos ceremoniales de Chan Chan. Lima: Instituto Cultural Peruano Norteamericano, 1982. 36 p.: bibl., ill.

Description of 16 silver and four gold ceremonial vessels from Chan Chan, purchased in 1924 and now in the Museo Nacional de Antropología y Arqueología, Lima. Each specimen is described individually, followed by discussion of the iconography and its significance.

881 Rowe, Ann Pollard. Textiles from the burial platform of Las Avispas at Chan Chan (IAS/NP, 18, 1980, p. 81–148, bibl., ill.)

Detailed analysis of textiles from burial platform permits defining techniques that appear to be distinctively Chimu as opposed to those characterizing the central coast. Specimens are classified by technique and described in detail. Garment types are loincloths, tunics, hats, and bands. Useful to specialists in textiles.

882 Rowe, John Howland. An account of the shrines of ancient Cuzco (IAS/NP, 17, 1979, p. 1–80)

Original manuscript, completed in 1653, of *Historia del Nuevo Mundo* by Bernabé Cobo was encountered in Biblioteca Capitular Colombina, Sevilla, in 1974. Chaps. 13–16 of Book 13 record shrines of Inca Cuzco. Spanish and English texts are provided on facing pages, preceded by evaluation of reliability, authorship, and previous editions of text, and a résumé of significance of data for interpreting Inca culture.

883 Sawyer, Alan R. Squier's "Palace of Ollantay" revisited (IAS/NP, 18, 1980, p. 63–72, bibl., ill.)

New ground plan and diagonal projections were prepared using more than 200 photographs, ground measurements, and observations. These reveal highly developed symmetry, not apparent from Squier's less accurate plan. Its limited access, labyrinthine plan, ramps, niches, and other features suggest a ceremonial-administrative function. Construction is distinct from Imperial Inca style and may predate Inca domination of area.

884 Schaedel, Richard P. and **Izumi Shimada.** Peruvian archaeology, 1946–80: an analytic overview (World Archaeology [Routledge and Kegan Paul, London] 13:3, Feb. 1982, p. 359–371, bibl.)

Trends in Peruvian (national) and Peruvianist (foreign) approaches to archaeology, examined by decades, show marked differences in goals, concepts, and cohesion. Improved communication between members of both groups is essential, but existing mechanisms are inadequate.

885 Shady Solís, Ruth. La cultura Nievería y la interacción social en el mundo andino en la época Huari (MNAA/A, 19, 1982, p. 5–108, bibl., ill., map)

Presents evidence in support of integration of central coast prior to Wari influence, which conflicts with commonly accepted interpretation that the latter reflects an expanding political control from the highlands.

886 ———— and Hermilio Rosas. El complejo Bagua y el sistema de establecimientos durante el formativo en la sierra norte del Perú (IAS/NP, 17, 1979, p. 109–142, bibl., ill., map)

Information from 22 sites on the Utcubamba near its juncture with the Marañón permits defining the Bagua complex. Combining archaeological, ethnographic, and ecological data, authors suggest sites represent small dispersed agricultural communities that were economically, socially, and ideologically independent. Communication with surrounding region was facilitated by river network and gradual environmental transitions. Elevation is about 520 m and tropical cultigens predominate today. Useful information on little known region.

887 Shimada, Izumi. Horizontal archipelago and coast-highland interaction in north Peru: archaeological models (*in* El Hombre y su ambiente en los Andes centrales. Edited by Luis Millones and Hiroyasu Tomoeda. Osaka, Japan: Senri, 1982, p. 137–210, bibl., ill., maps [Senri ethnological studies; 10])

Environmental and archaeological data from Lambayeque Valley reveal greater resource abundance and heterogeneity than has been assumed, making highland interaction unnecessary for development of state-level societies. Coastal self-sufficiency prevailed from 1300 BC until AD 700, when coastward expansion from Cajamarca occurred. Important contribution questions universality of "verticality" model dominating reconstructions of cultural development in Andean region.

888 ———. Temples of time: the ancient burial and religious center of Batán Grande, Peru (AIA/A, 35, Sept./Oct. 1981, p. 37–45, ill.)

Intensive investigations at Batán Grande, extensive site in Leche Valley, north coast of Peru, has produced remains from Chavín to Inca periods. Details of construction, deposition, style, architecture, murals, and artifacts imply contacts of varying kinds with highland and coastal groups, and raise questions about center's role during precolumbian times.

889 ———; **Carlos G. Elera;** and **Melody J. Shimada.** Excavaciones efectuadas en el centro ceremonial de Huaca Lucía-Chólope, del Horizonte Temprano, Batán Grande, costa norte del Perú: 1979–1981 (MNAA/A, 19, 1982, p. 109–210, bibl., ill.)

Describes environmental context, processes of site formation, architecture, organic remains, and pottery for a ceremonial center in the Valle de La Leche dating in the Early Horizon, between about 1300 and 600 BC. Unusual architectural features include a columnade with 24 columns constructed from conical adobes and painted solid red, and a staircase with 24 steps. Structure was covered with clean, pale sand, requiring transport of at least 300 cubic m of sand over large distance within a brief period. Features known elsewhere in Peru are reported for the first time from the far north coast.

890 ———; **Stephen Epstein;** and **Alan K. Craig.** Batán Grande: a prehistoric metalurgical center in Peru (AAAS/S, 216, 1982, p. 952–959, bibl., ill.)

Excavations at Batán Grande on north coast of Peru have revealed furnaces, slag, and other features indicating that smelting of copper was conducted on an industrial scale from about AD 1200 to 1532. Details of process are reconstructed from archaeological remains. Data provide "strong support" for independent development of metallurgy in central Andean region by AD 800.

891 Terada, Kazuo. Excavaciones arqueológicas en La Pampa, Ancash, realizadas por la Expedición Científica Japonesa a la América Nuclear en 1975 (*in* Congreso Peruano: El Hombre y la Cultura Andina, 3rd, 1977. El hombre y la cultura andina [see *HLAS 43:253*] v. 5, p. 1048–1078, maps)

Excavations during 1975 permitted defining four periods: 1) Yesopampa (1400–970 BC); 2) La Pampa (670–540 BC); 3) Tornapampa (AD 1310); and 4) Caserones (AD 1450). Describes and compares constructions and artifacts with other Peruvian complexes. Dating is provided by C14.

892 ——— and **Yoshio Onuki.** Excavations at Huacaloma in the Cajamarca Valley, Peru, 1979: report 2 of the Japanese scientific expedition to Nuclear America. Tokyo: University of Tokyo Press, 1982. 365 p., 140 plates: bibl., ill., tables.

Final report on excavation at site on margins of town of Cajamarca, which produced sequence of occupation from early formative until about AD 1300. Describes in detail stratigraphy, pottery types and their chronological patterning, and nonceramic (pottery, stone, metal, bone, shell) artifacts.

These data are used to reconstruct process of site formation. Appendixes provide technical studies of pottery, pollen, faunal remains, and a human skeleton. Thoroughly documented with tables, graphs, drawings, and photographs, this monograph maintains high standard set by previous works of Japanese Mission. It is indispensible for specialists on Andean archaeology.

893   Thatcher, John P., Jr. Early ceramic assemblages from Huamachuco, north highlands, Peru (IAS/NP, 17, 1979, p. 91–109, bibl., ill.)

Surface collection from some 60 sites in the vicinity of Huamachuco provide basis for recognizing three cultural phases attributed to the initial period and Early Horizon. Vessel shapes and decoration defining each phase are described and illustrated.

894   Tushingham, A. Douglas; Ursula M. Franklin; and Christopher Toogood. Studies in ancient Peruvian metalworking: an investigation of objects from the Museo Oro del Peru exhibited in Canada in 1976–77 under the title "Gold for the Gods." In cooperation with Kent C. Day, Carol Jack, and Elke Mutterer. Toronto, Canada: Royal Ontario Museum, 1979. 103 p.: bibl., ill. (History, technology, and art monograph; 3 0316–1269)

Nondestructive techniques (radiography, thickness measurements, X-ray diffraction, X-ray flourescence analysis, neutron activation analysis, and microscopic examination, both optical and scanning electron) were employed to establish composition, methods of manufacture, and other technological components of objects from the Mujica Gallo collection loaned for exhibit. Principal method of manufacture was cutting and shaping sheets, which were exceedingly uniform in thickness. Cutting, by contrast, is crudely done. Mechanical methods of joining pieces are characteristic, including crimping, lacing, and stapling. Welding, soldering, and casting were only adopted widely in Inca times, although they were used much earlier in Ecuador and Colombia. Concluding chapter explores hypothesis that textile techniques were the model for metal craftsmen.

895   von Schuler-Schömig, Immina. Die sogenannten Fremdkrieger und ihre weiteren ikonographischen Bezüge in der Moche-keramik (MV/BA, Neue Folge, 19, 1981, p. 207–239, bibl., ill.)

Further discussion of significance of so-called "friendly soldiers" depicted on Moche ceramics (see *HLAS 43:816*).

SURINAM

896   Boomert, Aad. Hertenrits: an Arauquinoid complex in north west Suriname: pt. 1 (Journal of Archaeology and Anthropology [Georgetown] 2:2, 1980 [i.e. 1983] p. 68–104, ill., map, tables)

Five habitation mounds connected with raised fields by paths submerged during rainy season define the Hertenrits complex. Four building stages are distinguishable at the Hertenrits site, which attains an elevation of 2.5 m and measures 200 by 320 m. Three $C14$ dates extend between 1265 ± 60 and 1130 ± 60 BP. Ten primary and two secondary urn burials were encountered. Describes pottery, stone, bone, and shell artifacts. Relative frequency of decorated pottery increased from 2.9 to 23.3 percent during site's occupation.

URUGUAY

897   Pinto, Milton and **Silvia V. de Pinto.** Sitio A.L.C. Los Cerros: un precerámico en el Depto. de Artigas, República Oriental del Uruguay (Sapiens [Museo Arqueológico Dr. Osvaldo F.A. Menghin, Chivilcoy, Argentina] 4, 1980, p. 93–99, bibl., ill.)

Classifies 663 lithics collected from the surface of a large site by technique, function, and varieties within functional categories. Distal portion of a biface is the only shaped artifact encountered.

898   Tuya de Maeso, Leila C. Consideraciones sobre la cerámica de yacimientos arqueológicos investigados en los Departamentos de Colonia, Soriano y Río Negro: decoración: expresiones zoomorfas. Montevideo: Editorial Talleres Don Bosco, 1980. 94 p.: bibl., ill.

Discusses sherds with drag-and-jab and zoomorphic modeled decoration from sites in the Depts. of Soriano and Río Negro.

Presentation emphasizes art and illustrations are crude. Of limited scientific value.

VENEZUELA

899 Nieves, Fulvia. La fase bañador: investigaciones arqueológicas en el Bajo Orinoco. Caracas: Universidad Central de Venezuela, Facultad de Ciencias Económicas y Sociales, División de Publicaciones, 1980. 237 p.: bibl., ill. (Colección Libros)

Description of excavations, ceramic and lithic artifacts, pottery types, and burials encountered in three stratigraphic excavations in a habitation site 2 km from the left bank of the lower Orinoco. Depth of refuse varied from 80 cm to 5 m. Sherds of post-classic Barrancas decorated types occurred in the lower levels and a single C14 date of AD 1430 falls near the middle of the seriated sequence. Bañador Phase pottery is characterized by abundance of corrugated surfaces. No other site with this complex has been encountered in the region and its affiliations are uncertain.

900 Pollak-Eltz, Angelina. The earthglyph of Chirgua, Carabobo, Venezuela (Journal of Archaeology and Anthropology [Georgetown] 3:2, 1980 [i.e. 1983], p. 111–112, bibl., ill.)

Description of a "glyph" about 50 m long produced by excavating ditches about 50 cm wide and 70 cm deep, located on a slope. It consists of three concentric circles. Two "antenea" with curved ends emanate from one side and straight diagonal "legs" emanate from the opposite side. The only other geoglyphs known occur in south Peru and Chile.

901 Sanoja, Mario and **Iraida Vargas.** New light on the prehistory of eastern Venezuela (*in* Advances in world archaeology. Fred Wendorf and Angela Close, editors. New York: Academic Press, 1983, v. 2, p. 205–244, bibl., ill.)

Relatively complete sequences from eastern coast, Orinoco delta, and middle Orinoco permit reconstructing cultural development, assessing effects of environmental differences, and recognizing kinds and directions of influences. Evaluating total picture in broader continental context leads to rejection of several early C14 dates and interpretation of Barrancas, Ronquín, and Saladero

traditions as derived from Andean antecedents, contrary to position taken by Roosevelt and Rouse (for monographs presenting complete data, see *HLAS 43:825, HLAS 43:828,* and *HLAS 43:831*).

902 Vargas Arenas, Iraida. Investigaciones arqueológicas en Parmana: los sitios de La Gruta y Ronquín, Estado Guarico, Venezuela. Caracas: Biblioteca de la Academia Nacional de la Historia, 1981. 574 p.: bibl., ill., tables (Serie Estudios, monografías y ensayos; 20)

Detailed, well illustrated monograph on sites and excavations on middle Orinoco. Defines two chronological phases: 1) Ronquín Phase, dating between about 650 BC and AD 600, is characterized by small settlements, vegetative agriculture, and pottery tempered with sand and decorated with white-on-red or polychrome painting and incision; 2) Corozal Phase, extending from AD 600 to European contact, is characterized by larger settlements, manioc and maize agriculture, and pottery tempered with sponge spicules and decorated using incision and modeling. After analyzing temporal and spatial distribution of white-on-red elsewhere in the hemisphere, author concludes Ronquín Phase represents intrusion from western highlands into Orinoco basin. A basic reference for specialists.

903 ———. Orígenes y filiaciones de la tradición Saladero del Orinoco medio (UCV/ECS, 18:4, oct./dic. 1979, p. 112–128, bibl.)

Review of geographical and chronological occurrence of diagnostic elements of the Saladero (white-on-red) tradition provides a basis for evaluating the three principal hypotheses of its origin: local development and dispersal from Venezuela; origin in the Nuclear areas and dispersal to Venezuela; and multiple independent origins. Second hypothesis best fits the existing data.

904 Wagner, Erika. La prehistoria de Mucuchíes. Caracas: Universidad Católica Andrés Bello, Instituto de Investigaciones Históricas, 1980. 28 p.: bibl., ill.

Summary of prehispanic culture in vicinity of Mucuchíes, Venezuelan Andes, including architecture, burials, pottery and other artifacts, subsistence, commerce, and demography, during the period extending from AD 450 to Spanish contact.

ETHNOLOGY: Middle America

JOHN M. INGHAM, *Associate Professor of Anthropology, University of Minnesota*

INTERESTING PUBLICATIONS ON FIESTA SPONSORSHIP have appeared in recent years. Rus and Wasserstrom (item **1010**) demonstrate that civil-religious hierarchies in highland Chiapas may have replaced a more egalitarian *cofradía* organization in the late 19th and early 20th centuries consequent to changing economic and political conditions. Chick (item **940**) finds in a Nahua community that fiesta sponsors do not as a rule progress from less to more important offices; rather, they enter the hierarchy at any level. Moreover, it may be noted that throughout the Nahua region—and in other parts of central Mexico as well—religious and political offices tend to be less closely connected than in Maya communities. Several studies (e.g., Brintnall, see *HLAS 43 : 842* and Smith, *see HLAS 41 : 947*) show that economic modernization tends to undermine sponsorship; Greenberg (items **964–965**) examines this effect in detail among the Chatino where traditional maize farmers of moderate wealth contribute the most to the fiestas and wealthy coffee farmers the least, apparently because they prefer to reinvest surplus funds in cash cropping. Brandes (item **926**) suggests that a broader sharing of ceremonial burdens may allow ritual festivities to persist in the face of modernization. The reexamination of the civil-religious hierarchy by Rus and Wasserstrom should alert us, however, to the possibility that the patterns described by Greenberg and Brandes may not be altogether recent. In Morelos the wealthiest villagers have always tended to exempt themselves from the *mayordomías* and ritual expenses have long been widely distributed among the common people in a pattern that recalls the 16th-century *cofradía* (item **1033**), although consistent with Brandes, the number of men in *mayordomías* is increasing.

Economy per se continues to be a source of interest. The present compilation includes significant works on craft industry (items **943–944** and **983–984**) and agricultural decision making (item **907**). Indeed, the economic research in Middle America is becoming quite sophisticated, although in some instances cumbersome applications of Marxist or neo-classical theory seem to confound rather than clarify ethnographic understanding. For scholars who favor cultural interpretations of economic behavior, rereading Malinowski and de la Fuente's study of Oaxaca markets, which is now available in English (item **990**), is recommended. Köhler's (item **980**) insightful examination of interethnic economic exchange in highland Chiapas also illustrates the virtues of solid, old-fashioned ethnography. Nonetheless, Warman's (item **1033**) brilliant analysis of relations of production in eastern Morelos shows that satisfactory syntheses of theory and ethnography are possible, although it could be argued that Warman succeeds precisely because his Marxist sensibilities inform rather than constrain his narrative.

Various publications attest to the resurgence of research on folk medicine and to the methodological resourcefulness of young scholars; they use rigorous sampling and statistical procedures to collect and interpret data on symptom syndromes, etiology, treatment selection, and therapeutic efficacy (items **913, 957–958, 985, 989, 1013, 1027–1028,** and **1036**). Again, one might wish for more attention to culture. Tousignant's (item **1026**) paper on *susto* in highland Chiapas, for example, makes a persuasive plea for the examination of the syndrome in terms of its cultural rationale rather than biomedical data.

These caveats about economic and medical anthropology aside, much of the compilation points to the continuing vitality of cultural anthropology in Middle America. Important work is being done on ritual (items **924, 927, 962, 994,** and **996**), myth (items **973** and **1018**), divination (items **942, 997,** and **1020**), dreaming (items **932** and **1019**), drinking behavior (item **968**), and violence (items **959** and **1019**). Especially commendable is Bricker's (item **929**) analysis of the interaction of myth and history in the Maya area.

905　Acheson, James M. Agricultural business choices in a Mexican village (*in* Agricultural decision-making: anthropological contributions to rural development [see item **907**] p. 241–264)

Population growth and land scarcity have stimulated non-agricultural business in a Tarascan village. Calculations of internal rates of return show that non-farming enterprises are more profitable but have limited potential for absorbing capital, so farming remains an important and valued component of economic strategy.

906　Adams, Richard N. The Sandinistas and the Indians: the "problem" of the Indian in Nicaragua (FIU/CR, 10:1, Winter 1981, p. 23–25, 55–56)

The histories of Nicaragua's Miskito and Guatemala's highland Indians are compared to elucidate the present adverse relations between the Miskito and Sandinistas.

907　Agricultural decision making: anthropological contributions to rural development. Edited by Peggy Bartlett. New York: Academic Press, 1980. 378 p.: bibl., index (Studies in anthropology)

Anthology of theoretical and empirical studies of economic behavior in rural areas that includes several papers on Middle America (see items **905, 912, 939, 951,** and **956**).

908　Aguirre Beltrán, Gonzalo. Formas de gobierno indígena. México: Instituto Nacional Indigenista, 1981. 221 p.: ill. (Clásicos de la antropología. Colección INI; no. 10)

Reissue of 1953 edition includes new prologue by Andrés Fábregas.

909　Alvarez Arévalo, Miguel. Etnografía de la Fiesta de Navidad en Guatemala (IAHG/AHG, 2:2, 1980, p. 105–147, bibl., ill.)

Notes on *posadas* and Nativity scenes in Guatemala. Discusses European origins of customs and their present distribution in Latin America.

910　Arnason, Thor; Feliz Uck; John Lambert; and **Richard Hebda.** Maya medicinal plants of San José Succotz, Belize (Journal of Ethnopharmacology [Elsevier Sequoia, Lausanne, Switzerland] 2:4, Dec. 1980, p. 345–364, bibl., tables)

Authors describe 64 medicinal plants and their uses.

911　Avila B., Alejandro de; A.L. Welden; and **Gaston Guzmán.** Notes on the ethnomycology of Hueyapan, Morelos, Mexico (Journal of Ethnopharmacology [Elsevier Sequoia, Lausanne, Switzerland] 2:4, Dec. 1980, p. 311–321, bibl.)

Presents scientific and local names of 53 species of fungi; brief notes describe plants' use and cultural significance.

912　Bartlett, Peggy F. Cost-benefit analysis: a test of alternative methodologies (*in* Agricultural decision-making: anthropological contributions to rural development [see item **907**] p. 137–160)

Evaluates qualitative analysis, traditional economic profit calculations, and Chayanovian profit calculations in relation to Costa Rican farmers' behavior. Observes difficulties of estimating opportunity costs and finds qualified utility in Chayanov's approach.

913　——— and **Setha M. Low.** *Nervios* in rural Costa Rica (Medical Anthropology [Redgrave Pub. Co., Pleasantville, N.Y.] 4:4, Fall 1980, p. 523–564, bibl., table)

Examines concept and epidemiology of *nervios* in two Costa Rican communities. A broad category, *nervios* encompasses various stress-related ailments and complaints.

Data show it occurs more often among women, married couples, and parents; contrary to expectations, it is not much more common among the poor than the rich. Folk beliefs tend to absolve victims of responsibility for the condition (see item **989**).

914 Bartolomé, Miguel Alberto. Narrativa y etnicidad entre los chatinos de Oaxaca. México: Instituto Nacional de Antropología e Historia, 1979. 60 p.: bibl., plates, tables (Cuadernos de los centros regionales)

Theoretical appeal for use of ethnography in the study of Indian ethnicity prefaces transcriptions of 33 Chatino myths and tales.

915 Beals, Ralph L. Economic adaptations in Mitla, Oaxaca (*in* Mesoamerica: homenaje al Doctor Paul Kirchoff. Coordinación: Barbro Dahlgren. México: INAH, 1979, p. 165–193)

Describes the changes in trading patterns and occupational specialization that have occurred since Parson's study as responses to modernization. Tables present variety of supporting statistical data.

916 Benítez, Fernando. Los indios de México. v. 5, El gran tiempo: tepehuanes y nahuas. México: Ediciones Era, 1980. 449 p.: map, plates (Serie Mayor)

Vol. 5 of Benítez's informal ethnography of Mexican Indians, focuses on the Tepehuanes and Nahuas of the western sierra's Santa María Ocotán-San Pedro Xicoras region. Benítez describes *mitote* ritual and shamanism, and drawing on materials collected by both himself and Preuss, undertakes an impressive study of myth. As always, Benítez's observations are fascinating, but the Tepehuan and San Pedro Xicoras Nahua mythical texts included here are especially valuable for the study of prehispanic Aztec mythology as well as postconquest syncretism.

917 Bizarro Ujpán, Ignacio. Son of Tecún Umán: a Maya Indian tells his life story. James D. Sexton, editor. Tucson: University of Arizona Press, 1981. 250 p.: bibl., index.

Autobiography conveys recurrent themes in subjective experience of Tzutuhil Maya Indian of Solola Dept., Guatemala: importance of family and communal solidarity, including ritual communion through use of alcohol, but also fragility of marriage, recourse to drunkenness as source of solace, struggle for a living, intercommunity conflict, and spectre of illness. Text incorporates diary kept over period of eight years, with numerous entries prompted by editor's questions.

918 Bock, Philip K. Tepoztlán reconsidered (UCLA/JLAL, 6:1, Summer 1980, p. 129–150)

Demonstrates remarkable persistence of traditional culture despite effects of modernization, thus supporting Redfield's view of folk culture and qualifying Lewis' critique of it. Shows that continuing strength of traditional barrio organization, ritual uses of the flower *pericón*, and symbolic dualism in barrio and Carnival organization all point to vitality of traditional symbols.

919 Boremanse, Didier. A comparative study of two Maya kinship systems (SOCIOL, 31:1, 1981, p. 1–37, bibl., graphs, tables)

Analysis of kinship terminologies and marriage practices in northern and southern Lacandon populations confirms that there is no necessary relation between formal implications of prescription in terminologies and actual mate selection.

920 Bort, John R. and **Philip D. Young.** New roles for males in Guaymi society (*in* Sex roles and social change in native lower Central American societies [see item **1011**] p. 88–102)

Population growth and resulting shortening of fallow cycles led to increasing dependence on wage labor and decline of subsistence-based redistribution. At the same time, leadership roles are being redefined by need to interact with external economy although female role, oriented toward domestic sphere, remains more traditional.

921 Bossen, Laurel. Plantations and labor force discrimination in Guatemala (UC/CA, 23:3, June 1982, p. 263–268)

Contrasts two Guatemalan plantations that differ in labor recruitment policies and explains hiring of women in one and not the other in relation to size and unity of work force. By excluding resident women, management may be seeking to minimize labor solidarity and militance.

922 Bourgois, Philippe. Class, ethnicity, and the state among the Miskitu Amerindians of northeastern Nicaragua (LAP, 8[2]:29, Spring 1981, p. 22–39, map, plate)

Informative historical and socio-economic analysis of difficulties confronting the Sandinistas in their attempt to develop an Indian policy with regard to the Miskito and others. Although author is a Sandinista supporter, his account of recent events is commendably well detailed.

923 Bozzoli de Wille, María Eugenia. Localidades indígenas costarricenses. 2. ed. aumentada y corr. San José: Editorial Universitaria Centroamericana, 1975. 231 p.: bibl., ill., maps, plates (Colección Aula)

Expanded version of 1969 edition.

924 ———. El nacimiento y la muerte entre los bribis. San José: Editorial Universidad de Costa Rica, 1979. 264 p.: bibl., ill., plates.

Interesting book in which good data and plausible structuralist analysis show that for Bribis, death and birth represent analogous but opposite movements between the other world and society (i.e., clans or society as a whole), nature and culture. Initial chapters describe Bribri clanship and interethnic relations while later chapters elaborate central thesis with detailed discussions of birth and funerary ritual as well as relevant myths. Two themes inform much of data: 1) correspondence between conceptions of seed, bone, and origin; and 2) connection between sexual relations and death.

925 ———. Symbolic aspects of Bribri roles on the occasions of birth and death (in Sex roles and social change in native lower Central American societies [see item **1011**] p. 142–165)

Insightful, well-documented analysis shows that pregnant women and buriers are alike in occupying liminal ground, respectively, entrances to and exits from society. Thus, both are the focus of pollution concerns, although birth is more a source of tension while funerary ritual is a means of resolving it.

926 Brandes, Stanley. Cargos versus cost sharing in Mesoamerican fiestas, with special reference to Tzintzuntzan (UNM/JAR, 37:3, Fall 1981, p. 209-225, bibl.)

Describes decline of individual sponsorships and financial responsibility and increasing importance of cost-sharing arrangements in religious festivities of Tzintzuntzan.

927 ———. Fireworks and fiestas: the case from Tzintzuntzan (UCLA/JLAL, 7:2, 1981, p. 171–190, bibl.)

Purchase, distribution, and display of fireworks in the Fiesta de Febrero exhibit unity and division among Tzintzuntzan and its outlying ranchos as well as power of clerical and administrative authorities.

928 ———. The household developmental cycle in Tzintzuntzan (in From Tzintzuntzan to the "image of limited good" [see item **960**] p. 13–23)

Field work in a Tzintzuntzan barrio confirms that extended-joint family is not the ideal but rather a stage in developmental cycle of domestic groups required by insufficient economic means. Brandes attributes high proportion of extended-joint households in barrio studied to greater poverty and relatively large house sites.

929 Bricker, Victoria Reifler. The Indian Christ, the Indian king: the historical substrate of Maya myth and ritual. Austin: University of Texas Press, 1981. 368 p.: bibl., ill., index, maps, plates, tables.

Book makes significant contribution to symbolic reading of historical process (e.g., Lafaye, Turner, Sahlins). Shows Maya first perceived conquest through own cyclical-cosmological conception of history and after assimilating Christianity, proceeded to formulate their separateness in terms of devotions to perspiring saints, talking stones and crosses, Virgins, and Indian Christs. Shows that contemporary myth and ritual are the cumulative effects of syncretism, nativistic movements, and cyclical conception of time. Postconquest ritual preserved form and content of indigenous and Catholic ritual but was permeable to novel events. Indeed, symbolic content that seems prehispanic in origin is often product of recent history.

930 Brintnall, Douglas. A model of changing group relations in the Mayan highlands of Guatemala (UNM/JAR, 36:3, Fall 1980, p. 294–315, bibl.)

Proposes model of change in which centripetal relations among Indian groups and paternalistic racial domination of Indians by Ladinos in *municipio* of Aguacatán are giving way—result of population pressure, cash cropping, elimination of vagrancy laws—to centrifugal tendencies among Indians and more competitive relations between Indians and Ladinos. Model is said to better account for Indian-Ladino relations than pluralist theory of Colby and van den Berghe.

931 Brown, Cecil H. and **Paul K. Chase.** Animal classification in Juchitan Zapotec (UNM/JAR, 37 : 1, Spring 1981, p. 61–70, bibl.)

Investigation of life-form classes elicited "fish" and "snake" but not "bird," "mug," or "mammal." Evidence for incipient categories is used to speculate about linguistic change.

932 Bruce S., Roberto D. Lacandon dream symbolism: dream symbolism and interpretation among the Lacandon Mayas of Chiapas, Mexico. v. 1, Dream symbolism and interpretation. v. 2, Dictionary, index, and classifications of dream symbols. México: Ediciones Euroamericanas, 1975/1979. 2 v.: bibl., ill.

There is less on Lacandon dreams and more digressions on the world views of ancient Maya and modern Europeans in this rather undisciplined work than one might expect, but nonetheless some data are interesting. Vol. 1 describes principles of interpretation (i.e., reversal, direct representation, and metaphor) in the use of dreams for prognostication. Vol. 2, the more informative, supplies a dictionary of dream symbols and prophesies.

933 Calderón Bárcena, Rita and **Patricia Emilia Salcido Cañedo.** Indigenismo: grupos étnicos, conciencia nacional, antropología social: hemerografía (UNAM/RMPCS, 25 : 97, julio/sept. 1979, p. 177–193, bibl.)

Bibliography of 175 items, mostly articles about Middle America.

934 Castile, Georges Pierre. On the Tarascanness of the Tarascans and the Indianness of the Indians (*in* Persistent peoples: cultural enclaves in perspective [see item 1005] p. 171–191)

Somewhat rambling but at times interesting reflections on ethnicity.

935 Chamoux, Marie Noëlle. Les savoir-faire techniques et leur appropriation: le cas des Nahuas du Mexique (EPHE/H, 21 : 3, juillet/sept. 1981, p. 71–94, bibl.)

Demonstrates that woman's role in Nahua village depends on wide range of implicit technical knowledge, and shows that women's skills receive only partial and distorted representation in traditional ideology.

936 Chavez, María Luisa and **James Loucky.** Caretaking and competence: siblings as socializers in rural Guatemala (Anthropology [University of California, Department of Anthropology, Los Angeles] 11 : 1/2, 1981, p. 1–23, bibl., tables)

Excellent observational data demonstrate that care and attention offered by older siblings vary with age and sex, and baby's age. Care given by older girls is found to be responsible and nurturing.

937 Chemin, Dominique. Rituales relacionados con la venida de la lluvia, la cosecha y las manifestaciones atmosféricas y telúricas maléficas en la región Pame de Santa María Acapulco, San Luis Potosí (UNAM/AA, 17, 1980, p. 67–97, plates)

Solid ethnographic report about beliefs and practices concerning crops and weather among the Pame. Catholic god is associated with sun, fire, and heat; he is subordinate to and struggles with a *padre paterno* (the father of maíces) who is in charge of rain, thunder, and water. Offerings are made to the *padre paterno* to bring rain.

938 Cheney, Charles C. Religion, magic, and medicine in Huave society (*in* From Tzintzuntzan to the "image of the limited good" [see item 960] p. 59–73)

Informative summary of Huave world view, supernatural figures, and ideas about illness and witchcraft.

939 Chibnik, Michael. The statistical behavior approach: the choice between wage labor and cash cropping in rural Belize (*in* Agricultural decision making: anthropological contributions to rural development [see item 907] p. 87–114)

Comparative analysis of two villages discloses preference for wage labor, rather than cash cropping, among men with high living costs. Trend may be due to greater speed of returns to wage labor and flexibility in allocating labor time it affords.

940 Chick, Gary E. Concept and behavior in a Tlaxcalan *cargo* hierarchy (UP/E, 20:3, July 1981, p. 217–228, bibl., ill., tables)

In Nahua community of San Rafael Tepatlaxco, there is a conceptual model of *cargo* hierarchy but no career pattern of progression upward through the hierarchy. Instead, data show that office holders enter at various levels.

941 Coe, Michael D. and **Richard A. Diehl.** In the land of the Olmec. v. 2, The people of the river. Austin: University of Texas Press, 1980. 198 p.: bibl., ill., map, plates, tables.

Reports results of Río Chiquito Project, an ecological study of San Lorenzo Tenochtitlán undertaken to shed light on rise of Olmec civilization. Discussions of methodology, regional history, natural setting, settlement patterns, land tenure, and village customs are followed by detailed treatments of agriculture, hunting and fishing, and pottery making. Authors conclude that highly productive river levee soils probably played decisive role in rise of Olmec: they allowed more elaborate ceremonialism and redistribution, thus promoting social hierarchy, and were focus of military competition in conformity with Carneiro's circumscription theory of rise of the state.

942 Colby, Benjamin N. and **Lore M. Colby.** The daykeeper: the life and discourse of an Ixil diviner. Cambridge, Mass.: Harvard University Press, 1981. 333 p.: bibl., ill., tables.

Substantive contribution in this work consists of transcriptions of a daykeeper's life history, moral philosophy, and folk tales, along with account of his divinatory techniques. Some insights are offered to elucidate cultural grammar of tales (one recurrent theme is a transgression sequence: transgression—imprisonment— appeal—release).

943 Cook, Scott. Crafts, capitalist development, and cultural property in Oaxaca, Mexico (IAMEA, 35:3, Winter 1981, p. 53–68)

Offers critique of culturalist views and policies regarding illicit traffic in precolumbian artifacts and contemporary craft production, and reviews author's ill-fated proposal to FONART recommending ways of rationalizing simple commodity production

while mobilizing big capital on its behalf. Concludes by questioning assumption often made in Mexico's ruling circles that development is better served by capital-intensive rather than labor-intensive production.

944 ———. Zapotec stoneworkers: the dynamics of rural simple commodity production in modern Mexican capitalism. Washington: University Press of America, 1982. 432 p.: bibl., ill., map, plates, tables.

Ambitious work on rural *metate* manufacturing presents most detailed and comprehensive description and analysis to date of craft production in rural Mexico. Covers production matrix, exchange, markets, means of production, labor relations, price, income, etc. Argues that rise in *metate* prices (1968–78) was related to cost of reproducing labor power which partly leads him to a not altogether convincing attempt to show that Marxist labor theory of value better explains *metate* pricing than neoclassical supply and demand. Final chapter favors class rather than ethnic analysis of peasant's predicament.

945 Cosminsky, Sheila and **Mary Scrimshaw.** Sex roles and subsistence: a comparative analysis of three Central American communities (*in* Sex roles and social change in native lower Central American societies [see item **1011**] p. 44–69)

Comparison of coastal, Guatemalan finca, a Highland Maya community, and a black Carib population in Belize to assess effects of economic roles and developmental cycle of domestic groups on status of women.

946 Costello, Richard W. New economic roles for Cuna males and females: an examination of socioeconomic change in a San Blas community (*in* Sex roles and social change in native lower Central American societies [see item **1005**] p. 70–87)

Increasing male and female labor migration is undermining traditional matriuxorilocal residence and traditional female focus on domestic tasks.

947 Crumrine, N. Ross. The dramatization of opposition among Mayo Indians of Northwest Mexico (*in* Persistent peoples: cultural enclaves in perspective [see item **1005**] p. 109–131)

Comments on Spicer's model of Yuto-Aztecan ceremonialism in light of Mayo data. Wet-dry distinction is not as clear as in the Huichol case but many underlying themes conform to the model.

948 ——. The Mayo southern Sonora: socioeconomic assimilation and ritual-symbolic syncretism—split acculturation (*in* Themes of indigenous acculturation in Northwest Mexico [see item **1021**] p. 22–35)

Shows that although forces are encouraging Mayo assimilation into the bottom stratum of mestizo society, Mayo myth and ceremonialism are being continuously revitalized in response to changes in kinship and community organization and economic circumstances.

949 **Dermarest, William** and **Benjamin D. Paul.** Mayan migrants in Guatemala City (Anthropology [University of California, Department of Anthropology, Los Angeles] 11:1/2, 1981, p. 43–73, bibl.)

Finds that San Pedro Indian migrants, located in Guatemala City, are generally young males who have gained economic niches either by entering military or by peddling or working in a textile factory. Results are compared and contrasted with Guatemalan and Mexican urban migration studies. Concludes that Guatemalan Indian migrants to urban areas may typically come from better educated and wealthier communities, even though they represent range of economic and educational levels within particular communities.

950 **Deverre, Christian.** Indiens ou paysans. Paris: Le Sycomore, 1980. 212 p.: bibl., ill., map, tables (Les Hommes et leurs signes)

Purports to show through an historical analysis of relations of production that Indianness in southern Mexico represents the effects of centuries of postconquest oppression, not a prehispanic heritage.

951 **DeWalt, Billie R.** and **Kathleen Musante DeWalt.** Stratification and decision-making in the use of new agricultural technology (*in* Agricultural decision-making: anthropological contributions to rural development [see item **907**] p. 289–317)

Instances of agricultural innovation in the Mazahua area fit models of middle-class conservatism elaborated by Homans and Cancian.

952 **Dunnigan, Timothy.** Adaptive strategies in peasant Indians in a biethnic community: a study of Mountain Pima assimilation (*in* Themes of indigenous acculturation in Northwest Mexico [see item **1021**] p. 36–49)

Lucid description of Mountain Pima adaptive strategies in the face of competition from mestizos. The Pima's lack of salable work experience and their reliance on family-centered exchange networks limit their mobility.

953 ——. *Indito* versus *blanco* in Mountain Pima Easter ceremonies (*in* Persistent peoples: cultural enclaves in perspective [see item **1005**] p. 132–150)

Solid ethnography discloses symbolic expressions of interethnic conflict in Easter ceremonialism. Rather than defusing conflict—an effect sometimes ascribed to rituals of rebellion—ritual in this case actually seems to exacerbate social tensions.

954 **Ensayos sobre el sur de Jalisco.** Guillermo de la Peña *et al.* 2. ed. México: Centro de Investigaciones Superiores del INAH, 1980. 206 p.: bibl., ill., maps, tables (Cuadernos de la casa chata; 4)

Includes the following: Guillermo de la Peña "Industrias y Empresarios en el Sur de Jalisco" (p. 1–36); Verónica Veerkamp "El Mercado Informal y la Industria: el Caso de Ciudad Guzmán" (p. 37–73); Pastora Rodríguez Aviñoá "El Complejo Industrial de Atenquique" (p. 74–156); Agustín Escobar "La Explotación Forestal en el Sur de Jalisco" (p. 157–176); and Luisa Gabayet "Economía Familiar de los Obreros de Atenquique" (p. 177–206).

955 **Faron, Louis C.** Micro-ecological adaptations and ethnicity in an Otomi municipio (UP/E, 19:3, July 1980, p. 279–296, bibl., map, tables)

Traces various differences between upland and lowland Otomi to the influence of the hacienda on the latter. Lowlanders are more apt to know Spanish and to have occupational skills characteristic of *gente de razón*, while in the uplands indigenous craft specialists have proved more persistent and folk Catholicism is more syncretic.

956 **Finkler, Kaja.** Agrarian reform and economic development: when is a landlord a client and a sharecropper a patron? (*in* Agricultural decision making: anthropological contributions to rural development [see item **907**] p. 265–288)

Describes an intriguing situation in Hidalgo, Mexico, where economic advantage lies with sharecroppers rather than land-holders. *Ejido* system, water distribution, and lack of access to credit all contribute to this situation, which departs in certain respects from Chayanov's model of peasant economic behavior.

957 ———. A comparative study of health seekers: or, why do some people go to doctors rather than to spiritualist healers? (Medical Anthropology [University of Connecticut, Storrs] 5 : 4, Fall 1981, p. 383–424, bibl., tables)

Compares 366 patients of spiritualists with 156 patients of medical doctors in Hidalgo, Mex. Multivariate statistical analysis reveals that females more than men seek spiritualist help, that such females show more evidence of emotional disorder than those consulting physicians, and that socio-economic measures show little difference between patients of spiritualists and physicians.

958 ———. Non-medical treatments and their outcomes (Culture, Medicine and Psychiatry [D. Reidel, Dordrecht, Netherlands] 4 : 3, Sept. 1980, p. 271–310, bibl., tables)

Sophisticated study of efficacy of treatment in spiritualist center in Hidalgo finds that patients presenting fewer symptoms show most improvement. Conditions amenable to nonmedical therapy include diarrheas not due to pathogens, simple gynecological disorders, somatized syndromes (e.g., hysterical conversion), and mild psychiatric disorders.

959 **Flanet, Véronique.** Viviré, si Dios quiere: un estudio de la violencia en la Mixteca de la Costa. Frontispicio, Ortolf Karla. Fotos, Véronique Flanet y Monique Vileyn. México: Instituto Nacional Indigenista, 1977. 238 p., 16 leaves of plates: bibl., ill., maps, plates (Colección INI; no. 55)

Pt. 1 presents general ethnography with interesting material on contracts with the devil and concepts of the person. Pt. 2 addresses violence as such. Considers various historical and social foundations of violence: warfare in prehispanic period, conquest, four centuries of *cacicazgo*, divisions within dominant class, and interethnic relations. Particularly valuable are discussions of intra-

family relations, attitudes toward death, and symbolic expressions of aggression (e.g., Carnival dancing, gossip, etc.).

960 **From Tzintzuntzan to the "image of the limited good:" essays in honor of George M. Foster.** Margaret Clark, Robert V. Kemper, Cynthia Nelson, editors. Berkeley: Kroeber Anthropological Society, Department of Anthropology, University of California, 1979. 181 p.: bibls. (The Kroeber Anthropological Society papers; no. 55–56)

Festschrift includes many interesting papers on Middle America (see items **928, 938, 976,** and **1023**).

961 **Fuller, Nancy** and **Brigitte Jordan.** Maya women and the end of the birthing period: postpartum massage-and-binding in Yucatán, Mexico (Medical Anthropology [University of Connecticut, Storrs] 5 : 1, Winter 1981, p. 35–50, bibl., ill.)

Informative paper on a subject which has had only cursory attention. Describes techniques of stroking the mother and locating her *tipte*, repositioning her uterus, and binding her head and pelvis. Also describes precautions taken to protect postpartum mother and child from cold influences and "evil winds."

962 **Galinier, Jacques.** *N'yũhũ*, les indiens otomis: hiérarchie sociale et tradition dans le sud de la Huasteca. Mexico: Mission archéologique et ethnologique française au Mexique, 1979. 615 p.: bibl., ill., index, maps, plates, tables (Etudes mésoaméricaines: Série II; 2)

Valuable ethnography of several communities, with interesting information on social organization, fiesta systems, *naguales*, and beliefs and practices relating to birth and death.

963 **Ghidinelli, Azzo.** La familia entre los caribes negros, ladinos y kekchíes de Lívingston. Lívingston?, Guatemala: Instituto Indigenista Nacional, 1975 [i.e. 1976]. 315 p.: bibl., ill., maps, tables (Guatemala indígena; v. 11, nos. 3–4, 1976)

Commendably solid study of family organization in a socially stratified, multiethnic Guatemalan community. Description of demography, stratification, and economic conditions sets context for treatment of residence, household composition, inheritance, kinship terminology, etc., all of which are discussed with an evident knowledge of the literature. Concludes with interesting investigation of role of ethnic stereotypes in the instability of interethnic unions.

964 Greenberg, James B. Santiago's sword: Chatino peasant religion and economics. Berkeley: University of California Press, 1981. 227 p.: bibl., ill., index, maps, tables.

Analysis of Chatino folk Catholicism and socioeconomic organization makes significant contribution to literature on closed corporate community and debate about its relation to wider economic order. Concepts of house, saint, cross, and candle are said to compose matrix of ritually significant pairs, and an examination of rites of passage and *barrio*, village, and regional fiestas perceptively demonstrates replication of ritual themes. Book contains very interesting analysis of economic and demographic dimensions of ritual behavior. Also discusses demographic effects of customary restrictions on sexual intercourse and surmises that restrictions tended to increase population because they concentrate births at time of year when infant mortality is lower.

965 ———. Social change and fiesta systems in Mexican Indian communities (ASU/LAD, 15:2, Spring 1981, p. 1–5, plates, tables)

Suggests that disagreement about economic functions of religious fiestas can be partly resolved by hypothesis that formation of new religious offices (alternatively, freezing of available offices) in response to population growth is related to economic and political adaptations to modernization. In Yaitepec, traditional, moderately wealthy corn planters give fiestas more support than wealthy, market-oriented coffee growers (see item **964**).

966 Griffen, William B. The question of enclavement in colonial central northern Mexico (*in* Persistent peoples: cultural enclaves in perspective [see item **1005**] p. 26–39)

Describes conditions that mitigated against formation of ethnic enclaves in Nueva Vizcaya.

967 ———. Some problems in the analysis of the native Indian population of northern Nueva Vizcaya during the Spanish

colonial period (*in* Themes of indigenous acculturation in Northwest Mexico [see item **1021**] p. 50–53)

Assesses 18th-century demography data.

968 Guerrero Guerrero, Raúl. El pulque: religión, cultura, folklore. México: Instituto Nacional de Antropología e Historia, 1980. 241 p.: bibl., ill., plates.

Unusual, fascinating book examines meaning and place of *pulque*, or *maguey* beer, in Mexican culture from prehispanic period through early 20th century. Demonstrates drink's preconquest associations with water, blood, fertility, and certain gods. Chronicles conflicting opinions on drink during colonial period and history of attempts to suppress it. Also describes pulque manufacture, haciendas, peluquerías or cantinas, drinking mugs, songs, and card games. Latter sections focus mainly on Hidalgo; a final chapter describes regional variations from Sonora to Maya area. Marvelous photographs.

969 Harman, Robert C. Enclavement, fusion, and adaptation in a Tzeltal Maya community (*in* Persistent peoples: cultural enclaves in perspective [see item **1005**] p. 212–227)

Finds that Protestantism is contribution to the erosion of traditional enclavement.

970 Hinton, Thomas B. Cultural visibility and the Cora (*in* Themes of indigenous acculturation in Northwest Mexico [see item **1021**] p. 1–3)

Describes the Cora strategy for minimizing mestizo cultural influence and economic exploitation.

971 Hobgood, John and **Carroll L. Riley.** Tepusilam and Chul: a comparison of Mexicanero and Tepehuan mythology (*in* Themes of indigenous acculturation in Northwest Mexico [see item **1021**] p. 54–61)

Similarities in Mexicanero and Tepehuan myths may have implications for understanding Aztec influence in Northwest Mexico.

972 Horcasitas, Fernando. Versos de la danza de Santiago de Taxco, Guerrero (UNAM/AA, 17:2, 1980, p. 99–157, bibl.)

Lengthy transcription of verse collected in Taxco by Donald Cordry, with notes and commentary by Horcasitas.

973 **Howe, James** and **Lawrence A. Hirsch-field.** The star girls' descent: a myth about men, women, matrilocality, and singing (AFS/JAF, 94:373, July/Sept. 1981, p. 292–322)

Series of distortions and inversions of customary residence rules and sexual division of labor in Kuna myth delineate, by implication, proper developmental cycle of Kuna domestic group and ideal balance of production and reproduction, cultivation of food and raising of children. Elegant, subtle exercise in symbolic and structuralist analysis, paper contains insights into Kuna concepts of medicine, hunting, attachment and separation, and maleness and femaleness.

974 **Hurwicz, Margo-Lea** and **Walter Goldschmidt.** Values in three Guatemalan villages (Anthropology [University of California, Department of Anthropology, Los Angeles] 11:1/2, 1981, p. 75–86, bibl., plates, tables)

Responses to dilemma-posing scenes of Indian life suggest significant relations between predominant values (i.e., respect, moderation, and hard work) and courses of action.

975 **Kaplan, Flora S.** and **David M. Levine.** Cognitive mapping of a folk taxonomy of Mexican pottery: a multivariate approach (AAA/AA, 83:4, Dec. 1981, p. 868–884, bibl., ill., tables)

Multivariate statistical analysis suggests that open/closed and multiple/non-multiple ears are principal factors in native taxonomy of pottery types in Valley of Puebla.

976 **Kemper, Robert V.** Compadrazgo in city and countryside: a comparison of Tzintzuntzan migrants and villagers (in From Tzintzuntzan to the "image of the limited good" [see item 960] p. 25–44)

Purports to show, among other things, that verticle compadre selection and secular types of compadrazgo are more common in Mexico City than in Tzintzuntzan.

977 ———. The compadrazgo in urban Mexico (CUA/AQ, 55:1, Jan. 1982, p. 17–30, table)

Survey of 21 studies suggests compadrazgo's viability in urban settings, although conclusions are weakened somewhat by incomplete coverage of literature and uneven data.

978 ——— and **Anya Peterson Royce.** Mexican urbanization since 1821: a macro-historical approach (Urban Anthropology [State University of New York, Brockport] 8:3/4, Winter 1979, p. 267–289)

Argues on basis of secondary sources that pace of urbanization in Mexico has been affected by transformations in national economy and political orientation.

979 **Kerns, Virginia.** Structural continuity in the division of men's and women's work among the black Carib: *Garífuna* (in Sex roles and social change in native lower Central American societies [see item 1011] p. 23–43)

Argues that discrimination against women in labor market keeps them in subsistence work and reinforces their traditionalism.

980 **Köhler, Ulrich.** Patterns of interethnic economic exchange in southeastern Mexico (UNM/JAR, 36:3, Fall 1980, p. 316–337, bibl., map)

Unusually rich description of economic relations in Chiapas highlands shows that Ladinos seek negative reciprocity while Indians settle for balanced reciprocity in their mutual relations. This in turn suggests that Ladino power is not based on class (i.e., ownership of means of production) or even accumulation of capital so much as on colonial pattern of exploitation that persists despite waning of repressive apparatus once associated with it.

981 **Kurtz, Donald V.** The Virgin of Guadalupe and the politics of becoming human (UNM/JAR, 38:2, Summer 1982, p. 194–210, bibl.)

Somewhat speculative paper hypothesizes that proclamation by Bishop Juan de Zumárraga on Virgin of Guadalupe's apparition was symbolic legitimation of Indian-Catholic syncretism which served to define Indians as human beings and thus aided the Bishop in his attempt to assert control over the First Audiencia.

983 **Littlefield, Alice.** The expansion of capitalist relations of production in Mexican crafts (JPS, 6:4, July 1979, p. 471–488, bibl.)

Simple commodity production by artisans is being replaced by capitalist relations of production. Although similar to processes that occurred in Europe during transition to capitalism, the present pattern of merchant exploitation of cottage industries in rural Mexico is a stable phenomenon that coexists with more advanced capitalist relations of production (see item **984**).

984 ———. La industria de las hamacas en Yucatán, México: un estudio de antropología económica. Traducción de Antonieta S. de Hope. México: Instituto Nacional Indigenista: Secretaría de Educación Pública, 1976. 231 p., 6 leaves of plates: bibl., ill., maps, plates, tables (Serie de antropología social. Colección SEP-INI; no. 52)

Examination of relation of hammock production to land tenure, cropping, and population growth suggests that peasants turn to making hammocks when they cannot sustain themselves through agriculture. After considering economic underpinnings of craft production, author describes in detail forces and relations of production in hammock industry and illustrates situation of hammock makers with study of families in Cacalchen, a community near Mérida. Data show that in present-day Yucatan traditional system of cottage artisans producing for local, periodic markets has given way to one in which capitalists increasingly control distribution and means of production.

985 **Logan, Michael H.** Variations regarding *susto* causality among the Cakchiquel of Guatemala (Culture, Medicine and Psychiatry [D. Riedel, Dordrecht, Netherlands] 3:2, June 1979, p. 153–166, bibl.)

In San Antonio, fright-illness is seen as the result of change or destiny whereas in Panajachel it is more often thought to result from witchcraft. The difference, which corresponds to a typology of illness-causation proposed by Foster, may be due to the greater prevalence of land scarcity and intracommunity competition and, hence, greater need for social control in Panajachel.

986 **Lomnitz, Larissa** and **Marisol Pérez-Lizaur.** Kinship structure and the role of women in the urban upper class of Mexico (UC/S, 5:1, Autumn 1979, p. 164–168)

Cohesion of upper class kindreds is reinforced by family business and by women, who organize ritual family reunions. Women increasingly participate in business although motherhood remains their primary occupation. Briefly describes socialization of girls.

987 **Love in the armpit: Tzeltal tales of love, murder, and cannibalism.** Compiled by Brian Stross. Columbia: Museum of Anthropology, University of Missouri-Columbia, 1977. 27 p.: map (Museum brief; no. 23)

Tales about primordial copulation, Lucifer, and hell.

988 **Loveland, Franklin O.** Watch that pot or the *waksuk* will eat you up: an analysis of male and female roles in Rama Indian myth (*in* Sex roles and social change in native lower Central American societies [see item **1011**] p. 124–141)

Convincingly shows that men and women are both associated with nature and culture in Rama myth.

989 **Low, Setha M.** The meaning of *nervios*: a sociocultural analysis of symptom presentation in San José, Costa Rica (Culture, Medicine and Psychiatry [D. Riedel, Dordrecht, Netherlands] 5:1, March 1981, p. 25–47, bibl., ill., table)

Competent article based on large samples from general medicine and psychiatry clinics implies that *nervios* is a dyscontrol syndrome that arises in disturbed family relations. Interprets the illness as help-seeking behavior aimed at social reintegration (see item **913**).

990 **Malinowski, Bronislaw** and **Julio de la Fuente.** Malinowski in Mexico: the economics of a Mexican market system. Edited with introduction by Susan Drucker-Brown. London: Routledge & Kegan Paul, 1982. 217 p.: bibl., ill., maps, plates, tables.

First English ed. of seminal work on Oaxaca markets. Drucker-Brown's valuable introduction reviews authors' careers and theoretical orientations, nature of their collaboration, and comments on its intellectual context and practical implications for applied anthropology in Mexico. While underscoring author's principal findings, she makes some perceptive remarks about types of buyers and sellers observed by Malinowski and de la Fuente. Also summarizes work of recent students of peasant economy in Oaxaca and chides them for not making better use of Malinowski's work. Text itself describes markets' internal organization, their distribution, timing, and economic and cultural contexts. Close attention is given to actual transactions.

991 Mason, J. Aldean and **Phil C. Weigand.**
The ceremonialism of the Tepecan Indians of Azqueltán, Jalisco (*in* Themes of indigenous acculturation in Northwest Mexico [see item **1021**] p. 62–76)

Brief but informative ethnography of neglected but very interesting Tepecan folk religion. Based on field work done during 1912–13, paper should prove interesting to students of prehispanic religion and contemporary syncretism.

992 La Mixteca Baja: algunos aspectos demográficos. México: Instituto Nacional de Antropología e Historia, Departamento de Etnología y Antropología Social, 1980. 77 p.: bibl. (Cuadernos de trabajo; 26)

Contains Teófilo Reyes C. "La Demografía en La Mixteca Baja," a compilation of demographic statistics covering 75 municipios, and Isabel Hernández G. "Migración en La Mixteca Baja Oaxaqueña: un Intento de Interpretación," a study of migration in relation to employment patterns.

993 Molina, Virginia. San Bartolomé de los Llanos: una urbanización frenada. México: Centro de Investigaciones Superiores, Instituto Nacional de Antropología e Historia, 1976. 239 p.: bibl., maps, tables.

Survey of actual and historical economic resources and activities in Chiapas municipio.

994 Moore, Alexander. Basilicas and king posts: a proxemic and symbolic event analysis of competing public architecture among the San Blas Cuna (AAA/AE, 8:2, May 1981, p. 259–277, bibl.)

Argues that the traditional Cuna house and congress house encapsulate and encode roles and relations of men and women in different contexts. Newer basilica-style meeting structure evinces effects of modernization and changing patterns of authority. Construction of such a basilica-like house provoked attempt by nativistic faction to build a traditional meeting house.

995 Nigh, Ronald B. El ambiente nutricional de los grupos mayas de Chiapas (III/AI, 40:1, enero/marzo 1980, p. 73–91, bibl., charts)

Argues that progressive destruction of natural habitat brought about by cattle raising and commercial agriculture has resulted in deterioration of diet and nutritional health

among Indian groups in Chiapas. Data gathered in Zinacantan point in particular to deficiencies in zinc and vitamins A and C.

996 Nutini, Hugo G. and **Betty Bell.** Ritual kinship: the structure and historical development of the compadrazgo system in rural Tlaxcala. v. 1. Princeton, N.J.: Princeton Univeristy Press, 1980- . 494 p.: bibl., ill., index, maps, tables.

Provides comprehensive and detailed description of sacramental and nonsacramental compadrazgo in Tlaxcala (remarkably, 31 types are described in all). Also notes statistical trends in selection patterns: wealthier villagers have more godchildren than poor villagers, and growth of migratory wage labor correlates with geographical expansion of intervillage compadrazgo network (but not with a change in proportion of intra- and intervillage ties). Unfortunately, the excellent ethnography is marred by prolixity and pretentious theorizing, along with lapses in scholarship. Authors stress importance of religious ideology and differentiate between sacred and social aspects of compadrazgo, but hardly acknowledge existing literature on institution's symbolic and ritual structure and relation of such structure to actual selection patterns. Moreover, their historical reconstruction of elaboration of compadrazgo in Tlaxcala seems rather speculative and poorly documented. Presumably, some of these deficiencies will be remedied in a forthcoming vol. 2.

997 Oettinger, Marion, Jr. Dos métodos de adivinación tlapaneca: medir el hueso y echar los granos de maíz (UNAM/AA, 16, 1979, p. 225–232, bibl., ill.)

Describes two methods of divination among Tlapanec, measuring the bone of the arm and casting maíz. Methods are similar to techniques found among Mixtec, Trique, and other groups.

998 Olivera, Mercedes. Huemitle de mayo en Citlala: ¿ofrenda para Chicomecoatl o para la Santa Cruz? (*in* Mesoamérica: homenajes al Doctor Paul Kirchoff. Coordinación Barbro Dahlgren. México: INAH, 1979, p. 143–158)

Fascinating paper about Santa Cruz ceremonies of Nahua community in Guerrero shows that the Cruz is conceptualized as a Virgin and that she is a latter-day version of Chicomecoatl.

999 O'Nell, Carl W. Nonviolence and personality dispositions among the Zapotec: paradox and enigma (Journal of Psychological Anthropology [Association for Psychohistory, New York] 2:3, Summer 1979, p. 301–322, bibl.)

Suggests that personality factors may account for difference between violent and nonviolent communities in Valley of Oaxaca. Research in one nonviolent community indicates that hostility may have a developmental origin in an abrupt transition from physical and emotional nurturance to mere instrumental care combined with parental teasing and deceit at age three or four. Speculates that socialization for social dependence—respect, responsibility, and cooperation—may inhibit actual expression of resulting hostility.

1000 Orellana, Sandra L. Idols and idolatry in highland Guatemala (ASE/E, 28:2, Spring 1981, p. 157–177, bibl., ill.)

Documents the persistence of prehispanic idol worship, religious offices, and festival organization.

1001 Peckenham, Nancy. Land settlement in the Petén (LAP, 7[25/26]:2/3, Spring/Summer 1980, p. 169–177)

Describes roles of the cattle and oil industries and the military in failure of Petén's colonization to solve Guatemala's land crisis.

1002 Pennington, Campbell W. The Pima Bajo of Central Sonora, Mexico. v. 1, The material culture. v. 2, Vocabulario en la lengua nevome [contains a revised version of a 17th-century manuscript ascribed to B.X. Loaiza]. Salt Lake City: University of Utah Press, 1979/1980. 2 v. (410, 129 p.): bibl., ill., plates, tables.

Vol. 1 draws on field and archival research to reconstruct the Pima Bajo's prehispanic material culture and to trace their postconquest history. Vol. 2 reproduces 18th-century grammar and vocabulary.

1003 Pensamiento antropológico e indigenista de Julio de la Fuente. Gonzalo Aguirre Beltrán *et al.* México: Instituto Nacional Indigenista, 1980. 267 p.: bibl., ill.

Homenaje to Julio de la Fuente, published on 10th anniversary of his death, contains following contributions: Félix Báez-Jorge "Introducción" (p. 9–18); Gonzalo Aguirre Beltrán "Julio de la Fuente: Antropólogo e Indigenista" (p. 23–27); Agustín Romano Delgado "Julio de la Fuente: el Hombre y el Antropólogo" (p. 31–43); Evangelina Arana de Swadesh "Julio de la Fuente: Destacado Maestro Indigenista" (p. 47–64); Alberto Beltrán "Julio de la Fuente: el Artista Gráfico" (p. 67–87); Félix Báez-Jorge "La Antropología Aplicada desde la Perspectiva Teórico-Práctica de Julio de la Fuente" (p. 93–139); Isabel Horcasitas de Pozas and Ricardo Pozas Arciniega "El Monolingüismo en Lengua Indígena al Bilingüismo en Lengua Indígena y Nacional" (p. 145–195); Laura Collin Harguindeguy "Julio de la Fuente a Través de su Obra" (p. 199–237); and Laura Collin Harguindeguy "Bibliografía de Julio de la Fuente" (p. 243–266).

1004 Pérez Castro, Ana Bella. Mitos y creencias en los movimientos mesiánicos y luchas campesinas en Chiapas (UNAM/AA, 17, 1980, p. 185–195, bibl.)

Examines role of supernatural visitations and talking saints in messianic movements and peasant struggles in Chiapas (see item **929**).

1005 Persistent peoples: cultural enclaves in perspective. George Pierre Castile and Gilbert Kushner, editors. Contributing authors, William Y. Adams *et al.* Tucson: University of Arizona Press, 1981. 274 p.: bibl., index.

Festschrift honoring Prof. Edward H. Spicer, with contributions from various students of Middle America (see items **934, 947, 953, 966,** and **969**).

1006 Pietri, Anne Lise and **René Pietri.** Empleo y migración en la región de Pátzcuaro. Traductores, Leticia Leduc Segura, Luis Enrique Délano D. México: Instituto Nacional Indigenista: Secretaría de Educación Pública, 1976. 270 p., 10 leaves of plates: bibl., ill., maps (Serie de antropología social. Colección SEP-INI; no. 46)

Pt. 1 focuses on employment in agriculture, crafts, and fishing in four municipios around Pátzcuaro, noting income levels, patterns of mixed occupations, etc., community by community. Pt. 1 examines migration and concludes that its frequency, duration, and finality are functions of occupation: ejidatarios are more likely to migrate than artisans. Indianness is associated with craft production but seems to have little impact in and of itself on migration.

1007 Rogoff, Barbara. Adults and peers as agents of socialization: a highland Guatemalan profile (Ethos [Society for Psychological Anthropology, University of California, Los Angeles] 9 : 1, Spring 1981, p. 18–36, bibl., ill.)

Finds that children's interaction with other children increases while that with adults decreases between ages one and 10, but observes that this pattern does not interfere with acquisition of adult skills because children engage in adult activities when they interact with adults.

1008 ———. The relation of age and sex to experiences during childhood in a highland community (Anthropology [University of California, Department of Anthropology, Los Angeles] 11 : 1/2, 1981, p. 25–41, bibl., tables)

Describes socialization and age-specific activities of children from infancy to age 10 in highland Guatemalan community of San Pedro, with special attention to sex differences. Includes especially interesting material on children's contributions to child care and other chores.

1009 Rosengarten, Frederic, Jr. A neglected Mayan galactagogue ixbut— *Euphorbia Lancifolia* (Journal of Ethnoparmacology [Elsevier Sequoia, Lausanne, Switzerland] 5 : 1, Jan. 1981, p. 91–112, bibl., ill., map, plates, table.

Describes use of *ixbut* by postpartum Guatemalan women to stimulate milk flow.

1010 Rus, Jan and **Robert Wasserstrom.** Civil-religious hierarchies in central Chiapas: a critical perspective (AES/AE, 7 : 3, Aug. 1980, p. 466–478, bibl., ill., tables)

Historical evidence shows that in late 19th and early 20th centuries, civil-religious hierarchies developed out of traditional cofradía organization and in response to changing economic and political circumstances: in Zinacantan, cash incomes from wage labor promoted competition in religious sponsorship; in Chamula, ascendancy of Cardenista scribes reinforced linkage between political and religious offices.

1011 Sex roles and change in native lower Central American societies. Edited by Christine A. Loveland and Franklin O. Loveland. Urbana: University of Illinois Press, 1981. 185 p.: bibl., ill., maps, plates, tables.

Volume includes introduction by Christine A. Loveland and overview by Regina Holloman. Seven papers are annotated separately in this section (see items **920, 925, 945–946, 979, 988,** and **1016**).

1012 Signorini, Italo. Los huaves de San Mateo del Mar, Oax. Con ensayos de Giorgio Raimondo Cardona, Carla M. Rita, Luigi Tranfo. 1. ed. en español. México: Instituto Nacional Indigenista, 1979. 375 p., 12 leaves of plates: bibl., ill. (Serie Antropología social. Colección INI; no. 59)

Comprehensive, traditional ethnography of little-studied Huave, with chapters on subsistence system, mayordomía organization, kinship terminology, and godparenthood. Chapter by Tranfo reviews Middle American literature on *tonal* and *nagual* and describes Huave versions of these notions. Signorini and Tranfo discuss traditional folk medicine; a valuable chapter by Rita examines beliefs and practices relating to conception, pregnancy, and birth; and Cardona considers connections between ethnobiological and human anatomical categories and other domains (e.g., house, trees, boats, village).

1013 ———. Patterns of fright: multiple concepts of susto in a Nahua-Ladino community in the Sierra of Puebla, Mexico (UP/E, 21 : 4, Oct. 1982, p. 313–323, bibl.)

Nahua and Ladino concepts of *susto* differ: the Nahua interpretation is more spiritual and the Ladino, more physiological. Evidently, the folk medical category of *susto* encompasses emotional and organic disorders, including parasitic infection.

1014 Singelmann, Peter. Structures of domination and peasant movements in Latin America. Columbia: University of Missouri Press, 1981. 246 p.: bibl., index.

Serious, systematic attempt to theorize about conditions underlying peasant movements in Latin America draws extensively on available theoretical and empirical literature. Argues for synthesis of macro and microstructural perspectives, in which latter employs concepts of such exchange theorists as Homans and Blau. Thus it is argued that stability in countryside is function of strong patron-client exchange relations which compete effectively with peasant-peasant exchanges. Specification of the traditional institutional parameters of a model of unilateral dependence in triadic exchanges permits a series of hypotheses about how imbalances in parameters promote peasant movements.

1015 Sitton, Salomon Nahmad. Some consideration of the indirect and controlled acculturation in the Cora-Huichol area (*in* Themes of indigenous acculturation in Northwest Mexico [see item **1021**] p. 4–8)

Details the pervasive pattern of mestizo exploitation in Huichol highlands and limited success of various INI programs.

1016 Swain, Margaret Byrne. Being Cuna and female: ethnicity mediating change in sex roles (*in* Sex roles and social change in native lower Central American societies [see item **1011**] p. 103–123)

Commercial mola production has reinforced Cuna ethnicity and traditional status of women although schooling and a hospital may affect traditional sex roles.

1017 Swetnam, John J. Ambidextros culturales: vendedores indígenas urbanos (III/AI, 41 : 1, enero/marzo 1981, p. 11–24, bibl., tables)

Describes success of Indian vendors in market of Antigua, Guatemala, made possible by inexpensive bus service. Indians commute from countryside to urban market, where they have established permanent sites, incorporated manufactured goods into their stocks, and established permanent clientele among Indians and Ladinos alike. Increasingly, Indian merchants are displacing Ladinos as economic middlemen.

1018 Taggart, James M. Class and sex in Spanish and Mexican oral tradition (UP/E, 21 : 1, Jan. 1982, p. 39–53, bibl., tables)

Drawing on data from community in central Spain and Nahuat-speaking community in central Mexico, uses cognate folktale comparison to delineate androcentric attitudes in both and then relates differences to socioeconomic variables. Findings support hypothesis that male-dominant ideology is

more likely among men in lowest strata of rigid class societies. Also suggests segregation of sexes and lack of complementarity in work activities further reinforces male dominance ideology.

1019 Tedlock, Barbara. Quiché Maya dream interpretation (IFP/E, 9 : 4, Winter 1981, p. 313–330, bibl., ill.)

Informative description of dream interpretation among Quiché Maya, with special reference to recruitment and training of calendrical diviners. Standardized rules, context of dreamer, mythical codes, and calendrical auguries all affect interpretations, as do dreamer's social status: different principles of interpretation are applied to dreams of daykeepers and ordinary persons.

1020 ———. Sound texture and metaphor in Quiché Maya ritual language (UC/CA, 23 : 3, June 1982, p. 269–272, bibl.)

Intriguing note on Quiché divination reveals that prognostications are not given by day signs as such but rather by their associated figurative phrases and paronomasia; precise interpretation of these in turn depends on contextual considerations.

1021 Themes of indigenous acculturation in Northwest Mexico. Thomas B. Hinton and Phil C. Weigand, editors. Contributors, N. Ross Crumrine *et al.* Tucson: University of Arizona Press, 1981. 76 p.: bibl., ill. (Anthropological papers of the University of Arizona; no. 38)

In addition to a preface by Phil C. Weigand, volume includes eight papers annotated elsewhere in this section (see items **948, 952, 967, 970–971, 991, 1015,** and **1034**).

1022 Thomas, John S. The socioeconomic determinants of political leadership in a Tojolabal Maya community (AAA/AE, 8 : 1, Feb. 1981, p. 127–138, bibl., ill., tables)

Multiple regression and path analysis delineate determinants of political leadership. Important independent variables are shown to be wealth, family size, and friendship networks although, curiously, the statistical results attribute little effect to compadrazgo ties.

1023 Thomas, Norman S. The Mesoamerican barrio: a reciprocity model for community organization (*in* From

Tzintzuntzan to the "image of the limited good" [see item **960**] p. 45–58)

Valuable survey of barrio systems in Middle America.

1024 Toledo, Víctor Manuel *et al.* Los purépechas de Pátzcuaro: una aproximación ecológica (III/AI, 40: 1, enero/marzo 1980, p. 17–55, bibl., charts, map)

Surveys ecological conditions and systems of economic adaptation (i.e., agriculture, fishing, hunting, etc.) found among Tarascan communities of Lake Pátzcuaro region. Concludes that adaption to local resources has reinforced the perpetuation of Tarascan ethnicity.

1025 Torres de Araúz, Reina. Panamá indígena. Panamá: Instituto Nacional de Cultura, Patrimonio Histórico, 1980. 383 p.: bibl., ill., maps, plates.

This handbook-life survey of Panama's Indians should prove indispensable to students of its indigenous cultures. There is detailed coverage of habitat, technology, family and social organization, rites of passage, religion, and politics for each Indian group and many excellent photographs and maps. Also discusses linguistic classification, history, and present dynamics of ethnicity.

1026 Tousignant, Michel. *Espanto*: a dialogue with the gods (Culture, Medicine and Psychiatry [D. Reidel, Dordrecht, Netherlands] 3: 4, Dec. 1979, p. 347–361, bibl., tables)

Reported symptoms in 109 cases of fright-illness in a Tzeltal community imply that condition is not coherent biomedical syndrome. Rather, its unity consists in its cultural meaning: fright is caused by *aires* sent by various supernatural beings inhabiting caves, ravines, lakes (i.e., passageways to the underworld) and, ultimately, by the Holy Earth herself. This Being causes earthquakes which are said to be like the trembling and chills associated with fear and other ailments.

1027 Trotter, Robert T., II. Folk remedies as indicators of common illnesses: examples from the United States-Mexico border (Journal of Ethnopharmacology [Elsevier Sequoia, Lausanne, Switzerland] 4: 2, Sept. 1981, p. 207–221, bibl., tables)

Large sample of home remedies illustrates ethnopharmacological resources presently in use along border and identifies ailments considered by informants to be most amenable to home remedy.

1028 ——— and **Juan Antonio Chavira.** *Curanderismo*: an emic theoretical perspective of Mexican-American folk medicine (Medical Anthropology [University of Connecticut, Storrs] 4: 4, Fall 1980, p. 423–487, bibl.)

Describes three categories of illness and treatment (i.e., material/natural, supernatural, and mental) with some interesting information on notion of "gift," therapeutic uses of candles, and spiritualism, but the criticisms of scholarly literature seem rather pretentious, particularly in view of article's own modest contribution.

1029 Tzeltal tales of demons and monsters. Compiled by Brian Stross. Columbia: Museum of Anthropology, University of Missouri-Columbia, 1978. 40 p.: bibl., map (Museum brief no. 24)

Series of tales and vignettes about Black Demon, Treemoss, Backwards Foot, Wall Demon, Flesh Droper, Whirling Arm, Rabid Demon, Alligator, Headache Woman, and others, with discussion of their classification, place in world view, and relation to demons in other Maya communities.

1030 Villa Rojas, Alfonso. Los elegidos de Dios: etnografía de los mayas de Quintana Roo. Prólogo de Miguel León Portilla. Apéndice: Howard F. Cline, Sobre la Guerra de Castas. México: Instituto Nacional Indigenista, 1978. 571 p., 10 leaves of plates: bibl., ill., maps, tables (Serie de Antropología social. Colección INI; no. 56)

Reprint of original 1945 edition with new prologue by Miguel León-Portilla.

1031 ———. La imagen del cuerpo humano según los mayas de Yucatán (UNAM/AA, 17, 1980, p. 31–46, bibl., ill.)

Data gathered in Yucatan indicates that contemporary Maya may preserve a conception of the body that replicates the four-part composition of the prehispanic cosmos.

1032 Vogt, Evon Zartman. Ofrendas para los dioses: análisis simbólico de rituales zinacantecos. Traducción de Stella Mastrangelo. 1. ed. en español. México: Fondo de Cultura Económica, 1979. 328 p., 7 leaves of plates: bibl., ill. (Sección de obras de antropología)

Spanish translation of English edition (see *HLAS 39:1164*).

1033 Warman, Arturo. *We come to object:* the peasants of Morelos and the national state. Translated by Stephen K. Ault. Baltimore: Johns Hopkins University Press, 1980. 319 p.: bilb., maps.

English translation of Warman's important monograph (see *HLAS 43:937*).

1034 Weigand, Philip C. Differential acculturation among the Huichol Indians (*in* Themes of indigenous acculturation in Northwest Mexico [see item **1021**] p. 9–21)

Scholarly treatment of the various exogenous cultural influences on the Huichol from prehispanic times to present, with plea for less concentration on shared symbolism and more attention to social and economic diversity.

1035 Wells, Marilyn McK. The symbolic use of Guseue among the Garif— black Carib—of Central America (CUA/AQ, 55:1, Jan. 1982, p. 44–55, tables)

Describes changes in use of guseue, a red body paint, by the Garif (black Carib) since 18th century. Present-day use of galati, a dilution of guseue, is seen as an accommodation to the wider society.

1036 Young, James Clay. Medical choice in a Mexican village. New Brunswick, N.J.: Rutgers University Press, 1981. 233 p.: bibl., ill., maps, tables.

Important study of medical treatment in a Tarascan community draws on blend of solid ethnography, sophisticated data-eliciting techniques, and statistical analysis. Presents interesting material on conceptions of body parts, blood, *fuerza*, hot and cold, etc. Cluster analysis suggests that classification of illnesses is influenced by source, seriousness, and patient's life stage as well as by hotness or coldness of offending agent. Selection of medical treatment is found to be a function of knowledge of home remedies, faith in folk medicine, gravity of illness, and expense of treament. Concludes that expense and relative unavailability of modern medicine are main obstales to its acceptance.

ETHNOLOGY: West Indies

LAMBROS COMITAS, *Professor of Anthropology and Education, Teachers College, Columbia University, and Director, Institute of Latin American and Iberian Studies, Columbia University*

FOR THIS VOLUME OF *HLAS*, I include annotations of publications in social and cultural anthropology and closely related disciplines that deal with 26 distinct Caribbean territories: Bahamas, Barbados, Barbuda, Belize, Cuba, Dominica, Dominican Republic, French Guyana, Grenada, Guadeloupe, Guyana, Haiti, Jamaica, Marie-Galante, Martinique, Montserrat, Nevis, Puerto Rico, St. Eustatius, St. John, St. Kitts, St. Lucia, St. Vincent, Suriname, Trinidad, and Venezuela. In addition, some 15 annotations of publications that deal generally with the Caribbean region, the Commonwealth Caribbean, the Lesser Antilles, or the French Antilles are included.

The two countries that received the most attention from researchers during this two-year report period were Guyana and Jamaica followed by Suriname, Belize, Haiti, and Trinidad.

As is always true for this section, the publications cited cover such an extraordinarily wide range of topics that organizing them under subject headings becomes a problematic venture. Nevertheless, for the convenience of the user, I have classified, somewhat arbitrarily, the bulk of the items into the following overlapping categories.

I. STUDIES WITH HISTORICAL ORIENTATION

Anthropologists and others working in the Caribbean region have increasingly turned their attention to certain questions of structure and process that can be resolved best by examining the records of the past. On precolumbian ceramic making in contemporary Martinique, see Roo Lemos (item **1130**). For publications on slave-related issues, consult the following: Handler (item **1081**) on slave revolts in Barbados; Brathwaite (item **1057**) on slave culture in Jamaica; and Olwig (items **1110** and **1111**) on slave family, women, and "matrifocality" in St. John. Schnakenbourg (items **1132** and **1133**) traces the history of the sugar industry in Marie-Galante and Martinique. For Belize, Bolland (items **1054** and **1055**) deals with land and labor control in the postabolition period; Grant Jones (item **1090**) on a 19th-century fiesta; and Helms (item **1082**) on Black Carib domestic organization in historical perspective. For specific populations, see Fouchard (item **1078**) on Haitian Maroons; Kopytoff (item **1094**) on the colonial treaties and Jamaican Maroons; and Thoden van Velzen and van Wetering (item **1138**) on female religious responses to male prosperity in Bush Negro societies. For Guyana, Menezes (item **1103**) deals with government policies toward the Amerindians; Edwards and Gibson (item **1073**) present an historical account of Amerindian immigration; and happily, the Hillhouse eye-witness account of early 19th-century Amerindians (item **1084**) was reprinted. Hill (item **1085**) writes about Howell and millenarian visions in early Rastafari; Guanche (item **1080**) offers a scheme for the analysis of the development of Cuban culture; and Hoetink (item **1086**) discusses, in English translation, the historical sociology of the Dominican Republic.

II. STUDIES OF CONTEMPORARY AMERINDIANS, BLACK CARIBS, AND MAROONS

On Amerindians, Layng (items **1097** and **1098**) deals with the Carib reserve in Dominica; Berte (item **1049**) with the peasant rationality of the K'eckchi Maya of Belize; Adams (item **1038**) with the socioeconomic role of Guyanese Carib children; Bennet, Colson, and Wavell (item **1046**) and Hennigsgaard (item **1083**) with the plight of the Guyanese Akawaio caused by the projected construction of a hydroelectric complex; and Rivière (item **1129**) with the Trio of Suriname. On Black Caribs, Foster (items **1076** and **1077**) discusses the *dugu* rite and spirit possession, while Wells describes the symbolic use of *guseue* powder. On contemporary Maroon societies, Bilby (items **1051** and **1052**) treats the Kromanti dance and the current identity crisis among Jamaican Maroons; Hurault (item **1087**) responds to the criticisms of his work raised by Köbben and Price; Vernon (item **1141**) comments on *Bakuu* possession among the Djuka; Counter and Evans (item **1063**) on their visits to the Surinamese Maroons; and Price and Price (items **1123–1126**) on various aspects of Surinamese Maroon art.

III. SOCIETY, CULTURE, AND POLITICAL PROCESS

Berleant-Schiller (item **1048**) writes on plantation society as a construct, while Masse (item **1102**) examines it against the reality of Martinique and Guadeloupe. Wout van der Bor (item **1140**) describes the social organization of the small island of St. Eustatius, and Bregenzer (item **1058**) presents an ethnography of the equally small Eleuthera. Streetlife is explored by Dodd (item **1069**) in Georgetown, Guyana, and by Lieber (item **1100**) in Port-of-Spain. Ehrlich (item **1074**) and Nevadomsky (items **1107–1109**) analyze socioeconomic changes among East Indians in Jamaica and Trinidad, respectively. Brockmann (item **1059**) discusses household composition and socioeconomic strategies in a rural Belizean town. The Spanish influence on the contemporary culture of the Dominican Republic is the subject of Dobal's essay (item **1067**). Annemarie de Waal Malefijt (item **1142**) treats symbolic aspects of Javanese puppet plays in Suriname, while Abrahams (item **1037**) delineates expressive devices in Vincentian ceremonies and festivities. Barros (item **1044**) deals with Haiti's linguistic destiny; and Fontaine (item **1075**) with the social and political nature of Haiti's language problem.

Interest in politics, political institutions and political process continues apace. On Guyana, Silverman (item **1136**) examines the factional politics among rural East Indians; Danns (item **1066**) the police and the current political system; and Serbin (item **1134**) nationalism, ethnicity, and politics. On Suriname, Brana-Shute (item **1056**) writes on the all-female Children's Police. Mars (item **1101**) deals with theoretical positions on race and class in the Caribbean as they relate to the political process.

IV. RELIGION AND MAGIC

The Rastafari are examined in several works: a special issue of the *Caribbean Quarterly* (item **1060**) that marks the 50th anniversary of this movement; by Chevannes (item **1061**), who describes Rasta youth in West Kingston; by Mandefro (item **1148**), who gives the canon law of Ethiopian Orthodox marriage in the Western Hemisphere; and by de Albuquerque (item **1041**), who discusses the spread of Rastafarianism in the Commonwealth Caribbean. Voodoo is examined by the following authors: van Sertima (item **1135**) on the African presence in ritual and art; Jiménez Lambertus (item **1089**) on historical and psychological dimensions of Dominican voodoo; and Agosto de Muñoz (item **1039**) on the phenomenon of possession. Pentecostalism is the subject of several books: Glazier's (item **1114**) compilation of Caribbean case studies; Austin's (item **1043**) examination of communitas and social change among urban Jamaicans; and Pollak-Eltz (items **1116** and **1117**) on magico-religious movements and magical operations in Venezuela. Finally, Dobbin (item **1068**) writes on the Jombee dance in Montserrat; Wooding (item **1146**) on Winti in Suriname; and Pozzi (item **1121**) offers a Durkheimian analysis of Jonestown. Beck (item **1045**) presents an autobiography of a St. Lucian fisherman and *obeahman*, and Owen (item **1112**) discusses personal involvement with witchcraft in Dominica.

V. APPLIED STUDIES

Studies of health are by Dressler (item **1072**) on hypertension and culture change in St. Lucia; Fredrich's (item **1079**) survey on St. Lucian folk medicine; Staiano (item **1137**) on alternative therapeutic systems in Belize; and Weniger *et al.* (item **1145**) on use of Haitian plants as antifertility agents. Marihuana use and manual work in rural Jamaica is examined by Dreher (items **1070** and **1071**); patterns of drinking in Barbados by Dann (item **1065**); crime, race, and culture in Guyana by Howard Jones (item **1091**); and small-scale fishing and development in Barbuda by Berleant-Schiller (item **1047**).

VI. IMMIGRATION AND EMIGRATION

For studies of population movement with a clear Caribbean locus, see Myers (item **1105**) on post-emancipation migrations in Dominica; Richardson (item **1128**) on environment and human survival in St. Kitts and Nevis; Stinner *et al.* (item **1127**) on Caribbean return migration and remittances; Pourraz (item **1120**) on ethnic diversity in French Guiana; and Ashton (item **1042**) on return and re-return of Puerto Rico migrants. For US-based study, see Jackson (item **1088**) on Puerto Rican culture in New York. For Canadian-based study, see the bibliography of Kemperneers and Masse (item **1092**).

Finally, for its intrinsic value to Amerindian research, the bibliographic effort of Myers (item **1105**) on the Amerindians of the Lesser Antilles is to be commended, as is the two-volume *The Complete Haitiana: a bibliography guide to the scholarly literature 1900–1980* (item **1096**) by Michel Laguerre.

I am indebted to Ellen Schnepel for her valuable contribution to the preparation of this section.

1037 Abrahams, Roger D. Symbolic landscapes on St. Vincent (Canadian Journal of Anthropology/Revue Canadienne d'Anthropologie [University of Alberta, Department of Anthropology, Edmonton, Canada] 2:1, Spring 1981, p. 45–53, bibl.)

Survey of Vincentian community's repertoire of expressive devices in ceremonies and festivities. Sharp distinction drawn between worlds of *yard* (related to household, respect-celebrating events, rules governing practices of privacy and family, etc.) and *road* (related to public world, male activities, friendship networks, license, rudeness, etc.).

1038 Adams, Kathleen J. The role of children in the changing socioeconomic strategies of the Guyanese Caribs (Canadian Journal of Anthropology/Revue Canadienne d'Anthropologie [University of Alberta, Department of Anthropology, Edmonton, Canada] 2:1, Spring 1981, p. 61–66, bibl., ill.)

Over 50-year period the Barama River Caribs have experienced considerable socioeconomic change, from subsistence horticulture to wage work and incorporation into money economy. Despite this, they continue to manage reproduction, that is, to plan the group's sex ratio. "This Carib example suggests that population adaptation is part of a strategy with which to confront forces in the social context and as such is subject to change in relation to those forces."

1039 Agosto de Muñoz, Nélida. El fenómeno de la posesión en la religión Vudú: un estudio sobre la posesión por los espíritus y su relación con el ritual en el Vudú. Río Piedras: Instituto de Estudios del Caribe, Universidad de Puerto Rico, 1975. 119 p. (Caribbean monograph series; no. 14)

Spanish version of author's bachelor's thesis offers a general description of the organization and belief system of Voodoo and context of Voodoo ritual.

1040 Aho, William R. Sex conflict in Trinidad calypsoes, 1969–1979 (RRI, 11:1, Spring 1981, p. 76–81)

Investigation of 311 calypso lyrics for evidence of male-female conflict. Of the one-fourth found to deal with male-female relationships, nearly all were detrimental to women.

1041 Albuquerque, Klaus de. Rastafarianism and cultural identity in the Caribbean (RRI, 10:2, Summer 1980, p. 230–247, bibl.)

Contends that Rastafarian movement is supranational and that larger cultural identity is emerging which poses serious challenge to West Indian leaders. Discusses factors influencing spread of Rastafarianism in English-speaking Caribbean.

1042 Ashton, Gay T. The return and re-return of long-term Puerto Rican migrants: a selective rural-urban sample (RRI, 10:1, Spring 1980, p. 27–45, bibl., tables)

Based on responses to 399 bilingual interviews, presents assessment of reasons why long-term Puerto Rican migrants to the US return to the island, how they readapt to their native society, and why a substantial number plan to return to the mainland.

1043 Austin, Diane J. Born again . . . and again and again: *communitas* and social change among Jamaican Pentecostalists (UNM/JAR, 37:3, Fall 1981, p. 226–246, bibl.)

Examination of ritual in one Kingston Pentecostal church which, according to the author, demonstrates that the nature of *communitas* in this congregation is indicative of their subordinate social position and is not a force for social change. ". . . the history of religious *communitas* in Jamaica suggests that the symbolic power of religion to represent the situation of the oppressed, even in the most persuasive and revealing modes, cannot in itself be a source of social change. Rather, the fascination with representation that constant religious innovation reveals, merely underlines the continuing political subordination of a working class."

1044 Barros, Jacques. Quel destin linguistique pour Haiti? (Anthropologie et Sociétés [Université Laval, Départment d'Anthropologie, Québec, Canada] 6:2, 1982, p. 47–58, bibl.)

Raises important question of Haiti's linguistic destiny. Given reevaluation of status and role of Creole in school system, along with recent rise of interest in English as vehicle for work and mobility, author questions future role of French, not only for Haiti but for the Americas. Notes need to maintain "Haitianity" in light of past imperialism and neoimperialism of today evident in the gallicanization or Americanization of the society.

1045 Beck, Jane C. To windward of the land: the occult world of Alexander Charles. Bloomington: Indiana University Press, 1979. 309 p.: bibl., plates.

Interesting oral autobiography of St. Lucian fisherman, part-time smuggler, and practitioner of bush medicine and obeah. Vignettes of lower-class life in St. Lucia, the Dominican Republic, and Dominica.

1046 Bennett, Gordon; Audrey Colson; and Stuart Wavell. The damned: the plight of the Akawaio Indians of Guyana. London: Survival International, n.d. 12 p.: plates (Survival International Document; 6)

Sharp attack by anthropologist and lawyer on official Guyanese plan to construct a hydroelectric complex in the Upper Mazaruni district, a plan that would flood 1000 sq. miles of Akawaio land and displace that Amerindian population.

1047 Berleant-Schiller, Riva. Development proposals and small-scale fishing in the Caribbean (SAA/HO, 40:3, Fall 1981, p. 221–230, bibl.)

Uses contemporary Barbudan fishery to illustrate need for considering "effective environment" and local conditions before initiating plans for techno-economic change. Argues innovations can upset delicate working balance. While value to local diet and economy of small fisheries such as Barbuda's

is important so are needs and aspirations of new, emerging states. "How these differing development needs are to be reconciled and made mutually supportive is one of the critical problems in economic development."

1048 ———. Plantation society and the Caribbean present: history, anthropology and the plantation (Plantation Society in the Americas [T. Fiehrer, New Orleans] 1:3, Oct. 1981, p. 387–409)

Exploration of problem of understanding the Caribbean present and processes that formed it. Offers some goals for Caribbean research and assesses usefulness of plantation construct for achieving these goals. Considers what history and anthropology can contribute to devising of useful, interpretive categories and fresh perceptions and discusses implications for Caribbean studies.

1049 Berte, Nancy A. Peasant rationality: a K'eckchi' example (BISRA/BS, 10:5, 1982, p. 2–11)

Explores effects of modern economic incentives on traditional relations among K'eckchi' Maya of Belize. They continue with traditional system of relationships in milpa cultivation but have developed new, modern set of relationships in their cash cropping activities.

1050 Berthelot, Jack and Martine Gaumé. Kaz Antiyé jan moun ka rété = Caribbean popular dwelling. Traduction anglaise, Karen Bowie. Traduction créole, Robert Fontès, Jean-Pierre et Juliette Sainton. Paris: Editions caribéennes: Pointe-à-Pitre, Guadeloupe: Editions perspectives créoles, 1982. 167 p.: ill. (some col.)

Begins with discussion of several definitive influences in Caribbean architecture, in which the hut, result of African and European syncretism, was determined by type of colonization on each island. Authors show how this architecture in Martinique and Guadeloupe is intimately linked to way of life (e.g., domination, resistance, expression).

1051 Bilby, Kenneth M. Jamaica's Maroons at the crossroads: losing touch with tradition (FIU/CR, 9:4, Fall 1980, p. 18–21, 49)

General statement on Windward Maroons with emphasis on current identity crisis in Moore Town, where the young are losing touch with Maroon tradition.

1052 ———. The Kromanti dance of the

Windward Maroons of Jamaica (NWIG, 55:1/2, Aug. 1981, p. 52–101, bibl.)

Full description of the Kromanti dance complex as practiced by limited number of Maroons from Moore Town area. Discusses several aspects of ceremonial organization of complex in detail: outsiders and outside influence in dance, relationship of dance to Afro-Jamaican cults, and the dance and Maroon identity.

1053 The Black woman cross-culturally.
Edited by Filomina Chioma Steady. Cambridge, Mass.: Schenkman Publishing Co., Inc., 1981. 645 p.: bibl.

Collection of 30 articles on African, American, Caribbean, and South American black women: Nancie Solien González "Household and Family in the Caribbean: Some Definitions and Concepts" and "West Indian Characteristics of the Black Carib;" Joyce Bennett Justus "Women's Role in West Indian Society;" Kenneth Bilby and Filomina Chioma Steady "Black Women and Survival: a Maroon Case;" Constance Sutton and Susan Makiesky-Barrow "Social Inequality and Sexual Status in Barbados;" Yolanda T. Moses "Female Status, the Family, and Male Dominance in a West Indian Community;" and Sidney W. Mintz "Economic Role and Cultural Tradition."

1054 Bolland, O. Nigel. Labour control in post abolition Belize (BISRA/BS, 9, 1979, p. 21–35)

Well-argued paper deals with Belizean economic situation between 1830–70, systems of labor control, and consequences of labor-control system and changes in economy in the second half of 19th century. Concludes "transition was not from slavery to freedom, but rather, from one system of labour control to another and the old struggle between former masters and slaves continued, although in new forms."

1055 ——. Systems of domination after slavery: the control of land and labor in the British West Indies after 1838 (CSSH, 23:4, Oct. 1981, p. 591–619)

Within context of labor-control attempts after 1838, interrelationship of land and labor control, and usefulness of dialectical theory, author examines differing degrees of success with which masters controlled former slaves. Argues for abandonment of conceptual opposition to slavery and freedom in

favor of comparative study of transition from slave to wage labor.

1056 Brana-Shute, Gary. Mothers in uniform: the children's police of Suriname (UA, 10:1, Spring 1981, p. 71–88, bibl.)

Description of severely circumscribed police activities of all-female Children's Police (*Kinderpolitie*): "the subordinate and nurturant roles females play as *Kinderpolitie* in the police force of Suriname are . . . complementary to and, ultimately, supportive of the larger roles (and expectations) women play in other sectors and social fields."

1057 Brathwaite, Edward Kamau. Folk culture of the slaves in Jamaica. 2. ed. rev. London: New Beacon Books, 1981. 56 p.: bibl.

Revised essay (in author's book on Jamaica's Creole society) deals with African orientation of Jamaican folk culture in life cycle, religious ideas and practices, African matrix of Jamaican folk religion, music, entertainments, etc.

1058 Bregenzer, John. Tryin' to make it: adapting to the Bahamas. Washington: University Press of America, Inc., 1982. 88 p.: bibl., tables.

Short ethnography of human adaptation in Eleuthera, island that is not "insular," that is, not isolated or insulated from world pressures. One result of this exposure is the development of an Eleutheran "covert culture" that remains unchanged by outward circumstances.

1059 Brockmann, C. Thomas. Household composition and socioeconomic strategies in Orange Walk Town, Belize (BISRA/BS, 10:5, 1982, p. 12–21)

Nuclear family household is statistically predominant and normatively preferred type for all "ethnic" groups (European, Mestizo, Creole, Garifuna, Asian) and social strata that make up a small, district governmental, agricultural, and retailing center.

1060 *Caribbean Quarterly*. University of the West Indies. Vol. 26, No. 4, Dec. 1980- . Mona, Jamaica.

Special issue, celebrating 50th anniversary of Rastafari movement, contains six articles by "persons who share the vision of Rastafari" on: history; women; religion to social theory; speech patterns; Rastafarians in Eastern Caribbean; and West Indian culture through Rastafarian prism.

1061 Chevannes, Barry. The Rastafari and the urban youth (*in* Perspectives on Jamaica in the seventies. Edited by Carl Stone and Aggrey Brown. Kingston: Jamaica Publishing House, 1981, p. 392–422, tables)

After vivid descriptions of Rasta and Rasta-like youth in West Kingston, concludes that since early 1960s Jamaica witnessed "creation and maturing of a *lumpenproletariat* far more dangerous than the mere delinquent. Human life values no more than it takes to keep it alive from one meal to the next. The urban youth . . . is little concerned with the niceties and subtleties of Rastafari doctrine and ritual. Physical survival is more critical to him than doctrine."

1062 Collinwood, Walter. Terra incognita: research on modern Bahamian society (Journal of Caribbean Studies [Association of Caribbean Studies, Coral Gables, Fla.] 2:2/3, Autumn/Winter 1981, p. 284–297)

Argues "that the paucity of research specifically designed to explain and understand contemporary Bahamian society is largely due to willful ostracism of the Bahamas—based on highly tenuous irrelevant grounds—from the consciousness of the Caribbean social scientific community." Gives reasons why Bahamas deserve serious research.

1063 Counter, S. Allen and **David L. Evans.** I sought my brother: an Afro-American reunion. Cambridge: The Massachusetts Institute of Technology Press, 1981. 276 p.: plates.

Richly illustrated, personal account by two black Americans of their several visits to the Maroons of Suriname.

1064 Cultural traditions and Caribbean identity: the question of patrimony. Edited by S. Jeffrey K. Wilkerson. Gainesville: University of Florida, Center for Latin American Studies, 1980. 445 p.

Papers from 1978 conference on patrimony and cultural identity focus on contemporary perspectives on patrimony, syncretism of traditions from European contact to 19th century, and folk culture and identity. Definition of patrimony is complex, given Caribbean ethnic diversity, and no adequate understanding of contemporary perspectives is possible without examining syncretic cultural processes operating since precolumbian past and intensified during European contact. Contributions cover religion, language, vernacular, architecture, archaeology, etc.

1065 Dann, Graham M.S. Patterns of drinking in Barbados: the findings of a sample survey of adult residents. Bridgetown: The Cedar Press, 1980. 157 p.: bibl., tables.

Results of survey taken in 1979 on attitudinal and behavioral patterns toward drinking alcohol.

1066 Danns, George K. Domination and power in Guyana: a study of the police in a Third World context. New Brunswick, N.J.: Transaction Books, 1982. 193 p.: bibl., figures, tables.

Valuable, ground-breaking study of Guyana's police, based on participant-observation, sample survey, interviews, archival research, and newspaper analysis. Author concludes that police have "to be understood as an integral sector of a formidable array of military institutions engaged in the 'administrative politics' of public institutional rivalry, politicized and penetrated by a dominant one party system and caught up in an orgy of loyalty to the political directorate that creatively destroys their conventional professionalism and organizational texture."

1067 Dobal, Carlos. Herencia española en la cultura dominicana de hoy (EME, 8:43, julio/agosto 1979, p. 67–107, bibl.)

Argues the considerable impact of Spain, in terms of social institutions, culture, personality, and individuals, on the development of contemporary Dominican culture. Useful bibliography.

1068 Dobbin, Jay D. The *Jombee* dance: friendship and ritual in Montserrat (Caribbean Review [Florida International University, Miami] 10:4, Fall 1981, p. 28–31, 51)

Description of Montserrat's *jombee* dance. In island's folk religion *jombees* are identified with the dead. Using Victor Turner's insights, author interprets ritual as social drama. Although dance focuses on afflictions and illnesses of one individual, these crises are not seen as purely personal and private but as focal points of intricate webs of relationships and histories, and as solutions sought to here-and-now problems.

1069 Dodd, David J. A day in Babylon: street life in Guyana (FIU/CR, 10:4, Fall 1981, p. 24–27, 50)

Excerpt from ethnographic and historical study of culture and social structure of Georgetown's black protoproletariat. Describes street-corner life of Babylon people (i.e., "lower class" in Guyana) in Georgetown's environs.

1070 Dreher, Melanie Creagan. Marihuana and work: cannabis smoking on a Jamaican sugar estate (SAA/HO, 42:1, Spring 1983, p. 1–8, bibl., table)

Systematic exploration of divergent claims about effect of marihuana use on work performance in Jamaica. Bases analysis on data generated from estate payroll tabulations and from observations of different managerial strategies or styles on three sugar estate farms.

1071 ———. Working men and ganja: marihuana use in rural Jamaica. Philadelphia: Institute for the Study of Human Issues, 1982. 216 p.: bibl., tables.

Major study of marihuana-linked behavior and variations in marihuana use in three rural communities.Author argues that *ganja* use at community level is dependent on local socioeconomic factors, explores relationship of level of *ganja* use to position in the local stratification systems. Dissects contrasting claims about relationship of *ganja* to work performance by comparing ganja-using and nonusing sugar cane cutters.

1072 Dressler, William W. Hypertension and culture change: acculturation and disease in the West Indies. South Salem, N.Y.: Redgrave Publishing Co., 1982. 158 p.: bibl., tables.

Study of hypertension in Soufrière, St. Lucia. Deals with sociocultural factors in disease's development (changing life styles; mating; family structure; psychological factors; etc.) and in response to it (Western medical system; ethnomedical beliefs; behaviors; stress; etc.). Emphasizes how changing socioeconomic environment affects health.

1073 Edwards, W. and **K. Gibson.** An ethnohistory of Amerindians in Guyana (ASE/E, 26:2, Spring 1979, p. 161–175, bibl.)

Using available sources, presents historical account of Amerindian tribal migra-

tion into Guyana. They posit that the Warran arrived first, when still "marginals," followed by Arawaks from Orinoco-Río Negro area, and then by Carib from Xingú-Tapajoz area.

1074 Ehrlich, Allen S. The interplay of rice and cane: East Indians in rural Jamaica (*in* East Indians in the Caribbean: colonialism and the struggle for identity. Millwood, N.Y.: Kraus International Publications, 1982, p. 141–157, bibl., tables)

In the past, East Indians in Westmoreland derived a comfortable existence from the cultivation of two crops—sugar cane and rice. In cane cultivation they sold labor outright to estates, while in rice cultivation they labored for themselves. Forced conversion of rice lands to cane led to breakdown of dual crop pattern and to proletarianizing of population.

1075 Fontaine, Pierre-Michel. Language, society and development: dialectic of French and Creole use in Haiti (LAP, 8:1, Winter 1981, p. 28–46, bibl.)

Exploration of profoundly social and political nature of linguistic problem in Haiti views it primarily as manifestation of imperial or neoimperial domination and thus linked to class, political power, and social status. Discusses how domination is manifested in relationship between French and Creole.

1076 Foster, Byron. Body, social and social structure at the Garifuna *dugu* (BISRA/BS, 9:4, July 1981, p. 1–11)

Deals with meaning and socioeconomic aspects of *dugu*, the ultimate rite of a sequence related to Garifuna ancestors.

1077 ———. Spirit possession in southern Belize (BISRA/BS, 10:2, 1982, p. 18–23)

Functional explanation of women's behavior under possession during *dugu* (Garifuna curing rite). At *dugu*, a female, possessed by ancestors, is able to extract cash from close male kin. *Dugu* ritual helps women make matrifocality and consanguineal household viable institutions.

1078 Fouchard, Jean. The Haitian Maroons: liberty or death. New York: Edward W. Blyden Press, 1981. 386 p.

English translation of rich, massively detailed 1972 French publication on Haitian Maroons and maroonage, based on materials culled from Saint-Domingue newspapers. C.L.R. James' preface claims that author "establishes that the Haitian nation, the result of the only successful slave revolt in history, was formed, organized and maintained by the Maroons, the slaves who had run away from the slave society organized by the Metropolitan forces and made a place for themselves in the inaccessible hills."

1079 Fredrich, Barbara E. Research note: a prospective St. Lucian folk medicine survey (Social Science and Medicine [New York] 15D:4, Nov. 1981, p. 435–437, table)

Reports steps being taken to preserve and further document St. Lucian medicinal plant usage through a program sponsored by the Folk Research Centre on the island and author's own field research.

1080 Guanche, Jesús. Hacia un enfoque sistémico de la cultura cubana (RYC, 90, feb. 1980, p. 35–40, table)

Utilizing concept of *ethnos* as developed by Yu. Bromlei and other Soviet ethnographers, author sketches formation or ethnogenesis of Cuban ethnocultural system from 1511 (beginning of the Spanish conquest) to 1868 when first "anticolonial" war of independence began. Indicates following ethnic processes and chronology: forced interethnic assimilation *iberoaborigen* (1511–1650); interethnic integration *iberica* (1511–1790); natural interethnic assimilation *abroaborigen* (1515–1650); interethnic integration *interafricana* (1515–1868); the interethnic integration *hispano-africano* (1515–1868); natural interethnic assimilation *canarioaborigen* (1550–1650); interethnic integration (*canariohispano-africana* (1550–1868); natural interethnic assimilation *crïollohispanofrancesa* (1790–1868); interethnic integration *franco-haitianoafricana* (1790–1868); and natural interethnic assimilation *criollohispanoafro-asiática* (1847–68).

1081 Handler, Jerome S. Slave revolts and conspiracies in seventeenth-century Barbados (NWIG, 56:1/2, 1982, p. 5–42, bibl.)

Description of important "incidents of collective slave resistance, or group actions or intentions of violence, against white authority during the formative years of Barbadian slave society." Also deals with white response to incidents and legislation they engendered.

1082 Helms, Mary W. Black Carib domestic organization in historical perspective: traditional origins of contemporary patterns (UP/E, 20:1, Jan. 1981, p. 77–86, bibl.)

On basis of ethnohistorical data, author argues that contemporary Black Carib domestic organization shows strong structural similarities not only with earlier Black Carib but also with Island Carib domestic arrangements as recorded in the mid-17th century. Suggests that contemporary format may be viewed not only as an adaptation to marginal involvement with modern industrial economy but also as traditional Carib marital and residential patterns in modern form.

1083 Henningsgaard, William. The Akawaio, the Upper Mazaruni hydroelectric project and national development in Guyana. Cambridge, Mass.: Cultural Survival, Inc. 1981. 37 p. (Occasional paper; 4)

Presents data that raises fundamental questions about social and environmental consequences of projected hydroelectric complex.

1084 Hilhouse, William. Indian notices: or, Sketches of the habits, characters, languages, superstitions, soil, and climate of the several nations; with remarks on their capacity for colonization, present government and suggestions for future improvement and civilization. Also the ic[h]thyology of the fresh waters of the interior. New ed. with an introd. and supplementary notes by M.N. Menezes. Georgetown: National Commission for Research Materials on Guyana, 1978. 153 p.

Reprint of interesting and useful 1825 publication of English advocate of British Guiana's Amerindians. Dubbed "pioneer scientist explorer who blazed the trail into the interior of Guiana," Hilhouse was a participant observer, amateur ethnographer, and applied scientist as well as a severe critic of colonial policy towards and administration of the Amerindian populations.

1085 Hill, Robert. Leonard P. Howell and the millenarian visions in early Rastafari (IJ/JJ, 16:1, Feb. 1983, p. 24–39, plates)

Sketch of emergence of millenarian visions in early Rastafari religion and Howell's role in context of Jamaican peasant origins of this millenarian impetus.

1086 Hoetink, H. The Dominican people 1850–1900: notes for a historical sociology. Baltimore: Johns Hopkins University Press, 1982. 243 p.: bibl., plates.

Welcome English translation of author's *El pueblo dominicano 1850–1900* (see *HLAS 31:1337*). Deals with critical social changes during first half century of Dominican Republic. "Beginning with an exposition of the changes in the agrarian and demographic structures, I compiled sufficient material through examination of the country's economic, political, and educational organization to be able to make a provisional analysis of social stratification, concluding the study with a description of the cultural 'superstructure' and of family life."

1087 Hurault, Jean. Analyse comparative d'ouvrages sur les noir réfugiés de Guyane: Saramaka et Aluku, Boni (L'Homme [Revue Française d'Anthropologie, La Sorbonne, Paris] 20:2, avril/juin 1980, p. 119–127)

A response, in part, to criticism raised by A.J.F. Köbben and R. Price of the author's work on the Aluku. Beginning with a summary of Price's analysis of Saramaka social structure and a re-examination of his own observations on the Aluku, author argues that his findings are not incompatible with those of his critics since, he claims, the societies each person studied are at different levels of evolution. Author posits that no society can maintain its structure indefinitely and disagrees with Price's explanation for matrilineality and uxorilocality among Maroons as a result of the competition for women. For the author, these developments are best understood in light of changes in the economic system and the emergence of a monetary economy. The study of the survival of African institutions, he argues, has hindered a full understanding of Maroons by ignoring the effect of environmental constraints such as population density and competition for natural resources.

1088 Jackson, Peter. A transactional approach to Puerto Rican culture (RRI, 11:1, Spring 1981, p. 53–68, bibl.)

Application of transactional perspective which emphasizes negotiable qualities of transactions to concept of Puerto Rican culture in N.Y.

1089 Jiménez Lambertus, Aberlardo. Aspectos históricos y psicológicos del culto a los luases en República Dominicana (MHD/B, 9:15, 1980, p. 171–182)

Part of results of medical/psychiatric team on historical and psychological aspects of voodoo in the Dominican Republic. Deals briefly with questions of origin, semantics, authenticating possession, process of ritual possession, identification of future *caballos*, apprenticeship and the process of becoming a *caballo*.

1090 Jones, Grant. Mayas, Yucatecans and Englishmen in the nineteenth century fiesta system of Northern Belize (BISRA/BS, 10:3/4, 1982, p. 25–42)

Description and analysis of fiesta held in Xaibe in 1865 and extraordinary court trial it generated. Events took place after arrival of Mayan and Yucatecan refugees from Caste War. Contends fiesta was ritualized reflection of class differences that characterized Yucatan and refugees' own society.

1091 Jones, Howard. Crime, race and culture: a study in a developing country. Chichester: John Wiley and Sons, 1981. 184 p.: bibl., tables.

Interesting study based on quantitative data, explores implications of pluralism (East Indian, Afro-Guyanese split), underdevelopment, demography, stratification, family, and unemployment on nonpolitical crime in Guyana.

1092 Kempeneers, Marianne and Raymond Masse. Les migrants antillaises: bibliographie sélective et annotée. Montréal: Université de Montréal, Centre de Recherches Caraïbes, 1981. 55 p.

Selected and annotated bibliography of Antillean migration, grouped according to principal immigration and emigration zones: Quebec (Canada), US, Europe (Great Britain and France).

1093 Kerns, Virginia. Women and the ancestors: Black Carib kinship and ritual. Urbana: University of Illinois Press, 1983. 229 p., 24 p. of plates: bibl., ill., index.

Substantial study of how older Black Carib mothers and grandmothers "perpetuate the primary makers of Black Carib culture:

music, dance, supernatural knowledge and a system of morality and exchange that centers on obligations to lineal kin." Covers historic antecedents, national setting, property ownership and exchange, interpersonal conflict, age and gender, household and family organization, and rituals for the dead.

1094 Kopytoff, Barbara Klamon. Colonial treaty as sacred charter of the Jamaican Maroons (ASE/E, 26:1, Winter 1979, p. 45–64, bibl.)

Treaties of 1739, signed by Jamaican Maroons and British, were and continue to be viewed differently by both sides. Suggests "that since it is impossible for either side [the present-day Jamaican government succeeds the English in the relationship] to accept the other's point of view or to give up its own, any settlement that is made (barring the destruction of the Maroon corporate communities) must rest on practical adjustments. And one of these adjustments must, in fact, be to obscure the principles behind the adjustments, or at least not to insist on agreement on the principles."

1095 LaFleur, Gérard. Bouillante: l'histoire et les hommes (SHG/B, 53/54:3/4, 1982, p. 35–47, bibl., map)

Short history of rural district Bouillante on west coast of Basse-Terre, Guadeloupe, from 17th century to beginning of the 20th. Includes origin of place names, demographic settlement, types of cultivation, and geographical-climatic constraints affecting region.

1096 Laguerre, Michel S. The complete Haitiana: a bibliographic guide to the scholarly literature 1900–1980. Millwood, N.Y.: KTO Press, 1982. 2 v. (1562 p., continuous pagination)

Welcome resource for the specialist on Haiti and for Caribbeanists in general, this two-volume guide to the literature, organized from an anthropologist's perspective, contains citations of all important publications relating to 20th-century Haiti. Divided into 65 subject chapters and extensively cross-referenced, work includes English translations of French titles as well as author index and code to libraries (for locating each citation). Major sections: introduction to Haiti; ecological setting; history of Haiti; population studies; Haitian culture; structure of

Haitian society; health and medicine; educational system; political and legal processes; socioeconomic system; and rural and urban development (for bibliographer's comment, see item 2).

1097 Layng, Anthony. The Carib reserve: identity and security in the West Indies. Washington: University Press of American, Inc., 1983. 177 p.: bibl., plates, tables.

Based on 1974–75 field research, author deals with following aspects of Dominica Carib reality: history of the reserve, demography, social structure, religion, education, economic resources and strategies, relationship to outsiders, and Carib identity.

1098 ———. Ethnic identity, population growth, and economic security on a West Indian reservation (RRI, 9:4, Winter 1979/1980, p. 577–584, bibl.)

Examines ethnic boundary-maintaining behavior of rapidly expanding Carib Reserve population in Dominica and identifies some economic consequences of this behavior. Carib reluctance to endorse government attempts to terminate their reservation is not viewed as outgrowth of Carib identity but as strategy to perpetuate their peculiar land tenure system and hence provide economic security.

1099 Levine, Robert M. Race and ethnic relations in Latin America and the Caribbean: an historical dictionary and bibliography. Metuchen, N.J.: Scarecrow Press, 1980. 252 p.: index.

Dictionary of terms, names, and events linked to racial and ethnic questions (relatively good coverage of Caribbean) accompanied by unannotated bibliography of 1,342 books and articles. Useful as a general work but lacks clearly stated selection criteria.

1100 Lieber, Michael. Streetlife: Afro-American culture in urban Trinidad. Cambridge, Mass.: Schenkman Publishing Co., 1981. 119 p.

Ethnographic account, based on observations collected in 1969 and 1970–71, of urban lifestyles in Port-of-Spain. Offers "naturalistic" vignettes of capital city; various styles and adaptations to "depressed urban setting;" and commentaries on how work, class, and ethnicity affect poor black males.

1100a Manning, Frank E. Celebrating cricket: the symbolic construction of Caribbean politics (AES/AE, 8:3, Aug. 1981, p. 616–632, bibl.)

Argues that cricket festivals in Bermuda, major public celebrations, and gambling, an important ancillary activity, "symbolically depict both a reflexive, assertive sense of black culture and a stark awareness of black economic dependency on whites—a dramatic tension that is also the semantic context of Bermudian politics." Useful descriptions and interesting analyses.

1100b ———. Risk taking in the stock market: gambling and politics in Bermuda (FIU/CR, 11:4, Fall 1982, p. 20–21, 45–47)

More than a gambling casino and a festive display of black style, the "stock market" in Bermuda is a kind of political theater which reveals much about the ordering of Caribbean society, notably the distribution of wealth and power.

1101 Mars, Perry. Race and class as determinants in the political process of the Caribbean: some methodological issues (RRI, 10:4, Winter 1980/1981, p. 507–526, tables)

Discusses inadequacies of both "plural society" and "social stratification" models and concludes that, with respect to understanding fundamental change and political behavior in the region, Marxist class analysis is both relevant and crucial but the relative importance of racial factors cannot be ignored in the explanation of change.

1102 Masse, Raymond. La fin des plantations? évolution des formes de soumission du travail dans deux sociétés néo-coloniales: Martinique et Guadeloupe. Montréal, Canada: Université de Montréal, Centre de recherches caraïbes, Fonds Saint-Jacques, Sainte-Marie, Martinique, 1980. 150 p.: bibl., tables.

Analysis of the structural changes in the 20th century which contributed to Guadeloupean and Martinican societies passing from colonial plantation societies, based largely on production for export, to neo-colonial peripheral societies of consumption with a focus on the evolution of the small agrarian farmer. Thesis is that agricultural peasantry is foundation on which urban, commercial, and civil servant sectors have developed on both islands.

1103 Menezes, Mary Noel. From protection to integration: the Amerindians of Guyana vis-à-vis the government, 1803–1973 (in Caribbean societies. London: University of London, Institute of Commonwealth Studies, 1982, v. 1, p. 93–112, bibl. [Collected seminar papers; no. 29])

Informative short review and analysis of colonial and postcolonial Guyanese policies toward the Amerindian population.

1104 Moretti C. and P. Grenand. Les *Nivrées* ou plantes ichtyotoxiques de la Guyane française (Journal of Ethnopharmacology [Elsevier Sequoia, Lausanne, Switzerland] 6:2, Sept. 1982, p. 139–160, bibl., ill., map)

Article on taxonomy, biogeography, and ethnobotany of fishing poisons of French Guiana and adjacent territories, and significance of those poisons on the forest economy of tropical America. For each drug the vernacular names and synonyms still used are given, as well as the most notable morphological characteristics, ethnological observations, and active constituents, when known.

1105 Myers, Robert A. Amerindians of the Lesser Antilles: a bibliography. New Haven, Conn.: Human Relations Area Files, Inc., 1981. 158 p. (HRAFlex books; ST1-001. Bibliography series)

Excellent bibliography on complex topic of island Amerindians divided into: 1) archaeology and prehistory; 2) archives, history, travel and description, and social science research; 3) languages; 4) biology, nutrition, and medicine; and 5) literature. Includes geographic and author indexes.

1106 ———. Post-emancipation migrations and population change in Dominica: 1834–1950 (RRI, 11:1, Spring 1981, p. 87–109, bibl., tables)

Useful description of population composition and shifts through chronological (post-emancipation period, 1870–90 move to Venezuelan gold fields, and 20th century) review of significant migrations in and out of the island and their socioeconomic contexts.

1107 Nevadomsky, Joseph. Changing conceptions of family regulation among the Hindu East Indians in rural Trinidad (CUA/AQ, 55:4, Oct. 1982, p. 189–198, bibl.)

Utilizing data generated 1972–73 on Hindu East Indian community first studied by Morton Klass in 1950s, author argues that socioeconomic conditions are critical in determining strategies of family formation.

1108 ———. Cultural and structural dimensions of occupational prestige in an East Indian community in Trinidad (UNM/JAR, 37:4, Winter 1981, p. 343–359, bibl.)

Social and economic change in an East Indian community led to "lengthening of the status hierarchy." New possibilities for urban and white-collar employment changed the community's social structure but did not transform the cognitive bases of social differentiation.

1109 ———. Economic organization, social mobility, and changing social status among East Indians in rural Trinidad (UP/E, 22:1, Jan. 1983, p. 63–79, bibl., tables)

Based on field research, author contends that rural East Indian economy has been structurally transformed, and new occupational patterns are linked to formal education and mobility into nonagricultural work.

1110 Olwig, Karen Fog. Finding a place for the slave family: historical anthropological perspectives (DEF/F, 23, 1981, p. 345–348, bibl.)

Contends that research on history of the Afro-American family has suffered from undue concentration on reconstituting family units. Given nature of available evidence, recommends delineating Afro-American social systems, one aspect of which involves the family. Using historical data from St. John, V.I., author concludes that slave family life did not revolve around the household or nuclear family but was based on network of relationships involving various consanguineal kin and spouses.

1111 ———. Women, "matrifocality" and systems of exchange: an ethnohistorical study of the Afro-American family on St. John, Danish West Indies (ASE/E, 28:1, Winter 1981, p. 59–78, bibl.)

Questions usefulness of concept of "matrifocality" by examining position of St. John's Afro-American women over 260-year period. Uses Engels' concept of social reproduction to examine women's role as agents

of production and reproduction in social economic units.

1112 Owen, Nancy H. Witchcraft in the West Indies: the anthropologist as victim (Anthropology and Humanism Quarterly [Society for Humanistic Anthropology, Tallahassee, Fla.] 6:2/3, June/Sept. 1981, p. 15–22)

Short account of personal encounter with witchcraft on the Carib Reserve in Dominica. Discusses implications for training field researchers.

1113 Oxaal, Ivar. Black intellectuals and the dilemmas of race and class in Trinidad. Cambridge, Mass.: Schenkman Publishing Co., 1982. 317 p.: plates.

Welcome reprint edition of author's two works: *Black intellectuals come to power* (1968) and *Race and revolutionary consciousness* (1971), with very short epilogue on final years of Eric Williams era (1971–81).

1114 Perspectives on Pentecostalism: case studies from the Caribbean and Latin America. Edited by Stephen D. Glazier. Washington: University Press of America, Inc., 1980. 197 p.

Volume on American Anthropological Association 1977 meeting session on growth of Pentecostalism consists of following papers of interest to Caribbeanists: Frederick J. Conway "Pentecostalism in Haiti: Healing and Hierarchy;" William Wedenoja "Modernization and the Pentecostal Movement in Jamaica;" Anthony L. LaRuffa "Pentecostalism in Puerto Rican Society;" Stephen D. Glazier "Pentecostal Exorcism and Modernization in Trinidad, West Indies;" Donna Birdwell-Pheasant "The Power of Pentecostalism in a Belizean Village;" and Thomas J. Chordas "Catholic Pentecostalism: a New Word in a New World."

1115 Pimenov, Vladimir. Cuba vista por etnógrafos (URSS/AL, 2[50], 1982, 5–120, ill.)

Report of Cuban-Soviet ethnographic team that worked in Matangas Province, Cuba, for a seven-week period in 1980. Expedition is seen as trial run for major Cuban-Soviet collaborative effort to produce an ethnographic atlas of Cuba. Target date is 1990. Short section on types of inhabited locations, housing, traditional instruments of work, dress, and other aspects of material culture.

1116 Pollak-Eltz, Angelina. Magico-religious movements and social change in Venezuela (Journal of Caribbean Studies [Association of Caribbean Studies, Coral Gables, Fla.] 2:2/3, Autumn/Winter 1981, p. 162–180)

"Social and economic changes foster the expansion of religious movements, as people search new resources to solve their problems, but at the same time these movements also may foster change, as may be seen in the religion." Deals with folk-Catholicism, the magico-religious movements (including Pentecostalism, spiritism, santería, cult of José Gregório Hernández, cult of María Lionza), and relationship of spirit cults to politics.

1117 ———. Magische operationen und ihre wirkung in Venezuela (Ethnomed [In Kommission H. Buske Verlag, Hamburg, FRG] 7:1/4, 1981/1982, p. 117–126)

Deals with magical operations performed by Venezuelan folk healers who receive spirit of a deceased doctor. Patient is touched by surgical instrument but not cut. Such operations are successful in cases of psychosomatic illness, hysterical blindness, etc.

1118 ———. Regards sur les cultures d'origine africaine au Vénézuela. Montréal, Canada: Université de Montréal, Centre de Recherches Caraïbes, Fonds Saint-Jacques, Sainte-Marie, Martinique, 1977. 54 p.: bibl.

Review of author's publications on diverse aspects of Afro-Venezuelan ethnography and sociology during 12 years of study among the coast's black populations. In spite of mixing, these people have conserved much of their heritage, as well as being influenced by other Afro-Caribbean groups. Topics include: history of slavery in Venezuela, structure and function of family, religion, and cultural forms.

1119 ———. Socialization of children among Afro-Venezuelans (UN/ISSJ, 31:3, 1979, p. 470–476)

General description of Afro-Venezuelan socialization process. Mother is household's primary parental socializer, father plays only marginal role.

1120 Pourraz, Robert. Le puzzle ethnique de la Guyane Française (CJN, 239, mai 1982, p. 7–10, graphs, ill., map)

Missionary priest, author discusses growing ethnic diversity in French Guiana, characterized by a history of immigration from all parts of the world— Latin America, Caribbean, Africa, Asia, Middle East. In spite of French Guiana's size, its population remains small, concentrated in urban area of Cayenne.

1121 Pozzi, Enrico. Sécularisation et déboires du Sacré: le suicide collectif de Jonestown (FS/CIS, 72, jan./juin 1982, p. 131–143)

Author applies Durkeimian analysis to People's Temple of Jonestown, Guyana: "Constituting a pseudo-cohesive group, that introduced within itself the very 'anomie' it sought to abolish. This situation, combined with intense millenary religiosity and loudly proclaimed secularism, led to a sacralization of the social, an autoconsecration of the group where the individual was annihilated and where ultimate collective suicide became an irrefutable demonstration of a totality without fault."

1122 *Présence Africaine.* Nos. 121/122, 1er./2d. trimestre 1982- . Paris.

Special issue (447 p.) devoted to French Antillean society and culture (Guadeloupe, Martinique, French Guiana) presents panorama of cultural research by more than 70 writers. Traces growing articulation of Antillean identity by examining folktales, literature, especially Creole, music, etc.

1123 Price, Sally. When is a calabash not a calabash? (NWIG, 56:1/2, 1982, p. 69–82, bibl.)

According to author, incorrect interchangeability of terms *calabash* and *gourd* by speakers of European languages has led to confusion in ethnographic literature. In elegant exposition, she differentiates both plants indicating scientific value of such distinction for understanding links between African and Afro-American *calabash* arts.

1124 ——— and **Richard Price.** Afro-American arts of the Suriname rain forest. Los Angeles: University of California, Museum of Cultural History, 1980. 235 p.: bibl., plates.

Handsomely illustrated book associated with Maroon art exhibition organized by the Museum of Cultural History. Authors deal expertly with art and aesthetics in Maroon life, personal adornment, woodcarving, *calabashes*, performance, iconography, and problems of continuity-in-change.

1125 —— and ——. Art of the rain forest (AMNH/NH, 90:9, Sept. 1981, p. 54–63, ill.)

General article on art of Suriname's Maroons, its role in their social life and institutions. Discusses development of Maroon artistry not as direct transmission of African forms from one generation to next but as continuity of aesthetic ideas.

1126 —— and ——. Exotica and commodity: the arts of the Suriname Maroons (FIU/CR, 9:4, Fall 1980, p. 13–17, 47, plates)

"Maroon women have consistently fought, not for higher prices, but for the right of possession, and the right to define the meaning and value of a particular object in their own way, and they have generally lost."

1127 Return migration and remittances: developing a Caribbean perspective. Edited by William F. Stinner, Klaus de Albuquerque, and Roy S. Bryce-Laporte. Washington: Research Institute on Immigration and Ethnic Studies, Smithsonian Institution, 1982. 322 p.: bibl. (RIIES occasional papers; no. 3)

Timely collection of 12 articles, drawn from three conferences. Papers on return migration focus on English-speaking Caribbean (H. Rubenstein), Leeward Caribbean (B. Richardson), East Indians to India (B. Samaroo), Dominican Republic (A. Ugalde and T.C. Langham), Costa Rica and El Salvador (G. Poitras), Puerto Rico (R.A. Johnson and B.B. Levine), and Suriname (Bovenkerk). Papers on remittances focus on rural English-speaking Caribbean (H. Rubenstein), eastern Caribbean (R. Brana-Shute and G. Brana-Shute) and Caribbean cane cutters in Florida (C.H. Wood). Separate bibliographies on each topic.

1128 Richardson, Bonham C. Caribbean migrants: environment and human survival and St. Kitts and Nevis. Knoxville: The University of Tennessee Press, 1983. 207 p.: bibl., ill., plates.

Useful historical geography of human migration from St. Kitts and Nevis stresses how African-descended population dealt with environmental and human-induced problems. Details historical and environmental factors affecting migration in Commonwealth Caribbean, and evolution of contemporary migration cultures over four different time periods (slavery, postslavery, intra-Caribbean movement, and the metropoles).

1129 Rivière, P.G. A report on the Trio Indians of Surinam (NWIG, 55:1/2, Aug. 1981, p. 1–38, bibl., plates)

Abbreviated version of report prepared for Surinam government based on 1978 fieldwork. Deals with external influences on Trio (Bush Negroes, coastal people, officials, etc.), and Trio society and culture (demography, economic organization, etc.). Concludes Trio have not changed significantly but have successfully adapted to change.

1130 Roo Lemos, Noëlle de. Les derniers potières de Sainte-Anne, Martinique. Montréal, Canada: Université de Montréal, Centre de recherches caraïbes, Fonds Saint-Jacques, Sainte-Marie, Martinique, 1979. 75 p.: bibl., glossary, plates.

Author describes precolumbian ceramic-making in Sainte-Anne, Martinique, one of few areas left in Antilles where it is still made by women. Detailed, illustrated description, placed in socioeconomic context. Examines possible continuity between prehistoric Carib ceramic complex and contemporary patterns in light of double problem of origins and survival.

1131 Sanz, Ileana. Características del proceso de transculturación en Jamaica (UH/U, 212, enero/dic. 1980, p. 15–24, bibl., ill.)

Uses Fernando Ortiz' concept of transculturation to sketch this process in Jamaica with brief notes on religion, dance, etc., during colonization and slavery, when island's English culture was homogeneous and African culture heterogeneous, and during postemancipation period, when English culture was major presence and direct influence. Notes consolidation of Jamaican national culture.

1132 Schnakenbourg, Christian. Note sur l'histoire de l'usine du Galion: Martinique, 1865–1939. Montréal, Canada: Université de Montréal, Centre de recherches caraïbes, Fonds Saint-Jacques, Sainte-Marie, Martinique, n.d. 27 p.: graphs, tables (Collection de reimpression; 7)

Study of history of Galion sugar factory discusses most significant features of and periods in its origins and evolution. Galion is important being one of last two factories still active on the island and only one belonging to metropolitan family (thus accounting for its archives in Paris).

1133 ———. Recherches sur l'histoire de l'industrie sucrière à Marie-Galante, 1664–1964 (SHG/B, 48/50:2/4, 1981, p. 3–144, appendix, bibl., tables)

Contends that importance of Marie-Galante's sugar industry in Guadeloupe's economic history has long been neglected. Lengthy and detailed article traces character and difficulties of this industry. Its 300-year history is divided into two periods (1664–1902, 1845-present) corresponding to distinct systems of production and types of social relations generated by each—family estates and centralized factories.

1134 Serbin, Andrés. Nacionalismo, etnicidad y política en la República Cooperativa de Guyana. Caracas: Editorial Bruguera Venezolana S.A., 1982? 276 p.: bibl., plates, tables.

From somewhat Marxist perspective, author offers analysis of Guyanese nationalism, ethnicity, and politics. Provides descriptions of social context; ethnic groups and ideologies; areas of ethnic socialization; ideological apparatus of the state (education and mass communication) and their control; interethnic relations; and interplay of politics, ethnicity, and national ideology.

1135 Sertima, Ivan van. The voodoo gallery: African presence in the ritual and art of Haiti (Journal of African Civilizations [Rutgers University, Douglass College, New Brunswick, N.J.] 3:2, Nov. 1981, p. 78–104, plates)

Author relates Haitian art to voodoo ritual and belief, examines voodoo's function as a revolutionary force or dynamic in Haitian history, and indicates differences and discontinuities between Haitian voodoo and the Dahomean cult.

1136 Silverman, Marilyn. Rich people and rice: factional politics in rural Guyana. Leiden: E.J. Brill, 1980. 240 p.: bibl., diagrams, maps, tables.

Considerable and detailed contribution to the study of factional politics and economic change of East Indians in the Caribbean based on 1969–70 field research in village of West Berbice.

1137 Staiano, Kathryn V. Alternative therapeutic systems in Belize: a semiotic framework (Social Science and Medicine [Pergamon Press?, Oxford, N.Y.] 15B:3, July 1981, p. 317–332, bibl.)

Pt. 1 deals with sociomedical system in Punta Gorda, Toledo District, with special emphasis on practices of Garifuna and with possible functions of alternative therapeutic systems. Pt. 2 presents semiotic approach to analysis of illness episodes.

1138 Thoden van Velzen, H.U.E. and W. van Wetering. Female religious responses to male prosperity in turn-of-the-century Bush Negro societies (NWIG, 56:1/2, 1982, p. 43–68, bibl.)

Males left tribal areas for relatively lucrative work in burgeoning national economy, disrupting sexual division of labor in traditional subsistence economy. Describes new religious movements of the time and notes relationship of specific movements to female religious responses or strategies to male affluence and distancing.

1139 Tobias, Peter M. The socioeconomic context of Grenadian smuggling (UNM/JAR, 38:4, Winter 1982, p. 383–400, bibl.)

Description of smuggling of taxable consumer goods into Grenada based on research in 1973–74. Includes smuggling pattern developed by these lower-class men, rough estimates of people involved, financial dimensions of the illegal trade, and process by which some smugglers become successful and gain reputations.

1140 van den Bor, Wout. Island adrift: the social organization of a small Caribbean community; the case of St. Eustatius. The Hague: Royal Institute of Linguistics and Anthropology, Department of Caribbean Studies, 1981. 439 p.: bibl., figures, tables.

Probably first full-length anthropologi-

cal study of this small unit of the Netherlands Antilles. Author deals with island's
history, economy, and social organization
with detailed sections on political relationships (patronage and two-party system); religious relationships; family and household;
and primary relationships (youth, adults, elderly, etc.). Conclusions concern psychological effects of the island's dependence on the
outside for socioeconomic development.

1141 Vernon, Diane. Bakuu: possessing spirits of witchcraft on the Tapanahony
(NWIG, 54:1, Feb. 1980, p. 1–38, bibl., ill.)
Reports on type of possessing spirits
called *Bakuu* which by 1978 became important among the Djuka of Tabiki village.
Bakuu phenomenon appear as visions in the
night, as interpretation of illness and death,
as witch accusation, and as spirit possession.
Includes detailed example of *Bakuu* inspired
social drama.

1142 Waal Malefijt, Annemarie de. From
wajang kulit to rock-and-roll in
Surinam (RRI, 10:3, Fall 1980, p. 391–397,
bibl.)
Argues that equivocations and "multi-
vocality" are prerequisites for survival of
meaningful symbol systems. If ambiguities
vanish and meanings become static, symbols
lose their power to adjust to changing social
situations. Analysis of *wajang kulit* (puppet
play), in Surinam's Javanese society, illustrates point.

1143 Warner, Keith Q. Kaiso! the Trinidad
calypso: a study of the calypso as oral
literature. Washington: Three Continents
Press, 1982. 153 p.: bibl., plates.
Informative book for anthropologist
covers evolution and language of calypso,
male/female interplay, humor and fantasy
in calypso, and impact of this art form on
Trinidadian literature.

1144 Wells, Marilyn McK. Spirits see red:
the symbolic use of *gusueue* among
the Garif (Black Caribs) of Central America
(BISRA/BS, 10:3/4, 1982, p. 10–16, bibl.)
Describes use of *gusueue* (deep red
powder derived from the *Bixa orellana*) by
Belizean and Honduran Garifs and analyzes
its ritual. While *gusueue* remains a dominant
symbol in Garif ritual, its usage has been
modified in respone to different and varying
social environments.

**1145 Weniger, B.; M. Haag-Berrurier; and R.
Anton.** Plants of Haiti used as antifertility agents (Journal of Ethnopharmacology
[Elsevier Sequoia, Lausanne, Switzerland]
6:1, July 1982, p. 67–84, bibl., tables)
Investigates traditional medical practice of "médecine-feuilles" (treatment-based
medicinal herbs) in Haiti, in particular those
indigenous to the island with reputed antifertility properties. Includes botanical identification of plants, chemical composition, and
pharmacological basis that could justify their
empirical use.

1146 Wooding, Charles J. Evolving culture:
a cross-cultural study of Suriname,
West Africa and the Caribbean. Washington:
University Press of America, Inc., 1981. 329
p.: bibl., plates, tables.
Study based on extensive depth interviews with Creole Surinamese in Para region.
Surinamese anthropologist gives comprehensive, systematic description of Winti, traditional religion in Suriname with almost no
relationship to Christianity, and attempts to
establish African origin of its gods based on
their names and terminology and institutions that have been preserved. Compares
Surinamese and other Afro-American data to
show that change results in different structures. Good descriptions of tribal origin, Para
region, and various aspects of the religion as
well as rich case studies and histories. Useful
Sranan glossary and comparison of Sranan
and West African words included.

1147 Wylie, Jonathan. The sense of time,
the social construction of reality, and
the foundations of nationhood in Dominica
and the Faroe Islands (CSSH, 24:3, July 1982,
p. 438–466)
Author examines local construction of
social order such as history, social reality,
and nationhood in two fishing villages (Casse
Dominica and Alvabour in Faroe Islands of
North Atlantic), ultimately in order to compare Afro-Caribbean and Scandinavian
societies.

**1148 Ya'Ityo.pyā 'ortodoks tawā.hedo béta
kerestiyān.** Order and canon law of
marriage of the Ethiopian Tewahedo Church.
Edited by Abba L. Mandefro. Kingston: Ethiopian Orthodox Church in the Western
Hemisphere, 1976. 17 p.: ill.
Translation from Amharic of order and

principle of marriage, including incest definitions, of Ethiopian Orthodox Church. Useful
for specialists.

1149 Yamaguchi, Masao. The elements of
Carnival in the myth of Caribbean Sea
(Journal of Asian and African Studies [Insti-
tute for the Study of Languages and Cultures
of Asia and Africa, Tokyo, Japan] 21, 1981,
p. 111–119)

Japanese anthropologist views continuities of African trickster myth, in particular Eshu-Elegba version of Yoruba, which
made it possible for New World blacks "to
maintain the dynamic balance between the
world of artificiality and that of spontaneity
through a carnivalistic engagement in the
world."

ETHNOLOGY: South America, Lowlands

WAUD H. KRACKE, *Associate Professor of Anthropology, University of Illinois, Chicago Circle*

BOTH RESEARCH AND POLITICAL ACTIVITY concerning South American Indians continue to increase in volume, intensity, and depth. The accelerated expansion of frontiers, stimulated by dismal economic conditions, leads to many new
contacts and an increased level of threat to numerous tribes. And so tasks of ever
increasing urgency are understanding Indian cultures and their problems, commu-
nicating such understanding to a wider public, and defending the interests of threatened indigenous peoples. These issues have generated new research interests and
orientations, as well as new types and degrees of organized action on the part of
indigenous peoples and new concepts of action on anthropology by anthropologists.
Amid all this activity, several thoughtful and searching ethnographies have appeared as well as papers on social structure. Interesting works on cosmology include an ambitious and provocative proposal by Roe (item **1314**) of a basic cosmological framework underlying all Amazonian cosmologies.

With the economic situation worse than ever in South America, especially in
Brazil on the eve of its return to electoral democracy and in Chile, the situation of
indigenous cultures looks grimmer than ever. The election of the Shavante leader
Mario Juruna to a congressional seat from Rio's Zona Sul has provided new focus
for indigenous self organizing but does not alleviate the basic problems. Despite
reports published in *Science* (214:755, 1984) and elsewhere of the failure of initial
settlement projects along the Transamazon Highway due to poor understanding of
the area's ecology (item **1169**), agricultural development and resettlement projects
continue at a rapid pace (item **1172**). The World Bank has signed an agreement with
Brazil for funding the Polonoroeste Project, which will isolate the Guapore Valley
Nambiquara communities and severely restrict their hunting territories (item
1154). FUNAI proposals for safeguards have been criticized as inadequate to protect
Nambiquara and other indigenous communities. Even if FUNAI's renewal proves
lasting, its inability to stem encroachments on the Aripuanã Park will be aggravated by Polonoroeste. Throughout eastern South America, especially Brazil, the

hard won reservation lands of numerous indigenous peoples are threatened with inundation by dams to produce electricity whose need by no means has been established. In addition to covering the hunting and living territories of many groups, the flooding could have serious health and environmental consequences.[1] In Guyana, the Akawaio are faced with the possibility of total dispossession by the Mazaruni River dam (item **1181**) and in both Brazil and Paraguay (item **1197**), indigenous and "indigenist" organizations vainly struggle to obtain at least resettlement aid from the government or the hydroelectric companies. (Resettlement of coastal populations in territory occupied by Indians is a major effort of the government of Brazil, but for resettlement of displaced Indian populations aid is scarcely forthcoming.) Two thousand Waimiri-Atroari will be left homeless by the Balbina Dam north of Manaus whose construction has begun. The Tucurui Dam on the lower Xingu River will flood or bisect three reservations for the Paracanã and Gaviões, thus inundating one of FUNAI's few success stories, the successful Gavião Brazil-nut trade (item **1169**). Over a dozen other major projected dams in Amazonian Brazil alone will threaten thousands more Brazilian Indians (see IWGIA Doc. 44, Indian Lands Threatened by Hydroelectric Dams in Brazil).

Nevertheless, there have been some victories. As of last year, possibilities of a compromise settlement on a border park for the Yanomami seemed promising (as reported in *Cultural Survival Quarterly*, 6:2, Spring 1982, p. 27–29), but unfortunately no such agreement has been reached as of this writing. In Peru there is an encouraging proposal to link an Amuesha reservation with a national park (item **1198**). The World Bank, partly instigated by the threat to Nambiquara groups in the Polonoroeste Project, has published policy guidelines[2] for safeguarding indigenous minorities in project areas, although the operative part of the guidelines—"Measures to Mitigate the Effects of Development on Tribal Groups"—was first available only by special request and has since been withdrawn from public circulation. These guidelines contain a useful bibliography and a list of "tribal protection groups," but their effect on actual Bank project policy has so far been nominal.

Perhaps the most important development in publication concerning endangered Amazonian cultures is CEDI's (Conselho Ecumênico de Documentação e Informação) project to survey the peoples of the Amazon and their conditions in 18 volumes of which one is annotated here (item **1167**). CEDI also issues a collection of news clippings on the situation of various Brazilian indigenous cultures entitled *Aconteceu: Fatos destacados da Imprensa*.

Recourse to the law has become increasingly frequent and sophisticated, and last year a major conference on the plight of the Indian and Brazilian law was convened by Silvio Coelho dos Santos. Recently published papers from this conference were not received in time to review for this *HLAS*. However, two very interesting papers on the topic are included (items **1159** and **1179**).

Inspired by the highly successful Barbados conference, additional meetings of indigenous leaders and anthropologists are being held. A forum hosted by the Universidad Central de Venezuela provides interesting reading and documents problems and the development of the country's indigenous movement (item **1182**).

1. Catherine Caulfield, "Dam the Amazon, Full Steam Ahead" in *Natural History* (Vol. 92, No. 7, July 1983, p. 60–67)

2. Robert Goodland, *Tribal peoples and economic development: human ecologic considerations* (available from Office of Enviromental Affairs, World Bank, 1818 H Street, N.W., Washington, D.C. 20433)

For further information on specific indigenous lowland societies, one should consult the first part of the bibliography listed below in which books and articles on the situation of Indians in the face of expanding national societies are arranged by countries.

ETHNIC IDENTITY AND SOCIAL STRUCTURE

Concern with the fate of indigenous peoples in contact with national society has spurred the development of several areas of investigation, most notably the fields of ethnic identity and interethnic relations and of ethnohistory. Conceptual development in the area of ethnicity and ethnic identity owes much to the work of Roberto Cardoso de Oliveira who has formulated complex models of interethnic contact (items **1230** and **1231**). These have been extended and elaborated in a fascinating comparison of three different situations of asymmetrical relations among different Brazilian Indian groups, published in an important study by Alcida Ramos with four coauthors for different chapters (items **1302** and **1304**). Another important and frequently cited article by Roberto Da Matta (item **1284**) develops Goffmanian concepts of the "cost" of ethnic identity, and an interesting paper by Seeger stresses the rapidity with which ethnic identifications may fluctuate in sensitive response to changing situations (item **1320**). Henley's ethnography of the Panare (item **1263**) applies Darcy Ribeiro's model of interethnic relations in analyzing the situation of contact. Whitten (item **1202** and see *HLAS 43 : 1222*) explores jungle Quechua identity in Ecuador (see also items **1296, 1321,** and **1326**).

Similar interests are also evident in a number of ethnohistorical studies which trace the process of contact of a particular culture, or of cultures in a particular area (items **1152, 1162, 1166, 1216, 1235,** and **1238**). While most of these ethnohistorical studies focus on the process of contact and acculturation, a few make considerable effort to reconstruct the past culture and trace internal changes in the culture or social structure (items **1216** and **1235**). Guss (item **1258**) traces the incorporation of historical events into myth. In historical sources, an important set of 16th- and 17th-century Jesuit reports by Father Fernão Cardim have been reissued (item **1229**) in a University of São Paulo series of historic reprints.

Turning to work on social structure, the Northwest Amazon continues to be a focus of new ethnographic studies, including some of general theoretical interest. Kaj Arhem's study of Makuna social organization (item **1213**) is one significant contribution listed in this bibliography (see also item **1212**). By focusing on actual behavioral patterns of lineage segmentation and marriage alliance, Arhem's study provides a balance to recent works emphasizing ideal patterns of social organization, most notably Christine Hugh-Jones' (see *HLAS 43 : 1129*). On the other hand, the work of Peter Silverwood-Cope (items **1304** and **1324**) concentrates on the hitherto neglected interfluvial "servants" of the riverine Tukanoan and Arawakan speaking Vaupes societies. The Sanuma, a Brazilian Yanomami subgroup, are discussed in interesting articles on social structure (items **1303** and **1329**), and Melatti (item **1285**) offers a structural analysis of Timbira plaza groups.

David Price provides a particularly illuminating perspective on Nambiquara leadership (item **1301**), correcting some of Lévi-Strauss' impressions and developing some significant observations of his own about contrasting leadership styles within the same society (see *HLAS 43 : 1142*). A different type of contribution on leadership by Dennis Werner offers empirical studies of Kayapó leadership that draw on the tradition of small group studies in sociology (items **1342** and **1343**). For other studies on social organization, see items **1212, 1263, 1283, 1285** and **1330**.

A number of articles annotated below, as well as in *HLAS 43*, deal with naming. The system of name transmission has been recognized for some time as a central structural element of Gê societies (see *HLAS 43: 1101, HLAS 43: 1148, HLAS 43: 1158*, and *HLAS 43: 1163*), providing the principle of social continuity that in many other societies is carried by unilineal descent groups. It is becoming increasingly evident that name transmission is an important principle of continuity in societies from the Northwest Amazon and Orinoco regions (items **1270** and **1303**) to the Chaco (item **1312**), as was in fact anticipated in the symposium on "Construction of the Self in South American Societies" reported in the preceding social sciences volume (see *HLAS 43: 1198*). In one intriguing case, naming (teknonymy) constitutes an early phase in the formation of lineage groups (item **1303**).

An unanticipated topic that has become pervasive, perhaps understandably so given the present conditions of lowland societies, is death. In *HLAS 43* (p. 143), we noted half a dozen studies on the subject and several more are annotated below (e.g., one on the Bororo, item **1291**; one on the Krahó, item **1243**; and three on cultures of Paraguay and Peru, items **1226–1227**, and **1325**). Novaes' (item **1291**) suggestion that Bororo funeral objects constitute the individual identity of the deceased follows reasoning suggested by Crocker's arguments (see *HLAS 43: 1094*). Finally, Da Cunha (item **1243**) proposes that ideas about death provide Krahó thinkers with a "free field of fabulations" (i.e., creativity).

DREAMING, SHAMANISM, AND COSMOLOGY

Dreaming, another area of personal significance that appears to have wide social importance in South America, is discussed in a number of works. Aguaruna find their magical garden stones in dreams (item **1223**) and Mataco fathers find names for their sons through them (item **1312**). More basically, or more widely, dreaming is associated with shamanism, and Guss (item **1259**) argues that the trances of Makiritare shamans are regarded as dream states in which and through which shamans perform their actions. (The same is true of Kagwahiv shamans, as I have been told by many informants; see *HLAS 43: 1141*.)

There is some interest in the part played by dreams in South American cultures. At a recent conference on dreams at the School of American Research, four of the 10 papers discussed were on South American cultures, three of them lowland. Papers on dreams include discussions of systems of dream beliefs (items **1254** and **1338**) and interpretations of the content of dreams, psychoanalytic (item **1273**) or statistical (item **1253**). A controversy concerning the interpretability of culturally patterned dreams has arisen, with Watson (item **1338**) taking issue with my view (see *HLAS 43: 1141*) that even dreams with culturally stereotyped symbols may have personal meanings. A reply will be forthcoming.

Other articles deal with culturally patterned psychic illnesses (items **1227** and **1296**), shamanic cure (items **1228** and **1328**), and witchcraft (items **1225** and **1268**). Of two articles on medicinal plants (items **1246** and **1265**), one evaluates the pharmacological effectiveness of contraceptive herbs. A third discusses hallucinogenic plants (item **1222**).

Several studies of shamanism and shamanic healing (items **1228, 1242, 1259, 1307–1308** and **1328**) attest to a rising interest in the subject that culminated in a series of symposia on shamanism in lowland South America, the first organized by

Joanna Kaplan at the 43rd International Congress of Americanists in Manchester, Sept. 1982.

Cosmology also commands as much or even greater interest as is evident in the publication of several outlines of the cosmologies of particular cultures (items **1314, 1324,** and **1345**) and studies of cosmologies through their myths (items **1215, 1240,** and **1300**). Bormida and his school have refined this latter approach to a near formula (items **1219, 1221, 1224, 1241, 1281–1282, 1297, 1313, 1322** and **1331**). Urban (item **1334**) argues interestingly that agent or patient centricity in myths may characterize the orientation of certain cultures. However, the landmark study of cosmology is Peter Roe's *Cosmic Zygote* (item **1314**), a bold attempt to identify a single cosmology underlying all Amazonian cultures. Starting with the Shipibo, among whom he did his field work, Roe sifts through cosmological data throughout the Amazon in order to formulate a consistent portrayal of an underlying universe. Although the attempt is bound to be controversial, I suspect that some of its aspects will hold up. In any case, it represents a major venture in the study of Amazonian religions.

ECOLOGY, RELATIONS OF PRODUCTION, AND THE QUESTION OF DETERMINISM

Although the familiar stridency still characterizes some cultural materialist writings (items **1237** and **1315**), in others there is now a discernible moderation in tone. For example, several methodological critiques by authors interested in ecology now emphasize the need for a cultural dimension in human ecology. Nugent (item **1292**) presents a Marxist critique of "vulgar materialists" like Harris who ignore relations of production (compare Bloch's critique of American materialists in *Marxism and anthropology*), while Allen Johnson's significant paper, a watershed in this controversy, demonstrates that "scarcity" of land or game animals is in itself culturally defined and not by UNESCO minimum standards (items **1269** and **1271**). Most of the current contributions concerning ecology are empirical studies of a particular culture and its relationship with its environment, many of them detailed and quantitative studies of food production (items **1217, 1232, 1234, 1239, 1250, 1260– 1261, 1267, 1274,** and **1277–1278**). Other studies discuss questions of food production in relation to mythology (items **1218, 1236,** and **1280**), magic (item **1223**), or other aspects of culture (items **1271** and **1309**). One publication on food taboos (item **1248**) is in part a reply to the narrow environmental determinism of Eric Ross' earlier paper (see *HLAS 41:1192*), while two others (items **1329** and **1335**) address the exploration of food taboos as markers of social categories. At last, this controversy has begun to shed some light instead of merely heat.

These, then, are the major issues addressed in the literature covered for this *HLAS*. The following few bibliographies on specific regions and topics provide additional guidance: Erika Wagner and Walter Coppens continue their annual coverage of Venezuela (item **1185**); Reátegui offers a selective guide to anthropology and archaeology of the Peruvian tropical forest (item **1305**); and Alba Zaluar Guimarães' survey of messianic movements in Brazil (item **1256**) provides good references on indigenous revitalization movements. John Hudelson's index of tribal appellations for indigenous groups in the montaña of northern Peru and Ecuador (item **1266**) also includes bibliographic references. Finally, the above mentioned World Bank paper on *Tribal peoples and economic development* can be obtained by writing the Bank's Office of Environmental Affairs (1818 H Street, N.W., Washington, D.C.

20433). The excellent bibliography included in this publication consists of books, articles and papers on problems and conditions of tribal peoples and provides good coverage for South America, especially Brazil. The bibliography is preceded by two "Guides" providing indexes by country and subject.

The following major organizations provide regular information on conditions of South America's indigenous peoples in their newsletters or bulletins:

ARC
37 Temple Place, No. 521
Boston, Massachusetts 02111
(617) 426-9286

Survival International (USA)
2121 Decatur Street, N.W.
Washington, D.C. 20008
(202) 265-1077

OXFAM America
P.O. Box 288
Boston, Mass. 02116
USA

AMAZIND
17, Rue des Sources
1205 Geneva
Switzerland

UNI (União das Nações Indigénas)
Regional Sul
Rua Caiubi, 126
05010 Perdizes
São Paulo, SP
Brazil

CTI (Centro de Trabalho Indigenista)
Rua Fidalga, 548—sl. 13
Vila Madalena
05432 São Paulo, SP
Brazil

Comissão Pró-India, SP
Rua Caiubi, 126
05010 Perdizes
São Paulo, SP
Brazil

Asociación de Parcialidades Indígenas
Defensa Nacional 849
Casilla Posta 1796
Asunción, Paraguay

Cultural Survival
11 Divinity Avenue
Cambridge, Masschusetts 02138
(617) 495-2962

Survival International (London)
29 Craven Street
London WC 2
United Kingdom

IWGIA (International Work Group for Indigenous Affairs)
Fiolstraede 10, DK-1171
Copenhagen K, Denmark

PORANTIN
Monthly newspaper of CIMI, Conselho Indigenista Misionario)
Caixa postal 11–1159
70084 Brasilia, DF
Brazil

CEDI (Conselho Ecumenico de Documentação e Informação)
Avenida Higienópolis, 983
02138 São Paulo, SP
Brazil

CCPY (Comisão pela Criação do Parque Yanomami) Rua São Carlos do Pinhal, 345
01333 São Paulo, SP
Brazil

CRIC (Consejo Regional Indígena del Cauca)
Aartado Aereo 516
Popayan, Cauca
Colombia

ORGANIZATION OF THE BIBLIOGRAPHY

The following bibliography is divided into two parts. Pt. I entitled "Threats to Survival and Problems of Integration" contains works on issues confronting Indian groups in the face of expanding national societies and is subdivided into: 1) Brazil; 2) Colombia, Venezuela, Guyana, and Surinam; 3) Ecuador, Peru, and Paraguay; and 4) Missionary Organizations. Pt. II entitled "Anthropological Studies of Indigenous Cultures: Theory and Ethnography" contains ethnographic writings and anthropological analyses of lowland Indian societies. This part is not subdivided geographically because the natural groupings of South American cultures do not respect national boundaries.

I. THREATS TO SURVIVAL AND PROBLEMS OF INTEGRATION

1. BRAZIL

1150 Amorim, Paolo Marcos de. Acamponesamento e proletarização das populações indígenas do Nordeste brasileiro (Boletim do Museu do Indio [Fundação Nacional do Indio, FUNAI, Rio de Janeiro] Antropologia 2, maio 1975, p. 1–19, bibl., charts)

Describes assimilation of major indigenous groups of Northeast into agricultural economy, concentrating on eight (including Potiguara, Fulnio, and Pankaruru (see also item **1171**). Warns of progressive proletarianization.

1151 Antropologia e indigenismo na América Latina. Organização, Carmen Junqueira, Edgard de A. Carvalho. São Paulo: Cortez Editora, 1981. 129 p.: ill.

Consists of eight articles "on aspects of the indigenous question in Brazil and in Latin America." First three by Assis Carvalho (item **1155**), Mindlin Lafer (item **1161**), and Davis and Menget (item **1157**), concern Brazil specifically. The rest deal with more general issues: Margarita Nolasco Armas "A Antropologia Aplicada no México en seu Destino Final: o Indigenismo;" Guillermo Bonfil "Do Indigenismo da Revolução á Antropologia Crítica;" M.A. Bartolomé and Scott S. Robinson "Indigenismo, Dialética e Consciência Etnica" with critique by Jacques Lafaye; and Stefano Varese "Estratégia Etnica ou Estratégia de Classe?."

1152 Arnaud, Expedito. Os índios Mirânia e a expansão Luso-Brasileira: Médio Solimões-Japurá, Amazonas. Belém, Brazil: Museu Paranaense Emílio Goeldi, 1981. 48 p.: bibl., ill., map (Boletim do Museu Paranaense Emílio Goeldi. Antropologia; 81)

Traces history of contact since 1758 of this formerly populous Solimões tribe, linguistic affiliation unknown, to their present reduced and deculturated status. Language lost.

1153 Broli, Carmen Nicolussi. Indios no Brasil (UFP/EB, 4:8, 1979, p. 249–258) Recalls Rondon's ideals to protect Indians against expanding frontier and briefly sketches decline of SPI, "replacement" by FUNAI, and recent development of Indian movement.

1154 Carelli, Vincent and **Milton Severiano.** Le sort des Indiens du Brésil à l'exemple des Nambiquara du Guaporé (SSA/B, 45, 1981, p. 55–60, bibl., ill., maps) French translation of *HLAS 43:1082*.

1155 Carvalho, Edgard de Assis. Pauperização e indianidade (*in* Antropologia e indigenismo na América Latina [item **1151**] p. 7–19, tables)

Wage labor and commercial production have transformed nature of the Indian problem from one of ethnicity to class. Author of *Terena: as alternativas dos vencidos* (not yet received) discusses mode of production of cultivation on Ariribá reservation (see item **1158** and *HLAS 43:1103*) as part of agrarian problem of "self-exploitation."

1156 Davis, Shelton. Vitimas do milagre: o desenvolvimento e os indios no Brasil. Rio de Janeiro: Zahar Editores, 1978. 1 v. Translation of important treatment of Brazilian Indian policy (see *HLAS 43:1099*).

1157 ——— and Patrick Menget. Povos primitivos e ideologias civilizadas no Brasil (*in* Antropologia e indigenismo na América Latina [see item **1151**] p. 37–65)

Traces contradiction between Rondon's ideals and the dream of developing the Amazon, with special attention to the bisection of the Xingú National Park by route BR-80.

1158 Diniz, Edson Soares. Aririba: uma reserva indígena em São Paulo (Boletim do Museu do Indio [Fundação Nacional do Indio, FUNAI, Rio de Janeiro] Antropologia 5, nov. 1976, p. 1–15, bibl., maps, tables)

Summarizes language groups living on the reservation—three Guaraní and one Terena—and briefly characterizes their differences and interactions (for fuller report, see *HLAS 43:1103* and also item **1155**).

1159 Halfpap, Luiz Carlos and **Remy Fontana.** Direito, ideologia e comunidades indígenas (Encontros com a Civilização Brasileira [Rio de Janeiro] 12, junho 1979, p. 115–128)

Examination of legal case against a Kaingang Indian reveals ambiguities and prejudices in Brazilian Indian law.

1160 Kietzman, Dale W. Factors favoring ethnic survival (in International Congress of Americanists, 42nd, Paris, 1976. Actes [see *HLAS 41:255*] v. 2, p. 528–536, bibl.)

Documents resistance of Brazilian indigenous groups to total assimilation and makes recommendations for fostering persistence of cultural identity.

1161 Lafer, Betty Mindlin. A nova utopia indígena: os projetos econômicos (in Antropologia e indigenismo na América Latina [see item **1151**] p. 19–35)

Describes projects to foster economic autonomy among Terêna, Guaraní, Kaingáng, Shokleng, and Gaviões, and some obstacles challenging such projects.

1162 Marcato, Sonia de Almeida. A repressão contra os Botocudos em Minas Gerais (Boletim do Museu do Indio [Fundação Nacional do Indio, FUNAI, Rio de Janeiro] 1, maio 1979, p. 1–59, bibl.)

Historical study that documents v lence since 1808 against "Botocudos" (lip plugged Gê-speaking peoples) of Minas Gerais. Also traces Krenak subgroup from contact to assimilation in 20th century through series of reports, one by Nimuend

Matta, Roberto da. Quanto custa ser indi Brasil. See item **1284**.

1163 Miguez, José Mario Guedes. Chaci do Meruri: a verdade dos fatos. São Paulo: Editora A. Gazeta Maçônica, n.d. 2

Proprietor of cattle ranch on Borot reservation, who attacked party demarcat reservation, killing a Salesian father, is pa sionately defended by enraged brother. D turbing book which documents anti-India prejudices and constitutes indictment of ernment vacillation and corruption that a lows exploitation of Indian lands.

1164 Moonen, Francisco José. Introduçã aos problemas dos índios no Brasil 1, Indios e brancos. v. 2, Problemas indíge

v. 3, Política indigenista. v. 4, Indigenismo e indiologia. João Pessoa: Centro de Ciências Humanas, Letras e Artes, 1975. 4 v.: bibl. (Série Antropologia; 1–4. Texto didático)

Four brief pamphlets for course texts on problems of contact, Indian policy, and "indigenism and indiology." Good elementary survey, though brevity and avoidance of controversy leads to superficial treatment of some topics.

1165 Oliveira, Roberto Cardoso de. Teses sobre o indigenismo brasileiro (Anuário Antropológico [Edições Tempo Brasileiro, Rio de Janeiro] 79, 1981, p. 171–178)

Consists of his address accepting the 1978 "International Prize for the Promotion of Human Understanding," a brief manifesto of pro Indian activities in Brazil which discusses FUNAI's Indian policies. Focuses on concept of "tutelage" and FUNAI's threat of "emancipation."

1166 Pacheco, Eliezer *et al.* O povo condenado. Rio de Janeiro: Editora Artenova, 1977. 226 p.: bibl., ill.

History of cultural subjugation of Indians of Brazil, with special attention given to role of Jesuit missions. Last two chapters sketch current situation of "the survivors" including summary of 1977 CIMI Ijui conference statement. Article by CIMI's Egidio Schwade ("Visão Panorámica da Atual Situação Indígena no Brasil") surveys situations of particular tribes. Book closes with congressional testimony of Tomas Balduino, CIMI's president.

1167 Povos indígenas no Brasil. v. 5 accompanied by supplement "Apresentação: Texto para Discussão/Circulação Interna" by Carlos A. Ricardo. São Paulo: Centro Ecumênico de Documentação e Informação, 1981. 1 v.: ill., maps, ports.

Vol. 5 of 18 projected by Centro Ecumênico de Documentação e Informação (CEDI) to document the cultures and current conditions of the indigenous peoples of Brazil. This volume covers Indians of Javari River area, including full accounts of Panoan-speaking Marubo, Mayoruna, and Matis, based on recent expedition by the Melattis and other field workers, and of the Kanamari, with briefer accounts of Arawakan Kulina and several lesser-known groups.

1168 Price, David. The Nambiquara, the Parecí, and the Indians of southern

Rondônia (*in* In the path of Polonoroeste. Cambridge, Mass.: Cultural Survival, 1982. 1 v. (Occasional paper; no. 6)

Details disastrous present and future effects of World Bank-funded "Polonoroeste Project" on Guapore Valley's Nambiquara, Parecis, and various tribes of southeastern Rondônia. Other articles by Moore, Lafer and Junqueira document tribes (including Cintas Largas and Surui) of Aripuana National Park.

1169 Ramos, Alcida R. Development, integration and the ethnic integrity of Brazilian Indians (*in* Land, people and planning in contemporary Amazonia. Françoise Barbira-Scazzocchio, editor. Cambridge, England: University of Cambridge, Centre of Latin American Studies, 198?, p. 222–229 [Occasional publication; no. 3])

After presenting descriptions of devastating effects on some indigenous groups of abrupt contact brought about by Transamazon Highway, cites example of Gaviões and Nambiquara to show that, given opportunity, native communities can be productively integrated into regional economies.

Ribeiro, Darcy. Os protagonistas do drama indígena. See *HLAS 41 : 1187.*

1170 Schmink, Marianne. Land conflicts in Amazonia (AAA/AE, 9 : 2, May 1982, p. 341–357, bibl.)

Amazonian frontier expansion breeds conflict as agricultural enterprises purchase land occupied by untitled subsistence farmers (*posseiros*). INCRA bureaucracy generally favors buyer. Church pressure and organized action by *posseiros* has pressured state to adopt local, palliative, administrative "solutions."

1171 Soares, Carlos Alberto Caroso. Pankararé de Brejo do Burgo: um grupo indígena aculturado (Boletim do Museu do Indio [Fundação Nacional do Indio, FUNAI, Rio de Janeiro] Antropologia 6, fev. 1977, p. 1–9, bibl., maps)

Revival of traditional customs among highly acculturated indigenous group in Bahia (see also item **1150**).

1172 Souza Martins, José de. Lutando pela terra: índios e posseiros na Amazônia legal (UPR/RCS, 11 : 1/2, 1980, p. 7–27, bibl.)

Enumerates Indian tribes involved in recent conflict over lands invaded by poor farmers and by large capitalist enterprises. Sees *posseiros* (squatters) as first phase of

"front of expansion" culminating in large cattle *fazendas* which displace them.

1173 Viana, Zelito. Terra dos índios. Fotografia e câmera, Affonso Beato. Direção, Zelito Viana. Rio de Janeiro: Embrafilme, 1979. 117 p.: ill.

Text and background of a powerful film documenting how Indian lands are being threatened and the growing indigenous leadership that emerged in response.

1174 Vieira Filho, João Paulo Botelho. Medicina indígena e medicina científica (USP/RA, 21 : 2, 1978, p. 171–174, bibl.)

Based on author's experience in programs of medical treatment and vaccination among the Xikrín, Gaviões, and Surui, this conference paper discusses relationship between indigenous treatment and scientific medicine. While acknowledging actual and potential debt of modern medicine to indigenous pharmacopeia, and citing therapeutic elements of shamanistic treatment, author stresses need for vaccination and scientific medical treatment against communicable diseases which devastate indigenous populations. Citing value of cooperation with the shaman in the Xikrin vaccination program, author denies conflict between systems.

1175 ———. Problemas da aculturação alimentar dos Xavante e Bororo (USP/RA, 24, 1981, p. 37–40, bibl.)

Physician recounts efforts to encourage planting of pigeon pea and broad beans to replace protein sources diminished with loss of traditional hunting territories.

1177 Zarur, George Cerqueira Leite. Envolvimento de antropólogo e desenvolvimento da antropologia no Brasil (Boletim do Museu do Indio [Fundação Nacional do Indio, FUNAI, Rio de Janeiro] Antropologia 4, abril 1976, p. 1–9, bibl.)

Discusses anthropologists' involvement in pro Indian action as a consequence of field work and as a basic theme of Brazilian anthropology since Nimuendaju.

2. COLOMBIA, VENEZUELA, GUYANA, AND SURINAM

1178 Adams, Kathleen J. Work opportunities and household organization among Barama River Caribs (AI/A, 74 : 1/2, 1979, p. 291–222, bibl., chart)

Summarizes traditional relationships among Barama-River Carib (Guyana) kin, and shows how work in mining has eroded these relationships.

1179 Deltgen, Florian. De la situación del indio en el derecho penal colombiano: reflexiones con motivo de un dictamen jurídico etnológico (AI/A, 76 : 5/6, 1981, p. 784–806)

Interesting study of Colombian law pertaining to Indians. Law leaves judgment of "semisavage" Indians to missionaries. Author records interviews with several Indian defendants and advocates justice for all indigenous peoples based on their own cultural law as established by anthropological investigation.

1180 Dieter Heinen, H. and Walter Coppens. Las empresas indígenas en Venezuela (III/AI, 41 : 4, 1981, p. 573–602, bibl., ill.)

Evaluates economic enterprises established with aid of Instituto Agrario Nacional among Warao, Piaroa, and other indigenous groups. Critique attributes failures and difficulties to cultural and ecological factors not foreseen in planning projects (see item **1182**).

1181 Henningsgaard, William. The Akawaio, the Upper Mazaruni Hydroelectric Project, and national development in Guyana. Cambridge, Mass.: Cultural Survival, Inc., 1981. 37 p.: bibl., maps (Cultural survival occasional paper; no. 4)

After brief description of Akawaio and their contact, cites detrimental effects of projected Mazaruni dam on environment, health, and on the Akawaio, adding new information since 1978 Survival International report *The Damned*. Documents appended.

1182 Indigenismo y autogestión: coloquio sobre indigenismo realizado en el Estado Bolívar. Con la participación de N. Arvelo de Jiménez *et al*. A. Serbín, O. González Náñez, compiladores. Caracas: Monte Avila Editores, 1980. 237 p.: bibl., ill. (Colección Estudios / Monte Avila Editores)

Universidad Central de Venezuela Anthropology Dept. colloquium provides forum for animated discussion of issues among indigenous leaders (Carlos Figueroa and Juvencio Fierro, both Pemón; A. Montiel, Guajiro; Rudoph Chance of Guyana, *et al*.), officials of the Instituto Agrario Nacional (Gerardo Clerac and Alberto Váldez), and anthropologists Nelly Arvelo-Jiménez, Esteban

Mosonyi and organizers Andrés Serbín and Omar Gonzáles Náñez. Focuses on indigenous initiative and problems of Indians of the Gran Sabana.

1183 Pinzón Sánchez, Alberto. Monopolios, misioneros y destrucción de indígenas. Bogotá?: Ediciones Armadillo, 1979. 215 p.: bibl., maps.

Book by Colombian anthropologist sketches social organization of Vaupes cultures (with interesting statistics on multilingual speakers and interlinguistic marriages); traces impact of Catholic and SIL missionaries and of rubber and other capitalistic enterprises.

1184 Rivière, Peter G. A report on the Trio Indians of Surinam (NWIG, 55, 1981, p. 1–38, bibl., photos)

Followup to 1966 report finds little changed in problems facing Trio. Cash economy has increased, Christianity replaced traditional beliefs, but social norms remain strong.

1185 Wagner, Erika and Walter Coppens. Octava bibliografía antropológica reciente sobre Venezuela (FSCN/A, 54, 1980, p. 167–180)

1186 Zerries, Otto. Los waika—yanoama: indígenas del Alto Orinoco, 1954–1974 (IAI/I, 3, 1975, p. 147–154, bibl., plates)

Brief notes on six-day return visit to the Yanomami noting acculturative changes since his previous field work.

3. ECUADOR, PERU, AND PARAGUAY

1187 Amazonia ecuatoriana: la otra cara del progreso. Edited by Norman Whitten. Cambridge, Mass.: Cultural Survival *with the collaboration of* Mundo Shuar, 1981. 229 p.: bibl., ill., maps, photographs.

Consists of papers translated from English into Spanish on aspects of ethnic identity and economic development selected from compilation entitled "Cultural Transformations and Ethnicity in Modern Ecuador." Those dealing with Shuar culture primarily are by: Norman Whitten (item **1202**); Salazar (item **1196**); Descola (item **1192**); Taylor (item **1199**); and Belzner (item **1188**); those on the Canelos Quichua by MacDonald (item **1194**) and Dorothea Whitten (item **1201**).

1188 Belzner, William. Música, modernación y occidentalización entre los Shuar de Macuma (*in* Amazonia ecuatoriana: la otra cara del progreso [see item **1187**] p. 145–166, bibl., ill.)

Describes traditional Shuar music, seen as conservative force in Shuar life, and traces changes.

1190 Castro de León, Mercedes. La desestructuración de la comunidad nativa en su relación con la penetración del capitalismo en los casos de dos comunidades nativas de la selva peruana: los bora y huitoto de la región del Ampiyacu (*in* Congreso Peruano: El Hombre y la Cultura Andina, 3d, Lima, 1977. El hombre y la cultura andina [see *HLAS 43:* 253] v. 3, p. 176–186)

General survey of postcontact relations of production for these two Northwest Peruvian tribes, mentioning patron system and "penetration of international capitalism." Little of specific ethnographic value.

1191 Chase-Sardi, Miguel. La antropología aplicada en el Chaco paraguayo (UCNSA/SA, 16:2, dic. 1981, p. 157–166, bibl., tables)

Summarizes population estimates and situations of the five major language families of the Chaco, and describes activities of Proyecto Marandu in stimulating formation of Indian organizations and in educating white population. Tables of tribal population and of Indian reserves, their size, and legal status.

1192 Descola, Philippe. Del habitat disperso a los asentamientos nucleados: un proceso de cambio socio-económico entre los Shuar (*in* Amazonia ecuatoriana: la otra cara del progreso [see item **1187**] p. 83–113, bibl., photo)

After calculating that agricultural potential could support much larger settlements than the traditional Achuar ones, describes tendency to increasing nucleation and cattle raising and their consequences (see also item **1195**).

1193 Gasche, Jürg. Un diálogo con la naturaleza: los indígenas Witoto en la selva amazónica: reflexiones sobre el significado y la importancia de un programa pluridisciplinario (*in* Etnicidad y ecología [see item **1247**] p. 119–129, bibl.)

Discursive account of multidisciplinary study of slash-and-burn agriculture, un-

der UNESCO "Man and the Biosphere" program, giving project goals and guidelines. Laments colonial desecration of tropical environment.

1194 MacDonald, Theodore, Jr. Respuesta indígena a una frontera de expansión: conversión económica de la selva quechua en hacienda ganadera (*in* Amazonia ecuatoriana: la otra cara del progreso [see item **1187**] p. 167–194, bibl.)

Describes changes in jungle Quechua culture resulting from adoption of cattle ranching.

1195 Rivera Chávez, Pedro Lelis. Procedimiento para determinar el requerimiento de tierras de una familia nativa sedentaria de la selva baja (*in* Congreso Peruano: El Hombre y la Cultura Andina, 3d, Lima, 1977. El hombre y la cultura andina [see *HLAS 43:253*] v. 3, p. 205–208)

Calculates amount of forested land needed to feed one family in swidden agriculture, to determine amount of land which must be allocated to Indians for raising cattle (99 ha). No provision for differences in time needed for regeneration with different soil qualities (see also item **1192**).

1196 Salazar, Ernesto. La Federación Shuar y la frontera de la colonización (*in* Amazonia ecuatoriana: la otra cara del progreso [see item **1187**] p. 59–82, bibl.)

Condensed and much rewritten Spanish version of *HLAS 43:1189*, describes organization and activities of Shuar Federation and traces its origins to "the frontier of colonization."

1197 Situación de comunidades indígenas avá-chiripá cuya ocupación de tierras se ve afectada por los trabajos de la Itaipú binacional (UCNSA/SA, 16:2, dic. 1981, p. 189–209, maps)

Brief account of effect of binational Itaipú dam on Avá Chiripá. Reports on attempts by indigenous organizations to get Itaipú to take responsibility for resettlement of affected communities, and outlines proposed resettlement project.

1198 Smith, Richard Chase. El proyecto amuesha/yanachaga (*in* Etnicidad y ecología [see item **1247**] p. 157–176, bibl., tables)

Describes history and current situation of Amuesha (central Peruvian montaña) contact, and presents data in support of proposal to form Amuesha reservation conjoined with a national park (Yanachaga).

1199 Taylor, Anne Christine. La riqueza de dios: los achuar y las misiones (*in* Amazonia ecuatoriana: la otra cara del progreso [see item **1187**] p. 115–143, bibl., photos)

Paper, whose title ("God Wealth") loses irony in translation, attributes' acceptance of missions and their message to economic and educational advantages they offer and to superficial congruence with Shuar beliefs.

1200 Varese, Stefano. Notas sobre el colonialismo ecológico (*in* Etnicidad y ecología [see item **1247**] p. 177–186, bibl.)

Critique of government policy of settling coastal and mountain people on small plots in Amazonia. Countering prejudiced views of Indians, points out success of their mode of agriculture, advocating its adoption.

1201 Whitten, Dorothea. Antiguas tradiciones en un contexto contemporáneo: cerámica y simbolismo de canelos quechua en la región amazónica ecuatoriana (*in* Amazonia ecuatoriana: la otra cara del progreso [see item **1187**] p. 195–227, bibl., ill.)

Describes manufacture and decoration of Canelos Quechua pots and contact with urban environment in marketing them.

1202 Whitten, Norman. La Amazonia actual en la base de los Andes: una confluencia étnica en la perspectiva ecológica, social e ideológica (*in* Amazonia ecuatoriana: la otra cara del progreso [see item **1187**] p. 11–58, bibl., map)

Describes "ethnic confluence" of Andean Quechua-speaking groups with lowland Jivaroan and other language groups. Spanish version of *HLAS 43:1220*.

4. MISSIONARIES AND INDIANS

1203 Espínola Benítez, Ebelio. Algunas anotaciones en torno a *Indios y Menonitas en el Chaco paraguayo* de Henk Hack (UCNSA/SA, 16:2, dic. 1981, p. 213–226)

Based on observations from Hack's carefully impartial study (see item **1204**), author criticizes Mennonites' ethnocentric educational goals and social and economic consequences of their domination of Paraguayan Indians groups in the Chaco.

1204 Hack, Henk. Indios y menonitas en el Chaco paraguayo: pts. 1/3 (UCNSA/SA, 13:1/2, dic. 1978, p. 207–260, graphs, ill., tables; 14:1/2, dic. 1979, p. 201–244, graphs, tables; 15:1/2, dic. 1980, p. 45–137, bibl., tables)

Extensive and detailed, three-part, historical-etnographic study of Mennonites in Paraguayan Chaco and their proselytization ("misionización") of Indians. Stresses separateness of Mennonite and Indian communities in "plural society" acknowledging caste-stratified nature of relationship (see item **1203**).

1205 Is God an American?: an anthropological perspective on the missionary work of the Summer Institute of Linguistics. Edited by Søøren Hvalkof and Peter Aaby. Copenhagen: International Work Group for Indigenous Affairs (IWGIA); London: Survival International, 1981. 192 p.: bibls., ill., index (Document / IWGIA / Survival International, 0105–4503; 43)

Group of articles by anthropologists sharply critical of SIL/Wycliffe Bible Translators. Robinson, Stoll, Pereira, and d'Ans survey SIL's activities in four articles on Ecuador, Colombia, Bolivia, and Peru. Five by Vickers, Arcand, Hahn, Smith and Moore, describe work with specific tribes or language groups: Western Tukanoans, Cuiva, Rikbakca, Amuesha, and Amaracaeri. Articles vary in tone: less militant Brazilian branch of SIL is moderately defended by Hahn while more evangelistic branches are sharply rebuked for aiding government repression of Indians.

1206 Mosonyi, Esteban E. *et al.* El caso Nuevas Tribus. Caracas: Editorial Ateneo de Caracas, 1981. 259 p.: bibl., ill. (Colección Testimonios)

Consists of 30 brief documents of testimony by Venezuelan anthropologists, indigenous leaders, and others condemning New Tribes Mission for undermining Venezuela's traditional cultures.

1207 Sevilla-Casas, Elías. Notes on Las Casas' ideological and political practice (*in* International Congress of Anthropological and Ethnological Sciences, 9th, Chicago, 1973. Western expansion and indigenous people: the heritage of Las Casas. Editor, Elías Sevilla-Casas. The Hague: Mouton, 1977, p. 15–29, bibl., indexes [World anthropology])

Discusses life and work of 16th-century activist proponent of the Indian cause, Bartolomé de Las Casas, appointed "Defender of the Indians" by the Spanish king in 1516. Draws from Las Casas' conclusions relevant to the defense of Indians against oppression in current South American sociopolitical systems.

II. ANTHROPOLOGICAL STUDIES OF INDIGENOUS CULTURES: THEORY AND ETHNOGRAPHY

1208 Alvarsson, Jan-Ake. Colección etnográfica del Gran Chaco boliviano nos recuerda del finado etnógrafo sueco Erland Nordenskiöld, ex-Director del Museo Etnográfico de Gotemburgo, Suecia (EM/A, 1979/1980, p. 15–20, ill.)

Brief account of Nordenskiöld's visits to the Mataco and discussion of materials and designs of Mataco woven artifacts. Asks what in Mataco spirit accounts for their survival.

1209 Anuário Antropológico 1977. Editora Tempo Brasileiro. 1979-. Rio de Janeiro.

Second issue of new annual which consists of articles, longer essays and article-length book reviews, and review articles includes following ones on Lowland Indians: Alcida Rita Ramos' "Tecnonomia e Conceitualização Social entre os Indios Sanuma" (item **1303**); Roque Laraia's review article of Charles Wagley's *Welcome of tears* (see *HLAS 41:1208*); Julio Melatti on Lux Vidal's *Morte e vida de uma sociedade indígena brasileira: os Kayapó-Xikrin* (see *HLAS 41:1204*), on Thomas Gregor's *Mehinaku* (see *HLAS 41:1145*), and on Betty Megger's *Amazonia* (see *HLAS 39:1349*); Alcida Ramos on Thomas Gregor's *Mehinaku* (see *HLAS 41:1145*); Ordep José Trindade-Serra on Roberto Da Matta's *Um mundo dividido* (see *HLAS 41:1174*); and Peter Silverwood-Cope on Portuguese translation of Shelton Davis' *Victims of the miracle* (see *HLAS 43:1099*). Each review constitutes a substantial critical discussion.

1210 ——— 1978. ———. 1980-. Rio de Janeiro.

Articles on lowland indigenous topics include: Anthony Seeger's "A Identidade Etnica como Processo: os Indios Suya e as Sociedades do Alto Xingú (item **1320**); Peter Silverwood-Cope's "Cosmologia Maku" (item **1324**); and Roberto Cardoso de Oliveira's "Identidade e Estrutura Social" (item **1231**).

1211 ——— 1979. ———. 1981-. Rio de Janeiro.

Includes articles on Lowland Indians: Julio César Melatti "Individuo o Grupo: à Procura de uma Classificação dos Personagems Mítico-Rituais Timbiras" (item **1285**) and by Roberto Cardoso de Oliveira "Teses sobre o Indigenismo Brasileiro" (item **1165**), and reviews by Paul Aspelin of E.G. Heath and Vilma Chiara's *Brazilian Indian archery* and by Edwardo Viveiros de Castro of Edgar de Assis Carvalho's *As Alternativas dos vencidos* and by João Pacheco de Oliveira of Ari Pedro Oro's *Tükuna: vida ou morte.*

1212 Århem, Kaj. Bride capture, sister exchange and gift marriage among the Makuna: a model of marriage exchange (SEM/E, 46:1/2, 1981, p. 47–63, bibl., charts, maps, tables)

Develops a model of Makuna (Vaupes River Tukanoan) marriages based on Sahlins' theory of exchange. Model relates three dimensions of spatial distance, affinal distance, and type of exchange involved in marriage. Last dimension related to three types of Makuna marriage: direct exchange, bride capture, or unreciprocated "gift marriage" to close ally.

1213 ———. Makuna social organization: a study in descent, alliance and the formation of corporate groups in the Northwest Amazon. Uppsala, Sweden: Acta Universitatis Upsaliensis, 1981. 379 p.: bibl., charts, ill., index, plates, tables (Uppsala studies in cultural anthropology; 4)

Detailed ethnographic kinship/descent study of Makuna (Tukanoan, on Vaupes). Focuses on behavioral social reality of Makuna alliance patterns and sib stratification, which differs significantly from abstract theory of ranked fivefold segmentation and triadic marriage categories. Makuna subscribe to ideal of linguistic exogamy, but now form a Cubeo-like two-phratry marriage system, both Makuna-speaking. Arhem develops model of "segmentary alliance system" with higher-level spatial units "alliance ordered rather than descent ordered." Thorough documentation in tables and in appendixes statistically and genealogically delineate marriages and segmentation of Makuna sibs and interspersed sibs of other language groups, making this a highly useful complement to more theoretical analyses such as Hugh-Joneses' (see *HLAS 43 : 1129–1130*).

1214 Banner, Horace. Uma cerimônia de nominação entre os Kayapó (USP/RA, 21 : 1, 1978, p. 109–116, plates)

Chronicle and photographs of naming ceremony without analysis.

1215 Becher, Hans. Poré/Perimbó: Einwirkungen der lunaren Mythologie auf den Lebensstil von drei Yanomámi-Stämmem —Surara, Pakudai und Ironasiteri Hannover: Völkerkunde-Abteilung des Niedersächsischen Landesmuseums, 1974. 215 p.: bibl., charts, ill., maps, photos (Völkerkundliche Abhandlungen; Band 6)

Comparison of cosmology and religious beliefs of three different North Brazilian Yanomami groups, stressing the centrality of worship of lunar deity Poré, approached through *hekula* spirits (see item **1300**).

1216 Beckerman, Stephen. Datos etnohistóricos acerca de los Bari (Motilones) (UCAB/M, 8, 1978, p. 255–327, bibl., maps, tables)

History of the Bari (Lake Maracaibo, Venezuela) from 1529. Guillen's diary of 1772, with visits to Bari villages, is extensively quoted and provides basis for interesting comparison with present-day Bari, revealing some significant changes. Also traces demographic trends and territorial shifts.

1217 Bergman, Ronald W. Amazon economics: the simplicity of Shipibo Indian wealth. Ann Arbor, Mich.: Published for Department of Geography, Syracuse University *by* University Microfilms International, 1980. 249 p.: bibl., ill., index (Dellplain Latin American studies; 6)

Very thorough study of Shipibo food production by geographer.

1218 Berlin, Brent. Bases empíricas de la cosmología botánica aguaruna (*in* Etnicidad y ecología [see item **1247**] p. 15–26, bibl., map, tables)

In Nungukui myth of the Aguaruna (Shuar, northern Peruvian montaña), 20 major crops are transformed into corresponding wild species. Article analyzes implications for folk plant taxonomy (see also items **1222** and **1223**).

1219 Bórmida, Marcelo. Ergon y mito: una hermenéutica de la cultural material de los ayoreo del Chaco Boreal (Scripta Ethnologica [Centro Argentino de Etnología Americana, Buenos Aires] 1 : 1, 1973, p. 9–68; 2 : 1, 1974, p. 40–107; 3 : 1, 1975, p. 73–130)

Study of Ayoreo material culture using phenomenological perspective, inferring Ayoreo perception of their artifacts (*erga*) through 312 texts of myths and accounts of ancestral transformations. Pts. 1/2 describe Ayoreo world view and present myths of metamorphosis of ancestors into entities of present world. Pt. 3 explores nature of power embodied in *erga*.

1220 ——— and Mario Califano. Los últimos pakawara: familia lingüística pano (Scripta Ethnologica [Centro Argentino de Etnología Americana, Buenos Aires] 2 : 2, 1974, p. 159–172, figure, ill., map, plates)

Notes on family of nine Pakawara, living in Bolivian Chaco, describe their material culture and former habitat. Linguistic difficulty precluded detail on social structure or religion.

1221 Braunstein, José. Dominios y jerarquías en la cosmovisión de los matakos tewokleyley (Scripta Ethnologica [Centro Argentino de Etnología Americana, Buenos Aires] 2 : 2, 1974, p. 7–30, bibl., figures, glossary)

Relates Mataco (Central Chaco) Tewokleyley myth to Mataco cosmology. Myth text, in Spanish, in appendix.

1222 Brown, Michael F. From the hero's bones: three Aguaruna hallucinogens and their uses (*in* The Nature and status of ethnobotany. Richard I. Ford, editor. Ann Arbor: University of Michigan, Museum of Anthropology, 1978, p. 118–136, bibl., charts, map, table [Anthropological papers; no. 67])

Notes that three hallucinogens with common origin myth (see title), though probably botanically similar, are held to give quite different visions. Depicts significance of these visions in Aguaruna (Peruvian montaña Shuar) life (compare with *HLAS 35 : 1272*).

1223 ——— and Margaret L. Van Bolt. Aguaruna Jívaro gardening magic in the Alto Rio Mayo, Peru (UP/E, 19 : 2, 1980, p. 169–190, bibl., tables)

Aguaruna women's garden magic includes spells addressed to spirits and magical stones inherited or found through dreams.

Explained through importance of spirit contact and perceived uncertainty of gardening, both distinctive of Jívaro world view.

1224 Califano, Mario. El ciclo de Tokjwaj: análisis fenomenológico de una narración mítica de los mataco costaneros (Scripta Ethnologica [Centro Argentino de Etnología Americana, Buenos Aires] 1, 1973, p. 157–186, bibl., glossary)

Translation of Central Chaco Mataco myth cycle of Tokjwaj is presented, with variants, and analyzed into "mythemes" (thematic units), concluding with a definition of essential characteristics of this culture hero.

1225 ———. El complejo de la bruja entre los mashco de la Amazonia sudoccidental, Perú (AI/A, 73:3/4, 1978, p. 401–433, bibl., map, plate)

Describes Mashco (Madre de Dios River, Peru) beliefs about witchcraft, imputed to unmarried girls in collaboration with mythical toad. Analyzes "complex" in terms of special narrative form ("narrative horizon") describing incidents, and other features.

1226 ———. El concepto de enfermedad y muerte entre los mataco costaneros (Scripta Ethnologica [Centro Argentina de Etnología Americana, Buenos Aires] 2:2, 1974, p. 33–71, bibl., charts, glossary, tables)

After deriving Mataco cosmology from their cosmic myth, author analyzes Mataco concepts of illness and death, concluding with discussions of "ontoloty and the notion of power" and of "fear as an existential structure."

1227 ———. Muerte, miedo y fascinación en la crisis de *embüye* de los mashco de la Amazonia sudoccidental (UBAIA/R, 13:1/2, 1976/1980, p. 125–151, bibl.)

After account of Amaracaire Mashco (SW Amazonia, Peru) beliefs about death, Califano describes an anxiety state with hallucinations of dead people called *embüye*, which occurs in personal crises, especially during bereavement, and is treated with therapeutic songs. Draws comparison with Ernesto de Martino's ideas on death in antiquity.

1228 ———. El shamanismo mataco (Scripta Ethnologica [Centro Argentino de Etnología Americana, Buenos Aires] 3:2, 1976, p. 7–60, appendix, bibl., ill., glossary, tables)

Describes shamanistic practices among riverine Mataco of Argentine Chaco, with extensive texts (in Spanish translation) on initiation and curing methods. Analysis relates them briefly to myths. Appendix describes briefly six principal informants.

1228a ——— and **Alicia Fernández Distel.** El empleo de la coca entre los mashco de la Amazonia del Perú (EM/A, 1977, p. 16–32, bibl., ill., maps, plates)

Details of coca cultivation and use among Mashko, with brief comparative notes on its use in other Arawakan groups in Peru (Machiguenga, Campa, Amuesha) and comments on the psychopharmacological effects of alkaline accompaniment.

1229 Cardim, Fernão. Tratados da terra e gente do Brasil. Introdução e notas de Batista Caetano, Capistrano de Abreu e Rodolfo Garcia. 3. ed. São Paulo: Companhia Editora Nacional, 1978. 259 p. (Brasiliana; v. 168)

Reissue of 1938 publication of three documents by 16th- and 17th-century Jesuit missionary, largely on coastal Tupi cultures, with 19th-century notes, comments by Capistrano de Abreu, and additional 1938 notes by Rodolfo García. Documents are: *Do clima e terra no Brasil, Do principio e origem dos indios do Brasil,* and *Narrativo epistolar de uma viagem e missão Jesuítica.*

1230 Cardoso de Oliveira, Roberto. Identidade, etnia e estrutura social. São Paulo: Livraria Pioneira Editora, 1976. 118 p.: bibl., tables.

Four essays develop the framework of Cardoso's principal areas of theoretical contribution to Brazilian ethnography by dealing with ethnic identity, interethnic friction and structures of interethnic articulation. Drawing on examples from his own previous ethnographic work (with Terena and Tukuna Indians) and other Brazilian ethnography, Cardoso examines concept of identity in its cultural and psychological dimensions, and different types of interethnic contact, stressing importance of ideology of contact as well as level of structural relations.

1231 ———. Identidade e estrutura social (Anuário Antropológico [Editora Tempo Brasileiro, Rio de Janeiro] 1978 [i.e. 1980] p. 143–363, chart)

Reviews his earlier definition and classification of ethnic identity, stressing that ethnic identity subsists in a group's external relations as well as its internal structure.

Discusses internal identity structure of Tukuna and Bororo, and several studies of interethnic relations among Brazilian Indians. Also stresses need for investigator's self awareness.

1232 Carneiro, Robert L. El cultivo de roza y quema entre los Amahuaca de éste del Perú (*in* Etnicidad y ecología [see item **1247**] p. 27–40, table)

General description of the cycle of clearing, burning, and abandoning fields among the Amahuaca, including figures on productivity. Footnote provides comparative soil analyses from virgin forest, a former field, and a plot cultivated consecutively for five years (see item **1277** and also *HLAS 39:1382*).

1233 ———. Factors favoring the development of political leadership in Amazonia (UNC/ED, 4:1, March 1979 [i.e. Dec. 1980] p. 86–94, bibl.)

Argues that chiefs in Amazonian cultures exercised far greater power in wartime than in peace (see *HLAS 43:1142*) and that their control over more than one village arose in situations of competition for scarce resources, as in rich river bottomlands. Cites historical sources on Tupinamba and others.

1234 ———. Forest clearance among the Yanomamö: observations and implications (FSCN/A, 52, 1979, p. 36–76, ill., plates, tables)

Presents detailed data on methods used and time taken by Yanomamö in clearing experimental garden tract. Calculates that stone axes would take eight to 10 times longer than steel ones to accomplish task (see items **1274** and **1277**).

1235 Casanova V., Jorge. Migraciones aidopaĩ; Secoya, Pioje (CAAAP/AP, 3:5, junio 1980, p. 75–102, bibl., ill., maps, plates)

Ethnohistorical-ethnographic study traces migrations of the W. Tukanoan Sekoya of the Yubineto and Putumayo Rivers from 1542, following fission and movements of individual clans and their segments (1950–79). Conclusion criticizes notion of "native community" used by government in land titling, suggesting more adequate criteria for legal adjudication of lands.

1236 ———. El sistema de cultivo sekoya (*in* Etnicidad y ecología [see item **1247**] p. 52–53, bibl., diagrams)

General discussion of Sekoya (Peruvian montaña) subsistence activities, with diagram of their seasonal round. Lunar myth central to Sekoya cosmology is related to lunar regulation of agricultural tasks.

1237 Chagnon, Napoleon and **Raymond B. Hames.** La "hipótesis proteica" y la adaptación indígena a la cuenca del Amazonas: una revisión crítica de los datos y de la teoría (AI/I, 5:6, nov./dic. 1980, p. 346–358, bibl., ill., maps, tables)

Overall review of ecological determinist arguments attributing Amazonian social organization to soil poverty (Meggers) or protein scarcity (Gross, Ross) and presenting counterevidence. Argues that scientific explanation should take account of whole biological and social nature of man, not be limited to nutrition (see also items **1223**, **1260**, and **1269**).

1238 Chaumeil, J.P. Historia y migraciones de los Yagua de finales del siglo XVII hasta nuestros días. Traducción, María del Carmen Urbano. Lima: Centro Amazónico de Antropología y Aplicación Práctica, 1981. 209 p.: bibl., ill., indexes, maps, plates (Serie Antropológica; no. 3)

Well-annotated factual history of contacts with Yagua from Orellana's 1542 expedition to 1976. Pt. 1 relates Yagua history to major social developments in Peru, and pt. 2 summarizes migrations of this Carib-speaking group (1693–1976). Closes with two-p. summary of "internal factors" and five-p. list of "external factors" in their migrations.

1239 Chernela, Janet M. Indigenous forest and fish management in the Uaupés Basin of Brazil (Cultural Survival Quarterly [Cultural Survival, Cambridge, Mass.] 6:2, Spring 1982, p. 17–18)

The Uanano (Uaupes Tukanoans) intentionally preserve riparian forest as part of riverine ecosystem which harbors margin wildlife as food for fish. This is a more effective use of resources than the developers' practice of using this zone for agriculture (see also item **1267**).

1240 Civrieux, Marc de. Watunna: an Orinoco creation cycle. Edited and translated by David M. Guss. San Francisco, Calif.: North Point Press, 1980. 195 p., 10 p. of plates: ill., maps.

In brief introduction that sets scene,

author describes Makiritare (So'to or Ye'kwana) and history of their contact, and portrays rite in which full, formal Watunna cycle is told. The reader is then introduced to Makiritare cosmology through this collaborative colloquial translation of Makiritare creation cycle presented in its everyday form.

1241 Cordeu, Edgardo J. La idea de mito en las expresiones narrativas de los indios chamacoco o ishir (Scripta Ethnologica [Centro Argentino de Etnología Americana, Buenos Aires] 2 : 2, 1974, p. 75–117, bibl.)

Discusses types of narrative of Chamacoco or Ishir Indians of central Chaco by relating them to Western concept of "myth."

1242 ——— **and José A. Braunstein.** Los aparatos de un shamán chamacoco: contribución al estudio de la parafernalia shamánica (Scripta Ethnologica [Centro Argentino de Etnología Americana, Buenos Aires] 2 : 2, 1974, p. 121–139, bibl.)

Describes apparatus and exegesis of one Chamacoco shaman.

1243 Cunha, Manuela Carneiro da. Eschatology among the Krahó: reflections upon society, free field of fabulation (in Mortality and immortality: the archaeology and anthropology of death. Edited by Sally Humphreys and H. King. New York: Academic Press, 1981, p. 161–174)

Describes Krahó beliefs about society of dead souls—harmonious but static—stressing diversity of versions. Author suggests eschatology provides (for this northern Gê group) a field for socially encouraged creativity.

1244 Denevan, William M. Los patrones de subsistencia de los campa del Gran Pajonal (in Etnicidad y ecología [see item 1247] p. 85–109, map, tables)

Survey of Campa (Peruvian montaña) subsistence patterns. Stresses importance of hunting for sufficient protein, which leads to unstable settlement pattern detrimental to agriculture.

1245 Dricot, Jean M. Ecología humana en el ambiente amazónico (in Etnicidad y ecología [see item 1247] p. 111–117, bibl.)

Defines general characteristics of Amazonian population in terms of ecological theory.

1246 Eakin, Lucille; Ervin Lauriault; and **Harry Boonstra.** Bosquejo etnográfico de los shipibo-conibo del Ucayali. Traduc-

ción, Marlene Ballena Dávila. Lima: I. Prado Pastor, 1980. 101 p.: bibl., ill.

Straightforward descriptive ethnography by Summer Institute of Linguistics team. Detailed treatment of kinship terms. Of special interest are (separate) lists of medicinal and "magical" plants, the former with botanical identification.

1247 Etnicidad y ecología. Alberto Chirif, compilador. Carátula, Aranzasu Iguiñez. Foto carátula, Raúl Gallegos. Lima: Centro de Investigación y Promoción Amazónica, 1979. 186 p.: bibl., ill.

Varied collection of papers on tropical agriculture, tropical forest, human ecology, indigenous knowledge of the environment, and ecological dangers of subjecting Indians to Western colonial concepts. Papers by following authors are annotated separately: Berlin (item **1218**), Carneiro (item **1232**), Casanova (item **1236**), del Pino (item **1299**), Denevan (item **1244**), Dricot (item **1245**), Gasche (item **1193**), Kramer (item **1274**), Scazzocchio (item **1319**), Smith (item **1198**), and Varese (item **1200**).

1248 Food taboos in Lowland South America. Kenneth M. Kensinger and Waud H. Kracke, editors. Bennington, Vt.: Bennington College, 1981. 198 p.: bibl., figures (Working papers on South American Indians; no. 3)

Papers from a symposium partly in response to Eric Ross (see *HLAS 41 : 1192*) take a variety of approaches such as structuralist, semiotic, and psychoanalytic and include attempts to integrate symbolic understanding to food taboos with ecological considerations. Recurrent themes are taboos as markers of social categories and consubstantiality of nuclear family: Menget "From Forest to Mouth: Reflections on the Txicão Theory of Substance;" Dumont and Hurlich "Protein, Protein, What is Done in Thy Name?;" Taylor "Knowledge and Praxis in Sanuma Food Prohibitions;" Langdon "Food Taboos and the Balance of Oppositions among the Barasana and Taiwano;" Urban "The Semiotics of Tabooed Food: Shokleng (Gê);" Kracke "Don't Let the Piranha Bite your Liver: a Psychoanalytic Approach to Kagwahiv (Tupi) Food Taboos;" Goldman "Cubeo Dietary Rules;" Kensinger "Food Taboos as Markers of Age Categories in Cashinahua;" Abelove and Campos "Infancy Related Food Taboos among the Shipibo;" Kelekna "Achuara Food Taboos;" and discussions by the New Guinea specialists Tuzin and Poole in "Protean Analyses of Food Taboos in Lowland South America: the Search for a Framework" (see also items **1329** and **1335**).

1249 Frikel, Protásio. Areas de arboricultura pré-agrícola na Amazônia: notas preliminares (USP/RA, 21 : 1, 1978, p. 45−52)
Various Amazonian cultures (Tiriyo, Munducurú, Xinguan, etc.) attribute particular concentrations of fruit trees to planting by pre-agricultural predecessors. Hence a pre-agricultural phase of arboriculture is postulated.

1250 Fuentes, Emilio. Los Yanomami y las plantas silvestres (FSCN/A, 54, 1980, p. 3−138, bibl., figures, ill., plates, tables)
Thorough ethnobotanical discussion of forest plants and their uses with quantitative data on time spent by the Yanomami gathering them. Includes list of Yanomami terms for plant parts and processes. Concludes with summaries of origin myths of forest plants (see also item **1278** and *HLAS 43 : 1076*).

1251 Galvão, Eduardo Enéas. Indios do Brasil, áreas culturais e áreas de subsistência. Artigos reunidos sob a responsabilidade de Pedro Agostinho. Salvador, Brazil: Universidade Federal da Bahia, Centro Editorial e Didático, 1973. 76 p., 8 p. of plates: ill. (Núcleo de recursos didáticos: 67)
Consists of 1960 and 1963 articles on "Indigenous Culture Areas of Brazil" and "Basic Elements of Indigenous Horticulture and Subsistence" reissued for teaching purposes under Pedro Agostinho's editorship. Includes curriculum vitae, bibliography and obituary appreciation of Galvão by Agostinho.

1252 Gasc, Jean-Pierre; Jürg Gasché; Jean Lescure; and Claude Sastre. Culture sur brûlis et évolution du milieu forestier en Amazonie du Nord-ouest (*in* International Congress of Americanists, 42nd, Paris, 1976. Actes [see *HLAS 41 : 255*] v. 2, p. 441−452, bibl.)
Interdisciplinary comparative study of swidden agriculture in five tribes of southern Colombia-northeastern Peru (Witoto, Bora-Miraña, Andoke, Sekoya, and Yagua). Among general considerations of method and philosophy, gives brief description of Witoto agriculture cycle (on same project, see item **1196**; see also item **1276**).

1253 Gregor, Thomas. A content analysis of Mehinaku dreams (Ethos [Society for Psychological Anthropology, Washington] 9 : 1, 1981, p. 353−390)
Applies Hall/Vandercastle's statistical analysis of themes to 276 Mehinaku dreams, by 15 different dreamers. Includes sequential list of dreams summarizing each briefly. Material with rich potential for further analysis.

1254 ———. "Far, far away my shadow wandered . . .:" the dream symbolism and dream theories of the Mehinaku Indians of Brazil (AAA/AE, 8 : 4, Nov. 1981, p. 709−720, tables)
Arawakan Mehinaku of the Xingú believe dreams are perceptions of a nocturnally wandering "eye soul," and that they symbolically predict the future. These beliefs are interpreted as expressing concern with the fluid boundaries of the self.

1255 Grossa, Dino J. Shori, camië ya jama = Amigo, quiero visitarte. Caracas: E. Armitano Editor, 1975. 459 p.: col. ill.
Popular book, half consisting of color photographs, by self-styled amateur ethnologist gives surface introduction to life of "Waica (Yanomami north of upper Orinoco). Brief chapters on aspects of social life alternate with "anecdotes."

1256 Guimarães, Alba Zaluar. Resenha bibliográfica: os movimentos "messiânicos" brasileiros; uma leitura (BIB: Boletim Informativo e Bibliográfico de Ciências Sociais [Suplemento de *Dados*, 20, Instituto Universitário de Pesquisa, Rio de Janeiro] 6, 1979?, p. 9−21, bibl.)
Well-constructed bibliographic essay has several paragraphs on Brazilian indigenous messianic movements. Outlines basic issues in the literature.

1257 Guss, David M. The enculturation of Makiritare women (UP/E, 21 : 3, July 1982, p. 259−270, bibl.)
Somewhat misleadingly titled article primarily discusses structural relationships between the sexes and position of women in Makiritare (Ye'kuana) society, a Carib-speaking group near the Orinoco in Venezuela. Only the description of the menarche ceremony, in which men whip girl initiates (along with boys), stresses enculturation of women. Guss argues that male ceremonial dominance and matricidal myths are male counterweights to importance of women in

food production, and to women's domestic control in this uxorilocal ("matrilocal") society. Male ceremonial dominance is redressed by role-reversal rites in which women attack men and appropriate the male central ceremonial space.

1258 ———. Historical incorporation among the Makiritare: from legend to myth (UCLA/JLAL, 7:1, Summer 1981, p. 23–36)

Shows how historical events of contact with the Spanish and Dutch are incorporated into two Ye'cuana myths that deal with events in ways reflecting their different social functions.

1259 ———. Steering for dream: dream concepts of the Makiritare (UCLA/JLAL, 6:2, Winter 1980, p. 297–312, bibl.)

Makiritare (Ye'cuana of the Orinoco, Venezuela) relate dreams to the experiences of wandering *akato* (spirit doubles). Unlike an ordinary dreamer's spirit, a shaman's (*damodede*) remains under his intentional control during trance. Magical action of mythical heroes also occurs through dreams.

1260 Hames, Raymond B. and **William T. Vickers.** Optimal diet breadth theory as a model to explain variability in Amazonian hunting (AAA/AE, 9:2, May 1982, p. 358–378, bibl., tables)

Concerns quantitative data on prey caught and distance traveled by hunters of the Tukanoan Siona-Sekoya (Ecuador) and Ye'cuana and Yanomami (Venezuela). Supports theory that hunters respond to local game depletion by increasing their catch of less valued species and/or hunting further afield.

1261 Hawkes, Kristen; Kim Hill; and **James F. O'Connell.** Why hunters gather: optimal foraging and the Ache of eastern Paraguay (AAA/AE, 9:2, May 1982, p. 379–398, bibl., charts, tables)

Extensive quantitative data gathered on Ache (Tupí, Paraguay) confirm that gathering food encountered during hunt is efficient.

1262 Heinen, H. Dieter; George Salas; and **Miguel Layrisse.** Migración y distancia cultural entre cinco subtribus del Delta del Orinoco, T.F. Delta Amacuro (FSCN/A, 46/48, 1977, p. 3–44, maps, tables)

Demographic study calculates cultural distance among Orinoco Delta Warao subtribes on basis of number of migrants exchanged among them. Argues that bands are exogamous but subtribes largely endogamous.

1263 Henley, Paul. The Panare: tradition and change on the Amazonian frontier. New Haven, Conn.: Yale University Press, 1982. 263 p.: bibl., figures, index, maps, photos, tables.

Well-written ethnography, a restudy of the Carib-speaking Panaré of Venezuela, focuses on ecology and subsistence, economic, and social organization, and especially relations with Creole neighbors. Following Ribeiro's model (*Os indios e a civilização*), last three chapters discuss structure of contact situation, contrasting Peru with Brazil. Complements Dumont's more structuralist (see *HLAS 39:1318*) and epistemological (see *HLAS 43:1105*) treatments of Panaré philosophy and of field work among them. See also *HLAS 43:1124.*

1264 Hern, Warren M. High fertility in a Peruvian Amazon Indian village (Human Ecology [Plenum, New York] 5:4, 1977, p. 355–368, bibl, chart, tables)

Physician who did field work in Ucayali Shipibo village as medical student explores reason for high fertility rate which accelerated cultural change.

1265 ———. Knowledge and use of herbal contraceptives in a Peruvian Amazon village (SAA/HO, 35:1, Spring 1976, p. 9–19, bibl., chart, tables)

Medical study of fascinating Amazonian phenomenon. Interviews with Shipibo women in Ucayali village give no evidence of biological effectiveness of traditional contraceptive herbs. Attributes contraceptive effects to sexual abstinence accompanying their use.

1266 Hudelson, John E. Indian groups of the Northern Montaña: the problem of appellation (UNC/ED, 4:3, Oct. 1979, p. 1–19, bibl., maps)

Useful list of names used to denote various indigenous groups in the Northern Montaña region of Peru and Ecuador. Distinguishes among names that are self-designations, designations by other cultures, and ambiguous terms with multiple referents. (Maps may follow p. 30.)

1267 Ibarra, Robert A. Cultural-ecological adaptations to black, white and blue-water rivers in Amazonia: a preliminary study (UNC/ED, 4:1, March 1979 [i.e. Dec. 1980] p. 1–27, bibl., tables)

Citing studies of distribution of fish

species and acidity levels in different Amazonian rivers and one comparative nutritional study, author concludes by tentatively supporting hypothesis that acidic "black water rivers" are nutritionally poorer than blue- and white-water rivers, and that this affects adaptations of cultures on different rivers.

1268 Idogaya Molina, Anatilde. El daño mediante la palabra entre los ayoreo del Chaco Boreal (EM/A, 1979/1980, p. 21–38, bibl.)

Negative power of mythic narrative (*kíkie uhuáide*) is discussed at length in terms of Bormida's analysis, noting how it can be used to harm others.

1269 Johnson, Allen. Reductionism in cultural ecology: the Amazon case (UC/CA, 23:4, Aug. 1982, p. 413–482, bibl., tables)

Author argues that despite apparently abundant garden land and protein supply, the Machiguenga (of the Upper Ucayali, Peru) *perceive* shortages of best land and prized game. Such cultural perceptions of scarcity must be included in assessment of resource abundance or scarcity. Advocates "bridging" structural and ecological approaches, arguing that any scientific explanation is "reductionist."

1270 Kaplan, Joanna Overing. Amazonian anthropology: review article (JLAS, 13:1, May 1981, p. 151–165, bibl.)

Review article places four recent books (see *HLAS 43:1101, 1105,* and *1129–1130*) in comparative perspectives. Stresses fundamental role of naming in lowland South American societies and concept of exogamy as mixing of differences essential for social/economic processes. Introduces Piaroa data to illustrate last point.

1271 Kensinger, Kenneth M. On meat and hunting (UC/CA, 24:1, Feb. 1983, p. 128–129, bibl.)

Brief but important contribution to the protein deficiency debate and to understanding tropical forest hunting. Suggests multiple reasons for importance of meat in tropical forest diet, including value placed on hunting for male identity, for release of tension and for achieving a "high" in strenuous activity (a non-nutritional biological factor, see item **1237**).

1272 Kracke, Waud H. Complementarity of social and psychological regularities:

leadership as a mediating phenomenon (Ethos [Society for Psychological Anthropology, Washington] 8:4, Winter 1980, p. 273–285, bibl.)

Analysis of instability of uxorilocal marriage in Kagwahiv society is juxtaposed with psychological studies of sources of strain in marriages of three Kagwahiv men. Illustrates point that anthropological analysis of social causes and psychological analysis of emotional reasons for the same event may lead in completely different directions. Compares contradiction with the principle of complementarity in physics.

1273 ———. Kagwahiv mourning: dreams of a bereaved father (Ethos [Society for Psychological Anthropology, Washington] 9:1, 1981, p. 249–257, bibl.)

Interprets dreams of a Kagwahiv father who lost his child as expressing conflicts over the loss. Argues that empathic understanding of psychological states of someone from a very different culture is possible.

1274 Kramer, Betty Jo. La agricultura de los urarina (*in* Etnicidad y ecología [see item **1247**] p. 131–136, bibl.)

Describes Urarina (Northern Peruvian Amazon region) variant of slash-and-burn agriculture: plantain rhizomes are planted *before* burning field, for maximum growth period during dry season (see also items **1232** and **1277**).

1275 Kühne, Heinz. Der Bodenbau der Kaingáng und Lakranó-Indianer und dessen Stellung im Rahmen der Gê-Völker: pt. 1, Der Bodenbau im Wechselwirkung zum geistigen Leben, zur Gesellung und zur; pt. 2, Sammelwirtschaft, Fischfang und Tierhaltung der Kaingáng-und Lakranó-Indianer (MVW/AV, 33, 1979, p. 61–84, bibl.; 34, 1980, p. 101–122)

First two of three-part series comparing subsistence of Kaingáng and "Lakrano" (Shokleng) with rest of Gê. Pt. 1 on agriculture, concludes that Gê agriculture is aboriginal but that Kaingáng-Shokleng agriculture differed substantially from other Gê. Pt. 2 compares collecting, fishing, and animal domestication.

1276 Lescure, Jean-Paul. Etudes interdisciplinaires sur le haut Oyapock: Guyane française (*in* International Congress of Americanists, 42nd, Paris, 1976. Actes [see *HLAS 41:255*] v. 2, p. 453–462)

Botanist of multidisciplinary team reports on study of agriculture of the Wayapi (upper Oyapock River, French Guiana) and its part in the local ecosystem.

1277 Lizot, Jacques. La agricultura yanomami (FSCN/A, 53, 1980, p. 3–93, ill., plates, tables)

Challenges assertion that Yanomami agriculture was introduced recently, by offering detailed description of agriculture among the Central Yanomami based on long field work. Includes discussion of each plant cultivated and its uses, quantitative case studies of area devoted to each crop and time spent in cultivating, soils, and productivity (see item **1234**).

1278 ———. Economie primitive et subsistence: essai sur le travail et l'alimentation chez les Yanomami (Libre [Petit bibliothèque Payot, Paris] 4, 1978, p. 69–113, bibl., charts, tables)

Quantitative study of time/energy devoted to food production among Venezuelan Yanomami supports Sahlins' image of abundance against more conventional (and orthodox Marxist) view of primitive scarcity (see also items **1234** and **1250** *HLAS 39:1388, HLAS 43:1076* and *1086*).

1279 Martínez-Crovetto, Raúl. Algunos juegos de los indios mataco-wichí de Pozo Verde, Formosa (UCNSA/SA, 14:1/2, dic. 1979, p. 249–258, bibl.)

Describes 27 Mataco games for adults and children observed while visiting this Paraguayan Chaco group.

1280 Mashnshnek, Celia Olga. Aportes para una comprensión de la economía de los mataco (Scripta Ethnologica [Centro Argentino de Etnología Americana, Buenos Aires] 3:1, 1975, p. 7–39, bibl., glossary)

Presents Matacos' own conception of their economy through myths of origin of food species and economic implements and techniques, and through explanations of food taboos.

1281 ———. Seres potentes y héroes míticos de los mataco del Chaco Central (Scripta Ethnologica [Centro Argentino de Etnología Americana, Buenos Aires] 1, 1973, p. 105–154, bibl., glossary)

Classifies and discusses major figures in Mataco (Central Chaco) mythology. Appendix includes selection of Mataco myths in Spanish translation.

1282 ———. Textos míticos de los chulupí del Chaco Central (Scripta Ethnologica [Centro Argentino de Etnología Americana, Buenos Aires] 3:1, 1975, p. 151–189, bibl.)

Presents 47 Chulupi (Central Chaco) myths grouped by subject matter (i.e., astral, animal, origin, catastrophe, etc.).

1283 Matta, Roberto da. A divided world: Apinayé social structure. Cambridge, Mass.: Harvard University Press, 1982. 186 p.: bibl., charts, index, notes.

Translation of da Matta's brilliant and controversial ethnography of Northern Gê Apinayé (see *HLAS 41:1174*) which stresses division between structured public, ceremonial domain and private, everyday domain marked by *communitas*. Also emphasizes dialectic of ideology and practice. Comparison with other Gê tribes throughout book generates broader theory of Gê societies. Concludes with general theory of dual organization.

1284 ———. Quanto custa ser índio no Brasil?: considerações sobre o problema de identidade étnica (IUP/D, 13, 1976, p. 33–54, bibl.)

Much-cited article places interethnic relations in context of theory of "paradoxical identity" and its high costs. An Apinayé myth serves as paradigm of multiple relationships involved in identity as "Indian" vis-à-vis "white man." Thus, the Indian can take advantage of the dominant society's contradictions in order to improve his condition. Includes summaries in English and French.

1285 Melatti, Julio Cesar. Indivíduo e grupo: à procura de uma classificação de personagems mítico-rituais Timbiras (Anuário Antropológico [Edições Tempo Brasileiro, Rio de Janeiro] 1979 [i.e. 1981] p. 99–147, bibl., figures, tables)

Discusses relations among "plaza groups" in three Timbira (Gê) tribes (Krahó, Ramkokamekra and Krikati), and the related classification of animals in system of omens. Argues that the eight plaza groups, in contrasting pairs, form a paradigm for choices in conflicts of individual loyalty to groups.

1286 Meliá, Bartoloméu; Georg Grünberg; and Friedl Grünberg. Los Paî-Tavyterã: etnografía guaraní del Paraguay contemporáneo. Asunción: Universidad Católica Nuestra Señora de la Asunción, Centro de Estudios Antropológicos, 1976. p. 152–295, bibl., ill.

Well-rounded descriptive ethnography of major Paraguayan Guaraní group emphasizes listing and definition of Guaraní terms. Historical introductory section traces development of Paraguayan identity and catechization. Pedagogical texts in Guaraní (13 p.) enhance book's didactic flavor.

1287 Méndez, Luis G. Calixto. Evolución étnica del Ucayali Central (*in* Congreso Peruano: El Hombre y la Cultura Andina, 3d, Lima, 1977. El hombre y la cultura andina [see *HLAS 43:253*] v. 3, p. 194–203)

Sketches successive waves of ethnic groups in Ucayali River: "Nahuas," Panos, Tupi groups, Andeans, Franciscan missionaries, and rubber gatherers.

1288 Miraglia, Luigi. Caza, recolección y agricultura entre indígenas del Paraguay (UCNSA/SA, 10:1/2, dic. 1975, p. 9–91, bibl., ill., tables)

Arguing that both Chaco and Parana environments of Paraguay offer abundant resources, zoologist compares hunting and gathering of Ache-Guayaki, the Chaco hunter-gatherers (Toba, Mak'a, and Ayoreo), and the agricultural Ava. Assigns Ache to non-Mongoloid race of "pygmoid hunter-gatherers" distinct from "Amazónid" Ava. Includes 40 sketches and photos of hunts, gathering equipment, and traps.

1289 Morey, Robert V. A joyful harvest of souls: disease and the destruction of the Llanos Indians (FSCN/A, 52, 1979, p. 77–108, map)

Chronicle documenting the toll taken by disease among Llanos Indian groups from 16th to 19th centuries.

1290 Nimuendaju, Curt. Os Indios Tukuna (Boletim do Museu do Indio [Fundação Nacional do Indio, FUNAI, Rio de Janeiro] Antropologia 7, dez. 1977, p. 1–69, bibl., glossary)

Previously unpublished report to Indian Protective Service written by father of Brazilian ethnography on his first field trip to Tukuna. Introduction by Carlos de Araujo Moreira Neto and Charlotte Emmerich.

1291 Novaes, Sylvia Caiuby. Tranças, cabaças e couros no funeral Bororo: a propósito de um proceso de constituição de identidade (USP/RA, 24, 1981, p. 25–36, bibl., tables)

Description of Bororo funeral, interpreting ritual objects used as markers of social identity of the deceased (see *HLAS 43:1094, 1149,* and *1214*).

1292 Nugent, Stephen. Amazonia: ecosystem and social system (RAI/M, 16:1, March 1981, p. 62–74, bibl.)

Criticizes recent ecological determinist writings on Amazonia (e.g., *HLAS 39:1331*) for neglecting crucial historical factors affecting social relations of production, and anthropologists and ecologists for ignoring long-standing non-Indian settlement that did not damage the environment. Recent irreversible degradation, Nugent asserts, is due to large scale capital-intensive ranching, mining, and timber operations.

1293 Oosten, J.G. Filiation and alliance in three Bororo myths: a reconsideration of the social code in the first chapters of *The raw and the cooked* (KITLV/B, 137, 1981, p. 106–125, bibl.)

Reinterprets Bororo myths using structural mode but in terms of Bororo culture. Sees them as concerning parent-child relationships.

1294 Ortiz, Francisco. Taxonomía de los grups guahibo (ICA/RCA, 20, 1976, p. 281–293, bibl.)

Based on some field work ("since August 1972") in mixed Guahibo-Cuiva community, supplemented by published sources, author sketches Guahibo and Cuiva classifications of social groups by various criteria.

1295 Ottaviano, John and **Ida Ottaviano.** Notas sobre la cultura tacana. Traducción de Pedro Plaza. Riberalta, Bolivia: Instituto Lingüístico de Verano; La Paz: Ministerio de Educación y Cultura, 1980. 52 p.: bibl., ill.

Simple descriptive ethnography, mostly devoted to superficial description of subsistence and material culture.

1296 Pagés Larraya, Fernando. Investigaciones de psiquiatría transcultural entre los aborígenes Maskoy del Chaco Boreal (UBAIA/R, 13:1/2, 1976/1980, p. 209–269, bibl., ill., tables)

After presenting epidemiological statistics on mental illness among Maskoy (Lengua-Maskoy, Angaite, Sanapana and Kashkiha) of Paraguayan Chaco, and noting early reports of distinctive Maskoy ethnic psychosis, author examines six cases of mental illness in the context of traditional belief and current conditions. Author's view of mental illness as response to profound loss of ethnic identity leads him to conception of "madness as hermeneutic of the culture."

1297 Pérez Diez, Andrés A. Noticia sobre la concepción del ciclo anual entre los matacos del noreste de Salta (Scripta Ethnologica [Centro Argentino de Etnología Americana, Buenos Aires] 2:1, 1974, p. 111–120, bibl.)

Relates mythical personalities of sun, moon, and other calendrical figures to seasonal round of the Mataco (Central Chaco).

1298 Peters, John F. The Shirishana of the Yanomami: a demographic study (SSSB/SB, 27:4, Winter 1980, p. 272–285, bibl.)

Missionary who lived since 1958 with small Yanomami dialect group documents rise in population over contact period despite epidemics, abortion, and infanticide.

1299 Pino, Fermín del. Migración y adaptación en Madre de Dios: el caso de los serranos (in Etnicidad y ecología [see item 1247] p. 55–83, bibl.)

Discusses problems of migrants from mountains to low tropical forest region.

1300 Polykrates, Gottfried. Beiträge zur Religionsfrage der Yanomámi-Indianer. Copenhagen: The National Museum of Denmark, 1974. 35 p.: bibl. (Publications of the National Museum; vol. 14)

Differentiates three "myth complexes," each centering on a different mythic hero, and discusses their distribution among Yanomami groups in Venezuela and Brazil (see item 1215).

1301 Price, David. Nambiquara leadership (AAA/AE, 8:4, Nov. 1981, p. 686–708, bibl, map, photo)

Important contribution outlines structure of Nambiquara villages and criteria for leadership, correcting some points in Lévi-Strauss' classic paper and in Tristes tropiques. While most leaders are egalitarian, a minority command greater authority— mostly along northern perimeter exposed to Cinta Larga raids (see HLAS 43:1142 and HLAS 41:1126).

1302 Ramos, Alcida R. Rumor: the ideology of an inter-tribal situation (FSCN/A, 51, 1979, p. 3–23, bibl.)

Analyzes rumor of Sanuma or Yanam killing of a Maiongong (Makiritare) Indian as expressing the "ideology of Maiongong-Sanuma contact" and anxieties by individuals who propagate the rumor, themselves in intermediate positions.

1303 ———. Tecnonomia e conceitualização social entre os índios Sanuma (Anuário Antropológico [Editora Tempo Brasileiro, Rio de Janeiro] 1977 [i.e. 1978] p. 148–167, bibl., charts)

Sanuma (Yanomami) teknonymy, extended to siblings and parents or to spouses and children, avoids insulting use of personal names. This practice delimits the nuclear family, distinguishes it from the wife's extended family within which it is submerged, and constitutes a stage in the formation of a named local lineage.

1304 ———; Peter Silverwood Cope; Ana Gita de Oliveira; and **Maria Luisa Mouro Pires.** Hierarquia e simbiose: relações intertribais no Brasil. São Paulo: Editora Hucitec, 19080. 246 p.: ill. (Ciências sociais. Série Realidade social)

Three case studies of asymmetrical interethnic contact between native Brazilian tribes stress symbiotic nature of these "hierarchical" relationships in contrast to exploitative nature of white domination. Pt. 1, study of Maiongong (Makiritare or Ye'kwana)-Sanuma relations in Roraima, includes studies of identity in cases of intermarriage, of Maiongong individual as well as of a rumor. Pt. 2 consists of shorter studies of relations between Vaupes River Indians and Makcú and between Kaingáng and Guaraní in Paraná.

1305 Reátegui G., Mirca. Bibliografía sobre antropología y arqueología de la selva del Perú (PEBN/B, 21/22:73/76, 1975/1976, p. 5–58, table)

Interesting though incomplete bibliography, partially annotated, divided into anthropology and archaeology sections and further subdivided into topical subsections. Concludes with "evidence of tropical forest themes in coastal and mountain Peru." Especially good on articles published in Peru.

1306 Regehr, Walter. Movimientos mesiánicos entre los grupos étnicos del Chaco paraguayo (USCN/SA, 16:2, dic. 1981, p. 105–117, bibl.)

Chaco groups have taken part in charismatic movements incorporating evangelical messages that were resisted initially. Describes one such movement initiated by Nivakle and analyzes it as response to food crisis.

1307 Reichel-Dolmatoff, Gerardo. Brain and mind in Desana Shamanism (UCLA/JLAL, 7 : 1, Summer 1981, p. 73–98, bibl., ill.)

Examines complex beliefs about mind and brain of Desana (Vaupes River, Colombia) shamans. Based on observation of brain-injured individuals, these beliefs include recognition of lateral specialization of hemispheres.

1308 ———. Some source materials on Desana shamanistic initiation (FSCN/A, 51, 1979, p. 27–61, bibl.)

Two texts on shamanic initiation by elderly Desana (Tukanoan, Vaupes River) shaman are presented in Desana and English translation with line-by-line commentary elucidating connotations and symbolism.

1309 Renard-Casevitz, France Marie. Su-açu: essai sur les cervidés de l'Amazonie et sur leur signification dans les cultures indiennes actuelles. Paris: Institut français d'études andines, 1979. 126 p., 4 leaves of plates: bibl., indexes, ill. (Travaux de l'Institut français d'études andines; t. 20)

Essay on Amazonian deer. First half is species-by-species zoological treatise. Second half, "Men and Deer," begins with "technical" aspects—hunting methods and uses of deer parts—and then turns to most interesting "Cultural Universe of the Hunt," beliefs and taboos about deer, and their place in myths and religious beliefs. Closes with section on "Semantic Position of the Deer" summarizing symbolic meaning, which combines "beauty and seduction" with "death." Sources limited, but well selected except for heavy dependence on outdated HSAI articles.

1310 Ribeiro, Berta G. Diário do Xingú. Capa e diagramação, Ana Luisa Escorel, Cynthia Leite Araújo. São Paulo: Paz e Terra, 1979. 265 p.: ill. (Coleção Estudos brasileiros; v. 42)

Account of ethnography as a personal experience, in diary form of two-and-a-half-week field trip to various Xingúan tribes (half of it with the Kayabí) studying basketry. More emotional self-reflection would enhance value as account of field experience. Includes brief introduction on development of Xingúan intertribal society.

1311 Ribeiro, Darcy. Kadiwéu: ensaios etnológicos sobre o saber, o azar e a beleza. 2. ed. Petrópolis, Brazil: Vozes, 1980. 318 p.: bibl., ill.

Ethnography of art and thought among the Kadiwéu (Caduveo), composed of two previously published books, *Religião e mitologia Kadiwéu* and *Arte Kadiwéu*. Three chapters (reflected in book's subtitle) suggest content: "Mythology: the Search for Knowledge," "Religion: the Control of Chance," and "Art: the Wish for Beauty."

1312 Ríos, Miguel Angel de los. Hacia una hermenéutica del nombre en la etnía mataco (Scripta Ethnologica [Centro Argentino de Etnología Americana, Buenos Aires] 3 : 2, 1976, p. 63–83, bibl.)

A Mataco name, revealed to a father (or shaman) by a supernatural being in a dream, constitutes a power and is an essential part of a person's being. Thus a dead child's name must be avoided in its father's presence. Interesting article discusses power inherent in names and its relation to name-giving power of father and nonhuman beings.

1313 ———. Temporalidad y potencia entre los grupos matacos (Scripta Ethnologica [Centro Argentino de Etnología Americana, Buenos Aires] 2 : 1, 1974, p. 7–38, bibl.)

Discusses concepts of time, being, and power among the Mataco of Paraguayan Chaco, and the "two ontological regions" of human and superhuman power.

1314 Roe, Peter G. The cosmic zygote: cosmology in the Amazon Basin. New Brunswick, N.J.: Rutgers University Press, 1982. 384 p.: bibl., index, ill.

Daring synthesis of materials on Amazonian/Orinoco cosmologies constructs underlying cosmological model for Amazonian cultures. Includes both structure of universe and central personages of mythologies, suggesting transformational equivalences among personages who play structurally equivalent roles in different mythologies. Begins book with 95-p. presentation of Shipibo cosmology based on his own field research, and extends model through review of other literature on Amazonian cosmologies (for specific cosmologies, see especially items **1219, 1226, 1240, 1281, 1324** and **1345**; for contrasting traditional compendium approach, see item **1341**).

1315 Ross, Jane Bennett. Ecology and the problem of tribe: a critique of the Hobbesian model of preindustrial warfare (*in* Beyond the myths of culture: essays in cultural materialism. New York: Academic Press, 1980, p. 33–60, bibl., map, table)

Branding Chagnon's and Sahlins' attribution of warfare to "the nature of tribal political organization" (*inter alia*) as "Hobbesian," Ross advances "Darwinian" explanation of warfare as extension of hunting strategy in competition for protein resources (see also items **1237, 1269, 1292,** *HLAS 43:1076, 1086, 1120,* and *HLAS 43,* p. 144–145).

1316 Sá, Cristina C. da Costa e and **Eduardo Henrique Bacellar Corrêa.** Habitação indígena no Alto Xingú (Encontros com a Civilização Brasileira [Editora Civilização Brasileiro, Rio de Janeiro] 12, junho 1979, p. 129–142, bibl., figures, ill., map, plates)

Architect and photographer combine their talents to study the style, construction, and use of traditional elliptical houses in Xingú Indian villages.

1317 Salas, George and **H. Dieter Heinen.** Algunos materiales para la demografía warao (FSCN/A, 46/48, 1977, p. 71–258, tables)

Census list of several Warao groups of the Orinoco Delta region includes appended tables of demographic statistics.

1318 Santos, Yolanda Lhullier dos; Helda Bullotta Barracco; and **Nubue Myazaki.** Textos-ritos do índio brasileiro: Xinguano e Kadiwéu. São Paulo: Ebraesp Editorial Ltda., 1975. 128 p.: ill., photos.

Examines designs, everyday objects, and rituals of Xingú and Kadiwéu face paintings, as "texts" which are "read" through unclear, universalistic (Jungian?) code. Based on limited field work and library research.

1319 Scazzocchio, Françoise. Informe breve sobre los lamistas (*in* Etnicidad y ecología [see item **1247**] p. 137, table)

On the basis of cultural traits, speculates that large native population of Lamas in montaña dept. of San Martín is of highland origin. Study probes cultural conservatism.

1320 Seeger, Anthony. A identidade étnica como processo: os índios Suya e as sociedades do alto Xingú (Anuário Antropológico [Edições Tempo Brasileiro, Rio de Janeiro] 1978 [i.e. 1980] p. 156–175)

Discussion of integration of Gê-speaking Suyá Indians into Xingúan society stresses that ethnic identity is a process that depends on the vicissitudes of intergroup relations and internal group processes. The Suyá themselves emphasize identity traits other than those noted by anthropologists.

1321 Siffredi, Alejandra. La autoconciencia de las relaciones sociales entre los Yojwaha-Chorote (Scripta Ethnologica [Centro Argentino de Etnología Americana, Buenos Aires] 1, 1973, p. 71–103, bibl., chart)

Considers ideas of ethnic identity of the Chorote (autodenomination: Yojwaha), including relevant myths, and briefly considers social structure.

1322 ———. La noción de reciprocidad entre los Yojwaha-Chorote (Scripta Ethnologica [Centro Argentino de Etnología Americana, Buenos Aires] 3:1, 1975, p. 41–70, bibl., figures)

After discussing notions of giving in this Central Chaco Matao group, author presents data (mythic and observational) on: the "pure (unreciprocated) gift," types of reciprocity in food, reciprocity in relation to rank, and kinds of reciprocity in various social contexts.

1323 Silva, Alcionilio Brüzzi Alves da. A civilização indígena do Uaupés: observações antropológicas, etnográficas e sociológicas. 2. ed. Roma: Centro Studi di Storia delle Missini Salesiane, 1977. 443 p., 26 p. of plates: bibl., ill. (some col.), index (Studi e richerche; 1)

Detailed but patronizing ethnographic survey of various cultures of Uaupes. Lists of *malocas* among major rivers, historical references to different tribes, descriptions of items of material culture, etc., may be useful; but chapter on "psychology" (and other passages) characterize them as indolent, dirty, irresponsible, etc.

1324 Silverwood-Cope, Peter. Cosmologia Maku (Anuário Antropológico [Edições Tempo Brasileiro, Rio de Janerio] 1978 [i.e. 1980] p. 176–239, bibl., tables)

Beginning with circumstantial descriptions of conditions and methods for gathering information, author narrates Macú (Northwest Amazon) accounts of origin and describes "structure of cosmos" in Macú belief—levels, space-time relations, and kinds of living beings. Analyzes cosmology in terms of several dynamically interacting oppositions of "insupportable extremes."

1325 Smith, Robert J. La vida en la muerte de los aché-guayakí (UCNSA/SA, 10:172, dic. 1975, p. 135–176, ill., tables)

Uses statistics on the cause of death of 330 deceased members of a band of Aché-Guayakí in Paraguay to reconstruct past social conditions.

1326 Stocks, Anthony Wayne. Los nativos invisibles: notas sobre la historia y realidad actual de los Cocamilla del Río Huallaga, Perú. Traducción, Annette Rosenvinge de Uriarte, Armando Valdés Palacios. Lima: Centro Amazónico de Antropología y Aplicación Práctica, 1981. 1 v. (Serie Antropológica; no. 4)

Presents history and current state of Tupi-speaking Cocamilla as example of problems facing partially detribalized indigenous cultures who still form ethnic enclaves but lack visibility of less acculturated Indians. Discusses problems of ethnic identity, of an egalitarian culture in adapting to political authority, and the economic stratification that ensues with "development." Dim forecast in closing chapter is somewhat mitigated by later developments described in epiloque.

1327 Straka, Hellmuth. Ocho años entre yucpas y japrerías. Caracas: Ediciones de la Presidencia de la República, 1980. 89 p.: bibl., ill.

Readable, well-informed, and sympathetic account of Indians with whom author lived during eight years of travels in Venezuelan *selva*.

1328 Taussig, Michael. Folk healing and the structure of conquest in Southwest Colombia (UCLA/JLAL, 6:2, Winter 1980, p. 271–278, bibl.)

Fascinating and provocative historical-ethnographic study of network of lowland and highland indigenous and mestizo shamanic healers in Colombia. Healers mediate (sometimes by inversion) oppositions created by colonial domination. Uses field data on *yagé* visions and curing as practiced by the Siona and Kopan of the Putumayo valley as well as data gathered by Jean Langdon (see *HLAS 43:1146–1147*) and Scott Robinson.

1329 Taylor, Kenneth Iain. Sanuma food prohibition and para-totemic classification (FSCN/A, 51, 1979, p. 63–92, bibl., graphs, maps)

Sanuma lineages are "para-totemically" marked by food prohibitions, but, at a second-order level. All lineages (and "agnatic cores," see item **1303**) share the same age-related food prohibitions, but in different lineages prohibitions of particular species extend to different age categories. This system (one of "differences of differences") is elaborated, and types of classification are discussed in relation to totemism (see also *HLAS 43:1206*).

1330 Thomas, David John. Order without government: the society of the Pemon Indians of Venezuela. Urbana: University of Illinois Press, 1981. 1 v.: bibl., index (Illinois studies in anthropology; no. 13)

Ethnography of the Carib-speaking, Venezuelan (Caroni River) Pemón. Interesting chapters on secular and religious leaders (including shamans and prophets), and on conflict ("forces of disharmony"). Concludes with chapter on how acculturative influences are destroying Pemón egalitarian ethic.

1331 Tomasini, Alfredo. Tanki: un personaje mítico de los toba de occidente (Scripta Ethnologica [Centro Argentino de Etnología Americana, Buenos Aires] 2:1, 1974, p. 133–150; and 3:1, 1975, p. 133–148)

Translated text of Eastern Toba (Argentine Chaco) myth cycle of 31 episodes. Brief commentary discusses Tanki's relation to other Toba mythic personages.

1332 Torre López, Fernando. Notas etnográficos sobre el grupo anti o campa de la Amazonia Peruana (IPGH/FA, 25, junio 1978, p. 43–72, bibl., plates)

Notes on material culture, food, state of health, and economic division of labor of the Arawakan-speaking Campa of the Upper Ucayali, Peru.

1333 Trupp, Fritz. Mythen der Makuna. Wien: Elisabeth Stiglmayr, 1977. 150 p., 8 leaves of plates: bibl., ill., map (Acta ethnologica et linguistica; Nr. 40: Series Americana; 8)

Collection of Makuna (Vaupes) myths collected in field work over a period of 10 months, transcribed in Spanish through an interpreter and published in German translation from Spanish, with commentary.

1334 Urban, Greg. Agent- and patient-centricity in myth (AFS/JAF, 94:373, 1981, p. 323–344)

On the basis of examples drawn from

myths of the Eastern Timbira (Gê), Bella Coola, and Shokleng (Southern Gê) whom Urban studied, he distinguishes myths according to whether an event's protagonist is active (agent) or acted upon (patient). Argues that patient-centricity is characteristic of Gê myths and agent-centricity of Northwest myths.

1335 ———. The semiotics of tabooed food: the Shokleng case (Social Science Information [Sage, London and Beverly Hills, Calif.] 20:3, 1981, p. 475–507)

Presents semiotic analysis of food taboos as indexing social categories among the Shokleng (Southern Gê), Sanuma (Yanomami), Cashinawa (Panoan), and in an Australian totemic system (see also items **1248** and **1329**).

1335a Vargas Arenas, Iraida. Introducción al estudio de las ideas antropológicas venezolanas: 1880–1936 (BBAA, 40:49, 1978, p. 25–48, bibl.)

Outline of development of 19th-20th century anthropological thought serves as background for sketches of seven 19th- and early 20th-century Venezuelan anthropologists, three contributors to the "ethnographic current" (Marcano, Alvarado, Jahn) and four to the "ethnohistoric current" (Salas, Fébres Cordero, Tavera Acosta and Arcaya).

1336 Vellard, Jehan Albert. Muñecas karajás de la Misión Vellard (UBAIA/R, 13:1/2, 1976/1980, p. 197–208, ill.)

Comments on Museo del Hombre collection of ceramic and wax Karajá figurines, in traditional and outside-influenced styles, relating shape and decoration to social status of person depicted by doll. Photos illustrate Karajá life scenes as well as dolls (see also *HLAS 43:1092*).

1338 Watson, Lawrence C. Dreaming as world view and action in Guajiro culture (UCLA/JLAL, 7:2, 1981, p. 239–254, bibl.)

Describes Venezuelan Guajiro belief in dreaming as experience of soul, and distinguishes ordinary dreams from "message" dreams prescribing action. Agrees with Lincoln that message dreams cannot be psychologically interpreted and attributes Kracke's contrary finding among Kagwahiv (see *HLAS 43:1141*) to cultural differences rather than to differences of research methodology.

1339 Watson-Franke, María Bárbara. Seclusion huts and social balance in Guajiro society (AI/A, 77:3/4, 1982, p. 449–460, bibl.)

Interprets seclusion in life-crisis rites (menarche, shamanic initiation, after killing) as protective retraction of social boundaries around person during period of spiritual danger. Women's key roles in such rites reflect their importance in matrilineal society.

1340 ———. The urbanization and liberation of women: a study of urban impact on Guajiro women in Venezuela (FSCN/A, 51, 1979, p. 93–117, bibl.)

Guajiro women may gain opportunities for schooling in Maracaibo, but lose kinship network which gives them power and education in their traditional matrilineal society.

1341 Wavrin, Robert, *marquis de.* Mythologie, rites et sorcellerie des Indiens de l'Amazonie. Monaco: Editions du Rocher, 1979. 392 p., 12 leaves of plates: ill. (Collection Itinéraires)

Old style compendium of religious beliefs of various tribes encountered by this adventurer Marquis during his South American expeditions (1913 to 1937), presented patchwork-fashion in chapters on deities, divinities, death, magic, sorcerers, and rites. Published posthumously (contrast with item **1314**).

1342 Werner, Dennis. Chiefs and presidents: a comparison of leadership traits in the United States and among the Mekranoti-Kayapo of central Brazil (Ethos [Journal of the Society for Psychological Anthropology, Washington] 10:2, Summer 1982, p. 136–148, bibl., tables)

Using projective tests, Werner rates sociometrically chosen Kayapó leaders on 15 social and personality traits. Compares these with Stogdill's 1950 review of disparate leadership trait studies for supposedly comparable US sample. Pioneering effort to apply leadership study techniques to a primitive culture marred by poorly chosen baseline for US comparison.

1343 ———. Gerontocracy among the Mekranoti of Central Brazil (CUA/AQ, 54:1, Jan. 1981, p. 15–27, bibl., tables)

Uses sociograms, TATs, genealogies, and interactional observations in order to explain political authority of age among

Kayapó. Influence correlates little with number of sons as intervening variable, but highly with accumulated knowledge, especially of ceremonies. Supports argument well with anecdotes of how knowledge is used for persuasion. (Fails to test for number of sons-in-law, important in this uxorilocal society.)

1344 ———. Trekking in the Amazon forest (AMNH/NH, 87:9, Nov. 1978, p. 42–55, photographs)

Nicely illustrated popular account of economic activities of Mēkranoti Kayapo, focusing on rainy season treks. Based on author's field work.

1344a Wiedemann, Inga. Brazilian hammocks (DGV/ZE, 104:1, 1979, p. 105–133, bibl., map, plates, tables)

This simple library paper, which describes the hammock types of both Indian tribes and Brazilian towns, is most useful for its exhaustive list of hammock types produced by different Indian tribes and for its extensive bibliography. Illustrated with seven photographic details of hammock weaves, four from museum collections. [L. Huyssen Kracke]

1345 Wilbert, Johannes. Warao cosmology and Ye'cuana roundhouse symbolism (UCLA/JLAL, 7:l, Summer 1981, p. 37–72, bibl., diagrams, map, photos)

Parallels between (Chibchan) Warao cosmology and cosmic symbolism of (Carib) Ye'cuana leads Wilbert to postulate early period of contact between these now separate Venezuelan tribes.

Zerries, Otto. Los waika-yanoama: indígenas del Alto Orinoco, 1954–1974. See item **1186**.

ETHNOLOGY: South America, Highlands

WILLIAM E. CARTER, *Chief, Hispanic Division, Library of Congress*

OVER THE PAST DECADE, ANDEAN ETHNOLOGY has reached ever greater maturity. It now constitutes one of the major bodies of ethnology within anthropology, and should be reaching the point of making major contributions to anthropological theory.

Surprisingly few monographs were published during the biennium; bound collections of articles dealing with single themes were almost as numerous. The traditional vehicle of the community study was becoming increasingly rare, one of the few exceptions being *Irpa Chico* (item **1388**), itself based on data some 20 years old, although updated with a lengthy epilogue. More common were studies of regions, some of which were of excellent quality. A model of this approach is Robin Shoemaker's *The peasants of El Dorado: conflict and contradiction in a Peruvian frontier settlement* (item **1478**). Here the author makes it eminently clear that what happens on the Peruvian frontier is highly dependent on the manipulation of political and economic power both at the national and the international level. Another superb study that looks at a series of communities and compares their response to the Peruvian agrarian reform is Harold O. Skar's *The War Valley people: duality and land reform among the Quechua Indians of highland Peru* (item **1479**). Of the few book-length ethnographies produced over the biennium, this may qualify as the best. Another excellent book-length ethnography is Anthony Wayne Stocks' *Los nativos invisibles: notas sobre la historia y realidad actual de los cocamilla del Río Huallaga, Perú* (item **1481**). Because the Cocamilla are Spanish speakers and are frequently indistinguishable from the surrounding populations, Stocks argues that marriage patterns, more than language, should be used as a primary defining feature of an ethnic group.

An innovative and welcome attempt to look at problems in the Andes as a whole is David Guillet's article "Land Tenure, Ecological Zone, and Agriculture Regime in the Central Andes" (item **1361**). In preparing it, Guillet reviewed all the community and regional studies he could find, and concluded that only 17 gave sufficient, detailed information to establish clear correlations among these three basic elements of Andean economy. His approach, more sophisticated than that of many who have blindly parroted the archipelago theory of John Murra, holds the promise of more empirical appraisals of the whole man land equation in the Andes. One of the finest pieces of research to be based on the Murra theoretical framework is Tristán Platt's "El Papel del Ayllu Andino en la Reproducción del Régimen Mercantil Simple en el Norte de Potosí" (item **1395a**), where he documents a relationship between social ranking and access to a variety of ecological niches.

There seems to be a surprising renewal of concern over the definition of "Indian." In large part, this reflects the fact that ever large numbers of Indians are receiving higher education, are occupying positions of authority in society, and still are resolved to retain their identification as Indians. Contrary to the movement of several years ago to obliterate the term *indio* from the vocabulary and to substitute for it *campesino* or *indígena*, there is now a counter movement to reinstate the term as the only one specific enough to describe the Indians' actual situation. Adolfo Colombres has brought together documents from Indian groups throughout the continent, most of which focus on the need for self determination; Yves Materne has produced a companion piece, more documentary and less polemic in orientation; Enrique Mayer has argued that "Indian" should be defined in positive rather than, as in the past, negative traits; Darcy Ribeiro has, once again, insisted on the need to maintain ethnic variety throughout Latin America as part of mankind's overall survival strategy; Ernesto Salazar has described the great leadership potential of the Shuar Federation of Ecuador; and Andrés Serbén has given us a unique and intriguing insight into the formation of indigenous organizations in Argentina, a country in which, from the beginning, the organizations have been pan-Argentinian because no single group was large enough or powerful enough to dominate. Finally, among the articles reviewed in this section, there is an interview with Nilo Cayuquo (item **1349**), a Mapuche Indian from Argentina who is coordinator of the Consejo Indio de Sud América, a communications center headquartered in Lima, Perú. In his interview, he is highly critical of international Marxism and its attempts to control the Indian movements of Latin America. His criticism seems to be shared increasingly by Indian groups throughout the continent. A cogent argument that such perceptions are wrong, however, is presented in Héctor Díaz-Polanco's "Indigenismo, Populism, and Marxism" (item **1353**). In his extremely well-reasoned argument, the author asserts that *indigenismo* is simply a subterfuge for eventual acculturation, that populism tries to reduce everyone to the same level, and that only Marxism can win out in the long run.

Perhaps the strongest message to come out of these Indian groups is that knowledge, insights, and skills transmitted through their cultures have great value and should be not only respected, but used. This message has become the *leitmotif* of an increasing number of studies by outside researchers. Stephen Brush, who for years has been demonstrating the richness of the Peruvian potato-growing heritage, has now produced "The Environment and Native Agriculture" (item **1348**), in which he argues that to allow the great variety of native tubers to lapse into extinction would bring on ecological disaster.

Also in line with the insistence on the value of traditional Andean cultures is the continuing work on coca. While less intense than it had been the previous biennium, interest continues high. Reviewed in this section is Oscar Crespo Soliz's "El Problema del Coqueo" (item **1350**), Juan M. Ossio's "La Sociedad Nacional, los Indígenas del Area Andina y la Coca" (item **1469**), Ruggiero Romano's "Problemi della Coca nel Perú del Secolo XX" (item **1474**), and William Carter's *Ensayos científicos sobre la coca* (item **1354**). All defend use of the coca leaf by Andean Indians, and distinguish between the coca leaf and cocaine. The latter work, by compiling in a single volume major articles written about the coca leaf over the past 30 years, attempts to provide policy makers with a rationale for defending Indian rights.

Interest in Andean religion continues unabated, with an increasing emphasis on cosmology. More and more evidence is being presented on the syncretic nature of the Andean system, a prime example of which is David D. Gow's "The Roles of Christ and Inkarrí in Andean Religion" (item **1459**). Another example is Fernando Fuenzalida Vollmar's "Santiago y el Wamani: Aspectos de un Culto Pagano en Moya" (item **1456**). At the heart of syncretism is, of course, the fiesta system of the Andes. We now have a major work dealing with the subject: Hans Buechler's *The masked media: Aymara fiestas and social interaction in the Bolivian highlands* (item **1387**) which argues that many social and economic messages are being transmitted through practically every act of the fiesta.

In terms of interest in cosmology and astronomy, the most interesting work has been done by Gary Urton ("Animals and Astronomy in the Quechua Universe," item **1484** and *At the crossroads of the earth and sky; an Andean cosmology*, item **1485**). The most encouraging breakthrough to come from the continued interest in religion and values, however, is in the form of a challenge to the theories of the cultural materialist, such as Marvin Harris. In Tomás R. Melville's "Los Mapuche de Chile: su Organización Social y su Ideología (item **1403**), we are told that social ideology can be and was deterministic in the Mapuche case, making it difficult for them to adapt to Hispanic society and economy. And in William T. Vicker's "Ideation as Adaptation: Traditional Belief and Modern Intervention in Siona-Secoya Religion" (item **1432**), we are told essentially the same. In other words, ideas and beliefs can constitute creative processes in the forming of cultures.

As can be seen from the review presented thus far, most anthropologists stayed with their traditionally defined topics, although there have been some exceptions. One of the most notable is the work of Dennis Gilbert, who studied cognatic descent groups among the two leading families of Lima, Peru: the Prado's and the Miró Quesada's. His description of the way corporate ownership is maintained within these extended family structures is first-class ethnography.

Perhaps the weightiest book to be produced over the biennium is the one edited on Ecuador by Norman E. Whitten, Jr., *Cultural transformations and ethnicity in modern Ecuador* (item **1412**). Like all edited volumes, it is uneven in both topic and quality, but it has many excellent chapters. One recurring theme in the book is the ecological disaster the expansion of cattle ranching is bringing to eastern Ecuador; another is the authors' fear that the cultures of eastern Ecuador are facing almost sure extinction; yet another is that the Hispanic minority in power is insensitive to the minority cultures of their country, and that unless that sensitivity is quickly developed, Ecuador is likely to face increasing and unnecessary difficulties and disasters.

A colleague of Whitten's, Frank Salomon (contributing editor for the ETHNO-HISTORY: SOUTH AMERICA section of *HLAS 46*), in addition to giving us an excellent history explaining why the weavers of Otavalo have been so exceptional among Andean peoples, has given us the service of reviewing the development of Andean ethnology in the 1970s. The review (item **1376**) is a good one. It concludes by saying that Andean ethnology is now mature, and that what is now needed is more internally comparative analysis. This contributor heartily agrees.

GENERAL

1346 Bloch, M. and **S. Guggenhelm.** Compadrazgo, baptism and the symbolism of a second birth (RAI/M, 16:3, Sept. 1981, p. 376–386)

Eureka! Authors rediscover Christian doctrine of original sin and conclude that baptism is essentially a cleansing rite representing an individual's spiritual, as opposed to carnal, birth. Perhaps social science is finally admitting the existence of theology.

1347 Browman, David L. El manejo de la tierra árida del altiplano del Perú y Bolivia (III/AI, 40:1, enero/marzo 1980, p. 143–159, bibl., ill.)

Naive, generalized discussion of the potential for agricultural development in the arid highlands of Peru and Bolivia. Author seems totally unaware of the dominant Andean pattern of simultaneously exploiting a variety of ecological niches.

1348 Brush, Stephen B. The environment and native Andean agriculture (III/AI, 40:1, enero/marzo 1980, p. 161–172)

Discusses genetic diversity of the domesticated, Andean potato. Author argues cogently for *in situ* strategies of genetic conservation, after clarifying the superior qualities of many "primitive" Andean tubers.

1349 Cayuquo, Nilo. Interview with Nilo Cayuquo (LAP, 9:2[33], Spring 1982, p. 100–109, plates)

Nilo Cayuquo, a Mapuche Indian from Argentina, is coordinator of the Consejo Indio de Sur América, a communications center headquartered in Lima, Peru. In the interview he is highly critical of international Marxism and Marxists' attempts to coopt indigenous movements.

1350 Crespo Soliz, Oscar. El problema del "coqueo" (*in* Congreso Panamericano de Criminología, Buenos Aires, 1979. Congreso Panamericano de Criminología. v. 1, Delincuencia juvenil, estupefacientes. Buenos Aires: Ediciones Universidad del Salvador, 1980, p. 229–239 [Colección Actas y documentos; 1])

Provocative article that raises some important issues underlying international attempts to reduce or eradicate coca production. Author suggests an approach that would respect long-standing Andean traditions but at the same time would tackle the problem of international drug trafficking realistically.

1351 Custred, Glynn. The place of ritual in Andean rural society (*in* Land and power in Latin America: agrarian economies and social processes in the Andes. Edited by Benjamin S. Orlove and Glynn Custred. New York: Holmes and Meier Publishers, 1980, p. 195–209, table)

Brief examination of Andean ritual attempts to demonstrate that it is flexible and may be used to reinforce values and relationships on a variety of social levels. Nothing extraordinary in this interpretation.

1352 Darío: un campesino antes y después de la reforma agraria. 2. ed. La Paz?: Centro de Información y Documentación Boliviano, 1979. 80 p., 2 leaves of plates: maps (Serie Testimonios de vida)

Autobiography of a Bolivian worker who, at various stages of his life, labored in Argentine cane fields, national oil refinery, series of tin mines, hat factories, and as agriculturalist exploiting his own land. Of value as representing views of a politically aware worker, but weak life history when compared with that of Domitila Chungara.

1353 Díaz-Polanco, Héctor. Indigenismo, populism, and Marxism (LAP, 9:2[44], Spring 1982, p. 42–61)

Well-reasoned, theoretical article that begins with a definition of indigenism, populism, and Marxist, proceeds to expose the fallacies of the first two, and ends by implicitly predicting the success of the latter. The arguments presented leave food for thought.

1354 Ensayos científicos sobre la coca. William E. Carter, compilador. La Paz: Librería Editorial Juventud, 1983. 246 p.: bibl., graphs, ill., tables.

Compilation of major articles written about the social, cultural, and biomedical aspects of coca leaf chewing, produced over the past 30 years. Purpose of book is to provide Andean policy makers with important data on the coca leaf, published in relatively obscure places.

1355 Esteva Fabregat, Claudio. El campesinado andino como clase social (RUC, 28:117, Jan. 1979, p. 391–429, bibl.)

Theoretical consideration of the class structure of Indian communities within Andean society. Raises question as to whether such communities are internally segmented by class. Article suffers from lack of concrete data and from confusing class with ranking.

1356 Faroux, Emmanuel. Le décline des cultures indigènes de la sierra équatorienne et le renouveau des mouvements indigenistes (*in* Indianité, ethnocide, indigénisme en Amérique latine. Toulouse-Le Mirail, France: Groupe de recherches sur l'Amérique latine Toulouse-Perpignan [GRAL], Centre interdisciplinaire d'études latinoaméricaines; Paris: Editions du Centre National de la Recherche Scientifique [CNRS], 1982, p. 87–203, bibl.)

Superficial historical review of the status and structure of indigenous groups in highland Peru from the time of the Incas onward. Makes weak argument that 20th-century education, hispanization, transportation, and foreign mission activity have brought decline to these cultures, but that indigenous organizations, national unions, and even groups such as the Confederación Ecuatoriana de Obreros Católicos are reviving them.

1357 Gallegos A., Luis. Previsión del clima entre los aymaras (III/AI, 40:1, enero/marzo 1980, p. 135–141, bibl.)

Although the title insinuates that the Aymara have developed a true "system" for predicting the weather, the contents of the article do little other than list omens, most of which have been mentioned in previous ethnographic reports. Cloud formations, winds, and the behavior of animals and birds figure among the most potent of the signs.

1358 Golte, Jurgen. Cultura y naturaleza andinas (IPA/A, 15:17/18, 1981, p. 119–132)

Paints in broad strokes traditional Andean technology, linked tightly to local ecologies, and contrasts this high degree of adaptation with the superimposing and transforming nature of Western technology. Argues that most Andean people today are increasingly caught up in Western technology, while at the same time suffering the indignities of domination by an elite minority. Protection of the Andean tradition of balance with nature is the challenge of scientific thinking today.

1359 González Ferreyra, Jorge A. Prohibición del coqueo: su institucionalización (*in* Congreso Panamericano de Criminología, 1979, Buenos Aires. Congreso Panamericano de Criminología. v. l, Delincuencia juvenil, estupefacientes. Buenos Aires: Ediciones Universidad del Salvador, 1980, p. 227–228 [Colección Actas y documentos; 1])

1360 Gros, Christian. Comptes rendus d'ouvrages récents sur les mouvements indiens paysans (CDAL, 23:1, 1981, p. 203–224)

Reviews presented at the 1978 Congress of Americanists of recent books dealing with the indigenous movements of Latin America: Henri Favre *Mouvement indiens paysans aux XVIII, XIX, et XXe siécles*; María Teresa Huerta and Patricia Palacios *Rebeliones indígenas de la época colonial*; Miguel Alberto Bartolomé and Alicia Mabel Barabas *La resistencia maya: relaciones interétnicas en el oriente de la península de Yucatán*; Segundo Moreno Yanez (sic) *Sublevaciones indígenas en la Audiencia de Quito, desde comienzos del siglo XVIII hasta finales de la Colonia*; Jürgen Golte *Repartos y rebeliones: Tupac Amaru y las contradicciones de la economía colonial*; *Movimientos campesinos* (special issue of *Allpanchis*, nos. 11/12); Javier Albó *Achacachi: rebeldes pero conservadores*; Roberto Choque Canqui *Sublevación y masacre de los comunarios de Jesús de Machaca*; Centro de Investigación y Educación Popular of Bogotá *Indígenas y represión en Colombia* and *Los bombardeos en El Pato*.

1361 Guillet, David. Land tenure, ecological zone, and agriculture regime in the Central Andes (AAA/AE, 8:1, Feb. 1981, p. 139–155, bibl., tables)

Analyzes interrelationships among land tenure, agricultural regime, and ecological zone in the Central Andes, using data from 17 community studies. Article represents type of pioneering synthesis, of which we need more.

1362 Hacia la autogestión indígena: documentos. Compilación, prólogo y notas de Adolfo Colombres. Quito: Ediciones del Sol, 1977. 294 p.: bibl. (Serie Antropológica)

Compilation of resolutions, declarations, and legal documents produced by indigenous groups throughout the Americas, introduced in each instance by the editor's belligerent prose. Instead of documents for Peru and Chile, editor presents sociopolitical history of exploitation within which he sees anthropology predicting either its demise or its absorption by sociology. Includes Ecuadorian documents that support this view and calls for a halt to all research by foreign anthropologists. Valuable book for insights on emerging indigenous leadership throughout the hemisphere.

1363 The Indian awakening in Latin America. Edited by Yves Materne. Postscript by Michel de Certeau. New York: Friendship Press, 1980. 127 p.: bibl.

Formal pronouncement by various indigenous organizations in Bolivia, Venezuela, Colombia, Mexico, Paraguay, Panama, and Brazil. The thread common to all is the desire for self determination and an end to exploitation.

1364 Long, Norman. Mine-based regional economies: Andean examples; historical and contemporary (*in* State and region in Latin America: a workshop. G.A. Banck, R. Buve, and L. Van Vroonhoven, editors. Amsterdam: Centrum voor Studie en Documentatie van Latijns-Amerika, 1981, p. 151–188, bibl. [CEDLA incidentele publicaties; 17])

General discussion of relationship between mining centers and peasant communities both in the 16th and 20th centuries. Poorly documented article reveals ignorance of much relevant ethnohistorical and ethnological research.

1365 Maltby, Laura. Colonos en Hacienda Picotani (*in* Land and power in Latin America: agrarian economies and social processes in the Andes. Edited by Benjamin S. Orlove and Glynn Custred. New York: Holmes & Meier, 1980, p. 99–112)

Historic case study demonstrating as false model of total domination of the peon by the hacendado, and isolation of the peon from the outside world. Author argues that, within hacienda, peon households often established wide and flexible networks with traders, officials, and members of nearby communities.

1366 Orlove, Benjamin S. El suicidio de Juanita (III/AI, 41:1, enero/marzo 1981, p. 25–52)

Takes case of young, female suicide victim as point of departure to explore subjugated status of many rural and small-town Latin American women, and to emphasize importance to such individuals of a solid, male kin network.

1367 —— and **Glynn Custred.** Agrarian economies and social processes in comparative perspective: the agricultural pro-

duction unit (*in* Land and power in Latin America: agrarian economies and social processes in the Andes. Edited by Benjamin S. Orlove and Glyn Custred. New York: Holmes & Meier, 1980, p. 13–29, maps)

Introductory essay to an edited volume, arguing that, because the type of closed, corporate communities and manorial type haciendas found in the Andes are found elsewhere in the world, insights from the Andes can help us understand world-wide problems.

1368 —— and ——. The alternative model of agrarian society in the Andes: households, networks, and corporate groups (*in* Land and power in Latin America: agrarian economies and social processes in the Andes. Edited by Benjamin S. Orlove and Glynn Custred. New York: Holmes & Meier, 1980, p. 31–54)

Argues that the household, rather than hacienda and community, should be considered the basic unit of social and economic organization in the Andes. Communities and haciendas are seen as the product of social and economic activity, rather than the context that limits such activity.

1369 Palomino, Aquiles; Duane G. Metzger; and Christine von Glascoe. Aspectos de socialización en la adquisición de una realidad de la coca (*in* Congreso Peruano: El Hombre y la Cultura Andina, 3d, Lima, 1977. El hombre y la cultura andina [see *HLAS 43:253*] v. 4, p. 518–520)

Brief summary of authors' work on the ethnosemantics of coca, with special reference to patterns of socialization to use.

1370 Paredes de Salazar, Elssa. La mujer y su época. La Paz: Ediciones ISLA, 1972. 175, 8 p.: bibl. (Colección Ensayo)

General treatise of women, ranging from the myths of the Amazons, to women in oriental antiquity, Christianity, the Crusades, French Revolution, and first women's movements. Devotes only a few pages to a discussion of the status of women in South America, and these focus principally on Bolivia and Chile. No mention is made of women in traditional Andean society.

1371 Primov, George. The political role of mestizo school teachers in Indian communities (*in* Land and power in Latin America: agrarian economies and social processes in the Andes. Edited by Benjamin S.

Orlove and Glynn Custred. New York: Holmes & Meier, 1980, p. 153–163)

Sees school teachers as bypassing certain blockages in the regional power structure, and argues that the use peasants make of teachers' abilities varies in accordance with the existence or lack of existence of alternative avenues of access to power.

1372 Ribeiro, Darcy. Etnicidad: indígenas y campesinos (*in* Perú, identidad nacional. César Arróspide de la Flor *et al.* Lima: Centro de Estudios para el Desarrollo y la Participación, 1979, p. 37–55 [Serie Realidad nacional])

Appeal to reaffirm the ethnic variety of Latin America as part of a necessary long-term survival strategy for all mankind. Author concludes, pessimistically, that the old, dominant classes of Latin America may impede the resurgence of ethnic identity in an effort to retain their sterile power.

1373 Rivière, Gilles. Evolution des formes d'échange entre altiplano et vallées: l'exemple de Sabaya, Bolivie (CDAL, 20:2, 1979, p. 145–158, maps, tables)

Historical sketch of how traditional exchange of agricultural products between Carangas region of Oruro, Bolivia, and valleys of northern Chile, set stage for and gave rise to present, large-scale contraband trade between Carangas and Chilean port of Arica.

1374 Ryn, Zdzislaw. El coqueo y la vida en las grandes alturas (UCCEA/A, 2:3, 1981, p. 34–41, bibl.)

Superficial, general statement emphasizing importance of coca leaf for persons who live and work in the cold of the high Andes. Article based entirely and uncritically on secondary sources.

1375 Sallnow, M.J. *Communitas* reconsidered: the sociology of Andean pilgrimage (RAI/M, 16:2, June 1981, p. 163–182, bibl., maps)

Well-reasoned analysis of the divisive as well as the unifying aspects of Andean pilgrimage ritual. Author presents solid challenge to Victor Turner's argument that the pilgrimage process is based on the concept of *communitas*.

1376 Salomon, Frank. The Andean contrast (CU/JIA, 36:1, Spring/Summer 1982, p. 55–71)

Informative review of the traditional

fragmentation of the Quechua and Aymara-speaking groups of Ecuador, Peru, and Bolivia. Assesses relative success of emerging indigenous movements and organizations, and suggests that for them to have maximum impact, they must seek coalition with non-indigenous groups.

1377 ———. Andean ethnology in the 1970s: a retrospective (LARR, 17:2, 1982, p. 75–128, bibl.)

First-class review of the development of Andean ethnology during the decade of the 1970s. Concludes that Andean studies are now sufficiently developed to form a core area of ethnographic literature, and the challenge of the future is for more comparative analysis and for the development of a "distinctly Andean current in the human sciences."

1378 Singelmann, Peter. Structures of domination and peasant movements in Latin America. Columbia: University of Missouri Press, 1981. 246 p.: bibl., index.

General overview of situation of peasants in Latin America, especially during 20th century. Heavily laden with social science jargon, book often belabors the obvious and offers relatively few new insights to readers familiar with specific studies of peasants throughout the area.

1379 Urbano, Henrique-Osvaldo. Dios Yaya, Dios Churi y Dios Espíritu: modelos trinitarios y arqueología mental en los Andes (UCLA/JLAL, 6:1, Summer 1980, p. 111–127)

Exploration of concepts of the deity, the soul, and social segmentation among Quechua and Aymara-speakers of the Andes. Although article tends to ignore important English language source materials, it confirms much that may be found therein, such as the concept of multiple souls.

1380 Varese, Stefano. Restoring multiplicity: Indianities and the civilizing project in Latin America (LAP, 9:2[33], Spring 1982, p. 29–41)

Exploration of the theory underlying the emergence of Indian movements and organizations in Latin America today. Article is flawed by uncritical use of terms and equally uncritical interpretation of history.

1381 Yambert, Karl A. Thought and reality: dialectics of the Andean community

(*in* Land and power in Latin America: agrarian economies and social processes in the Andes. Edited by Benjamin S. Orlove and Glynn Custred. New York: Holmes & Meier, 1980, p. 55–78)

Historical overview of Andean rural communities that includes their relationship to governments and elites. Author also examines relationship between actual organization of communities and images of them found in social theory and policy.

ARGENTINA

1382 Cagliotti, Carlos Norberto. Algunas consideraciones sobre la masticación de la hoja de coca en la República Argentina (*in* Congreso Panamericano de Criminología, 1979, Buenos Aires. Congreso Panamericano de Criminología. v. l, Delincuencia juvenil, estupefacientes. Buenos Aires: Ediciones Universidad del Salvador, 1980, p. 332–343 [Colección Actas y documentos; 1])

Diatribe against coca leaf and coca chewing. Article written in pseudo-scientific style that presents opinion as fact and contains series of uncritical references to questionable studies. In all, what one would expect from a "medical" paper presented to a criminology conference.

1383 Merlino, Rodolfo J. Pastoreo y agricultura en el altiplano meridional: aspectos cosmovisionales y religiosos (UBAIA/R, 13:1/2, 1976/1980, p. 113–120, bibl.)

On the basis of herding practices and religious ceremonial in the puna of northwestern Argentina, author asks whether one determines the other. Reflecting an apparent total ignorance of the elaborate theories of cultural ecology, concludes that either religion or economies can be seen as deterministic, and that the choice of either would simply reflect the researcher's bias.

1384 Millan de Plavecino, María Delia. Las migraciones actuales de los indígenas (Revista Nacional de Cultura [Ediciones Culturales Argentinas, Buenos Aires] 2:7, 1980, p. 67–84, bibl., ill.)

Brief sketch of patterns of culture in the Argentine Chaco, with little reference to migration.

1385 Serbín, Andrés. Las organizaciones indígenas en la Argentina (III/AI, 3:41, julio/sept. 1981, p. 407–434, bibl.)

Detailed, well-researched historical review of the development of indigenous movements in Argentina. Among other unusual features, these movements tended to be multi-ethnic, bringing together members from widely scattered indigenous groups. Article updates status of the movements to present day.

BOLIVIA

1386 Aguiló, Federico. Los cuentos: ¿tradiciones o vivencias? La Paz: Editorial Los Amigos del Libro, 1980. 256 p.: bibl.

One of the best collections of Bolivian folktales ever come to light. Each tale is given in the original Quechua, accompanied by faithful Spanish translation. First half consists of interpretation of major motifs of tales, drawing on both structural and functional theory and spiced with occasional Freudianism.

1387 Buechler, Hans C. The masked media: Aymara fiestas and social interaction in the Bolivian highlands. The Hague; New York: Mouton, 1980. 399 p.: ill. (Approaches to semiotics; 59)

Landmark study of Aymara fiesta system. Argues that fiesta complex constitutes medium of communication by means of which all sorts of social relationships are expressed or represented. Through complex, "individuals display their positions in the community, whole or parts of communities represent their changing mutual relationships, outsiders pay tribute to community members, and migrants give recognition to continuing ties with their home communities."

1388 Carter, William E. and **Mauricio Mamani P.** Irpa Chico: individuo y comunidad en la cultura aymara. La Paz: Librería-Editoria Juventud, 1982. 460 p.: ill.

Community study of the "old school" attempts to present full round of Aymara life. Last chapter is an epilogue describing frustrated attempts at directed culture change in the community from 1920s to present. Latest of such attempts is major World Bank "Proyecto Ingavi."

1389 Crandon, Libbet. Why *susto*? (UP/E, 22:2, April 1983, p. 153–167, bibl., graphs)

New and powerful analysis of the concept and role of *susto* in Andean disease. It is strange that author completely neglects three of the more instructive articles on Andean, and particularly Aymara *susto*: Carter's "Secular Reinforcement in Aymara Death Ritual," same author's "Coca Use as a Medicinal Substance," and his recent published book *Irpa Chico* (item **1388**).

1390 Instituto Andino de Antropología. La Paz: s.n., 1978. 71 leaves: ill.

Proposal submitted by National Institute of Culture of Bolivia for creation of Andean Institute of Culture, to be located in La Paz, but to coordinate development of anthropology throughout Andean region. Already approved in principle by Andean Pact countries, Institute would act as information clearing house, publishing bulletin and monographic series, seeking to stimulate graduate training in anthropology, and setting standards for protection of cultural patrimony of all the Andean countries. For its first year of operation (1979), Bolivian government committed to it a budget of $150,000. Yet Institute was never founded, and the Bolivian author of the proposal emigrated to Venezuela.

1391 Kimura, Hideo. La mitología de los ese ejja del Oriente Boliviano: el dueño imaginario de los animales silvestres (UCCEA/A, 2:3, 1981, p. 1–22, bibl.)

Small collection of myths from the Ese Ejja group of eastern Bolivia, accompanied by brief analytical interpretation. Because Ese Ejja are so acculturated, best author can conclude is that their aboriginal religion was based on idea of balance between man and nature.

1392 Lebot, Yvon. Etrangers dans notre propre pays: le mouvement indien en Bolivie dans les années soixante-dix (*in* Indianité, ethnocide, indigénisme en Amérique latine. Toulouse-Le Mirail, France: Group de recherches sur l'Amérique latine Toulouse-Perpignan [GRAL], Centre interdisciplinaire d'études latino-américaines; Paris: Editions du Centre National de la Recherche Scientifique [CNRS], 1982, p. 155–165, bibl.)

Brief discussion of the growth of indigenous movements in Bolivia during decade of 1970s. Aymara speakers are seen as spearheading movements, and as resisting assimilation by country's dominant Hispanic culture.

1393 Lindert, Paul van and Otto Verkoren. Segregación residencial y política urbana en La Paz, Bolivia (CEDLA/B, 33, dic. 1982, p. 127–138, bibl., maps)

Valuable article, in spite of disappointingly poor historical background, that describes what has been happening in city of La Paz over past 60 years and what is likely to happen through the end of the century. One thing made clear is that the rich grow constantly richer at the expense of the poor. Another is that land values in La Paz have inflated beyond all reasonable relation with the wage economy.

1394 Macera, Pablo. Arte y lucha social: los murales de Ambaná, Bolivia (IPA/A, 15:17/18, 1981, p. 23–40, map, plates)

Brief article on secular murals in Ambaná, Bolivia. Argues, rather weakly, that these reflect changes in local social structure and economy over a period of more than 100 years.

1395 Paredes Candia, Antonio. Costumbres matrimoniales indígenas. La Paz: Ediciones Isla, 1980. 63 p.

Brief descriptions of marriage practices and ritual among various ethnic groups in Bolivia. Far more detailed descriptions are available elsewhere.

1395a Platt, Tristán. El papel del ayllu andino en la reproducción del régimen mercantil simple en el Norte de Potosí (III/AI, 41:4, 1981, p. 665–728, bibl., ill., tables)

Lengthy article, giving unusually clear description of how an archipelago arrangement actually works in a modern Andean setting. Platt shows clearly that: 1) only a minority of households continue to have access to both Puna and Valley lands; 2) those who exploit both types of land tend not to have small children; and 3) those who exploit both types of land are more successful economically than those who do not.

1396 Plaza Martínez, Pedro and Luis Oporto Ordóñez. El Tinku de Macha (Revista Boliviana de Etnomusicología y Folklore [Instituto Nacional de Antropología, La Paz] 11:2, 1981, p. 17–26, bibl.)

Detailed account of a mock battle held yearly in canton of Macha, in conjunction with *fiesta de La Cruz*. Authors promise future monograph on subject.

1397 Quiroga, Néstor Hugo and **Javier Albó.** La radio, expresión libre del aymara. La Paz: Centro de Investigación y Promoción del Campesinado, 1976. 28 p.: bibl., diagrams (Cuadernos de investigación—CIPCA; 4)

Practical suggestions as to how best to communicate by radio with Aymara speakers. *Jaqi* (person) Aymara is differentiated from *q'ara* (mestizo or white) Aymara, and the former is recommended for all radio broadcasts. Because of the fact that Aymara has no real written tradition, simple outlines rather than detailed librettos are suggested as guides for actors and announcers.

1398 Rojas, Antonio. Land and labor in the articulation of the peasant economy with the hacienda (LAP, 7[4]:27, Fall 1980, p. 67–82, tables)

Description of peasant conditions on haciendas near Achacachi, Bolivia, immediately prior to and following the 1953 agrarian reform. Similarity to conditions described nearly 20 years ago in Carter's *Aymara communities and the Bolivian agrarian reform* (see *HLAS 29:1587*) is striking.

1399 Suárez Añez, Manuel. Mayorías marginadas. La Paz: Offset Millán, 1980. 142 p., 10 leaves of plates: ill.

Layman's appeal for Bolivia to become self-sufficient in foodstuffs and fuels. Book is utopian, rambling, disorganized, and almost totally lacking in technical knowledge.

1400 Vellard, Jehan. Une ethnie de guérisseurs Andins: les Kallawaya de Bolivie (AISA/TA, 41, dic. 1980, p. 25–38, ill., plates)

Yet another somewhat romanticized treatment of the Kallawaya of Bolivia, containing partial listing of maladies they cure and short inventory of main herbs and rituals they employ. Article contains little that is not available in greater detail elsewhere.

1401 Virreira Guzmán, Jaime. Sexto sol y octavo día: apuntes para una reflexión sobre la cultura en la realidad boliviana. La Paz: Centro de Promoción Social, Arzobispado de La Paz, 1982. 156, 38 p.: ill.

Odd mixture of theology, pseudo-history, pseudo-anthropology, and sheer speculation. Author pleads for mutual respect among Bolivia's various cultures.

1402 Weil, Jim. National socioeconomic integration of Quechua pioneer settlers in the tropical Chapare of Bolivia (Anthropology [State University of New York at Stony Brook] 5:1, May 1981, p. 3–28, bibl., ill., graphs, maps, tables)

Fairly lengthy, yet superficial study of colonization of the Chapare region in Bolivia, more in the tradition of cultural geography than of ethnography. One basic point made is that though the Chapare is producing immense fortunes through coca growing, very few of the growers realize more than a few hundred dollars a year profit.

CHILE

1403 Melville, Thomas R. Los mapuche de Chile: su organización social y su ideología (*in* Congreso Peruano: El Hombre y la Cultura Andina, 3d, Lima, 1977. El hombre y la cultura andina [see *HLAS 43:253*] v. 4, p. 501–517, bibl.)

Excellent examination of Mapuche ideology and its relationship to social structure and economics. Author challenges cultural materialists such as Marvin Harris, and argues that social ideology can, itself, be deterministic. Presents Mapuche as his case in point.

COLOMBIA AND VENEZUELA

1404 Clarac de Briceño, Jacqueline. Dioses en exilio: representaciones y prácticas simbólicas en la cordillera de Mérida: ensayo antropológico. Caracas: FUNDARTE, 1981. 259 p., 1 folded leaf of plates: bibl., ill. (Colección Rescate; 2)

Study of myth, ritual, and traditional Andean elements of social structure in a sequence of communities in the Mérida valley. [W. Kracke]

1405 Ortiz, Sutti. The structure and regional articulation of dispersed rural settlements in Colombia (*in* Land and power in Latin America: agrarian economies and social processes in the Andes. Edited by Benjamin S. Orlove and Glynn Custred. New York: Holmes & Meier, 1980, p. 129–151)

Argues that remote populations are as strongly affected by their links to markets and central government as are less isolated groups, though their forms of social and economic linkages may differ markedly. Argument strengthens view of social organization as adaptation to structural constraints rather than as continuity of cultural traditions.

ECUADOR

1406 Belote, Linda Smith and **Jim Belote.** Development in spite of itself: the Saraguro case (*in* Cultural transformations and ethnicity in modern Ecuador [see item **1412**] p. 450–476, bibl.)

Case study of vagaries of attempts to implement directed culture change. Whereas outside agencies did not achieve all their goals in Saraguro, they did play pivotal roles in community's recent transformation.

1407 Belzner, William. Music, modernization, and westernization among the Macuma Shuar (*in* Cultural transformations and ethnicity in modern Ecuador [see item **1412**] p. 731–748, bibl.)

Unusual exploration of symbolic role music can play in matter of cultural acceptance or rejection. In Shuars' case, after initial acceptance of western music, they turned back to their own traditions, for within those traditions they saw the possibility of greater control of power.

1408 Bromley, Ray. Market center and market place in highland Ecuador: a study of organization, regulation, and ethnic discrimination (*in* Cultural transformations and ethnicity in modern Ecuador [see item **1412**] p. 233–259, bibl., maps)

Useful overview of market systems of highland Ecuador. Point is made and well illustrated that Ecuadorian marketplace can be understood only through combination of economic, sociocultural, and politico-administrative perspectives.

1409 Brownrigg, Leslie A. Economic and ecological strategies of Lojano migrants to El Oro (*in* Cultural transformations and ethnicity in modern Ecuador [see item **1412**] p. 303–326, bibl., map, tables)

Study of push-pull factors accounting for migration from Lija to El Oro, ends with appraisal of El Oro's developmental poten-

tial. Concern is expressed over effects of deforestation and expansion of cattle ranching.

1410 Casagrande, Joseph B. Strategies for survival: the Indians of highland Ecuador (*in* Cultural transformations and ethnicity in modern Ecuador [see item **1412**] p. 260–277, bibl.)

Brief review of contrasts among six highland Indian communities is followed by account of seminar where two men from each community interpreted their own community life to other. Results are in accord with much of dependency theory.

1411 Crespi, Muriel. St. John the Baptist: the ritual looking glass of hacienda Indian ethnic and power relations (*in* Cultural transformations and ethnicity in modern Ecuador [see item **1412**] p. 477–505, bibl., tables)

Diachronic, functional analysis of roles played by fiesta of St. John the Baptist in Atahualpa hacienda of northern Ecuador.

1412 Cultural transformations and ethnicity in modern Ecuador. Edited by Norman E. Whitten, Jr. Urbana: University of Illinois Press, 1981. 811 p.: bibl., ill., index, maps, tables.

Major collection of essays on modern Ecuador by 27 contributors that reads like a "Who's Who" of anthropologists who have worked in that country: Norman E. Whitten, Jr. (item **1436**), Ronald Stutzman (item **1430**), Marcelo F. Naranjo (item **1421**), Frank Salomon (items **1423** and **1424**), DeWight R. Middleton (item **1419**), Ray Bromley (item **1408**), Joseph B. Casagrande (item **1410**), Susan C.M. Scrimshaw (item **1428**), Leslie A. Brownrigg (item **1409**), J. Peter Ekstrom (item **1414**), Theodore Macdonald, Jr. (item **1418**), Louisa R. Stark (item **1429**), Niels Fock (item **1415**), Linda Smith Belote and Jim Belote (item **1406**), Muriel Crespi (item **1411**), Blanca Muratorio (item **1420**), Constance García Barrio (item **1416**), Grace Schubert (item **1427**), Ernesto Salazar (item **1422**), Philippe Descola (item **1413**), Anne-Christine Taylor (item **1431**), James A. Yost (item **1437**), William T. Vickers (item **1432**), William Belzner (item **1407**), and Dorothea S. Whitten (item **1435**). Although a number of articles deal with theoretical issues, most are ethnographic and processual in their orientation, with strong emphasis on ethnicity. For anyone planning to do serious research in Ecuador or to be involved in any way with economic or social policy, the book is a must.

1413 Descola, Philippe. From scattered to nucleated settlement: a process of socioeconomic change among the Achuar (*in* Cultural transformations and ethnicity in modern Ecuador [see item **1412**] p. 614–646, bibl.)

Socioeconomic change described here is an unhappy one, with Achuar culture possibly headed for extinction. All results from the pressures of "modernity."

1414 Ekstrom, J. Peter. Colonist strategies of verticality in an eastern valley (*in* Cultural transformations and ethnicity in modern Ecuador [see item **1412**] p. 327–355, bibl., ill., map)

Descriptive account of migration into Cuyes valley from Jima valley, accompanied by minimum of analysis. Makes weak argument that the situation has much in common with Murra's model of verticality.

1415 Fock, Niels. Ethnicity and alternative identification: an example from Cañar (*in* Cultural transformations and ethnicity in modern Ecuador [see item **1412**] p. 402–419, bibl., ill., maps)

Author ponders how Indians of highland Ecuador have maintained separate ethnic identification in spite of years of Spanish domination, and concludes that they have done so by reinterpreting Hispanic cultural institutions in terms of indigenous symbols and values. Even where they accepted foreign structures, they have created their own content for those structures.

1416 García-Barrio, Constance. Blacks in Ecuadorian literature (*in* Cultural transformations and ethnicity in modern Ecuador [see item **1412**] p. 535–562, bibl.)

In spite of the existence of a rich literature reflecting the black culture of coastal Ecuador, author finds increasing prejudice against black people, and economic and political disenfranchisement. She expresses particular concern over the future role of blacks in Esmeraldas province, traditional stronghold for Ecuadorian black society.

1417 Iturralde, Diego G. Nacionalidades étnicas y política cultural en Ecuador (III/AI, 3:41, julio/sept. 1981, p. 387–397, bibl.)

Idealistic apology for Ecuador's minorities. Written within Marxist theoretical framework, article somewhat naively demands economic development coupled with total ethnic respect.

1418 Macdonald, Theodore, Jr. Indigenous response to an expanding frontier: jungle Quechua economic conversion to cattle ranching (*in* Cultural transformations and ethnicity in modern Ecuador [see item **1412**] p. 356–383, bibl.)

After documenting successful adaptation of jungle Quechua group to cattle raising, author makes impassioned argument that large-scale cattle raising has no long-term future in lowland tropics. Pleads for more diverse use of environment and acceptance of "wealth of knowledge based on centuries of accumulated experience" that Quechua bring to situation.

1419 Middleton, DeWight R. Ecuadorian transformations: an urban view (*in* Cultural transformations and ethnicity in modern Ecuador [see item **1412**] p. 211–232, bibl.)

Traces history of urban development in Ecuador, with special attention to ethnic and regional cleavages that make generalization difficult. Concludes that Ecuador's cities are stage upon which "drama of change is unfolding."

1420 Muratorio, Blanca. Protestantism, ethnicity, and class in Chimborazo (*in* Cultural transformations and ethnicity in modern Ecuador [see item **1412**] p. 506–534, bibl.)

Description of changes brought about by peasant conversion to Protestantism in Chimborazo. Though Protestant workers are increasingly known for their sobriety and dependability, Protestant leaders of peasant *comunas* see need to fight against all forms of exploitation, whereas leaders of indigenous churches tend to see most conflicts as "moral individual issues."

1421 Naranjo, Marcelo F. Political dependency, ethnicity, and cultural transformations in Manta (*in* Cultural transformations and ethnicity in modern Ecuador [see item **1412**] p. 95–120, bibl.)

Paints dismal picture of both macro- and micro-dependency in Manta, and concludes that "each day the asymmetry of political, economic, and social relations increases." No solutions are offered; only a diagnosis of the disease.

1422 Salazar, Ernesto. The Federación Shuar and the colonization frontier (*in* Cultural transformations and ethnicity in modern Ecuador [see item **1412**] p. 589–613, bibl.)

Chronicles emergence of remarkably successful Shuar Federation, explaining it as an adaptive mechanism to expanding Ecuadorian frontier. In spite of problems faced by the Federation, author believes it holds great potential for leadership in a pan-Ecuadorian movement of Indian liberation.

1423 Salomon, Frank. Killing the Yumbo: a ritual drama of northern Quito (*in* Cultural tranformations and ethnicity in modern Ecuador [see item **1412**] p. 162–208, bibl., tables)

In syncretistic religious dancing on the outskirts of Quito, author sees one group's interpretation of meanings of nationalism and ethnicity. Argues that such groups demonstrate that two are not mutually incompatible, but that subnational identity can and should be maintained simultaneously with development of national identity.

1424 ———. Weavers of Otavalo (*in* Cultural transformations and ethnicity in modern Ecuador [see item **1412**] p. 420–449, bibl.)

Useful historical review of development of textile industy in Otavalo. Clarifies how Otavalan region has been favored for centuries, and proposes that it provides important model for local development growing out of local creativity.

1425 ———. La "yumbada:" un drama ritual quechua en Quito (III/AI, 41 : 1, enero/marzo 1981, p. 113–134, bibl., ill.)

Examines role of folk dance in preserving and reinterpreting indigenous culture in a contemporary urban setting. The "yumbo" dance simultaneously draws on both the jungle and city experience, representing some facets of this experience directly and others in reverse or mirror image.

1426 Santana, Roberto. En la sierra del Ecuador: reivindicaciones étnicas y agrarias; el caso de un movimiento indígena (*in* Indianité, ethnocide, indigénisme en Amérique latine. Toulouse-Le Mirail, France:

Groupe de recherches sur l'Amérique latine Toulouse-Perpignan [GRAL], Centre interdisciplinaire d'études latino-américaines; Paris: Editions du Centre national de la recherche scientifique [CNRS], 1982, p. 205–219)

Defends importance of the Ecuarunari movement in highland Ecuador. More information for lay reader on how movement began, what it represented, and what is accomplished, would have been welcome. Other writers (Frank Salomon, *The Andean contrast*) argue that the movement has already lost its thrust.

1427 Schubert, Grace. To be black is offensive: racist attitudes in San Lorenzo (*in* Cultural transformations and ethnicity in modern Ecuador [see item **1412**] p. 563–585, bibl., tables)

Documents how economic development and highland migration to coastal community led to steadily increasing racism. Highlanders, because of their more direct ties to national systems, have prospered at the expense of locals, and have come increasingly to deprecate the latter.

1428 Scrimshaw, Susan C.M. Adaptation and family size from rural Ecuador to Guayaquil (*in* Cultural transformations and ethnicity in modern Ecuador [see item **1412**] p. 278–302, bibl., tables)

Compares family size between highlands and lowlands, and between rural and urban settings. A most interesting conclusion is that highland family size, whether rural or urban, tends to be smaller than lowland family size. No satisfactory explanations are given for the differences.

1429 Stark, Louisa R. Folk models of stratification and ethnicity in the highlands of northern Ecuador (*in* Cultural transformations and ethnicity in modern Ecuador [see item **1412**] p. 387–401, bibl., tables)

Linguist looks at ethnic labeling by persons from different strata in Cotachi, and concludes that: 1) social classification is based primarily on one's leverage, or *palanca*; 2) top and bottom strata are most stable and therefore most closely correlated ethnic and social categories; and 3) when individuals (usually from middle sector) wish to move upward socially, they use same ethnic labels to refer to themselves as they do to refer to those *above* them, while maintaining different labels for those below them.

1430 Stutzman, Ronald. *El mestizaje*: an all-inclusive ideology on exclusion (*in* Cultural transformations and ethnicity in modern Ecuador [see item **1412**] p. 45–94, bibl., table)

Laments urban and Hispanic bias in Ecuadorian society, and calls for more equitable distribution of resources in country's rural areas. Racial and ethnic classifications used in argument are, at times, questionable.

1431 Taylor, Anne-Christine. Gold-wealth: the Achuar and the Missions (*in* Cultural transformations and ethnicity in modern Ecuador [see item **1412**] p. 647–676, bibl.)

Fascinating account of how indigenous belief in spiritual source for all material wealth can act as stimulus to Christian conversion. But conversion then brings conflict with other traditional values.

1432 Vickers, William T. Ideation as adaptation: traditional belief and modern intervention in Siona-Secoya religion (*in* Cultural transformations and ethnicity in modern Ecuador [see item **1412**] p. 705–730, bibl., map)

Important paper that cogently argues that religious systems are fundamental components of human adaptation, and that among the Siona-Secoya religion traditionally promoted settlement dispersion and movement, and thus was consistent with their tropical forest adaptation. Author expresses concern that land development practices of Ecuadorian government threaten survival of societies like the Siona-Secoya.

1433 Walter, Lynn. Otavaleño development, ethnicity, and national integration (III/AI, 41:2, abril/junio 1981, p. 319–337)

Perceptive examination of challenge presented by economically successful Otavaleños to traditional cleavages of race, ethnicity, and class in Ecuadorian society. Notes, however, that Otavaleños have succeeded in challenging these traditional structures only when they remained within strictly defined economic niches.

1434 ———. Social strategies and the fiesta complex in an Otavaleño community (AAA/AE, 8:1, Feb. 1981, p. 172–185, bibl.)

In this consideration of latent and manifest functions of fiesta system, concludes that system works as both a leveling and stratifying mechanism, thus agreeing with previous analyses of system made by Cancion (1965), Smith (1977), and others. Predicts that, as alternative uses for cash surplus expand, popularity of fiesta system will wane.

1435 Whitten, Dorothea S. Ancient tradition in a contemporary context: Canelos Quichua ceramics and symbolism (*in* Cultural transformations and ethnicity in modern Ecuador [see item **1412**] p. 749–775, bibl.)

Sketchy history of how Canelos Quichua ceramics came to be a serious market commodity, interspersed with diverse tangents on aspects of recent culture change.

1436 Whitten, Norman E., Jr. Amazonia today at the base of the Andes: an ethnic interface in ecological, social, and ideological perspectives (*in* Cultural transformations and ethnicity in modern Ecuador [see item **1412**] p. 121–161, bibl., map)

Excellent survey of major ethnic groups in eastern Ecuador, followed by a dismal appraisal of their prospects. Argues for "the indigenous power source of biosphere knowledge as a logical alternative to developmentalism leading to destruction, degradation, and annihilation."

1437 Yost, James A. Twenty years of contact: the mechanisms of change in Wao—"Auca"—culture (*in* Cultural transformations and ethnicity in modern Ecuador [see item **1412**] p. 677–704, bibl., map)

Specific, detailed examination of effects of 20 years of contact with the outside world, largely through Summer Institute of Linguistics missionaries. Presentation is purely descriptive and lacks analysis.

PERU

1438 Alberts, Tom. Agrarian reform and rural poverty: a case study of Peru. Lund, Sweden: University of Lund, Research Policy Institute; Stockholm: Institute of Latin American Studies, 1981. 306 p.: bibl., maps, tables (Lund economic studies; no. 12)

Sweeping, national-level study of impact of Peruvian agrarian reform, from economist's viewpoint. Makes and substantiates argument that even under great push of military government beginning in 1968, Peruvian rural dwellers went backwards rather than forwards. Gross economic inequalities of Peruvian system are amply documented, as is increasing pauperization of the already impoverished.

1439 Allen, Catherine J. To be Quechua: the symbolism of coca chewing in highland Peru (AAA/AE, 8:1, Feb. 1981, p. 157–171, bibl.)

Refreshingly new theoretical interpretation of the symbolism of coca reciprocity, in which the leaf is seen as key ethnic identifier among highland Quechua speakers. Descriptors used in article are unusually perceptive.

1440 Altamirano, Teófilo. Aportes antropológicos al estudio de los movimientos campesinos en el Perú (PUCP/DA, 2, mayo 1978, p. 53–73, bibl.)

Instructive review of the various theories of culture change that have been applied to peasant movements in Peru. Reader is told that simultaneous application of these various theories has led to confusion, but he is not told which is of greater value and why.

1441 Andrews, David H. Un caso de migración interandina (in Congreso Peruano: El Hombre y la Cultura Andina, 3d, Lima, 1977. El hombre y la cultura andina [see HLAS 43:253] v. 5, p. 893–902)

Brief case study of migration to Paucartambo, marred by poorly developed theory and overly literal translation.

1442 Baquerizo, Manuel J. El quechua en el mundo andino de hoy (IPA/A, 15:17/18, 1981, p. 61–76, bibl., tables)

Laments relative loss of monolingual Quechua speakers in Peru, and argues that this is due to penetration of capitalist system throughout country's interior. Sees only long-term salvation for the language as coming from the triumph of socialism.

1443 Berghe, Pierre L. van den. Ccapana: the demise of an Andean hacienda (in Land and power in Latin America: agrarian economies and social processes in the Andes. Edited by Benjamin S. Orlove and Glynn Custred. New York: Holmes & Meier, 1980, p. 165–178)

Examines processes of transformation in the hacienda Ccapana near Cuzco, and correlates changes in hacienda organization with shifts in regional and national economic and political systems.

1444 Bourque, Susan Carolyn and **Kay Barbara Warren.** Women of the Andes: patriarchy and social change in two Peruvian towns. Ann Arbor: University of Michigan Press, 1981. 241 p., 16 p. of plates: bibl., ill., index (The Women and culture series)

Exposé of oppressed conditions of women in two towns in highlands of Lima Dept. Title is unfortunate, in that patterns described are Hispanic and/or coastal, rather than highland Andean. At some point in history, both towns lost their Andean heritage. Authors seem unaware of either occurrence or importance of such a loss.

1445 Brush, Stephen B. Peru's invisible migrants: a case study of inter-Andean migration (in Land and power in Latin America: agrarian economies and social processes in the Andes. Edited by Benjamin S. Orlove and Glynn Custred. New York: Holmes & Meier, 1980, p. 211–258, bibl., index, map, tables)

Report on a seldom studied topic: migration from one rural area to another in Peruvian highlands. Concludes that relative scarcity of land is primary variable in determining emergent social structures.

1446 Cáceres, Baldomero. El problema de la coca en el Perú (Socialismo y Participación [Centro de Estudios para el Desarrollo y la Participación, CEDEP, Lima] 21, marzo 1982, p. 51–67, bibl., maps, tables)

Major article reviews present patterns of coca leaf production and use in Peru, giving major emphasis to nutritional aspects of coca leaf, and pleading for more rational approach to whole matter of international narcotics control. Author clearly thinks that present programs are a total failure.

1447 Caro, Deborah A. and **Félix Palacios Ríos.** Pastizales y propiedad: tensiones normativas en la organización social de los pastores (in Congreso Peruano: El Hombre y la Cultura Andina, 3d, Lima, 1977. El hombre y la cultura andina [see HLAS 43:253] v. 3, p. 155–166, bibl.)

Contrasts access rights for different types of pasture in Aymara community. Noting that, in less favored lands, access is granted to bilateral and affinal kin, whereas in more favored it tends to be restricted to agnatic kin. Concludes that it is unrealistic to expect a single organizational principle to explain a culture. Makes brief comparison with similar structure among the Nuer.

1448 Collins, Jane L. Seasonal migration as a cultural response to energy scarcity at high altitude (UC/CA, 24:1, Feb. 1983, p. 103–104, bibl.)

Brief field report and analysis argues that Andean peasants use variety of environments for agriculture and animal husbandry only at particular phases in life cycle when they have unusual financial and sustance demands made upon them. If so, this considerably reduces the universality of the applicability of Murra's archipelago theory.

1449 Contreras Hernández, Jesús. La valoración del trabajo en una comunidad campesina de la sierra peruana (UB/BA, 22:30, 1980, p. 41–68, bibl.)

Detailed analysis of importance attached to good work habits in highland, Quechua-speaking community. Article solidly refutes any allegation that the Indian is "lazy." Unfortunately, proposes dubious hypothesis that the "work elite" is the result of recent adaptation to land scarcity and technological impoverishment.

1450 Cornejo, Walter. La *mipa*: una creencia social de los campesinos (*in* Congreso Peruano: El Hombre y la Cultura Andina, 3d, Lima, 1977. El hombre y la cultura andina [see *HLAS 43:253*] v. 4, p. 745–765, bibl.)

Pioneer description of belief system employed by mothers to explain the behavior appearance, and health peculiarities of their children. Article is strengthened by inclusion of results of questionnaire administered to 180 rural and 120 urban women in Huancayo province as well as inventory of 29 different types of *mipa*.

1451 Deustua Carvallo, José. Intelectuales y campesinos en el sur andino (IPA/A, 15:17/18, 1981, p. 41–60)

Traces leverage exercised by local intellectuals and *indigenistas* in opening doors to greater land equity and respect for human rights in area surrounding Cuzco, Peru, in early 1920s. Article documents a still-born social reform movement.

1452 Doughty, Paul L. A Latin American specialty in the world context: urban primacy and cultural colonialism in Peru

(UA, 8:3/4, Winter 1979, p. 383–397, tables)

After raising questions regarding theory of primate cities, author provides illustrative data from Lima, Peru. Missing from his discussion of Latin America's primate cities is the hemisphere's most extreme case: Montevideo, Uruguay.

1453 Flores Ochoa, Jorge A. and **Félix Palacios Ríos.** La protesta de 1909: un movimiento de pastores de la Puna Alta a comienzos del siglo XX (PUCP/DA, 2, mayo 1978, p. 75–88, bibl.)

History of successful resistance on the part of shepherds inhabiting the high Puna country near Chucuito, Peru. Explores reasons for success through functional analysis.

1454 Fonseca Martel, César. El proceso de cambio de cultivos en un comunidad campesina de los Andes (*in* Congreso Peruano: El Hombre y la Cultura Andina, 3d, Lima, 1977. El hombre y la cultura andina [see *HLAS 43:253*] v. 3, p. 85–106, bibl.)

Traces movement from a system of numerous, highly dispersed, small parcels to consolidated pastures as response to changing economy of the upper Cañete River basin. Argues for the natural history approach toward understanding change in rural Peru.

1455 —— and Enrique Mayer. Sistemas agrarios y ecología en la cuenca del Río Cañete (PUCP/DA, 2, mayo 1978, p. 25–59, bibl., maps)

General overview of different ecological zones represented by Cañete River basin. Because of article's general approach, it is lacking in both detail and analysis.

1456 Fuenzalida Vollmar, Fernando. Santiago y El Wamani: aspectos de un culto pagano en Moya (PUCP/DA, 5, julio 1980, p. 155–187)

Pure descriptive ethnography of the fiesta of Santiago which, author tells us, is really a fiesta in honor of Andean spirit, Wamani, a figure that can be both capricious and the cause of evil. Includes detailed description of ceremonies associated with the fiesta. Concludes with appendix consisting of lyrics of 14 fiesta songs.

1457 Gilbert, Dennis. Cognatic descent groups in upper-class Lima, Peru (AAA/AE, 8:4, Nov. 1981, p. 739–757, tables)

Illuminating study of structure and functions of cognatic descent group among the Prado and Miró Quesada families of Peru. Well-researched and cogently argued article.

1458 González Carré, Enrique. La antropología en Ayacucho: informe preliminar (PUCP/DA, 8, mayo 1982, p. 128–140)

Detailed history of development of anthropology in Huamanga Univ. Includes sensitive evaluation of prior emergence of anthropology in other parts of Peru, contribution of US scholars, and present trend toward social and political action in lieu of theory.

1459 Gow, David D. The roles of Christ and Inkarrí in Andean religion (UCLA/ JLAL, 6:2, Winter 1980, p. 279–296, bibl.)

Important and unusual article, relating the popular "Christs" of southern Peruvian highlands with indigenous and precolumbian concepts and spirits. Presents convincing argument that Christianity of southern Peru is nothing more than a reworking of long-standing Andean religious belief.

1460 Guillet, David. Surplus extraction, risk management and economic change among Peruvian peasants (JDS, 18:1, Oct. 1981, p. 3–24)

Pretentious attempt to apply economic theory to peasant production decisions. Data are sparse and theory somewhat unimaginative.

1461 Haboud de Ortega, Marleen. La educación informal cono proceso de socialización en San Pedro de Casta (PUCP/ DA, 5, julio 1980, p. 71–114, bibl., maps, tables)

Describes child-rearing practices in highland Peruvian community (e.g., pre-natal role of child, his/her incorporation into kindred, work assignments as learning situations, games, and gradual incorporation into community decision making). Concludes that system is effective because child's play world is one and the same as the adult's work world.

1462 Martínez, Héctor. Reforma agraria peruana: empresas asociativas (CEDLA/B, 30, junio 1981, p. 103–123, tables)

Critique of the associative model used for the Peruvian agrarian reform. Agrees with many of the points made in Alberts' *Agrarian reform and rural poverty*, though the focus of the critique is more sociostructural than economic.

1463 Mayer, Enrique. Consideraciones sobre lo indígena (*in* Perú, identidad nacional. César Arróspide de la Flor *et al.* Lima: Centro de Estudios para el Desarrollo y la Participación, 1979, p. 79–108, ill. [Serie Realidad nacional])

Provocative article, first part of which was produced 10 years before second. After reviewing past definitions of *indio*, *cholo*, and *mestizo*, Mayer concludes that Peruvian Indian's situation today is amazingly varied, and that any future definition of "Indian" should emphasize the positive rather than, as in the past, the negative.

1464 Millones Santa Gadea, Luis. Las religiones nativas del Perú: recuento y evaluación de su estudio (*in* Congreso Peruano: El Hombre y la Cultura Andina, 3d, Lima, 1977. El hombre y la cultura andina [see *HLAS 43:253*] v. 3, p. 3–26, bibl.)

Rather uncritical review of studies of indigenous religion and folk Catholicism in Peru. Article is, additionally, flawed by remarkable number of typographical errors.

1465 Mróz, Marcin. José María Arguedas como representante de la cultura quechua: análisis de la novela *El zorro de arriba y el zorro de abajo* (IPA/A, 15:17/18, 1981, p. 133–160, charts)

Critique of Arguedas' perception of culture in his novel *El zorro de arriba y el zorro de abajo*. Concludes that Arguedas wrote as Quechua thinker rather than as *indigenista*. Anthropologists, with more precise definitions of culture, might question this conclusion.

1466 Orlove, Benjamin S. Landlords and officials: the souces of domination in Surinama and Quehue (*in* Land and power in Latin America: agrarian economies and social processes in the Andes. Edited by Benjamin S. Orlove and Glynn Custred. New York: Holmes & Meier Publishers, 1980, p. 113–128, map, tables)

Controlled comparison of historical development of relationships between peasants and elites in two adjacent areas in Cuzco Dept.

1467 ———. The position of rustlers in regional society: social banditry in the Andes (*in* Land and power in Latin America:

agrarian economies and social processes in the Andes. Edited by Benjamin S. Orlove and Glynn Custred. New York: Holmes & Meier, 1980, p. 179–194)

Brief report on activity of rustlers in a province of Cuzco dept. Argues that, to carry out their activities, rustlers need extensive peasant networks; therefore their victims are almost invariably of the landlord class.

1468 Ortiz Rescaniere, Alejandro. Arguedas y la antropología (PUCP/DA, 5, julio 1980, p. 25–30)

Brief and superficial discussion of the influence of anthropological training on the writings of the Peruvian novelist, José María Arguedas.

1469 Ossio, Juan M. La sociedad nacional, los indígenas del área andina y la coca (PUCP/DA, 2, mayo 1978, p. 137–141)

Appeal that the law prohibiting the sale of coca leaves below 1,500 m. be rescinded, based on respect for cultures that have withstood 400 years of onslaught by the Spanish-speaking minority of Peru. Argues that a pluri-cultural Peru will be a stronger Peru.

1470 Osterling, Jorge P. De campesinos a profesionales: migrantes de Huayopampa en Lima. Lima: Pontificia Universidad Católica del Perú, Fondo Editorial, 1980. 203 p.: bibl., maps.

Case study of a Spanish-speaking rural community in the Peruvian sierra that, having fewer than 200 families, had, by 1975, produced more than 140 professionals. Author explains this phenomenon, as well as others such as the fact that Huayopampinos never succeeded in establishing a permanent regional association in Lima, in purely historical terms.

1471 ———. San Agustín de Pariác: su tradición oral (PUCP/DA, 5, julio 1980, p. 189–224)

Collection of 30 folktales recorded in the highland Peruvian community of San Agustín de Huayopampa, accompanied by a minimum of interpretation. One searches in vain in the collection for suggestions of theoretical significance.

1472 Ramírez Villacorta, Yolanda. La penetración capitalista en una comunidad campesina: el caso de San Pedro de Casta,

Huarochirí (PUCP/DA, julio 1980, p. 39–70, maps, tables)

Cursory review of the impact of a hydroelectric plant and a paved road on a highland Peruvian community. Author insists that basic community structure has remained intact, yet admits that one of the spin-offs of this "development" has been nightly drinking bouts in canteens, which now accounts for one of every six houses!

1473 Robles Mendoza, Román. Evolución económica de las comunidades pastoras de la Sierra Central del Perú (in Congreso Peruano: El Hombre y la Cultura Andina, 3d, Lima, 1977. El hombre y la cultura andina [see HLAS 43:253] v. 3, p. 107–119)

Documents the movement of two central Peruvian herding communities toward a fully market-oriented economy and an increasingly stratified internal socioeconomic order. Article argues that agencies of the agrarian reform such as SAIS increase rather than decrease differential access to strategic resources.

1474 Romano, Ruggiero. Problemi della coca nel Perú del secolo XX (GEE/NA, 4, 1981, p. 67–106, maps, tables)

Review of the literature dealing with production, external and internal use of coca in Peru. Concludes that use of coca leaf should never be equated with use of cocaine, and that the driving force behind present anti-coca campaigns in Peru is the US.

1475 Schaedel, Richard P. From homogenization to heterogenization in Lima, Peru (UA, 8:3/4, Winter 1979,p. 399–421)

Provocative article suggesting that urban model developed in Lima over past 20 years is multi-ethnic or heterogeneous. Argues that barriada residents are consciously resisting assimilation and have, through independent marketing system, laid claim to their own share of gross national product.

1476 Scurrah, Martin J. and Guadalupe Esteves. Reflexiones sobre experiencias autogestionarias en el Perú (III/AI, 41:4, 1981, p. 627–664, bibl., tables)

Explores relative success of formal cooperative ventures in Peru. Based on more than 200 interviews, authors conclude that rural ventures, exemplified by ERPS, SAIS, and CAP, are more successful than urban ventures, as exemplified by EATS. Decisive factors accounting for this difference are seen as external.

1477 Seligman, Linda J. and Elayne Zorn.
Visión diacrónica de la economía de la producción textil andina (III/AI, 41:2, abril/junio 1981, p. 265–287)

Brief overview of the role of textiles in rural economy of southern Peru from conquest onward. Abandonment of weaving tradition is attributed to exploitative market of the past, and experience of weavers on Titicaca Lake island of Taquile is held up as example of what should be done.

1478 Shoemaker, Robin. The peasants of El Dorado: conflict and contradiction in a Peruvian frontier settlement. Ithaca, N.Y.: Cornell University Press, 1981. 265 p.: bibl., index.

Middle-range analytic perspective on problems of economic and social change in Peruvian montaña. Author cogently argues that such areas are not "marginal," nor are they examples of a "plural society" configuration. Rather, they are tightly integrated with and exploited by national and international structures. Solid, well-reasoned study.

1479 Skar, Harold O. The War Valley people: duality and land reform among the Quechua Indians of highland Peru. Foreword by Norman Long. Oslo, Norway: Universitetsforlaget, 1982. 350 p.: bibl., ill., maps, plates, tables (Oslo studies in social anthropology; 2)

One of best books of Andean ethnology to be produced over the biennium. Skar looks at effects of agrarian reform on Pincos Valley of Peru, concluding that, in spite of very favorable base, reform brought loss of productivity and technology. Some Andean scholars will raise eyebrows at author's definitions of *ayllu*, for it is ego-centered and floating: "people classed together and recruited on diverse principles in relation to a conceptionalized opposition." For Pincos Valley, however, author's definition is well defended.

1480 Smith, Richard Chase. Liberal ideology and indigenous communities in post-independence Peru (CU/JIA, 36:1, Spring/Summer 1982, p. 73–82)

Sketchy historical summary of the application of liberal ideas and policies, à la Adam Smith, to indigenous communities. Discusses both impact of these policies on communities' landholding practices and remarkable resistance to this impact over more than 150 years.

1481 Stocks, Anthony Wayne. Los nativos invisibles: notas sobre la historia y realidad actual de los cocamilla del Río Huallaga, Perú. Traducción, Annette Rosenvinge de Uriarte, Armando Valdés Palacios. Lima: Centro Amazónico de Antropología y Aplicación Práctica, 1981. 1 v. (Serie Antropológica; no. 4)

Extraordinarily rich ethnohistorical and ethnographic study that argues that marriage patterns, more than language, determine whether a given ethnic group remains unassimilated. Author pleads for Peruvian government's recognition of Cocamilla as a tribal group. Suggests that, in developing upper Amazon, the white man should learn from such groups' millenia of experience.

1482 Strugg, David L. The foreign politics of cocaine: comments on a plan to eradicate the coca leaf in Peru (Journal of Drug Issues [Drug Issues Inc.?, Tallahassee, Fla.] 13:1, Winter 1983, p. 135–145, bibl.)

Succinct analysis of the influence of US government in attempting to eradicate coca leaf in Peru, accompanied by brief references to cultural and economic impact of such a move. Author argues that effort increases dependency relationship between Peru and US.

1483 Urbain, Jean-Didier. Le système quechua de l'échange: développements métaphoriques et adaptation d'un "vocabulaire de base" (EPHE/H, 20:1, jan./mars 1980, p. 71–90, bibl., charts, ill.)

Argues, from standpoint of semiology, that indigenous Andean systems of labor recruitment and exchange can be compatible with dominant, Hispanic market system. Author appeals for reciprocal adaptation of two different cultural universes.

1484 Urton, Gary. Animals and astronomy in the Quechua universe (APS/P, 125:2, April 1981, p. 110–127, ill., plates)

First-class exploration of concept of "dark cloud" animal constellations among Peru's Quechua. Discusses specifically constellations representing serpent, toad, *tinamou*, llama, and fox. Articles such as this are beginning to help us understand the Andean mind.

1485 ——. At the crossroads of the earth and the sky: an Andean cosmology. Austin: University of Texas Press, 1981. 248 p.: bibl., ill., index (Latin American monographs)

Although this book presents much information on Inca and Quechua cosmology, it falls somewhat short of presenting it as an internally consistent and meaningful system. In surprising short supply are references to concepts of disease, misfortune, healing, and magic. Also missing is sort of tight analysis that would tie the ethnohistorical to the ethnographic.

1486 ——. Celestial crosses: the cruciform in Quechua astronomy (UCLA/JLAL, 6:1, Summer 1980, p. 87–110, facsim., ill., plates)

Argues that model of the cross (though not the Latin cross) was indigenous to precolumbian Andes, and that it was related to interpretation of star clusters. Underlying principle of Andean concept of the cross is the *chaka*, an axis along which a state of equilibrium is established and maintained.

1487 Valderrama Fernández, Ricardo and **Carmen Escalante Gutiérrez.** Apu Qorpuna: visión del mundo de los muertos en la comunidad de Awkimarca (PUCP/DA, 5, julio 1980, p. 233–264, ill.)

Unusually full account of concepts of afterlife among Quechua speakers in Apurímac Dept., Peru. No attempt is made to clarify underlying patterns, to relate these beliefs to other facets of the culture, or to explore theoretical implications of belief structure.

1488 Villafuerte R., Jorge E. La tierra y sus contradicciones en el régimen cooperativo (*in* Congreso Peruano: El Hombre y la Cultura Andina, 3d, Lima, 1977. El hombre y la cultura andina [see *HLAS 43:253*] v. 3, p. 215–228, bibl.)

Negative and wordy critique of Peruvian agrarian reform and cooperative movement, lacking in both data and analysis.

1489 Wallis, Cristóbal. Pastores de llama en Cailloma, Arequipa, y modelos estructuralistas para la interpretación de su sociedad (*in* Congreso Peruano: El Hombre y la Cultura Andina, 3d, Lima, 1977. El hombre y la cultura andina [see *HLAS 43:253*] v. 3, p. 248–257)

On the basis of case study of interrelations between agriculturalists and herders, author challenges validity of John Murra's archipelago hypothesis, and suggests that a strictly structuralist approach would have more universal applicability.

1490 Webster, Steven. Interpretation of an Andean social and economic formation (RAI/M, 16:4, Dec. 1981, p. 616–633, bibl.)

Novel analysis of relationships between *colonos* and their hacienda *patrón*, based on case study in southern Peru. Author offers hypothesis that "nominally dominant regimes have had to compromise for the sake of consent, or even suffer cynical exploitation at the hands of their nominal subordinates."

1491 Yaranga Valderrama, Abdón. Migración de las comunidades de Huancaraylla, Llusita y Circamarca a Lima (*in* Congreso Peruano: El Hombre y la Cultura Andina, 3d, Lima, 1977. El hombre y la cultura andina [see *HLAS 43:253*] v. 3, p. 229–247, tables)

Preliminary report of migration to Lima from three Ayacucho rural communities. At most, article offers few case-specific facts and figures.

1492 Zorrilla E., Javier. Sueño, mito y realidad en una comunidad ayacuchana (PUCP/DA, 2, mayo 1978, p. 119–124, ill.)

Attempt to relate two revelations received by resident of the Ayacucho community of Acoco, with subsequent construction by community of an irrigation ditch. Author states that he makes an "anthropological" analysis of the "revelations," but it is unclear to just what anthropology he refers.

ANTHROLINGUISTICS

LYLE CAMPBELL, Associate Professor of Anthropology, Latin American Studies, and Linguistics, State University of New York, Albany

ERNESTO C. MIGLIAZZA, Consultant in Anthrolinguistics, Washington, D.C.

IN RECENT YEARS INTEREST IN the native languages of Mexico and Central America has increased. Perhaps most striking is the appearance of a large number of basic reference works—grammars, dictionaries, and texts—many more extensive and more useful than earlier publications. Good examples of dictionaries are: Barrera's for Popoloco (item **1501**); Clark's for Oluta (item **1509**); *Diccionario maya Cordemex* for Yucatec Maya (item **1513**); Grimes' for Huichol (item **1516**); Haeserijn's for Kekchi (item **1519**); Harrison, Harrison, and Cástulo García's for Zoque (item **1520**); Henne's for Quiché (item **1522**); von Houwald's for Sumu (item **1523**); Lenkersdorf's for Tojolabal (item **1532**); Margery Peña's for Bribri (item **1535**); and Stairs Kreger and Scharfe de Stairs' for Huave (item **1548**). Some of the several detailed grammars are: Alexander's for Mixtec (item **1494**); Butler's for Zapotec (item **1506**); Guzmán Betancourt's for Nahuatl (item **1518**); Haviland's for Tzotzil (item **1521**); Launey's for Nahuatl (item **1531**); Mondloch's for Quiché (item **1538**); Warkentin and Scott's for Chol (item **1557**); and Wolgemuth's for Mecayapan Nahuatl (item **1558**).

More evidence of the interest in basic reference works is the republication of several colonial (sometimes called "classical") language sources that include: Alvarez' for Yucatec Maya (item **1495**); Arenas' for Nahuatl (item **1499**); *Diccionario maya Cordemex* for Yucatec Maya, both colonial and modern (item **1513**); Carochi's for Nahuatl (item **1508**); López Austín's for Nahuatl (item **1534**); Pennington's for Eudeve (item **1500**); Pennington's for Pima Bajo or Lower Pima (item **1542**); Ramírez' for Nahuatl (item **1546**); plus colonial texts such as Chávez' *Quiché Popol Vuh* (item **1544**); and Edmonson's Yucatec Maya *Chilam Balam of Tizimín* (item **1497**). The growing interest is also evident in new serials such as *The Journal of Mayan Linguistics* (item **1526**) and *Amerindia* (item **1496**).

Historical and comparative studies include works by Canger (item **1507**), Dakin (item **1511**), Merrifield (item **1537**), and Sullivan (item **1551**), plus several articles from the *Proceedings* of the Berkeley Linguistics Society (item **1545**) and the *International Journal of American Linguistics* (item **1525**).

Special mention should be made of several uniform volumes issued by the Archivo de Lenguas de México devoted to the description of several languages (item **1498**).

That there is a great diversity of interests is exemplified by works such as Knorozov and Schele's on Mayan hieroglyphic writing (item **1528**), Lastra and Suárez', Mejías', Suárez', and Vásquez' on interferences between Spanish and Indian languages (items **1513, 1530, 1536,** and **1550**); Burns' on Yucatec Mayan oral literature (item **1505**), Tapia's on Amuzgo ethnobotany (item **1552**), and Wilhite's on acquisition of language routines by Cakchiquel children (item **1557**). [LC]

SOUTH AMERICAN INDIAN LANGUAGES

The fact that anthrolinguistic publications on South America have declined is compensated by the appearance of some important theoretical papers of excellent quality on Quechua by Cole and Hermon (item **1575**); Cole, Harbert and Hermon (item **1576**); Jake (item **1594**); Dextre (item **1581**); and Cordoba (item **1577**); one in Capanahua by Safir (item **1612**); and another on Aymara by Martin and Briggs (item **1598**). We hope that papers of equal merit will be written by scholars working in other languages.

Discourse analysis continues to be the exclusive province of the Summer Institute of Linguistics. Outstanding are their studies on Guahibo (item **1584**), Guajiro by Mansen (item **1585**), and Kaiwa by Bridgeman (item **1567**), as well as their studies of five Peruvian languages edited by Wise (item **1574**).

Quite a few publications deal with partial descriptions and didactic grammars: Allin for Resigaro (item **1560**); Fast for Achuar (item **1586**); Metzger for Carapana (item **1601**); Tovar for Mataco (item **1619**); Pontes for Tupi (item **1609**); Pino Duran for Quechua (item **1606**); and West for Tucano (item **1627**).

Sociolinguistic and applied linguistics are the most productive areas. A number of recent publications deal with bilingualism or diglossia situations. Most notable are works by Miño-Garcés (item **1602**), Corvalán and Granda (item **1615**), Escobar (item **1583**), and Corvalán (item **1578**). Among works in sociolinguistics and related areas, the following publications are noteworthy: Garvin (item **1588**); Guzmán (item **1592**); Weber (item **1626**); Granda (item **1590**); Masson (item **1600**); and Cerron (item **1571**).

There are vocabularies and dictionaries of various length and usefulness. Some include grammatical notes, sketches or summaries: Montag on Cashinawa (item **1603**); Torres on Ecuadorian Quechua (item **1618**); Jusayu on Guajiro (item **1595**); Vegamián on Yupa (item **1623**); Velie on Orejon (item **1624**). Some are preliminary vocabularies such as Kindberg's on Campa Ashaninca (item **1596**); and the Summer Institute of Linguistics' work on Siriano (item **1625**). Others are new editions such as Barral's on Warao (item **1563**) and Guardía's on Quechua (item **1591**).

While many folk stories and myths have appeared only a few publications include texts in native languages such as Capanahua (item **1616**); Guajiro (item **1606**); Chulupi (item **1573**); Araucanian (item **1587**); Kawesqar (item **1617**); and Quechua San Martín (item **1559**). Other publications include only the free Spanish or Portuguese version of folk tales translated from the following languages: Canela and Guajajara (item **1579**); Mataco (item **1580**); Shipibo (item **1566**); and Quechua (item **1621**). Some publications consist of analyses of folk narratives in Aymara (item **1564**); Neengatu-Guaraní (item **1565**); Huachipaire (item **1568**); and a study of time in Andean myths (item **1605**).

It is regrettable that so few comparative studies have been published, although Ritchie Key's paper (item **1611**) is a stimulating contribution to the field. One explanation could be that such papers are usually presented at meetings or international congresses and are still in manuscript form.

Of interest are publications on history and bibliography exemplified by González (item **1589**); Armellada (item **1562**); Rey (item **1610**); Campo (item **1569**); Carrocera (item **1570**); linguistic studies by missionaries in Venezuela (item **1569**); Landaburu (item **1597**); and Silva (item **1613**).

Worthy of special mention are the study of Guarani proverbs by Bersabe Ruiz (item **1565**), an analysis of color of terms in Jaqaru by Hardman (item **1593**), and a good Lengua-Maskoy ethnobotany by Arenas (item **1561**). [ECM]

MEXICAN AND CENTRAL AMERICAN INDIAN LANGUAGES

1493 Aguirre Beltrán, Gonzalo. El Instituto Lingüístico de Verano (III/AI, 3:41, julio/sept. 1981, p. 435–461, bibl.)
Brief history of linguistic and applied linguistic activities of Summer Institute of Linguistics (SIL) in Mexico. It is also a defense against accusations of Mexican anthropologists who would like to expel SIL missionary-linguists from Mexico. [ECM]

1494 Alexander, Ruth Mary. Gramática mixteca de Atatlahuca = Gramatica yuhu sasau jee cahan ñayuu San Estevan Atatlahuca. México: Instituto Lingüístico de Verano, 1980. 156 p.: bibl., ill. (Serie de gramáticas de lenguas indígenas de México; no. 2)
Grammar of Mixtec of Atatlahuca, excellently done, good examples, easy to use, but also sophisticated, with treatment of sounds and their allophones, tones and their changes, and with short texts at end of each chapter. Grammar is presented first in Spanish, then in Mixtec for native readers.

1495 Alvarez, Cristina. Diccionario etnolingüístico del idioma maya yucateco colonial. v. 1, Mundo físico. México: Universidad Autónoma de México, Instituto de Investigaciones Filológicas, Centro de Estudios Mayas, 1980. 385 p.: bibl., charts.
Compilation of terms referring to physical world gathered from several colonial Yucatec dictionaries. Arranged according to semantic domains (e.g., astronomy, geography, botany, zoology, man).

1496 Amerindia. Revue d'éthnolinguistique amérindienne. Equipe de Recherche associée du Centre national de la recherche scientifique. No. 3, 1978 [through] No. 7, 1980- . Paris.
Relatively new journal dedicated to all aspects of American Indian languages. Seven available issues also include many articles on North and South American languages. Those on Mexican and Central American languages are: Juan A. Hasler "Semántica Mesoamericana" (No. 3); Sybille de Pury-Toumi "La Logique de l'Emprunt en Mexicano (Nahuatl)" (No. 4); also by Pury-Toumi "Le Saltillo en Nahuatl" (No. 5); Michel Launey "Une Interprétation Linguistique des Schémes Relationnels: Passifs-Impersonnels et Causatifs en Nahuatl Classique" (No. 6); and André Lionnet "Un Dialecte Méridional du Tarahumar" (No. 7).

1497 The Ancient future of the Itza: the *Book of Chilam Balam of Tizimin.* Translated and annotated by Munro S. Edmonson. Austin: University of Texas Press, 1982. 220 p.: ill. (The Texas Pan American series)
Translation of *Book of Chilam Balam of Tizimin*, with Yucatec Maya text and considerable commentary and interpretation in copious notes. Index is detailed and useful. Edmonson's translation pays particular attention to text's poetic structure.

1498 *Archivo de Lenguas Indígenas de México.* v. 1- . México. Centro de Investigación para la Integración, 197?- .
Monographic series reflects Archivo's goal to document systematically the languages of Mexico. Several volumes have appeared to date following uniform format and extensive questionnaire. Archivo and Center are directed by Gloria Ruiz de Bravo Ahuja, Archivo itself by Jorge Suárez, and questionnaire was framed by Ray Freeze. Each volume contains examples of phonological contrasts and allophones, a text with translation, sentences with translations which illustrate most important syntactic categories and rules that a language can contain plus maps and word list of approximately 500 items, including Swadesh's 100-word list. Examples of volumes are: *Mixteco de Santa María Peñoles* (No. 3); *Mazateco de Chiquihuitlán* (No. 5); *Chontal de la Sierra (Tequistlateco)* (No. 7); *Chinanteco de San Juan Lealao* (No. 9); and *Náhuatl de Acaxochitlán* (No. 10). Others are in production. Uniform presentation of linguistic material on native languages proves extremely valuable, partly because some are very poorly known and also because it facilitates comparisons among languages.

1499 Arenas, Pedro de. Vocabulario manual de las lenguas castellana y mexicana, en que se contienen las palabras, preguntas y respuestas más comunes y ordinarias que se suelen ofrecer en el trato y comunicación entre españoles e indios. With an introduction and notes by Ascención H. de León-Portilla. México: Universidad Nacional Autónoma de México, Instituto de Investigaciones Históricas y Filológicas, 1982. 260 p.: bibl.

Facsimile reproduction of 1611 edition of Arenas' *Vocabulario* of Nahuatl, with information about Arenas and about vocabulary.

1500 *Arte y vocabulario de la lengua dohema, heve, o eudeva*: anónimo; siglo XVII. Campbell W. Pennington, editor. México: Universidad Nacional Autónoma de México, Instituto de Investigaciones Filológicas, 1981. 259 p., 2 leaves of plates: bibl., ill.

Presents 17th-century anonymous grammar (*Arte*) and dictionary (*Vocabulario*) of Eudeve (Uto-Aztecan), together with a "doctrina cristiana" in the language. Book is introduced with copious historical notes and commentary on the manuscript in both English and Spanish versions.

1501 Barrera, Bartolo and **Karen Dakin**. Vocabulario popoloca de San Vicente Coyotepec, popoloca-español, español-popoloca. México: Centro de Investigaciones Superiores del INAH, 1978. 147 p.: bibl. (Cuadernos de la Casa Chata; 11)

Popoloca (Otomanguean) vocabulary of San Vicente Coyotepec, Puebla, based on word list of 1400 items (p. 7–90 Popoloco-Spanish, p. 91–147 Spanish-Popoloca).

1502 Barrera-Vásquez, Alfredo. Estudios lingüísticos. Obras completas. t. 1. Mérida, México: Fondo Editorial de Yucatán, 1980. 1 v.

Collection of several of Barrera Vásquez's articles on Yucatec Maya and on mutual influences of Maya and Spanish on each other in Yucatán.

Bartolomé, Miguel Alberto. Narrativa y etnicidad entre los chatinos de Oaxaca. See item **914**.

Benítez, Fernando. Los indios de México. v. 5, El gran tiempo: tepehuanes y nahuas. See item **916**.

1503 Bibliografía anotada sobre fonología, dialectología y ortografía naua. Compiled by James L. Fidelholtz. México: Instituto Nacional Indigenista (INI), Programa de Etnolingüística, 1982. 121 p.

Bibliography of over 200 entries on Nahuatl language and linguistics.

1504 Bibliography of Mayan languages and linguistics. Compiled by Lyle Campbell, Pierre Ventur, Russell Stewart, and

Brant Gardner. Albany: University of New York at Albany, 1978. 182 p.: index (Institute for Mesoamerican Studies; publication no. 3)

Contains 2513 bibliographic entries on Mayan languages and linguistics, plus an index arranged primarily according to language.

1505 Burns, Allan Frank. An epoch of miracles: oral literature of the Yucatec Maya. Translated with commentaries by Allan F. Burns. Foreword by Dennis Tedlock. Austin: University of Texas Press, 1983. 266 p.: bibl., ill. (The Texas Pan American series)

Presents Yucatec Maya oral literature following ethnopoetics (verbal-art) approach, where performance is dominant characteristic. Selections are taken from many of the genre which represent native Yucatec Mayan conception of speech and their oral tradition. These include ancient conversations (about origins), stories, counsels, secret (esoteric) knowledge, playful speech (riddles and jokes), a song, and a feathered-serpent story. All are translated but only very few include Maya text.

1506 Butler H., Inez M. Gramática zapoteca: zapoteca de Yatzachi el Bajo. México: Instituto Lingüístico de Verano, 1980. 350 p.: bibl., ill., maps (Serie de gramáticas de lenguas indígenas de México; no. 4)

Presents rather comprehensive grammar of Zapotec of Yatzachi el Bajo, Oaxaca, including abundant examples and a detailed phonological description.

1507 Canger, Una. Five studies inspired by Nahuatl verbs in -oa. With a summary in Spanish. Copenhagen: The Linguistic Circle of Copenhagen, 1980. 255 p.: bibl., ill., maps (Travaux du Cercle linguistique de Copenhague; v. 19)

Extremely careful and excellent study of Nahuatl verbs ending in -oa which involves, in effect, an explanation of Nahuatl verb types and verbal morphology in general. Study represents most accurate dialectology of Nahuatl to date, and offers brilliant solutions to several long-standing problems in Nahuatl linguistics. Contains appendix of all verb roots in Molina's (1571) *Vocabulario*, comprehensive bibliography, and Spanish summary.

1508 Carochi, Horacio. Arte de la lengua mexicana: gramática náhuatl. Edited by Ignacio Paredes. México: Editorial Innovación, 1979. 202 p.: ill.

Republication of Carochi's famous *Gramática náhuatl* of 1645.

1509 Clark, Lawrence E. Diccionario popoluca de Oluta: popoluca-español, español-popoluca. México: Instituto Lingüístico de Verano, 1981. 162 p.: appendices, bibl., ill., map (Serie de vocabularios y diccionarios indígenas Mariano Silva y Aceves; no. 25)

Dictionary of Oluta Popoluca (Mixean language) includes statement of the grammar in appendix, plus appendices on animals, birds, insects, reptiles, trees and plants.

Colby, Benjamin N. and **Lore M. Colby.** The daykeeper: the life and discourse of an Ixil diviner. See item **942.**

1510 Coronado de Caballero, Gabriela; Víctor Manuel Franco Pellotier; and **Héctor Muñoz Cruz.** Bilingüismo y educación en el Valle del Mezquital. México: Centro de Investigaciones y Estudios Superiores en Antropología Social, 1981. 208 p.: ill. (Cuadernos de la casa chata; 42)

Description of Indian education in Valle del Mezquital, with social and educational problems in Otomí-Spanish contact and response to bilingual education. Study is a contribution to language policy in Mexico, focusing on evaluating sociolinguistic conditions of the distribution and use of Otomí and Spanish, on linguistic attitudes of bilingual Otomis, with criticism of pedagogical materials designed for Otomí population.

1511 Dakin, Karen. La evolución fonológica del protonáhuatl. México: Universidad Nacional Autónoma de México, Instituto de Investigaciones Filológicas, 1982. 237 p.: bibl., indexes.

Reconstructs Proto-Nahuatl, with sound changes in series of rules. Contains considerable information on historical morphology, with 315 reconstructed roots and 56 reconstructed grammatical morphemes.

1512 Díaz Olivares, Jorge. Manual del tseltal. San Cristóbal de las Casas, México: Universidad Autónoma de Chiapas, 1980. 338 p.

Pedagogical work with complicated organization, intended to facilitate learning of Tzeltal. Includes long Spanish-Tzeltal and Tzeltal-Spanish word list at end.

1513 Diccionario maya Cordemex: maya-español, español-maya. Director, Alfredo Barrera Vásquez. Redactores, Juan Ramón Bastarrachea Manzano, William Brito Sansores. Colaboradores, Refugio Vermont Salas, David Dzul Góngora, Domingo Dzul Poot. Mérida, México: Ediciones Cordemex, 1980. 1 v. (69, 984, 360 p.): bibl.

Massive dictionary of Yucatec Maya compiled from 12 colonial and 17 modern sources, indicated by number within text. It represents the work of a team of Yucatec scholars/speakers over several years and is a truly monumental achievement. Modern linguists might wish for more accurate information concerning Yucatec vowel length, tones, and glottal stops, or for more consistency in the representations. Nevertheless, this dictionary stands out among those of native languages and will prove extremely useful for all sorts of interests.

1514 *Estudios de Cultura Náhuatl*. Universidad Nacional Autónoma de México, Instituto de Investigaciones Históricas. Vol. 14, 1980- . México.

Contains several articles on Nahuatl linguistics, including: Frances Karttunen and James Lockhart "La Estructura de la Poesía Náhuatl Vista por sus Variantes;" Thelma Sullivan "Tlatoani and Tlatocayotl in the Sahagún Manuscripts;" Tim Knab "Algunos Apuntes Acerca del Pochuteco;" Una Canger "Ochpaniztli and Classical Nahuatl Syllable Structure;" and Tim Knab "Lenguas del Soconusco, Pipil y Náhuatl de Huehuetán," etc.

Gossen, Gary H. The *Popul Vuh* revisited: a comparison with modern Chamula narrative tradition. See *HLAS 44:1523.*

1515 Gramática de la lengua zapoteca. Por un autor anónimo. La edición ha sido dirigida por Antonio Peñafiel. México: Editorial Innovación, 1981. 148 p.

Anonymous Zapotec grammar, originally published in 1886 by Peñafiel. Contains bibliography of writings on Zapotec, an *Arte* of Zapotec by Valdespino, additions to the *Arte*, a *Confesionario*, and selections of a Zapotec *Catecismo*, and ends with three pages of word lists called "Cartilla de la Ideoma (sic) Sapoteca."

1516 Grimes E., José. El huichol: apuntes sobre el léxico. Ithaca, N.Y.: Cornell University, Department of Modern Languages and Linguistics, 1982. 295 p.: appendices, bibl., ill.

Excellent two-way dictionary (Huichol-Spanish, Spanish-Huichol), which represents tone and vowel length. Contains English summary, appendix of biological names in Latin, and second appendix on morphosemantic functions in lexicon.

1517 Guatemalan Maya texts. Paul G. Townsend, editor. Guatemala: Summer Institute of Linguistics, 1980. 231 p.: bibl., ill.

Collection of texts in various Guatemalan Mayan languages, predominantly of Mamean subgroup, partial results of textual grammar and analysis workshop held by Summer Institute of Linguistics in 1979. Objective was to make available accurate and representative data in broad textual context with minimum of terminological trappings. Texts are from Tacaná Mam, Tectitec (Teco), Aguacatec, Ixil, Cantel Quiché, Sipacapa, Chinautla Pokomam and San Luis Jilotepeque Pokomam. They include folk narratives, procedures, personal experience and exposition.

1518 Guzmán Betancourt, Ignacio. Gramática del náhuatl de Santa Catarina, Morelos. México: Instituto Nacional de Antropología e Historia (INAH), Departamento de Lingüística, 1979. 109 p.: bibl.

Describes in some detail structure of Santa Catarina Nahuatl phonology and morphology. Contains vocabulary.

1519 Haeserijn V., Padre Esteban. Diccionario k'ekchi' español. Guatemala: Editorial Piedra Santa, 1979. 489 p.

Excellent dictionary, K'ekchi'-Spanish and Spanish-K'ekchi' (Mayan), introduced with phonological and morphological notes.

1520 Harrison, Roy; Margaret Harrison; and **Cástulo García H.** Diccionario zoque de Copainalá. México: Instituto Lingüístico de Verano, 1981. 489 p.: appendices, bibl., ill., maps (Serie de vocabularios y diccionarios indígenas Mariano Silva y Aceves; no. 23)

Extensive Zoque-Spanish, Spanish-Zoque dictionary, with reasonably comprehensive appendix on grammar, plus numerals, geographical names, kinship terms, and sayings.

1521 Haviland, John Beard. Skop sotz'leb: el tzotzil de San Lorenzo Zinacantán. México: Universidad Nacional Autónoma de

México, Instituto de Investigaciones Filológicas, Centro de Estudios Mayas, 1981. 385 p.: bibl., ill.

Excellent, comprehensible, and extensive grammar of Tzotzil (Mayan). Includes clear presentation of both basic and very complicated aspects of Tzotil grammar and syntax.

1522 Henne Pontious, David. Diccionario quiché-español. Investigadores, Abraham García Hernández, Santiago Yac Sam. México: Instituto Lingüístico de Verano, 1980. 270 p.: ill.

Excellent Quiché-Spanish, Spanish-Quiché dictionary, the best currently available, prepared for both native and non-native speakers. Begins with sketch of Quiché grammar.

Horcasitas, Fernando. Versos de la danza de Santiago de Taxco, Guerrero. See item **972.**

1523 Houwald, Götz Dieter, Freiherr von. Diccionario español-sumu, sumu-español. Managua: Ministerio de Educación, 1980. 133 p.: appendix.

Dictionary of Sumu (Misumalpan), with an appendix on the grammar of the language. This is an especially welcome reference, since Sumu is relatively unknown.

1524 Indigenismo y lingüística: documentos del foro "La Política del Lenguaje en México." México: Universidad Nacional Autónoma de México, Instituto de Investigaciones Antropológicas, 1980. 193 p. (Serie Antropológica; 35)

Contains 21 papers on Indian language policy (Mexico, 1980). Although of uneven quality, they reflect very well the sensitive and, indeed, highly emotional nature of the topic. While some papers are grounded on a sound scholarly base and address important linguistic and anthropological issues in Indian language policy, others unfortunately engage in rather empty political rhetoric often against the Summer Institute of Linguistics. Unbiased but critical readers will find little of substance in these criticisms. One hopes that something as important as Mexico's linguistic policy will not be decided without careful documentation.

1525 *International Journal of American Linguistics.* University of Chicago Press. Vol. 46, No. 1, Jan. 1980 [through] Vol. 49, No. 1, March 1983- . Chicago.

This is the leading journal for linguistic studies of native American languages. Important articles on Mexican and Central American languages are: Donald G. Nellis and Barbara E. Hollenbach "Fortis versus Lenis in Cajonos Zapotec Phonology;" Doris Bartholomew "Otomanguean Influence on Pochutla Aztec;" Doris Bartholomew and David Mason "The Registration of Transitivity in the Guerrero Aztec Verb;" Lyle Campbell and David Oltrogge "Proto-Tol (Jicaque);" Douglas Taylor and Berend Hoff "The Linguistic Repertory of the Island-Carib in the Seventeenth Century: the Men's Language—a Carib Pidgin?;" Jane and Kenneth Hill "Regularities in Vocabulary Replacement in Modern Nahuatl;" Douglas Biber "The Lexical Representation of Contour Tones" (examples primarily from Otomanguean languages); Jeri Jaeger and Robert Van Valin "Internal Consonant Clusters in Yatée Zapotec;" Carole Ann Jamieson "Conflated Subsystems Marking Person and Aspect in Chiquihuitlán Mazatec Verbs;" Elizabeth Willett "Reduplication and Accent in Southeastern Tepehuan;" John Robertson "The History of the Absolutive Second-Person Pronoun from Common Mayan to Modern Tzotzil;" Nora England "Ergativity in Mamean (Mayan) Languages;" and Glen Ayres "The Antipassive 'Voice' in Ixil."

1526 *Journal of Mayan Linguistics.* University of Iowa, Anthropology Department. Vol. 1, 1979- . Iowa City.

New journal, devoted to all aspects of Mayan linguistics, has issued three volumes since its inception in 1979. Many articles to date have dealt with formal description of aspects of grammar in a large number of different Mayan languages, employing insights of recent linguistic theory.

1527 Kimball, Geoffrey. A dictionary of the Huazalinguillo dialect of Nahuatl with grammatical sketch and readings. New Orleans: Tulane University, Latin American Studies Curriculum Aids, Center for Latin American Studies, 1980. 131 p.

Useful Nahuatl-English, English-Nahuatl dictionary with sketch of grammar, primarily its morphology, plus several folkloric texts and translations as readings.

1528 Knorozov, Yurii. Maya hieroglyphic codices. Translated from Russian by Sophie D. Coe. Albany: State University of New York at Albany, 1982. 429 p.: bibl., index (Institute for Mesoamerican Studies; publication no. 8)

Analysis and commentary of four extant Mayan codices, rich in ideas and interpretations.

1529 Lardé y Larín, Jorge. Toponimia autóctona de El Salvador occidental. San Salvador: Ediciones del Ministerio del Interior, 1977. 441 p., 36 leaves of plates: ill., index.

Concerns place names of western El Salvador and serves as companion volume to two previous ones on names of native origin for eastern and central El Salvador. While useful, this collection of names' origins and etymologies is frequently mistaken (e.g., there were no Mixe or Jicaque names in El Salvador). Includes Pipil (Nahuatl) word list of Izalco (p. 344–346).

1530 Lastra, Yolanda and **Jorge Suárez.** La investigación de las interferencias entre las lenguas amerindias y el español (*in* Perspectivas de la investigación lingüística en Hispanoamérica. Edited by Juan M. Lope Blanch. México: Universidad Nacional Autónoma de México, Instituto de Investigaciones Filológicas, 1980, p. 31–43)

Considers ways of investigating interinfluences of native languages and Spanish, with several examples of interference and contact.

1531 Launey, Michel. Introduction à langue et à la littérature aztèques. v. 1, Grammaire. Paris: L'Harmaltan, 1979. 416 p.: index.

Excellent work on classical Nahuatl; it is well organized and comprehensive and has been much praised. Includes exercises and lexical index.

1532 Lenkersdorf, Carlos. B'omak'uman tojol ab'al-kastiya. v. 1, Diccionario tojolabal-español. v. 2, Diccionario español-tojolabal. México: Editorial Nuestro Tiempo, 1979/1981. 2 v. (425, 812 p.)

Lenkersdorf's extensive Tojolabal (Mayan) dictionary is introduced with notes on phonology and brief sketch of morphology. Designed to be of service to the Tojolabal people and to show that Tojolabal is not inferior but equal to Spanish. Both introduction and many sample sentences suggest a

Marxist orientation. Pro-Indian rhetoric is unfavorable to linguists, anthropologists, and ladinos.

1533 Lionnet, Andrés. El idioma tubar y los tubares: según documentos inéditos de C.S. Lumholtz y C.V. Hartman. México: Universidad Iberoamericana, 1978. 132 p.: bibl.

Pt. 1 contains description of Tubar (Uto-Aztecan) language, based on unpublished notes taken by Carl Lumholtz in 1890s. Includes treatment of phonetics, phonology, morphology, and syntax, plus two versions of *Padre nuestro*, with Tubar-Spanish and Spanish-Tubar vocabulary. Pt. 2 consists of brief Tubar ethnography, based on notes from Hartman and Lumholtz. Pt. 3 treats Tubar history.

1534 López Austin, Alfredo. Cuerpo humano e ideología: las concepciones de los antiguos nahuas. México: Universidad Nacional Autónoma de México, Instituto de Investigaciones Antropológicas, 1980. 2 v. (490, 334 p.): bibl., glossaries, ill.

Investigates human body in Nahuatl world view, a philological study of an ideological system. Contains paleography and translation of several Nahuatl texts, colonial sources, and vocabulary lists according to body parts, age, and sex.

Luckenbach, Alvin H. and **Richard S. Levy.** The implications of Nahua Aztecan lexical diversity for Mesoamerican culture-history. See item **324** and *HLAS 44:1535.*

Manuscritos de Tekax y Nah. Edited by Héctor M. Calderón. See item **572.**

Marcus, Joyce. Zapotec writing. See item **472.**

1535 Margery Peña, Enrique. Diccionario bribri-español, español-bribri. San José: Editorial Universidad de Costa Rica, 1982. 160 p.

Welcome dictionary of Bribri (Chibchan) of Costa Rica. Contains preliminary information on Bribri phonology, morphology, and syntax (ergative pattern).

1536 Mejías, Hugo A. Préstamos de lenguas indígenas en el español americano del siglo XVII. México: Universidad Nacional Autónoma de México, Instituto de Investigaciones Filológicas, 1980. 182 p.: bibl., index, map (Publicaciones del Centro de Lingüística Hispánica; 11)

Studies influence of Indian language on 17th-century Spanish, based on Boyd-Bowman's corpus of Spanish colonial documents. Discusses 538 loans involving Aymara, Carib, Cumanagoto (Carib), Chibcha-Cuna, Guaraní, Mapuche, Maya-Quiché, Nahuatl, Quechua, Taino, and Tarascan.

1537 Merrifield, William R. Proto-Otomanguean kinship. Dallas, Tex.: Summer Institute of Linguistics, 181. 396 p.: bibl.

Reconstructs Proto-Otomanguean kinship system, justifies reconstruction, discusses cognate sets, and summarizes developments from Proto-Otomanguean in each of the daughter subfamilies.

1538 Mondloch, James L. Basic Quiché grammar. Albany: State University of New York at Albany, 1978. 222 p. (Institute for Mesoamerican Studies; publication no. 2)

Thorough and easily understood pedagogical grammar of Quiché (Mayan), with vocabulary lists and folktales. Serves as best introduction to the language appearing to date, perhaps only one which clearly describes Quiché's complicated verb morphology, particularly its ergativity and voices.

1539 Nahuatl studies in memory of Fernando Horcasitas. Edited by Frances Karttunen. Austin: University of Texas, Department of Linguistics, 1981. 277 p.: bibl. (Texas linguistics forum; 18)

Collection of articles on Nahuatl linguistics: Richard Andrews "Directionals in Classical Nahuatl;" Jeff Burnham "The Innovation of a Plural Suffix in Aztecan;" Una Canger "Reduplication in Nahuatl, in Dialectal and Historical Perspective;" Karen Dakin "The Characteristics of a Nahuatl *Lingua Franca*;" F.R. Higgins "Proleptic Objects and Verbs of Perception in Zacapoaxtla Nahuatl;" Jane and Kenneth Hill "Variation in Relative Clause Construction in Modern Nahuatl;" Frances Karttunen "Nahuatl Lexicography;" Yolanda Lastra de Suárez "Stress in Modern Nahuatl Dialects;" Miguel León-Portilla "Place Names in Nahuatl: the Morphology of the Place Name;" James Lockhart "Toward Assessing the Phoneticity of Older Nahuatl Texts . . .;" Judith Maxwell "Vowels in the Nahuat-Pipil of El Salvador;" Jane Rosenthal "How Uto-Aztecan is the Nahuatl Possessive?;" William Sischo "The Double Causative in Michoacan Nahuatl;" David

Tuggy "Epenthesis of *i* in Classical and Tetelcingo Nahuatl: Evidence for Multiple Analyses." Collection attests to both upsurge of interest in Nahuatl and welcome linguistic sophistication in its study.

1540 Palafox Vargas, Miguel. La llave del huichol. México: Instituto Nacional de Antropología e Historia (INAH), 1978. 89 p.: glossaries, ill.

Brief description of Huichol grammar, particularly of sounds and morphology, with vocabulary lists.

1541 Papers in Mayan linguistics. Edited by Nora C. England. Columbia: University of Missouri, Department of Anthropology, 1978. 310 p.: ill., maps.

Collection contains many excellent papers on Mayan historical linguistics and structure (pt. 1) and studies in Mayan language and culture (pt. 2): Victoria Bricker "Antipassive Constructions in Yucatec Maya;" Colette Craig "On the Promotion of Instrumentals in Mayan Languages;" Marshall Durbin and Fernando Ojeda "Basic Word-Order in Yucatec Maya;" Thomas Lengyel "Ergativity, Aspect and Related Perplexities of Ixil-Maya;" Katherine Martin "A Preliminary Survey of Modals in Mayan Languages;" Laura Martin "Maya Influence in Guatemalan Spanish: a Research Outline and Test Case;" Judie Maxwell "Chuj Clause Collapsing;" William Norman and Lyle Campbell "Towards a Proto-Mayan Syntax: a Comparative Perspective on Grammar;" Sandra Pinkerton "Word Order and the Antipassive in K'ekchi;" Thom Smith-Stark "The Mayan Antipassive: Some Facts and Fictions;" Jill Brody "To Have and to Hold— Gapping in Tojolabal;" Sandra Derrig "Universals as Specifics: the Yucatecan Case;" Nora England "Space as a Mam Grammatical Theme;" Anne Farber "The Spread of Spanish in a Cakchiquel-Speaking Population;" Mary Prindiville Tenner "A Problem of Pre-Columbian Tzeltal Kinship;" Margaret Wilhite "The Lexicon of Weaving in Cakchiquel: Acquisition and Development;" and Louanna Furbee-Losee "Comments."

1542 Pennington, Campbell W. Vocabulario en la lengua nevome. v. 2, The Pima Bajo of Central Sonora, México. Salt Lake City: University of Utah Press, 1979. 129 p.: bibl., index.

Consists of a Pima Bajo (Uto-Aztecan) dictionary, Spanish to Pima Bajo (Nevome) including detailed description and history of the manuscript (*Vocabulario*) prepared by an anonymous Jesuit in late 17th century.

1543 Po'ot Yah, Eleuterio. Yucatec Maya verbs: Hocaba dialect = Los verbos de maya yucateco: dialecto de hocaba. Grammatical introduction, Victoria R. Bricker. Traducido por James Ward. New Orleans, La.: Tulane University, Center for Latin American Studies, 1981. 35 p. (American studies curriculum aids)

Presents Yucatec Maya verbs in dictionary form, including long and very useful grammatical introduction to Yucatec verbs— both in English and Spanish.

1544 *Pop wuj* = Libro de acontecimientos. Traducción directa del manuscrito del padre Jiménez por Adrián I. Chávez. México: Ediciones de la Casa Chata, 1979. 112, 112a p.: 1 port.

New and "unusual" translation of the *Popol Vuh*, which employs geometrically shaped orthographic symbols invented by Chávez (not found in conventional printing). Includes comparison of both Ximénez's original Quiché and Spanish texts with Chávez's transliteration and new translation. Translation lacks linguistic, literary, and cultural perspective and is off the mark when compared to others.

1545 *Proceedings of the Annual Meeting of the Berkeley Linguistics Society.* University of California, Department of Linguistics. Vol. 1, 1975- . Berkeley.

Several articles have appeared in vols. 1–8 (1975–1982) of the Berkeley Linguistics Society's *Proceedings* available to date: Mauricio Mixco "The Linguistic Response of Kiliwa to Hispanic Culture" (vol. 3); William Norman "Advancement Rules and Syntactic Change: the Loss of Instrumental Voice in Mayan" (vol. 4); Mauricio Mixco "The Evolution of Certain Cochimí Aspectuals and the Cochimí-Yuman Hypothesis" (vol. 5); Wick Miller "Speaking for Two: Respect Speech in the Guarijo of Northwest Mexico" (vol. 6); William Norman "Grammatical Parallelism in Quiché Ritual Language" (vol. 6); Tom Larsen "Functional Correlates of Ergativity in Aguacatec" (vol. 7); Stephen Marlett "The Abstract Consonant in Seri" (vol. 7); Leanne

Hinton "How to Cause in Mixtec (vol. 8); Monica Macaulay "Verbs of Motion and Arrival in Mixtec (vol. 8).

1546 Ramírez, José Fernando. Las partículas nahuas: estudio basado en la gramática de Horacio Carochi, *Arte de la lengua mexicana*. México: Editorial Cosmos, 1980. 114 p.
Republication of work on particles (i.e., affixes and grammatical words) of Nahuatl, based on Carochi's colonial grammar. This originally appeared in four parts in *Anales del Museo Nacional* (1903).

1547 Schele, Linda. Maya glyphs, the verbs. Austin: University of Texas Press, 1982. 427 p.: bibl., ill.
Extremely useful and up-to-date study of verbs in Mayan hieroglyphic writing. First eight chapters describe Mayan glyphic verbs and syntax, combining results of latest findings in a variety of areas. Bulk of work is a verb catalogue, which presents the known (and suspected) glyphic verbs, with information about their location, date, patient (object) and agent (subject), etc. Appendices on affix patterns and their co-occurrence and distribution are of great value. Important basic reference for future advances in decipherment.

1548 Stairs Kreger, Glenn Albert and **Emily Florence Scharfe de Stairs.** Diccionario huave de San Mateo del Mar. México: Instituto Lingüístico de Verano, 1981. 423 p.: appendices, bibl., ill., maps (Serie de vocabularios y diccionarios indígenas Mariano Silva y Aceves; no. 24)
Large Huave-Spanish, Spanish-Huave dictionary, which has reasonably extensive grammar appended, plus appendices of numerals, time, flora and fauna.

Stoll, David. The Summer Institute of Linguistics and indigenous movements. See item **259**.

1549 Studies in Uto-Aztecan grammar. v. 1, Overview of Uto-Aztecan grammar. v. 2, Modern Aztec grammatical sketches. v. 3, Uto-Aztecan grammatical sketches. Edited by Ronald W. Langacker. Dallas, Tex.: Summer Institute of Linguistics; Arlington, Tex.: University of Texas at Arlington, 1977/1982. 3 v. (199, 380, 393 p.) (Summer Institute of Linguistics publications in linguistics; no. 56)

Vol. 1 is Langacker's overview of Uto-Aztecan, including phonology and grammar, which serves as the formula followed by sketches of other two volumes. Vol. 2 has detailed sketches of four relatively different varieties of Nahuatl. Vol. 3 contains sketch of Northern Paiute, Papago, and Northern Tepehuan. Set is extremely useful for understanding Uto-Aztecan languages and will prove a significant reference.

1550 Suárez, Víctor M. El español que se habla en Yucatán: apuntamientos filológicos. 2. edición corregida y aumentada. Mérida, México: Ediciones de la Universidad de Yucatán, 1979. 225 p.: bibl., index, maps.
Important reedition of book first published in 1945, but much changed in this edition. Contains much on the influence of Yucatec Maya on the Spanish of Yucatán.

1551 Sullivan, Thelma D. Reconstrucción de las consonantes del protonáhuatl: estudio preliminar y el origen del conectivo -kā. México: Instituto Nacional de Antropología e Historia (INAH), Centro de Investigaciones Superiores, 1980. 104 p. (Cuadernos de la casa chata; 31)
Reconstructs Proto-Nahua consonants by comparing classical Nahuatl, Pochuteco, Tetelcingo, and Pipil showing sound changes. Lists 269 cognate sets with their reconstructions, and establishes origin of connective *-kā- as retention of proto suffix -kā of the preterite.

1552 Tapia, Fermín. Etnobotánica de los amuzgos. v. 1, Los árboles. v. 2, Los bejucos, zacates, yerbas y otras plantas. México: Instituto Nacional de Antropología e Historia (INAH), Centro de Investigaciones, 1978/1980. 2 v. (157, 228 p.) (Cuadernos de la casa chata; 14, 28)
Presents Amuzgo (Otomanguean) folk classification of its ethnobotany, with comments about meaning and etymology of plant names, uses and characteristics. Vol. 1 deals with 144 tree names; vol. 2 with 183 other plant names.

Tedlock, Barbara. Sound texture and metaphor in Quiché Maya ritual language. See item **1020**.

1553 *Tlalocan*. Revista de fuentes para el conocimiento de las culturas indígenas de México. Universidad Nacional Autónoma de México. Vol. 9, 1982- . México.

This issue contains several Nahuatl texts from different locations, material from Pima Bajo, texts from several Mayan languages, a Highland Chontal (Tequistlatec) text, stories in Huave, Zapotec, and others.

1554 Troike, Rudolf C. Subject-object concord in Coahuilteco (Language [Baltimore, Md.] 57, 1981, p. 658–673)

Coahuilteco is an extinct language of northeast Mexico which had SOV (subject-object-verb) order, in which non-subject noun phrases showed concord with subject noun phrases, serving some of the same functions as switch-reference.

1555 Vermont Salas, Refugio. Primer curso radiofónico de lengua maya. Mérida, México: Universidad de Yucatán, 1980. 46 p.

"Simplified" pedagogical grammar published for use in conjunction with radio programs of instruction in Yucatec Maya, based on Robert W. Blair's and Refugio Vermont Salas' *Spoken Yucatec Maya* (Chicago: University of Chicago, 1965).

1556 Warkentin, Viola and Ruby Scott. Gramática chól. México: Instituto Lingüístico de Verano, 1980. 134 p.: appendices, bibl., ill., maps (Serie de gramáticas de lenguas indígenas de México; no. 3)

Presents good grammar of Chol (Mayan), with appendices on cardinal and ordinal numbers, noun classifiers, kinship, body parts.

1557 Wilhite, Margaret. Children's acquisition of language routines: the end-of-meal routine in Cakchiquel (Language in Society [Commissioner of Official Languages?, Ottawa, Canada] 12, 1982, p. 47–64)

Deals with how Cakchiquel children learn to use their language—appropriate usage in context routines.

1558 Wolgemuth, Carl. Gramática náhuatl de Mecayapan. México: Instituto Lingüístico de Verano, 1981. 222 p.: bibl., ill., map (Serie de gramáticas de lenguas indígenas de México; no. 5)

Presents detailed, but usable grammar of Nahuatl of Mecayapan, Veracruz, with abundant examples. Contains long vocabulary list (p. 159–208).

SOUTH AMERICAN INDIAN LANGUAGES

1559 Aku parlanakuypachi: cuentos folklóricos de los quechua de San Martín. Lima: Instituto Lingüístico de Verano, 1981. 90 p. (Comunidades y culturas peruanas; no. 14)

Collection of 36 short folk narratives is Quechua (San Martín, Peru). Texts are followed by Spanish free translation.

1560 Allin, Trevor Reginald. A grammar of Resigaro. Horsleys Green, England: Summer Institute of Linguistics, 1976. 3 v. (533 p.): bibl., ill.

Partial tagmemic description of Resigaro (Arawak), an almost extinct language of Peru. Three volumes contain: v. 1, description of phonemes and syllables; v. 2, six morphosyntactic levels from roots to sentences; and v. 3, vocabulary and comparative basic lexicon (Resigaro, Bora, Ocaina, and Huitoto). A possible genetic relationship between Resigaro and the Bora-Huitoto family is proposed.

1561 Arenas, Pastor. Etnobotánica lengua-maskoy. Ilustración, Josefina Lacour. Buenos Aires: Fundación para la Educación, la Ciencia y la Cultura, 1981. 358 p.: bibl., ill., indexes.

Classification of Paraguayan Chaco plants and their place in Lengua-Maskoy culture. Descriptive list of 268 classified plants (with illustrations) is preceded by ethnohistorical introduction and a chapter with different cultural aspects such as curing and shamanism, material culture and life cycle within which plants were used. Excellent ethnobotanical description also invaluable for the historical anthrolinguist interested in the center of dispersal of South American languages and tribes.

1562 Armellada, Cesáreo de. Las lenguas indígenas venezolanas y el castellano. Caracas: Universidad Católica Andrés Bello, Centro de Lenguas Indígenas, 1978. 88 p.: bibl. (Serie Lenguas indígenas de Venezuela. Serie menor; 14)

Lecture given by author summarizes history of missions, education and linguistic studies of most indigenous groups in Venezuela.

1563 **Barral, Basilio María de.** Diccionario
warao-castellano, castellano-warao. 2.
ed. Caracas: Universidad Católica Andrés
Bello, 1979. 730 p., 1 leaf of plates: bibl, ill.
(Serie Lenguas indígenas de Venezuela; 8)
Second editon of Warao (unclassified
language of Venezuela and Guyana) dictionary. A contribution to study of Warao and
useful to Warao themselves as they become
bilinguals in Spanish.

1564 **Barstow, Jean R.** Marriage between human beings and animals: a structuralist discussion of two Aymara myths
(Anthropology [State University of New York
at Stony Brook, Department of Anthro-
pology] 5 : 1, May 1981, p. 71–88, bibl.)
Lévi-Straussian analysis of two Aymara
narratives, "The Condor and the Hum-
mingbird" and "Juanito, Son of the Fearless
Bear," carried out in terms of contrasting oppositions found in the narratives. Offers an
insight into the Aymara world view in which
the natural and supernatural are taken as
ordinary human experience.

1565 **Bersabé Ruiz Ovelar, Clara.** La comprensión del *ñe'ēnga* y su relación con
el aprendizaje del guaraní (UCNSA/SA, 16 : 1,
junio 1981, p. 115–329, bibl., ill.)
Study of specific sentences of *ñe'ēnga*
type (saying, adage, proverb) very common in
Guaraní. In attempt for wider application,
author also considers multiplicity of factors
in connection with *ñe'ēnga* that may condition process of language learning.

1566 **Bertrand-Rousseau, Pierrette.** Cinco
fábulas shipibo (PUCP/DA, 5, julio
1980, p. 225–232)
Five Shipibo (Panoan) folk tales in free
Spanish translation. No Shipibo text nor
commentary is given.

Braunstein, José. Dominios y jerarquías en la
cosmovisión de los matakos tewokleley. See
item **1221**.

1567 **Bridgeman, Loraine Irene.** O parágrafo
na fala dos Kaiwá-guaraní. Brasília:
Summer Institute of Linguistics, 1981. 131 p.
Revision and Portuguese translation of
author's PhD. dissertation (Indiana University, 1966). Tagmemic analysis of Kaiwa
(Tupi) paragraphs includes classification and
distribution of three levels: discourse, paragraphs and periods (sentences). Analysis is
followed by three Kaiwa texts.

Califano, Mario. El ciclo de Tokjwaj: análisis
fenomenológico de una narración mítica de
los mataco costaneros. See item **1224**.

1568 ———. El mito de Atunto y la poten-
cia amorosa: análisis de una práctica
ritual de los huachipaire, Mashco (Cuadernos
Prehispánicos [Seminario Americanista de la
Universidad Casa de Colón, Valladolid,
Spain] 9, 1981, p. 33–90, bibl., ill., table)
Analysis of "Atunto" myth of the
Huachipaire (Arawak) of Peru and its relation
to actual tribal behaviour. No original text,
only Spanish free translation.

1569 **Campo del Pozo, Fernando.** Los
agustinos y las lenguas indígenas de
Venezuela. Caracas: Universidad Católica
Andrés Bello, Instituto de Investigaciones
Históricas, Centro de Lenguas Indígenas,
1979. 253 p.: bibl.
Historical summary of work of Augus-
tinian Missionaries in Venezuela. Includes
among other non-ethnolinguistic information, references to their linguistic work especially with the "Saliva" and "Goahiva"
languages, a catalogue of 70 indigenous
groups and subgroups noting their location,
subdivision, population, and impressionistic
information on their language relationship
and dialects. Most of the volume is devoted
to biographical sketches of missionaries
since 1527. A few pages are dedicated to language classification according to the Augus-
tinians and includes useful bibliography.

1570 **Carrocera, Buenaventura.** Lingüística
indígena venezolana y los misioneros
capuchinos. Caracas: Universidad Católica
Andrés Bello, Instituto de Investigaciones
Históricas, Centro de Lenguas Indígenas,
1981. 333 p.: bibl. (Colección de lenguas
indígenas)
History of Capuchin missionary work
(since mid 17th century) in Venezuela. Four
main chapters cover their four geographical missionary regions: Cumaná, Caracas,
Guyana and Maracaibo. Each chapter includes ethnographical informaton on local
indigenous groups, and references to vocabularies and small grammars of some local
languages.

1571 **Casamiquela, Rodolfo M.** The deluge
myth in Patagonia (UP/LAIL, 6 : 2, Fall
1982, p. 91–101, bibl.)
Analysis of provenience of various

versions of Patagonian deluge myth, with emphasis on myth's diffusion throughout southern Chile and Argentina.

1572 Cerrón Palomino, Rodolfo. La cuestión lingüística en el Perú: notas metodológicas (CPES/RPS, 17:47, enero/abril 1980, p. 121–130)

Appeals for multilingual and multicultural society in Peru, by allowing economic, cultural, and political autonomy to minority groups. Revitalization of their language is essential first step.

1573 Chase-Sardi, Miguel; Martha Teresa Ortiz Faitmann; and José Seelwische. El mito Nasuc y su transcripción fonética (UCNSA/SA, 15:1/2, dic. 1980, p. 139–169, bibl.)

The phonetic transcription and translation of a Nivacle (Chulupi) myth called Nasuc (Gayacan tree).

1574 Cohesión y enfoque en textos y discursos. Editoras, Mary Ruth Wise, Anne Stewart. Lima: Ministerio de Educación, Instituto Lingüístico de Verano, 1981. 273 p.: ill. (Serie Lingüística peruana; no. 17)

Contains five studies on textual and discourse analysis in five Peruvian languages: Amuesha (Arawak), Chayahuita (Jebero-Cahuapanan), Arabela (Zaparoan), Candoshi (Jivaroan), and Quechua of Rio Pastaza. Discourse analysis includes: focus; cohesiveness; participants identification (referential); tense and aspects; phonology at the discourse level. These papers are a significant contribution not only to the structure of language but also for the study of universals.

1575 Cole, Peter and Gabriella Hermon. Subject to object raising in an EST framework: evidence from Quechua (Studies in the Linguistic Sciences [University of Illinois at Urbana-Champaign, Department of Linguistics, Urbana] 9:1, Spring 1979, p. 65–89, bibl.)

Description of certain aspects of complement clauses in Imbabura Quechua. Also argues in favour of a modified "raising" analysis.

1576 ———; Wayne Harbert; and Gabriella Hermon. Headless relative clauses in Quechua (IU/IJAL, 48:2, April 1982, p. 113–124, bibl.)

Attempt to show that an analysis of three Quechua languages supports hypothesis that relative clauses derive from underlying headless constructions.

1577 Córdoba-Guimaray, Jacinto. La expresión de la categoría de posesión en el quechua ancashino (Lenguaje y Ciencias [Universidad Nacional de Trujillo, Departamento de Idiomas y Lingüística, Lima] 22:3, sept. 1982, p. 82–90)

Description of possessive particles, their peculiarity and selection in Quechua of Ancash.

1578 Corvalán, Grazziella. El bilingüísmo en la educación en el Paraguay: ¿es creativo u opresivo? (CPES/RPS, 18:52, sept./dic. 1981, p. 179–200, tables)

Analysis of Spanish-Guaraní bilingualism, including discussion of creative and oppressive aspects of bilingualism and role that both languages play in educational system. Also considers influence of rapid social change on bilingualism.

1579 Cruz, Olímpio and Maria de Lourdes Reis. Lendas indígenas. Brasília: Thesaurus, 1981. 64 p.: ill.

Collection of seven Canela (Gê) and seven Guajajara (Tupi) myths given only in Portuguese preceded by notes about respective tribal people.

1581 Dextre, Pompeyo Yábar. Sobre la relación *tema-rema* en algunas lenguas sin artículos (Lenguaje y Ciencias [Universidad Nacional de Trujillo, Departamento de Idiomas y Lingüística, Lima] 22:3, sept. 1982, p. 71–81)

Presentation of examples showing how Japanese, Quechua, and Russian (languages without articles) express the *tema-rema* (determinate-indeterminate) relation.

Eakin, Lucille; Ervin Lauriault; and Harry Boonstra. Bosquejo etnográfico de los shipibo-conibo del Ucayali. See item **1246.**

1582 Encina Ramos y Tatayyvá, Pedro. Las cien mejores poesías en Guaraní. Asunción: Escuela Técnica Salesiana, 198?. 279 p.

Gathering of 100 selected poems in Guarani "from the origin of Guarani poetry (last century) in Paraguay to the present." Author's short biographical summary accompanies each poem. Lack of translations limits book to those who know Guarani.

1583 Escobar, Alberto. Situación multilingüe y planeamiento lingüístico en el Perú (*in* Indianité, ethnocide, indigénisme en Amérique latine. Toulouse-Le Mirail, France: Groupe de recherches sur l'Amérique latine Toulouse-Perpignan [GRAL], Centre interdisciplinaire d'études latino-américaines; Paris: Editions du Centre national de la recherche scientifique [CNRS], 1982, p. 95–104, bibl.)

Survey of Andes multilingual situation before and after Spanish conquest. Peru's current sociolinguistic situation is discussed more specifically including language planning and bilingual education.

1584 Estudios guahibos. Bogotá: Ministerio de Gobierno, Dirección de Integración y Desarrollo de la Comunidad, División Operativa de Asuntos Indígenas: Instituto Lingüístico de Verano, 1978. 22 p.: ill. (Serie Sintáctica; no. 11)

Contains two papers on discourse analysis with few analyzed texts as examples in two related languages, Cuiba and Guahibo of Colombia. First paper shows how "dialogue" is basic linguistic behaviour while "discourse" can be viewed as type of dialogue. Second study on Guahibo narrative discourse presents various types of paragraphs as well as system expressing participant reference.

1585 Estudios en guajiro. Bogotá: Ministerio de Gobierno, Dirección General de Integración y Desarrollo de la Comunidad, División Operativa de Asuntos Indígenas: Instituto Lingüístico de Verano, 1979. 163 p. (Serie Sintáctica; no. 10)

"Narrative" discourse analysis of Guajiro text, *Couyatalima*. Includes classification and structure of paragraph and sentence types. Guajiro, Arawak language with various dialects, is spoken in Colombia by about 8,000 individuals (about 20,000 in Venezuela.)

1586 Fast Mowitz, Gerhard and **Ruby Fast.** Introducción al idioma achuar. Lima: Ministerio de Educación: Instituto Lingüístico de Verano, 1981. 144 p. (Documento de trabajo; no. 20)

Preliminary "practical" grammar with exercises for learning Achuar, a Jivaroan language of about 3,000 people in Peru. Only most productive aspects of Achuar grammar are given: verb forms in the present, past and future; interrogative and imperative forms;

pronouns. Each of 20 lessons contains small conversation or dialogue to be memorized, exercises for learning certain key vocabulary and finally basic grammatical rules with examples.

1587 Fernández G., Germán M.A. The Araucanian deluge myth (UP/LAIL, 6:2, Fall 1982, p. 102–113, bibl.)

Literal interlinear text translation of Araucanian deluge myth, including free translations into Spanish and English, with brief analysis.

1587a Folk literature of the Mataco Indians. Domenico Del Campana, *et al.* Johannes Wilbert and Karin Simoneau, editors. Introduction by Niels Fock. Los Angeles: University of California, Latin American Center Publications, Los Angeles, 1982. 507 p.: 1 p. of plates: bibl., ill., indexes (Folk literature of South American Indians. UCLA Latin American studies; v. 52)

Collection of folk stories of the Mataco Indians reprinted from works of diverse authors. Narratives are not in Mataco but only in English free translation and of limited interest to the linguist. Introduction gives ethnographic account of the Mataco and provides useful cultural background for narratives that follow.

1588 Garvin, Paul L. La lingüística como recurso en la planificación del lenguaje (CPES/RPS, 16:50, enero/mayo 1981, p. 7–23, bibl.)

Translation of paper originally presented in 1973, focuses on language planning. Principal topics are alphabetization, standard language, and national language.

1589 González de Pérez, María Stella. Trayectoria de los estudios sobre la lengua chibcha o muisca. Bogotá: Instituto Caro y Cuervo, 1980. 225 p. (Publicaciones del Instituto Caro y Cuervo. Series Minor; 22)

Historical summary of cultural and linguistic studies of Muisca (extinct Chibchan language of Colombia). Book divided into: 1) cultural information; 2) linguistic studies; 3) brief hypothesis on some aspects of the language; and 4) Loukotka classification of Chibchan languages and bibliography.

1590 Granda, Germán de. Actitudes sociolingüísticas en el Paraguay (CPES/RPS, 18:51, junio/sept. 1981, p. 7–22)

Discusses attitudes regarding relative prestige of Spanish and Guaraní among various sectors of Paraguayan population.

1591 Guardia Mayorga, César Augusto. Diccionario kechwa-castellano, castellano-kechwa: contiene además, vocabulario del chinchaysuyu y toponimias. 6. ed. Lima: Ediciones Populares Los Andes, 1980. 219 p.: bibl., ill.

Sixth ed. of original 1959 dictionary. Contains also historical background of Quechua especially in Peru, a word list of Chinchaysuyu, place names and bibliography.

1592 Guzmán de Rojas, Iván. Problemática lógico-lingüística de la comunicación social con el pueblo aymara. Ottawa, Canada: International Development Research Centre, 1982. 158 p.: bibl., ill., tables (Manuscript reports)

Analysis of problems of communication in Aymara, a language of Peru and Bolivia. Shows interrelationship of certain morpho-syntactic aspects with logic and mechanisms of understanding among speakers. Includes analysis of "logical suffixes" in Aymara, statistical tables and useful bibliography of related studies in Aymara and Quechua.

1593 Hardman, Martha J. Jaqaru color term (IU/IJAL, 47:1, Jan. 1981, p. 66–68)

Description of color terms in Jaqaru (Jaqi), language spoken in Andean Mountains of Peru. Brief comparison of Jaqaru color system with universal order of color-terms proposed by Berlin and Kay reveals almost no correspondence between the two.

Idogaya Molina, Anatilde. El daño mediante la palabra entre los ayoreo del Chaco Boreal. See item **1268.**

Is God an American?: an anthropological perspective on the missionary work of the Summer Institute of Linguistics. See item **1205.**

1594 Jake, Janice. Some remarks on relativization in Imbabura Quechua (Studies in the Linguistic Sciences [University of Illinois at Urbana Champaign, Department of Linguistics, Urbana] 9:2, Fall 1979, p. 109–129, bibl.)

Description of relativization in Imbabura Quechua. Includes some arguments against hypothesis that relative clauses are underlyingly headless.

1595 Jusayú, Miguel Angel and Jesús Olza Zubiri. Diccionario de la lengua guajira. v. 1, Guajiro-castellano. v. 2, Castellano-guajiro. Caracas: Universidad Católica Andrés Bello, Centro de Lenguas Indígenas; Maracaibo: Biblioteca Corpozulia, 1977/1981 (Serie Lenguas indígenas de Venezuela; 18)

Vol. 2 of Guajiro dictionary (Spanish-Guajiro) includes grammatical notes and appendix containing a vocabulary of plants and animals.

1596 Kindberg, Lee. Diccionario asháninca. Recopilación de Lee Kindberg. Ed. provisional. Yarinacocha, Perú: Instituto Lingüístico de Verano, 1980. 466 p. (Documento de trabajo. Instituto Lingüístico de Verano; no. 19)

Preliminary edition of bilingual vocabulary Campa Ashaninca-Spanish for use of native Campa (Arawak) or for Spanish-speakers interested in Campa. Verbal entries are given with their pronominal prefix thus majority of verbs are found under the letter i- (he) or n- (I) or a-/o- (she). However, translation is given with the infinitive Spanish. Appendix includes useful list of verbal affixes.

1597 Landaburu, Jon. Les indiens de Colombie: perspectives sur leur situation lingüistique et éducative (in Indianité, ethnocide, indigénisme en Amérique latine. Toulouse-Le Mirail, France: Groupe de recherches sur l'Amérique latine Toulouse-Perpigan [GRAL], Centre interdisciplinaire d'études latinoaméricaines; Paris: Editions du Centre national de la recherche scientifique [CNRS], 1982, p. 105–112)

Paper consists mostly of historical information on Arhuaco Indians of Sierra Nevada de Santa Marta (Colombia). Also mentions other nearby groups. Conclusion addresses present state of their education program.

1598 Martín, Eusebia Herminia and Lucy Therina Briggs. Aymara syntactic relations and derivational verb suffixes; revised version (IU/IJAL, 47:3, July 1981, p. 236–242)

Description of four derivational suffixes in Aymara (Bolivia nd Peru) complement constructions.

1599 Masica, Colin P. Joseph H. Greenberg, *Universals of human language*: review essay (General Linguistics [Pennsylvania State University Press, University Park] 21 : 2, Summer 1981, p. 126–141, bibl.)

Extensive and useful review of Greenberg's three volumes on language universals. Includes methodology, phonology, word morphology and syntax.

1600 Masson, Peter. Aspectos de cognición y enculturación en el habla interétnica: términos de referencia y tratamiento interétnicos en Saraguro, Ecuador (IAA, 9 : 1, 1983, p. 73–129)

Analyzes terms used by three sectors of "whites," "Indians," and "rural whites" in Saraguro, Ecuador, to designate themselves and other groups in the population. Study ranges over terms of address and of references and is based on different social contexts, including family life, schools, religious ceremonies, god-parent relationships, commercial and work relationships.

Mélia, Bartoloméu; Georg Grünberg; and Friedl Grünberg. Los Paĩ-Tavyterã: etnografía guaraní del Paraguay contemporáneo. See item **1286**.

1601 Metzger, Ronald G. Gramática popular del carapana. Traducción de Nancy L. Morse, Olga Trujillo R. Bogotá: Ministerio de Gobierno, Dirección General de Integración y Desarrollo de Comunidad, División Operativa de Asuntos Indígenas: Instituto Lingüístico de Verano, 1981. 240 p.: ill.

"Popular grammar" of Carapana (Tukanoan), primary language of 250 aborigines of Colombia. Although not intended as pedagogical grammar, it could well be used (with additional exercises) for this purpose since it includes features found in contrastive grammars. Descriptive of Carapana tends to be more classificatory than theoretical but in spite of the "popular" presentation (for general audience) the linguist can find useful morphological and syntactic information for testing recent claims about words and sentence formation as well as for comparative purposes.

1602 Miño-Garcés, Fernando. Enfoques teóricos sobre alfabetización dicultural: el programa MACAC, Ecuador (III/AI, 42 : 2, abril/junio 1982, p. 221–234, tables)

Discussion and description of Ecuador's MACAC educational project. Quechua-

speaking individuals themselves (not "mestizos") prepared the educational material for their project. It is a significant step which should be taken throughout Latin America in any diglossia situation.

1603 Montag, Susan. Diccionario cashinahua. 2. ed. Yarinacocha, Perú: Ministerio de Educación: Instituto Lingüístico de Verano, 1981. 2 v. (621 p.) (Serie Lingüística peruana; no. 9)

Dictionary of Cashinawa (Panoan) language in two volumes: 1) Cashinawa-Spanish, and 2) Spanish-Cashinawa followed by grammatical notes and list of local birds.

1604 Orjuela, Héctor H. Yurupary: epopeya indígena suramericana (ICC/T, 37 : 1, enero/abril 1982, p. 107–119)

Commentary on reconstruction of Yurupary myth of Colombian Vaupés region, based on recent translation of Italian text recorded by Stradelli in late 19th century. There follows brief analysis of myth's contents and of rites associated with it.

1605 Ortíz Rescaniere, Alejandro. El tratamiento del tiempo en los mitos andinos (PUCP/DA, 8, mayo 1982, p. 66–76, tables)

Although article has no data useful for the linguist per se, it is a significant contribution for studies in fields of folklore, literature, and mythology.

1606 Perrin, Michel. Sükuaitpa wayuu: los guajiros: la palabra y el vivir. Caracas: Fundación La Salle, 1979. 255 p.: ill. (some col.) (Monografía / Fundación La Salle; no. 25)

Presentation of Guajiro (Arawak) oral literature in three languages: Guajiro original and Spanish and French free translations. The 27 myths are organized in three groups attempting to reflect prehistoric cultural evolution of the Guajiro. While book's value as record of Guajiro knowledge and world view is unquestionable, a morpheme by morpheme translation would have been more helpful for the linguist.

1607 Pino Durán, A. Germán. Runasimi: gramática quechua crítico-comparada: lecciones teórico-prácticas del idioma incaico. 3. ed., refundida, corr. y aum. Huancayo, Perú: Tall. Gráf. de Editorial San Fernando, 1980. 169 p.: bibl., index.

Third and revised edition of didactic

grammar of Quechua first published in 1968. Main parts include extensive morphology, rather short syntax, and vocabulary.

1608 ——. Runasimi bilingüe, gramática castellano-quechua: lecciones teórico-prácticas del idioma incaio en español y quechua. Concepción, Perú: OCOPA, 198?. 123 p.

Short pedagogical grammar of Quechua which is summary of author's previous work *Runasimi*. Text is presented in a Latin model of grammatical terms. Includes small vocabulary at end.

Pinzón Sánchez, Alberto. Monopolios, misioneros y destrucción de indígenas. See item **1183**.

1609 Pontes, Salvador Pires. Noções da gramática tupi: vocabulário de verbos, nomes e corruptelas tupis e guaranis, afinidades lingüísticas, vocabulario, lembretes, lingüísticos, aymará kéchua ou quichua, raças de índios. Belo Horizonte, Brasil: Impr. Oficial de Minas Gerais, 1981. 138 p.: port.

Short traditional grammar of Tupi followed by vocabulary, quotes and sayings (some impressionistic) related to language, its origin and history.

Reichel-Dolmatoff, Gerardo. Some source materials on Desana shamanistic initiation. See item **1308**.

1610 Rey Fajardo, José del. Los jesuitas y las lenguas indígenas venezolanas. Caracas: Universidad Católica Andrés Bello, Instituto de Investigaciones Históricas, Centro de Lenguas Indígenas, 1979. 126 p.: bibl.

Discussion of achievements of Jesuit order in studies of Venezuelan indigenous languages. Contains valuable list of 113 groups missionized by the Jesuits including their habitat and population number. Also includes extensive list of Jesuit linguistic works.

1611 Ritchie Key, Mary. North and South American linguistic connections (La Linguistique [Presses Universitaires de France, Paris] 17:1, 1981, p. 3–18, bibl.)

Presents examples of resemblances suggesting relationship among some South American and North American languages: Quechumaran, Tacanan, Panoan, Chon, Uto-Aztecan, Aztec, Mosetene, Mapuche and Alacaluf.

1612 Safir, Ken. Nasal spreading in Capanahua (Linguistic Inquiry [MIT, Cambridge] 13:4, Fall 1982, p. 689–694, bibl.)

"Nondirectional" descriptive analysis of nasality in Capanahua (Panoan). Shows how this analysis is to be preferred to more traditional one and how it fits within larger "Domain" analysis not allowing use of variables as environments for phonological rules.

1613 Silva, J. Romão da. Os índios bororos: família etno-lingüística. Rio de Janeiro: Editora e Distribuidora Valverde, 1980. 46 p.: 1 folded leaf: bibl., ill.

In spite of title, subject of this booklet is not linguistic but ethnohistorical summary of western and eastern Bororo groups in Mato Grosso (Brazil) near Bolivian border. Of interest is information on some exogamic clans and subgroups at end of last century. Author estimates about 2,000 acculturated Bororo still living today.

1614 Situación lingüística y educación (CPES/RPS, 17:47, enero/abril 1980, p. 131–146, tables)

Contains selected statistical tables reflecting sociolinguistic and educational situation in Paraguay during past three decades. Useful summary for language planning and educators.

1615 Sociedad y lengua: bilingüismo en el Paraguay. Grazziella Corvalán y Germán de Granda, compiladores. Asunción: Centro Paraguayo de Estudios Sociológicos, 1982. 2 v. (865 p.) (Serie Estudios)

Two-volume collection of articles concerning bilingual situation in Paraguay on following topics: Models of Historical Evolution of Bilingualism; The Sociolinguistic Configuration; Linguistic Studies of Bilingualism in Paraguay; and Bibliography and Statistical Tables. Most articles are reprints and some go back to 1950s.

Stark, Louisa R. Folk models of stratification and ethnicity in the highlands of northern Ecuador. See item **1429**.

1616 Textos capanahua. v. 2. Recopilados por Betty Hall Loos y Eugene E. Loos. 2. ed. Yarinacocha, Perú: Instituto Lingüístico de Verano, 1980. (Comunidades y culturas peruanas; no. 17)

Vol. 2 of Capanahua (Panoan) folk narratives. Includes various versions of three texts followed by sentence-by-sentence Spanish translation. Useful publication for studying variations in which oral literature is transmitted to next generation by various narrators.

1617 Textos kawésqar. v. 1/2. Compilador, Oscar Aguilera F. Santiago de Chile: O. Aguilera F., 1979/1980. 2 v.: bibl., ill., index.
Vol. 2 of 19 Kawesqar short texts (typewritten) without introduction. Texts are first available in Kawesqar and followed by literal translation and two free translations. Useful work for those interested in Kawesqar language.

1618 Torres Fernández de Córdova, Glauco. Diccionario, kichua-castellano, yurakshimi-runashimi. Cuenca: Casa de la Cultura Ecuatoriana, Nucleo del Azuay, 1982. 1 v.: bibl., ill.
First part of Ecuadorian Quechua-Spanish dictionary with about 100,000 entries. For some words like place names and historical figures, it is more of an encyclopedia than dictionary. Includes grammatical and other linguistic information as well as extensive bibliography.

1619 Tovar, Antonio. Relatos y diálogos de los matacos: seguidos de una gramática de su lengua. Madrid: Ediciones Cultura Hispánica del Instituto de Cooperación Iberoamericana, 1981. 225 p. (Colección Amerindia)
Traditional description of Mataco language of Argentinian Chaco preceded by 18 interlinear texts in Mataco and Spanish. Grammar includes short phonemic statements, good morphology and short syntax.

Trupp, Fritz. Mythen der Makuna. See item **1333.**

1620 Urioste F. de C., Miguel. Educación popular en el altiplano boliviano: el programa ECORA (III/AI, 42:2, abril/junio 1982, p. 253–268)
Describes Bolivia's ECORA project in bilingual education consisting of radio transmissions in Aymara and Spanish.

1621 Valderrama Fernández, Ricardo and **Carmen Escalante Gutiérrez.** Mitos y leyendas de los quechuas del sur del Perú: Apurimac-Cusco (PUCP/DA, 2, mayo 1978, p. 125–135)
Consists of 10 Quechua myths collected in department of Cusco and Apuri-

mac (Peru) in Spanish free translation. No Quechua text.

1622 Vega Centeno, Imelda. La visión del mundo andino en López Antay: una aproximación socio-lingüística (Socialismo y Participación [Centro de Estudios para el Desarrollo y la Participación, Lima] 19, 1982, p. 73–83, tables)
Attempt to formalize world view of Andean society through textual analysis of "Battle of Ayacucho." Although of marginal interest for linguist, it is of value for our historical and social understanding of the Andean people and their culture.

1623 Vegamián, Félix María, *padre.* Diccionario ilustrado yupa español, español yupa: con onomástica y apuntaciones gramaticales. Guarenas, Venezuela: Formateca, 1978. 383 p., 1 folded leaf of plates: ill (some col.)
Dictionary of Yupa (Carib)-Spanish and vice versa preceded by 100 p. of some grammatical aspects presented in traditional style. Orthography used makes it difficult to decide on proper pronunciation or phonetic value of symbols.

1624 Velie, Daniel and **Virginia Velie.** Vocabulario orejón. Yarinacocha, Peru: Ministerio de Educación, Instituto Lingüístico de Verano, 1981. 128 p. (Serie Lingüística peruana; no. 16)
Vocabulary (56 p., two columns per page) of Orejon (Tukanoan) followed by grammatical notes intended primarily for Orejon Indians (about 180 people) who would like to learn Spanish. Also useful for anthrolinguistics for comparative purposes.

1625 Vocabulario siriano y español. Bogotá: Ministerio de Gobierno, Dirección General de Integración y Desarrollo de la Comunidad, División Operativa de Asuntos Indígenas: Instituto Lingüístico de Verano, 1980. 128 p.: ill.
Preliminary word list in Siriano (Tukanoan) with Spanish translation. About 250 people speak Siriano in Colombia near Brazil border.

1626 Weber, David J. Un aspecto del quechua de Ancash (PUC/L, 4:2, dic. 1980, p. 191–200, bibl.)
Attempt to explain why Spanish word *Cachillo* was borrowed in all Quechua dialects except that of Ancash (Peru).

1627 West, Birdie. Gramática popular del tucano. Traducción de Anne Pilat de Galvis. Bogotá: Ministerio de Gobierno, Dirección General de Integración y Desarrollo de la Comunidad, División Operativa de Asuntos Indígenas, Instituto Lingüístico de Verano, 1980. 249 p.: ill.

Simplified grammar of Tukano (Eastern Tukanoan, branch of Tukanoan) not intended for linguists nor as pedagogical grammar but rather as aide for teaching or learning Tukano. Provides description of basic structure of Tukano in traditional grammatical style without using too many specialized linguistic terms, so that native Tukano speakers can also find it useful. Also attempts to present Tukano structural forms in relation to Spanish ones.

HUMAN BIOLOGY

ROBERT M. MALINA, *Professor, Department of Anthropology, and Associate Director, Institute of Latin American Studies, University of Texas, Austin*

PHYSICAL ANTHROPOLOGY CONCERNS the biology of human populations of the past and the present. Hence, it is commonly called human biology or biological anthropology. A central theme is the understanding of human biological variation, its nature, distribution and significance within the context of evolutionary theory and of course culture. Human biology thus operates in a biocultural framework. This is especially evident in numerous studies of nutritional and medical problems in Latin American populations.

The literature dealing with biological aspects of Latin American populations has increased considerably in scope and thus in volume since *HLAS 43*. This is due in part to an inclusion of a variety of biologically-related topics in the domain of physical/biological anthropology. Hence, a significant portion of materials included do not fall in the context of traditional physical anthropology. Nevertheless, it serves to illustrate the broad basis of human biology in Latin American populations.

This overview considers materials published between 1980 and early 1983. Earlier materials are occasionally included, depending on their relevance to developments in human biology of Latin American populations. The overview is divided into seven sections: 1) General; 2) Earlier Populations; 3) Demography; 4) Population Genetics; 5) Human Adaptability; 5) Nutritional Anthropology; and 6) Biomedical Considerations.

EARLIER POPULATIONS

Interest in the skeletal and dental characteristics of precolumbian populations continues, as evidenced in reports dealing with precolumbian sites in Chile (item **1644**), Peru (items **1631, 1642, 1645,** and **1647**), and Venezuela (items **1630, 1639,** and **1641**). The interest in earlier populations of Latin America extends also to more recent historical times, as is apparent in three reports dealing with slave populations (items **1633** and **1637–1638**). The health status of earlier groups is still a primary focus, and the volume edited by Buikstra (item **1643**) offers an excellent account of prehistoric tuberculosis in the Americas. Methodological improvements in the study of precolumbian skeletal and mummified materials may provide information on the more subtle metabolic disorders affecting the earlier residents of Latin America (item **1648**).

DEMOGRAPHY

Studies of demographic parameters are prominent and include most Latin American countries. Given population growth in Latin America (item **1683**), reproductive performance, fertility control, and related factors are more or less regularly monitored. Latin American populations also have high mortality rates, especially at the preschool ages. Hence, mortality statistics serve as an index of the health status of the populations. The relationship between fertility and mortality, and between these indicators and various cultural and biological factors is complex. It emphasizes the need for a biocultural approach in human biology.

Many country-specific surveys of fertility and mortality have been published over the past few years and are included in this section. Two comprehensive reviews (items **1655** and **1706**) offer statistical summaries of the status of children and youth in Latin America, and address issues of social policy. The relationship of lactation and fertility (item **1678**), the effects of infant mortality on fertility (items **1684, 1694,** and **1707**), types of marital unions and fertility (items **1671, 1675,** and **1679**), and the role of women in the work force relative to fertility (items **1661** and **1664**) are common themes in biodemographic research in Latin American populations.

Methodological concerns are also common. Mazess and Mathisen (item **1685**) consider the age exaggeration among the supposed longevous population of Vilcabamba, Ecuador. Several reports (items **1650, 1658, 1688,** and **1692**) emphasize difficulties and deficiencies in utilizing civil registries as sources of raw data, and the discrepancies between estimated and observed mortality rates. The use and development of models in examining and predicting demographic trends are also common (items **1660, 1687,** and **1698**).

POPULATION GENETICS

Research dealing with genetic aspects of Latin American population continues to expand, including data for many genetic polymorphisms in a number of populations, and specifically for Indian groups (items **1716, 1721–1722, 1728,** and **1736**). A significant portion of genetic research deals with population admixture and divergence, genetic distances, comparisons of tribal populations, and associations with cultural traits. As such research efforts continue, new genetic variants (items **1720** and **1741**), rare phenotypes (items **1740** and **1742**), and occasional clinical syndromes (item **1732**) are identified. Studies of Brazilian populations are more common in genetic research than in other Latin American groups.

Several studies of skin color, anthropometric dimensions, and cranio-dental characteristics are also included in the genetics section as these generally have as their focus admixture estimates, population/racial comparisons, or correlations with genetic traits.

HUMAN ADAPTABILITY

The area of human biology labeled human adaptability is perhaps the most diverse, commonly including studies of Man under different climatic, ecological, disease and nutritional circumstances. For the sake of convenience, this section will focus on selected aspects of human adaptability research, while separate sections on nutritional and biomedical aspects are considered subsequently.

The study of altitude stress in Latin American populations continues to be significant, including primarily developmental studies (items **1745–1746, 1760,** and **1780**). The Quechua-Aymara comparison of hematological parameters (item **1744**) suggests greater adaptability of the latter to the high altitude environment.

Studies of response to exercise stress (working capacity) have increased considerably in Latin American samples, and include data for high altitude groups (items 1757–1758) and of nutritional relevance (item 1752). Torun and colleagues (item 1781) offer a concise summary of the energy costs of selected domestic and agricultural activities for Guatemalan women, while Spurr *et al.* (item 1779) summarize a good portion of their Colombian work which suggests that malnutrition in young children may result in depressed work capacity as adults (see also the Nutritional Anthropology section).

Growth studies comprise a significant portion of human adaptability research since these serve as indicators of the health and nutritional status of a population and since a good deal of the variation observed in adults has its origin during the years of growth and development. The Cuban Growth Study (item 1761) is a comprehensive analysis of the growth and maturation of a representative sample of Cuban children, while initial reports from a comprehensive growth study of São Paulo children (item 1772) are also available. Growth studies illustrate clearly the impact of socioeconomic differentials in Latin America (items 1743 and 1747–1748).

The secular trend refers to the tendency of contemporary children and youth to be larger in size and mature earlier, and of adults to be taller than samples from several generations ago. This developmental phenomenon has been examined in a number of Latin American populations (items 1748, 1753, 1756, 1765–1767, and 1783).

Several studies of behavioral development are also included in this section as they are related to problems of human adaptability to different environmental situations (items 1750, 1762–1763, 1774, and 1777).

NUTRITIONAL ANTHROPOLOGY

Given the significant percentage of the Latin American population which lives under marginal or suboptimal nutritional circumstances, and given the role of nutritional stress in human adaptability research, a separate section on nutritional anthropology is included. The nutritional literature for Latin America is vast and comprises a broad spectrum, ranging from biochemical studies of the composition of lesser known edible plants (items 1833–1834) to the "protein hypothesis" for tribal warfare (item 1798). By and large, the majority of the nutritional literature is of the survey type, i.e., surveys of nutritional status (especially of preschool and school children), dietary intake, and familial factors influencing nutritional status and malnutrition. Undernutrition is common in Latin America and is most often viewed as the result of a complex of factors including environmental stress; social, economic, and political inequalities; and cultural practices (items 1788, 1814–1815, 1817, 1835, and 1841).

Many specific foci of nutritional research in Latin America are evident. The excellent series of papers of Spurr, Barac-Nieto and colleagues (items 1849-1851, 1794–1795, and the Human Adaptability section) focuses on the functional consequences of undernutrition on growth, body composition and working capacity. The series of papers by Immink and colleagues (items 1819–1821) focuses on the economic and food production consequences of undernutrition and the effects of dietary supplementation of workers. The series of studies from Colombia (items 1831–1832, 1836, and 1844) considers the combined effect of nutritional supplementation and education programs on the nutritional status and development of children, while the studies from the Institute of Nutrition of Central America and Panama (items **1800–1801**, and **1829**) consider the effects of supplementation on pregnancy and lactation, and on child growth. Pollitt's critical reviews (items **1838–1839**) of intervention programs and strategies are a significant contribution to the literature on the effects of such programs on growth and cognitive development.

Torun and colleagues (item **1853**) give an exhaustive review of 194 publications dealing with lactose intolerance or malabsorption. Surprisingly, papers dealing with nutritional anemias (a common problem in Latin America) and with obesity (an emerging problem in some segments of the Latin American population) are not well-represented in the literature.

BIOMEDICAL CONSIDERATIONS

Infectious disease has been and is a significant agent in the adaptive process. And, given the "Columbian exchange," the disease history of Latin American populations is of interest to many disciplines. Human biologists who focus on disease-related research in human populations are relatively small in number, but the area of biomedical anthropology has expanded significantly.

One of the major areas of interest in biomedical anthropology is ethnomedicine, with emphasis on traditional medicine and its interface with modern, western medicine. The 1979 translation of the writings of Martius (item **1882**), a German naturalist, offers an interesting account of the characteristics, disease and medicine of Brazilian Indians as observed in the early 19th century. Ramírez (item **1889**) provides an annotated bibliography of studies of traditional medicine in Mexico between 1900 and 1978, while the volume edited by Bastien and Donahue (item **1864**) includes 11 papers on aspects of health in the Andes. Many of the other works are rather specific in focus such as the medical practices of the Guajiro Indians (item **1888**); attitudes towards and beliefs about traditional and modern medicine in rural Ecuador (item **1879**); medical choice in a Mexican community (item **1898**); hot-cold classification in Mexico (item **1883**); and so on. Several excellent compendia of medicinal plants and their specific uses in Paraguay (item **1873**), Colombia (item **1884**), and the West Indies (item **1863**) have also been published.

A number of reports dealing with specific illnesses and diseases attest to the significance of infectious diseases in Latin American populations. Ashcroft (item **1862**) gives a brief discussion of three non-infectious diseases endemic to the West Indies, illustrating their association with dietary (i.e., cultural) practices, while Lewellen (item **1880**) provides a comprehensive reevaluation of the association between aggression and hypoglycemia in populations in the Lake Titicaca basin.

RECENT DOCTORAL DISSERTATIONS
Biological Anthropology in Latin America (1980–1982)

Berlin, Elois Ann. Migrants to Amazonia: a study of the nutrition and health of settlers on the Santiago River, Peru. Univ. of California, Berkeley, 1981.

Buschang, Peter H. Growth status and rate of school children 6 to 13 years of age in a rural Zapotec-speaking community in the Valley of Oaxaca, Mexico. Univ. of Texas at Austin, 1980.

Chapin, Frances White. The tides of migration: a study of migration decision-making and social process in São Miguel, Azores. Univ. of Wisconsin, Madison, 1980.

Collins, Jane. Kinship and seasonal migration among the Aymara of southern Peru: human adaptation to energy scarcity. Univ. of Florida, 1981.

Fredlund, Eric. Shitari Yanomamo incestuous marriage: a study of the use of structural, lineal, and biological criteria when classifying marriages. Pennsylvania State Univ., 1982.

Fry, Petty. Changing patterns of marriage and reproduction in a depopulating Caribbean society. Pennsylvania State Univ., 1981.

Hull, Cindy V. The strategies of migration and return migration: a Yucatecan case study. Wayne State Univ., 1980.

Melancon, Thomas. Marriage and reproduction among the Yanomamo Indians of Venezuela. Pennsylvania State Univ., 1982.

Meswick, Susan A. Migration, health and schooling: a case study of Puerto Rican adolescents in urban Connecticut. Univ. of Connecticut, 1982.

Murray, Breen. The relevance of anthropology in medical education: a Mexican case study. McGill Univ., 1981.

Nations, Marilyn K. Illness of the child: the cultural context of childhood diarrhea in northeast Brazil. Univ. of California, Berkeley, 1981.

Palacio, Joseph Orlando. Food and social relations in a Garifuna village. Univ. of California, Berkeley, 1981.

Richards, Nancy. Erythoxylon cocoa in the Peruvian highlands: practices and beliefs. Univ. of California, Irvine, 1980.

Scheder, Joanne C. Diabetes prevalence among Mexican-American migrants. Univ. of Wisconsin, Madison, 1981.

Schuman, Debra. Fertility and economic strategy in a southern Mexican ejido. Southern Methodist Univ., 1982.

Scott, Russell P. Between captivity and the middle of the world: household organization and migration among rural workers in Pernambuco, Brazil. Univ. of Texas, Austin, 1981.

Sponsel, Leslie E. The hunter and the hunted in the Amazon: an integrated biological and cultural approach to the behavioral ecology of human predation. Cornell Univ., 1981.

Strongin, Jonathan David. Machiguenga, medicine and missionaries: the introduction of western health aids among a native population of southeastern Peru. Columbia, Univ., 1982.

Weller, Susan. A cross-cultural comparison of illness concepts: Guatemala and the United States. Univ. of California, Irvine, 1980.

GENERAL

1628 Villanueva S., María. Estadísticas, ideas y comentarios en torno a un inventario bibliográfico de antropología física en México, 1930–1979 (UNAM/AA, 17, 1980, p. 209–232, tables)

General statistical inventory of physical anthropology in Mexico over past 50 years. Based on 1420 entries and organized according to specific branches of physical anthropology (e.g., prehistory, medical anthropology, etc.).

EARLIER POPULATIONS

Allison, Marvin J. et al. La práctica de la deformación craneana entre los pueblos andinos precolombinos. See item **678.**

1629 Antúnez de Mayolo R., Santiago E. La nutrición en el antiguo Perú (in Congreso Peruano: El Hombre y la Cultura Andina, 3d, 1977. El hombre y la cultura andina [see HLAS 43:253] v. 5, p. 811–828)

General review of foods and nutrients used in prehispanic Peru, with comments on climatic influences, food conservation and food preservation (for archaeologist's comment, see item **839**).

1630 Arechabaleta, Gentzane Z. de. Cráneos deformados de La Pica (UCV/ECS, 18:4, oct./dic. 1979, p. 29–55, bibl., tables)

Of 211 skulls from the basin of Lago de Valencia, Venezuela, 61 showed intentional deformation. Presents detailed craniometry for subsample of 30 deformed skulls.

1631 Benfer, Robert A. and **Sarah Gehlert.** Los habitantes precolombinos de La Paloma: un estudio osteológico (*in* Congreso Peruano: El Hombre y la Cultura Andina, 3d, 1977. El hombre y la cultura andina [see *HLAS 43:253*] v. 5, p. 792–801, tables)

Description of skeletal population from La Paloma, Peru, covering five cultural periods between 6000 and 4500 years ago. Includes little data, appears to be text of presentation with occasional references to slides.

1633 Corruccini, Robert S.; Jerome S. Handler; Robert J. Mutaw; and **Frederick W. Lange.** Osteology of a slave burial population from Barbados, West Indies (AJPA, 59:4, Dec. 1982, p. 443–459, bibl., graphs, plates, tables)

Examination of craniodental characters in relation to ethnohistoric data for a 17th/19th-century slave cemetery population.

1634 Dricot, Jean M. Cálculo de distancias en poblaciones prehispánicas del Perú. Lima: Museo Nacional de Antropología y Arqueología, 1976. 16 p.: bibl., map (Serie Antropología física; no. 1)

Reports distance statistics based on craniometric dimensions of 10 samples of adult males from prehistoric sites. Derives data from reports published 1916–1968. Sample sizes range from six to 67. Uses general Penrose distance statistics, and its components of size and shape.

1635 El-Najjar, Mahmoud Y. Human treponematosis and tuberculosis: evidence from the New World (AJPA, 51:4, Nov. 1979, p. 599–618, bibl., plates, tables)

Critical review of evidence for presence of human treponematosis and tuberculosis in prehistoric New World skeletons is followed by description of nine new cases

dated before contact.

1636 Feldman, Robert A. Two additional cases of lumbar malformation from the Peruvian coastal preceramic (UC/CA, 22:3, June 1981, p. 286–287, bibl.)

Briefly describes two cases of lumbar malformations (among seven burials). Individuals are from Aspero site, coastal preceramic village dated 4360–3950 years BP. Both malformations involved arches of lumbar vertebrae: one was separate from vertebral body; there was lack of closure of two lumbar vertebral arches in the other.

1637 Handler, J.S.; R.S. Corruccini; and **R.J. Mutaw.** Tooth mutilation in the Caribbean: evidence from a slave burial population in Barbados (Journal of Human Evolution [Academic Press, London] 11, 1982, p. 297–313, ill., plates, tables)

Evidence from slave burials in a sugar plantation suggests that dental mutilation disappeared among New World black slaves.

1638 Kiple, Kenneth F. and **Virginia H. Kiple.** Deficiency diseases in the Caribbean (JIH, 11:2, Autumn 1980, p. 197–215, table)

Examines mortality of slave populations relative to deficiency diseases. Bases analysis upon investigation of West African nutritional heritage, analysis of slave diet, and matching of nutritional deficiencies evident in reconstructed diets to symptoms of diseases which plagued the slave population.

1639 Lagrange de Castillo, Helia. Cráneos no deformados de La Pica (UCV/ECS, 18:4, oct./dic. 1979, p. 8–28, bibl., tables)

Presents craniometric data and summary statistics for sample of 60 nondeformed skulls (39 male, 21 female) from total of 211 found in Lago de Valencia, Venezuela.

1640 Mansilla Lory, Josefina. Las condiciones de la población prehispánica de Cholula, Puebla: estudios de las líneas de Harris. México: INAH, 1980. 77 p.: bibl., ill., plates, tables (Colección Científica; 82. Antropología física)

Prehistoric diseases and dietary deficiencies arrested skeletal growth at Cholula, according to X-ray study of human long bones. 86 percent of population retained linear traces of growth interruptions, best observed on the distal tibia and femur. Examines correlation of Harris lines with age, sex, temporal phase, and observable pathology. [Suzanne Lewenstein]

1641 Ortega de Mancera, Alicia. Evaluación odontométrica y morfológica de la dentición de los antiguos habitantes del Lago de Valencia (UCV/ECS, 18:4, oct./dic. 1979, p. 56–88, bibl., tables)

Presents results of odontological and morphological analysis of 70 precolumbian skulls from La Pica (Venezuela). Compares with other indigenous populations.

1642 Pezzia Assereto, Alejandro. La paleopatología iqueña (in Congreso Peruano: El Hombre y la Cultura Andina, 3d, 1977. El hombre y la cultura andina [see HLAS 43:253] v. 5, p.770–774)

Descriptive paleopathologic overview of precolumbian inhabitants of Ica, Peru, based on collection of specimens in Ica's Museo Regional. Identifies several diseases (e.g., tuberculosis, hydrocephaly, goiter, pneumonia, etc.). However, offers little quantitative data.

1643 Prehistoric tuberculosis in the Americas. Edited by Jane E. Buikstra. Evanston, Ill.: Northwestern University Archeological Program, 1981. 182 p.: bibl., graphs, ill., tables (Scientific papers - Northwestern University Archeological Program; no. 5)

Eleven papers consider diagnosis, ecology, and etiology of prehistoric tuberculosis in the Americas, although only Allison's and colleagues' focus on precolumbian Andean populations.

1644 Rothhammer, Francisco; José A. Cocilovo; Silvia Quevedo; and Elena Llop. Microevolution in prehistoric Andean populations: pt. 1, Chronologic craniometric variation (AJPA, 59:4, Aug. 1982, p. 391–396, bibl., tables)

Mahalanobis D^2 statistics (with size and shape components) were computed for nine craniometric variables among five prehistoric groups comprising steps in the microevolution of coastal population in northern Chile.

1645 Sawyer, Danny R.; Marvin J. Allison; Alejandro Pezzia; and Adeyemi Mosadomi. Crown dimensions of deciduous teeth from precolumbian Peru (AJPA, 59:4, Dec. 1982, p. 373–376, bibl., tables)

Presents mesiodistal and buccolingual diameters for deciduous teeth from precolumbian Peru, and compares them to those of modern populations.

1646 Uribe, Rafael Fragoso. Algunos observaciones que apoyan el origen precolombino de la "enfermedad de Robles" en América (Salud Pública de México [México] 21:6, nov./dic. 1979, p. 697–706, bibl., tables)

Considers various data relative to precolumbian origin of Roble's disease in the Americas. Of particular interest is suggestion that Monte Albán's "danzantes" represent diseased individuals, some with manifestations that could well be facial edema by oncocerosis (erisipela de la costa).

Vásquez Leiva, Ricardo. Consideraciones generales sobre un población de huesos humanos encontrados de Bahía Culebra, Guanacaste. See item 673.

——— and **David S. Weaver.** Un análisis osteológico para el reconocimiento de las condiciones de vida en Sitio Vidor. See item 674.

1647 Vidal Vidal, Hilda and **Tamotsu Ogata.** Estudio de tres esqueletos de Lauricocha (in Congreso Peruano: El Hombre y la Cultura Andina, 3d, 1977. El hombre y la cultura andina [see HLAS 43:253] v. 5, p. 775–791, bibl., tables)

Describes three prehistoric skeletons (all adults, two males and one female) from Lauricocha, Peru. Presents their osteometric dimensions and indices.

Weaver, David S. An osteological test of changes in subsistence and settlement patterns at Casa Grandes, Chihuahua, Mexico. See item 533.

1648 Weinstein, Robert S.; David J. Simmons; and C. Owen Lovejoy. Ancient bone disease in a Peruvian mummy revealed by quantitative skeletal histomorphometry (AJPA, 54:3, March 1981, p. 321–326, bibl., plates, tables)

Histomorphometric analysis of undecalcified transileal bone core from adult male, precolumbian, Peruvian mummy (Chancay, AD 400-1600) indicated low trabecular bone volume and trabecular atrophy suggestive of skeletal pathology. Results emphasize importance of subtle metabolic disorders which are not ordinarily detected by quantitative analyses limited to cortical bone.

Wilkinson, Richard G. and **Richard J. Norelli.** A biocultural analysis of social organization at Monte Alban. See item **536.**

1649 Zimmerman, Michael R. *et al.* Trauma and trephination in a Peruvian mummy (AJPA, 55:4, Aug. 1981, p. 497–501, bibl., plates)

Results of detailed examination of colonial era mummy (young adult male) indicated multiple cranial and facial wounds and fractures, and death soon after trephination. Lungs showed anthracosilicosis. Observed pathology may be related to two health hazards of early colonial era, physical trauma and silver mining.

DEMOGRAPHY

1650 Aguirre M., Alejandro and **Sergio Camposortega C.** Evaluación de la información básica sobre mortalidad infantil en México (CM/DE, 14:4[44], 1980, p. 447–466, bibl., graphs, ill.)

Considers deficiencies in using civil registry as source of raw data for estimates of infant mortality in Mexico. Reviews alternate methods and implications of differences in estimates for examining directions of demographic trends.

1651 Anderson, John E.; Leo Morris; Antonieta Pineda; and **Roberto Santiso.** Determinants of fertility in Guatemala (Social Biology [Society for the Study of Social Biology, New York] 27:1, Spring 1980, p. 20–35, bibl., table)

Based upon 1978 Contraceptive Prevalence Survey, Ladinos had higher rate of contraceptive use than Indians, but both groups had similar birth rates. Attributes lack of difference in fertility to pattern of prolonged breast feeding among Indians and perhaps to differences in rate of conception related to nutrition, coital frequency and other factors.

1652 Arias de Blois, Jorge. La mortalidad en Guatemala hacia fines del siglo XIX (SGHG/A, 50:50, enero/dic. 1977, p. 133–149, tables)

Uses new techniques to estimate Guatemala's mortality rate in late 1800s. Shows deficiency and incompleteness of data drawn from other sources (e.g., civil registry, rudimentary censuses from 1800s).

1653 Behm, Hugo *et al.* La mortalidad en los primeros años de vida en países de la América Latina. Argentina, 1966–1967.

Nicaragua, 1966–1967. Honduras, 1969–1970. Guatemala, 1968–1969. San José: Centro Latinoamericano de Demografía (CELADE), 1978. 4 v.: bibl., ill. (Serie A. Centro Latinoamericano de Demografía [CELADE]; nos. 1036–1039)

Series of reports by Behm and colleagues considers child mortality in the first two years of life in Argentina, Nicaragua, Honduras and Guatemala.

1654 Beisso, Serrano Garat. Análise sócio-econômica da fecundidade no Brasil. Rio de Janeiro: Ministério da Indústria e do Comércio, Banco Nacional do Desenvolvimento Econômico, 1981. 154 p.: bibl., ill.

Analyzes high levels of fertility coupled with large interregional differences in Brazil within macro socioeconomic framework in attempt to measure impact of socioeconomic structures on regional fertility patterns.

1655 Blasco, Juan Carlos. Indicadores sobre la situación de la infancia en América Latina y el Caribe = Indicators on the situation of children in Latin America and the Caribbean. Trabajo realizado por Juan Carlos Blasco, bajo la supervisión y apoyo técnico de la División de Estadística y Análisis Cuantitativo de la CEPAL. Traducción, Marjorie Casassus. Dirección de arte, Mary Ann Streeter-Prieto. s.l.: UNICEF; s.l.: CEPAL, 1979. 279 p.: bibl., ill.

Statistical summary of the status of children in Latin America and the Caribbean devotes one-half to infant mortality and factors associated with it (nutrition, health resources, environmental conditions), the other to school-age children, youth, educational status, educational opportunity and labor. Also includes complementary statistics relating to demography, urbanization, and economic activity.

1656 Bravo Carrada, Teodoro. Observaciones sobre las condiciones de salud en las regiones rurales de Tamaulipas, México (Salud Pública de México [México] 22:1, enero/feb. 1980, p. 45–74, bibl., plates, tables)

Reasonably comprehensive overview of health conditions in Tamaulipas' rural regions emphasizes prevalence of malnutrition, contagious diseases, alcoholism and violent crimes. Effects of insecticide poisoning is apparent in some areas.

1657 Brody, Eugene B. Sex, contraception, and motherhood in Jamaica. Cambridge, Mass.: Harvard University Press, 1981. 278 p.: bibl., ill., index (A Commonwealth Fund book)

Carefully presents and discusses results of reasonably comprehensive analysis of personal data, sociocultural factors and fertility-related behaviors. Primary sample was 150 women, with related supplementary data for 183 men.

1658 Canales M., José Luis; Patricia López P.; José Narro R.; and Ignacio Almada B. El subregistro de la natalidad y la mortalidad en una comunidad rural en México (Salud Pública de México [México] 22:2, marzo/abril 1980, p. 123–134, bibl., tables)

Using rural community in Morelos state, compares records from household survey of total population and official registry. Results indicate poor quality of vital statistics. There was underregistration of 31 percent births and 83 percent deaths. For deaths in children under five, registry records only 10 percent.

1659 Carvalho, José Alberto Magno de. Evolução demográfica recente no Brasil (IPEA/PPE, 10:2, agôsto 1980, p. 527–554, tables)

Analysis of demographic trends in Brazil (1930–1970) reports decrease in mortality with constant fertility rate fueling population growth, after which (1970s) fertility rate rapidly decreases. Discusses implications for population growth and demands for services (e.g., housing, schools, jobs, etc.).

1660 Castañeda, Tarcisio. Determinantes del cambio poblacional en Colombia (CEDE/DS, 4, julio 1980, p. 309–334, bibl., tables)

Attempts empirically based model of relationship between fecundity and several socioeconomic changes (e.g., education, income, health, etc.). In general, associates increasing socioeconomic welfare with reduced fecundity.

1661 Costa, Manoel Augusto. Reprodução e mortalidade em cidades de porte médio: 1960–1970 (in Encontro Nacional Estudos Populacionais, 2d, Aguas de São Pedro, Brasil, 1980. Anais. São Paulo: Associação Brasileira de Estudos Populacionais [ABEP], Secretaria Geral o Tesouraria, 1981, p. 953–977, bibl., tables)

Calculates levels, tendencies, and differentials of fecundity and mortality. Also examines effects of progressive entrance of women into labor force upon fecundity and mortality for Brazilian cities with populations between 100,000 and 500,000 for period 1960–70.

1662 Costa, Veloso; Manoel Ricardo da Costa Carvalho; and Maria Dolores Paes da Silva. Aspectos de saúde de Nordeste do Brasil (Revista da Fundação Serviços de Saúde Pública [Rio de Janeiro] 25:2, 1980, p. 5–22, tables)

Describes and discusses health conditions in Northeast Brazil. Presents data relative to life expectancy (ca. 50 years), infant mortality (about 120/1000 live births), preschool mortality (about 50 percent of deaths occur in children under five), and mortality for contagious diseases (about 400/100,000 population). These conditions are related to malnutrition, poor sanitary conditions, poor health services, and lack of education.

1663 D'Aloja, Ada. La población del Valle del Mezquital (UNAM/AA, 17, 1980, p. 187–198, bibl., map, tables)

Descriptive survey of Valle del Mezquital population based upon census data. Considers distribution of population, age and sex, and indices of nuptiality and fertility.

1664 Davidson, Maria. Female work status and fertility in urban Latin America (UWI/SES, 27:4, Dec. 1978, p. 481–506, bibl., tables)

Examines relationship of selected socioeconomic characteristics of married women to fertility in eight capital cities of Latin America. There was considerable variability and the most important factors affecting fertility were wife's age at marriage and her education.

1665 Díaz, S. et al. Fertility regulation in nursing women: pt. 1, The probability of conception in full nursing women living in an urban setting (Journal of Biosocial Science [Oxford, England] 14, 1982, p. 329–341, bibl., tables)

Sample of 130 full nursing women in Santiago, Chile, was followed during first postpartum year to assess fertility, lactation and bleeding pattern. By end of six months and one year, respectively, cumulative probability of pregnancy was 10 percent and 33.9 percent.

1666 Díaz-Briquets, Sergio. Determinants of mortality transition in developing countries before and after the Second World War: some evidence from Cuba (LSE/PS, 35:3, Nov. 1981, p. 399–411, tables)

Examines mortality trends in Cuba (1900–53) by age, sex, and cause. Compares specific years: 1901, 1919, 1931, 1943, and 1953. Considers factors involved in mortality decline including significant effect of Cuba's proximity to US (distance, political and economic).

1667 ———. The health revolution in Cuba. Austin: University of Texas Press, 1983. 227 p.: bibl., ill., index.

Rather detailed analysis of trends in mortality over approximately the last 100 years in Cuba, focusing on the secular trend in mortality per se, disease-specific death rates, and determinants of the decline in mortality.

1668 ——— and Lisandro Pérez. Fertility decline in Cuba: a socioeconomic interpretation (Population and Development Review [Population Council, New York] 8:3, Sept. 1982, p. 513–537, tables)

Analyzes fertility for period 1953–80, focusing on recent fertility decline. Emphasizes social and economic factors but also effects of poor performance of the Cuban economy.

1669 Dutt, James S. Altitude and fertility: the confounding effect of childhood mortality, a Bolivian example (Social Biology [Society for the Study of Social Biology, New York] 27:2, Summer 1980, p. 101–113, bibl., tables)

Studies fertility of 906 Bolivian women of lower socioeconomic status residing at low, medium, and high altitudes. Data shows no significant altitude-related differences in number of live births. However, childhood mortality rates increase at higher altitudes so that there were significantly less living children.

1670 Encuesta nacional de fecundidad: República del Paraguay. Asunción: Dirección General de Estadística y Censos, 1981. 623, 40 p.: ill.

Summary of 1979 national fertility survey includes data on type of union, place of residence, level of education, fertility, preferences (i.e., sex and number of children), knowledge and use of contraceptives, and mother-child health.

1671 Goldman, Noreen and Anne R. Pebley. Legalization of consensual unions in Latin America (Social Biology [Society for the Study of Social Biology, New York] 28:1/2, Spring/Summer 1981, p. 49–61, bibl., tables)

Examines legalization of consensual unions in rural areas of Colombia, Mexico, Peru, and Costa Rica based on data from 1969 PECFAL rural survey. Legalization is frequent in rural Latin America especially among women who enter consensual unions after age 17 and who have some education.

1672 Guerra, Federico. Determinantes de la mortalidad infantil en Panamá, 1940–1974. Santiago de Chile: CELADE, 1981. 87 p.: bibl., ill. (Serie D. CELADE; no. 99)

Detailed analysis of infant mortality in Panama (1940–74). Considers maternal characteristics, urban-rural differentials, birth intervals, and other factors.

1673 Gutiérrez, J.H.; Antonio Villalobos Olivas; and Javier Contreras Lemus. La mortalidad en el período perinatal I (Salud Pública de México [México] 22:3, mayo/junio 1980, p. 261–268, bibl., ill., tables)

Analyzes social and physiological characteristics of infants dying in perinatal period (first week of life). Social indicators include unmarried mother and no prenatal care. Physiological indicators include low birth weight, gestational age less than 37 weeks and suspected diabetes. Note, social and physiological indicators are related.

1674 Guzmán, José Miguel. Evaluation of the *Dominican Republic National Fertility Survey: 1975.* The Hague, Netherlands: International Statistical Institute; London: World Fertility Survey, 1980? 55 p. (Scientific reports. International Statistical Institute; no. 14)

Using information collected in Dominican Republic's national fertility survey, report attempts to ascertain quality of data relative to nuptiality, fertility, and infant and childhood mortality.

1675 Henriques, Maria Helena F.T. Uniões legais e consensuais: incidência e fecundidade na América Latina (IBGE/RBE, 41:164, out./dez. 1980, p. 499–529, tables)

Data indicate marked difference in fecundity between common-law and legal unions in Latin American capitals, former having higher values. Brief section focuses on several regions of Brazil which represent different stages of economic development. These regions indicate an exception to general pattern.

1676 Hernández García, Alberto and **Carmen Elisa Flórez N.** Tendencias y diferenciales de la fecundidad en Colombia. Bogotá: Corporación Centro Regional de Población, Area Socioeconómica, 1979. 134 p.: bibl., graphs (Monografías de la Corporación Centro Regional de Población; v. 15)

Complete description and analysis of Colombia's national fertility survey of 1976 includes methods, urban-rural comparisons, analysis of impact of education and knowledge of family planning procedures, etc. Also offers concise summary.

1677 Hobcraft, John. Illustrative analysis: evaluating fertility levels and trends in Colombia. The Hague, Netherlands: International Statistical Institute; London: World Fertility Survey, 1980. 52 p. (Scientific reports. WFS; no. 15)

Examination of data from Colombian national fertility survey indicates that data are generally high quality, enabling fairly satisfactory estimation levels and trends of fertility. There are, however, several problems and errors (e.g., in comparisons of household and individual samples.)

1678 Jain, Anrudh K. and **John Bongaarts.** Lactancia: esquemas, correlaciones y efectos sobre la fecundidad (ACEP/EP, 6:1/6, enero/junio 1981, p. 3–35, tables)

Reports on cross-cultural study of effect of lactation on fertility based upon data from world Fertility Census (1976). Includes Peru, Colombia, and Panama among eight countries analyzed.

1679 Leridon, H. and **Y. Charbit.** Patterns of marital unions and fertility in Guadeloupe and Martinique (LSE/PS, 35:2, July 1981, p. 235–245, tables)

Authors first consider relationship between union patterns and fertility, and then offer age-union-specific fertility rates. All estimates show that legitimate fertility slightly exceeds that of consensual unions. Analysis was based on experience of birth cohorts of 1926–40, so that conclusions might be different for later cohorts (1940–60).

1680 Llano Saavedra, Luis. Bolivia, diferenciales de fecundidad según el *Censo de Población de 1976.* La Paz: Ministerio de Planeamiento y Coordinación, Instituto Nacional de Estadística, 1980. 1 v. (various foliations): bibl., graphs, ill., tables.

Reports differences in fertility according to area of residence (urban/rural), level of education, language spoken (Spanish, indigenous dialect, or both), and level of economic activity.

1681 Loza Saldívar, Arnoldo de la *et al.* Evaluación de los programas de salud para la niñez en México (Salud Pública de México [México] 22:6, nov./dic. 1980, p. 631–654, bibl., graphs, tables)

Examines childhood mortality and compares it to indicators from other countries. Provides detailed data for 1975 and for individual states.

1682 Madrigal Hinojosa, Romeo E. La mortalidad en el Noreste de México. Monterrey, México: Universidad Autónoma de Nuevo León, Facultad de Economía, Centro de Investigaciones Económicas: Gobierno del Estado, Oficialía Mayor, Dirección de Estadística y Procesamiento de Datos, 1980. 145 p.: bibl., graphs.

Presents age and sex specific mortality data for three states in northeast Mexico: Coahuila, Nuevo León, and Tamaulipas, covering 1940–70.

1683 Marcilio, Maria Luiza. A população da América Latina de 1900 a 1975 (SBPC/CC, 32:9, set. 1980, p. 1155–1176, graphs, maps, tables)

Examines population growth in Latin America (1900–75) using statistics from census information and estimates. Comparisons include considerations of natality, mortality, natural increase, internal migration, life expectancy, spatial distribution and urbanization.

1684 Martorell, Reynaldo; Hernán L. Delgado; Víctor Valverde; and **Robert E. Klein.** Maternal stature, fertility and infant mortality (WSU/HB, 53:3, Sept. 1981, p. 303–312, bibl., tables)

Analyzes relationship between maternal stature, parity, offspring mortality and number of surviving children in 380 malnourished Guatemalan Indian women. After adjusting for age and/or parity, association between maternal stature and number of surviving children was significant. Mortality rates were higher for children of shorter mothers.

1685 Mazess, Richard B. and Ralph W. Mathisen. Lack of unusual longevity in Vilcabamba, Ecuador (WSU/HB, 54:3, Sept. 1982, p. 517–524, bibl., tables)

Evaluates mortality records for population of Vilcabamba and nearby urban center of Loja for period 1907–79. Although life expectancy has increased in Vilcabamba over past 70 years, it is still 15–30 percent below US. Age exaggeration was apparently responsible for supposed increased longevity in Vilcabamba.

1686 Mexico. Coordinación General del Sistema Nacional de Información. Encuesta mexicana de fecundidad. México: Secretaría de Programación y Presupuesto, Coordinación General del Sistema Nacional de Información, 197? 3 v.: bibl., ill.

These three volumes summarize the methods and first reports of the Mexican fertility survey of 1976.

1687 Mina V., Alejandro. Aplicación del modelo estándar de nupcialidad de A.J. Coale al caso de México (CM/DE, 14:4[44], 1980, p. 421–446, bibl., graph, table)

Describes female nuptiality levels and trends using A.J. Coale's model and data from two fecundity surveys (1970, 1976) and three censuses (1950, 1960, 1970). Estimates future frequencies of entrance into married state.

1688 ———. Estimaciones de los niveles, tendencias y diferenciales de la mortalidad infantil en los primeros años de vida en México, 1940–1977 (CM/DE, 15:1[45], 1981, p. 85–142, graphs, tables)

Reports on levels, tendencies and differentials in infant mortality for 1940, 1950, 1960, and 1970. Considers sources and quality of data and factors associated with high mortality.

1689 Müller, María S. and Silvia Caronia de Jouliá. Mortalidad infantil en Misiones, 1968 a 1977: datos para el estudio de la natalidad y la mortalidad infantil. Posadas, Argentina: Provincia de Misiones, Secretaría de Planeamiento, Dirección General de Estadística y Censos, Centro de Estudios de Población Misiones, 1980. 79 leaves: bibl., ill.

Concerns infant mortality relative to total mortality and variation by province and zones in Argentina.

1690 Natalidad-fecundidad: comentarios, atención profesional, fecundidad, variación estacional, legitimidad, peso al nacer, edad gestacional, etc.: cuadros estadísticos, Uruguay, 1977. Estadísticas nacionales de natalidad y fecundidad elaboradas con el apoyo del Fondo de Naciones Unidas para Actividades de Población. Montevideo: Ministerio de Salud Pública, División Higiene, Departamento de Estadística, 1979. 150 p.: ill., tables.

Reports Uruguay's birth rates, birth weights, gestational ages, and related factors (e.g., type of union, age of mother, seasonal variation) in 1977.

1691 Odell, Mary E. The domestic context of production and reproduction in a Guatemalan community (Human Ecology [Plenum, N.Y.] 10:1, 1982, p. 47–69, tables)

Analysis of demographic variables among three productive sectors shows that greatest changes in fertility have occurred in families of labor intensive garlic producers and in those of poor basket-makers.

1692 Partida B., Virgilio. Patrones modelo de mortalidad para México (CM/DE, 15:1[45], 1981, p. 27–58, bibl., graphs, tables)

Based upon discrepancy between estimated and observed mortality rates by age for Mexico, author offers new model of mortality estimates with detailed consideration of underlying methodology.

1693 Pebley, Anne R. The age at first birth and timing of the second in Costa Rica and Guatemala (LSE/PS, 35:3, Nov. 1981, p. 387–397, graphs, tables)

Data for Costa Rica indicate significant relationship between age at first birth and timing of subsequent fertility. Association is weaker and less consistent in Guatemalan data.

1694 ———; Hernán Delgado; and Elena Brineman. El ideal de fecundidad y mortalidad infantil experimentada entre mujeres guatemaltecas (ACEP/EP, 4:1/6, enero/junio 1979, p. 30–39, bibl., tables)

Examines effects of decrease in infant mortality on fertility for two areas of Guatemala. Finds perception of possibility of infant survival to be realistic but not to influence

1695 **Peru. Instituto Nacional de Estadística. Oficina Nacional de Estadística. Dirección General de Censos, Encuestas y Demografía. Dirección de Demografía.** Encuesta nacional de fecundidad del Perú, 1977–1978: informe general. Lima: 1979. 487 p., 1 fold. leaf of plates: forms.

Comprehensive summary of objectives, methods and results of Peruvian fertility survey of 1977–78, including data on marriage, types of unions, risk of pregnancy, fertility, knowledge and use of contraceptives, preferred number and sex of offspring, and mother-child care.

1696 ———. ———. ———. ———. ———. ———. La mortalidad en los primeros años de vida, 1967–1968. Lima: La Dirección, 1977. 79 p.: bibl., ill. (Boletín de análisis demográfico; no. 17)

Examines in detail mortality during first two years of life using mortality data for late 1960s and census data for 1972. Makes geographic and urban/rural comparisons, and includes several maternal characteristics.

1697 **Peters, John F.** The Shirishana of the Yanomami: a demographic study (Social Biology [Society for the Study of Social Biology, New York] 27 : 4, Winter 1980, p. 272–285, bibl., map, tables)

Analyzes group's social change over 23-year period. At contact in 1958, population was 118 with sex ratio of 149. In 1980, group numbered 280 with sex ratio of 93. Attributes population increase to immigration, medical care and absence of warfare, and interprets it in terms of modern demographic transition theory.

1698 **Petruccelli, José Luis; María Helena Rato; and Sérgio Luiz Bragança.** The socioeconomic consequences of a reduction in fertility: application of the ILO-IBGE national model, BACHUE-Brazil (ILO/R, 119 : 5, Sept./Oct. 1980, p. 623–635, tables)

Uses BACHUE-Brazil simulation model to examine hypothesis that reduction in population growth rate should result in drop in manpower surplus and underemployment. Model's demographic subsystem includes mortality, fertility, migration and education; economic subsystem includes final demand and production, labor market, wages and other income, and income distribution. Uses 1970 as starting point and projects simulation to year 2000. Results sug-

gest that sudden reduction in fertility would not have significant effect on Brazilian economy and would not tend to improve income distribution.

1699 **Quilodrán, Julieta.** Algunas características de la fecundidad rural en México (CM/DE, 14 : 4[44], 1980, p. 397–410, graphs, ill., table)

Using data from 1969–70 Rural Survey of Fecundity, shows how rural sector did not significantly limit its birth rate nor significantly use contraceptive methods during 1960s decade.

1700 ———. Tablas de nupcialidad para México (CM/DE, 14 : 1[41], 1980, p. 27–89, graphs, maps, tables)

Using data from 1930, 1960, and 1970 censuses and National Fecundity Survey of 1976, presents Mexico's nuptiality tables for 1930, 1960, 1970, and 1976 by sex and region.

1701 **Ramos, Héctor.** Mortalidad infantil y atención infantil en el Perú. Auspiciado por la Oficina Nacional de Estadística, República del Perú. Santiago de Chile: CELADE, Seminario de Análisis y Capacitación, Encuesta Mundial de Fecundidad, 1981. 57 p.: bibl.

This is a reasonably detailed summary of infant mortality and maternal-child care for the mid-1970s, with comparative data for earlier periods. Data related to maternal-child care are derived from 1977–1978 fertility survey of Peru.

1702 **Rosero Bixby, Luis.** Dinámica demográfica, planificación familiar y política de población en Costa Rica (CM/DE, 15 : 1[45], 1981, p. 59–84, bibl., graphs, tables)

Presents Costa Rica's demographic trends (natality, mortality, growth) relative to their causes and consequences. Reviews migration, urban/rural differences, and Costa Rica's family planning program.

1703 **Sawyer, Donald R.** Fecundidade e mortalidade na Amazônia: notas sobre estimativas e interpretações (in Encontro Nacional Estudos Populacionais, 2d, Aguas de São Pedro, Brasil, 1980. Anais. São Paulo: Associação Brasileira de Estudos [ABEP], Secretaria Geral o Tesouraria, 1981, p. 115–183, map, tables)

Methodological study attempts to estimate changes in fecundity and mortality rates of the Brazilian Amazon by micro-region.

1704 Stinson, Sara. The interrelationship of mortality and fertility in rural Bolivia (WSU/HB, 54:2, May 1982, p. 299–313, bibl., tables)

Demographic information was collected from 149 families of school aged children from rural Aymara population. This group showed lower sex ratio at birth than other Andean groups. Family size had little effect on child mortality.

1705 Stycos, J. Mayone. The decline of fertility in Costa Rica: literacy, modernization, and family planning (LSE/PS, 36:3, March 1982, p. 15–30, graphs, tables)

Attempts to analyze causal sequence in differential fertility. High level of literacy apparently led to decline, perhaps resulting from increased secondary school education and shift to non-agricultural occupations. Modernization, especially improved health and economic circumstances, throughout 1950s became significant factor, followed by National Family Planning program in 1968.

1706 Terra, Juan Pablo. Situación de la infancia en América Latina y el Caribe (ACEP/EP, número especial, abril 1980, p. 45–80, tables)

Overview of situation of children in Latin America is divided into five sections: 1) growth of the child population and related issues; 2) situation in marginal communities and populations; 3) primary problems of children; 4) issues of social policy; and 5) future trends and strategies.

1707 Trussell, T.J. and K. Hill. Fertility and mortality estimation from the Panama Retrospective Demographic Survey, 1976 (LSE/PS, 34:3, Nov. 1980, p. 551–563, tables)

Preliminary analysis of results from retrospective survey focuses on marriage, fertility, childhood, and adult mortality. Authors emphasize methodological utility of retrospective survey for indirect demographic estimation procedures.

1708 Valle Prieto, María Eugenia del. Parto y aborto en algunas "ciudades perdidas" de México (UNAM/AA, 17, 1980, p. 197–222, bibl., tables)

Analyzes childbirth and abortion in urban marginal population (i.e., residents on fringes of cities). Based on 2173 families from

five urban centers: Monterrey, Tijuana, Coatzacoalcos-Minatitlán, Lázaro Cárdenas-Las Truchas, and México-Netzahualcoyotl. Focuses largely on mother's physical and mental health and families in marginal environmental circumstances (i.e., poor health, nutritional, housing and sanitary services).

1709 Villa Posse, Eugenia. Salud y enfermedad en tierradentro (PUJ/UH, 11, dic. 1979, p. 7–96, bibl.)

Presents comprehensive overview of present social, political, economic, cultural, and medical status of Colombia's Paeces Indians, based on one semester field work in 1976. Stresses consequences of contacts with "white civilization."

1710 Wood, Charles H. The political economy of infant mortality in São Paulo, Brazil (International Journal of Health Services [Baywood Publishing Co., Farmingdale, N.Y.] 12:2, 1982, p. 215–229, tables)

Using economic and mortality statistics, author emphasizes association between declining purchasing power of minimum wage and increase in infant mortality observed from early 1960s through 1970s. Trend is especially strong among urban poor.

1711 Wood, Harold A. Mortality in three departments of Colombia: a preliminary assessment (Social Science and Medicine [Pergamon Press, New York] 15D, 1981, p. 439–447, bibl., ill., tables)

Evaluation of causes of death shows that prior to 45 years of age, most causes were susceptible to public health programs. Apparently, sanitation and infectious disease control would benefit children and elderly, while social and economic measures would reduce young adults' death rate.

POPULATION GENETICS

1712 Aréchiga, Julieta. Tipología sanguínea--sistema ABO y Rh--en población Tojolabal y mestiza (UNAM/AA, 17, 1980, p. 199–208, bibl., tables)

Describes phenotypic frequencies for Tojolabal (Chiapas) Mayan population and Las Margaritas mestizo community using ABO and Rh systems. Interprets differences in terms of admixture with populations of European and African ancestry.

1713 Azevedo, Eliane S. *et al.* Genetic and anthropological studies in the island of Itaparica, Bahia, Brazil (HH, 31, 1981, p. 353–357, bibl., tables)

Ongoing racial admixture was studied in this island population using several genetic markers (Hb, PGD, Gd), death certificates, and surnames.

1714 ——— *et al.* Spread and diversity of human populations in Bahia, Brazil (WSU/HB, 54:2, May 1982, p. 329–341, bibl., graphs, map, tables)

School children (n=29,755) from 60 localities in Bahia state were studied for proportion of black admixture and type of family names. Racial classification based on phenotypic and cultural indices showed significant association between physical type and proportion of black admixture estimated from cultural index.

1715 Barbosa, C.A.A.; N.E. Morton; D.C. Roa; and **H. Krieger.** Biological and cultural determinants of immunoglobulin levels in a Brazilian population with Chagas disease (Human Genetics [Springer-Verlag, Hamburg, FRG] 59, 1981, p. 161–163, bibl., ill., tables)

Under general model, genetic heritability of immunoglobin levels in a Brazilian population was 0.33 for IgA, 0.34 for IgG, and 0.12 for IgM. Cultural heritability was much smaller.

1716 Barrantes, Ramiro *et al.* Migration and genetic infrastructure of the Central American Guaymi and their affinities with other tribal groups (AJPA, 58:2, June 1982, p. 201–214, bibl., ill., maps, tables)

Reports on genetic data on 40 red cell enzymes, antigenic blood groups and serum proteins representing 42 separate loci for two Guaymi communities of recent origin in southeastern Costa Rica. Compares results with data for other tribal groups and relates them to settlement patterns.

1717 Byard, P.J. and **F.C. Lees.** Skin colorimetry in Belize: pt. 2, Inter- and intra-population variation (AJPA, 58:2, June 1982, p. 215–219, bibl., tables)

Skin colorimetry readings on Black Caribs and Creoles are related to variation in African, Indian, and European admixture as estimated from serological markers.

1718 Champin, J.; J. Pinto-Cisternas; A. Rodríguez; and **G. Muller.** Some variables of the craniofacial complex in a Venezuelan population of negroid ancestry (AJPA, 59:1, Sept. 1982, p. 9–19, bibl., ill., maps, tables)

Considers 33 craniofacial and dental variables in 226 individuals, eight-60 years, from Venezuelan Negro isolated community, and compares them to African Negroes, Caucasians and Amerindians.

1719 Crawford, Michael H. *et al.* The Black Caribs (Garifuna) of Livingston, Guatemala: genetic markers and admixture estimates (WSU/HB, 53:1, Feb. 1981, p. 87–103, bibl., maps, tables)

Documents genetic variation for 24 blood group, red cells and serum protein systems in Black Carib community. Admixture estimates (based upon Gm) suggest 70 percent African, 29 percent Indian, and one percent European parental population contributions.

1720 Elizonda, J. *et al.* G6PD-Puerto Limón: a new deficient variant of glucose-6-phosphate dehydrogenase associated with cogenital nonspherocytic hemolytic anemia (Human Genetics [Springer-Verlag, Hamburg, FRG] 62, 1982, p. 110–112, bibl., ill., tables)

Describes new glucose-6-phosphate dehydrogenase variant with total deficiency associated with congenital non-spherocytic hemolytic anemia in Costa Rican family.

1721 Erdtmann, B.; F.M. Salzano; and **Margarete S. Mattevi.** Size variability for Y chromosome distal C-band in Brazilian Indians and Caucasoids (Annals of Human Biology [Taylor and Francis, London] 8:5, Sept./Oct. 1981, p. 415–424, bibl., tables)

Densitometric measurements of the Y chromosome distal heterochromatin were done on 183 Indians and 21 Caucasians. No significant intratribal and intervillage variation was observed, tribal averages ranging from 0.81 to 1.32 microns. Caucasian mean was intermediate. There was positive correlation between this variable and C-band size of chromosome 16.

1722 ———; ———; ———; and **R.Z. Flores.** Quantitative analysis of C Bands in chromosomes 1, 9, and 16 of Brazilian Indians and Caucasoids (Human Genetics [Springer-Verlag, Hamburg, FRG] 57, 1981, p. 58–63, bibl., ill., tables)

Reports densitometric C-band measurements in chromosomes 1, 9, and 16 for 394 Indians and 40 Caucasians. No significant intratribal variability in average lengths of regions was observed, and intertribal variation showed no consistent patterns. Lower mean values were consistently present in Caucasians.

1723 Franco, M. Helena L.P.; Tania A. Weimer; and F.M. Salzano. Blood polymorphisms and racial admixture in two Brazilian populations (AJPA, 58:2, June 1982, p. 127–132, bibl., tables)

Studies 12 and eight genetic systems respectively in 1000 individuals of Pôrto Alegre (south) and 760 individuals of Natal (Northeast). Ancestry of total sample was estimated as 58 percent white, 25 percent black, and 17 percent Indian.

1724 Frisancho, A. Roberto; Robert Wainwright; and Anthony Way. Heritability and components of phenotypic expression in skin reflectance of mestizos from the Peruvian lowlands (AJPA, 55:2, June 1981, p. 203–208, bibl., ill., tables)

Considers parent-child, sibling and spouse similarities in skin reflectance measurements of 209 mestizos, two-64 years. Data indicates high degree of assortative mating, no evidence of X-linkage, and heritability estimates which suggest that about 55 percent of total variance in skin reflectance can be attributed to additive genetic factors.

1725 García, M. *et al.* Glyoxalase I polymorphism and racial admixture in the Cuban population (Human Genetics [Springer-Verlag, Hamburg, FRG] 61, 1982, p. 50–51, 91–92, bibl., tables)

Polymorphism of glyoxalase was demonstrated in Cuba's three main racial groups. GLO[1] frequencies were 0.4129 in Caucasians, 0.3530 in mulattoes, and 0.2441 in Negroes.

1726 Halberstein, R.A.; J.E. Davies; and A.K. Mack. Hemoglobin variations on a small Bahamian island (AJPA, 55:2, June 1981, p. 217–221, bibl., map, tables)

Detects adnormal hemoglobin variants in 20.3 percent of 492 specimens from small island community (1450 inhabitants). Vari-

ants include genotypes AS, AC, AF (A/HPFH), SC and SF. Historical migrations and genetic drift (especially founder effect) were apparently key factors influencing variants.

1727 Hutchinson, Janis and Michael H. Crawford. Genetic determinants of blood pressure level among the Black Caribs of St. Vincent (WSU/HB, 53:3, Sept. 1981, p. 453–466, bibl., tables)

In 421 Black Caribs (tri-ethnic origin: African, Arawak, Carib), there was no relationship between African ancestry and blood pressure, but Black Caribs were apparently more similar to American blacks regarding age changes in blood pressure.

1728 Jobim, Luiz F. *et al.* HLA antigens in Tukuna Indians (AJPA, 56:3, Nov. 1981, p. 285–290, bibl., tables)

HLA antigens were typed for 99 Tukuna Indians of high Amazon, and cross-matched with 240 other multiparous Indians. Latter were also cross-matched with Caucasoid individuals. Most frequent antigens for the HLA-A locus were A2, Aw24, and Aw31, and for the HLA-B locus were B5, Bw39, and B40.

1729 Keiser, Julius A. and Charles B. Preston. The dentition of the Lengua Indians of Paraguay (AJPA, 55:4, Aug. 1981, p. 485–490, bibl., plates, tables)

Describes crown morphology (as per dental casts) of 202 living Indians, 18–30 years, and compares them with other populations. The Lengua dentition shows Mongoloid affinities with little effect of European admixture. Data suggests sexual dimorphism in Carabelli's cusp.

1730 Laska-Mierzejewska, Teresa. Dymorfizm Płciowy Człowieka odmiany białej i czarnej na Kubie. Warsaw: Akademie Wychowania Fizycznego, 1982. 160 p.: bibl., graphs, tables (Studia Monografie; 1)

Anthropometric data and indices for 370 men and 499 women, representing blacks, whites, and mulattoes, from Havana, Cuba, were analyzed relative to sexual dimorphism and racial differences.

1731 Lathrop, G.M. Evolutionary trees and admixture: phylogenetic inference when some populations are hybridized (UCGL/AHG, 46, 1982, p. 245–255, bibl., ill., tables)

Develops maximum likelihood estimation of admixture parameters and divergence times for evolutionary tree in which some populations may be hybridized and applies it to gene frequency data from Makiritare Indians of southern Venezuela.

1732 Pinheiro, M. *et al.* Christ-Siemens-Touraine syndrome: investigations on two large Brazilian kindreds with a new estimate of the manifestation rate among carriers (Human Genetics [Springer-Verlag, Hamburg, FRG] 57, 1981, p. 428–431, bibl., ill., tables)

Reports on two large Brazilian families with 34 males and 32 females presenting Christ-Siemens-Touraine syndrome.

1733 Pollitzer, W.S. *et al.* Characteristics of a population sample of Jacobina, Bahia, Brazil (WSU/HB, 54:4, Dec. 1982, p. 697–707, bibl., tables)

Physical measurements were taken on adult members of 200 families. Adults were classified by appearance into gradations of white, black, and Indian ethnic groups. Head measurements varied with race, but stature and lower segments did not. Mahalanobis' D^2 measure of distance suggested some similarity to Seminole Indians of Florida.

1734 Relethford, John H. and **Francis C. Lees.** Admixture and skin color in the transplanted Tlaxcaltecan population of Saltillo, Mexico (AJPA, 56:3, Nov. 1981, p. 259–267, bibl., tables)

Skin colorimetry was used to assess interpopulational affinities in two barrios. Admixture estimated for Indian-Spanish model (dihybrid) derived from skin reflectance tended to underestimate Spanish admixture compared to blood group estimates, but trihybrid model incorporating West African admixture gave similar estimates based on blood groups, immunoglobins and skin color.

1735 Rothhammer, Francisco; Elena Llop; and **James V. Neel.** Dermatoglyphic characters and physique: a correlation study (AJPA, 57:1, Jan. 1982, p. 99–101, bibl., tables)

Analyzes associations between certain anthropometric (middle finger and hand breadth and length, stature, weight) and dermatoglyphic (finger and palm prints) characteristics in middle class population (105

adults, 108 children) of Santiago, Chile. Evidence indicates small correlation.

1736 Salzano, F.M.; E. Butler-Brunner; and **R. Butler.** Ag groups of the Krahó Indians of Brazil (HH, 31, 1981, p. 61–64, bibl., tables)

Sera from 73 Krahó Indians were tested for nine Ag factors. They were uniformly $(x-y+)$, (a_1-d+), $(t+z-)$, and $(h-)$, but showed polymorphism at the c, g site, the frequency of Ag^g being 0.63. These frequencies are different than those observed in one Caucasian, one Oriental, and one African population.

1737 Santos, Maria Concepción and **Eliane S. Azevedo.** Generalized joint hypermobility and black admixture in school children in Bahia, Brazil (AJPA, 55:1, May 1981, p. 43–46, bibl., ill., tables)

Studies joint hypermobility in 3000 school children, six-17 years of age. Classified five racial subgroups to assess proportion of black admixture. Overall frequency of generalized joint hypermobility was 2.3 percent, and darker children had lower frequency. Apparent racial effect, however, was associated with age.

1738 Schuler, Lavinia *et al.* Demographic and blood genetic characteristics in an Amazonian population (Journal of Human Evolution [Academic Press, London] 11, 1982, p. 549–558, bibl., ill., plates, tables)

Reports on demographic, epidemiological, and genetic studies of 595 persons living in Parintins, extreme east of Amazonia state. Includes marital distances, parent-offspring distances, and genetic data for nine systems (ABO, Rh, Hb, ESD, CA_2, Hp, Tf, Cp, A1). Preliminary admixture estimates were 67 percent white, 29 percent Indian, four percent black.

1739 Silva, M. Isabel A.F. da; F.M. Salzano; and **F.A.M. de Lima.** Migration, inbreeding, blood groups and hemoglobin types in Natal, Brazil (Studies in Physical Anthropology [Polish Academy of Sciences, Warsaw] 7, 1981, p. 3–11, map, tables)

Studies A_1A_2BO, MN, Ph and hemoglobin systems in 807 individuals from Natal, Northeast Brazil. Attempts to relate data from genetic markers to migration history, marital distances, parent-offspring distances and inbreeding coefficients generally yielded negative results.

**1740 Silva, Rosilda S.; Tania A. Weimer;
and F.M. Salzano.** Rare and common types of phosphyglucomutase in two Brazilian populations (WSU/HB, 53 : 2, May 1981, p. 227–238, bibl., ill., tables)

PGM types were determined in 695 whites and 1032 blacks from Porto Alegre and in 38 Xikrin Indians. Whites showed higher frequency of PGM_1^2 (0.21 to 0.29 in three age groups) than blacks (0.22–0.23), while frequency of this marker was 0.26 in Xikrin. Two rare phenotypes were also found: PGM_1 6–2 and PGM_1 3–1. Whites were all homozygous for PGM_2^1, and its allele PGM_2^2 had frequency of 0.01 in blacks and 0.05 in Xikrin.

1741 Vaca, G. *et al.* G-6-PD Guadalajara: a new mutant associated with chronic nonspherocytic hemolytic anemia (Human Genetics [Springer-Verlag, Hamburg, FRG] 61, 1982, p. 175–175, bibl., tables)

Describes new glucose-6-phosphate dehydrogenase variant found in Mexican boy suffering from chronic hemolytic anemia. Red cell enzyme activity was about 14 percent.

**1742 Weimer, Tania A.; F.M. Salzano; and
Mara H. Hutz.** Erythrocyte isozymes and hemoglobin types in a southern Brazilian population (Journal of Human Evolution [Academic Press, London] 10, 1981, p. 319–328, bibl., plates, tables)

Four red cell isoenzymes and hemoglobin types were tested in 710 white and 1070 black individuals from Porto Alegre. Results were consistent with those expected in populations of these ethnic groups with some admixture. Two rare phenotypes were identified: one involving "null" adenosine deaminase allele, and the other a G6PD nondeficient variant tentatively named Gd (+) "Guaiba."

HUMAN ADAPTABILITY

1743 Ariza Macías, J. *et al.* Estudio seccional de crecimiento y desarrollo de niños y niñas colombianas de dos clases socioeconómicas de los seis a los veinte años (SLN/ALN, 28 : 1, marzo 1978, p. 5–90, bibl., graphs, tables)

Presents data from study of height and weight and age at menarche in cross-sectional sample of 3473 Bogotá children and youth (6–20 years) from two socioeconomic strata (high and very low). Results are consistent with other such economic comparisons.

**1744 Arnaud, J.; J.C. Quilici; and G.
Riviére.** High-altitude haematology: Quechua-Aymara comparisons (Annals of Human Biology [Taylor and Francis, London] 8 : 6, Nov./Dec. 1981, p. 573–578, bibl., tables)

Hematological studies carried out at altitudes between 450 m and 4800 m on 1885 Quechua and Aymara (64 percent men, 36 percent women) suggest Aymara's greater adaptability to high altitude (characterized by increase in red cell count and concentration and decrease in red cell volume). Adaptive phenomena observed in Quechua were reversible whereas they persisted in Aymara when they migrated to lowlands.

1745 Beall, Cynthia M. A comparison of chest morphology in high altitude Asian and Andean populations (WSU/HB, 54 : 1, Feb. 1982, p. 145–163, bibl., tables)

Compares chest widths and depths of Nepalese Tibetans (3800 m) and Peruvian Quechua (4000 m). Tibetan population had small chest dimensions during growth, perhaps reflecting their shorter statures. As adults, Tibetan males had similar statures and chest depths as Quecha, but smaller widths. Females did not differ in chest dimensions, but Quechua were taller.

1746 ———. Optimal birthweights in Peruvian populations at high and low altitudes (AJPA, 56 : 3, Nov. 1981, p. 209–216, bibl, graphs, tables)

Examines concept of "optimum" birthweight in high (3860 m) and low (600 m) altitude areas of Peru in data derived from hospital records. High altitude population had lower mean birth weight and lower optimum birth weight which suggests that it is closer to its optimum birthweight distribution than sea level population. Results were interpreted in context of stabilizing selection.

1747 Bogin, Barry and Robert B. MacVean. Body composition and nutritional status of urban Guatemalan children and high and low socioeconomic class (AJPA, 55 : 4, Aug. 1981, p. 543–551, bibl., graphs, tables)

Analyzes socioeconomic differences in

anthropometric estimates of body composition in two samples of 981 urban children seven-13 years of age. High SES children fatter (skinfolds) and more muscular (estimated mid-arm muscle area) than low SES children.

1748 —— and ——. Ethnic and secular influences on the size and maturity of seven year old children living in Guatemala City (AJPA, 59:4, Dec. 1982, p. 393–398, bibl., tables)

Examines stature, weight, and skeletal maturity of high socioeconomic children in three ethnic groups and across two decades. Evidence indicates ethnic differences but no secular changes.

1749 —— and ——. Nutritional and biological determinants of body fat patterning in urban Guatemalan children (WSU/HB, 53:2, May 1981, p. 259–268, bibl., tables)

In sample of high and low socioeconomic status urban children, former had thicker skinfolds. Skinfolds of low socioeconomic children (chronic moderate energy malnutrition) showed greater reduction in triceps site (extremity) than in subscapular site (trunk). Discusses physiological significance of site differences in undernourished children.

1750 —— and ——. The relationship of socioeconomic status and sex to body size, skeletal maturation, and cognitive status of Guatemala City schoolchildren (SRCD, 54:1, Feb. 1983, p. 115–128, bibl., tables)

Analyzes influence of socioeconomic status (SES) on physical and cognitive growth in longitudinal data for 144 children. Middle and low SES children showed delayed growth and skeletal maturation compared to high SES children. When SES was controlled, there was no significant correlation between physical and cognitive growth status of girls and only few significant correlations for boys.

1751 Demographic and biological studies of the Warao Indians. Johannes Wilbert and Miguel Layrisse, editors. Los Angeles: Univeristy of California, Latin American Center Publications, 1980. 252 p.: appendix, ill., index, tables.

Collection of papers focuses on Warao Indians of Venezuela, and includes biological section. Variables considered include blood groups, HLA, red cell phosphates, immunoglobins, physical working capacity, anthropometry and biomedical observations.

1752 Desai, I.D. *et al.* Anthropometric and cycloergometric assessment of the nutritional status of the children of agricultural migrant workers in southern Brazil (ASCN/J, 34, Sept. 1981, p. 1925–1934, bibl., ill., tables)

Compares physical growth and work performance of 455 slum children and 475 private school children. Former showed consistently poorer anthropometric and ergometric status.

1753 Farid-Coupal, Nancy.; Mercedes López Contreras; and Hernán Méndez Castellano. The age at menarche in Carabobo, Venezuela with a note on the secular trend (Annals of Human Biology [Taylor and Francis, London] 8:3, May/June 1981, p. 283–288, bibl., tables)

Mean age of menarche (estimated by logits) in 955 sample from Carabobo was 12.68 ± 0.08 years. Comparisons with other Venezuelan data indicated secular trend.

1754 Faulhaber, Johanna. Correlaciones entre la talla de niños mexicanos y la de sus padres (UNAM/AA, 17, 1980, p. 233–248, bibl., tables)

Presents parent-child correlations for stature for sample of middle-class children born in Mexico City and followed longitudinally from one month to 10 years.

1755 García de Alba, G.J.E. *et al.* Algunos aspectos de la presión arterial en el área rural de Jalisco: pt. 1 (Salud Pública de México [México] 22:5, sept./oct. 1980, p. 487–500, bibl., graphs, map, tables)

Blood pressure was measured in 6010 persons, 15+ years of age, in 43 rural towns in Jalisco state. Weight and stature were related to blood pressure, data indicating no difference between blood pressures in overweight and underweight. There was a positive association between altitude above sea level and blood pressure.

1756 González, Gustavo; Isaac Crespo-Retes; and Roger Guerra-García. Secular change in growth of native children and adolescents at high altitudes: Puno, Peru, 3800 meters (AJPA, 58:2, June 1982, p. 191–195, bibl., tables)

Compares growth status (stature, weight, sitting height, leg length, chest circumference) of 969 native males, seven-70 years, from Puno (3800 m) measured in 1980 to similar data for 992 native males from same place measured in 1945. Although there is no secular increase in adult body size, stature and weight are larger at all ages between seven and 19 years in 1980 than in 1945. Differences may reflect earlier sexual maturation.

1757 Greksa, Lawrence P. *et al.* Maximal aerobic power in trained youths at high altitude (Annals of Human Biology [Taylor and Francis, London] 9 : 3, May/June 1982, p. 201–209, bibl., tables)

Measures maximal aerobic power in 25 male and 19 female well-nourished, trained swimmers (eight-19 years) resident in La Paz (3700 m) in effort to provide normative values for work capacity of high altitude youth. Values increased with age in males but not in females, and were 10–20 percent lower than in sea level athletes.

1758 ——— and Jere D. Haas. Physical growth and maximal work capacity in preadolescent boys at high-altitude (WSU/HB, 54 : 4, Dec. 1982, p. 677–695, bibl., graphs, tables)

Maximal exercise tests were given to 67 boys (eight-13 years) of European ancestry in La Paz, Bolivia. About half were born at high altitude, other half at low. Except for fatness and chest circumferences, samples were morphologically similar, and were also similar in weight and stature to US reference data. Maximal aerobic power did not differ between the groups, although high-altitude born boys had greater maximal work output.

1759 Guimarey, Luis Manuel; Aquiles Eugenico Piedrabuena; and Antonio de Azevedo Barros Filho. Treinamento e padronização do pessôal para realização de um estudo antropométrico em escolares (SLN/ALN, 31 : 2, junio 1981, p. 303–313, bibl, tables)

Methodological study aimed at developing model for training and standardization of personnel involved in anthropometric survey of school children.

1760 Haas, Jere D. *et al.* Altitude and infant growth in Bolivia: a longitudinal study (AJPA, 59 : 3, Nov. 1982, p. 251–262, bibl., graphs, tables)

Growth of 79 healthy, well-nourished lowland and highland infants was followed longitudinally through first postnatal year. Highland infants were shorter and lighter at birth and at certain measurement points during first year, but were fatter in triceps and subscapular skinfolds.

1761 Jordan, José R. Desarrollo humano en Cuba. La Habana: Editorial Científico-Técnica, 1979. 282 p.: bibl., graphs, ill., maps, tables.

Comprehensive summary of physical growth and maturation of representative sample of Cuban children (birth to 20 years of age). All regions of country are represented. Data include number of anthropometric dimensions, skeletal maturity (10 percent of national sample were X-rayed), secondary sex characteristics and age at menarche.

1762 Lasky, Robert E. *et al.* The relationship between physical growth and infant behavioral development in rural Guatemala (SRCD, 52, 1981, p. 219–226, bibl., tables)

Considers relationship between number of anthropometric indices and behavioral development during first two years of life in rural Guatemalan children. Strongly correlates length and weight with behavioral development. When these are statistically controlled, no anthropometric variable explains a significant proportion of the variance.

1763 ———; Robert E. Klein; Charles Yarbrough; and Kenneth D. Kallio. The predictive validity of infant assessments in rural Guatemala (SRCD, 52, 1981, p. 847–856, bibl., tables)

Assesses behavioral development in rural Guatemalan infants shortly after birth and at six, 15, and 24 months of age, and related to cognitive performance at three-seven years of age. Composite scale of infant development was modestly correlated with later cognitive performance. Results were similar to those for samples from developed nations.

1764 López Contreras, Mercedes *et al.* Estudios comparados de la estatura y edad de la menarquia segun estrato socioeconómica en Venezuela (SLN/ALN, 31 : 4, dic. 1981, p. 740–757, bibl., graphs, tables)

Retrospective overview of data for Venezuelan children (1936–78). Data indicate social class differences in growth and maturation and clear secular trend. Results are related to improved environmental conditions, particularly nutrition and hygiene.

1765 McCullough, John M. Secular trend for stature in adult male Yucatec Maya to 1968 (AJPA, 58:2, June 1982, p. 221–225, bibl., tables)

Compares statures of 64 Yucatecan Mayan males (18+ years of age) to results of previous studies. Evidence indicates no significant changes in mean stature since 1895, but decrease over past two centuries.

1766 Malina, Robert M. Human biology of urban and rural communities in the valley of Oaxaca, Mexico (*in* Ekologia populacji ludzkich. N. Wolański, editor. Wrocław, Poland: Ossolineum, 1982, p. 469–503)

Overview of growth and maturity status of urban and rural school children in Valley of Oaxaca includes selected comparisons with studies of Latin American children.

1767 —— and **Anthony N. Zavaleta.** Secular trend in the stature and weight of Mexican-American children in Texas between 1930 and 1970 (AJPA, 52:4, May 1980, p. 453–461, bibl., graphs, tables)

Stature and weight comparisons of school-aged Mexican-American children in Texas in 1930 and 1970 suggest only small secular change and rates which were considerably less than those for American blacks and whites, Europeans and Japanese.

1768 —— and **B.B. Little.** Comparison of TW1 and TW2 skeletal age differences in American black and white and in Mexican children 6–13 years of age (Annals of Human Biology [Taylor and Francis, London] 8:6, Nov./Dec. 1981, p. 543–548, bibl., tables)

Compares differences in Tanner-Whitehouse (TW) skeletal ages as derived from original (TW 1) and revised (TW 2) systems in American black and white and Mexican children, six-13 years. Within given chronological age and sex group, differences were similar in better-off black and white and in disadvantaged Mexican children.

1769 ——; **Peter H. Buschang; Wendy L. Aronson;** and **Henry A. Selby.** Aging in selected anthropometric dimensions in a rural Zapotec-speaking community in the valley of Oaxaca, Mexico (Social Science and Medicine [Pergamon Press, London] 16, 1982, p. 217–222)

Describes age changes and sex differences for stature, weight, arm circumference, triceps skinfold, mid-arm muscle circumference and grip strength in cross-sectional sample of 116 men and 113 women, 20–82 years. Secular changes in stature, after adjusting for aging effects, were minor.

1770 ——; ——; ——; and ——.
Childhood growth status of eventual migrants and sedentes in a rural Zapotec community in the valley of Oaxaca, Mexico (WSU/HB, 54:4, Dec. 1982, p. 709–716, bibl., tables)

Results of comparison in 306 children suggest no apparent selection for physical characteristics (23 in males, 20 in females) at ages six-15 years. If changes occur between sedentes and migrants, they apparently develop after migration.

1771 Maniero Alfert, Rogelio; Alma Armisen Penichet; and **Oscar Fregel Quesada.** Un método para estimar la capacidad física de trabajo (Revista Cubana de Higiene y Epidemiología [La Habana] 18:3, julio/sept. 1980, p. 222–226, bibl., graphs)

Presents nomogram for estimating peak oxygen consumption in Cuban males, 17–40 years of age. Similar to that offered by others, it is adjusted for Cuban climatic conditions and workers' anthropometric characteristics.

1772 Marcondes, Eduardo *et al.* Crescimento e desenvolvimento pubertario em crianças e adolescentes brasileiros. v. 1, Metodologia. v. 2, Altura e peso. Rio de Janeiro: Editora Brasileira de Ciências, 1982. 2 v. (206, 117 p.): bibl., graphs, ill., tables.

Vol. 1 describes methodology used to develop growth charts for São Paulo's Santo André municipality. Notes procedures for sampling (n=6794 youth, 10–20 years of age), measuring for several anthropometric dimensions, and for assessing secondary sex characteristics. In addition, presents region's selected demographic and sociological characteristics. Vol. 2 presents tables and graphs of reference data for stature and weight of Brazilian children (birth to 20 years). Includes comparisons to US and Cuban surveys, and to 1968 Brazilian survey.

1773 **Ramos Rodríguez, Rosa María.** El
ritmo estacional en la aparición de la
menarquía de un grupo de adolescentes mexicanas (UNAM/AA, 17, 1980, p. 269–279,
tables)
Describes seasonal occurrence of
menarche in sample of 808 (12–20 years of
age) from Mexico City. Relative frequency of
occurrence of menarche was greatest in June
(12.3 percent), with five months varying between 9.2 percent and 9.8 percent (May, July,
August, Sept., Dec.) and four months varying
between 6.1 percent and 6.8 percent (Feb.,
March, April, Nov.).

1774 **Saco-Pollitt, Carmen.** Birth in the
Peruvian Andes: physical and behavioral consequences in the neonate (SRCD,
52, 1981, p. 839–846, bibl., tables)
Full-term neonates (20 males and
20 females in each altitude group) born to
healthy mothers at 4300 m and 150 m were
evaluated at 24–36 and 48–60 hours of life.
High altitude infants were shorter and lighter,
had smaller arm circumferences, and presented more signs of behavioral immaturity
in interactive and motoric processes compared to sea-level neonates. There were
no differences in head circumference and
skinfolds.

1775 **Sáenz Faulhaber, María Elena.** Crecimiento y maduración diferencial en
una zona marginada de la capital mexicana
(UNAM/AA, 17, 1980, p. 281–294, tables)
Considers relationship between skeletal maturation and several anthropometric
dimensions in 400 children, eight and 10
years of age.

1776 **Sandoval Arriaga, Alfonso.** Variaciones
de algunos carácteres antropométricos
en relación con la clase social y el tamaño de
la familia (UNAM/AA, 17, 1980, p. 249–268,
bibl., tables)
Examines effects of social class, family
size and birth order on the stature, weight
and ponderal index of 185 Mexico City
males, 18–25 years of age. One-half were upper class, other semi-skilled laborers. In contrast to other studies, sample showed no
significant family size differences in stature.

1777 **Solomons, Hope C.** Standardization of
the Denver developmental screening
test on infants from Yucatán, Mexico (International Journal of Rehabilitation Research

[G. Schindele, Heidelberg, FRG] 5:2, 1982,
p. 179–189, bibl., tables)
Denver Developmental Screening Test
was standardized on 288 Yucatán infants,
two-54 weeks, divided equally by age, sex,
and sociocultural group.

1778 **Spurr, G.B.; J.C. Reina; M. Barac-
Nieto; and M.G. Maksud.** Maximum
oxygen consumption of nutritionally normal
white, mestizo and black Colombian boys,
6–16 years of age (WSU/HB, 54:3, Sept.
1982, p. 553–574, bibl., tables)
Maximum oxygen consumption (absolute and per unit body weight) of 106 white,
217 mestizo, and 70 black males showed no
racial nor socioeconomic differences.

1779 ———; **M. Barac-Neito; and M.G.
Maksud.** Childhood undernutrition:
implications for adult work capacity and productivity (in Environmental stress: individual human adaptations. L.J. Folinsbee et al.,
editors. New York: Academic Press, 1978,
p. 165–181, bibl., graphs, tables)
On basis of detailed anthropometric
and working capacity data for Colombian
children and supplementary information for
several Latin American countries, draws implication that malnutrition in young children
may result in depressed work capacities as
adults and further exacerbate depressed productivity of populations in developing countries due to their smaller size.

1780 **Stinson, Sara.** The effect of high altitude on the growth of children of
high socioeconomic status in Bolivia (AJPA,
59:1, Sept. 1982, p. 61–71, bibl., graphs,
tables)
Examines growth status of 323 well-off
children of European ancestry (eight-14
years) resident at 3200–3600 m altitude for
varying periods. Although children who always lived at high altitude were smaller, evidence indicated only small effect of altitude
relative to socioeconomic and genetic factors.

1781 **Torun, Benjamin; Judith McGuire;
and Rubén D. Mendoza.** Energy cost of
activities and tasks of women from a rural
region of Guatemala (Nutrition Research
[Pergamon Press, New York] 2:2, 1982,
p. 127–136, appendix, bibl., tables)
Energy costs of various domestic and
agricultural activities was measured by indirect calorimetry in 56 women, 16–49 years
of age, from rural village.

1782 Van Wering, Elisabeth R. The anthropometric status of Aruban children: 1974 (WSU/HB, 53 : 1, Feb. 1981, p. 117–135, bibl., graphs, tables)

Presents results of cross-sectional study of 2659 Aruban children, zero-14 years. Variables include stature, weight, sitting height, skinfold thickness, arm circumference, pubertal stages, and menarche. Growth and maturity status of Aruban children is comparable to other Caribbean ethnic groups of high socioeconomic background.

1783 ———. The secular growth trend on Aruba between 1954 and 1974 (WSU/HB, 53 : 1, Feb. 1981, p. 105–115, bibl., tables)

Compares stature, weight, and sitting height in Aruban children measured in 1954 and 1974. Secular trend has occurred, but growth of Aruban children still lags behind reference data for Dutch children.

1784 Villanueva, María and Vivian L. Villaseñor. Brote dental en un grupo de niños de nivel socioeconómico medio de la Ciudad de México y panorama general sobre la primera dentición en distantos grupos humanos (UNAM/AA, 17, 1980, p. 295–306, bibl., tables)

Presents general overview of factors which may influence dental age and data for eruption of first incisor in sample of Mexican children. Taller and heavier children had earlier eruption of this tooth.

1785 Zavaleta, Anthony N. and Robert M. Malina. Growth and body composition of Mexican-American boys 9 through 14 years of age (AJPA, 57 : 3, March 1982, p. 261–271, bibl., tables)

Describes growth status (19 dimensions) and densitometric estimates of body composition for 95 Mexican-American boys, nine-14 years, from lower socioeconomic background. Boys are smaller than US reference data and have greater body density, thus less fatness. Offers equations for prediction of body density in Mexican-American boys.

NUTRITIONAL ANTHROPOLOGY

1786 Alvarez, María de la Luz; Dora Mikacic; Anna Ottenberger; and María Ester Salazar. Características de familias urbanas con lactante desnutrido (SLN/ALN, 29 : 2, junio 1979, p. 220–232, bibl., graphs, tables)

Examines characteristics of families with malnourished infants in Santiago, Chile. Following features were characteristic: low socioeconomic level; low maternal affectivity index; deficient parent-child communication; isolation from rest of community; and physical environment deficient in color stimuli.

1787 ———; J. Alvear; L. Cousino; and M.T. Saitúa. Influencia del medio en la desnutrición infantil (SLN/ALN, 30 : 2, junio 1980, p. 254–263, bibl., graphs)

Studies socioeconomic and cultural characteristics of families in Santiago, Chile, as conditioning factors of malnutrition in 63 full-term infants. Compares experimental (45 infants, small-for-date) and control (18 infants, adequate weight for gestational age) groups at three years of age.

1788 Amat y León, Carlos. La alimentación en el Perú. Lima: Centro de Investigacion de la Universidad del Pacífico, 1981. 306 p.: ill.

Comprehensive analysis of nutritional status of Peru based primarily upon National Survey of Food Consumption (Aug. 1971-Aug. 1972) consists of four sections: 1) family budget and food consumption; 2) econometric analysis of demand by expense and foods; 3) nutritional diagnosis per calories and nutrients; and 4) political-economic applications of results and nutritional policies.

1789 Araya, Héctor and Guillermo Arroyave. Relación del contenido energético proveniente de grasas y de proteínas como indicador de la potencialidad energética-proteínica de las dietas de poblaciones (SLN/ALN, 29 : 1, marzo 1979, p. 103–112, bibl., tables)

Presents fat-calorie to protein-calorie ratio as complementary index in evaluating potential of diets to meet population's protein and calorie needs, especially where diet's energy density is low (e.g., rural areas of developing countries).

1790 ———; Bertha García; and Guillermo Arroyave. Estudio dietético en embarazadas de Santa María Cauque, Guatemala: pt. 1, Variabilidad de los indicadores proteínicos y su análisis por tiempo de comidas (SLN/ALN, 31 : 1, marzo 1981, p. 108–117, bibl,. tables)

Studies distribution of protein energy ratio, amino acid score, and protein value in three daily meals (breakfast, lunch, dinner) of the diet of pregnant women from Santa María Cauque, Guatemala. Variability of protein energy ratio indicators was similar to that for developed countries.

1791 Arroyave, Guillermo; Luis A. Mejía; and Juan R. Aguilar. The effect of vitamin A fortification of sugar on the serum vitamin A levels of preschool Guatemalan children: a longitudinal evaluation (ASCN/J, 34:1, Jan. 1981, p. 41–49, bibl., figures, tables)

Analyzes results of a vitamin A fortification program. Natural dietary vitamin A intake remained unchanged throughout, but fortification of sugar significantly increased serum vitamin A levels.

1792 Arteaga, Antonio *et al.* Cambios en el estado nutricional de la nodriza durante lactancia exclusiva (SLN/ALN, 31:4, dic. 1981, p. 766–781, bibl., graphs, tables)

Measures several anthropometric and nutritional parameters in attempt to examine effects of breast feeding on 54 lactating women during interval between 40 and 180 days. Only one significant change was detected, loss of body weight. No changes were detected in hemoglobin levels or in serum protein and albumin.

1793 Bailey, Wilma. Clinical undernutrition in the Kingston/St. Andrew metropolitan area: 1967–1976 (Social Science and Medicine [Pergamon Press, New York] 15D, 1981, p. 471–477, bibl., figures, tables)

Incorporates variety of sociocultural information using simple and stepwise multiple regression models. Unemployment of mothers accounted for 87 percent of variation in spatial distribution of undernutrition. Relatively unimportant variables were infant feeding practices, family stability, family size, etc.

1794 Barac-Nieto, M. *et al.* Body composition during nutritional repletion of several undernourished men (ASCN/J, 32, May 1979, p. 981–991, bibl., graphs, tables)

Studies body composition in 19 severely undernourished adult males (mean age 39.2 years, mean stature, 156.4 cm) from rural area of Colombia to evaluate extent and time course of changes occurring with nu-

tritional repletion. Major compositional changes occurred in body fat and body cell mass, independently of each other.

1795 ———; G.B. Spurr; H.W. Dahners; and M.G. Maksud. Aerobic work capacity and endurance during nutritional repletion of severely undernourished men (ASCN/J, 33, Nov. 1980, p. 2268–2275, bibl., tables)

Maximal oxygen consumption increased during nutritional rehabilitation of severely undernourished sedentary adult males from rural Colombia only when dietary protein was increased from 27 to 100 g/day. Adequate caloric intake maintained prior to increased protein content of diet had no effect on maximal oxygen consumption.

1796 Blank, Paul W. Wet season vegetable protein use among riverine tropical American cultures: a neglected adaption? (Social Science and Medicine [Pergamon Press, New York] 15D, 1981, p. 463–469, figures)

Macusi Indians of northern Amazonia depend on maize, beans and vegetable proteins during rainy season. Such use may represent selective adoption of maize and other Mesoamerican crops by tropical lowland groups who use them to overcome seasonal scarcities of animal protein.

1797 Cerqueira, María T.; Martha McMurry Fry; and William E. Connor. The food and nutrient intakes of the Tarahumara Indians of Mexico (ASCN/J, 32, April 1979, p. 905–915, tables)

Diet of 174 adults and 198 children, obtained by interviews and field observations and composed primarily of beans and corn, provided high intake of complex carbohydrate and was low in fat and cholesterol.

1798 Chagnon, Napoleon A. and **Raymond B. Hames.** La "hipótesis protéica" y la adaptación indígena a la Cuenca del Amazonas: una revisión crítica de los datos y de la teoría (Interciencia [Washington] 5:6, Nov./Dec. 1980, p. 346–358, bibl., table)

Reviews literature on cultural ecology, stressing methodological deficiencies in "protein hypothesis" for tribal warfare (i.e., war results from competition over scarce animal protein resources). Special attention is given to Yanomama who apparently have higher animal protein intake per capita than many industrialized areas.

1799 Dahners, H.W.; M. Barac-Nieto; and G.B. Spurr. Development of standards for rapid assessment of nutritional status: Colombian children (ASCN/J, 34, Jan. 1981, p. 110–112, appendix, table)

Describes method for deriving polynomial equations which describe weight and height for age and weight for height of children between six and 16 years of age.

1800 Delgado, Hernán; Reynaldo Martorell; Elena Brineman; and Robert E. Klein. Nutrition and length of gestation (Nutrition Research [Pergamon Press, New York] 2:2, 1982, p. 117–126, figures, tables)

Examines effect of a food supplementation on length of gestation in 830 singleton births to rural Guatemalan women. Those who consumed more protein-energy or energy supplement had significantly longer lengths of gestation.

1801 ———; ———; and Robert E. Klein. Nutrition, lactation, and birth interval components in rural Guatemala (ASCN/J, 35, June 1982, p. 1468–1476, figure, tables)

Examines effect of maternal nutritional status and food supplementation ingested by infant on duration of postpartum amenorrhea and duration of menstrual interval. By determining amount of breastmilk available, hence frequency, duration and intensity of suckling, hypothesis that maternal nutritional status is indirectly negatively related to length of postpartum amenorrhea. No association with length of menstruating interval.

1802 Fagundes-Neto, Ulysses et al. Observations of the Alto Xingu Indians, Central Brazil, with special reference to nutritional evaluation in children (ASCN/J, 34:10, Oct. 1981, p. 2229–2235, figures, tables)

Anthropometric assessments of nutritional status (weight for height and arm circumference for height) showed that approximately 96–97 percent of preschool children were adequately nourished.

1803 Fajardo, Luis F.; Hermilson Leal; Fanny Victoria; and Carmen E. González. Intolerancia a la leche en niños colombianos, su prevalencia y relación con la mala absorción de lactosa (SLN/ALN, 29:3, sept. 1979, p. 329–339, bibl., tables)

Evaluates gastrointestinal symptoms in response to graded amounts of milk intake in sample of 121 children, two-10 years, from orphanage. Prevalence of milk intolerance varied, but was minimal when milk was given in usual amounts. Ethnic background, sex or state of malnutrition were not related to lactose malabsorption.

1804 Flores, Marina and José Aranda-Pastor. Evaluación dietética a nivel nacional en Costa Rica: cambios en una década (SLN/ALN, 30:3, sept. 1980, p. 432–450, bibl., tables)

Compares dietary data from two nutritional evaluations of Costa Rican population (1966–67 and 1978) for food consumption, and energy and nutrient intakes for families and children and for urban and rural areas. Substantial improvements were especially apparent in rural areas and among preschool children.

1805 ——— and Vernon W. Bent. Canasta familiar de alimentos: definición y metodología (SLN/ALN, 30:1, marzo 1980, p. 58–74, bibl., tables)

Explains definition and methodology of "family food basket" concept in nutritional programs. Uses El Salvador's national survey data to define "family food basket of El Salvador."

1806 Fraser, H.S. An overview of obesity in the Caribbean: its prevalence, prevention and treatment (Cajanus [St. Augustine, Trinidad and Tobago] 13:3, 1980, p. 131–138, tables)

Reviews causes and complications of obesity in the Caribbean. Prevalence of obesity varies from five to 13 percent among men and from 24 to 63 percent among women in Barbados, Guyana, Trinidad and Jamaica.

1807 García García, Jorge. La situación de desnutrición en Colombia (CEDE/DS, 4, julio 1980, p. 337–356, tables)

Incidence of malnutrition in Colombia is indirectly estimated at about 40 percent of the population (20 percent urban, 70 percent rural). Magnitude of effective effort to eradicate malnutrition (given present socioeconomic organization) is estimated as considerably larger.

1808 García Ulloa, Aura. Valoración de dos procedimientos para estimar el consumo de alimentos en niños de edad preescolar (SLN/ALN, 30:3, sept. 1980, p. 384–399, bibl., tables)

Studies food consumption of preschool children (61 families and 61 children under six years) from urban area of three small towns in Boyacá and Cauca Depts., Colombia. Discusses data for certain nutrients in terms of average "equivalent child" and family average, and their utility in surveys.

1809 González Vigil, Fernando; Carlos Parodi Zevallos; and Fabián Tume Torres. Alimentos y transnacionales: los complejos sectoriales del trigo y avícola en el Perú. Lima: DESCO, Centro de Estudios y Promoción del Desarrollo, 1980. 286 p.: bibl., ill.

Two-part book deals with Peru's wheat and poultry industries and covers their history, international capitalist system, and multinationals' control. Interesting statistics: food production volume in 1979 fell 11 percent relative to 1973; in 1972–78 cost of unit of protein increased by factor of six, while cost of poultry tripled; per capital caloric intake in Lima decreased from 2031 in 1972 to 1538 in 1979; per capital protein intake over same period fell from 58 to 45 grams.

1810 Gordon, Antonio M., Jr. Nutritional status of Cuban refugees: a field study on the health and nutriture of refugees processed at Opa Locka, Florida (ASCN/J, 35, March 1982, p. 582–590, tables)

Describes nutritional status and foods consumed by 138 Cuban refugees.

1811 Graham, George G. *et al.* Determinants of growth among poor children: effect of expenditure for food on nutrient sources (ASCN/J, 34:4, April 1981, p. 562–567, figure, tables)

Compares diets of 111 children from 20 typically poor urban families in Lima, Peru, and of 12 children from six economically better-off families. Significant portion of variation related to milk and meat consumption.

1812 —— *et al.* Determinants of growth among poor children: nutrient intake-achieved growth relationships (ASCN/J, 34:4, April 1981, p. 539–554, tables)

Seven-day individual weighed dietary intakes and anthropometric dimensions were determined in 123 children, two-19 years,

from 26 urban poor families in Lima, Peru. Polynomial regression analysis identified percentage protein from animal sources and percentage fat calories as having significant quadratic as well as linear correlations with achieved growth.

1813 —— *et al.* Determinants of growth among poor children: relation of nutrient intakes to expenditure for food (ASCN/J, 34:4, April 1981, p. 555–561, tables)

Growth status and nutrient intake of 123 children from 26 urban poor families in Lima, Peru, were related to per capita expenditure for food. Those from better-off families were taller and heavier, and had significantly higher calorie and protein intake. Availability of money for food means increase in animal and protein fat intakes.

1814 Gueri, Miguel. Childhood malnutrition in the Caribbean (Cajanus [St. Augustine, Trinidad and Tobago] 15:2, 1982, p. 76–83, bibl., graphs, tables)

One-fourth to one-half of the children under five years of age in the English-speaking Caribbean community are malnourished (underweight for age). Discusses factors related to undernutrition and implications for food and nutritional policy.

1815 ——. Some economic implications of breast-feeding (Cajanus [St. Augustine, Trinidad and Tobago] 13:2, 1980, p. 85–94, tables)

Cost of breastmilk substitutes in Caribbean is four to five times higher than cost of supplementing mother's diet during lactation. In terms of foreign exchange, data suggest that it costs a country about twice as much to import breastmilk substitutes as it does to import commodities required to provide supplementary food for mothers.

1816 Gurney, J. Michael. The problems of feeding the weaning age group: an overview of available solutions (Cajanus [St. Augustine, Trinidad and Tobago] 12:1, 1979, p. 43–51, bibl.)

Briefly reviews history of weaning foods with Caribbean emphasis. Describes characteristics of ideal weaning foods: energy dense, nutrients in proportion, digestible, reasonably germ-free, given frequently, cheap enough and labor-saving. Weaning children receive inadequate food because there's a lack of resources, knowledge, and facilities.

1817 **Hakim, Peter** and **Giorgio Solimano.** Development, reform, and malnutrition in Chile. Cambridge, Mass.: MIT Press, 1978. 91 p.: bibl., index (International nutrition policy series; 4)

Historical review of nutritional deprivation in Chile (1930–70). Briefly examines food consumption, clinical surveys of nutritional status, and patterns of development and reform. More attention is given to nutritional programs and specifically milk distribution program. Emphasizes influence of political and economic factors.

1818 **Hernández, Mercedes; Judith Aguirre; Leticia Serrano;** and **José del Carmen Moreno.** Evaluación de las actividades de campo del plan educativo para la alimentación de la población rural (Salud Pública de México [México] 21:2, marzo/abril 1979, p. 135–143, bibl., graphs, maps)

Concerns nutrition education program aimed at improving child feeding practices, increasing maternal food consumption and diversifying family diets in 27 rural regions of Mexico. Samples of 50–60 families were interviewed. Changes were more prominent in northern and gulf coast regions than in south and Yucatan peninsula.

1819 **Immink, Maarten D.C.** and **Fernando E. Viteri.** Energy intake and productivity of Guatemalan sugarcane cutters: pts. 1/2 (Journal of Development Economics [North-Holland Publishing Co., Amsterdam] 9, 1981, p. 251–271, bibl., graphs, tables)

Studies of 158 sugarcane cutters who were moderately energy deficient indicates that energy supplementation program was generally effective in raising daily energy intake and expenditure levels. However, increased energy availability did not result in increased energy expenditure at work, or in an increased supply of work units.

1820 ——; ——; and **Ronald W. Helms.** Energy intake over the life cycle and human capital formation in Guatemalan sugarcane cutters (UC/EDCC, 30:2, Jan. 1982, p. 351–372, bibl., tables)

Examines size and estimated body composition, daily energy intake and productivity, and earnings (harvest, annual, lifetime) in 158 adult sugarcane cutters. Increased energy intake during childhood and adolescence had positive effect in adulthood.

1821 ——; ——; and ——. Food substitution with worker feeding programs: energy supplementation in Guatemalan sugarcane workers (ASCN/J, 34, Oct. 1981, p. 2145–2150, bibl., graphs)

In sample of 518 moderately energy deficient workers, significant increases in total daily energy intake were obtained with high energy supplement, but by less than energy content of supplement. Degree of substitution with energy supplementation was not related to energy intake status of workers' households.

1822 **Jenkins, Carol L.** Factors in the aetiology of poor growth in Belize (Cajanus [St. Augustine, Trinidad and Tobago] 15:3, 1982, p. 172–184, bibl., tables)

Reports results of investigation of demographic, dietary and health-related factors in nutritional status of Belizean preschool children. Three variables correctly classified poor and better-than-average growth classes: frequency and severity of diarrhea, age at introduction of solid foods, number of children in household.

1823 ——. Patterns of growth and malnutrition among preschoolers in Belize (AJPA, 56:2, Oct. 1981, p. 169–178, bibl., graphs, tables)

In anthropometric survey (stature, weight, arm circumference) of two districts, about 25 percent of children, birth to five years, showed growth stunting and 25 percent showed wasting. Maya and Garifuna (Black Carib) showed more malnutrition than other groups.

1824 ——. A report on contemporary Belizean foodways (BISRA/BS, 10:3/4, 1982, p. 2–9)

Brief descriptive overview of Belizean food patterns. Traditional patterns of food consumption still in evidence are being eroded by general acculturative process by which native foods and values are replaced with imported ones.

1825 **Johnson, Allen** and **Clifford A. Behrens.** Nutritional criteria in Machiguenga food production decisions: a linear-programming analysis (Human Ecology [Plenum, New York] 10:2, 1982, p. 167–189, tables)

Examines degree of fit between observed food production and that predicted with linear model of "diet problem" and discusses factors underlying discrepancies for Machiguenga Indians of Peruvian Amazon.

1826 Johnston, Francis E. *et al.* An analysis of environmental variables and factors associated with growth failure in a Mexican village (WSU/HB, 52:4, Dec. 1980, p. 627–637, bibl., tables)

Principal components analysis of growth records of 276 rural children indicate that malnourished children came from poorer families with less educated parents who were smaller in linear dimensions. Results suggest utility of parental variables as screening device.

1827 Kohn de Brief, Fritzi. Evaluación nutricional de la comunidad indígena Chaparro, tribu Yukpa de la Sierra de Perijá. Caracas: Universidad Central de Venezuela, Facultad de Ciencias Económicas y Sociales, División de Publicaciones, 1976. 63 p.: ill. (Colección Antropología y sociología)

Summary of nutritional survey of Chapparo subtribe of Yukpa, in Perijá, Zulia, Venezuela. Protein malnutrition and caloric imbalance are common in children. Diet had little meat, milk products, green vegetables, and fruit. Discusses interrelationship of social, economic, and cultural factors in public health and nutritional status.

McKay, Harrison *et al.* Improving cognitive ability in chronically deprived children. See item **4399**.

1828 McMurry, Martha P.; William E. Conner; and **María T. Cerqueira.** Dietary cholesterol and the plasma lipids and lipoproteins in the Tarahumara Indians: a people habituated to a low cholesterol diet after weaning (ASCN/J, 35, April 1982, p. 741–744, ill., table)

Eight Tarahumara men participated in metabolic study to measure responsiveness to their plasma cholesterol levels to dietary cholesterol.

1829 Martorell, R.; C. Yarbrough; and **R.E. Klein.** Protein-calorie supplementation, body size, and skeletal maturity in three-year old Guatemalan children (Studies in Physical Anthropology [Institute of Anthropology, Polish Academy of Sciences, Warszawa] 6, 1980, p. 23–32, tables)

Protein-calorie intake was more strongly related to growth in length than to

skeletal maturity, so that effect of supplementation on body size was largely independent of changes in maturity.

1830 Mejía, Luis A. and **Guillermo Arroyave.** The effect of vitamin A fortification of sugar on iron metabolism in preschool children in Guatemala (ASCN/J, 36:1, July 1982, p. 87–93, ill., tables)

Evaluation of national vitamin A fortification program indicated that fortification of sugar with vitamin A had favorable effect on iron metabolism and nutritional status.

1831 Mora, José O. *et al.* The effects of nutritional supplementation on physical growth of children at risk of malnutrition (ASCN/J, 34, Sept. 1981, p. 1885–1892, ill., tables)

Studies effect of food supplementation on physical growth during last trimester of pregnancy and first three years of life in families at risk of malnutrition in Bogota's urban slums. Growth status improved but not sufficiently to close gap between low and high socioeconomic groups.

1832 ——; Stephen G. Sellers; Jorge Suescun; and **M. Guillermo Herrera.** The impact of supplementary feeding and home education on physical growth of disadvantaged children (Nutrition Research [Pergamon Press, New York] 1:3, 1981, p. 213–225, ill., tables)

Effectiveness of supplementary feeding and home education in augmenting physical growth of children during first three years of life was assessed longitudinally in urban Colombian families with malnourished children.

1833 Omawale. Energy and major nutrients in some of Guyana's less known edible plants (Cajanus [St. Augustine, Trinidad and Tobago] 12:3, 1979, p. 150–154)

Reports results of chemical analysis of Guyana's less known edible plants. *Kuru* (*Astrocaryum tucuma*) is possibly good source of edible oil, while *sijan* leaves (*Moringa oleifera*) may contribute significant quantities of protein to coastal groups' diet. *Bura bura* (*Solanum stramonifolium*) and wild cocoa seeds (*Bombax aquaticum*) may be significant sources of energy for children.

1834 ——. The nutritional significance of root and tuber crop development as staples in the Caribbean community (SLN/

ALN, 29:3, Sept. 1979, p. 311-325, bibl., tables)

Describes competition between cereals and root crops as staples. Cites evidence to show essential adequacy of protein in root crops, except plantain and cassava, and for all human groups except perhaps some infants.

1835 ———. Political constraints to nutritional improvement: the case of Guyana (International Journal of Health Services [Baywood Publishing Co., Farmingdale, N.Y.] 12:2, 1982, p. 231–247, tables)

Among important factors underlying malnutrition in Guyana are low national production, inequitable income distribution, and maladaptive cultural practices. Concludes that for Guyana, the political process is a limiting factor which must be altered before significant nutritional improvement can occur.

1836 Overholt, Catherine *et al.* The effects of nutritional supplementation on the diets of low-income families at risk of malnutrition (ASCN/J, 36, Dec. 1982, p. 1153–1161, ill., tables)

Studies effects of food supplementation program on family diet patterns and protein-energy intake in families nutritionally at risk in Bogotá.

1837 Plail, Roger O. and **Janet M.S. Young.** A nutritional haematological and sociological study of a group of Chilean children under the age of five years (Journal of Biosocial Science [Blackwell's, Oxford, England] 9, 1977, p. 35 3–369, ill., tables)

In a sample of 108 children from Renaico, Malleco, Chile, undernutrition of the first degree (Gómez scale) was present in 41.5 percent, second degree in 11.4 percent, and third degree in 1.0 percent. About 46 percent of the children were anemic, presumably due to iron deficiency.

1838 Pollitt, Ernesto. Child poverty in South America: reflections on its magnitude, and the basic-need developmental approach; a retrospect on the International Year of the Child (SLN/ALN, 31:2, junio 1981, p. 235–249, bibl., graphs, tables)

Overview postulates that intervention programs (e.g., nutrition, health, and education) directed to economically deprived children will not be successful and are not representative of basic-needs approach unless they also attend to broader economic and social needs of families and communities.

1839 ———; **Robert Halpern;** and **Patricia Eskenasy.** Poverty and malnutrition in Latin America: early childhood intervention programs: a report to the Ford Foundation. New York: Praeger, 1980. 162 p.: bibl.

Comprehensive report on interrelationships between poverty, malnutrition, and cognitive development in South America. Evaluates intervention programs and results of three case studies (Antioquia, Colombia; Puno, Peru; Caracas, Venezuela).

1840 Quiroz, Sara Eugenia *et al.* Aspectos sociales del consumo de energia y proteina en un grupo de gestantes (SLN/ALN, 31:1, marzo 1981, p. 118–132, bibl., tables)

Reports results of dietary survey (weighed intake/24 hours) of 64 pregnant women living in Huamantla, Tlaxcala, Mexico and its environs. Family organization had significant relationship to levels of energy and protein intake, extended families presenting better energy/protein ratio than nuclear families.

1841 Ramsey, Frank C. Protein-energy malnutrition in Barbados: the role of continuity of care in management. New York: Josiah Macy, Jr. Foundation, 1979. 173 p.: bibl., ill. (Macy Foundation series on international problems of health care and medical education)

Overview of health and nutritional status of Barbados' population, with specific focus on problems relating to protein-energy malnutrition (i.e., policy, intervention programs, care, etc.). Chapters dealing with Barbados' history and its health problems, and with history of concepts related to preschool malnutrition are especially interesting.

1842 Riley, Robert A. A dietary survey of downward Indian migrants and long-term coastal residents living in southern coastal Peru (SLN/ALN, 29:1, marzo 1979, p. 69–102, bibl., tables)

Studies alterations in food consumption patterns of downward Indian migrants in three southern coastal communities in Valley of Tambo. Results indicate that dietary levels of calories and nutrients were adequate; dietary intakes of more recent migrants were less; there was a minimal retention of highland foodstuffs in total food inventory; residents in Valley of Tambo had higher intakes than highland residents.

1843 Rivera, Roberto *et al.* Bioavailability of iron- and copper-supplemented milk for Mexican school children (ASCN/J, 36, Dec. 1982, p. 1162–1169, ill., tables)

Examines issue of fortification of dairy products with trace metals in school lunch programs. Results indicate that milk can be excellent vehicle for iron and copper supplementation.

1844 Sellers, Stephen G.; José O. Mora; Charles M. Super; and M. Guillermo Herrera. The effects of nutritional supplementation and home education on children's diets (Nutrition Reports International [Los Altos, Calif.] 26:4, Oct. 1982, p. 727–714, ill., tables)

Experimental program of diet supplementation and home education was attempted on children (18 and 36 months) at risk for malnutrition in Bogotá.

1845 Sheffer, M.L.; S.M. Grantham-McGregor; and S.J. Ismail. The social environment of malnourished children compared with that of other children in Jamaica (Journal of Biosocial Science [Blackwell's, Oxford, England], 13, 1981, p. 19–30, tables)

Jamaican mothers of malnourished children are characterized by poverty rather than poor maternal-child relationships. Comparisons with other countries suggest that ecology of malnutrition varies in different cultures.

1846 Sigulem, Dirce Maria and Eliete Salomon Tudisco. Aleitamento natural em diferentes classes de renda no municipio de São Paulo (SLN/ALN, 30:3, sept. 1980, p. 400–416, bibl., tables)

High percentage of malnutrition in São Paulo's low income families is related in part to early weaning. Examines relationship between breast feeding and income, including maternal attitudes, reasons for early weaning, and role of health services.

1847 Simmons, William K. *et al.* A survey of the anemia status of preschool age children and pregnant and lactating women in Jamaica (ASCN/J, 35, Feb. 1982, p. 319–326, ill., tables)

Island-wide anemia survey was conducted on pregnant and lactating women and preschool children. Sixty-one and six/tenths

percent of pregnant women had Hb levels below 11.0 g/dl, while 58.7 percent of lactating women had Hb levels below 12 g/dl. Among preschool children, 69.1 percent had Hb levels below 11 g/dl.

1848 —— and **J. Michael Gurney.** Nutritional anemia in the English-speaking Caribbean and Suriname (ASCN/J, 35, Feb. 1982, p. 327–337, ill., tables)

Reviews nutritional anemia in the English-speaking Caribbean and Surinam. Anemia effects primarily preschool children and lactating women, and most common cause is iron deficiency.

1849 Spurr, G.B.; J.C. Reina; and M. Barac-Nieto. Marginal malnutrition in school-aged Colombian boys: anthropometry and maturation (ASCN/J, 37, Jan. 1983, p. 119–132, ill., tables)

Size attained, growth velocities, skinfolds, mid-arm and head circumferences, and sexual maturation were all depressed in nutritionally deprived boys (six-16 years) compared to Colombian reference data.

1850 ——; **M. Barac-Nieto; H. Lotero; and H.W. Dahners.** Comparisons of body fat estimated from total body water and skinfold thicknesses of undernourished men (ASCN/J, 34, Sept. 1981, p. 1944–1953, ill., tables)

Among Colombian adult males, body composition estimates based on total body water and skinfolds were quite good in mildly undernourished subjects, but were progressively poorer as nutritional compromise became more severe.

1851 ——; ——; and **M.G. Maksud.** Functional assessment of nutritional status: heart rate response to submaximal work (ASCN/J, 32, April 1979, p. 767–778, bibl., graphs, tables)

Heart rate response to submaximal treadmill work was calculated using heart rates and oxygen intakes during maximal oxygen consumption test in 88 normally nourished Colombian adults (sugarcane cutters and loaders) and 49 nutritionally compromised Colombian adults from rural areas. Age range was 18–56 years. Increased severity of malnutrition was associated with increased heart rate response to same submaximal work loads.

1852 Stetler, Harrison C. and Alan Y. Huong. Epidemiología de la anemia en niños de edad preescolar y sus madres en El Salvador (SLN/ALN, 31:4, dic. 1981, p. 679–697, bibl., map, tables)

Surveyed representative sample of preschool children in each of country's four major ecological regions for protein-calorie malnutrition using anthropometric procedures. Hemoglobin determinations were done in subsample. Countrywide prevalence of anemia was 12.6 percent, with similar prevalence in three of four regions. Prevalence was lower in northern marginal agricultural region.

1853 Torun, Benjamin; Noel M. Solomons; and Fernando E. Viteri. Lacatose malabsorption and lactose intolerance: implications for general milk consumption (SLN/ALN, 29:4, dic. 1979, p. 445–494, bibl., tables)

Comprehensive review of 194 publications dealing with lactose malabsorption or intolerance. Not sufficient scientific or epidemiological support to justify discouraging use of milk in food supplementation programs.

1854 Valverde, Víctor; Reynaldo Martorell; William Owens; and Robert E. Klein. Problems in the estimation of corn consumption in longitudinal studies in rural Guatemala (SLN/ALN, 30:3, sept. 1980, p. 353–368, bibl., graphs, tables)

Methodological study evaluates sources of variability in corn tortilla weights and validates a method for accurately estimating corn consumption in 24-hour-dietary recall surveys.

1855 Vandale, Susan. Factores sociales y culturales que influyen en la alimentación del lactante menor en el medio urbano (Salud Pública de México [México] 20:2, marzo/abril 1978, p. 215–230, bibl., graphs, tables)

Describes infant feeding practices of 90 low-income women in south Mexico City. Maternal characteristics associated with breastfeeding for 16 weeks or more included lower education level (primary school or less) and age of oldest child. Extended family was associated with short-term breastfeeding.

1856 Varea, José and Mauro Rivadeneira. Bocio y sal yodada en el Ecuador: si-

tuación actual. Quito: Fundación Ciencia para Estudios del Hombre y la Naturaleza, 1980. 104 p.: bibl., ill.

Two studies are presented: 1) incidence of endemic goiter and relationship to altitude. Anthropometric and hormonal data suggest altitude per se does not have negative impact on growth and maturation, rather, socioeconomic conditions are determining factor; and 2) production, distribution, and consumption of iodized salt, quality of salt, and attitudes towards the beliefs about goiter (note: 19 percent of population surveyed believed iodized salt caused goiter!).

1857 Ward, John O. and John H. Sanders. Nutritional determinants and migration in the Brazilian Northeast: a case study of rural and urban Ceará (UC/EDCC, 29:1, Oct. 1980, p. 141–163, tables)

Considers nutritional effects of Brazil's chosen pattern of economic growth noting potential underinvestment in human capital resulting from preoccupation with physical capital formation. Reviews magnitude of malnutrition as well as factors determining nutritional status in econometric model. Analysis suggests nutritional crisis, principally caloric, in Northeast.

1858 Whiteford, Michael B. and Karen S. Hanrahan. Dietary factors and nutritional well-being: a comparison of two Costa Rican villages (Nutrition Reports International [Los Altos, Calif.] Sept. 1982, p. 26:3, p. 303–318, tables)

Considers factors which influence nutritional well-being of pre-school children from two Costa Rican villages relative to types and amounts of food consumed and nutrient intakes.

1859 Wolfe, Barbara L. and Jere R. Behrman. Determinants of child mortality, health, and nutrition in a developing country (Journal of Development Economics [North-Holland Publishing Co., Amsterdam] 11, 1982, p. 163–193, tables)

Building upon economic models of household behavior, estimates of determinants of child mortality, health and nutrition in Nicaragua varied significantly across regions. Income was not important factor, there was inverse relation with number of siblings, and there were positive associations with caloric intake, schooling, availability of refrigeration and quality of sewage systems.

1860 Wolfe, Phyllis and **Frederick L. Trowbridge.** Dietary intakes of preschool children in La Paz, El Salvador, Central America (SLN/ALN, 30:1, marzo 1980, p. 49–57, bibl., tables)

Average daily energy intake of children one–four years was only 60 percent of 1973 level recommended by INCAP and 76 percent of that recommended on body weight basis. Average daily protein intake was 110 percent and 136 percent respectively. Estimated retinol equivalent was only 36 percent of recommended allowance. Results were similar to those obtained in 1965 survey by INCAP.

1861 Yañez, Enrique *et al.* Capacity of the Chilean mixed diet to meet the protein and energy requirements of young adult males (British Journal of Nutrition [London] 47:1, Jan. 1982, p. 1–10, ill., tables)

Evaluates capacity of Chilean mixed diet to meet protein-energy requirements of young adult males from lower socioeconomic stratum in eight subjects (20–31 years) using nitrogen balance method.

BIOMEDICAL CONSIDERATIONS

Arnason, Thor; Feliz Uck; John Lambert; and **Richard Hebda.** Maya medicinal plants of San José Succotz, Belize. See item **910**.

1862 Ashcroft, M.T. Some non-infective diseases endemic in the West Indies (Cajanus [St. Augustine, Trinidad and Tobago] 12:3, 1979, p. 155–164, bibl.)

Describes three non-infectious diseases of particular interest to medical geography: vomiting sickness (related to the *ackee* fruit); veno-occlusive disease (perhaps related to alkaloids in teas made from the *Crotalaria* bush); and tropical sprue (apparently related to use of re-heated pork fat in frying).

1863 Ayensu, Edward S. Medicinal plants of the West Indies. Algonac, Mich.: Reference Publications, 1981. 282 p.: bibl., ill., indexes, map (on lining papers).

Excellent compendium of West Indies' medicinal plants and data (e.g., uses and chemical constituents). Includes excellent illustrations, glossary, and medicinal, common name and species indexes.

Barlett, Peggy F. and **Setha M. Low.** *Nervios* in rural Costa Rica. See item **913**.

1864 Bastien, Joseph W. Exchange between Andean and western medicine (Social Science and Medicine [Pergamon Press, New York] 16, 1982, p. 795–803, ill., tables)

Given reliance of rural Andeans on traditional medicine, author discusses how specialists (diviners and herbalists) from different communities complement each other in providing for health care of Andeans.

1865 Bonilla, L. Chacin; E. Chacin-Martínez; E. Espinoza; and **B. Cárdenas.** A seroepidemiological study of amebiasis in children of low socioeconomic level in Maracaibo, Venezuela (ASTMH/J, 31:6, 1982, p. 1103–1106, ill., tables)

Sera from 606 children from low socioeconomic background were screened for *Entamoeba histolytica*. Seropositivity rate was 7.7 percent. Stool examinations of 516 children showed cysts or trophozoites in 4.4 percent.

1866 Bravo Carrada, Teodoro and **Georgina Velázquez Díaz.** El impacto del sarampión en México (Salud Pública de México [México] 22:4, julio/agosto 1980, p. 359–408, bibl., ill., tables)

Comprehensive overview of measles in Mexico, offering historical considerations and detailed evaluation of morbidity and mortality statistics for period 1961–79. Emphasizes link to malnutrition.

1867 Browner, Carole. The management of early pregnancy: Colombian folk concepts of fertility control (Social Science and Medicine [Pergamon Press, New York] 14B, 1980, p. 25–32, tables)

Presents case materials from Cali, Colombia, to show one way in which women influence frequency and timing of births without modern contraceptives. Colombian folk pharmocopeia contains large number of substances to bring on late menstrual period and to induce early abortion.

1868 Campos, Teresa de María. Los animales en la medicina tradicional mesoamericana (UNAM/AA, 16, 1979, p. 183–223, bibl., ill., tables)

Analysis of different ways in which animal is used in symbols, and in etiology, diagnosis and treatment of several ailments, with specific information from north (Michoacán), center (Mexico City, Chimalhuacán), and south (Chiapas and Honduras).

Dressler, William W. Hypertension and culture change: acculturation and disease in the West Indies. See item **1072**.

1869 Estado actual del conocimiento en plantas medicinales mexicanas. Xavier Lozoya L., editor. México: Instituto Mexicano para el Estudio de las Plantas Medicinales, 1976. 255 p.: bibl., ill.

Collection of several reports and essays dealing with current status of historical, botanical, and chemical studies of medicinal plants in Mexico. Includes five reports from institutions involved study of plants and possible development of industrial uses.

1870 Estrella, Eduardo. Medicina aborigen: la práctica médica aborigen de la Sierra ecuatoriana. Quito: Editorial Epoca, 1978. 239 p.: bibl, maps.

Complete and well-structured study of traditional folk medicine in Ecuador's Pichincha prov. Based on extensive field observations, considers basic concepts about Man and health, supernatural and natural causes, traditional typology of illnesses, and therapeutics.

1871 Fernández de Castro, Jorge. Historia de la oncocercosis (Salud Pública de México [México] 21 : 6, nov./dic. 1979, p. 683–696, bibl.)

Presents chronological summary on "natural" history of onchocerciasis, including several hypothesis on source of disease in Americas. Includes summary of onchocerciasis campaign in Chiapas.

Finkler, Kaga. A comparative study of health seekers: or, why do some people go to doctors rather than to spiritualist healers? See item **957**.

———. Non-medical treatments and their outcomes. See item **958**.

Fuller, Nancy and **Brigitte Jordon.** Maya women and the end of the birthing period: postpartum massage-and-binding in Yucatán, Mexico. See item **961**.

1872 García, Silvia Perla and **Sara Josefina Newbery.** Formas tradicionales de la medicina vigentes en el area pampeana (IPGH/FA, 27, junio 1979, p. 97–119, bibl.)

Review of Argentine popular medicine and popular religion with many examples. Reviews elements of traditional medicine, kinds of practitioners, illnesses treated, and

both empirical and magic-religious medicines and treatments.

1873 González Torres, Dionisio M. Catálogo de plantas medicinales (y alimenticias y útiles) usadas en Paraguay. Asunción: Editorial Comuneros, 1981. 456 p., 28 plates: bibl., ill.

Catalogue of plants used for medicinal and other purposes (e.g., nutritional) in Paraguay. Data are drawn from old manuscripts, modern compilations and field observations. Entries are alphabetized by common name, botanic name, classification; properties, virtues, and uses; variant names if any; chemical composition if known; etc. Final list includes medicinal virtues as primary entries, followed by plants which exhibit said qualities. Includes pronunciation guide, annotated bibliography, and limited number of illustrations.

1874 Guderian, Ronald H. *et al.* Report on a focus of onchocerciasis in Esmeraldas province of Ecuador (ASTMH/J, 31 : 2, 1982, p. 270–274, ill., tables)

Results based upon several clinical tests showed a 73 percent prevalence of onchocerciasis in isolated 20 km section of Cayapa, River, Esmeraldas prov.

1875 Health in the Andes. Edited by Joseph W. Bastien and John M. Donahue. Washington: American Anthropological Association, 1981. 251 p.: bibl., graphs, ill., maps, tables (Special publication; no. 12)

Consists of 11 papers on issues related to Andean ethnomedicine, altitude, nutrition and coca use, and health conditions and services.

1876 Hurtado V., Juan José. Práctica relacionada con el embarazo, parto y crianza del niño y su efecto sobre la salud y el estado nutricional de las madres y niños de edad baja en Latinoamérica (GIIN/GI, 14 : 1/2, enero/julio 1979, p. 149–234, bibl., table)

Comprehensive review of customs, beliefs, and practices surrounding pregnancy, child birth, and maternal nutrition in Latin America from precolumbian times to present. Emphasizes low-income families, especially Guatemala.

1877 Jorg, Miguel Eduardo and **Ignacio Zalazar Rovira.** Encephalopathic forms of chronic Chagas' disease in Argentina

(IOC/M, 76:4, Oct./Dec. 1981, p. 353–360, bibl., graph)

Among 420 patients, diagnosed 22 cases (14 males, eight females) of true try-panosomic encephalopathy (Chagas' disease). Documents signs and symptoms (e.g., depression, mental confusion, weak muscular-tendinous reflexes, speech disturbance).

1878 Kozek, Wieslaw J.; Antonio D'Alessandro; Juan Silva H.; and Silvia N. Navarette. Filariasis in Colombia: prevalance of mansonellosis in the teenage and adult population of the Colombian bank of Amazon, Comisaría del Amazonas (ASTMH/J, 31:6, 1982, p. 1131–1136, ill., tables)

Prevalence and distribution of mansonellosis was studied among inhabitants of 16 villages and towns along Colombian bank of Amazon (Comisaría del Amazonas) and in neighboring Peruvian village. Average prevalance rate among blood samples of 535 residents was 47.1 percent; in individual villages 15.6 percent to 84.6 percent. Infection was more common in males and increased with age in both sexes.

1879 Kroeger, Axel. South American Indians between traditional and modern health services in rural Ecuador (PAHO/B, 16:3, 1982, p. 242–254, bibl., ill., tables)

Presents results of 1978 survey of 727 heads of households in rural Ecuador. Indian attitudes towards traditional and modern health services showed a marked preference for latter, but also marked tendency to multiple use of different healing systems and lack of confidence in existing services.

1880 Lewellen, Ted C. Aggression and hypoglycemia in the Andes: another look at the evidence (UC/CA, 22:4, Aug. 1981, p. 347–361)

Reevaluates evidence for and essentially refutes hypothesis that low blood sugar is primary cause of high levels of conflict among natives of Lake Titicaca basin in Peru and Bolivia. Report includes 16 equally interesting comments.

Logan, Michael H. Variations regarding *susto* causality among the Cakchiquel of Guatemala. See item **985**.

Low, Setha M. The meaning of *nervios*: a sociocultural analysis of symptom presentation in San José, Costa Rica. See item **989**.

1881 Loza-Balsa, Gregorio. La medicina aymara (UCCEA/A, 2:3, 1981, p. 43–61)

Summary of Aymara medicine includes world-vision, religion, and culture relative to death and illness. More focused discussion notes Aymara use of scientific method and medical training of future doctors. Closes with Aymara surgical treatment of phlebitis.

1882 Martius, Karl Friedrich Philipp von. Natureza, doenças, medicina e remédios dos índios brasileiros: 1844. Translation of *Das Naturell, die Krankheiten, das Arztthum und die Heilmittel der Urbewohner Brasiliens*. Tradução, pref. e notas de Pirajá da Silva. Apresentação de Egon Schaden. 2. ed. São Paulo: Companhia Editora Nacional, 1979. 183 p.: bibl., ill. (Brasiliana; v. 154)

Translation of German naturalist's 1844 writings on his travels through Brazil (1817–20). Discusses physical characteristics, diseases, and medicine of Indians as observed in early 1800s.

1883 Messer, Ellen. Hot-cold classification: theoretical and practical implications of a Mexican study (Social Science and Medicine [Pergamon Press, New York] 15B, 1981, p. 133–145, appendix, ill.)

Examines hot-cold food and medicinal categories in Mitla, Oaxaca, to describe general principles of classification, dimensions of age, and potential for change. Compares Mitla findings with those from other Latin American communities and with data from Near East, Far East, and other Old World communities.

1884 Montes Giraldo, José Joaquín. Medicina popular en Colombia: vegetales y otras sustancias usadas como remedios. Bogotá: Instituto Caro y Cuervo, 1981. 295 p.: ill. (Publicaciones del Instituto Caro y Cuervo; 58)

Compendium of various plants and medicinal substances used to treat/cure sicknesses in Colombia. Illnesses are arranged alphabetically. Includes detailed glossary and maps.

1885 Montolíu, María. Los dioses de los cuatro sectores cósmicos y su vínculo con la salud y enfermedad en Yucatán (UNAM/AA, 17, 1980, p. 47–65, bibl., tables)

Excursion into ethnomedicine considers four cosmic squares and associated gods among Maya traditions. Notes links with health, illness, and traditional curing systems.

1886 Mora, Xinia. La medicina pre y post colombina aplicada en la herborística (*in* Congreso sobre el Mundo Centroamericano de su Tiempo, 5th, Nicoya, Costa Rica, 1978. Memoria. Centenario de Gonzalo Fernández de Oviedo. Nicoya?, Costa Rica: Comisión Nacional Organizadora, 1978, p. 433–439, bibl.)

After general introduction, offers list of plants and herbs for which medicinal properties have been claimed in pre- and postcolumbian times.

Nigh, Ronald B. El ambiente nutricional de los grupos mayas de Chiapas. See item **995**.

1887 Perrin, Michel. Un succès bien relatif: la médecine occidentale chez les Indiens Guajiro (Social Science and Medicine [Pergamon Press, New York] 14B, 1980, p. 279–287, ill.)

Describes Guajiro traditional medical practices and general practice of western medicine in Guajiro environment in Venezuela.

1888 ———— and José Uliyuu Machado. El arte Guajiro de curar frente a la medicina occidental (VMJ/BIV, 19:16, enero/junio 1980, p. 39–200, bibl., ill., tables)

Very complete and detailed study of medical understandings and practices of Guajiro Indians (Venezuela and Colombia). Of special significance is fact that co-author is a Guajiro Indian. Includes catalogues of Guajiro names and treatments for sicknesses, and various medical herbs and compounds.

1889 Ramírez, Axel. Bibliografía comentada de la medicina tradicional mexicana: 1900–1978. México: Instituto Mexicano para el Estudio de las Plantas Medicinales (IMEPLAM), 1979. 147 p.: indexes.

Annotated bibliography of anthropological studies of traditional medicine (ethnomedicine) in Mexico (1900–78). Lists 500 entries alphabetically. Includes topical, author, and geographic (place) indexes.

1890 Ramírez de Lara, Leticia and Héctor Lara Tapia. La epidemiología neurológica en México: un estudio completo (Salud Pública de México [México] 22:5,

sept./oct. 1980, p. 501–511, bibl., tables)

Considers epidemiology of neurological diseases in Mexico. Most common diseases are cerebrovascular accidents, epilepsy, and infectious and parasitosis of the nervous system.

1891 Salud y nutrición en sociedades nativas. Alberto Chirif, compilador. Lima: Centro de Investigación y Promoción Amazónica, 1979. 128 p.: bibl., ill.

Collection of field studies of health care among Indians in Amazon basin criticizes current health care which tends to isolate medical aspects from sociocultural and economic contexts. Studies report on Aguaruna Jíbaro nutrition; health care in Peru's Río Cenepa region of Peru; relationship of witchcraft to psychosomatic disease; health care at "Clínica Cahuapana;" sociocultural factors influencing health of Venezuelan Indians; and medical aspects of Amuesha community.

1892 Sánchez M., Fernando *et al.* Medicina folklórica y atención primaria. Santo Domingo: Secretaría de Estado de Salud Pública y Asistencia Social (SESPAS), División de Recursos Humanos en Salud, 1980. 59 p.: bibl., ill. (Colección SESPAS. Serie Salud y medicina popular; 1)

Proceedings of 1980 symposium on traditional folk medicine in Dominican Republic includes six interdisciplinary essays with common theme of incorporating western medicine into traditional practices. No original research is included.

Signorini, Italo. Patterns of fright: multiple concepts of susto in a Nahua-Ladino community in the Sierra of Puebla, Mexico. See item **1013**.

1893 Souza Novelo, Narciso. Farmacopea maya (UY/R, 22:131/132, sept./dic. 1980, p. 67–85)

Overall survey of state of knowledge and research about Mayan folk medicine in 1940. Describes Mayan botanical/medical gardens and professional herbalists, including extensive quotes from older manuscripts and Mayan prescriptions (e.g., eye diseases, snake bites, biliousity, blood vomiting, and dog bites). Successful substances used to treat diseases are included as interesting annotated bibliography.

1894 Tay, Jorge *et al.* La enfermedad de Chagas en la República Mexicana (Salud Pública de México [México] 22 : 4, julio/agosto 1980, p. 400–450, bibl., maps, tables)
Reasonably thorough review of literature on Chagas disease in Mexico (1939–76).

1895 Testimonios sobre medicina de los antiguos mexicanos. Selección de textos y transcripción de las ilus., Zita Basich. Presentación, Arsenio Farell Cubillas. Introd., Antonio Pompa y Pompa. México: Instituto Mexicano del Seguro Social, 1980. 150 p.: ill. (some col.).
Promotional book aimed at salvaging . . . "values of the Nahuatl world." Modern reproductions of selected illustrations from the Florentine Codex are accompanied with edited texts from Fray Bernardino de Sahagún dealing with Nahuatl medicine in general.

Tousignant, Michel. *Espanto*: a dialogue with the gods. See item **1026**.

Trotter, Robert T., II. Folk remedies as indicators of common illnesses: examples from the United States-Mexico border. See item **1027**.

──── and **Juan Antonio Chavira.** *Curanderismo*: an emic theoretical perspective of Mexican-American folk medicine. See item **1028**.

1896 Vieira Filho, João Paulo Botelho. Diabetes mellitus entre os indios dos Estados Unidos e os do Brasil (USP/RA, 21 : 1, 1978, p. 53–60, bibl.)
Presents evidence documenting relatively high incidence of *diabetes mellitus* among North American and Brazilian Indians. Stresses Neel's hypothesis that disease may be advantageous to primitive societies and disadvantageous to sedentary ones.

────. Medicina indígena e medicina científica. See item **1174**.

1897 Villa Rojas, Alfonso. La imagen del cuerpo humano según los mayas de Yucatán (UNAM/AA, 17, 1980, p. 31–46, bibl., ill., plate)
Presents concepts of body held by Maya groups from Chiapas and Guatemala, followed by more recent data from Mayas of Yucatan. Latter shows that they still retain old ideas which attribute to human body structure similar to that of cosmos.

Weniger, B.; M. Haag-Berrurier; and R. Anton. Plants of Haiti used as antifertility agents. See item **1145**.

1898 Young, James Clay. Medical choice in a Mexican village. New Brunswick, N.J.: Rutgers University Press, 1981. 233 p.: bibl., ill., index.
Ethnographic study of medical choice in Pichátaro, Michoacán, rural community in west-central Mexico. Informants include members of about one-fifth of 500 households in community. Includes medical beliefs, folk medical knowledge, alternative treatments, and analysis of choice of medical treatment (for ethnologist's comment, see item **1036**.)

1899 ──── and **Linda Young Garro.** Variation in the choice of treatment in two Mexican communities (Social Science and Medicine [Pergamon Press, New York] 16, 1982, p. 1453–1465, ill., tables)
Considers relationship among lay illness beliefs, accessibility of Western health care sources, and rates of physician utilization in two rural communities in Mexico (Pichataro and Uricho).

JOURNAL ABBREVIATIONS
ANTHROPOLOGY

AAA/AA American Anthropologist. American Anthropological Association. Washington.

AAA/AE American Ethnologist. American Anthropological Association. Washington.

AAAS/A *See* AAAS/S.

AAAS/S Science. American Association for the Advancement of Science. Washington.

AAC/AJ Anthropological Journal of Canada. Quarterly bulletin of the Anthropological Association of Canada. Quebec.

ACEP/EP Estudios de Población. Asociación Colombiana para el Estudio de la Población. Bogotá.

AES Archives Européennes de Sociologie. Paris.

AES/AE American Ethnologist. American Ethnological Society. Washington.

AFS/JAF Journal of American Folklore. American Folklore Society. Austin, Tex.

AGS/GR The Geographical Review. American Geographical Society. New York.

AHL/B Boletín de la Academia Hondureña de la Lengua. Tegucigalpa.

AI/A Anthropos. Anthropos-Institut. Psoieux, Switzerland.

AI/I Interciencia. Asociación Interciencia. Caracas.

AIA/A Archaeology. Archaeological Institute of America. New York.

AISA/TA Terra Ameriga. Associazione Italiana Studi Americanistici. Genova, Italy.

AJPA American Journal of Physical Anthropology. American Association of Physical Anthropologists and the Wistar Institute of Anatomy and Biology. Philadelphia, Pa.

AMNH/NH Natural History. American Museum of Natural History. New York.

ANC/B Boletín de la Academia Nacional de Ciencias. Córdoba, Argentina.

APS/P Proceedings of the American Philosophical Society. Philadelphia, Pa.

ARCHEO Archeologia. Paris.

ASCN/H *See* ASCN/J.

ASCN/J American Journal of Clinical Nutrition. American Society for Clinical Nutrition. New York.

ASE/E Ethnohistory. Journal of the American Society for Ethnohistory. Buffalo, N.Y.

ASHG/J American Journal of Human Genetics. The American Society of Human Genetics. Baltimore, Md.

ASTMH/J American Journal of Tropical Medicine and Hygiene. Published by Waverly Press for the American Society of Tropical Medicine and Hygiene. Baltimore, Md.

ASU/LAD Latin American Digest. Arizona State Univ., Center for Latin American Studies. Tempe.

AT/A Antiquity. A quarterly review of archaeology. The Antiquity Trust. Cambridge, England.

BBAA Boletín Bibliográfico de Antropología Americana. Instituto Panamericano de Geografía e Historia, Comisión de Historia. México.

BISRA/BS Belizean Studies. Belizean Institute of Social Research and Action and St. John's College. Belize City.

BNB/REN Revista Econômica do Nordeste. Fortaleza, Brazil.

BNBD Boletín Nicaragüense de Bibliografía y Documentación. Banco Central de Nicaragua, Biblioteca. Managua.

BNJM/R Revista de la Biblioteca Nacional José Martí. La Habana.

BRMN/B Boletim do Museu Nacional. Compôsto e impresso na Oficina Gráfica da Univ. do Brasil. Rio de Janeiro.

CAAAP/AP Amazonía Peruana. Centro Amazónico de Antropología y Aplicación Práctica, Depto. de Documentación y Publicaciones. Lima.

CBR/BCB Boletín Cultural y Bibliográfico. Banco de la República, Biblioteca Luis-Angel Arango. Bogotá.

CDAL Cahiers des Amériques Latines. Paris.

CEDE/DS Desarrollo y Sociedad. Univ. de los Andes, Facultad de Economía, Centro de Estudios sobre el Desarrollo Económico (CEDE). Bogotá.

CEDLA/B Boletían de Estudios Latino-americanos. Centro de Estudios y Documentación Latinoamericanos. Amsterdam.

CEM/ECM Estudios de Cultura Maya. Univ. Nacional Autónoma de México, Centro de Estudios Mayas. México.

CEPAL/R CEPAL. Review/Revista de la CEPAL. Naciones Unidas, Comisión Económica para América Latina. Santiago.

CJN Croissance des Jeunes Nations. Paris.

CLACSO/ERL Estudios Rurales Latino-americanos. Consejo Latinoamericano de Ciencias Sociales, Secretaría Ejecutiva y de la Comisión de Estudios Rurales. Bogotá.

CLASCO/ERL *See* CLACSO/ERL.

CM/DE Demografía y Economía. El Colegio de México. México.

CMALS/B Boletín. Publicaciones del Museo y de la Sociedad Arqueológica de La Serena. Museo Arqueológico de La Serena. La Serena, Chile.

CNRS/ASR Archives de Sociologie des Religions. Centre Nationale de la Recherche Scientifique. Paris.

CPES/RPS Revista Paraguaya de Sociología. Centro Paraguayo de Estudios Sociológicos. Asunción.

CPS Comparative Political Studies. Northwestern Univ., Evanston, Ill. and Sage Publications, Beverly Hills, Calif.

CPU/ES Estudios Sociales. Corporación de Promoción Universitaria. Santiago.

CRCA/A Anthropologica. Canadian Research Centre for Anthropology. St. Paul Univ. Ottawa.

CSSH Comparative Studies in Society and History. An international quarterly. Society for the Comparative Study of Society and History. The Hague.

CU/JIA Journal of International Affairs. Columbia Univ., School of International Affairs. New York.

CUA/AQ Anthropological Quarterly. Catholic Univ. of America, Catholic Anthropological Conference. Washington.

DEF/F Folk. Dansk Etnografisk Forening. Koøbenhavn.

DGV/ZE Zeitschrift für Ethnologie. Deutschen Gesellschaft für Völkerkunde. Braunschweig, FRG.

EANH/B Boletín de la Academia Nacional de Historia. Quito.

EAZ Ethnographisch-Archäologische Zeitschrift. Deutscher Verlag Wissenschaften. East Berlin.

EHESS/C Communications. École des Hautes Études en Sciences Sociales, Centre d'Études Transdisciplinaires. Paris.

EM/A Årstryck. Etnografiska Museum. Göteborg, Sweden.

EME Revista Eme-Eme. Estudios dominicanos. Univ. Católica Madre y Maestra. Santiago de los Caballeros, República Dominicana.

EPHE/H L'Homme. Revue française d'anthropologie. La Sorbonne, l'École Pratique des Hautes Études. Paris.

ERS Ethnic and Racial Studies. Routledge & Kegan Paul. London.

FAIC/CPPT Comunicaciones Proyecto Puebla-Tlaxcala. Fundación Alemana para la Investigación Científica. Puebla, México.

FFCL/EL Estudos Leopoldenses. Faculdade de Filosofia, Ciências e Letras. São Leopoldo, Brazil.

FIU/CR Caribbean Review. Florida International Univ., Office of Academic Affairs. Miami.

FS/CIS Cahiers Internationaux de Sociologie. La Sorbonne, École Pratique des Hautes Études. Paris.

FSCN/A Antropológica. Fundación La Salle de Ciencias Naturales, Instituto Caribe de Antropología y Sociología. Caracas.

GEE/NA Nova Americana. Giulio Einaudi Editore. Torino, Italy.

GIIN/GI Guatemala Indígena. Instituto Indigenista Nacional. Guatemala.

HAHR Hispanic American Historical Review. Duke Univ. Press *for the* Conference on Latin American History of the American Historical Association. Durham, N.C.

HH Human Heredity. Basel, Switzerland.

IAA Ibero-Amerikanisches Archiv. Ibero-Amerikanisches Institut. Berlin, FRG.

IAHG/AHG Antropología e Historia de Guatemala. Instituto de Antropología e Historia de Guatemala. Guatemala.

IAHR/N Numen. International review for the history of religions. International Association for the History of Religions. Leiden, The Netherlands.

IAI/I Indiana. Beiträge zur Volker-und Sprachenkunde, Archäologie und Anthropologie des Indianischen Amerika. Ibero-Amerikanisches Institut. Berlin, FRG.

IAMEA Inter-American Economic Affairs. Washington.

IAP/P Pesquisas. Anuário do Instituto Anchietano de Pesquisas. Porto Alegre.

IAS/ÑP Ñawpa Pacha. Institute of Andean Studies. Berkeley, Calif.

IBEAS/EA Estudios Andinos. Instituto Boliviano de Estudio y Acción Social. La Paz.

IBGE/RBE Revista Brasileira de Estatística. Ministério do Planejamento e Coordenação Geral, Instituto Brasileiro de Geografia e Estatística. Rio de Janeiro.

ICA/RCA Revista Colombiana de Antropología. Ministerio de Educación Nacional, Instituto Colombiano de Antropología. Bogotá.

ICC/T Thesaurus. Boletín del Instituto Caro y Cuervo. Bogotá.

ICS/JCCP Journal of Commonwealth and Comparative Politics. Univ. of London, Institute of Commonwealth Studies. London.

IFCH/R Revista do Instituto de Filosofia e Ciências Humanas. Univ. Federal do Rio Grande do Sul. Porto Alegre.

IFEA/B Bulletin de l'Institut Français d'Etudes Andines. Paris.

IFH/C Conjonction. Institut Français d'Haïti. Port-au-Prince.

IFP/E Ethos. Revista de filosofía práctica. Instituto de Filosofía Práctica. Buenos Aires.

IGME/RG Revista Geográfica. Instituto Geográfico Militar del Ecuador, Depto. Geográfico. Quito.

IGFO/RI Revista de Indias. Instituto Gonzalo Fernández de Oviedo and Consejo Superior de Investigaciones Científicas. Madrid.

IGM/U L'Universo. Rivista bimestrale dell'Istituto Geografico Militare. Firenze, Italy.

IIE/A Anales del Instituto de Investigaciones Estéticas. Univ. Nacional Autónoma de México. México.

III/AI América Indígena. Instituto Indigenista Interamericano. México.

IJ/JJ Jamaica Journal. Institute of Jamaica. Kingston.

ILO/R International Labour Review. International Labour Office. Geneva.

INAH/A   Anales del Instituto Nacional de Antropología e Historia. Secretaría de Educación Pública. México.

INAH/B   Boletín del Instituto Nacional de Antropología e Historia. Secretaría de Educación Pública. México.

INEP/RBEP   Revista Brasileira de Estudos Pedagógicos. Instituto Nacional de Estudos Pedagógicos. Centro Brasileiro de Pesquisas Educacionais. Rio de Janeiro.

IOC/M   Memórias do Instituto Oswaldo Cruz. Rio de Janeiro.

IPEA/PPE   Pesquisa e Planejamento Econômico. Instituto de Planejamento Econômico e Social. Rio de Janeiro.

IPGH/FA   Folklore Americano. Instituto Panamericano de Geografía e Historia, Comisión de Historia, Comité de Folklore. México.

IRR/RC   Race and Class. A journal for black and Third World liberation. Institute of Race Relations and The Transnational Institute. London.

IUP/D   Dados. Publicação semestral do Instituto Universitário de Pesquisas do Rio de Janeiro. Rio de Janeiro.

JBA   Journal of Belizean Affairs. Belize City, Belize.

JDS   The Journal of Development Studies. A quarterly journal devoted to economics, politics, and social development. London.

JEHM/R   Revista de la Junta de Estudios Históricos de Mendoza. Mendoza, Argentina.

JIH   The Journal of Interdisciplinary History. The MIT Press. Cambridge, Mass.

JLAS   Journal of Latin American Studies. Centers or institutes of Latin American studies at the universities of Cambridge, Glasgow, Liverpool, London and Oxford. Cambridge Univ. Press. London.

JPS   The Journal of Peasant Studies. Frank Cass & Co. London.

KITLV/B   Bijdragen tot de Taal-, Landen Volkenkunde. Koninklijk Instituut voor Taal-, Landen Volkenkunde. Leiden, The Netherlands.

LALR   Latin American Literary Review. Carnegie-Mellon Univ., Dept. of Modern Languages. Pittsburgh, Pa.

LAP   Latin American Perspectives. Univ. of California. Riverside.

LARR   Latin American Research Review. Univ. of North Carolina Press *for the* Latin American Studies Association. Chapel Hill.

LSE/PS   Population Studies. London School of Economics, The Population Investigation Committee. London.

MEMDA/E   Etnía. Museo Etnográfico Municipal Dámaso Arce. Municipalidad de Olavarría, Provincia de Buenos Aires, Argentina.

MH/OM   Objets et Mondes. Musée de l'Homme. Paris.

MHD/B   Boletín del Museo del Hombre Dominicano. Santo Domingo.

MLV/T   Tribus. Veröffentlichungen des Linden-Museums. Museum für Länder- und Völkerkunde. Stuttgart, FRG.

MNAA/A   Arqueológicas. Museo Nacional de Antropología y Arqueología, Instituto Nacional de Cultura. Lima.

MNCR/V   Vínculos. Revista de antropología. Museo Nacional de Costa Rica. San José.

MOBR/B   Boletín. Museo del Oro; Banco de la República. Bogotá.

MP/R   Revista do Museu Paulista. São Paulo.

MPEG/B   Boletim do Museu Paraense Emílio Goeldi. Nova série: antropologia. Conselho Nacional de Desenvolvimento Científico e Tecnológico, Instituto Nacional de Pesquisas da Amazônia. Belém, Brazil.

MV/BA   Baessler-Archiv. Museums für Völkerkunde. Berlin.

MVW/AV   Archiv für Völkerkunde. Museum für Völkerkunde in Wien und von Verein Freunde der Völkerkunde. Wien.

NAS/P   Proceedings of the National Academy of Sciences. Washington.

NCFR/JFH   Journal of Family History. Studies in family, kinship and demography. National Council on Family Relations. Minneapolis, Minn.

NGS/NGM   National Geographic Magazine. National Geographic Society. Washington.

NMJS   Nature. A weekly journal of science. Macmillan & Co. London.

NWIG   Nieuwe West-Indische Gids. Martinus Nijhoff. The Hague.

NYAS/A   Annals of the New York Academy of Sciences. New York.

OAS/AM   Américas. Organization of American States. Washington.

OAS/CI   Ciencia Interamericana. Organization of American States, Dept. of Scientific Affairs. Washington.

OCLAE   OCLAE. Revista mensual de la Organización Continental Latinoamericana de Estudiantes. La Habana.

PAA/D   Demography. Population Association of America. Washington.

PAHO/B Bulletin of the Pan American Health Organization. Washington.

PAIGH/G Revista Geográfica. Instituto Panamericano de Geografía e Historia, Comisión de Geografía. México.

PAN/ES Estudios Latinoamericanos. Polska Akademia Nauk (Academia de Ciencias de Polonia), Instytut Historii (Instituto de Historia). Warszawa.

PEBN/B Boletín de la Biblioteca Nacional. Lima.

PEMN/R Revista del Museo Nacional. Casa de la Cultura del Perú, Museo Nacional de la Cultura Peruana. Lima.

PMK Paideuma. Mitteilungen zur Kulturkunde. Deutsche Gesellschaft für kultur- morphologie von Frobenius Institut au der Johann Wolfgang Goethe—Universität. Wiesbaden, Germany.

PUC/L Lexis. Revista de lingüística y literatura. Pontificia Univ. Católica del Perú. Lima.

PUC/V Veritas. Revista. Pontifícia Univ. Católica do Rio Grande do Sul. Porto Alegre, Brazil.

PUCIRA/BSA Boletín del Seminario de Arqueología. Pontificia Univ. Católica del Perú, Instituto Riva Agüero. Lima.

PUCP/DA Debates en Antropología. Pontificia Univ. Católica del Perú, Depto. de Ciencias Sociales. Lima.

PUCP/H Histórica. Pontificia Univ. Católica del Perú, Depto. de Humanidades. Lima.

PUJ/UH Universitas Humanistica. Pontificia Univ. Javeriana, Facultad de Filosofía y Letras. Bogotá.

RAI/M Man. A monthly record of anthropological science. The Royal Anthropological Institute. London.

RRI Revista/Review Interamericana. Univ. Interamericana. San Germán, Puerto Rico.

RUC Revista de la Universidad Complutense. Madrid.

RYC Revolución y Cultura. Publicación mensual. Ministerio de Cultura. La Habana.

SA Scientific American. Published monthly by Scientific American, Inc. New York.

SA/J Journal de la Société des Américanistes. Paris.

SAA/AA American Antiquity. The Society for American Archaeology. Menasha, Wis.

SAA/HO Human Organization. Society for Applied Anthropology. New York.

SAA/HQ *See* SAA/HO.

SAA/R Relaciones de la Sociedad Argentina de Antropología. Buenos Aires.

SAH/J Journal of the Society of Architectural Historians. Amherst, Mass.

SAR/P El Palacio. School of American Research, the Museum of New Mexico, and the Archaeological Society of New Mexico. Santa Fe.

SBPC/CC Ciência e Cultura. Sociedade Brasileira para o Progresso da Ciência. São Paulo.

SEB/EB Economic Botany. Devoted to applied botany and plant utilization. *Published for* The Society for Economic Botany *by the* New Botanical Garden. New York.

SEM/E Ethnos. Statens Ethnografiska Museum. Stockholm.

SF Social Forces. *Published for the* Univ. of North Carolina Press *by the* Williams & Wilkins Co. Baltimore, Md.

SGHG/A Anales de la Sociedad de Geografía e Historia de Guatemala. Guatemala.

SGL/B Boletín de la Sociedad Geográfica de Lima. Lima.

SHG/B Bulletin de la Société d'Histoire de la Guadeloupe. Archives Départamentales *avec le concours du* Conseil Général de la Guadeloupe. Basse-Terre, West Indies.

SLN/ALN Archivos Latinoamericanos de Nutrición. Sociedad Latinoamericana de Nutrición. Caracas.

SO Society. Social science and modern society. Transaction, Rutgers—The State Univ. New Brunswick, N.J.

SOCIOL Sociologus. Zeitschrift für empirische Soziologie, sozialpsychologische und ethnologische Forschung (A journal for empirical sociology, social psychology and ethnic research). Berlin.

SRCD Child Development. Society for Research in Child Development. Chicago, Ill.

SSA/B Bulletin. Société Suisse des Américanistes. Geneva.

SSSB/SB Social Biology. Society for the Study of Social Biology. New York.

TU/CCM Cerámica de Cultura Maya. Temple Univ., Dept. of Anthropology. Philadelphia, Pa.

UA Urban Anthropology. State Univ. of New York, Dept. of Anthropology. Brockport.

UB/BA Boletín Americanista. Univ. de Barcelona, Facultad de Geografía e Historia, Depto. de Historia de América. Barcelona.

UBAIA/R   Runa. Archivo para las Ciencias del Hombre. Univ. de Buenos Aires, Facultad de Filosofía y Letras, Instituto de Antropología. Buenos Aires.

UC/A   Anales de la Universidad de Cuenca. Cuenca, Ecuador.

UC/AT   Atenea. Revista de ciencias, letras y artes. Univ. de Concepción. Concepción, Chile.

UC/CA   Current Anthropology. Univ. of Chicago. Chicago, Ill.

UC/EDCC   Economic Development and Cultural Change. Univ. of Chicago, Research Center in Economic Development and Cultural Change. Chicago, Ill.

UC/EE   Estudios de Economía. Univ. de Chile. Facultad de Ciencias Económicas y Administrativas, Depto. de Economía. Santiago.

UC/S   Signs. Journal of women in culture and society. The Univ. of Chicago Press. Chicago, Ill.

UCAB/M   Montalbán. Univ. Católica Andrés Bello, Facultad de Humanidades y Educación, Institutos Humanísticos de Investigación. Caracas.

UCC/CE   Cuadernos de Economía. Univ. Católica de Chile. Santiago.

UCC/NG   Norte Grande. Revista de estudios integrados referentes a comunidades humanas del Norte Grande de Chile, en una perspectiva geográfica e histórica-cultural. Univ. Católica de Chile, Instituto de Geografía, Depto. de Geografía de Chile, Taller Norte Grande. Santiago.

UCCEA/A   Antropología. Revista del Centro de Estudios Antropológicos. Univ. de Chile. Santiago.

UCGL/AHG   Annals of Human Genetics (Annals of Eugenics). Univ. College, Galton Laboratory. London.

UCL/CD   Cultures et Développement. Revue internationale des sciences du développement Univ. Catholique de Louvain *avec le concours de la* Fondation Universitaire de Belgique. Louvain, Belgium.

UCLA/JLAL   Journal of Latin American Lore. Univ. of California, Latin American Center. Los Angeles.

UCLV/I   Islas. Univ. Central de las Villas. Santa Clara, Cuba.

UCNSA/SA   Suplemento Antropológico. Univ. Católica de Nuestra Señora de la Asunción, Centro de Estudios Antropológicos. Asunción.

UCV/ECS   Economía y Ciencias Sociales. Revista de la Facultad de Economía de la Univ. Central de Venezuela. Caracas.

UFP/EB   Estudos Brasileiros. Univ. Federal do Paraná, Setor de Ciências Humanas, Centro de Estudos Brasileiros. Curitiba, Brazil.

UH/U   Universidad de La Habana. La Habana.

UK/SE   *See* UK/SR.

UK/SR   The Sociological Review. Univ. of Keele. Staffordshire, England.

UMUP/E   Expedition. The bulletin of the University Museum of the Univ. of Pennsylvania. Philadelphia.

UN/ISSJ   International Social Science Journal. United Nations Educational, Scientific, and Cultural Organization. Paris.

UNAM/AA   Anales de Antropología. Univ. Nacional Autónoma de México, Instituto de Investigaciones Históricas. México.

UNAM/AL   Anuario de Letras. Univ. Nacional Autónoma de México, Facultad de Filosofía y Letras. México.

UNAM/ECN   Estudios de Cultura Náhuatl. Univ. Nacional Autónoma de México, Instituto de Historia, Seminario de Cultura Náhuatl. México.

UNAM/RMS   Revista Mexicana de Sociología. Univ. Nacional Autónoma de México, Instituto de Investigaciones Sociales. México.

UNAM/RMCPS   Revista Mexicana de Ciencias Políticas y Sociales. Univ. Nacional Autónoma de México, Facultad de Ciencias Políticas y Sociales. México.

UNAM/RMPCS   *See* UNAM/RMCPS.

UNC/ED   El Dorado. Univ. of Northern Colorado, Museum of Anthropology. Greeley.

UNC/K   Katunob. Univ. of Northern Colorado, Museum of Anthropology. Greeley.

UNCIA/R   Revista del Instituto de Antropología. Univ. Nacional de Córdoba. Córdoba, Argentina.

UNESCO/CU   Cultures. United Nations Educational, Scientific and Cultural Organization. Paris.

UNLPM/R   Revista del Museo de La Plata. Univ. Nacional de La Plata, Facultad de Ciencias Naturales y Museo. La Plata, Argentina.

UNM/JAR   Journal of Anthropological Research. Univ. of New Mexico, Dept. of Anthropology. Albuquerque.

UNTIA/R Revista del Instituto de Antropología. Univ. Nacional de Tucumán. San Miguel de Tucumán, Argentina.

UNV/ED *See* UNC/ED.

UP/E Ethnology. Univ. of Pittsburgh. Pittsburgh, Pa.

UP/EA Estudios Andinos. Univ. of Pittsburgh, Latin American Studies Center. Pittsburgh, Pa.

UP/LAIL Latin American Indian Literatures. A new review of American Indian texts and studies. Univ. of Pittsburgh, Dept. of Hispanic Languages and Literatures. Pittsburgh, Pa.

UPB Universidad Pontificia Bolivariana. Medellín, Colombia.

UPR/CS Caribbean Studies. Univ. of Puerto Rico, Instituto of Caribbean Studies. Río Piedras.

UPR/RCS Revista de Ciencias Sociales. Univ. de Puerto Rico, Colegio de Ciencias Sociales. Río Piedras.

UR/L Lateinamerika. Univ. Rostock. Rostock, GDR.

URL/ES Estudios Sociales. Univ. Rafael Landívar, Institute de Ciencias Políticas y Sociales. Guatemala.

URSS/AL América Latina. Academia de Ciencias de la URSS (Unión de Repúblicas Soviéticas Socialistas). Moscú.

USP/RA Revista de Antropologia. Univ. de São Paulo, Faculdade de Filosofia, Letras e Ciências Humanas and Associação Brasileira de Antropologia. São Paulo.

UTIEH/C Caravelle. Cahiers du monde hispanique et luso-brésilien. Univ. of Toulouse, Institut d'Études Hispaniques, Hispano-Americaines et Luso-Brésiliennes. Toulouse, France.

UUAL/U Universidades. Unión de Universidades de América Latina. Buenos Aires and México.

UWI/CQ Caribbean Quarterly. Univ. of the West Indies. Mona, Jamaica.

UWI/SES Social and Economic Studies. Univ. of the West Indies, Institute of Social and Economic Research. Mona, Jamaica.

UY/R Revista de la Universidad de Yucatán. Mérida, México.

VMJ/BIV Boletín Indigenista Venezolano. Ministerio de Justicia, Comisión Indigenista. Caracas.

WD World Development. Pergamon Press. Oxford, U.K.

WM Westermann Monatschefte. Georg Westermann Verlag. Braunschweig, FRG.

WRU/JMF Journal of Marriage and the Family. Western Reserve Univ. Cleveland, Ohio.

WSU/HB Human Biology. Official publication of the Human Biology Council. Wayne State Univ., School of Medicine. Detroit, Mich.

YAXKIN Yaxkin. Instituto Hondureño de Antropología e Historia. Tegucigalpa.

ZMA Zeitschrift für Morphologie und Anthropologie. E. Nägele. Stuttgart, Germany.

ECONOMICS

GENERAL

JOHN M. HUNTER, *Director Emeritus, Latin American Studies Center, Michigan State University*

WRITING A MEANINGFUL, COMPLETE, and *short* account of a two-year flow of economic literature on Latin America is a formidable task: its publication continues to grow in quantity, quality, and in scope. All that I can do here is to report on some facets, relate some impressions; summary and comprehensiveness are not possible.

I lamented years ago the lack of attention being given to the most important of all markets, the labor market. Recently, the ILO's regional agency, Programa Regional del Empleo para América Latina y el Caribe (PREALC), has taken the lead in doing some first-rate, analytic work in labor as exemplified by PREALC entries (items **2923–2927**) and those of its various staff members such as Tokman (items **2962–2966**), Szretter (item **2959**), Alvaro García (item **2830**), Macedo (item **2883**), and Klein (item **2863**). ECIEL has also done good work along these lines, mostly reported earlier, but see Buttari (item **2780**), and Salazar-Carrillo (item **2939**). Other important contributors include Peter Gregory (items **2842-2843**), and Meller and Mizala Cieplan (item **2890**). Bergquist (item **2774**) reviews 11 studies on the urban working class and organized labor—if encapsulated information is desired.

Either the Russians became much more prolific in this biennium or circumstances were such that I was made aware of their writing. See Bereznoi (item **2773**), Karaváiev (item **2860**), Keshisvev (item **2861**), Kistanov (item **2862**), and Volkov (item **2982**). This material appeared in one journal, translated into Spanish. It is appreciable in quantity, but one should not assume that it is necessarily representative of Soviet research.

Several studies gave serious attention to the effects of shock and responses thereto which resulted from dramatic increases in oil prices in the early 1970s—clearly an instructive period. See particularly Balassa (items **2768–2769**), Bacha (item **2765**), and Aranda (item **2759**).

The "public enterprise" is a relatively new, serious topic. Córdova (item **2796**) explored their labor relations. *The Journal of Inter-American Studies and World Affairs* (item **2857**) devoted an entire issue to the matter; in it, Saulliers (item **2944**) produced an annotated list of research papers. Glade (items **2838–2839**), Vernon (item **2979**), Pennano (item **2912**), and Boneo (item **2778**), all published papers on special topics related to public enterprises; and the Escuela Interamericana de Administración Pública (FGV) has a thorough, general study (item **2751**).

Agriculture got fewer "pages" this biennium, but three works in particular merit attention here. De Janvry's book (item **2797**) is a serious, analytic look at the agrarian question and unequal growth. Schejtman (item **2945**) has an interesting piece on differences between peasant and other types of production units. Preston (item **2814**) has a volume on the environment and rural change.

External debt and the problems associated with it are also beginning to get attention. García-Zamor (item **2821**) has a general work on financing development. Wionczek (item **2875**) produced an early volume on the relation of LDC debt to the world economy. Fishlow has one piece (item **2822**); Devlin, one (item **2802**); and the Centro de Estudios Monetarios Latinoamericanos (item **2762**), one.

Four miscellaneous works caught my eye—either because they were particularly good or because they plowed new ground. The Centro de Investigaciones Económicas (item **2836**) produced a pilot study of the relationships between military expenditures and development in Latin America. Nugent and Glezakos (item **2903**) studied time series for 15 years and 16 countries to determine the relevance of Philipps curves. Conference papers on short-term macro-planning (ILPES, item **2794**), also deal empirically with Philipps curves and other quantitative relationships. CEPAL, among its usual informative output, had an interesting volume, ¿Se puede superar la pobreza? (item **2947**), a collection of 1979 seminar papers focusing on the causes and cures of poverty.

2751 Administración de empresas públicas.
Banco Interamericano de Desarrollo, Escuela Interamericana de Administración Pública, Fundación Getúlio Vargas. México: Editorial Limusa, 1979. 674 p.: bibl., ill.

Very much a "how-to-do-it" volume with wide range of discussion—rate setting, decentralization, personnel management, systems theory, with frequent "cases." Designed as teaching tool. Includes instructor's manual.

2752 Aguilar Monteverde, Alonso. La crisis del capitalismo: ensayos. México: Editorial Nuestro Tiempo, 1979. 359 p. (Colección Desarrollo)

Series of essays (1975–79) describing fundamental crisis of capitalism, amelioration of which requires a "victorious revolution," and a new social order.

2753 ——— et al. Capitalismo, atraso y dependencia en América Latina. 2. ed., corregida y aum. México: Instituto de Investigaciones Económicas, 1980. 245 p. (Seminario de teoría del desarrollo)

Built around Antonio García's Atraso y dependencia en América Latina. Hacia una teoría latinoamericana del desarrollo (1972).

2754 Albert, Bill and Paul Henderson. Latin America and the Great War: a preliminary survey of developments in Chile, Peru, Argentina and Brazil (WD, 9:8, Aug. 1981, p. 717–734, tables)

Some results of comparative study of effects of World War I on Latin America which authors feel have much to teach about capitalist development.

2755 Alcalde Cardoza, Javier. Bibliografía anotada sobre aspectos políticos de la integración andina. Lima: Junta del Acuerdo de Cartagena, Biblioteca, 1977. 34 p.: index.

Consists of 174 items (some far afield) by broad topics. Author index.

2756 Allen, Elizabeth A. The state and region: some comparative development experiences from México and Brazil (in State and region in Latin America: a workshop. G.A. Banck, R. Buve, and L. Van Vroonhoven, editors. Amsterdam: Centrum voor Studien en Documetatie van Latijns-Amerika, 1981, p. 231–264, bibl., tables [CEDLA incidentele publicaties; 17])

Compares two very different programs: Mexico's regional development agency for Papaloapan River basin and Brazil's Brazilian Legion of Assistance (recently absorbed into Ministry of Social Welfare and Assistance with task of providing social welfare at various levels and throughout country—especially to those in acute poverty). Conclusion: programs work least well when assistor and assistee try to work independently.

2757 Alzamora C., Lucía. Bibliografía, planificación regional en América Latina. Caracas: Junta Nacional de Planificación y Coordinación Económica, Sección Publicaciones: Instituto Latinoamericano de Investigaciones Sociales, Fundación Friedrich Ebert, 1977. 55 p.: bibl. (Materiales de trabajo; no. 13)

Includes 438 unannotated items divided into broad subject matter areas. No indexes.

2758 **Amsden, Alice H.** The industry characteristics of intra-Third World trade in manufactures (UC/EDCC, 29:1, Oct. 1980, p. 1–19, tables)

Seeks to determine extent to which "South-North" trade represents harmful diversion, with particular concern over degrees of labor-intensity and employment-creation.

2759 **Aranda, Sergio** *et al.* América Latina en crisis. Caracas: Instituto Latinoamericano de Investigaciones Sociales, 1980. 394 p.: bibl.

"Crisis" is recession of 1974–75, phenomenon of capitalistic system of post-war period, symptomatic of prolonged crisis particularly of industrialization pattern. Country chapters deal with Argentina (Fernando Porta), Brazil (Jorge Fontanais), Jamaica (Porta, Fontanais), Mexico (José Cademartori).

2760 **Argüello, Omar.** Estrategias de supervivencia: un concepto en busca de su contenido (CM/DE, 15:2[46], 1981, p. 190–203)

Analysis of many dimensions of "survival."

2761 **Arroyo, Gonzalo.** Problemas agrarios, seguridad alimentaria y desarrollo en América Latina (CEESTEM/L, 1:2, 1981, p. 64–75, tables)

Analyzes agricultural development and proposes policies concerning it as well as industrialization strategies designed to provide national food security.

2762 **Aspectos técnicos de la deuda externa de los países latinoamericanos.** México: Centro de Estudios Monetarios Latinamericanos, 1980. 159 p.: ill. (Reuniones y seminarios)

Five essays with wide range, more "general" aspects than "technical" ones. Presented to seminar of central bank functionaries in Quito, 1979.

2763 **Astudillo Espinosa, Carlos T.** Realidad socioeconómica latinoamericana (IGME/RG, 16, abril 1981, p. 27–48)

Stresses need for "harmonic" integration of Latin American policies for economic and social development. Special emphasis on Andean group. Approach is philosophic.

2764 **The Automotive industry in Latin America.** Edited by Jan M. Herd. Erie, Pa.: Mercyhurst College, 1980. 181 p. (Institute of Latin American Studies monograph; no. 12)

Three papers: Charles A. Ford, "Mexico with Implications for US-Mexican Trade" (p. 1–120); George A. Westacott, "Brazil—Development and Outlook" (p. 121-149); and John H. Hoagland "Possible Trends, 1980–85" (p. 150–178).

2765 **Bacha, Edmar L.** O impacto da flutuação cambial sobre os países subdesenvolvidos: experiências latinoamericanas nos anos 70 (IPEA/PPE, 10:2, agosto 1980, p. 409–434, tables)

Develops methodology to examine effects of exchange rate changes on effective rates in real terms. Examples: Brazil, Chile, Costa Rica, Guatemala. Some policy conclusions.

2766 ——— and **Carlos F. Díaz Alejandro.** Mercados financeiros internacionais: uma perspectiva latino-americana (IPE/EE, 11:3, set./dez. 1981, p. 53–92, tables)

Recounts private financial arrangements, details events and evolution of 1970s, studies impact in Latin America, and raises various analytic issues. Effort to fill gap in literature regarding reemerging and massive private finance.

2767 **Báez, René.** Las transnacionales y América Latina. Bogotá: Ediciones Tercer Mundo, 1970. 91 p.

Crises of capitalist world in producing new forms of imperialism of which transnationals are one (and changing division of labor of which they are a part).

2768 **Balassa, Bela.** The newly-industrializing, developing countries after the oil crisis (CAUK/WA, 117:1, 1981, p. 142–194, bibl., tables)

Empirical study of effects of oil crisis shock, policy responses, and evaluations of policy. Not Latin America-specific but includes some such countries.

2769 ———. Reações de políticas econômicas aos choques externos em alguns países latino-americanos (IPE/EE, 11:2, abril/junho 1981, p. 11–49, tables)

Effects of oil pricing shocks (1974) and world recession (1974–75) in Brazil, Mexico, Uruguay. Analysis of policy responses. Analytic. Methodological appendix with extensive statistics.

2770 Baranson, Jack. North-South technology transfer: financing and institution building. Mt. Airy, Md.: Lomond Publications, 1981. 160 p.: bibl., index.

Short introduction. Deals with *issues* of technology transfer. Three country studies: Colombia, Brazil, Mexico. Conclusions.

2771 Bawa, Vasant K. Latin American integration. Atlantic Highlands, N.J.: Humanities Press, 1980. 244 p.: bibl., index, map.

Careful study of integration in Latin America primarily from the point of view: What is there here to be learned by Asians?

2772 Berberoglu, Berch. The nature and contradictions of state capitalism in the Third World: a re-examination of dominant conceptions and an alternative formulation (UWI/SES, 28:2, June 1979, p. 341–363, bibl, tables)

Examines three theories (Maoist, Soviet, dependency) of state capitalism and finds them wanting. Synthesis provides beginning of "general" theory. Considerable attention to Latin America.

2773 Bereznoi, Alexei. Prácticas restrictivas de comercio de las corporaciones transnacionales en América Latina (URSS/AL, 3[39], 1981, p. 52–64, tables)

Restrictive effects of multinationals on development in Latin America. A sort of "catalog" of sins.

2774 Bergquist, Charles. What is being done?: some recent studies on the urban working class and organized labor in Latin America (LARR, 16:2, 1981, p. 203–223)

Review article covers 11 works, some country-specific and including wide variety of purpose and approach.

2775 Bienefeld, Manfred. Dependency in the eighties (Bulletin [Institute of Development Studies, Sussex, England] 12:1, Dec. 1980, p. 5–10)

Issue's lead article is devoted to dependency theory. Concludes that while criticisms have shown some propositions untenable, experiences of 1970s strengthen main propositions although further refinement is required.

2776 Bilson, John F.0. Civil liberty: an econometric investigation (KYKLOS, 35:1, 1982, p. 94–114, tables)

Relates economic variables with civil liberties in large sample of countries. Correlations are not great but positive relation found between civil liberties and real per capita income and high ratios of wages and salaries to total income.

2777 Board of the Cartagena Agreement. Programa sectorial de desarrollo de la industria automotriz. Lima: Junta del Acuerdo de Cartagena, 1980. 157 p.: graphs.

Basic document explains Andean group's intent with respect to joint development of automotive industry. Includes "Decision 120" of 1977, and various modifications to it in subsequent decisions.

2778 Boneo, Horacio. Planificación, presupuesto y empresas públicas en América Latina. Buenos Aires: Centro de Estudios de Estado y Sociedad, 1979. 49 p.: bibl., ill. (Estudios CEDES; v. 2, no. 4)

Theoretical examination of organizational and behavioral patterns of public enterprises.

2779 Buira Seira, Ariel. Recesión, inflación y sistema monetario internacional (BCV/REL, 16:62, 1981, p. 79–118)

Reviews elements of world monetary crisis and urges that approach to solution will require philosophy similar to that of Marshall Plan—avoidance of North-South confrontation and participation and sacrifice by all.

2780 Buttari, Juan J. Aspectos relativos a la disponibilidad de mano de obra en América Latina (ECIEL, 5, julio 1978, p. 51–65, tables)

Examines relation between total population, labor force, distribution of labor force in various categories, and educational level.

2781 Butterworth, Douglas and **John K. Chance.** Latin American urbanization. New York: Cambridge University Press, 1981. 243 p.: bibl., index, map (Urbanization in developing countries)

Concerned with process of urbanization in demographic, sociocultural, economic, political dimensions. Avoids policy discussion.

2782 Calcagno, Alfredo Eric. Informe sobre las inversiones directas extranjeras en América Latina. Santiago: CEPAL, 1980. 114 p.: bibl. (Cuadernos de la CEPAL; no. 33. E/CEPAL/G.1108)

Essentially empirical, concludes with overview of policies adopted.

2783 Calili Padis, Pedro *et al.* América Latina: cincuenta años de industrialización. 2. ed. México: Premia Editora, 1978. 205 p.

Originally published in French. Series of essays evaluates industrialization. Considerable attention to role of US. One chapter on state militarization, another on agriculture.

2784 Cardoso, Ciro Flamarion Santana and **Héctor Pérez Brignoli.** Historia económica de América Latina. v. 1, Sistemas agrarios e historia colonial. v. 2, Economías de exportación y desarrollo capitalista. Barcelona, Spain: Crítica, 1979. 2 v.: bibl., ill. (Crítica/Historia; 10/11)

Vol. 2 studies history of economies since independence in two parts: 1) transition into peripheral capitalism (and its attendant frustrations); and 2) period 1870–1970 which was marked by more complete integration into the world economy (analysis goes beyond export sector). Vol. 1 concerns colonial period.

2785 Cardoso, Eliana A. Celso Furtado revisited: the postwar years (UC/EDCC, 30:1, Oct. 1981, p. 117–128)

Examines Furtado-Huddle controversy over whether expansion of real output in post-war years was due to exchange rate policy (Furtado, yes) or whether these were restrictive (Huddle). A Cardoso model suggests Furtado more nearly correct, but Huddle improves as term lengthens.

2786 Cardoso, Fernando Henrique. As idéias e seu lugar: ensaios sobre as teorias do desenvolvimento. Petrópolis, Brazil: Editora Vozes; São Paulo: CEBRAP, 1980. 163 p.: bibl. (Cadernos CEBRAP; no. 33)

A collection of essays which had appeared (1972–79) elsewhere in publications of varying difficulties to obtain.

2787 Cat and mouse on the coffee market? (BNCE/CE, 27:11, Nov. 1981, p. 474–478)

Quick review of machinations in international coffee market—and attempts to "regularize" it—since mid 1950s.

2788 Chang, Ligia and **María Angélica Ducci.** Realidad del empleo y la formación profesional de la mujer en América Latina. Montevideo: CINTERFOR, 1977. 124 p. (Estudios y monografías CINTERFOR; no. 24)

Bibliographic work of immense potential value. Annual series began in 1976 with vol. 1 which contained 742 references and their summaries. Vol. 2 has 500 summaries, and vol. 3, 504. References appear in eight subject-matter groupings with extensive indexing and cross-references.

2789 Chudnovsky, Daniel. The changing remittance behaviour of United States manufacturing firms in Latin America (WD, 10:6, June 1982, p. 513–521, bibl., tables)

Examines remittance policies, 1966–79, and finds remittances were reduced absolutely after 1975, the result of retained earnings.

2790 Cline, William R. International economic reform and income distribution (CEPAL/R, 10, April 1980, p. 103–112, tables)

Examines various NIEO proposals from point of view of their impact on the distribution of income both within and between countries.

2791 Cohen, Robert B. La reorganización internacional de la producción en la industria automotriz (FCE/TE, 48(2):190, abril/junio 1981, p. 383–404, tables)

Multinationals have begun process of world integration of automobile production as extension of policy of diversifying supply sources. Examines effects of national policy on this phenomenon.

2792 *Comercio Exterior.* Banco Nacional de Comercio Exterior. Vol. 27, No. 5, mayo 1981- . México.

This publication is one worth noting. Its section "Monthly Report" reviews events in the hemisphere in a professional and comprehensive manner. Convenient source of many topics.

2793 Conference on Commodity Models in Latin America, *Lima, Peru, 1978.* Commodity markets and Latin American development, a modeling approach. Sponsored by the Escuela de Administración de Negocios para Graduados (ESAN) and the National Bureau of Economic Research. Edited by Walter C. Labys, M. Ishaq Nadiri, and José Núñez del Arco. Cambridge, Mass.: Published for National Bureau of Economic Research by Ballinger Pub. Co., 1980. 280 p.: bibl., ill., index.

Papers presented at 1978 conference designed to provide perspective on relationship between primary commodity production and development by quantitative or modeling methods. Proceeds from general discussion, to specific commodity models, relation of commodities to national economies, and problems of stabilization.

2794 Conferencia sobre Planificación y Política Macroeconómica en el Corto Plazo en América Latina, *Contadora Island, Panama, 1975.* Planificación de corto plazo: la dinámica de los precios, el empleo y el producto. Sponsored by the Instituto Latinoamericano de Planificación Económico y Social (ILPES), the Ministerio de Planificación y Política Económica de Panamá, and the National Bureau of Economic Research (NBER). Santiago: Instituto Latinoamericano de Planificación Económica y Social, 1977. 129 p.: bibl., graphs (Cuadernos del ILPES; no. 25)

Although dated, contains several empirical pieces of considerable interest: explorations of Phillips curves, relationships between money quantity changes and production, case studies of Mexico, Colombia, Brazil, Argentina.

2795 Cordero S., Fernando. El proceso de integración y cooperación económico físico en América Latina. Stockholm: Institute of Latin American Studies, 1979. 28 p.: ill. (Research paper series; no. 13)

Overview of integration efforts whose results he finds disappointing.

2796 Córdova, Efrén. Labour relations in the public service in Latin America (ILO/R, 119:5, Sept./Oct. 1980, p. 579–593)

While public service has grown in numbers and types of employment, little change has occurred in the *de facto* treatment of labor relations. Change is noted, however, in liberalization of attitudes toward rights of public employees.

2797 De Janvry, Alain. The agrarian questions and reformism in Latin America. Baltimore: The Johns Hopkins University Press, 1981. 311 p.: bibl., index (The Johns Hopkins studies in development)

Important study. Deals with unequal agricultural growth and rural poverty and finds neo-classical theory not very helpful

either with respect to explanation or policy. Carefully done.

2798 Delorme, Robert. Latin America: social science information sources, 1967–1979. Santa Barbara, Calif.: ABC—Clio Press; Oxford, England: Clio Press, 1980. 262 p.: bibl., indexes.

About 5600 unannotated items with author and subject index. Includes books, monographs and articles selected from about 125 journals.

2798a Democracia & economía de mercado: ponencias y debates de un simposio. San Isidro, Perú: Instituto Libertad y Democracia, 1981. 436 p., 16 p. of plates: ill.

Powerful collection of papers and comments by such distinguished liberals as Von Hayek, Jean François Revel and others, presented at a symposium on democracy and the market economy. [M. Mamalakis]

2799 Democracy and development in Latin America. Edited and introduced by Louis Lefeber and Liisa L. North. Toronto: LARU, 1980. 193 p.: bibl., ill. (CERLAC-LARU studies on the political economy and culture of Latin America and the Caribbean; v. 1)

Outcome of a 1978 conference on "Democracy and Development: Latin America and Canada." Topics are important but have little centrality (e.g., dynamics of peripheral capitalism [Prebisch], external sector, international crisis, relations with world economy, spatial population distribution, technical change in agriculture, Cuba, education).

2800 El Desarrollo de América Latina en los años ochenta. Santiago: Naciones Unidas, Secretaría de la CEPAL, 1981. 183 p.: bibl. (Estudios informes de la CEPAL; 5. E/CEPAL/G.1150)

Basic ECLA document no. 5 in monographic series devoted to studies related to planning for 1980s (e.g., no. 6, projections; no. 7, external economic relations; no. 8, integration and regional cooperation; no. 9, strategies of sectoral development; and no. 10, dynamics of underemployment). New approach to development: integral and organic planning for economic development and social transformation).

2801 Development strategies and basic needs in Latin America: challenges for the 1980s. Originally presented as papers at the Symposium on Development Strategies in Latin America and the New International Order, held at the University of Lund, Sweden, Sept. 21–23, 1979. Edited by Claes Brundenius and Mats Lundahl. Boulder, Colo.: Westview, 1982. 180 p.: ill. (Westview special studies on Latin America and the Caribbean)

Good deal less general than title suggests but has broad coverage nonetheless. Three chapters are general. Five are country-specific: population in Haiti, employment in the Dominican Republic, needs and production in Peru, direction of Brazil, needs and strategies in Cuba.

2802 Devlin, Robert. Commercial bank finance from the North and the economic development of the South: congruence and conflict (CEPAL/R, 9, Dec. 1979, p. 69–93, bibl, tables)

Develops four important areas when banking interests and recipients do not have a "harmony of interests" and suggests alternatives to bank-provided international finance.

2803 Di Filippo, Armando. Economic development and theories of value (CEPAL/R, 11, Aug. 1980, p. 77–114)

Examines Marxian and neo-classical theories of "value" and particularly of market behavior and results. These markets do not have self-regulating forces leading to equilibrium accompanied "by a socially 'open' distribution of the fruits of development." Author's alternative is analysis of "power."

2804 Diálogo Norte-Sur: informe de la Comisión Brandt. Introducción de Willy Brandt. México: Editorial Nueva Imagen, 1981. 346 p.

Complete report of the Brandt Commission.

2805 Diálogo ou confronto?: América Latina e a Nova Ordem Econômica Internacional: debate de Canela sobre o Relatório Brandt. Organizado por Sergio C. Buarque. Rio de Janeiro: Paz e Terra, 1980. 216 p. (Coleção O mundo, hoje; v. 38)

Carefully edited result of seminar in Brazil (1980) including wide range of participants to analyze the Brandt report of 1979 (see item **2804**). Includes pieces (woven together) of several well-known contributors to thought about Latin American development.

2806 Díaz Alejandro, Carlos F. A América Latina em depressão: 1929/39 (IPEA/PPE, 10:2, agosto 1980, p. 351–382, tables)

Describes shocks, policy responses, effects of Great Depression on development in Latin America. Concentrates on exchange/trade policy. Concludes that advice was faulty to formulate policy as if countries were small or as if world economy did not matter.

2807 Díaz M., Luis. El Sistema Económico Latinoamericano, proposiciones para un modelo subregional. Santiago: Instituto de Estudios Internacionales, Universidad de Chile, 1977. 129 p.: bibl. (Serie de publicaciones especiales; no. 24)

Examination of SELA as potential factor in region's development. Second portion deals mostly with juridical-organizational aspects.

2808 Dickinson, Joshua. Una perspectiva ecológica sobre el desarrollo (AI/I, 6:1, enero/feb. 1981, p. 30–41)

Techniques transplanted from mid-latitudes to tropics as well as some values (e.g., prestige to cattle-owning) have far-reaching ecological effects. Planners, economists, ecologists must react together in designing viable systems.

2809 Distribución regional del producto interno bruto sectorial en los países de América Latina. Santiago: Naciones Unidas, 1981. 68 p.: bibl., tables (Cuadernos estadísticos de la CEPAL; 8. E/CEPAL/G. 115)

Effort to collate material on geographic subdivision participation in national product both per capita and by activity. Explores methodology and provides bibliography. Most data are, however, less than current.

2810 Economía de los países latinoamericanos. Bajo la redacción general de L. Klochkovski. Traducido del ruso por L. Vladov. Autores, P. Anániev et al. Moscú: Editorial Progreso, 1978. 504 p.: bibl. (Progreso, problemas de los países en desarrollo)

"A step on the way toward a Marxist study of [some] problems of vital importance to the present and future of Latin America." Principal themes: struggle for economic independence, Cuban conversion experiences, foreign capital and development, industrialization, agriculture, trade and integration, monetary problems.

2811 Elías, Víctor Jorge. Un estudio comparativo del desarrollo económico de Argentina, Brasil y Estados Unidos en el período 1940–1973 (UNLP/E, 25:1/3, enero/dic. 1979, p. 43–55, tables)

Comparative study of growth in Argentina, Brazil, and US and principal input sources of that growth. Technology found to be particularly important.

2812 ———. Government expenditures on agriculture in Latin America. Washington: International Food Policy Research Institute, 1981. 68 p.: tables (Research report; no. 23)

For nine countries (1950–78) seeks to relate government expenditures on agriculture to GDP, agricultural output; analyzes trends and variability; assesses effectiveness.

2813 Las Empresas públicas en América del Sur y México. v. 2. Banco Interamericano de Desarrollo, Escuela Interamericana de Administración Pública, Fundación Getúlio Vargas. México: Editorial Limusa, 1979. 1 v.: bibl., indexes.

More general than vol. 1. Consists of one chapter characterizing public enterprises, another very detailed one describing them in Latin America and by countries, others describing their international activities, and bibliography.

2814 Environment, society, and rural change in Latin America: the past, present, and future in the countryside. Edited by David A. Preston. Chichester, N.Y.: J. Wiley, 1981. 256 p.: bibl., indexes, maps.

Wide range of original essays discussing issues concerning rural people themselves, issues which will remain important even though the agricultural sector is in decline. Includes 11 country-specific chapters of 14 (e.g., Mexico, Peru, Ecuador, Brazil, Argentina).

2815 Estévez, Jaime and Belfor Portilla. El desarrollo agroindustrial: ¿agronegocio o Nuevo Orden Económico Internacional? (CEESTEM/L, 1:2, 1981, p. 83–96, tables)

Examines agro-business as possible contributor to goals of NIEO, especially full employment and food security, and finds it badly deficient. Proposes principles for organizing agriculture.

2816 Estilos de desarrollo y medio ambiente en la América Latina. Selección de Osvaldo Sunkel y Nicolo Gligo. México: Fondo de Cultura Económica, 1980. 2 v.: bibl., indexes, maps (El Trimestre económico. Lecturas; 36)

Vol. 1: introduction (Sunkel) treats inter-relationships between development and environment. Pt. 1 consists of nine essays (Prebisch *et al.*) on general topics; pt. 2 includes eight essays on forestry-agricultural sector, several of them with country focus. Vol. 2: urbanization and marginality; energy and industrialization; policy, strategy, and planning. For geographer's comment, see item **5013**.

2817 Estimating accounting prices for project appraisal: case studies in the Little [Mirrlees] Squire-van der Tak method. Terry A. Powers, editor. Washington: Inter-American Development Bank, 1981. 483 p.: tables.

Case studies are Paraguay, El Salvador, Ecuador, Barbados. Chaps. 1/3 explain and critique method which deals largely with "efficiency accounting price" rather than "social accounting price," which is even more complex. More "economics" than "accounting" in usual sense. Interesting methodologically and for data.

2818 Ferber, Robert. Distribución de ingreso y desigualdad de ingresos en algunas áreas urbanas (ECIEL, 3, agosto 1976, p. 67–125, tables)

Evaluation of data and methodology. Invaluable source of information with developing solid picture of urban incomes.

2819 Financiamiento del comercio exterior y seguro de crédito a las exportaciones. Lima: Asociación Latinoamericana de Instituciones Financieras de Desarrollo, 1979. 431 p.: ill.

Papers from 1979 seminar tend to be pragmatic, cases, country reports. Three themes: non-traditional exports, financial resources for export sector, credit insurance.

2820 Financiamiento y asistencia a la pequeña y mediana empresa: experiencia en Canadá y América Latina. Proceedings of the Seminario sobre Financiamiento y Asistencia a la Pequeña y Mediana Empresa, held in Arequipa, Peru, on December 5–9, 1977. Lima: ALIDE: publicado con la colaboración del Federal Business Development Bank y la Canadian International Development Agency, 1980. 520 p.: ill.

Papers from 1977 seminar in Peru. Brief, mostly descriptive presentations by a large number of participants. Contribution of Federal Development Bank of Canada is substantial (p. 61–232).

2821 Financing development in Latin America. Edited by Jean-Claude García-Zamor and Stewart E. Sutin. New York: Praeger, 1980. 354 p.: bibl., index.

Seeks to cover processes of public and private lending (mostly from abroad). Covers variety of topics not frequently seen (e.g., risk assessment, problem of industrial financing, accounting and reporting, legal aspects).

2822 Fishlow, Albert. A new Latin America in a new international capital market (CEPAL/R, 10, April 1980, p. 49–58)

Capital flows have increased, been productive but not without problems. Period has been characterized by "muddling through."

2823 Foreign debt and Latin American economic development. Papers presented at a conference on Latin American External Debt and Economic Growth held on February 23–25, 1982, at Miami, Florida, organized by the Department of Economics and the International Banking Center of Florida International University. Edited by Antonio Jorge, Jorge Salazar-Carrillo, and René P. Higonnet. New York: Pergamon Press, 1983. 183 p.: bibl.

Essentially papers presented at Miami conference (Feb. 1982). Seven discuss, in general way, relation between growth and external debt. Others cover specific areas/countries: Jamaica, Commonwealth Caribbean, Dominican Republic, Central America, Brazil, Mexico, Haiti, Venezuela, Costa Rica.

2824 Fossati Rocha, Humberto. El Nuevo Orden Económico: ensayo. La Paz: Talleres-Escuela de Artes Gráficas del Colegio Don Bosco, 1980. 243 p.: bibl.

Seeks to redevelop general economic theory that distinguishes between "temporal" and more usual "atemporal" economics. His version is more *real* and less *monetary*, more objective and less subjective, etc. Anticipates great benefits especially from the elimination of all but "neutral" money.

2825 Foxley, Alejandro. Experimentos neoliberales en América Latina. Santiago:

Corporación de Investigaciones Económicas para América Latina, 1980. 149 p.: tables (Estudios CIEPLAN)

Examines efficacy of "neo-liberal" economic policy in Chile after 1973, Uruguay after 1974, and Argentina after 1976. Principal objectives: 1) to explain why stabilization policies of 1970s and 1980s were more radical than in 1950s and 1960s; 2) to clarify nature of ultraliberal economic focus; and 3) to deal with techniques of stabilization. Major work by major observer.

2826 ———— and Laurence Whitehead. Economic stabilization in Latin America: political dimensions (WD, 8 : 11, Nov. 1980, p. 823–832)

Background summary for workshop on politics of stabilization, a comparative case study approach. Other contributors: Dell on international environment; Whitehead on Mexico; Augell and Thorp on Peru; Foxley on Chile; Canitrot on Argentina. Examines in detail relations between degrees of popular acceptance and stabilization policies.

2827 Franklin, Bruce. Debt peonage: the highest form of imperialism? (MR, 33 : 10, March 1982, p. 15–31, tables)

Analyzes possible effects of $500 billion external debts of developing countries. Concludes "debt imperialism" cannot long survive unless it can put armies in the field as "enforcers" and demonstrate its superiority ("more advanced form of political economy") to socialism.

2828 Freyssinet, Jacques. L'emploi en Amérique Latine: analyses et politiques (FDD/NED [Problèmes d'Amérique Latine, 59] 4609/4610, 10 mars 1981, p. 42–63)

Covers broad range of topics on employment and employment policy.

2829 From dependency to development: strategies to overcome underdevelopment and inequality. Edited by Heraldo Muñoz. Boulder, Colo.: Westview Press, 1981. 336 p.: bibl., index (Westview special studies in social, political, and economic development)

Collection of original and previously published papers pointed at theme of "dependency reversal"—the means of overcoming dependency and underdevelopment. Begins with thorough airing of dependency theory.

2830 García, Alvaro. Criterios y

metodologías para la satisfacción de necesidades básicas. Santiago: Programa Regional del Empleo para América Latina y el Caribe (PREALC), 1980. 81 p. (Documento de trabajo; 190)

Careful methodological examination of definition and measurement of "basic necessities" and "poverty."

2831 García, Norberto E. Necesidades básicas y crecimiento económico. Santiago: Oragnización Internacional del Trabajo (OIT), Programa Mundial del Empleo, Programa Regional del Empleo para América Latina y el Caribe (PREALC), 1979. 21 leaves: tables (Trabajo ocasional; no. 27)

Correlated per capita GDP with various welfare measures (e.g., life expectancy); also uses Spearman rank-order correlation. Seeks to answer question: does growth improve welfare?

2832 García G., Rigoberto. Algunos elementos para una geografía del bienestar: la distribución del ingreso en América Latina. Stockholm: Institute of Latin American Studies, 1979. 44 p. (Research paper series; no. 2)

Deals mostly with income distribution, little with geography. Notes failure of modern sector to reduce inequality and suggests it is not likely to do so autonomously.

2833 ———. Evolución de la industria manufacturera latinoamericana, 1850–1930. Stockholm: Institute of Latin American Studies, 1980. 85 p. (Research paper series; no. 26)

One must get behind aggregate data to understand changes which occurred. Approach is several country studies.

2834 ———. The planning process in Latin America. Stockholm: Institute of Latin American Studies, 1978. 25 p.: tables (Research paper series; no. 8)

Overview of planning process. Not a failure for power groups but others have not benefitted much.

2835 Garzón Valdés, Ernesto. SELA—Eine Organisation der Lateinamerikanischen Entwicklungspolitik (DDW, 8:1, 1980, p. 86–101)

Reviews various organizations of Latin American economic integration and their shortcoming. Examines 1975–80 period in Sistema Económico Latinoamericano (SELA),

stressing need for greater coordination of international commerce. [G.M. Dorn]

2836 Gastos militares y desarrollo en América del Sur. Lima: Universidad de Lima, Centro de Investigaciones Económicas y Sociales (CIESUL). 312 p.: ill.

Pilot study. Projects arms expenditures, develops a model to suggest limits, explores resources to be freed and possible uses. A first step.

2837 Gilhodes, Pierre. Les relations economiques entre les Etats-Unis et l'Amérique Latine: 1975–1979 (FDD/NED [Problèmes d'Amérique Latine, 60] 4619/4620, 12 Mai 1981, p. 87–122, tables)

Thorough review of Latin America-US relations. Emphasis is economic.

2838 Glade, William P. Economic policy making and the structures of corporatism in Latin America (*in* Institutional economics: contributions to the development of holistic economies. Boston: Martinus Nijhoff Publishing Co., 1979, p. 217–238)

Traces growth of technocratic class, autonomous and semi-autonomous agencies, and examines other reasons for the emergence of corporatist economies in Latin America which he expects to endure for some time. Article available from University of Texas, Austin, Offprint Series No. 208.

2839 ———. La política económica de los controles en la empresa pública: un enfoque contextual (Anuario Jurídico [Universidad Nacional Autónoma de México, Instituto de Investigaciones Jurídicas, México] 8, 1981, p. 269–295)

Public enterprise plays a particular role in Latin America. Article examines basically the institutional matrix which produced public enterprise. Article available from University of Texas, Austin, Offprint Series No. 223.

2840 Glaser, William A. and G. Christopher Habers. The brain drain: emigration and return: findings of a UNITAR multinational comparative survey of professional personnel of developing countries who study abroad. New York: Pergamon Press, 1978. 324 p.: bibl., indexes (UNITAR research report; no. 22)

Not Latin America-specific but a general problem and includes several Latin American countries. Calls for more, and country-specific, research.

2841 Gligo Viel, Nicolo. The environmental dimension in agricultural development in Latin America (CEPAL/R, 12, Dec. 1980, p. 129–143)

Examines impact of agriculture on environment (over-use of land), causes therefore, and implications of so continuing.

2842 Gregory, Peter. An assessment of changes in employment conditions in less developed countries (UC/EDCC, 28:4, July 1980, p. 673–700, tables)

Systematic attempt to test widely accepted hypothesis that employment conditions in LDC's have deteriorated generally. Data do not support the hypothesis, but this is not definitive and even if it were, there would be cause for concern because of continuing poor conditions.

2843 ———. Employment, unemployment, and underemployment in Latin America. Albuquerque: University of New Mexico, Latin American Institute, 1981. 45 p.: bibl., tables.

Very careful analysis of data sources, definitions, conceptual problems related to title topics. Concludes data do not support conventional wisdom that conditions have been deteriorating in the labor markets.

2844 Grosse, Robert. Foreign investment regulation in the Andean Pact: the first ten years (IAMEA, 33:4, Spring 1980, p. 77–92, tables)

Restrictive effects of early years are disappearing and investment now growing. More general than title suggests.

2845 Halperin-Donghi, Tulio. "Dependency theory" and Latin American historiography (LARR, 17:1, 1982, p. 115–130)

Reviews principal contributors (particularly Cardoso and Faletto, André Gunder Frank) to dependency theory and their impacts from an historian's point of view (see also item **2905**).

2846 Hardoy, Jorge E. International cooperation for human settlements (LARR, 17:3, 1982, p. 3–28)

Studies relations between governments and multilateral agencies in general area of human settlements. Draws largely from Latin America.

2847 Heller, Peter S. Impact of inflation on fiscal policy in developing countries (IMF/SP, 27:4, Dec. 1980, p. 712–748, tables)

Analysis of factors influencing speed of reaction of various revenue and expenditure policies to inflation and test of Aghevli-Khan hypothesis that inflation is self-sustaining through inflation-caused deficits. Not Latin America specific but most countries included in 60-country sample.

2848 Hirschman, Albert O. Essays in trespassing: economics to politics and beyond. New York: Cambridge University Press, 1981. 310 p.: bibl., index.

Consists of 14 Hirschman essays, trespassing disciplinary boundaries, on broad theme of development. They have appeared elsewhere, but are grouped around topics of author's book-length studies. Useful, as usual.

2849 Iglesias, Enrique V. The economic evolution of Latin America in 1981 (BNCE/CE, 28:3, March 1982, p. 96–106, tables)

Thorough review of 1981 economy.

2850 ———. Latin America on the threshold of the 1980s (CEPAL/R, 9, Dec. 1979, p. 7–43, graphs, tables)

Review of recent past. Statement of objectives: improving distribution gains of growth, increasing growth. . . reducing dependence. Discusses, then, requisites to attain objectives.

2851 La Industrialización de América Latina y la cooperación internacional. Santiago: Naciones Unidas, 1981. 170 p.: bibl., ill. (Estudios e informes de la CEPAL; 3. E/CEPAL/G.1140)

Actually, two separate 1979 studies: l) *Análisis y perspectivas del desarrollo industrial latinoamericano* which treats three decades, points up problems and suggests alternatives for policy; and 2) *Cooperación internacional para el desarrollo industrial de América Latina* which examines subregional, regional, inter-regional, and world possibilities. Good source of data.

2852 Infante B., Ricardo. Heterogeneidad estructural, empleo y distribución del ingreso (FCE/TE, 48[2]:190, abril/junio 1981, p. 319–340, tables)

Interrelationships among segments of the "structurally heterogeneous" economies. Discusses appropriate policies.

2853 Inotai, Andrés. Integración regional en el Nuevo Mundo: el ámbito económico (UNAM/L, 14, 1981, p. 293–314, tables)

Explores "new" economic environment for regional integration. Concludes that there is a place for regional organizations but they should not be pursued at "any cost."

2854 Integración y cooperación en América Latina. Antonio Jorge and Jorge Salazar-Carrillo, editores. Campinas, Brasil: CARTGRAF, 1982. 358 p.: tables (Coleção; 4)

Particularly valuable compendium in broad review of integration experience in Latin America at this rather critical time, assesses future prospects. Among authors are the editors, Eduardo R. Conesa, Elvio Baldinelli, Ricardo Ffrench-Davis, Felipe Herrera, Wolf Grabendorff.

2854a Jackman, Robert W. Dependence on foreign investment and economic growth in the Third World (PUCIS/WP, 34:2, Jan. 1982, p. 175–196, tables)

Econometric study. Conclusions: "Mathew effect" greater within Third World than between it and developed countries; impact of foreign investment on growth appears limited although growth of investment is positively associated.

2855 Jiménez, Emmanuel. The value of squatter dwellings in developing countries (UC/EDCC, 30:4, July 1982, p. 739–752, tables)

Sample is from Philippines but methodology is applicable elsewhere. Of interest where urban "squatting" is important.

2856 Jiménez C., Edgar. Reflexiones acerca del nuevo modelo de acumulación en Latinoamérica (UNAH/RCE, 1:1, sept. 1979, p. 140–153, tables)

Analyzes internal effects of flows of international capital into Latin American economies—considerable effect on the classic entrepreneurial groups.

2857 *Journal of Inter-American Studies and World Affairs.* Sage Publications. Vol. 22, No. 4, Nov. 1980- . Beverly Hills, Calif.

Six short essays on public enterprise (i.e., introduction, two on Brazilian banks, Peru's ENCI, Mexico's CONASUPO, bibliography).

2858 Junta del Acuerdo de Cartagena. Evaluación del proceso de integración, 1969–1979. Lima: 1979? 172 p.: bibl.

Thorough review of integration over 10 years. Recommendations and conclusions.

2859 Kádár, Béla. Problems of economic growth in Latin America. Translated from the Hungarian by Pál Félix. Translation rev. by David Biró. New York: St. Martin's Press, 1989. 267 p.: bibl., index.

Pt. 1 is general, and besides providing background information, seeks to distinguish Latin America from other parts of Third World. Pt. 2 considers five country cases: Peru, Argentina, Brazil, Colombia, Mexico.

2860 Karaváiev, Alexandr. La estrategia de la modernización capitalista de la economía (URSS/AL, 4:28, 1980, p. 9–36)

Chicago "school" is responsible for new wave of integration of Latin American countries into capitalist sphere and of exploitation of labor; production for export is the primary mode. Brazil, Mexico, Venezuela are discussed in some detail.

2861 Keshishev, Vladimir. La pesca en la solución del problema de los alimentos (URSS/AL, 8:32, 1980, p. 67–78)

Notes dietary deficiencies in Latin America, reviews experience in Peru and Cuba, and suggests that a fishery industry could alleviate much misery.

2862 Kistanov, Valeri. El capital japonés en América Latina (URSS/AL, 1/2:37/38, 1981, p. 123–137, tables)

Sketch of Japanese investment experience in Latin America in recent decades. Covers trade, investment, investment strategy with most attention to aggregates rather than individual countries.

2863 Klein, Emilio. Diferenciación social: tendencias del empleo y los ingresos agrícolas. Santiago: Organización Internacional del Trabajo (OIT), Programa Mundial del Empleo, Programa Regional del Empleo para América Latina y El Caribe (PREALC), n.d. 17 leaves: bibl., tables (Trabajo ocasional; 28)

Agriculture is generally the sector of the poor. The modern, wage-earning, permanent agriculturalist, though, is becoming differentiated from the seasonal worker without land of his own.

2864 Klochkovski, Lev. América Latina: problemas en el desarrollo del comercio exterior (URSS/AL, 3:39, 1981, p. 28–51, tables)

Review of Latin American trade since World War II with emphasis on US role and intra-Latin American policy.

2865 ———. Estrategia económica de los monopolios de Estados Unidos en la región latinoamericana (URSS/AL, 5 : 29, 1980, p. 4–20)

Sketches history of multinationals in Latin America, their participation in import substitution, manufacturing for export, direct investment patterns, the need for Latin American countries to stand together.

2866 Koehler, Wallace C., Jr. A multinational fuel-cycle proposal for Latin America (AI/I, 5 : 2, marzo/abril 1980, p. 92–95)

Proposal to test the idea of multinational nuclear fuel center in Latin America as possible model to use elsewhere.

2867 Kosobchuk, Svetlana. El capital extranjero privado en los mercados de crédito (URSS/AL, 4 : 28, 1980, p. 37–54)

Private bank credit is relatively new and rapidly growing means for "private foreign monopoly capital" to influence decisive development patterns in Latin America. Includes European as well as US banks in analysis.

2868 Kovaliov, Evgueni. Las reformas agrarias y el desarrollo agrícola (URSS/AL, 9 : 33, 1980, p. 69–82)

Surveys experiences of "bourgeois" land reforms and concludes they are only partial, neglecting as many problems as they solve.

2869 ———. La revolución verde y las transformaciones agrarias (URSS/AL, 1 : 49, 1982, p. 34–47)

Traces "green revolution" in Latin America and its problems as a means of transforming agriculture.

2870 Kulakov, Mijail. Cuestiones de modernización de la agricultura (URSS/AL, 1 : 49, 1982, p. 48–60, ill.)

Traces evolution of agriculture in the area, notes its importance and tendency to lag. Discusses problems associated with "green revolution" and other changing technologies.

2871 Labarca, Guillermo. Los bancos multinacionales en América Latina y la cri-

sis del sistema capitalista. México: Editorial Nueva Imagen, 1979. 201 p.: bibl. (Serie Sociedad, proceso, coyuntura)

Thoughtful book which seeks to analyze capital's role in the "crisis" and how this affects Latin America through multinationals and, particularly, private international banking. Closes with chapter on unresolved theoretical questions.

2872 Lall, Sanjaya. The international automotive industry and the developing world (WD, 8 : 10, Oct. 1980, p. 789–812, tables)

Post-oil-crisis development of automobile industry seems to be changing toward greater concentration of ownership and greater geographic dispersion.

2873 The Latin American integration process in 1980. Buenos Aires: Inter-American Development Bank, Institute for Latin American Integration, 1980. l v.: tables.

Reminder of this annual publication which this year is of special significance since it records the demise of LAFTA and the emergence of LAIA. Comprehensive summary of regional and subregional cooperation.

2874 Lazo, Jaime. El desarrollo rural en el agro de América Latina (Boletín de Antropología Americana [Instituto Panamericano de Geografía e Historia, México] 2, dic. 1980, p. 61–76, ill., tables)

Survey of "state" of Latin American rural sector and assessment of tendencies.

2875 LDC external debt and the world economy. Proceedings of a private international meeting organized October 1977 in Mexico City under the auspices of El Colegio de México and the Center for Economic and Social Studies of the Third World. Miguel S. Wionczek, editor. México: El Colegio de México: Center for Economic and Social Studies of the Third World, 1978. 477 p.: bibl.

Proceedings of 1977 meeting which treats topic in considerable depth as one principal theme for the NIEO. Reports summary conclusions. Important volume.

2876 Leff, Nathaniel H. El "capitalism monopólico" y la política pública de los países en desarrollo (FCE/TE, 48[2]:190, abril/junio 1981, p. 363–382)

Analysis of extent and effects of concentration of manufacturing in developing countries ànd public policy alternatives to ameliorate distortions. Not Latin America specific. For English version, see *Kyklos* (32:4, 1979).

2877 Lejavitzer, Moisés. Evolución y estructura de la balanza de pagos de América Latina y el Caribe. México: Centro de Estudios Monetarios Latinoamericanos, 1979. 177 p.: bibl., graphs (Serie Estudios)

Covers two periods 1969–73, 1974–76, and region as a whole rather than country-by-country. Is particularly careful in managing and explaining concepts.

2878 Lichtensztejn, Samuel and **Edgardo Lifschitz.** Impacto de las empresas transnacionales sobre las políticas económicas de América Latina. México: Instituto Latinoamericano de Estudios Transnacionales, 1978. 48 leaves.

In a variety of ways, transnationals affect (negatively) economic policies related to development.

2879 Lifschitz, Edgardo. Bibliografía analítica sobre empresas transnacionales = Analytical bibliography on transnational corporations. México: Instituto Latinoamericano de Estudios Transnacionales, 1980. 607 p.: indexes.

Elaborate 3800 item compilation. Extensive indexing includes indication of availability at select Mexican libraries. "Annotation" consists of listing major topics covered for many entrys (in language of entry). Very useful publication.

2880 Lord, Montague J. Commodity export instability and growth in Latin American economies (*in* Commodity markets and Latin American development: a modeling approach. Cambridge, Mass.: Published for National Bureau of Economic Research by Ballinger Publishing Co., 1980, p. 213–244)

Demonstrates instability but less certain as to how it affects growth and whether or not buffer stock schemes would in fact improve producer economies. Article available from Inter-American Development Bank, Washington, D.C., as Bank Reprint Series No. 103.

2881 Lustig, Nora. Underconsumption in Latin American economic thought: some considerations (Review of Radical Political Economics [Union for Radical Political Economics, New York] 12:1, Spring 1980, p. 35–43, bibl.)

Careful analysis of "underconsumption," its relevance to Latin American development, and characterization of Latin American writers by their views on subject.

2882 McCulloch, Rachel. A posição da América Latina em relação as medidas de liberalização do comércio (IPE/EE, 11:2, abril/junho 1981, p. unavailable, bibl., tables)

Analyzes effects of external trade policies (of developed and developing countries) on Latin America. Sub-questions: how important are such policies on Latin American development? What are effects of recent policy changes at the international level? What strategies can most effectively be employed by Latin American countries?

2883 Macedo, Roberto Brás Matos. Elasticidad de sustitución: evaluación crítica e implicaciones para políticas de empleo en América Latina. Santiago: Organización Internacional del Trabajo, Programa Mundial del Empleo, Programa Regional del Empleo para América Latina y el Caribe, 1980. 37 p.: bibl., graphs (Documento de trabajo PREALC; 192)

Careful assessment of literature regarding elasticity of substitution between labor and capital. This has important employment policy implications. Finds that there is considerable methodological and empirical ambiguity.

2884 McGaughey, Stephen E. Investment criteria for agricultural and rural development projects. Washington: Inter-American Development Bank, 1981. 62 p.: bibl. (Inter-American Development Bank reprint series; 105)

Seeks to provide usable, intervening stage of project evaluation between present practice of little evaluation (particularly when there are multiple objectives) and widespread use of social cost-benefit analysis, which may be possible in the future.

2885 Malan, Pedro. The Latin American countries and the New International Economic Order (CEPAL/R, 10, April 1980, p. 66–80, diagram)

Deals with NIEO issues trade, direct foreign investment, capital flows and assesses Latin American interest in these issues and their resolution.

2886 Mansilla, H.C.F. Crítica a las teorías de la modernización y la dependencia (CSIC/RIS, 37:31, julio/sept. 1979, p. 329–349)

Criticizes general theories of modernization and dependency (as being over-simple) and suggests lines of thought for improvement *and* synthesis.

2887 Martner, Gonzalo. Una estrategia tercermundista para América Latina (NSO, 51, nov./dic. 1980, p. 7–32)

Stresses control of resources, regional integration, South-South trade.

2888 Massad, Carlos. Latin America and the international monetary system: some comments and suggestions (CEPAL/R, 10, April 1980, p. 59–65, table)

Present working of monetary system, effects of system on LDCs, changes which could help minimize difficulties.

2889 Mattos, Carlos Antonio de. Crecimiento y concentración espacial en la América Latina: algunas consecuencias (FCE/TE, 48[2]:190, abril/junio 1981, p. 341–362, tables)

Concerned primarily with effects of the spatial inequality in the distribution of fruits of growth.

2890 Meller, Patricio and **Alejandra Mizala.** US multinationals and Latin American manufacturing employment absorption (WD, 10:2, Feb. 1982, p. 115–126, tables)

Concerns seven countries (1966–70). Conclusions: growth rate of employment neither high nor low, industrial differences in employment-generation are not great, exports were not major employers, technology tended to be labor-saving.

2891 ———; Soledad Léniz; and Carlos Swinburn. Comparaciones internacionales de concentración industrial en América Latina (ECIEL, 3, agosto 1976, p. 27–65, tables)

Pioneer effort: comparative study in Latin America of structure of concentration in industrial sectors. Data interesting and conclusions important.

2892 Méndez, Jorge. El estado de la planificación en América Latina y el Caribe. Santiago: Naciones Unidas, CEPAL, Instituto Latinoamericano de Planificación Económica y Social, 1980. 343 p.: ill.

Thorough study of planning—styles of planning, character of plans, planning techniques, policies in several areas as means of executing plans, the emerging dimensions of planning.

2893 Miller, Rory. Latin American manufacturing and the First World War: an exploratory essay (WD, 9:8, Aug. 1981, p. 707–716, tables)

Concerned with lack of industrial development (particularly textile) in five countries—Argentina, Brazil, Chile, Colombia, Peru—during World War I when incentives were great and expansion and diversification were, a priori, expected.

2894 Monetary policy and balance-of-payments adjustment: three studies. Santiago: Naciones Unidas, 1980. 60 p.: bibl. (Cuadernos de la CEPAL. Document—Naciones Unidas; E/CEPAL/1088)

Demand for imported goods; balance of payments adjustment, credit policy, debt control; monetary approach to exchange rates. Serious papers.

2895 Money and monetary policy in less developed countries: a survey of issues and evidence. Edited by Warren L. Coats, Jr. and Deena R. Khatkhate. New York: Pergamon Press, 1980. 827 p.: bibl., ill., index (Readings in money and banking in the LDCs)

Collection of 46 journal articles on money, monetary policy and development. Latin America treated incidentally. Editors have provided an important service in producing this volume.

2896 Morgan, Theodore and **Albert Davis.** The concomitants of exchange-rate depreciation: less developed countries, 1971–73 (UC/EDCC, 31:1, Oct. 1982, p. 101–129)

Sample of 42 LDCs studied for efficacy of depreciation. Conclusions: 1) official rates are misleading; 2) effective depreciation correlates more highly with capital flows than goods-service flows; 3) terms-of-trade changes were dominated by other effects; and 4) inflationary effects not clear.

2897 Morris, Arthur Stephen. Latin America: economic development and regional differentiation. Totowa, N.J.: Barnes & Noble, 1981. 256 p.: bibl., index.

Heavily "spatial" with "regional" generally meaning "subnational." Puts "development" in historical context and also stresses desirability of planning on levels lower than "central."

2898 Multinational corporations and international investment in Latin America: a selection and annotated bibliography with an annotated film bibliography. Compiled, edited, and introduced by Harold Molineu. Contributors, Steven M. Jongewaard *et al.* Athens: Ohio University, Center for International Studies, Latin American Program, 1978. 98 p.: indexes (Papers in international studies: Latin American series; no. 3)

Useful, annotated bibliography of English-language works on multinationals (108 items), foreign investment (24 items). Pt. 3 offers 24 official publications, pt. 4, 24 films.

2899 Muñoz, Heraldo. The strategic dependency of the centers and the economic importance of the Latin American periphery (LARR, 16:3, Fall 1981, p. 3–29)

Although the share of Latin America in US trade has declined, strategic dependency may have increased. This involves critical minerals, cheap labor, large markets, giving Latin American countries increased bargaining power.

2900 Nelson, Nici. Actividades productivas y generadoras de ingreso para mujeres del Tercer Mundo. Santiago: UNICEF, Proyecto de Promoción y Desarrollo de la Mujer en América Latina y el Caribe, Oficina Regional para las Américas, 1980. 63 p. (Documentos de trabajo sobre programas para la mujer = Working documents on programmes benefitting women. Proyecto Regional de Promoción y Desarrollo de la Mujer en América Latina y el Caribe; UNICEF/TARO/PAM/80/4. Documento—Grupo de Estudio de UNICEF sobre Mujer y Desarrollo; no. 3)

Sort of primer on "programs for women:" Why have them? What will women gain? What kinds of income-generating programs? Principles for starting such programs.

2901 Nevin, Paul F. The survival economy: micro-enterprises in Latin America Cambridge, Mass.: Acción International/AITEC, 1982. 86 p.

Good deal of case material and some generalization therefrom on small, urban business.

2902 Novak, Michael. Why Latin America

is poor (The Atlantic [Boulder, Colo.] 249:3, March 1982, p. 66–75, ill.)

Largely a critical examination of "Catholic Latin American economics." Concludes that "blame" for poverty is not so much external as internal.

2903 Nugent, Jeffrey B. and **Constantine Glezakos.** Phillips curves in developing countries: the Latin American case (UC/EDCC, 30:2, Jan. 1982, p. 321–334)

Using 15-year time series for 16 countries, authors find that Philipps curves are positively sloped and that the premise of negative slopes does not hold; increases in inflation are likely to be associated with decreases rather than increases in output. This is because of the nature and dominance of agriculture. Article has important policy implications.

2904 Oyeca, Ikewelugo C.A. An analysis of some determinants of agricultural productivity in developing countries (AI/A, 7:1, enero/feb. 1982, p. 30–36, bibl., tables)

Land and labor intensification, rather than capital intensification, are found to be effective (fertilizer possible exception). In Latin America (and elsewhere) best means to increasing *per capita* agricultural productivity is to increase proportion of non-agricultural to agricultural labor.

2905 Packenham, Robert A. Plus ça change: . . .: the English edition of Cardoso and Faletto's *Dependencia y desarrollo en América Latina* (LARR, 17:1, 1982, p. 131–151)

Examines in detail the unadvertised and substantial changes in the English version and assesses their significance. This is an early and key work on dependency (see *HLAS 41:2773–2774*, and item **2845**).

2906 Pagano, Carlos O. External financing prospects of Latin America's development banking system. Washington: Inter-American Development Bank, 1980. 96 p.: bibl., graphs.

Comprehensive examination of development banks and sources of funding available to them. Sketches their growing importance and also proposes a "package" of funding experience: local development banking, regional institutions, private system. Also available in Spanish as *Evolución y perspectivas del financiamiento externo de la banca de fomento latinoamericano.*

2907 Los Países en desarrollo en lucha por un Nuevo Orden Económico Internacional (URSS/AL, 3[51], 1982, p. 93–100, ill.)
Informal and interesting report of second meeting of Association of Third World Economists (April 1981, Havana).

2908 Pantelides, Edith A. Estudio de la población femenina económicamente activa en América Latina, 1950–1970. Santiago: Centro Latinoamericano de Demografía, 1976. 99 p.: bibl., ill. (Serie C. CELADE; no. 161)
Essentially statistical study based on censuses of 1950, 1960, 1970. Carefully done and well documented. Dated but likely to be a benchmark study.

2909 Parques industriales en América Latina: Bolivia, Brasil, Colombia, Chile, Ecuador. Instituto Latinoamericano de Investigaciones Sociales (ILDIS), Centro de Desarrollo Industrial del Ecuador (ENDES). Bogotá: Grupo Editorial Dobry, 1979. 274 p.: bibl.
Papers from 1978 seminar on role of industrial park in development. Covers many aspects: macroeconomic, localization, administration. Reports experiences in Bolivia, Brazil, Colombia, Chile, Ecuador.

2910 Parra Peña, Isidro. Leyendo a Raúl Prebisch (Desarrollo Indoamericano [E. Salazar F., Bogotá] 15:66, marzo 1981, p. 7–16, ill., tables)
Competent essay on Prebisch's contributions.

2911 Peña, Rosa María de la. Las preferencias del comercio internacional: el sistema generalizado de preferencias para las exportaciones mexicanas. México: Universidad Nacional Autónoma de México, 1980. 165 p. (Estudios de derecho económico; no. 7. Serie I)
Review and analysis of the NIEO with respect to the "generalized system of preferences" under the GATT particularly concerning Mexico.

2912 Pennano, Guido. Empresas públicas y desarrollo económico: la polémica continúa (UP/A, 6:11, 1981, p. 99–10, bibl.)
Public firms are increasingly important. Examines role, effectiveness, and new relationships which emerge.

2913 Pensamiento latinoamericano: CEPAL, R. Prebisch y A. Pinto. Víctor M. Bernal Sahagún *et al.* México: Universidad Nacional Autónoma de México, Seminario de Teoría del Desarrollo, Instituto de Investigaciones Económicas, 1980. 178 p.: bibl.
Principal essays on ECLA, Prebisch, Pinto with comments thereon by others. Interesting work retains flavor of seminar.

2914 La Pequeña empresa en el desarrollo de América Latina. Autores, Eliseo Salas P. *et al.* Caracas: Fundación para el Desarrollo de la Comunidad y Fomento Municipal (FUNDACOMUN), 1979. 403 p.: bibl., ill.
Product of 1978 Venezuela conference. Covers wide range of topics: theoretical-methodological and country reports (Bolivia, Costa Rica, Chile, Ecuador, Honduras, Mexico, Venezuela).

2915 Pinto, Aníbal. La internacionalización de la economía mundial: una visión latinoamericana. Madrid: Ediciones Cultura Hispánica del Instituto de Cooperación Iberoamericana, 1980. 142 p.: ill.
Explores two questions: 1) nature and scope of so-called "internationalization of the world economy" particularly from Center-Periphery analytic considerations; and 2) degree and form of inserting Latin America into the international complex with present and future prospects.

2916 ———. The opening up of Latin America to the exterior (CEPAL/R, 11, Aug. 1980, p. 31–56, tables)
Reasons for, varieties of and changes in the policy of "openness." Significance, options, and problems of industrializing through integration with the world economy (see also *HLAS 43:2900–2901*).

2917 *Planindex*. Resúmenes de documentos sobre planificación. Naciones Unidas, Comisión Económica para América Latina (CEPAL), Centro Latinoamericano de Documentación Económica y Social. Vol. 1, No. 2, 1980- . Santiago.
Summaries of 353 planning documents from Latin American countries, arranged by subject and with several indexes. To be published twice annually. Very useful tool.

2918 Pollitt, Ernesto; Robert Halpern; and Patricia Eskenasy. Poverty and malnutrition in Latin America: early childhood intervention programs: a report to the Ford Foundation. New York: Praeger, 1980. 162 p.: bibl.

Seeks to evaluate "interventions" in general and "cases" from Peru, Colombia, and Venezuela, in particular (for anthropologist's comment, see item **1839**).

2919 Posner, Joshua L. and **Malcolm F. McPherson.** Agriculture on the steep slopes of tropical America: current situation and prospects for the year 2000 (WD, 10:5, May 1982, p. 341–353, bibl., tables)

Examines situation of very important steep-slope agriculture (also associated with poverty) and considers policies for alleviation of resource erosion and poverty.

2920 Prado, Eleutério F.S. Crescimento econômico, pobreza e distribuição de renda em países subdesenvolvidos (IPE/EE, 11:1, jan./março 1981, p. 83–91, bibl., tables)

Discusses income distribution in general and closes with empirical study of Brazil's Northeast.

2921 Prebisch, Raúl. Obras escogidas. t. l, Teoría económica general: crecimiento y desarrollo económico de América Latina. Selección, introducción y comentarios de Isidro Parra-Peña. Bogotá: Ediciones Colibrí, 1981. 1 v.: bibl., ill. (Antología del pensamiento económico y social de América Latina; v. 3)

Apparently vol. 1 of two or more. Includes wide selection of writings (1940s–70s) on two general themes: general theory (Keynes) and Latin American development. Lengthy introduction puts selections in perspective. Useful effort.

2922 Programa de Estudios Conjuntos sobre Integración Económica Latino-americana (ECIEL). Cinco anos ao serviço acadêmico da América Latina, 1974–1979: atividades do Programa ECIEL. Felipe Herrera. Rio de Janeiro: 1979. 117 p.: bibl.

Good account of an excellent and innovative activity. Bibliography is both impressive and useful.

2923 Programa Regional del Empleo para América Latina y el Caribe (PREALC). Employment in Latin America. New York: Praeger, 1978. 193 p.: bibl.

Prepared for 1976 meeting; important enough to include even now. Covers: employment situation, review of employment

policies, long-term perspectives, strategy proposals, quantitative aspects.

2924 ———. Heterogeneous rural labor markets and employment. Santiago: Organización International del Trabajo, Programa Mundial del Empleo, 1979. 37 leaves: bibl., graphs (Monograph—PREALC; 11)

Theoretical and not Latin America specific. Builds model of agricultural sector, demonstrates that only way for real change to occur is in structure. Utilizes "land reform" as an example of structural change.

2925 ———. Identificación de sectores claves para la generación de empleo: metodologías alternativas. Santiago: Organización Internacional de Trabajo, 1979. 95 p.: bibl. (Investigaciones sobre empleo; 15)

Essentially a methodological piece on the study of "key sectors" and "linkages" for employment generation.

2926 ———. Necesidades esenciales y políticas de empleo en América Latina: un estudio del Programa Regional del Empleo en América Latina y el Caribe. Ginebra: Oficina Internacional del Trabajo, 1980. 137 p.: bibl.

Study of relationships of employment, incomes, and basic needs. These are related to development strategies, employment policies, and new alignments of the international division of labor.

2926a ———. Participación femenina en la actividad económica en América Latina: análisis estadístico. Prepared by Manuel Barrera. Santiago: Organización Internacional del Trabajo, 1978. 25, 11 leaves: bibl. (Documento de trabajo -PREALC; 161)

Role of women in the Latin American labor force, small relative to other areas, is increasing, will continue to do so, and will leave a larger reserve even as it increases. Much more detailed data are needed.

2927 ———. El problema del empleo en la región andina: elementos para un diagnóstico y una estrategia. Santiago: Organización Internacional del Trabajo, 1978. 35 p.: bibl. (Documento de trabajo—PREALC; 147)

Documents situations country-by-country and makes suggestions toward problem solutions.

2928 Proyectos de desarrollo: planificación, implementación y control. Banco

Interamericano de Desarrollo, Escuela Interamericana de Administración Pública, Fundación Getúlio Vargas. México: Editorial Limusa, 1979. 5 v.: bibl., ill.

Product of teaching since 1964, these text-manuals are comprehensive, lengthy, and organized primarily for didactic purposes. Readers of specialized volumes should at least browse vol. 1 as reference before undertaking others. Major effort.

2929 Puig, Juan Carlos. Integración latinoamericana, derecho interno y derecho de la comunidad internacional: falacia de los enfoques tradicionales (MN, 2:4, abril/junio 1979, p. 139–161)

Examines in depth the legal relationships involved in integration agreements and the various approaches to the problem.

2930 Puyana, Alicia. La política económica de la integración en América Latina, analizada a la luz de las experiencias del Grupo Andino (UNAM/L, 14, 1981, p. 477–528, charts)

Concerns fundamental decisions. Concludes that for a regional arrangement involving economies of different levels to work would require more of a supernational structure and individual loss of sovereignty.

2931 Randall, Laura et al. Symposium: energy policy in Latin America (LARR, 17:3, 1982, p. 119–172)

Introduction, study of three responses to shock, and brief summary of nations' energy planning constitute symposium.

2932 Ranis, Gustav. Desafios e oportunidades colocados pelos superexportadores da Asia: implicações para a exportação de manufaturados da América Latina (IPE/EE, 11:2, abril/junho 1981, p. 51–84, bibl., graphs, tables)

Experiences of East Asia (Korea, Taiwan, Hong Kong, Singapore) which may be applicable to Latin American situation. Analytic, much data.

2933 Resúmenes analíticos en economía agrícola latinoamericana. Cali, Colombia: Centro Internacional de Agricultura Tropical, Documentación Económica para América Latina, 1978. 3 v.: indexes (Serie Centro Internacional de Agricultura Tropical; HS-30, HS-33, 08SE-3)

Comprehensive, solid study based largely on censal data but in part on surveys in five countries.

2934 Revista de Economía Latinoamericana. Banco Central de Venezuela. Vol. 59, enero/marzo 1980- . Caracas.

Very substantial issue (390 p.) devoted entirely to NIEO. Includes bibliography, citations, documents, original articles—considerable variety.

2935 Rimez, Marc. Politique commerciale et modèle d'accumulation en Amérique Latine (UCL/CD, 12:3/4, 1980, p. 441–476, tables)

Thorough examination of changing commercial policy in 1970s, that is toward "opening" up economies to world trade. Discusses reasons therefore, effects, and makes preliminary evaluation. For Spanish version, see "Las Experiencias de Apertura Externa y Desprotección Industrial en América Latina" (Economía de América Latina, México, 2, marzo 1979).

2936 Roberts, Bryan R. Cities of peasants: the political economy of urbanization in the Third World. London: E. Arnold, 1978. 207 p.: bibl., indexes (Explorations in urban analysis)

Historical in approach, deals primarily with Latin America, and seeks to show how urbanization (in various characteristics) is the product of dependency. Further seeks to differentiate results of dependency on Great Britain and on US.

2937 Robinson, Richard and **Deborah Holtzman.** Comparative dependence and economic development (YU/IJCS, 22:1/2, March/June 1981, p. 86–101, bibl., tables)

Systematic studies (based on others' research), relationships between trade, investment, and development in hierarchical system of interdependent capitalistic economies.

2938 Rovetta, Vicente. El capital extranjero en el comercio desigual y la comercialización de azúcar y lácteos en América Latina (Desarrollo Indoamericano [Barranquilla, Colombia] 67, abril 1981, p. 43–52, ill., tables)

Surveys marketing practices (dumping, etc.) in dairy products, world sugar market, and significance of foreign capital in associated problems.

2939 Salazar-Carrillo, Jorge. La estructura salarial en el sector manufacturero de la ALALC (ECIEL, 5, julio 1978, p.68–84, tables)

Concentrates on three aspects: differences between countries, differences in wages according to skills, differences in occupational remuneration.

2940 ——— and **Juan José Buttari.** The structure of wages in Latin American manufacturing industries. Gainesville: University Presses of Florida, 1981. 1 v.: bibl., index (A Florida International University book)

English translation of *Estructura de los salarios industriales en América Latina* (see *HLAS 43:2928*).

2941 Sánchez G., Walter. Estratificación entre los países andinos: un examen cuantitativo. Santiago: Universidad de Chile, Instituto de Estudios Internacionales, 1978. 104 leaves: bibl., graphs (Serie de publicaciones especiales; no. 26)

Consists of wide range of comparisons of data on Andean countries (including Chile) with rationale for making those comparisons.

2942 Santos, Theotonio dos. Dependence relations and political development in Latin America: some considerations (NOSALF/IA, 7:1, 1977, p. 11–19)

Abstract, philosophical treatment of dependency.

2943 ———. Notas sobre la teoría del desarrollo, la dependencia y la revolución: algunas reflexiones metodológicas e históricas. México: Seminario Permanente sobre Latino América, 1978. 37 p. (Documento de trabajo)

Bourgeois development theory has shortcomings overcome by Marxist theory. Pt. 2 deals with dependency. Finally, national structures are examined *vis-à-vis* world revolution and revolutionary theory.

2944 Saulniers, Alfred H. Public enterprises in Latin America: an annotated list of recent research papers (SAGE/JIAS, 22:4, Nov. 1980, p. 463–470, bibl.)

Briefly annotated list of 49 items, unpublished and available after Jan. 1978. Also notes availability of papers through compiler.

2945 Schejtman, Alexander. The peasant economy: internal logic, articulation and persistence (CEPAL/R, 11, Aug. 1980, p. 115–134, graphs, ill.)

Surveys recent view of peasant economy that it is "different" from other production units. Synthesizes and spells out differences in logical operation and implications for peasant economy.

2946 Schwartz, Hugh H. Problems of industrial financing in Latin America (*in* Financing development in Latin America [see item **2821**] p. 108–140, tables)

Essay on basics of industrial finance: need for disaggregated demand and supply data, shortcomings of currently available data, new problems for industry, some proposals to alleviate analytic difficulties. Available from Inter-American Development Bank, Washington, D.C., as Bank Reprint Series No. 104.

2947 ¿Se puede superar la pobreza?: realidad y perspectivas en América Latina. Coordinador: Sergio Molina S. Santiago: Naciones Unidas, Comisión Económica para América Latina, Programa de las Naciones Unidas para el Desarrollo, 1980. 286 p.: bibl., ill. (E/CEPAL/G. 1139)

First-rate papers presented at 1979 seminar convened to look specifically at poverty. Five main topics, rural and urban, factor market considerations, redistributive policies, international trade and employment.

2948 El Sector agrario en América Latina: estructura económica y cambio social. Magnus Mörner *et al.* Includes Separata: comentarios (36 p.) Stockholm: Instituto de Estudios Latinoamericanos de Estocolmo, 1979. 187 p: bibl. (Skrifter utgivna av Latinamerika-institutet i Stockholm. Serie A., Monografier; 4)

Series of papers delivered (1977) in Stockholm. Four are general, six are country specific (three on Chile, one each on Brazil, Peru, Argentina), and two deal with international organisms.

2949 Seminario sobre el Nuevo Orden Económico Internacional, Viña del Mar, Chile, 1979. América Latina y el Nuevo Orden Económico Internacional. Editores: Eduardo Hill, Luciano Tomassini. Autores: Aldo Ferrer *et al.* Santiago: Corporación de Promoción Universitaria, 1979. 306 p.: bibl.

Contributions to 1979 seminar. Four main topics: 1) developing countries in the international system; 2) Latin American prospects in North-South dialogue; 3) Latin America as middle-income region; and 4) priorities. Among contributors: Sunkel, Massad, Tironi, Iglesias, Jaguaribe, Ferrer.

2950 Shea, Donald; Frank W. Swacker; Robert J. Radway; and Stanley T. Stairs. Reference manual on doing business in Latin America. Milwaukee: University of Wisconsin-Milwaukee, Center for Latin America, 1979. 210 p.: bibl.

Practical "how-to" reference with bibliography, check-lists, particular attention to legal aspects, lists of organizations and services they provide. More emphasis on investment than trade.

2951 Silva Colmenares, Julio. La crisis económica del capitalismo y el Tercer Mundo (URSS/AL, 12:48, 1981, p. 24–42)

General restatement of Marxist analysis, for the most part related to Latin America.

2952 Slater, David and **Jean Stroom.** Capitalist development and issues of urban and regional research in Latin America (CEDLA/B, 27, dic. 1979, p. 3–7)

"State of the art" piece on urban and regional research in Latin America. Introduces five other articles on same general theme in this issue of *Boletín de Estudios Latinoamericanos y del Caribe.*

2953 Socialismo democrático y reforma agraria. Jacques Chonchol *et al.* San José: Centro de Estudios Democráticos de América Latina, 1981. 167 p.: ill. (Colección Seminários y documentos)

Major presentations and Commission reports from seminar under sponsorship of Friederich Ebert Foundation on agricultural reform and democratic socialism. Among contributors: Jacques Chonchol, Antonio García, Guillermo Maldonado Lince. Some specific attention to the Dominican Republic, the seminar site.

2954 Statistical summary of Latin America: 1960–1980. New York: United Nations, CEPAL, 1981?. 7 leaves: graphs, maps, tables.

Some important and readily available indicators of social and economic class.

2955 Story, Dale. Sectoral clash and industrialization in Latin America. Syracuse, N.Y.: Syracuse Univeristy, Maxwell School of Citizenship and Public Affairs, 1981. 1 v.: bibl. (Foreign and comparative studies. Latin American series; no. 2)

Analyzes conflicts between emerging industrial sectors and traditional export sectors, agricultural or mineral. Cases: Argentina, Brazil, Chile, Mexico, Venezuela.

2956 ———. Time-series analysis of industrial growth in Latin America: political and economic factors (SSQ, 61:2, Sept. 1980, p. 293–307, bibl., tables)

Argentina, Brazil, Chile, Mexico, Venezuela—since World War II. Findings: per capita income and population are crucial factors in industrialization; government expenditures and sectoral discrimination are also important.

2957 Sunkel, Osvaldo. La dimensión ambiental en los estilos de desarrollo de América Latina. Santiago: Naciones Unidas, Comisión Económica para América Latina, Programa de las Naciones Unidas para el Medio Ambiente, 1981. 136 p.: ill. (United Nations; E/CEPAL/G.1143)

This document synthesizes an ECLA-UN seminar on Development Styles and the Environment in Latin America. Individual studies appear in *Revista de la CEPAL* (Dec. 1980), and in a volume *Estilos de desarrollo y medio ambiente en América Latina* (Mexico: Fondo de Cultura Económica, 1981). Some will appear as monographs in series "Estudios e Informes de la CEPAL."

2958 Symposium on *Dependencia y desarrollo en América Latina* by Cardoso and Falleto (LARR, 17:1, 1982, p. 115–172)

Four separate pieces on the above book constitute the "symposium:" Halperin-Donghi (item **2845**) compares Cardoso and Falleto with other strains of dependency, particularly André Gunder Frank; Packenham (item **2905**) meticulously compares the book's English and Spanish editions; Marcelo Cavarozzi's "El 'Desarrollismo' y las Relaciones entre Democracia y Capitalismo Dependiente en *Dependencia y desarrollo en América Latina*" (p. 152–165) treats of populism, its rise and decline; and Christopher K. Chase-Dunn's "A World-System Perspective on *Dependency and development in Latin America* (p. 166–171) subjects the topics to global views.

2959 Szretter, Héctor. Asalariados de bajos ingresos y salarios mínimos en América Latina. Santiago: Oficina Internacional del Trabajo, PREALC, 1980. 137 p. (Investigaciones sobre empleo; 18)

Characteristics of low-wage earners (other than in agriculture). Empirical.

2960 Teitel, Simón. Productivity, mechanization and skills: a test of the Hirschman hypothesis for Latin American industry (WD, 9:4, April 1981, p. 355–371, tables)

Empirically tests hypothesis for seven countries—Argentina, Brazil, Chile, Colombia, Mexico, Peru, Venezuela—and finds little evidence that capital-intensive industries do better than more traditional ones in developing economies (see also *HLAS* 43:2950).

2961 Third World migration and urbanization: a symposium (UC/EDCC, 30:3, April 1982, p. 463–670, graphs, tables)

Eight articles, complete issue, devoted to topic from various perspectives. Even general articles (e.g., Jacques Ledent, "Rural-Urban Migration, Urbanization, and Economic Development") include considerable attention to Latin America. Two are country-specific: T. Paul Schultz "Lifetime Migration within Educational Strata in Venezuela" and Gary S. Fields "Place-to-Place Migration in Colombia."

2962 Tokman, Víctor E. Dinámica de los mercados de trabajo y distribución del ingreso en América Latina. Santiago: Organización Internacional de Trabajo, Programa Mundial del Empleo, Programa Regional del Empleo para América Latina y el Caribe (PREALC), 1979. 47 leaves: bibl., tables (Trabajo ocasional; 26)

Using little data available, seeks conclusions regarding income distribution.

2963 ———. Dinámica del mercado de trabajo urbano: el sector informal urbano en América Latina. Santiago: Organización Internacional del Trabajo, Programa Mundial del Empleo, Programa Regional del Empleo para América Latina y el Caribe (PREALC), 1977. 45 p.: bibl. (Documentos de trabajo; no. 135)

"State of the arts" piece, rich in literature review, references, and suggestions for further research.

2964 ———. Empleo y distribución del ingreso en América Latina: ¿avance o retroceso? Santiago: Organización Internacional del Trabajo, Programa Mundial del

Empleo, Programa Regional del Empleo para América Latina y el Caribe (PREALC), 1979. 58 p.: bibl., tables (Trabajo ocasional; 24)

Reviews data, literature, methodologies, seeking empirical answers 1960–1970–1976. Also asks: Is the pattern "natural" or perverse?

2965 ———. The influence of the urban informal sector on economic inequality. Santiago: Organización Internacional del Trabajo, Programa Mundial del Empleo, Programa Regional del Empleo para América Latina y el Caribe (PREALC), 1980. 33 leaves: tables (Monograph; 15)

Carefully analytical piece concludes that existence and operation of informal urban sector tend to increase inequalities and also to lengthen time required for low incomes to increase in growth processes. For Spanish version, see *El Trimestre Económico* (México, 48[4]:192, oct./dic. 1981, p. 931–964).

2966 ———. Urban poverty and employment in Latin America: guidelines for action. Santiago: Programa Regional del Empleo para América Latina y el Caribe (PREALC), 1977. 41 leaves: bibl. (Occasional paper; 1)

Analyses of informal labor markets in urban areas—conditions expected to deteriorate relatively—with suggestions on improving outcomes.

2967 Tolosa, Hamilton C. Asuntos claves en el desarrollo espacial latinoamericano (Revista Latinoamericano de Estudios Urbano Regionales, EURE [Instituto de Planificación del Desarrollo Urbano y Regional, Santiago] 7:20, dic. 1980, p. 9–23, tables)

Concerned with spatial inequities in planning. Main topics: import substitution and redistribution, poverty and urban centers, political and institutional changes required to effect redistribution.

2968 Transferencia de tecnología de empresas extranjeras hacia el Grupo Andino. Prepared by the Board of the Cartagena Agreement, Grupo de Política Tecnológica. Lima: Junta del Acuerdo de Cartagena, Unidad de Comunicaciones, 1981. 34 p.: bibl.

Study country-by-country of effects of Decision 24. Includes interesting data on why some investments were denied.

2969 Transnacionalización y dependencia.
Edición a cargo de Vicente Donoso.
Osvaldo Sunkel *et al.* Madrid: Ediciones
Cultura Hispánica del Instituto de Coopera-
ción Iberoamericana, 1980. 425 p.: bibl., ill.
(Estudios económicos)
"Collection" of essays and comments
thereon. Some deal primarily with Latin
America. Major part deals with "the Euro-
pean periphery and the economy of the Med-
iterranean countries" and another with
Spain.

**2970 Trends in the Latin American econ-
omy in 1979** (*in* United Nations.
Economic Commission for Latin America.
Economic survey of Latin America: 1979.
Santiago: 1981, p. 1–48, graphs, tables)
Careful attention to the international
setting. Growth, the external sector, and inflation are given separate analysis. Debt problems also receive attention. Laced with data.

**2971 United Nations. Economic Commis-
sion for Latin America.** El balance de
pagos de América Latina, 1950–1977. Santiago: Naciones Unidas, 1979. 164 p.: tables
(Cuadernos estadísticos de la CEPAL; no. 5)
Excellent reference. Contains brief
methodological notes, a few regional and subregional summaries, and annual country data.

2972 ———. ———. The economic relations of Latin America with Europe.
v. 1, Latin America: a case of contradictory
development. v. 2, Latin American trade
with Europe. v. 3, Direct private investment.
v. 4, Financing. v. 5, The future of these relations: notes for an analysis. New York: The
Commission, 1979. 5 v. (35, 67, 52, 13, 29 p.):
bibl., tables (Document—United Nations;
E/CEPAL/L.190–194)
Invaluable, pithy studies which are
difficult for outsiders to learn of and to ac-
quire. They represent serious attention to an
important topic.

2973 ———. ———. Regional programme of
action for Latin America in the 1980s:
resolution 422 (XIX) adopted by CEPAL at its
nineteenth session, Montevideo, Uruguay,
1981. Santiago: Naciones Unidas, 1981. 66 p.
(Cuadernos de la CEPAL; 40. E/CEPAL/
G.1189)
Official statement of program for the
"Latin American Development Decade."
Stresses economic and social development
and is organized around national policies, re-

gional policies, cooperation with other developing countries, and "international"
cooperation.

2974 ———. ———. Projections Centre.
Latin America and the New International Development Strategy (CEPAL/R, 11,
Aug. 1980, p. 7–30)
Based on 1970s, analyzes principal
problems and strategies. Stress is placed on
importance of regional cooperation and cooperation among LDCs.

2975 ———. Research Institute for Social
Development. The quest for a unified
approach to development. Geneva: 1980.
180 p. (UNRISD report; no. 80.3)
Account of UN's 20-year search for a
"unified approach to development"— how it
came about, how "search" was carried on,
and evaluation. Last item is an effective synthesis by Marshall Wolfe and makes fascinating reading. ECLA plays a role.

**2976 United States. Department of Agri-
culture. Economic Research Service.**
World indices of agricultural and food production. Washington: 1981. 161 p.: tables
(Statistical bulletin; no. 669)
Detailed data by country, region, crop,
with specialized data such as per capita output. Valuable source of highly specialized
information.

2977 ———. ———. Economic Statistics
and Cooperatives Service. Global food
assessment. Washington: 1980. 119 p.: tables
(Foreign agricultural economic report; 159)
Excellent source of data with global,
regional, and country summaries.

2978 Vacchino, Juan Mario. Integración económica regional. Caracas: Universidad
Central de Venezuela, Facultad de Ciencias
Jurídicas y Políticas, Instituto de Derecho
Público, Sección Integración, 1981. 602 p.:
bibl.
Rather exhaustive. Covers in major
parts: theory of integration; integration for
developed capitalism; integration and socialism; integration and peripheral capitalism. Numerous case studies, pt. 4 deals
with Latin America specifically.

2979 Vernon, Raymond. A participação das
empresas estatais nas exportações
latino-americanas (IPE/EE, 11:2, abril/junho
1981, p. 85–101, bibl., tables)
Explores potentials and limits to state

enterprise exporting, minerals and petroleum, manufacturing and transformation industries.

2980 Villarreal, René. El FMI y la experiencia latinoamericana: desempleo, concentración del ingreso, represión (BNCE/CE, 30:8, agosto 1980, p. 889-899, tables)

Focus of IMF not only does not solve problems of international disequilibria but contributes to inequality in distribution of income and employment.

2981 ———. Problemas y perspectivas del comercio y las finanzas internacionales: los puntos de vista del Sur (FCE/TE, 48[4]:192, oct./dic. 1981, p. 903–929)

Review of world trade and monetary policies since World War II, a critique of their effects in the Third World, and suggestions for reform.

2982 Volkov, Mai. Investigaciones económicas de los latinoamericanistas soviéticos (URSS/AL, 5[41], 1981, p. 22–42)

Interesting review of USSR interests in economies of Latin America and of Soviet research on them.

2983 Weaver, Frederick Stirton. Class, state, and industrial structure: the historical process of South American industrial growth. Westport, Conn.: Greenwood Press, 1980. 247 p.: bibl., index (Contributions in economics and economic history; no. 32 0084–9235)

Seeks to synthesize "history" and "development" as is seldom done, particularly against backdrop of European economic history. Distinguishes between "financial and competitive capitalism" and "monopoly capitalism" which predominates in Latin America. Provocative volume.

2984 Wheaton, William C. and **Hisanobi Shishido.** Urban concentration, agglomeration economies, and the level of eco-

nomic development (UC/EDCC, 30:1, Oct. 1981, p. 17–30)

Relates optimal city size and level of economic activity and considers that notion of one or two primal cities may develop into an explained decentralization.

2985 Wilkins, Mira. Multinational corporations (LARR, 17:2, 1982, p. 185–198) Review of 11 books (1975–79) on MNCs.

2986 Wionczek, Miguel. The major unresolved issues in the negotiations on the UNCTAD Code of Conduct for the transfer of technology (CEPAL/R, 10, April 1980, p. 95–102)

Explains issues which remain unresolved after some years of negotiations.

2987 ———. El mundo subdesarrollado y las corporaciones transnacionales: el conflicto acerca de la tranferencia de tecnología y sus principales puntos negociables (FCE/TE, 48[1]:189, enero/marzo 1981, p. 45–85)

Study of present means of technology transfer, particularly by multinationals, with eye to improving the situation.

2988 Wolfe, Marshall. Elusive development. Geneva: United Nations, Research Institute for Social Development and Economic Commission for Latin America, 1981. 265 p.

Examines 40 years of experience to identify those elements that seem now to offer the greatest hope for LDCs. Pragmatic. Largely based on and related to Latin American experience.

2989 Zuk, Gary and **William R. Thompson.** The post-coup military spending question: a pooled cross-sectional time series analysis (APSA/R, 76:1, March 1982, p. 60–74, bibl., graphs, tables)

Elaborate examination of military spending. Find that the distribution and timing of regime types is not helpful in predicting behavior of post-coup spending.

MEXICO

SERGIO ROCA, *Associate Professor of Economics, Adelphi University*

MOST OF THE IMPROVEMENTS and many of the shortcomings in the economic literature on Mexico noted in *HLAS 43* (p. 271–273) are still apparent in works annotated below. The flood of publications dealing with the antecedents and the potential consequences of the 1976 crisis shows little, if any, decline. The contributions by Ortiz (item **3041**) and Solís (items **3051–3052**), being more theoretical and empirical, provide a salutary contrast to the political-economic nature of pieces by Cordera and Tello (item **3007**) and Yúnez-Naude (item **3063**). Critical commentary on economic policymaking is a hallmark of this literature and many writers are probably now at work examining the 1982 episode. In this connection, first-rate studies on the causes and implications of the massive foreign debt and the attending external disequilibrium by Green (item **3020**) and Quadri (item **3044**) represent timely anticipations of the coming wave. Green's book provides solid empirical background of the conditions leading to last year's devaluation, while Quadri's article evaluates alternative policies to manage the crisis.

The quality of the works dealing with the oil sector shows definite improvement. Carrada-Bravo (item **3002**) undertakes a macro-econometric analysis of the impact of oil revenues on several key sectors and Villareal (item **3059**) emphasizes how a country with oil reserves can exercise international leverage.

Several excellent studies examine the relationship between transnational enterprises (TNEs) and Mexican development. Gereffi and Evans (item **3017**) compare public policies vis-à-vis TNEs in Brazil and Mexico, Fajnzylber (item **3012**) presents a comprehensive analysis of the role of TNEs in the industrial sector, and Bennett and Sharpe (item **2996**) examine the logic behind national policies to control the behavior of multinationals. Green's work (item **3020**) on the foreign debt also traces the incursion of international banks into the domestic financial system.

It is gratifying to note a rising concern with comparative country studies. Hewlett and Weinert (item **2999**) undertake such a task by examining several aspects (foreign investment, labor unions, income distribution) of late economic development in Brazil and Mexico.

Possibly the best work reviewed here is Herrera's book (item **3023**) on Mexican foreign trade in the 19th century. It is a model of scholarly research and lucid writing. Equally impressive is Bazant's massive study (item **2995**) of the economics of low-cost housing and urbanization in Mexico City.

Several notable works examine issues related to income distribution and poverty. In novel fashion, Lustig (item **3031**) estimates family income requirements for an adequate diet and spells out some policy implications. Hers is an important piece. Nugent and Tarawneh (item **3039**) reach surprising conclusions about the determinants of sectoral income inequality and question the impact of government policies aimed at redistribution. Bergsman's monograph (item **2997**), part of the World Bank series on the topic, evaluates the Mexican experience with redistribution and attempts some comparative intercountry assessments.

Fairly detailed work is now available on some of the areas identified last year as meriting further research attention. Maldonado (item **3032**) examines the female workforce in tobacco farms, and Rendón (item **3047**) studies female labor-force participation in the state of Mexico. In an excellent case-study of technology transfer, Mercado (item **3035**) analyzes the degree of technological dependency at several levels of the textile industry from basic inputs to final outputs. Finally, Hilger (item **3024**) undertakes a pioneering review of the functioning of CONASUPO, the government's food distribution system.

Clearly, additional research is still needed in areas mentioned in the previous *Handbook*, especially in wealth distribution, investment decision-making in the private sector, and US-Mexican economic interdependence. Furthermore, much remains to be done in assessing Mexico's economic relations with the developing world and in examining the process of Mexican negotiations with international economic organizations such as the IMF.

For an invaluable summary of sources related to research and publications on the Mexican economy, see *HLAS 43:271–273*.

2990 Alba-Hernández, Francisco. La población de México: evolución y dilemas. 2. ed. México: Colegio de México, Centro de Estudios Económicos y Demográficos, 1979. 189 p.: graphs.

Brief but rewarding study of population characteristics and projections of demographic change. Argues that business interests and public policy in the past encouraged rapid population growth which now must be curtailed by comprehensive socioeconomic development and family planning measures.

Alfaro Santacruz, Melchor de *et al.* Relaciones histórico geográficas de la Provincia de Tabasco. See item **5083.**

Antuñano, Estevan de. Obras: documentos para la historia de la industrialización en México, 1833–1846. See *HLAS 44:1986.*

2991 Baerresen, Donald W. Mexico's assembly program: implications for the United States (Texas Business Review [Bureau of Business Research, University of Texas at Austin] 55:6, Nov./Dec. 1981, p. 253–257, tables)

Informative piece on assembly program in border cities and states. Concludes that labor-intensive portions occur in Mexico while capital-intensive steps are conducted in US.

2992 Barkin, Donald and **Adriana Zavala.** Desarrollo regional y reorganización campesina: La Chontalpa como reflejo del problema agropecuario mexicano. México: Editorial Nueva Imagen, 1978. 173 p., 9 fold. leaves of plates: bibl., ill.

Reports on development plan to incorporate large humid tropical land into modern agricultural systems. Concludes costs have been high; production has been lower than expected; conflicts among peasant groups, private landowners, and governmental officials have plagued the project. Believes problem is subordination of Mexican interests, particularly campesino interests, to world market requirements. [R. E. Greenleaf]

2993 ———— and Blanca Suárez. El complejo de granos en México. México: Centro de Ecodesarrollo: Instituto Latinoamericano de Estudios Transnacionales, 1981. 237

p.: bibl., ill. (Serie Estudios. Centro de Ecodesarrollo; 5)

Analysis of changes in grain production as a result of increasing oil specialization. Examines mode and extent of foreign capitalist penetration in the sector and implications for national economic policymaking.

———— and Gustavo Esteva. Inflación y democracia: el caso de México. See *HLAS 44:2146.*

2994 Bassols Batalla, Angel. México, formación de regiones económicas: influencias, factores y sistemas. México: Universidad Nacional Autónoma de México, Instituto de Investigaciones Económicas, 1979. 625 p., 2 fold. leaves of plates: bibl., ill., maps.

Exhaustive analysis of regional economics from colonial times onward. Regional disequilibrium worsened under Díaz and after 1940 to benefit of capitalists and to detriment of economic independence and social equity. Argues for policies to decentralize industrial development.

2995 Bazant, Jan. Rentabilidad de la vivienda de bajos ingresos: aspectos microeconómicos del financiamiento del desarrollo urbano-habitacional en México metropolitano. México: Editorial Diana, 1979. 339 p.: bibl., ill.

Excellent study of economics of low-cost housing and urbanization in Mexico City. Detailed description of several characteristics of different types of urban settlements from squatters to public housing. Provides criteria for provision and maintenance of acceptable urban housing. Superb bibliography. Major contribution to urban economics literature.

2996 Bennett, Douglas and **Kenneth Sharpe.** El control sobre las multinacionales: las contradicciones de la mexicanización (CM/FI, 21:4, abril/junio 1981, p. 388–427, bibl., tables)

Examines logic behind national policies to control multinationals, especially equity participation schemes. Exhaustive discussion of three logical premises: paralelism, control, and identification. Excellent review of literature and arguments. Must reading.

2997 Bergsman, Joel. Income distribution and poverty in Mexico. Washington: World Bank, 1980. 46 leaves: bibl., tables (World Bank staff working paper; no. 395)

Careful evaluation of difficult topic deals with size distribution, characteristics of the poor, and causes of inequality. Examines Mexican case in comparison with other countries. Concludes that Mexico has one of most unequal distributions among LDCs.

2998 Blanquel, Eduardo. Nuestras historias, México y el Grupo Nacional-Provincial. México: Grupo Nacional-Provincial, 1979. 216 p., 164 p. of plates: bibl., ill. (some col.)

Internally commissioned history of one of largest insurance companies in the country (founded 1901). Interesting work because it analyzes development of government economic policies from perspective of private sector.

2999 Brazil and Mexico: patterns in late development. Editors, Sylvia Ann Hewlett and Richard S. Weinert. Philadelphia: Institute for the Study of Human Issues, 1982. 349 p.: bibl., ill., index (Inter-American politics series; v. 3)

Excellent collection of articles dealing with characteristics and consequences of late development in Brazil and Mexico. Examines the role of the state, foreign capital, demographic factors, labor organizations and social structures and impact on social equity and political rights. Concludes that late developers pay heavier costs and over longer time horizons.

3000 Bueno, Gerardo M. Desarrollo y petróleo: la experiencia de los países exportadores (FCE/TE, 47[2]:186, abril/junio 1980, p. 283–301, tables)

Studies effects of increased oil revenues in 14 countries. Finds gains were dissipated rapidly and, thus, shares lack of optimism for oil as a panacea in Mexico. [J. M. Hunter]

3001 ———. Petróleo y planes de desarrollo en México (BNCE/CE, 31:8, agosto 1981, p. 831–840)

Assessment of government's petroleum policies contained in Global Plan, Energy Program, and National Industrial Development Plan, in terms of objectives,

export-import goals, policy instruments, and sectoral relationships.

3002 Carrada-Bravo, Francisco. Oil, money, and the Mexican economy: a macroeconomic analysis. Boulder, Colo.: Westview Press, 1982. 146 p.: bibl., ill. (A Westview replica edition)

Econometric model traces impact of oil revenues upon the economy under several simulation scenarios. Based on doctoral thesis, book illustrates many shortcomings implicit in use of modelling techniques.

3003 Chapoy Bonifaz, Alma de María. Ruptura del sistema monetario internacional. México: Universidad Nacional Autónoma de México, 1979. 215 p.: bibl.

Serious study of failure of post-World War II monetary system and its effects in Third World. Short pt. 2 deals specifically with Mexico. [J. M. Hunter]

3004 Clavijo, Fernando. Reflexiones en torno a la inflación mexicana (FCE/TE, 47[4]:188, oct./dic. 1980, p. 1023–1054, bibl., tables)

Lucid analysis of Mexico's inflation process using model of open/oligopolistic economy. Concludes that inflation is associated with structural factors (development style, external dependency) and not with short-run cyclical fluctuations. Solution requires structural change and fair distribution of adjustment costs. Despite some methodological shortcomings, a worthwhile article.

3005 Coatsworth, John H. Growth against development: the economic impact of railroads in Porfirian Mexico. DeKalb: Northern Illinois University Press, 1981. 249 p.: bibl., ill., index (The Origins of modern Mexico)

Well documented study of the economic and social impact of railroads on 19th-century Mexico using theoretical concepts of social savings and linkage effects. Freight savings contributed greatly to economic growth during the Porfiriato, but effects on land ownership, income distribution, and institutional development were detrimental (see *HLAS 43:2988*).

3006 Connor, John M. and **Willard F. Mueller.** Market power and profitability of multinational corporations in Brazil and Mexico: report to the Subcommittee on Foreign Economic Policy of the Committee on Foreign Relations, United States Senate. Washington: GPO, 1977. 136 p.: bibl.

Badly dated but nonetheless important. Analyzes extent of multinationals' power in Brazil and Mexico and structural determinants of profitability. Important conclusion: determinants of profitability were about the same in both countries. [J. M. Hunter]

3007 Cordera, Rolando and **Carlos Tello.** México, la disputa por la nación: perspectivas y opciones del desarrollo. México: Siglo Veintiuno Editores, 1981. 149 p.: bibl. (Sociología y política)

Starting from present system, lucid discussion of two future options for economic and political development: neoliberal (pro-market and US ties) and nationalist (advance vision of 1917 Constitution and Cárdenas). Authors strongly favor nationalist road and outline its requirements, among which full and active participation of workers and popular forces is paramount.

3008 Desarrollo y crisis de la economía mexicana: ensayos de interpretación histórica. Selección de Rolando Cordera con la colaboración de Ernesto Camacho. México: Fondo de Cultura Económica, 1981. 818 p.: ill. (El Trimestre económico. Lecturas; 39)

Comprehensive but uneven collection of mostly previously published essays by Mexican social scientists on antecedents and implications of mid-1970s economic crisis. Best are works by Blanco, Ros, Pereyra and Ayala. Overlapping coverage of some topics allows appreciation of different methodological and political perspectives.

Documentos para el estudio de la industrialización en México: 1837–1845. See *HLAS 44:2023.*

3009 Eckaus, Richard S. La estructura del sistema bancario comercial de México: 1940–1970 (BHEL/R, 12:3, julio/sept. 1978, p. 309–367, bibl., tables)

Exploratory study of commercial banking system dealing with market shares, net profitability, lending practices of small, medium, and large institutions. Tentative conclusions raise questions about ability of financial authorities to properly regulate banking sector.

3010 The Economic evolution of the indi- vidual countries: Mexico (*in* United Nations. Economic Commission for Latin America. Economic survey of Latin America, 1979. Santiago: 1981, p. 351–380, tables)

Comprehensive review of economic conditions and trends (1974–79).

3011 Esteva, Gustavo and **David Barkin.** La batalla en el México rural. México: Siglo Veintiuno Editores, 1980. 243 p.: bibl. (Sociología y política)

Discusses agricultural crisis in Mexico (starvation, rural violence, poverty) which results from Mexico's subservience to needs of world capitalism in which multinational corporations control economic decisions and the Mexican government. Solution is to return land to the peasants, but we've heard this solution for 70 years. [R. E. Greenleaf]

3012 Fajnzylber, Fernando and **Trinidad Martínez Tarragó.** Las empresas transnacionales: expansión a nivel mundial y proyección en la industria mexicana. México: Fondo de Cultura Económica, 1976. 423 p.: bibl., tables (Sección de obras de economía)

Well presented analysis of role of transnational enterprises in Mexican industrial sector. Clear differentiation among competing variables (size, sector, market concentration) provides basis for policy recommendations affecting control over financial markets and technology transfer. Excellent tables (over 150) and bibliography.

3013 García, Citlali and **Guillermo Sánchez.** Impacto socioeconómico del cooperativismo en el ejido mexicano (EDTM, 3:1, marzo 1980, p. 151–208)

Analysis of 1970–76 "Ejido" policy shift from low-yielding individual farming to higher productivity cooperative enterprise. Micro data collected from two collective "ejidos" and macro data compiled from several samples of "ejidos" and other farm units. Concludes that collective agriculture represents on-the-job training for next stage of socialized agribusiness.

3014 García de Fuentes, Ana. Cancún, turismo y subdesarrollo regional. México: Universidad Nacional Autónoma de México, Instituto de Geografía, 1979. 128 p., 1 folded leaf of plates: bibl., ill., tables (Serie Cuadernos)

Critical assessment of regional development planning in Cancún tourist area. Maintains that plan objectives were not clearly specified and resources were not allocated for its implementation. Local needs were disregarded and negative effects on employment and housing remain uncorrected.

3015 García Rodríguez, Elizabeth and **Leticia Barraza Silva.** Inventario de estadísticas laborales. México: Secretaría del Trabajo y Previsión Social, Centro Nacional de Información y Estadísticas del Trabajo, 1981. 251 p.: bibl., tables.

Indispensable source on availability of statistical information about labor/employment. Contains data on coverage, frequency, topic, and official source of vast statistical literature ranging from general publication census to highly specialized surveys (strikes, female workforce in extractive industry).

3016 Garza, Gustavo. Industrialización de las principales ciudades de México: hacia una estrategia espacio-sectorial. México: El Colegio de México, 1980. 155 p.: apéndice estadístico, bibl. (Colección Centro de Estudios Económicos y Demográficos; 12)

Based on premise that excessive economic-demographic concentration in a few Mexican cities entails high costs, proposes a realistic strategy for industrial decentralization around Saltillo, Querétaro and Mexicali. Formula acknowledges impact of spatial economic factors and financial limitations of the state upon plan implementation. Useful data on regional economic activities.

3017 Gereffi, Gary and **Peter Evans.** Transnational corporations, dependent development, and state policy in the semiperiphery: a comparison of Brazil and Mexico (LARR, 16:3, 1981, p. 31–64, bibl., tables)

Analysis of role of direct foreign investment and transnational corporations in process of dependent development. Discussion of several types of import-substitution strategies and response of local power elites to issues raised by their success. One conclusion: such development path impedes resolution of welfare and equity issues.

3018 Gollás, Manuel. La migración, el ingreso y el empleo urbanos (CM/DE, 14:1[41], 1980, p. 1–26, bibl., tables)

Econometric model to determine relative contribution of rural-urban income differentials and urban employment opportunities upon migration to Mexico's metropolitan area. Finds that income is more determinant than employment. Solution to urban employment is rural jobs.

3019 Gordon, Peter and **Peter Theobald.** Migration and spatial development in the Republic of Mexico (JDA, 15:2, Jan. 1981, p. 239–250, charts)

Based on Glesjer-Dramais flow models of migration, authors test effectiveness of policy seeking to channel migratory flows away from large centers by promoting other destinations (counter-magnets) and introducing migrant interceptors. Critical finding: no evidence of flow diversion to Distrito Federal.

3020 Green, Rosario. Estado y banca transnacional en México. México: Centro de Estudios Económicos y Sociales del Tercer Mundo: Editorial Nueva Imagen, 1981. 430 p.: bibl.

Well researched and well written study of the foreign debt incurred by Mexico's government, providing excellent background of 1982 crisis. Increased foreign debt is attributed to inability of government to tap domestic savings and to excessive international liquidity due to petrodollar recycling. Negative consequences include foreign penetration of domestic economy and increased impotence of the state. Required reading.

3021 Greenwood, Michael J.; Jerry R. Ladman; and **Barry S. Siegel.** Long-term trends in migratory behavior in a developing country: the case of Mexico (PAA/D, 18:3, Aug. 1981, p. 369–387, tables)

Examines trends in socioeconomic factors that determined internal lifetime migration (1950–70). Significant changes are reported in responsiveness of migrants to various stimuli over time and across space. Key finding: up to 340 miles higher origin earnings deter migration, but beyond this limit encouragement results.

3022 Gutiérrez R., Roberto. Cambios de matiz en la estrategia económica de México: los años setenta y ochenta (BNCE/CE, 31:8, agosto 1981, p. 864–875, tables)

Concise analysis of economic-policy changes since 1960: from import-substitution to crude-oil specialization. Argues for diversification of petroleum exports and for more decisive state role in conducting external negotiations and setting domestic agenda.

3023 Herrera Canales, Inés. El comercio exterior de México, 1821–1875. México:

Colegio de México, 1977. 193 p.: bibl., ill., maps, tables (Nueva serie. Centro de Estudios Históricos; 25)

Superb piece of scholarly research and writing. Analyzes incorporation of newly independent Mexico to expanding world economy already in midst of industrial revolution. Traces impact of trade patterns upon domestic economic structure and vice-versa. Excellent bibliography, notes, charts, and maps. An important work.

3024 Hilger, Marye Tharp. Decision-making in a public market and enterprise CONASUPO in Mexico (SAGE/JIAS, 22:4, Nov. 1980, p. 471–494, bibl.)

One of the first studies of CONASUPO, dealing with factors affecting its marketing decisions. Discusses goals and organization of the enterprise as well as its political context.

3025 Huache. Toluca, México: Universidad Autónoma del Estado de México, Facultad de Economía, Centro de Investigación, 1979. 139 p.: ill.

Detailed report of social and economic conditions in the municipality of Tlatlaya, State of Mexico, including land tenure patterns, distribution of income and consumption goods, employment and migration. Useful statistical data.

3026 Las Huastecas en el desarrollo regional de México. Angel Bassols Batalla *et al*. México: Editorial Trillas, 1977. 436 p.: bibl., ill.

Attempts to use Marxist approach in presenting productive activities of region, in discussing exploitation, and in identifying factors which contribute to class struggle. [R.E. Greenleaf]

3027 Jiménez de Ramos, María Teresa. Características de la demanda de mano de obra femenina en la industria de transformación (STPS/R, 1:2, mayo/agosto 1978, p. 37–76, tables)

Exhaustive study of female workforce in light industry around Mexico City in 1975. Data show employment level, salary, mobility and hiring practices. Concludes that over entire range of indicators, females are in "disadvantageous position" vis-à-vis males.

Juárez, Antonio. Las corporaciones transnacionales y los trabajadores mexicanos. See *HLAS 44:2207*.

3028 Kate, Adriaan ten *et al*. Protection and development in Mexico. New York: St. Martin's Press, 1980. 318 p.: bibl., tables.

Analyzes consequences of protectionist policy conducted through tariff schemes and direct controls for year 1970. Concludes that success was achieved in stimulating industrial growth and promoting import substitution. Also resulted in greater regional concentration of economic activity.

Krauze, Enrique. La reconstrucción económica. See *HLAS 44:2211*.

3029 Looney, Robert E. Mexico's economy: a policy analysis with forecasts to 1990. Boulder, Colo.: Westview Press, 1978. 250 p.: bibl., index, tables (Westview special studies on Latin America)

Identifies forces underlying high economic growth rate through early 1970s and maintains that prime sources of expansion are indefinitely sustainable while adverse side effects are remediable. Analyzes economic policies of Echeverría administration and examines economic strategy proposed by López Portillo. Suggests measures to attract foreign investment and to control external financial disequilibrium.

3030 López Rosado, Diego G. Curso de historia económica de México. México: Universidad Nacional Autónoma de México, 1981. 529 p.: bibl., tables (Textos universitarios)

Detailed narrative of Mexico's economic history from pre-colonial times to 1925. Reprint of 1954 ed.

3031 Lustig, Mora. Distribución del ingreso y consumo de alimentos en México (CM/DE, 14:2[42], 1980, p. 214–245, tables)

From basic needs perspective, presents relationship between actual food consumption and family income distribution and estimates money redistribution required to guarantee an adequate diet to lowest 40 percent of population under several assumptions. Important work.

3032 Maldonado Lee, Gabriel. La mujer asalariada en el sector agrícola: consideraciones sobre la fuerza del trabajo en el cultivo de tabaco. México: Centro Nacional de Información y Estadísticas del Trabajo, 1977. 149 p.: bibl., tables (Serie Avances de investigación; 2)

Pioneering study of paid female workers in tobacco farms discusses sex-assigned tasks, substitutability with males, benefit differentials. Argues for greater state role to protect workers' rights, especially labor contracts and minimum wages.

3033 Manrique, Irma. La política monetaria en la estrategia del desarrollo: su impacto en América Latina y México. Méxco: EDAMEX, 1979. 263 p.: bibl., tables.

Superficial structuralist analysis of monetary policy since 1920s, and its mostly negative impact on Mexican development. Blames capitalist system and IMF for Mexico's continued underdeveloped dependency. Strong defense of exchange and price controls as policy instruments.

3034 Matriz nacional de las ventajas comparativas en la industria manufacturera a nivel estatal. v. 1, Presentación y bases metodológicas. v. 2, Información por industrias. v. 3, Información por entidad federativa. México: Coordinación General de los Servicios Nacionales de Estadísticas, Geografía e Informática, 1980. 3 v.: bibl., tables.

Elaborates efficiency indicators for manufacturing sector arranged in matrix form to show comparative advantage by industry (vol. 2), and by state (vol. 3). Vol. 1 contains study objectives and methodology. Discusses implications for industrial decentralization.

3035 Mercado García, Alfonso. Estructura y dinamismo del mercado de tecnología industrial en México: los casos del poliéster, los productos textiles y el vestido. México: El Colegio de México, 1980. 287 p.: ill., tables (Colección Centro de Estudios Económicos y Demográficos; 9)

Well done study of technology transfer in textile industry (based on entire "column") from inputs to outputs. Examines changes in technological dependency at different development levels caused by monopoly elements, R&D efforts, and government policies. Solid microeconomic empirical base.

3036 Mexico. Secretaría de Programación y Presupuesto. Plan global de desarrollo, 1980–1982. 3. ed. México: 1980. 543 p.: ill., index, tables.

López Portillo's contribution to the implementation of a system of indicative economic planning. Essential document for analysis of current problems and proposed policies.

3037 ———. Centro Nacional de Información y Estadísticas del Trabajo. Encuesta de ingresos y gastos familiares, 1975. México: Centro Nacional de Información y Estadísticas del Trabajo, 1977. 160 p.: ill., tables (Serie Estudios. Centro Nacional de Información y Estadísticas del Trabajo; no. 1)

Collection of over 50 statistical tables related to 1975 family income distribution including structure, explanatory factors, and social implications. Clearly specifies methodological bases.

3038 ———. Comisión Consultiva del Empleo. Programa nacional de empleo, 1980–1972: proyecto que la Comisión Consultiva del Empleo presenta a la consideración del Ejecutivo Federal. v. 1, Presentación y diagnóstico: objetivos, estrategias, y políticas: programas sectoriales, sus efectos en el empleo. v. 2, Algunas propuestas para la acción. v. 3, Presentación resumida. v. 4, Síntesis. México: Secretaría del Trabajo y Previsión Social, 1979. 4 v.: tables.

Very useful government report on employment: characteristics of labor force, sectoral variations, future strategies. Highly disaggregated data by economic sector and by region. Four volumes contain current analyses, program objectives, and summary.

3039 Nugent, Jeffrey B. and **Fayez A. Tarawneh.** Anatomía de los cambios ocurridos en la distribución del ingreso y de la pobreza entre la población económicamente activa de México en el período de 1950–1970 (FCE/TE, 49[3]:195, julio/sept. 1982, p. 731–769, bibl., tables)

Using decomposition analysis, identifies determinants of growing income inequality and poverty. In surprising conclusion, almost 80 percent of increased sector inequality is attributable to intra-sectoral changes (especially in agriculture). Because of continued existence of rural poverty, raises questions about efficacy of government policies and effects of migration trends on sectoral distribution.

3040 Opciones de políticas económicas en México después de la devaluación. Gerardo M. Bueno, coordinador. Saúl Trejo et al. Prólogo, David Ibarra. México: Editorial Tecnos, 1977. 245 p.: bibl., graphs, tables.

Collection of excellent articles which, after providing economic review of 1950–76 period, discuss policy options in several areas including foreign trade, private sector relations, government spending, taxation, and labor. Clearly written with pragmatic policy recommendations.

3041 Ortiz Martínez, Guillermo. Acumulación de capital y crecimiento económico: perspectivas financieras en México. México: Centro de Estudios Monetarios Latinoamericanos, 1979. 176 p.: bibl., ill.

Superb combination of institutional description and methodological rigor to examine capital formation, financial markets, and economic growth in 1970–76. Uses general equilibrium model based on Tobin's asset-choice theory. Prescient conclusion: development strategy largely based on foreign borrowing is untenable in long-run. Important addition to the literature.

3042 Padilla Aragón, Enrique. México: hacia el crecimiento con distribución del ingreso. México: Siglo Veintiuno Editores, 1981. 208 p.: bibl., ill.

Cogent and plausible argument for growth with redistribution. Analyzes government policy and economic performance since 1939 to suggest required changes in tax structure and provision of basic needs. Oil wealth presents unique opportunity for the state to take charge of Mexico's economic destiny to realize above goals.

Peña, Rosa María de la. Las preferencias del comercio internacional: el sistema generalizado de preferencias para las exportaciones mexicanas. See item **2911.**

3043 Las Perspectivas del petróleo mexicano. Papers presented at a symposium sponsored by the Colegio de México, July 6–7, 1978. México: Colegio de México, Centro de Estudios Internacionales, 1979. 403 p.: bibl., ill., tables.

Collection of papers and commentaries of 1978 symposium on the future of Mexico's oil industry. Examines positive and negative impact on economic growth, financial markets, and social equity. Important record of fears and hopes at a time of great expectations to be contrasted with eventual developments and 1982 crisis.

3044 Quadri de la Torre, Gabriel R. Efectos intersectoriales del manejo de la deuda externa en un modelo de la teoría de control para México (FCE/TE, 49[4]:196, oct./dic. 1982, p. 895–919, bibl., graphs, ill.)

Using econometric model with realistic institutional assumptions and applying sensible policy alternatives, presents effects of changes in external debt upon gross domestic product and several main sectors (agriculture, manufacturing, social services). Concludes that reducing external financial dependency may be achieved by increasing agricultural exports, perhaps at expense of domestic food production.

3045 Ramírez Brun, J. Ricardo. Estado y acumulación de capital en México, 1929–1979. México: Universidad Nacional de México, Escuela Nacional de Estudios Profesionales Aragón, 1980. 189 p., 5 folded leaves: ill.

Orthodox Marxist interpretation of the state's role in process of capital accumulation and implementation of economic policy. Warns about excessive dependency on oil and recommends gradual nationalization of private banking system.

3046 Ramos G., Sergio; Margarita Camarena L.; and Benito Terrazas. Spicer, S.A.: monografía de una empresa y de un conflicto. México: Universidad Nacional Autónoma de México, 1979. 205 p., 1 folded leaf of plates: bibl., ill., tables.

Study of labor conflict in a privately-owned automotive equipment firm. Concludes that foreign capital destroys domestic capital and manipulates state power to crush worker demands. Labor unions should do well to learn this sad lesson.

3047 Rendón G., Jorge Leopoldo. Participación de la mujer en la fuerza de trabajo, significado e implicaciones: el caso específico del Estado de México. México: Centro Nacional de Información y Estadísticas del Trabajo, 1977. 110 p.: appendices; bibl., graphs, tables (Serie Avances de investigación; 1)

Informative monograph on female labor-force participation in the state of Mexico. Depicts well-known links among labor-intensive sectors and underemployment. Concludes that women work largely to compensate for deteriorating family living standards and suggests that housework be considered a productive activity.

3048 Roldán, Eduardo. La economía mexicana: auge, crisis y perspectivas: hemerografía internacional. México: Universidad Nacional Autónoma de México, Dirección General de Publicaciones, 1980. 76 p.: bibl., tables (Cuaderno -Centro de Relaciones Internacionales; 9)

Comprehensive international bibliographic listing of almost 900 articles on the Mexican economy published in 114 economic journals (1945–70). Forthcoming issue to cover items published 1971–77.

3049 Sánchez Burgos, Guadalupe. La región fundamental de economía campesina en México. México: Centro de Investigaciones del Desarrollo Rural: Editorial Nueva Imagen, 1980. 157 p.: bibl., maps.

Well done study of the economics of small-scale private farming in south-central region, including data on land tenure, production techniques, and output composition. Presents concept of region defined by several factors in addition to geographic continuity. Examines implications for labor migration to and absorption into urban areas.

Serrón, Luis A. Scarcity, exploitation, and poverty: Malthus and Marx in Mexico. See *HLAS 44:2267*.

3050 Smith, Stanley K. Determinants of female labor force participation and family size in Mexico City (UC/EDCC, 30:1, Oct. 1981, p. 129–152, tables)

Adapts household decision-making model by adding social and cultural variables to determine effect of wife's potential wage on her labor force participation and family size: finds that opportunity cost of children is low, because women continue to perform traditional work without income loss. Fertility decline is tied to reduction in traditional sector jobs.

3051 Solís M., Leopoldo. Alternativas para el desarrollo. México: Editorial J. Mortiz, 1980. 126 p.: bibl. (Cuadernos de Joaquín Mortiz)

General discussion of the total economic environment: endowments and policies. Perceptive analyses of alternative models (liberal and socialist) and development strategies (stabilizing and shared) leading to an outline of "integral option" for the achievement of both efficiency and equity goals. Refreshing analysis of hard political choices.

3052 ———. Economic policy reform in Mexico: a case study for developing countries. New York: Pergamon Press, 1981. 223 p.: bibl., ill., index, tables (Pergamon policy studies on international development)

Clearly written and well documented study of economic policy from period of "stabilizing development" to attempt at reform in 1970s from a top policymaker's perspective. Pragmatic analysis concentrates on problem-solving rather than on ideological structures. Must reading for development specialists. Extensive statistical materials.

3053 Tello, Carlos. La política económica en México, 1970–1976. México: Siglo Veintiuno Editores, 1979. 209 p.: bibl., tables (Economía y demografía)

Superb concise analysis of economic policy during Echeverría administration, leading to 1976 *peso* floating exchange rate. Maintains that financial crisis was precipitated not by statist and populist policies but by failure to reform monetary system, a measure that would have served genuine domestic economic objectives.

Thompson, John K. Inflation, financial markets, and economic development: the experience of Mexico. See *HLAS 44:2275*.

3054 Torres Gaitán, Ricardo. Un siglo de devaluaciones del peso mexicano. México: Siglo Veintiuno Editores, 1980. 427 p.: bibl., graphs; tables (Economía y demografía)

Monetary history of Mexico since 1870. Based on dependency theory, analyzes effects of successive *peso* devaluations upon main economic sectors, banking system, and income distribution. Conclusion speculates on possibilities of transforming oil and gas revenues into the foundation for economic growth, national independence, and social equity. Informative but somewhat simplistic work (for historian's comment, see *HLAS 44:2277*).

Torres Ramírez, Blanca. México en la Segunda Guerra Mundial. See *HLAS 44:2278*.

3055 Trajtenberg, Raúl and **Blanca Suárez San Román.** El empleo y las exportaciones de frutas y legumbres de México 1960–1975. México: Instituto Latinoamericano de Estudios Transnacionales, 1977. 108 leaves: bibl., ill., tables (DEE/R/10 preliminar)

Examines effects of exports of fruits and vegetables on rural employment and income. Argues that Mexico's comparative cost advantage is not allowed full play due to US trade restrictions. Solid microeconomic study.

3056 Urías, Homero. Economic and social conditions in Mexico: finance; the devaluation, a review of facts and opinions (BNCE/CE, 28 : 3, March 1982, p. 71–80)

Useful review of main factors and key documents related to 1982 devaluation, with brief comments on the situation by business and labor groups, and political parties.

3057 Van Ginneken, Wouter. Socioeconomic groups and income distribution in Mexico. New York: St. Martin's Press, 1980. 37 p.: bibl., index.

Discusses education as an accurate predictor of income equality. Pays slight attention to labor migration and the effects of earnings on the economy. Calls for tax reforms and urges development of small manufacturing and small farmers.

3058 Vera, Gabriel; Oscar Vera; and Francisco Núñez. Dos estudios: Seis perfiles de la pobreza en México [and] Caracterización de la distribución del ingreso en México a partir de las encuestas de ingresos y gastos familiares: 1963, 1968 y 1975. México: Centro Nacional de Información y Estadísticas del Trabajo, 1979. 66 p. (Serie Estudios. CENIET; 5)

Two brief but excellent compilations of studies of poverty and income distribution related to age, family size, occupation, education, and location. A summary of "Estudios de ingresos y gastos de familias," a monographic series sponsored by the Office of the President.

3059 Villarreal, René. El petróleo como instrumento de desarrollo y de negociación internacional: México en los ochenta (FCE/TE, 48[1]:189, enero/marzo 1981, p. 3–44, tables)

Detailed analysis of how to maximize benefits of oil wealth—several means including conservation of reserves and maintenance of market price. Emphasis on international negotiation using oil to obtain bilateral concessions to increase export of manufactured goods.

3060 Whitehead, Laurence. Mexico from bust to boom: a political evaluation of the 1976–1979 stabilization programme (WD, 8 : 11, Nov. 1980, p. 843–864, tables)

Examines Mexican experience under 1976 IMF regime from comparative perspective. Presidential cycle and "resilience" of political managers explain largely why economic outcome was more favorable here than in South American cases. Concluding comments assess the scope and limits of Mexican "reformism."

3061 Williams, Edward J. The rebirth of the Mexican petroleum industry: developmental directions and policy implications. Lexington, Mass.: Lexington Books, 1979. 218 p.: bibl., ill., index.

Analyzes political and developmental impact of oil industry. Suggests, as if it needs stating, that future paths of economic and social development will proceed differently because of oil. Fails to discuss more fully future distribution patterns on how much political clout will remain with PEMEX. [R.L. Greenleaf]

3062 World Conference on Agrarian Reform and Rural Development, Rome, 1979. Conferencia Mundial sobre Reforma Agraria y Desarrollo Rural. México: Centro Nacional de Investigaciones Agrarias, 1980. 219 p.: bibl., tables.

Central theme is FAO sponsored 1979 world conference on agricultural reform. Volume is heavy on documentation, especially as related to Mexican participation. Includes documents from preceding conferences and interesting summary chapter on status of Mexico's agricultural sector. [J.M. Hunter]

3063 Yúnez-Naude, Antonio. Los dilemas del desarrollo compartido: la política económica de 1971 a 1976 (FCE/TE, 48[2]: 190, abril/junio 1981, p. 273–302)

Interpretation of economic events and policies during Echeverría administration designed to answer this question: Is it likely that capitalist development will result in domestic social equity and national independence from the great powers? Basic conclusion is that "shared development" strategy was a failure.

CENTRAL AMERICA, PANAMA, AND THE CARIBBEAN (except Cuba and Puerto Rico)

MANUEL J. CARVAJAL, *Associate Professor of Economics, Florida International University*

ALTHOUGH THE PROBLEMS AFFLICTING Central America and the Caribbean encompass a myriad of issues and almost as many manifestations as the national fragmentation of their territory, change can be easily discerned as the common denominator affecting the entire region. And the many facets of change are found in this small albeit heterogeneous area approximately the size of Texas and New Mexico combined.

One manifestation of this change is the emergence of a national and regional identity that rejects colonialism (items **3082, 3085,** and **3089**) and dependency (items **3068, 3071, 3107, 3117, 3166, 3213,** and **3217**), a phenomenon addressed by many sources annotated below. Since the beginning, the area has been known for its grim history of neglect and exploitation, first by European powers and more recently by the US. Often major decisions concerning investment, levels of production, and technology have been made by outsiders disregarding the region's welfare, a fact that has prevented the development of a self-reliant structure. Thus, it is not surprising to find a substantial number of publications dealing with the historical evolution of economic dependency and general economic history (items **3065, 3092, 3125, 3151, 3161, 3228, 3230,** and **3232**). The extent of both past and present US influence (items **3100** and **3152**) and control by transnational corporations (items **3073** and **3131**) are subjects of intense study. Transnational corporations are viewed as a major impediment to economic development for they syphon the natural wealth of less developed countries in their attempt to maximize global profits, so the rationale for regulating their activities by virtue of host country legislation or, ultimately, expropriation, responds not solely to a capricious exercise of sovereignty, but more fundamentally to the promotion of national development goals.

A second manifestation of change is evident in the internationalization of the region. One can no longer think of Central America and the Caribbean exclusively as remote tropical lands suited for holiday travel or as mere appendages within the US *mare nostrum's* sphere of influence. The push to break with all forms of dependency has resulted in greater attention to foreign trade issues (items **3200, 3208–3209,** and **3225**), most noticeably import substitution (items **3111–3112,** and **3138**) and export promotion (items **3077, 3088, 3099,** and **3146**) experiments. Of paramount importance are the integration-related literature (items **3067, 3075, 3080, 3083–3084, 3090, 3194, 3216,** and **3218**), particularly after the disappointing results of both CACM and CARICOM, and the political turmoil experienced throughout the region. The islands are currently experiencing a rare peaceful (although, according to many observers, highly volatile) interlude in their tumultuous contemporary history, but violence and military confrontation have spread to most of the isthmus, interrupting normal economic activity and affecting virtually every household. Most analyses of the armed conflict (items **3098, 3120,** and **3124**) conclude that as long as violence continues there is no point in normalizing economic life. The Nicaraguan government, in an attempt to institutionalize its revolution along ideological lines, has chosen to generate a large volume of propaganda with little, if any, objective content, while at the other extreme, most studies issued by the government of El Salvador appear altogether oblivious to the fighting. Guatemala and Honduras are subject to their share of subversion and even Costa Rica, apparently untouched by political upheaval and immersed in its own economic crisis, has experienced some hostilities on its northern border.

Amidst the vicissitudes of the Caribbean Basin is a rapidly growing indigenous school of economic and social thought, largely eclectic in nature, which coexists with more traditional approaches ranging from USAID studies (items **3123**, **3144**, **3204**, and **3226**) to Marxist analysis (items **3074**, **3173**, and **3215**). Major topics of consideration include quasi-philosophical matters such as capitalism (items **3129–3130**, and **3160**), capital accumulation (items **3114**, **3133**, and **3142–3143**), and the role of the State (items **3086-3087**, **3145**, and **3147**) as well as more empirical and applied issues such as employment (items **3132**, **3140**, and **3190**), investment (items **3104** and **3188**), inflation (items **3203**, **3222**, and **3227**), industrial development (items **3108**, **3176**, **3184**, and **3195**), housing (items **3115** and **3189**), and monetary and fiscal policies (items **3118**, **3186**, and **3202**). Agricultural development (items **3110**, **3122**, **3126**, **3172**, and **3180**) receives a great deal of attention, as do related areas like land tenure and distribution (items **3066**, **3093**, **3157**, **3164**, and **3175**); displacement of peasants (items **3078** and **3156**); specific problems confronted by small farmers (items **3105** and **3207**); agrarian reform (items **3106** and **3154**); agroindustry (items **3096** and **3153**); and studies of individual crops (e.g., coffee, item **3113**; bananas, items **3116** and **3155**; sugarcane, items **3103**, **3179**, **3187**, and **3221**; tobacco, item **3192**; and rice, item **3185**).

Finally, there is the ever-present concern with economic growth (items **3158**, **3196**, and **3198**), especially since some evidence indicates that the quality of life has declined for the middle and lower population strata. There may be some validity to the assertion that the region's primarily agroexport model encompasses an undue portion of arable land in detriment of production of basic grains and other essential commodities, thereby making their availability scarce and their prices unbearably high. Proponents of the comparative-advantage principle of international trade contend that the agroexport model optimizes resource utilization, and this may indeed be the case in the aggregate. The problem, however, is that the revenue and profits accruing from increased efficiency are not redistributed in order for lower- and middle-income groups to benefit either directly or indirectly by becoming more active participants in the exchange process. Instead, revenue and profits are retained by the corporations, which further accelerates capital accumulation and exacerbates an already disparate distribution of wealth. For this reason, poverty and income distribution (items **3072**, **3101**, **3167**, and **3182**) are prominent themes, along with elements necessary for their alleviation, institutional development (item **3199**) and human capital formation (items **3081**, **3119**, and **3170**). The most notable instances of human capital investment analyzed in the literature are in the areas of education and health (items **3095**, **3137**, and **3169**), nutrition (item **3168**), population growth (item **3181**), and migration and urban expansion (items **3097**, **3127**, **3150**, and **3193**).

Listed below is a representative compendium of relevant writings on Central America and the Caribbean. It is evenly divided between journal articles and other publications including books and reports. The major journals of the area are *Estudios Sociales Centroamericanos* (items **3064** and **3128**), *Estudios Centroamericanos* (items **3069**, and **3148–3149**), and *Social and Economic Studies* (items **3212**, **3214**, **3220**, and **3223–3224**); *Nueva Sociedad* (item **3079**), *Eme Eme Estudios Dominicanos* (items **3183**), and *Conjonction* are important, too. Various articles also appear in *El Trimestre Económico* (item **3070**), *América Indígena* (item **3141**),

América Latina (item **3197**), *The Developing Economies* (item **3205**), *International Social Science Journal* (item **3206**), and *Croissance des Jeunes Nations* (item **3231**). Publications by both local universities (items **3076, 3139, 3159, 3162,** and **3191**) and commercial publishers (items **3177–3178,** and **3219**) are proliferating and constitute further evidence of the development of an indigenous and original strain of social and economic thought. The public sector continues to publish its share of meaningful works (items **3109, 3134–3136,** and **3174**). Complementing these entries are sources by regional and international organizations (items **3091, 3094, 3102, 3121, 3201,** and **3210**).

The references annotated below are classified into six groupings: 1) *General* contains 30 regional publications; 2) *Central America* consists of 67 entries related to Costa Rica, El Salvador, Guatemala, Honduras, and Nicaragua; 3) *Panama*, containing seven references, constitutes a separate subsection (although geographically Panama is the continuation of Central America, there are significant differences between it and the other five nations with respect to ethnic composition, historical development, socioeconomic structures, and other fundamental aspects to warrant a separate classification); 4) *Hispaniola*, shared by the Dominican Republic and Haiti, contains 22 items; 5) *British Caribbean* including noninsular Belize and Guyana, comprises 34 publications; 6) *French* and *Dutch Caribbean* which includes five works. All 165 entries were published during the 1979–83 period and, in addition to meeting the *HLAS*'s permanent-value criterion, either have or will contribute to the formulation of public policies.

GENERAL

3064 Acuña, Víctor Hugo. Capital comercial y comercio exterior en América Central durante el siglo XVIII: una contribución (CSUCA/ESC, 9:26, mayo/agosto 1980, p. 71–102)

Between 16th and 19th centuries indigo (añil) was a main Central American export product and driving force of commercial sector. Dye was capital generator, but both procedures and workers were exploited to the extreme by merchants, who lent money to producers and in the process kept full control over trade. Article relates how the exploitation took place.

3065 Andrews, Kenneth R. The Spanish Caribbean: trade and plunder, 1530–1630. New Haven: Yale University Press, 1978. 267 p.: maps.

Argues that Spanish Caribbean's economy during this period was largely based on smuggling and that spectacular naval assaults on San Juan, Santo Domingo, and Panama had little bearing on course of Caribbean history. Real reason for establishment of Northern European colonial enclaves was less the challenge of power than the challenge of profit (for historian's comment, see

HLAS 42:1826).

3066 Arias Peñate, Salvador. Las perspectivas del desarrollo agropecuario y la tenencia de la tierra (UJSC/ECA, 379, mayo 1980, p. 445–462, tables)

Reviews production and financing in agricultural sector during 1960–78, analyzes export-subsistence model, and proposes an alternative agricultural development strategy.

3067 Axline, Andrew W. Caribbean integration: the politics of regionalism. New York: Nichols Publishing Company, 1979. 233 p.: bibl.

Maintains that development will not proceed automatically from elimination of obstacles which impede sustained economic growth, but that this situation is closely linked to historical relationship with (and conditioned by) the external world. Analyzes political behavior based on benefits and costs of integration. Some topics discussed are: CARIFTA's establishment, decision to move to a customs union, failure to adopt measures to control foreign investment, and transfer of technology at regional level.

3068 Aybar, José M. and **Raúl Moncarz.**

Tecnócratas: agentes para el mantenimiento de la "nueva dependencia" en Centroamérica (Revista de la Integración y el Desarrollo de Centroamérica [Banco Centroamericano de Integración Económica, Tegucigalpa] 28, enero/junio 1981, p. 69–101, tables)

Establishes link between US-sponsored development ideas and Central American technocrats, especially in Honduras and El Salvador, who implement these ideas in government agencies and multinational corporations.

3069 Boyle, William A. Termodinámica, ecología y proceso económico (UJSC/ECA, 405, julio 1982, p. 665–682, bibl., graphs)

Thorough discussion of ecological-economic systems, utilizing thermodynamic theory as an explanatory tool. Uses commonly accepted economic-process and economic-development models to point out absence of ecological component, thereby creating imbalances.

3070 Cáceres, Luis René and **Stephen F. Seninger.** Redes inter-regionales, estructuras jerárquicas y fuga de la riqueza en Centroamérica: un análisis de cadena de Markov (FCE/TE, 49[3]:195, julio/sept. 1982, p. 623–644, bibl., tables)

Based on complex quantitative model, article estimates, for each of five Central American countries, extent of income diffusion and probabilities for income units to remain in Central America or be transferred outside region.

3071 Cárdenas, Osvaldo. La viabilidad de la integración del Caribe (CSUCA/ESC, 10:30, sept./dc. 1981, p. 33–48, map, tables)

Views foreign dependency, underdevelopment, and political heterogeneity as main obstacles to integration efforts.

3072 Castillo Rivas, Donald. Acumulación de capital y empresas transnacionales en Centroamérica. México: Siglo XXI Editores, 1980. 177 p.: appendices, bibl.

Studies three models of transnational penetration, evaluating their socioeconomic impact and policymaking consequences. The three models under scrutiny are import substitution, agribusiness, and export promotion. Argues that benefits of transnational corporations to Central America are limited and far from offsetting their responsibility for

large foreign debts, disequilibria in the balance of payments, high unemployment rates, heavy rural-to-urban migration flows, and extreme poverty.

3073 ———. Características del nuevo modelo de acumulación de capital en América Latina, con ilustración del caso centroamericano (CSUCA/ESC, 9:25, enero/abril 1980, p. 145–182, bibl., tables)

Probes creation and impact of multinational corporations on Central American economic development, with emphasis on the role of the State and the allegedly inevitable conflict between the rural and industrial oligarchies' interests. Argues that fiscal policy, duty exemptions, and many other privileges enjoyed by foreign investment have hindered development in the region.

3074 Cross, Malcolm. Urbanization and urban growth in the Caribbean: an essay on social change in dependent societies. New York: Cambridge University Press, 1979. 174 p.: bibl., index, map (Urbanization in developing countries)

Using plantation as center of analysis in neo-Marxist framework, author develops effective application of dependency theory to different socioeconomic problems in region. Move towards enhancing economic role of government is interpreted as attempt to overcome structural discontinuity between influence and accountability. Dependency and weakness it implies for local administrators have bred centralizing tendency in which government officials vest in themselves economic power through nationalizing enterprises or undertaking joint public-private ventures.

3075 Dada Hirezi, Héctor. La crisis de la integración centroamericana (UNAM/RMS, 42:2, abril/junio 1980, p. 731–747)

Summary of origins, performance, and breakdown of the Central American Common Market. Emergence of mixed economies in Nicaragua and El Salvador further complicates renewed attempts at economic integration. [G.W. Grayson]

3076 Documentación socioeconómica centroamericana. San José: Confederación Universitaria Centroamericana, Centro de Documentación Económica y Social de Centroamérica, 1982. 235 p.

Annotated socioeconomic bibliography contains 300 entries and indices of geographical location, author, topics, institutions, and conferences.

3077 Doggart, Caroline. Industrial investment incentives in the Caribbean. Washington: World Bank, 1979. 66 p.: appendices, bibl.

Review of incentive sytems to attract investment in industry, especially export-oriented enterprises, and assessment of different incentives as tools of development policy.

3078 Durham, William H. Scarcity and survival in Central America. Stanford, Calif.: Stanford University Press, 1979. 209 p.: bibl., graphs, ill., tables.

Views 1969 "Soccer War" between El Salvador and Honduras not as a conflict between these countries, but between latifundia owners, supported by both US and big corporations, and peasants who were consistently, and sometimes violently, displaced from their land.

3079 Fermín, Claudio. La descolonización y la reestructuración de la economía caribeña (NSO, 48, mayo/junio 1980, p. 54–66, tables)

Exposition of interests and resources of Caribbean states vis-à-vis rest of world. Discusses reasons for integration and identifies heterogeneity as main obstacle. Also calls for more land ownership by agricultural workers.

3080 Fonseca Zúniga, Gautama. Lecciones de integración económica centroamericana. San José: Escuela Aduanera Regional, 1979. 173 p.: bibl., tables.

Traces development of Central American integration movements since its beginning. Provides interesting historical framework all the way back to colonial administration and in-depth analysis of price stabilization of basic grains, incentives for industrial development, determination of common tariff policy, and role of major institutions such as BCIE and SIECA.

3081 Gabbin, Alexander L. The use of regional resources in shaping the economic development of the Caribbean (in Development issues, Caribbean-American dialogue: proceedings and papers from the Caribbean-American exchange program conducted by the Phelps-Stokes Fund. New York: The Fund, 1980, p. 55–66, bibl., tables)

Contends that region's most abundant

and underutilized resource is its human element and that answers to future economic problems lie in people's will and commitment to a strong economy, which means that they must perform productive functions. Provides good insight into motivation, risk, satisfaction, and power as policy variables toward greater involvement of human resources in development efforts.

3082 Langley, Lester D. The United States and the Caribbean, 1900–1970. Athens: University of Georgia Press, 1980. 324 p.: bibl., index, map (on lining papers)

Second of two books in which the author relates US efforts to secure and maintain hegemony in the region by virtue of exerting economic, political, and cultural pressure. Contends that the failure of US policy can be traced to violation of sovereignty, denigration of institutions, and disparagement of culture.

3083 Lizano, Eduardo. Reflexiones en torno al proyecto de tratado de la Comunidad Económica y Social Centroamericana (FCE/TE, 46[2]:182, abril/junio 1979, p. 255–284)

Surveys institutional framework of integration movement and assesses impact of its agricultural, wage, and monetary policies.

3084 ——— and Maritza Huertas. Bibliografía sobre el Mercado Común Centroamericano (CSUCA/ESC, 8:24, sept./dic. 1979, p. 271–330)

Comprehensive bibliography on Central American integration through 1977 contains 498 references.

3085 Manley, Michael. La importancia estratégica de la Cuenca del Caribe en términos políticos y económicos (NSO, 63, nov./dic. 1982, p. 5–20)

Focuses on economic and geopolitical importance of Caribbean Basin to European countries in the past and to US today. After analyzing transition from past open exploitation (by Europe) to present disguised exploitation (by US), author provides suggestions for breaking economic and cultural dependency cycle.

3086 Molina Chocano, Guillermo and Diego Palma. Estado y desarrollo agrario en Centroamérica (NSO, 41, marzo/abril 1979, p. 48–67, ill., table)

Marxist analysis views the Central American State as one that increasingly intervenes in economic affairs while attempting to legitimize its existence by holding regular elections characterized by absenteeism and fraud allegations.

3087 Molina Chocano, Miguel. Crisis, capitalismo, inflación y papel económico del Estado (CSUCA/ESC, 10:28, enero/abril 1981, p. 9–41, tables)

Contends that government participation in economic activity is key factor of capital accumulation process which tends to reactivate the economy in crisis situations. Bases analysis on 1970–79 economic events.

3088 Murga Frassinetti, Antonio. Economía primaria exportadora y formación del proletariado: el caso centroamericano, 1850–1920 (CSUCA/ESC, 11:32, mayo/agosto 1982, p. 49–73, tables)

Historical exposition of various developmental phases in Central American economies. Discussion centers around international trade, with emphasis on behavior of elites, role of the State, and cultivation of coffee and bananas.

3089 Pierre-Charles, Gérard. El Caribe contemporáneo. México: Siglo XXI Editores, 1981. 413 p.: bibl.

Views Caribbean history as series of frustrated attempts to gain autodetermination. Colonialism, through its various phases of exploitation, mercantilism, and incorporation of territories, manages to destroy local organizations and native traditions. After Monroe Doctrine, focus of influence shifts from Europe to US, which supports governments that are favorable to its own economic and political interests.

3090 Problemas del Caribe contemporáneo = Contemporary Caribbean issues. Conferencias sobre el Caribe contemporáneo auspiciado por el Colegio Universitario de Cayey de la Universidad de Puerto Rico. Angel Calderón Cruz, editor. Río Piedras: Universidad de Puerto Rico, Instituto de Estudios del Caribe, 1979. 180 p.: bibl.

Collection of 11 articles by prominent Caribbean writers such as Gordon Lewis, Sir Phillip Sherlock, Basil Ince, and Fuat Andic. Covers economic integration, contemporary political and economic change, role of education, international relations, etc.

3091 Salazar-Carrillo, Jorge; Jorge Borstcheff; and Enrique Delgado. Estudio comparativo centroamericano de niveles y estructuras de precios: años de 1973, 1977 y 1981. Guatemala: Secretaría Permanente del Tratado General de Integración Económica Centroamericana, 1983. 194 p.: appendices, bibl., tables.

Inquiry into impact of economic integration on price structure of each country as evidenced by changes in consumption of final goods and services, utilization of factors of production, internal marketing, and both intraregional trade and trade with rest of the world.

3092 Solórzano Fonseca, Juan C. Centroamérica en el siglo XVII: un intento de explicación económica y social (CSUCA/ESC, 11:32, mayo/agosto 1982, p. 11–22)

Discusses various hypotheses explaining fundamental characteristics of Central American production structure in 18th century.

3093 Tenencia de la tierra y desarrollo rural en Centroamérica: estudio elaborado por expertos de CEPAL et al. 3. ed. Ciudad Universitaria Rodrigo Facio, Costa Rica: Editorial Universitaria Centroamericana, 1980. 199 p.: bibl., tables (Colección Seis)

Probe into Central American land tenure, distribution, productivity, and utilization patterns; labor absorption capability; rural income distribution; education, housing, and nutrition; migration flows; and colonization policies.

3094 United Nations. Economic Commission for Latin America. Economic survey of Latin America, 1979. Santiago: 1981. 499 p.: graphs, ill., tables.

Follows uniform format for all countries. Covers Costa Rica, Barbados, Dominican Republic, Guyana, Haiti, Honduras, Jamaica, Nicaragua, Panama, Suriname, and Trinidad and Tobago. After reviewing recent economic trends (aggregate supply and demand, growth of main sectors, and employment and unemployment trends), analyzes external sector (exports, imports, terms of trade, and financing and evolution of external indebtedness), prices and wages, and monetary and fiscal policies. Provides excellent framework for intercountry comparison of economic performance.

CENTRAL AMERICA

3095 Arias Sánchez, Oscar. Nuevos rumbos para el desarrollo costarricense. Ciudad

Universidad Rodrigo Facio, Costa Rica: Editorial Universitaria Centroamericana, 1979. 150 p.: tables (Colección Seis)

Reviews recent developments in areas of education; health and social security; housing; monetary policy and credit facilities; fiscal policy and public debt; exchange rates; agriculture, industry, and tertiary sector; commercial, financial, and technological dependence; and income distribution.

3096 Bello, Juan Carlos del. El sector agroindustrial en Costa Rica (CSUCA/ ESC, 8 : 22, enero/abril 1979, p. 36–69, tables)

In-depth analysis of nature and importance of industrialization of agricultural products, which amounts to 36 percent of industrial value added. Focuses individually on meat, bread, dairy products, oils, sugar, fruits and vegetables, candy, and seafood, providing useful information on source and concentration of capital, employment generation, wages, export, and utilization of raw materials.

3097 Bogan, Marcos W. La migración internacional en Costa Rica. Heredia, Costa Rica: Universidad Nacional, Instituto de Estudios Sociales y de Población, 1980.

Study of the demographic, economic, and occupational impact of foreigners migrating into Costa Rica. Also analyzes outmigration trends.

3098 Bran, Salvador O. Algunos lineamientos para lograr la reactivación económica en El Salvador (UJSC/ECA, 410, dic. 1982, p. 1109–1115)

Sees traditional economic principles of supply and demand, terms of trade, and comparative advantage as obsolete and incapable of providing proper solution to current crisis. Roots of country's problems, according to author, are not economic but political and military. Attributes economic chaos to civil war.

3099 Brodersohn, Victor. Estructura y desarrollo social en El Salvador (IDES/ DE, 20 : 77, abril/junio 1980, p. 121–134, bibl., tables)

Analyzes relationships between economic system and social structure based on premise that development schemes throughout last two decades have revolved around promotion of exports. Recommends more active role for public sector in matters of resource allocation.

3100 Bulichiov, Ilia. Guatemala: nuevo modelo de la economía y viejos problemas (URSS/AL, 7 : 82, julio 1982, p. 13–19, table)

Critical analysis of Guatemala's economy. Views current crisis as stemming from country's capitalistic structure, endemic to the system and aggravated by world recession. Blames US capital for introducing rigidities that work against people's welfare.

3101 Carvajal, Manuel J. Report on income distribution and poverty in Costa Rica. Washington: Agency for International Development, Bureau for Latin America and the Caribbean, Rural Development Division, 1979. 74 p.: ill. (Working document series Costa Rica. General working document; 2)

Describes income distribution and poverty through a variety of quantitative measures. Notes regional differences and particularly differentiates rural and urban households. [J.M. Hunter]

3102 Castillo, Margarita and **María José Galrão.** Bibliografía agrícola de Costa Rica. San José: IICA, Centro Interamericano de Documentación e Información Agrícola: SEPSA, Centro Nacional de Información Agropecuaria, 1980. 431 p.: index (Serie Documentación e información agrícola, 0301–438X; no. 83)

Extensive bibliography contains 8,100 references published 1945–80 and divided into: 1) agricultural sciences; 2) geography and history; 3) education and extension; 4) administration and legislation; 5) economics, development, and rural sociology; 6) vegetable production; 7) plant protection; 8) forestry; 9) animal husbandry; 10) fishing; 11) machinery and construction; 12) natural resources; 13) bromatology; 14) home economics; 15) human nutrition; 16) environmental protection; and 17) related areas.

3103 Cid, José R. del. El cultivo de la caña de azúcar en Honduras (CSUCA/ESC, 11 : 32, mayo/agosto 1982, p. 97–129, bibl., tables)

Study based on observation of 200 small farms and 50 medium and large corporate farms.

3104 Córdoba, Julio. La capacidad inversionista del sector público en Costa Rica. San José: Instituto Centroamericano de

Administración Pública, 1978. 91 p.: tables
(Serie Economía y finanzas; no. 421)

Establishes methodology for evaluating investment capacity and applies it to public sector in 1974. Focuses on physical, financial, and human resources as well as organizing and technological capacity.

3105 Davis, L. Harlan and **David E. Weisenborn.** Small farmer market development: the El Salvador experience (JDA, 15:3, April 1981, p. 407–416, ill., table)

Discussion of practical experience of designing a market development program and implications it has for directly helping small producer and, indirectly, small consumer. Argues that effective market development program must go beyond construction of facilities as it requires a price stabilization policy, working capital fund, regional storage network, and institutional support.

3106 Deere, Carmen Diana and **Peter Marchetti.** The worker-peasant alliance in the first year of the Nicaraguan agrarian reform (LAP, 8[2]:29, Spring 1981, p. 40–73, table)

Examines role of worker-peasant alliance in Nicaraguan Revolution and its impact on first year of Sandinista agrarian reform under premise that transition to socialism in countries where process of capitalist development has not generated a substantial industrial proletariat must necessarily be based on worker-peasant alliance. Contends that organization of new productive structures in agriculture, such as state farms, production cooperatives, and service and credit cooperatives, has been based on changed relations of production, especially socialization of labor.

3107 DeWitt, R. Peter. The Inter-American Development Bank and policy making in Costa Rica (JDA, 15:1, Oct. 1980, p. 67–82, tables)

Describes impact of US national interest in IDB and its effect on the policy making process in Costa Rica. Argues that an increase in international lending also increases host country's dependence, which is likely to have long-term negative consequences.

3108 Díaz Pérez, Alvaro. El desarrollo industrial y el Estado en Costa Rica. Ciudad Universitaria Rodrigo Facio: Universidad de Costa Rica, Facultad de Ciencias

Económicas, Instituto de Investigaciones en Ciencias Económicas, 1979. 35 p.: tables (Documentos)

Inquiry into the increasingly oligopolization nature of the Costa Rican industry, its importance in generating employment, and its effect on income distribution. Also reviews industry-related public policies 1959–75.

3109 El Salvador. Ministerio de Planificación y Coordinación del Desarrollo Económico y Social. Plan Trienal, 1981–1983. San Salvador: El Ministerio, 1980. 142 leaves: bibl., tables.

Establishes priorities for agricultural, industrial, and tourism development policies; education, housing, nutrition, and health; energy, transport, and communication; regional, community, and technological development; and monetary, fiscal, labor, and population policies. Defines as "fundamental priority" programs those in economic reconstruction, agrarian reform, nutrition, municipal development, adult education, population and human development, urban growth, and environmental protection.

3110 Erazo, Benjamín and **Allan Fajardo.** El proceso de colectivización del agro hondureño (EDTM, 3:1, marzo 1980, p. 11–57, tables)

Inquiry into collectivization experience in agricultural sector. Stresses importance of organization of production into banana plantation enclaves, reviews objectives and legal framework of cooperatives, explains social participation at the enterprise and global society levels, and analyzes role of training in collective enterprises using experimental laboratory method. Concludes that collectivization has contributed to both consolidating triumphs of the peasant movement and modernizing agriculture in a country where support for the individual farmer has failed.

3111 Evolución socioeconómica de Costa Rica, 1950–1980. San José: Presidencia de la República, Oficina de Planificación Nacional y Política Económica: Editorial Universidad Estatal a Distancia, 1982. 470 p.: ill., tables.

Comprehensive study of contemporary economic forces and events, focusing on components of aggregate demand and aggregate supply, employment sectors, savings and investment, availability of human resources, capital accumulation, international trade and import-substitution attempts, income distribution, population growth and composition, energy pressures, and expansion of public sector.

3112 Fallas, Helio. Crisis económica en Costa Rica: un análisis económico de los últimos 20 años. San José: Editorial Nueva Década, 1981. 139 p.: ill., tables.

Assessment of socioeconomic events occurring during 1960s and 1970s within context of import substitution model adopted by Central America. Focuses on performance of both agricultural and industrial sectors, employment, exports and imports, public policy, inflation, and poverty.

3113 Fernández A., Miguel Francisco. El café en estadísticas. Ed. rev., ampliada y mejorada. San José: Oficina del Café, Departamento de Estudios Técnicos y Diversificación, 1981. 1 v.: bibl., ill.

Provides valuable data on coffee production and processing, domestic consumption, export volume and prices, taxes, and credit availability.

3114 Figueroa Ibarra, Carlos. Algunas consideraciones preliminares sobre la acumulación capitalista en el agro guatemalteco (Alero [Universidad de San Carlos, Guatemala] 1:4, mayo/junio 1979, p. 58–85, plates, tables)

Explores ties between agricultural development and capital accumulation, with emphasis on size of holding and mode of production.

3115 Flores, R. Producción de la vivienda y el papel del Estado hondureño. San José: Universidad de Costa Rica, 1981. 154 p.

Discusses housing shortages, attributing them to capital accumulation and US monopolies protected by Honduran government. Compares urban and rural dwellings and different types of housing tenure.

3116 Gaspar, Jeffrey Casey. Limón: 1880–1940, un estudio de la industria bananera en Costa Rica (CSUCA/ESC, 8:23, mayo/agosto 1979, p. 245–279)

Socioeconomic analysis of impact of Limón's banana-industry enclave on Costa Rican historical development. Based on author's master's thesis at Universidad Nacional, Heredia.

3117 Gutiérrez Espeleta, Nelson. Notas sobre la evaluación del Estado costarricense: 1821–1978 (CSUCA/ESC, 10:28, enero/abril 1981, p. 69–86, bibl.)

Analyzes factors that contributed to formation of the State since attainment of political independence, with emphasis on capital accumulation and economic dependence.

3118 Hernández, Carlos. Banca central. San José: Editorial Universidad Estatal a Distancia, 1980. 146 p.: bibl., ill., tables.

Probe into nature and mechanisms of central banking, with specific application to Costa Rica. After tracing its origin to Bank of England, analyzes objectives of central banking (economic growth, full employment, and price stability), functions and policy tools (open market operations, discount rate, reserve requirements). Concludes with inquiry into international financial relations, with emphasis on IMF.

3119 Immink, Maarten D.C.; Fernando E. Viteri; and Ronald W. Helms. Energy intake over the life cycle and human capital formation in Guatemalan sugarcane cutters (UC/EDCC, 30:2, Jan. 1982, p. 351–372, tables)

Precursory study indicates that increased energy intake during childhood and adolescence appears to have positive effect on sugarcane cutting once adulthood is reached, thus implying that increased energy intake during the preproductive phase of life cycle may be a significant form of human capital investment.

3120 Instituto de Investigaciones Económicas, San Salvador. Evaluación de las reformas (UJSC/ECA, 403/404, mayo/junio 1982, p. 507–539, tables)

Argues that fundamental roots of economic, social, and political problems in El Salvador lie in extreme concentration of land and other sources of wealth in a few families. Once control of land was secured, these families moved to control industry, commerce, services, and finance. Also presents evidence that social and economic reforms introduced after Oct. 15, 1979 military coup have been poorly administered, adversely affected by the war, and consistently rejected by oligarchy.

3121 Instituto Interamericano de Ciencias

Agrícolas, *Tegucigalpa.* Proyecto de Planificación Agraria y Análisis de Políticas en América Latina y el Caribe, PROPLAN: la etapa de instrumentación de la ejecución del proceso de planificación agrícola en Honduras. Tegucigalpa: 1979. 68 p.

Assesses agricultural sector using socioeconomic, political, administrative, and planning criteria and describes PROPLAN's contributions toward improving situation.

3122 Jiménez, Dina. Bibliografía retrospectiva sobre política agraria en Costa Rica, 1948–1978. San José: Universidad de Costa, Vicerrectoría de Investigación, Instituto de Investigaciones Sociales, Centro de Documentación: Consejo Nacional de Investigaciones Científicas y Tecnológicas (CONICIT), 1981. 528 p.: indexes.

Partially annotated bibliography containing 2,750 references and divided into seven areas: economic development and history; institutional framework; agrarian structure; agricultural production; commerce, prices, and consumption; banking and public finance; and living conditions, labor, and social security.

3123 Kusterer, Kenneth C.; María Regina Estrada de Batres; and Josefina Xuyá Cuxil. The social impact of agribusiness: a case study of ALCOSA in Guatemala. Washington: Agency for International Development (AID), 1981. 83 p.: tables (AID Evaluation special study; 4)

Reports results of in-depth case study of single case of agribusiness growth, operations of Alimentos Congelados Monte Bello, S.A., designed to improve understanding of social consequences of development process. Provides detailed data on problems and successes encountered by an agribusiness firm in its operations with small farmers.

3124 Lindo Fuentes, Héctor. La economía en época de guerra (UJSC/ECA, 403/404, mayo/junio 1982, p. 493–506, graphs, tables)

Exposition of all-pervasive nature of El Salvador civil war, which has affected all aspects of economic activity. Concludes that as long as war continues there is no possibility of reconstructing the economy.

3125 ———. La extinción de ejidos y la eficiencia económica (UJSC/ECA, 386, dic. 1980, p. 1135–1143, graph)

Views extinction of common land

holdings in El Salvador as necessary conclusion of liberal reforms implemented in second half of 19th century. Uses econometric model to show that the driving force behind such extinction was not a search for greater economic efficiency, but tendency toward land and wealth concentration.

3126 Lizano Fait, Eduardo. Agricultura y desarrollo económico. San José: Editorial Universidad Estatal a Distancia, 1980. 315 p.: bibl., ill., tables (Serie de estudios nacionales; no. 1)

Collection of nine articles dealing with institutional organization of agricultural sector, interest rate subsidies and income distribution, the National Production Council's activities with respect to basic grains, determination of crop prices, and other agricultural concerns.

3127 McIntosh, Terry L. Economic crisis and progress in spatial integration: the case of Guatemala (CQ, 26:3, Sept. 1980, p. 18–23, tables)

Maintains that increases in international prices of petroleum and basic grains have motivated Guatemalan government to develop policies of rational utilization of domestic resources in order to raise national self-sufficiency levels. Urban-rural dichotomy in living standards has stimulated rise in urbanization and inflow of peasants from densely populated highlands to capital. Drive toward self-sufficiency has increased public and private investment in previously neglected portions of country.

3128 Maloney, Thomas J. El impacto social del esquema de desarrollo de la franja transversal del Norte sobre los maya-kekchí en Guatemala (CSUCA/ESC, 10:29, mayo/agosto 1981, p. 91–106, bibl.)

Portrait of Indians who account for approximately 40 percent of country's population. Argues that Kekchí are forced out of their land and traditional environment into proletarian labor force, thus contributing to capitalist export-oriented economic scheme.

3129 Mendizábal, Ana B.; Rokael Cardona; and R.A. Zepeda López. Empleo rural, estado y políticas públicas en Guatemala. Guatemala: Universidad de San Carlos de Guatemala, 1979. 294 p.: tables.

Probes structure and mechanisms of rural employment in light of capital accumulation process experienced by agriculture sector since 1960s. Examines labor supply and demand as function of area cultivated with a variety of crops and changes in population growth. Estimates rural unemployment rates at departmental level.

3130 Menjívar, Rafael. Acumulación originaria y desarrollo del capitalismo en El Salvador. San José: Editorial Universitaria Centroamericana, 1981. 169 p.

Probe into country's experiences with policies which encourage accumulation of private capitals and lead to external economic dependence.

3131 Moncada Valladares, E. El desarrollo del capitalismo en la agricultura de Honduras (URSS/AL, 3[39], 1981, p. 65–78)

Exposition of country's development of the agricultural sector, with emphasis on capitalistic modernization, new strategies of international monopolies, farmers' plight, and struggle for agrarian reform. Blames latifundia and dependency on banana transnational interests that hindered industrial growth.

3132 Montes, Segundo. El agro salvadoreño: 1973–1980. San Salvador: Universidad Centroamericana José Simeón Cañas, 1980. 395 p.: bibl., tables (mimeo) (Publicaciones del Departamento de Sociología y Ciencias Políticas, Universidad Centroamericana José Simeón Cañas)

Inquiry into past and present land tenure patterns, with emphasis on farming income and expenses, housing, education, migration, unemployment, poverty, and impact of agrarian reform on these variables. Areas under study are presumably representative of country's land tenure patterns, crop distribution, and population composition (i.e., Aguilares, Coatepeque, Comasagua, La Herradura, and Opico).

3133 Moreno, Francisco A. El Salvador: acumulación del capital industrial en la década del 70; un ejercicio empírico (CSUCA/ESC, 10:28, enero/abril 1981, p. 87–108, tables)

Attributes national industry crisis to absence of self-sustaining growth due to external dependence of many factors of production. Crisis is perceived as structural in nature, linked to participation by El Salvador in international capital accumulation process.

3134 Nicaragua. Instituto Nacional de Estadísticas y Censos. Indicadores socioeconómicos: 1970–1980. Managua: 1981. 48 p.: tables.

Provides information on institutional performance, population, gross internal product, money and credit, balance of payments, government expenditures and taxes, output, employment, wages and salaries, education, health and social welfare, energy, transport and communication, and construction.

3135 ———. Ministerio de Planificación. Plan de reactivación económica en beneficio del pueblo. Managua: Secretaría Nacional de Propaganda y Educación Política, FSLN, 1980. 142 p.

Detailed outline of goals and objectives, phases, and components of revolutionary government's major economic recovery programs such as agriculture, industry, foreign trade, investment, fulfillment of basic needs, employment, salaries, and social services.

3136 ———. Secretaría Nacional de Propaganda y Educación Política del Frente Sandinista de Liberación Nacional. Datos básicos sobre Nicaragua. Managua: 1980. 40 p.: tables.

Provides data on the country's socioeconomic structure during 1975–80. Indicators include population, labor force, employment classified by economic sector, gross internal product, agricultural and industrial output, foreign trade, external debt, and education.

3137 Oduber, Daniel. El nuevo modelo económico en Costa Rica (NSO, 48, mayo/junio 1980, p. 5–21, tables)

Warns against experiments conducted by Chicago-School economists, explaining that their assumptions do not conform to Costa Rican reality. Calls for comprehensive resource-allocation strategy based on utilization of all resources, including education, health, water, and agriculture.

3138 Ortiz-Buonafina, Marta. The impact of import substitution policies on marketing activities: a case study of the Guatemalan commercial sector. Washington: University Press of America, 1982. 158 p.: bibl., tables.

Explains how in late 1950s and early 1960s Guatemala began major development effort based on import-substitution industrialization as means to strengthen economy and improve welfare of majority of population. Although initial results were positive, mostly due to establishment of the Central American Common Market, industrialization soon reached its limits and policy makers failed to promote new markets for output.

3139 Perfil del sector pesquero costarricense. Ciudad Universitaria Rodrigo Facio: Universidad de Costa Rica, Instituto de Investigaciones en Ciencias Económicas, 1981. 68 p. (Documentos de trabajo; no. 27)

Study of nature and importance of fishing industry, with emphasis on seafood prices, processing, and marketing.

3140 Programa Regional del Empleo para América Latina y el Caribe. Honduras, el empleo en el Plan Nacional de Desarrollo, 1979–1983. Prepared by Héctor Szretter, Conrado Osorio, and Fausto Lazo. Santiago: Organización Internacional del Trabajo, Programa Mundial del Empleo, Programa Regional del Empleo para América Latina y el Caribe (PREALC), 1980. 116 p.: bibl., tables (Documento de trabajo—PREALC; 181)

Assessment of impact on labor force participation and employment generation by National Development Plant. Areas researched are agriculture (including forestry, fishing, and hunting), industry (manufacturing, energy, mining, construction, and tourism), and provision of basic services.

3141 Quiroga, Eduardo R. La transformación de la agricultura de subsistencia mediante riego en El Salvador (III/AI, 40:3, julio/sept. 1980, p. 499–525, bibl., tables)

Case study of Zapotitán Irrigation Project illustrates problems of attempting to transform subsistence agriculture by irrigation investment without proper institutional changes. Project's main aim was to improve small farmers' welfare by enhancing fresh vegetable production through irrigation. Author concludes that although vegetable crops have potential to improve income because of their high market value and labor-intensive nature, results for small farmers are disappointing insofar as large landowners become Project's real beneficiaries.

3142 Reuben Soto, Sergio. Capitalismo y crisis económica en Costa Rica: treinta años de desarrollo. San José: Editorial Por-

venir, 1982. 266 p.: tables (Colección Debates)

Views socioeconomic development during 1948–78 as proof of consolidation of capitalist system. Pays special attention to development indicators, labor for utilization, capital accumulation, agricultural colonization, and oligopolistic nature of the manufacturing sector.

3143 Rodríguez Fernández, Silvia. La reproducción de la fuerza de trabajo de los peones cafetaleros: estudio del caso de San Pablo de Heredia, Costa Rica (CSUCA/ESC, 10:29, mayo/agosto 1981, p. 55–78, tables)

Discusses close correlation that exists between coffee production and country's economy in attempt to relate capital accumulation to maintaining a sizeable labor force capable of responding to crop's needs.

3144 Rourk, Phillip W. Equitable growth: the case of Costa Rica. Washington: Agency for International Development, 1979. 93 p.: appendices, bibl., tables.

Provides historical perspective for Costa Rica's development and evaluates various public sector programs such as physical infrastructure (roads, electricity, and housing), human resources (education, health care, and nutrition), land reform, and wage policy.

3145 Rovira Mas, Jorge. Costa Rica: economía y estado; notas sobre su evolución reciente y el momento actual (CSUCA/ESC, 9:26, mayo/agosto 1980, p. 37–70, tables)

Author contends that a tendency toward agriculture and fiscal discipline began after events and reforms following the 1948 Revolution. Also warns that in the near future real wages will decline, economy will record slower expansion rate, and unemployment will increase, all of which will lead to the emergence of a more combative work force.

3146 Ruiz Granadino, Santiago. Modernización agrícola en El Salvador (CSUCA/ESC, 8:22, enero/abril 1979, p. 71–100, tables)

Contends that agricultural development in El Salvador is manifested through concentration of land, disproportionate growth of export crops, deterioration of rural income distribution, and consolidation of power in the hands of few producers-exporters of agricultural products.

3147 Sarti Castañeda, Carlos A. and **J. Godoy.** Nicaragua: aproximación al estudio del carácter de la Revolución y la naturaleza del Estado, 1979–1981. San José: Consejo Superior Universitario Centroamericano, 1981. 33 p.

Examines manifestations of class struggle during capitalism-to-socialism transition and new role of the State after the Revolution's triumph.

3148 Sebastián, Luis de. Algunas directrices para organizar una economía popular (UJSC/ECA, 377/378, marzo/abril 1980, p. 207–218, bibl., ill.)

Criticizes Salvadoran economic structure and proposes new socioeconomic and political system based on people's direct participation. Focuses on growth, efficiency, social relations, economic independence, technology transfer, transnational corporations, and organizations of international cooperation.

3149 ———. La economía nacional un año después del 15 de octubre de 1979 (UJSC/ECA, 384/385, oct./nov. 1980, p. 953–954, tables)

Analysis of Salvadoran economic situation a year after 1979 coup based on official statistical data, newspaper articles, and discussion of current and past events.

3150 Sermeño Lima, José. Los movimientos de población y sus relaciones socioeconómicas en El Salvador (UJSC/EA, 387/388, enero/feb. 1981, p. 33–42, bibl., ill., maps, tables)

Relates migration flows, which apparently have been considerable, to the production capacity and socioeconomic potential of various regions. Analytical framework is predominantly historical and conducted at the departmental level.

3151 Silva, Jorge E. Estudios de moneda y banca de El Salvador. San Salvador: Banco Agrícola Comercial de El Salvador, 1979. 2 v.: tables.

Economic history of Salvadoran monetary and banking system. Vol. 1 consists of an exposition of systems prior to 1934, when the Central Bank of Reserve was founded, while vol. 2 focuses on post-1934 developments.

3152 Simon, Laurence and **James C.**

Stephens, Jr. Reforma agraria en El Salvador, 1980–1981: su impacto en la sociedad salvadoreña (UJSC/ECA, 389, marzo 1981, p. 173–185)

Concludes that more than 60 percent of rural population does not benefit from agrarian reform, as workers without land are excluded. Program is perceived as having been imposed on the Salvadoran people and government by US agencies, without consulting peasants, the Church, or domestic academicians, and without adequate planning or provisions for regulation.

3153 Slutsky, Daniel. La agroindustria de la carne en Honduras (CSUCA/ESC, 8:22, enero/abril 1979, p. 101–205, tables)

Extensive and thorough inquiry into production, marketing, and export of Honduran beef. Provides information on slaughtering and packing, employment generation, and credit availability.

3154 ———. Notas sobre empresas transnacionales, agroindustrias y reforma agraria en Honduras (CSUCA/ESC, 8:23, mayo/agosto 1979, p. 35–48)

Analysis of public policy role in foreign investment process of multinational corporation. Emphasizes agricultural sector. Presents current phenomena in light of historical developments.

3155 ——— and **Esther Alonso.** Empresas transnacionales y agricultura: el caso del enclave bananero en Honduras. Tegucigalpa: Editorial Universitaria, 1980. 141 p.: bibl.

Among topics analyzed in this publication are the enclave's characteristics: export-oriented production, horizontal and vertical integration, patterns of growth, income generation and distribution, and prospects for agricultural cooperatives.

3156 Taylor, J. Edward. Peripheral capitalism and rural-urban migration: a study of population movements in Costa Rica (LAP, 7[25/26]:2/3, Spring/Summer 1980, p. 75–90, map, tables)

Maintains that rural-to-urban migration and subsequent growth of shantytowns in metropolitan center reflect response of subpopulation, marginalized by disarticulated capitalist development, to economic system's inability to satisfy its most basic human needs. Displaced Costa Rican peasants are left with no option but to migrate to urban centers, where availability of jobs is severely restricted by foreign-dominated industrial growth.

3157 La Tenencia de la tierra en Honduras. Tegucigalpa: Instituto Nacional Agrario, 1981. 75 p.: ill., tables (Colección Siembra; 1)

Assessment of land redistribution through agrarian reform in country's eight administrative regions using Lorenz curve and Gini concentration ratio.

3158 Universidad Centroamericana. Departamento de Economía. Seminario Permanente de la Realidad Nacional. Análisis crítico e interpretativo de la plataforma programática del Gobierno Democrático Revolucionario, en sus aspectos económicos y sociales (UJSC/ECA, 35, marzo/abril 1980, p. 294–328, ill.)

Summarizes major policies implemented in El Salvador since 1945, showing their inability to bring about equilibrium and growth. Develops new model for revolution-oriented economy. Analyzes international relations, new forms of ownership of factors of production, central planning, and guidelines for development scheme.

3159 Universidad Nacional Autónoma de Honduras. Postgrado Centroamericano en Economía y Planificación del Desarrollo: prospecto. Tegucigalpa: 1981. 66 p.

Contains information on postgraduate degree on Economics and Development Planning financed by Central American governments. Describes admission requirements, courses, faculty credentials, and research and extension activities.

3160 Vega, Mylena. El Estado Costarricense de 1974 a 1978: CODESA y la fracción industrial. San José: Editorial Hoy, 1982. 184 p.

Studies interaction of Corporación Costarricense de Desarrollo (CODESA) and industrial sector in Costa Rica. CODESA was created to assist and complement private sector, but its results have been less than satisfactory because of ideological struggle within the organization. Promoters of State capitalism have gained preponderance at expense of industrialists, who advocate subsidiary role for CODESA rather than direct competition with private sector.

3161 Villalobos Vega, Bernardo. Bancos emisores y bancos hipotecarios en Costa Rica, 1850–1910. San José: Editorial Costa Rica, 1981. 460 p.: bibl., ill., index.

Excellent economic history treatise traces development of major banking institutions and their involvement with provision of legal tender and mortgages during second half of 19th and early part of 20th centuries.

3162 Villasuso, Juan Manuel and **Juan Diego Trejos.** Evolución reciente de la estructura salarial en Costa Rica. Ciudad Universitaria Rodrigo Facio: Universidad de Costa Rica, Instituto Investigaciones en Ciencias Económicas, 1982. 71 p.: ill., tables (Documentos de trabajo; no. 32)

Probe into nature and determinants of recent changes in both money and real wage earnings by economic sector. Wage earnings in each sector are presented as function of labor productivity, occupational structure, number of hours worked, and sector's unionization.

PANAMA

3163 Foro sobre Proyecto Minero de Cerro, *Panama, Panama, 1979.* Foro sobre Proyecto Minero de Cerro Colorado. Panamá: Cámara de Comercio Industrias y Agricultura de Panamá, 1981. 100 p., 2 p. of plates: ill. (Biblioteca empresarial; 5)

Presents proceedings of debate held on feasibility of Cerro Colorado mining project. Chamber of Commerce goes on record warning against undertaking of such a huge project which demands enormous financial commitment on the government's part.

3164 Gandásegui, Marco A. Situación actual del agro en Panamá. Panamá: Centro de Estudios Latinoamericanos Justo Arosemena, 1980. 24 p.

Analyzes performance and characteristics of agriculture sector (1961–78) focusing on land distribution, agricultural land use, and levels of production by crop. Also looks into marketing practices and other regional differentials.

3165 Gorostiaga, Xabier. Los centros financieros internacionales en los países subdesarrollados. México: Instituto Latinoamericano de Estudios Transnacionales, 1978. 149 p.: bibl., ill. (Estudios ILET;

DEE/E/3)
Serious study of relatively new financial center in LDC's with particular attention to Panama. [J.M. Hunter]

3166 Manduley, Julio. Panama: dependent capitalism and beyond (LAP, 7[25/26]:2/3, Spring/Summer 1980, p. 57–74)
Describes manifestations of Panamanian dependent capitalism as limiting sphere of circulation, an excessively open economy, hypertrophy of tertiary sector, foreign control of most dynamic sectors, relegation of local bourgeoisie, and regional disarticulation.

3167 Panamá, estrategia de necesidades básicas y empleo. Santiago: Organización Internacional del Trabajo, Programa Regional del Empleo para América Latina y el Caribe, 1980. 115 p.: ill. (Documento de trabajo—PREALC; 189)
Maintains that in spite of accelerated rate of economic growth experienced between 1960–73, in 1970 more than one-third of all households were unable to satisfy their basic needs adequately. After 1973 rate of growth declines, unemployment increases, and basic needs disequilibrium, a fundamentally rural problem, deteriorates. Provides interesting information on income distribution, relative importance of various economic sectors, employment, investment, credit availability, and population growth and distribution.

3168 Pereira, A. Alimentación infantil: ¿negocio con el niño panameño? Panamá: CEASPA, 1980. 157 p.
Relates decline in breastfeeding practices to marketing practices of transnational pharmaceutical and agroindustrial corporations distributing baby food. Also discusses latter's import cost.

3169 Smith, D. Modelo de desarrollo y políticas educativas en Panamá bajo el Régimen de Torrijos: 1968–1980. San José: Consejo Superior Universitario Centroamericano, 1981. 332 p.
Interprets educational policies as promoting human capital investment and increasing in labor force's long-term productivity.

3170 United States. Agency for International Development. Panama project paper: Guaymí area development. Washington: 1979. 61 p.: appendices, tables.

Project's goal is to raise standard of living of more than half of severely disadvantaged Guaymí Indians, concentrated in three westernmost provinces, by responding to Guaymí-identified needs and increasing levels of productivity, health, education, and nutrition. Project seeks to institutionalize a coordinated, participatory system for providing Panamanian government services.

HISPANIOLA (Dominican Republic and Haiti)

3171 Bell, Ian. The Dominican Republic. Boulder, Colo.: Westview Press, 1981. 392 p.: bibl., maps, photographs, tables (A Nations of the modern world book)
Comprehensive survey from precolumbian times to present focuses on composition of population, history, social conditions, and economy in general.

3172 Développement rural en Haïti et dans la Caraïbe. Papers presented at the 1st Colloque international sur le développement rural en Haïti et dans le Caraïbe, sponsored by the Département des sciences du développement of the Université d'Etat d'Haïti in Port-au-Prince, Oct. 29-Nov. 10, 1979. Port-au-Prince: Imprimerie M. Rodríguez, 1980. 424 p., 15 p. of plates: bibl., ill. (Revue de la Faculté d'éthnologie; nos. 34/55. Bulletin de l'Académie des sciences humaines et sociales; nos. 9/10)
Proceedings of conference on rural development discuss literacy, community development, appropriate technology, rural health, religion, specific development projects, regional organizations, and agricultural credit.

Doré y Cabral, Carlos. Problemas de la estructura agraria dominicana. See *HLAS 44:2055a.*

3173 Duarte, Isis and **Jorge Cela.** Capitalismo y superpoblación en Santo Domingo: mercado de trabajo rural y ejército de reserva urbano. 2. ed. Santo Domingo: Colegio Dominicano de Ingenieros, Arquitectos y Agrimensores (CODIA), 1980. 553 p.: bibl., ill.
Marxist interpretation of population growth and flows views capital accumulation and concentration of land as major peasant expulsion factors that force them to migrate

to overpopulated, urban shantytowns.

3174 Estrategias energéticas para la República Dominicana: informe de la evaluación energética nacional. Preparado, Comisión Nacional de Política Energética *et al.* Santo Domingo: La Comisión, 1980. 109 p., 5 leaves of plates: ill. (some col.)

Studies energy-management policies needed under seven different sets of assumptions. Includes an inventory of energy resources and consumption centers.

3175 Fernández Rodríguez, Aura C. Origen y evolución de la propiedad y de los terrenos comuneros en la República Dominicana (EME, 9:51, dic. 1980, p. 5–45, bibl., tables)

Terrenos comuneros were indivisible pieces of land co-owned by two or more persons. Each co-owner had his/her rights represented in shares acquired either by heredity or purchase and could use any part of land, but only as much as shares in his/her possession. Origin of this practice is traced to colonial times, when land rights were granted in exchange for services to the Crown. Practice evolved into significant type of land tenure and cattle production system requiring large extensions of land.

3176 Garrity, Monique P. The assembly industries in Haiti: causes and effects: 1967–1973 (NEA/RBPE, 11:2, Winter 1981, p. 203–215)

Analyzes industries based on American made components for reexport to US markets and their increasingly important role in the Haitian economy's monetization. Assessment is based on contribution to GDP, job and skill creation, purchasing power, and generation of foreign exchange earnings.

3177 Guiliani Cury, Hugo. Reflexiones acerca de la economía dominicana. Santo Domingo: Editora Alfa y Omega, 1980. 411 p.

Comprehensive assessment of the Dominican economy with emphasis on regional development, the agricultural and industrial sectors, the role of sugar production, identification of future markets, inflation, tourism, and implementation of economic policy.

3178 Honorat, Jean J. Le Manifeste du dernier monde. Port-au-Prince: Imprimerie Henri Deschamps, 1980. 219 p.

Philosophical study searches for new form of integrated development transcending mere social, cultural, and economic transformation of structures.

3179 Latorre, Eduardo. Hacia una política azucarera dominicana en la década de los 80 (Ciencia y Sociedad [Instituto Tecnológico de Santo Domingo] 5:2, julio/dic. 1980, p. 253–268, bibl.)

Brief analysis of sugar industry focuses on production and productivity, marketing, diversification, employment, social justice, and role of public policy.

3180 Lois Malkún, José E. Evolución, estructura y organización del subsector ganadero en la República Dominicana. Santo Domingo: Secretaría de Estado de Agricultura, 1979. 174 p.: bibl.

Detailed analysis of livestock subsector, focusing on regional distribution, marketing, prices, exports, animal health, genetic improvement, extension, and research.

3181 Lundahl, Mats. Peasant strategies for dealing with population pressure: the case of Haiti (NOSALF/IA, 10:1/2, 1981, p. 19–38, bibl.)

Insightful paper warns that only long-term solution to population pressure in rural Haiti is economic development. Otherwise, increase mortality may become chief mechanism for maintaining an equilibrium between people and natural resources close to subsistence levels. Partly attributes peasant inefficiency in searching for adjustment mechanisms to lack of government support.

3182 ———. Peasants and poverty: a study of Haiti. New York: St. Martin's Press, 1979. 699 p.

After showing that peasants' standard of living has fallen over past several decades, author maintains that economic decline cannot be attributed to market deficiencies. Also describes in detail mechanisms of circular causation which exacerbate retrogression of peasant sector, namely, soil erosion, land fragmentation, government corruption, malnutrition, and inadequacy of educational system.

3183 Moreno, Guillermo. De la propiedad comunera a la propiedad privada moderna: 1844–1924 (EME, 9:51, nov./dic. 1980, p. 47–129, bibl., charts)

Relates how common land holdings (*propiedades comuneras*) were consistent with trade forms and needs existing until late 19th century. Around 1875 new forms of agricultural production and trade (cocoa, sugarcane, coffee, and tobacco) were introduced in Dominican Republic, disrupting land tenure organization in favor of private property. Growing importance of foreign concerns and the economy's enormous external dependency accelerated trend in 20th century.

3184 Rencontre avec les industriels d'Haïti, 22 avril 1979. Port-au-Prince: 4VRD Radio nationale, 1979. 237 p.

Collection of interviews with 11 top industrialists and decision makers whose purpose is to share their experiences, profit from their suggestions, and understand their problems. Most industries represented in interviews consist of new endeavors presumably indicative of economic growth and diversification.

3185 Sang Ben, Miguel. La existencia de un mercado político en el proceso de la política pública: el caso de la política de precios del arroz en la República Dominicana (Ciencia y Sociedad [Instituto Tecnológico de Santo Domingo] 5 : 2, julio/dic. 1980, p. 197–222, bibl., tables)

Inquiry into nature of agricultural public policy emphasizes minimum prices of rice, along T.W. Schultz's and University of Chicago guidelines.

3186 Santana Rivera, Félix. Moneda, banca y las instituciones financieras de la República Dominicana. 3. ed. Santo Domingo: Publicaciones América, 1981. 287 p.: bibl., ill.

Comprehensive study of Central Bank and its implementation of monetary policy with special reference to classical-Keynesian controversy, inflation, foreign trade, and role of banks and other financial institutions.

3187 Seminario Nacional La Industria Azucarera y el Desarrollo Dominicano, *Universidad Central del Este, 1980.* La industria azucarera y el desarrollo dominicano. San Pedro de Macorís: Asociación Dominicana de Rectores de Universidades [y] Universidad Central del Este [y] Asociación de Tecnólogos Azucareros de la República Dominicana (ATAREDO), 1981. 273 p.: tables.

Proceedings of multidisciplinary seminar on sugar industry's role in Dominican economic development, production, market-ing, transportation, employment generation, ecological considerations, soil requirements, human resource training, potential application as an energy source, and determination of social justice criteria.

3188 Serrulle Ramia, José and **Jacqueline Boin.** La inversión de capitales imperialistas en la República Dominicana: elementos de crítica a la "teoría de la dependencia." Artículos publicados en el matutino *El Sol* durante los meses de abril-agosto de 1981. Santo Domingo: Ediciones Gramil, 1981. 172 p.: tables.

Collection of 13 articles divided into: 1) hard data on US investment in Dominican Republic; 2) concentration of capital and formation of monopolies; 3) consequences of US investment in terms of foreign dependence; and 4) impact of US investment on social stratification.

3189 United States. Agency for International Development. Office of Housing. Dominican Republic shelter sector assessment. Washington: 1980. 2 v.: tables.

Estimates that, in order for housing demand to satisfy population growth, an annual average of 32,900 units (29,300 urban and 3,600 rural) are needed. Provides excellent insight into nature and extent of internal migration, household income and expenditure, powers and responsibilities of housing-related institutions, and effect of varying interest rates on proposed housing solutions.

3190 Vargas G., Rosemary. Unemployment, underemployment and labor imports in the Dominican Republic: a sketch of some of the problems (NOSALF/IA, 10 : 1/2, 1981, p. 39–61, bibl., tables)

Concludes that both backwardness of agrarian structure and inability of modern sector to provide employment and income constitute insurmountable obstacles in the attainment of self-sustaining growth.

3191 Vega, Bernardo. La coyuntura económica dominicana: 1980–1981. Selection of articles published in *Listín Diario* in 1980–1981. Santiago, República Dominicana: Universidad Católica Madre y Maestra (UCMM), 1981. 146 p. (Colección Estudios)

Collection of 22 articles published in *Listín Diario* (1980–81) presents different aspects of Dominican economy, government, and culture (e.g., absence of coherent agroindustrial policy, agrarian reform, import duties, formation of middle class).

3192 Zaldívar Luna, Iturbides G. Producción y comercialización de tabaco negro en la República Dominicana. Santiago de los Caballeros, República Dominicana: Universidad Católica Madre y Maestra (UCMM), 1979. 116 p.: bibl., graphs, ill., indexes, tables (Colección Estudios; 28)

Summarizes many and complex aspects of tobacco's production and marketing, country's fourth most important agroexport activity, which employs 300,000 people in its full cycle and generates 40 million pesos in income. Numerous tables and graphs provide plethora of hard data.

BRITISH CARIBBEAN

3193 Albuquerque, Klaus de; Wesley Van Riel; and J. Mark Taylor. Uncontrolled urbanization in the developing world: a Jamaican case study (JDA, 14:3, April 1980, p. 361–386, map, tables)

Reviews research on uncontrolled urbanism and compares some substantial findings with results of study conducted in West Kingston shantytown based on 679 resident sample.

3194 Atkinson, Glen W. Fiscal harmonization in the Caribbean community (IAMEA, 36:1, Summer 1982, p. 13–21, tables)

Focuses on Agreement for the Harmonization of Fiscal Incentives to Industry among 12 CARICOM member countries, designed to reduce self-defeating competition for industry among members and rationalize criteria for granting incentives by relating amount of incentive to contribution made by beneficiary industry to the national (regional) economy.

3195 Ayub, Mahmood Ali. Made in Jamaica: the development of the manufacturing sector. Baltimore, Md.: Published for the World Bank by Johns Hopkins University Press, 1981. 128 p.: bibl., tables (World Bank staff occasional papers; no. 31)

Comprehensive account of manufacturing sector's key characteristics, with emphasis on legislation for industrial incen-

tives, nominal and effective protection, prospects for exports, capacity utilization, pricing in domestic market, employment, and impact of government policies.

3196 Bennett, Karl. Mobilizing foreign exchange reserves for economic growth in CARICOM (UWI/SES, 30:4, Dec. 1981, p. 172–186, bibl., tables)

Explores extent to which foreign exchange constraints hinder attainment of economic growth targets, using Jamaica as case in point. Suggests policies which may be taken by CARICOM states to mobilize foreign exchange reserves.

3197 Borozdina, Raisa. La economía de Guyana a los quince años de desarrollo independiente (URSS/AL, 2[50], 1982, p. 55–67, ill., tables)

Assessment of Guyanese economy 15 years after political independence. Focuses on nationalization, performance of public sector, and role of planning.

3198 Bourne, Compton. Government foreign borrowing and economic growth: the case of Jamaica (UWI/SES, 30:4, Dec. 1981, p. 52–74, bibl., tables)

Examines connection between government foreign borrowing and country's 1970s recession, concluding that economic problems of this period could have been mitigated by early adoption of appropriate policies of consumption restraint and export promotion.

3199 ———. Issues of public financial enterprises in Jamaica: the case of the Jamaican Development Bank (UWI/SES, 30:1, March 1981, p. 197–208, bibl., tables)

Examines objectives and decision-making framework, JDB influence on credit supply, and its funding and viability. Concludes that development banks can improve quantity of long-term risk capital and provide financial advisory and other services. However, recommends that quality of credit services be improved by provision of short-term loans and by changes in lending procedures. Also cautions that concessionary interest rate policies practiced by JDB compromise its institutional viability and confer large subsidies on borrowers.

3200 Brown, Adlith. Economic policy and the IMF in Jamaica (UWI/SES, 30:4, Dec. 1981, p. 1–51, tables)

Assessment of economic performance

of Jamaica and government strategies to deal with monetary crises and currency devaluation.

3201 The Caribbean Community in the 1980s: report. By a group of Caribbean experts appointed by the Caribbean Common Market Council of Ministers. Georgetown: Caribbean Community Secretariat, 1981. 157 p.: index.

Seeks to provide additional development opportunities and increased bargaining power for CARICOM member states as part of national development effort. After extensive review of rationale for integration, focuses on harmonization of tax incentives and tax systems, possibility of full monetary integration, common policy of foreign investment and technology transfer, joint development of natural resources, and monetary and exchange-rate policies.

3202 Downes, Andrew S. Government policy actions and the balance of payments of Barbados (CEDLA/B, 32, junio 1982, p. 87–102, bibl., tables)

Evaluation of performance of economic authorities in trying to achieve favorable balance-of-payments position using monetary and fiscal policies (1973–77). Government should eliminate possibility of conflict between balance-of-payments performance and economic growth by encouraging local production of substitutes for foreign products, educating public about products easily developed from local materials, regulating foreign products advertising, and strengthening selective import restrictions and tariffs.

3203 ——. A wage index for Barbados: an exploratory note (UPR/CS, 20:2, June 1980, p. 77–80, bibl., tables)

Develops Lespeyres index to examine effect of wages on inflation, balance of payments, and other economic variables.

3204 Erickson, Frank A. and **Elizabeth B. Erickson.** An annotated bibliography of agricultural development in Jamaica. Washington: Agency for International Development, 1979, 197 p.

Comprehensive bibliography divided into following sections: 1) overall economy and regional agriculture; 2) socioeconomic characteristics; 3) surveys, censuses, and statistics; 4) extension, education, and organizations; 5) land, natural resources, and credit;

6) markets and marketing; 7) technology, techniques, and research; 8) policy and planning; 9) projects; 10) commodities; 11) nutrition; and 12) bibliographies and proceedings.

3205 Gafar, John. Price responsiveness of tropical agricultural exports: a case study of Jamaica, 1954–72 (IDE/DE, 18:3, Sept. 1980, p. 288–297, tables)

Develops and empirically tests model of supply response applied to sugar, bananas, coffee, and cocoa. Concludes that supply of agricultural exports responds positively and significantly to price changes, and that lagged output is also an important factor influencing supply response of farmers. Finds short-run supply price elasticities low because of time farmer needs to adjust to instantaneous price changes. Long-run supply price elasticities being greater suggest that remunerative prices can be relied upon as policy instrument to stimulate agricultural output and deal with problem of resource allocation and output mix. Recommends stimulation of agricultural exports in short-run as additional stabilization policy.

3206 Greene, J.E. and **Reive Robb.** National primary socioeconomic data structures: No. 9, Barbados, Jamaica, Trinidad and Tobago (UN/ISSJ, 33:2, 1981, p. 393–414, ill., tables)

Analysis of availability and quality of regional data, with emphasis on development of censi, labor force, government statistical services, confidentiality and legal provisions, and regional organizations. Concludes that major deficiency related to primary socioeconomic data system is lack of coordinating agency and infrastructure for adequately processing and disseminating information.

3207 Griffith, Anthony D. A geographical perspective on scale of farming in a developing economy (CQ, 26:3, Sept. 1980, p. 24–35, tables)

Argues that in Barbados, as Third World, expansion of existing small-farm operations carry significant implications for local and world food production, employment, and rural development. Agricultural development is attained by improving quality of inputs and striving for efficiency rather than by adopting alien technologies solely on basis of their successes elsewhere. Application of technology is viewed as dependent on type of crop, nature of terrain, and population density.

Henningsgaard, William. The Akawaio, the Upper Mazaruni hydroelectric project and national development in Guyana. See item **1083.**

3208 Hope, Kempe R. and R.M. Walters.
Recent performance and trends in the Caribbean economy: a study of selected Caribbean countries. Imperialism: a contemporary study. St. Augustine, Trinidad: University of the West Indies, Institute of Social and Economic Research, 1980. 118 p. (Occasional papers; 4)
Pt. 1 by Kempe (p. 1–61) examines recent performance and trends in economies of Barbados, Guyana, Jamaica, and Trinidad and Tobago. Study is both descriptive and analytical, focusing on population, labor, and employment; sector development (agriculture, manufacturing, mining, tourism); and external trade, with emphasis on the development of CARIFTA and CARICOM. Also offers policy solutions for future development efforts of the four countries.

3209 Humes, Dorla. Foreign reserves management in Belize: an assessment of liquidity constraints (UWI/SES, 30:4, Dec. 1981, p. 187–200, bibl., tables)
Maintains that because of open nature of Belizean economy, both supply of and demand for foreign exchange reserves are closely related to foreign trade. Urges policymakers to exercise control over, and establish guidelines on, expansion of domestic credit.

3210 Ifil, Max B. Report on a farm survey conducted in Grenada. Port-of-Spain: Economic Commission for Latin America, Office for the Caribbean, 1979. 76 p., 12 leaves (CEPAL/CARIB;79/12)
Report on 1976 farm survey warns that farming population is aging. Recommends youths be attracted into farming; mass communication changes via extension service; development of producer cooperatives; introduction of simple record systems which can be used by farmers; implementation of soil conservation practices; and provision of financial incentives to produce specific commodities on minimum size acreages.

3211 Long, Frank. Is size a disadvantage in dealing with transnational corporations? (IAMEA, 33:4, Spring 1980, p. 61–75)

Smallness is not necessarily a disadvantage. Case: Cooperative Republic of Guyana in areas of sugar, bauxite, commercial banking. Technology transfer regulation, though, remains a problem. [J.M. Hunter]

3212 McBain, Helen. External financing of the Water Commission of Jamaica (UWI/SES, 30:1, March 1981, p. 171–196, bibl., tables)
Using Water Commission as case in point, paper probes into extent to which World Bank exercises leverage through financing of development projects in Third World.

3213 ———. The political economy of capital flows: the case of Jamaica (UWI/SES, 30:4, Dec. 1981, p. 75–100, bibl., tables)
Examines relationship between domestic policy and reliance on foreign capital for pursuing economic development. Also analyzes changes throughout 1970s in governmental perception of growth in light of unsuccessful industrialization efforts and influence of radical ideologies.

3214 Mitchell, Ivor S. and Richard R. Still.
Correlates of consumer banking behaviour in the Socialist Cooperative Republic of Guyana (UWI/SES, 28:2, June 1979, p. 397–430, bibl., tables)
Identifies sociodemographic correlates which may predict media usage, economic and information banking criteria, service (patronizing) and convenience (of location) of banks' criteria, and optimism-pessimism toward indigenous Guyana National Cooperative Bank.

3215 Morrissey, Marietta. Towards a theory of West Indian economic development (LAP, 8[1]:28, Winter 1981, p. 4–27, bibl., tables)
Argues how Marxists can bring needed dialectical dimension to labeling of modes of production. Shows ties between latter and existing theoretical and empirical statements about capitalist development as realized historically in Western metropoles, recently restored to study of Third World development by proponents of "dependent development."

3216 Muller, Arnold A. and Raúl Moncarz.
Proceso de integración en el Caribe (CSUCA/ESC, 21, sept./dic. 1978, p. 101–113, bibl., tables)
Views economic integration as sole an-

swer to protecting regional markets from unfavorable competition; planning common strategies for resources that may not be detrimental to smaller countries; and coordinating external economic policies for purposes of strengthening terms of world trade. Discusses process and implications of transition from CARIFTA into CARICOM and analyzes volume, direction, and weaknesses of British Caribbean trade.

3217 Parris, Carl D. Joint Venture I: the Trinidad-Tobago Telephone Company, 1968–1972 (UWI/SES, 30:1, March 1891, p. 101–126, bibl.)

Contends that partnership with foreign capital thwarts development. After brief analysis of problems arising from partnership relation between Trinidad-and-Tobago Telephone Company (public domestic corporation) and US Continental Telephone Company (transnational corporation), concludes that modes of utilization of company's limited funds were heavily biased in interest of both foreign capital and its local representatives.

3218 Payne, Anthony. The politics of the Caribbean Community, 1961–79: regional integration among new states. New York: St. Martin's Press, 1980. 299 p.: bibl., map, tables.

After review of Caribbean intraregional relations from early British rule to Federation's collapse in 1961, examines community system aspects (economic integration, functional cooperation, and foreign policy coordination) and analyzes decision-making within integration movement. Concludes with assessment of overall experience of the Caribbean Community.

3219 Paz Salinas, María Emilia. Belize: el despertar de una nación. México: Siglo XXI Editores, 1979. 188 p.

Emphasizes Belize's independence as it reviews country's historical development since time of English pirates. Although economic and political considerations are scarce, book is important because of scarcity of related material.

3220 Rai, Khemraj. Worker participation in public enterprise in Guyana (UWI/SES, 30:1, March 1981, p. 209–244, bibl., graphs, tables)

Study of attitudes, perception, and behavior of people in work situations based on interviews conducted with 300 workers, 20 management personnel, and 20 trade unionists. Interviewees presumably represent cross section of work force randomly selected from among agricultural workers, bauxite workers, and people in retail and wholesale trade, all in public enterprises.

3221 Ramlogan, Vishnu. The sugar industry in Trinidad and Tobago: management, challenges and responses (IAMEA, 33:4, Spring 1980, p. 29–59, tables)

Reveals that problems within industry's sphere of influence are: personnel management; planning/budgeting/information/control; effectiveness of wet season activities; factory and equipment; maintenance; speed of decision making; union-management relationships; compensation; and packages.

3222 St. Cyr, E.B.A. Wages, prices and the balance of payments: Trinidad and Tobago, 1956–1976 (UWI/SES, 30:4, Dec. 1981, p. 111–133, bibl., tables)

Exposition of export-propelled model suggests that capital inflows and exports exert strongest positive impact on balance of payments, while domestic credit has negative effect. Balance of payments is far more sensitive to capital movements than to exports or domestic credit.

3223 Swaby, Raphael A. The rationale for State ownership of public utilities in Jamaica (UWI/SES, 30:1, March 1981, p. 75–107, bibl., tables)

Focuses on foreign capital utilization for expansion of public utility infrastructure in attempt to discover rationale for transferring into public ownership some utilities between 1971–73, a decade after attaining political independence. Examines three case studies: urban transportation, electricity, and telecommunications.

3224 Theodore, Karl. The economics of water treatment: a Caribbean case study (UWI/SES, 28:2, June 1979, p. 364–396, bibl., ill., tables)

Explores extent to which water treatment activity of water supply system could be subjected to meaningful economic analysis. Identifies and discusses factors of production relevant to water treatment, tests various hypotheses concerning nature of treatment costs, and delineates a simple model of water treatment costs.

3225 United States. Agency for International Development. Caribbean Development Facility. Washington: 1979. 48 p.: appendices.

AID assists governments of English-speaking Caribbean countries participating in the Caribbean Development Facility (CDF) to maintain adequate levels of development investment by providing resources needed to carry out essential donor-assisted socioeconomic programs. CDF was created by Caribbean Group for Cooperation in Economic Development to provide supplementary financing of projects and programs for which international institutions are providing funds.

3226 ———. ———. Guyana Project Paper: agriculture sector planning. Washington: 1980. 32 p.: appendices, tables.

Description of project which seeks to improve agriculture sector planning capacity of Statistics Bureau, National Data Management Authority, and Ministry of Agriculture. Specific objectives of agriculture plan are to reduce unemployment and its associated problems of unequal distribution of income; reduce dependence on bauxite, sugar, and rice as foreign exchange sources; mobilize internal financial resources; and improve productivity of investment concentrated on infrastructure.

3227 Worrell, Delisle. External influences and domestic policies: the economies of Barbados and Jamaica in the 1970s (UWI/SES, 30:4, Dec. 1981, p. 134–155, bibl., tables)

Analyzes impact of external forces on domestic economies of both countries using framework which divides system into traded and non-traded goods sectors, with prices of traded goods determined by international arbitrage and prices of non-traded goods depending on real aggregate demand and returns to factors of production. Compares economic growth, inflation, balance of payments, and unemployment during 1960–72 and 1973–78, as well as adjustment policies (fiscal, credit, and exchange rate) implemented in both countries.

DUTCH AND FRENCH CARIBBEAN

3228 Dekker, Jeroen J.H. Curaçao zonder/met Shell. Zutphen, Nederlands: De Walburg Pers, 1982. 240 p.: bibl., ill., tables.

Study of socioeconomic and demographic evolution during 1900–29, focusing on 1915 establishment of refinery.

3229 Gemengde Commissie van Deskundigen. Aanzet tot een integraal beleidskader voor de Nederlandse Antillen in de jaren tachtig. Gravenhage, Nederlands en Willemstad, Curaçao: 1979. 281 p.: graphs, tables.

In-depth inquiry into socioeconomic conditions in Netherlands Antilles concludes that public sector is plagued by shortage of funds and unreproductive civil service, while private sector shows too much consumption and wage structure rising too rapidly in relation to labor productivity. Provides specific recommendations for improvements in both sectors in preparation for the islands' independence.

3230 Goslinga, Cornelis Christian. Short history of the Netherlands Antilles and Surinam. The Hague: Martinus Nijhoff, 1979. 198 p.

Contemplates historical, economic, and social aspects of Dutch Caribbean's bid for independence. Bound by sentiments of political inferiority and economic dependency vis-à-vis Holland, the Dutch Caribbean evolved through colonial phases of exploitation, either benign neglect or destructive policies of restriction, emerging in 20th century as self-sustaining, financially solvent, and politically maturing dominions in search of autonomy (for historian's comment, see *HLAS 44:2485*).

3231 Lerie, Adrien. Martinique, Guadeloupe: une économie sous le boisseau: la situation économique des Antilles françaises est catastrophique; des réformes seraient possibles; mais trop d'interêts particuliers s'emploient à maintenir les choses en l'état (CJN, 242, sept. 1982, p. 29–32, plates)

Charges that economic development attempts are systematically hindered by small white elite. Poverty and high unemployment levels force migration to France, where more than half of French Antilles population resides.

3232 Römer, René A. Een volk op weg: un pueblo na kaminda. Zutphen, Nederlands: De Walburg Pers, 1979. 144 p.: bibl., map, tables.

Historical probe into conditions prevailing immediately prior to emancipation of slaves. Master-slave relationship continued in post-emancipation period which resulted in social and economic dependence of free mulattoes and blacks vis-à-vis native elite. Also focuses on economic and cultural changes set in motion as result of modernization in wake of Shell Oil Co.'s establishment.

CUBA

JORGE F. PEREZ-LOPEZ, *Bureau of International Labor Affairs, United States Department of Labor*

THE MOST SIGNIFICANT DEVELOPMENT concerning the economic literature on Cuba is the recent appearance of five volumes written by scholars outside the country that attempt to provide long-term analyses of the economy. These works, which use different methodologies and focus on different mixes of socioeconomic indicators, are of uneven quality. Carmelo Mesa-Lago's *The economy of socialist Cuba* (item **3247**), comprehensive, up-to-date and replete with statistical data and insightful analyses, might well be the definitive volume on the Cuban economy in the first two decades of the Revolution. The volumes by Recarte (item **3251**) and Brundenius (items **3235–3236**), methodologically different from Mesa-Lago's, provide other perspectives and are also worthy of careful consideration. For reasons mentioned in the annotations, the contributions by MacEwan (item **3244**) and Theriot (item **3258**) fall short of the mark and are of more limited use.

Other trends worth mentioning are the continued availability of statistical data and the appearance of assessments of the first Five-Year Plan and of a new journal. The Comité Estatal de Estadísticas continues to publish regularly a statistical yearbook (item **3237**) that has improved on its timeliness (about an 18-month lag for the 1980 volume, a respectable record by Latin American standards). The Comité also has initiated the publication of data on the 1981 population and housing census (item **3238**), and released a useful volume with some historical statistics (item **3239**). Among recent assessments of the 1976–80 plan we might mention two studies by the Banco Nacional de Cuba (items **3233–3234**) and papers by Mesa-Lago (item **3246**), Rodríguez García (item **3254**), and Rodríguez Mesa (item **3256**). Finally, in early 1982 the Centro de Investigaciones de la Economía Mundial began publication of a promising journal, *Temas de Economía Mundial* (item **3257**), which provides a Cuban perspective on international economic issues.

3233 Banco Nacional de Cuba. Cuba: economic and social development 1976–80 and first half 1981. La Habana: 1981. 39 p.: tables.

Updates earlier Banco Nacional de Cuba report (item **3234**) and discusses preliminary information on the development of the Cuban economy during first half of 1981.

3234 ———. Highlights of Cuban economic and social development 1976–80 and main targets for 1981–85. La Habana: 1981. 20 p.: tables.

Preliminary official assessment of economic and social development during the first five-year plan (1976–80) and objectives of second (1981–85). Based on official data from the Comité Estatal de Estadísticas and from main report submitted to the Second Congress of the Cuban Communist Party (Dec. 1980, see *HLAS 43:3207*).

3235 Brundenius, Claes. Economic growth, basic needs and income distribution in revolutionary Cuba. Lund, Sweden: University of Lund, Research Policy Institute, 1981. 232 p.: bibl., charts, map, tables (Ekonomisk-historiska föreningens skriftserie; nr. 32)

Serious effort to analyze quantitatively economic and social performance in revolutionary Cuba. Author develops indexes of material product and basic needs satisfaction for period 1958–80 and discusses their behavior. Research suggests that Cuba has performed better in satisfaction of basic needs than in economic growth.

3236 ——. Growth and equity: the Cuban experience: 1959–1980 (WD, 9:11/12, Nov./Dec. 1981, p. 1083–1096, bibl., tables)

Elaboration of basic arguments made by Brundenius in his earlier work (item **3235**). Article focuses on Cuba's experience with redistribution of income and satisfaction of basic needs during 1959–80. Also appears as Chap. 8 under title "Development Strategies and Basic Needs in Revolutionary Cuba" in *Development strategies and basic needs in Latin America: challenges for the 1980s* (edited by Claes Brundenius and Mats Lundahl, Boulder, Colo.: Westview Press, 1982, p. 143–164).

3237 Cuba. Comité Estatal de Estadísticas. Anuario estadístico de Cuba: 1980. La Habana: 1981. 342 p.: index, tables.

Comprehensive statistical yearbook following format of earlier volumes (see *HLAS 43:3208*). In most cases, contains data through 1980; exceptions are labor statistics for which the latest reported data is for 1979 and imports which run through 1978. Contains subject index.

3238 ——. ——. Censo de población y viviendas 1981: cifras preliminares. La Habana: 1981. 196 p.: tables.

Preliminary report of population and housing census conducted on 10 Sept. 1981. Publication contains data on following: population growth; total population by provinces; urban and rural population; structure of population according to sex and age groups; population density and rural and urban housing.

3239 ——. ——. Estadísticas quinquenales de Cuba: 1965–1980. La Habana: 1982. 115 p.: appendix, tables.

Special publication of the Comité Estatal de Estadísticas (CEE) containing much economic data for five-year periods (1966–70, 1971–75, and 1976–80). First effort by CEE to provide consistent data for extended time period; limited in usefulness, however, since it provides only averages of each of the five-year periods. Contains an appendix describing the series.

3240 Díaz Vázquez, Julio A. Cuba: colaboración económica y científico-técnica con países en vías de desarrollo de Africa, Asia y América Latina (UH/ED, 68, mayo/junio 1982, p. 26–43, tables)

Survey of Cuban economic and scientific-technical cooperation with developing countries. Contains useful quantitative and qualitative information on Cuba's foreign aid and export of services.

3241 ——. Cuba: integración económica socialista y especialización de la producción (UH/ED, 63, julio/agosto 1981, p. 132–165)

After discussing Cuba's benefits from trading with COMECON countries, author reviews in considerable detail Cuba's scientific-technical cooperation with COMECON.

3242 Forster, Nancy. Cuban agricultural productivity: a comparison of State and private farm sectors (UP/CSEC, 11:2/12:1, julio 1981/enero 1982, p. 105–125)

Relying on official production and acreage data, author compares private and state productivity on a crop-by-crop basis. For the limited number of crops and years for which comparison can be made, author finds that private-sector yields were consistently higher than in state farms.

3243 Kondrashov, Piotr. En beneficio de los pueblos hermanos (URSS/AL, 6:54, 1982, p. 4–22, plates)

Reviews Cuban scientific-technical cooperation with the Soviet Union and other COMECON members.

3244 MacEwan, Arthur. Revolution and economic development in Cuba. New York: St. Martin's Press, 1981. 265 p.

Unbalanced work, long on Marxist reinterpretations of Cuban economic history but short on serious analyses of Cuba's economic development. Although volume appeared in early 1981, data and analyses are badly out-of-date, stopping with 1975 (except for brief discussion on sugar production in 1978). Conceivably, Marxists might profit from this work, but those interested in learning about the Cuban economy and its problems would do well to turn to other available works.

3245 Marrero y Artiles, Leví. Cuba: economía y sociedad. v. 8, Del monopolio
hacia la libertad comercial: pt. 3, 1701–1763.
Madrid: Editorial Playor, 1980. 295 p.: ill.,
index, maps, tables.

Vol. 8 of projected 14-volume work on
Cuban economic history, begun by author in
1972. Deals with developments in ship-
building, finance, money, prices and salaries
in Cuba in first half of 18th century. Complements other aspects of the economy dealt
with in vols. 6/7 (see *HLAS 43:3222*).

3246 Mesa-Lago, Carmelo. The economy:
caution, frugality, and resilient ideology (*in* Cuba: internal and international affairs. Edited by Jorge I. Domínguez. Beverly
Hills, Calif.: Sage Publications, 1982,
p. 113–166)

Careful evaluation of performance of
the Cuban economy during the first five-year
plan (1976–80) and prospects for second
(1981–85). Concludes that during 1976–80
economic performance fell short of goals for
a variety of internal and external factors and
is skeptical of the feasibility of the relatively
modest plan targets for 1981–85.

3247 ———. The economy of socialist
Cuba: a two-decade appraisal. Albuquerque: University of New Mexico Press,
1981. 235 p.: bibl., index, tables.

Undoubtedly the most authoritative
and comprehensive treatment of Cuba's economic development in the last two decades.
Analyzes Cuba's performance in the attainment of five major socioeconomic goals
sought by most developing countries: 1) sustained economic growth; 2) diversification of
production; 3) relative external economic independence; 4) full employment; and 5) more
equal distribution of income and social services. Concludes that Cuba performed relatively well in the areas of full employment,
more equitable distribution of income, and
delivery of social services to the population,
and less so in the others. Required reading for
serious students of the Cuban economy.

3248 Pérez-López, Jorge F. Energy production, imports, and consumption in
revolutionary Cuba (LARR, 16:3, 1981,
p. 111–137)

Using fragmentary data, author develops an energy balance for revolutionary
Cuba.

3249 Pollitt, Brian. Transformación en la
agricultura cañera de Cuba: 1959-1980
(AR, 8:30, 1982, p. 13–17, plates, tables)

Analyzes rationale for, and Cuban experience with, mechanization of sugar cane
harvest.

**3250 Principales características laborales de
la población de Cuba:** *Encuesta demográfica nacional de 1979.* La Habana:
Comité Estatal de Estadísticas, Dirección de
Demografía, 1981. 81 p.: tables.

Report on characteristics of Cuba's labor force based on data from the *National
demographic survey of 1979.* Contains 12
tables dealing with labor force participation,
economically active population, characteristics of employed workers, etc.

3251 Recarte, Alberto. Cuba: economía y
poder, 1959–1980. Madrid: Alianza
Editorial, 1980. 235 p.

Insightful book written from perspective of foreign observer with first-hand information on the Cuban economy and its
external relations. Recarte served as Commercial Officer of the Spanish Embassy in
Havana during most of 1970s. Consists of five
essays dealing with shifts in economic policies, standard of living, Cuban-Spanish commercial relations, Cuban-Soviet economic
and commercial relations, and organizational
changes in the agricultural sector. Chapter
on Cuban-Spanish commercial relations
presents fascinating view of complex bargaining that has taken place between the two
countries.

3252 Roca, Sergio. Moral incentives in socialist Cuba (ACES Bulletin [Associa-
tion for Comparative Economic Studies,
DeKalb, Ill.] 22:2, Summer 1980, p. 33–52)

Cogent and concise summary of
Cuba's experimentation with moral and material economic incentives in 1960s and
1970s.

3253 Rodríguez, Carlos Rafael. Problemas
prácticos de la planificación cen-
tralizada (BNCE/CE, 30:11, nov. 1980,
p. 1214–1219)

Important article reviews Cuban experience with central planning within a
developing-countries planning context. Concludes that while rigid centralization can
lead to misallocation of resources, decentralization (as practiced by some Eastern Euro-

pean nations) gives rise to disadvantages of capitalism without attaining latter's efficiency. Characterizes the new Cuban economic planning and management system as viable alternative between the two extremes.

3254 Rodríguez García, José Luis. La economía cubana entre 1976 y 1980: resultados y perspectivas (UH/ED, 66, enero/feb. 1982, p. 108–149)

Assessment of Cuba's economic policies and performance during the 1976–80 five-year plan.

3255 ———. La economía de Cuba socialista (UH/ED, 61, marzo/abril 1981, p. 112–148)

Useful overview of Cuban economic policies with emphasis on Revolution's early years.

3256 Rodríguez Mesa, Gonzalo M. El desarrollo industrial de Cuba y la maduración de inversiones (UH/ED, 68, mayo/junio 1982, p. 108–139)

Important article describes industrialization process in Cuba and prospects up to year 2000. Author differentiates between 1959–75 period in which bases for rapid industrialization were established and 1976–80 period in which previous investments began to be productive. Investment guidelines for the five-year plan (1981–85) and appear unrealistically ambitious.

3257 *Temas de Economía Mundial.* Centro de Investigaciones de la Economía Mundial. No. 1, 1982- . La Habana.

Quarterly journal sponsored by Centro de Investigaciones de la Economía Mundial (CIEM), a relatively new institution dealing with research on international economic relations. Publication is primarily devoted to disseminating research by CIEM staffers. Issue No. 1 (1982) contains analysis of proposals in the Brandt Commission Report, an essay on economic development models and a critique of Western international trade theory. No. 2 (1982) reviews economic relations between socialist and Third World nations, expansion of multinational corporations, food crisis in Latin America, and limitations of the NIEC. No. 3 (1982) contains a critique of the US Caribbean Basin Initiative and a study of developing countries and the international monetary system.

3258 Theriot, Lawrence H. Cuba faces the

economic realities of the 1980s: a study prepared for the use of the Joint Economic Committee of the United States Congress. Washington: GPO, 1982. 49 p.

Brief but ambitious monograph in which author first summarizes Cuban economic performance during 1960s and 1970s, then analyzes magnitude and role of Soviet assistance, and finally discusses Cuban development prospects to 1986 in the context of Cuban relations with COMECON. Of limited value since footnotes are not used. Also appeared as chapter in US Congress' Joint Economic Committee's *East-West trade: the prospects to 1985* (Washington: GPO, 1982, p. 104-135).

3259 United Nations. Consejo Económico y Social. Comisión Económica para América Latina (CEPAL). Cuba: notas para el estudio económico de América Latina, 1980. México: 1981. l v.: tables (CEPAL/MEX/1044).

Reviews Cuban economic developments during 1980 following same format as earlier studies (see *HLAS 43:3215* and *3231–3232*). Also available under title "Cuba: Evolución Reciente de su Economía" in *Comercio Exterior* (México, 32:1, enero 1982, p. 25–35).

3260 United States. Central Intelligence Agency. National Foreign Assessment Center. The Cuba economy: a statistical review. Washington: GPO, 1981. 54 p.: tables (ER-81–10052; PA 81–10074)

Compendium of Cuban economic statistics particularly useful for those who do not have access to official statistical yearbooks. Almost all data are culled from Cuban sources and organized as follows: 1) agricultural and industrial output; 2) transportation; 3) distribution; 4) foreign trade; and 5) population and labor force. Also contains estimates of Cuban GNP in dollars, hard currency balance of payments and value of Soviet assistance.

3261 Valdés Paz, Juan. La pequeña producción agrícola en Cuba (CNC/RMA, 15:1, enero/marzo 1982, p. 125–155, tables)

Despite collectivization, small farmers continue to play key role in revolutionary Cuba's agricultural sector.

3262 Valdés Suárez, Pedro. Crecimiento de población y economía. La Habana: Edi-

torial de Ciencias Sociales, 1980. 79 p.
    Using different hypotheses concerning female fertility, author projects Cuban demo-graphic structure through 2070 and relates it to different economic growth scenarios to analyze manpower supply and demand.

COLOMBIA AND ECUADOR

FRANCISCO E. THOUMI, *Chief, International Economics Section, Inter-American Development Bank*
THOMAS B. HUTCHESON, *Economist, The World Bank*

COLOMBIA
A SURVEY OF RECENT PUBLICATIONS on the Colombian economy reveals some interesting features. The increase in the number of authors now working in the country can be attributed to the large crop of Colombians who, after undergoing graduate training in the US and Europe, have returned to study their nation's economy. A parallel development has been the increase in the number of research institutions. Some are affiliated with universities, but a number of important ones are independent from academia, and combine the functions of economic research centers and consulting institutions. Their turnover is high as principal researchers often change institutional affiliation and assume temporary positions in the government.

Research activities received considerable outside support in the 1960s and early 1970s, but as these sources dried up, the financing of long-term projects became increasingly difficult. The Colombian government has appropriated funds for research through COLCIENCIAS and the Banco de la República, but the country still lacks the type of government-supported institutions exemplified by Brazil's Fundação Getúlio Vargas and El Colegio de México, organizations in which researchers are granted the security of a permanent commitment, so important for long-term basic research.

The large number of empirical studies reflecting the needs of institutions that generate them can be attributed to the above factors as can the trend to produce short seminar-type papers. The 42 works annotated below can be classified as follows: 15 sector studies; two surveys of the Colombian economy; 11 policy formulation and critique volumes; four analyses of foreign trade; four economic history books; and 11 collections of essays, most of which were papers presented at seminars. The heavy emphasis on policy-oriented works is evident in this breakdown.

The quality of many studies is good. The final version, however, is often unpolished as the pre-publication process is not well developed in Colombia. Moreover, financial pressures on authors force them to turn in a quick product in order to move on to the next project.

The literature covers a broad ideological spectrum, with writers on the left generating works of a wider scope, and those who lean towards the right concentrating on narrower topics that are easier to fund. Left-oriented economists tend to remain in the academic environment, while their colleagues on the right use universities as stepping stones to attain policy-making positions in the government, or high paying jobs in private "think-tanks."

The heavy emphasis on empirical work is evident in the limited number of theoretical studies. Most are being generated by a handful of economists of various ideological persuasions and the result is that very few Colombian economists have had an impact on the development of Latin American economic thought.

The number of journals devoted to economic issues has also grown. Among the better known are *Coyuntura Económica* published by FEDESARROLLO, which emphasizes short-term policy analysis of the economy; *Revista de Planeación y Desarrollo* of the National Planning Department which has fluctuated between serving as an organ for policy statements and as a regular economic development journal; and the *Revista del Banco de la República* which publishes monetary and trade data and contains research articles chiefly concerned with money and banking. Among more recent academic journals is *Desarrollo y Sociedad*, issued by the Universidad de Los Andes, and which publishes quality papers on economics and other social sciences. Unfortunately, space limitations have prevented us from including annotations of articles in this section which is devoted entirely to monographs. However, in *HLAS 47* we shall include a representative sample of the periodical literature on the Colombian economy.

Lack of interest in the Colombian economy is evident in academic communities abroad. In the US, the Colombian economy is studied at multilateral institutions, particularly the World Bank. Among works annotated below, only five were published in the US: two were sponsored by the World Bank, one by the International Food Policy Research Institute, another was the Ph.D. dissertation of a full-time IMF employee, and the last consists of a collection of essays edited under the sponsorship of the Center for Inter-American Relations. A survey of economists affiliated with academic institutions in North America reveals that there is only one "Colombianist," at a Canadian University. One would surmise that the middle-of-the-road policies followed by Colombian governments over the last 25 years have produced substantial growth and stability, but not enough drama to attract the interest of North American academics.

In brief, in the recent past we have seen a remarkable growth of empirical and policy-oriented research on the Colombian economy by Colombians, their continual changing of institutional affiliation and research interests notwithstanding. While the quality of research has increased, the field's future is uncertain given the weakness and instability of Colombian academic institutions. Finally, it is clear that North American interest in the Colombian economy (outside of multilateral financial institutions) is virtually non-existent at this time. [FET]

ECUADOR

The most notable aspects of the economic literature on Ecuador are scarcity and weakness. Little is published on economic subjects and that little tends towards superficiality. Economics in Ecuador is almost wholly descriptive rather than analytic. Consequently, publications on economic history, where description is most appropriate, are the strongest. Particularly surprising is the lack of discussion of either what economic changes can be expected (e.g., the "Dutch disease") from the oil boom or how oil revenues should be managed. This lack of an analytic tradition will be keenly felt as petroleum exports decline and the country is forced to make adjustments throughout the economy. At this time, the best, perhaps the only, solid work is being generated by economists of a consulting firm, the Corporación de Estudios Económicos (e.g., Francisco Swett, Carlos Julio Emanuel, Alberto Dahik). Their output, however, tends to be proprietary and is published in newspapers and magazines of general interest. [TBH]

COLOMBIA

3263 Alvarez Atehortua, Orión. Antioquia ante el futuro. Bogotá: Ediciones Tercer Mundo, 1981. 184 p.: ill. (Colección Universidad y pueblo)

Short economic history of Antioquia which recommends several regional policy alternatives highly influenced by limits of growth theories of early 1970s. Strong regionalist tone reveals longing for greater regional autonomy.

3264 Arango, Mariano. El café en Colombia, 1930–1958: producción, circulación y política. Bogotá: C. Valencia Editores, 1982. 300 p.: bibl., tables.

Good recent history of Colombia's coffee industry provides revealing insights into coffee growers' role in country's policy-making process. Discusses domestic and external markets, and distribution of coffee income.

3265 Arango F., Juan Ignacio. La inversión extranjera en la industria manufacturera colombiana. Bogotá: Editográficas, 1982. 346 p.: bibl., ill., tables.

Comprehensive study of increasing role of transnational corporations in the development of manufacturing sector, of manufactured exports, and introduction of new goods and technologies during 1970s. Concludes that increasing importance of foreign capital in manufacturing could not be stopped under current capitalist system.

3266 Arango Londoño, Gilberto. Estructura económica colombiana. 4. ed. rev. y actualizada. Bogotá: Ediciones Colibrí, 1981. 561 p.: bibl., ill., tables.

Updated edition of very useful and comprehensive study of Colombian economy. Discusses main economic sectors and describes most important economic policies during 1970s. Excellent reference volume.

3267 Bejarano, Jesús A. El régimen agrario: de la economía exportadora a la economía industrial. Bogotá: La Carreta, 1979. 370 p.: bibl., ill.

Economic history of Colombian concentrates on period around 1930—the watershed between agricultural-exporting and industrialization. Three principal divisions: 1) conditions of the transition; 2) dissolution of agrarian sector; and 3) social transforma-

tions of 1930s. [J.M. Hunter]

3268 Bustamante Roldán, Darío. Efectos económicos del papel moneda durante La Regeneración. 2. ed. Bogotá: La Carreta Inéditos, 1980. 159 p.: graphs.

Careful study of impact which the elimination of the gold standard and establishment of paper money system in 1886 had on the Colombian economy. Covers period up to 1898. This monetary system change led to 1900 outbreak of the "1,000 Days" War.

3269 Castro, Yesid; Juan J. Echavarría; and Miguel Urrutia. El sector comercio en Colombia: estructura actual y perspectivas. Bogotá: FEDESARROLLO, 1979. 172 p.: bibl., graphs, tables.

Important analysis of understudied commerce sector. Questions conventional assumptions about sector's inefficiency and lack of productivity.

3270 Colombia, vivienda y subdesarrollo urbano. Editor, Humberto Molina. Colaboradores, Luz Angela Mondragón, Eduardo Toro, Martín Reig. Bogotá: Universidad de los Andes, Centro de Planificación y Urbanismo, 1979. 530 p.: ill.

Very extensive analysis of several housing related issues (i.e., costs, household expenditures, physical characteristics, different construction systems, employment in housing industry, housing problem in Bogotá, and housing policies of five presidential periods during 1958–78).

3271 Colombia y la crisis energética. Compilación y presentación de Diego Otero y Edgar Reveiz. Bogotá: Universidad de los Andes, Facultad de Economía, Centro de Estudios sobre Desarrollo Económico, 1982. 327 p.: bibl., ill. (Colección Debates CEDE; no. 2)

Collection of essays, given at 1979 seminar, surveys world energy problems, conventional and non-conventional energy sources. Analyzes Colombian situation with help of econometric models, and offers country projections up to year 2,000.

3272 La Cuestión cafetera: su impacto económico, social y político: Colombia, Costa Rica, Costa de Marfil. Compilación y presentación de Edgar Reveiz. Bogotá: Universidad de los Andes, Facultad de Economía, Centro de Estudios sobre Desarrollo Económico, 1980. 370 p.: ill. (Colección Debates;

no. 1)

Compilation of papers and comments given at coffee issues seminar. Covers the following: history of Colombia's, Costa Rica's and Ivory Coast's coffee economies; mid-1970s coffee boom and its impact on Colombian society; world coffee market; and, coffee sector's institutional problems.

3273 Currie, Lauchlin Bernard. The role of economic advisers in developing countries. Westport, Conn.: Greenwood Press, 1981. 270 p.: bibl., index (Contributions in economics and economic history, 0084–9235; no. 44)

Distilled wisdom from several decades as an "adviser." Weighted heavily toward Colombia. [J.M. Hunter]

3274 La Economía colombiana en la década de los ochenta. 2. ed. Bogotá: Fundación para la Educación Superior y el Desarrollo (FEDESARROLLO), 1980. 394 p.: bibl., ill.

Collection of sectoral essays on Colombian economic perspectives for 1980s, written by FEDESARROLLO economists. Main issues are: employment, income distribution, agriculture, industry, energy, and foreign sector.

3275 Ensayos sobre historia económica colombiana. Bogotá: FEDESARROLLO, 1980. 242 p.: bibl., ill.

Very good collection of quality essays on Colombian economic history of the 18th, 19th, and 20th centuries. Topics do not follow unified theme although there is substantial emphasis on analysis of foreign trade data.

3276 Fondo Colombiano de Investigaciones Científicas y Proyectos Especiales Francisco José de Caldas. División de Recursos Científicos y Tecnológicos. La fundición en Colombia: proyecto de mecanismos institucionales y organizacionales de política científica y tecnológica. Autores, Miguel Infante D. *et al.* Asesores, Pedro Amaya P. *et al.* Bogotá: Ministerio de Educación Nacional, Fondo Colombiano de Investigaciones Científicas y Proyectos Especiales Francisco José de Caldas, COLCIENCIAS, Sub-dirección de Asuntos Científicos y Tecnológicos, División de Recursos Científicos y Tecnológicos, 1979. 307 p.: bibl., diagrams.

Very detailed study of about 100

foundries in 1977. Examines technologies used, cost and availability of inputs, labor organizations and costs, and domestic and international demands.

3277 Fondo de Promoción de Exportaciones (PROEXPO). Colombia y su comercio con los países socialistas. Bogotá: República de Colombia, Ministerio de Desarrollo, PROEXPO: Banco de la República, 1978. 252 p.: bibl., tables.

Study of Colombian trade (1955–76) with Eastern European socialist countries describes its nature and characteristics, experience of Colombian importers and exporters and draws recommendations for improvement.

3278 Garay, Luis J. El Pacto Andino: ¿creación de un mercado para Colombia? Bogotá: Fundación para la Educación Superior y el Desarrollo (FEDESARROLLO), 1981. 343 p.: bibl., ill.

Evaluation of Colombian experience as member of Andean group (1970–77). Study argues that Andean group has been important for Colombia but unsuccessful in several aspects.

3279 García, Antonio. ¿A dónde va Colombia?: de la república señorial a la crisis del capitalismo dependiente. Bogotá: Tiempo Americano Editores, 1981. 120 p. (Textos populares)

Collection of three essays by leading radical economist in which he discusses inward tendencies of Colombian society and resulting ineffectiveness in dealing with changing and powerful capitalist powers.

3280 García García, Jorge. The effects of exchange rates and commercial policy on agricultural incentives in Colombia, 1953–1978. Washington: International Food Policy Research Institute, 1981. 88 p.: bibl., graphs.

Very careful econometric study of impact of commercial policy on production incentives of traded and non-traded goods during 1953–78. Author uses general equilibrium framework and concentrates on agricultural sector.

3281 El Grupo Andino y sus relaciones con la Comunidad Europea. Bogotá: Fundación Friedrich Naumann, 1979. 125 p.: bibl. (Enfoques colombianos, temas latinoamericanos. Serie Monografía; no. 12)

Basically a Colombian-German dialogue on three subtopics: 1) alternatives in North-South relationships; 2) transnationals and the industrial sector in the Andean Pact; and 3) trade problems. [J.M. Hunter]

3282 El Intercambio comercial entre Colombia y Venezuela: rasgos característicos y principales limitantes. Estudio realizado para el Fondo de Promoción de Exportaciones (PROEXPO) bajo la dirección del economista Isidro Parra-Peña, Bogotá, 1981. Bogotá: A. Pineda Editores, 1982. 300 p.: bibl.

Complete study of international trade between Colombia and Venezuela during 1970s. Discusses importance of trade for each country, role of Andean group and importance of trade on foodstuffs, cattle as well as border trade and contraband. Also surveys existing public transportation systems between both countries and their joint investment and international payments systems.

3283 Jaramillo, Samuel. Producción de vivienda y capitalismo dependiente: el caso de Bogotá. Bogotá: Editorial Dintel, 1980? 240 p.: appendices, bibl., ill.

Very serious study of housing construction in Bogotá between 1930–77. Emphasizes link between government financial policies and housing construction, and impact of several policy changes on housing.

3284 Lecturas sobre desarrollo económico colombiano. En honor de Alvaro López Toro. Editores: Hernando Gómez Otálora and Eduardo Wiesner Durán. Bogotá: Fundación para la Educación Superior y el Desarrollo (FEDESARROLLO), 1974. 624 p.: tables.

Set of readings by leading Colombian, Latin American, and North American economists concern income distribution; employment, demography; planning; money and credit; fiscal, foreign trade, and economic growth policies; and agricultural sector. Essays focus on 1960s and early 1970s.

3285 Lleras Restrepo, Carlos. Política cafetera, 1937–1978. Bogotá: Osprey Impresores, 1980. 333 p.: bibl.

Collection of Lleras Restrepo's journalistic and official writings over 40 years on coffee issues. The statesman analyzes, evaluates and notes features of coffee's influence on Colombia's economy and politics.

McGreevey, William Paul. Reinterpreting Colombian economic history. See *HLAS*

44:2857.

3286 Machado C., Absalón. El problema agrario en Colombia y sus soluciones. Bogotá: Fundación Mariano Ospina Pérez, 1981. 151 p.: bibl., ill. (Publicaciones; 21)

Study of rural sector during 1960s and 1970s discusses marketing, credit, and tenancy problems. Study's main value lies in its description of institutional framework and markets of several products.

3287 Los Medios de pago y la base monetaria en Colombia: 1923–1979. Bogotá: República de Colombia, Federación Nacional de Cafeteros de Colombia, División de Investigaciones Económicas, 1980. 152 p., 5 folded leaves of plates: ill. (some col.).

Study makes quarterly estimates of money supply (M1) during 1923–79. Argues that government policies toward coffee sector in 1970s are responsible for only about 10 percent of money supply increase during period, despite large increase in foreign reserves induced by coffee boom of late 1970s.

3288 Meldau, Elke C. Benefit incidence: public health expenditures and income distribution: a case study of Colombia. North Quincy, Mass.: Christopher Pub. House, 1980. 224 p.: bibl., graphs, index.

Estimate of benefit incidence of health expenditures of the Colombian Institute of Social Security and of the Ministry of Health in 1970. Using two approaches to measure benefit incidence, author shows that the poor enjoy higher benefits from these programs, although not as high as expected.

3289 Méndez Q., Rodolfo. Introducción a la economía de los recursos naturales de Colombia. Bogotá: Ediciones Fundación Educacional Autónoma de Colombia, 1980. 237 p.: bibl.

Natural resources sector study analyzes their mismanagement in Colombia and resulting ecological problems which are affecting the country.

3290 Mendoza Morales, Alberto and Angela Mendoza. Retorno al campo. Bogotá: Editorial Orbs, 1981. 185 p.: ill.

Studies history and current condition of Colombian peasantry. Authors emphasize anthropological aspects, land tenure systems, relationship between land ownership and power, technology and government's Indian policy.

3291 Michelsen Niño, Pablo. Estudio sobre banca de desarrollo. Bogotá: Pontificia Universidad Javeriana, Facultad de Ciencias Jurídicas y Socio-Económicas, 1980. 126 p.: bibl., ill., tables.

Descriptive analysis of characteristics of development banking institutions is followed by survey of institutional and legal aspects that are relevant to Colombian development banks. Study also analyzes Instituto de Fomento Industrial (IFI) and large Nacional Financiera de México (NAFINSA).

3292 Morawetz, David. Why the emperor's new clothes are not made in Colombia: a case study in Latin American and East Asian manufactured exports. Washington: Published for the World Bank by Oxford University Press, 1981. 192 p.: bibl., ill., index (A World Bank research publication)

Detailed case study of Colombian clothing exports identifies main reasons for 1971–74 export success and failure after 1975. Author emphasizes exchange rate role, difficulties in achieving a rapid importation of intermediate products, domestic pricing of textiles, quality control, and the unreliability of domestic suppliers, as leading factors in the turnabout export performance of this sector.

Ocampo, José Antonio. Las exportaciones colombianas en el siglo XIX. See *HLAS 44:2861.*

3293 Parra Escobar, Ernesto. La economía colombiana, 1971–1981. Bogotá: Centro de Investigación y Educación Popular, 1982. 102 p.: bibl., ill., tables (Serie Controversia; no. 100)

Concise discussion of evolution of Colombian economy during 1971–81 period emphasizes increasing role of foreign sector and of development plans of three governments during period.

3294 ———. Económica colombiana, 1979 [i.e. mil novecientos setenta y nueva]: la nueva política económica. Bogotá: Centro de Investigación y Educación Popular, 1979. 108 p.: bibl., graphs, tables (Serie Controversia; nos. 75/76)

Good description of economic policies followed during first two years of Turbay government using as framework "the cyclical process of capitalistic production." Study

does not use econometric analysis and is based on traditional explanations of business cycle.

3295 Pensando en Colombia. Bogotá: Asociación Nacional de Instituciones Financieras (ANIF), 1979. 288 p.: ill. (Biblioteca de economía)

Compilation of most important studies and policy statements made by Asociación Nacional de Instituciones Financieras' (ANIF) research group. It is a relevant reference for understanding several policies of the current Betancur government.

3296 Pizano Salazar, Diego. Expansión del comercio exterior de Colombia, 1875–1925. Bogotá: Fondo Cultural Cafetero, 1981. 102 p.: ill.

Theoretical discussion of validity of several international trade theories in explaining growth of primary commodity exports between 1875–1925.

3297 ———. Procesamiento y mercado del café en la República Federal Alemana. Bogotá: Fondo Cultural Cafetero, 1980. 151 p.: bibl., tables.

Study of processing and marketing of coffee in Germany during 1970s. Examines consumption trends, processing capacity and technology, market structure, taxes and government policies.

3298 Politics of compromise: coalition government in Colombia. Edited by R. Albert Berry, Ronald G. Hellman, Mauricio Solaún. New Brunswick, N.J.: Transaction Books, 1980. 488 p.: ill.

Collection of essays mostly by leading Colombian experts and North American Colombianists on the controversial National Front period (1958–72). They discuss it from historical, political, and economic perspectives.

3299 Power, Alejandro *et al.* Modelos de desarrollo económico: Colombia, 1960–1982. Edición preparada por Cristina de la Torre. Bogotá: Editorial La Oveja Negra: Asociación de Profesionales de la Educación Superior, 1982. 293 p.

Collection of essays on economic plans implemented by Colombian governments since 1960 were given at seminar organized by the left wing of the Liberal Party. Essays trascend formal development plans and discuss general policies of recent governments and would-be policies of presidential candidate Alfonso López.

3300 Recursos para el futuro: Colombia, 1950–2000. Bogotá: Instituto de Estudios Colombianos, 1981. 358 p.: bibl., tables (Biblioteca Banco Popular. Divulgación económica y social; 3)

Study of use of basic economic resources between 1950–74 with projections to year 2,000. Surveys energy; air and water pollution; urban requirements; agriculture; forestry; demography; the public and the external sectors.

3301 Rojas H., Fernando. Hegemonía del capitalismo monopolista. Bogotá: Centro de Investigación y Educación Popular, 1978. 169 p.: bibl., tables (Constituyente; 2. Controversia; nos. 61/62)

Marxist critique of the economic policies followed by the Alfonso López administration (1974–78), especially of the 1974 tax reform.

3302 Selowsky, Marcelo. Who benefits from government expenditures?: a case study of Colombia. New York: Published for the World Bank [by] Oxford University Press, 1979. 186 p.: bibl., index, tables.

Excellent study of redistributive effects of public subsidies for education, health, electricity, piped water and sewage, and of the loans of the Caja Agraria. Study is based on 1974 survey data of over 4,000 households.

3303 Seminario sobre Evaluación y Perspectivas de la Estructura Fiscal Colombiana, los Impuestos y el Gasto Público, *Universidad Javeriana, Bogotá, 1978.* La estructura fiscal colombiana: los impuestos y el gasto público, evaluación y perspectivas. Seminario organizado por el Programa de Postgrado en Economía de la Facultad de Estudios Interdisciplinarios y la Facultad de Ciencias Económicas y Administrativas de la Universidad Javeriana, con la colaboración de la Universidad de Harvard. Editores, Sebastián Arango Fonnegra, Jaime Bueno Miranda, and Florángela Gómez de Arango. Bogotá: Universidad Javeriana, Facultad de Estudios Interdisciplinarios, 1979. 356 p.: graphs.

Collection of essays on issues related to overall Colombian tax structure, impact of inflation on tax incidence, taxes on transnational corporations, the "presumed income" tax, and on the planning and implementation

of public expenditures in the country.

3304 Sierra Jaramillo, Francisco. Cooperativismo colombiano. Bogotá: Editorial Temis Librería, 1980. 332 p.: appendix, bibl., indexes, tables.

Textbook surveys theory of cooperativism and summarizes Colombian legislation and institutions which affect cooperatives.

3305 Simposio sobre Inflación y Política Económica, *Cali, Colombia, 1980.* Inflación y política económica. Mauricio Cabrera Galvis, editor. Bogotá: Asociación Bancaria de Colombia, 1980. 392 p.: ill.

Collection of essays on inflation and economic policies during 1970s. Essays deal with causes of inflation, relationships between inflation and political system, exchange rate, monetary controls and development of economic and financial conglomerates.

3306 Simposio sobre Mercado de Capitales, *Cali, Colombia, 1979.* El sector financiero en los años ochenta. Carlos Caballero Argáz, editor. Bogotá: Asociación Bancaria de Colombia, 1979. 477 p.: bibl., ill., tables (Biblioteca Asociación Bancaria de Colombia)

Compilation includes essays on various kinds of financial institutions in Colombia, financing of various sectors, financial systems of US, Brazil, and Mexico. Concludes with three essays that examine financial needs during 1980s.

3307 Sistema financiero y políticas anti-inflacionarias, 1974–1980. Mauricio Cabrera Galvis, editor. Bogotá: Asociación Bancaria de Colombia, 1980. 278 p.: bibl., ill.

Comprehensive collection of essays dealing wth several types of financial institutions of the country, and institutional changes that took place during 1970s.

3308 Vélez de Sierra, Cecilia; Liliana Jaramillo Velosa; and **Roberto Forero Báez.** ¿Cuánto vale el carbón de El Carrejón? Bogotá: Ediciones Tercer Mundo, 1980. 258 p.: bibl., maps, tables.

Discussion of large coal project of "El Carrejón" criticizes government's contracts with transnational corporations to develop this mine and questions advisability of exporting Colombian coal in the future.

3309 Vélez M., Hugo E. Factores de inflación en la economía colombiana, 1971–1977. Bogotá: Inéditos, 1979. 204 p.:

bibl., tables (La Carreta)

Discussion of relative changes of various components of consumer price index in 1971–77 period. Finds that products of modern agricultural sector and increase in interest rates due to indexation of savings deposits were index's fastest growing components. Accumulation of international reserves and growth in monetary base are discussed in appendix. There is no discussion of the part played by deficits in generating inflation.

3310 Wiesner Durán, Eduardo. Devaluación y mecanismo de ajuste en Colombia. México: Centro de Estudios Monetarios Latinoamericanos (CEMLA), 1980. 64 p.: bibl., tables (Colección Investigaciones. Ensayos CEMLA; 43)

Good study of adjustment process of the Colombian economy induced by instability in its foreign sector. Analyzes exchange rate and other relevant policies beginning in 1948, and emphasizes 1975–78 period.

3311 Zamosc, León and Juan G. Gavira. El fique y los empaques en Colombia. Bogotá: Editorial Dintel, 1981. 237 p.: tables (Publicaciones de la Fundación Mariano Ospina Pérez; 22)

Detailed sector study of production and use of sisal. Study is based on survey, and describes location of production, type of production units, uses and socioeconomic impact of sisal production on peasant families that work in it.

3312 Zuleta Jaramillo, Luis Alberto and Jorge Valencia Restrepo. Sector financiero colombiano: un análisis del desarrollo de la intermediación financiera. Medellín: Universidad de Antioquia, Facultad de Ciencias Económicas, Centro de Investigaciones Económicas, 1981. 196 p.: bibl., ill., tables.

Surveys historical development of financial sector, emphasizing developments during 1970s. Authors develop econometric model to measure changes in financial intermediation during that decade.

ECUADOR

3313 Estadísticas fiscales. v. 1/2. Quito: Ministerio de Finanzas, Subsecretaría de Presupuesto y Crédito Público, Departamento de Estadísticas Fiscales, 1979? 2 v.:

col. ill., tables.

Vols. 1/2 of what could become a useful statistical handbook if continued and if present format is maintained.

3314 Fernández, Iván. Estado y desarrollo capitalista en el Ecuador (NSO, 45, nov./dic. 1979, p. 89–103, ill.)

Historical overview, from Marxist perspective, of five stages in transition from a "liberal oligarchy" state to a "modern underdeveloped" state. Sensible stages and interesting insights. Expects no fundamental change to result from new constitutional regime. Does not consider whether import dependent (i.e., petroleum export dependent) economic mode is sustainable.

3315 Handelman, Howard. Development and misdevelopment in Ecuador (SAGE/JIAS, 24:1, Feb. 1982, p. 115–122)

Sympathetic review essay discusses from a left or center-left perspective two books on Ecuador which deal with economic issues: *Ecuador hoy* (whose papers are annotated in *HLAS 43:3367–3368, 3370* and *6421*), and current President Osvaldo Hurtado's *Political power in Ecuador* (see item **6281**). Calls attention to social science research by FLACSO and CEPAL.

3316 Invest in Ecuador. Quito: Banco Central del Ecuador, 180. 76 p.: ill. (some col.)

Short and useful publication includes basic data on infrastructure and development laws. Designed to attract foreign investment in industry, book highlights possibilities of Andean Group Industrial Programs. Unfortunately, 1982–83 economic crisis has made much of its economic information outdated.

3317 Montaño Pérez, Galo and Eduardo Wygard. Visión sobre la industria ecuatoriana. Quito: COFIEC, 1981. 488 p.: bibl., ill., tables.

Mid-1970s outlook on Ecuador's industrial possibilities. One of authors was Minister of Industry for several years. Argues for capital intensive import substitution projects. Also contains proceedings of nontechnical conference held in 1976, to discuss industrialization of Ecuador. Technically weak study.

Roberts, Lois Crawford de. El Ecuador en la época cacaotera: respuestas locales al auge y colapso en el ciclo monoexportador. See

HLAS 44:2904.

3318 Salgado Peñaherrera, Germánico. Crisis y activación en una economía regional: la experiencia de Cuenca y su zona de influencia, 1950–1970. Caracas; Quito: Instituto Latinoamericano de Investigaciones Sociales; República Federal de Alemania: Fundación Friedrich Ebert, 1978. 100 p.: bibl., tables (Serie Materiales de trabajo; no. 18)

Explains ways in which Cuenca's economy recovered from collapse of the straw hat export market after World War II. Highlights importance of infrastructure investments that reduced province's economic isolation stimulated by regional development authority, CREA.

3319 Tama Paz, Cyrano. Escándalos petroleros ecuatorianos. Guayaquil, Ecuador: Universidad de Guayaquil, Departamento de Publicaciones, 1979. 444 p.: ill., tables.

Collection of author's newspaper articles written between 1975–78 on petroleum and other economic issues, with introduction. Analysis in most articles is superficial and tone emotional. Of more political than economic interest.

VENEZUELA

JORGE SALAZAR-CARRILLO, *Chairman and Professor of Economics, Florida International University, Non-Resident Staff Member, Brookings Institution*

THIS IS THE FIRST TIME SINCE 1972, when I began reviewing the economic literature of Venezuela for *HLAS*, that I notice a decline in the quantity and quality of publications. Perhaps this is another consequence of the "petro-crisis" that hit oil producers in the 1970s and early 1980s.

The proposed creation in 1984 of a new government funded economic research center, the Instituto de Investigaciones Científicas en Economía, reflects the concern of Venezuelan leaders over this crisis. Unfortunately, the Institute's budget will be affected by declining oil prices.

During this biennium, there have been a few commendable research efforts. As expected, the Central Bank of Venezuela continued to support researchers in and out of government, through publication of its various monographic series, notable among which is a public policy analysis by Constantino Quero Morales in *Imagen: objetivo de Venezuela* (item **3354**).

The two most productive universities in terms of research were once again the Universidad de los Andes in Mérida and the Universidad Central de Venezuela in Caracas. Several important articles and monographs were sponsored by these educational institutions (items **3328–3329, 3337, 3346, 3349–3350, 3356, 3358, 3360, 3365,** and **3369**).

US economic research on Venezuela has dwindled reflecting the decline in generous funding for US-Venezuelan cooperative efforts that characterized much research in the past. Again, the decline reflects Venezuela's mounting economic problems. In contrast to their American counterparts, European researchers are taking a more active interest in Venezuelan economic topics. However, it is unlikely that European investigators will outdistance those in the US given the frequency of contact between Venezuelan and American researchers.

Two other distinct trends that despite their opposition may end by reinforcing one another, are the emphasis on political economy and the recurrence of statistical-econometric models. These two tendencies attest to a growing sophistication in research and a consistency of output, qualities that have prevailed despite a trying period for the field of economics in Venezuela.

Not unrelated to the above phenomenon is the new rigor and reasoning of much of the Marxist literature on the nation's economy, characterized mostly by rhetoric in the past. In contrast, Marxist publications annotated below reflect the work of a new breed of economists who, though radical in training and conviction, are also aware of the importance of a strong theoretical base, a sound statistical presentation and hypotheses that have been tested (item **3337**).

In closing I would like to express my gratitude, especially to Manuel Chávez but also to Adriana Correa, for their help in reviewing the economic literature that follows.

3320 Aguirre, Antonio. Crecimiento de las instituciones financieras de Venezuela: 1960–1980 (Revista de Hacienda [Ministerio de Hacienda, Dirección de Investigaciones Económicas, Caracas] 44 : 78 enero/dic. 1981, p. 7–38, bibl., tables)

Study of origin and evolution of Venezuela's financial system. Lists and describes different kinds of financial intermediaries and studies financial flow of funds involving these institutions. Shows which financial instruments have been more important. Author is a professor of economics at Universidad Católica Andrés Bello.

3321 Anuario Estadístico Agropecuario. Ministerio de Agricultura y Cría, División de Estadística. 1977/1978- . Caracas.

Yearly statistical abstract on Venezuela's agricultural sector corresponding to 1977–1978.

3322 Banco Central de Venezuela. Las tasas de interés y la balanza de pagos: el caso venezolano (ABM/RB, 29 : 2, feb. 1981, p. 1–4)

Central Bank of Venezuela's President at the time, Carlos Rafael Silva, addresses meeting of Central Bank governors of Latin America and Spain on topic of interest rates and international capital movements. Regards persistent and rising inflationary process of 1970s as culprit. Briefly discusses defensive measures introduced by Venezuela to stem outflow of short-term funds seeking higher yields abroad.

3323 Casas González, Antonio. La crisis energética mundial y la América Latina: el papel de Venezuela (FCE/TE, 48[2]: 190, abril/junio 1981, p. 405–421)

Former Planning Minister of Venezuela and currently Director of PDVSA (Petroven), author is knowledgeable on basic characteristics of the energy problem. Defines its nature in inter-temporal terms. His messsage is one of cooperation rather than confrontation, between OPEC and non-OPEC countries, particularly in Latin America which is rich in untapped resources. In conclusion, unveils new plan, sponsored by Venezuela, for Latin American coordination and cooperation to develop these resources regionally.

3324 Cerpe, Equipo. El ciclo diversificado industrial en Venezuela (CEE/RL, 11 : 2, Primavera 1981, p. 87–119, bibl., tables)

Examination and discussion of implementation of flexible secondary school track that would train students for possible involvement in industrial activities. Approach is part of Venezuela's educational reform undertaken in early 1970s.

3325 Chaves, Luis Fernando. Patrones y funcionamiento del espacio socioeconómico en una economía subdesarrollada: el caso venezolano (ULA/RG, 13 : 28/29, enero/dic. 1972, p. 22–50, tables)

Regional economist at University of Los Andes in Mérida, author examines developmental patterns of Venezuela's economy from regional perspective. Study is based on assumption that underdevelopment is the state of peripheral countries during the imperialist phase of the capitalist system. Considers and tests for Venezuela several regional models of development within the center and periphery framework of international division of labor.

3326 Colmenares Zuleta, Juan Carlos. El control de las percepciones tributarias contempladas en la Ley de Impuesto sobre Sucesiones, Donaciones y demás Ramos Conexos (Revista de Control Fiscal [Contraloría General de la República, Caracas] 23 : 104, enero/marzo 1982, p. 149–154)

Reviews laws concerning estate and gift taxation in Venezuela. Author is the law professor at Universidad Católica Andrés

Bello, Caracas.

3327 Colts, Manuel; Orlando Sánchez; and Henry Sarmiento. La transferencia de tecnología al agro venezolano. Caracas: Instituto Latinoamericano de Investigaciones Sociales, Fundación Friedrich Ebert, 1977. 51 leaves: ill. (Serie Materiales de trabajo; no. 9)

Studies transfer of technology in developing countries, with special reference to agricultural production in Venezuela. Authors argue that both external factors and internal factors determine technology transfer. Among latter, authors single out the educational system and planning mechanisms.

3328 Córdova Cañas, Víctor. Capitalismo, subdesarrollo y modo de vida en Venezuela. Caracas: Universidad Central de Venezuela, Facultad de Ciencias Económicas y Sociales, División de Publicaciones, 1980. 204 p.: bibl. (Colección Libros)

Socioeconomic analysis of life styles in Venezuela is divided into: 1) introduction to essence of development and underdevelopment and socioeconomic problems implied; 2) detailed examination of characteristics of developed and underdeveloped countries, especially Venezuela; and 3) theoretical background in which economic systems (i.e., capitalism) are tied to particular life styles.

3329 Corrales, Werner. La capitalidad de Venezuela (Urbana [Universidad Central de Venezuela, Instituto de Urbanismo, Caracas] 2, feb. 1980, p. 105–131)

Study of problems brought about by concentration of development in Venezuela's capital. Rapid development of Caracas is contrasted with slow development in rest of the country. Criticizes elementary suggestions advanced by writers and policy-makers to solve the problem. Proposes instead to consider problem within conceptual confines of a capital city's role and function, implying a reconsideration of governmental activities and objectives of the State in Venezuela.

3330 Correa R., César R. Venezuela: 25 [i.e. veinticinco] años de industria férrica y su nacionalización. Caracas: s.n., 1977? 151 p.: ill., tables.

Covers succinctly process of Venezuelan iron and steel industries from early origin until mid-1970s nationalization. Organized in a chronological fashion, study ends in 1976.

3331 Delahaye, Olivier. Formation de la propriété rurale et rapports fonciers au Venezuela: les cas de Portuguesa (UP/TM, 21:84, oct./déc. 1980, p. 721–733)

Using Portuguesa state as case study, author considers evolution of Venezuela's land-ownership system. Attributes critical importance to government policies in determining land rent in agriculture and believes they have fostered establishment of capitalistic mode of production in rural sector.

3332 Dietzman, William D.; Naim R. Rafidi; and Arthur J. Warner. Venezuela, Trinidad and Tobago: crude oil potential from known deposits. Washington: U.S. Department of Energy, Energy Information Administration, Office of Oil and Gas, 1981. 122 p.: bibl., ill., 2 col. maps.

Analyzes future oil supply potential of known fields of Venezuela and Trinidad and Tobago. Estimates original oil in place, ultimate recovery, remaining reserves and projected supply patterns. Presents discussion of metodology for projecting future supply.

3333 The Economic evolution of the individual countries: Venezuela (*in* United Nations. Economic Commission for Latin America. Economic survey of Latin America, 1979. Santiago: 1981, p. 516–534, tables)

Appraisal of Venezuela's economic performance in 1979, as part of traditional survey of Latin America undertaken by CEPAL. Of all surveys annotated here, this is certainly the most professional evaluation of the economy in a given year. Statistics of previous years are used as aid to highlight principal traits of 1979, and to establish trends or their reversal.

3334 Escovar, Janet Kelly de. Empresas del estado, negociación y el balance del poder económico (Argos [Universidad Simón Bolívar, División de Ciencias Sociales y Humanidades, Caracas] 1, 1981, p. 69–95)

Article examines role of state enterprises, particularly in mineral products by using Venezuela mostly, but not exclusively, as illustrative case. Steel, bauxite and aluminum are studied in detail. Considers state enterprises, from viewpoint of developing world's economic independence, as possible challenge to multinational or transnational firms.

3335 Fariñas, Guillermo. Tributos petroleros venezolanos, antes y después de la nacionalización de tal industria (Revista de Control Fiscal [Contraloría General de la República, Caracas] 23 : 104, enero/marzo 1982, p. 135–147, charts)

Informative article by professor of law and political science at Venezuela's Central University considers tax measures for the nation's oil industry.

3336 Fermín, Pedro J. La tasa subyacente de inflación en Venezuela (Revista de Hacienda [Ministerio de Hacienda, División de Investigaciones Económicas, Caracas] 44:78, enero/dic. 1981, p. 39–67, bibl., graphs, ill., tables)

Econometric investigation of structural rate of inflation in Venezuela uses stochastic time-series techniques (i.e., Box and Jenkins). Separates transitory from systematic part of cost-of-living changes experienced in the country (1975–81) and attempts to explain underlying causes of inflationary process.

3337 Flores D., Max. Aspectos de la contradicción capital-trabajo en Venezuela (Economía y Ciencias Sociales [Universidad Central de Venezuela, Facultad de Ciencias Económicas y Sociales, Instituto de Investigaciones, Caracas] 18 : 3, julio/sept. 1979, p. 15–26, tables)

Marxist oriented critique of the functional distribution of income in Venezuela, which highly favors the capital share. Blames the State for favoring a model which supports monopoly position of dominant economic classes. Arguments are well presented and documented in contrast to the usual cursory economic criticisms that emanate from Venezuelan universities. At end, author reinforces argument by showing that the country's personal income distribution is deficient as well.

3338 García Martín, José Lorenzo. Venezuela: plataforma para la penetración comercial en América Latina. Madrid: Banca Mas Sardá, 1977? 24 p.

Statement by Secretary General of Venezuela Chamber of Commerce in Spain discusses his country's participation in the Andean Pact, its foreign investment policy, and most promising technology transfer fields.

3339 Gutiérrez, Freddy. La contratación de mano de obra migrante en Venezuela (STPS/R, 1 : 2, mayo/agosto 1978, p. 27–35)

Law professor at Simón Bolívar University, Caracas, discusses legal requirements and procedures for hiring migrant workers in Venezuela, on both temporary and permanent basis.

3340 *Informe de Coyuntura.* Ministerio de Industria, Turismo e Integración, Secretaría de Estado de Integración, Dirección General de Asuntos Económicos, Dirección de Estudios Económicos. Vol. 6, 1979- . Caracas.

Analysis (80 p.) of Venezuela's economic performance in 1979, and of economic policies implemented during the year. Based on secondary sources.

3341 Karlsson, Weine. Evolución y localización de la industria manufacturera en Venezuela y América Latina. Stockholm: Institute of Latin American Studies, 1979. 79 p.: tables (Research papers series; no. 21)

Brief survey of growth of manufacturing sector in Latin America, followed by more detailed report on Venezuela. Provides a good bird's-eye view of evolution of manufacturing therein from late 19th century to middle 1970s.

3341a López Pérez, Eduardo. Marco conceptual para el análisis del endeudamiento externo en el caso venezolano (Revista de Hacienda [Ministerio de Hacienda, División de Investigaciones Económicas, Caracas] 44:78, enero/dic. 1981, p. 39–67, bibl., graphs, ill., tables)

Consists of preface on constituent parts of model of external debt, adjusted to Venezuelan case. Serves as general guideline for future investigations in the 1980s at Economic Research Unit, Finance Ministry of Venezuela.

3342 McAllister, Donald M. Report on productivity in relation to housing conditions in Ciudad Guayana, Venezuela. Los Angeles: University of California, Graduate School of Business Administration, 1968. 48 leaves: ill., tables.

Describes efforts to analyze effects on health and productivity of improved housing. Tests two hypotheses: 1) improved housing leads to improved health; and 2) improved housing leads to increased labor productivity.

Evidence uncovered in study neither supports nor rejects either hypothesis.

3343 Maza Zavala, D.F. *et al.* El petróleo y la cuestión de superar la deformación de las estructuras económicas (URSS/AL, 12, 1980, p. 59–78)

Journalistic account of present and future impact of the oil industry on Venezuela's economic development.

3344 Mommer, Bernard and **Ramón A. Rivas A.** El petróleo en la transformación burguesa de Venezuela (BCV/REL, 16:62, 1981, p. 206–233)

Historical examination of the process of granting and modifying concessions for petroleum exploration and exploitation in Venezuela. Discusses conditions, fiscal and otherwise, spelled in such concessions from early 1900s to 1943.

3345 Montiel Ortega, Leonardo. Crisis mundial del petróleo. Caracas: Publicaciones Seleven, 1980. 175 p.: bibl., graphs, tables.

Examines oil crisis and its impact on economies of Venezuela, US, and rest of world. Attempts to predict trends in world oil market, which author regards as foreseeable. Also exudes faith on the predictive accuracy of oil trends on the Venezuelan economy. Engineer trained at John Hopkins, author's exceptations exemplify the unreaaliability of long-run projections as such expectations were soon disappointed by unexpected glut of oil markets.

3346 Oficina Metropolitana de Planeamiento Urbano (OMPU), *Caracas.* Simulación y evaluación de escenarios económicos de la región capital (Urbana [Universidad Central de Venezuela, Instituto de Urbanismo, Caracas] 2, feb. 1980, p. 27–103, graphs, tables)

Paper presented at seminar on quantitative methods in economics, by Urban Planning Group of Caracas Metropolitan Goverment. In cooperation with consulting firm, group conducted simulation study attempting to resolve problems of increasing concentration in Venezuela's capital city. This exercise on futurology is taken up to year 2,000.

3347 Palma C., Pedro A. Venezuela: la nueva bonanza petrolera; perspectivas para 1980–1983 (Comercio Exterior [Banco Nacional de Comercio Exterior, México] 30:6, junio 1980, p. 587–600, bibl., charts, graphs)

Reviews macroeconomic behavior of the Venezuelan economy during 1974–79 period, and makes forecasts for 1980–83. Author uses macroeconometric model he developed (MODVEN) for this purpose. Palma is professor at IESA (Institute of Higher Studies in Administration), and head of Metro Económica, an econometric forecasting firm.

3348 Panorama de la economía venezolana en el año 1980 (BCV/REL, 16:62, 1981, p. 8–35, tables)

Usual yearly analysis of Venezuelan economy by Central Bank. Uses data presented in statistical appendix.

3349 Pardo, Carlos Arturo. La contratación colectiva en Venezuela (Economía y Ciencias Sociales [Universidad Central de Venezuela, Facultad de Ciencias Económicas y Sociales, Instituto de Investigaciones, Caracas] 18:3, julio/sept. 1979, p. 55–65)

Sociohistorical analysis of process of collective bargaining in Venezuela. Criticizes abolishment of right to strike as having constrained collective bargaining process. Author would prefer if process would de-emphasize economic matters (e.g., wage settlementts, etc.) in favor of class struggle.

3350 Pareles, Sarah Orestes de. La cooperativa de consumo y el salario real (Economía y Ciencias Sociales [Universidad Central de Venezuela, Facultad de Ciencias Económicas y Sociales, Instituto de Investigaciones, Caracas] 18:3, julio/sept. 1979, p. 49–54, bibl.)

Advocates consumer cooperatives in Venezuela by noting their advantages as means for fighting inflation and as preferable alternatives to wage increases.

3351 Pinto Cohen, Gustavo. Visión general de la agricultura venezolana (Revista de Control Fiscal [Contraloría General de la República, Caracas] 23:104, enero/marzo 1982, p. 73–81, graph)

Concerns evolution of Venezuelan agriculture, some of whose problems can be attributed to policy mistakes, influence of petroleum exploitation, and inappropriate technological adaptation to the country's bio-climatic conditions. Author was Minister of Agriculture and long-standing researcher in field.

3352 Prishkolnik, Dorina. Fomento económico de la zona tropical: la experiencia venezolana (URSS/AL, 3:19, 1978, p. 151–165, tables)

Description and appraisal of Venezuelan government's attempt to develop its tropical land mass rich in mineral resources. Development of industrial complex based on heavy industry receives mixed reviews.

3353 *Quarterly Bulletin.* Ministry of Energy and Mines. Vol. 15, No. 3, July/Sept. 1980 [and] Vol. 15, No. 4, Oct./Dec. 1980- . Caracas.

Two issues of journal published in English by Venezuela's Ministry of Energy and Mines. Covers mostly current affairs related to Venezuelan oil activities, sometimes reprinting material from other sources.

3354 Quero Morales, Constantino. Imagen-objetivo de Venezuela: reformas fundamentales para su desarrollo. Caracas: Banco Central de Venezuela, 1978. 2 v. (1657 p., 3 fold. leaves of plates): ill. (Colección de estudios económicos; 6)

Magnum opus by Venezuelan official of manifold abilities who has observed his country's problems from various perspectives: Minister of Development, President of the Venezuelan Investment Fund and Director of the Central Bank. In the tradition of Latin American works of political economy, book leaves no socioeconomic issue untouched. After introducing several themes with a diagnostic purpose, author examines them more fully within the context of a hypothetical Venezuela. Concludes by stating a number of objectives with their concomitant policy recommendations. The two volumes are enhanced by an outstanding bibliography and summary section which gathers the study's main conclusions.

3355 Quintana Llamozas, José. Abastecimiento y desarrollo rural en América Latina: el caso de Venezuela (Boletín de Antropología Americana [Instituto Panamericano de Geografía e Historia, México] 2, dic. 1980, p. 77–86, bibl, plates, tables)

Analyzes present situation of agriculture in Latin America, and factors that have conditioned its development. Stresses importance of policies adapted to particular country conditions, especially adaptation of technologies to Venezuela's tropical eco-

systems. Despite subtitle, not much attention is given to Venezuela.

3356 Quintero, Rodolfo. La contratación colectiva de trabajo en Venezuela hoy (Economía y Ciencias Sociales [Universidad Central de Venezuela, Facultad de Ciencias Económicas y Sociales, Instituto de Investigaciones, Caracas] 18:3, julio/sept. 1979, p. 7–14, tables)

Criticizes collective bargaining process and labor relations in Venezuela as well as attempt to present a false picture of serenity and conciliation. Examines how contract bargaining by CTV (Confederation of Workers of Venezuela) actually betrayed working class interests. Believes accumulation of such agreements is tantamount to an abdication of political rights.

3357 Rada, Juan. The development of the money market in Venezuela (*in* Financing development in Latin America [see item **2821**] p. 207–221, tables)

Discusses development of Venezuela's financial markets from 1973 til late 1970s. Money markets and capital markets are discussed separately, since the latter have not progressed as much. Article consists of chapter in book covering Latin American countries which should allow for some interesting comparisons.

3358 Ramírez, Erasmo. Región de los Andes, estimaciones y proyecciones de población. Mérida, Venezuela: Universidad de los Andes, Facultad de Economía, Instituto de Investigaciones Económicas, 1978. 14 leaves.

Population of four states (1973–71, with projections to 1980) to include those "economically active" by sectors. [J.M. Hunter]

3359 Rebelledo, Guillermo. La inflación en el V Plan de la Nación (Economía y Ciencias Sociales [Universidad Central de Venezuela, Facultad de Ciencias Económicas y Sociales, Instituto de Investigaciones, Caracas] 18:3, julio/sept. 1979, p. 71–100, tables)

Examines fifth development plan of Venezuela in light of world inflationary trends, and their impact on country's economy. Believes that plan increases rather than diminishes changes for success in fighting inflation in Venezuela. Author's critical appraisal of Venezuelan planning is part of longer study of the nation's structural inflation.

Reyes Baena, Juan Francisco. Dependencia, desarrollo y educación. See item **4514.**

3360 Rivero M., Luis E. Los determinantes de la oferta monetaria venezolana. Mérida, Venezuela: Universidad de los Andes, Facultad de Economía, Instituto de Investigaciones Económicas, 1974. 101 p.: bibl., ill., tables.

Book's objective is to study money supply and its determinants in Venezuela (1950–69). Determines that, in the Venezuelan case, monetary policy is endogenous in a critical fashion, and discusses conduct of monetary policy during period.

3361 Rodríguez, Gumersindo. El nuevo modelo de desarrollo venezolano. Caracas: Ediciones Corpoconsult, 1979. 536 p.: bibl., tables.

Discusses economic and social framework which justified economic policies during the Carlos Andrés Pérez administration (1974–79) as well as the formulation of the Fifth National Plan. Evaluates results of these measures. Author was Minister of Planning in Pérez regime (1974–77) and his book is attempt to justify and explain planning decisions made and economic policies adopted at the time.

3362 Rodríguez, José Egidio. Necesidad de un nuevo periodismo económico. Prólogo, Héctor Mujica. Caracas: Ediciones Centauro, 1979. 193 p.: bibl. (Serie azul; no. 5)

Journalist stresses need to improve reporting and coverage of economic news in Venezuela. Discusses what elements should be included for economic news to be meaningful. Criticizes current presentation of such items in Venezuelan news reporting.

3363 Santos, Milton. Société et espace transnationalisés dans la Venezuela actuel (UP/TM, 21:84, Oct./Dec. 1980, p. 709–720, tables)

Geographer writes about Venezuelan regional development, noting the country's rapid growth, its modernization in last two decades, and profound socioeconomic changes that have occurred. Stresses concentration of population and important factors such as employment, income, industrial output, government expenditures, etc., over central axis of Caracas-Valencia and Maracaibo region.

3364 Silva Michelena, José A. La situation socio-économique du Venezuela (UP/TM, 21:84, oct./déc. 1980, p. 779–792)

Discusses socioeconomic and political history of Venezuela, and describes main characteristics of a system that, according to author, is presently engaged in a transnational economy.

3365 Sindicato UTIT. El papel de la contratación colectiva en la relación capital-trabajo (Economía y Ciencias Sociales [Universidad Central de Venezuela, Facultad de Ciencias Económicas y Sociales, Instituto de Investigaciones, Caracas] 18:3, julio/sept. 1979, p. 101–127)

Labor union position paper, written from Marxist perspective, on role of collective bargaining in chanelling labor-capital relations.

3366 Sines, Richard H. "Financial deepening" and industrial production: a microeconomic analysis of the Venezuelan food processing sector (UWI/SES, 28:2, June 1979, p. 450–474, bibl., tables)

Analyzes role of financial markets in determining efficiency of small firms in LDCs. Small unincorporated companies cannot invest in more productive technologies because of their more limited access to financial markets. Uses micro-econometric analysis of food processing industry in Venezuela to support conclusion.

3367 Sivesind, Erik J. Outlook on Venezuela's petroleum policy: a study prepared for the use of the Subcommittee on Energy of the Joint Economic Committee, Congress of the United States. Washington: US GPO, 1980. 111 p.: bibl., ill., tables.

Study by Library of Congress' Congressional Research Service requested by Joint Economic Committee of Congress. Provides background for US-Venezuela energy relations. Bases recommendation for changes in US policies on technical study of prospects for oil production in Venezuela into mid 1980s and on realization of past mistakes made by US government. Assumes continuation of world's energy shortage.

3368 Sonntag, Heinz R. and **Rafael de la Cruz.** Estado e industrialización en Venezuela (UNAM/RMS, 43:2, abril/junio 1981, p. 905–939)

Socioeconomic analysis of State's role in Venezuela's industrialization. Covers chiefly 1920–80 period, with references to 19th century. Authors trace interrelations between public sector, various private capital subsectors, and foreign capital. They believe that predominance of industrialization that became apparent in early 1950s, was fostered by the State since 1930s and was based on oil sector resources.

3369 Valencillos T., Héctor. Notas sobre la significación económico-revindicativa de las prácticas sindicales en Venezuela (Economía y Ciencias Sociales [Universidad Central de Venezuela, Facultad de Ciencias Económicas y Sociales, Instituto de Investigaciones, Caracas] 18 : 3, julio/sept. 1979, p. 27–48, tables)

On basis of hypothesis of labor market segmentation, author examines evolution of wages, employment and other related factors during 1960s and 1970s. Considers role of unions in achieving worker benefits in different segments of the labor market.

3370 Valery S., Rafael. Las comunidades petroleras. Caracas: Cuadernos Lagoven, 1980. 59 p., 11 p. of plates: bibl., ill. (some col.) (Cuadernos Lagoven)

Historical study of the development of oil communities in Venezuela. Shows impact of discovery of oil and of company activities on the environment. Illustrates how oil companies created their own towns.

3371 Venezuela. Oficina Central de Coordinación y Planificación. Venezuela, VI Plan de la Nación, 1981/1985: resumen. Caracas: Oficina Central de Coordinación y Planificación de la Presidencia de la República de Venezuela, 1981? 75 p., 7 leaves of plates: ill. (some col.), tables.

Summary of Sixth National Plan of Venezuela is divided into: 1) overview of country's socioeconomic developments during 1970–80 period; 2) definition of goals and strategies for 1980s and their planing period; 3) policy variables that will be used to comply with strategies and attain objectives; and 4) discussion of implementation of these policies through public sector projects and programs.

3372 ———. Oficina Central de Estadística e Informática. Encuesta industrial: resultados nacionales. Caracas: Presidencia de la República, Oficina Central de Estadística e Informática, 1976? 1 v.: tables.

Detailed tables from Sixth Industrial Survey of Venezuela, conducted in 1976.

3373 Venezuela, estadísticas de comercio exterior: importaciones, 1979. Montevideo: La Asociación Latinoamericana de Libre Comercio, 1981. 192 p. in various pagings: ill., tables (Serie B. Asociación Latinoamericana de Libre Comercio; no. 7)

Latest publication of statistical summaries of Venezuelan imports that LAFTA (Latin American Free Trade Association) has been publishing since early 1960s. This one refers to 1979, and has as its most important element intra-regional flows.

3374 Wilkins, Mira. Venezuelan investment in Florida: 1979 (LARR, 26 : 1, 1981, p. 156–165, tables)

Research report of Venezuelan investments in parts of Florida, principally Dade County. Uses information obtained through Agriculture Foreign Investment Disclosure Act, Federal Reserve, Comptroller of the Currency and Securities and Exchange Commission. Uses Florida case as example to illustrate the flight of capital from Venezuela.

3375 Zavala, D.F. Maza. Venezuela: coexistence de l'opulence et du dénuement: la difficile accumulation de l'excédent pétrolier (UP/TM, 21 : 84, oct./déc. 1980, p. 761–778, bibl., tables)

Blazing criticism of Venezuelan government use of petroleum export windfalls in 1970s. Also assails conduct of economic policy eventually as leading to fiscal deficits, high external debt, inflation, and economic stagnation. Draws a picture of sharp contrast between, on the one hand, the wealth of government sector, native capitalists and foreign investors, and on the other, the poverty of most Venezuelans.

CHILE AND PERU

MARKOS MAMALAKIS, *Professor of Economics, University of Wisconsin-Milwaukee*

CHILE: IN 1983, CHILE'S ECONOMIC, POLITICAL, and even social fabric began to fall apart under the impact of the worst economic depression on record. In an attempt to stem and possibly reverse the downward drift, Gen. Augusto Pinochet Ugarte tried four ministers of finance (De Castro, De la Cuadra, Lüders, and Cáceres) in less than 12 months and his government was forced to relinquish basic tenets of its 1973–81 free trade, free market, and private sector-based development strategy. The by now infamous fixed exchange rate of 1979 was scuttled in June 1983, private foreign capital inflows were stampeding out of Chile, foreign exchange controls were reinstated and by early 1983, panic and insolvency had crippled its financial system. The "economic miracle" of 1973–81, degenerated into the world's most self-inflicted disaster of 1982, by which time government and fiscal policy resumed their traditional role as protectors of national welfare and engines of growth.

No book or article annotated below contains a comprehensive review of these events and their underlying causes. However, publications of the Central Bank, the Planning Office and the Ministry of Finance are invaluable sources that explain the official point of view. Also, some publications issued by universities, research institutes, and individual academics are worth reading as they begin to expose some of the weaknesses that led to the partial collapse of Chile's free market experiment in 1982.

The following five publications stand out in terms of their insights or lasting contributions to Chilean historiography: 1) the latest edition of Encina's classic *Nuestra inferioridad económica* (item **3396**); 2) Isabel Heskia's study of income distribution (item **3401**); 3) vol. 7 of *Estudios Monetarios* of the Central Bank concerning financial policies (item **3377**); 4) O'Brien's study of the nitrate sector (item **3412**); and 5) vol. 3 of *Historical statistics of Chile: forestry and related activities* (item **3407**).

PERU: The literature on Peru is chiefly concerned with the return to political democracy and economic pluralism. Even though the ruling Belaúnde-Ulloa political movement strongly favors and largely follows a liberal path towards development, Peru's government never locked itself into a doctrinaire commitment to abstract economic principles such as the one that ruined Chile in 1982–83.

The majority of writings reviewed in this section reveal a profound disillusionment with Velasco Alvarado's Peruvian road to stagnation. A reaction to it is apparent in the number of books, articles, and documents that explore and advocate economic liberalism. However, the commanding theme of the large body of literature on the Peruvian economy is *land reform* regarded neither as an end in itself nor as a sufficient means for eradicating rural misery. A critical lesson drawn from the Velasco experiment is that agrarian reform (i.e., agricultural land, price, water, and investment reforms) can eliminate absolute poverty. However, what has not as yet been fully recognized is that agrarian reform will not guarantee overall rural prosperity. Only a comprehensive *rural reform*, that is the transformation and modernization of *all* rural activities, namely agricultural, industrial, mineral and service ones, can usher in lasting prosperity.

Among many excellent Peruvian publications, the following stand out: 1) the liberal treatise *Democracia & economía de mercado: ponencias y debates de un simposio* published by the Instituto Libertad y Democracia (item **3445**); Boggio's reference volume *El Perú minero: yacimientos* (item **3469**); 3) Witzel de Ciudad's analysis of the *Comunidad industrial* (item **3478**); 4) Oscar Ugarteche's edited work evaluating the Belaúnde-Ulloa development plan (item **3476**); 5) Shane Hunt's analysis of real wages in Peru, 1900–40 (item **3457**); and 6) the *Economía social de mercado* published by the Coloquio Peruano-Alemán (item **3440**).

Overall, the economic literature on Chile and Peru is of high quality and offers a balanced treatment of the production, income distribution, and capital formation structural features of these economies.

CHILE

3376 Arellano, José Pablo. Elementos para el análisis de la reforma de la previsión social chilena (FCE/TE, 49[3]:195, julio/sept. 1982, p. 563–605, bibl., tables)

Very important examination of Chile's social security system.

3377 Banco Central de Chile. Dirección de Política Financiera. Alternativas de políticas financieras en economías pequeñas y abiertas al exterior: seminario realizado por el Banco Central de Chile, los días 21 y 22 de enero de 1980. Santiago: 1981. 192 p.: tables (Estudios monetarios; 7)

Chilean economic policies (1973–83) have not as yet been either adequately understood or thoroughly analyzed. Articles by McKinnon, Frenkel, Harberger, and Edwards published in this volume provide many important insights into theoretical and practical issues raised by the 1973–83 "free" market experiment.

3378 Bravo, Juan Alfonso. Inversiones norteamericanas en Chile: 1904-1907 (UNAM/RMS, 43:2, abril/junio 1981, p. 775–818, table)

Very solid examination of North American investments in Chile during 1904–07.

3379 Carkovíc S., Maruja. Estabilidad de la demanda por dinero en Chile: período 1947 a 1970 (UCC/CE, 18:53, abril 1981, p. 65–87, bibl., graphs, tables)

Very careful examination of money demand in Chile (1953–56).

3380 Carrière, Jean. Los terratenientes organizados y la modernización capi-
talista de la agricultura: comentarios teóricos y un estudio del caso chileno (*in* El sector agrario en América Latina: estructura económica y cambio social [see item **2948**] p. 82–107, tables)

Fascinating article analyzes role of Chile's National Society of Agriculture in defending the sector's interests. Author presents ample evidence in support of Mamalakis' theory of sectoral clashes between agriculture and industry. Carrière attributes Chile's sectoral clashes to the contradictions of dependent industrial capitalism in a small peripheral economy.

3381 Cauas Lama, Jorge and **Alvaro Saieh B.** Política económica, 1973–1979. Santiago: Departamento de Informaciones Económicas y Estadísticas del Banco Central de Chile, 1979. 17 p.

Review of Chile's economic policy (1973–79) by two members of the "Chicago boys" team that formulated and implemented it.

3382 Cereceda, Luz Eugenia and **Fernando Dahse.** Dos décadas de cambios en el agro chileno. Santiago: Pontificia Universidad Católica de Chile, Instituto de Sociología, 1980. 170 p.: tables (Cuadernos del Instituto de Sociología; 2)

Examination of changes and tendencies in the Chilean agricultural system during past two decades. Detects trends towards homogenization of rural markets.

3383 Chile. Comisión Nacional de Energía. Balance de energía, 1961–1980. Santiago: La Comisión, 1982. 187 p.: col. ill.

Comprehensive survey of Chile's

energy sector.

3384 ——. **Ministerio del Interior.** Programa Socio-Económico, 1981–1989. Santiago: El Ministerio, 1981. 54 p.

Outline of social and economic plans of the government of Gen. Pinochet for 1981–89 period.

3385 ——. **Presidencia. Oficina de Planificación Nacional (ODEPLAN).** Informe económico anual, 1977. Santiago: 1978? 134 leaves: tables.

Broad governmental review of Chilean economic development (1974–77).

3386 **Chile, liberalismo económico y dictadura política.** Sergio Bitar, compilador, *et al.* Lima: Instituto de Estudios Peruanos, 1980. 181 p.: bibl. (América problema; 11)

Collection of essays subjects Chile's 1974–79 free market experiment to a critique from the left.

3387 **Chilean economic and social development, 1973–1979.** Santiago: National Planning Office, ODEPLAN, 1981. 91 p.: ill.

Government view of Chilean development (1973–79).

3388 **Chilean external debt, 1979.** Santiago: Central Bank of Chile, 1980. 42 p., 5 leaves of plates: col. ill.

Detailed examination of Chile's external debt (1960–79).

3389 **Chonchol, Jacques.** Organización económica y social del sector reformado durante el gobierno de la Unidad Popular (*in* El sector agrario en América Latina: estructura económica y cambio social [see item **2948**] p. 67–81)

Lucid and accurate presentation of the social and economic organization of the reformed agricultural sector during the Popular Unity Government of Salvador Allende.

3390 ——. El sistema burocrático: instrumento y obstáculo en el proceso de reforma agraria chileno (NOSALF/IA, 7/8:2/1, 1978, p. 55–67)

In this excellent article, Salvador Allende's ex-Minister of Agriculture describes difficulties encountered trying to make the bureaucracy serve the farmers' interests.

3391 **Cordo, Vittorio** and **Patricio Meller.** Alternative trade strategies and employment implications: Chile (*in* Trade and employment in developing countries. v. 1, Individual studies. Edited by Anne O. Krueger *et al.* Chicago: University of Chicago Press, 1981, p. 83–134, bibl., tables)

Examination of impact of alternative trade strategies on Chilean employment.

3392 —— and ——. Sustitución de importaciones, promoción de exportación y empleo: el caso chileno (FCE/TE, 48[1]:189, enero/marzo 1981, p. 157–196, tables)

Careful examination of impact of import substitution and export promotion on employment in Chile.

3393 **Cuentas nacionales de Chile, 1960–1980.** Santiago: Dirección de Política Financiera, Banco Central de Chile, 1982. 122 p.: col. ill., tables.

Comprehensive set of Chile's new national accounts estimates.

3394 **Desarrollo energético en América Latina y la economía mundial.** Trabajos presentados al Seminario sobre los Factores Internacionales del Desarrollo Energético, organizado por el Instituto de Estudios Internacionales de la Universidad de Chile entre el 7 y el 9 de noviembre de 1979. Obra editada bajo la dirección de Heraldo Muñoz. Santiago: Universidad de Chile, Instituto de Estudios Internacionales, 1980. 245 p.: bibl., ill. (Estudios internacionales)

Papers (in English and Spanish) presented to late 1979 seminar. Covers scattered range of topics with considerable attention to macro-problems and to Chile. [J.M. Hunter]

3395 **La Economía campesina chilena.** E. Boeninger *et al.* Editor, Hugo Ortega. Santiago: Editorial Aconcagua, 1981. 185 p.: bibl., tables (Colección Lautaro)

Six short essays on rural Chile attempt to formulate a base for rural development.

3396 **Encina, Francisco Antonio.** Nuestra inferioridad económica: sus causas, sus consecuencias. 4. ed. Santiago: Editorial Universidad, 1978. 245 p. (Colección Imagen de Chile)

This classic study (4th ed.) by Francisco Encina is a must for anyone interested in Chile.

3397 **Espinosa, Juan G.** and **Andrew S. Zimbalist.** Economic democracy: workers' participation in Chilean industry, 1970–1983. New York: Academic Press,

1981. 211 p.: bibl., index, tables (Studies in social discontinuity)

Examination of workers; participation in Chilean industry during the Allende presidency.

3398 Fazio, Hugo and **Pedro Felipe Ramírez.** El carácter de la política económica de la Junta Militar. México: Casa de Chile en México, 1981. 54 p.: bibl. (Cuadernos Casa de Chile; no. 7)

Marxist critical review of Chilean economic policies (1973–76).

3399 Ffrench-Davis, Ricardo. Exportaciones e industrialización en un modelo ortodoxo: Chile, 1973–1978 (NOSALF/IA, 8/9:1/2, 1980, p. 7–35, tables)

Ffrench-Davis correctly argues that Chilean economic policy during 1973–78 was successful in promoting nontraditional exports but failed to create new productive capacity or generate employment.

3400 Foxley, Alejandro. Inflación con recesión: las experiencias del Brasil y Chile (FCE/TE, 47[4]:188, oct./dic. 1980, p. 919–979, tables)

This comparative analysis of price stabilization through orthodox means in Brazil (1964–66) and Chile (1973–77) is full of useful insights concerning major developmental issues. For English version of this article, see *World Development* (Oxford, UK, 8:1, Nov. 1980, p. 887–912).

3401 Heskia, Isabel. Distribución del ingreso en el Gran Santiago, 1957–1979. Santiago: Departamento de Economía, Universidad de Chile, 1980. 223, 12 p.: tables (Documentos Serie Investigación; no. 53)

Heskia, one of Chile's best economists, has produced here an excellent study of income distribution in Greater Santiago (1957–79). Hopefully, she will publish a more comprehensive study for all of Chile.

3402 Huerta de Pacheco, María Antonieta. Reforma agraria chilena 1938–1978: evaluación histórica (PUJ/UH, 11, dic. 1979, p. 159–188, bibl.)

Descriptive account of various phases of agrarian reform in Chile.

3403 Illanes Benítez, Fernando. Política económica y desarrollo. Santiago: Editorial Jurídica de Chile, 1979. 382 p.: bibl.

Comparative study of economic development policies for university students and the general public.

3404 Kay, Cristóbal. Política económica, alianza de clases y cambios agrarios en Chile (PUCP/E, 3:5, junio 1980, p. 125–160)

Long-term examination of agrarian change and economic policy in Chile. Argues that because Chilean working class is unwilling to accept bourgeois democracy, only alternatives are dictatorship or socialism.

3405 Lasaga, Manuel. The copper industry in the Chilean economy: an econometric analysis. Lexington, Mass.: Lexington Books, 1981. 198 p.: bibl., index, tables (The Wharton econometric studies series)

In this solid study, Lasaga specifies a detailed econometric model that incorporates direct as well as indirect linkages to the copper sector. By using model to analyze various copper scenarios, author establishes a basis for the formulation of copper policy recommendations.

3406 Lavados M., Ivan and **Sergio Montenegro A.** Evolución de la cooperación técnica internacional en Chile (CPU/ES, 24:2, 1980, p. 77–134)

Analyzes evolution of international technical cooperation in Chile, important modifications achieved therein, and how it has been strongly influenced by prevailing development ideologies and role of science and technology.

3407 Mamalakis, Markos J. Historical statistics of Chile. v. 3, Forestry and related activities. Westport, Conn.: Greenwood Press, 1982. 443 p.: bibl., tables.

Comprehensive presentation, review and analysis of quantitative and qualitative historical evidence of Chile's forestry, forestry-based industry and forestry-related services (for vols. 1/2, see *HLAS 41:3229* and *HLAS 43:3473*).

3408 Marshall Lagarrigue, Isabel. Políticas de acción en el mercado del cobre: análisis y evaluación. Santiago: Pontificia Universidad Católica de Chile, Instituto de Economía, Oficina de Publicaciones, 1980. 399 p.: bibl., ill., tables (Documento de trabajo; no. 68)

Systematic, thorough examination of Chile's copper sector. Presents different action courses to increase and stabilize returned value from copper.

3409 Meller, Patricio; René Cortázar; and

Jorge Marshall. Employment stagnation in Chile: 1974–1978 (LARR, 16:2, 1981, p. 144–155, tables)

By including alternative sources of information in their analysis, authors show that increase in employment in Chile is "practically nil" contrary to that country's official reports.

3410 Méndez G., Juan Carlos. Panorama socio-económico de Chile. Santiago: Impresora Printer, 1980. 165 p.: bibl.

Document provides many major philosophical, theoretical, and empirical foundations for Chile free market experiment.

3411 Monardes T., Alfonso. El empleo en la pequeña agricultura: un estudio del Valle Central de Chile. Santiago: Universidad de Chile, Departamento de Economía, 1979. 176 p.: bibl., tables (Publicación del Departamento de Economía; no. 72)

Analysis of employment and underemployment in small-scale farming in Chile.

3412 O'Brien, Thomas F. The nitrate industry and Chile's crucial transition, 1870–1891. New York: New York University Press, 1982. 211 p.: bibl., index, tables.

In this excellent study, O'Brien makes a significant contribution to Chilean historiography by explaining causes, patterns, and effects of dependency. His extremely scholarly, synthetic, and evidence-oriented approach leads to a balanced presentation of Chile's relationship to the nitrate industry (1870–91).

3413 Ominami, Carlos. Un nouveau type de financement extérieur pour un nouveau modèle de croissance: un exemple, le Chili, 1974–1979 (FDD/NED [roblèmes d'Amérique Latine, 60] 4599/4600, 31 déc. 1980, p. 102–127, tables)

Excellent treatment of foreign capital inflows into Chile during 1970–78.

Oppenheimer, Robert. Chile's Central Valley railroads and economic development in the nineteenth century. See *HLAS 44:3100.*

———. National capital and national development: financing Chile's Central Valley railroads. See *HLAS 44:3101.*

Ortega, Luis. Acerca de los orígenes de la industrialización chilena, 1860–1879. See *HLAS 44:3102.*

———. The first four decades of the Chilean

coal mining industry, 1840-1879. See *HLAS 44:3103.*

3414 Ossa, Fernando José. La balanza de pagos: aspectos contables. Santiago: Pontificia Universidad Católica de Chile, Instituto de Economía, Oficina de Publicaciones, 1980. 37 leaves: bibl., tables (Trabajo docente; no. 29)

Explanation of economic transactions (balance of payments) of Chile with rest of world (1960–79).

3415 Passicot, Andrés and **Julio Acevedo.** Indicadores económicos de corto plazo. Editores, Fernando Contreras A., Elsa Valladares O. Santiago: Oficina de Planificación Nacional (ODEPLAN): Universidad de Chile, Facultad de Ciencias Económicas y Administrativas, Departamento de Economía, 1975. 126 p.: appendix, forms, ill. (Publicación del Departamento de Economía; no. 21)

Review and analysis of short-term macroeconomic indicators.

3416 Pinto S.C., Aníbal. El modelo ortodoxo y el desarrollo nacional (FCE/TE, 48[4]:1982, oct./dic. 1981, p. 853–902, tables)

Lucid treatment of origin and effects of Chile's orthodox economic policies during 1973–80.

3417 Pizarro C., Crisóstomo. Políticas públicas y grupos de presión en Chile, 1965–1970: un análisis exploratorio. Santiago: Corporación de Investigaciones Económicas para Latinoamérica, 1978. 35 p.: bib., tables (Estudios CIEPLAN; 26)

Careful analysis of the relationship between public policy and pressure groups in Chile during 1965–70.

3418 Portales, Diego. Heterogeneidad industrial en la prensa de Santiago de Chile. México: Instituto Latinoamericano de Estudios Transnacionales, 197? 64, 29 leaves.

Examines highly heterogeneous press of Santiago in a novel, thoroughly empirical manner.

Pregger Román, Charles, G. Economic interest groups within the Chilean government, 1851 to 1891: continuity and discontinuity in economic and political evolution. See *HLAS 44:3109.*

3419 Progama Regional del Empleo para América Latina y el Caribe (PREALC). Antecedentes sobre el trabajo de los menores en Chile. Prepared by María de la Luz Silva. Santiago: Organización Internacional del Trabajo, Programa Mundial del Empleo, Programa Regional del Empleo para América Latina y el Caribe (PREALC), 1978. 43 leaves: bibl., tables (Documento de trabajo PREALC; 163)

Analysis of employment of miners in Chile.

3420 ———. Efecto ocupacional de la política de subsidio a la contratación adicional de mano de obra en Chile. Prepared by Jorge Tamblay. Santiago: Organización Internacional del Trabajo, Programa Mundial del Empleo, Programa Regional del Empleo para América Latina y el Caribe (PREALC), 1979. 81 leaves: bibl., graphs (Monografía PREALC; 14)

Analysis of formulation, application and effectiveness of the Chilean government's efforts to reduce unemployment by subsidizing hiring of additional labor.

3421 ———. Efectos de la política de comercio exterior sobre el empleo en algunas ramas industriales: Chile, período 1974–1977. Prepared by Pablo Wilson. Santiago: Organización Internacional del Trabajo, Programa Mundial del Empleo, Programa Regional del Empleo para América Latina y el Caribe (PREALC), 1979. 92 leaves: bibl., graphs, tables (Monografía PREALC; 12)

Analysis of foreign trade policies utilized in Chile since 1973 and their effects on employment.

3422 ———. El plan de empleo mínimo en Chile. Prepared by Roberto Urmeneta. Santiago: Organización Internacional del Trabajo, Programa Mundial del Empleo, Programa Regional del Empleo para América Latina y el Caribe (PREALC), 1979. 87 leaves: bibl., tables (Monografía PREALC; 13)

Informative treatment of Chile's minimum employment program (1975–78).

3423 ———. Los trabajadores por cuenta propia en Santiago. Prepared by Alois Möller. Santiago: Organización Internacional del Trabajo, Programa Mundial del Empleo, Programa Regional del Empleo para América Latina y el Caribe (PREALC),1980. 199 p.: tables (Documento de trabajo PREALC; 184)

Very informative study of the self-employed in Santiago.

3424 Reyes, F. Armando. A guide to the spreading and analysis of Chilean bank statements. Philadelphia, Pa.: Robert Morris Associates, 1982. 60 p.: forms.

Short but useful introduction to Chile's financial system in effect in 1981.

3425 Silva, Ricardo. Inflación reprimida en Chile: el período 1970–1973 (UCC/CE, 18:53, abril 1981, p. 97–106, graphs, tables)

Solid examination of repressed inflation in Chile (1970–75).

3426 Solimano, Andrés. Composición factorial de exportaciones para filiales de empresas multinacionales. Santiago: Pontificia Universidad Católica de Chile, Instituto de Economía, 1980. 122 p.: bibl., tables (Documento de trabajo; no. 67)

Author undertakes empirical and theoretical analysis of factorial composition of exported goods of multinational businesses.

3427 Uthoff, András B. Distribución del ingreso familiar según características de jefe, Gran Santiago, 1969 (ECIEL, 5, julio 1978, p. 106–130, tables)

First rate analysis of distribution of family income in Greater Santiago, Chile, in terms of education and employment of head of family.

PERU

3428 Alcántara, Elsa. La seguridad social en el Perú: revisión y ampliación de los trabajos presentados al Seminario sobre Seguridad Social en el Grupo Andino. Lima: Centro Latinoamericana de Trabajo Social, 1979. 40 p., 20 p. of plates: ill. (Cuadernos Celats; no. 20)

Presents orderly and systematic description of history of social security in Peru.

3429 Amat y León Ch., Carlos; Héctor León Hinostroza; and Luis Monroy Rojas. La desigualdad interior en el Perú. Lima: Centro de Investigación de la Universidad del Pacífico, 1981. 40 p., 5 fold. leaves, 1 leaf of plates: ill.

In effort to remove widespread rural poverty, authors develop a methodology for identifying basic needs of deprived rural groups. They also suggest corrective policies.

3430 Angell, Alan and Rosemary Thorp. Inflation, stabilization and attempted re-democratization in Peru, 1975–1979 (WD, 8:11, Nov. 1980, p. 865–886, bibl., tables)

Careful examination of major economic events in Peru (1975–79).

3431 Aramburú, Clemencia and Carlos Monge. Cronología agraria, 1980. Cusco, Perú: Centro de Estudios Rurales Andinos Bartolomé de Las Casas, 1981. 329 p.: bibl., ill.

Day-by-day account of agricultural events in 1980 arranged in chronological order and grouped according to subthemes important to Peruvian agriculture.

3432 Asentamientos humanos. Colegio de Arquitectos del Perú. México: Fundación de las Naciones Unidas para el Hábitat y los Asentamientos Humanos, 1978. 64 p.

General, solid review of Peru's housing problem.

3433 Barreto, Emilio G. Perú: los desarrollos económicos y financieros, 1970–1980. Lima: Talleres Gráficos de Editorial Andina, 1980. 368 p.

Systematic analysis of Peru's economic and financial situation (1970–80).

3434 Bellido Sánchez, Alberto. Aspectos tributarios vinculados con las empresas asociativas del sector agrario peruano. Lima: Universidad Nacional Agraria, Taller de Coyuntura Agraria, Centro de Investigaciones Socio-Económicas, 1979. 54 p.: bibl., tables.

Review of taxation system of Peru's cooperative farms.

3435 Biesinger, Brigitte. Der Bergbausektor im peruanischen Reformprozess, 1968–1975. Heidelberg: Esprint, 1981. 163 p.: bibl., tables (Heidelberger Dritte Welt Studien; Bd. 9)

In this analysis of mining during Peru's 1968–75 reform process (the third route to development), Biesinger correctly argues that the only road to less dependency is elimination of internal structural defects.

3436 Billone, Jorge; Daniel Carbonetto; and Daniel Martínez. Términos de intercambio ciudad-campo, 1970–1980: precios y excedente agrícola. Lima: Centro de Estudios para el Desarrollo y la Participación, 1982. 96 p.: ill. (Serie Desarrollo rural)

Examines Peru's agricultural terms of trade during 1970–80. Recommends more government intervention in all facets of rural life.

3437 Caballero, José María. Economía agraria de la sierra peruana antes de la reforma agraria de 1969. Lima: Instituto de Estudios Peruanos, 1981. 426 p.: ill., tables (Estudios de la sociedad rural; 7)

Lengthy review of agrarian economy of Peruvian highlands prior to 1969.

3438 Centro Nacional de Capacitación e Investigación para la Reforma Agraria (CENCIRA). Diagnóstico microregional de Huancavelica. Lima: 1980. 300 p.: bibl., ill., tables.

Detailed and thorough multidisciplinary micro-regional study of Huancavelica Dept. Analyzes region's extreme rural poverty and proposes solutions.

3439 CERTEX: resultados y alternativas. Lima: Universidad del Pacífico, Centro de Investigación: Fundación Friedrich Ebert-Stiftung, 1980. 451 p.: appendix, ill., tables.

Excellent description and analysis of Peru's policy of promoting non-traditional exports through tax incentives (CERTEX).

3440 Coloquio Peruano-Alemán, *Lima, 1979.* Economía social de mercado. Organizado en Lima durante los días 29 y 30 de junio y 1° de julio de 1979, con el apoyo de la Fundación Konrad Adenauer. Lima: Cámara de Comercio de Industria Peruano-Alemana, 1980. 435 p.: bibl., tables.

Excellent treatment of social market economy from a Peruvian perspective.

3441 Couriel, Alberto. Estado, estrategia de desarrollo y necesidades básicas en el Perú. Lima: DESCO, 1981. 222 p.: bibl., tables.

Solid, balanced review of Peruvian economic development (1968–77).

3442 Crisis económica y democracia: a propósito de la exposición del Primer Ministro Manuel Ulloa, 27-VIII-80. Oscar Ugarteche *et al.* Lima: Instituto de Estudios Peruanos, 1980. 93 p.: bibl., ill., tables.

Evaluation of the Belaúnde-Ulloa plan for Peruvian development.

3443 Cuentas nacionales del Perú, 1950–1980. Lima: Instituto Nacional de Estadística, Dirección General de Cuentas Nacionales, 1981. 129 p.: tables.

Comprehensive collection of Peruvian national accounts statistics for 1950–80 period.

3444 Dammert, Alfredo. Economía minera. Lima: Universidad del Pacífico, Centro de Investigación, 1981. 159 p.: ill. (Cuadernos)

Describes and analyzes Peruvian mining industry and its relationship to the international market.

3445 Democracia & economía de mercado: ponencias y debates en un simposio. San Isidro, Perú: Instituto Libertad y Democracia, 1981. 436 p., 16 p. of plates: ill.

Powerful collection of papers and comments by such distinguished liberals as Von Hayek, Jean François Revel, and others, presented at a symposium on democracy and the market economy.

3446 Descentralización financiera y políticas de desarrollo regional. Seminario realizado por el CIESUL el 23 y 24 de octubre de 1980. Lima: Universidad de Lima, Centro de Investigaciones Económicas y Sociales, 1981. 140 p.: bibl., tables (Serie Seminarios; no. 1)

Authors discuss processes of financial decentralization and regional development paying particular attention to role of banking institutions. Includes section devoted to authors' questions, answers, and comments.

3447 Economía peruana: ¿hacia dónde? Amat y León et al. Guido Pennano, editor. Lima: Universidad del Pacífico, Centro de Investigación, 1981. 192 p.: bibl., tables.

Edited volume contains diverse opinions and ideas relating to the Peruvian economy.

3448 Estrategias y políticas de industrialización. Proceedings of Seminario sobre Estrategias y Políticas de Industrialización, held 18–22 Aug. 1981. Sánchez Albavera et al. Lima: Centro de Estudios y Promoción del Desarrollo (DESCO), 1981. 492 p.: bibl., ill., tables.

Economists of diverse backgrounds comment on industrialization.

3449 Fernández-Baca, Jorge; Fernando González Vigil; and Félix Portocarrero Maisch. El complejo automotor en Perú. México: Instituto Latinoamericano de Estudios Transnacionales, 1979. 3 v.: tables (mimeo)

This is a comprehensive and thorough study of Peru's automotive industry. Mimeographed.

3450 Ferrand Inurritegui, Alfredo and **Arturo Salazar Larraín.** La década perdida. Lima: Sociedad de Industria, 1980. 112 p.: bibl., graphs, tables.

Harsh criticism of socialism in Peru describes its negative effects.

3451 Geng T., Luis. Consumo histórico de derivados del petróleo: alternativas futuras. Lima: Universidad de Lima, Centro de Investigaciones Económicas y Sociales, 1981. 118 p.: ill., tables.

Solid historical analysis of the demand for petroleum and petroleum products in Peru. Attempts to estimate future demand of this nonrenewable resource in order to determine its most efficient use.

3452 González Vigil, Fernando; Carlos Parodi Zevallos; and Fabián Tume Torres. Alimentos y transnacionales: los complejos sectoriales del trigo y avícola en el Perú. Lima: Centro de Eetudios y Promoción del Desarrollo (DESCO), 1980. 286 p.: bibl., ill., tables.

Authors analyze effects of international capitalist system on food-producing industries at both the global and national levels noting how it affects the Peruvian economy. Also describes ways in which food resources are used to apply political pressure at an international level (for anthropologist's comment, see item **1809**).

3453 ——; ——; and ——. El complejo sectorial lácteo en el Perú. México: Instituto Latinoamericano de Estudios Transnacionales, 1979. 3 v. (325 leaves): bibl., ill., tables.

Excellent review and analysis of Peru's dairy products complex.

3454 Gordon, Dennis R. The Andean auto program and Peruvian development: a preliminary assessment (JDA, 16:2, Jan. 1982, p. 233–248, tables)

Carefully examines relationship between Peru's auto program and the mystique of industrialization.

3455 ——. Developmental nationalism and international finance: Peru and the IMF (PCCLAS/P, 8, 1981/1982, p. 93–107)

According to Gordon, IMF has become the primary instrument of advanced capitalist states to influence policies of less developed ones. Examines only selective aspects of this old but provocative thesis. As author himself admits, his critique is in the spirit of "muckraking and informational activity" (p. 93).

3456 Hopkins, Raúl. Desarrollo desigual y crisis en la agricultura peruana, 1944–1969. Lima: Instituto de Estudios Peruanos, 1981. 209 p.: ill., tables (Estudios de la sociedad rural; 9)

Highly informative, panoramic examination of the performance of Peruvian agriculture (1944–69).

3457 Hunt, Shane. Evolución de los salarios reales en el Perú: 1900–1940 (PUCP/E, 3:5, junio 1980, p. 83–123, tables)

Excellent analysis of the evolution of real wages in the capitalist and traditional sectors of Peru (1900–40).

3458 Kay, Cristóbal. Achievements and contradictions of the Peruvian agrarian reform (JDS, 18:2, Jan. 1982, p. 141–170, bibl.)

In this excellent review of the Peruvian agrarian reform, Kay correctly concludes that rural development can be achieved only through land reform plus proper price, marketing, credit, and investment policies.

3459 Kuczynski, Pedro-Pablo. The Peruvian external debt: problem and prospect (SAGE/JIAS, 23:1, Feb. 1981, p. 3–28, tables)

Outstanding article on Peru's foreign debt problem examines it within and relates it to the nation's economic structure.

3460 Laite, Julian. Industrial development and migrant labour in Latin America. Austin: University of Texas Press, 1981. 229 p.: bibl., ill., indexes, tables (The Texas Pan American series)

Examines idiosyncratic features of migration and industrialization in Peru.

3461 Maletta, Héctor and **Jesús Foronda.** La acumulación de capital en la agricultura peruana. Lima: Universidad del Pacífico, Centro de Investigación, 1980. 267 p.: bibl., tables (Serie Cuadernos. Trabajo de investigación; no. 11)

Excellent discussion of capital accumulation in Peruvian agriculture.

3462 Martínez, Daniel and **Armando**

Tealdo. El agro peruano, 1970–1980: análisis y perspectivas. Lima: Centro de Estudios para el Desarrollo y la Participación, 1982. 187 p.: ill., tables (Serie Desarrollo rural)

The 1970–76 agrarian reform did not solve the problems of rural Peru. This extremely careful and comprehensive analysis of the agro-rural sector reveals the complexity of its development process.

3463 Ogata Schmokawa, Clara. Políticas explícitas de tratamiento al capital extranjero en el Perú. Lima: Centro de Estudios y Promoción del Desarrollo (DESCO), 1981. 93 p. (Serie Publicaciones previas; 1)

Pragmatic review of Peru's treatment of foreign capital during 1970–80.

3464 Pinto, Aníbal and **Héctor Assael.** Perú, 1968–1977: la política económica en un proceso de cambio global. Santiago: Naciones Unidas, 1981. 166 p.: bibl., ill., tables (Estudios e informes de la CEPAL; 2)

Lucid structuralist analysis of economic policy in Peru (1968–77).

3465 Pinzas García, Teobaldo. La economía peruana, 1950–1978: un ensayo bibliográfico. Lima: Instituto de Estudios Peruanos, 1981. 156 p.: tables (Análisis económico; 4)

Provides careful examination of role of exports, industrialization and the State in shaping Peruvian development.

3466 Problemática de la producción y comercialización del trigo en el Perú. Lima: Centro Nacional de Capacitación e Investigación para la Reforma Agraria, Dirección de Investigación, 1980. 141 p.: bibl., ill., tables.

Systematic, empirical review and analysis of wheat production and commercialization in Peru (1960–75).

3467 Programa Regional del Empleo para América Latina y el Caribe (PREALC). Perú, estrategia de desarrollo y grado de satisfacción de las necesidades básicas. Prepared by Alberto Couriel. Santiago: Organización Internacional del Trabajo, Programa Mundial del Empleo para América Latina y el Caribe (PREALC), 1978. 231 p.; bibl., graphs; tables (Documentos de trabajo PREALC; 127)

Examination of the satisfaction of Peru's basic needs.

3468 Rodríguez Campos, Orestes; Carlos Capuñay Mimbela; and Félix Merino Landakay. Ensayos económicos. Análisis del presupuesto del sector público para 1980. La economía y las finanzas públicas en la nueva Constitución. Lima: Universidad Nacional Federico Villareal, Vice-Rectorado, Dirección Universitaria de Investigación, 1980. 27 p.: tables.

These two essays discuss the public sector budget for 1980 and evaluate Peru's new Constitution of 1979. Second article states that the "social market economy" principles of the new Constitution are either incomplete or inconsistent with the ideas of Raúl Haya de la Torre and should be reformed.

3469 Samamé Boggio, Mario. El Perú minero. v. 4, Yacimientos. Lima: INCITEMI, 1980. 992 p.: maps, tables.

Excellent geological reference treatise on Peru's mining bed (for historian's comments on vols. 1/2, see *HLAS 44:2980*).

3470 Sánchez Albavera, Fernando. Minería, capital transnacional y poder en el Perú. Lima: Centro de Estudios y Promoción del Desarrollo, 1981. 412 p.: ill., tables (Serie Estudios)

Analysis of Peruvian mining industry, its structure, development and role in the world market.

3471 Saulniers, Alfred H. ENCI: Peru's bandied monopolist (SAGE/JIAS, 22:4, Nov. 1980, p. 441–462, tables)

Excellent analysis of Peru's public National Enterprise for the Commercialization of Inputs. Extremely valuable for understanding how the public sector functions.

3472 Schydlowsky, Daniel M.; Jorge González Izquierdo; and Roberto Abusada-Salah. Propuestas para el desarrollo peruano, 1980–1985. Lima: Asociación de Exportadores, 1980. 98 p.: tables.

Includes three sets of recommendations for achieving economic development in Peru.

3473 Scott, C.D. Agrarian reform and seasonal employment in coastal Peruvian agriculture (JDS, 17:4, July 1981, p. 282–306, bibl., graphs, tables)

Excellent treatment of seasonal employment in three coastal valleys of Peru.

3474 Scurrah, Martin J. El empleo intelectual en el Perú: el sobre-empleo de la minoría y el subempleo de la mayoría (UP/A, 7:12, 1982, p. 19–31, bibl., tables)

Carefully examines facts of over-employment of a minority and underemployment of the majority of Peru's intellectual.

3475 Susano Lucero, Aurelio Reynaldo. La concentración bancaria: análisis de la desigual competencia entre bancos en el Perú. Lima: Universidad de Lima, Centro de Investigaciones Económicas y Sociales, 1980. 114 p.: bibl., ill. (mimeo) (Serie Investigaciones; no. 3)

Essay deserves special mention because it deals with the neglected topic of competition in Peru's banking system. Mimeographed.

3476 Ugarteche, Oscar. Teoría y práctica de la deuda externa en el Perú. Lima: Instituto de Estudios Peruanos, 1980. 167 p.: bibl., ill., tables (Colección mínima; 11)

Systematic review of interrelationship between external debt, international banks and Peru's institutional structure.

3477 Webb, Richard. Tendencias del ingreso real en el Perú, 1950–1966 (PUCP/E, 2:4, dic. 1979, p. 147–218, tables)

Excellent analysis of real income trends in Peru (1950–66) is part of author's prize-winning Harvard PhD dissertation.

3478 Witzel de Ciudad, Renate. Die peruanishe Unternehmensreform in Industriesektor: zur ökonomischenund politischen Bedeutung der "Comunidad industrial" für den globalen Reformprozess 1970–1977. Heidelberg: Esprint-Verlag, 1981. 303 p.: bibl., tablesd (Heidelberger Dritte Welt Studien; Bd. 2)

In this fascinating analysis of Peruvian industrial communities, author shows how industrial reform benefitted the already well-to-do workers and was accepted by large firms while it did very little for the underprivileged workers and was fought by medium and small enterprises.

BOLIVIA, PARAGUAY, AND URUGUAY

STEPHEN M. SMITH, *Associate Professor of Agricultural Economics, University of Idaho*

ALTHOUGH THE GENERAL CHARACTERISTICS NOTED for the economic literature on Bolivia, Paraguay, and Uruguay in *HLAS 41* and *HLAS 43* are still evident in this volume, a number of different themes are apparent as well. The continuing characteristics are: 1) lack of scholarly analytical work originating within all three countries; 2) numerous non-controversial government and semiofficial studies of a descriptive nature; and 3) statistical publications. The emerging issues are: 1) women's participation in the labor market and their role in the economy; 2) concern over rising foreign debts; 3) foreign trade; and 4) criticism of current and recent economic policies. Most of these works are by scholars residing outside their respective countries (exiles), buttressed by foreign researchers.

BOLIVIA: A noteworthy feature of its literature is the criticism and analysis of past government policies and of the nationalized mining sector. The attack by Ramos Sánchez (item **3495**) on the economic policies of the Banzer military government is interesting, and would not have appeared while that government was in power. The PREALC study (item **3494**) and the Musgrave report (item **3492**) provide valuable perspectives on the 1976–80 economic plan and offer suggestions for future policy directions. A popular subject for Bolivian authors continues to be the mining sector. Beyond descriptions of its various aspects, the studies by Ruiz González (item **3498**) and Canelas Orellana (item **3484**) examine the failure of the nationalized mines to contribute to the economy as expected and required. These authors reach similar conclusions by noting that upper and middle management, along with government meddling, are at the roots of the problem. Bolivian statistics also register an improvement in depth, breadth, and quality, with more of them available by department and for urban areas. Much of this data is drawn from the 1976 *Census of population and housing* (see *HLAS 43 : 3573*).

PARAGUAY: Its economic literature is scarce with very little being generated within the country and that which is, being of little research value. Pleasant exceptions are several critical/analytical publications that focus on the economy and economic policies, written by Paraguayan nationals living abroad and by foreign scholars. Required initial reading is the World Bank Country Study, covering Paraguay's economy in the 1970s (item **3500**). Much of the other work centers around the Itaipú and Yacyretá hydroelectric developments and their impacts. One result of these developments appears to be an opening of the economy and society, a trend that should lead to more information and research. I rank the Julia Carísimo Báez article (item **3503**) as the best, but good and valuable complements are those by Rodríguez Silvero (items **3510–3511**), Nickson (item **3507**), and Canese (item **3502**). Women's participation in Paraguay's workforce is examined in a book by Galeano containing seven studies (item **3506**), and in two analyses of secondary data (items **3513** and **3515**).

URUGUAY: As noted in *HLAS 43*, the trend is to concentrate on the economic history of the country and neglect the period since 1973, (see *HLAS 43*, p. 351–352). However, articles annotated below reflect a change. The Anichini *et al.* (item **3517**) and Barbato de Silva (item **3518**) publications present a noncontroversial, government viewpoint whereas articles by Behar (items **3519–3521**) provide the only critical analysis of current government policies. International trade issues constitute the other major area of concentration, consisting of both statistical publications and policy analyses.

In conclusion, there are interesting and encouraging new trends in the economic literature on and from these three countries. One looks forward to their continuing to provide broader and more in-depth analysis of the issues mentioned above.

BOLIVIA

3479 Argandoña Calderón, José. Las cooperativas mineras de Bolivia, especialmente las estañíferas. La Paz: Universidad Católica Boliviana, Departamento de Estudios Cooperativos, 1978? 222 p.: bibl., ill. (Serie Estudios; no. 3)

Analysis of economic aspects of mining cooperatives, as entities distinct from large nationalized and private mines. Discusses financing, management, production, and dependency situation vis-à-vis COMIBOL and Banco Minero as sources of problems and failures.

3480 Banco Central de Bolivia. Instituto Nacional de Estadística. Indices de comercio exterior de Bolivia, período 1970–1979. La Paz: El Instituto, 1981. 37 p.: ill.

Detailed tables of foreign trade statistics (1970–79). No text.

3481 Bartlema, Johannes and **Augusto Soliz Sánchez.** Bolivia, estudio de la población económicamente activa a nivel departamental según el censo de 1976, con algunas comparaciones intercensales. La Paz: Instituto Nacional de Estadística, Departamento de Estadísticas Sociales, 1980. 62 leaves: bibl., ill.

National and departmental analysis of employment and unemployment by age, sex, occupation based on 1976 *Population and housing census* (see *HLAS 43:3573*).

3482 Bolivia, proyecciones de la población por áreas urbana-rural, según sexo y edad, 1975–2000. Documento elaborado por Vilma Médica, Augusto Soliz Sánchez. Con la asesoría de Eduardo E. Arriaga. La Paz: República de Bolivia, Ministerio de Planeamiento y Coordinación, Instituto Nacional de Estadística, Departamento de Estadísticas Sociales, 1980. 50: bibl., ill.

Detailed projections of population migration, life expectancies, morality by sex, age groups, and urban-rural residence under intermediate growth rate hypothesis.

3483 Camacho Omiste, Edgar. Bolivia y la integración andina. 2. ed. actualizada. La Paz; Cochabamba, Bolivia: Editorial Los Amigos del Libro, 1981. 437 p. (Enciclopedia Boliviana)

Review of theory, background and process of regional economic integration, focusing on the Latin American experiences. Particular attention paid to the Andean Pact and Bolivia's participation, concluding that this regional grouping has been the most successful.

3484 Canelas Orellana, Amado. ¿Quiebra de la minería estatal boliviana? La Paz: Editorial Los Amigos del Libro, 1981. 333 p. (Colección Texto y documento)

Review of performance of nationalized mining sector since 1952, with a thesis similar to Ruiz González' (item **3498**), in that bad management and organization, and politically motivated policies underlie the sector's problems.

3485 Echazú A., Luis Alberto. La deuda externa de Bolivia. La Paz: s.n., 1980. 30 leaves.

Statistical review and critical analysis of the growth of Bolivia's foreign debt (1970–77), showing type and source of loans, particularly growth of "hard" loans from private banks, and receiving entities in Bolivia. Makes comparisons with rest of Latin America and discusses short and long term prospects under the weight of the debt.

3486 The Economic evolution of the individual countries: Bolivia (*in* United Nations. Economic Committee for Latin America. Economic survey of Latin America: 1979. Santiago: 1981, p. 94–111, tables)

Review of national economic, financial, and trade statistics (1974–79), showing the economy's progressive deterioration.

3487 Empleo en el sector informal de la ciudad de La Paz. La Paz: Ministerio de Trabajo y Desarrollo Laboral, Dirección General de Empleo, 1980. 169 p.

Very detailed study of the socially and economically important "informal" business and labor sectors of La Paz, based on 1977 survey. "Informal" means owner-operated, with less than five paid workers. Sector comprises the small service and comercial businesses which abound in large Latin American cities.

3488 Hiraoka, Mario. Settlement and development of the upper Amazon: the East Bolivian example (JDA, 14:3, April 1980, p. 327–348, maps, tables)

Comprehensive literature review of historical process of land settlement/ colonization in upper Amazon Basin areas of Bolivia through mid-1970s. Based on field research, describes settlement characteristics and farming system, and extent of success in meeting government goals.

3489 Instituto Nacional de Estadística (Bolivia). Boletín demográfico departamental: análisis de los resultados del *Censo nacional de población y vivienda de 1976.* v. l, Chuquisaca. La Paz: El Instituto, 1981. 68 p.: bibl., ill., tables.

Analysis of population statistics from 1976 *Population and housing census.* Text and tables.

3490 ———. Estadísticas regionales. v. 1, Beni, Bolivia. v. 2, Oruro, Bolivia. v. 3, Tarija, Bolivia. v. 4, Cochabamba, Bolivia. v. 5, Santa Cruz, Bolivia. La Paz: El Instituto, 1978/1980. 5 v.: ill, tables.

Data, covering varying periods in 1970s, for population, agriculture, forestry, fisheries, transportation, health, and education. No text.

3491 Medinaceli, Juan. Reforma al sistema financiero en Bolivia. La Paz: Banco Central de Bolivia, División Técnica, Unidad de Investigaciones Económicas, 1981. 27 leaves.

Outline of role, functioning and interrelationships of financial institutions which make up Bolivia's financial structure.

3492 Musgrave, Richard Abel. Fiscal reform in Bolivia: final report of the Bolivian Mission on Tax Reform. Cambridge, Mass.: Law School of Harvard University, 1980. 1 v.

In-depth study of fiscal policies, including expenditure, budgetary and taxation aspects, and economic implications, pri-

marily from conservative viewpoint. Report is based on 36 papers by US and Latin American economists, and contains policy suggestions which relate to 1976–80 Five-Year Economic Plan. Final report, English version, of *HLAS 43:3559.*

3493 Peláez R., Segundino and **Marina Vargas S.** Estaño, sangre y sudor: tragedia del minero locatario. Oruro, Bolivia: Editorial Universitaria, 1980. 69 p., 7 p. of plates: ill.

Description of subsidiary mining sector, which is made up largely of unorganized workers who work under highly exploitative conditions by contracting to mine abandoned sites. Discusses importance of such production for nationalized sector's performance.

3494 Programa Regional de Empleo para América Latina (PREALC). El impacto ocupacional de la inversión pública en Bolivia. Prepared by Guido Reyes, Percy Jiménez, and Joseph Ramos. Santiago: Organización Internacional del Trabajo, Programa Mundial del Empleo, Programa Regional del Empleo para América Latina (PREALC), 1980. 86 p. in various pagings: bibl., tables (Documento de trabajo PREALC; 182)

Analysis of direct and indirect impacts on regional employment and income distribution of public investments programmed in the 1976–80 economic plan. Concludes plan would not be successful because of emphasis on capital intensive, high technology investment, rather than on infrastructure and agriculture and rural investment, where greater employment and income impacts would result.

3495 Ramos Sánchez, Pablo. Siete años de economía boliviana. La Paz: Universidad Mayor de San Andrés, 1980. 258 p.: bibl., ill.

Political-economic analysis of Bolivian economic policy during the Banzer government (1971–78). Thrust is that the latter was not simply another run-of-the-mill military government, but one guided by coherent, classic fascist principles, part of a continental strategy.

3496 Resultados de la encuesta de empleo, segundo semestre de 1978: ciudades La Paz, Cochabamba, Santa Cruz. La Paz: República de Bolivia, Ministerio de Planeamiento y Coordinación, Instituto Nacional de Estadística, 1980. 89 p.: tables.

Part of series, including Oruro in 1979, provides detailed statistics on economically active population by age, sex, education, occupation, and amount worked. Includes definitions and survey methodology.

3497 Romero Bedregal, Hugo. Desarrollo histórico, movimientos sociales y planeamiento andino en Bolivia. La Paz: Ediciones Populares Camarlinghi, 1980. 163 p.: bibl. (Colección Mundo andino; 1)

Well written and interesting discussion of economic and social planning concepts and their application to realities of Bolivia and Andean peoples. If planning is to be a successful process of facilitating human action and behavior, particularly in rural areas, it will require knowledge of present society and of its past character as well.

3498 Ruiz González, René. La administración empírica de las minas nacionalizadas. 2. ed. actualizada. La Paz: Librería Editorial Juventud, 1980. 322 p.: bibl.

Long-time student of mining in Bolivia presents comprehensive review of the sector's history, focusing particularly on the organization and administration since the 1952 nationalization. Believes failure of mining to contribute its required share to the nation's development is due to persistent failure of upper and middle management.

3499 Zavaleta, René. El proletariado minero boliviano entre 1940 y 1980 (CEDLA/B, 32, junio 1982, p. 29–37, bibl.)

Sociopolitical treatment of development and national role of the organized mining labor force.

PARAGUAY

3500 Agarwal, Manmohan and **Hugo Zea-Barriga.** Paraguay, economic memorandum. Washington: World Bank, Latin America and the Caribbean Regional Office, 1979. 178 p., 1 folded leaf of plates: map, tables (A World Bank country study)

Study identifies sources of recent economic growth and economic sectors in which more action is necessary. Includes over 120 p. of economic statistics. Comprehensive and very informative assessment of Paraguay's public and private economies in 1970s.

3501 Campos Ruiz Díaz, Daniel. Escolaridad y fuerza de trabajo en el Paraguay: economía de la educación (UCNSA/EP, 8:2, dic. 1980, p. 67–124, bibl., tables)

Cross-tabular analysis of active workforce with occupation, industry sector and other socio-demographic variables by education level, from perspectives of several labor market theories. Well-done and interesting study.

3502 Canese, Ricardo. El petróleo: su relación con la energética en el Paraguay (UCNSA/EP, 8:2, dic. 1980, p. 125–213, bibl., graphs, tables)

Presents general review of energy situation and costs in world, Paraguay, Brazil, and Argentina in 1970s, and projections for Paraguay. Criticizes role of Refinería Paraguaya S.A., and recommends its nationalization.

3503 Carísimo Baéz, Julia. Crisis energética: su impacto en Paraguay (UNAM/PDD, 12:46, mayo/julio 1981, p. 113–144)

Good review and examination of development of hydroelectric resources and resulting economic growth. Criticizes the former because of dominance by transnational firms and the resulting greater domination of Paraguayan economy by these firms, particularly Brazilian, with benefits not going to Paraguayan workers and small farmers.

3504 The Economic evolution of the individual countries: Paraguay (*in* United Nations. Economic Commission for Latin America. Economic survey of Latin America, 1979. Santiago: 1981, p. 425–438, tables)

General assessment of the Paraguayan economy from mid-to-late 1970s. Not of the quality of the World Bank study (item **3500**).

3505 Morínigo A., José N. Hacia una cuantificación de la población pobre en Asunción (UCNSA/EP, 9:1, junio 1981, p. 181–228, maps, tables)

Develops theoretical and methodological framework for empirically describing poverty, using 1972 and 1980 data. Describes location of poor in Asunción, income distribution by various factors, and reasons for poverty.

3506 Mujer y trabajo en el Paraguay. Luis Galeano, comp. Fulvia Brizuela de Ramírez *et al.* Asunción: Centro Paraguayo de Estudios Sociológicos, 1982. 503 p.: bibl.

(Serie Estudios)

Seven studies by different authors of various aspects of women's participation in the workforce. Topics covered are general supply of and demand for female labor, changing participation rates, relationship between work and fertility, changing family and social roles, and types of employment and occupations.

3507 Nickson, Andrew. Brazilian colonization of the eastern border region of Paraguay (*in* State and region in Latin America: a workshop. G.A. Banck, R. Buve, and L. Van Vroonhoven, editors. Amsterdam: Centrum voor Studie en Documetatie van Latijns-Amerika, 1981, p. 201–229, bibl., tables [CEDLA incidentele publicaties; 17])

Describes growing Brazilian migration to Paraguay's Eastern Border Region (EBR) in 1970s, and assesses political and economic reasons for it, both in Brazil and Paraguay. Examines Brazilian advantages over Paraguayans, effects on Paraguayans, and resulting economic change in EBR in 1960s and 1970s. Good article, complements Carísimo Baéz's (item **3503**).

3508 Panorama económico del Paraguay. Elaborado por el Gabinete Técnico del Ministerio de Industria y Comercio. Asunción: El Ministerio, 1980. 59 p., 13 leaves of plates: ill., maps.

Compendium of general economic statistics for 1970s, and assessment of prospects for various sectors in 1980s.

3509 Rodríguez Silvero, Ricardo. El desarrollo y el crecimiento económico (UNCSA/EP, 7:2, dic. 1979, p. 9–36, tables)

General and unoriginal discussion of worth of GNP vs. other statistics to provide information on growth and development, particularly poverty, hunger, social and political aspects. Uses some Paraguayan data to support case.

**3510 ———. Paraguay: defectos estructurales en el modelo de acumulación capitalista periférico y dependiente (CPES/RPS, 17:48, mayo/agosto 1980, p. 77–100, bibl., tables)

Using dependency model, describes how production is not geared to long run development needs of Paraguay or most of its population. Criticizes particularly import, export, and capital goods sectors, which though linked together are not linked to ma-

jority of populace.

**3511 ———. Paraguay: la balanza de pagos oficial y la real (UCNSA/EP, 9:1, junio 1981, p. 160–179, bibl., tables)

Estimates foreign trade not accounted for by official statistics (i.e., resulting from contraband and through binational entities created to construct Itaipú and Yacyretá dams). Concludes that official statistics underestimate trade deficit by up to two-thirds, and are thus useless for any analysis of Paraguay's economy.

3512 Rovetta, Vicente. El capitalismo extranjero es propietario de la mayoría de las tierras y domina el 80 por ciento de la economía del Paraguay (Desarrollo Indoamericano [E. Salazar F., Bogotá] 15:66, marzo 1981, p. 41–47, ill.)

Popular article presents Marxist view of Paraguay's history. Focuses on intervention of foreign business to take over Paraguayan economy and by restructuring it to their own needs, leading to the country's current major problems.

3513 Silva, Juan Andrés *et al.* Participación de la mujer en la fuerza de trabajo (CPES/RPS, 13:36, mayo/agosto 1976, p. 143–171, charts, graphs, tables)

Presentation of data on women's work force participation with percentage and numerical breakdowns by economic sector, education level, and salary.

3514 Sosa, Horacio C. El desarollo del Chaco paraguayo (UCNSA/EP, 8:1, junio 1980, p. 143–258, map, plate, tables)

Reprints of newspaper articles (1976–80) on issues of water in the Chaco's economy and development. Includes some general articles on region's economy.

3515 Wainerman, Catalina and Zulma Recchini de Lattes. Trabajadoras latinoamericanas: un análisis comparativo de la Argentina, Bolivia y Paraguay. Buenos Aires: Centro de Estudios de Población, 1980. 117 p.: bibl., ill. (Cuadernos del CENEP; no. 13–14)

Using primarily census data, describes labor market for women in 1970s. Compares Argentina and Bolivia, on basis of sociodemographic characteristics of labor market participants and the nature of their work.

URUGUAY

3516 Alonso, José María. Proceso histórico de la agricultura uruguaya. Montevideo: Fundación de Cultura Universitaria: Centro Interdisciplinario de Estudios sobre el Desarrollo Uruguay, 1981. 50 p., 7 leaves of plates: bibl., ill., tables (Colección Temas nacionales; 3)

Brief history of agricultural development in Uruguay. Tables of historical data. Good bibliography. First in planned series of five short books on issues and aspects of Uruguay's agricultural sector designed for people and institutions working in rural areas.

3517 Anichini, Juan J.; Jorge Caumont; and Larry Sjaastad. La política comercial y la protección en el Uruguay. 2. ed. Montevideo: Banco Central del Uruguay, Secretaría General, 1978. 211 p.: bibl., ill.

Discusses evolution of industrial protectionist policies from 1875 through mid-1970s, divided into five periods. Interesting and thorough examination of various justifications for these policies, and their negative long-run economic consequences. Emphasizes 1970s and benefits and costs of those policies, concluding that freer trade is a better alternative.

3518 Barbato de Silva, Celia. Política económica y tecnología: un análisis de la ganadería vacuna uruguaya. Montevideo: Centro de Investigaciones Económicas: Banda Oriental, 1981. 179 p.: bibl., ill. (Estudios CINVE; 2)

Reviews government policies over last 20-plus years for their impact on the economics and levels of technology in the cattle industry. Although pro-livestock, the government had to consider urban power groups and other economic sectors, thus leading to restrictive and inconsistent policies which did not encourage the desired technological change.

3519 Behar, Jaime. Economía política de la integración regional uruguaya. Stockholm: Institute of Latin American Studies, 1980. 137 p.: bibl., tables (Research paper series; 24)

Criticizes within anti-capitalist framework, the more market oriented, freer trade economic policy adopted after 1973, focusing on regional economic integration and its effects on Uruguay's industrial development. Concludes that new policy will worsen internal problems and result in subordination to Brazil and especially Argentina. Good complement to study by Anichini *et al.* (item 3517), and good bibliography.

3520 ———. La promoción y el desarrollo de las exportaciones no tradicionales en el Uruguay: 1973–1977 (NOSALF/IA, 8/9:1/2, 1980, p. 36–67, bibl., tables)

Detailed examination and critical analysis of policy of non-traditional export promotion which is key part of new economic policy adopted after 1973. Although successful, author concludes the policy had negative effects on internal market, employment and income distribution, and other industries.

3521 ———. Uruguay: exportaciones no tradicionales y políticas monetaristas. Stockholm: Institute of Latin American Studies, 1979. 104 p.: bibl., tables (Research paper series; 12)

More general study than items 3519–3520 covering economic crisis of early 1970s, its antecedents, and new economic policy.

3522 Bensión, Alberto and Jorge Caumont. Uruguay: alternative trade strategies and employment implications (*in* Trade and employment in developing countries. v. 1, Individual studies. Edited by Anne O. Krueger *et al.* Chicago: University of Chicago Press, 1981, p. 499–529, bibl., tables)

Review of economy and economic policies from early 1950s to early 1970s, focusing on analysis of effects of import substitution policy on industrial development and trade. Chiefly examines micro-level aspects (factor use) of industrial development, but does conclude that freer trade would be beneficial.

3523 COMCORDE. Secretaría Técnica. El comercio exterior del Uruguay. v. 1, 1971–1977. v. 2, Análisis de la política comercial, 1973–1980. Montevideo: La Secretaría, 1980. 2 v.: bibl., ill., tables.

Description of international trade policy from 1973–80, compares formal policies and their implementation through government actions and instruments with policy objectives of freer trade and de-emphasis on import substitution. Discusses general policy, tariffs, actions to promote exports and exchange policy. Some tables.

3524 The Economic evolution of the individual countries: Uruguay (*in* United Nations. Economic Commission for Latin America. Economic survey of Latin America, 1979. Santiago: 1981, p. 500–515, tables)

Summary of economic performance (1974–79). Reviews main macroeconomic indicators plus major industrial sectors, with emphasis on agriculture, manufacturing, foreign trade, prices, wages, and the government.

3525 Endeudamiento externo del Uruguay.
Montevideo: Banco Central del Uruguay, Departamento de Investigaciones Económicas, 1980. 18 p.

Statistics on and discussion of evolution of foreign private and public debt from mid-1960s to 1979. Examines changes in types of loans and their amounts, and compares debt and debt service with other economic indicators.

3526 Finch, Martin Henry John. Historia económica del Uruguay contemporáneo. Traducción de José de Torres Wilson y Benjamín Nahum. Montevideo: Ediciones de la Banda Oriental, 1980. 280 p.: bibl.

Overview of economic development from 1870–1970, divided into four periods, but emphasizing 1955–70 period of "economic crisis." Contains chapters on agriculture, industry, foreign trade, services and public enterprises, and government fiscal policies (for English version, see *HLAS 44:3453*).

3527 *Informaciones y Estadísticas Nacionales e Internacionales.* Centro de Estadísticas Nacionales y Comercio Internacional del Uruguay (CENCI). Nos. 7/10, mayo/julio 1981- . Montevideo.

Selected trade and economic statistics for 1979 and 1980, emphasizes Uruguay, but includes information for other Latin American countries. Not as complete nor detailed as other sources reviewed in this section.

3528 Jacob, Raúl. Inversiones extranjeras y petróleo: la crisis de 1929 en el Uruguay. Montevideo: Fundación de Cultura Universitaria, 1979. 186 p.: bibl., tables.

Historical description of foreign penetration into key economic sectors, with emphasis on energy industries, primarily for 1920–33 period.

3529 ———. Uruguay, 1929–1938: depresión ganadera y desarrollo fabril.

Montevideo: Fundación de Cultura Universitaria, 198? 431 p.: bibl., tables.

Detailed economic history of Uruguay during the Great Depression. Discusses: 1) economic policies; 2) effects of Depression on major economic sectors of livestock, agriculture, banking, and manufacturing; and 3) penetration of foreign capital. Well documented, but somewhat rambling and unfocused.

3530 Lineamientos básicos de política económica y social: cónclave gubernamental, Piriápolis, 1981. Montevideo: República Oriental del Uruguay, Presidencia de la República, Secretaría de Planeamiento, Coordinación y Difusión, 1982. 109 p.: ill.

Updated official government economic and social policies for major economic and social sectors and various ministries. Restates adherence to free-market orientation begun in 1973.

3531 Pérez Arrarte, Carlos. El agro uruguayo y el mercado internacional. Montevideo: Fundación de Cultura Universitaria; Centro Interdisciplinario de Estudios sobre el Desarrollo Uruguay, 1982. 74 p.: ill. (Colección Temas nacionales; 4)

Brief review of role and development of agricultural trade from colonial times to present, and its dependence on markets in more developed nations. Second monograph in series on issues and aspects of Uruguay's agricultural sector (see item **3516**).

3532 Prates, Suzana and **Graciela Taglioretti.** Participación de la mujer en el mercado de trabajo uruguayo: características básicas y evolución reciente. Montevideo: Centro de Informaciones y Estudios del Uruguay, 1979 or 1980. 62 p.: bibl. (Centro de Informaciones y Estudios del Uruguay; no. 27)

Description of changing character of workforce, focusing on women's participation and related sociocultural characteristics of urban-versus-rural residence, age, sex, marital status, and type of employment and occupation. Covers periods 1908–63, and 1963–75 in more detail, as more data is available.

3533 Rial Roade, Juan. Estadísticas históricas de Uruguay, 1850–1930: población, producción agropecuaria, comercio, industria, urbanización, comunicaciones, calidad de vida. Montevideo: Centro de Informaciones y Estudios del Uruguay, 1980. 168 p.: bibl., ill. (Cuaderno / Centro de Informaciones y Estudios del Uruguay; no. 40)

This very useful publication combines data accumulated during several research projects on urban and demographic history and rural structures. The tables and graphs present general and specific demographic characteristics, agricultural land use and production data, and statistics on foreign trade and foreign investment, railroads, health and literacy, disaggregated by departments and urban areas where possible.

3534 Seminario sobre Política Cambiaria, *Montevideo, 1978.* Seminario sobre Política Cambiaria. Montevideo: Banco Central del Uruguay, Comisión Económica para América Latina (CEPAL), 1978. 4 v.: ill.

Four-volume set made up of 17 papers from conference on issues of monetary exchange policy and internal monetary policy. They comprehensively treat theory and practice of exchange policy within the context of the open economies of Uruguay, Paraguay, Brazil, and Chile.

3535 Taglioretti, Graciela. La participación de la mujer en el mercado de trabajo: Uruguay, 1963–1975. Montevideo: Centro de Informaciones y Estudios del Uruguay, 1981. 86 p.: bibl., ill. (Cuaderno / Centro de Informaciones y Estudios del Uruguay; no. 43)

Expansion of study by Prates and Taglioretti (item **3532**), with more detail and analysis. Women's workforce participation increased markedly, in both rural and urban areas, during period studied. Analyzes historical process of change, sociocultural demographic characteristics, and hypothesizes on reasons for changes.

3536 Uruguay. Dirección de Investigaciones Económicas Agropecuarias. División de Estudios Econométricos and Inter-American Institute of Agricultural Sciences. Información histórica de precios agrícolas y pecuarios. 3. ed. rev. y actualizada. Montevideo: La División, 1980. 54 p.: tables (Serie Informativa; no. 13)

Real and nominal wholesale and producer prices of major crop and livestock commodities, covering various periods between late 1940s-79. Valuable research document.

3537 ———. Dirección General de Estadística y Censos. V [i.e. Quinto] censo general de población. Fasc. 3, Características económicas. Montevideo: La Dirección, 1980. 93 p.: tables.

Statistics on economically active population from 1975 *General census of population and housing,* by age, sex, activity, functional categories, occupation, and other comparisons.

3538 ———. Ministerio de Economía y Finanzas. Dirección General de Comercio Exterior. Estadísticas: comercio exterior, 1976–1980. Montevideo: El Ministerio, 1981. 39 p.

Gross dollar value of exports by destination, value of exports by detailed commodity, value of exports by aggregated commodity and country of destination.

ARGENTINA

MICHAEL B. ANDERSON, *Chief of the Economic Sector, Institute for the Integration of Latin America, Inter-American Development Bank, Buenos Aires*

BY FAR THE MOST INTERESTING ISSUE addressed by Argentine economists during the past two years concerned the failure of the so-called liberal experiment of the Minister of Economy, José Alfredo Martínez de Hoz. Some commentators such as Rodríguez (item **3572**), Uriarte (item **3578**), Tchinnosian (item **3576**), and Martínez de Hoz himself (item **3564**) thought that many of the reforms or modifications introduced were correct and if carried out consistently would have permitted a higher and more stable long-term growth path. But other authors pointed to inconsistencies which created uncertainty, cut down investments and led to increasing speculation and instability. The "successes" of the government program such as the halving of the rate of inflation, the rapid increase in foreign reserves and the low rate of unemployment turned out to be short-lived or simple statistical illusions.

Canitrot (item **3547**) and Ferrer (item **3556**) never thought the Martínez de Hoz program would work. For Canitrot the program could not succeed given the military's unwillingness to permit high rates of unemployment "a la chilena" and the economic team's underestimation of the importance of this variable in the stabilization program. Even if successful the liberal program would eventually come into conflict with the industry's demand for protection and subsidies. According to Ferrer, (item **3556**) the government was not addressing the right issues (e.g., the impact of transnational firms on Argentina, new technologies and their effects on international relations, hegemony of the OECD on international commerce).

In addition to works on the above debate at the global level, there are also many interesting and well done studies that scrutinize the liberal program in detail. R. Frenkel (item **3558**) looks critically at the financial reforms of 1977 and asks if the reliance on the domestic rate of interest as part of the stabilization effort was appropriate. According to him, the answer is not straightforward and depends on inflationary expectations as well as on an adjustment process that seeks a new equilibrium. Another key element of the liberal program, perhaps the only stabilization instrument used towards the end, was the *tablita* or pre-announced minidevaluations. Ana María Martirena-Mantel (item **3565**) just touches on the first phase of the liberal program in her fine study of minidevaluations. But her work provides a sound basis for analyzing different classes of minidevaluations, and I think it is correct to conclude from her work that minidevaluations by themselves cannot serve as the only stabilization instrument without provoking drastic consequences on real activity.

A rich body of theoretical studies covering a wide variety of subjects has been produced by Argentine economists during the past several years. Many of these concern themes important to the Argentine economy and several were published in the *Anales de la XVII Reunión de la Asociación Argentina de Economía Política* (not available at press time for review in this *HLAS*).

A number of studies have taken advantage of the recent availability of high-quality statistics to reexamine old themes such as the relation between wages, inflation, and employment and the stop-go business cycle. Much of this information is derived from the Economic Commission for Latin America's or CEPAL's program "Información y Análisis de Corto Plazo de la Economía Argentina." The Central Bank is also improving its own statistics and some important empirical works such as those of Heymann (item **3561**), Martín (item **3563**), and Tchinnosian (item **3576**), were produced as a result. Some rather sophisticated general equilibrium models such as those by Baliño *et al.* (item **3543**) and Feltenstein (item **3554**) have been built using this new data to deal with (what else) real wages and inflation and trade restrictions and their effects on domestic prices. Finally, there are at least two studies by Beccaria (item **3544**) and by Diéguez and Petrecolla (item **3551**) that have made use of a rich source of raw information contained in household surveys collected regularly by the National Institute of Statistics.

Any article written about economic events prior to 1976 can be considered historical in Argentina. Still, despite the paucity of such studies, the period is interesting, and some intriguing works are annotated below. Finally, studies by Escude (item **3552**) and Capie (item **3548**) support Ferrer's thesis (item **3556**) regarding the importance of international relations in Argentina's economic history.

3539 Archetti, Eduardo P. The process of capitalization among Argentinian peasants (*in* Mörner, Magnus *et al.* El sector agrario en América Latina: estructura económica y cambio social [see item **2948**] p. 138–150, bibl., tables)

Interesting description of the historical transformation of the agricultural sector in the northeastern part of Santa Fe prov. Examines three periods of importance to region: colonization (1872–1936/37); 2) introduction of cotton (1936–37); and 3) mechanization and growing use of fertilizers from 1956. Author indicates that as accumulation of capital became the critical factor in region's growth, land and labor ceased to be crucial elements in the production process.

3540 Argentina. Banco Central. Centro de Estudios Monetarios y Bancarios. Política monetaria y crediticia (Información Comercial Española [Ministerio de Comercio y Turismo, Secretaría General Técnica, Madrid] 562, junio 1980, p. 73–79, tables)

Describes situation at beginning of 1976, reaction of the Martínez de Hoz team and results obtained. Reflecting official opinion, review is as interesting for what is left out as for its contents. To be fair, no one has yet offered a reasonable explanation for the 1977–80 high rate of inflation. But considering that its reduction was the main policy objective of the Martínez de Hoz team, the results were a dismal failure.

3541 Arnaudo, Aldo A. Rentabilidad bancaria y política monetaria en el régimen argentino de nacionalización de depósitos (UNC/REE, 21:1/4, 1977–1978, p. 67–80, tables)

Review and analysis of effects of 1973 "nationalization" of deposits in the banking system. Nationalization implied that banks held deposits as agents of the Central Bank; interest rates, lending policy and profits to the banking system being determined by CB directives. Results depended on type of banks and type of financial instrument employed.

3542 Baliño, Tomás José Teodoro. Evolución de las tasas de interés en la Argentina: un análisis de series temporales (BCRA/EE, 18, junio 1981, p. 51–95, graphs, tables)

Following financial reform of 1977, interest rates were freed and quickly rose to positive (real) levels. Baliño seeks to explain movements in these rates using Box-Jenkins techniques to eliminate noise and autocorrelation. Findings, unfortunately, are quite limited, but Baliño does provide reader with some interesting data which could be worth examining by others.

3543 ———; Ke-young Chu; and Andrew Feltenstein. El salario real y la inflación: un análisis de la experiencia argentina (BCRA/EE, 14, junio 1980, p. 5–48, bibl., graphs, tables)

Within context of general equilibrium model, authors examine relation between industrial real wages and inflation (1963–76). They attempt to determine whether price controls actually increased real wages or just the opposite. In addition, they investigate long-run impact of inflation on real wages on an industry-by-industry basis. Simulation results are interesting; unfortunately, the wage series used in study is conceptually a poor representation of the wage rate.

3544 Beccaria, Luis A. Los movimientos de corto plazo en el mercado de trabajo urbano y la coyuntura 1975–78 en la Argentina (IDES/DE, 20:78, julio/sept. 1980, p. 155–182, bibl., tables)

Fall in real wages in 1976 resulted in lowest unemployment rates since the compilation of such statistics began in late 1960s. Using data from household surveys, author points to reduction in the active work force as a principal factor in the decline.

3545 Bour, Juan L. and Jorge H. Meier. Tamaño de establecimientos, intensidad de factores y productividad del trabajo en la industria manufacturera argentina (ECIEL, 5, julio 1978, p. 1–36, graph, tables)

Using census data from 1963, authors investigate relation between firm size, measured by number of employees and productivity. Study is intended to complement studies for other Latin American countries sponsored by the Program of Joint Studies on Latin American Economic Integration (ECIEL). While interesting methods are used, study is limited by old and unreliable information. Findings do not indicate any clear overall tendencies.

3546 Canitrot, Adolfo. Discipline as the central objective of the economic programme of the Argentine government since 1976 (WD, 8:11, Nov. 1980, p. 913–928)

Brilliant, penetrating critic of the "liberal" economic program. Major conclusion is that the government can pursue this program for a short time, in a period of generally recognized economic emergency. Once order has been reestablished, pressure for a program of expansion requiring a degree of industrial protection and subsidized investments will grow. The "liberal" program, being in conflict with the program of expansion, will "self-destruct."

3547 ———. Teoría y práctica del liberalismo: política antiinflacionaria y apertura económica en la Argentina, 1976–1981. Buenos Aires: Centro de Estudios de Estado y Sociedad, 180. 78 p.: bibl., ill., tables (Estudios CEDES; v. 3, no. 10)

Author presents detailed and critical review of the liberal program of Minister Martínez de Hoz. Insists that economic aspects of the program cannot be separated from the armed forces' political goals to reach long-term solution to the social crisis which the country faced during first half of 1970s through a radical modification of country's institutions and economic organization.

3548 Capie, Forrest. Invisible barrier to trade: Britain and Argentina in the 1920s (IAMEA, 35:3, Winter 1981, p. 91–96, table)

While GATT works hard to reduce tariff barriers, the developed countries replace them with clever non-tariff barriers especially for agricultural goods from developing countries. Such trade barriers are not new as article makes clear. Argentina supplied almost half the wheat imported by England in 1920 and increased its share to 70 percent by 1927. Pressure from other suppliers caused England to impose tight controls on Argentine imports causing a fall in Argentina's share of English market. No wonder future Argentine governments favored a more autarkic form of development.

3549 Colome, Rinaldo Antonio. Importancia estratégica de la agricultura pampeana en el desarrollo económico argentino (UNC/REE, 21:1/4, 1977/1978, p. 39–65, bibl., tables)

Supply of agricultural output is determined mainly by relative prices. Compares relative prices of industrial to agricultural goods and cereals to meat. Estimates supply functions dependent on relative prices of

goods competing for same scarce factor (land).

3550 Di Marco, Luis E.; Eduardo González Olguín; and E. Altamira Gigena. Recursos y gastos en Córdoba: análisis interjurisdiccional (UNC/REE, 21:1/4, 1977/1978, p. 191–217, bibl., tables)

During 1976–81 period, national government promoted "fiscal federalism," redistribution of the federal budget towards provinces. Article attempts to identify appropriate governmental level at which federal expenditures should be made using cost-benefit techniques by placing a monetary value on public services. Article attempts to convert political rhetoric into an operational plan.

3551 Diéguez, Héctor L. and Alberto Petrecolla. Distribución de ingresos en el Gran Buenos Aires. Buenos Aires: Instituto Torcuato Di Tella, 1979. 146 p.: bibl. (Serie ocre, Economía. Cuaderno—Instituto Torcuato Di Tella; no. 102 0325–8483)

Taking advantage of rich source of information, conducts thorough examination of income distribution across families in Buenos Aires' greater metropolitan area. Statistical methods are excellent. Unfortunately, findings of close correlation between distribution and occupation and education of head of household are now merely of historical interest.

3552 Escude, Carlos. Las restricciones internacionales de la economía argentina: 1945–1949 (IDES/DE, 20:77, abril/junio 1980, p. 3–40)

Documents US efforts, often successful, to boycott Argentina and prevent England from trading with her as well during World War II.

3553 Feldman, Ernesto V. Empleo, sucursalismo y represión financiera en el sistema bancario argentino (BCRE/EE, 15, sept. 1980, p. 5–28, tables)

Interesting study of competition and labor demand in the financial sector under conditions of price controls. Also reviews 1977 financial reforms' effects on sector.

3554 Feltenstein, Andrew. A general equilibrium approach to the analysis of trade restrictions, with an application to Argentina (IMF/SP, 27:4, Dec. 1980, p. 749–784, tables)

While paper is oriented more to

method than application, model would have been useful to Argentine policy makers, since it deals with means to neutralize effects of tariff reductions on internal prices.

3555 Ferrer, Aldo. Las grandes perspectivas económicas de la Argentina (Información Comercial Española [Ministerio de Comercio y Turismo, Secretaría General Técnica, Madrid] 526, junio 1980, p. 19–24, ill.)

Brief introduction to Argentine economy. Author points out that by 1930 Argentina had obtained a per capita income of $1500 (in 1980 prices), had abundant resources, exports, and sophisticated manufactured goods. Argentina's future, according to author, does not lie with agricultural sector but with continued production and export of high technology goods. Article reflects a segment of *desarrollista* school of thought.

3556 ———. Nacionalismo y orden constitucional: respuesta a la crisis económica de la Argentina contemporánea. México: Fondo de Cultura Económica, 1981. 238 p.: bibl.

Long-term view of short-term problem. Author takes position that liberal as well as popular experiments before were inadequate responses to the problems affecting the Argentine economy. Examines latter from the historical as well as international perspective, and presents his own interpretation of problems which Argentine policy makers must confront.

3557 Frenkel, Roberto. Decisiones de precio en alta inflación. Buenos Aires: Centro de Estudios de Estado y Sociedad, 1979. 58 p.: bibl., graphs (Estudios CEDES; v. 2, no. 3)

Models (includes prices, expectations, risks) short-term entrepreneurial behavior in the context of high uncertainty. Theoretical but related to the Argentina experience (1975–78). [J.M. Hunter]

3558 ———. El desarrollo reciente del mercado de capitales en Argentina. Buenos Aires: Centro de Estudios de Estado y Sociedad, 1980. 55 p.: bibl., ill., tables (Estudios CEDES; v. 2, no. 10)

Good descriptive and analytical treatment of Argentine capital market after 1976 financial reform. Focuses particular attention on importance of inflationary expectations and on how the speculative demand for goods affected the economy's behavior. Includes

bibliography and tables. See also author's article on subject in *Desarrollo Económico* (20:78, julio/sept. 1980, p. 215–247).

3559 Guadagni, Alieto Aldo. Hacia un modelo económico para la década del ochenta (CRIT, 53:1849/1850, 15 dic. 180, p. 770–780)

While at present most Argentine economists are interested in the country's short-run problems, Guadagni's concerns here are more fundamental and long-term. He emphasizes important policy questions for future statesmen.

3560 Guissarri, Adrián C. and **Carlos E. Zarasaga.** Algunas evidencias sobre la política fiscal y monetaria en la Argentina (BCRA/EE, 21, marzo 1982, p. 1–13, graph, tables)

Authors present results of their investigation on effects of Argentina's fiscal and monetary policy on output's growth and variations. They find that fiscal policy is not (at least statistically) an effective instrument while monetary policy is. Their results are based on annual data for 1962–79 and quarterly data between 1964 (II) and 1979 (IV).

3561 Heymann, Daniel. Las fluctuaciones de la industria manufacturera argentina, 1950–1978. Santiago: CEPAL, 1980. 240 p.: bibl., ill. (Cuadernos de la CEPAL; no. 34. Documento—Naciones Unidas; E/CEPAL/G.1114)

While Argentina's "stop-go" economic cycle has been described by many economists, few have provided as much empirical detail as Heymann. He identifies three epochs in which manufacturing sector followed quite distinct patterns of growth: 1) transformation from light to medium size industry through 1958; 2) preeminence of automotive industry through mid 1960s; followed by 3) universal growth in almost all manufacturing sectors through 1974. Using National Bureau of Economic Research's reference cycle methodology describes stop-go pattern of growth. Finds some correspondence with economic policies especially at peak of cycle, but does not see relation as straightforward nor does he accept hypothesis advanced by some economists.

3562 Katz, Jorge. Creación de tecnología en el sector manufacturero argentino (Información Comercial Española [Ministerio de Comercio y Turismo, Secretaría General

Técnica, Madrid] 562, junio 1980, p. 111–122, ill., tables)

Katz produces convincing evidence that firms are not passive consumers of imported technology. They provide technology locally as complement to imports. Generation of local technology, according to author, is critical for industry's future growth.

3563 Martín, Juan. Desarrollo regional argentino: la agricultura. Santiago: Naciones Unidas, 1981. 119 p.: bibl., graphs, ill., tables (Cuadernos de la CEPAL; 38)

Fine statistical survey of agricultural sector at provincial level and contribution of sector to overall output. Takes good advantage of census data as well as host of other sources. Includes original tables and graphs.

3564 Martínez de Hoz, José Alfredo. Bases para una Argentina moderna, 1976–80. Buenos Aires: Cía. Impresora Argentina, 1981. 244 p.

Insider's view of the liberal government. Reviews overall objectives and actual policies, paying special attention to important investment projects initiated during author's tenure as Minister of Economy (1976–80).

3565 Martirena-Mantel, Ana María. Minidevaluaciones y estabilidad macroeconómica: el caso argentino, 1971–78. Buenos Aires: Instituto Torcuato Di Tella, 1980. 68 p.: bibl., tables (Cuaderno; no. 104. Serie ocre, Economía, 0325–8483)

Author develops macro model which permits more rigorous analysis of minidevaluations. Given a fixed set of objectives, model results in a convergence to equilibrium only under a limited set of conditions. Looks at Argentina's experience and identifies three types of minidevaluations and examines impact of each on the economy.

3566 Montuschi, Luisa. Crecimiento, empleo y las estrategias del sector externo: Argentina 1953–1970 (UNLP/E, 26:3, sept./dic. 1980, p. 185-205, tables)

As to the two major external sector strategies employed in Argentina from 1953: import substitution or export promotion, which gave better results in terms of growth and employment? Neither strategy appears superior and author suggests that an appropriate external sector strategy would employ elements of each.

3567 Neyra, Raúl. Las inversiones extranjeras en Argentina (Información Comercial Española [Ministerio de Comercio y Turismo, Secretaría General Técnica, Madrid] 562, junio 1980, p. 99–108, ill., tables)

Brief overview of foreign investments in Argentina. Contains good historical summary as well as some statistics on situation through 1979.

3568 Nogués, Julio J. Distorsiones en mercados de factores, empleo y ventajas comparativas en el sector manufacturero argentino (BCRA/EE, 20, dic. 1981, p. 23–80)

Attempts to measure changes in relative prices brought about by economic policies designed to promote industrialization. Analyzes 1970 with complete and detailed description of policies. Concludes that model of industrial growth then pursued in Argentina was not labor intensive as a result of direct intervention to maintain wages above their (probable) equilibrium level. Well done.

3569 Ordenamiento económico-social (IDES/DE, 20:77, abril/junio 1980, p. 93–120, tables)

Originally published in 1945, article contains wealth of statistical material for 1939–43 period. Analysis of data reflects prevalent concerns and provides interesting backdrop to ensuing peronist period.

3570 Piekarz, Julio A. Desequilibrio monetario e ingresos fiscales (UNLP/E, 26:1/2, enero/agosto 1980, p. 35–83, tables)

Using historical data published by Fiscal Taxing Authority, author investigates influence of monetary variables on fiscal income (1935–75). Tax evasion and delays in payments are found to be important determinants of real fiscal income. However, no clear causal relation was found between monetary variables, particularly inflation, and tax revenues.

3571 Reca, Lucio G. Características estructurales y posibilidades de crecimiento del sector agro-alimentario argentino (Información Comercial Española [Ministerio de Comercio y Turismo, Secretaría General Técnica, Madrid] 562, junio 1980, p. 27–32, plates)

Excellent general introduction to agricultural sector since 1950s.

3572 Rodríguez, Carlos Alfredo and **Larry A. Sjaastad.** El atraso cambiario en Argentina (Información Comercial Española [Ministerio de Comercio y Turismo, Secretaría General Técnica, Madrid] 562, junio 1980, p. 81–95, tables)

Perhaps most controversial of policy measures proposed by Martínez de Hoz and adopted by the government was the slowing down in the speed of exchange rate devaluations from 1978, causing the Argentine peso to increase in value vis-à-vis US dollar. The uninitiated might have thought something wrong when paying two dollars for a cup of coffee but according to authors, real reevaluation of the peso reflected a fundamental change in the structure of production in Argentina. Authors use some high powered tools to support their position but unfortunately do not generate significant debate on such a critical issue. Same article published in *Ensayos Económicos* (13, marzo 1980, p. 9–51).

3573 **Rofman, Alejandro B.** Notas teórico-empíricas sobre el proceso de desigualdades regionales en la Argentina (CEDLA/B, 27, dic. 1979, p. 9–28, tables)

Significant contribution to debate on regional inequalities. Article critically examines some interpretations of these inequalities, solutions proposed and why they have failed. Author's own conception of problem relies on a global "system wide" viewpoint.

3574 ———. La promoción industrial en la Argentina: propuestas y resultados de los objetivos de descentralización regional (CPES/RPS, 13:36, mayo/agosto 1976, p. 117–142, charts)

Dominance of Buenos Aires metropolitan area has led numerous politicians to promote decentralization as cure-all for Argentina's economic ills. One example is industrial promotion legislation that forbade industrial enterprises from locating near the capital and created fiscal incentives to relocalizing in provinces. Unfortunately, legislation designed for industrial promotion, as Rofman points out, was complex, contradictory, expensive and not very successful.

3575 **El Sector externo: indicadores y análisis de sus fluctuaciones: el caso argentino.** Santiago: Naciones Unidas, 1982. 216

p.: bibl., graphs, ill., tables (Estudios e informes de la CEPAL; 14)

Three-part study takes detailed look at Argentine external sector. Effort and care which went into construction of the basic series by itself makes this work valuable. Pt. 1 describes evolution of exports and imports (1953–78, with some series extending to 1980); pt. 2 relates external sector to industrial cycle extending analysis by Heymann (item **3561**); and pt. 3 deals with services and methods.

3576 **Tchinnosian, Beatriz A.** Una estimación de la demanda de bienes durables (BCRE/EE, 15, sept. 1980, p. 67–95, tables)

Using original data of production of durable goods, author estimates equation explaining behavior of demand. Relative prices, income distribution, real rates of interest of the stock of money were found to explain movements in durable goods demand in Argentina.

3577 **Teijeiro, Mario O.** Inversión británica en Argentina: causas y consecuencias del pánico Baring (BCRA/EE, 13, marzo 1980, p. 87–108, tables)

Estimates model representing causes of Argentine devaluations in 1890s, the result of which was the Baring crisis.

3578 **Uriarte, José A.** and **Beatriz A. Tchinnosian.** Aspectos empíricos del enfoque monetario de la balanza de pagos de la Argentina (BCRA/EE, 13, marzo 1980, p. 53–86, tables)

After reviewing monetary approach to balance of payments, authors estimate an equation to explain changes in level of foreign reserves using 1969–77 data. Data is published to make possible further work on topic.

Wainerman, Catalina and **Zulma L. Recchini de Lattes.** Trabajadoras latinoamericanas: un análisis comparativo de la Argentina, Bolivia y Paraguay. See item **3515**.

3579 **Wynia, Gary W.** Illusion and reality in Argentina (CUH, 80:463, Feb. 1981, p. 62–65, 84–85)

Article reviews economic and political aims of Videla-Martínez de Hoz government. Good overview for foreign readers.

BRAZIL

DONALD V. COES, *Associate Professor of Economics, University of Illinois at Urbana-Champaign*

THE RECENT ECONOMICS LITERATURE dealing with Brazil reflects several continuing and developing trends. Since the publication of *HLAS 43*, the atmosphere of economic crisis has worsened, particularly on the international front. As had been the case in earlier periods, much of the literature has focused on the implications and potential solutions for some of the most pressing current problems. The external debt, the links between internal macroeconomic policies and the balance of payments, inequities in the regional and the personal distribution of income, and the continuing pressure of high energy prices are among the issues most frequently discussed.

One favorable trend in the literature, already underway for a decade, but probably accelerating in recent years, is the growing number of contributions based on recent doctoral and masters theses, as an increasing number of Brazilians complete graduate work. In the past, the shortage of Brazilians with graduate training in economics and allied fields, as well as the demands of a political system in which decision-making was done by "technocrats" and their assistants, rather than by elected officials, drew many potential scholars into the public sector, with relatively less incentive to research and to publish. The growth of the human capital stock in the economics area, however, now seems to have had the welcome effect of increasing both the quantity and quality of economic analysis of Brazilian experience, both past and present. In the annotations that follow, I have noted those books or articles based on theses and dissertations when the author made it clear that this was the case. It is likely that an even larger number of the entries belong in this category.

One consequence of this trend is an increase in the critical standards which Brazilian economists apply to themselves and their peers. The specification of hypotheses in empirically testable forms has become much commoner than was the case a decade or two ago; as a result a few sacred cows have been sacrificed, or at least seriously gored. Conventional theories of the way a currency devaluation actually works in a Brazilian context, for example, have been called into question by Eliana Cardoso (item **3622**). The widely accepted notion that multinational firms use more capital intensive techniques than do local firms engaged in the same activity is challenged by Reinaldo Gonçalves (item **3635**). The efficiency of minimum wage legislation to reduce poverty is questioned by Roberto Macedo (item **3646**), while the common premise that exposure to the international market increases uncertainty is shown by Fernando Homem de Melo (item **3651**) not to be generally true for agricultural commodities.

Another favorable trend is the appearance of a number of articles based on newly available data. The most productive data in terms of the articles based on them are those coming from the Instituto Brasileiro de Geografia e Estatística's national household survey corresponding to the years 1974–75 (item **3626**). Given the richness of this body of information, it appears that works already published and based on it may be only the beginning of an important body of literature. A continuing trend in recent publications is provided by the regional disparities in the Brazilian economy, most notably the Northeast. Northeasterners themselves (e.g., Celso Furtado, items **3628** and **3629**; Manuel Correia de Andrade, items **3580** and

3581; or Pedro Vianna, item 3693) are the primary contributors. The Amazon region is the focus of several studies. Of particular note is Roberto Santos' (item 3675) extensive economic history of the region between 1800 and 1920, based on his masters thesis at the University of São Paulo.

Brazilian writing on economics does not occur in isolation, and with the large number of economists, particularly younger ones, in contact with academic economists in other countries, it is to be expected that many of the themes and approaches familiar in the US and other countries should appear in Brazilian works as well. The concept of labor market segmentation is employed by José Pastore (item 3663), while Basilia Aguirre Salomon (item 3672) has masterfully applied contemporary microeconomic time allocation models to study low income family labor decisions in rural São Paulo. Rational expectations appear in a recent macroeconomic analysis of Brazilian policies by Antonio Carlos Lemgruber (item 3642). The monetary approach to the balance of payments is applied to Brazil by Antonio C. Porto Gonçalves (item 3634) while dynamic programming is applied in an econometric model by João Luiz Mascolo (item 3650).

In short, one must be impressed by recent developments in Brazilian economic literature. Although traditional themes are not neglected, an increasing level of methodological and theoretical sophistication has brought new insights to old problems. As the society moves toward more open and democratic discussion of its basic and largely economic problems, the economists' direct role as "technocrats" may decline, but their indirect role in clarifying the functioning of the economy and the choices faced by their society may prove far more valuable in the future.

3580 Andrade, Manuel Correia de Oliveira. Estado, capital e industrialização do Nordeste. Rio de Janeiro: Zahar Editores, 1981. 101 p.: ill., tables (Biblioteca de ciências sociais)

Examination of Northeastern development and industrialization, from colonial roots to present. Traces aspects of development which have been present in Northeast over several centuries such as role of foreign capital, concentration of income, and regional inequality.

3581 ———. Latifúndio e reforma agrária no Brazil. São Paulo: Livraria Duas Cidades, 1980. 115 p. (Coleção História e sociedade)

Three essays by one of the Northeast's best-known geographers. Contemporary policy is characterized as being "responsible for the great social and spatial concentration of income in Brazil and the continually decreasing standard of living of the Brazilian population." Third essay addresses some ecological aspects of current economic trends.

3582 ———. Nordeste: a reforma agrária ainda é necessária? Recife: Editora Guararapes, 1981. 119 p.: bibl. (Coleção Guararapes; vol. 2)

Collection of six revised and updated essays written 1978–80. They present a critical view of recent Brazilian economic development since 1964, which author argues has been characterized by "inhuman planning, which aimed at maximizing the concentration of income in certain groups, the majority of them foreign."

3583 Assis, Christine Ann and **Luis de Barros Rodrigues Lopes.** A ineficiência da política de preços para conter o consumo dos derivados de petróleo (IBE/RBE, 34: 3, 417–428, bibl., tables)

Questions whether price increases were the appropriate way to restrain demand for petroleum in Brazil. Estimates of very low demand price elasticities for gasoline and deisel fuel, based on annual data from 1970s, suggest that policies based on manipulation of real relative price will not produce the desired results in Brazil.

3584 Authoritarian capitalism: Brazil's contemporary economic and political development. Edited by Thomas C. Bruneau and Philippe Faucher. Boulder, Colo.: Westview Press, 1981. 272 p.: bibl., tables (Westview special studies on Latin America and the Caribbean)

Ten essays by a group of specialists in Latin American economics and politics. Common theme of many essays is the development of the Brazilian economy in a politically centralized, authoritarian context, which has given the government and state a relatively more important role in development than in other periods of industrialization.

3585 Azzoni, Carlos Roberto. Incentivos municipais e localização industrial no Estado de São Paulo. São Paulo: Universidade de São Paulo, Instituto de Pesquisas Econômicas, 1981. 103 p.: ill., tables (Série Ensaios econômicos / Instituto de Pesquisas Econômicas de Faculdade de Economia e Administração da Universidade de São Paulo; v. 6)

Prize-winning masters thesis submitted 1975 to University of São Paulo, work analyzes location decisions of firms in São Paulo state. Among potentially relevant factors identified by author's study are proximity to metropolitan São Paulo, local population, tax incentives, and municipal tax incentives.

3586 Baer, Werner and **Paul Beckerman.** The trouble with index-linking: reflections on the recent Brazilian experience (WD, 8:9, Sept. 1980, p. 677–703, bibl., tables)

Reviews some consequences of monetary correction in Brazil since 1965. Argues that the system created two units of account, nominal and index-linked, with funds fleeing to the latter sector, creating financial instabilities. Concludes that index-linking replaced some inflationary distortions with different type of distortions.

3587 Barzelay, Michael and **Scott R. Pearson.** The efficiency of producing alcohol for energy in Brazil (UC/EDCC, 31:1, Oct. 1982, p. 131–144, tables)

Analyzes efficiency of sugarcane-based alcohol production in São Paulo and Paraná region to determine the price of imported petroleum which would make alcohol fuel production economically viable. Concludes that the current program costs rather than saves foreign exchange, and that oil prices would have to increase significantly to make alcohol fuel socially profitable.

3588 Baumgarten, Alfredo Luiz, Jr. A aritmética perversa da política salarial (IBE/RBE, 35:4, out./dez. 1981, p. 317–337, tables)

Brazilian wage-adjustment policy, which since 1965 had been aimed in part at reducing inflation was modified significantly in 1979 to pursue distributive aims. Analyzes functioning of new system in adjusting wages in the presence of inflation and concludes that present wage policy must be abandoned.

3589 Behrends, Alfredo. A distribuição da renda real no contexto urbano: o caso da cidade do Rio de Janeiro (IPEA/PPE, 1:2, agosto 1981, p. 499-536, tables)

Study enlarges conventional concept of "income" for urban residents to include number of intangible amenities ("commodidades") such as public security, parks and recreational areas, and public transport. Concludes that in Rio de Janeiro, income defined in this broad sense may be even more concentrated than is income defined more narrowly.

3590 Berndt, Alexander and **Heron Carlos E. do Carmo.** 37 [i.e. Trinta-e-seis] anos de custo de vida. São Paulo: Universidade de São Paulo, Faculdade de Economia e Administração, Instituto de Pesquisas Econômicas, 1979. 92 p.: tables (IPE-USP relatórios de pesquisa; 4)

Cost-of-living and related price indices play crucial role in a highly indexed economy like Brazil's. This monograph discusses problems associated with the construction of meaningful cost-of-living indices in Brazil, presents an index for city of São Paulo for 1939–78 period, and concludes with analysis of index's major components.

3591 Bonelli, Régis and **Eduardo Augusto A. Guimarães.** Taxas de lucro de setores industriais no Brasil: uma nota sobre sua evolução no período 1973–1979 (IPE/EE, 11:3, sep./dez. 1981, p. 93–114, graphs, tables)

Analyzes evolution of profitability in Brazilian industry in post-"boom" period, focusing primarily on return to the firm's own capital, and using data from the VISAO register of major companies. In most of 47 sectors analyzed, there was a measurable decline in profitability after 1975, as the pace of economic growth slowed.

3592 Boschi, Renato Raul. Elites industriais

e democracia: hegemonia burguesa e mudança política no Brasil. Traduzido por Patrick Burglin. Rio de Janeiro: Graal, 1979. 249 p.: bibl., tables (Série Sociologia; v. no. 13. Biblioteca de ciências sociais)

Penetrating study of attitudes and perspectives of Brazil's industrial elite in post-1964 period, this study was author's 1978 Michigan political science doctoral dissertation. Pt. 1 consists of historical and theoretical examination of industrial elite; pt. 2 analyzes contemporary elite and the State, based on extensive interviews.

3593 Braga, Helson Cavalcante. Estrutura de mercado e desempenho da indústria brasileira, 1973–75. Rio de Janeiro: FGV-Instituto de Documentação, Editora da Fundação Getúlio Vargas, 1980. 169 p.: ill. (Série Teses EPGE/Escola de Pós-Graduação em Economia; no. 6)

Based on Fundação Getúlio Vargas doctoral dissertation, study applies carefully developed model explaining the rate of return to cross-section of Brazilian industry and to sample of individual firms. Results suggest that market power and economies of scale have a significantly positive effect on the rate of return.

3594 Brazil, human resources special report. Washington: World Bank, Latin America and the Caribbean Regional Office, 1979. 578 p. in various pagings, 1 fold. leaf of plates: bibl., ill. (A World Bank country study)

Extensive report on Brazil's population and development of human resources by World Bank team headed by Peter T. Knight. Special attention is given to population dynamics and uneven growth of the Brazilian economy. Valuable for large quantity of statistical information and for detailed projections through year 2000.

Brazil and Mexico: patterns in late development. See item **2999.**

3595 Bueno, Ricardo. A farsa do petróleo: por que querem destruir a Petrobrás. Petrópolis: Vozes, 1980. 109 p.: bibl.

Spirited and sometimes polemical defense of Brazil's state petroleum enterprise, PETROBRAS, argues that its efficiency is comparable to that of the best multinational petroleum companies, and that risk contracts with the latter should be revoked.

3596 Cano, Wilson. Raízes da concentração

industrial em São Paulo. Rio de Janeiro: Difel, 1977. 317 p.: bibl. (Corpo e alma do Brasil; 53)

Examination of industrial growth in São Paulo state up to 1930, originally written as author's Campinas dissertation, argues that São Paulo's industrial expansion did not occur at the cost of other Brazilian regions, at least before 1930.

3597 Cardoso, Eliana A. Celso Furtado revisited: the postwar years (UC/EDCC, 30:1, Oct. 1981, p. 117–128, graphs)

Examines effect of exchange rate policy and selective import control on the economy's level and rate of growth in post-World War II period. Generally supports Furtado's contention that policies stimulated industrial growth, but argues that these policies were far from optimal, due in part to their anti-agricultural bias.

3598 ———. The Great Depression and commodity-exporting LDCs: the case of Brazil (JPE, 89:6, Dec. 1981, p. 1239–1250, bibl., graphs, tables)

Analyzes macroeconomic policies in a model of an economy dependent on export of major commodity, assuming both idle capacity and unemployment. Model is then applied to Brazil in 1930s. Concludes that expansion of output in periods of both real appreciation and depreciation was due to relative strength of expenditure effects.

3599 ——— and Rudiger Dornbusch. Uma equação para as exportações brasileiras de produtos manufaturados (IBE/RBE, 34:3, julho/set. 1980, p. 429–437, bibl., tables)

Estimates a supply equation for Brazilian exports of manufactures, using data from 1960–77 period. Exports are found to respond with an approximately unitary price elasticity to changes in real remuneration of exporting relative to domestic sales. Time lag is about one year.

3600 Cardoso, Fernando Henrique and Geraldo Müller. Amazônia: expansão do capitalismo. São Paulo: Editora Brasiliense, 1977. 205 p.: bibl., maps, tables.

Viewing recent development in Amazonia is part of general process of capitalist expansion in Brazil, authors argue that style of colonization and settlement of region must be understood in terms of relations of production. They conclude with a number of suggestions for alternative public policies.

3601 Carvalho, Joaquim de and **José Goldemberg.** Economia e política da energia. Rio de Janeiro: Livraria J. Olympio Editora em convênio com o Núcleo Editorial da UERJ, 1980. 118 p.: bibl., ill.

Former official of Brazil's nuclear program and one of the country's leading physicists review technologies and energy sources appropriate for Brazil. They argue convincingly that policy should be directed at consumption as well as supply, and that greater emphasis should be placed on alternative energy sources.

3602 Carvalho, José L. and **Cláudio L.S. Haddad.** Foreign trade strategies and employment in Brazil (*in* Trade and employment in developing countries. v. 1, Individual studies. Edited by Anne O. Krueger *et al.* Chicago: University of Chicago Press, 1981, p. 29–81, bibl., tables)

Part of larger international project sponsored by the NBER to evaluate trade and industrialization policies in a number of LDCs. Analyzes employment implications of Brazilian trade policies and finds that shift from import substitution to export promotion in mid-1960s benefitted labor, since Brazilian exports are relatively labor intensive.

3603 Castro, Hélio Oliveira Portocarrero de. As causas econômicas de concentração bancária. Rio de Janeiro: Instituto Brasileiro de Mercado de Capitais, 1981. 172 p.: bibl., ill., tables.

Three related essays examine different aspects of increase in degree of concentration in Brazil's banking industry since 1946: 1) microeconomic analysis of banking industry that incorporates economies of scale; 2) graphical analysis of banking controls; and 3) examination of monetary policy and banking concentration in Brazil.

3604 Chiesa, Dirceu Antônio. O mercado financeiro, suas variações com os títulos mais negociados. 2. ed. atualizada. Porto Alegre: Editora Sulina, 1980. 190 p.: graphs, tables (Coleção universitária)

Intended to acquaint the Brazilian public with variety of assets traded in the country's capital markets, this work may also be valuable for economists interested in institutional features of Brazil's financial system. Includes discussions of federal obligations

(ORTN and LTN), state obligations, certificates of deposit, "letras de cambio," and other instruments.

3605 Cline, William R. *et al.* World inflation and the developing countries. Washington: The Brookings Institution, 1981. 266 p.: tables.

Econometric studies of inflation and contraction (1972–75), primarily as they were transmitted to developing countries, their effects, and effectiveness of policy responses. Contains case studies of Brazil, Central America (Guatemala, El Salvador), India, Malaysia. [J.M. Hunter]

3606 Coes, Donald V. The impact of price uncertainty: a study of Brazilian exchange rate policy. New York: Garland Pub.,1979. 261 p.: bibl., graphs, indexes (Outstanding dissertations in economics)

Based on 1977 Princeton dissertation, study examines effect of the "crawling peg" or "mini-devaluation" exchange-rate policy instituted by Brazil in 1968. Using both a microeconomic expected utility model and econometric estimates, it argues that reduction in real exchange rate uncertainty after 1968 may have been an important stimulant to exports.

3607 *Comércio Exterior do Brasil.* Secretaria da Receita Federal, Centro de Informações Econômico-Fiscais. Ano 8, Tomo 1, 1979- . Rio de Janeiro.

Issue contains computer-generated tables of 1979 Brazilian imports, disaggregated by: 1) locality of the importer; 2) port of entry; 3) country of origin; 4) exchange coverage; 5) tariff classification; 6) country of origin; 7) currency of invoice; and a number of other classifications, based on import documentation.

3608 A Compra da Light: o que todo brasileiro deve saber. A. Veiga Fialho, compilador. Rio de Janeiro: Civilização Brasileira, 1979. 188 p.: bibl.

Collection of articles by Fialho and others relating to the purchase of the Canadian-owned Rio Light and Power Company by Eletrobras in 1978 for approximately a billion dollars. Transaction is criticized in a populist, almost muckraking style as unnecessary, irregular, and injurious to the national interest, and a judicial investigation of the transfer is suggested.

3609 Condições de vida da população de baixa renda na Região Metropolitana de Porto Alegre. Secretaria de Planejamento da Presidência da República, Fundação Instituto Brasileiro de Geografia e Estatística, Diretoria Técnica. Rio de Janeiro: A Diretoria Técnica, 1981. 371 p.: bibl., ill., tables (Série Estudos e pesquisas; 7)

Survey of living conditions of lower-income groups in one of Brazil's principal metropolitan areas, based in large part on data from ENDEF (National Household Survey) of 1974–75 and from 1970 *Demographic census*. Includes abundance of detailed tables on economic activities, hours worked, nutrition, expenditure patterns, and demographic variables.

3610 Connolly, Michael and **José Danta da Silveira.** Exchange market pressure in postwar Brazil: an application of the Girton-Roper monetary model (AEA/AER, 69:3, June 1979, p. 448–454)

Uses approach originally developed for Canadian exchange market to study "exchange market pressure" in Brazil (1955–75). Authors argue that their monetary model appears to work well, especially in 1962–75 period, to explain movements in reserves and exchange rates.

3611 Connor, John M. and **Willard F. Mueller.** Market structure and performance of US multinationals in Brazil and Mexico (JDS, 18:3, April 1982, p. 329–353, bibl., tables)

Presents results of regression analysis of profitability and market structure for 70 Brazilian and Mexican branches of US multinationals, based on 1972 data. Seller concentration, product differentiation, and relative market share appeared to explain market power in both countries (see also item **3006**).

3612 Contador, Claudio R. Ciclos econômicos e indicadores de atividade no Brasil. Rio de Janeiro: Instituto de Planejamento Econômico e Social (IPEA), Instituto de Pesquisas (INPES), 1977. 237 p.: bibl., ill. (Relatório de pesquisa; no. 35)

Pathbreaking attempt to improve quality of economic forecasting in Brazil, based in part on identification of "leading indicators" like those of the NBER. Also discusses surveys and indicators provided by Fundação Getúlio Vargas and evaluates predictive capacity of different approaches.

3613 Correia, Serzedello. O problema econômico no Brasil: 1903. Brasília: Senado Federal; Rio de Janeiro: Fundação Casa de Rui Barbosa, 1980. 326 p. (Coleção Bernardo Pereira de Vasconcelos; 24)

First published in 1903, this collection of essays was an important early manifestation of economic nationalism by one of the leading political figures of the Old Republic. Many of the essays, first appearing as editorials, deal with Brazilian industries at the turn of the century.

3614 Delfim Netto, Antônio. O problema do café no Brasil. Rio de Janeiro: Fundação Getúlio Vargas (FGV), Instituto de Documentação: Ministério de Agricultura/SUPLAN, 1979. 259 p.: bibl., ill., index.

This work, originally Universidade de São Paulo doctoral thesis of Brazil's present Planning Minister, is a careful study of Brazil's coffee sector and the international market. Includes historical examination and econometric study of the market.

3615 ———. A recuperação da economia em 1980/1981. Brasília: Presidência da República, Secretaria de Planejamento, 1981. 55 p.: ill. (Publicação / Presidência da República, Secretaria de Planejamento, Coordenadoria de Comunicação Social; 05/81)

Text of Planning Minister's speech to Escola Superior da Guerra (June 1981), published with ensuing questions and answers. Among issues addressed by Minister are balance of payments deficit and external borrowing, inflation and salary indexation, and Brazil's response to the energy crisis.

3616 Dib, Maria de Fátima S. Pombal. Equações para a demanda de importações no Brasil: 1960–79 (IBE/RBE, 35:4, out./dez. 1981, p. 373–386, tables)

Attempts to estimate an aggregate demand function for imports by Brazil, in which real income and relative prices are the explanatory variables. Estimates were based on data for 1960–79 period, and permit a lagged adjustment. They suggest that the long-run income elasticity is greater than unity, while the long-run price elasticity may be around -2.0.

3617 Dornbusch, Rudiger *et al.* The black market for dollars in Brazil (QJE, 98:1, Feb. 1983, p. 25–40)

Develops a stock-flow asset market equilibrium model of the black market for dollars in Brazil, using it to explain the percentage level of the premium above the official rate. Shows role of expectations, seasonal factors, and interest rate differentials and successfully tests model with empirical data.

3618 A Economia política da crise: problemas e impasses da política econômica brasileira. Organizadores, Maria da Conceição Tavares, Maurício Dias David. Rio de Janeiro: Vozes, 1982. 141 p.

Group of eight essays on contemporary Brazil by economists from universities and research institutes in Rio de Janeiro ranges from external debt to energy policy and inflation. Essays represent interesting cross-section of current thinking among Brazilian economists, combining clear preference for a more democratic decision process with a high level of technical competence.

3619 Em discussão, o Brasil. São Paulo: O Estado de São Paulo, 1981. 281 p.: bibl. Proceedings of series of public debates about Brazilian economy sponsored by a leading Brazilian newspaper (Aug. 1981). Among topics discussed were the foreign debt, the international economy, and short-term government policy. Participants included Albert Fishlow, Celso Furtado, Mario Simonsen, and Michael Piore.

3620 Ensaios sobre política agrícola brasileira. Coordenação, Alberto Veiga. São Paulo: Governo do Estado de São Paulo, Secretaria de Agricultura, 1979. 294 p.: bibl., graphs.

Seven essays on various aspects of Brazilian agriculture by nine leading scholars (e.g., Ruy Miller Paiva, J.R. Mendonça de Barros, Claudio Contador, Affonso Celso Pastore). Topics included agricultural credit policy, minimum price supports, agricultural exports, and technological change.

3621 Exchange rate rules: the theory, performance, and prospects of the crawling peg. Proceedings of a conference sponsored by the Ford Foundation, the Associação Nacional de Centros de Pos-Graduação em Economia, and the Pontifícia Universidade Católica do Rio de Janeiro, held in Rio de Janeiro, Oct. 1979. Edited by John Williamson. New York: St. Martin's Press, 1981. 410 p.: bibl., ill., index.

Conference proceedings at which economists examined theoretically and empirically the use of a "crawling peg" exchange rate like that adopted by Brazil in 1968. Links between exchange rate policy and macroeconomic policies are the focus of several papers.

3622 Export diversification and the new protectionism: the experiences of Latin America. Edited by Werner Baer, Malcolm Gillis. Cambridge, Mass.: National Bureau of Economic Research; Champaign: University of Illinois, Bureau of Economic and Business Research, 1981. 301 p.: ill.

Proceedings of conference (São Paulo, 1980), deal in part with move away from import substitution and toward both export promotion and greater exchange rate realism in several Latin American countries. In one paper, Eliana Cardoso argues that a devaluation like that of 1979 transfers income from unskilled to skilled labor without affecting the trade deficit.

3623 Ferreira, Léo da Rocha. Um modelo de programação com risco para a agricultura do Nordeste (IBE/RBE, 34:3, julho/set. 1980, p. 333–363, bibl., tables)

Based on author's 1978 Florida doctoral dissertation, study analyzes sharecropping in Northeast's arid regions with explicit consideration of role of risk in decision-making. Linear and quadratic programming models were used, with results suggesting that cotton production is a relatively less risky agricultural activity.

3624 Fields, Gary S. Who benefits from economic development?: a reexamination of Brazilian growth in the 1960s (AEA/AER, 67:4, Sept. 1977, p. 570–582)

Argues that despite relative worsening of income distribution among individuals in Brazil (1960–70), the absolute level of welfare of poorest groups improved, with an increasing number of individuals rising above the "poverty line." Comments and criticism of article by seven economists, together with Fields' reply, appear in *American Economic Review* (Vol. 70, No. 1, March 1980).

3625 Fishlow, Albert. A dívida externa latino-americana: um caso de desenvolvimento com incerteza (IPEA/PPE, 11:2, agosto 1981, p. 283–322, tables)

Concerns the debt: magnitude and composition, cost, implications for future policy. Emphasizes Brazil and, for planning purposes, uncertainty involved. [J.M. Hunter]

Foxley, Alejandro. Inflación con recesión: las experiencias del Brazil y Chile. See item **3400.**

3626 Fundação IBGE. Estudo nacional de despesa familiar-ENDEF. v. 1, Dados preliminares. t. 1, Consumo alimentar, antropometria. t. 2, Despesas das famílias. v. 3, Publicações especiais. t. 1, Tabelas de composição dos alimentos. t. 2, Tabelas seleccionadas. Rio de Janeiro: Secretaria de Planejamento da Presidência da República, Fundação Instituto Brasileiro de Geografia e Estatística, 1979. 2 v. in 11: tables.

Basic summary tables of data resulting from the IBGE's ENDEF (National Household Survey, 1974–75) based on an extensive survey of 55,000 households nationwide. Survey includes data on occupation, family expenditures, durable ownership, nutrition, and household's demographic characteristics.

3627 ———. Matriz de relações intersetoriais, Brasil-1970. 2. ed. rev. e ampliada (versão final). Rio de Janeiro: Secretaria de Planejamento da Presidência da República, Instituto Brasileiro de Geografia e Estatística (IBGE), 1979. 266 p.: bibl.

Final version of input-output table for Brazilian economy, based on 1970 data. Matrix distinguishes 87 productive sectors and 160 product groups, based on industrial, service, agricultural, and construction data collected by IBGE. Introductory chapters provide extensive discussion of methodology used, as well as data sources.

3628 Furtado, Celso. O Brasil pós-"milagre." 2. ed. Rio de Janeiro: Paz e Terra, 1981. 152 p. (Coleção Estudos brasileiros; v. 54)

Spirited and sometimes impassioned group of essays by one of Brazil's leading economists. Among other topics, Furtado discusses social and ecological costs of rapid economic growth in past decade. Concludes that future development, especially in Northeast, will require "institutional alternatives" to present policies.

3629 ———. Pequena introdução ao desenvolvimento: enfoque interdisciplinar. São Paulo: Companhia Editora Nacional, 1980. 161 p.: bibl., ill.

Exploiting distinction between economic "growth" and economic "develop-

ment," author advances broad theory of development, emphasizing its interdisciplinary aspects. Although not specifically concerned with Brazil, due to its abstract and general nature, students of the Brazilian economy will be interested in seeing how one of the country's best-known economists views development.

3630 Furuguem, Alberto Sozin. Controle monetário no Brasil, o papel do "Open Market" e da dívida pública (Revista de Finanças Públicas [Ministério da Fazenda, Secretaria de Economia e Finanças, Rio de Janeiro] 39:338, abril/junho 1979, p. 11–31, tables)

Examines monetary control process in Brazil and attempts to identify instruments which should be manipulated, in context of Brazilian financial market development. Concludes that unsatisfactory performance of monetary instruments requires deeper analysis of available ones.

3631 Galvêas, Ernane. Brasil, economia aberta ou fechada? 2. ed. rev. e ampliada. Rio de Janeiro: APEC, 1982. 203 p.: ill.

In this second edition of his 1977 work, Brazil's present Finance Minister examines country's situation in world economy. Reviews recent trends and argues that the Brazilian economy has in general benefitted from an increase in degree of openness and inflow of foreign investment.

3632 Gattás, Ramiz. A industria automobilística e a 2a. revolução industrial no Brasil: origens e perspectivas. São Paulo: Prelo Editora, 1981. 532 p., 16 p. of plates: ill., ports.

Wide-ranging and sometimes anecdotal account of origins and development of Brazilian automobile and autoparts industry from 1930 to late 1970s by a participant. Potentially valuable source of information on government policies, industry strategies, and market conditions affecting one of Brazil's principal dynamic sectors in post-World War II period.

3633 Gibbon, Virgílio Horácio Samuel. Distribuição de renda e mobilidade social: a experiência brasileira. Rio de Janeiro: Fundação Getúlio Vargas, Instituto de Documentação, 1979. 103 p.: bibl., ill. (Série Teses; no. 5)

Author's Fundação Getúlio Vargas doctoral thesis, study analyzes Brazilian income distribution in 1970 and 1975. Despite worsening of income inequality in Brazil in recent decades, author argues that there are indications that social mobility for some groups may have increased.

3634 Gonçalves, Antônio Carlos Pôrto. O problema brasileiro de balanço de pagamentos e de endividamento externo (IBE/RBE, 34:4, out./dez. 1980, p. 533–540, bibl., tables)

Develops model for Brazil along lines of the "monetary approach to the balance of payments." Equilibrium solution permits a payments deficit and growing external debt. Model is then applied to petroleum price shock to examine appropriate policy responses in the Brazilian case.

3635 Gonçalves, Reinaldo. Proporção de fatores, escolha de técnicas e empresas multinacionais na indústria de transformação no Brasil (IBE/RBE, 36:2, abril/junho 1982, p. 161–181, tables)

Tests hypothesis that multinational firms in Brazil use more capital intensive techniques than do local private firms, using 1972, 1975, and 1978 data for several 100 firms. Concludes that in the Brazilian case the capital-labor ratios for the two types of firms are not significantly different.

3636 Gordon-Ashworth, Fiona. Agricultural commodity control under Vargas in Brazil, 1930–1945 (JLAS, 12:1, May 1980, p. 87–105, tables)

Examines Brazilian agricultural sector under Vargas, focusing on *autarquias* which administered agricultural policies. Discusses coffee, manioc, sugar, and cotton and concludes that there was little obvious change in quantitative terms, but that *autarquias* were socially and politically important.

3637 Graham, Douglas H. Interstate migration and the industrial labor force in center-south Brazil (JDA, 12:1, Oct. 1977, p. 31–46)

Uses manpower data base of Ministry of Labor to analyze interstate migration in industrial labor force development. Concludes that migratory process is reasonably efficient in allocating long distance migrants to most rapidly growing industrial labor markets. Suggests further refinements in data

collection and collation to permit evaluation of other hypotheses.

3638 Hewlett, Sylvia Ann. The cruel dilemmas of development: twentieth-century Brazil. New York: Basic Books, 1980. 243 p.: bibl., ill., index.

Sweeping review of poverty, inflation, ideology, the State, inequality, multinationals, and other themes in Brazil's "late development." Maintains that recent Brazilian economic performance "has depended upon massive poverty and political repression." Concludes that "there are no easy routes to the modern world."

3639 Industrialização rural no Nordeste do Brasil. Fortaleza: Banco do Nordeste do do Brasil, 1978- . 2 v.: bibl., ill.

Extensive report of results of two-year interdisciplinary study by eight Brazilian and Israeli investigators of prospects for industrialization in the Northeast rural areas. Six areas, including 19 *municípios* were studied, primarily through detailed questionnaires administered in nearly 12,000 interviews, covering variety of economic and social questions.

3640 Instituto Roberto Simonsen. A problemática da industrialização no Brasil: resenhas bibliográficas. Equipe de trabalho, coordenação, Maria Antonieta Lancellotti Del Priore. Colaboração, Paulo Celso Miceli. Resenhas, Antônio Favrin Filho, Paulo Celso Miceli e Paulo Sérgio Cappuzo. São Paulo: O Instituto, 1979. 192 p.

Collection of brief bibliographic essays on works related to Brazilian industrialization by both local and foreign authors, mostly published in past two decades. Over 80 works are discussed, with volume divided into eight subject areas.

3641 Kutcher, Gary P. and Pasquale L. Scandizzo. The agricultural economy of Northeast Brazil. Baltimore: Published for the World Bank [by] the Johns Hopkins University Press, 1981. 271 p.: bibl., ill., index (A World Bank research publication)

World Bank-sponsored study uses data from SUDENE/Bank study of 8,000 farms to examine land tenure, capitalization, seasonal employment and sharecropping, and number of other characteristics of Northeastern agriculture. Linear programming and other quantitative techniques are then employed to analyze number of agricultural policies.

3642 Lemgruber, Antônio Carlos. Expectativas racionais e o dilema produto real/inflação no Brasil (IBE/RBE, 34 : 4, out./ dez. 1980, p. 497–531, bibl., tables)

Examines relation between rate of inflation and output growth in the short and long run under a number of hypotheses, including rational expectations, using macroeconomic models suggested by Laidler and Parkin and by Lucas. Concludes that short-run inflation-output tradeoff in Brazil may be asymmetrical, so that "stop and go" policies should be avoided.

3643 ———. Inflação, moeda e modelos macroeconômicos: o caso do Brasil. Rio de Janeiro: Editora da Fundação Getúlio Vargas, 1978. 141 p.: bibl., graphs, index.

Five studies in which macroeconomic models are used to analyze inflation and monetary policy in Brazil. The approach is monetarist in spirit, and suggests that there is a tradeoff between inflation and recession in Brazil only in the short run. Econometric model for Brazil based on 1953–74 data is estimated and used to stimulate 1975–78 period.

Lewin, Helena. Educação e força de trabalho feminina no Brasil. See item **4557.**

3644 Longo, Carlos Alberto. Ajustamentos de impostos na fronteira e a alocação de receitas tributárias: o caso do ICM. São Paulo: Instituto de Pesquisas Econômicas, 1979. 208 p.: bibl. (Série Ensaios econômicos; v. 3)

Originally written as author's 1978 Rice doctoral dissertation, study examines functioning of Brazilian state value added tax (ICM), with special reference to state border tax adjustments. As major source of state revenue in Brazil, the distribution of revenues among states is a major interest of state governments.

3645 Macedo, Roberto. Salário mínimo e distribuição da renda no Brasil (IPE/EE, 11 : 1, jan./março 1981, p. 43–56, bibl., tables)

Argues that importance of the "salário mínimo" or minimum wage has been overestimated in debate over reasons for a worsening of Brazilian income distribution since 1960. Uses national household survey (PNAD) data to conclude that minimum wage legislation will not succeed as a policy to reduce poverty in Brazil.

3646 ———. Salário mínimo e pobreza no Nordeste (BNB/REN, 13 : 2, abril/junho 1982, p. 241–282, tables)

Examines minimum wage as policy for reducing income inequality, particularly in Northeast. Argues that there is little evidence that reductions in differences between regional minimum wages have contributed to reducing regional income inequality, and suggests some alternative approaches.

3647 Magalhães, João Paulo de Almeida. A economia e abertura política: bases para um novo pacto social. Rio de Janeiro: Livros Técnicos e Científicos Editora, 1981. 112 p.

Written in context of increasing hopes for greater degree of political liberalization, this group of essays examines some implications for economic policy and policy-makers of political liberalization in a period of economic crisis. Among issues discussed is labor, salary, and balance of payments policy, as well as technological dependency.

3648 Mantega, Guido and **Maria Moraes.** Acumulação monopolista crisis no Brasil. Rio de Janeiro: Paz e Terra, 1980. 106 p.: bibl. (Coleção Economia; v. 7)

Authors characterize Brazilian economic development in past two decades as movement dominated by the growth of monopolistic power. Critical period of early 1960s is examined, followed by discussion of 1968–73 expansion and succeeding economic difficulties.

3649 Martins Filho, Amilcar Vianna. A economia política do café com leite, 1900–1930. Belo Horizonte: Universidade Federal de Minas Gerais, PROED, 1981. 145 p.: bibl., ill. (Série Dissertações e teses; 2)

Revision of author's 1978 Master's thesis, which examines conventional view that history of Old Republic was dominated by alliance between *paulista* and *mineiro* economic interests. Argues that unlike coffee-based São Paulo oligarchy, Minas' ruling groups were much more dependent on the Federal government and its expenditures.

3650 Mascolo, João Luiz. Um estudo econométrico da pecuaria de corte no Brasil (IBE/RBE, 33 : 1, jan./março 1979, p. 65–105)

Summary of 1978 Fundação Getúlio Vargas dissertation, in which a dynamic model of beef cattle sector was specified. Data limitation precluded a test of the full theoretical model, but work is good example of use of careful theory to partially circumvent this problem.

3651 Melo, Fernando B. Homem de.
Abertura ao exterior e estabilidade de preços agrícolas (IBE/RBE, 35 : 2, abril/junho 1981, p. 189−205, bibl., tables)
Addresses issue of whether greater openness to international markets increases or decreases price instability. Using data for Brazilian agricultural products, which include both exportables and "non-tradables," concludes that for various food crops, greater exposure to world market has resulted in less price instability.

3652 ——— and Adolpho Walter P. Canton.
Risco na agricultura brasileira: Nordeste "versus" Sul (BNB/REN, 11 : 3, julho/set. 1980, p. 471−483, tables)
Focuses on production uncertainty in Brazilian agriculture. Various statistical measures are used to compare productivity fluctuations in Northeast and South for a group of products, among them cotton, rice, beans, corn, sugar cane, and manioc. Concludes that with a few exceptions, instability is greater in Northeast.

3653 Moreira, Marcílio Marques. Poder, liberdade, desenvolvimento: indicações para o debate brasileiro. Rio de Janeiro: Tempo Brasileiro, 1980. 196 p.: bibl., index (Biblioteca Tempo universitário; 58)
Wide-ranging group of essays dealing with contemporary Brazilian political and economic development, mostly speeches or articles published in 1970s. Among those addressing economic questions are "A Economia Brasileira: 1977−78," "Economistas na Berlinda," and "Sistema Financeiro de Cibernética."

3654 Morley, Samuel A. Labor markets and inequitable growth: the case of authoritarian capitalism in Brazil. New York: Cambridge University Press, 1982. 316 p.: bibl., ill., index.
Examines apparent worsening of personal income distribution in Brazil over the last two decades. Study questions consensus view, arguing that the poor benefitted more from economic growth than income distribution statistics would appear to indicate.

3655 Motta, José do Patrocínio. Economia mineira nacional. Porto Alegre: Uni-

versidade Federal do Rio Grande do Sul; São Paulo: Editora McGraw-Hill do Brasil, 1977/1981. 3 v.: bibl., ill., index, tables.
Vol. 3, *Economia mineira nacional,* examines technology and economy of Brazil's principal mining and energy sectors. Study includes processing and activities as well as primary extraction. Abundant statistics provided on costs, reserves, price trends, and infrastructure for iron, non-ferrous metals and non-metallic minerals.

3656 Motta, Ronaldo Serôa da. Custo social da mão-de-obra na região metropolitana do Rio de Janeiro (IBE/RBE, 35 : 3, julho/set. 1981, p. 251-272, bibl., tables)
Uses data from national household survey (PNAD) to estimate social cost of unskilled labor in Rio's metropolitan area. Concludes that social cost of labor in informal sector is approximately 63 percent of wage paid in formal sector. Estimate has important implications for analysis of investment projects in Brazil.

3657 Multinacionais, os límites da soberania. Getúlio Carvalho, coordenação. 3. ed. Rio de Janeiro: Fundação Getúlio Vargas, Instituto de Documentação, 1980. 387 p.: bibl., index.
Eight stimulating essays by group of social scientists, seven of them Americans, dealing with different aspects of multinational corporations and their political implications. Samuel Huntington's "O Brasil e as Multinacionais" and Theodore H. Moran's "Atomos para o Brasil" deal specifically with Brazil. Five essays have been published elsewhere in English.

3658 Musalem, Alberto Roque. Política de subsídios e exportações de manufaturados no Brasil (IBE/RBE, 35 : 1, jan./março 1981, p. 17−41, bibl., graphs, tables)
Complexity of Brazilian export incentives and other instruments of commercial policy raises severe problems for investigators trying to determine effects of these policies. Study presents improved time series for 1964−78 period, including several instruments ignored in earlier studies, which although not definitive, should be useful for studies of export promotion.

3659 Ness, Walter L., Jr. Vantagens financeiras das empresas multinacionais. Rio de Janeiro: Instituto Brasileiro de Mercado de Capitais, 1979. 219 p.: bibl., graphs (Relatório de estudos e pesquisas; 2)

Sponsored by IBMEC, the Brazilian Capital Markets Institute, study attempts to determine if multinational enterprises in Brazil have relatively greater access to financial resources than other firms. Concludes that government favoring local enterprises has been relatively successful in counterbalancing financial access enjoyed by multinationals.

3660 Nicholls, William Hord and Ruy Miller Paiva. Changes in the structure and productivity of the Brazilian agriculture, 1963/73: ninety-nine "fazendas" revisited. t. 1, Brazil South and Southeast. Rio de Janeiro: Instituto de Planejamento Econômico e Social, Instituto de Pesquisas (IPEA/INPES), 1979. 1 v.

Sequel to authors' 1963 study of Brazilian agriculture (see *HLAS 29:3959*) based on return visits to the 99 farms of the original survey. Penetrating study of agriculture at farm level by two leading specialists, providing wealth of detailed information on farm size, production, employment, and mechanization.

3661 Oliveira, Fabrício Augusto de. A reforma tributária de 1966 e a acumulação de capital no Brasil. São Paulo: Brasil Debates, 1981. 161 p.: ill. (Coleção Brasil estudos; no. 3)

Based on the author's 1978 Campinas Master's thesis, this is an examination of 1966 tax reforms and their consequences for the Brazilian economy. Intended to promote both greater saving and economic efficiency, author argues that they introduced a bias in taxation of labor income, relative to capital.

3662 Padis, Pedro Calili. Formação de uma economia periférica: o caso do Paraná. São Paulo: Editora HUCITEC; Curitiba, Brasil: Governo do Estado do Paraná, Secretaria da Cultura e do Esporte, 1981. 235 p.: bibl., ill. (Economia & planejamento. Série Teses e pesquisas)

Published posthumously, study was author's 1970 doctoral dissertation at Pontifícia Universidade Católica de São Paulo. Beginning in colonial times, growth of Paraná's economy and its response to external forces is examined. Author argues that its degree of autonomy has decreased, particularly since 1950.

3663 Pastore, José. Mobilidade social sob condicões de segmentação do mercado

no Brasil (IPE/EE, 11:1, jan./março 181, p. 21–41, bibl., tables)

Analyzes labor markets in Brazil in context of segmented markets, following recent work in labor economics, and using data from national household survey (PNAD). Brazilian labor law tends to maintain a degree of segmentation, which in turn has a measurable effect on the degree of social mobility.

3664 Pesquisa industrial: 1976/1977. t.2, Região Nordeste. t. 3, Região Sudeste. t. 5, Brasil. Rio de Janeiro: Fundação Instituto Brasileiro de Geografia e Estatístia, 1981. 3 v. (349, 245, 184 p.) tables.

Annual industrial survey of establishments in manufacturing, mining, and processing sectors, presented by *município*, as well as in aggregate form. Among variables included are capital structure, labor force, salaries and other costs, energy use, and inventories (vols. 1 and 4 not available for review at present time).

3665 Petruccelli, José Luis; Maria Helena Rato; and Sergio Luiz Bragança. The socioeconomic consequences of a reduction in fertility: application of the ILO-IBGE national model; BACHUE-Brazil (ILO/R, 119:5, Sept./Oct. 1980, p. 623–635, tables)

Uses simulation model developed jointly by ILO and IBGE to investigate effects of a reduction in fertility on a series of social and economic variables. Among them are the age structure of the population, wages in different sectors, investment and consumption. Results fall short of those predicted by many birth control advocates.

3666 Pinto, Mauricio Barata de Paula. Os efeitos dos incentivos sobre a estrutura das exportações brasileiras de manufaturados (IPE/EE, 11:3, sep./dez. 1981, p. 115–132, bibl., tables)

Based on author's 1979 Johns Hopkins PhD dissertation, this article analyzes effect of export promotion of Brazilian manufactured goods since 1964. Uses concept of domestic resource cost to attempt to measure efficiency of export promotion system.

3667 Prado, Eleutério Fernando da Silva. Estrutura tecnológica e desenvolvimento regional. São Paulo: Universidade de São Paulo, Faculdade de Economia e Administração, Instituto de Pesquisas Econômicas, 1981. 257 p.: ill. (part folded) (Série Ensaios econômicos; v. 10)

Originally written as a doctoral dissertation at São Paulo University, study focuses on geographical concentration of production in certain regions. Argues that there is a role for public policy and programming to improve distribution of social benefits of economic growth.

3668 Queiroz, Carlos Alberto Reis. A política monetária num contexto de indexação: o caso brasileiro. Rio de Janeiro: Fundação Getúlio Vargas, Instituto de Documentação, 1980. 165 p.: bibl., ill., index (Série Teses / Escola de Pós-Graduação em Economia; no. 4)

Originally submitted to Fundação Getúlio Vargas as Doctoral thesis, study adapts Federal Reserve Bank of St. Louis' econometric model to Brazil's inflation indexing system. Concludes that introduction of indexing after 1965 did not have a role in accelerating inflation.

3669 Rangel, Ignácio. Recursos ociosos e política econômica. São Paulo: Editora HUCITEC, 1980. 140 p. (Economia & planejamento. Série Obras didáticas)

In this collection of previously published essays, updated and supplemented by new chapter, author suggests that excess capacity is the rule rather than exception in the Brazilian economy. Advocates active role for the State in promoting economic development.

3670 Resende, André Lara. Incompatibilidade distributiva e inflação estrutural (IPE/EE, 11:3, sep./dez. 1981, p. 133–150, bibl., graphs)

Develops theory of inflation as outcome of struggle for distributive shares. Assuming an oligopolistic "mark up" pricing mechanism and incompatible demands by capital and labor, model leads to inflation when supply shocks hit the economy. Interesting linkage of economic and social structure in a fully-specified model.

3671 Rosenn, Keith S, Trends in Brazilian regulation of business. Washington: American Enterprise Institute for Public Policy Research, Center for Hemispheric Studies, 1981. 75 p. (Occasional papers series; no. 1)

Study takes as its point of departure the complexity of Brazil's legal environment, which some have estimated to consist of more than 40,000 laws. Author argues that

sheer profusion of laws, many of them in potential conflict, have exacted high economic cost, but for many reasons situation is not likely to improve.

3672 Salomon, Basilia M. Aguirre. A utilização da mão-de-obra familiar entre agricultores de baixa renda (IPE/EE, 11:3, sep./dez. 1981, p. 27–52, bibl., tables)

Uses microeconomic model to analyze time allocation and labor supply in low-income families in agricultural sector. Model is then applied to data from 106 families collected over two years from one of São Paulo's poorest regions. Good combination of theory and data, this work is based on a 1977 São Paulo Master's thesis.

3673 Sampaio, Plínio. Capital estrangeiro e agricultura no Brasil. Petrópolis: Editora Vozes em co-edição com CEBRAP, 1980. 140 p.: ill., tables (Cadernos CEBRAP; no. 31)

One of author's stated aims in this study is to provide information to those "sectors of the population who have interests to defend against the predatory exploitation of our labor force and our natural resources." Students of Brazilian economy, however, will find this a convenient source of potentially useful statistical information on foreign investment in agriculture, culled from a variety of sources.

3674 Santos, Dinaldo Bizarro dos and Sergio Alberto Brandt. Estimativa da função consumo agregado para o Brasil (BNB/REN, 13:1, jan./março 1982, p. 219–228, tables)

Attempts to consider explicitly both the dynamic and simultaneous aspects of the determination of aggregate consumption. Two-stage least squares estimates yield .96 for the marginal propensity to consume, but no evidence of dynamic adjustment in aggregate consumption.

3675 Santos, Roberto. História econômica da Amazônia: 1800–1920. São Paulo: T.A. Queiroz, 1980. 338 p.: bibl., ill. (Biblioteca básica de ciências sociais: Série 1a., Estudos brasileiros; v. 3)

Valuable historical survey of the economic growth of the Amazon region (1800–1920) by University of Pará, Belém, economist. Study focuses on growth cycles of regional economy, especially those associated with rubber production. Work is based on University of São Paulo economics thesis.

3676 Sayad, João. Energia e inflação (IPE/EE, 11, 1981, p. 35–60, graphs, tables)

Analyzes key role of controlled domestic energy prices in the Brazilian inflationary process in the past decade. A model relating energy prices and inflation is used to study pricing policies. Concludes that large simultaneous price increases have little of the desired relative price effect but do accelerate inflation.

3677 Schliemann, Peter-Uwe. The strategy of British and German direct investors in Brazil. Farnborough, England: Gower, 1981. 193 p.: bibl., facsim., forms, ill., 1 map.

Based on author's London Business School doctoral thesis, this is a descriptive study of British and German direct investment in Brazil since 1930s. Many conclusions are based on responses of 43 firms to questionnaire about their structure and management strategies.

3678 Schmitz, Hubert. Manufacturing in the backyard: case studies on accumulation and employment in small-scale Brazilian industry. London: F. Pinter; New Jersey: Allanheld, Osmun, 1982. 232 p.,: bibl.

Case studies of three small-scale manufacturing activities in Brazil are used to draw conclusions about employment, investment, income levels, and social mobility. Examines knitting and clothing industry in Petrópolis, hammock industry in Fortaleza, and weaving industry of Americana (São Paulo).

Seminario sobre Política Cambiaria, *Montevideo, 1978.* Seminario sobre Política Cambiaria. See item **3533.**

3679 Silva, Fernando Antônio Rezende de and **Dennis Mahar.** Saúde e previdência social: uma análise econômica. Rio de Janeiro: Instituto de Planejamento Econômico e Social, Instituto de Pesquisas (IPEA/INPES), 1974. 222 p.: bibl., graphs (Relatório de pesquisa; no. 21)

In last two decades Brazil has built one of the most ambitious and extensive health and social security systems in the developing world. Study analyzes macroeconomic aspects of this group of programs, concluding that their continued viability will require a number of reforms.

3680 Silva, Francisco Antônio Calvancanti da. Tecnologia e dependência: o caso do Brasil. Fortaleza, Brasil: Edições UFC; Rio de Janeiro: Civilização Brasileira, 1980. 98 p.

Based on Federal University of Paraiba Master's thesis, work focuses on relation between technological development in Brazil and dependence on foreign sources of technology. Author characterizes Brazil as "technologically dependent," with foreign technology dominant in many of the most productive sectors of the economy.

3681 Silva, José Francisco Graziano da. Progresso técnico e relações de trabalho na agricultura. São Paulo: Editora HUCITEC, 1981. 210 p. (Coleção Economia & planejamento. Série Teses e pesquisas)

Study is revision of author's Campinas doctoral thesis. Using Marxist approach to examine relations between capital and labor in *paulista* agriculture, he argues that partial modernization and accompanying increase in number of temporary workers is part of broader process of proletarization of agricultural labor.

3682 Silva, Peri Agostinho da. O controle monetário e a contribuição do open market (IBE/RBE, 35:2, abril/junho 1981, p. 105–155, bibl., graphs, tables)

Analyzes increasingly complex Brazilian financial market and implications of recent financial innovations for monetary control. Concludes that the performance of monetary authorities has been limited by these changes, using data for 1970–77 period. Good integration of theory and institutional considerations.

3683 ————. Desenvolvimento financeiro e política monetária. Rio de Janeiro: Editora Interciência, 1981. 201 p.: bibl., ill.

Presents wealth of information on structure of Brazil's financial system. Covers topics such as available financial instruments, primary and secondary markets, bank portfolio behavior and liquidity, and links between monetary policy and financial markets.

3684 Silva, Sergio. Expansão cafeeira e origens da indústria no Brasil. São Paulo: Editora Alfa Omega, 1976. 120 p.: bibl., tables (Biblioteca Alfa-Omega de ciências sociais; Série 1, Economia; v. 1)

Based on author's 1973 thesis at Ecole Pratique des Hautes Etudes in Paris, this study of the Brazilian coffee sector and industrialization before 1930 emphasizes the "form of accumulation of capital" in the coffee sector and "contradictions of development" based on this sector.

3685 Simon, David N. *et al.* Energia nuclear em questão. Rio de Janeiro: Instituto Euvaldo Lodi, 1981. 75 p.: bibl., ill. (Coleção Universidade & indústria. Monografias)

Six leading Brazilian engineers and physicists critically examine present nuclear policy. The focus of their criticisms is the Brazilian-West German nuclear accord, under which eight reactors are to be built. All argue that the accord in its present form is not in the national interest and that superior alternative policies exist.

3686 Simonsen, Mário Henrique. Novos aspectos da inflação brasileira. São Paulo: ANPES, 1970. 81 leaves (Estudos ANPES; no. 19)

Examines inflation in Brazil (1967–70), following assumption of Costa e Silva government and marked change from Castello Branco administration's stabilization program (1964–67). Written in 1970, it is an interesting analysis by a scholar who was to become one of Brazil's top economic policymakers in 1970s.

3687 ———. Palestras e conferencias. v. 1, 1974. v. 2, 1° semestre de 1975. v. 3, 2° semestre de 1975. v. 4, 1° semestre de 1976. v. 5, 2° semestre de 1976. v. 6, 1977. v. 7, 1978. Rio de Janeiro: República Federativo do Brasil, Ministério da Fazenda, Gabinete do Ministro, 1978. 7 v.

Consists of 11 speeches and lectures given by Finance Minister in 1977 to audiences such as Escola Superior de Guerra, Governors of the IMF and IBRD, exporters, bankers, and the Federal Congress. Among topics are balance of payments, economic policy and social development, and monetary policy and inflation.

3688 Singer, Paul Israel. Dominação e desigualdade: estrutura de classes e repartição da renda no Brasil. Rio de Janeiro: Paz e Terra, 1981. 185 p. (Coleção Estudos brasileiros; v. 49)

Based on 1960–70 census data, as well as household survey data, study examines distribution of personal income in Brazil, emphasizing links between class structure and income distribution. Special attention is given to evolution of income among lowest income groups.

3689 Smith, Charles H., III. Japanese technology transfer to Brazil. Ann Arbor, Mich.: UMI Research Press, 1981. 168 p.: bibl., ill., index (Research for business decisions; no. 42)

Originally submitted as doctoral dissertation in business administration at George Washington University, study is based on questionnaire responses by 33 Japanese manufacturing firms operating in Brazil. Among questions addressed are motivations for technology transfer, linguistic and cultural barriers to transfer, and ownership and control.

3690 Spindel, Cheywa R. Homens e máquinas na transição de uma economia cafeeira: formação e uso da força de trabalho no Estado de São Paulo. Rio de Janeiro: Paz e Terra, 1980. 184 p.: bibl. (Coleção Estudos brasileiros; v. 40)

Investigation of changes in social relations and production in coffee-based economy of São Paulo (1850–1930). Interdisciplinary in a political economy spirit, work focuses on "process of accumulation, or capitalist development."

3691 Taylor, Lance *et al.* Models of growth and distribution for Brazil. New York: Published for the World Bank [by] Oxford University Press, 1980. 355 p.: bibl., graphs, index (A World Bank research publication)

Study is outgrowth of World Bank-supported research on Brazilian income distribution and growth over past two decades. Using computable general equilibrium model, authors conclude that part of observed deterioration in income distribution can be attributed to public policy.

3692 Tyler, William G. The Brazilian industrial economy. Lexington, Mass.: Lexington Books, 1981. 152 p.: bibl., index.

Four studies of Brazilian industrial growth by a leading American student of the Brazilian economy, two of them previously unpublished or unavailable in English. Chap. 4, "Technical Efficiency in the Industrial Sector" uses an analysis of covariance approach to analyze micro-level industry data and concludes that foreign firms in Brazil were generally not technically more efficient than local ones.

3693 Vianna, Pedro Jorge R. Nordeste: a 79a. Nação (BNB/REN, 12:1, jan./março 1981, p. 53–87, tables)

Uses data on income per capita, industrial production, installed energy, road, water and other infrastructure supply, education and health levels to compare Northeast with the rest of Brazil and other countries. Using 1976 world data, concludes that Northeast's relative position has changed little in two decades.

3694 Villela, Annibal V. and **Werner Baer.**
O setor privado nacional: problemas e políticas para seu fortalecimento. Rio de Janeiro: Instituto de Planejamento Econômico e Social, Instituto de Pesquisas (INPEA/INPES), 1980. 369 p. (Relatório de pesquisa; no. 46)

Of three major sectors of Brazilian economy (i.e., government enterprises, multinationals, and locally-owned private firms), the last appears weakest. Study examines position of local private sector in national economy and analyzes number of government institutions and programs intended to strengthen it.

3695 Wöhlcke, Manfred. Abhängige Industrialisierung und sozialer Wandel: der Fall Brasilien. München: Fink, 1981. 262 p.: ill. (Beiträge zur Soziologie und Sozialkunde Lateinamerikas; Bd. 16)

Critical socioeconomic analysis of Brazil's dependent development which has produced enclaves of rapid progress and prosperity while contributing to further "underdevelopment" of country as a whole. While application of dependency model appears useful, author tends to overlook rapid expansion of broad middle class and Brazil's capacity to excell in technological fields traditionally the preserve of advanced countries. [Jan Peter Wogart]

3696 Zagha, Nessim Roberto. Política fiscal no Brasil, 1948–1968: avaliação de seus efeitos estabilizadores. São Paulo: Instituto de Pesquisas Econômicas, 1981. 110 p.: bibl., ill. (Série Ensaios econômicos; v. 11)

Based on 1979 Universidade de São Paulo Master's thesis, this examination of Brazilian Fiscal policy uses both historical data and a simplified macroeconomic model. Concludes that fiscal policy (1948–68) was slightly expansionary and that it had an output-stabilizing effect.

JOURNAL ABBREVIATIONS
ECONOMICS

AAA/AE   American Ethnologist. American Anthropological Association. Washington.
ABM/RB   Revista Bancaria. Asociación de Banqueros de México. México.
AEA/AER   American Economic Review. Journal of the American Economic Association. Evanston, Ill.
AGRO   Agrociencia. Secretaría de Agricultura y Recursos Hidráulicos, Colegio de Postgraduados de la Escuela Nacional de Agricultura. Chapingo, Mexico.
AI/A   Anthropos. Anthropos-Institut. Psoieux.
AI/I   Interciencia. Asociación Interciencia. Caracas.
AJES   The American Journal of Economics and Sociology. Francis Neilson Fund and Robert Schalkenbach Foundation. New York.
ANCE/A   Anales de la Academia Nacional de Ciencias Económicas. Buenos Aires.
APSA/R   American Political Science Review. American Political Science Association. Columbus, Ohio.
AR   Areíto. Areíto, Inc. New York.
BCRA/EE   Ensayos Económicos. Banco Central de la República Argentina. Buenos Aires.
BCRE/EE   *See* BCRA/EE.
BCV/REL   Revista de Economía Latinoamericana. Banco Central de Venezuela. Caracas.
BHEL/R   Revista del Banco Hipotecario de El Salvador. San Salvador.
BID/INTAL   Revista de Integración. Banco Interamericano de Desarrollo. Washington.
BNB/REN   Revista Econômica do Nordeste. Banco do Nordeste do Brasil, Depto. de Estudos Econômicos do Nordeste. Fortaleza.
BNCE/CE   Comercio Exterior. Banco Nacional de Comercio Exterior. México.
CAUK/WA   Weltwirtschaftliches Archiv. Zeitschrift des Instituts für Weltwirtschaft an der Christians-Albrechts-Univ. Kiel. Kiel, FRG.
CEDE/DS   Desarrollo y Sociedad. Univ. de Los Andes, Facultad de Economía, Centro de Estudios sobre el Desarrollo Económico. Bogotá.
CEDLA/B   Boletín de Estudios Latinoamericanos. Centro de Estudios y Documentación Latinoamericanos. Amsterdam.
CEE/RL   Revista Latinoamericana de

Estudios Educativos. Centro de Estudios Educativos. México.

CEESTEM/L Lecturas del CEESTEM. Centro de Estudios Económicos y Sociales del Tercer Mundo. México.

CEMLA/M Monetaria. Centro de Estudios Monetarios Latinoamericanos. México.

CEPAL/R CEPAL Review/Revista de la CEPAL. Naciones Unidas, Comisión Económica para América Latina. Santiago.

CJN Croissance des Jeunes Nations. Paris.

CLAEH Centro Latinoamericano de Economía Humana. Montevideo.

CM/DE Demografía y Economía. El Colegio de México. México.

CM/FI Foro Internacional. El Colegio de México. México.

CNC/RMA Revista del México Agrario. Organo teórico de la Confederación Nacional Campesina. México.

CPES/RPS Revista Paraguaya de Sociología. Centro Paraguayo de Estudios Sociológicos. Asunción.

CPS Comparative Political Studies. Northwestern Univ., Evanston, Ill., and Sage Publications, Beverly Hills, Calif.

CPU/ES Estudios Sociales. Corporación de Promoción Universitaria. Santiago.

CQ Caribbean Quarterly. Government Printing Office. Port of Spain.

CRIT Criterio. Editorial Criterio. Buenos Aires.

CSIC/RIS Revista Internacional de Sociología. Consejo Superior de Investigaciones Científicas. Instituto Balmes de Sociología. Madrid.

CSUCA/ESC Estudios Sociales Centroamericanos. Consejo Superior de Universidades Centroamericanas, Confederación Universitaria Centroamericana, Programa Centroamericano de Ciencias Sociales. San José.

CUNY/CP Comparative Politics. The City Univ. of New York, Political Science Program. New York.

DDW Die Dritte Welt. Verlag Anton Hain. Meisenheim, FRG.

EHA/J Journal of Economic History. New York Univ., Graduate School of Business Administration *for* The Economic History Association. Rensselaer.

ECIEL Ensayos ECIEL. Programa de Estudios Conjuntos sobre Integración Económica Latinoamericana, Brookings Institution. Washington.

EDTM Estudios del Tercer Mundo. Centro de Estudios Económicos y Sociales del Tercer Mundo. México.

EME Revista Eme-Eme. Estudios dominicanos. Univ. Católica Madre y Maestra. Santiago de los Caballeros, República Dominicana.

FCE/TE El Trimestre Económico. Fondo de Cultura Económica. México.

FDD/NED Notes et Études Documentaires. Direction de la Documentation. Paris.

FGV/CE Conjuntura Econômica. Fundação Getúlio Vargas, Instituto Brasileiro de Economia. Rio de Janeiro.

HAHR Hispanic American Historical Review. Duke Univ. Press *for the* Conference on Latin American History of the American Historical Association. Durham, N.C.

IAA Ibero-Amerikanisches Archiv. Ibero-Amerikanisches Institut. Berlin, FRG.

IAMEA Inter-American Economic Affairs. Washington.

IASI/E Estadística. Journal of the Inter American Statistical Institute. Washington.

IBE/RBE Revista Brasileira de Economia. Fundação Getúlio Vargas, Instituto Brasileiro de Economia. Rio de Janeiro.

IDE/DE The Developing Economies. The Journal of the Institute of Developing Economies. Tokyo.

IDES/DE Desarrollo Económico. Instituto de Desarrollo Económico y Social. Buenos Aires.

IEAS/R Revista de Estudios Agro-Sociales. Instituto de Estudios Agro-Sociales. Madrid.

IEERAL/E Estudios. Instituto de Estudios Económicos sobre la Realidad Argentina y Latinoamericana. Córdoba.

IEI/EI Economia Internazionale. Rivista dell'Istituto di Economia Internazionale. Genova, Italy.

IFH/C Conjonction. Institut Français d'Haïti. Port-au-Prince.

IG Information Geographique. Paris.

IGME/RG Revista Geográfica. Instituto Geográfico Militar del Ecuador, Depto. Geográfico. Quito.

IHGB/R Revista do Instituto Histórico e Geográfico Brasileiro. Rio de Janeiro.

IIDC/C Civilisations. International Institute of Differing Civilizations. Bruxelles.

III/AI América Indígena. Instituto Indigenista Interamericano. México.

ILO/R International Labour Review. International Labour Office. Geneva.

IMF/SP Staff Papers. International

Monetary Fund. Washington.

INTAL/IL Integración Latinoamericana. Instituto para la Integración de América Latina. Buenos Aires.

IPA/A Allpanchis. Instituto de Pastoral Andina. Cuzco, Perú.

IPE/EE Estudos Econômicos. Univ. de São Paulo, Instituto de Pesquisas Econômicas. São Paulo.

IPEA/PPE Pesquisa e Planejamento Econômico. Instituto de Planejamento Econômico e Social. Rio de Janeiro.

IRR/RC Race & Class. A journal for black and Third World liberation. Institute of Race Relations and The Transnational Institute. London.

ISTMO Istmo. Revista del pensamiento actual. México.

JDA The Journal of Developing Areas. Western Illinois Univ. Press. Macomb.

JDS The Journal of Development Studies. A quarterly journal devoted to economics, politics and social development. London.

JLAS Journal of Latin American Studies. Centers or institutes of Latin American studies at the universities of Cambridge, Glasgow, Liverpool, London and Oxford. Cambridge Univ. Press. London.

MPE Journal of Political Economy. Univ. of Chicago. Chicago, Ill.

JPR Journal of Peace Research. Edited at the International Peace Research Institute. Universitetforlaget. Oslo.

KYKLOS Kyklos. International review for social sciences. Basel, Switzerland.

LAP Latin American Perspectives. Univ. of California. Riverside.

LARR Latin American Research Review. Univ. of North Carolina Press *for the* Latin American Studies Association. Chapel Hill.

MN Mundo Nuevo. Instituto Latinoamericano de Relaciones Internacionales. Paris.

MR Monthly Review. An independent Socialist magazine. New York.

MSTPS/R Revista Mexicana del Trabajo. Secretaría del Trabajo y Previsión Social. México.

NACLA NACLA: Report on the Americas. North American Congress on Latin America. New York.

NACLA/LAER NACLA's Latin America & Empire Report. North American Congress on Latin America. New York. *See also* NACLA.

NCFR/JFH Journal of Family History. Studies in family, kinship and demography.

National Council on Family Relations. Minneapolis, Minn.

NEA/RBPE The Review of Black Political Economy. National Economic Association (and) Atlanta Univ. Center. Atlanta, Ga.

NOSALF/IA Ibero Americana. Scandinavian Association for Research on Latin America (NOSALF). Stockholm.

NSO Nueva Sociedad. Revista política y cultural. San José.

OAS/CI Ciencia Interamericana. Organization of American States, Dept. of Scientific Affairs. Washington.

OUP/OEP Oxford Economic Papers. Oxford Univ. Press. London.

PAA/D Demography. Population Association of America. Washington.

PAN/ES Estudios Latinoamericanos. Polska Akademia Nauk [Academia de Ciencias de Polonia], Instytut Historii [Instituto de Historia]. Warszawa.

PCCLAS/P Proceedings of the Pacific Coast Council on Latin American Studies. Univ. of California. Los Angeles.

PCE/TE *See* FCE/TE.

PP Past and Present. London.

PUCIS/WP World Politics. A quarterly journal of international relations. Princeton Univ., Center of International Studies. Princeton, N.J.

PUCP/E Economía. Pontificia Univ. Católica del Perú, Depto. de Economía. Lima.

PUJ/U Universitas. Ciencias jurídicas y socioeconómicas. Pontificia Univ. Javeriana, Facultad de Derecho y Ciencias Socioeconómicas. Bogotá.

PUJ/UH Universitas Humanistica. Pontificia Univ. Javeriana, Facultad de Filosofía y Letras. Bogotá.

RBMC Revista Brasileira de Mercado de Capitais. Instituto Brasileiro de Mercado de Capitais. Rio de Janeiro.

RES/EJ Economic Journal. Quarterly journal of the Royal Economic Society. London.

RU/MP Marxist Perspectives. Transaction Periodicals Consortium. Rutgers Univ. New Brunswick, N.J.

RU/SCID Studies in Comparative International Development. Rutgers Univ. New Brunswick, N.J.

SAGE/JIAS Journal of Inter-American Studies and World Affairs. Sage Publications for the Center for Advanced International Studies, Univ. of Miami. Coral Gables, Fla.

SS Science and Society. New York.

SSQ   Social Science Quarterly. Southwestern Social Science Association. Austin, Tex.

STPS/R   *See* MSTPS/R.

UC/EDCC   Economic Development and Cultural Change. Univ. of Chicago, Research Center in Economic Development and Cultural Change. Chicago, Ill.

UC/EE   Estudios de Economía. Univ. de Chile, Facultad de Ciencias Económicas y Administrativas, Depto. de Economía. Santiago.

UCC/CE   Cuadernos de Economía. Univ. Católica de Chile. Santiago.

UCC/NG   Norte Grande. Revista de estudios integrados referentes a comunidades humanas del Norte Grande de Chile, en una perspectiva geográfica e histórico-cultural. Univ. Católica de Chile, Instituto de Geografía, Depto. de Geografía de Chile, Taller Norte Grande. Santiago.

UCL/CD   Cultures et Développement. Revue internationale des sciences du développement. Univ. Catholique de Louvain avec le concours de la Fondation Universitaire de Belgique. Louvain, Belgium.

UCNSA/EP   Estudios Paraguayos. Univ. Católica Nuestra Señora de la Asunción. Asunción.

UCV/ECS   Economía y Ciencias Sociales. Univ. Central de Venezuela, Facultad de Economía. Caracas.

UFMG/DCP   Cadernos DCP. Univ. Federal de Minas Gerais, Faculdade de Filosofia e Ciências Humanas, Depto. de Ciência Política. Belo Horizonte, Brazil.

UH/ED   Economía y Desarrollo. Univ. de La Habana, Instituto de Economía. La Habana.

UJSC/ECA   Estudios Centro-Americanos. Revista de extensión cultural. Univ. José Simeón Cañas. San Salvador.

ULA/RG   Revista Geográfica. Univ. de Los Andes. Mérida, Venezuela.

UM/JIAS   *See* SAGE/JIAS.

UN/ISSJ   International Social Science Journal. United Nations Educational, Scientific, and Cultural Organization. Paris.

UNAH/RCE   Revista Centroamericana de Economía. Univ. Nacional Autónoma de Honduras, Programa de Postgrado Centroamericano en Economía y Planificación. Tegucigalpa.

UNAM/L   Latinoamérica. Anuario de estudios latinoamericanos. Univ. Nacional Autónoma de México, Facultad de Filosofía y Letras, Centro de Estudios Latinoamericanos.

México.

UNAM/PDD   Problemas del Desarrollo. Univ. Nacional Autónoma de México, Instituto de Investigaciones Económicas. México.

UNAM/RMS   Revista Mexicana de Sociología. Univ. Nacional Autónoma de México, Instituto de Investigaciones Sociales. México.

UNC/REE   Revista de Economía y Estadística. Univ. Nacional de Córdoba, Facultad de Ciencias Económicas. Córdoba, Argentina.

UNESCO/CU   Cultures. United Nations Educational, Scientific and Cultural Organization. Paris.

UNLP/E   Económica. Univ. Nacional de La Plata, Facultad de Ciencias Económicas, Instituto de Investigaciones Económicas. La Plata, Argentina.

UP/A   Apuntes. Univ. del Pacífico, Centro de Investigación. Lima.

UP/CSEC   Cuban Studies/Estudios Cubanos. Univ. of Pittsburgh, Univ. Center for International Studies, Center for Latin American Studies. Pittsburgh, Pa.

UP/TM   Tiers Monde. Problèmes des pays sous-développés. Univ. de Paris, Institut d'Étude de Développement Économique et Social. Paris.

UPR/CS   Caribbean Studies. Univ. of Puerto Rico, Instituto of Caribbean Studies. Río Piedras.

UPR/RCS   Revista de Ciencias Sociales. Univ. de Puerto Rico, Colegio de Ciencias Sociales. Río Piedras.

UR/L   Lateinamerika. Univ. Rostock. Rostock, GDR.

URSS/AL   América Latina. Academia de Ciencias de la URSS (Unión de Repúblicas Soviéticas Socialistas). Moscú.

USC/SSR   Sociology and Social Research. An international journal. Univ. of Southern California. University Park.

UTIEH/C   Caravelle. Cahiers du monde hispanique et luso-brésilien. Univ. de Toulouse, Institut d'Études Hispaniques, Hispano-Americaines et Luso-Brésiliennes. Toulouse, France.

UWI/CQ   Caribbean Quarterly. Univ. of the West Indies. Mona, Jamaica.

UWI/SES   Social and Economic Studies. Univ. of the West Indies, Institute of Social and Economic Research. Mona, Jamaica.

WD   World Development. Pergamon Press. Oxford, United Kingdom.

YU/IJCS International Journal of Comparative Sociology. York Univ., Dept. of Sociology and Anthropology. Toronto, Canada.

EDUCATION

LATIN AMERICA (except Brazil)

EVERETT EGGINTON, *Professor, School of Education, University of Louisville* *

AT FIRST BLUSH IT WOULD APPEAR THAT this year's material is not strikingly different from publications of recent years. On the one hand, the literature on the university and on education and development continue to predominate; on the other hand, the day-by-day operations of schools, the teaching-learning process, and early childhood and elementary education remain largely unexplored. Historical studies are plentiful and publications on educational planning and educational reform are well represented. The issue of educational equity continues to intrigue scholars.

A more careful appraisal, however, reveals some variation. For example, science and technology have received more attention. Bernal and Javier's examination of COLCIENCIAS, Colombia's official scientific and technological institution (item **4391**), Wionczek's analysis of developments in science and technology in Mexico (item **4475**), Grigorián's analysis of the consequences of Latin American unwillingness to invest in science and technology (item **4322**), and the UNESCO report on its 1980 regional seminar on science and technology (item **4500**) exemplify the high quality of many of this year's contributions. Other good examples include Lalor's comparative study on the productivity of Jamaican and other Latin American scientists (item **4445**), and Velasco's discussion of obstacles to the development of science and technology in Mexico (item **4474**).

Educational technology has also received more attention from scholars. Chadwick and Magendzo's examination of educational technology in government, in higher education, in multinational institutions as well as in a variety of other institutions (item **4375**) and Valenzuela's analysis of the effectiveness of learning resource centers in Chilean schools (item **4388**) warrant scrutiny.

Educational research in Latin America is the focus of several publications. In the past, scholars have not adequately addressed issues germane to the educational research process in Latin America—its problems and promises, its strengths and weaknesses. Escobar's analysis of the financial status of educational research (item **4314**) addresses one of the problems while Kreimer's description of the research activities of OAS's Multinational Educational Research Project demonstrates one promising approach to research—international collaboration (item **4327**). Schiefelbein's analysis of research and its effects on Chilean educational policy is extremely important although his conclusions are somewhat disheartening (item **4386**).

* I should like to gratefully acknowledge my indebtedness to Sheree Koppel, my graduate assistant, for her general assistance, and to Wynn De Bevoise of the University of Oregon and Alice Flynn, formerly of the US Department of Health and Human Services, for their comments on earlier drafts of this chapter.

Egginton's content analysis of the education sections of recent volumes of the *Handbook of Latin American Studies* revealed specific strengths, weaknesses, and trends of Latin American educational research (item **4313**). Item **4348** summarizes with recommendations a UNESCO-sponsored meeting on research in Latin America and the Caribbean; item **4387** does the same for an international seminar on educational research in Chile. Other works focusing on educational research are items **4386, 4400, 4426** and **4511**.

A measure of the effectiveness of educational research is its dissemination; a barometer, published bibliographies. Recent *Handbook* volumes have noted both the increased number and the improved quality of bibliographies on Latin American education. This trend continues. *Resúmenes Analíticos en Educación* (item **4385**) continues to be the best of a general nature; the best of a topical nature are those published by UNESCO's Regional Office for Education in Latin America and the Caribbean (items **4303, 4311, 4325** and **4353**). Two exceptional bibliographies focus on specific countries (item **4380** on Chile and item **4409** on Cuba). Additional bibliographies include items **4346, 4357** and **4397**.

Publications on the university and on development will be treated separately after a look at the material on the role of the university in development. Literature again this year points to a strong relationship between higher education and development. In 1978, the Corporación de Promoción Universitária (CPU) sponsored an international seminar on higher education and development in Latin America; item **4324** contains seminar essays on various facets of this topic including one on science and technology in development and another on the limitations on higher education in development. Additional literature includes Lema and Márquez's piece containing conclusions and recommendations on higher education and development stemming from several OAS- and UNESCO-sponsored meetings of education ministers (item **4329**), Rama's article on a UNESCO-sponsored regional study of higher education and development in diverse Latin American countries (item **4344**) and the Irvine study on the University of Guyana, which argues that certain conditions are necessary if a university is to be an effective instrument of national development (item **4440**).

National development, or lack thereof, can be only partially explained by the variation among national systems of higher education. The issue, however, is too complex to analyze from this single perspective. Current literature reflects the complexity. For example, an entire issue of *Educación Hoy* focuses on the relationship between education and poverty (item **4310**). Volume no. 11 of *Geosur* contains a wide-ranging analysis of education and human development and cites specific OAS activities in this area (item **4320**). Irizarry's study of education and employment in Third World countries concedes a relationship between educational investment and industrialization but argues that the general welfare of a people does not improve as a consequence of increasing resources for education (item **4326**). Several works focus on education and development in specific areas: the Río de la Plata countries (item **4351**); the Dominican Republic (item **4423**); and Venezuela (item **4514**).

Current literature contains numerous publications on higher education that do not discuss national development. Writings on problems that afflict higher education in general (item **4319**), by country (items **4367, 4446, 4487, 4494, 4508** and **4513**), and by specific university (items **4406, 4464** and **4488**) are plentiful. University reform literature is again well represented, including one of particular interest: Almuiñas Rivero's analysis of Cuba's post-Revolution reforms (item **4408**). Good companion pieces concern Colombia (item **4403**) and the Universidad Nacional Autónoma de México (item **4457**).

A new topic in higher education literature is university extension (item **4338**). In this article, Ontiveros posits that extension services are widely misunderstood yet are as important to higher education as are the university's principal functions—teaching and research. By far the most striking publication reviewed in this year's collection (not only among the materials on higher education but compared to the literature as a whole) is the multivolume series which commemorates the 50th anniversary of official autonomy for the Universidad Nacional Autónoma de México. Comprehensive in scope and lucid in style, this collection is a masterpiece (items **4448** and **4472**).

For readers uninitiated in the complexities of Latin American education and interested in the more general picture, Allard's review of Latin American developments in education over the last two decades provides an excellent overview (item **4304**); we also recommend the UNESCO study on a number of interrelated educational issues (item **4312**). The literature also includes high-quality overviews by country, including publications on Costa Rica (item **4405**), Cuba (items **4410** and **4419**), Ecuador (items **4429** and **4431**), Mexico (items **4459** and **4466**), Nicaragua (item **4483**), Panama (item **4484**), Peru (items **4492** and **4493**) and Venezuela (item **4510**).

The educational planning literature is extensive this year, showing an increase over recent years. Not only is the topic well represented, but the quality of the material is good and its scope is broad. For example, Fernández and Aguerrondo's discussion of educational planning from a theoretical perspective is excellent (item **4316**) as is Moncada's discussion of a more practical planning issue—how to expand educational opportunities without jeopardizing quality or efficiency (item **4337**). Country plans on Cuba (item **4411**); Costa Rica (item **4404**); and Venezuela (item **4519**), planning models (items **4450** and **4471**), and analyses of educational plans (items **4382** and **4414**) round out the literature in this area.

Nine publications focus on educational reform, including four on the Peruvian Educational Reform of 1972 (items **4491, 4495-4496** and **4499**). Hanson's analysis of the Colombian Ministry of Education's administrative reform is well documented (item **4396**) and Paulston's treatment of the Cuban educational reform model merits attention (item **4420**). Unlike others who have applauded this model, Paulston recognizes its remarkable accomplishments but questions its transferability.

Several works considering the issue of educational equity reflect a position consistent with that of previous years: despite the expansion of educational opportunities, inequities prevail and social justice is not served. Gómez argues that the expansion of educational systems in Latin America has resulted in even greater educational inequities and even more severe class polarization (item **4321**). Rama points to the increased educational opportunities in Latin America on the one hand and to limited political participation and inequitable income distribution on the other (item **4343**). Another work describes the persistent inequities which prevail in Mexico despite the premium which that government has placed on education (item **4452**). Gómez's analysis of the compensatory potential of the Cuban educational model concludes that while equity is the rule in Cuban education, equality in terms of social compensation remains elusive (item **4414**).

Current literature in the history of education is disappointing. As a rule, the topics seem too trivial or too broad; the documentation, inadequate or missing entirely; the footnotes, scarce or nonexistent. Brevity is unknown. The flow of university histories continues unabated (items **4373, 4381, 4442, 4447, 4456** and **4458**). The most ambitious study is Castillo's five-volume history of Mexican education (item **4451**). Other comprehensive historical studies include one on public education in Argentina (item **4361**), one on education in Tamaulipas, Mexico (item **4455**), and one on Guatemalan education (item **4437**). The most interesting items in this literature are Weinberg's intriguing but obscure comparative analysis of key historical periods (item **4356**) and Conte Porras' history of the Panamanian student movement (item **4485**).

Finally, there are the publications that do not lend themselves to easy classification. Two good examples include Déleon's intriguing work on folklore in the Guatemalan classroom, a rationale for inclusion and a proposal for implementation (item **4435**), and Escudero Burrows' analysis of problems in orthography among Chilean primary school students (item **4376**). Publications on somewhat more conventional and timely topics such as lifelong education (items **4302, 4318** and **4340**), special education (items **4334** and **4399**), parent education (item **4374**), teachers' unions (item **4393**) and teachers' strikes (item **4467**), women in education (items **4339, 4427** and **4507**), and moral education (item **4512**) were also among the literature reviewed.

In summary, the literature on Latin American education continues to be abundant in quantity, varied in scope, and diverse in range of topics explored. Generally, its methodology is either descriptive or historical, rarely experimental. Lacunae exist and there is little research that is rigorously designed and convincingly argued. However, publications that are largely polemical and based on narrow ideological grounds have also declined. There is light at the end of the Latin American educational research tunnel, and that light is research grounded in theory, based on adherence to accepted methods, focused on important issues, and directed toward the goal of high quality education. Let us then proceed.

GENERAL

4301 Acevedo C., Jairo. Educación y alienación: contribución al análisis de la función reproductora de la escuela. Medellín, Colombia: Ediciones Hombre Nuevo, 1980. 171 p.

Author argues that private ownership of means of production results in alienation among the working class. Marxist interpretation further contends that education serves the interests of the elite (owners of the means of production) by promoting acquiescence and passivity among the working class. The solution: education for liberation, not for domination; in other words, Paulo Freire warmed over.

4302 Alarcón Armendáriz, Alicia. La educación permanente (STPS/R, 1:2, mayo/agosto 1978, p. 77–88, bibl.)

Analysis of concept "permanent education:" its implications for curriculum, its development in historical context, its relationship to other "educational alternatives," and its role in a "new strategy for education."

4303 Alfabetización y educación de adultos. Santiago: Organización de las Naciones Unidas para la Educación, la Ciencia y la Cultura, Oficina Regional de Educación de la UNESCO para América Latina y el Caribe, 1980. 48 p. (Resúmenes OREALC; 3)

Consists of 97 annotations of publications (1975–80) related to literacy and to adult education in Latin America.

4304 Allard, Raúl. Educación, capacitación y recursos humanos (OAS/LE, 25:85, 1981, p. 3–37, tables)

Five-part review of developments in education in Latin America over last two decades: 1) education and development; 2/3) problems which afflict education at each level; 4) four OAS-sponsored inter-American educational materials programs; and 5) summary and conclusions. Author is Director of OAS's Department of Educational Affairs. Provides excellent overview of recent developments.

4305 Bieliaev, Viktor. Las tendencias actuales en la educación (URSS/AL, 3 : 19, 1978, p. 73—93)

Marxist interpretation of educational growth and development in Latin America. While acknowledging considerable growth in its educational infrastructure (albeit disproportionate with respect to social class and region), author argues that area's economic and social needs cannot be met by North American model of education. Latter, he argues, serves needs of wealthy capitalists. Cuba is cited as example of truly progressive educational reform.

4306 Blasier, Cole. The Soviet Latin Americanists (LARR, 26 : 1, 1981, 107—123)

Cuban Revolution provided impetus behind formal establishment of Latin American studies in the Soviet Union. Today, Blasier argues, the USSR's Institute of Latin America is the largest and probably most prolific research center on Latin America. Article describes it.

4307 Blat Gimeno, José. La educación en América Latina y el Caribe en el último tercio del siglo XX. Paris: UNESCO, 1981. 210 p.: bibl.

Summary of perspectives compiled from Regional Conference of Ministers of Education and of Economic Planning held in Mexico City, Dec. 1979. Sponsored by UNESCO with ECLA and OAS assistance, conference consisted of 27 delegations. Focus was on need to democratize education in Latin America and the Caribbean.

4308 Castro, Cláudio de Moura et al. A educação na América Latina: um estudo comparativo de custo e eficiência: Programa ECIEL, Projecto Educação e Desenvolvimento. Rio de Janeiro: FGV-Instituto de Documentação, Editora da Fundação Getúlio Vargas, 180. 225 p.: ill. (part fold.) (Série Educação/FGV/IESAE; 02)

Compares efficiency and equity of primary and secondary education in nine Latin American countries. Provides detailed information on school characteristics, educational costs and learning outcomes. Documents precariousness of school installations and poor utilization of existing resources. Indicates regressiveness of educational finance and suggests that programs created to redistribute opportunities have opposite effect. Contends that high drop-out rates are function of high private costs of public schooling. Concludes by presenting evidence that learning results for the poor can be significantly improved by increasing educational expenditures. Study is based on survey data collected as part of what is, according to authors, largest educational investigation ever conducted in Latin America. Important work. [R. Verhine]

4309 Dirección de Investigaciones de IASEI (Instituto Ajijic sobre Educación Internacional), *Mexico*. Evolución cuantitativa de nivel post-secundario en América Latina, 1960—1977: resumen y proyecciones para el año 2000 (UAG/D, 9 : 3, mayo/junio 1981, p. 15—36, tables)

Latin American school enrollment analysis by level of schooling for 1960—77. Also analyzes issues of personnel, finance, and literacy and presents enrollment projections to year 2000.

4310 *Educación Hoy: Perspectivas Latinoamericanas.* Asociación Educación Hoy. Año 10, No. 57, mayo/junio 1980– . Bogotá.

Volume explores relation between education and poverty. Latter affects physical and mental health of children which in turn affects school performance. Entire issue prepared by ECLA intended to help educators comprehend poverty's effects on learning.

4311 Educación sobre población. Santiago: Organización de las Naciones Unidas para la Educación, la Ciencia y la Cultura, Oficina Regional de Educación de la UNESCO para América Latina y el Caribe, 1980. 12 p. (Resúmenes OREALC; 2)

Consists of 25 annotations of publications related to sex education, health and ecology, and family planning in Latin America.

4312 Educación y sociedad en América Latina y el Caribe: Proyecto Desarrollo y Educación en América Latina y el Caribe. Compilador, Germán W. Rama. s.l.: UNICEF, 1980. 276 p.

Book is culmination of UNESCO/CEPAL/PNUD project entitled "Development and Education in Latin America and the Caribbean." Themes include education and social structure, education and development, education and rural society, and problems in education.

4313 Egginton, Everett. Educational research in Latin America (CES/CER, 27:1, Feb. 1983, p. 119–127)

By reviewing the content of education items in the *HLAS* during last 12 years, article analyzes, traces, and documents trends in research on Latin American education. Among its conclusions: educational topics change markedly from volume to volume; in like manner, countries emphasized in certain years are barely heard from in subsequent years. Includes brief history of *HLAS*.

4314 Escobar, Ismael. Financiamiento de la investigación educativa en América Latina (OAS/LE, 24:83, 1980, p. 22–47, tables)

Brief analysis of financial status of educational research in Latin America. Reveals that it has a low priority in most countries. Lack of recognition of need for such research resulted in no investment in it. Includes recommendations.

4315 Estudios e investigaciones sobre educación evaluacional. Consejo de redacción, Josefina Aragoneses Alonso, Luis Bravo Valdivieso, Cecilia Beuchat Reichardt. Editora, Erika Himmel. Santiago: Pontificia Universidad Católica de Chile, 1980. 115 p.: bibl., ill. (Anales de la Escuela de Educación; 3. época, no. 2)

Consists of seven articles on various aspects of educational evaluation (e.g., curriculum evaluation, measurement and academic achievement, evaluation and learning, formative evaluation).

4316 Fernández Lamarra, Norberto and **Inés Aguerrondo.** Some thoughts on educational planning in Latin America (Prospects: Quarterly Review of Education [UNESCO, Paris] 8:3, 1978, p. 352–361)

Educational planning in Latin America has not produced expected results. From a theoretical perspective discusses educational planning in order to understand its problem in Latin America.

4317 Filgueira, Carlos. Educational development and social stratification in Latin America, 1960–70 (Prospects: Quarterly Review of Education [UNESCO, Paris] 8:3, 1978, p. 332–344, tables)

Description of and reasons behind recent unprecedented development of educa-

tion in Latin America; an expansion which cuts across all countries and social strata.

4318 Freire, Pedro. La educación permanente. Montevideo: s.n., 1980. 125 p.: bibl.

There is a crisis in schooling; quite simply, schools do not serve fundamental human needs. Basic to the human condition is change; basic to traditional schools is stability. Permanent education is "educación para el cambio;" its focus is on the present condition and on the means to change the present condition.

4319 Garibay Gutiérrez, Luis. Reflexión y perspectivas de la educación superior en América Latina (UAG/D, 9:3, mayo/junio 1981, p. 5–9)

Author lists most urgent needs which Latin American universities will have to address.

4320 *Geosur*. Asociación Sudamericana de Estudios Geopolíticos e Internacionales. No. 11, julio 1980– . Montevideo.

Wide-ranging analysis of education and human development. Argues that education's contribution to development is limited by political and economic constraints; reviews OAS activities in human development; and describes several innovative human development programs.

4321 Gómez, Víctor Manuel. Expansión, crisis y prospectiva de la educación en la América Latina (FCE/TE, 48[1]:189, enero/marzo 1981, p. 121–155)

Argues that expansion of educational systems in Latin America since 1950 resulted in even greater educational inequities and severe class polarization. Manpower training needs dictated greater expenditures on secondary and university education at the expense of primary and adult education; thus, advantaged classes continued to reap benefits disproportionately to their numbers.

4322 Grigorián, Yuri. Industria, ciencia, tecnología (URSS/AL, 6:42, 1981, p. 22–40, ill., tables)

Highlights limited and unequal development of science and technology in Latin American countries and continued dependence on industrialized countries for manufactured goods. Among causes behind dependence are governments' unwillingness to invest in sufficient resources to achieve scientific and technological independence.

4323 Hanson, E. Mark. Field research methodology for the study of Latin American Ministries of Education (UNESCO/IRE, 27:3, 1981, p. 247–270, bibl.)

Framework for field study of Ministries of Education in Latin America. Assumes direct relationship between efficiency and effectiveness of Ministries and quantity and quality of school outcomes. Assumes potential to improve Ministry operations would improve school outcomes.

4324 Herrera Lane, Felipe *et al.* Universidad contemporánea: antecedentes y experiencias internacionales. Obra editada por Iván Lavados Montes. Santiago: Corporación de Promoción Universitaria, 1980. 306 p.: ill.

Consists of papers presented at seminars sponsored (1978–79) by Corporación de Promoción Universitaria (CPU) on higher education and development in Latin America and by CPU and Yale University on university politics.

4325 Inovaciones en radio educacional. Santiago: Organización de las Naciones Unidas para la Educación, la Ciencia y la Cultura, Oficina Regional de Educación de la UNESCO para América Latina y el Caribe, 1980. 25, 4 p. (Resúmenes OREALC; 1)

Consists of 63 annotations of publications (1975–79) concerning use of radio for educational purposes in Latin America.

4326 Irizarry, Rafael L. Overeducation and unemployment in the Third World: the paradoxes of dependent industrialization (CES/CER, 24:3, Oct. 1980, p. 338–351)

Third World development strategies emphasize educational policies that provide for high-level manpower training. Supposedly process of modernization would thus be accelerated. While acknowledging some industrial growth in Third World countries, author argues that there have not been commensurate improvements in welfare and standard of living.

4327 Kreimer, Osvaldo. La investigación educativa en Latinoamérica y el PREDE: sumario y perspectivas (UAG/D, 8:5, sept./oct. 1980, p. 5–54, bibl., table)

Profile of OAS's PREDE (Multinational Educational Research Project) includes a detailed description of current research activities and proposes future plan of action.

4328 The Latin American brain drain to the United States. Carlos E. Cortés, editor. New York: Arno Press, 1980. 508 p.: bibl., ill. (Hispanics in the United States)

Three studies report on Latin American professional "brain drain" to US: 1) comprehensive PAHO study focuses on motivating forces; 2) examines effect of US immigration laws; and 3) discusses impact on Latin American nations.

4329 Lema, Vicente and **Angel D. Márquez.** What kind of development and which education? (Prospects: Quarterly Review of Education [UNESCO, Paris] 8:3, 1978, p. 295–300)

Reflections on international technical cooperation and development in Latin America and the Caribbean. Focuses on conclusions reached at various OAS- and UNESCO-sponsored inter-American meetings of education ministers beginning with the one held in Caracas, 1948.

4330 Lima, Lauro de Oliveira. Pedagogia: reprodução ou transformação. São Paulo: Brasiliense, 1982. 110 p.: ill. (Primeiros vôos; 9)

Essay by noted educator-philosopher which argues that modern schooling serves interests of power rather than human development. Sees educator under capitalism and socialism as equally misguided and contends that solution lies in pedagogy based on scientific principles, especially those associated with "psycho-genetics" and "genetic epistomology." Provocative and controversial. [R. Verhine]

4331 McGinn, Noel. Autonomía, dependencia y la misión de la universidad (CPU/ES, 25:3, 1980, p. 121–134, bibl.)

University's *raison d'être* is truth, its transmission, application, and search. Analyzes academic policies in light of this function from perspective of two distinct university models: Napoleonic and Humboldtian. Concludes that while both models concern truth, their academic policies differ.

4332 Mamontov, Stepan. El estudio de la cultura como factor de formación de la conciencia nacional (URSS/AL, 5:41, 1981, p. 62–75)

Intriguing argument for interdisciplinary and multidisciplinary approaches to the study of Latin American culture. Argues Latin American culture cannot be understood without a multidimensional approach.

4333 Marquínez Argote, Germán *et al.* Educación y cultura popular latinoamericana. Bogotá: Editorial Nueva América, 1979. 201 p.: bibl., ill. (Contestación; 4)

Eight mostly doctrinaire, unoriginal Marxist essays by Universidad de Santo Tomás professors examine popular culture in Latin America from different perspectives. The exception is Germán Marquínez Argote's contribution which draws a striking parallel between oppression in Macondo (García Márquez's *Cien años de soledad*) and popular cultures in general.

4334 Martínez, María L. Educación especial en las Américas: metas para el año 2000 y desafíos para la década del 80 (OAS/LE, 27:89, 1982, p. 46–53)

Argument for universal special education for the handicapped in Latin America; problem areas described and goals established.

4335 Melfo, Hugo Daniel. Marginalidad, un enfoque educativo. Caracas: Centro Regional de Educación de Adultos, CORDIPLAN: Organización de los Estados Americanos, 1979 or 1980. 76 p.: bibl.

"Marginality" is not a problem but *the* problem in Latin America. Author argues coordination of institutions' services and programs to address the needs— including educational—of those living on the margin.

4336 Millas, Jorge *et al.* El rol de la ciencia en el desarrollo: seminario latinoamericano: 1977. Ataliva Amengual S., Jaime Lavados M., editores. Santiago: Corporación de Promoción Universitaria, 1978. 279 p.

Consists of 14 essays prepared for Corporación de Promoción Universitaria's (CPU) Latin American Seminar on the Role of Science in Development held in Viña del Mar, Chile, Sept. 1977. Essays organized into: 1) Science, Culture and Society; 2) Science and Development; 3) Organization for the Promotion of Science; 4) Science and the University; and 5) Scientists. Consensus among participants was: study and application of science is essential for economic and social development, science and technology

are essential to each other, and essential to a university is rigorous scientific activity.

4337 Moncada, Alberto. La crisis de la planificación educativa en América Latina. Madrid: Tecnos, 1982. 221 p. (Ventana abierta)

To plan for expansion of educational opportunities in Latin America without jeopardizing quality or efficiency of educational systems presents challenge to educational planners. Book analyzes results of study undertaken by Interamerican Center for the Study and Investigation of Educational Planning (CINTERPLAN) in 1980.

4338 Ontiveros, Eleazar. Extensión universitaria, un compromiso con la historia. Mérida, Venezuela: Universidad de los Andes, 1980. 126 p: bibl.

Two major functions of higher education are teaching and research. Third is extension services, equally important but not fully understood and at best only marginally implemented. Director of Extension Services of Venezuela's University of the Andes defends extension services, analyzes failure to provide them and describes measures to improve them. Message is germane to universities throughout Latin America.

4339 Ossadón, Josefina and **Paz Covarrubias.** Elementos para el análisis integrado del medio rural y, en particular, de la situación de la mujer en lo concerniente a educación, familia, salud y ocupación. Santiago: Organización de las Naciones Unidas para la Educación, la Ciencia y la Cultura, Oficina Regional de Educación para América Latina y el Caribe, 1980. 20, [16] p.: bibl.

Background material for UNESCO conference on rural women's educational needs. Reports on their level of poverty, employment, and education, technical and homemaking skills. Principal conclusion: in Latin America rural women carry lion's share of family responsibilities; yet, educational opportunities available to them are very limited.

4340 Prada, Abner. Towards a realistic approach to rural education (Prospects: Quarterly Review of Education [UNESCO, Paris] 8:3, 1978, p. 345–351)

Examines problems of impoverished rural areas (e.g., food and protection) and how educational systems should respond. Suggests lifelong education and community governance of local schools.

4341 Puiggrós, Adriana. Imperialismo y educación en América Latina. México: Editorial Nueva Imagen, 1980. 247 p. (Serie Educación)

Imperialist model of education (i.e., US model) has largely failed in Latin America because capitalist ideology on which it is based is unacceptable to the majority of Latin Americans. Well-presented Marxist interpretation.

4342 Purcell, John M. The preparation of modern language teachers in Latin America (MLTA/MLJ, 65:3, Autumn 1981, p. 269–272)

US professor of Spanish and trainer of teachers describes variety of modern language teacher preparation programs in Latin America. Observations are based on his short visits to these programs.

4343 Rama, Germán W. Education, social structure and styles of development (Prospects: Quarterly Review of Education [UNESCO, Paris] 8:3, 1978, p. 306–319, table)

Author argues that despite increase in educational opportunities in Latin America, political participation and income distribution remain very restricted. Country's social forces determine level of political participation, income distribution, and access to education. Thus, functions of education are limited (e.g., to transmit culture of dominant class, to preserve the status quo).

4344 ———. The project for development and education in Latin America and the Caribbean (Prospects: Quarterly Review of Education [UNESCO: Paris] 8:3, 1978, p. 301–305)

Reports on regional program sponsored by UNESCO, ECLA, UNDP, and 13 Latin American governments to study models of education and development in Latin American countries.

4345 Rivas Balboa, Celso. Educadores para un desarrollo autónomo: ensayo de pedagogía crítica. Caracas: Equinoccio, Editorial de la Universidad Simón Bolívar, 1979. 165 p.: bibl.

Argues that expansion of educational opportunities in Latin America will not contribute to dual goals of economic develop-

ment and social justice. Proposes new educational "paradigm" in which student and teacher through a mixture of study, work and research could achieve both goals. Author's analysis is convincing; his solution is not.

4346 Rossi Etchelouz, Nelly Yvis; María Teresa Recardininde León; María del Carmen D'Angelo; and Daniel Mernes Orbe. Bibliografía analítica (UJMS/U, 93, mayo/agosto 1979, p. 187–250, bibl.)

Annotated bibliography on the Latin American university.

4347 Sanz Adrados, Juan José. Educación y liberación en América Latina. Bogotá: Universidad Santo Tomás, 1979. 272 p.

Explores education issues from Marxist perspective. Looks at dependency of education on political and economic systems and reviews alternative models. Examines different educational ideologies vis-à-vis varied Latin American political contexts. Final discussion about potential of education to liberate is done with appropriate reference to Paulo Freire.

4348 Situación del investigador científico en América Latina (Ciencia y Sociedad [Instituto Tecnológico de Santo Domingo] 4:1, enero/junio 1979, p. 69–75)

Summary and recommendations of UNESCO-sponsored meeting held in Montevideo, Nov. 1978.

4349 Tareas y perspectivas de la latinoamericanística soviética (URSS/AL, 5:41, 1981, p. 4–21)

Prepared for XXVI Congress of USSR's Communist Party, article highlights Soviet Union's growing influence in Latin American affairs, particularly in the literacy movement, educational reforms, and "anti-imperialist" ideology.

4350 Tedesco, Juan Carlos. Conceptos de sociología de la educación. Buenos Aires: Centro Editor de América Latina, 1980. 126 p.: bibl. (La Nueva biblioteca; 34)

Sociological analysis of educational issues from Latin American perspective (e.g., literacy, social change, finance, personnel).

4351 Triviños, Augusto Silva; Richard George Wright; and Maria Carmen Rosa de Souza. Analfabetismo, evasão escolar e produto interno bruto per capita nos países da Bacia do Prata: Argentina, Bolívia, Brasil,

Paraguai e Uruguai (Educação e Realidade [Universidade Federal do Rio Grande do Sul, Faculdade de Educação, Porto Alegre] 5:1, jan./abril 1980, p. 31–53, bibl., tables)

River Plate Treaty signed by Argentina, Bolivia, Brazil, Paraguay, and Uruguay in 1969 addressed common development goals. Reports on progress toward one such goal: education.

4352 Tünnermann Bernheim, Carlos. Ensayos sobre la universidad latinoamericana. Universitaria Rodrigo Facio, Costa Rica: Editorial Universitaria Centroamericana, 1981. 223 p. (Colección Aula)

Six essays on the Latin American university explore its role in scientific and technological development and analyze problems of university autonomy and democratization of higher education.

4353 UNESCO. Regional Office for Education in Latin America and the Caribbean. Bibliografía sobre construcciones escolares y equipamiento educativo. Santiago: UNESCO, OREALC, Servicio de Biblioteca y Documentación, 1980. 25 p. (OREALC/ bibliografías; 20)

Brief unannotated bibliography on school construction and equipment in Latin America and the Caribbean has no analysis.

4354 Velázquez, María del Carmen. Situación de la investigación historiográfica en América (PAIGH/H, 90, julio/dic. 1980, p. 93–97)

Speech to Historical Commission of Latin America asks: Where is significant historical research in Latin America conducted? How is it conducted? What is its focus?

4355 Vólov, Boris. Centro de la latinoamericanística soviética (URSS/AL, 5:41, 1981, p. 76–96, ill.)

Soviet Academy of Science's Institute for Latin America consists of four sections: 1) Economics; 2) Social and Political Problems; 3) Geography and International Relations; and 4) Dissemination. Article provides detailed description of their organization, staffing, accomplishments, and agenda.

4356 Weinberg, Gregorio. Educational models in the historical development of Latin America (Prospects: Quarterly Review of Education [UNESCO, Paris] 8:3, 1978, p. 320–331)

Examines and compares key historical periods in Latin America where educational systems and philosophies differed according to country and circumstances during 19th century. Argues that differences can be understood *only* by considering each country's development model or style. Author's logic is not altogether clear.

ARGENTINA

4357 Córdoba, Argentina. Universidad Nacional. Biblioteca Mayor. Aportes para una bibliografía sobre la Universidad Nacional de Córdoba. Córdoba: División Publicidad de la Biblioteca Mayor, 1979. 73 leaves: index.

Consists of annotated entries on all aspects of the University of Córdoba compiled mostly from its publications.

4358 Estadísticas de la educación: síntesis.
Buenos Aires: Ministerio de Cultura y Educación, Departamento de Estadística, 1977. 1 v.

Statistical abstracts of enrollment in Argentine educational institutions (1970–77) cover preschool, primary, secondary, and higher by category of educational institution (national, provincial, municipal, private) and by jurisdiction. Includes other education-related data.

4359 Fainholc, Beatriz. La educación rural argentina. Buenos Aires: Librería del Colegio, 1980. 158 p.: bibl., ill. (Biblioteca Nueva Pedagogía)

Author argues that single system of education cannot meet both urban and rural needs. Traditional Argentine educational system is urban-oriented, based on models from technologically advanced countries and does not address rural needs. Recommends alternative systems that provide universal primary education for children and basic and functional education for adults; secondary-level and university-level technical and agricultural training; and lifelong community-based education.

4360 Levin, Emanuel. Los jóvenes argentinos y la investigación científico-tecnológica. Buenos Aires?: Ediciones Lihuel, 1981. 158 p.: ill.

World renowned cancer research specialist wrote this book to improve conditions for scientific and technological study. Years ago Argentina attracted greatest scientific minds; today it shares the lead in the Latin American "brain drain" with Colombia. Dr. Levin, whose own work has suffered from his country's hostility to science, hopes to stem this scientific and intellectual exodus. Should be required reading for the military junta.

4361 Martínez Paz, Fernando. El sistema educativo nacional: formación, desarrollo, crisis. Córdoba, Argentina: Universidad Nacional de Córdoba, Dirección General de Publicaciones, 1980. 254 p.: bibl.

History of public education in Argentina organized into: 1) formation, or time when public education evolved (1863–84); 2) development characterized by expansion and consolidation (1884–1916); and 3) crisis (1916 to present).

4362 La Regionalización educativa en la República Argentina (OAS/LE, 87:25, 1981, p. 49–71, tables)

Careful analysis examines Argentine educational system with specific focus on regionalization. Considers development of regional model in context of Argentina's economic, legislative, and political history. Excellent overview includes detailed description of contemporary system.

4363 Taquini, Alberto C., hijo. Analfabetismo y deserción; condicionantes para la superación: pts. 1/2 (CRIT, 54:1865, agosto 1981, p. 449–458, graphs, tables; 54:1866, sept. 1981, p. 485–489, bibl.)

Comprehensive report on extent of illiteracy and school desertion in Argentina by age, region, and residence (urban/rural). Includes both comprehensive data and sophisticated analysis.

BOLIVIA

4364 Cisneros C., Antonio and H.C.F. Mansilla. Las ciencias sociales en Bolivia: perfil sectorial y política científica. La Paz: Ediciones CIS, 1978. 37 leaves (Serie Estudios de recursos humanos; no. 1)

Three marginally related essays examine: 1) failure of social sciences to promote

Bolivian social change; 2) proposals to promote social sciences; and 3) science and reason in a philosophical essay that is unrelated and incomprehensible.

4365 Evaluación educativa: República de Bolivia. Servando Serrano Torrico, compilador. Cochabamba, Bolivia: S. Serrano Torrico, 1981. 62 p.

Bolivian decree established major educational objectives for all levels and types of schools. Law required regular, systematic, and comprehensive evaluations consistent with aforementioned objectives. Reproduces 1973 decree in its entirety as well as regulations governing required evaluations.

4366 Halconruy, René. Georges Rouma, pionero de las relaciones pedagógicas belgo-bolivianas. Traducción y prefacio de Guillermo Francovich. Sucre, Bolivia: Universidad Mayor, Real y Pontificia de San Francisco Xavier de Chuquisaca, 1980. 102 p.: bibl., port.

Biography of Belgian (d. 1976) who founded first normal school in Bolivia—Escuela Normal de Sucre—in 1909. Also founded Instituto Normal Superior de La Paz and was Bolivia's Director General of Primary, Secondary, and Normal Schools.

4367 Ortiz Lema, Edgar. Universidad boliviana: un enfoque crítico. Tarija: Universidad Boliviana "Juan Misael Saracho," 1980. 115 p.: ill.

Discussion of various crises which afflict higher education in Bolivia (e.g., student enrollments, finance, credibility, curriculum, autonomy, governance). Treats all universities collectively by referring to them as "the Bolivian university."

4368 Pilone, Jorge. La situación educativa en Bolivia según la información del censo nacional de 1976. La Paz: Ministerio de Planeamiento y Coordinación, Instituto Nacional de Estadística, 1979? 22 leaves: ill.

Analysis of educational data from 1976 Bolivian census. Includes comparison of enrollment data from 1950 and 1976 censuses by sex and by age. Compares enrollment data from 1976 census by age, by sex, by residence (rural/urban), by native language (Spanish/indigenous), and by employment status (employed/unemployed). Purely descriptive study.

4369 Villa-Gómez, Guido. El pensamiento pedagógico de Guido Villa-Gómez. La Paz: Instituto Boliviano de Cultura, 1979. 354 p.: bibl.

Selection of works (position papers, essays, educational plans) of noted Bolivian educator (1917–68).

THE CARIBBEAN AND WEST INDIES

4370 *Caribbean Journal of Education.* University of the West Indies, School of Education. Vol. 4, No. 3, Sept. 1977– . Mona, Jamaica.

Articles on Caribbean education examine issues such as relationship between classroom space and learning; academic motivation among Jamaican high school students; school expenditures of 12 Caribbean countries; and rationale for a West Indian language arts course.

4371 Fergus, Howard A. Restructuring education in Montserrat and St. Kitts (Caribbean Journal of Education [University of the West Indies, School of Education, Mona, Jamaica] 5 : 1/2, Jan./April 1978, p. 32–46, bibl.)

Suggestions on restructuring education in the English-speaking Caribbean, specifically in Montserrat and St. Kitts, to address development needs. Allows that task is difficult in light of questionable assumption that education promotes socioeconomic development.

CHILE

4372 Alarcón Quezada, Dina. La educación de párvulos en Chile: algunos datos sobre su trayectoria (Enfoques Educacionales [Universidad de Chile, Facultad de Educación, Santiago] 3, 1978, p. 40–50, bibl., facsim., ill., table)

Brief but excellent review of preschool education in Chile. Focuses on factors influencing development; legislation, regulations, plans, and programs shaping and defining its structure; and enrollment data describing its programs.

4373 Avila Martel, Alamiro de. Reseña histórica de la Universidad de Chile, 1622–1979. Santiago: Ediciones de la Universidad de Chile, 1979. 79 p.: ill., ports.

Brief history of the University of Chile by Alamiro de Avila Martel of the Chilean Academy of History. Concise yet comprehensive; however, no footnotes or bibliography.

4374 Balmaceda, Carmen *et al.* Parents help to educate their children: an experiment in Chile (Prospects: Quarterly Review of Education [UNESCO, Paris] 7 : 4, 1977, p. 557–564)

Rationale for Chile's Parent-and-Children Project sponsored by CIDE and located in rural village 600 km from Santiago, is to compensate for an educationally deprived environment by enriching the learning potential of the home and the community through parent education. Well worth reading, especially by rural education policy makers.

4375 Chadwick, Clifton B. and **Abraham Magendzo.** Tecnología educativa en Latinoamérica y la instrucción personalizada en Chile: una visión panorámica (Enfoques Educacionales [Universidad de Chile, Facultad de Educación, Santiago] 4, 1979, p. 42–51, table)

Interesting, wide-ranging examination of educational technology (e.g., in government, universities, multinational and private institutions). Also includes interesting description of manner in which Chilean universities have begun to implement "personalized instruction" to replace traditional instruction.

4376 Escudero Burrows, Ethel *et al.* Enseñanza de la ortografía significación de los grupos flexibles de nivelación permanente en la enseñanza de la ortografía (Enfoques Educacionales [Universidad de Chile, Facultad de Educación, Santiago] 2, 1978, p. 83–99, tables)

Analysis of problems in orthography among Chilean primary school students and proposed curriculum to resolve them.

4377 ——— and **Aída Barrueto Latapia.** Antecedentes sobre la investigación en Chile (Enfoques Educacionales [Universidad de Chile, Facultad de Educación, Santiago] 2, 1978, p. 100–114)

Examination of state of educational research in Chile from historical and contemporary perspectives.

4378 **Gajardo, Marcela.** Ruptura y permanencia: dos dimensiones de la educación de adultos en la sociedad chilena (CPU/ES, 26:4, 1980, p. 111–130)

As of 1960s, societal changes in Chile required increased attention to adult education. Discusses these changes in light of the country's manpower needs and examines adult education as means to alleviate manpower shortages.

4379 **Garretón, Manuel Antonio.** Universidad y política en los procesos de transformación y reversión en Chile 1967–1977 (CPU/ES, 26:4, 1980, p. 83–109)

Analysis of Chilean university reform distinguishes four stages in reform process. The latter abruptly ended with the 1973 military coup after which university authority was delegated to military appointees.

4380 **Grossi, María Clara** and **Ernesto Schiefelbein.** Bibliografía de la educación chilena, 1973–1980. Santiago: Corporación de Promoción Universitaria, 1980. 335 p.: ill., indexes (Serie Documentos de trabajo C.P.U.)

Annotated bibliography of Chilean education includes works published 1973–80. Entries are classified by educational topic and level, and by author.

4381 **Kirberg B., Enrique.** Los nuevos profesionales: educación universitaria de trabajadores: Chile, UTE, 1968–1973. Guadalajara, México: Instituto de Estudios Sociales, Universidad de Guadalajara, 1981. 506 p.: ill. (Colección Aportaciones)

Comprehensive history of the Universidad Técnica del Estado (Chile) focuses on its pre-military coup reforms which resulted in: triple enrollment, dramatic increase in lower-class representation, numerous new and technologically oriented courses, and new technological institutes. Author, incarcerated by Chilean military regime for so-called subversive activities, was University's Rector (1968–73).

4382 **Livacic G., Ernesto** and **Josefina Aragoneses A.** Nuevos planes y programas de educación general básica: dos análisis (UCC/RU, 5, abril 1981, p. 121-134, tables)

Two separate analyses of Chilean Ministry of Education Decree (1980) which established country's plan for General Basic Education, find positive and negative aspects (e.g., more freedom but less structure).

4383 **Luco, Joaquín V.** De lo que aconteció a un científico del siglo XX en lo que fuera el Reyno de Chile (UCC/RU, 5, abril 1981, p. 86–96, ill.)

General description of development of science in Chile by professor of neurophysiology and pharmacology at Pontifical Catholic University of Chile since 1931.

4384 **Nazar, Víctor.** El ingreso a la Universidad de Chile y a las carreras de pedagogía en el año 1978 (CPU/ES, 25:3, 1980, p. 135–172, graphs, tables)

Compares socioeconomic status and social class of students in education and students in other fields at University of Chile in 1978. Differences are not statistically significant but they point in one direction: education students come from more disadvantaged backgrounds.

4385 *Resúmenes Analíticos en Educación.* Centro de Investigación y Desarrollo de la Educación (CIDE). Nos. 1810/1929, 2. semestre, 1980 [through] Nos. 2050/2209, 2. semestre 1981– . Santiago.

These issues contain 280 well-annotated entries which focus on a variety of educational topics (see also *HLAS 39:4341* and *HLAS 41:4350*).

4386 **Schiefelbein, Ernesto.** Research, policy and practice: the case of Chile (UNESCO/IRE, 27:2, 1981, p. 153–162, bibl.)

Author reflects on why only certain research has had significant and lasting impact on educational policies and practices in Chile. Most likely to be influential is research requested by high-level officials and/or of interest to the media. Concludes that decision-making is highly political.

4387 **Seminario sobre el Futuro de la Investigación Educacional en Chile,** *Santiago, 1980.* Conclusiones y resúmenes de los trabajos, Santiago, 10 al 12 de enero de 1980. Santiago: CIDE, 1980. 296 p.: bibl., ill. (Documentos de trabajo/CIDE; 1–1980)

Worthwhile papers from seminar on educational research held in Santiago, Jan. 1980. Include a noteworthy one by Schiefelbein on the impact of educational research in Chile.

4388 **Valenzuela F., Alvaro M.** Los centros de recursos para el aprendizaje (OAS/LE, 24:84, 1980, p. 3–34, tables)

Argues for increased emphasis on

"learning resource centers" for improving instruction. Describes scope and organization of model centers.

COLOMBIA

4389 A dónde va la educación colombiana.
Editor, Juan Antonio Gómez. Bogotá: Centro de Investigaciones Científicas de la Fundación Universidad de Bogotá Jorge Tadeo Lozano, 1980. 436 p.: bibl., ill. (Colección Grandes problemas ignorados; no. 3)

High-quality papers presented at Colombia's First National Forum on Education (Bogotá, 1980) covered preschool, basic, and higher education and future values. Foremost educational leaders recognize crisis of Colombian education at all levels.

4390 Aldana Valdés, Eduardo. Planeación en entidades de educación superior. Bogotá: Instituto SER de Investigación, 1980. 141 leaves: bibl., ill.

Guide for systematic, permanent, and cyclical planning for Colombian institutions of higher education.

4391 Bernal, Campo Elías and **Luis Javier Jaramillo.** Gestión de programas nacionales de desarrollo tecnológico (Revista del Convenio Andrés Bello [Secretaría Ejecutiva Permanente del Convenio Andrés Bello, Bogotá] 4:8, abril 1980, p. 97–120, bibl.)

Examines problems and promises of Colombia's official scientific and technological institution (COLCIENCIAS); specifically, its efforts to work with other national scientific and technological institutions in promoting science and technology in the Andean region.

4392 Bernal Alarcón, Hernando. Educación fundamental integral: teoría y aplicación en el caso de ACPO. Bogotá: Acción Cultural Popular, 1978. 285 p.: bibl., ill. (Serie Educación fundamental integral; 2)

Outstanding book concerns history and structure of Colombia's well-known nonformal rural education project Acción Cultural Popular (ACPO). Also describes how project applied the philosophy of Fundamental Integral Education (EFI).

4393 Coral Quintero, Laureano. Historia del movimiento sindical de magisterio. Bogotá: Fondo Editorial Suramérica, 1980. 260 p.: bibl. (Colección Historia)

Reveals serious gaps in studies of Colombian teachers' unions (e.g., forces behind legislation affecting them as well as their role in the labor union movement and Colombian history). Pt. 1 focuses on theory (e.g., social stratification, class origins of teachers); pt. 2 looks at history of these unions (1930–60 and 1960–74).

4394 La Educación post-secundaria en Colombia: 1979 primer período académico (Boletín Mensual de Estadística [Departamento Administrativo Nacional de Estadística, Bogotá] 29:345, abril 1980, p. 4–43, tables)

First attempt to compile a statistical profile of post-secondary education in Colombia. Reveals that although approximately 72 percent of post-secondary institutions are private, they attract only 50 percent of applicants. Exhaustive data compiled in 1979 are largely unanalyzed.

4395 Fondo Colombiano de Investigaciones Científicas y Proyectos Especiales Francisco José de Caldas. División de Estadística Científica. La investigación en la universidad colombiana. Bogotá: Subdirección de Asuntos Científicos y Tecnológicos, División de Estadística Científica, 1978. 780 p.: bibl., graphs, index (Serie Información sobre investigaciones en proceso—COLCIENCIAS, División de Estadística Científica)

Five-part report on COLCIENCIAS' major survey of university research provides: 1) overview of study; 2) statistical information on finances, type, utility and personnel; 3) list of research projects by university; 4) summary of ongoing research projects by university; and 5) alphabetical listing of researchers by university.

4396 Hanson, E.M. Administrative development in the Colombian Ministry of Education: a case analysis of the 1970s (CES/CER, 27:1, Feb. 1983, p. 89–107)

Describes and analyzes Colombian Ministry of Education's effort at administrative reform. Data from this 12-year longitudinal study were gathered from an analysis of documents and in-depth interviews.

4397 Instituto Colombiano para el Fomento de la Educación Superior. Centro de Documentación. ICFES, diez años de producción bibliográfica. Compilado por Victoria Galofre Neuto y María Cristina de Arango. Bogotá: División de Documentación e Información de ICFES, Sección de Documentación en Educación Superior, 1979. 59 p.: index (Serie bibliográfica/Ministerio de Educación Nacional, Instituto Colombiana para el Fomento de la Educación Superior, División de Documentación e Información, Centro de Documentación, 0120–0259; v. 4, no. 1)

Partial unannotated listing of publications issued (1969–78) by Instituto Colombiana para el Fomento de la Educación Superior (ICFES) arranged by ICFES administrative division.

4398 La Investigación en la universidad colombiana. Bogotá: Subdirección de Asuntos Científicos y Tecnológicos, División de Estadística Científica, 1978. 780 p.: ill. (Información sobre investigaciones en proceso)

Five-part, useful, and comprehensive analysis of university research (1972–77) in Colombia—its scope, orientation, and distribution—covers: 1) research priorities and problems; 2) statistical profile of projects with data aggregated nationally and by university; 3) projects by university, faculty, and department; 4) summary of each project; and 5) list of researchers and their projects.

4399 McKay, Harrison *et al.* Improving cognitive ability in chronically deprived children (AAAS/S, 200:4339, 21 April 1978, p. 270–278, graphs, tables)

Reports on longitudinal quasi-experimental study conducted in Cali, Colombia, designed to assess effects of nutritional, health care, and educational program on severely undernourished children (ages 3 to 7). Reveals that participation enhanced cognitive abilities especially among the youngest children. Well-designed and convincing study.

4400 Pinto Vega, Santiago. Un nuevo centro superior de estudios para Colombia (Negritud [Centro para la Investigación de la Cultura Negra, Bogotá] 3, mayo/junio 1978, p. 22–23)

Describes and proposes agenda for new research center devoted to Colombian black culture.

4401 Regionalización de la educación en Colombia (OAS/LE, 87:25, 1981, p. 96–120)

General description of Colombian educational system and discussion of potential

effects of a proposed decentralization of its financial and administrative structure as well as its curricula.

4402 Stansfield, Charles W. English teaching and economic growth in Latin America: a case study (English Language Teaching Journal [Oxford University Press, London] 32:2, Jan. 1978, p. 138–143)

Attempt to document need for more intensive English training for Colombian students based on country's dependence on study abroad.

4403 Timaná Velásquez, Queipo Franco and **Víctor Manuel Calle Patiño.** La política educativa oficial, la reforma postsecundaria: análisis crítico. Medellín: Gráphicas Profesionales, 1980. 221 p.: bibl., ill.

Reproduces legislation on post-secondary educational reform and Instituto Colombiano para el Fomento de la Educación Superior. Also analyzes other educational issues (e.g., role of schools, education and socialization, secondary and post-secondary reform). Informative but lacks unifying theme.

COSTA RICA

4404 Consejo Nacional de Rectores, *Costa Rica.* **Oficina de Planificación de la Educación Superior.** PLANES II, Plan nacional de educación superior, 1981–1985: documentos de referencia. San José: CONARE, 1979. 6 v.: bibl.

Official five-year higher education plan for Costa Rica (1981–85) consists of six volumes: 1) university autonomy; 2) recent history of post-secondary education; 3) higher education's problems and recommended solutions; 4) higher education in light of manpower needs; 5) Costa Rica's four principal universities; and 6) summary of projected higher education enrollments for 1981–85.

4405 Gill, Clark C. The educational system of Costa Rica. Washington: U.S. Department of Education, 1980. 30 p.: 1 map (Education around the world)

Brief but informative general summary of Costa Rican educational system includes developments through 1978.

4406 *Universidades.* Unión de Universidades de America Latina. Año 21, No. 84, abril/junio 1981– . Buenos Aires.

Essays and speeches concerning idea

of University of Peace, first proposed by President Rodrigo Carazo (27 Sept. 1978) to the UN General Assembly and approved in principle by UN Resolution.

4407 Yogev, Abraham. Modernity and aspirations: youth organizations in the Third World (CES/SER, 24 : 3, Oct. 1980, p. 353–369, tables)

National youth organizations are a prime example of nonformal education. Participation in these organizations increases the status aspirations of their members therefore, when status attainment is explained in part by status aspirations, participation contributes to changes in occupational stratification. These findings are confirmed in this well-designed study of a Costa Rican youth organization.

CUBA

4408 Almuiñas Rivero, José Luis. Algunas particularidades del desarrollo de la educación superior en Cuba (La Educación Superior Contemporánea [Revista Internacional de Países Socialistas, La Habana] 3 : 27, 1979, p. 49–54, tables)

Discusses higher education prior to the Revolution (e.g., responsive only to elite interests; insensitive to country's political, economic, moral needs). Describes changes and major reforms initiated after 1960 creation of Consejo Superior de Universidades.

4409 Centro de Documentación e Información Pedagógicas, *Cuba.* Bibliografía nacional de educación, 1959–1969. La Habana: El Centro, 1974– . 2 v.: indexes.

Annotated bibliography of materials on Cuban education published in Cuba 1959–69. Includes journal and magazine articles, newspapers, textbooks, flyers, and nonprint media.

4410 Cuba. Cuba, organización de la educación, 1976–1978: XXXVII Conferencia Internacional de Educación, OIE, Ginebra, Suiza, septiembre 1979. La Habana: Editorial de Libros para la Educación, 1979. 171 p.: ill.

Report on 37th Meeting of UN's International Conference of Education. Includes synopsis of organization and structure of Cuban educational system as well as summary of developments in education during 1976–78.

4411 ———. Ministerio de Educación. Plan de perfeccionamiento y desarrollo del sistema nacional de educación de Cuba. La Habana: Ministerio de Educación, 1976. 192 p.: bibl., ill. (some col.)

Comprehensive Ministry of Education plan to improve Cuban educational system in accordance with Marxist-Leninist ideology. Castro requested this plan in 1971, citing fundamental problems in Cuban educational system (e.g., low rate of retention and high rate of repeating, high absenteeism among 13- to 16-year-olds).

4412 Currás López, Gonzalo and **Cándido López Pardo.** Causa de ausentismo escolar en la enseñanza primaria: estudio exploratorio en una escuela de la ciudad de La Habana (Revista Cubana de Administración de Salud [Centro Nacional de Información de Ciencias Médicas, La Habana] 7 : 1, enero/marzo 1981, p. 86–100, tables)

Study attempts to determine causes of student absenteeism at primary school in Havana. Health problems found to be primary cause although other factors were determined significant. Gender of child not an important factor but boarding status (externo, semi-interno) was relevant.

4413 García Alzola, Ernesto. Ramiro Guerra como crítico de la educación cubana (BNJM/R, 71[22]:1, 3. época, enero/abril 1980, p. 93–111, chart)

Biographical sketch of Cuban educator, noted proponent and critic of his country's primary educational system, both pre- and post-Revolution.

4414 Gómez C., Víctor Manuel. Igualdad y equidad social en educación: el caso de Cuba (CEE/RL, 11 : 2, Primavera 1981, p. 33–71, bibl., diagrams, table)

Three-part paper focuses on compensatory potential of Cuban education model (i.e., equal educational opportunity from the output perspective): 1) posits difference between equity and equality; 2) examines concept of social compensation; and 3) analyzes Cuban education with respect to its social compensation potential. Concludes that while equity within Cuban education is the rule, equality in terms of social compensation for graduates remains elusive.

4415 Hernández Valdés, Mario. Algunas consideraciones sobre el prognóstico de desarrollo de la base técnico-material para la formación de especialistas de nivel superior en Cuba (La Educación Superior Contemporánea [La Habana] 31, marzo 1980, p. 87–96)

Describes evolution of Base Técnico Material (BTM) and its current role in Cuban higher education. BTM, Cuba's basic strategy for scientific training and research and for higher education planning, is implemented by Centros de Estudios Superiores.

4416 Howard, Mary. Work and study: Cuba and the U.S. (Journal of Cooperative Education [Cooperative Education Association, Drexel University, Philadelphia, Pa.] 14:1, Nov. 1977, p. 24–33, bibl.)

Article examines Cuban work-study program, circumstances which prompted its development and overall objectives. US and Cuban work-study models are compared. Offers suggestions for improving US model.

4417 Kozol, Jonathan. How Cuba fought illiteracy (Learning: the magazine for creative teaching [Education Today Company, Palo Alto, Calif.] 5:9, May/June 1977, p. 26–29, 87)

Describes Cuba's 1961 literacy campaign on basis of interviews conducted during brief visit.

4418 López Sánchez, José. Breve historia de la ciencia en Cuba (BNJM/R, 7[22]:1, 3. época, enero/abril 1980, p. 21–49)

According to author, science and medicine in Cuba have not been subject to historical inquiry. In light of this claim, this is a very useful if conventional history, chronologically presented with major works and personages highlighted.

4419 Mickey, Lois. Education in Cuba: an American's report (Kappa Delta Pi Record [Kappa Delta Pi, West Lafayette, Ind.] 14:1, Oct. 1977, p. 29–30)

Elementary school teacher's brief and somewhat critical description of Cuban educational system. Author participated in abbreviated Cuban seminar for US educators (May 1977).

4420 Paulston, Rolland G. Impacto de la reforma educativa en Cuba. Pittsburgh, Pa.: University of Pittsburgh, University Center for International Studies, Center for

Latin American Studies, 1982. 124 p.: bibl., tables (Latin American reprint series; 17)

Analyzes Cuban revolutionary educational process (objectives, efforts, results). Concludes Cuba's educational reform model is not applicable to other Latin American countries without radical changes in their socioeconomic structures.

4421 Pérez Guerra, Santiago and **Maritzela Díaz Lorenzo.** Aspectos preliminares al estudio de la estructura sociológica de la población estudiantil de la Universidad (Revista Cubana de Educación Superior [Universidad de Camagüey] 1:1, 1981, p. 16–34, bibl., tables)

Study of socioeconomic origins of 1,294 Universidad de Camagüey students involved 23 sociodemographic variables in the administered questionnaire.

4422 Sahoy, Pauline. Cuban educational strategies (Caribbean Journal of Education [University of the West Indies, School of Education, Mona, Jamaica] 5:1/2, Jan./April 1978,p. 135–152, bibl.)

Analyzes first four years of post-Revolutionary educational expansion in Cuba along four dimensions: 1) manpower strategy; 2) adult education; 3) rural education; and 4) flexibility in education. Concludes that although Cuban strategies have been radical and largely successful, they are not transferrable to other countries.

DOMINICAN REPUBLIC

4423 Antonini, Gustavo A. and **Mason A. York.** Integrated rural development and the role of the university in the Caribbean: the case of Plan Sierra, Dominican Republic (Caribbean Educational Bulletin [Association of Caribbean Universities, San Juan] 7:3, Sept. 1980, p. 15–36, maps, tables)

Four-part examination of development policies and rural poverty: 1) surveys contemporary views on rural development in general; 2) focuses on Sierra region; 3) analyzes country's integrated rural development plan; and 4) projects university's role in rural development.

4424 Fernández, Jorge Max. Sistema educativo dominicano: diagnóstico y perspectivas. Santo Domingo: Instituto

Tecnológico de Santo Domingo, 1980. 182 p.: bibl., diagrams (Serie Educación; no. 1)

Excellent, well-documented book in two parts: 1) very good data-based analysis of Dominican educational system; and 2) thought-provoking strategy for improvement. Critique of current system—which is based on extensive documentation— is harsh; strategy for change is explicit, realistic and promising.

4425 Latorre, Eduardo. Sobre educación superior. Santo Domingo: Instituto Tecnológico de Santo Domingo, 1980. 235 p.: bibl. (Serie Educación/INTEC; no. 2)

Three-part collection of 11 essays: 1) Dominican education; 2) higher education for the Third World; 3) INTEC (Instituto Tecnológico de Santo Domingo) model. Argues that challenges to higher education differ between lesser developed and developed countries and that small universities (i.e., INTEC) can contribute to development. Absence of unifying theme, however, results in lack of cohesion.

4426 Sánchez Hernández, Antonio *et al.* Perspectivas de la investigación en la Universidad Autónoma de Santo Domingo. Santo Domingo: Editora de la UASD, 1979. 87 p.: ill. (Publicaciones de la Universidad Autónoma de Santo Domingo; v. 276. Colección Educación y sociedad; no. 12)

Includes official policy and planning documents which govern research at Universidad Autónoma de Santo Domingo as well as specific research proposals.

4427 Viezzer, Moema. A methodology for research training of women's groups, Dominican Republic. Port-au-Prince: UNICEF, Project for the Promotion and Development of Women in Latin America and the Caribbean, Regional Office for the Americas, 1980. 30 p. (Working documents on programmes benefitting women. Working document/UNICEF)

Final report of Educational Research Project for Women carried out in the Dominican Republic (1977–78). Conducted at UNICEF's request, this is a case study on research training of Dominican women.

ECUADOR

4428 Pozo de Ruiz, Gladys and **Ernesto Schiefelbein.** Los problemas de la expansión acelerada: el caso del desarrollo del sistema educacional del Ecuador (CPU/ES, 26:4, 1980, p. 131–165, tables)

Analyzes consequences of rapidly increasing school enrollments in Ecuador on factors such as cost and quality, stressing relationship between this expansion and its effect on the quality of higher education.

4429 Renner, Richard. Imágenes de la educación secundaria en Ecuador: propuestas reformistas entre 1955 y 1965 (CEE/RL, 11:2, Primavera 1981, p. 121–128)

Interesting content analysis of 1955–65 writings by Ecuadorians—journalists, educators, government officials—about country's educational system. Among criticisms leveled: secondary schools do not contribute to country's economic development, inclusion of technical education in the curriculum ought not be at expense of general education, country's educational facilities are inadequate.

4430 Ribadeneira, Edmundo. Universidad, arte y sociedad. Quito: Editorial Universitaria, 1980. 262 p.

Collection of 21 erudite essays by Vicerector of Ecuador's Central University focusing on the university, art, and society. Allows that he has been intellectually enriched through his association with the university and expresses his gratitude with these essays.

4431 Swett M., Francisco X. Los factores determinantes de la escolarización y el aprovechamiento en la educación ecuatoriana. Quito: Junta Nacional de Planificación y Coordinación Económica, Sección Publicaciones, 1979. 211 p.: ill.

Data-based, comprehensive, and detailed description of all levels of education in Ecuador. Analysis of data reveals significant problems. Recommends changes which would have major impact—financial, structural—on Ecuadorian society.

4432 Yépez Villalba, Eduardo. 150 [i.e. Ciento cincuenta] años de la Facultad de Medicina: 1827–26 de octubre 1977. Quito: Editorial Universitaria; Cuenca, Ecuador: Suministrado por Libros Ecuatorianos, 1979. 333 p.: bibl.

Supposedly a history of the Facultad de Ciencias Médicas of Ecuador's Central University. By including major sections on its origins, on history of medicine in Ecuador, as well as on the evolution of society, book suffers from lack of focus.

EL SALVADOR

4433 McGinn, Noel F. and Ernesto Toro Balart. Una evaluación de la educación media técnica en El Salvador (CEE/RL, 10:2, 2. trimestre, abril 1980, p. 1–31, tables)

Reports results of evaluation of Diversified High School Program initiated 1971 in El Salvador. Results suggest that demand for secondary school graduates is more a function of credentialism than a need for trained manpower.

4434 Speagle, Richard E. Educational reform and instructional television in El Salvador: costs, benefits, and payoffs. New York: Academy for Educational Development, 197?. 242 p.

One of series of research reports on El Salvador's Educational Reform Program focuses on instructional television and is designed to assess its costs and affordability.

GUATEMALA

4435 Déleon, Ofelia. Folklore aplicado a la educación guatemalteca. Ciudad Universitaria: Centro de Estudios Folklóricos, Universidad de San Carlos de Guatemala, 1977. 233 p.: ill. (Colección Problemas y documentos; v. 6)

Author's goal is to incorporate Guatemalan folklore into nation's preschool, primary, and middle level curricula. Supports plea with strong documentation based on extensive bibliographic search, and on analysis of Guatemalan educational laws, plans, and programs.

4436 Engle, Patricia Lee *et al.* Cognitive performance during middle childhood in rural Guatemala (Journal of Genetic Psychology [Journal Press, Provincetown, Mass.] 131, 2. half, Dec. 1977, p. 291–307, bibl., tables)

Developmental changes in selected cognitive processes as function of age and schooling were examined in 160 rural Guate-

malan children aged five, seven, nine, and 11 years. Data support assertion that school performance is related to various memory processes.

4437 González Orellana, Carlos. Historia de la educación en Guatemala. Ciudad Universitaria, Guatemala: Editorial Universitaria, 1980. 564 p.: bibl., index (Colección Historia nuestra; v. no. 1)

Six-part comprehensive history of Guatemalan education: 1) Mayan and Maya-Quiché; 2) colonial period; 3) 30 years of post-Independence; 4) liberal reform and organization of public education; 5) 1900–40; and 6) revolutionary decade: 1944–54. Excellent bibliography.

4438 Irwin, Marc *et al.* The relationship of prior ability and family characteristics to school attendance and school achievement in rural Guatemala (Child Development [University of Chicago Press for the Society for Research in Child Development, Chicago, Ill.] 49:2, June 1978, p. 415–427, bibl., tables)

Report on longitudinal study in progress which looks at relationship between family and home characteristics and school attendance and performance in three Guatemalan communities.

4439 Luján Muñoz, Jorge. Situación de la enseñanza superior de la historia y de la investigación histórica en Guatemala (PAIGH/H, 90, julio/dic. 1980, p. 119–141)

Examination of the teaching of history and of the condition of historical research in Guatemalan universities.

GUYANA

4440 Irvine, D.H. The university and national development: case history, Guyana (Higher Education and Research in the Netherlands [Netherlands Universities Foundation for International Co-operation (NUFFIC), The Hague] 22:1/2, Winter/Spring 1978, p. 29–38)

Argues that for a university to be an effective instrument of national development, three major issues need resolution— its relationship with the government, with the community, and who and what to teach. University of Guyana is discussed in this context.

HAITI

4441 Clesca, Eddy. L'éducation non formelle en Haiti (ASHSH/B, 33:8, 1979, p. 56–76, bibl.)
Cites need for closer collaboration between nonformal and formal education agencies to begin to address Haiti's education and training needs.

HONDURAS

4442 Reina Valenzuela, José. Historia de la universidad. Tegucigalpa: Universidad Nacional Autónoma de Honduras, 1976. 252 p.: bibl.
Comprehensive and chronologically organized history of Universidad Nacional Autónoma de Honduras (UNAH) fails to integrate documentation and narrative. Interesting sidelight: history was completed despite 1973 fire which destroyed irreplaceable documents essential to complete UNAH's history.

JAMAICA

4443 Howells, C.A. Authoritarianism in Jamaican teachers' colleges (Caribbean Journal of Education [University of the West Indies, School of Education, Mona, Jamaica] 5:1/2, Jan./April 1978, p. 71–80, bibl., tables)
Provides evidence to support assertion that Jamaican teachers are authoritarian but does not reveal sources of this attitude.

4444 King, Ruby. Teaching about teaching: a strategy (Caribbean Journal of Education [University of the West Indies, School of Education, Mona, Jamaica] 5:1/2, Jan./April 1978, p. 81–90, bibl.)
Brief hypothetical "case study" of uniformly poor teaching practices gleaned from over 300 lessons taught by student teachers in Jamaican rural schools. Intended for use in teacher training programs.

4445 Lalor, Gerald. The productivity of Jamaican scientists (IJ/JJ, 44, 1980, p. 52–59, bibl., tables)
Urges greater scientific and technological independence among lesser developed countries. Focuses on productivity of Jamaican scientists as indicator of potential for technological independence and reveals they are competitive with other Latin American scientists.

MEXICO

4446 Alba Alcaraz, Edmundo de et al. La crisis de la educación superior en México. Gilberto Guevara Niebla, coordenador. México: Editorial Nueva Imagen, 1981. 334 p.: bibl., ill. (Serie Educación)
Series of general and more specific papers prepared for 1979 seminar "The Crisis of Higher Education in Mexico" sponsored by UNAM and Universidad Autónoma Metropolitana-Xochimilco.

4447 Appendini, Guadalupe. Historia de la Universidad Nacional Autónoma de México. México: Editorial Porrúa, 1981. 446 p., [48] p. of plates: ill.
Another comprehensive history of UNAM includes innovative and interesting section on UNAM as seen through journalists' eyes. Good photographs.

4448 La Autonomía universitaria en México. México: Universidad Nacional Autónoma de México, 1979. 424 p.: ill. (Colección Cincuentenario de la autonomía de la Universidad Nacional de México; v. 1)
Vol. 1 of extensive series commemorates 50th anniversary of UNAM's official autonomy. Contains addresses, essays, lectures, and testimonies which focus on the importance of this milestone event.

4449 Bazant, Jan. La escuela primaria de la hacienda de San Bartolomé Tepetates: alumnos, maestros, equipo (CM/HM, 29:1, julio/sept. 1979, p. 163–179, tables)
Case study of important hacienda school in Mexico. Hacienda schools have played an important role in the history of Mexican education.

4450 Bazbaz y Mizrahi, Isaac et al. Planeación educativa integral: la ingeniería química. Presentación de Rudi-Primo Stivalet Corral. México: Universidad Nacional Autónoma de México, 1979. 475 p.: bibl., ill.
Provides excellent comprehensive planning model with potential application to educational programs at all levels. Thesis submitted for chemical engineering degree (UNAM, 1970).

4451 Castillo, Isidro. México, sus revoluciones sociales y la educación. México: Gobierno del Estado de Michoacán, 1976. 5 v.: bibl., ill.

Five-volume detailed history of Mexican education stresses social, political, philosophical influences on educational change from "origin of American man" to President José López Portillo. Scarce footnotes in 2,000 p.

4452 D'Argent, Charles *et al.* Alfabetismo funcional en el medio rural. México: Colegio de México, 1980. 205 p.: forms, ill. (Colección Centro de Estudios Económicos y Demográficos; 10)

Despite premium Mexican government places on education and increasing educational opportunities, major problems and inequities continue. Survey looks at rural/urban disequilibrium and finds three factors which explain disproportionately low achievement in rural areas: 1) inadequate school systems; 2) low socioeconomic conditions; and 3) lack of vital services in communities.

4453 Davis, Charles L. and **Kenneth M. Coleman.** Discontinuous educational experiences and political and religious nonconformity in authoritarian regimes: Mexico (Social Science Quarterly [University of Texas Press in cooperation with the Southwestern Social Science Association, Austin] 58 : 3, Dec. 1977, p. 489–497, bibl., table)

Survey conducted in Mexico City explores relationship between discontinuities in formal educational experiences (e.g., attendance in public and parochial schools as opposed to public schools exclusively) and level of opposition to conventional religious and political norms.

4454 Drake, Diana Mack. Bilingual education programs for Indian children in Mexico (MLTA/MLJ, 62 : 5/6, Sept./Oct. 1978, p. 239–248, bibl.)

Describes philosophy and practice of bilingual educational programs provided for Indian children throughout Mexico by Dirección General de Educación Extraescolar en el Medio Indígena.

4455 García García, Raúl. Apuntes para la historia de la educación en Tamaulipas. Ciudad Victoria, Tamaulipas: Universidad Autónoma de Tamaulipas, Instituto de Investigaciones Históricas, 1980. 168 p.

Comprehensive history of all levels of education in Tamaulipas, Mexico. Concludes that educational development came on the heels of major liberating movements (e.g., Independence, Revolution).

4456 Gómez, Marte R. Episodios de la vida de la Escuela Nacional de Agricultura. Chapingo, México: Centro de Economía Agrícola, Colegio de Postgraduados, Escuela Nacional de Agricultura, 1976. 316 p., [10] leaves of plates (some folded): ill., ports.

Comprehensive, detailed history of Chapingo's Escuela Nacional de Agricultura. Founded 1854 in San Jacinto, school moved to Chapingo in 1923. Published posthumously, book is testimony to author's affection for the school.

4457 González Oropeza, Manuel. Génesis de la Ley Orgánica de la Universidad Nacional Autónoma de México. México: Universidad Nacional Autónoma de México, 1980. 316 p.: ill.

History of UNAM's Ley Orgánica which became official university governance policy in 1945. Book should be of special interest to scholars of university governance for it represents the first time an official policy document was developed and passed by a university community (UNAM) instead of by the Mexican government. Includes documents, minutes, notes.

4458 Hermida Ruiz, Angel J. La fundación de la Escuela Normal Veracruzana. Jalapa, México: Ediciones Normal Veracruzana, 1978. 277 p.: bibl., ill. (Colección Difusión cultural; no. 5)

Well written and comprehensive institutional history based on newspaper articles designed to commemorate 90th anniversary of Escuela Normal Veracruzana Enrique C. Rébsamen.

4459 Latapí, Pablo. Mitos y verdades de la educación mexicana, 1971–1972: una opinión independiente. 2. ed. México: Centro de Estudios Educativos, 1979. 237 p.

When one considers education in Mexico, it is difficult to distinguish myth from reality. Latapí's book consists of his *Excelsior* editorials written 1970–72 and reprinted by Centro de Estudios Educativos in order to clarify the "muddied" educational waters.

4460 ———. Las prioridades de investigación educativa en México (CEE/RL, 11:2, Primavera 1981, p. 73–86)

In three parts: 1) summarizes nine key Marxian educational studies conducted 1972–80; 2) lists and ranks recommendations which stem from these studies; and 3) proposes series of research priorities for Mexico's Master Plan for Educational Research (Consejo Nacional de Ciencia y Tecnología, CONACYT).

Lerner, Victoria. Historia de la reforma educativa: 1933–1945. See *HLAS 44:2219.*

———. Historia de la Revolución Mexicana, período 1934–1940: la educación socialista. See *HLAS 44:2220.*

4461 Levy, Daniel. University autonomy in Mexico: implications for regime authoritarianism (LARR, 14:3, 1979, p. 129–152)

Argues that UNAM remains substantially autonomous and independent of government control. Analyzes possibilities for government control in terms of selection of University's rector, students, finances and tuition. Concludes that, in the context of UNAM, the catch-all label of "authoritarian rule" in Mexico may be misleading. [R.E. Greenleaf]

Llinás Alvarez, Edgar. Revolución, educación y mexicanidad: la búsqueda de la identidad nacional en el pensamiento educativo. See *HLAS 44:2222.*

4462 López Portillo, José. Educación y magisterio. 2. ed. actualizada. México: Secretaría de Programación y Presupuesto, Dirección General de Documentación y Análisis, 1980. 46 p.: bibl., index (Cuadernos de filosofía política; no. 2)

President López Portillo focuses on education as constitutional right, and in relation to sovereignty, social democracy, human development, and teachers.

4463 ———. Universidad y estado. 2. ed. México: Secretaría de Programación y Presupuesto, Dirección General de Documentación y Análisis, 1980. 38 p. (Cuadernos de filosofía política; 20)

President López Portillo discusses the university: concept of unity and diversity within it; its autonomy; its responsibilities to society; and its finance.

4464 Mora, Juan Miguel de. Muera de inteligencia: la UNAM es el botín. México: Editores Asociados Mexicanos, 1979. 97 p.

Clarion call to Mexicans and UNAM faculty to take action to quell crisis and to realize: it is governed by the elite; interests of Mexicans are not served; academic freedom is a sham. Do not be cowards, author implores.

4465 Mora Forero, Jorge. Los maestros y la práctica de la educación socialista (CM/HM, 29:1, julio/sept. 1979, p. 133–162, bibl.)

Describes violence and other demonstrations (*paros*) during President Cárdenas' administration which were directed at teachers who allegedly embraced socialism as a political ideology. For historian's comment, see *HLAS 44:2239.*

4466 Muñoz Izquierdo, Carlos. El problema de la educación en México: ¿laberinto sin salida? México: Centro de Estudios Educativos, 1979. 206 p. (Colección Estudios educativos; 3)

Compilation of newspaper editorials (1978–79) on educational policy organized by chapters on following themes: educational planning and national development; primary, adult, secondary, higher, and private education; and educational research.

4467 La Nueva insurgencia de los trabajadores de la educación. México: Ediciones Movimiento, 1980. 47 p.: ill. (Educación democrática; 11)

General review of series of related Mexican teachers' strikes (May 1979–June 1980) organized by Movimiento Revolucionario del Magisterio. While union won some concessions—salaries, voice in educational policy—major victory was increased recognition given by teachers to the union.

4468 Pallán Figueroa, Carlos. Bases para la administración de la educación superior en América Latina: el caso de México. México: Ediciones INAP, 1978. 177 p.: bibl.

Reports on conceptual study on higher education administration which won 1977 award. Approaches educational administration from systems perspective, administration being considered part of a subsystem (the university) which influences society and is also part of a system (education). Thus, higher education administration is influenced by and influences the system.

4469 Robles, Martha. Apuntes sobre el problema educativo en México (CAM, 226:5, sept./oct. 1979, p. 44–48)

Criticizes the gap between theory and reality concerning education in Mexico, which suffered from lack of equal opportunity for all. [R.E. Greenleaf]

4470 Seminario Regional sobre Universidad y Sociedad, *Monterrey, México, 1975.* Seminario Regional sobre Universidad y Sociedad, del 8 al 13 septiembre de 1975, Monterrey, N.L., México. Monterrey, México: Instituto de Administración Pública de Nuevo León, 1979. 276 p., [12] leaves of plates: ill. (Cuadernos de administración pública; 3)

Published proceedings include addresses with responses in nine topical areas including university autonomy, open university, university finance, and university's role in development.

4471 UNESCO. Oficina Regional de Educación para América Latina y el Caribe. Informaciones estadísticas de la educación y análisis cuantitativo. Santiago: 1980. 25 leaves: tables (OREALC/Estadísticas/21)

Three-part outline of variety of educational planning models: 1) examines relevance of models to educational planning; 2) describes general characteristics of planning models; and 3) reviews selected Mexican models.

4472 Universidad Nacional Autónoma de México (UNAM). La Ciudad Universitaria de México. Las Facultades y Escuelas de la UNAM, 1929–1979. La investigación en los Institutos y Centros de Humanidades, 1929–1979. La Universidad Nacional y los problemas nacionales. Memoria de la Exposición sobre la Universidad. México: UNAM, 1979. 5 v.: bibl., ill. (Colección Cincuentenario de la autonomía de la Universidad Nacional de México; v. 3, 4, 7–9, 10, 11)

Consists of five volumes of possibly 10 or more issued to commemorate the 50th anniversary of UNAM's autonomy. They examine history, organization, curricula, student body, faculty, and numerous other aspects of the institution.

4473 Valdés Olmedo, J. Cuauhtémoc. Consideraciones sobre el crecimiento de población escolar. 2. ed. México: Universidad Nacional Autónoma de México, Dirección General de Planeación, 1980. 70 p.: bibl., ill. (Cuadernos de planeación universitaria; 1)

Projects educational enrollments, justifies projections based on national trends, presents model to estimate enrollments, and discusses germane policy issues (e.g., the effect of selective admissions).

4474 Velasco, Ibélis. Algunos hechos y muchos impresiones sobre la ciencia y la tecnología en México (AI/A, 7:1, enero/feb. 1982, p. 37–44, ill.)

Discusses contradictions afflicting science and technology in Mexico in which impressive centers exist despite little government support, inadequate cooperation among them and poor dissemination of research results. All have retarded scientific progress. Describes in detail Colegio de México, a research center founded 1940.

4475 Wionczek, Miguel S. On the viability of a policy for science and technology in Mexico (LARR, 26:1, 1981, p. 57–78)

Explores two hypotheses: 1) Mexico has no national scientific/technological policy; and 2) formulation of such a policy is not viable in Mexico. Author's careful analysis of developments since the 1976 National Plan for Science and Technology confirms both hypotheses: knowledge is imparted in a disorganized manner; and adoptive capacity links among scientific, technological, productive, and educational systems are weak.

4476 Zúñiga, Leonel. México. Santiago: Oficina Regional de Educación de la UNESCO para América Latina y el Caribe, 1980. 1 v.: bibl., ill. (Estudio de cambios e innovaciones en la educación técnica y la formación profesional en América Latina y el Caribe; v. 12)

UNESCO country study on Mexico cites enrollment data, and documents disequilibrium between country's educational opportunities and economic needs.

NICARAGUA

4477 Arnove, Robert F. The Nicaraguan National Literacy Crusade of 1980 (CES/CER, 25:2, June 1981, p. 244–260)

Detailed description of Nicaragua's National Literacy Crusade (CNA) of 1980 includes its scope, content, organization, and results. Contends that political aspects of literacy crusade were least critical to its success; unfortunately, his evidence for this claim and others is scanty.

4478 Blum, Leonor. The literacy campaign: Nicaragua style (FIU/CR, 10:1, Winter 1981, p. 18–21, ill.)

Compares Nicaraguan and Cuban literacy campaigns. Although Nicaragua's was based on Cuban model, author is most impressed with differences she highlights. Argues in favor of US-sponsored literacy campaigns.

4479 Castilla Urbina, Miguel de. La alfabetización: un proyecto prioritario en Nicaragua (CEE/RL, 10:2, 2. trimestre, abril 1980, p. 103–123, ill., tables)

Extensive description of Nicaragua's National Literacy Crusade launched by Carlos Fonseca, head of La Revolución Popular Sandinista, barely two weeks after his accession to power. Interesting account of remarkable undertaking; clearly one of the Sandinistas' crowning achievements.

4480 Nicaragua. Ministerio de Educación. Gobierno de Reconstrucción Nacional. La Educación en el primer año de la Revolución Popular Sandinista. Managua: El Ministerio, 1980. 238 p., [13] leaves of plates: ill. (Publicaciones del Ministerio de Educación "19 de julio")

Report on Nicaragua's "Año de Alfabetización" prepared by country's Ministry of Education. Calling education under Somoza ". . . one of the most unjust privileges [afforded the elite] . . . and one of the most powerful instruments of domination and legitimation," book describes pitiful educational system prior to Gobierno de Reconstrucción Nacional, educational advances during its first year, and its agenda for the future.

4481 Roche, Marcel. Algunos hechos y muchas impresiones sobre ciencia y educación en Nicaragua/Some facts and many impressions on science and education in Nicaragua (AI/I, 6:3, May/June 1981, p. 161–164)

At the invitation of Nicaragua's Minister of Education, Venezuelan reporter summarizes observations of life under the Sandinistas in Nicaragua: state of disrepair of Managua; favorable treatment of and privileges afforded to military officers; unbridled

freedom enjoyed by press and radio; total absence of "science;" and impressive advances made in education, especially in literacy training.

4482 Seminario Político Miguel Bonilla, *1st, Universidad Nacional Autónoma de Nicaragua, 1980.* Primer Seminario Político Miguel Bonilla: la Universidad y la Revolución. Por Víctor Tirado, Omar Cabezas, Carlos Núñez. León, Nicaragua: Comisión Político Universitaria, U.N.A.N., 1980. 158 p.

Essays, interviews, and speeches by FSLN representatives delivered Jan. 1980 focus on the role of the university in the Revolution. Particularly noteworthy is Omar Cabezas Lacayo's argument on university autonomy: it is a specious concept unless the university serves the revolutionary process.

4483 Tünnermann Bernheim, Carlos. Hacia una nueva educación en Nicaragua. Managua: Ministerio de Educación, 1980. 187 p.

Seven essays by the Sandinista Minister of Education. First two are interesting discussions on Sandinista educational philosophy and Gen. Augusto César Sandino's educational vision.

PANAMA

4484 Céspedes, Francisco. La educación en Panamá: panorama histórico y antología. Panamá: Presidencia de la República, 1981. 470 p. (Biblioteca de la cultura panameña; t. 4)

Vol. 4 of 16-vol. series on various aspects of Panamanian life and culture provides overview and describes Panamanian educational system. Pt. 1 traces history of education from origins to present; pt. 2 focuses on country's educational theory and philosophy.

4485 Conte Porras, Jorge. La rebelión de Las Esfinges: historia del movimiento estudiantil panameño. Panamá?: Litho-Impresora Panamá, 1977 [i.e. 1978]. 177 p.: bibl., ill., index.

History of Panamanian student movement with specific emphasis on Federación de Estudiantes de Panamá. Focuses on period since 1940 but provides brief background. Of particular interest is Federación's posture toward US military presence in Panama.

4486 Isos, Ramón. Production schools in Panamá (Prospects: Quarterly Review of Education [UNESCO, Paris] 7:3, 1977, p. 395–400)

Panama's Integrated Educational Development Program, initiated by decree Feb. 1975, was to promote "general basic education" in poverty-stricken areas. Designed for children age 6–15, it is community based, provides for core curriculum, and encourages work-study.

4487 Rodríguez P., Raúl R. and Ornel Urriola. Educación superior y liberación nacional. Panamá: Huaca Editores, 1979 [i.e. 1980]. 67 p.

Panamanian university's crisis caused by growth. In last eight years, number of university students has quadrupled while courses and professors have tripled. Discusses consequences of growth on: teaching methods; recruitment, selection, and training of faculty and students; and curriculum.

PARAGUAY

4488 Palau Viladesau, Tomás. Universidad, desarrollo y autoritarismo (CPES/RPS, 17:49, sept./dic. 1980, p. 125–146, charts)

Following analysis of enrollment trends (1966–78) of Paraguay's two principal universities—Universidad Católica and Universidad Nacional—author asserts their power to make curriculum decisions and provide for social mobility is minimal. The Paraguayan university, he continues, marches to the tune of the political elite.

4489 Ruiz Díaz, Daniel Campos. Escolaridad y fuerza de trabajo en el Paraguay: economía de la educación (UCNSA/EP, 8:2, dic. 1980, p. 67–124, bibl., tables)

Using secondary data provided by Centro Latinoamericano de Demografía (CELADE), study confirms association between educational level and type and location of occupation, as well as age, gender, and residence.

4490 Schiefelbein, Ernesto and Carlos Clavel. Comparación de los factores que inciden en la demanda por educación en Paraguay y Chile (CPES/RPS, 17:48, mayo/agosto 1980, p. 23–45, bibl., ill., tables)

Authors replicate in Paraguay a study in which they analyzed factors that generated demand for education in Chile (see *HLAS 43:4409*). Results of both studies are compared. In both countries, demand for primary education is explained principally by cultural factors and demand for subsequent education by economic factors.

PERU

4491 Centro de Información, Estudios y Documentación, *Lima*. Perú, la reforma educativa en una sociedad de clases. Lima: Centro de Información, Estudios y Documentación, 1980. 85, [11] p.: bibl., ill. (Serie Las Barriadas)

Analyzes failure of 1972 law for Reforma de Educación in Peru which was eventually abandoned. Questions utility of educational reform imposed by ruling elite. Concludes that by placing excessive premium on efficacy of formal education, general population plays directly into elite's hands. Thus, faith in formal education guarantees continued subjugation of the masses.

4492 Delgado, Kenneth. Reforma educativa, ¿qué pasó? Lima: Ediciones SAGSA, 1981. 228 p.: bibl.

Full-scale assessment of all levels and types of Peruvian education—formal and nonformal—from the passage of the country's educational reform law in 1972–79. Author was Peruvian Ministry of Education specialist (1973–77). Conclusions: despite progress in developing preschool education, access is limited to privileged classes.

4493 Instituto Nacional de Investigación y Desarrollo de la Educación. Subdirección de Investigaciones Educacionales and **Centro Nacional de Documentación e Información Educacional.** Diagnóstico de la documentación e información educacional en el Perú: estudio para el establecimiento de una red de centros regionales de documentación e información educacional, CREDIES. Lima: Instituto Nacional de Investigación y Desarrollo de la Educación, 1978. 225 p.: diagrams.

General study of Peruvian education by region designed to recommend appropriate sites for Ministry's regional documentation and information centers. Good overview of Peruvian educational system.

4494 Ismodes Cairo, Aníbal. Tragedia de la universidad en el Perú. s.l.: s.n., between 1979 and 1981. 83 p.

Very strong critique of higher education in Peru. Despite gratuitous and offensive remarks about "Yanqui" university and doomsday prognostication regarding current state of Peruvian university (on verge of total liquidation), book contains well documented analysis of multitudinous problems confronting higher education. Argues that future legislation must focus on following five areas: autonomy, democracy, finance, structure, and relationship to society. Includes draft for proposed legislation.

4495 Malpica, Carlos. Education and the community in the Peruvian educational reform (UNESCO/IRE, 26 : 3, 1980, p. 357–367)

Article describes 1972 Peruvian educational reform; compares it to earlier ones; reports on evaluation studies in progress; and predicts a future for "educational nuclearization," the modus operandi of this reform.

4496 Maslankowski, Willi. La formación profesional en el contexto de la reforma educativa peruana (Boletín CINTERFOR [Centro Interamericano de Investigación y Documentación sobre Formación Profesional, Montevideo] 71, sept./oct. 1980, p. 11–22)

Analysis of effects of 1972 Peruvian educational reform on country's apprenticeship training program (SENATI). Warns of need to consider labor union demands if reform's professional training goals are to be achieved.

4497 Primov, George. The school as an obstacle to structural integration among Peruvian Indians (Education and Urban Society [Sage Publications, Beverly Hills] 10 : 2, Feb. 1978, p. 209–222, bibl.)

Argues Peruvian schools are used by ruling elite to impede integration of minorities into Peruvian society while simultaneously fostering among them a sense of identification with that society.

4498 Román de Silgado, Manuel; Alejandro Ortiz; and Juan Ossio. Educación y cultura popular: ensayo sobre las posibilidades educativas del folklore andino. Lima: Universidad del Pacífico, Centro de Investigación; Santiago: UNESCO, 1980. 158 p. (Serie Cuadernos; ensayo no. 15)

Focuses on need to develop entirely new educational model to meet needs of Peru's indigenous Andean population (Incaicos). Basic premise is that traditional schools are meaningless to native Andean child. Believes in need for "verbalization" based on mutual respect between white and native Andean. Thus, similarities and differences would become apparent and educational goals could be defined and achieved.

4499 Romero, Paulino. Formulación de la nueva política educativa (LNB/L, 291, junio 1981, p. 68–74)

Believes principal reason for failure of 1972 Peruvian educational reform was an educational system determined to impose a single ideology. Proposes series of doctrines for developing a new national educational policy.

4500 Seminario sobre Enseñanza Integrada de las Ciencias en América Latina, 3rd, Huaráz, Perú, 1980. Enseñanza integrada de las ciencias en América Latina: informe del Seminario sobre Enseñanza Integrada de las Ciencias en América Latina realizado en Huaráz (Perú) del 19 al 28 de marzo de 1980. Santiago: UNESCO, Oficina Regional de Educación para América Latina y el Caribe; Montevideo: UNESCO, Oficina Regional de Ciencia y Tecnología para América Latina y el Caribe, 1981. 187 p.: bibl., ill.

Contains complete proceedings of UNESCO regional seminar on science and technology (Huaráz, Peru, March 1980). Excellent overview; thought-provoking recommendations.

4501 Vargas Vega, Raúl. Educación e identidad nacional (in Perú: identidad nacional. Lima: Ediciones CEDEP, 1979, p. 365–377)

Discusses structural aspects of Peruvian society which preclude country's schools from promulgating an honest national identity and from providing true means of social mobility.

PUERTO RICO

4502 Cafferty, Pastora San Juan and Carmen Rivera-Martínez. The politics of language: the dilemma of bilingual education for Puerto Ricans. Boulder, Colo: Westview

Press, 1981. 119 p.: bibl. (A Westview replica edition)

Examination of bilingual education policies as they affect the Puerto Rican child. Argues that Puerto Rican immigrant's situation is unique and characterized by regular interaction—communication and travel—between Puerto Rico and the mainland. Thus, education must make Puerto Rican child literate and capable of functioning in both. Describes current bilingual educational policies in US and Puerto Rico, describes migration patterns, presents case studies, and recommends new language policy for Puerto Rican child.

4503 Montes, Carlos E. ¿Cuándo es la escolaridad útil para el desarrollo económico? (UPR/LT, 22:85/86, julio/dic. 1974, p. 131–166)

Studies relationship between education and employment in Puerto Rico. Unemployment remains high despite impressive quantitative gains in education; thus, suggests focus on qualitative considerations. Concludes motivation is single most important factor affecting educational and occupational success.

4504 Petrovish, Janice. Dependencia, estratificación social y la expansión de la educación postsecundaria en Puerto Rico (UCR/RCS, 21:3/4, sept./dic. 1979, p. 413–437, bibl., tables)

Convincingly argues that private Puerto Rican universities are in particularly precarious position because of their students' excessive dependence on US guaranteed student loans. Elitist stratification built into Puerto Rican system of education is furthered by its dependence on "mainland" sources of funds.

TRINIDAD AND TOBAGO

4505 Stauble, Ann-Marie. English-language teaching and learning problems in Trinidad (PCCLAS/P, 8, 1981/1982, p. 63–74)

Overview of English-language teaching and learning problems in Trinidad, in which diversity of languages and basic structure of Trinidad Creole vernacular render teaching and learning of standard English very problematical. Describes and supports a new language policy.

4506 Stewart, Sandra M. Nationalist educational reforms and religious schools in Trinidad (CES/CER, 25:2, June 1981, p. 183–201)

Explores potential effects of proposed national school reforms in Trinidad on traditional roles of denominational educators. If fully implemented, denominational educators and denominational schools would be eliminated.

URUGUAY

4507 Labadie, Gastón J. La mujer universitaria uruguaya. Montevideo: Dirección General de Extensión Universitaria, División de Publicaciones y Ediciones, 1980. 79 p.: bibl. (Serie Investigación; no. 5)

Examines Uruguayan women in higher education: numbers, proportions, families, and sociodemographic characteristics which set them apart from other women.

4508 Papa Blanco, Sergio. Alegato por una universidad sin trabas. Montevideo: MZ/Editor, 1981. 80 p. (Tribuna libre)

Ten newspaper articles (1979–81) examine multiple problems which confront higher education in general and university students in particular (e.g., implementation of required university admissions test which resulted in unforeseen and unfortunate consequences for thousands of university aspirants).

4509 Uruguay. Presidencia de la República Oriental del Uruguay. Secretaría de Planeamiento, Coordinación y Difusión. Dirección General de Estadísticas y Censos. Anuario estadístico: 1970–78. Montevideo: 1978? 45 p.: tables.

Consists of education section of Uruguay's official census (1970–78).

VENEZUELA

4510 Fernández Heres, Rafael. La instrucción de la generalidad: historia de la educación en Venezuela, 1830–1980. Caracas: Ediciones del Ministerio de Educación, 1981. 2 v. (1381 p., [8] leaves of plates): bibl., ill.

Prepared to commemorate centennial of Venezuelan Ministry of Education (1881–1981). From 1830 to present, the Minister of

Education, according to Venezuelan law, has reported to Congress on the state of education. These reports have been published in five volumes entitled *Memoria de cien años.* Each includes an introductory section all of which have been reprinted here.

4511 Jaspe G., Ramón A. El Instituto Venezolano de Investigaciones Científicas, IVIC: veintitrés años trazándole rutas a la ciencia en Venezuela (AI/I, 7 : 5, sept./oct. 1982, p. 295–300, plates)

Comprehensive description of Venezuela's Instituto Venezolano de Investigaciones Científicas (IVIC), history and development, position among similar Latin American centers, facilities, accomplishments, goals, and personnel.

4512 Lerner de Almea, Ruth. Los valores morales en el contenido de la educación: estudio de caso en Venezuela. Santiago: Organización de las Naciones Unidas para la Educación, la Ciencia y la Cultura, Oficina Regional de Educación de la UNESCO para América Latina y el Caribe, 1980. 61, 24 p.: bibl.

One of four case studies on moral education sponsored by UNESCO. Author's premise is that there has been a subversion of traditional values and a loss of national identity among Venezuelan youth. Argues that although principles of morality and national values are clearly articulated in country's constitution, laws, and regulations, they are not effectively taught by nation's schools.

4513 Marta Sosa, Joaquín. Problemas de la educación superior en Venezuela. Caracas?: Ediciones Papeles Universitarios, between 1979 and 1980. 145 p. (Colección Los Libros de la educación venezolana)

Unparalleled growth of higher education in Venezuela—in number of students and in total cost—has created serious problems: excessively high costs and exceedingly high drop-out rate, low levels of academic achievement, and preponderance of marginally qualified teachers. Solutions will require integrated approach to planning (i.e., planning for higher education in the context of national needs).

4514 Reyes Baena, Juan Francisco. Dependencia, desarrollo y educación. 2. ed. Caracas: Universidad Central de Venezuela, Ediciones de la Biblioteca, 1979. 301, [19] p.: bibl. (Colección Educación; 1)

Examination of issues related to development is part of large-scale multidisciplinary effort entitled *La Venezuela que necesitamos* by Universidad Central de Venezuela team. Meticulous and useful analysis of social classes, industrialization, employment, education, and other development issues. Complex interrelationships among issues are highlighted.

4515 Roche, Marcel and **Yajaira Freites.** Producción y flujo de información científica en un país periférico americano: Venezuela (AI/I, 7 : 5, sept./oct. 1982, p. 279–290, tables)

Reports on a study of research dissemination patterns in Venezuela. Concludes that English language publications disseminate most research findings, a practice with mixed consequences for the Latin American research community.

4516 Seminario sobre Investigación y Planificación de los Costos de la Educación, *2d, Ciudad Guayana, Venezuela, 1973.* Los estudios de costos de la educación en Venezuela. Caracas: Ministerio de Educación, Dirección de Administración, Departamento de Imprenta, 1975. 607 p.: bibl., ill.

Consists of 12 studies on educational costs and benefits in Venezuela: relationship of educational costs to development (Carnoy, Levin); comparative costs of primary and secondary education (Mollejas); rural and urban education (Andrade P.); rate of return (Barrios); relation of costs and achievement (Elivia de Sánchez and Carbo de Proano); cost/benefit methodology (Andrade P., Elivia de Sánchez, and Vogeler); cost/benefit terminology (de Quintero); and additional cost/benefit studies (de Quintero).

4517 Universidad Central de Venezuela. Vicerrectorado Académico. Centro de Estudios del Desarrollo. Coordinación Central de Estudios para Graduados. Situación de los postgrados en la Universidad Central de Venezuela, 1976–1977: funcionamiento, organización académico-docente y recursos. Caracas: La Coordinación, 1980. 141 p.

Examination of development and current status of graduate programs at Universidad Central de Venezuela (UCV). Employed two methodologies: documents were examined to trace development, and division (academic) directors were surveyed to assess current status. Finds many problems in

UCV's graduate programs can be traced to their rapid expansion.

4518 Universidad Simón Bolívar. Instituto de Investigaciones Educativas. El rendimiento estudiantil universitario: influencia de la condición socio-económico de los padres en el rendimiento de los alumnos del primer año universitario, región Capital: síntesis comparativa. Caracas: Equinoccio, Editorial de la Universidad Simón Bolívar, 1978. 229 p. (Colección Paramentros)

Summary and synthesis of six-volume study on socioeconomic determinants of academic success among students at five major Venezuelan universities. Well-designed study yielded few unexpected conclusions; recommendations, however, warrant serious consideration by policy makers.

4519 Venezuela. Ministerio de Educación. VI [i.e. Sexto] plan de desarrollo de la nación, 1981–1985: sector educación. Caracas: El Ministerio, 1981. 85, [29] p.

Venezuela's five-year plan for education (1981–85) analyzes current condition of Venezuelan education and proposes major changes to resolve problems and to meet current needs. Excellent and comprehensive plan is candid in its appraisal and ambitious in its recommendations.

4520 ――――. ――――. Oficina Sectorial de Planificación y Presupuesto. Anuario estadístico del Ministerio de Educación. Caracas: El Ministerio, Oficina Sectorial de Planificación y Presupuesto, 1979. 693 p.: fold. tables, tables.

Exhaustive compilation of statistical data on Venezuelan education from 1969–79. Includes summary tables as well as complete tables for the following levels of education: preschool, primary, secondary, higher, and adult.

BRAZIL

ROBERT E. VERHINE, *Faculdade de Educação, Universidade Federal da Bahia, Salvador, Brazil*
THOMAS J. LABELLE, *Graduate School of Education, University of California, Los Angeles*

NEW JOURNALS (items **4522, 4529** and **4541**) and anthologies in the field of education (items **4527, 4535, 4571, 4577, 4580** and **4582**) attest in part to the growing emphasis on scholarship in Brazil's many master's level graduate education programs and in part to the continuation of the *abertura* with its accompanying relaxation of censorship. The *abertura* has stimulated highly critical analyses based on a class-conflict or dependency orientation. One valuable example is Salm's book (item **4576**) on education and work which cogently attacks the popular neo-marxist principle of correspondence. The opposite point is made by Torino (item **4581**) in a book that examines the Southeast and Northeast regions using census data. Another noteworthy contribution to the radical critiques is a participant-observation study by Vieitez (item **4587**) conducted between 1968–72 which examines teacher conflict and the effects of political repression in a single private school.

A field of educational research which has particularly benefitted from critical, class-conflict analysis is the history of education. Examples are two works by Luiz Antônio Cunha, one (item **4538**) tracing the emergence of the Brazilian university from colonial times to the Vargas era and the other (item **4537**) reviewing the history of educational conferences in Brazil. Célio de Cunha's study (item **4536**) of educational reforms during Vargas' Estado Novo and Casemiro dos Reis Filho's analysis (item **4573**) of public education in São Paulo during the 1890s are two other histories which deserve mention.

Popular topics of recent educational history in Brazil are the vocational oriented reform of secondary level instruction (Lei 5692) and the 1968 reforms of the structure of the university (Lei 5540). Studies showing how industrial capitalism was supported by the secondary reform include Mirian Warde's (item **4588**) analysis of the mandates of the Federal Council of Education, José Arapiraca's (item **4523**) study of the influence of USAID in the reform process, and Lucília Machado's examination (item **4559**) of the ideological role of the technician in the factory. Notable contributions on the university reform are Veiga's study (item **4584**) showing the competing interests which led to the Reform, Graciani's work (item **4552**) focusing on the Reform's relationship to university bureaucratization and the centralization of authority, and Paiva's insightful essay (item **4566**) which places the reform in the context of the state's struggle for hegemony. Related to these efforts are a series of works which focus on the privatization of higher education and plans to charge tuition at now free (for the student) public institutions. The government's position is well stated by Melchior (item **4562**) while Carlos Martins (item **4561**) states the case against privatization and Teodoro Vahl (item **4583**) provides a more balanced picture.

Another controversial matter is pre-school education. Since the mid-1970s pre-school policy is intended to increase the educational opportunities of the poor. This compensatory policy is bitterly attacked by Ferrari and Gaspary (item **4544**) and Kramer (item **4556**). Both studies make similar points: pre-school programs are based on foreign models of dubious success, the opportunities provided are weighted in favor of the privileged, and such efforts will merely teach the poor to accept their inferior status.

Out-of-school programs—an area in which Brazil is a pioneer—have also received considerable attention from scholars. Di Ricco (item **4540**) provides an overview of national adult literacy campaigns between 1947–71, Sá (item **4575**) offers useful information on programs for adults in the late 1950s and early 1960s, Moacyr Góes presents a well documented personal memoir (item **4548**) of an innovative program for youth and adults sponsored by the mayor of Natal between 1961–64, and an INEP research report (item **4579**) inventories current extra-school activities.

Of course, the leading spirit behind most adult educational activities in Brazil continues to be Paulo Freire. Now back in Brazil after many years of exile, he is writing and speaking extensively, focusing on worldwide practical applications of his approach (item **4531, 4545** and **4555**). His work and thinking continue to be investigated by others. Vanilda Paiva (item **4567**) provides an excellent analysis of Freire's intellectual origins and the early evolution of this thought, and Maria van der Poel (item **4570**) offers an empirical evaluation of the impact of the Freire method among a group of prisoners in João Pessoa (Paraiba). Current thinking in the field of "popular" education is summarized in the first issue of *Cadernos de CEDES* (item **4529**). Meanwhile, the government's major effort in the field of adult education—the MOBRAL literacy program—is criticized in, among others, a study by Govoni (item **4551**) which concludes that it has little impact.

Much of the popular education literature has either a rural bias or a bias toward serving marginal populations. Two useful works on rural education are a collection of readings edited by Werthein and Bordenave (item **4580**) and a study of the innovative family school program in Espírito Santo by Passotti (item **4568**). As to marginal populations, the education of the Indian is examined in an edited volume by the Pro-Indian Commission (item **4535**) while women as a class have been dealt with in a number of articles on education, including those by Gouveia (item **4550**) and Lewin (item **4557**).

Another aspect of out-of-school education is manpower training. As Machado (item **4559**) makes clear, there is an increasing tendency for this form of education to be interpreted as serving narrow ideological and technical interests of dominant capitalist groups. Still, it is worth pointing to Agudelo's detailed review (item **4521**) of the methodology used by Brazil's National Industrial Training Service (SENAI) and Verhine and Lehmann's empirical study in Northeastern Brazil (item **4585**) which indicates that nonformal education—especially long courses focusing on basic skills—contribute to factory job acquisition.

In the areas of educational planning and educational technology, Horta (item **4554**) documents the role of the Federal Council of Education in macro planning efforts of the 1960s and the OAS (item **4572**) defends the government's current emphasis on participative planning even though it may be costly, inefficient and difficult to manage. Both Oliveira (item **4564**) and García (item **4525**) indicate the difficulties in implanting new educational technology and the need to attend to the context into which the technology is introduced.

While the current literature is dominated by thought pieces and position papers, as opposed to empirical field investigations, there are a number of the latter works of value, and one is directed to *Cadernos de Pesquisa*, published in São Paulo by the Fundação Carlos Chagas, to locate the best of them. One notable empirical investigation of size is that conducted by the Programa ECIEL (item **4308**) which examines educational costs and efficiency in nine Latin American countries (including Brazil), and suggests that learning outcomes for the poor can be augmented by increasing school expenditures.

We are grateful for the assistance rendered by Walter C. García of CNPQ and A. Virgílio Bastos and M. Amélia Verhine, both of the Universidade Federal de Bahia.

4521 Agudelo Mejía, Santiago. Formación individual: sistema utilizado en el SENAI de Rio de Janeiro. Montevideo: CINTERFOR, 1977. 136 p.: appendixes, bibl., ill. (Estudios y monografías—CINTERFOR; no. 26)

Detailed presentation of method of individualized vocational instruction developed by SENAI, Brazil's National Industrial Training Service. Includes description of method, analysis of program outcomes at SENAI center in Rio de Janeiro, and proposed approach for evaluating systems of individualized learning. Appendixes include lesson plans, handouts, and control and evaluation forms used in the SENAI apprenticeship course. Important work given current worldwide interest in the SENAI model.

4522 *Anuário de Educação.* Universidade Federal do Ceará; Tempo Brasileiro. 1981– . Fortaleza.

First issue of annual publication, volume contains variety of texts related to aspects of current educational policy in Brazil. Includes essays, articles and documents on higher education, UNESCO conference, research, the university and teaching profession. Most contributors held important positions in Brazil's federal educational hierarchy. Provides useful statistical information on educational trends.

4523 Arapiraca, José Oliveira. A USAID e a educação brasileira: um estudo a partir de um abordagem crítica da teoria do capital humano. São Paulo: Editora Autores Associados: Cortez Editora, 1982. 190 p.: ill. (Coleção Educação contemporânea. Série Memória da educação)

Argues that USAID funds given to Brazilian education after 1964 represented attempt to insure return on invested capital by promoting school system designed to produce efficient industrial manpower. Focuses on secondary level and on such USAID supported programs as EPEM, PREMEM, and Escolas Polivalentes. Includes detailed theoretical critique of concept of human capital. Somewhat disjointed and very polemical, but contains useful historical information and is helpful to those wishing to better understand anti-Americanism among Brazilian educators.

4524 Barretto, Elba Sa; Guiomar Namo de Mello; Lisete Arelaro; and Maria M. Malta Campos. Ensino de 1.° e 2.° graus: intenção e realidade (Cadernos de Pesquisa [Fundação Carlos Chagas, São Paulo] 30, set. 1979, p. 21–40, appendix, bibl., graphs, tables)

Compares data concerning primary and secondary education in Brazil with official goals defined for 1975–79 period. Concludes that distance between stated objective of equal opportunity and reality of extreme selectivity reflects contradictions between adopted model of economic development and ideal of democratic education. Provides useful statistical information.

4525 Barroso, Carmen *et al.* Inovação educacional no Brasil: problemas e perspectivas. Walter E. Garcia, coordenador. São Paulo: Editora Autores Associados: Cortez Editora, 1980. 264 p.: bibl. (Coleção Educação contemporânea)

Collection of 13 essays on educational innovation in three sections: 1) dimensions of educational innovation; 2) experiences in educational innovation; and 3) critical assessment of educational innovation in Brazil. From variety of theoretical perspectives, articles discuss history of phenomenon in Brazil, relationship to legislation and ideology, alternative procedures for evaluation, and four actual case studies. Illustrates problems associated with transference and maintenance of change. Reveals how administrative centralism and concern for form over substance have impeded effective educational innovation. Valuable work whose importance is not limited to Brazil.

4526 Braga, Helena. Política educacional e racionalidade econômica: o caso do ensino de 1.° e 2.° graus (Forum Educacional [Fundação Getúlio Vargas, Instituto de Estudos Avançados em Educação, Rio de Janeiro] 4:1, jan./março 1980, p. 45–74, bibl., tables)

Examines role of private initiative in provision of primary and secondary schooling in Brazil and suggests ways of improving effectiveness of this educational component. Includes analysis of Brazil's educational sector, contribution to economic development, and division of responsibility between private and public domains. Contends that country's educational policy discriminates against private schooling sector, especially on lower levels, and recommends remedying this situation via fiscal interventions.

4527 Brandão, Carlos Rodrigues *et al.* O Ecuador, vida e morte: escritos sobre um espêcie em perigo. Rio de Janeiro: Graal, 1982. 137 p.: bibl.

Collection of essays concerning social and political role of school supervisor in modern Brazil by Paulo Freire, Rubem Alves and Miguel Arroyo, etc. Common theme is that educator can overcome prospect of social death at hands of authoritarian state tied to capitalist interest if he emphasizes humanism, dialogue and community while incorporating political activism into his pedagogical activity.

4528 Brazil. Secretaria de Ensino Superior. Coordenação de Avaliação e Controle. O Ensino superior no Brasil, 1974/1978: relatório. Ministério da Educação e Cultura. Equipe de elaboração, Cláudio Cordeiro Neiva *et al.* Equipe de apoio, Victor Lopes de Oliveira *et al.* Brasília: Departamento de Documentação e Divulgação, 1979. 210 p.

Detailed report on Brazilian higher education documents its 1968–78 growth (public and private). Focuses on quantitative changes in such indicators as number of courses offered, number of matriculants, level of faculty qualification, spatial distribution of services and amount of public expenditures. Also describes nature and outcome of principal projects and activities promoted by Department of University Affairs (1974–78). Useful reference.

4529 *Cadernos do CEDES*. Concepções e experiências de educação popular. Cortez Editora. Ano 1, No. 1, 1980– . São Paulo.

First issue of new journal edited by Center of Education and Society Studies (CEDES) consists of three articles on: 1) fundamentals of popular education (C. Brandão); 2) methodology of popular education (L. Blass, S. Manfredi, and S. Barros); and 3) use of popular education as strategy for permanent education (A. Melo). Writers see popular education as extra-school process of promoting class consciousness among the poor and their analyses draw heavily from Freire and MEB experiences, among others. Good introduction to subject.

4530 Camargo, Nelly de. Televisão na praça: redefinição cultural e nova sintax do lazer (Comunicações e Artes [Escola de Comunicações e Artes da Universidade de São Paulo] 9, 1980, p. 1–19, tables)

Study of impact of television in traditional community setting is based on 1280 interviews (recent migrants) of outdoor public sets in São Luis. Reports that TV affected audiences' perceptions and expectations as well as patterns of social interaction, allocation of time, and use of leisure. Also notes that television fosters passivity, meaning that the use of TV for educational purposes can only succeed if programming is linked to recipient's needs, motives and frame of reference.

4531 Castro, Célia Lúcia Monteiro de. Mestre: E daí? (Forum Educacional [Fundação Getúlia Vargas, Instituto de Estudos Avançados em Educação, Rio de Janeiro] 5 : 4, oct./dez. 1981, p. 17–40, tables)

Evaluation of Masters programs in Brazil based on questionnaire responses from 463 graduates of 26 different programs in the Rio de Janeiro-São Paulo area. Finds that many graduates are underemployed and few continue to conduct research after thesis. Suggests that graduate study in Brazil serves more a social than a technical function, conferring elite status but not preparing human resources for national development.

4532 ———. Pesquisa em educação: vale a pena? (Forum Educacional [Fundação Getúlio Vargas, Instituto de Estudos Avançados em Educação, Rio de Janeiro] 4 : 1, jan./março 1980, p. 19–44, bibl., tables)

Compares educational research produced between 1960–77 with the government's official research and planning priorities for same period. Finds little relationship between what has been studied and what public authorities consider relevant. Notes that topics investigated are limited, most important being: 1) organization of school experiences; 2) teaching methodolgy; 3) student, teacher, and administrator characteristics; 4) student evaluation; and 5) student educational and vocational counseling.

4533 Castro, Cláudio de Moura; Eliane Mota Soriano; Margarida Maria Gomes de Melo; and Miguel Naccareto. O enigma do supletivo. Fortaleza, Brazil: Universidade Federal do Ceará, 1980. 220 p.: ill., tables.

Results of major study of 200 secondary level equivalency tests (exames supletivos) conducted in Rio de Janeiro: 1) estimates levels of validity and reliability of tests; 2) identifies personal characteristics which explain exam success; and 3) compares college entrance test performances of equivalency graduates with those of regular secondary system completers. Concludes that high equivalency exam failure rate (about 70 percent) is due more to weaknesses in candidates than to deficiencies in tests. Important (albeit controversial) investigation of type of program (i.e., equivalency) for which Brazil is pioneer.

4534 Centro de Integração Empresa-Escola (CIE-E). Dicionário das profissões: estudos ocupacionais referentes a profissões e cursos de formação em 2.° e 3.° graus: nível médio e superior. 2. ed. São Paulo: CIE-E, 1978. 4 v.

Designed to aid vocational guidance of adolescent students, this four-volume dictionary covers 64 professions, requiring either secondary or university level education, divided into five sections: 1) historical background; 2) characteristics of the job; 3) career prospects; 4) necessary academic preparation; and 5) additional notes. Contains useful insights into relationship between education and Brazil's labor market.

4535 Comissão Pró-Indio/SP. A questão da educação indígena. São Paulo: Brasiliense, 1981. 222 p.: bibl., ill., ports.

Contains papers presented at 1979 conference plus four articles and a partly annotated bibliography on relationship between the Indian and popular education, language policy, and alternative pedagogical approaches in various regions of Brazil. Bibliography distinguishes works on Brazil from those on the Americas in general. Important work on neglected aspect of Brazilian education.

4536 Cunha, Célio da. Educação e autoritarismo no estado novo. São Paulo: Cortez Editora: Autores Associados, 1981. 176 p.: bibl. (Coleção Educação contemporânea: Série Memória da educação)

Well written historical study of educational reforms launched during Estado Novo (1937–45) of Getúlio Vargas. Emphasizes historical antecedents and sociocultural context of these reforms, and provides bibliographic sketches of major personalities involved.

Concludes that reforms were basically conservative, protecting privilege and promoting centralization. They were not, however, as anti-democratic as the regime's authoritarian philosophy.

4537 Cunha, Luiz Antônio. A organização do campo educacional: as conferências de educação (Educação & Sociedade [Centro de Estudos Educação e Sociedade (CEDES), Cortez Editora: Autores Associados, São Paulo] 4:9, maio 1981, p. 5–48, appendix)

Lucid historical analysis of educational conferences in Brazil, ranging from first one recorded (1873) to present. Differentiates between those organized by the State to coopt the educator and those set-up by educators to influence the State. Depicts political-ideological struggles between competing factions of educators. Places each gathering in broader sociohistorical context and indicates that, even in times of political repression, conference served as means for educator participation in educational policy-making. Important addition to Brazil's history of education.

4538 ———. A universidade temporã: o ensino superior da colônia a era de Vargas. Rio de Janeiro: Civilização Brasileira, Edições UFC, 1980. 295 p. (Coleção Educação e transformação)

Interpretive history of higher education in Brazil emphasizes four periods: colony, empire, First Republic, and Vargas years. Places higher education within socio-political contexts and tries to identify its role in societal transformation. Through selective use of original documents and previous studies, examines course organization, curriculum content and implicit ideology of early Brazilian colleges and universities, considering also political-economic determinants of their objectives and power structures.

4539 Demo, Pedro. Educação, cultura e poder: hipótesis sobre a importância de educação para o desenvolvimento (Cadernos de Pesquisa [Fundação Carlos Chagas, São Paulo] 41, maio 1982, p. 12–21, bibl., tables)

One of first articles on education to present data drawn from 1980 census, this work demonstrates maintenance of low rates of schooling for Brazilian population. Questions relationship between economic growth and school attendance, suggesting that education has more importance for democratic participation than for economic development.

4540 Di Ricco, Gaetano Maria Jovino. Educação de adultos: uma contribuição para seu estudo no Brasil. São Paulo: Edições Loyola, 1979. 130 p.: bibl. (Coleção Realidade educacional; 5)

Three-chapter historical overview of adult literacy efforts in Brazil emphasizes 1947–71 by: 1) reviewing relevant theoretical literature; 2) summarizing federal legislation pertaining to six national literacy campaigns; and 3) documenting UNESCO's influence on adult education in Brazil. Concludes that Brazilian efforts in adult literacy have failed, but offers little insight as to why. Useful work, however, because of descriptive information it provides.

4541 *Educação e Seleção.* Fundação Carlos Chagas, Departamento de Seleção de Recursos Humanos. Nos. 1/5, julho 1980– . São Paulo.

Bi-annual new journal issued by Brazil's equivalent to the Educational Testing Service. Focuses on human resource selection, with particular attention to aspects of testing and evaluation. Most articles deal with improving college admission examination (O Vestibular). One of few technically-oriented educational journals in Brazil.

4542 Erber, Fábio Stefano. Science and technology policy in Brazil: a review of the literature (LARR, 26:1, 1981, p. 3–55, bibl.)

Extensive review of the literature on development of science and technology, as applied to manufacturing sector. Discusses works dealing with: role of science and technology in the process of capitalist development, technological dependency, diffusion of innovation, state's role in promoting science and technology in Brazil, economic consequences of use of technology in Brazil, etc. Concludes that though much research is of high quality, remaining gaps reflect institutional framework in which studies were done.

4543 Estudio de cambios e innovaciones en la educación técnica y la formación profesional en América Latina y el Caribe. v. 11, Brasil. Divonzir A. Gusso. Santiago: Oficina Regional de Educación de la UNESCO para América Latina y el Caribe, 1980. 1 v.: bibl., ill.

Descriptive overview of vocational-technical education in Brazil. Very detailed, but provides incomplete picture because relies much more on official documents than on actual observations. Considers both formal and nonformal programs. Important conclusion: impressive expansion of vocational system in 1970s had little effect on workers' employability or salary levels.

4544 Ferrari, Alceu R. and Lúcia Beatriz Velloso Gaspary. Distribuição de oportunidades de educação pré-escolar no Brasil (Educação & Sociedade [Centro de Estudos Educação e Sociedade (CEDES), Cortez Editora: Autores Associados, São Paulo] 2 : 5, jan. 1980, p. 63–79, bibl., tables)

Analysis of quantity and quality of pre-school education in Brazil, based on census data. Compares distribution of pre-school opportunities by region and social class, revealing that access is both limited and unequally allocated. Trends have aggravated in recent years, indicating government's stated policy of using pre-school education for compensatory purposes is merely rhetoric designed to obfuscate more basic structural problems. Useful information source.

4545 Freire, Paulo. A importância do ato de ler: em tres artigos que se completam. 2. ed. São Paulo: Editora Autores Associados: Cortez Editora, 1982. 96 p. (Coleção Polêmicas do nosso tempo; 4)

Recent papers deal with political significance of act of reading, use of people's libraries as cultural centers, and nature of author's literacy work in São Tome and Príncipe (Africa). Most important to Freire students is second half of third article, which includes sections of exercise book used by author in Africa along with explanatory comments. This last portion is designed to complement previous Freire article in *Harvard Educational Review* (Feb. 1981).

4546 Gadotti, Moacir. Educação e poder: introdução à pedagogia do conflito. São Paulo: Cortez Editora: Autores Associados, 1980. 143 p. (Coleção Educação contemporânea)

Three-part collection of essays by noted educational philosopher: 1) philosophical aspects of education; 2) practices of pedagogy; and 3) ideological and political components of pedagogy in Brazil today. Articles present author's conception of pedagogy as designed to unmask and confront conflict, rather than hide it. Critical, provocative work.

4547 Gersdorff, Ralph von. Educação brasileira: problemas e soluções possíveis. Rio de Janeiro: Livraria Agir Editora, 1981. 171 p.: bibl.

Listing of Brazilian educational problems and possible solutions, from perspective of experienced educational planner: formal education (all levels), nonformal education, educational planning and administration, educational finance, and compilation of educational statistics. Solutions offered emphasize technical rather than socio-political considerations and thus many seem simplistic. Useful, nevertheless, in providing insight into operational aspects of Brazil's educational structure.

4548 Góes, Moacyr de. De Pé no Chão Também Se Aprende a Ler (1961–64): uma escola democrática. Revisão, Umberto F. Pinto, Mário Elber dos S. Cunha, Cristina M. Paes da Cunha. Rio de Janeiro: Civilização Brasileira, 1980. 209 p., [12] p. of plates: bibl., ill. (Coleção Educação e transformação; v. 3)

Historical account of popular, basic education movement in Natal (Rio Grande do Norte, 1961–64). Program, whose name gave title to book (roughly: "shoeless ones can also learn to read"), was directed at both youths and adults and had a nationalistic, social change focus. Before 1964 "revolution" ended it, it reached 17,000 students at estimated cost of $2 per pupil. Although a personal account written by one intimately involved, book is well documented and places movement in appropriate historical and geographical context.

4549 Goldberg, Maria Amélia *et al.* Seletividade socio-econômica no ensino de 1.° grau. Rio de Janeiro: Associação Nacional de Pós-Graduação em Educação (ANPED): Patrocínio CNPQ, 1981. 115 p.

Proceedings of 3d Meeting of National Association of Graduate Study in Education (Salvador, 1980) are devoted to socioeconomic selectivity in primary education. Points out importance of extra-school variables in socioeconomic selection process and need for non-traditional, non-quantitative investigations in this area.

4550 Gouveia, Aparecida Joly. Origem social, escolaridade e ocupação (Cadernos de Pesquisa [Fundação Carlos Chagas, São Paulo] 32, fev. 1980, p. 3–17, bibl., tables)

Using data from 1973 labor market survey, investigates relation between social origin, education and occupation in São Paulo and Northeast. Finds that although levels of schooling are higher in São Paulo, similar pattern of educational inequality associated with social background is evident in both regions. Reveals that social origins interact with education/occupation linkage and that being a woman, though not detrimental to schooling attainment, has negative consequences in labor market.

4551 Govoni, Ilário. Alfabetização de adultos como mudança socio-cultural: pesquisa no MOBRAL, de Salvador e Teresina. Teresina, Brazil: Edições Punaré, 1980. 350 p.: appendixes, bibl., ill., index, tables.

Ambitious, well designed evaluation of impact of MOBRAL literacy courses. Using data from in-depth interviews, compares living conditions and sociocultural attitudes of program graduates and illiterates in two Northeastern cities and concludes that course participation has little effect on lives and thinking of urban adults. Also provides detailed background information on MOBRAL and literacy efforts in general.

4552 Graciani, Maria Stela Santos. O ensino superior no Brasil: a estrutura de poder na universidade em questão. Petrópolis: Vozes, 1982. 164 p.: bibl.

Describes and analyzes internal organization and decision-making process of Brazilian university after 1968 Reform. Also includes sections dealing with rise of bureaucracy in Brazil, student protest movement preceding Reform, and backgrounds of those occupying key university positions. Most data collected from primary and secondary sources at 29 institutions of higher learning. Major conclusion is that Reform preserved university's autocratic authority system by strengthening bureaucratic tendencies.

4553 Hendricks, Craig and Robert M. Levine. Pernambuco's political elite and the Recife Law School (AAFH/TAM, 37:3, Jan. 1981, p. 291–313)

Biographical data are used to characterize composition and continuity in Pernambuco's political elite in the Brazilian federation (1889–1937). Authors indicate that membership in political elite was limited to rural aristocracy or urban commercial elite trained at prestigious Recife Law School which is said to have had profound influence on public career patterns.

4554 Horta, José Silvério Baia. Liberalismo, tecnocracia e planejamento educacional no Brasil: uma contribuição à história da educação brasileira no período 1930–1970. São Paulo: Editora Autores Associados: Cortez Editora, 1982. 226 p. (Coleção Educação contemporânea. Série Memória da educação).

Historical study of influence of Federal Council of Education on evolution of educational planning in Brazil. Contrary to title, focuses on period from 1962 (when Council was established) to 1971 (when Sector Plan for Education and Culture was incorporated into First National Development Plan). Indicates that Council's influence was marginal, as planning prerogatives were usurped by Ministry of Education. Shows how during 1960s, educational planning moved from expansionist to contentionist emphasis and how responsibility for planning passed from pedagogues to technocrats. Well documented analysis.

4555 Institut d'action culturelle. Vivendo e aprendendo: experiência do IDAC em educação popular. Paulo Freire *et al.* São Paulo: Brasiliense, 1980. 125 p.: ill.

Another work by Freire and associates on efforts to implement pedagogy of the oppressed. Contains six articles relating specific experiences of Cultural Action Institute (IDAC), research and social intervention center created (Geneva, 1970) by Freire and other Brazilian exiles. Experiences described include consciousness-raising activities with workers in Italy, women in Switzerland, and peasants in Guiné-Bissau. Aimed at practitioners and cleverly illustrated. Contribution to Brazilian educational literature but does not deal with Brazilian education.

4556 Kramer, Sonia. A política do pré-escolar no Brasil: a arte do disfarce. Rio de Janeiro: Achiamé, 1982. 131 p. (Série Universidade; v. 20)

Highly critical analysis of pre-school education in Brazil, from class-conflict, dependency perspective. Includes nation's history of child care and review of politics of pre-school education. Concludes that preschool education is not panacea for social ills and, as currently implemented, serves to enhance inequality through restricted access and compensatory bias (of foreign origin) which marks participants as inferior. Provocative study of topical issue.

4557 Lewin, Helena. Educação e força de trabalho feminina no Brasil (Cadernos de Pesquisa [Fundação Carlos Chagas, São Paulo] 32, fev. 1980, p. 45–59, bibl., tables)

Analyzes women's participation in Brazilian work force, focusing on distribution by occupations, wages in relation to men, and college career options. Discusses problem of female work in terms of capitalist society dynamics, for which, according to author, use of women in low-prestige and payment occupations is highly functional. Useful information source.

4558 Língua e literatura: o professor pede a palavra. Organização, Valéria de Marco, Lígia Chiappini M. Leite, Suzi Frankl Sperber. São Paulo: Cortez Editora, 1981. 184 p.: bibl.

Collection of 30 papers presented by public school teachers of writing and literature. Primarily case studies and thought pieces, they offer insight into experiences and thinking of this professional class.

4559 Machado, Lucília R. de Souza. Educação e divisão social do trabalho. São Paulo: Autores Associados: Cortez Editora, 1982. 154 p.; bibl. (Coleção Educação contemporânea)

Radical analysis of function of technical education in capitalist society. Includes history of technical education in Brazil, interpretation of role of factory technician, and critique of theories (functionalist, human capital, modernization) which serve to justify investments in this form of instruction. Argues that current emphasis on technical education in Brazil is due less to technical needs than to political-ideological importance of technician as link between management and labor in industrial workplace. Informative and topical.

4560 Marques, Gladis A. Bottaro. Aplicación de un currículo flexible en el proyecto de educación ambiental de Ceilandia, Brasil. Santiago: Oficina Regional de Educación de la UNESCO para América Latina y el Caribe, 1980. 42 p.: bibl., ill.

Case study of UNESCO-supported project of school-community integration, implemented on outskirts of Brasília (Ceilandia, 1978). Focuses on use of Integrated Learning Units (UAIs) to create flexible curriculum related to needs and interests of clients. Notes that project suffered from parental skepticism and inadequate teacher preparation, but considers it on the whole a success, warranting application in other areas.

4561 Martins, Carlos Benedito. Ensino pago: um retrato sem retoques. São Paulo: Global Editora, 1981. 210 p.: bibl., tables (Teses; 2)

Case study of private university in São Paulo written to illustrate problems inherent in current movement away from free public higher education in Brazil. Using as backdrop neo-marxist theory of reproduction, views institution under study as "cultural industry" designed to serve structures of dependent capitalism. Supports argument with interpretive analysis of university's structure, students and faculty members. Topical and provocative.

4562 Melchior, José Carlos de Araújo. Financiamento da educação no Brasil numa perspectiva democrática (Cadernos de Pesquisa [Fundação Carlos Chagas, São Paulo] 34, agôsto 1980, p. 39–83, bibl., ill., tables)

Analysis of educational finance in Brazil, including description of how system operates and suggestions for improvement. Discusses legalities of financing, budgetary procedures, system of special funds, taxes and incentives, and politics of additional resource obtainment. Concludes with 28 recommendations, including involvement of education councils in budgetary planning, placement of school taxes on profits, inheritances and financial transactions, and charging of tuition (for those who can pay) at secondary and university levels. Important and influential.

4563 Mendes Júnior, Antônio. Movimento estudantil no Brasil. São Paulo: Brasiliense, 1981. 92 p.: ill. (Coleção Tudo e história; 23)

Short but informative history of student movement in Brazil from colonial times to early 1970s. Identifies four historical periods according to type of action: 1) individual (until 1840); 2) collective (until 1937); 3) organized (until 1968); and 4) clandestine. Argues that although transitory and sporadic, student political activity had moments of major influence, most important of which involved Brazil's entry into World War II, nationalization of oil, and resistance to post-1964 dictatorship.

4564 Oliveira, João Batista Araújo e. Tecnologia educacional no Brasil (Cadernos de Pesquisa [Fundação Carlos Chagas, São Paulo] 33, maio 1980, p. 61–69, bibl., tables)

Presents overview of educational technology in Brazil and analyzes examples of successful and unsuccessful projects, particularly in educational TV field. Final section presents critical assessment of contributions and shortcomings of Brazil's educational technology, suggesting that such efforts have failed to solve critical problems of educational quality and quantity. Good background piece.

4565 Oliveira, Raimundo Sobreira Goes de.
A crise do ensino, Brasília. Brasília: Horizonte Editora, 1980. 131 p.: bibl., ill. (Movimento cultural brasileiro)

Although Oliveira is listed as author, work belongs equally to major Brazilian educator Lauro de Oliveira Lima. Consists of their separate reactions to 24 topical educational issues (e.g., school organization, curriculum content, vocational education, and parent-teacher associations). Both contributions are better at identifying problems than indicating solutions, though Lima's observations, reflecting strong nationalistic-democratic bent, are more incisive. While ostensibly directed at Brasília, issues apply to entire country.

4566 Paiva, Vanilda Pereira. Estado, sociedade e educação no Brasil (ECB, 3:4, abril 1980, p. 37–58, bibl.)

Lucid, class-conflict analysis of politics of Brazilian higher education which summarizes and interprets events of 1960s and 1970s and considers likely developments in 1980s. Argues that new political and economic realities will cause regime, as part of ongoing quest for legitimacy, to revert to pre-1964 policies of restricting investments in higher education and giving priority to primary level. Insightful work, buttressed by extensive notes.

4567 ———. Paulo Freire e o nacionalismo-desenvolvimentista. Rio de Janeiro:

Civilização Brasileira: Edições UFC, 1980. 208 p.: bibl. (Coleção Educação e transformação; v. 2)

Scholarly analysis of evolution of Paulo Freire's pedagogical thinking between 1959–65, emphasizing origins of his philosophy. Argues that Freire's literacy method is product of Brazil's nationalist-developmentalist intellectual movement of 1950s, as expressed by affiliates of Higher Institute of Brazilian Studies (ISEB), links three essays: 1) contribution of ISEB to existential-culturalist nature of Freire's thought; 2) inter-relationship of Freire's, ISEB's, and Karl Mannheim's ideas; and 3) Freire's shift from a directive to a non-directive pedagogical focus. Valuable contribution towards understanding both Freire's approach and Brazil's intellectual climate prior to 1964.

4568 Passotti, Alda Luzia. Escola-família: a pedagogia de alternancia no meio rural (Forum Educacional [Fundação Getúlio Vargas, Instituto de Estudos Avançados em Educação, Rio de Janeiro] 5:2, abril/junho 1981, p. 39–59, bibl.)

Analysis of family-school program (MEPES) of rural education implanted 1969 in Espírito Santo. Program proposes to tie student to family and rural life by alternating instruction between school and home. Indicates that innovative effort succeeds despite problems of: 1) student age and geographic dispersion; 2) lack of financial resources; and 3) need to adhere to governmental norms.

**4569 Pesquisa e realidade no ensino de 1.°
grau.** Gizelda Santana Morais, organizador. São Paulo: Cortez Editora, 1980. 159 p.: bibl.

Presents results of research project conducted in Salvador, Bahia, to study primary school learning and instruction via classroom observations. Seven interrelated articles, drawing from same data, address issues such as student-teacher verbal interaction, and teacher perceptions of school objectives and student social behavior. Useful insight into primary-level classroom dynamics.

4570 Poel, Maria Salete van der. Alfabetização de adultos: sistema Paulo Freire: estudo de caso num presídio. Petrópolis: Vozes, 1981. 223 p: ill.

Well presented case study of 60-day course based on Freire's literacy approach given to group of prison inmates in João

Pessôa. Carefully details steps taken, materials used, and theoretical principles involved. Concludes with evaluation (based on pretest/post-test comparisons) which indicates substantial gains in reading and writing skills and small but significant advances in critical awareness (measured along seven dimensions). Findings indicate that these outcomes are independent of student age. Important empirical investigation.

4571 Psicologia educacional: contribuições e desafios. Organização e comentários de Juracy C. Marques. Porto Alegre: Editora Globo, 1980. 378 p.: bibl.

Well organized anthology of 12 articles on educational psychology grouped under: 1) psychology and education; 2) theories of learning and instruction; 3) creativity; and 4) educational problems. Most contributions based on bibliographic research rather than primary data and only two—on cognitive psychology (D. Cavicchia) and urban marginality (G. Morais)—focus specifically on Brazil.

4572 Regionalização educacional a nível nacional: notas sobre a experiência brasileira (OAS/LE, 87:25, 1981, p. 72–95)

Reviews governmental efforts to regionalize educational administration in Brazil. Provides historical background, alternative systems of regionalization, and case study of regionalization in Pernambuco state. Analyzes relationship between regionalization and participative educational planning. Concludes that regionalization promotes administrative efficiency and is a pre-condition for participative planning, though this latter process has suffered from high costs and internal conflicts.

4573 Reis Filho, Casemiro dos. A educação e a ilusão liberal. São Paulo: Cortez Editora: Autores Associados, 1981. 214 p.: appendixes: bibl. (Coleção Educação contemporânea: Série Memoria da educação)

Well documented historical study of public school system in São Paulo state in Republic's early years (1890–96). Notes that although public system was promoted in name of democratic-liberalism, it was in fact quite selective, with excessively high standards and encyclopedic approach to teaching. Argues that many inadequacies can be traced to an over reliance on foreign models. Considers all educational levels and emphasizes sociocultural context variables.

4574 Rezende, Antônio Muniz de. O saber e o poder na universidade: dominação ou serviço. São Paulo: Editora Autores Associados: Cortez Editora, 1982. 88 p. (Coleção Polêmicas do nosso tempo; 3)

Essays on administrative aspects of Brazilian higher education written by noted educational philosopher with university policy-making experiences. Focuses on: 1) pedagogical dimension of educational administration; 2) distinction between educational and business administration; 3) political and cultural role of higher education; and 4) need to "de-stateize" the university and to return institutional learning to civil domain.

4575 Sá, Nicanor Palhares. Política educacional e populismo no Brasil. 2. ed. São Paulo: Cortez Editora: Editora Autores Associados, 1982. 107 p.: bibl. (Coleção Educação contemporânea)

Adopting radical, class-analysis approach, author conceptualizes educational policy as political/ideological phenomenon and on this basis examines non-traditional, populist-based educational programs promoted by religious and student groups in 1950s and early 1960s. Argues that, though short-lived, programs illustrated how social conflict creates openings in which active, change-oriented, people-focused education flourishes. Sees education (in broad sense) as instrument not only of domination but also of resistance and liberation. Highly interpretive, but contains useful historical information.

4576 Salm, Claudio L. Escola e trabalho. São Paulo: Livraria Brasiliense Editora, 1980. 112 p.: appendixes, bibl.

Marxist analysis of education/labor market relationship attacks dominant neo-Marxist contention that under capitalism school reflects and serves system of production. Contends that the education which interests the firm is provided via on-the-job learning accompanied by simplication, through specialization, of work itself. Sees school's relative independence from economy as indicative of its potential to prepare individuals for democracy and social bargaining. Important publication within the context of Brazilian literature because it criticizes radical thinking (vulgar Marxism, in author's words) from radical perspective.

4577 Schwartzman, Simon. Ciência, universidade e ideologia: a política do cohecimento. Rio de Janeiro: Zahar Editores, 1981. 166 p.: bibl.

Articles on science, the university, and the politics of knowledge, are linked by author's concern with the nature and political use of alternative forms of knowledge— mainly science, technology and ideology— and with the conditions necessary for promoting science in underdeveloped countries, such as Brazil. A supporter of scientific inquiry, author warns against "scientific imperialism" and "technocratic domination." Valuable contribution to sociology of knowledge.

4578 Souza, Alberto de Mello e. Despesas familiares em educação: um estudo empírico (IBE/RBE, 34:3, julho/set. 1980, p. 387–399, bibl., tables)

Sophisticated quantitative analysis of relationship between family expenditures on education and variables defining family socioeconomic situation. Whereas family income and size are most important predictors, origin of income and zone of residence are also significant, suggesting that family outlays for schooling are influenced by perceived relevance of education to father's employment and by unequal geographic distribution of public schools. Extension of author's previous publication (see *HLAS 43 : 4623*).

4579 Tipologia da educação extra-escolar. Ministério da Educação e Cultura, Instituto Nacional de Estudos e Pesquisas Educacionais. Coordenador do equipe de trabalho: Osmar Favero. Rio de Janeiro: Fundação Getúlio Vargas, Instituto de Estudos Avançados em Educação, 1980. 115 p.: appendixes, bibl. (Série Estudos e pesquisa; 5)

Inventories Brazilian nonformal education programs (educação extra-escolar) and develops typological framework for classification. Conceptualizes nine basic types of nonformal education and groups them according to two intersecting dimensions: 1) degree of institutionalization (in relation to school system, other systems, social groups); and 2) priority (in relation to productive work, social organization, and sociocultural life). Includes extensive bibliography and appendixes on 128 extra-school institutions. Valuable reference.

4580 Tombim, Ana *et al.* Educação rural no Terceiro Mundo: experiências e novas alternativas. Organização de Jorge Werthein e

Juan Díaz Bordenave. Prefácio de Paulo Freire. Tradução de Paulo Roberto Kramer e Lúcia Teresa Lessa Carregal. Rio de Janeiro: Paz e Terra, 1981. 370 p.: bibl.; ill. (Coleção Educação e comunicação; v. 5)

Apparently original contributions on Third World rural education divided into: 1) theoretical aspects; 2) educational policies; and 3) experiences and new alternatives. Of 14 articles, only five concern Brazil of which noteworthy are a study of educational demand and achievement in São Paulo (L. Fukui) and an analysis of an integrated development program in Pernambuco (J. Werthein). Valuable resource.

4581 Torino, Malena Talayer. Educação e estrutura de produção: estudo de desigualdades educacionais regionais. São Paulo: Editora Autores Associados: Cortez Editora, 1982. 111 p.: ill. (Coleção Teoria e prática sociais)

Examines relationship between structure of production and schooling opportunities by comparing economic and education indicators in two Brazilian regions—Southeast and North—during a 50-year period (1920–70). Adopts dependency framework and basis analysis on census data. Concludes that widening disparity between both regions with regard to educational attainment is result of evolving capitalism which offsets development in one locale (e.g., Southeast) with underdevelopment in another (e.g., North).

4582 Tragtenberg, Maurício. Sobre educação, política e sindicalismo. v. 1, Educação. São Paulo: Editora Autores Associados: Cortez Editora, 1982. 163 p.: bibl. (Coleção Educação contemporânea: Série Teoria e prática sociais)

Vol. 1 of four by important Brazilian sociologist deals with education (others on labor sindicalism, politics, political economy). Covers wide range of educational issues though emphasis is on university level. One interesting contribution, titled "O Saber e o Poder," analyzes link between US academic community and Washington's Latin American policy. Perspective throughout is nationalistic and anti-authoritarian.

4583 Vahl, Teodoro Rogério. A privatização do ensino superior no Brazil: causas e conseqüências. Florianópolis, Brazil: Editora Lunardelli, 1980. 313 p.: bibl., ill. (Coleção Comunicação e educação; v. 5)

Balanced, well documented analysis of causes and consequences of privatization of higher education in Brazil. Covers history of Brazilian higher education; current situation; factors responsible for trend toward privatization; public vs. private systems; and specification of outcomes of privatization. Identifies consequences as increase in opportunities to study, stratification of higher education quality (private institutions are generally inferior to public), and weakening of student movement. Good information source.

4584 Veiga, Laura da. Os projetos educativos como projetos de classe: Estado e Universidade no Brasil, 1954–1964 (Educação & Sociedade [Centro de Estudos de Educação e Sociedade (CEDES): Cortez Editora, São Paulo] 7 : 11, jan. 1982, p. 25–71, figures)

Well conceived analysis of interaction between university and class conflict examines positions of social groups with relation to three university reform proposals (traditional, modern, radical) which emerged in 1954–64. Demonstrates that each proposal corresponds to interests of groups dominant in different phases of Brazil's development. Based on author's Phd dissertation (Stanford, 1981).

4585 Verhine, Robert E. and Rainer H. Lehmann. Nonformal education and occupational obtainment: a study of job seekers in Northeastern Brazil (CES/CER, 26 : 3, Oct. 1982, p. 374–390, figures, tables)

Study of contribution of nonformal education (NFE) to obtainment of skilled manual employment, based on data derived from job seekers in Salvador, Bahia and João Pessôa, Paraíba. Results indicate that NFE exerts positive impact, while formal education and work experience have only indirect influence, affecting level of job candidate chooses to seek. Observed NFE effect, however, is restricted to long courses, leading authors to hypothesize that employers prefer applicants with evidence of basic skills and "proper" socialization.

4586 Victória, Cesar Gomes; José Carlos Martins; and Juvenal Dias da Costa. Fatores socio-econômicos, estado nutricional e rendimento escolar: um estudo em 500 crianças da primeira série (Cadernos de Pesquisa [Fundação Carlos Chagas, São Paulo] 41, maio 1982, p. 38–48, bibl., tables)

Based on study of 511 first-graders, re-

ports only weak association between nutritional status and school performance. Among variables studied, those measuring socio-economic level—especially family income—are most important determinants of academic success. Contributes to current controversy over effect of hunger on learning.

4587 Vieitez, Cândido Giraldez. Os professores e a organização da escola: a nova hegemonia na escola. São Paulo: Editora Autores Associados: Cortez Editora, 1982. 164 p.: bibl. (Coleção Educação contemporânea)

Participant-observation study of educational activity in private secondary school in São Paulo during 1968–72. Documents effects of era's political repression on classroom environment and analyzes in-school conflict between teachers of three political inclinations: modernizers, reformers and transformers. Drawing heavily from Gramsci's writings, author sees school not as mere reproducer of dominant interests but as arena in which constant struggle for hegemony takes place. High quality study.

4588 Warde, Mirian Jorge. Educação e estrutura social: a profissionalização em questão. São Paulo: Cortez & Moraes, 1977. 190 p.: appendixes, bibl. (Coleção Educação universitária)

Provides detailed comparative analysis of two legal documents mandating vocationalization of Brazilian secondary schools. Argues that apparent contradictions (one document calls for integration of theory and practices, the other stresses only theory) reflects historical contradiction in Brazilian education resulting from class conflict dynamic. Concludes that separation of theoretical and practical learning is inevitable, given the dominant class' interest in driving wedge between intellectual and manual work.

JOURNAL ABBREVIATIONS
EDUCATION

AAFH/TAM The Americas. A quarterly publication of inter-American cultural history. Academy of American Franciscan History. Washington.

AI/A Anthropos. Anthropos-Institut. Psoieux.

AI/I Interciencia. Asociación Interciencia. Caracas.

ASHSH/B Bulletin de l'Académie des Sciences Humaines et Sociales d'Haiti. Port-au-Prince.

BCV/REL Revista de Economía Latinoamericana. Banco Central de Venezuela. Caracas.

BISRA/BS Belizean Studies. Belizean Institute of Social Research and Action /and/ St. John's College. Belize City.

BNJM/R Revista de la Biblioteca Nacional José Martí. La Habana.

BRP Beiträge zur Romanischen Philologie. Rütten & Loening. Berlin.

CAM Cuadernos Americanos. México.

CEE/RL Revista Latinoamericana de Estudios Educativos. Centro de Estudios Educativos. México.

CES/CER Comparative Education Review. Comparative Education Society. New York.

CH Cuadernos Hispanoamericanos. Instituto de Cultura Hispánica. Madrid.

CM/FI Foro Internacional. El Colegio de México. México.

CM/HM Historia Mexicana. El Colegio de México. México.

CP Cuadernos Políticos. Revista trimestral. Ediciones Era. México.

CPES/RPS Revista Paraguaya de Sociología. Centro Paraguayo de Estudios Sociológicos. Asunción.

CPU/ES Estudios Sociales. Corporación de Promoción Universitaria. Santiago.

CRIT Criterio. Editorial Criterio. Buenos Aires.

CUNY/CP Comparative Politics. The City Univ. of New York, Political Science Program. New York.

CYC Comunicación y Cultura. La comunicación masiva en el proceso político latinoamericano. Editorial Galerna. Buenos Aires y Santiago.

DESCO/Q Quehacer. Realidad nacional: problemas y alternativas. Revista del Centro de Estudios y Promoción del Desarrollo (DESCO). Lima.

EC/M Mapocho. Biblioteca Nacional, Extensión Cultural. Santiago.

ECB Encontros com a Civilização Brasileira. Editora Civilização Brasileira. Rio de Janeiro.

FCE/TE El Trimestre Económico. Fondo de Cultura Económica. México.

FH Folia Humanística. Ciencias, artes, letras. Editorial Glarma. Barcelona.

FIU/CR Caribbean Review. Florida International Univ., Office of Academic Affairs. Miami.

IAEERI/E Estrategia. Instituto Argentino de Estudios Estratégicos y de las Relaciones Internacionales. Buenos Aires.

IBE/RBE Revista Brasileira de Economia. Fundação Getúlio Vargas, Instituto Brasileiro de Economia. Rio de Janeiro.

IBGE/R Revista Brasileiro de Geografia. Conselho Nacional de Geografia, Instituto Brasileiro de Geografia e Estatística. Rio de Janeiro.

IDES/DE Desarrollo Económico. Instituto de Desarrollo Económico y Social. Buenos Aires.

III/AI América Indígena. Instituto Indigenista Interamericano. México.

IJ/JJ Jamaica Journal. Institute of Jamaica. Kingston.

INEP/RBEP Revista Brasileira de Estudos Pedagógicos. Instituto Nacional de Estudos Pedagógicos, Centro Brasileiro de Pesquisas Educacionais. Rio de Janeiro.

LAP Latin American Perspectives. Univ. of California. Riverside.

LARR Latin American Research Review. Univ. of North Carolina Press *for the* Latin American Studies Association. Chapel Hill.

LNB/L Lotería. Lotería Nacional de Beneficencia. Panamá.

MLTA/MLJ Modern Language Journal. The National Federation of Modern Language Teachers Associations. Univ. of Pittsburgh. Pittsburgh, Pa.

NSO Nueva Sociedad. Revista política y cultural. San José.

NYAS/A Annals of the New York Academy of Sciences. New York.

OAS/CI Ciencia Interamericana. Organization of American States, Dept. of Scientific Affairs. Washington.

OAS/LE La Educación. Organization of American States, Dept. of Educational Affairs. Washington.

PAIGH/H Revista de Historia de América.

PCCLAS/P Proceedings of the Pacific Coast Council on Latin American Studies. Univ. of California. Los Angeles.

SBPC/CC Ciência e Cultura. Sociedade Brasileira para o Progresso da Ciência. São Paulo.

SGHG/A Anales de la Sociedad de Geografía e Historia de Guatemala. Guatemala.

STPS/R Revista Mexicana del Trabajo. Secretaría de Trabajo y Previsión Social. México.

UAG/D Docencia. Univ. Autónoma de Guadalajara. México.

UASD/U Revista Dominicana de Antropología e Historia. Univ. Autónoma de Santo Domingo, Facultad de Humanidades, Depto. de Historia y Antropología, Instituto de Investigaciones Antropológicas. Santo Domingo.

UC/EE Estudios de Economía. Univ. de Chile, Facultad de Ciencias Económicas y Administrativas, Depto. de Economía. Santiago.

UCC/CE Cuadernos de Economía. Univ. Católica de Chile. Santiago.

UCC/RU Revista Universitaria. Anales de la Academia Chilena de Ciencias Naturales. Univ. Católica de Chile. Santiago.

UCLV/I Islas. Univ. Central de las Villas. Santa Clara, Cuba.

UCNSA/EP Estudios Paraguayos. Univ. Católica Nuestra Señora de la Asunción. Asunción.

UCR/RCS Revista de Ciencias Sociales. Univ. de Costa Rica. San José.

UFP/EB Estudos Baianos. Univ. Federal da Bahia, Centro Editorial e Didático, Núcleo de Publicações. Bahia, Brazil.

UJMS/U Universidad. Revista de la Univ. Juan Misael Saracho. Tarija, Bolivia.

UMG/RBEP Revista Brasileira de Estudos Políticos. Univ. de Minas Gerais. Belo Horizonte, Brazil.

UN/ISSJ International Social Science Journal. United Nations Educational, Scientific, and Cultural Organization. Paris.

UNAM/RMCPS Revista Mexicana de Ciencias Políticas y Sociales. Univ. Nacional Autónoma de México, Facultad de Ciencias Políticas y Sociales. México.

UNC/BCPS Boletín de Ciencias Políticas y Sociales. Univ. Nacional de Cuyo, Facultad de Ciencias Políticas y Sociales. Mendoza, Argentina.

UNESCO/IRE International Review of Education. United Nations Educational, Scientific and Cultural Organization, Institute for Education. Hamburg, FRG.

UNPHU/A Aula. Univ. Nacional Pedro Henríquez Ureña. Santo Domingo.

UP/TM Tiers Monde. Problèmes des pays sous-développés. Univ. de Paris, Institut d'Étude du Développement Économique et Social. Paris.

UPB Universidad Pontificia Bolivariana. Medellín, Colombia.

UPN/RCE Revista Colombiana de Educación. Univ. Pedagógica Nacional, Centro de Investigaciones. Bogotá.

UPR/CS Caribbean Studies. Univ. of Puerto Rico, Institute of Caribbean Studies. Río Piedras.

UPR/LT La Torre. Univ. de Puerto Rico. Río Piedras.

UPR/RCS Revista de Ciencias Sociales. Univ. de Puerto Rico, Colegio de Ciencias Sociales. Río Piedras.

UPR/RO Revista de Oriente. Univ. de Puerto Rico, Colegio Universitario de Humacao. Humacao.

URL/ES Estudios Sociales. Univ. Rafael Landívar, Instituto de Ciencias Políticas y Sociales. Guatemala.

URSS/AL América Latina. Academia de Ciencias de la URSS Unión de Repúblicas Soviéticas Socialistas. Moscú.

UUAL/U Universidades. Unión de Universidades de América Latina. Buenos Aires.

UWI/CQ   Caribbean Quarterly. Univ. of the West Indies. Mona, Jamaica.

WJC/JJS   The Jewish Journal of Sociology. The World Jewish Community. London.

WD   World Development. Pergamon Press. Oxford, United Kingdom.

ZMR   Zeitschrift für Missionswissenschaft und Religionswissenschaft. Lucerne, Switzerland.

GEOGRAPHY

GENERAL

CLINTON R. EDWARDS, *Professor of Geography, University of Wisconsin-Milwaukee*

ALMOST ALL OF THE ENVIRONMENTAL CONCERNS recognized in North America and Europe can now be identified in the geographical and related literature of Latin America. The human impact on resources for food production is now receiving major attention, with agriculture and related rural development the primary themes. Commentators like Charles F. Bennett, who for long has warned of the adverse ecological consequences of ill-advised land use, now have their counterparts in Latin America, for example Nicolo Gligo (items **5018** and **5019**). There seems no doubt that the enthusiasm for "development" that has characterized the last few decades is now tempered increasingly sharply by the realization that the long-term price may be too high. Latin American geographers are participating in this view, not only with individual contributions to this burgeoning literature, but with papers in national and international symposia on such themes as "development and the environment" (items **5013** and **5025**).

The reduction of forest area to make space for farms and especially pasture land is a concern now fully recognized by some Latin American scholars. Along with North American colleagues, they ask, will the substitution of meat production for the harvesting of forest products prove more beneficial in the long run? The benefits or losses in question are not only immediately economic, but much more long range, for example the possibility of losing important sectors of botanical genetic pools. Also, useful species such as oil palms (item **5002**) are endangered by deforestation. The monitoring of deforestation can be aided immensely by the use of remote sensing techniques, particularly data represented in satellite imagery (item **5039**).

An apparent lull in the momentum of growth in the literature of population and over-population in Latin America may mean that available data have for the time being been subjected to as much analysis as possible. What appears now is a strengthening trend to relate over-population to resource utilization (item **5004**). This theme joins the well-entrenched one of urban population problems. The latter is represented in the selections for this *Handbook* by only a few of the numerous contributions by individual scholars, and by a collective effort to identify and analyze the major factors in the growth of urban population in Latin America (item **5021**).

The geography of Latin America as presented by Latin Americans is available further in a new textbook (item **5014**).

The Humboldt literature in Spanish has been expanded by publication of his correspondence during his American travels (item **5022**). Extracts from the original French have been assembled to form Humboldt's itinerary (item **5023**).

Prehistoric geography of Latin America is eliciting much more than antiquarian interest, as is evident in the analysis of various archaeologically identified landforms related to agriculture. In many places within the humid tropics it seems now probable that elaborate techniques of agricultural production, far more sophisticated than shifting field farming, supported large populations at acceptable levels of supply for long periods of time. Some investigators (Turner and Denevan come readily to mind) do not necessarily see in modern "development" the answer to the inability of shifting field farming to support increasing numbers in the Latin American tropics. However, they are beginning to look for viable models in the more remote agricultural experience of the prehispanic cultures. Discoveries of aboriginal agricultural landforms ("raised fields," terraces, etc.) are now sufficient to warrant some ordering in their typology and terminology (item **5011**).

5001 Bähr, Jürgen and **Günter Mertins.** Idealschema der sozialräumlichen Differenzeirung lateinamerikanischer Großstädte (GZ, 69:1, 1981, p. 1-33, bibl., maps)

Presents model to explain changes in large Latin American cities from colonial times to present. Original colonial structure of more or less concentric circles (central business district, residential, industrial, etc.) has been subjected to sectoral expansion, with subsequent cell-like development around the periphery.

5002 Balick, Michael J. Palmas neotropicales: nuevas fuentes de aceites comestibles (AI/A, 7:1, enero/feb . 1982, p. 25–29, bibl., ill., tables)

Many useful species of oil palms exist in Latin America. They are endangered by deforestation, but could be rendered extremely beneficial through establishment of plantation growth and commercial production.

5003 Bennett, Charles F. Deforestation in the neotropics: causes, consequences, prospects (PCCLAS/P, 8, 1981/1982, p. 55–61)

Major causes of forest clearance in the humid tropics are the use of wood for fuel, construction material, and, above all, clearing to make space for agriculture and livestock husbandry. Consequences are loss of biological diversity, extinctions, and deterioration of soils. In view of present rates of clearing, conflicting legislation, lack of trained foresters and ecologists, as well as demographic and political factors, the outlook is not encouraging.

5004 Bonifaz, Emilio. La tragedia del trópico (IGME/RG, 15, dic. 1981, p. 35–55, graphs, maps, tables)

The "tragedy of the tropics" comprises poverty, lack of development, and irrational use of resources, but above all, overpopulation. Cites a brief inventory of minerals, energy, and agricultural land, in relation to population, concluding that the major "tropical policy" that impedes solution of problems is the "taboo" on discussing birth control.

5005 Busto Duthurburu, José Antonio del.
Historia de los descubrimientos geográficos: siglos V al XV. Lima: Editorial Arica, between 1972 and 1981. 302 p.: bibl., maps.

Brief commentaries on a large number of travelers from the age of Viking expansion to the Portuguese discovery of the sailing route to India, also including the Celts, Arabs, and travelers originating in Mediterranean lands. Includes individuals not mentioned commonly in such collections, a few with tenuous American connections.

5006 Caraci, Ilaria Luzzana. Colombo e le longitudini (SGI/B, 10:9, ott./dic. 1980, p. 517–529, bibl.)

Until the 16th century, longitude had relatively little importance for European navigators, who depended mainly on latitude sailing to reach their destinations. Columbus was concerend with longitude for fixing the positions of newly discovered lands, in terms of his geographical conceptions.

5007 Conference of Latin Americanist Geographers, 10th, Muncie, Ind., 1980. Geographic research on Latin America: benchmark 1980, proceedings. Edited by Tom L. Martinson and Gary S. Elbow. Muncie, Ind.: Ball State University, Department of Geography, 1981. 482 p.: bibl., ill., maps, plates, tables.

Consists of papers presented at the April 1980 meeting and annotated in the corresponding *HLAS* sections. CLAG's 10th anniversary volume groups them as follows: *Opening Session*: Robert C. West "The Contribution of Carl Sauer to Latin American Geography."

Ecology: James J. Parsons "The Ecological Dimension: Ten Years Later;" Charles F. Bennett "Environmental Awareness and Conservation of Natural Resources in Latin America: a Brief Review;" Clinton R. Edwards and Norman R. Stewart "Recent Intensification of Resource Use in Quintana Roo, Mexico."

Population and Settlement: Robert N. Thomas and Osvaldo Muñiz "Population Research in Latin America: Retrospect and Prospect;" Richard W. Wilkie "The Dynamics of Human Settlement and Migration;" Alfonso González "Latin America's Population and Development in the 1970s;" Thomas D. Boswell "An Inventory of Migration Research Dealing with Caribbean Topics;" Richard C. Jones "The Impact of Perception on Urban Migration in Latin America;" Harold E. Jackson "The Impact of Cityward Migration on Urban Environments: Slums of Cities and Squatter Settlements;" Philip H. Allman, Jr. "A New Form of International Migration: US Military Retirees in Central America;" Luc J.A. Mougeot "Frontier Population Absorption and Migrant Socioeconomic Mobility: Evidence from Brazilian Amazonia;" Oscar H. Horst "Teaching the Evolution of Population Distribution."

Aboriginal and Peasant Cultures: William M. Denevan "Recent Research on Traditional Food Production in Latin America;" Larry L. Patrick "Geographic Research on the Pre-Hispanic Period with Emphasis on Agriculture;" William V. Davidson "Recent Ethnography on Historic Latin America;" James S. Kus "Recent Research on Pre-Hispanic Agriculture in Coastal Peru;" Gregory Knapp "The Full Extent of the Field: a Commentary on the 'New Cultural Geography' in Latin America;" B.L. Turner, II "Research Roles and Goals: a Commentary on the Study of Aboriginal and Peasant Cultures by Latin Americanist Geographers."

Primary Activities: Ernst Griffin and Don R. Hoy "Geographic Research on Commercial Agriculture in Latin America in the 1970s;" Clarence W. Minkel and Vernon M. Smith "Latin America in the Seventies: the Geography of Minerals;" François J. Belisle "Forest Uses in Latin America;" John Thompson "Publications of Livestock Production

and Marketing in Latin America and the Caribbean by North American Geographers."

Physical Geography: Dieter Brunnschweiler "On Nature in Latin America: Progress and Problems of Physical Geography;" César Caviedes "Natural Hazards in Latin America: a Survey and Discussion;" Gerald W. Olson "Progress in Use of Soil Resource Inventories in Latin America;" Alan K. Craig and Ramiro Lagos A. "Geomorphological Research in Western South America: the Surprising Seventies;" Robert H. Schmidt, Jr. "Literature and Data Sources for the Study of Weather and Climate in the Arid Zones of Mexico."

Social Geography: Homer Aschmann "The Immortality of Latin American States;" Charles H. Richardson "The Political Geography of Latin America: a Decade of American Research;" Robert C. Mings, "Tourism Development in Latin America and Related Research Needs;" Tom L. Martinson "Interrelationships between Landscape Art and Geography in Latin America: First Response to a Challenge."

Economic Geography and Development: Lawrence A. Brown and Rickie S. Gilliard "On the Interrelationships between Development and Migration Processes;" Marvin F. Gordon "Development Policy and the Disadvantaged, Subsistence Sector of Agriculture;" Gary S. Elbow "Modernization and Change in Latin American Towns: Geographical Research from the 1970s;" Frank C. Innes "Economic History and Historical Geography of the Caribbean: the Last Ten Years Reviewed;" Richard C. Jones and Ronald D. Garst "Rural-to-Urban Migration in Latin America and Africa: a Comparative Analysis of Trends and Motives;" Wayne T. Enders "Regional Development in Brazil, Research Trends in the Seventies;" Joshua C. Dickinson, III "The Ecological Factor in Regional Development: a Venezuelan Case Study."

Research Methodology: Barry Lentnek "Reality and Research: Some Relationships for the Eighties;" Julio Quan "Geographic Method: a Latin American Perspective;" Edward L. Hillsman "The Planning of Biomass Energy Systems in Latin America;" Robert E. Nunley, Pamela J. Nebgen, and Michael A. Fisher "Simulating the Dynamics of Urban Impact on Middle America from 1600 to the year 2000." *Closing Session*: John P. Augelli "Latin American Geography in the Seventies: Inventory and Prospects."

5008 Córdova Aguilar, H. Las decisiones de localización en las actividades agrícolas: comparación entre Alonso y Chisholm (IFEA/B, 7 : 3/4, 1978, p. 95–107, bibl., ill.)

Analizes two approaches toward explaining agricultural localization, one based on an economic theory of urban land use (Alonso), and the other based on considerations of rural experience and the role of distance from markets (Chisholm). Several premises of the theories discussed do not exist in the real world.

5009 Denevan, William M. Hydraulic agriculture in the American tropics: forms measures, and recent research (*in* Maya subsistence. Kent V. Flannery, editor. New York: Academic Press, 1982, p. 181–203)

Describes various modes of water management for aboriginal agriculture, and reviews recent research on precolumbian "raised field" farming.

5010 ———. Latin America (*in* World systems of traditional resource management. Gary A. Klee, editor. New York: Halsted Press, 1980, p. 217–244)

Reviews traditional methods and modern problems in Latin American agriculture. Suggests adaptations of traditional methods as workable substitutes for inappropriate "modernization" of agriculture. Major criterion of suitability of an agricultural system is its permanence, which "modern" systems do not exhibit as applied in Latin America. Intelligent variation of traditional modes holds the best promise for the future.

5011 ———. Tipología de configuraciones agrícolas prehispánicas (III/AI, 40 : 4, oct./dic. 1980, p. 619–652)

Provides typology and terminology for agricultural landforms and other rearrangements of the natural scene for agricultural purposes in precolumbian Latin America.

5012 Diffusion of plantation traits in the New World. Compiled by Roland Chardon. Baton Rouge, La.: Department of Geography and Anthropology, Louisiana State University, 1981. 145 p.: bibl., ill. (Studies in historical geography; 1)

Eight papers by various authors cover "plantation traits" such as the sugar industry, land units, slavery, architecture, "free villages," political units, coffee replacement crops, and the anomaly of Belize as a non-plantation colony.

5013 Estilos de desarrollo y medio ambiente en la América Latina. Selección de Osvaldo Sunkel y Nicolo Gligo. México: Fondo de Cultura Económica, 1980. 1 v.: bibl., indexes, maps (El Trimestre económico. Lecturas; 36)

Results of a project (1978 to mid-1980) and seminar (19–23 Nov. 1979, Santiago, Chile) on development and the environment in Latin America, sponsored by ECLA and the UN Program for the Environment. Deals with general considerations and development of forestry and agricultural resources, with final chapter on oceans and fishing.

5014 Flores Silva, Eusebio; Florencio Magallón; and Esther Jimeno. La tierra y el hombre en las Américas: una geografía crítica. San José: Editorial Universidad Estatal a Distancia, 1981. 300 p.: bibl., ill., maps.

The Latin American chapters are arranged topically, with general physical geographical data followed by sections on population, economic life, and urbanization. Strong historical orientation.

5015 Geografía descriptiva. v. 1, Europa y los países del Mediterráneo europeos. v. 2, Africa, Asia, Australia y Nueva Zelanda. v. 3, América. Dirigida por José Manuel Casas Torres. Madrid: E.M.E.S.A., 1979. 3 v.: bibl., col. maps, index.

Chapters by a number of authors and arranged by country and region. Latin American sections contain material on environmental conditions, population, economic resources, agriculture, industry, transport, and modern colonization.

5016 Gilbert, Alan G. Planning for urban primacy and large cities in Latin America: a critique of the literature (ISA/CUR, 8:1, 1980, p. 105–116, bibl.)

Local research on urban growth and planning in Latin American cities is of recent development. Reviews practical contributions that urban planners can use for analysis of problems in primate cities.

5017 ——— and **Peter M. Ward.** Residential movement among the poor: the constraints on housing choice in Latin American cities (Transactions [Institute of British Geographers, London] 7 : 2, 1982, p. 129–149, ill., maps, tables)

Tests theories of intra-city migration using examples of 13 "low-income settlements" in Bogotá, Mexico City, and Valencia,

Venezuela. Concludes that constraints on land and housing markets, conditioned by particular local sociopolitical structures, play greater roles than migrants' choices in determining residential patterns.

5018 Gligo, Nicolo. Estilos de desarrollo, modernización y medio ambiente en la agricultura latinoamericana. Santiago: Naciones Unidas, 1981. 130 p.: bibl., ill. (Estudios e informes de la CEPAL; 4)

Commentary on the relationships between environment and agricultural development. Modernization of agriculture includes changes in social structure, production modes, and land tenure. All have consequences for the environment, which is in danger of serious deterioration.

5019 ———. Implicancias medioambientales del modelo tecnológico predominante en la agricultura latinoamericana (Revista Latinoamericana de Estudios Urbano-Regionales, EURE [Pontificia Universidad Católica de Chile, Instituto de Planificación del Desarrollo Urbano y Regional, Santiago] 6:18, agosto 1980, p. 11-23, tables)

Modernization and increased capitalization of agricultural development in Latin America are often resulting in environmental difficulties and wastage of natural resources. A basic problem is the continued growth of the low-income peasant population.

5020 Hargreaves, George C. Climate and Third World agricultural development (AI/I, 6:4, 1981, p. 234-238, bibl., tables)

Truism that needs occasional recall is that in "Third World" regions agriculture is often marginal because climate and soil conditions are marginal. Thus, sound development planning requires much more data on environmental factors than are generally available.

5021 Herrera, Ligia and Waldomiro Pecht. Crecimiento urbano de América Latina. Con la colaboración de Fernando Olivares. Washington: Banco Interamericano de Desarrollo; Santiago: Centro Latinoamericano de Demografía, 1976. 2 v.: bibl., ill., maps (Serie E / Centro Latinoamericano de Demografía; no. 22)

Pt. 1 deals with individual cities in Brazil, Mexico, Colombia, Venezuela, Peru, Chile, and Argentina. Pt. 2 analyzes urban growth and presents models of projection of population growth. Includes separate atlas of maps and city plans.

5022 Humboldt, Alexander von. Cartas americanas. Compilación, prólogo, notas y cronología, Charles Minguet. Traducción, Marta Traba. Caracas: Biblioteca Ayacucho, 1980. 428 p.: bibl. (Biblioteca Ayacucho; 74)

First edition in Spanish of Humboldt's correspondence within and from the Americas during his travels, and about the Americas after his return to Europe. Also contains documents, including official decrees, travel arrangements, brief reports, and letters and notes to and about Humboldt by various notables. There is a list of the correspondents with brief biographical notes, and a detailed chronology of Humboldt's life, emphasizing his Latin American travels and interests.

5023 ———. Voyages dans l'Amérique équinoxiale. v. 1, Itinéraire. v. 2, Tableaux de la nature et des hommes. Introduction, choix de textes et notes de Charles Minguet. Paris: F. Maspero, 1980. 2 v.: bibl., ill. (La Découverte, 0224-1285; 23—24)

Extracts from Humboldt's works to form a continuous itinerary of his travels in the Americas.

5024 Ingram, Gregory K. and Alan Carroll. The spatial structure of Latin American cities (Journal of Urban Economics [Academic Press, New York] 9:2, March 1981, p. 257—273, appendix, bibl., tables)

Census data from 1950, 1960, and 1970 are used to compare various characteristics of Latin American and North American cities. While newer North American cities are more decentralized, Latin American cities have centralized population densities similar to those of older North American cities. Concentrations of high-status groups still occur in metropolitan areas of Latin American cities, but they are declining.

5025 International Meeting on the Use of Ecological Guidelines for Development in the American Humid Tropics, *Caracas, 1974.* Proceedings of International Meeting on the Use of Ecological Guidelines for Development in the American Humid Tropics, held at Caracas, Venezuela, 20—22 February 1974. Sponsored by I.U.C.N. and the United Nations Environment Programme, with the co-sponsorship of the United Nations Development Programme *et al.* Morges, Switzerland: International Union for Conservation of Nature and Natural Resources, 1975. 249 p.: bibl., ill. (IUCN publications; new series; no. 31)

General summary of conclusions of international conference on development in humid tropics (20–22 Feb. 1974, Caracas). Contains sections on wildlife, logging, freshwater fisheries, shifting field and plantation agriculture, livestock, pesticides, and infrastructure.

5026 Kaczynski, Wlodzimierz. Problems of long-range fisheries (OCEANUS, 22:1, Spring 1979, p. 60–66, bibl., ill., tables)

Discusses effects of recently established 200-mile limits or "economic zones" on long-range fleets that formerly fished inshore waters. Among examples is the Patagonian Shelf, controlled by Argentina, where foreign fleets made large catches before fishing was restricted to licensees.

5027 McClung, Robert M. Vanishing wildlife of Latin America. Illustrated by George Founds. New York: Morrow, 1981. 160 p.: bibl., ill., index.

Brief discussion of evolution of South American wildlife, migrations, early and aboriginal man, and aspects of European conquests, followed by regional treatment of extinct and threatened species: the Caribbean, Mexico and Central America, Andean lands, Amazon rainforest, southern grasslands and plains, and Galapagos Islands.

5028 Meijer, Willem. A new look at the plight of tropical rain-forests (Environmental Conservation [*Published for the Foundation for Environmental Conservation by* Elsevier Sequoia S.A., Lausanne, Switzerland] 7 : 3, Autumn 1980, p. 203–206, map)

Brief, but useful review of recent literature of concern over forest destruction in humid tropics. The "new look" expresses need for a global environmental ethic modeled after cultural attitudes and life styles of vegetarian societies and intensive farmers of tropical lowlands (e.g., Southeast Asia).

5029 New themes in instruction for Latin American geography. Edited by Oscar H. Horst and Joseph P. Stoltman. Muncie, Ind.: Conference of Latin Americanist Geographers, 1982. 116 p.: ill., maps, tables (Special publication of the Conference of Latin Americanist Geographers; v. 2)

Themes that can be identified substantively are ethnic conflict, agricultural geography, maintenance of natural environment, population, and agrarian reform. Other issues treated are teaching about Latin America in social science curricula, and instructional materials.

5030 Olivier, Santiago Raúl. Ecología y subdesarrollo en América Latina. México: Siglo Veintiuno Editores, 1981. 225 p.: ill.

General commentary on causes of various ecological problems, pollution, and environmental damage, with emphasis on consequences of resource exploitation in under-developed areas.

5031 Papers in Latin American geography in honor of Lucia C. Harrison. Edited by Oscar H. Horst. Muncie, Ind.: Conference of Latin Americanist Geographers, 1981. 92 p.: bibl., ill., maps, ports. (Special publications of the Conference of Latin Americanist Geographers; v. 1)

Although Lucia Harrison's contributions to Latin American geography were somewhat more potential than actual, her contributions "to the role of women in geography" are here celebrated with five papers by female geographers, and an essay on Miss Harrison and two responses to the papers by male geographers.

5032 Pariser, E.R. Reducing postharvest losses of fish in the Third World (OCEANUS, 22:1, Spring 1979, p. 47–53, bibl., ill.)

By weight, about 35 percent of the fish destined for human consumption is wasted. Strategies for reducing this loss are proposed, including improved communication with fishermen, better methods of preparation, reduction of losses to insects, and various training and assistance programs. Not oriented to Latin America, but with broad application there.

5033 Peña, Orlando. Información climatológica para la planificación urbana (PAIGH/G, 91/92, enero/dic. 1980, bibl., figures, table)

Air pollution is not the only facet of urban climates worthy of study. Also important are various thermodynamic and hydromechanical processes that affect Latin American cities. Proposes a methodology for the geographical study of urban climates.

5034 Pesticides in South America and Mexico. New York: Frost & Sullivan, 1981. 338 p.

Analyses of agricultural and general economic situation, pesticide use and policy, arranged by country. Lists and comments on major pesticide manufacturers, and discusses future implications of energy production from agricultural biomass.

5035 Pyle, Jane. The selection of national parks and equivalent reserves in Latin America (*in* Papers in Latin American geography in honor of Lucia C. Harrison [see item 5031] p. 57–76)

There is need of a systematic basis for selecting sites or regions for national parks and reserves that are more representative of the varied habitats and environments characteristic of each country. Presents a model for selection, with application in Guatemala.

5036 Rengert, Arlene C. Some sociocultural aspects of rural out-migration in Latin America (*in* Papers in Latin American geography in honor of Lucia C. Harrison [see item 5031] p. 15–27)

Discusses differences between male and female rural-urban migration, with example from Mexico. More females than males migrate, because of "push" factors such as the lack of need for females in agriculture, and because of "pull" factors such as more opportunity to establish in cities, by marriage or as domestic servants.

5037 Schärfe, Joachim. Fishing technology for developing countries (OCEANUS, 22:1, Spring 1979, p. 54–59, ill.)

Presents an organizational structure for national institutes for fishing technology in less developed countries, which are necessary for effective development of fisheries resources.

5038 Smith, Leah J. and **Susan Peterson.** Pitfalls in Third World aquaculture development (OCEANUS, 25:2, Summer 1982, p. 31–39, plates, tables)

Constraints on successful aquaculture are appropriate choice of species, weather, disease, predation, and general lack of capital for materials, trained labor, and experience. Discusses a number of problems, some of which are material in nature, but equally important are cultural problems, perhaps more difficult to overcome.

5039 Talbot, James J. and **Lawrence R. Pettinger.** Use of remote sensing for monitoring deforestation in tropical and subtropical latitudes (OAS/CI, 21:1/4, 1980, p. 63–72, bibl., ill., maps)

Notes urgent need for monitoring human impact on tropical forests, by use of aerial photography, radar imagery, and Landsat data. Case studies of remote sensing programs in different parts of the world, including Hispaniola and the Peruvian Amazon, are discussed, with conclusion that Landsat offers the greatest potential for identifying and monitoring deforestation over extensive areas.

5040 United Nations. Economic Commission for Latin America. Water management and environment in Latin America: analysis and case studies of water management, including new approaches through simulation modelling and the environmental consequences of past and potential trends in water use: a report. Oxford; New York: *Published for the* United Nations *by* Pergamon Press, 1979. 327 p.: bibl., ill. (Water development, supply, and management; v. 12)

Subtitle: "Analysis and case studies of water management, including new approaches through simulation modelling and the environmental consequences of past and potential trends in water use." Pt. 1 deals with relationships among water, development, and environment; water management; institutional factors and decision making; and socioeconomic and biophysical factors. Case studies in pt. 2 include San Lorenzo, Peru; Guri, Venezuela; Chontalpa, Mexico; Caño Mánamo, Venezuela; Guanabara Bay, Brazil; Bogotá River, Colombia; Maipo, Chile; São Paulo, Brazil; and Aconcagua Valley, Chile.

MIDDLE AMERICA
(Caribbean Islands, Central America and Mexico)

TOM L. MARTINSON, *Professor of Geography, Ball State University*
GARY S. ELBOW, *Professor of Geography, Texas Tech University*

NOTABLE AMONG THE ENTRIES IN THIS YEAR'S section on Middle America are many studies pertaining to the changing ecology of the region. Especially prominent are works on Panama that accentuate ecological problems related to the Canal by Lecompte and Schachar (item **5080**), Jaén Suárez (item **5079**), and Alba (item **5074**), and to the Darién by Méndez (item **5081**) and Holz (item **5077**). This concern extends to other countries in the area that are promoting conservation of their natural resources, as exemplified by Boza's treatment of Costa Rican national parks (item **5061**) and by the Ecologic Committee of the Universidad Madre y Maestra on environmental pollution in the Dominican Republic (item **5049**).

Welcome additions to the literature concerning the role of women in the socioeconomic development of the Caribbean have been made by Henshall (item **5042**) on agriculture and by Monk (item **5056**) on migration, both in a special publication by the Conference of Latin Americanist Geographers (CLAG).

Rounding out the special features of this section are two items: the first printing of a study by Sauer on ecological balance in the precolumbian Caribbean (item **5045**) and a highly perceptive view by Sandner of the political geography of the Caribbean as it has changed since the Conquest (item **5044**). [TLM]

By far the most significant contribution among the selections for the Mexico and Guatemala subsections is Herbert Wilhelmy's book on the Maya (item **5121**). This comprehensive analysis of lowland Maya civilization has the earmarks of a classic. One hopes it will be translated into English and made available to wider readership.

Other noteworthy contributions are the encyclopedic regional physical description of the State of Michoacán written under the direction of Genaro Correa Pérez (item **5091**) and a study of agricultural colonization in the Papaloapan project by Ewell and Poleman (item **5095**).

It is gratifying to see a continuing number of monographs, research reports, proceedings, and journal articles coming from Mexico. Several of these publications are annotated below, but many others were omitted for lack of space. Two series of *municipio* monographs are especially worthy of mention. Fourteen volumes covering 24 separate *municipios* were published between 1977−80 under the series title "Monografías Municipales, Gobierno del Estado de Michoacán." The second series, published as a serial by the Instituto de Geografía y Estadística of the Universidad de Guadalajara, presents *análises geoeconómicos* of many *municipios* in the state of Jalisco. These series contain useful and sometimes hard to locate data and maps for small communities.

A new journal, *Mesoamérica*, is published in Spanish by the Centro de Investigaciones Regionales de Mesoamérica, in Antigua, Guatemala. It contains articles on southern Mexico and Central America that will be of interest to geographers and others. [GSE]

CARIBBEAN
GENERAL

5041 Brierley, J.S. Kitchen gardens in the West Indies, with a contemporary study from Grenada (USM/JTG, 43, Dec. 1976, p. 30–40, maps, tables)

Kitchen gardens have become more diverse and efficient in recent years as inflation has increased the price of food.

5042 Henshall, Janet D. Women and small-scale farming in the Caribbean (*in* Papers in Latin American geography in honor of Lucia C. Harrison [see item **5031**] p. 44–56, bibl., charts)

Women farmers will meet the basic nutritional needs of the growing Caribbean, although the characteristics of their farms remain poorly understood.

5043 Pollard, H.J. Geographical variation within the tourist trade of the Caribbean (USM/JTG, 43, Dec. 1976, p. 49–62, graphs, tables)

The slow starters in the Caribbean tourist movement occupy a desirable position because they can control the type and number of visitors.

5044 Sandner, Gerhard. Politisch-geographische Raumstrukturen und Geopolitik im karibischen Raum (GZ, 69:1, 1981, p. 34–56, bibl., maps)

Six means of regional political organization for the Caribbean arranged in chronological sequence.

5045 Sauer, Carl O. Indian food production in the Caribbean (AGS/GR, 71:3, July 1981, p. 272–280)

One more example of Sauer's agro-historical scholarship, dedicated to an explanation of ecological balance in the precolumbian Caribbean.

CAYMAN ISLANDS

5046 Considine, James L. and **John J. Winberry.** The green sea turtle of the Cayman Islands (OCEANUS, 21:3, Summer 1978, p. 50–55, ill.)

Sea turtles face extinction unless mariculture is established, such as the new complex on Grand Cayman Island.

CUBA

5047 González, María de los Angeles *et al.* Provincia La Habana. Santiago de Cuba: Editorial Oriente, 1978. 224 p.: bibl., ill.

Compendium of data, graphs, maps, and photos illustrating the condition of rural Havana province.

DOMINICAN REPUBLIC

5048 Aquino Camarena, Andrés. La estrategia de los asentamientos humanos en la República Dominicana (PAIGH/G, 91/92, enero/dic. 1980, p. 41–68, maps, tables)

Description of regional planning as applied to population distribution.

5049 Universidad Católica Madre y Maestra, *Dominican Republic.* **Comité Ecológico.** Inventario del potencial de contaminación en la República Dominicana (EME, 8:44, sept./oct. 1979, p. 117–141, maps, tables)

Inventory of air, water, and land contamination offers a basis for decision-making.

5050 Vega, Bernardo. Quinientos años de cambio ecológico en Santo Domingo (MHD/B, 9:13, 1980, p. 153–158, bibl.)

Descriptions of landscapes by early residents are compared with present conditions, indicating great changes.

5051 Yunén, Rafael Emilio. Consideraciones antropogeográficas sobre la integración hombre-medioambiente en la Hispaniola (MHD/B, 9:15, 1980, p. 113–125)

Philosophical justification for the geographical study of the people-environment interface.

HAITI

5052 Harza Engineering Company, *Chicago.* Water resources study for Haiti: final report. Submitted to Agency for International Development. Chicago: Harza Engineering Co., 1979. ca. 450 p. (various pagings), 4 fold. leaves of plates: bibl., ill.

Investigation concludes that additional ground-water exploration and development is justified in 23 selected areas.

JAMAICA

5053 Berg, Robert J. *et al.* Jamaica feeder roads: an evaluation. Washington: Agency for International Development, 1980. 1 v. (various pagings): bibl., ill., 2 maps (Project impact evaluation; no. 11)

Documents failure of AID-sponsored rural roads project, citing inadequate supervision and evaluation.

5054 Sibley, Inez Knibb. Dictionary of place-names in Jamaica. Kingston: Institute of Jamaica, 1978. 184 p., 5 leaves of plates: ill.

First attempt at a comprehensive dictionary compiles useful landscape descriptions along with historical records.

PUERTO RICO

5055 Gómez-Gómez, Fernando and **James E. Heisel.** Summary appraisals of the nation's ground-water resources: Caribbean region. Washington: US G.P.O., 1980. 32 p.: bibl., ill. (2 fold. in pockets) (Geological Survey professional paper; 813-U)

Study urges more thorough knowledge of water resources in this rapidly urbanizing and industrializing island, including the development of a computerized water budget data bank.

5056 Monk, Janice. Social change and sexual differences in Puerto Rican rural migration (*in* Papers in Latin American geography in honor of Lucia C. Harrison [see item 5031] p. 28–43, bibl., charts, map)

Sexual differences play an important yet largely unexplained role in migration in Puerto Rico and elsewhere in Latin America.

TRINIDAD AND TOBAGO

5057 Niddrie, David L. Tobago. Midleton, Ireland; Gainesville, Fla.: Litho Press, 1980. 243 p., 1 fold leaf of plates: bibl., ill., index.

Comprehensive review of Tobago's landscape by a veteran observer of the Caribbean.

CENTRAL AMERICA
GENERAL

5058 Nuhn, Helmut. Struktur und Entwicklung des Stadtesystems in den Kleinstaaten Zentralamerikas und ihre Bedeutung fur den Regionalen Entwicklungsprozess (UBGI/E, 35:4, Dez. 1981, p. 303–320)

Rank-size ordering of Central American cities shows primate distributions. There is little evidence of evolution toward a more regular distribution of cities by size. Concludes with comments on the implications of the findings for decentralization plans.

BELIZE

5059 Frost, Marvin D. Patterns of human influence on landscape and wildlife: selected case studies in Belize (PAIGH/G, 94, dic. 1981, p. 89–100, bibl., maps)

Two contrasting examples are used to determine impact of forest clearing and settlement on wildlife. Construction of roads encourages settlement, changing the wildlife species composition. Author notes agricultural development in Belize is still limited enough to permit implementation of a successful wildlife management program.

COSTA RICA

5060 Bonilla, Alexander. Situación ambiental en Costa Rica (Tiempo Actual [Junta de Pensiones y Jubilaciones del Magisterio Nacional, San José] 6:21, mayo 1981, p. 107–115)

Development and environment do not balance; ecological destruction proceeds apace in Costa Rica.

5061 Boza, Mario A. Los parques nacionales de Costa Rica. San José: Servicio de Parques Nacionales, Ministerio de Agricultura y Ganadería, 1978. 80 p.: bibl., col. ill.

Extensive description and photographs, designed to inform public opinion on the value of parks.

5062 Pan American Institute of Geography and History. Costa Rica. San José: Instituto Panamericano de Geografía e Historia: Editorial Universidad Estatal a Distancia, 1978. 90 p.: ill., maps (some col.) (Cuadernos panamericanos de información geográfica; vol. 1, no. 1)

Teaching manual based on the interpretation of Costa Rican maps and aerial photographs. Worthy of emulation.

EL SALVADOR

5063 Arocha, Antonio R. La República de El Salvador, Departamento de Santa Ana. San Salvador: Editorial CODICE, between 1981 and 1980. p. 85–172: ill. (Colección Antropología, fasc. no. 2)

Municipio-by-municipio description of this northwesternmost state of El Salvador.

GUATEMALA

5064 Elbow, Gary S. Agricultural practices on a cultural frontier in the western highlands of Guatemala (*in* Conference of the Rocky Mountain Council on Latin American Studies, 29th, Las Cruces, N.M., 1981. Proceedings of the 29th annual meeting of the Rocky Mountain Council on Latin American Studies, Las Cruces, New Mexico, February 12–14, 1981. Edited by John J. Brasch and Susan R. Rouch. Lincoln: University of Nebraska, Bureau of Business Research, 1981, p. 68–76)

Case study within community of Zaragoza compares responses of Ladino and Indian farmers to innovative agricultural practices. Finds that Indians are generally more willing than Ladinos to adopt new practices and, accordingly, their yields are somewhat higher.

5065 ———. Determinants of land use change in Guatemalan secondary urban centers (AAG/PG, 35:1, Feb. 1983, p. 57–66, bibl., maps)

Tests theory explaining Latin American urban structure in small towns. Observations indicate actions of public agencies have a significant impact on shaping the urban structure of Guatemalan towns.

5066 Farfán, Oscar Manolo. Vocación agrícola y prioridades de acción en las Verapaces (USC/U, 9, 2. época, 1978, p. 186–215, tables)

Agricultural land use placed in its environmental setting in central highland Guatemala.

5067 Harp, Edwin L.; Raymond C. Wilson; and Gerald F. Wieczorek. Landslides from the February 4, 1976, Guatemala earthquake. Washington: US G.P.O., 1981. 35 p.: bibl., graphs, ill., maps (Geological Survey professional paper; 1204-A)

Surveys landslides in Guatemala's tuff barranca topography following severe earthquake. Volume includes two 1:50,000 scale contour maps locating landslides.

5068 Johnson, Dennis. Agricultural zonation using production data: the example of beans in Guatemala (PAIGH/G, 94, dic. 1981, p. 117–121, bibl., map)

Uses data from 1964 agricultural census of Guatemala to develop eight production regions. Emphasizes methods of data collection and analysis; provides very little information on bean production as an agricultural activity.

5069 Lovell, W. George. The Cuchumatan highlands of Guatemala on the eve of the Spanish Conquest (UNC/K, 11:4, nov. 1979, p. 1-41, ill., map)

Lovell expands the work of Robert Carmack and his students on the Quiché into a new region of Guatemala. Study is a valuable contribution to the preconquest historical geography of a little known part of Middle America.

5070 Luján Muñoz, Luis. Nueva información sobre los terremotos de 1773 (SGHG/A, 50:50, enero/dic. 1977, p. 195–225, map, plates)

New documentary sources reveal details of destruction from the 1773 earthquake that resulted in the transfer of Guatemala's capital from Antigua to Guatemala City. Lengthy first person accounts will be of interest for students of natural hazard perception.

5071 Thomas, Robert N. and James L. Mulvilhill. Temporal attributes of stage migration in Guatemala (*in* Internal migration systems in the developing world. Edited by Robert H. Thomas and John M. Hunter. Boston: G.K. Hall; Cambridge, Mass.: Schenkman Pub. Co., 1980, p. 51–61, ill., table)

Research verifies hypothesis that today most migrants arriving in a primate city have come directly from a rural area.

HONDURAS

5072 Dawson, Frank Griffith. Mosquito shore settlement expedition (EJ, 60:2, June 1982, p. 62–65, map, plates)

Explorers plan a return to Black River, a prosperous 18th-century British colony in coastal northeastern Honduras.

NICARAGUA

5073 Massajoli, Pierleone and **Gian Franco de Stefano.** La regione orientale del Nicaragua (IGM/U, 61:1, gen./feb. 1981, p. 9–46, maps, plates, tables)

Pt. 1 of general description of eastern Nicaragua, environmental and cultural, in three parts.

PANAMA

5074 Alba, Georgina A. de. Implicaciones ecológicas de las transformaciones geográficas ocasionadas por la construcción del Canal de Panamá (LNB/L, 292, julio 1980, p. 74–79, bibl.)

Plea for ecological awareness in development projects undertaken in canal's vicinity.

5075 Gordón, Antonio. Los corregimientos y sus límites (LNB/L, 277, marzo 1979, p. 6–18, maps, tables)

Contains valuable maps showing location of smallest political units of Panama.

5076 Gutiérrez, Roberto F. Poder local y desarrollo rural en Panamá: el ejemplo del distrito de Guararé (UTIEH/C, 36, 1981, p. 41–61, maps, tables)

Study points to spatial disequilibrium in land use related to politics of planning.

5077 Holz, Robert K. The Darien of Panama: the twilight of a unique environment (EJ, 58:4, Dec. 1980, p. 158–164, map, plates)

Enormous ecological changes, particularly the burning of tropical forest, are rapidly altering this area's landscape.

5078 Jaén Suárez, Omar. Análisis regional y Canal de Panamá: ensayos geográficos. Panamá: EUPAN, Editorial Universitaria, 1981. 235 p.: bibl., ill., maps (Sección Geografía. Serie Ensayo)

Successor to 1974 volume, this work consists of six essays on the regional economic geography of Panama.

5079 ———. Creación de una franja pionera en las riberas del Canal de Panamá (LNB/L, 290, mayo 1980, p. 1-14, maps, plates, tables)

The Canal might have been responsible for widespread ecological destruction except for the active protection measures taken to maintain the efficiency of the route.

5080 Lecompte, Dominique and **Arie Schachar.** La récupération de la Zone du Canal et ses conséquences géographiques pour la République de Panama (SGB/COM, 33, 1980, p. 23–47, maps, tables)

Restoration of the Canal to Panama offers the opportunity to correct economic, ecologic, and regional economic distortions.

5081 Méndez, Teodoro E. El Darién: imagen y proyecciones. Panamá: Ediciones Instituto Nacional de Cultura, 1979. 553 p.: ill. (Colección Patrimonio histórico)

Comprehensive review of historical development, natural resources, and use of Panama's Darién region, with the object of encouraging its rational development.

5082 Sosa, Juan B. Límites de Panamá (LNB/L, 303/304, junio/julio 1981, p. 1-44)

Detailed examination of Panama's boundaries, based on original sources.

MEXICO

5083 Alfaro Santacruz, Melchor de et al. Relaciones histórico geográficas de la Provincia de Tabasco. Villahermosa, México: Consejo Editorial del Gobierno del Estado de Tabasco, 1979. 52 p.: fold. map in pocket (Serie Año del centenario Instituto Juárez. Colección de archivo; no. 5)

Publication of the *Relación Geográfica de Tabasco*. This small book would have been enhanced by the addition of commentary and notations of contemporary place name equivalents. Includes interesting map.

5084 Allen, Elizabeth A. The state and region: some comparative development experiences from Mexico and Brazil (*in* State and region in Latin America: a workshop. G.A. Banck, R. Buve, and L. Van Vroohoven, editors. Amsterdam: Centrum voor studie en Dicumetatie van Latijns-Amerika, 1981,

p. 231–264, bibl., tables [CEDLA incidentele publicaties; 17])

Examines roles of state agencies and beneficiary populations in successful implementation of development programs. Concludes that the highest rate of success is with projects that have high degree of cooperation between state agency and beneficiaries from initial planning stages through implementation.

5085 Anaya Garduño, Manuel *et al.* La desertificación en México. Editado por Fernando Medellín-Leal. Críticos estudiantiles, José Refugio Ballín-Cortés *et al.* San Luis Potosí, México: Instituto de Investigación de Zonas Desérticas, Universidad Autónoma de San Luis Potosí, 1978. 130 p.: bibl., maps.

Reviews problem of desertification in Mexico with lengthy list of recommendations for slowing the expansion of deserts in the country. Prepared as the Mexican position paper for the UN Conference on Desertification of 1977.

5086 Arreola, Daniel D. Landscapes of nineteenth-century Veracruz (LAND, 24:3, p. 27–31, ill.)

Reports on changing perceptions of travelers to Veracruz. Initial impressions of surprise at the apparent size of the city from the sea rapidly gave way to disappointment when the traveler actually landed. The urban landscape is a collection of changing images, not a single view from one perspective.

5087 ———. Nineteenth-century townscapes of eastern Mexico (AGS/GR, 72:1, Jan. 1982, p. 1-19, ill., map)

Travelers' observations of landscapes in the cities of Veracruz, Jalapa, Orizaba, and Puebla. Travel accounts provide valuable insights into the colonial towns that preceded the development of modern cities.

5088 Bassols Batalla, Angel. Geografía económica de México: teoría, fenómenos generales, análisis regional. 4. ed. México: Editorial Trillas, 1980. 431 p., 12 p. of plates: bibl., ill. (some col.), maps.

Latest edition, revised and updated, of standard Mexican college-level economic geography text. Includes many maps and tables with data through mid-1970s.

5089 Clark, Colin G. and **Peter M. Ward.** Stasis in makeshift housing: perspec-

tives from Mexico and the Caribbean (ISA/CUR, 8:1, 1980, p. 117–127, bibl.)

Distinguishes between squatter settlements and *ciudades perdidas* or rent yards. Former are located on public land, the latter on privately owned land. Ciudades perdidas and rent yards lack the promise of eventual improvement that exists in squatter settlements. Short but useful paper.

5090 Cordero, Fernando. La influencia de los ferrocarriles en los cambios económicos y espaciales de México, 1870–1910. Stockholm: Institute of Latin American Studies, 1981. 89 p.: bibl., ill. (Research paper series / Institute of Latin American Studies, Stockholm; paper no. 29)

Well documented paper with many tables. Should be of particular interest for economic historians and historical geographers.

5091 Correa Pérez, Genaro. Geografía del Estado de Michoacán: física, humana, económica. v. l, Geografía física. Morelia, México: Gobierno del Estado, 1974- . 1 v.: bibl., ill.

Vol. 1 of four consists of comprehensive description of the physical environment and is unlikely to be surpassed as a Mexican state regional reference work for many years. Vol. 2 will cover human geography; vol. 3, economic geography; and vol. 4 will be a state atlas.

5092 Crist, Raymond E. and **Louis A. Paganini.** Pyramids, derricks, and mule teams in the Yucatán Peninsula: a second effort in 2,500 years to develop a jungle and forest area (AJES, 39:2, July 1980, p. 217–226)

Optimistic review of Mexican efforts to develop Yucatan and integrate the region and its people into the Mexican state.

5093 Economic and social conditions in Mexico: communications and transport (BNCE/CE, 27:7, July 1981, p. 261–278, tables)

Misleading title for a paper that reviews current status and plans for future development of Mexico's railroad network. Tabular data current through 1979 will be useful for those with an interest in Mexican railroads.

5094 Edwards, Clinton R. and **Norman R. Stewart.** Recent intensification of resource use in Quintana Roo, Mexico (*in* Conference of Latin Americanist Geographers, 10th, Muncie, Ind., 1980. Geographic research on Latin America [see item 5007] p. 48–57, bibl., maps, photographs, tables)

Large-scale landscape modification is taking place in a formerly little populated area. Plans are to introduce commercial agriculture and cattle raising. Results of agricultural projects have been disappointing, cattle ranching may offer more promise. To date there has been little concern with possible impacts of forest clearing.

5095 Ewell, Peter T. and Thomas T. Poleman. Uxpanapa: agricultural development in the Mexican tropics. New York: Pergamon Press, 1980. 207 p.: bibl., index, ill. (Pergamon policy studies on international development. Pergamon policy studies)

Comprehensive study of the development and early progress of an agricultural colonization program on Mexico's east coast.

5096 Frederich, Barbara E. Folk remedies in modern pharmacies: examples from Tijuana, Mexico (*in* Papers in Latin American geography in honor of Lucia C. Harrison [see item 5031] p. 77–87, bibl., ill., photos, table)

Report on the medicinal plants found in 26 pharmacies in Tijuana, Mexico. Stores offering greatest variety of medicinal plants were located in the city center, not in poor residential neighborhoods where new migrants would be expected to live.

5097 Gilbert, Alan G. and Peter M. Ward. Residential movement among the poor: the constraints on housing choice in Latin American cities (IBG/TP, 7:2, April 1982, p. 129–149, bibl., maps, tables)

Study of intra-city migration in Mexico City, Bogotá, and Valencia (Venezuela) tests current migration theories. Residential patterns in Latin American cities appear to be more influenced by land and housing markets than by migrant free choice. Several factors affecting land and housing markets are noted.

5098 González Cortés, Ambrosio. Los recursos naturales de México. v. 5, Recursos naturales del Estado de Nuevo León. México: Instituto Mexicano de Recursos Naturales Renovables (IMERNAR), 1979. 147 p.: bibl.

Essentially a physical geography of Nuevo León, book includes chapters on geol-

ogy, climate, soils, agricultural activities, etc. Final chapter deals briefly with economic and social conditions. Comprehensive bibliography that accompanies this work will be especially valuable.

5099 Gormsen, Erdmann. Die Städte im Spanischen Amerika (UBGI/E, 35:4, Dez. 1981, p. 290–303, bibl., map, photos., tables)

A model of development for Spanish-American cities during the last century is proposed. Three developmental stages are identified: 1) pre-industrial, 2) early modernization, 3) recent expanding urban. The model is tested in Puebla, Mexico.

5100 Helgren, David M. and Conrad J. Bahre. Reconnaissance geomorphology of the central coast of Sonora, Mexico (ZG, 25:2, Jun. 1981, p. 166–179, maps, plates)

Descriptive paper that will be of interest for physical geographers. Some maps have been reduced to the point of marginal legibility.

5101 Jones, Richard C. Channelization of undocumented Mexican migrants to the the U.S. (CU/EG, 58:2, April 1982, p. 156–176, bibl., maps, tables)

Mexican migrants to the US tend to follow channels from certain Mexican states of origin to certain US points of destination. Discusses several factors accounting for the channelization of migration.

5102 ———. Undocumented migration from Mexico: some geographical questions (AAG/A, 72:1, March 1982, p. 77–87)

Analysis of undocumented migrant flows from Mexican origins to US destinations. Migrant flows are expanding in space with respect both to origin and destination.

5103 Kreth, Ruediger. Características socioeconómicas y organización regional de la población de Acapulco como consecuencia del turismo y de la migración urbano-rural (*in* International Congress of Latin Americanist Geographers, 1st, Paipa, Colombia, 1977. The role of geographical research in Latin America: proceedings. General editors, William M. Denevan and Hector F. Rucinque. Muncie, Ind.: Conference of Latin Americanist Geographers, 1978, v. 2, p. 8–12 [CLAG publication; no. 7])

Preliminary survey of impact of population growth in response to tourism on the city of Acapulco. Author notes efforts made by municipal and national government to plan for rapid growth and calls for additional studies of growth in other tourist centers.

5104 Kurjack, Edward B. and **Silvia Garza T. de González.** Una visión de la geografía humana en la región serrana de Yucatán (in Congreso Interno del Instituto Nacional de Antropología e Historia, Centro Regional del Sureste, Mérida, Yucatán, 1979. Memoria del Congreso Interno, 1979. México: INAH, 1981, p. 39–54, bibl.)

Interesting and well researched paper concludes that control of productive agricultural land was key factor in the evolution of Yucatan Maya social stratification.

Licate, Jack A. Creation of a Mexican landscape: territorial organization and settlement in the eastern Puebla basin, 1520–1605. See *HLAS 44:1914.*

5105 Longwell, A. Richard. The literature on Mexico's agrarian reform (in New themes in instruction for Latin American geography. Oscar H. Horst and Joseph P. Stoltman, editors. Muncie, Ind.: Conference on Latin Americanist Geographers, 1982, p. 100–110 [Special publications of the Conference of Latin Americanist Geographers; v. 2]

Reviews literature on Mexico's agrarian reform in order to provide summaries for teachers and students. Will be of interest for anyone wishing to find a broad perspective on the Revolution.

5106 Michaels, Patrick J. The climatic sensitivity of "Green Revolution" wheat culture in Sonora, Mexico (Environmental Conservation [Foundation for Environmental Conservation, Geneva] 8:4, Winter 1981, p. 307–312, map, tables)

High yielding varieties (HYV) of wheat developed in Mexico are tested for responses to interannual climatic variability. HYV wheat shows greater yield response to climatic variability than do older varieties. Author concludes greater reserves should be set aside to cover fluctuation in yield as HYV planting increases.

5107 Ortiz Ramos, Carlos. Cultivos asociados o intercalados en México: evaluación (Econotecnia Agrícola [Secretaría de Agricultura y Recursos Hidráulicos, Subsecretaría de Agricultura y Operación, Direc-

ción General de Economía Agrícola, México] 3:7, julio 1979, p. 3–40, map, tables)

Encyclopedic presentation of data on intercultivated crops in Mexico. The data in this work will be of great value for anyone interested in Mexican agriculture. Many tables with data at *municipio* level.

5108 Pérez Borges, Manuel. Origen y desarrollo de la agricultura de riego en el sur del estado (in Congreso Interno del Instituto Nacional de Antropología e Historia, Centro Regional del Sureste, Mérida, Yucatán, 1979. Memoria del Congreso Interno, 1979. México: INAH, 1981, p. 339–350)

Largely descriptive study of the development and impact of irrigation/commercialization in Yucatecan agriculture. Field investigations and interviews were conducted in three different types of agricultural holding: the Oxkutzcab irrigation district, the Emiliano Zapata cooperative, and Yaax-Hom, an agricultural colony.

5109 Rengert, Arlene C. Some sociocultural aspects of rural outmigration in Latin America (in Papers in Latin American geography in honor of Lucia C. Harrison [see item 5031] p. 15–27, bibl., ill., photos, tables)

Argument for disaggregating migration data by sex to identify social and spatial processes in each group. Case study data are from Ojuelos, Mexico.

5110 Sander, Hans-Jörg. Beziehungen zwischen tourismus, ländlichem kunsthandwerk und agrarstruktur in einigen Dörfern zentralmexikos (UBGI/E, 35:3, Sept. 1981, p. 201–209, map, tables)

Three villages near Puebla are studied to determine the relationship between tourism, handicraft development, and agrarian structure. Promotion of artisan industries is intended to supplement income from small farmer agriculture. Evidence suggests handicraft development may divert labor away from agriculture, in some cases reducing productivity.

Sandos, James A. International water control in the lower Rio Grande basin, 1900–1920. See *HLAS 44:2258.*

5111 Schmidt, Robert H., Jr. Literature and data sources for the study of weather and climate in the arid zones of Mexico (in Conference of Latin Americanist Geographers, 10th, Muncie, Ind., 1980. Geographic research on Latin America [see item **5007**] p. 312–322, bibl., maps, photographs, tables)

Review of research with lengthy and useful bibliography.

5112 Scott, Ian. Urban and spatial development in Mexico. Baltimore: *Published for the* World Bank *by* Johns Hopkins University Press, 1982. 328 p.: bibl., index, maps.

In-depth review of Mexican urban development from conquest to present. Emphasizes the 1940–70 period. Section on developing policy to govern future urban growth. Many useful tables with data through 1970.

5113 Simposio Binacional sobre el Medio Ambiente del Golfo de California, 3rd, *La Paz, Baja California Sur, México, 1978.* Memoria-Proceedings: Ecodesarrollo. México: Instituto Nacional de Investigaciones Forestales, 1979. 224 p.: bibl., ill. (Publicación especial / Instituto Nacional de Investigaciones Forestales, SARH; no. 14)

Over 40 papers, some in English, most in Spanish only, dealing with such topics as water conservation, plant resources, wildlife, gulf islands, environmental pollution, and conservation education. Focuses on northwestern Mexico and Gulf of California littoral in particular.

5114 Simposio sobre el Medio Ambiente del Golfo de California, 4th, *Mazatlán, Sinaloa, México, 1979.* Memoria-Proceedings: la producción sostenida de alimentos, materias primas y empleos. México: SFF, SARH, Instituto Nacional de Investigaciones Forestales, 1979. 395 p.: bibl., ill. (Publicación especial / SFF, SARH, Instituto Nacional de Investigaciones Forestales; no. 17)

Collection of over 40 papers, in both English and Spanish, covering various aspects of resource utilization and conservation in northwestern Mexico. Themes include resource use in arid zones, development of forests, rangeland, and agriculture, wildlife, marine resources, and tourism.

5115 Soto, Margarita. Contribución al conocimiento del clima de la Sierra de Nanchititla, México (SMHN/R, 36, dic. 1975, p. 29–76, graphs, maps, tables)

Descriptive study of the climate of a part of Michoacán state north of the Balsas depression. Contains temperature and precipitation data for 19 climate stations.

5116 Swan, Susan L. Mexico in the Little Ice Age (JIH, 11:4, Spring 1981, p. 633–648, graphs)

Late 18th and early 19th-century Mexican climate fluctuations parallel similar events ascribed to the "little ice age" in Europe. This study differs from earlier attempts at correlating European and Mexican historic climate patterns by using hacienda records as a primary source of climate information.

Tibón, Gutierre. Historia del nombre y de la fundación de México. See *HLAS 44:1854.*

5117 Trautmann, Wolfgang. Agrarstruktur und rezente Wandlungen in der Henequén-Landschaft Yucatáns (Zeitschrift für Wirtsdaftsgeographie [Pick-Verlag, Hagen, FRG] 6:19, 1975, p. 172–181, map)

Reviews history of henequen production in Yucatan and offers careful analysis of production units and efforts at diversification from henequen production into other activities.

5118 Turner, B.L., II. La agricultura intensiva de trabajo en las tierras mayas (III/AI, 40:4, oct./dic. 1980, p. 653–670)

Precolumbian agricultural techniques utilized by ancient Maya of Quintana Roo State, Mexico, could provide an alternative to mechanized agriculture that is currently being introduced in the region by the Mexican government.

5119 Vanneph, Alain. La pétrochimie mexicaine (FDD/NED [Problème d'Amérique Latine, 60] 4619/4620, 12 mai 1981, p. 123–140, maps, tables)

Rather lengthy "note" reviews status of Mexican petrochemical production with plans for future development. Includes tabular data for 1979.

5120 Vidal Zepeda, Rosalía. Algunas relaciones clima-cultivos en el estado de Morelos. México: Universidad Nacional Autónoma de México, 1980. 95 p.: bibl., ill.

Interesting and innovative research monograph correlates average annual precipitation with yields of maize, beans, and tomatoes. Analysis of precipitation by month and conclusions regarding relationship of precipitation and yield will be useful to climatologists, agricultural geographers, and others.

5121 **Wilhelmy, Herbert.** Welt und Umwelt der Maya: Aufstieg und Untergang einer Hochkultur. München; Zürich: Piper, 1981. 541 p., 32 p. of plates: bibl., ill. (some col.), index, maps.

Cultural geographer reviews current state of knowledge on the Maya and places it in a spatial/ecological context. Recommended for anyone with a serious interest in the Maya. For an excellent summary in English, see *Geographical Review* (vol. 72, no. 2, April 1982, p. 223–227).

5122 **Williams, Barbara J.** and **Carlos A. Ortiz-Solorio.** Middle American folk soil taxonomy (AAG/A, 71 : 3, Sept. 1981, p. 335–358)

Folk classifications of soils used by Mexican and Guatemalan traditional farmers recognize statistically observable and valid soil variations, but they correspond poorly with formal, technical soil taxonomies. Article contains useful lists of native soil classification terms.

SOUTH AMERICA (except Brazil)

ROBERT C. EIDT, *Professor of Geography, University of Wisconsin-Milwaukee*

PUBLICATIONS ON SOUTH AMERICAN GEOGRAPHY attest to a growing interest in themes listed in declining order of importance: 1) physical geofactors followed by rural settlement, general economic and urban phenomena; 2) political, regional, and population studies; and 3) exploration-travel, energy, conservation, and transportation. In contrast to past years, there are very few publications on cartography and methodology.

Argentina led all countries in number of publications followed by Chile, Colombia, and Venezuela after which come Ecuador, Bolivia, and Peru. The least number of works were devoted to Uruguay, The Guianas, and Paraguay. A separate group, consisting of international studies (i.e., works dealing with more than one country), was sizeable and divided along lines outlined above but with exploration as the commanding theme.

Nearly half (40 percent) of all publications annotated in this section were drawn from foreign sources with English-language in the lead, followed by French and German. Indeed, France's interest in South America has taken such precedence over Germany's that of the total publications annotated, one-third were French and one-fifth German. Only one Dutch article appeared on The Guianas (item **5211**).

Most English language items appear in the South America: General, Colombia, and Venezuela subsections. French studies are most numerous in the South America: General and Peru subsections, with most German works devoted to Bolivia, Chile, and Ecuador. The remaining studies are spread about equally among all countries excepting The Guianas, Paraguay, or Uruguay.

Interest in physical geofactors such as mineral resources, soils, and climate are exemplified by an excellent study from Peru (item **5217**) and an outstanding regional soils contribution from Colombia (item **5181**).

Ongoing investigations of "empty" spaces for soils and settlement attest to a continuing trend toward occupying underused or unused areas as in the case of Amazonia. President Belaúnde Terry's idea of opening up this region is still alive as proven by at least one article which mentions the importance of completing the marginal highway east of the Andes.

GENERAL

5123 Alvarez Q., Víctor Julio. Un sistema de servicios como base de las relaciones ciudad-campo (PAIGH/G, 91/92, enero/dic. 1980, p. 89–98, bibl., charts)

Attempt to develop an infrastructure to permit integration of the smallest rural settlements into larger networks.

5124 Charnay, Désiré. América pintoresca: descripción de viajes al Nuevo Continente por los más modernos exploradores, Carlos Wiener, Doctor Crevaux, D. Charnay, etc. v. 2. Cali, Colombia: Carvajal, 1981. 1 v.: ill., maps, plates.

Vol. 1 of three first published in 1884, and dealing with observations of three French explorers in Latin America: Wiener about the Amazon, Charnay about Mexico, and André about Colombia and Ecuador. Each will be published separately. This tome by Charnay is well illustrated with drawings and descriptions of interest to historical geographers.

5125 Cochrane, Thomas T. and **Luis F. Sánchez.** Clima, paisajes y suelos de las sabanas tropicales de Suramérica (AI/I, 6:4, julio/agosto 1981, p. 239–244, bibl., graphs, ill., maps, tables)

Summarizes findings of the International Center for Tropical Agriculture (CIAT) on South American grasslands of which there are two types, each determined by drainage conditions. Evaluates the agricultural potential of both kinds of savannas. [M. Hiraoka]

5126 Cusack, David F. The transfer of computer-based technology in agroclimate information systems (AI/I, 6:4, 1981, p. 261–267, bibl., ill., tables)

Projects based on the so-called technological fix do not succeed in Latin America because of different environments, both physical and human, within short distances.

5127 Dalmatrac, Bernard et al. La chaine hercynienne d'Amérique du Sud: structure et évolution d'un orogene intracratonique (GV/GR, 69:1, 1980, p. 1-21, bibl., ill., maps)

Model for explaining the Hercynian Foldbelt of the Central Andes explains its presence in terms of global tectonics.

5128 Geyer, Otto F. von. Die mesozoische Magnafazies-Abfolge in den nördlichen Anden: Peru, Ekuador, Kolumbien (GV/GR, 69:3, 1980, p. 875–891, map, table)

More than 100 sedimentary formations and groups of the Mesozoic are found in the Andean Region of Peru, Ecuador, and Colombia. A uniform development occurred, although coastal cordilleras in the north (Colombia, Ecuador) are geologically different from those in Peru and Chile.

5129 Mazo, Gabriel del. Proyecto de un canal Sudamericano (IAEERI/E, 61/62, nov. 1979/feb. 1980, p. 30–39, bibl., maps)

Possibility of linking the Plata, Amazon, and Orinoco rivers in a gigantic canalization scheme presented with historical data concerning the project.

5130 Middleton, Dorothy. Stout hearts in South America (GM, 52:6, March 1980, p. 434–438, facsims.)

Brief survey of important travelers in South America, many of whom left scientific records.

5131 Power, Robert H. The Drake conundrum, Cape Horn discovered—and then to San Francisco Bay (GM, 52:8, May 1980, p. 537–543, facsims., ill., maps)

Discussion of whether Drake named Henderson Island or Cape Horn, and Point San Quentin or Point Reyes on his voyage to the Pacific in 1578.

5132 Sauer, Carl Ortwin. Andean reflections: letters from Carl O. Sauer while on a South American trip under a grant from the Rockefeller Foundation, 1942. Edited by Robert C. West. Boulder, Colo.: Westview Press, 1982. 139 p. (Dellplain Latin American studies; no. 12)

Interesting reading from 25 letters written by Sauer during a trip to South America at the outbreak of World War II. Observations on climate and soils in relation to land use.

5133 Simpson, George Gaylord. Splendid isolation: the curious history of South American mammals. New Haven: Yale University Press, 1980. 266 p.: bibl., ill., index.

Fascinating account of the fauna of South America with detailed discussion of the contribution made by the Ameghino brothers and others.

5134 The South American Handbook. Bath, England: Trade & Travel Publications, 1980? 1 v.: fold. map, ill.

Probably the best of the travel guides on South America with information on numerous hotels and pensiones of all types.

5135 Thery, Hervé. Les conquètes de l'Amazonie: 4 siècles de luttes pour le controle d'un espace (CDAL, 18, 2. semestre, 1978, p. 129–146, map)

Political vs. economic control of the region called Amazonia is discussed up to the renewed international activities begun in the 1970s.

ARGENTINA

5136 Barros, Vicente. Algunos aspectos de las fluctuaciones climáticas de los últimos 50 años en la provincia del Chubut (OAS/CI, 19:1, enero/marzo 1978, p. 18–21)

In the 1940s, higher rainfall occurred in the arid zone of Chubut than in other decades. Vegetation changes have also occurred.

5137 Beyna, Jean-Michel. L'hydroélectricité dans le Bassin de La Plata (FDD/NED [Problèmes d'Amérique Latine, 53] 4533/4534, 31 oct. 1979, p. 119–145, tables)

Importance of region's hydroelectric potential is evident in recent binational agreements of the La Plata Basin. Sources of capital and possible conflict are discussed as development of water energy continues.

5138 Castiello, Nicolino. La pesca in Argentina e Mar del Plata (SGI/B, 7[10]:1/6, gen./giugno 1978, p. 81–112, ill., tables)

Argentina's fishing industry is backward and restricted by unionization. Furthermore, Mar del Plata has a monopoly on unloading the catch—a feature which results in less of a market and poor distribution of the product.

5139 Cogliatti, Daniel H. Algunos datos preliminares sobre deficiencias de nutrientes minerales es un suelo de la depresión del Salado, provincia de Buenos Aires (Revista de la Universidad Nacional del Centro de la Provincia de Buenos Aires [Argentina] 8/9, mayo/dic. 1979, p. 97–106, bibl., graphs)

The practice of fertilization for improving yields is based on previous knowledge of soil chemistry. Article demonstrates phosphate and sulfur deficiencies in the Salado depression, Province of Buenos Aires.

5140 Cuevas Acevedo, Huberto. Tandilia: una interpretación de su geomorfología (Revista de la Univesidad Nacional del Centro de la Provincia de Buenos Aires [Argentina] 8/9, mayo/dic. 1979, p. 53–68, diagrams, map)

Attempt to explain geomorphology of the hilly Pampean Tandil sector south of Buenos Aires.

5141 Denis, Paul-Yves. Espacio agrario y centros urbanos de la provincia de Córdoba: conceptualización geográfica y problemática actual de las relaciones ciudad-campo al nivel regional (PAIGH/G, 91/92, enero/dic. 1980, p. 101–139, bibl., figures, graphs, maps)

The function of regionalism seen through the competition of cities in the Province of Córdoba, Argentina.

5142 Ellis, Richard. Argentina's Valdés Peninsula. Photographs by Ricardo Mandojana (OAS/AM, 32:9, Sept. 1980, p. 13–21, plates)

Interesting account of native wild life on the Valdés Peninsula and a plea for its preservation as a natural reserve zone.

5143 Federico, Antonio Pedro. Las posibilidades de aprovechamientos mareomotrices en la República Argentina (UNL/U, 89, enero/abril 1978, p. 83–110, bibl,. tables)

Possibility of achieving energy from water movements along coasts of the Peninsula de Valdés, Argentina.

5144 Guevara, Carlos Noé Alberto. La problemática marítima argentina. Secretaría de Estado de Intereses Marítimos. 2. ed. corregida y aum. Buenos Aires: Fundación Argentina de Estudios Marítimos, 1981. 3 v.: bibl., ill.

A compendium in three volumes of marine resources of Argentina. Legislation, physical aspects, and politics of geological and fishing as well as navigational aspects of the economy. Useful bibliographies.

5145 Mársico, Alfredo D. Estudio de las condiciones de higiene del aire de la ciudad de Buenos Aires. Buenos Aires: Universidad de Buenos Aires, 197? 155 p.: ill.

Meteorological aspects of air contamination, analytical determinations, standards, and actual conditions of the air in Buenos Aires are scrutinized. Recommendations such as the control of emissions from automobiles take standard forms.

5146 Oviddio Zavala, Juan. El transporte en la Argentina: cuadro de situación (IAEERI/E, 54, sept./oct. 1978, p. 77−93)

Economic influence, status of different methods of transport, and problems of planning in Argentina are major aspects of this study.

5147 Perié, Julio César. Fronteras y el desarrollo nacional: el caso Misiones (IAEERI/E, 58, mayo/junio 1979, p. 27−47, maps, tables)

Discusses dangers of allowing a frontier zone to deteriorate, as is occurring in Misiones Province.

5148 Raymundo, Basilio Adrián. Argentina 2000: una nación semidesierta. 2. ed. corr. y aum. Buenos Aires: Ediciones LIHUEL, 1981. 249 p.: bibl.

Author laments Argentina's slow rate of population growth and feels compelled to propagandize an economy based on rapid population growth. His goal is for Argentina to keep up with the rest of the underdeveloped world's population rates of increase.

5149 Reboratti, Carlos E. Migraciones y frontera agraria: Argentina y Brasil en la cuenca del Alto Paraná-Uruguay (IDES/DE, 19 : 74, julio/sept. 1979, p. 189−209, bibl., map)

Stages of settlement are identified for the Upper Paraná region. Misiones is described as an indecisive frontier area, whereas Paraná is called an explosive frontier.

5150 Stingl, Helmut and Karsten Garleff. Gletscherschwankugen in den subtropisch-semiariden Hochanden Argentiniens (ZG, 30, 1978, p. 115−131, bibl., maps, plates, tables)

Variations in glaciation in the high cordillera of Argentina (35A8S) are believed due to effects of changes in humidity.

5151 Torres, Horacio A. El mapa social de Buenos Aires en 1943, 1947 y 1960: Buenos Aires y los modelos urbanos (IDES/DE, 18 : 70, julio/set. 1978, p. 163−204, maps, tables)

The growth of Buenos Aires is set at these dates: 1935, 1943−47, and 1960, the last year analyzed by this article. The extension of the transport net and the appearance of small holdings on the outskirts of the city

are reasons for the changes. Maps illustrate the phenomena for periods examined.

5152 Vecchio, Ofelio. Mataderos, mi barrio. 2. ed. Buenos Aires: Editora Nueva Lugano, 1981. 350 p.: ill.

One of the several studies of barrios in Buenos Aires which have gained popularity in recent years. Largely personalized historical and geographical views about cultural progress and events within the city of Buenos Aires.

5153 Vedoya, Juan Carlos. La primera comisión para el trazado de Tandil (Revista de la Universidad Nacional del Centro de la Provincia de Buenos Aires, 8/9, mayo/dic. 1979, p. 173−180, ill., photos)

Historical geography of the city of Tandil according to planning which emerged first in 1849.

5154 Werckenthien, Cristian G. El transporte en Buenos Aires, 1870−1880. Buenos Aires: Asociación Amigos del Tranvía, 1981. 117 p.: ill. (Publicación/Asociación Amigos del Tranvía; no. 1)

Deals with rail and tram services in Buenos Aires during 1870−80. Discusses contribution of each to the development and extention of settlement in the city.

BOLIVIA

5155 Arc, Hélène Rivière d'. Espace national et périphéries frontaliéres en Bolivie (FDD/NED [Problèmes d'Amérique Latine, 53] 4533/4534, 31 oct. 1979, p. 109−118, map)

Discussion of Bolivia's loss of territory to Peru, Brazil, and others from 1879−1933, and the existing need for a corridor to the sea.

5156 Hiraoka, Mario. Agricultural colonization in the Bolivian Upper Amazon (Annual Report [Latin American Special Project, University of Tsukuba, Ibaraki, Japan] 2, 1979 [i.e. March 1980] p. 39−46, bibl., tables)

Analyzes unsatisfactory attempts to settle Bolivia's eastern interior. Concludes that if present trends continue, area will fall under control of large land holders and emerge with same pattern found in pre-revolutionary highland Bolivia.

5157 López Avila, Miguel. Sud Cinti: historia y tradición. La Paz: Librería-Editorial Popular, 1981. 134 p.

Account of the city of Cinti, in southern Chuquisaca. Indian vocabulary and customs lend flavor to the human occupation of the landscape.

5158 Monheim, Felix and **Gerrit Köster.** Die wirtschaftliche Erschliessung des Departement Santa Cruz, Bolivien, seit der Mitte des 20. Jahrhunderts. Wiesbaden, FRG: Steiner, 1982. 152 p.: ill. (Erdkundliches Wisen; Heft 56. Geographische Zeitschrift. Beihefte)

Settlement in eastern Bolivia has been severely affected since the 1970s by the crisis in the cotton, sugar cane, and oil economies. Establishment of an industrial park in Santa Cruz has not brought promising results because of distance to interior markets. Finally, political disinterest in the region and the beginning of cocaine manufacture further aggravated the situation.

5159 Parejas Moreno, Alcides J. Colonias japonesas en Bolivia. La Paz: Talleres-Escuela de Artes Gráficas del Colegio Don Bosco, 1981. 195 p.: bibl., ill.

Japanese emigration to Bolivia and discussion of modern colonies in that country are presented with statistics.

5160 Pinto Parada, Rodolfo. Rumbo al Beni. Trinidad, Bolivia: s.n., 1878 [i.e. 1978]. 245 p.

Popularized account of the settlement of the area around Trinidad, eastern Bolivia. Includes documents.

5161 Rivière, Gilles. Les zones de colonisation en Bolivie (FDD/NED [Problèmes d'Amérique Latine, 62] 4649/4650, 28 déc. 1981, p. 55–77, bibl., chart)

Population explosion in the Andes cntinues to find outlet in the tropical lowlands of Bolivia. Reviews colonization schemes since the revolution of 1952.

5162 Unterladstatter Knorn, Roberto. Consideraciones generales sobre erosión y la situación actual en el Depto. de Santa Cruz. Santa Cruz, Bolivia: Universidad Gabriel René Moreno, Instituto de Investigaciones Agrícolas y de Recursos Naturales Renovables, 1979 [i.e. 1980]. 31 p.: ill.

General discussion of soil erosion presented with special comments about eastern Bolivia.

5163 Villarroel, Carlos and **Kurt Graf.** Zur Entstehung des Talkessels von La Paz/ Bolivien und Umgebung (GH, 34:1, 1979, p. 43–49, plates, tables)

Geological explanation of landforms in the vicinity of La Paz are explained in detail. Geomorphological reshaping of terrain took place since the late Pliocene, following which uplift of some 3300 feet occurred.

CHILE

5164 Chile. Instituto de Investigaciones Geológicas. Catálogo de informes inéditos del Instituto de Investigaciones Geológicas: diciembre 1957-junio 1978: preprint. Santiago: El Instituto, 1978. 164 p.: index.

Catalogue of geological investigations conducted in Chile during 1960s-70s and prepared as reports without publication.

5165 Cunill Grau, Pedro. La geografía social histórica en el empobrecimiento paisajístico chileno (*in* Encuentro de Historiadores Latinoamericanos y del Caribe, 2d, Caracas, 1977. Los estudios históricos en América Latina: ponencias, acuerdos y resoluciones: Caracas, 20–26 de marzo de 1977. Caracas: Universidad Central de Venezuela, Facultad de Humanidades y Educación, Escuela de Historia, 1979, v. 1, t. 2, p. 392–407, maps)

Describes degradation of original landscapes of the coast of central Chile by mining, farming, and grazing activities. For historian's comment, see *HLAS 44:3076.*

5166 Grenier, Philippe. Le différend frontalier chileno-argentin (CDAL, 18, 2. semestre, 1978, p. 87–92)

Discusses major aspects of dispute between Chile and Argentina over their national frontiers. Reveals clash between Chilean nationalism and Argentine policy of peopling frontier regions.

5167 Ilabaca Guajardo, Pedro. Las condiciones naturales del sitio de Concepción metropolitano (PAIGH/G, 91/92, enero/dic. 1980, p. 141–152, maps)

Analysis of physical geofactors which influence function and growth of Concepción, Chile, with emphasis on terrace sites and flooding along the Río Bío-Bío.

5168 Larraín, Horacio. Identidad cultural e indicadores eco-culturales del grupo étnico Chango (UCC/NG, 6, 1978/1979, p. 63–76, bibl.)

Identification of Chilean ethnic group by use of eco-cultural indicators.

Martinic Beros, Mateo. Los alemanes en Magallanes. See *HLAS 44:3094.*

5169 Morales A., Miguel and **Pedro Labra A.** Condicionantes naturales, metropolización y problemas de planificación del Gran Santiago, Chile (PAIGH/G, 91/92, enero/dic. 1980, p. 179–221, bibl., graphs, maps, tables)

Discussion of growth of Santiago, which already contains over half the actively employed people of Chile. Not as constructive an approach as found in item **5239.**

5170 Núñez A., Lautaro. Emergencia y desintegración de la sociedad tarapaqueña: riqueza y pobreza en una quebrada del Norte chileno (UC/AT, 439, 1979, p. 163–213, graphs, maps)

Detailed account of the changes caused in pre-Spanish Indian society in the Quebrada de Tarapacá, Chile. Maps of Indian settlement distribution. Population deterioration graph.

5171 Paskoff, Roland. Sobre la evolución geomorfológica del gran acantilado costero del Norte Grande de Chile (UCC/NG, 6, 1978/1979, p. 7–22, bibl., map, plates, tables)

The high cliff of the northern coastal part of Chile is some 800 km long. It appears to have formed from faulting in the Upper Miocene.

5172 Riesco J., Ricardo. Antecedentes preliminares sobre la relación entre el "smog" de la ciudad de Santiago y la circulación general de la atmósfera (UCC/RU, 3, abril 1980, p. 9–29, bibl., plate, tables)

Meteorological explanation of Santiago's smog problem.

5173 ———. Vergrünlandung in der Bodennutzung Süd-Chiles: Dargestellt am Beispiel des jüngsten Kulturlandschaftswandels in der Frontera (IAA, 6:1, 1980, p. 29–52, bibl., tables)

Land use in the Chilean *frontera* is turning from cereal production to milk cattle. The process is independent of the region's population dynamics.

5174 Salinas Messina, Rolando. Uso del suelo y estructura urbano de Valpa-raíso (PAIGH/G, 91/92, enero/dic. 1980, p. 153–177, bibl., maps, plates)

Analysis of the various functions of the port of Valparaíso.

5175 Santiago, Jacques. Les transport en commun à Santiago du Chili: problèmes et perspectives (SGB/COM, 31:122, avril/juin 1978, p. 152–170, map, tables)

In Greater Santiago, 90 percent of the movement of people is by public vehicles. Problems of congestion, limitations of new transport systems such as the subway, and financial difficulties are investigated.

5176 Santibañez, Fernando; Mario Silva; and Alberto Mansilla. Desarrollo de un modelo de productividad para la zona mediterránea árida de Chile (OAS/CI, 19:1, enero/marzo 1978, p. 3–10)

Productivity of dry material is simulated for nine different rainfall regions in an arid part of Chile.

5177 Zapater E., Horacio. Cinco relaciones sobre San Pedro de Atacama (UCC/NG, 5, 1976/1977, p. 49–64, bibl., maps)

Human geography of the Atacama analyzed according to five different reports written over several centuries since the conquest. Included are studies by Jerónimo de Vivar (1558), Vásquez de Espinosa (1629), Juan del Pino Manrique (1787), R. Philippi (1860), and A. Bertrand (1885).

5178 Zolezzi Velásquez, Silvia M. Demografía y antecedentes socio-económicos de Arica entre los años 1824 y 1879 (UCC/NG, 6, 1978/1979, p. 46–61, bibl., tables)

Population analysis of Arica during the period 1824–79, after which dependence was on trade rather than agriculture and industry.

5179 Zuñiga Ide, Jorge. Fray Jorge: un relicto boscoso natural de probable origen Terciario en el Norte Chico de Chile (UC/AT, 440, 2. semestre 1979, p. 11-37, bibl.)

Speculates that a 9000 ha. forest reserve in the north of Chile has survived from the beginning of the Holocene.

COLOMBIA

5180 Alfredo, Tomás. El Macizo Colombiano: arca limnológica de Colombia (SGC/B, 33:113, 1978, p. 73–94, maps, plates)

Survey investigation of lakes in the Macizo Colombiano, southern Colombia.

5181 Bibliografía nacional de suelos, 1930–1980. Bogotá: Ministerio de Hacienda y Crédito Público, Instituto Geográfico Agustin Codazzi, 1981. 376 p.

Useful bibliography of publications dealing with soils of Colombia. Lengthy section on references about soils-related articles and other works will be of help to physical geographers.

5182 Brucher, Wolfgang and **Wilfried Korby.** Zur Standortfrage von integrierten Hüttenwerken in außereuropäischen Entwicklungsländern: Die Beispiele Aryamahr/ Iran und Paz del Río/Kolumbien (GZ, 1:67, 1979, p. 77–94, plates)

Although much smaller than the steel mill at Aryamahr, Iran, the one at Paz del Río, Colombia, shares characteristics with the former such as interior location, and important political and developmental influence in an underdeveloped country. Examines various aspects of growth and of the industry in general and compares them with steel projects in developed countries.

5183 Colombia. Instituto Geográfico Agustín Codazzi. Subdirección Agrológica. Estudio general de suelos del sector El Aguila, Yotoco, Cordillera Occidental (Departamento del Valle del Cauca). Realizado con la colaboración de la C.V.C. Bogotá: La Subdirección, 1977. 406 p.: appendix, bibl., ill., maps (8 fold.)

Outstanding example of soils studies carried out on a regional basis by the Colombian government. Employs US soil taxonomy and presents thorough analysis of soil types.

5184 Convers Pinzón, Rafael. El oriente colombiano (SGC/B, 31:112, 1978, p. 41–44)

Reports on an OAS plan for improving cattle raising in the Colombian llanos principally along roads.

5185 Estudio de planeación nucleoeléctrica para Colombia: mediante el uso del Programa WASP II del Organismo Internacional de Energía Atómica. Bogotá: Instituto de Asuntos Nucleares, 1981. 283 p.: bibl., ill.

Planning study for the integration of Colombian energy networks. Natural resource availability of petroleum, natural gas, coal, uranium, and hydroelectric potentials are investigated. Includes discussion of atomic power.

5186 García Jacome, Eduardo. El oro en Colombia (SGC/B, 33:113, 1978, p. 23–62, bibl., ill., maps, plates, tables)

Colombia is fourth in gold production in the hemisphere, first in South America. Discusses methods of production, locations (with maps), and politics of the gold industry.

5187 Griffin, Ernst C. and **Lynden S. Williams.** Social implications of changing population patterns: the case of rural depopulation in Colombia (*in* International migration systems in the developing world. Edited by Robert H. Thomas and John M. Hunter. Boston: G.K. Hall; Cambridge, Mass.: Schenkman Pub. Co., 1980, p. 17–25)

Radical change in the relationship between rural and urban populations is occurring in Colombia. By 1975, an estimated 61 percent lived in cities, and the numbers are increasing explosively. Furthermore, there is no longer an absolute increase in rural population because of high birth rate.

5188 Guhl, Ernesto. Los páramos circundantes de la sabana de Bogotá. Bogotá: Litografía Arco, 1982. 127 p.: maps, photos.

Well written study of the páramos around Bogotá is replete with color photographs of high quality. Author discusses climatic and vegetational aspects of the páramo in central Colombia, as well as use of the land at higher elevations.

5189 ———. La sabana de Bogotá: sus alrededores y su vegetación. Bogotá: Jardín Botánico José Celestino Mutis, 1981. 106 p.: maps, photographs.

Book reveals interrelationships of climatic and vegetation, with peculiarities found in a tropical highland region. Edaphic factors are not treated.

5190 Mosquera Rivas, Ramón. Pasado, presente y futuro de la minería en el Chocó (SGC/B, 31:112, 1978, p. 65–68)

Reviews mining characteristics in western Colombia and suggests effort to locate the mother lode areas of platinum.

5191 Ordoñez, Temístocles. Subsistencia versus conservación: el caso de La Macarena (SGC/B, 31:112, 1978, p. 5–14, bibl., map)

Plea for the preservation of the reserve

zone of La Macarena in eastern Colombia, which is being invaded by colonists.

5192 Pagney, Pierre. Aspects climatiques des Andes de Colombie Climatological aspects of Colombian Andes (AGF/B, 55:456/457, nov./déc. 1978, p. 321-327, map, table)

Influence of intertropical convergence zone and of low pressure trend on Colombia's Pacific side are used to explain precipitation regimes.

5193 Paynter, Raymond A. and **Melvin A. Traylor, Jr.** Ornithological gazetteer of Colombia. Cambridge, Mass.: Bird Department, Museum of Comparative Zoology, Harvard University, 1981. 311 p.: bibl., maps (Ornithological gazetteers of the neotropics)

Gazetteer of places in Colombia contains altitude and exact location for use in finding country's birds. Useful information for geographers and others.

5194 Restrepo Uribe, Jorge and **Luz Posada de Greiff.** Medellín: su origen, progreso y desarrollo. Medellín: Servigráficas, 1981. 655 p.: ill. (some col.)

Historical and political treatment of the evolution of the modern city of Medellín. Includes city planning, industrial expansion, transportation, and is filled with statistics.

5195 Rosas García, Humberto. Estudio sobre los depósitos de bauxita en Cauca y Valle, especialmente en el área de Morales y Cajibio (COIGN/BG, 22:1, 1979, p. 57–84, bibl., maps, tables)

Detailed study of geological conditions in western Colombia with emphasis on presence of bauxite.

5196 Ruiz, José Ignacio. Dos ilustres geógrafos (SGC/B, 33:113, 178, p. 65–72) Describes contributions to geography by two Colombians: Ruiz Wilches, who founded the Instituto Geográfico, and Rozo Martínez, who made important contributions to Colombia's Geographical Society.

5197 Tobón Toro, Guillermo and **Fernando Alzate Amaya.** Uraba: diario de fronteras (UA/U, 52:200/201, enero/junio 1977, p. 47–54, ill., map, plate)

Analysis of the fishing and coconut villages and towns along the Colombian-Panamanian border with emphasis on contraband trade activities.

5198 Ulloa Melo, Carlos and **Erasmo Rodríguez Martínez.** Geología del cuadrángulo K-12, Guateque (COIGN/BG, 22:1, 1979, p. 3–56, bibl., maps, tables)

Study of stratigraphy, tectonics, and historical geology, including mineral resources, in an area of sedimentary rocks 50 km east of Bogotá. Useful maps.

ECUADOR

5199 Aguilar Moscoco, Cristina and **Gladys Agustoni Olivera.** Calderón un centro urbano-rural al margen de Quito (PAIGH/G, 84, 1976, p. 171–182, map, plate, table)

Analysis of urban and rural attributes of a community located 15 km from Quito. The settlement suffers from having spontaneous origins without benefit of a proper infrastructure.

5200 Behrends, Alfredo. Geopolítica de la energía (Geopolítica [Instituto Uruguayo de Estudios Geopolíticos, Montevideo] 10, dic. 1980, p. 37–56, maps, tables)

Ecuador must rely entirely on hydroelectric and solar energy for domestic fuel. Article suggests a continued search for fossil fuel in the north and along the continental shelf, as well as integrated urban energy nets.

5201 Benavides Solís, Jorge. El conflicto urbano: crónicas. Quito: Facultad de Arquitectura y Urbanismo de la Universidad Central, 1979. 121 p., 16 leaves of plates: ill.

Problems of urban architecture and planning with special emphasis on Quito, Ecuador.

5202 Borchart de Moreno, Christiana. Landbesitz im Machachi-Tal am Ende des 17. Jahrhunderts (IAA, 5:3, 1979, p. 243–266, bibl.)

Land tenure development in the Audiencia de Quito, based on a report made in 1692 by Antonio de Ron.

5203 Céspedes, Arabella and **Julio Urbáes B.** Los inmigrantes asiáticos y su impacto en la economía de la ciudad de Quevedo (IGME/RG, 11, 1979, p. 121–149, bibl., maps, tables)

Asiatics (Chinese) make up about five percent of the population of the city of Quevedo, Ecuador. The origin of these immigrants is mainly Peru, from which most have come illegally. Economic contributions are discussed.

5204 Collin Delavaud, Anne. Nouvelles transformations des zones de colonisation agricole sur la côte de l'Equateur: Quininde (UTIEH/C, 34, 1980, p. 99–115, bibl., col. plates)

Discusses changes on the western Ecuadorian colonization front from banana plantings to mixed crops, and the difficulties of integration with the national economy.

5205 Durán Abad, César. Algunas relaciones entre la geomorfología y la vegetación en la región morfoclimática ecuatorial (IGME/RG, 11, 1979, p. 63–71, maps, tables)

Satellite information reveals that tree species prefer undulating terrain; and that in Ecuador shrubs and palms appear more frequently on level land.

5206 Eibl-Eibesfeldt, Irenäus. Galápagos-Inseln: Arche Noah im Pazifik; der Evolution auf der Spur (WM, 8, Aug. 1980, p. 72–81, plates)

Description of certain forms of animal and bird life in the Galápagos by well known expert.

5207 Feininger, Tomás and C. Roger Bristow. Cretaceous and Paleogene geologic history of coastal Ecuador (GV/GR, 69:3, 1980, p. 849–874, maps, tables)

Sufficient geological information has been gathered to make a modern interpretation of the formative history of Ecuador. The basement problem, the lack of volcanic contamination of the Napo Formation, lack of intervening rocks of Paleocene-Eocene age over the Cayo Formation in the Santa Elena Peninsula, and origin of the Azúcar rocks in the Santa Elena Peninsula are all explained by lateral displacements and presence of an unrecognized Bolívar plate.

5208 Garayar Coppelli, Miguel A. Sangolqui: ciudad de estructura y función dual (IGME/RG, 11, 1979, p. 3–28, bibl., maps, tables)

After improved road construction in 1956, the growth of Sangolqui (near Quito) accelerated and was partly attributed to immigration from rural areas and Quito.

5209 Terán, Francisco. Nuevas páginas de geografía e historia. Quito: Instituto Panamericano de Geografía e Historia, Sección Nacional del Ecuador, 1982. 189 p. (Biblioteca Ecuador)

Historical overview of foreign inter-

ests in Ecuador during colonial period, of physical geographical factors of significance, and of politics.

THE GUIANAS

5210 Shaw, Paul. Cave development on a granite inselberg, South Rupununi Savannas, Guyana (ZGP, 24:1, März 1980, p. 68–76, bibl., col. plates)

Cave formation in granite is unusual, and in this case is explained by postulating intensive runoff during more arid conditions. Latter are substantiated by calcrete banks nearby.

5211 Varma, F.H.R. Oedayrajsingh. Van savannen tot natuurreservaten en hun betekenis voor het Surinaamse landschap: een geografische verhandeling. Amsterdam: F.H.R.O. Varma, 1980? 111 p.; bibl., maps.

Description of savanna landscapes in Surinam.

PARAGUAY

5212 Bailby, Edouard. Paraguay: un barrage aux conséquences imprévisibles (CJN, 220, sept. 1980, p. 4–7, ill., map)

Political-economic changes are expected in Paraguay as a result of the opening of the Itaipú electrical facility.

5213 Gutiérrez, Ramón. Un conjunto inédito de planos paraguayos (UCNSA/EP, 61:l, sept. 1978, p. 115–131, ill., maps)

Discussion of a series of 50 maps drawn at the end of the 18th century while Brazil was at war with Paraguay. The maps are located in the national library of Rio de Janeiro.

PERU

5214 Collin-Delavaud, Claude. Le Pérou et ses frontières non consolidées: les difficultés de l'integration économique (FDD/NED [Problèmes d'Amérique Latine, 53] 4553/4534, 31 oct. 1979, p. 99–107, maps)

Problems of economic integration and with international frontiers, especially in the north and south, hold development back in Peru.

5215 Krzanowski, Andrzej and Jan Szemiński. La toponimía indígena en la cuenca del Río Chicama, Perú (PAN/ES, 4, 1978, p. 11–51, maps, tables)

Divides Chicama valley into three regions with populations which were differentiated linguistically in prehispanic times.

5216 Lima Año 2000, *Lima,* 1977. Lima Año 2000. Lima: Colegio de Arquitectos del Perú, 1977. 4 v.: bibl., ill.

The College of Architects of Lima has produced this four-volume work of planning for the year 2000. It is predicted that Lima will have over 12,000,000 people by that year, with present population growth rate proportions of three percent per year. Historical, physical, social, and economic conditions are reviewed. Authors are somewhat optimistic in spite of water shortage, transport, and in-migration problems.

5217 El Perú minero. Edited by Mario Samamé Boggio. Lima: INCITEMI, 1979. 14 v.: bibl., ill.

Valuable series of 14 volumes which constitutes a modern summary in detail of metallic and non-metallic minerals in Peru. Includes, for example, maps of sources of gold for entire country as well as for specific mining areas.

5218 Saccasyn della Santa, Elisabeth. Sous le froid tropical: notes sur le Pérou du sud, entremêlées des récits d'Abelino. Séville: Edition E. della Santa, 1976. 222 p., 4 leaves of plates: ill.

Problems of geography and society, especially in southern Peru, are discussed by an educated traveler.

5219 Villarejo, Avencio. Así es la selva. Mapa, Abelardo Mozombite. 3. ed. ampliada y totalmente reformada con la colaboración de un equipo de especialistas en temas amazónicos. Iquitos, Perú: Publicaciones CETA, 1979. 348 p., 21 leaves of plates (1 fold.): bibl., ill., index.

Third edition of a study of the Department of Loreto in the lower Amazon region of Peru. Physical geography and population studies are emphasized.

5220 White, Stuart. Cedar and mahogany logging in eastern Peru (AGS/GR, 68:4, Oct. 1978, p. 394–416)

Types of logging, environmental factors, and consequences of such activities in eastern lowland Peru.

URUGUAY

5221 Mandracho, Héctor. El acuífero infrabasáltico del noroeste uruguayo (Geopolítica [Instituto Uruguayo de Estudios Geopolíticos, Montevideo] 3:6, dic. 1978, p. 22–28, map)

Water resources are not lacking in northwest Uruguay, as commonly supposed. By drilling over 1000 m. deep, aquifers may be reached.

5222 Musso, Carlos. Acondicionamiento del espacio rural (CLAEH, dic. 1978, p. 5–40)

Studies restructuring of Uruguay's rural activities and the need for equilibrium of the rural population. Details types of service centers with different functions, and other aspects of infrastructure.

5223 Wettstein, Germán. Hacia una tipología de los paisajes humanizados: el caso de los paisajes agrarios en el Uruguay (ULA/RG, 13:28/29, enero/dic. 1972, p. 51–80, bibl., tables)

Uses labor and other statistics in order to determine what is happening to the regional development of Uruguay. Unfortunately, no maps were prepared.

VENEZUELA

5224 Aguilera, Jesús Antonio. Venezuela y sus ambientes naturales. Caracas: Facultad de Humanidades y Educación de la Universidad Central de Venezuela: Colegio Universitario de Carupano, 1981. 122 p., 8 p. of plates: ill. (some col.)

Consists of physical geography of Venezuela in short sections dealing with geomorphology, climate, soils, hydrography, and vegetation. Includes colored maps of each phenomenon.

5225 Barrios, Sonia. Les inégalités régionales dans le Vénézuela actuel (UP/TM, 21:84, oct./déc. 1980, p. 749–759, maps)

Political approach to explain regional economic differences in Venezuela. Urban-rural inequalities will persist.

5226 Bauman, Janice *et al.* Guide to Venezuela. Caracas: E. Armitano, 1981. 856 p.: ill., indexes.

Popularized guide to Venezuela's points of interest for the traveler. Maps and numerous details.

5227 Curiel Rodríguez, José. Secretos del mundo perdido: la gran aventura del Amazonas. Portada de Régulo Pérez. Caracas: Publicaciones Seleven, 1980. 265 p.: bibl., ill.

Account of the economic potential of the Territory of Amazonas, Venezuela, with specific examples of plants, minerals, and other items of exploitable quality.

5228 Ellenberg, Ludwig. Coastal types of Venezuela: an application of coastal classifications (ZG, 22:4, Dez. 1978, p. 439–456)

Classification of coastal types varies, depending on the system used. This article compares three classifications of the coast of Venezuela from Cumaná to the Colombian border.

5229 ———. Jungholozäne Künstenverän- derungen im nördlichen Falcón, Vene- zuela (ZG, Supplementband 30, 1978, p. 104–114, maps, plates)

Changes along the coastline of Vene- zuela were caused by uplifting between the coast and the island of Paranaguana.

5230 Geigel Lope-Bello, Nelson. La defensa de la ciudad. Caracas: Equinoccio, 1979. 233 p.: bibl. (Colección Temas de urbanismo)

Review of city problems in Caracas, with attention to social and legal remedies.

5231 Hoyos, Jesús. El manglar y su eco- sistema (SCNLS/N, 67, sept. 1979, p. 7–14, bibl., plates)

Formation of mangrove swamps in Venezuela, with attention to animal and bird life supported by the four genera in that country.

5232 Jones, Richard D. Behavioral causes and consequences of rural-urban mi- gration: special reference to Venezuela (*in* Internal migration systems in the develop- ing world. Edited by Robert H. Thomas and John M. Hunter. Boston: G.K. Hall; Cam- bridge, Mass.: Schenkman Pub. Co., 1980, p. 26–50, bibl., ill., maps, tables)

Argues that the literature portrays mi- gration from rural areas into large cities as rational; however, he finds that living condi- tions may well be negative in cities and more positive for movement into resource frontiers.

5233 León, José-Balbino. Ecología y am- biente en Venezuela. Caracas: Editorial Ariel-Seix Barral Venezolana, 1981. 233 p.: bibl., ill. (Colección Geografía de Venezuela nueva; 2)

Highly original contribution to the study of environmental conditions with spe- cial reference to those in Venezuela and to atmospherics. Vol. 1 of 15 planned for a se- ries covering Venezuelan geography.

5234 Rojas, Temístocles. Geografía de la re- gión nororiental. Caracas: Editorial Ariel-Seix Barral Venezolana, 1981. 206 p.: bibl., ill. (Colección Geografía de Venezuela nueva; 8)

Geography of Venezuela's northeast with emphasis on physical regions. Includes some economic geography.

5235 Román, Benigno. Peces marinos de Venezuela. Ilustraciones de Giorgio Voltolina. Caracas: Sociedad de Ciencias Naturales la Salle, 1980. 408 p.: ill.

Catalogue of marine fish from the coast of Venezuela with scientific and popu- lar names and brief descriptions.

5236 Skoczek, Maria. La reforma agraria y las transformaciones de la agricultura en Colombia y Venezuela (PAN/ES, 4, 197, p. 181–203, maps)

Until 1970, Venezuela's agrarian re- form involved twice as much land as Colom- bia. Useful maps show colonization areas and discussion of results.

5237 Wilbert, Johannes. Geography and tel- luric lore of the Orinoco Delta (UCLA/ JLAL, 5:1, Summer 1979, p. 129–150, bibl., plates)

Discusses the moveable universe of the Warao Indians. Physical and abstract fea- tures characterize the geography of this universe.

5238 Santos, Milton. Société et espace transnationalisés dans le Venezuela actuel (UP/TM, 21:84, oct./déc. 1980, p. 709–720, tables)

Petroleum problems and more interest in scientific development of resources means that Third World countries such as Vene- zuela must make use of unoccupied territory.

5239 Segini, Isbelia *et al.* Algunos aspectos del conflicto urbano-rural: casos espe- cíficos en Venezuela (PAIGH/G, 91/92, enero/ dic. 1980, bibl., maps)

Recognizing the growth conflict between urban and rural segments of society as urban expansion proceeds more rapidly authors propose integrated network of settlements of varying functions with minimum disruption of agriculturally needed land.

BRAZIL

MARIO HIRAOKA, *Associate Professor, Millersville University of Pennsylvania*

GEOGRAPHIC RESEARCH ABOUT BRAZIL is as diverse as the multiple regions of the country, a trend noted in past volumes and corroborated by a review of the literature published in the past biennium. Nevertheless, certain topics such as population and agricultural changes, energy production, environmental imbalance, and urbanization command the interest of most researchers. Among regions, Amazônia outranks all others in the extent of coverage. In contrast, the South and Southeast, the country's leading agricultural, industrial, and demographic regions, where major transformations are occurring, receive scant attention, especially from foreign researchers.

Increasingly, topics with practical applications or concerned with specific problems command the attention of most geographers. Attempts to offer guidelines for solving many of the country's socioeconomic problems are evident in several studies. Some works express concern for the country's unevenly distributed and rapidly growing population (items **5260** and **5261**). Other studies examine the rising demand for energy and declining terms of trade which have led planners to search for alternate sources such as biomass and solar energy (item **5326**) with ethanol production receiving the most attention (items **5284** and **5309**). A number of stimulating topics treated from a variety of theoretical and methodological perspectives were the spatial concentration of industries, the population's unequal access to urban resources, the efficiency of transport networks, and the role of the state in organizing urban structures (items **5240, 5266, 5276, 5282, 5292, 5303, 5306, 5312, 5330–5331, 5345** and **5356**). The growing interest of agricultural geographers in applied research is exemplified by studies of sustained yield agricultural systems, ecologically-sound farming, and technologies appropriate for small farmers (items **5263, 5267, 5286–5287** and **5294**).

The growing awareness among scholars and the general public of the extent of environmental deterioration have led to a proliferation of ecological studies many of them analytical and based on sound principles (items **5311, 5334** and **5352**) and mostly focusing on Amazonian colonization zones. Hecht (item **5281**), and Smith (items **5342** and **5343**) offer some insights on changes in forest cover, edaphic base, fauna, and drainage systems.

Significant contributions to historical geography and climatology are included in this volume. Books by Taunay (item **5329**) and Magalhães (item **5301**) should be of interest to historical geographers. The former furthers understanding of colonial trade and transportation between São Paulo and Mato Grosso's gold mines, while the latter offers a synthesis of the expansion of colonial territories and settlement. The Portuguese edition of Bates' and Wallace's books (items **5247** and **5359**) on 19th-century Amazonian natural history will be of value to Brazilian students of the region. Nimer's volume on the climatology of Brazil (item **5319**) uses an expanded data base in order to provide a summary of diverse climates.

Amazônia's agro-mineral development continues to attract the attention of both specialists and laymen. Fascination with the region and concern with changes therein are evident in the flood of publications, as well as in the number of international meetings on the subject. For example, in Sept. 1979, a Conference on the Development of Amazônia in Seven Countries was held at Cambridge (item **5290**); in Feb. 1982, specialists gathered at the Univ. of Florida for: Conference on Frontier Expansion in Amazônia, and in July 1983, there will be in Belém an International Symposium on Amazônia. Topics range from ecological assessments (items **5259, 5274, 5278** and **5339**), socioeconomic evaluation of development activities (items **5277, 5288, 5316, 5321** and **5343**) to concern about the role of multinationals (items **5245, 5257** and **5275**). However, most of the research is restricted to the interfluvial areas where most activities have taken place in recent years. Studies of the riparian habitat, the traditional areas of human occupation, are still limited (items **5248, 5293** and **5342**).

A region of drought and poverty whose image has been exaggerated by politicians, the popular press and students of the area is the Northeast. Nevertheless, its history and culture continue to generate much writing and to stir further debate. Changes in the uses of land in the *agreste* are noted by Hiraoka and Yamamoto (item **5283**), while irrigation projects and water allocation schemes are evaluated by Pebayle (item **5325**), and Thèry (item **5350**). In contrast to the North and Northeast, there is considerably less research on the South, Southeast, and Center-West. However, recent agricultural development efforts in the *cerrado* are beginning to attract the attention of specialists to the Center-West region (items **5289** and **5333**).

5240 Abreu, Mauricio de Almeida. Contribuição ao estudo do papel do estado na evolução da estrutura urbana (IBGE/R, 43:4, out./dez. 1981, p. 577–585)

The concentration of income and urban resources in Brazil's metropolitan areas is a reflection of the country's present economic and political systems. The dominant factor, according to Abreu, is the state and its influence on the present imbalance in spatial organization.

5241 Adamo, Francesco. Il Nordeste brasiliano nel processo d'integrazione nazionale e internazionale (SGI/B, 9[10]:7/9, luglio/set. 1980, p. 257–289, tables)

Increasingly, Northeast Brazil's economic and spatial organization is bèing determined by international forces, through São Paulo's manufacturing interests. From a national perspective, it is evident that development plans for the Northeast are subordinated to the regional interests of the Southeast.

5242 Almeida, Valter Jesus de. Geomorfologia do estado do Acre (IBGE/R, 43:1, jan./março 1981, p. 87–97, bibl., plates, tables)

Concise description of Acre's landforms, a state divided into three physiographic regions: Amazon lowlands, Acre-

Javarí depression, and the low western-Amazonian plateau. Characteristics of each are mentioned.

5243 Alvim, Paulo de T. A perspective appraisal of perennial crops in the Amazon Basin (AI/I, 6:3, mayo/junio 1981, p. 139–145, bibl.)

Summary and assessment of perennial crop production in Amazônia. In addition to items like rubber, oil palm, cacao, and sugar cane, it is believed that little-known local perennials such as Brazil nut, *achiote, guaraná, pupunha, buriti,* and *copaíba* offer great potentials for cultivation in the region.

Anderson, Robin L. A government-directed frontier in the humid tropics: Pará, Brazil, 1870–1920. See *HLAS 44:3547.*

5244 Andrade, Manoel Correia de Oliveira. Recife: problemática de uma metrópole de região subdesenvolvida: pesquisa realizada no curso de mestrado em desenvolvimento urbano desta Universidade Federal de Pernambuco, sob o patrocínio da CNPU. Recife, Brazil: Universidade Federal de Pernambuco, Editora Universitária, 1979. 115 p., 7 fold. leaves of plates: bibl., maps.

Description of Recife that reconstructs the evolution of its urban area and explains main problems associated with its rapid growth.

5245 Arruda, Marcos. Daniel Ludwig e a exploração da Amazônia (Encontros com a Civilização Brasileira [Rio de Janeiro] 11, maio 1979, p. 35–56)

Uses Daniel K. Ludwig's Jarí Project in Amazônia to illustrate how multinationals exploit the resources of a Third World country.

5246 Barbiére, Evandro Biassi. O fato climático nos sistemas territoriais de recreação (IBGE/R, 43:2, abril/junio 1981, p. 145–265, bibl., ill., maps, plates)

Doctoral thesis examines climatic influences on leisure activities and recreational land uses in selected coastal resorts of Rio de Janeiro.

5247 Bates, Henry Walter. Um naturalista no Rio Amazonas. Tradução, Regina Regis Junqueira. Apresentação, Mário Guimarães Ferri. Belo Horizonte, Brazil, Livraria Itatiaia Editora; São Paulo: Editora da Universidade de São Paulo, 1979. 300 p., 1 folded leaf of plates: ill. (Coleção Reconquista do Brasil; v. 53)

Translation of unabridged English version originally published in 1876 and reprinted in 1975. Companion volume to Alfred Russel Wallace's book (see item **5359**), it provides a wealth of information on the flora, landforms, and people. Excellent sourcebook on 19th-century Amazon from river's estuary to Peruvian borders.

5248 Beretta, Pier Luigi. L'Isola di Marajó, Pará, Brasile (SGI/B, 10:9, ott./dic. 1980, p. 479–515, ill., maps, tables)

Outlines changing demographic and economic characteristics of Marajó-Island on the Amazon estuary. Also comments on the implementation and effects of Projeto Marajó, a socioeconomic development scheme.

5249 Berti, Pietro. Appunti per lo studio della jangada brasiliana (AISA/TA, 41, dic. 1980, p. 65–72, bibl., ill., plates)

Brief account of *jangadas* (i.e., Pernambuco sailing rafts) describes their structural characteristics and speculates on possible origins.

5250 Bibliografia sobre a baixada fluminense e Grande Rio (IBGE/R, 43:3, out./dez. 1981, p. 631–634)

Bibliography of 68 entries about metropolitan Rio de Janeiro and its surroundings focuses on urban-related topics.

5251 *Boletim Geográfico do Estado do Rio Grande do Sul.* Secretaria da Agricultura, Departamento de Comandos Mecanizados, Divisão de Geografia e Cartografia. Anos 22/25, Nos. 20/23, jan. 1977/julho 1980-Pôrto Alegre, Brazil.

Issue includes much selected geographic information (e.g., demographic data, urban characteristics, national security regions) but few interpretive articles.

5252 Botelho, Carlos de Castro; Edna Mascarenhas Sant'Anna; and Maria Helena Whately. Utilização de imagens orbitais no gerenciamento de bacias hidrográficas (IBGE/R, 42:2, abril/junho 1980, p. 382–401, bibl., plates)

Uses sample images from diverse ecological regions of the country in order to explain the value of LANDSAT images for interpreting physical and man-made changes on drainage basins.

5253 Braga, Robério. Benjamin Constant. Manaus, Brazil: Fundação Cultural do Amazonas: ICOTI, 1978. 54 p.: ill.

Synopsis of a border town along the Solimões River in western Amazon.

5254 Brooks, Reuben H. The adversity of Brazilian drought (Geojournal [Akademische-Verlagsgesellschaft, Wiesbaden, FRG] 6:2, 1982, p. 121–128)

Analyzes drought problems in Northeast Brazil in the context of four regional sub-units. Survey of drought perception and adjustments among residents indicates considerable variability according to socioeconomic group, age, sex, and marital status.

5255 Brown, Lester R. Food or fuel: new competition for the world's cropland (AI/I, 5:6, nov./dic. 1980, p. 365–372, bibl., tables)

Examines possible effects of cropland conversion for fuel production and postulates environmental and socioeconomic impacts of producing ethanol from sugarcane.

5256 Campos, Humberto de; Norberto A. Lavorenti; Luiz Sávio de Almeida; and Hamilton de Barros Soutinho. Estruturação de uma amostra de fornecedores de cana-de-açúcar das usinas do Estado de Alagoas (IAA/BA, 48[95/96]:6, junho 1980, p. 6–18, bibl., tables)

Brief study of *fornecedores* (i.e., Alagoas small-scale sugarcane suppliers) consists of preliminary inquiry into their role in the regional sugarcane industry.

5257 Campuzano, Joaquín Molano. As multinacionais na Amazônia (Encontros com a Civilização Brasileira [Rio de Janeiro] 11, maio 1979, p. 21–34, bibl., table)

Poorly conceived explanation of the role of multinationals in Amazônia.

5258 Casemiro, Alzira Magalhães. Cultivo do algodão no Nordeste (IBGE/R, 43:1, jan./março 1981, p. 133–135, plate)

Synopsis of cotton cultivation in Brazil, especially the Northeast.

5259 Castro, Martha Pimentel de. A complexidade da vegetação amazônica (IBGE/R, 43:2, abril/junho 1981, p. 283–300, bibl., ill., map, plates)

Classification and regionalization of plant communities in Amazônia.

5260 Costa, Manoel Augusto. Política demográfica para o Brasil (VOZES, 74:1, jan./fev. 1980, p. 5–24, bibl., tables)

Consists of proposals for demographic planning in Brazil based on past and present population dynamics. Three objectives are sought: a) to reduce spatial differences in mortality rates; b) to decrease birth rates; and c) to divert urbanward migrations to small and medium-sized cities.

5261 Costa, Rubens Vaz da. O censo de 1980 (ACSP/DE, 38:280, maio 1981, p. 21–33, graphs, maps)

Vignettes on population changes based on 1980 demographic census' preliminary results.

5262 Delson, Roberta. Land and urban planning: aspects of modernization in early nineteenth-century Brazil (UW/LBR, 16:2, Winter 1979, p. 191–214, maps)

Rebuttal of Oscar Yujnovsky's thesis that the urbanization process in Latin America occurred in the 1850–1930 period. Delson contends that the expansion and modernization of Brazilian cities began in the late colonial period. For historian's comment, see *HLAS 44:3485.*

5263 Denevan, William M. Swiddens and cattle versus forest: the imminent demise of the Amazon rainforest reexamined (*in* Where have all the flowers gone?: deforestation in the Third World. Williamsburg, Va.: Department of Anthropology, College of

William and Mary, 1981, p. 25–44 [Studies in Third World societies; publication no. 13]

Revised, updated, and expanded version of earlier essay about shifting cultivation. The most common type of land opening in Amazônia, it will affect cattle ranching and ultimately ecological stability.

5264 O Despovoamento do território amazônico: contribuições para a sua interpretação. Organizadores: Luc J.A. Mougeot e Luis E. Aragón. Belém, Brazil: Universidade Federal do Pará, 1981. 1 v. (Cadernos NAEA [Núcleo de Altos Estudos Amazônicos]; 6)

Collection of six essays analyzes migration processes and patterns of marginal and family farmers in Amazônia: Mougeot and Aragón explain major migration tendencies, while M. Serra Filho propose a theory of migration patterns in Amazônia. R. Wesche, C.H. Wood, and M. Schmink discuss characteristics of colonization in Rondônia, and along the Transamazon highways, respectively. Aragón describes mobility and occupational patterns among settlers of Northern Goiás, while in the last article, Mougeot proposes a model of migration processes along the settlement frontier.

5265 Duarte, Haidine da Silva Barros. Estrutura urbana do Estado do Rio de Janeiro: uma análise no tempo (IBGE/R, 43:4, out./dez. 1981, p. 477–560, bibl., maps, tables)

Historical-structural analysis of urbanization in Rio de Janeiro notes causes of its increasing hegemony.

5266 Enders, Wayne T. Regional disparities in industrial growth in Brazil (CU/EG, 56:4, Oct. 1980, p. 300–310, tables)

Attempts to explain spatial patterns of industries in Brazil as well as regional disparities in industrial growth by using growth method components.

5267 Fearnside, Philip M. Deforestation in the Brazilian Amazon: how fast is it occurring? (AI/I, 7:2, marzo/abril 1982, p. 82–88, map, tables)

Assesses rate and magnitude of rainforest clearing in Amazônia. Trends indicate that deforestation is occurring at an exponential rate and that process is spatially concentrated in places like Acre, Rondônia, Southern Pará, Western Maranhão, Northern Goiás, and Northern Mato Grosso. Considers clearings in Rondônia, where deforestation rates are monitored, as examples of pace at which rainforest is disappearing.

5268 ———. The development of the Amazon rainforest: priority problems for the formulation of guidelines (AI/I, 4:6, nov./dic. 1979, p. 338–342)

Identifies research priority areas in order to formulate development guidelines for Amazônia. Six rather vague ones are presented.

5269 **Fernandes, Liliana Laganá.** Introdução a um estudo geográfico de bairros rurais em São Paulo (AGB/BPG, 55, nov. 1978, p. 31–46, bibl., map)

Essay on genesis and evolution of rural *bairros*, one of rural Brazil's basic socio-spatial units.

5270 **Ferrarini, Sebastião Antônio.** Transertanismo: sofrimento e miséria do nordestino na Amazônia. Diagramação, Valdecir Mello. Petrópolis, Brazil: Editora Vozes, 1979. 94 p., 2 leaves of plates: bibl., ill.

Impressionistic discussion of life among the rubber gatherers of Western Amazônia.

5271 **Ferreira, Manoel Rodrigues.** A ferrovia do diabo: história de uma estrada de ferro na Amazônia. São Paulo: Melhoramentos, 1981. 400 p.: ill.

Interesting and well-written account of the new defunct Madeira-Mamoré Railroad. Journalist author describes historical circumstances leading to construction, engineering problems, economic failure, and demise of the short-lived railroad. Book should be of value to travelers, as well as Amazônia specialists.

5272 **Ferri, Mário Guimarães.** Vegetação brasileira. Belo Horizonte, Brazil: Editora Itatiaia, 1980. 157 p., 12 leaves of plates: col. ill. (Coleção Reconquista do Brasil; v. 26)

Pt. 1 explains principal Brazilian plant formations; pt. 2 presents ecological questions such as the influences of man and fire on vegetation.

5273 **Filgueiras, Tarciso S.** O fogo como agente ecológico (IBGE/R, 43:3, julho/set. 1981, p. 399–404, bibl., plates)

Brief review of fire as agent of ecological changes in Brazil. Stresses need for better understanding and use of fire as a tool in agriculture.

5274 *Garden.* Garden Society. Vol. 6, No. 1, Jan./Feb. 1982- . New York.

Special issue devoted to current concerns about Amazonia discusses five topics in non-technical language: 1) rainforest; 2) soil; 3) natives; 4) agricultural activities; and 5) attempts at controlling ecological damages.

5275 **Garrido Filha, Irene Braga de Miguez.** O Projeto Jari e os capitais estrangeiros na Amazônia. 2. ed. Petrópolis, Brazil: Editora Vozes, 1980. 98 p.: ill.

Informative monograph discusses two Amazonian subjects of current concern: Jarí Project and multinationals.

5276 **Geiger, Pedro Pinchas** *et al.* Questões da concentração geográfica dos estabelecimentos industriais (IBGE/R, 42:2, abril/junho 1980, p. 310–331, bibl., maps, tables)

Notes government planners' increasing concern with spatial concentration of industries in Brazil. Explains dynamics of industrial location by using 1960 and 1970 censuses.

5277 **Godfrey, Brian J.** Xingu Junction: rural migration and land conflict in the Brazilian Amazon (PCCLAS/P, 9, 1982, p. 71–81, map, tables)

Describes rural migration and land conflicts in Xinguará, frontier community in Southeast Pará. Illustrates by case study the pattern of edaphic base deterioration and farm size changes, a pan-Amazônian phenomenon.

5278 **Goulding, Michael.** The fishes and the forest: explorations in Amazônian natural history. Berkeley: University of California Press, 1980. 280 p.: bibl., ill., index.

Author's purpose is the "study of the ecosystemic role of the flooded forests in nourishing fishes and the effects of river-level fluctuations on the food supply and local migrations of fishes" (p. 2). Findings indicate that Amazon fauna is dependent on flood forests for food and protection, and that large scale deforestation of this ecological zone may have detrimental effects on the fauna and to people who depend on it.

5279 **Guimarães, Laís de Barros Monteiro.** Bairro de Chá-novo centro de São Paulo (AM/R, 42:192, jan./dez. 1979, p. 237–298, bibl., ill., maps)

Describes changes in urban patterns of

city of São Paulo. Focuses on urban expansions that occurred in late 19th century.

5280 Haller, Archibald O. A socioeconomic regionalization of Brazil (AGS/GR, 72:4, Oct. 1982, p. 450–464)

Numerous regionalization attempts have been tried in Brazil, each with varying degrees of success. Author proposes a new macroregional delineation based on socio-economic and demographic data compiled at the microregional level.

5281 Hecht, Susanna B. Deforestation in the Amazon Basin: magnitude, dynamics, and soil resource effects (*in* Where have all the flowers gone?: deforestation in the Third World. Williamsburg, Va.: Department of Anthropology, College of William and Mary, 1981, p. 61–108 [Studies in Third World societies; publication no. 13]

Summarizes Amazônian ecosystems, magnitude of forestation, and effects of forest clearing on agricultural activities.

5282 Hicks, James F., Jr. and **Sérgio Seelenberger.** Metodologia para a identificação de sistemas, problemas e diretrizes de transporte metropolitano: uma aplicação na Região Metropolitana do Rio de Janeiro (IBGE/R, 43:4, out./dez. 1981, p. 561-576, maps, tables)

Offers methodology for classifying metropolitan transportation systems. Believes approach identifies functional, operational, and spatial constraints of transportation systems.

5283 Hiraoka, Mario and **Shozo Yamamoto.** Changing agricultural land use in the Agreste of Northeast Brazil (Latin American Studies [University of Tsukuba, Special Research Project on Latin America, Sakura Mura, Japan] 2, 1981, unpaged)

Rural land uses are changing rapidly in the Agreste of Northeast Brazil. Authors point to labor legislation, improved transport and communication, urbanward migrations, and conversion of land to cattle ranches as agents responsible for the current changes.

5284 Holanda, Arylo Aguiar. O crédito e o desenvolvimento de fontes renováveis de energia (BNB/REN, 11:3, julho/set. 1980, p. 355–380)

Brief evaluation of the National Alcohol Program. After description of national energy policies, outlines local and technological peculiarities of alcohol production.

5285 Ichikawa, Tadao. Cattle production in Brazil (Latin American Studies [University of Tsukuba, Special Research Project on Latin America, Sakura Mura, Japan] 7, 1983, p. 189–212)

Informative essay on economic and status of cattle raising activities.

5286 Johnson, Dennis. Zoneamento agroclimatológico do milho e do sorgo granífero no Nordeste do Brasil (BNB/REN, 11:3, julho/set. 1980, p. 461-470, maps, tables)

Integration of crops with appropriate agroclimatic zones is accepted as a strategy to increase agricultural productivity with minimum investments. Replacement of maize by grain sorghum may increase the output in the marginal lands of the Northeast.

5287 Kageyama, A.A. and **J.F. Graziano da Silva.** A propósito da expansão da agricultura paulista (AGB/BPG, 56, março 1979, p. 29–59, bibl., ill., table)

Debates expansion of capitalist farming outward from São Paulo and its effects on the agrarian structure of the region (e.g., land tenure) and land use changes.

5288 Ketteringham, William. Amazonian roads and the Brazilian economic miracle (PCCLAS/P, 6, 1977/79, p. 119–137, maps, tables)

Assesses highway construction and colonization programs in Amazônia and analyzes demographic and economic impacts along the Belém-Brasília and Transamazon highways.

5289 Kuhlmann, Edgar and **Zélia Lopes da Silva.** Subsídios aos estudos da problemática do cerrado (IBGE/R, 42:2, abril/junho 1980, p. 361–381, bibl., plates)

Although one-fifth of Brazil is covered by a vegetation formation named *cerrado*, a number of questions about it remains unanswered. Authors discuss four topics on the bases of existing data and their field experiences: a) relationship between soil fertility and phytophysiognomy; b) xerophytic nature of vegetation; c) consequences of repeated burnings; and d) *cerrado* enclaves.

5290 Land, people and planning in contemporary Amazônia. Francoise Barbira-

Scazzocchio, editor. Cambridge: Cambridge University, 1980. 1 v. (Center of Latin American Studies occasional publication; no. 3)

Volume includes 35 papers revised from the originals presented at the "Conference on the Development of Amazônia in Seven Countries," held Sept. 1979, in Cambridge, England. Papers are loosely grouped as follows: 1) ecological impact of developments; 2) colonization activities; and 3) effects of land openings and settlement on aboriginal inhabitants.

5291 *Latin American Studies*. University of Tsukuba, Special Research Project on Latin America. v. 4, 1982- . Sakura Mura, Japan.

Issue consists of six papers, originally presented as part of a Symposium on the Environment and Society in Brazil, at University of Tsukuba, Nov. 1980: Mutsuo Yamada "Settlement and Economic Development in Northeast Brazil;" Kiichi Hanada and Keisaburo Oda "Crop Prduction in Northeast Brazil;" Eiji Matsumoto "Changes of Soil Properties through Agricultural and Pastoral Land Uses in Northeast Brazil;" Ichiroku Hayashi "Changing Aspects of the Caatinga Vegetation by Agricultural Land Uses in Northeast Brazil;" Takashi Fukuchi "Economic Development of Brazil and the Nordeste Problem;" and Takashi Maeyama "Identity and Strategy of the Japanese in Brazil."

5292 Lima, Maria Helena Beozzo de. Condições de habitação da população de baixa renda da região metropolitana do Rio de Janeiro (IBGE/R, 43 : 4, out./dez. 1981, p. 605–629, tables)

Presents residential characteristics of low income population, based on 1970 data. Explains housing strategies of the poor, and impact of government policies on housing.

5293 Lobato, Eládio. Caminho de Canoa Pequena. Belém, Brazil: Gráfica Falangola Editora, 1976. 134 p., 1 leaf of plates: ill (some col.)

History of the município of Igarapé-Mirí, an estuarine community, located near the mouth of Rio Tocantines in Pará.

5294 Lombardi, Antonio Cláudio *et al.* Agricultura energética e produção de alimentos: avaliação preliminar da experimentação da cana-de-açúcar rotacionada con milho,

feijão, amendoim, arroz e soja no estado de São Paulo (IAA/BA, 50[1]:99, jan. 1982, p. 29–44, bibl., tables)

Discusses productivity, output, and financial results of cultivating food crops like maize, beans, peanuts, rice, and soybeans in rotation with sugarcane in selected locations of São Paulo. There are increasing attempts to produce food items in traditional plantation regions, either in association with plantation crops or in the fields after harvests of plantation crops.

5295 Loureiro, Antonio José Souto. Amazônia: 10,000 anos. Manaus, Brazil: Editoria Metro Cúbico, 1982. 206 p.: bibl., ill.

Summary of human activities of Amazônia since pre-historic times is too general and unsubstantiated to be of use to serious students.

5296 Loureiro, Maria Amélia Salgado. A cidade e as áreas verdes. Ilustrações, Emilia Fernandes Caldas Moroni. São Paulo: Prefeitura do Município de São Paulo, Secretaria de Serviços e Obras, Departamento de Parques e Areas Verdes, 1979. 185 p.: bibl., ill.

Describes origin and evolution of green spaces in urban São Paulo.

5297 McConnell, Anita. Sojourn in the Brazilian Pantanal (GM, 53:1, Oct. 1980, p. 63–65, ill.)

Consists of traveler's impression of the *pantanal* in southwest Mato Grosso.

5298 Machado, Nonnato. A multiplicação dos peixes será possível? (Interior [Ministério do Interior, Brasília] 6 : 31, março/abril 1980, p. 22–27, plates, table)

Outlines activities conducted by São Francisco Valley Development Corporation (CODEVASF) to increase aquatic fauna in São Francisco River, especially portions affected by construction of Tres Marias and Sobradinho reservoirs.

5299 Maeyama, Takashi. Religion, kinship, and the middle classes of the Japanese in urban Brazil (Latin American Studies [University of Tsukuba, Special Research Project on Latin America, Sakura Mura, Japan] 5, 1983, p. 57–82)

Discusses role of religion among the Japanese urban middle class in Brazil.

5300 ——— and **R.J. Smith.** Otomo: a Japanese new religion in Brazil (Latin American Studies [University of Tsukuba, Special Research Project on Latin America, Sakura Mura, Japan] 5, 1983, p. 83–102)

Account of origin and diffusion of a "New Religion" of Japan in Brazil.

5301 Magalhães, Basílio de. Expansão geográfica do Brasil colonial. 4. ed. São Paulo: Companhia Editora Nacional, 1978. 348 p.: bibl. (Brasiliana; v. 45)

Originally published in 1915, and expanded in subsequent editions, book offers information basic to understanding territorial expansion and settlement during the colonial period. Based on sound documentation, Magalhães carefully reconstructs processes of frontier expansion and identifies distinctive economic cycles associated with them.

5302 Marques, Manuel Eufrazio de Azevedo. Apontamentos históricos, geográficos, biográficos, estatísticos e noticiosos da Província de São Paulo seguidos da cronologia dos acontecimentos mais notáveis desde a fundação da Capitania de São Vicente até o ano de 1876. Publicados por deliberação do Instituto Histórico e Geográfico Brasileiro. Capa, Cláudio Martins. Belo Horizonte, Brazil: Editora Itatiaia; São Paulo: Editora da Universidade de São Paulo, 1980. 2 v.: bibl., ill. (Coleção Reconquista do Brasil; nova série, v. 3–4)

Alphabetical listing of São Paulo Province's historical, biographical, and statistical data prior to 1876. Volumes may be of assistant to those interested in the historical reconstruction of landscapes in southern Brazil.

5303 Marques, Moacyr. A estruturação da rede viária terrestre de São Paulo (ABG/BPG, 55, nov. 1978, p. 47–73, bibl., graphs, map)

Reviews overland transport network developments in state of São Paulo. Existing asymmetric radial pattern evolved in response to distinctive economic cycles. Evaluates social and economic costs of existing rail and highway networks.

Martinière, Guy. Les stratégies frontalières du Brésil colonial et l'Amérique Espagnole. See *HLAS 44: 1770.*

5304 Matsumoto, Eiji. A note on the tabuleiros in the coastal region of the Brazilian Northeast (Latin American Studies [University of Tsukuba, Special Research Project on Latin America, Sakura Mura, Japan] 6, 1983, p. 1–13)

Describes possible origins of level uplands in coastal Northeast, locally called *tabuleiro.* Two geomorphic surfaces characterize the tabuleiros: a higher one formed by the pediplanation process similar to those of the interior, and a lower one resulting from deposition.

5305 Mattos, Raymundo José da Cunha. Corografia histórica da Província de Minas Gerais, 1837. Colaboração com o I.H.G.B. Introd. e notas de Tarquínio J.B. de Oliveira. Belo Horizonte, Brazil: Arquivo Público Mineiro, 1979. 1 v. (416 p.): tables (Publicações do Archivo Público Mineiro; no. 3)

Vol. 1 of three, book is based on a 1837 manuscript that provides valuable data on man-environment relations in late colonial Minas Gerais. This volume is limited to descriptions of administrative districts and biophysical characteristics.

5306 Matznetter, Josef. O sistema urbano no Norte e Nordeste do Brasil e a influência das novas estradas (IBGE/R, 43:1, jan./março 1981, p. 99–122, bibl., map, tables)

Describes results of experiment applying central place theory to service centers in Northern and Northeast Brazil.

5307 Mello, José Carlos. Planejamento dos transportes urbanos. Pref., Josef Barat. Rio de Janeiro: Editora Camus, 1981. 261 p.: ill. (Contribuições em desenvolvimento urbano; 3)

Useful reference book on Brazilian metropolitan transport systems, planning, and characteristics.

5308 Menezes, Mário Assis. O atual estágio de conhecimento sobre os recursos ais da Amazônia: pressuposto para definição de uma política de ocupação (*in* Encontro Nacional Estudos Populacionais, 2nd, Aguas de São Pedro, Brazil, 1980. Anais. São Paulo: Associação Brasileira de Estudos Populacionais, 1981, v. 1, p. 11–80, maps, tables)

Based on current knowledge of Amazônia's ecosystems, offers plans for environmentally-compatible occupation of the region.

5309 Menezes, Tobias José Barretto de.
Etanol, o combustível do Brasil. São Paulo: Editora Agronômica Ceres, 1980. 233 p.: bibl., ill. (Edições Ceres; 24)
Reference book on the Brazilian ethanol program notes raw materials, production processes, and prospects in Brazil. Of special value to those interested in technical aspects of ethanol as an alternate energy source.

5310 Mertins, Gunter. Determinanten, Umfang und Formen der Migration Nordostbrasiliens (GR, 34:8, Aug. 1982, p. 352–358, maps, tables)
Summary of migration patterns in Northeast Brazil.

5311 Miranda, Cláudio da Rocha. Economia e meio ambiente: uma abordagem de insumoproduto (IPEA/PPE, 10:2, agôsto 1980, p. 601–626, charts, maps, tables)
Continued concentration of manufacturing activities in Paraíba do Sul Valley, São Paulo state, poses a major threat to the inhabitants of downstream communities, including Rio de Janeiro, who utilize the water for drinking purposes.

5312 Miranda, Maria Helena Palhares de. Crescimento periférico da cidade do Rio de Janeiro: padrões espaciais da ocupação residencial (IBGE/R, 42:2, abril/junho 1980, p. 265–309, bibl., maps, tables)
Scrutinizes urban expansion of metropolitan Rio de Janeiro. Examines spatial pattern of residential growth in Rio's western suburbs using the Poisson and negative binominal distribution methods.

5313 Miranda Neto, Manoel José de. O dilema da Amazônia. Apresentação, Arthur Cezar Ferreira Reis. Petrópolis, Brazil: Editora Vozes, 1979. 230 p.: bibl.
Account of human settlements in Amazônia, with comments on current developments.

5314 Monteiro, Carlos Augusto de Figueiredo. A geografia no Brasil, 1934–1977: avaliação e tendências. São Paulo: Universidade de São Paulo, Instituto de Geografia, 1980. 155 p.: bibl., ill. (Série Teses e monografias; no. 37)
Reviews geography as an academic discipline in Brazil since 1934 according to three topics: a) evolution of the field; b) its attributes and limitations; and c) evaluation of geography as a discipline.

5315 Morán, Emilio F. Ecological, anthropological, and agronomic research in the Amazon Basin (LARR, 17:1, 1982, p. 3–41, bibl., maps)
Well-documented review of current state of knowledge of Amazônia. Examines topics such as rainforest ecology, forest productivity and traditional exploitation techniques, and present-day development activities.

5316 ———. Developing the Amazon. Bloomington: Indiana University Press, 1981. 292 p.: bibl., ill., index.
After a decade of large-scale family farming on Amazônia's terra firma, substantive findings are beginning to emerge. Unlike early studies that were pessimistic about officially-sponsored colonization programs, Moran argues that some planned projects did succeed but that their official support may have been withdrawn prematurely.

5317 Moura, Paulo Cursino de. São Paulo de outrora: evocações da metrópole. Belo Horizonte, Brazil: Editora Itatiaia; São Paulo: Editora da Universidade de São Paulo, 1980. 306 p.: bibl., ill. (Coleção Reconquista do Brasil; nova série, vol. 25)
Chronicle of urban São Paulo includes interesting vignettes on the origins of major districts and streets.

5318 Nickson, Andrew. Brazilian colonization of the eastern border region of Paraguay (in State and region in Latin America: a workshop. G.A. Banck, R. Buve, and L. Van Vroonhoven, editors. Amsterdam: Centrum voor Studie en Documetatie van Latijns-Amerika, 1981, p. 201–229, bibl., tables [CEDLA incedentele publicaties; 17]
Paraguay's eastern border region is rapidly being developed by Brazilian farmers from Paraná. Much of the land has been allocated to large Brazilian operators who practice commercial farming similar to that of Paraná. Attributes land allocation and creation of a minifundia class among Paraguayan farmers to Instituto de Bienestar Rural policies.

5319 Nimer, Edmon. Climatologia do Brasil. Rio de Janeiro: Secretaria de Planejamento da Presidência da República, Fundação Instituto Brasileiro de Geografia e Estatística, Directoria Técnica, Superintendência de Recursos Naturais e Meio Ambiente, 1979. 421 p., 8 fold. leaves of plates:

bibl., ill. (some col.) (Série Recursos naturais e meio ambiente; no. 4)

Uses principles of dynamic climatology which emphasize air mass analysis in order to interpret Brazil's climatic regions. Presents atmospheric circulation and precipitation characteristics of selected areas prior to discussing each climatic region.

5320 Nishizawa, Toshie and José Arnaldo Sales. The urban temperature in Rio de Janeiro, Brazil (Latin American Studies [University of Tsukuba, Special Research Project on Latin America, Sakura Mura, Japan] 5, 1983, p. 29–38)

Contribution to the study of a tropical city's urban climatology. Briefly discusses urban temperature differences, resulting from environmental peculiarities and pollutant concentration.

5321 Norgaard, Richard B. Desenvolvimento agrícola e transformação ambiental na terra firme amazônica (SBPC/CC, 33:1, jan. 1981, p. 48–56, bibl.)

Agricultural development attempts on Amazônia's terra firma has failed economically and ecologically. Uses two conceptual perspectives (eco-technological and center-periphery) to explain farming failure and argues that a third (neoclassical economic) offers a better understanding of the problem.

5322 Palheta, Iraci Gomes de Vasconcelos. O uso da terra em Tauá-Vigia, Estado de Pará. São Paulo: Universidade de São Paulo, Instituto de Geografia, 1980. 1 v.: bibl. (Série Teses e monografias; no. 38)

Doctoral dissertation concerns agricultural land use changes in one of Amazônia's oldest areas of settlement (i.e., Pará's Northeast).

5323 Pandolfo, Clara. Uma política florestal para a Amazônia brasileira (Interior [Ministério do Interior, Brasília] 7:36, jan./ fev. 1981, p. 32–33, map)

Outlines Amazonian forestry policy.

5324 Paschoal, Adilson D. Pragas, praguicidas e a crise ambiental: problemas e soluções. Rio de Janeiro: Instituto de Documentação, Editora da Fundação Getúlio Vargas, 1979. 102 p.: bibl., index.

Ecologist's view of the use and abuse of pesticides in Brazil.

5325 Pebayle, Raymond. L'irrigation dans le Nordeste du Brésil (FDD/NED [Pro-

blèmes d'Amérique Latine, 59] 4609/4610, 10 mars 1981, p. 84–109, graphs, maps, tables)

Evaluates semi-arid Northeast's irrigation projects and presents case studies of several irrigated areas. Reviews drought-related government programs.

5326 Pereira, Armand F. and Seymour Warkov. Energy for development in semi-arid areas of Northeastern Brazil (AI/I, 4:5, sept./oct. 1979, p. 272–281)

Reports work on progress concerning alternate energy system, primarily solar and biomass sources. Notes relevance of non-conventional energy sources in rural developments, especially Brazil's Northeast.

5327 Plantas ensinam Nordeste a tirar vantagem da aridez: cientistas e técnicos se voltam para a agricultura que convive com a dureza do clima (Interior [Ministério do Interior, Brasília] 7:39, julho/agôsto 1981, p. 30–33, plates)

Brief description of the role xerophytic plants play in the life of rural *nordestinos*.

5328 Puhl, José. Os loteamentos rurais (PUC/V, 26:104, dez. 1981, p. 503–510)

Rio Grande do Sul's food demands, especially for diary products and vegetables, have increased as a result of rapid rural-to-urban migrations. In order to meet the challenge, proposed that the state enact major land use changes along the von Thünen model.

5329 Relatos monçoeiros. Introdução, coletânea e notas de Afonso de E. Taunay. Belo Horizonte, Brazil: Editora Itatiaia; São Paulo: Editora da Universidade de São Paulo, 1981. 292 p.: ill. (Coleção Reconquista do Brasil; v. 33)

Collection of essays on the *monções* riparian expeditions carried out between São Paulo and Mato Grosso during the 18th and 19th centuries. Useful book for historical geographers interested in reconstructing colonial transport and trade networks.

Rendón, José Arouche de Toledo. Obras. See *HLAS 44:3531.*

5330 Ribeiro, Miguel Angelo Campos and Roberto Schmidt de Almeida. Padrões de localização espacial e estrutura de fluxos dos estabelecimentos industriais da área metropolitana de Recife (IBGE/R, 42:2, abril/junho 1980, p. 203–264, bibl., maps, tables)

Analyzes location patterns and linkages among Recife's industries. In the late 1940s, a decentralization process began with modern industries, based in Southeast Brazil, building plants in Recife's outskirts.

5331 Rocha, Sônia. Evolução das indústrias de transformação de Pernambuco entre 1970 e 1974 (IBGE/R, 42:1, jan./março 1980, p. 52–78, bibl., tables)

Despite government programs and policies aimed at developing the Northeast's economy, the region's share of national wealth continues to decline. Analyzes Pernambuco's industrial sector in order to interpret its lack of dynamism.

5332 Romeiro, Adhemar Ribeiro and Fernando José Abrantes. Meio ambiente e modernização agrícola (IBGE/R, 43:1, jan./março 1981, p. 3–45, plates, tables)

Attributes the accelerated deterioration of the environment to modernization of farming practices begun after the 1960s. State agricultural credit policies which forced farmers to increase productivity exacerbated ecological problems such as soil erosion and chemical pollution.

5333 Ronick, Volker. Polocentro: Brasiliens Entwicklungsprogramm für die Region der *Cerrados* (GR, 34:8, Aug. 1982, p. 360–366, maps, tables)

Abbreviated explanation of the Polocentro, a program designed to develop Central Brazil's *cerrados* region.

5334 Rosa, Sidney Augusto Gonçalves and Joaquim Caetano de A. Júnior. Uso racional e integrado dos recursos hídricos da bacia do Rio das Velhas (IBGE/R, 42:2, abril/junho 1980, p. 332–358, maps, tables)

Water quality analysis of the Rio das Velhas, Minas Gerais, is highly polluted, with drainage areas of heavy mining and rapid urban growth. Assesses causes of its deteriorating water quality and consequences on the drainage basin.

Roteiros e notícias de São Paulo colonial, 1751–1804. See *HLAS 44:3534.*

Salles, Francisco José Monteiro. Joaquim Corrêa de Mello, sua vida e sua obra. See *HLAS 44:3628.*

5335 Salles, Waldemar Batista de. O Amazônas: o meio físico e suas riquezas naturais. 3. ed. Manáus, Brazil: Impr. Oficial do Estado do Amazônas, between 1977 and 1980. 261 p.: ill.

Valuable compilation of information on the Brazilian Amazon for those seeking a general knowledge of the region.

5336 Sant'Anna, Edna Mascarenhas and Maria Helena Whately. Distribuição dos manguezais do Brasil (IBGE/R, 43:1, jan./março 1981, p. 47–63, bibl., plates, tables)

Brief essay on mangrove distribution in Brazil. Provides locational and floral characteristics of the mangrove but lacks the maps to show its distribution.

5337 Schacht, Siegfried von. Agrarkolonisation in der Zona da Mata Nordostbrasiliens am biespiel der Kolonie Pindorama (GZ, 68:1, 1980, p. 54–76, ill., maps, tables)

Analysis of colonization project in Zona da Mata, Alagoas. Field work reveals how difficult is the successful development of colonization projects, even in a country with long experiences in such activities.

5338 Secas: a mesma idade da história do Brasil; no seu terceiro ano consecutivo de falta de chuvas o Nordeste enfrente o 72° período do estiagem desde que recebeu a visita de Cabral (Interior [Ministério do Interior, Brasília] 7:39, julho/agôsto 1981, p. 24–29, plates)

Short, informative article on drought history of Northeast Brazil contains information on folklore of drought prediction.

5339 Seiler-Baldinger, Annemarie. Boundaries, peoples, and the cultural landscape on the Upper Amazon (Regio Brasiliensis [Geographisch-Ethnologische Gesellschaft, Basel, Switzerland] 2/3, 1981, p. 277–290)

Well documented, perceptive explanation of demographic and cultural changes that are happening on the western Amazon's tripartite frontier region of Brazil that borders on Colombia and Peru.

5340 Shaw, James H. and Tracey S. Carter. Giant anteaters (AMNR/NH, 1980, p. 62–67, plates)

Short explanation of the giant South American anteater emphasizes specimens found in Serra da Canastra.

5341 Silva, Solange Tietzmann. Os estudos de classificação na agricultura: uma revisão (IBGE/R, 42:1, jan./março 1980, p. 3–30, bibl.)

Reviews agricultural regionalization methodologies that are used in Brazil.

5342 Smith, Nigel J.H. Man, fishes, and the Amazon. New York: Columbia University Press, 1981. 180 p.: bibl., index.

Study of fisheries in Itacoatiara, an Amazon River town, downstream from Manáus. Presents fishing methods, output, biotopes, and species. Also discusses cultural traits associated with fishing, such as folklore, taboos, and food preparation techniques.

5343 ———. Rainforest corridors: the Transamazon colonization scheme. Berkeley: University of California Press, 1982. 1 v.: bibl., index.

Evaluates planned colonization carried out along the Transamazon Highway. Attributes failure of official projects to a lack of understanding among planners of the diversity of Amazônian habitats and their influence on both human and agricultural commodities.

5344 Soro, Yassoungo. O café em São Paulo e na Costa do Marfim: um estudo comparativo. São Paulo: Universidade de São Paulo, Instituto de Geografia, 1978. 152 p., 2 folded leaves of plates: bibl., ill. (Série Teses e monografias; no. 33)

Comparative study of coffee farming in São Paulo and the Ivory Coast. Describes and analyzes contrasts between both regions (e.g., environment, historical and cultural variables, technological levels, and agrarian landscapes).

Sternberg, Hilgard O'Reilly. Frontières contemporaines en Amazonie brésilienne: quelques consequences sur l'environment. See *HLAS 44:1679.*

5345 Strauch, Lourdes Manhães de Mattos. Educação e comportamento espacial (IBGE/R, 42:1, jan./março 1980, p. 31–51, bibl.)

Study of the role of space in the diffusion and differentiaton of educational opportunities is based on the commuting pattern of students at Campos, Rio de Janeiro state.

5346 Tadokoro, Kiyokatsu. Os factores geográficos na literatura do Nordeste Brasileiro (*in* Colóquio de Estudos Luso-Brasileiros, XIII, Tóquio, 1979. Anais. Tóquio: Associação Japonesa de Estudos Luso-Brasileiros, 1979, p. 12–33, bibl., maps)

The literature of Northeast Brazil strongly reflects regional geographical characteristics. Argues that local literature provides much insight into both man and land.

5347 Takahashi, Nobuo and **Nelson M. Yoshikae.** Structure de l'éspace financier au Brésil (Latin American Studies [Tsukuba University, Special Research Project on Latin America, Sakura Mura, Japan] 7, 1983, p. 77–102)

Studies origins and effects of spatial concentration of financial institutions in Southeast Brazil.

5348 Tavares, Paulo. A situação açucareira do Brasil (IAA/BA, 48[95/96]:6, junho 1980, p. 65–71, bibl., ill., tables)

Summary of sugarcane production. Unfortunately, data does not establish regional differences between sugar and alcohol output.

5349 Théry, Hervé. Routes transamazoniennes et réorganisation de l'éspace: le cas de Rondônia (SGB/COM, 133/134, jan./mars 1981, p. 5–22, maps)

In the last two decades highways were extended into Amazónia in order to integrate it with the rest of the country. Process is illustrated by colonization activities along the Cuibá-Pôrto Velho highway where a new spatial organization has emerged. It closely reflects the needs and plans of Brazil's Center-South region.

5350 ———. O Vale do São Francisco: uma região subdesenvolvida e sua valorização (SBPC/CC, 32:8, agôsto 1980, p. 1010–1027, maps, tables)

Reviews planned development activities in the São Francisco River Valley. Expresses concern about how increasing demands for hydroelectric energy and farming irrigation have intensified competition for water use.

5351 Tigner, James L. Japanese settlement in eastern Bolivia and Brazil (SAGE/JIAS, 24:4, Nov. 1982, p. 496–517, tables)

Well written review essay discusses immigration and agricultural settlement of Japanese in Bolivia and Brazil.

5352 Tundisi, J.G. Ecologia aquática no Brasil: problemas e perspectivas (AI/I, 5:6, nov./dic. 1980, p. 373–379, bibl., ill., maps, tables)

Reviews status of Brazilian aquatic ecological studies. Discusses problems and prospects of interior and coastal water studies. Proposes outline for an aquatic ecology program.

5353 Une, Michiko Y. An analysis of the effects of frosts on the principal coffee areas of Brazil [Geojournal [Akademische Verlagsgesellschaft, Wiesbaden, FRG] 6:2, 1982, p. 19–140]

Brazilian coffee regions have undergone major changes in farm size, land and labor use, and cultivation practices. Outlines effects of frosts on these new agricultural patterns.

5354 Vanin, V.R.; G.M.G. Graça; and J. Goldemberg. Padrões de consumo de energia: Brasil 1970 (SBPC/CC, 33:4, abril 1981, p. 477–486, bibl., graphs)

Analyzes household energy consumption patterns according to income levels.

5355 Vasco Neto. Problemas das secas do Nordeste (Política [Fundação Milton Campos, Brasília] 14/15, out. 1979/março 1980, p. 75–92, ill., tables)

Politician's view of western Bahia's drought problems includes brief review of implemented public works projects and an appeal for plans that would guarantee an adequate water supply for the region.

5356 Vetter, David Michael. A segregação residencial da população economicamente ativa na região metropolitana do Rio de Janeiro: segundo grupos de rendimento mensal (IBGE/R, 43:4, out./dez. 1981, p. 587–603, bibl., tables)

Analyzes Rio de Janeiro's residential spatial segregation according to income level. Hypothesizes that land use patterns can be explained in terms of a center-periphery model. Findings suggest, however, that nuclei and peripheries are often the result of a greater than assumed variety of urban structures.

5357 ——— et al. A apropriação dos benefícios das açãos do Estado em áreas urbanas: seus determinantes e análise através de ecologia fatorial (IBGE/R, 43:4, out./dez. 1981, p. 457–476, bibl., map, tables)

The state's expanding role in urban areas has led to increasing politization in the allocation of resources. Uses a factorial ecology technique to demonstrate who benefits from the state's intervention in urban affairs.

5358 Walde, D.H.G.; E. Gierth; and O.H. Leonardos. Stratigraphy and mineralogy of the manganese ores of Urucum, Mato Grosso, Brazil (GR, 70:3, 1981, p. 1077–1085, bibl., ill., maps)

Presents preliminary findings of geological mapping and microscopic studies of iron and manganese deposits at Urucum, western Mato Grosso. It is believed that these mineral deposits are younger than most banded iron formations of Brazil and that their origins are the result of both weathering and volcanic processes.

5359 Wallace, Alfred Russel. Viagens pelos Rios Amazonas e Negro. Tradução, Eugênio Amado. Apresentação, Mário Guimarães Ferri. São Paulo: Editora da Universidade de São Paulo; Belo Horizonte: Livraria Itatiaia Editora, 1979. 317 p.: ill. (Coleção Reconquista do Brasil; v. 50)

Description of man and environment in 19th-century Amazônia as seen through the eyes of a naturalist. Book complements Bates' observations of the lower Amazon (item **5247**), and adds new information on the Negro and Uaupés Rivers.

5360 World Bank. Latin America and the Caribbean Regional Office. Brazil, integrated development of the Northwest frontier. Washington: Latin America and the Caribbean Regional Office, World Bank, 1981. 2, 101 p., 1 folded leaf of plates: bibl., ill. (some col.) (A World Bank country study)

Report based on findings of World Bank mission to Brazil (15 Oct.-7 Nov. 1979). Reviews current agricultural developments in western Mato Grosso and Rondônia and offers general assessments on the viability of certain projects.

CARTOGRAPHY

ANDREW M. MODELSKI, *Geography and Map Division, The Library of Congress*

THE BASIC WORKING CONCEPTS AND GOALS for selection of cartographic materials presented in this issue of the *Handbook* has remained unchanged. The continued use of the current cartographic accessions of the Library of Congress Geography and Map Division as the major source for the listing has helped in establishing a uniform criteria for selection of items to be included in this section.

As in the past it requires selection of approximately 10 percent of the two-year Latin American cartographic accessions to provide an adequate spectrum of the most useful and important maps and atlases for this socioeconomic region.

The support provided by the Organization of American States and the United Nations, for inventories of natural resources and collection of basic mapping data, have helped to stimulate mapping activities. The training of professional cartographers, the increased use of sophisticated modern mapping technology, and the continued effort in surveying the economic potential of remote regions has stimulated interest in the graphic portrayal of the findings.

Topics depicted in both maps and atlases reflect the scope of these activities. Transportation systems still predominate as an important feature to show mobility and access to the economic bases, and many other aspects of the socioeconomic environment are also well documented. Many of the maps and atlases depict aspects of physical geography, the extractive industries, agriculture, manufacturing, population, electric power, the urban and rural landscape, history, and recreational geography.

As usual the highest production of maps and atlases is noted for Argentina, Brazil, Colombia, Mexico, and Venezuela, and increases have also been noted in Bolivia, Chile, Ecuador, Guatemala, and Panama. Noteworthy atlases reviewed for this section include the *Atlas del desarrollo territorial de la Argentina* (item **5458**); *Mapa cultural: artesanato, folclore, patrimônio ecológico, patrimônio histórico* (Brazil, item **5478**); *Atlas lingüístico-etnográfico de Colombia* (item **5498**); *Atlas cartográfico del Reino de Chile* (item **5490**); *Atlas preliminar de Costa Rica* (item **5396**); *Atlas del Ecuador* (item **5509**); *Atlas geográfico del Ecuador* (item **5521**); *Atlas nacional del medio físico, 1981* (item **5431**); and *El Territorio mexicano* (item **5436**).

CARIBBEAN
GENERAL

5361   Ashdown, Peter. Caribbean history in maps. Scales differ. Port-of-Spain, Trinidad?: Longman Caribbean, 1979. 1 atlas (84 p.): maps, 22 x 28 cm.

"Notable West Indian: Old and New" (p. 53–63). Includes index.

5362   Mairs Geographischer Verlag. Karibik, Strassen und Sehenswürdigkeiten: Shell Reisekarte Caribbian [sic], roads and places of interest: Shell road map. 1. Aufl. Stuttgart: Mair, 1981? 1 map: col.; 72 x 107 cm.

Relief shown by shading and spot heights. Depths shown by bathymetric tints and soundings. Title and legend in German, English, French, and Spanish. Cover title. Includes inset of Bermuda.

5363   Mesloh, David. Hurricane map: Caribbean area. Corpus Christi, Tex.: DM Graphics, 1980. 1 map: col.; 41 x 56 cm.

Hurricane plotting chart.

5364   National Geographic Society. Cartographic Division. West Indies and Central America. Washington: 1981. 1 map: col.; 53 x 82 cm.

"Supplemental to the National Geographic, February 1981, page 224A, vol. 159, no. 2- . West Indies." Includes lists of geographical equivalents and abbreviations. Includes 40 maps of islands, with text, on verso.

5365 **National Ocean Survey.** Bathymetric map, Caribbean region. Bathymetry was compiled from surveys and tracklines dating from 1939 to 1972 and ranging in scale from 1:500,000 to 1:1,000,000 and rev. in 1976 at the US Naval Oceanographic Office and the US Naval Ocean Research and Development Activity by Joseph P. Flanagan *et al.* Washington: US Department of Commerce, National Oceanic and Atmospheric Administration, National Ocean Survey; Denver: Geological Survey, 1981. 1 map on 2 sheets: col.; 83 x 165 cm.

Depths shown by contours and gradient tints.

5366 **Petroconsultants S.A.** Haiti and Dominican Republic, synopsis 1979 (including current activity). Geneva, Switzerland: Petroconsultants, 1980. 1 map: photocopy; 54 x 83 cm.

Oil and gas leases. Depths shown by contours. At head of title: Foreign Scouting Service. Includes "List of Rightholders," table of "Summary of Activity during 1979" and location map.

THE BAHAMAS

5367 **Bahamas flight planning chart.** Nassau: Bahamas Tourist Office, 1980. 1 map; on sheet 46 x 61 cm., folded to 23 x 16 cm.

Bahamas flight planning chart includes island aeronautical profiles of Grand Bahama, New Providence, Bimini, Abaco, Andros, Long Island, Eleuthera, Exuma, Berry, Cat Island.

5368 **Map of the Commonwealth of the Bahamas.** s.l.: s.n., 1981? 1 map: col.; 83 x 86 cm., folded in cover 26 x 17 cm.

Relief shown by spot heights. Cover title: *The Commonwealth of the Bahamas, the country of 700 islands.* Inset, 1:110,000: New Providence Island. Tables of "Classification of Accommodations" on verso.

5369 **Petroconsultants S.A.** Bahama Islands with southern Florida, synopsis 1979

(including current activity). Geneva, Switzerland: Petroconsultants, 1980. 1 map: photocopy; 43 x 60 cm.

Depths shown by contours. At head of title: Foreign Scouting Service. "April 1980." Includes location map, "Key to Wildcats," "Activity during 1979," and inset of Southern Florida.

5370 **William G. Browning, Weaver Inc.,** *Atlanta, Ga.* Bahamas Air Navigation Chart. Bahamas Tourist Office, 1980. 1 map: col.; on sheet 76 x 86 cm., folded to 26 x 17 cm.

Data in this chart was obtained from the Department of Lands and Surveys and the Department of Civil Aviation and is current as of June 15, 1978. Includes text. Map of Bahamas with list of accommodations, text, directory of Bahamas Tourist Office, and col. ill. on verso.

BARBADOS

5371 **Banks, G.R.** Map & visitor's guide to Barbados. Designed and produced in Barbados by G.R. Banks. Typography and filmwork by Chomagraphics. Augmented with co-operation of Ministry of Communication & Works *et al.* Bridgetown?, Barbados: Banks Barbados Breweries Ltd., 1981? 1 map: col.; 55 x 42 cm.

Relief shown by shading. Panel title. Includes location map. Text, descriptive index to points of interest, telephone directory, advertisement, ill. (some col.), and maps of "Central Bridgetown" and "South Coast Detail" on verso.

5372 **Petroconsultants S.A.** Barbados, synopsis 1979 (including current activity). Geneva, Switzerland: Petroconsultants, 1980. 1 map: photocopy; 54 x 40 cm. "April 1980." Includes "List of Rightholders," table of "Summary of Activity during 1979," statistical data, and location map.

CUBA

5373 **Defense Mapping Agency. Aerospace Center.** Cuba JPC-12. St. Louis, Mo.: 1980. 1 map: col.; on sheet 44 x 56 cm. Scale 1:3,568,451. "January 1980."

Aeronautical plotting chart.

5374 **Instituto Cubano de Geodesia y Cartografía.** Ciudad de La Habana, mapa turístico Tourist Map. Redactor, Mario del Valle Díaz. Redactor técnico, José L. Veiga Delgado. 2. ed. en 1980 "Ano del Segundo Congreso." La Habana: El Instituto, 1980. 1 map on 4 sheets: col.; 91 x 119 cm.

Depths shown by bathymetric tints. Legend and text in Spanish, English, French, and Arabic. Cover title. Text, col. ill., and ancillary map on verso of each sheet.

5375 **Soviet Union. Glavnoe upravlenie geodezii i kartografii.** Kuba, spravochnaia karta: masshtab 1:1 500 000. Karta sostavlena i podgotovlena k kartosostavitel' skim ob edineniem "Kartografiia" GUGK v 1981 g. Chetvertoe izd. Moskva: Glavnoe upravlenie geodezii i kartografii pri Sovete Ministrov SSSR, 1982. 1 map: col.; 40 x 79 cm.

Relief shown by shading, gradient tints, and spot heights. Depths shown by gradient tints and soundings.

DOMINICAN REPUBLIC

5376 **TRIUNFO (Firm).** Mapa turístico de la República Dominicana. Santo Domingo: TRIUNFO, 1981. 1 map: col.; 57 x 64 cm., folded to 21 x 12 cm.

Relief shown by shading. Legend in Spanish and English. Panel title. "Revisado y aprobado por el Instituto Cartográfico Universitario." Includes location map, distance chart, inset of "Rutas de Autobuses," and col. ill. Indexed "Mapa Metropolitano" of Santo Domingo with inset.

5377 **William G. Browning, Weaver, Inc.,** *Atlanta, Ga.* The Dominican Republic, northern Caribbean, air navigation chart. Santo Domingo: Ministry of Tourism, 1980. 1 map: both sides; on sheet 69 x 101 cm., folded to 23 x 17 cm.

Includes text, location map, ancillary map of Dominican Republic with index to points of interest and distance chart, and col. ill. Also covers Haiti, Puerto Rico, and Virgin Islands. "3–30–78." "Printed . . . DR 13 2/80." Relief shown by contours, hypsometric tints, shading, and spot heights. Depths shown by bathymetric tints.

GRENADA

5378 **Great Britain. Directorate of Overseas Surveys.** Grenada. Ed. 4-D.O.S. 1979. 4 ed. rev. by D.O.S. 1978. Tolworth, England: D.O.S.; St. George's, Grenada: Lands and Surveys Department, Office of the Prime Minister, 1979. 2 maps: col.; 63 x 102 cm. (Its Series; E803) (D.O.S.; 342) Scale 1:25,000.

"Projection: Transverse Mercator." "Grid: British West Indies." Relief shown by contours, spot heights, and land form drawings. Includes "Index to Sheets and Parish Boundaries." Contents: Grenada North.—Grenada South.

HAITI

5379 **Anglade, Georges.** Sé péyi pa nou, fok sé jéografi-li nou pi konnin: Haiti. Montréal: Presses de l'Université du Québec, 1980? 1 map: col.; 46 x 61 cm.

Shows economic conditions in Haiti. Includes indexed inset of "L'Espace Social de Port-au-Prince." Bibliography.

5380 **L'Isle, Guillaume de.** Haïti en 1722-Hispaniola in 1722-Española en 1722. Ithaca, N.Y.: Historic Urban Plans, 1980. 1 map: col.; 36 x 48 cm.

Facsimile reproduced from an engraving in the collection of Historic Urban Plans.

5381 **Publicités Rossard.** Haïti, plan-guide: carte d'Haïti, plan de Port-au- Prince et de Pétion-ville, historique et renseignements divers. Port-au-Prince: Rossard, 1981. 1 map: col.; 35 x 45 cm. Scale ca. 1:700,000.

Relief shown by hachures and spot heights. Includes indexed map of Pétionville, advertisements, and col. ill. Tourist information in French and English, indexed map of Port-au-Prince, and advertisements on verso.

JAMAICA

5382 **Cardozo, D.N.** Jamaica. s.l.: Phoenix Printery Ltd., 1981? 1 map: col.; 50 x 75 cm., folded in cover 27 x 20 cm.

Detailed tourist map.

PUERTO RICO

5383 **United States. Department of the Interior.** El viejo San Juan. Washington:

The Department, 1980. 1 map: col.; 46 x 39 cm.

Shows historic sites.

5384 ———. Soil Conservation Service. Guayanes River watershed, Puerto Rico with project. Lanham, Md.: USDA-SCS, 1981. 1 map: col.; 54 x 84 cm.

Shows flood control. "Base source: USGS 1:20,000 Punta Guayanes and Yabucoa, Puerto Rico, 1960, and Aerial Photography flown 1977." Includes location map.

5385 ———. ———. Project map: Guayanes River watershed, Puerto Rico. Lanham, Md.: USDA-SCS, 1981. 1 map: col.; 25 x 37 cm.

"July 1981." Watershed management map. "Base source: USGS 1:100,000 Humacao, P.R., 1979, and aerial photography flown 1977." Includes location map.

TRINIDAD AND TOBAGO

5386 **Denoyer-Geppert Company.** Trinidad and Tobago: cultural-economic map 11516. Produced for Educational Services by Denoyer-Geppert Co. Chicago: Denoyer-Geppert, 1980. 1 map: col.; 89 x 102 cm.

Relief shown by shading, hypsometric tints, and spot heights. Depths shown by bathymetric tints. Includes location map, inset of Tobago and island inset of Solado Rock.

5387 **Petroconsultants S.A.** Trinidad offshore, synopsis first half 1980. Geneva, Switzerland: Petroconsultants, 1981. 1 map: photocopy; 54 x 61 cm.

Covers Trinidad and Tobago. "January 1981." Map showing oil and gas leases. Depths shown by contours. At head of title: Foreign Scouting Service. Includes "List of Rightholders," table of "Summary of Activity during First Half of 1980," statistical data, and location map.

5388 **Trinidad and Tobago Tourist Board.** Guide map to Trinidad. Port-of-Spain: Trinidad and Tobago Tourist Board, 1980. 1 map: on sheet 25 x 40 cm. 25 x 10 cm.

Relief shown pictorially. Panel title: Trinidad, a brief guide to sightseeing and shopping. "A Trinidad and Tobago Tourist Board Publication." Includes index to points of interest and text. Map of Port-of-Spain with index to points of interest, text, and ill. on verso.

VIRGIN ISLANDS

5389 **Better Boating Association.** Chart kit BBA, The Virgin Islands. Scales differ. Needham, Mass.: Better Boating Association, 1980. 1 atlas (23 p.): col. ill., col. maps; 44 x 56 cm.

Includes indexes. Nautical chart atlas.

CENTRAL AMERICA
GENERAL

5390 **Atlas of Central America.** Stanley A. Arbingast *et al.* Cartography by William L. Hezlep. Austin: Bureau of Business Research, University of Texas at Austin, 1979. 1 atlas (62 p.): col. maps; 28 x 37 cm.

Includes bibliographical references.

5391 **Ellsworth, Robert Blair.** An interpretation of Zarahemla and the Land Northward as described in the *Book of Mormon* and overlayed on an earth resource satellite image of present-day lands in Central America. Ogden, Utah: Rob-Ell, 1980. 1 map: co.; 59 x 39 cm.

Oriented with north toward upper right. Includes text, index, *Book of Mormon* references, and maps of "The Travels of Moroni" and "Nephite and Lamanite Political Kingdoms between 90 and 77 BC (Alma 22:27−33)" on verso.

5392 **Kümmerly + Frey.** Zentralamerika-Mexiko-Karibik: Strassenkarte. Bern: Kümmerly + Frey, 1980. 1 map: col.; 89 x 126 cm.

Also covers southern US and portion of northern South America. Relief shown by shading and spot heights. Legend in seven languages. Title from publisher's catalog. Index and location map on verso.

5393 **United States. Central Intelligence Agency.** Central America. Washington: Central Intelligence Agency, 1982. 1 map: col.; 87 x 117 cm.

General map with relief shown by shading and spot heights. Gazetteer on verso.

BELIZE

5394 **Cubola** (Firm). Atlas of Belize. 7. ed. Belize City: s.n., 1982. 1 atlas (36 p.): ill.; 28 cm.

Atlas of the country.

5395 ———. Belize, Central America, tourist map. Produced by Cubola for Belize Tourist Board. Belize City: The Board, 1981.map: col.; 45 x 30 cm. on sheet 51 x 76 cm., folded to 26 x 16 cm.

Belize facilities map and guide for visitors. Includes text and 11 ancillary maps. Text and eight maps on verso.

COSTA RICA

5396 **Nuhn, Helmut.** Atlas preliminar de Costa Rica. Colaboración en la traducción al español por M. Lyew. San José: Instituto Geográfico Nacional *en colaboración con la* Oficina de Planificación Nacional y Política Económica, 1978, i.e. 1979. 47 p., 54 leaves of plates (1 folded): ill. (some col.); 30 x 31 cm.

Atlas includes section entitled: "Información Geográfico Regional."

5397 **Sánchez Chinchilla, Luis Angel.** Atlas estadístico de Costa Rica, no. 2. 2. ed. San José: Dirección General de Estadística y Censos: Oficina de Planificación Nacional y Política Económica, 1981. 1 atlas (ca. 200 p.): ill. (some col.); 30 x 45 cm.

Statistic atlas of country.

EL SALVADOR

5398 **United States. Central Intelligence Agency.** El Salvador. Washington: Central Intelligence Agency, 1980. 1 map: col.; 27 x 45 cm.

Relief shown by shading and spot heights. Includes distance map, comparative area map, graph showing "Ethnic composition,: and three subject maps of "Economic Activity," "Vegetation and Land Use," and "Population."

GUATEMALA

5399 **Guatemala. Consejo Nacional de Planificación Económica.** Area de Planificación Intersectorial. Mapa de capacidad productiva de la tierra: Guatemala. Secretaría General del Consejo Nacional de Planificación Económica (SGCNPE), Area de Planificación Intersectorial. Instituto Nacional Forestal (INAFOR), Sección de Ecología. Instituto Geográfico Nacional (IGN), División de Estudios Geográficos. Elaborado con el Apoyo Técnico del PNUD y el Departamento de Cooperación Técnica para el Desarrollo de Naciones Unidas. Guatemala: Instituto Geográfico Nacional de Guatemala, 1981. 1 map on 4 sheets: col.; 111 x 109 cm., on sheets 58 x 59 cm. Scale 1:500,000.

Detailed soil map.

5400 ———. Dirección General de Estadística. Sección de Cartografía y Dibujo. República de Guatemala, Centro América, Departamento Chimaltenango, Municipio Chimaltenango, Ciudad Chimaltenango. Guatemala: Sección de Cartografía y Dibujo, Departamento de Estadística Agrícolas, Dirección General de Estadística, 1980. 1 map: photocopy; 102 x 168 cm.

City map shows buildings in Chimaltenango.

5401 ———. Instituto Geográfico Nacional. Mapa de la República de Guatemala. Ministerio de Comunicaciones y Obras Públicas. Guatemala: El Instituto, 1981. 1 map: col.; 56 x 54 cm.

Good general reference map.

5402 ———. ———. Mapa preliminar de la ciudad de Esquipulas. Dibujo sept. 1980. Guatemala: El Instituto, 1980. 1 map; 49 x 48 cm.

Blue line print. Alternate title: Esquipulas Municipio del Departamento de Chiquimula, Guatemala, C.A. Indexed.

5403 ———. Instituto Nacional de Sismología, Vulcanología, Meteorología e Hidrología. Informe final, estudio de aguas subterráneas en el valle de la Ciudad de Guatemala: mapas. Instituto Geográfico Nacional, Programa de las Nacionales Unidas para el Desarrollo, INSIVUMEH. Guatemala: El Instituto, 1978, i.e. 1980. 1 atlas (22 leaves [some folded]): ill., col. maps; 68 x 58 cm. Scale 1:50,000 (W 90°44'50"—W 90°27'18"/ N 14°48'55"—N 14°21'25")

Cover title. Date on presentación: 1980. To accompany: *Informe final del estudio de aguas subterráneas en el valle de la Ciudad de Guatemala. 1978.*

5404 **Petroconsultants S.A.** Guatemala, synopsis 1979 (including current activity). Geneva, Switzerland: Petroconsultants, 1980. 1 map: photocopy; 74 x 61 cm.

Oil and gas lease map with depths shown by contours. At head of title: Foreign

Scouting Service. "May 1980." Includes table of "Summary of Activity during 1979," "List of Rightholders," and location map.

5405 República de Guatemala. Mapa de la red vial. Guatemala: s.n., 1981? 1 map: photocopy; 112 x 100 cm.
Road map with a list of distances.

HONDURAS

5406 Honduras. Dirección General de Estadística y Censos. Departamento de Cartografía. División Territorial Administrativa. Posición aproximada de los municipios: República de Honduras. Ministerio de Economía. Dibujo, César R. Ortego. Tegucigalpa: La Dirección, 1980. 1 map: photocopy; 55 x 95 cm.
Administrative map.

5407 ———. Instituto Geográfico Nacional. Mapa general, República de Honduras. Ministerio de Comunicaciones, Obras Públicas y Transporte. 8. ed. Tegucigalpa: El Instituto, 1981. 1 map: col.; 45 x 71 cm.
Relief shown by contours and spot heights. "Basado en hojas del mapa topográfico escala 1:50,000 . . ." Includes compilation diagrams, two insets, and col. ill.

5408 ———. Ministerio de Educación Pública. Densidad de población segun denso 1974: Honduras. Divulgación del Ministerio de Educación Pública. Impreso en el Instituto Geográfico Nacional. Tegucigalpa: El Ministerio, 1980. 1 map: col.; 45 x 71 cm.
Population map.

NICARAGUA

5409 Nicaragua. Instituto Geográfico Nacional. Atlas de la lucha de liberación nacional. Nicaragua libre: primer aniversario del triunfo de nuestra revolución popular Sandinista, 19 de julio 1980. Scales differ. Managua: El Instituto, 1980. 1 atlas (20 p.): ill. (some col.), col. maps; 27 x 35 cm.
Cover title. "El presente documento Atlas de Nuestra liberación nacional, es el esfuerzo colectivo del Instituto Geográfico Nacional (I.G.N.) y del Centro de Investigaciones Geográficas" Presentación.

5410 ———. ———. República de Nicaragua. Managua: El Instituto, 1981. 1 map: col.; 50 x 63 cm.

Relief shown by gradient tints and spot heights. Includes relief profile, distance chart, and island inset.

5411 ———. ———. República de Nicaragua: 1980 año de la alfabetización. Preparado por el Instituto Geográfico Nacional, Ministerio de la Construcción y el Instituto Nicaragüense de Turismo. Managua: Instituto Geográfico Nacional, 1980. 1 map: col.; 51 x 69 cm.
Alternate title: Nicaragua Libre 1980: año de la Alfabetización. Relief shown by spot heights. Depths shown by contours. Includes relief profile, distance chart, and location map. On verso with index: Mapa guía de la ciudad de Managua.

5412 Petroconsultants S.A. Nicaragua, synopsis 1979. Geneva, Switzerland: Petroconsultants, 1980. 1 map: photocopy; 53 x 97 cm. Depths shown by contours. "April 1980." At head of title: Foreign Scouting Service. Oil and gas lease map. Includes "List of Rightholders," statistical data, and location map.

PANAMA

5413 Panama. Instituto Geográfico Nacional Tommy Guardia. República de Panamá. 6. ed. Panamá: El Instituto, 1980. 1 map: col.; 26 x 56 cm.
Administrative and general reference maps. Relief shown by spot heights. Includes two insets and ill. (some col.). Map of "Ciudad de Panamá," map of Panama showing population data, distance diagrams, and tables of statistical data on verso.

5414 ———. ———. República de Panamá, mapa físico. 12. ed. Panamá: El Instituto, 1980. 1 map on 2 sheets: col.; 56 x 134 cm.
Relief shown by shading, hypsometric tints, and spot heights. Depths shown by contours and bathymetric tints. Includes col. ill.

5415 Petroconsultants S.A. Panama, synopsis 1979 (including activity). Geneva, Switzerland: Petroconsultants, 1980. 1 map: photocopy; 54 x 82 cm.
At head of title: Foreign Scouting Service. "June 1980." Map shows oil and gas leases. Depths shown by contours. Includes "Geological Sketch Map of Panama," "List of

Rightholders," table of "Summary of Activity during 1979," "Key to Wildcats," statistical data, and location map.

5416 United States. Central Intelligence Agency. Panama. Washington: Central Intelligence Agency, 1981. 1 map: col.; 24 x 54 cm.

Relief shown by shading and spot heights. Includes distance map, comparative area map, ancillary map of "Panama Canal area," graph showing "Ethnic Composition," and four subject maps of "Population," "Ethnic Groups," "Vegetation," and "Economic Activity."

5417 World Bank. Panama, hydro resources and main electric systems. Washigton: World Bank, 1980. 1 map: col.; 21 x 40 cm. Includes location map.

5418 ——. Panama, petroleum concessions and drillings. Washington: World Bank, 1980. 1 map: col.; 24 x 40 cm.

Includes index to existing concessions and location map.

MEXICO

5419 Cartógrafos y Publicistas. Ciudad de México. Este mapa fué elaborado por Cartógrafos y Publicistas S.A. y la Coordinación General Técnica de Servicios y Especiales de la Dirección General de Turismo del Departamento del Distrito Federal. México: La Dirección, 1980. 1 map: col.; 93 x 67 cm.

Map of central Mexico City with text and descriptive indexes to points of interest in Spanish and English on verso.

5420 Coggeshall Map Service. See! Monterrey, Mexico. Alamo, Tex.: Coggeshall Map Service, 1980? 1 map: col.; 43 x 59 cm.

Includes indexes to points of interest, directory of Sanborn's Mexico Insurance Agencies, distance list from cities in Texas to Monterrey, and insets of central city and region between San Antonio and Monterrey showing highway routes and locations of Sanborn's offices.

5421 Enlaces cortos de televisión y telefonía: México. s.l.: s.n., 1980? 1 map: photocopy; 28 x 36 cm.

Telephone and television map of Mexico.

5422 García de Miranda, Enriqueta and **Zaida Falcón de Gyves.** Atlas: nuevo atlas Porrúa de la República Mexicana. 5. ed. Scales differ. México: Editorial Porrúa, 1980. 1 atlas (197 p.): col. maps; 34 cm.

"Cifras preliminares del X Censo de Población"—Prólogo. Spine title: *Nuevo atlas Porrúa de la República Mexicana.* Includes index. Partial contents: Mapas históricos; Monografías y mapas de las entidades federativas; Mapas temáticos.

5423 Garza Tarazona de González, Silvia and **Edward Barna Kurjack Basco.** Atlas arqueológico del Estado de Yucatán. México: SEP, Instituto Nacional de Antropología e Historia, Centro Regional del Sureste, 1980. 1 atlas (2 v.): ill. (some col.), maps; 26 cm.

Archaeological atlas of Yucatán.

5424 General Drafting Company, Inc. Mexico. Houston, Tex.: Exxon Co., 1980. 1 map: col.; 60 x 84 cm.

Includes index, distance chart, tourist information, insets of "Mexico, D.F. and vicinity" and "Relief Map of Mexico," and island inset. Road sign chart, tourist information, indexed maps of "Downtown Monterrey" and "Mexico D.F. (central area)," and nine local route maps on verso.

5425 Guía Roji, S.A. Ciudad de México. México: Guía Roji, 1981. 1 map: col.; 117 x 81 cm.

City map with postal zone information.

5426 ——. México, mapa turístico Mexico, tourist map. México: Guía Roji, 1981. 1 map: col.; 42 x 65 cm.

Includes distance chart and inset of Mexico City region. Tourist information and map of Mexico showing distances and time on verso.

5427 Mairs Geographischer Verlag. Mexiko, Strassen und Sehenswürdigkeiten: Shell Reisekarte Mexico, roads and places of interest: Shell road map. Stuttgart: Mair, 1981? 1 map: col.; 71 x 107 cm.

Relief shown by shading and spot heights. Title and legend in German, English, French, and Spanish. Includes inset of "México, Distrito Federal."

5428 Mexico. Coordinación General de los Servicios Nacionales de Estadística, Geografía e Informática. Síntesis geográfica de Guanajuato. Scales differ (W 102°35'— W99°22'/N 22°00'—N 19°45'). México: Secretaría de Programación y Presupuesto, Coordinación General de los Servicios Nacionales de Estadística, Geografía e Informática, 1980. 1 atlas (2 v.): ill. (some col.), col. maps; 40 cm. Portfolio v. 2: Anexo cartográfico. Scale 1:500,000 (17 folded leaves of plates; all col. maps; 40 cm.

Bibliography: v. 1 (p. 198). Partial contents: División municipal y principales localidades; Vías de comunicación; Climatología; Geología; Hidrología; Las regiones fisiográficas del estado.

5429 ————. **Departamento de Pesca.** Carta nacional de información pesquera: Estados Unidos Mexicanos. México: El Departamento, 1981. 1 map: col.; 43 x 63 cm.

"Los datos contenidos en esta carta fueron actualizados al 31 de diciembre de 1980." Includes text, tables of statistical data, lists, and island inset.

5430 ————. **Dirección General de Análisis de Inversiones.** México, mapa turístico de carreteras Mexico, tourist road map. México: La Secretaría, 1981. 1 map: col.; 60 x 93 cm.

Includes inset of Mexico City region, diagram of "Approximate Driving Time," distance chart, road sign charts, and index. Tourist information and col. ill. on verso.

5431 ————. **Secretaría de Programación y Presupuesto.** Atlas nacional del medio físico, 1981. Lambert Conformal Conic Projection (W 118°—W 86°/ N 33°—N 14°). México: La Secretaría, 1981. 1 atlas (224 p.); all col. maps; 71 cm. Scale 1:1,000,000.

Includes index. Contents: Imágenes Landsat; Carta topográfica; Carta hipsográfica; Carta geoestadística; Carta de climas; Carta de temperaturas medias anuales; Carta de precipitación total anual; Carta geológica; Carta edafológica; Carta de uso del suelo; Carta turística.

5432 **National Geographic Society. Cartographic Division.** Visitor's guide to the Aztec world. Richard J. Darley, chief cartographer. John F. Shupe, associate chief cartographer. Washington: The Society, 1980. 3 maps on sheet: both sides, col.; sheet 51 x 66 cm., folded to 13 x 17 cm.

Relief shown by shading and spot heights. Depths shown by bathymetric tints

and soundings. Panel title. Supplement "Mexico and Central America" in *The National Geographic* (vol. 158, no. 6, Dec. 1980, p. 704-A).

5433 **Red federal de microondas: México.** s.l.: s.n., 1980? 1 map: photocopy; 28 x 36 cm.

Microwave communication systems map.

5434 **Red nacional de servicios radio-marítimos: México.** s.l.: s.n., 1980? 1 map: photocopy; 28 x 36 cm.

Radio navigation map.

5435 **Red nacional de telegrafía armónica por corrientes portadoras: México.** s.l.: s.n., 1980? 1 map: photocopy; 28 x 36 cm.

Telegraph map of Mexico.

5436 **Ruiz Naufal, Víctor** *et al.* El territorio mexicano. México: Instituto Mexicano del Seguro Social, 1982. 2 v.: ill. (some col.); 39 cm. Accompanied by "Planos y Mapas" (36 sheets: col. ill., map, plans; 78 x 46 cm., folded to 46 x 41 cm.) issued in a case.

Authors of vol. 1: Víctor Ruiz Naufal, Ernesto Lemoine, and Arturo Gálvez Medrano; of vol. 2: Cecilia Brown Villalba, Lourdes Celis Delgado Salgado, and Miguel Messmacher. Very detailed historical geography exquisitely illustrated with maps throughout the two volumes. Includes test and accompanying atlas folio. Made in a limited edition for presentation. Not offered for sale.

SOUTH AMERICA
GENERAL

5437 **Bartholomew (John) and Son, Ltd.** South America. Edinburgh: Bartholomew, 1981. 1 map: col.; 86 x 61 cm. (Bartholomew world travel series) Scale 1:10,000,000.

Cover title: World travel map, America, South. Lambert azimuthal equal area projection. Relief shown by gradient tints and spot heights. Depths shown by gradient tints. Inset: Galapagos Islands. List of points of interest in cover.

5438 **Cook, Hammond & Kell Ltd.** The Oilman South American oil and gas map 1981. London: Maclean-Hunter Ltd., 1981. 1 map: col.; 86 x 80 cm.

Includes seven insets and advertisements: 1) Oil and gas leases, South America, Maps; 2) Oil fields, South America, Maps; 3) Gas, Natural, South America, Maps; 4) Petroleum, South America, Pipe Lines, Maps; 5) Gas, Natural, South America, Pipe lines, Maps; 6) Petroleum shipping terminals, South America, Maps; and 7) Petroleum refineries.

5439 Geografic International Inc. South America. Montreal: Geografic International, 1980. 1 map: col.; 95 x 67 cm. folded in cover. Scale 1:9,000,000.

Good general map on Lambert's azimuthal equal area projection. Relief shown by spot heights. Insets: Galapagos Islands (Archipiélago de Colón); Central America and the Caribbean; Panama Canal.

5440 Geographia Ltd. América del Sur. Frankfurt am Main: Ravenstein Verlag, 1982. 1 map: col. Scale ca. 1:10,000,000.

Legend in English, German, and French. Relief shown by spot heights. Includes insets showing economy, land use, and major relief.

5441 Hueck, Kurt. Carta da vegetação da América do Sul. São Paulo: s.n., 1981. 1 map; 56 x 45 cm.

General vegetation map.

5442 Kümmerly und Frey, *Bern.* Südamerika. Berne: Kümmerly + Frey, 1982. 1 map: col.; 114 x 76 cm. Scale 1:8,000,000.

General map with cover title: *Südamerika, Kontinentkarte mit Landerlexikon.* Relief shown by shading and spot heights. Legend in six languages. Includes two insets.

5443 National Geographic Society. Cartographic Division. South America. Richard J. Darley, chief cartographer. Washington: The Society, 1982. 1 map: col.; 145 x 108 cm. Scale 1:5,540,000.

General reference map with relief shown by shading and spot heights. Depths shown by bathymetric tints and soundings. Includes lists of geographical equivalents and abbreviations.

5444 Oyarzún Muñoz, Jorge. Carte des gisements mineraux des pays andins. Compilée par Jorge Oyarzun Muñoz. Desinée par Arnaldo Ruiz, avec la collaboration de Miguel Ubilla. Santiago: Universidad de Concepción, Departamento de Geología y Paleontología, 1980. 1 map on 2 sheets; 152 x 57 cm.

Shows mines and mineral resources in the Andes.

5445 Petroleum Publishing Co. Mapa de oleoductos, gasoductos y poliductos de Latinoamerica 1980. Compilado y editado por Petroleo Internacional. Tulsa, Okla.: Petroleum Publishing Co., 1980. 3 maps on 1 sheet: col.; sheet 57 x 59 cm.

Relief shown by shading. Includes six insets and advertisement. Contents: South America; Mexico and Central America; and West Indies. Good general map of Latin America showing oil and gas pipelines and refineries.

5446 Soviet Union. Glavnoe upravlenie geodezil i kartografii. Chili, Argentina, Paragvai, Urugvai. Glavnoe upravlenie geodezii i kartografii pri Sovete Ministrov SSR. Redaktor N.I. Arep eva. Tekhnicheskii redaktor N.V. Khvedchenia. 3. izd., ispravlena v 1979g. Moskva: GUGK, 1980. 1 map: col.; 87 x 52 cm. Scale 1:5,000,000.

Cover title: *Chili, Argentina, Paragvai, Urugvai, spravochnaia karta.* Relief shown by shading, gradient tints, and spot heights. Depths shown by gradient tints and soundings. Includes place name index.

5447 ———. ———. IUzhnaia Amerika, fizicheskaia uchebnaia karta: dlia srednei shkoly. Karta sostavlena i podgotovlena k pechati Proizvodstvennym kartosostavitel' skim ob' edineniem "Kartografii" GUGK v 1972 g. Ispravlena v 1979 g. Moskova: Glavnoe upravlenie geodezii i kartografii pri Sovete Ministrov SSSR, 1980. 1 map: col.; 133 x 94 cm.

Shows mineral deposits and ocean currents. Relief shown by shading, gradient tints, and spot heights. Depths shown by gradient tints and soundings.

5448 Visintin, Luigi. America del Sud, fisico-politica. Novara, Italia: Instituto geografico De Agostini, 1981. 1 map: col.; 91 x 87 cm.

Physical and political map with relief shown by shading and hypsometric tints. Depths shown by bathymetric tints. Includes ancillary maps of "Densita di Popolazione," Rilievo," "Precipitazioni Annue," and "Vegetazione."

ARGENTINA

5449 Argentina. Subsecretaría de Turismo. Argentina: todos los climas y bellezas del mundo. Buenos Aires: Secretaría de Estado de Deportes y Turismo, Subsecretaría de Turismo, 1981? 1 map: col.; 46 x 31 cm.

Relief shown by hypsometric tints and spot heights. Depths shown by bathymetric tints. Includes inset of "Territorio Nacional de la Tierra del Fuego, Antártica e Islas del Atlántico Sur," list of distances and times by air, index to points of interest.

5450 Auto Mapa (Firm). Departamento de Producción. Rutas, República Argentina Road map. Buenos Aires: Automapa, 1981? 1 map: both sides, col.; 154 x 58 cm. Scale 1:2,500.000.

Relief shown by shading and spot heights. Title in six languages. Legend in Spanish and English. Includes index, two location maps, distance chart, and eight insets.

5451 ———. Provincia de Buenos Aires. Buenos Aires: Editorial Automapa, 1981? 1 map: col.; on sheet 81 x 58 cm.

Includes inset of "La Plata" and location map. Maps of "Accesos," "Bahía Blanca," "Zona Atlántica, San Clemente del Tuyu-Necochea," and "Zona Atlántica, Necochea-Bahía Blanca," and indexed map of "Mar del Plata" on verso.

5452 Automóvil Club Argentino. Area de Cartografía Vial y Turística. República Argentina: red caminera principal. Dibujo, Juan C. Corso. Buenos Aires: El Club, 1982. 1 map: col.; 96 x 57 cm.

Relief shown by shading. Depths shown by gradient tints. Includes three insets. Text, index, map of "Esquema de Distancias," map showing distances from Buenos Aires, col. ill., and directories of Automovil Club Argentino's lodgings, recreational facilities, and automobile service stations on verso.

5453 Buenos Aires. Dirección de Catastro. Ciudad de Buenos Aires, capital de la República Argentina. Municipalidad de la Ciudad de Buenos Aires. Confeccionado en la Dirección Fiscalización de Obras y Catastro, Dirección de Catastro. Buenos Aires: Dirección Fiscalización de Obras y Catastro, 1980. 1 map on 6 sheets: col.; 212 x 191 cm., sheets 81 x 117 cm. Scale 1:10,000.

Detailed city plan.

5454 Difrieri, Horacio A. Atlas de Buenos Aires. Buenos Aires: Municipalidad de la Ciudad de Buenos Aires, Secretaría de Cultura, 1981. 1 atlas (2 v.): ill. (some col.); 33 cm.

5455 Guías Riema (Firm). Plano "Trio" de la ciudad de Buenos Aires. Buenos Aires: Guías Riema, 1981? 1 map: col.; 86 x 98 cm., folded in cover 24 x 14 cm. Scale 1:20,000.

Cover title: *Nuevo plano "Trío" de la Ciudad de Buenos Aires.* Accompanied by: Nuevo plano "Trío" de la ciudad de Buenos Aires, nomenclatura de calles (95 p.; 24 cm.). Includes inset of "Policía Federal-Comisarías Seccionales" and advertisements.

5456 Ildefonso V. Torres (Firm). Nuevo plano general de la ciudad de Bahía Blanca, año 1980. Buenos Aires: Ildefonso V. Torres, 1980. 1 map: photocopy; 99 x 124 cm.

Partial cadastral map. Oriented with north toward the upper left.

5457 Peuser (Firm). Guía Peuser para el turista: Buenos Aires-Para o turista-For the tourist. 2. ed. 1981. Buenos Aires: Editorial Circulation Latinoamericana, 1980. 1 map: col.; 43 x 50 cm.

Accompanied by indexes: Guía Peuser planos de subtes, colectivos, calles, autopistas (159 p.; 15 cm.). Includes text, inset, index of transit routes, ancillary maps with indexes of "Guía de teatros y cines: and "Guía de compras," ancillary map showing routes of "No cars." On verso: Guía Peuser combinaciones de subterráneos y colectivos; Cambios en el sentido de circulación de algunas calles, Red de autopistas.

5458 Randle, Patricio H. Atlas del desarrollo territorial de la Argentina. Buenos Aires: OIKOS, 1981. 1 atlas (313 leaves of plates): all col. maps; 55 cm. Scale ca. 1:10,000,000 a 10000000

Atlas accompanied by two anexos: *Memoria* and *Serie de estadísticas históricas* (37 cm.). El territorio se configura; La producción y la población; El equipamiento territorial; El proceso de urbanización.

5459 San Juan, *Argentina* (Province). Departamento Planificación Vial. Mapa de la Provincia de San Juan, 1980. Dibujó, M.A. Galante. San Juan, Argentina: Dirección Provincial de Vialidad, 1980. 1 map: photocopy; 61 x 51 cm.

Relief shown by hachures and spot heights. Includes location map.

BOLIVIA

5460 Bolivia. Instituto Geográfico Militar. Departamento de Geografía y Recursos Naturales. Mapa del Departamento de La Paz. Preparado en base a imagenes Landsat, ajustadas al control geodésico y posicionamiento de puntos mediante el sistema Doppler. La Paz: El Departamento, 1981. 1 map on 3 sheets: col.; 150 x 69 cm., sheets 58 x 75 cm. and 56 x 75 cm. Scale 1:500,000.

Photo map. Relief shown by spot heights. Includes table of "Altitudes de las Capitales de Provincias," inset of "Cobertura del Departamento de La Paz con imágenes Landsat 2–3," location map, sheet index, and relief cross section.

5461 Carnero Albarrán, Nadia. Mapas campesinos en Bolivia. Lima: Universidad Nacional Mayor de San Marcos, Dirección de Proyección Social, Seminario de Historia Rural Andina, 1980. 1 atlas (57 leaves): chiefly maps; 21 x 30 cm. Scale 1:1,000.

Real property atlas of Chaqui region.

5462 La Paz, *Bolivia.* **Asesoría de Planificación y Evaluación.** Esquema urbano de la ciudad de La Paz, distribución poblacional, equipamiento básico y vialidad. La Paz: La Asesoría, 1980? 13 maps on 1 sheet: both sides, col.; sheet 45 x 70 cm., folded to 23 x 10 cm.

Includes text, 11 graphs, and two tables. Contents: Estado actual, 1977; Primera etapa de realización, 1990; Largo plazo, 2010; Mapa de constructibilidad; Renovación urbana y vivienda; Industria; Comercio y administración; Agua potable y alcantarillado; Electrificación y teléfonos; Pavimentación y arborización; Canalización y consolidación de suelos; La nueva estructura urbana metropolitana; and Crecimiento histórico de La Paz.

5463 Programa del Satélite Tecnológico de Recursos Naturales, *Bolivia.* Mapa de cobertura y uso de la tierra, Ciudad de La Paz. Elaborado por el Programa ERTS-GEOBOL. Dirección Programa ERTS, Carlos E. Brockmann H. Dirección técnica, Clarence W. Minkel. Autor, Erwin Galoppo V. Colaboración, Jorge Córdova *et al.* Dirección

cartográfica y separación a colores, Oscar Torrez Wilde. Grabado y operación separación a colores, Eduardo Pacheco Arzadum. Dibujos originales, Rodolfo Coronel Cabrera. P.E.B.-DNUSUC (preliminar). La Paz: El Programa, 1980? 1 map on 3 sheets: col.; 101 x 181 cm., sheets 110 x 65 cm. or smaller.

Urban land use maps with relief shown by contours and spot heights.

BRAZIL

5464 Administração do Porto de Rio Grande. Area e instalações portuárias: Rio Grande. Porto Alegre: Departamento Estadual de Portos, Rios e Canais, Gabinete de Planejamento e Coordenação, Administração do Porto de Rio Grande, 1981. 1 map: photocopy; 74 x 101 cm.

Harbor facilities map.

5465 Brazil. Departamento Nacional de Estradas de Rodagem. Directoria de Planejamento. Grupo de Projetos Cartográficos. Plano nacional de viação: sistema rodoviário federal: República Federativa do Brasil. Diretoria de Planejamento, Divisão de Planos e Programas, Grupo de Projetos Cartográficos. Brasília: República Federativo do Brasil, Ministério dos Transportes, Departamento Nacional de Estradas de Rodagem, 1980. 1 map: col.; 66 x 96 cm.

Includes table of "Relação Descritiva das Rodovias do Sistema Rodoviário Federal" and three insets. Representative map.

5466 ———. ———. Grupo de Projetos Cartográficos. Mapa rodoviário, Rondônia. Mapa elaborado na Diretoria de Planejamento, Divisão de Planos e Programas, Grupo de Projetos Cartográficos. Planejamento, preparo para impressão e impresso por Aerofoto Cruzeiro S.A., Rio de Janeiro. Brasília: República Federativa do Brasil, Ministério dos Transportes, Departamento Nacional de Estradas de Rodagem, 1980. 1 map: col.; 66 x 96 cm.

Representative map of the state road system. Other states are covered by this series of maps.

5467 Companhia de Engenharia de Tráfego, *São Paulo, Brazil.* São Paulo, POT, Programa de Orientação de Tráfego, CARTRAN, Sistema Cartográfico Referencial de Trânsito. Prefeitura do Município de São Paulo, Secretaria Municipal de Transportes, Departamento de Operação do Sistema Viário, Companhia de Engenharia Tráfego; Comissão Nacional das Regiões Metropolitanas e Política Urbana; Empresa Brasileira dos Transportes Urbanos. São Paulo: O Departamento, 1981? 2 maps on 1 sheet: both sides, col.; 54 x 64 cm.

São Paulo city plan and vicinity indicating major road, street, and express highway systems.

5468 Companhia Paranaense do Energia Eléctrica. Sistema eléctrica do Paraná, 1980. Curitiba, Brazil: A Companhia, 1980. 1 map: col.; 28 x 41 cm.

Electric power distribution map. Includes inset of "Area Metropolitana de Curitiba."

5469 Editora Geográfica Paulini. Grande Rio político e rodoviário. Cartógrafo, Victor Alves de Castro. Revisão, Fernando de Castro Velloso. Rio de Janeiro: Paulini, 1980. 1 map: col.; 80 x 121 cm.

Relief shown by contours and spot heights. Includes list of distances from local areas to Rio de Janeiro with routes and index to regional administrative divisions.

5470 Fundação de Amparo à Pesquisa do Estado do Rio de Janeiro (FAPERJ). Atlas do Estado do Rio de Janeiro: referências gerais. Scales vary. Rio de Janeiro: O Fundação, 1982. 1 atlas (6, 16 p.): col. maps; 54 x 73 cm.

Atlas of Rio de Janeiro state. Colored maps.

5471 Fundação Estadual de Planejamento Agrícola do Rio Grande do Norte. Zoneamento edafoclimático: Rio Grande do Norte. Governo do Estado do Rio Grande do Norte, Fundação Estadual de Planejamento Agrícola-CEPA/RN. Natal, Brazil: Fundação Instituto de Desenvolvimento do Rio Grande do Norte-IDEC, 1981. 1 atlas (55 leaves): maps (some col.); 43 x 58 cm.

Climatic atlas of Rio Grande do Norte.

5472 Geomapas (Firm). Brasil. São Paulo: Geomapas Produções Cartográficas, 1981. 1 map: col.; 94 x 89 cm., folded in cover 23 x 16 cm.

Cover title: Brasil, mapa rodoviário e político. Includes inset, table of statistical data, and distance chart.

5473 ———. Goiás, mapa do estado, político-administrativo-rodoviário, 1981.

São Paulo: Geomapas Produções Cartográficas, 1980. 1 map: col.; 118 x 76 cm.

Administrative and political map. A representative example of state maps published by this firm.

5474 Instituto Brasileiro de Geografia e Estatística. República Federativo do Brasil. Secretaria de Planejamento de Presidência da República, IBGE. Rio de Janeiro: IBGE, 1981. 1 map: col.; 32 x 36 cm.

Good general map showing state boundaries and the drainage and transportation networks.

5475 Instituto de Pesquisa e Planejamento Urbano de Curitiba. Cidade de Curitiba. Curitiba, Brazil: O Instituto, 1982? 1 map: col.; on sheet 79 x 54 cm.

Shows city planning.

5476 ———. Sistema de transportes coletivos, cidade de Curitiba. Curitiba, Brazil: O Instituto, 1982? 1 map: col.; 107 x 75 cm.

Subway transportation map.

5477 Instituto de Terras e Cartografia, *Paraná, Brazil.* Estado do Paraná. Vinculado a Secretaria da Agricultura, Governo do Paraná; Departamento de Engenharia. Curitiba, Brazil: O Instituto, 1980. 1 map: col.; 94 x 135 cm.

Shows administrative divisions. Relief shown by hachures and spot heights.

5478 Mapa cultural: artesanato, folclore, patrimônio ecológico, patrimônio histórico. Ministério da Educação e Cultura (MEC), Fundação Movimento Brasileiro de Alfabetização (MOBRAL), Centro Cultural (CECUT). Rio de Janeiro: MOBRAL, 1980. 1 atlas (2 v.: 1043 p.): ill., maps; 22 x 30 cm.

Cultural atlas of Brazil covers arts, crafts, folklore, historical patrimony and protected ecological zones.

5479 Minas Gerais, *Brazil.* **Instituto de Geociências Aplicadas. Diretoria de Cartografia e Geografia.** Mapa geográfico: Estado de Minas Gerais. Belo Horizonte, Brazil: O Instituto, 1980. 1 map: col.; 98 x 119 cm.

Detailed general map of the state.

5480 Moreno, José Alberto. Diagrama morfológico: Estado do Rio Grande do Sul. Organização, José Alberto Moreno, geógrafo. Miron Zaions, desenhista. Perfis geológicos, Nelson Amoretti Lisboa, geólogo. Carci de

Souza Picada, geólogo. 2. ed. Pôrto Alegre: Governo do Estado do Rio Grande do Sul, Secretaria da Agricultura, Departamento de Comandos Mecanizados, Divisão de Geografia e Cartografia, 1982. 1 diagram; 40 x 58 cm.

Geomorphological map with relief shown by hachures and land form drawings.

5481 Polimapas Editora. Mapa polivisual do Brasil, político, turístico, escolar, regional, rodoviário. Equipe técnico, José Nönoya Filho, Natanael Alves da Silva, e Manuel Salvador de Silva. 20. ed. São Paulo: Polimapas Editora, 1982. 1 map: col.; 76 x 93 cm.

Includes lists of "Municipios Brasileiros com mais de 25 mil habitantes C.E.P. e Distância em km por Rodovia a Partir de São Paulo,: statistical data, distance chart, text, and col. ill. of national and state flags. Insets: Brasil, físico; Distrito Federal; Distribuição geográfica da hora legal no Brasil.

5482 ———. Nova planta da cidade de Campinas. Desenho do José Nönoya Filho *et al.* 2. ed. São Paulo: Polimapas Editora, 1982. 1 map: col.; 112 x 85 cm. Scale 1.12,687.

Representative example of city plans and urban maps published by this firm.

5483 ———. República Federativa do Brasil, região norte, Amazônia legal. Desenho de José Nönoya Filho, Natanael Alves da Silva, e Manuel Salvador da Silva. São Paulo: Polimapas Editora, 1980. 1 map: col.; 83 x 110 cm.

Includes list of "Extração Vegetal e Mineral."

5484 ———. Rondônia, Território Federal, político, rodoviário, turístico, escolar polivisual. Equipe técnica, José Nönoya Filho *et al.* São Paulo: Polimapas Editora, 1981. 1 map: col.; 64 x 90 cm. Scale 1: 1,000,000.

Good general map showing roads and administrative divisions. Other states and territories are also covered by this map series.

5485 Quatro Rodas. Brasil, tourist maps. Rio de Janeiro: EMBRATUR, Brazilian Tourist Authority, 1981? 1 map: col.; 42 x 39 cm.

On verso: Brazil (regional division); Northern region; Northeast region; Southeast region; Central-west region; Southern region.

5486 ———. Departamento Cartográfico. Brasil, mapa rodoviário. Confeccionado especialmente para Auto Mapa. São Paulo: Quatro Rodas, 1981? 1 map: both sides, col.; 149 x 88 cm.

General road and transportation map.

5487 Rêde Ferroviário Federal, S.A. Sistema Regional/Curitiba. Departamento de Via Permanente e Obras. Esquema das linhas da SR-5: Curitiba regional. Desenhista, Miriam. Rio de Janeiro: O Departamento, 1980. 1 map: col.; 39 x 41 cm.

Good railroad map.

5488 Schaeffer, Juan E. Rio, cidade do Rio de Janeiro, Estado do Rio de Janeiro. 14. ed. Rio de Janeiro: Editora Presidente: Editora Geográfica Paulini, 1982. 1 map: col.; 80 x 113 cm.

General street map with relief shown by shading. Representative example of city maps published by this firm.

CHILE

5489 Chile. Fuerza Aérea. Servicio Aerofotogramétrico. Carta aeronáutica mundial: Chile. 4. ed. Santiago: El Servicio, 1980. 6 maps: col.; on sheets 92 x 90 cm. Scale 1:1,000,000.

Relief shown by contours, hypsometric tints, and spot heights. Includes index map. Contents: 1) Arica-Antofagasta; 2) Antofagasta-La Serena; 3) La Serena-Concepción; 4) Concepción-Isla de Chiloé; 5) Isla de Chiloé-Cerro Guido; and 6) Cerro Guido-Punta Arenas.

5490 ———. Instituto Geográfico Militar. Atlas cartográfico del Reino de Chile: siglos XVII-XIX. Santiago: El Instituto, 1981. 1 atlas (266 p.): chiefly ill. (some col); 41 x 60 cm.

Atlas of colonial Chile (1660–1800).

5491 ———. ———. Atlas escolar de Chile con la regionalización actualizada. Lallemand modified polyconic proj. (W 76°—W 65°/S 17°—S 56°. Santiago: El Instituto, 1980. 1 atlas (64 p.): col. ill., col. maps; 35 cm. Scale 1:1,500,000.

Rev. ed. published as: *Atlas regionalizado de Chile* (2. ed., 1981, bibliography, p. 2).

5492 ———. Servicio Nacional de Turismo. Chile, mapa rutero de la V Región y Area Metropolitana. Santiago: El Servicio, 1981? 1 map: col.; on sheet 54 x 36 cm.

Includes location map and five insets. Descriptive lists of routes, distance chart, and chart of road signs on verso.

5493 ———. ———. Chile, mapa rutero de la XII Región. Santiago: El Servicio, 1980? 1 map: col.; 53 x 36 cm.

Includes distance chart and location map. Three maps showing tourist routes, distance chart, chart of road signs, and col. ill on verso. Other regions are covered by this map series.

5494 Grohmann y Cía. Valparaíso, una ciudad diferente. Valparaíso, Chile: Ilustre Municipalidad de Valparaíso, Departamento de Turismo, 1980? 1 map: col.; 40 x 37 cm.

Indexed for points of interest. Tourist information, directories, map of Plaza Sotomayor area, and ill. on verso.

5495 INUPAL (Firm). Plano de Santiago. Santiago: INUPAL, 1980? 1 map: col.; 52 x 70 cm.

Relief shown by formlines and spot heights. Index and directories on verso.

5496 ———. Plano de Santiago INUPAL. Cartografía, Jorge Casanova Otero. Santiago: INUPAL, 1981? 1 map: col.; 71 x 71 cm.

Relief shown by formlines. Panel title: *Plano de Santiago, guía de calles.* Index, directory of "Carabineros comisarías," and advertisements on verso.

COLOMBIA

5497 Arango Cálad, Jorge Luis. Landsat-Colombia: mosaico no controlado de imágenes de satélite Landsat I y II, banda. Con la colaboración de IGAC y CIAF. Bogotá: República de Colombia, Ministerio de Minas y Energía, Instituto Nacional de Investigaciones Geológico-Mineras, División de Sensores Remotos, 1980. 1 map; 95 x 68 cm.

Accompanied by text (14 p.). Includes "Indice de Orbitas y puntos, sistema W.R.S. (World Reference System)" and table of "Imágenes Landsat utilizadas para la Elaboración de este Mosaico."

5498 Atlas lingüístico-etnográfico de Colombia. Bogotá: Instituto Caro y Cuervo, 1981/1982. 1 atlas (v. 1-2): ill. (some col.); 50 cm.

Specialized linguistic atlas.

5499 Cartur (Firm). República de Colombia, mapa vial. Bogotá: Cartur, 1981. 1 map: col.; 95 x 67 cm.

Relief shown by spot heights. Includes location map, four insets, index, distance chart, and chart of road signs.

5500 ———. República de Colombia, mapa vial. Preparado para Texaco. Bogotá: Cartur, 1982. 1 map: col.; 71 x 53 cm. Scale 1:2,000,000.

Relief shown by spot heights. Includes text, index, distance chart, ancillary map of "Mapa de Colombia, Carreteras Principales," and three island insets. Indexed map of Bogotá and maps of Barranquilla, Cartagena, Medellín, Cali, and San Andrés on verso.

5501 Instituto Geográfico Agustín Codazzi. Comisaría del Guainía. Bogotá: El Instituto, 1981. 1 map: col.; 67 x 95 cm.

Includes location map, two tables of statistical data, and index map to 1:200,000 sheets. Representative example of Comisaría maps published by this authority.

5502 ———. Departamento Valle del Cauca. Bogotá: El Instituto, 1982. 1 map: col.; 77 x 70 cm.

Relief shown by contours and hypsometric tints. At head of title: República de Colombia. "Proyección conforme de Gauss." Includes inset of Cali, table of coordinates, compilation diagram, index to 1:100,000 sheets, and location map. Representative example of department maps published by this authority.

5503 ———. Intendencia de Casanare. 2. ed. Bogotá: El Instituto, 1981. 1 map: col.; 50 x 87 cm.

Relief shown by contours and hypsometric tints. Includes location map, table of "Coordenadas de los Puntos Geodésicos," and index map to 1:000,000 sheets. Representative example of intendency maps published by this authority.

5504 ———. Mapa de la Ciudad de Buenaventura. Bogotá: El Instituto, 1981. 1 map: col.; 40 x 98 cm. Scale 1:10,000.

Relief shown by contours. Indexes, text, map of Buenaventura region, and col. ill. on verso. Representative example of city maps published by this authority.

5505 ———. República de Colombia: mapa vial y turístico. Bogotá: El Instituto, 1981. 1 map: col.; 96 x 63 cm.
Relief shown by gradient tints and spot heights. Depths shown by contours. Panel title: *Colombia, mapa vial y turístico.* Includes four insets, distances chart, and index map. Text, map of Colombian Amazonas region with index map, location map, and col. ill. on verso.

5506 **Petroconsultants S.A.** Colombia, synopsis first half 1980. Geneva, Switzerland: Petroconsultants, 1980. 1 map: photocopy; 109 x 60 cm.
Oil and gas lease map. Depths shown by contours. At head of title: Foreign Scouting Service. Includes "List of Rightholders," table of "Summary of Activity during First Half 1980," "Tectonic Sketch map," and location map.

5507 **Rodríguez C., César** and **Ary Pernett M.** Mapa de recursos minerales del Departamento de Antioquia, 1980. Elaboración cartográfica y edición INGEOMINAS. Bogotá: República de Colombia, Ministerio de Minas y Energía, Instituto Nacional de Investigaciones Geológico-Mineras (INGEOMINAS), 1980. 1 map: col.; 94 x 70 cm. Scale 1:500,000.
Accompanied by text: "Mapa de Recursos Minerales de Antioquia: por César J. Rodríguez y Ary Pernett M. (14 p.). Includes location map. "Listado de Ocurrencias y Explotaciones Minerales del Mapa Minero de Antioquia" on verso.

5508 **Unidad DER.** Mapa brillo solar, horas promedio anual. Recopilación e información de datos por Instituto de Meteorología e Hidrología y Adecuación de Tierras. Bogotá: Unidad DER, 1982? 1 map: col.; 95 x 68 cm.
Solar radiation map published on "Base Cartográfica del Mapa Físico Político de Colombia 1977 por I.G.A.C." Includes three island insets and location map. Text, statistical data, two maps, and ill. on verso.

ECUADOR

5508a **Centro Panamericano de Estudios e Investigaciones Geográficas.** Ecuador: división política-territorial del Ecuador. s.l.: El Centro, 1980. 1 map: 33 x 55 cm.

"División política-territorial, según el Instituto Nacional de Estadística y Censos 1979." Includes index and inset of "Archipiélago de Colón (Provincia de Galápagos)."

5509 **Delavaud, Anne Collin.** Atlas del Ecuador. Paris: Les Editions J.A., 1982. 1 atlas (80 p.): col. maps, ill; 29 cm.
Topographic data provided by Instituto Geográfico Militar. Other information compiled by authors. Islands Darwin, Wolf and Galápagos appear only on large scale maps. Includes information on vulcanism, geology, geomorphology, soils, agriculture, hidrography, climate, and vegetation compiled by various government agencies.

5510 **Ecuador. Instituto Geográfico Militar.** Ambato, plano de sectorización. Quito: El Instituto, 1981. 1 map: col.; 77 x 60 cm.
Relief shown by contours, gradient tints, and spot heights. Includes inset of central city, indexes, and coat of arms.

5511 ———. ———. Mapa didáctico de la República del Ecuador. Quito: El Instituto, 1980. 1 map on 2 sheets: col.; 62 x 159 cm.
Relief shown by shading, hypsometric tints, and spot heights. Includes text, location map, two relief profiles, statistical table, and col. ill.

5512 **Ecuador. Instituto Geográfico Militar.** Provincia de Cotopaxi. Quito: El Instituto, 1981? 1 map: col.; 56 x 70 cm.
Relief shown by contours, gradient tints, and spot heights. Includes location map, text, panoramic profile, and coat of arms.

5513 ———. ———. Provincia de Pichincha. Límites de jurisdicción político-administrativos revisados ror [sic] la Comisión Especial de Límites Internos de la República. Revisado. Quito: El Instituto, 1981. 1 map: col.; 75 x 100 cm.
Relief shown by contours, hypsometric tints, and spot heights. Includes compilation diagram, list of administrative divisions, population statistics, inset of "Vista Panorámica de una Area de la Provincia de Pichincha, perfil diagonal A.B." coats of arms, location map, and island inset.

5514 ———. ———. República del Ecuador. Quito: El Instituto, 1981. 1 map: col.; 83 x 111 cm.

Relief shown by contours, shading, hypsometric tints, and spot heights. Depths shown by contours and bathymetric tints. Includes two relief profiles, location map, compilation diagram, and coat of arms. Insets: Provincia de Galápagos Archipiélago de Colón (territorio insular); Situación del Archipiélago de Galápagos con relación al territorio continental.

5515 ────. **Programa Nacional de Regionalización Agraria.** Delimitación de las zonas agrícolas: Ecuador. Ministerio de Agricultura y Ganadería, Programa Nacional de Regionalización Agraria y Office de la recherche scientifique et téchnique outre-mer. Realización, Departamento de Estudios Integrados y Síntesis. Asesoramiento técnico, Michel Portais, Pierre Gondard. Datos, Síntesis de Datos Analíticos Establecidos por todos los departamentos de PRONAREG. Dibujo y proyección, Departamento de Cartografía. Quito?: El Programa, 1980. 2 maps: col.; 96 x 48 cm.

Contents: Delimitación de las zonas agrícolas, sierra, 1) grupos de parroquias con caracteres comunes zonificación teórica: traducción cartográfica del procesamiento matricial; Delimitación de las zonas agrícolas para la programación integrada, 2) sierra.

5516 Ediciones Amaya S.A. Plano de la Ciudad de San Francisco de Quito. Quito: Ediciones Amaya, 1980. 2 maps on 1 sheet: both sides, col.; 44 x 70 cm. and 44 x 57 cm.

Relief shown by contours. Panel title: *Plano informativo, ciudad de Quito: patrimonio de la humanidad: bienvenidos a las ferias.* "Información cartográfica tomada del plano de Quito a escala 1:15.000 editada por el Instituto Geográfico Militar en 1978 y reproducidad por su autorización." Includes 1980 calendar, index, and advertisements.

5517 Instituto Ecuatoriano de Reforma Agraria y Colonización. Departamento de Ingeniería. Areas de intervención en reforma agraria y colonización: Ecuador. Compilación de Gualberto Cortés. Reviso, Fabian Torres Z. Quito: IERAC, Departamento de Ingeniería, 1980. 1 map: col.; 42 x 56 cm.

Relief shown by contours and spot heights. Base map prepared by Instituto Geográfico Militar. Stamped on: Ministerio de Relaciones Exteriores, Sección Mapoteca,

Quito, Ecuador. Includes two insets and ill. Graphs and statistical data on verso.

5518 Landívar Viteri, Nantier. Mapa geográfico de la Provincia del Guayas: escala 1:300.000. Guayaquil, Ecuador: Consejo Provincial de Guayas, 1980? 1 map on 2 sheets; photocopy; 95 x 74 cm.

General map of the province.

5519 Paladines P., Agustín. Mapa metalogénico de la República del Ecuador. Colaboración, Héctor Sanmartin D. Dibujo, Homero Suárez L. Quito: Ministerio de Recursos Naturales y Energéticos, Dirección General de Geología y Minas, 1980. 1 map: col.; 84 x 111 cm.

Accompanied by text: *Mapa metalogénico del Ecuador, escala 1:1.000.000* (56 p.). Includes coat of arms. Insets: Provincia de Galápagos, Archipiélago de Colón; Zonas geotectónicas del Ecuador; Provincias y subprovincias metalogénicas del Ecuador.

5520 Rivadeneira G., F. Ecuadorian Oriente base map of hydrocarbon activities. Quito?: City Ecuatoriana Production Co., 1980. 1 map on 2 sheets: photocopy; 111 x 90 cm.

Oil field map of Ecuador.

5521 Sampedro V., Francisco. Atlas geográfico del Ecuador "SAM:" con las básicas nociones históricas de la nacionalidad. Editor, Vicente Wilfrido Maldonado Polo. Revisado y aprobado por el Instituto Geográfico Militar y por el Ministerio de Relaciones Exteriores. Ed. actualizada. Scales differ. Quito: Gráficas Claridad, 1979. 1 atlas (87 p.): ill. (some col.), 22 maps; 22 x 32 cm.

Contents: El Universo; Geografía cultural aborigen histórica; Descubrimiento y conquista española del Reino de Quito; Límites del territorio ecuatoriano; Geografía física; Geografía política y social; Geografía económica; Mapa de las provincias.

5522 Texaco Petroleum Company. Ecuadorian Division. Plano de carreteras preliminar: Provincia de Napo. Revisions, 16/5/80. New York: Texaco Petroleum Company, Ecuadorian Division, 1980. 1 map: photocopy; on sheet 144 x 61 cm.

Shows area in Napo Province.

FALKLAND ISLANDS

5523 Great Britain. Directorate of Overseas Surveys. Falkland Islands. 2. ed. Tolworth, Great Britain: The Directorate, 1977. 2 maps: col.; 87 x 64 cm. (Series D.O.S.; 653)

Relief shown by contours, gradient tints, and spot heights. Includes index map showing property boundaries. Sheet east includes inset.

5524 Guía Peuser. Islas Malvinas: mapa especial. Malvinas Argentinas: 1982. Buenos Aires: Editorial Circulación Latinoamericana S.R.L., 1982. 1 map: col.; 58 x 79 cm.

Accompanied by 14 p. booklet.

5525 Ryder Geosystems (Firm). Satellite photomap of the Falkland Islands, jointly claimed by Great Britain and Argentina. Denver, Colo.: Ryder Geosystems, 1982. 1 map: 22 x 35 cm. Scale (ca. 1:728,640). 1" approx. 11½ miles.

Map of Falkland Islands drawn from satellite compiled data.

FRENCH GUIANA

5526 France. Etablissement Public Régional. Office Departemental du Tourisme de Guyane. Guyane: carte touristique et routière. M. Cartigny, editor. Paris: Le Office, 1972. 1 map: col; on sheet 82 x 77 cm. Carte topographique au 1:500:000.

French Guiana tourist and road map.

GUYANA

5527 Guyana. Lands Department. Topographic Division. Co-operative Republic of Guyana. Georgetown: The Department, 1981. 1 map: col.; 86 x 56 cm.

A good general map with relief shown by hachures and spot heights. Includes indexed inset of "Administrative divisions" and location map.

5528 Venezuela. Ministerio de Relaciones Exteriores. Región limítrofe con la Guyana. Caracas: República de Venezuela, Ministerio de Relaciones Exteriores, 1981? 1 map: col.; 20 x 28 cm.

Area of boundary dispute.

PARAGUAY

5529 Paraguay. Instituto Geográfico Militar. Paraguay. 2. ed. Asunción: El Instituto, 1981. 1 map: col.; 62 x 53 cm.

General information map with roads, railroads, and administrative divisions. Relief shown by shading. Includes location map.

5530 Petroconsultants S.A. Paraguay, synopsis 1979 (including current activity). Geneva, Switzerland: Petroconsultants, 1980. 1 map: photocopy; 53 x 65 cm.

Oil and gas lease map. At head of title: Foreign Scouting Service. Includes "Structural Sketch Map," table of "Summary of Activity during 1979," "List of Rightholders," statistical data, and location map

PERU

5531 Editorial Navarrete. Mapa político del Perú. Lima: Navarrete, 1980. 1 map: col.; 86 x 61 cm.

Includes location map, statistical tables, distance chart, and col. ill.

5532 Embajada del Viajero S.A. Trujillo-Cajamarca. Lima?: Embajada del Viajero, 1982? 1 map: col.; 42 x 32 cm.

Shows roads in regions of Trujillo and Cajamarca. On verso: Valle de Chicama; Cajamarca y sus alrededores; Plano de Chimbote; Mapa político administrativo.

5533 Góngora Perea, Amadeo. Plano de la ciudad de Lima metropolitana. Lima: Cartográfica Nacional, 1981. 1 map: col.; 60 x 87 cm.

Relief shown by hachures. Cover title: Ciudad de Lima metropolitana. Accompanied by: índice de avenidas y jirones.

5534 Instituto Geográfico Nacional, *Peru.* Mapa físico, político, vial-Perú. 3. ed. Lima?: Librería Internacional del Perú, 1982. 1 map: col.; 95 x 66 cm.

Relief shown by shading. Includes location map, distance chart, and diagram showing roads. Indexed maps of "Centro de Lima" and "Lima metropolitana y alrededores," chart of road signs, and 23 local maps on verso.

5535 Petroconsultants S.A. Peru, synposis 1979. Geneva, Switzerland: consultants, 1980. 1 map: photocopy; 110 x 82 cm.

Oil and gas lease map. Depths shown by contours. At head of title: Foreign Scouting Service. Includes table of "Summary of Activity during 1979," "List of Rightholders," statistical data, and location map.

5536 Touring y Automóvil Club del Perú. Departamento de Cartografía. Mapa vial del Perú. Cartografía, dibujo, G. Paucarcaja B., C. Rincón P., A. Cano S. Lima: El Club, 1980. 1 map: col. 68 x 48 cm.
Relief shown by shading. Includes location map and distance chart.

5537 ———. ———. Zonas turísticas de Lima. Dibujo, G.P.B.-C.R.P. Lima: El Club, 1982? 1 map: col.; 68 x 46 cm.
Includes index, inset, and col. ill. Maps of "Caminos Principales" and "Balnearios y Playas de Veraneo," indexed maps of "Lima Metropolitana" and "Zona Céntrica,: and col. ill. on verso.

5538 United States. Central Intelligence Agency. Peru-Ecuador: area of boundary dispute. Washington: CIA, 1981. 1 map: col.; 21 x 17 cm.
Relief shown by shading. Includes location map.

SURINAM

5539 Aktiviteitenkaart bosbouw noord Suriname. Paramaribo?, Surinam: s.n., 1981. 1 map: photocopy; 41 x 93 cm.
Foresting map.

5540 Petroconsultants S.A. Surinam & French Guiana, synopsis 1979. Geneva, Switzerland: Petroconsultants, 1980. 1 map: photocopy; 62 x 81 cm.
Oil and gas lease map. Depths shown by contours. At head of title: Foreign Scouting Service. Includes "List of Rightholders," statistical data, and location map.

5541 Surinam. Bureau voor Waterkrachtwerken. Republiek Suriname: projekt kaart Kabalebo hydro-electric schema. Paramaribo, Surinam: Bureau voor Waterkrachtwerken, 1981? 1 map: photocopy; 64 x 93 cm.
Water power map.

5542 Surinam. Centraal Bureau Luchtkaartering. Kaart van de Republiek Suriname-Map of the Republic of Suriname. 7.

druk 1980. Paramaribo, Surinam: Het Bureau, 1980. 1 map: col.; 65 x 55 cm.
Relief shown by hypsometric tints and spot heights. "Issued on the occasion of the independence jubilee at Paramaibo 25th of November 1980."

URUGUAY

5543 Petroconsultants S.A. Uruguay, synopsis 1979. Geneva, Switzerland: Petroconsultants, 1980. 1 map: photocopy; 54 x 40 cm.
Oil and gas lease map. Depths shown by contours. At head of title: Foreign Scouting Service. Includes "List of Rightholders," table of "Summary of Activity during 1979," statistical data, and location map.

5544 Rubens Grub, Ulises. Atlas geográfico de la República Oriental del Uruguay. Montevideo: Mosca Hnos., 1980. 1 atlas (56 p.): ill., maps; 33 cm. Scales differ (W 58°30'—W 53°00'/S 30°30'—S 35°30')
"Ariel, contornos geográficos—colección Prof. Grub," on most maps.

5545 Uruguay. Dirección Nacional de Turismo. Plano de la ciudad de Montevideo. Montevideo: La Dirección, 1980. 2 maps on 1 sheet: both sides, col.; sheet 49 x 79 cm.
Includes index, text, ancillary map of "Montevideo capital y balneario, principales salidas viales," and col. ill.

VENEZUELA

5546 Aeromapas Seravenca. Mapa de carreteras de Venezuela. Caracas?: Lagoven, 1980. 1 map: col.; 65 x 102 cm.
Relief shown by shading and spot heights. Panel title: Rutas de Venezuela; Planos de Maracaibo y Barquisimeto. Includes index, distance chart, and four insets. On verso with indexes: Plano de Barquisimeto; Plano de Maracaibo.

5547 ———. Nuevo plano de Caracas. Caracas: Aeromapas de Seravenca: Distribuidora Santiago C.A., 1981? 1 map: both sides, col.; 93 x 154 cm.
Detailed city plan.

5548 Colegio Universitario de Carúpano. Centro de Investigaciones. Atlas del Estado Sucre. Coordinador, Jesús Antonio

Aguilera. Equipo de trabajo, María del Valle Azocar Silva *et al.* Carúpano, Venezuela: El Colegio, 1980. 1 atlas (31 *[i.e. 68]* p.): col. maps; 24 x 33 cm.

Includes bibliography (p. 31).

5549 CONZUPLAN. Región Zuliana, subregionalización: división político administrativa. Maracaibo?, Venezuela: CONZUPLAN, 1981? 1 map: col.; 64 x 46 cm.

Map showing administrative and political divisions.

5550 Fiedler, G. República de Venezuela, mapa sísmico, 1530–1980. Coordinación, geógrafo Lourdes Rivero, 1980. Caracas: s.n., 1981. 1 map: col.; 72 x 89 cm.

"Auspiciado por Fundación Venezolana de Investigaciones Sismológicas (FUNVISIS)." Includes text, diagram, and table of "Los Terremotos de Mayor Magnitud Ocurridos en Venezuela entre los Años 1530–1980."

5551 Kissenbeck, E. Caracas, plano directorio. Caracas: Interamericana Técnica, C.A.: Distribuidora Santiago C.A., 1981? 1 map: both sides, col.; 65 x 127 cm.

Good city plan with index. Panel title: Caracas, plano directorio: edición totalmente actualizada con el trazado y ubicación de las estaciones del metro de Caracas.

5552 Mérida, *Venezuela* (state). **Dirección de Turismo.** Mérida suya: informaciones turísticas. Mérida, Venezuela: La Dirección, 1981. 2 maps on 1 sheet: 1 col.; sheet 46 x 60 cm.; folded to 24 x 15 cm.

Includes index to points of interest for the city of Mérida. Text, tourist information, and ill. on verso. Contents: Mapa vial y sitios de interesnt [sic] del Estado Mérida.

5553 Petroconsultants S.A. Venezuela, synopsis 1979 (including current activity). Geneva, Switzerland: Petroconsultants, 1980. 2 maps: photocopies: 81 x 83 cm. and 81 x 80 cm.

Oil and gas lease maps. Depths shown by contours. At head of title: Foreign Scouting Service. Includes table of "Crude Oil Production 1978–1979," "List of Rightholders," table of "Exploratory Wells Drilled during 1979," indexed list of "South Lake Maracaibo Service Contract Area," table of "Summary of Activity during 1979," and index map.

5554 Venezuela. Dirección de Aeronáutica Civil. Indice de aerodromos Aerodrome index: AIP Venezuela: AIS Venezuela. Caracas: La Dirección, 1981. 1 map; 35 x 45 cm.

Map showing airports.

5555 ——. ——. Mapa físico y político de la República de Venezuela. Caracas: República de Venezuela, Ministerio del Ambiente y de los Recursos Naturales Renovables, Dirección General de Información e Investigación del Ambiente, Dirección de Cartografía Nacional, 1980. 1 map: col.; 72 x 89 cm.

Good general map. Relief shown by spot heights. Includes island inset, location map, and coat of arms.

5556 ——. ——. Regionalización administrativa de Venezuela. Caracas: República de Venezuela, Ministerio del Ambiente y de los Recursos Naturales Renovables, Dirección General de Información e Investigación del Ambiente, Dirección de Cartografía Nacional, 1980. 1 map: col.; 72 x 90 cm.

Relief shown by shading. Includes island inset, text, and coat of arms.

5557 ——. Dirección de Geología. Mapa geológico estructural y de recursos minerales del Estado Zulia. Caracas: República de Venezuela, Ministerio de Energía y Minas, La Dirección, 1980. 1 map: photocopy; 82 x 66 cm. Scale 1:500,000.

Includes island inset, sheet index of 1:500,000 geologic maps, and location map.

5558 ——. Dirección General de Vialidad. Mapa vial con otros de comunicaciones terrestres, marítimas y aéreas, región norte de la República de Venezuela. Preparado para Corpoven. Reed. 1981. Caracas: República de Venezuela, Ministerio de Transporte y Comunicaciones, La Dirección, 1981. 1 map: both sides, col.; 70 x 167 cm. on sheet 70 x 99 cm.; folded to 24 x 10 cm. Scale 1:1,000,000.

Relief shown by shading and spot heights. Panel title: Mapa vial de Venezuela. Includes distance chart, island inset, and inset of "Mapa político de la República de Venezuela."

5559 ——. Oficina Central de Estadística e Informática. Sector de Planificación y Control de Operaciones. Departamento de

Geografía y Cartografía. República de Venezuela, mapa de la división político-territorial 1981. Caracas: La Oficina, 1981. 1 map: photocopy; 72 x 89 cm.

Blue line print. Includes index, note, and inset.

JOURNAL ABBREVIATIONS GEOGRAPHY

AAAS/S Science. American Association for the Advancement of Science. Washington.

AAG/A Annals of the Association of American Geographers. Lawrence, Kan.

AAG/PG Professional Geographer. Journal of The Association of American Geographers. Washington.

ACH/BHA Boletín de Historia y Antigüedades. Academia Colombiana de Historia. Bogotá.

ACSP/DE Digesto Econômico. Associação Comercial de São Paulo e Federação do Comércio do Estado de São Paulo. São Paulo.

AGB/BCG Boletim Carioca de Geografia. Associação dos Geógrafos Brasileiros, Secção Regional do Rio de Janeiro. Rio de Janeiro.

AGB/BPG Boletim Paulista de Geografia. Associação dos Geógrafos Brasileiros, Secção Regional de São Paulo. São Paulo.

AGF/B Bulletin de l'Association de Géographes Français. Paris.

AGRO Agrociencia. Secretaría de Agricultura y Recursos Hidráulicos, Colegio de Postgraduados de la Escuela Nacional de Agricultura. Chapingo, México.

AGS/GR The Geographical Review. American Geographical Society. New York.

AGS/SG Soviet Geography: Review and Translation. American Geographical Society. New York.

AHGH/R Revista de la Academia Hondureña de Geografía e Historia. Tegucigalpa.

AI/A Anthropos. Anthropos-Institut. Psoieux, Switzerland.

AI/I Interciencia. Asociación Interciencia. Caracas.

AISA/TA Terra Ameriga. Associazione Italiana Studi Americanistici. Genova, Italy.

AJES The American Journal of Economics and Sociology. Francis Neilson Fund and Robert Schalkenbach Foundation. New York.

AM/R Revista do Arquivo Municipal. Prefeitura do Município de São Paulo, Depto. Municipal de Cultura. São Paulo.

AMNH/NH Natural History. American Museum of Natural History. New York.

AMNR/NH *See* AMNH/NH.

BCV/REL Revista de Economía Latinoamericana. Banco Central de Venezuela. Caracas.

BESPL Berichte zur Entwicklung in Spanien, Portugal, Lateinamerika. München, FRG.

BNB/REN Revista Econômica do Nordeste. Banco do Nordeste do Brasil, Depto. de Estudos Econômicos do Nordeste. Fortaleza.

BNBD Boletín Nicaragüense de Bibliografía y Documentación. Banco Central de Nicaragua, Biblioteca. Managua.

BNCE/CE Comercio Exterior. Banco Nacional de Comercio Exterior, S.A. México.

CDAL Cahiers des Amériques Latines. Paris.

CFC/RBC Revista Brasileira de Cultura. Ministério da Educação e Cultura, Conselho Federal de Cultura. Rio de Janeiro.

CJN Croissance des Jeunes Nations. Paris.

CLAEH Centro Latinoamericano de Economía Humana. Montevideo.

COIGN/BG Boletín Geológico. Ministerio de Minas y Petróleos, Instituto Geológico Nacional. Bogotá.

CP Cuadernos Políticos. Revista trimestral. Ediciones Era. México.

CU/EG Economic Geography. Clark Univ. Worcester, Mass.

DRG/BG Boletim Geográfico do Estado do Rio Grande do Sul. Diretório Regional de Geografia e da Secção de Geografia. Porto Alegre, Brazil.

EJ Explorers Journal. New York.

EME Revista Eme-Eme. Estudios dominicanos. Univ. Católica Madre y Maestra. Santiago de los Caballeros, Dominican Republic.

FAIC/CPPT Comunicaciones Proyecto Puebla-Tlaxcala. Fundación Alemana para la Investigación Científica. Puebla, México.

FCE/TE El Trimestre Económico. Fondo de Cultura Económica. México.

FDD/NED Notes et Études Documentaires. France, Direction de la Documentation. Paris.

GEB/E Die Erde. Zeitschrift der Gesellschaft für Erdkunde zur Berlin. Walter de Gruyter & Co. Berlin.

GH Geographica Helvetica. Schweizerische Zeitschrift für Länder- und Völkerkunde. Kümmerly & Frey, Geographischer Verlag. Bern.

GR Geographische Rundschau. Zeitschrift für Schulgeographie. Georg Westermann Verlag. Braunschweig, Germany.

GV/GR Geologische Rundschau. Internationale Zeitschrift für Geologie. Geologische Vereinigung. Ferdinand Enke Verlag. Stuttgart, Germany.

GZ Geographische Zeitschrift. Franz Steiner Verlag. Wiesbaden, Germany.

HAHR Hispanic American Historical Review. Duke Univ. Press *for the* Conference on Latin American History of the American Historical Association. Durham, N.C.

IAA Ibero-Amerikanisches Archiv. Ibero-Amerikanisches Institut. Berlin, FRG.

IAA/BA Brasil Açucareiro. Instituto do Açucar e do Alcool. Rio de Janeiro.

IAEERI/E Estrategia. Instituto Argentino de Estudios Estratégicos y de las Relaciones Internacionales. Buenos Aires.

IBE/RBE Revista Brasileira de Economia. Fundação Getúlio Vargas, Instituto Brasileiro de Economia. Rio de Janeiro.

IBG/TP Transactions and Papers. Institute of British Geographers. London.

IBGE/R Revista Brasileiro de Geografia. Conselho Nacional de Geografia, Instituto Brasileiro de Geografia e Estatística. Rio de Janeiro.

ICC/I Itaytera. Instituto Cultural do Cariri. Crato, Brazil.

IDES/DE Desarrollo Económico. Instituto de Desarrollo Económico y Social. Buenos Aires.

IFH/C Conjonction. Institut Français d'Haïti. Port-au-Prince.

IFEA/B Bulletin de l'Institut Français d'Études Andines. Lima.

IGM/U L'Universo. Rivista bimestrale dell'Istituto Geografico Militare. Firenze, Italy.

IGME/RG Revista Geográfica. Instituto Geográfico Militar del Ecuador, Depto. Geográfico. Quito.

III/AI América Indígena. Instituto Indigenista Interamericano. México.

IJ/JJ Jamaica Journal. Institute of Jamaica. Kingston.

INAH/A Anales del Instituto Nacional de Antropología e Historia. Secretaría de Educación Pública. México.

IPEA/PPE Pesquisa e Planejamento Econômico. Instituto de Planejamento Econômico e Social. Rio de Janeiro.

IPN/EP Economía Política. Instituto Politécnico Nacional, Escuela Superior de Economía. México.

ISA/CUR Comparative Urban Research. International Sociological Association, Committee for Community Research. College Park, Md.

JDA The Journal of Developing Areas. Western Illinois Univ. Press. Macomb.

JIH The Journal of Interdisciplinary History. The MIT Press. Cambridge, Mass.

JLAS Journal of Latin American Studies. Centers or institutes of Latin American studies at the universities of Cambridge, Glasgow, Liverpool, London and Oxford. Cambridge Univ. Press. London.

LAND Landscape. Published three times a year. Santa Fe, N. Mex.

LARR Latin American Research Review. Univ. of North Carolina Press *for the* Latin American Studies Association. Chapel Hill.

LNB/L Lotería. Lotería Nacional de Beneficencia. Panamá.

MHD/B   Boletín del Museo del Hombre Dominicano. Santo Domingo.

NGS/NGM   National Geographic Magazine. National Geographic Society. Washington.

NSO   Nueva Sociedad. Revista política y cultural. San José.

OAS/CI   Ciencia Interamericana. Organization of American States, Dept. of Scientific Affairs. Washington.

OAS/AM   Américas. Organization of American States. Washington.

OCEANUS   Oceanus. Oceanographic Institution. Woods Hole, Mass.

PAIGH/G   Revista Geográfica. Instituto Panamericano de Geografía e Historia, Comisión de Geografía. México.

PAIGH/RC   Revista Cartográfica. Instituto Panamericano de Geografía e Historia, Comisión de Cartografía. México.

PAN/ES   Estudios Latinoamericanos. Polska Akademia Nauk (Academia de Ciencias de Polonia). Instytut Historii (Instituto de Historia). Warszawa.

PCCLAS/P   Proceedings of the Pacific Coast Council on Latin American Studies. Univ. of California. Los Angeles.

PGM   Petermanns Geographische Mitteilungen. Geographische-Kartoggraphische Anstalt. Gotha, Germany.

PUC/V   Veritas. Revista. Pontificia Univ. Católica do Rio Grande do Sul. Porto Alegre, Brazil.

SAGE/JIAS   Journal of Inter-American Studies and World Affairs. Sage Publication *for the* Center for Advanced International Studies, Univ. of Miami. Coral Gables, Fla.

SBPC/CC   Ciência e Cultura. Sociedade Brasileira para o Progresso da Ciência. São Paulo.

SCNLS/N   Natura. Revista de divulgación científica. Sociedad de Ciencias Naturales de La Salle. Caracas.

SG/AG   Annales de Géographie. Société de Géographie. Paris.

SGB/COM   Les Cahiers d'Outre-Mer. Publiée par l'Institut de Géographie de la Faculté des Lettres de Bordeaux, par l'Institut

de la France d'Outre-Mer, par la Société de Géographie de Bordeaux *avec le concours* de Centre National de la Recherche Scientifique et de la VI. Section de l'École Pratique des Hautes Études. Bordeaux.

SGC/B   Boletín de la Sociedad Geográfica de Colombia. Academia de Ciencias Geográficas. Bogotá.

SGHG/A   Anales de la Sociedad de Geografía e Historia de Guatemala. Guatemala.

SGI/B   Bollettino della Società Geografica Italiana. Roma.

SGL/B   Boletín de la Sociedad Geográfica de Lima. Lima.

SMHN/R   Revista de la Sociedad Mexicana de Historia Natural. México.

SSAG/GA   Geografiska Annaler. Svenska Sällskapet för Antropologi och Geografi. Stockholm.

TESG   Tijdschrift voor Economische en Sociale Geographie. Netherlands Journal of Economic and Social Geography. Rotterdam, The Netherlands.

UA/U   Universidad. Univ. de Antioquia. Medellín, Colombia.

UBGI/E   Erdkunde. Archiv für Wissenschaftliche Geographie. Univ. Bonn, Geographisches Institut. Bonn.

UC/AT   Atenea. Revista de ciencias, letras y artes. Univ. de Concepción. Concepción, Chile.

UCC/NG   Norte Grande. Revista de estudios integrados referentes a comunidades humanas del Norte Grande de Chile, en una perspectiva geográfica e histórico-cultural. Univ. Católica de Chile, Instituto de Geografía, Depto. de Geografía de Chile, Taller Norte Grande. Santiago.

UCC/RU   Revista Universitaria. Anales de la Academia Chilena de Ciencias Naturales. Univ. Católica de Chile. Santiago.

UCLA/JLAL   Journal of Latin American Lore. Univ. of California, Latin American Center. Los Angeles.

UCNSA/EP   Estudios Paraguayos. Univ. Católica Nuestra Señora de la Asunción. Asuncion.

UCR/AEC Anuario de Estudios Centro-americanos. Univ. de Costa Rica. Ciudad Universitaria "Rodrigo Facio." San José.

UCR/CT Ciencia y Tecnología. Revista semestral de la Univ. de Costa Rica. San José.

ULA/RG Revista Geográfica. Univ. de Los Andes. Mérida, Venezuela.

UNC/K Katunob. Univ. of Northern Colorado. Museum of Anthropology. Greeley.

UNL/U Universidad. Univ. Nacional del Litoral. Santa Fe, Argentina.

UNPHU/A Aula. Univ. Nacional Pedro Henríquez Ureña. Santo Domingo.

UP/CSEC Cuban Studies/Estudios Cubanos. Univ. of Pittsburgh, Univ. Center for International Studies, Center for Latin American Studies. Pittsburgh, Pa.

UP/TM Tiers Monde. Problèmes des pays sous-développés. Univ. de Paris, Institut d'Étude du Développement Économique et Social. Paris.

USC/U Universidad de San Carlos de Guatemala. Guatemala.

USM/JTG The Journal of Tropical Geography. Univ. of Singapore and Univ. of Malaya, Depts. of Geography. Singapore.

UTIEH/C Caravelle. Cahiers du monde hispanique et luso-brésilien. Univ. de Toulouse, Institut d'Études Hispaniques, Hispano-Americaines et Luso-Brésiliennes. Toulouse, France.

UW/LBR Luso-Brazilian Review. Univ. of Wisconsin Press. Madison.

UWI/CQ Caribbean Quarterly. Univ. of the West Indies. Mona, Jamaica.

VOZES Vozes. Revista de cultura. Editora Vozes. Petrópolis, Brazil.

WM Westermann Monatshefte. Georg Westermann Verlag. Braunschweig, FRG.

ZG Zeitschrift für Geomorphologie. Gebrüder Borntraeger. Berlin.

ZGP Zeitschrift für Geopolitik. Herausgegeben von Institut für Geosoziologie und Politik Bellnhausen über Gladenbach. Hessen, Germany.

GOVERNMENT AND POLITICS

GENERAL

6001 Alisky, Marvin. Latin American media: guidance and censorship. Ames: Iowa State University Press, 1981. 265 p.: bibl., index.

Informative survey of the treatment of Latin American media by governments during past two decades with chapters organized by country (two on Mexico; the rest divided among Peru, Brazil, Venezuela, Colombia, Cuba, Argentina, Uruguay, and Chile). Though not especially well organized and lacking consistent theme, work offers substantial information on fate of most major newspapers under democratic and authoritarian regimes. [G. Wynia]

Burns, E. Bradford and **Thomas E. Skidmore.** Elites, masses, and modernization in Latin America, 1850–1930. See *HLAS 44:1821*.

6002 Catholic Church. Consejo Episcopal Latinoamericano. Puebla, grandes temas. Bogotá: Consejo Episcopal Latinoamericano, 1979 or 1980. 1 v.: bibl. (Documentos CELAM; 38)

Very important work for students of Church doctrine in which several clergymen who participated in Puebla's 1979 CELAM conference offer their interpretations of what was discussed and agreed upon. Essential for anyone who wants to understand how Church leaders interpret their own actions. [G. Wynia]

Child, John. Unequal alliance: the inter-American military system, 1938–1979. See *HLAS 44:1823*.

6003 Comblin, Joseph. El poder militar en América Latina. Salamanca, Spain: Ediciones Sígueme, 1978. 286 p.: bibl. (Tierra dos tercios)

Belgian theologian offers another study of the national security state in Latin America. Although published a year before his *Church and the national security state* (see *HLAS 43:6023*), book shares much with it. Focuses more on one source of the doctrine, US military, and its propagation in several countries, most complete application being Chile after 1973. Though not well integrated, book is informative and valuable, especially for its description of military thinking. [G. Wynia]

6004 Conferencia General del Episcopado Latinoamericano, 2nd, *Bogotá, and Medellín, Colombia, 1968.* The Church in the present-day transformation of Latin America in the light of the Council. Second General Conference of Latin American Bishops. 3. ed. Washington: National Conference of Catholic Bishops, Secretariat for Latin America, 1979-. 2 v.: bibl.

Third edition of English translation of conclusions of first conference of Latin American bishops (Bogotá, 1968). Because conference accepted some of the more progressive theological and social doctrines espoused by Latin American clergy, it played a crucial role in development of doctrinal reform within the Church. [G. Wynia]

6005 Congreso Iberoamericano de Derecho Constitucional, 2nd, *México, 1980.* Partidos políticos y democracia en Iberoamérica. II Congreso Iberoamericano de Derecho Constitucional, México, 1980. Jorge Mario García Laguardia, compilador. México: Universidad Nacional Autónoma de México, Instituto de Investigaciones Jurídicas, 1981. 197 p. (Serie B., Estudios comparativos. d, Derecho latinoamericano; no. 19)

Compilation of the results of Second Iberoamerican Congress of Constitutional Law (Mexico City, 1980). Findings on relationship between political parties and democratic rule are varied but central theme of these reports focuses on importance of constitutionalism for stable, orderly, and progressive development in Latin America. [D.W. Dent]

6006 Conniff, Michael L. Introduction: toward a comparative definition of populism (*in* Latin American populism in comparative perspective [see item **6016**] p. 3–30, bibl.)

Excellent historical and political treatment of Latin American populism including origins, characteristics, and research tasks for the next decade. [D.W. Dent]

6007 Cordero, Fernando. Importaciones y exportaciones de armas livianas en Argentina, Brasil, Colombia, Costa Rica, Chile, República Dominicana, Perú, México y Venezuela: 1970–1979. Stockholm: Institute of Latin American Studies, 1981. 26 p.: ill. (Occasional papers)

Informative study contains substantial data on quantities of light arms traded among several Latin American countries during 1970s. No effort made to examine impact within individual countries, however. [G. Wynia]

6008 Democracy and dictatorship in Latin America. Edited by Thomas Draper. New York: H.W. Wilson, 1981. 230 p.: bibl. (The Reference shelf; v. 53, no. 3)

Edited compilation of articles on Latin American conditions in late 1970s previously published in US magazines. Gathers contrasting points of view as well as basic information, with primary attention to US-Latin American relations and differences of opinion on Carter's human rights policy. [G. Wynia]

6009 Fagor Aviel, JoAnn. Political participation of women in Latin America (UU/WPQ, 34:1, March 1981, p. 156–173, tables)

Systematic effort to draw conclusions about women's political participation using many monographs written during past decade. Examines voting, organizational activities, political leadership, and labor union involvement in several Latin American countries. [G. Wynia]

6010 Forero Ramírez, Yamile. Estado y política económica internacional. Bogotá: Editorial Temis Librería, 1979. 149 p.: bibl., ill., index.

Applies decision-making theory and system analysis to trade, tariff, and exchange policy in an effort to analyze state's role in a multinational environment. [J.M. Hunter]

6011 La Formación de los periodistas en América Latina: México, Chile y Costa Rica. José Baldivia Urdininea, coordinador. San José: Centro de Estudios Económicos y Sociales del Tercer Mundo; México: Editorial Nueva Imagen, 1981. 393 p.

Valuable empirical study of the press, reporters, and journalistic training in Mexico, Chile, and Costa Rica. [D.W. Dent]

6012 Geller, Daniel S. Economic modernization and political instability in Latin America: a causal analysis of bureaucratic-authoritarianism (UU/WPQ, 35:1, March 1982, p. 33–49, bibl., tables)

Empirical analysis of relationship between socioeconomic development and political structure (bureaucratic-authoritarianism). Author is rather cautious in his conclusions but his data supports both O'Donnell and Collier concerning absolute size of modern sector and inception point of development process. [D.W. Dent]

6013 Guerrilla strategies: an historical anthology from the Long March to Afghanistan. Edited, with an introduction, by Gérard Chaliand. Berkeley: University of California Press, 1982. 353 p.: bibl.

Examines revolutionary warfare and counterinsurgency through writings of major participants and theoreticians (e.g., Héctor Béjar, Peru; Abraham Guillén, Uruguay; Ernesto "Che" Guevara, Bolivia; anonymous Colombian guerrillero). Each offers stories and insights into Latin American experience. Author claims that ". . . a fascination with death, rooted in Hispanic machismo and accentuated by their organizational fragility, explains why so few of the Latin American guerrilla leaders of the past twenty years are still alive." [D.W. Dent]

6014 Harmel, Robert. Environment and party decentralization: a cross-national analysis (CPS, 14:1, April 1981, p. 75–99, bibl., tables)

Causal, cross-national study of relationship between environmental factors (country size, type of polity, power distribution, sectionalism, and social heterogeneity) and party decentralization. Author's data and analysis supports conclusion that 68 percent of variance in party decentralization can be attributed to environmental causes. [D.W. Dent]

6015 Johnson, Kenneth F. The 1980 image-index survey of Latin American political democracy (LARR, 17:3, 1982, p. 193–201, tables)

Current update of "democratic weathervane" started by Russell Fitzgibbon in 1945. Most recent scores show Costa Rica first, Venezuela second, and Mexico third of 20 nations. Since 1975, Argentina, Uruguay, Guatemala, and El Salvador show a reputational decline while Nicaragua, Peru, and Cuba show a reputational increase. [D.W. Dent]

6016 Latin American populism in comparative perspective. Edited by Michael L. Conniff. Albuquerque: University of New Mexico Press, 1982. 248 p.: bibl., index.

Historians look backward at populist politics—its roots, rise, and demise— using both a case study and comparative framework. Resurgence of populism should not be ruled out given economic and political problems facing Latin America in 1980s. Helpful in mapping research tasks ahead. [D.W. Dent]

6017 Levy, Daniel. Comparing authoritarian regimes in Latin America: insights from higher education policy (CUNY/CP, 14:1, Oct. 1981, p. 31–52, tables)

A primary target for repression by authoritarian governments is higher education. Examines policies in five countries during past decade and gives evidence of differences among them, illustrating variability of policy under authoritarian rule and suggesting causes. [G. Wynia]

Library of Congress. Hispanic Division. Human rights in Latin America, 1964–1980: a selective annotated bibliography. See item 18.

6018 Military government and the movement toward democracy in South America. Edited by Howard Handelman and Thomas G. Sanders. Bloomington: Indiana University Press; Hanover, N.H.: American Universities Field Staff, 1981. 388 p.: bibl.

Reports written by editors and Norman Gall while AUFS members in Ecuador, Peru, Brazil, Uruguay, and Chile during late 1970s. As with AUFS reports, these are informative accounts of politics within each country that fill in press gaps concerning military rule and transitions from military to civilian government. [G. Wynia]

6019 Millas, Orlando. La vigencia del leninismo en América Latina (URSS/AL, 4:28, 1980, p. 4–18)

Interesting Russian study of the past century of what it terms "capitalist dependency economics" in Latin American trade. [W.R. Garner]

6020 Needler, Martin C. An introduction to Latin American politics: the structure of conflict. 2. ed. Englewood Cliffs, N.J.: Prentice-Hall, 1983. 213 p.: bibl., index, maps.

Country-by-country approach to Latin American politics with emphasis on political cleavages, conflict, and conflict management. Author's theory of development tends to avoid such concepts as "dependency," "corporatism," and "internal colonialism." Useful introduction with interesting reference to similarities and differences although a "stable democratic order" is the preferred political system. [D.W. Dent]

6021 O'Donnell, Guillermo. Apuntes para una teoría del estado (CSUCA/ESC, 20, mayo/agosto 1978, p. 177–219)

Exercise in political theory develops structuralist concept of the State, stressing modes of domination, organization, externalization, and social relations. Project merits careful reading by students of the State in capitalist societies. [G. Wynia]

6022 ———. Comparative historical formations of the state apparatus and socioeconomic change in the Third World (UN/ISSJ, 32:4, 1980, p. 717–729)

Compares state formation in Latin America to other Third World societies. Speculates about contrasting effects of Latin America's earlier decolonization on diversity of patterns and how linkages to international market have created economic dependency not unlike that found throughout Third World. [G. Wynia]

6023 Oszlak, Oscar. The historical formation of the State in Latin America (LARR, 16:2, 1981, p. 3–32)

Proposes neo-marxist approach that puts new labels on familiar phenomena such as national integration after independence and use of State power to foster capital accumulation. [G. Wynia]

6024 Pasquino, Gianfranco. Inclusive and exclusive regimes and the corporatist model (Politica Internazionale [Nova Italia,

Firenze, Italy] 2:2, Winter 1981/Spring 1982, p. 36—50)

Examines corporatist model of bureaucratic-authoritarian rule in terms of inclusive and exclusive regimes. Thinks new traits have been introduced which will dominate future development of state structures in Brazil, Argentina, Chile, Peru, and Uruguay. For example, near future will bring about more decisive role for military, more complex and dynamic state apparatus, and less social peace. [D.W. Dent]

6025 Pease García, Henry *et al.* América Latina 80, democracia y movimiento popular. Lima: Centro de Estudios y Promoción del Desarrollo, 1981. 508 p.: bibl.

Series of 15 papers on democracy and mass movements in Latin America in 1980s presented at Univ. of the Pacific (Lima). Discusses theoretical and methodological themes while soundly denouncing military rule in Argentina, Brazil, and Chile, and Uruguay. [D.W. Dent]

Pensamiento conservador, 1815–1898. See *HLAS 44:7603.*

6025a Pérez del Castillo, Alvaro. Bolivia, Colombia, Chile y el Perú. La Paz: Editorial Los Amigos del Libro, 1980. 396 p., 4 p. of plates: ill.

Historical study of socioeconomic and political differences among the four countries which have placed strains on the Andean Pact and the common factors that have strengthened it. Emphasizes the geographical and military developments which aided in bringing about the Pact of Cartagena as an attempt "to prevent the Balkanization" of the four countries covered. Obviously a warning to Bolivia related to her Southern Cone relationships.

6026 Petras, James. Political change, class conflict and the decline of Latin American fascism (MR, 31:2, June 1979, p. 26—37)

Challenges conventional explanations of collapse of military regimes. Argues for increasing class conflict as primary cause and for conflicts within national bourgeoisie as secondary one. [G. Wynia]

6027 Pierce, Robert N. and **John Spicer Nichols.** Keeping the flame: media and government in Latin America. New York:

Hastings House, 1979. 270 p.: bibl., index (Studies in public communication)

Pathbreaking comparative analysis of media-government relations in nine Latin American nations. Devotes considerable attention to ethnocentricity involved in measuring press freedom. Four categories (i.e., disclosive-adversary, cautious, collaborative, and absorbed) serve to explain relationship between keepers of the flame and government. [D.W. Dent]

6028 Puebla en décimas: texto oficial, versión popular: cómo vivir la fe hoy en América Latina. Santiago: Conferencia Episcopal de Chile, 1979. 708 p.: ill., index.

Two-part book: 1) official text of conclusions of 1979 Puebla Episcopal Conference, progressive controversy over social and political Church doctrine and Pope John Paul II's visit to settle it; and 2) popular version of Puebla text prepared by Chilean clergy. Especially helpful is volume's analytical index to official Puebla document. [G. Wynia]

6029 Restrepo, Antonio. El periodismo frente al país: de la libertad de expresión al derecho a la comunicación. s.l.: Centro de Investigación Popular, 1981. 90 p. (Serie Controversia; no. 93)

Polemical discussion of freedom of expression and ability of media to communicate views contrary to those of governments and powerful private economic interests. Third World themes of need for more sympathetic system of international communication is major concern in this critical investigation. [D.W. Dent]

6030 Riding, Alan. The sword and cross (NYRB, 28:9, 28 May 1981, p. 3—8, ill.)

Review of four contemporary works focusing on role of the Catholic Church in the Latin American context. Brief, but insightful for layperson. [R.A. Camp]

6031 Saarbach, Stefan. Einige Aspekte der aktuellen Lateinamerikapolitik der Sozialdemokratie (Lateinamerika: Analysen und Bericht [Verlag Olle & Wolter, Berlin] 4, 1980, p. 120—160, bibl.)

Reviews recent developments in left-of-center social democratic parties in Latin America and interest toward such parties in West Germany. Discusses need to promote more communication between parties with social democratic tendencies. [G.M. Dorn]

6032 Salinas Bascur, Raquel. Communication policies: the case of Latin America. Stockholm: Institute of Latin American Studies, 1978. 39 leaves: bibl. (Research paper series; paper no. 9)

Believes present communication processes in Latin America are inordinately controlled by US commercial interests. Calls for "truly free and balanced flow of information" to and throughout Latin America. Believes ideal would be Latin American regional organization, free from US networks (see also item **6033**). [W.R. Garner]

6033 ———. Estudio exploratorio sobre receptividad posible de ALASEI (Agencia Latinoamericana de Servicios Especiales de Información en América Latina): informe final. Estocolmo: Universidad de Estocolmo, Instituto de Estudios Latinoamericanos, 1980. 52 p. (Occasional papers)

Tentative report on five-year feasiblity study towards creating a Latin American regional information service or center for coordinating newspaper, radio, and TV news that would combat lack of information and/or disinformation. Notes some success in discussing prospects. Interesting monograph. [W.R. Garner]

6034 Sanders, Thomas G. The politics of Catholicism in Latin America (SAGE/JIAS, 24:2, May 1982, p. 241–258)

Review essay of three "high quality" books on the politics of the Catholic Church in Brazil (Bruneau), Venezuela and Colombia (Levine), and Chile (Smith). Examines complexity and changing role of the Church since Medellín and Puebla with considerable insight and analytical imagination. [D.W. Dent]

6035 Sloan, John E. Bureaucracy and public policy in Latin America (IAMEA, 34:4, Spring 1981, p. 17–47)

Four-part analysis of influence of Latin American bureaucracies on developmental policies examines: 1) commitment to bureaucracies as developmental strategy; 2) structure and functions of modern bureaucracies; 3) their weaknesses; and 4) consequences for public policy. Concludes by stressing inability of Latin American policy makers to modernize the State as instrument of development. Inherent dilemma for Latin American development is that "the Weberian bureaucracy is antithetical to the dominant social values in Latin America." [D.W. Dent]

6036 Tarrow, Sidney. Transforming enemies into allies: non-ruling communist parties in multiparty coalitions (SPSA/JP, 44:4, Nov. 1982, p. 924–954, bibl.)

Investigates three "paradoxes" concerning Communist Party behavior when attempting to function within coalition government: 1) entering coalitions but then withdrawing as opposition; 2) inability to form alliances with others often perceived as "tools of capital;" and 3) first and second lead to CP's meager influence on government policy. Sees ineffectiveness as result of tension between CP's "Western" character (i.e., desire for political participation and power-sharing) and "leftist" nature (i.e., retention of orthodoxy, resistance to compromise). In delineating this major conflict, author makes significant contribution to theoretical literature on CP practice. [W.R. Garner]

MEXICO AND CENTRAL AMERICA

RODERIC A. CAMP, *Professor of Political Science, Central College, Pella, Iowa*

MEXICO: FROM A METHODOLOGICAL and analytical point of view, research on Mexico is still strongest among academic works on these countries. Two studies are especially noteworthy, Claude Pomerleau's analysis of "The Changing Church in Mexico and its Challenge to the State" (item **6074**), an outstanding analysis of a Mexican political topic as neglected as are the intellectuals and the military. In addition, Miguel Basáñez's *La lucha por la hegemonía en México: 1968–80* (item

6038), offers many valuable insights on the interrelationships among economic elites, cultural leaders, and the State.

CENTRAL AMERICA: General works on this region as a whole are on the rise and the best are written by Mexicans or published in that country as exemplified by *Centroamérica en crisis* (item **6089**), a compilation issued by Colegio de México's Centro de Estudios Internacionales. However, the most outstanding change taking place in the literature on Central America has been the plethora of articles and monographs on El Salvador and Nicaragua. As recently as 1979, *HLAS 41* had only two entries each for both of these countries. Academics are inclined to criticize journalists for focusing on a geographic area of topical interest thereby fanning too much attention on one subject. But as bibliographic listings show, scholars themselves are equally attracted to the hemisphere's trouble spots. As might be expected, much of the literature on the above mentioned countries is shallow and propagandistic (approximately half of the publications scanned for inclusion in this section). Nevertheless, one welcomes the fact that two countries so thoroughly neglected in the past are finally the subject of scholarly interest. The best sources for an insightful and objective view of the situation in El Salvador through 1982 are provided by Enrique A. Baloyra's *El Salvador in transition* (item **6113**) and by Mexico's notable poet Gabriel Zaid's article (item **6131**). More scholarly interpretations based on longer perspectives, undoubtedly will appear on Nicaragua, a country which will continue its own dynamic process of change despite the revolutionary victory. At present, much of the literature presents a Sandinista or official government view, as is evident from the annotations that follow. Among them, however, is a work sympathetic to the revolution which includes the best collection of essays on the topic and an original analysis by Thomas Walker (item **6175**). Scholars wishing for some assistance in the now prolific literature on Nicaragua should also examine the bibliographic review of Spanish sources by John A. Booth (item **6144**).

A development parallel to the increase in the literature on Central America is the noticeable cross-national emphasis of works on the trade union movement. This topic, which had not received much serious attention until recently, was spurred on by the V Conference of Mexican-US Historians held in Pátzcuaro, Mexico, 1977, whose subject was labor as exemplified by many publications annotated below. This new emphasis is apparent in some of the best works issuing from individual countries as for example in Marco A. Gandásegui Jr.'s "Las Luchas Obreras en Panama" (item **6179**); Silvia Gómez Tagle's "Insurgencia y Democracia en los Sindicatos Electricistas" (item **6055**), an important Mexican union; and Rafael Menjívar's "Formación y Lucha del Proletariado Industrial Salvadoreño" (item **6124**).

Overall, we can be pleased with the increase of careful analyses on Mexico and the Central American countries. In the case of Central America, however, there are still a number of gaps, especially with regard to Panama, Honduras, and Guatemala. One exception is Steve Ropp's work on the Panamanian National Guard (item **6182**).

The most potentially threatening methodological problem is the ideological and polemical tendency of the literature on Nicaragua, El Salvador, and to a lesser extent, on Guatemala. Let us hope that scholars will have learned from the Cuban Revolution that clear-headed analyses of these regimes' strengths and weaknesses can best serve our understanding of the processes of development in all societies.

MEXICO

6037 Bailey, John F. Agrarian reform in Mexico: the quest for self-sufficiency (CUH 80:469, Nov. 1981, p. 357–360)

Brief, but excellent explanation of recent changes in agrarian reform laws, and consequences of present agricultural situation for Mexico's development.

Barkin, David and **Gustavo Esteva.** Inflación y democracia: el caso de México. See *HLAS 44:2146.*

6038 Basañez, Miguel. La lucha por la hegemonía en México. México: Siglo XXI, 1982. 143 p.

Best overall analysis of Mexican political situation by a Mexican since Pablo González Casanova's work appeared in mid-1960s. Describes in detail interrelationships between important groups, especially cultural leaders and entrepreneurs, and the State (1968–80).

6039 Basurto, Jorge. The late populism in Luis Echeverría (*in* Latin American populism in comparative perspective. [see item **6016**] p. 93–111, chart)

Argues that Echeverría attempted to introduce populist goals typical of Cárdenas era (1934–40), but failed to accomplish significant changes for middle classes, peasants, and labor. Complements Susan W. Sanderson's *Land reform in Mexico: 1910–1980* (New York: Academic Press, 1983).

6040 Bringas, Guillermina and **David Mascareño.** La prensa de los obreros mexicanos, 1870–1970: hemerografía comentada. México: Universidad Nacional Autónoma de México, 1979. 289 p.

Excellent reference tool for locating newspapers in archives and the type of materials each has on the labor movement. Includes detailed annotations.

6041 Camp, Roderic Ai. Family relationships in Mexican politics: a preliminary view (SPSA/JP, 44, Aug. 1982, p. 848–862)

Argues that kinship ties among Mexican political leaders has not declined in the last 40 years and that implications of such ties must be taken into account in assessment of continuity and turnover in Mexico's leadership.

6042 ———. La formación de un gobernante: la socialización de los líderes políticos en México post-revolucionario. México: Fondo de Cultura Económica, 1981. 268 p.: bibl., tables.

Analysis, based on extensive interviews, of sources of socialization of Mexican politicians governing Mexico (1940–70). Suggests some commonalities in such experience which have contributed to political stability.

6043 ———. Intellectuals: agents of change in Mexico? (UM/JIAS, 23:3, Aug. 1981, p. 297–320)

Examines structural relationships between intellectuals and the State (1920–80) and speculates about potential of intellectuals to influence governmental policies.

6044 Camposeco, Miguel Angel. El proceso político de renovación en México (NSO, 35, marzo/abril 1978, p. 90–102)

Interesting analysis, using voting statistics, of growth of apathy and abstention in the Mexican electoral process. Comments on recent changes in election laws and the media and their possible consequences for political participation.

6045 Carpizo, Jorge. Algunos aspectos de la organización del Ejecutivo Federal Mexicano (UNAM/RFD, 28:110, mayo/agosto 1978, p. 367–384)

Essentially an historical and legalistic analysis of provisions in the 1917 Constitution focusing on the Mexican president. Presents some interesting comparisons with US chief executive on issue of no-reelection and presidential terms.

6046 Carrillo Castro, Alejandro. Evolución de la reforma administrativa en México: 1971–1979. México: M.A. Porrúa, 1980. 274 p., 5 folded leaves of plates: bibl., ill. (La Reforma administrativa en México; 2)

Series of essays on 1970s administrative reforms. Because the editor is considered to be source of those reforms for 1976–83 administration, there is some value in his selections and presentations.

6047 Castillo, Heberto *et al.* 1968 [i.e. Mil novecientos sesenta y ocho], el principio del poder. México: *Proceso*, 1981. 310 p.: ill.

Fascinating collection of essays and interviews of what took place during the 1968 massacre 10 years after it. Includes some very useful interview material with participants and observers, including Gen. José Hernández Toledo, who claims "no one was killed."

6048 ——— and **Francisco J. Paoli Polio.** El poder robado. México: EDAMEX, 1980. 253 p.: ill.

Interpretation of the Mexican political scene from the viewpoint of one of Mexico's leading leftist intellectuals and leader of the opposition Mexican Workers Party. Lengthy appendix provides declarations of party principles.

6049 **Chávez, Elías.** Los priistas. México: Proceso, 1980. 263 p.: ill., ports.

Collection of articles published by one of Mexico's leading political journalists, Elías Chávez of Proceso. Some have been published elsewhere, and focus is on the official party and its leaders.

6050 **50 [i.e. Cincuenta] años de PRI.** Equipo de escritores y reporteros de Proceso. México: Editorial Posada: CISA, 1980. 348 p.: ill.

Selection of essays taken from magazine Proceso through 1979. Interesting collection, especially interview with former Governor of Campeche, José Ortiz Avila.

6051 **Cochrane, James D.** Occupants of elite positions in the Mexican diplomatic community (JDA, 15:4, July 1981, p. 605–620, tables)

Careful analysis of Mexican diplomatic leaders (1935–79). Reaches some interesting conclusions about recruitment process on basis of background data and career experiences.

6052 **Corrales Ayala, Rafael** and **Pericles Namorado Urrutia.** Ensayos sobre la reforma política III. v. 3. México: Gaceta Informativa de la Comisión Federal Electoral, 1979. 78 p.: tables (Serie Ensayos; 9)

Second half of this short work contains excellent explanation of the proportional representation system introduced by new electoral laws.

Davis, Charles L. and **Kenneth M. Coleman.** Discontinuous educational experiences and political and religious nonconformity in authoritarian regimes: Mexico. See item **4453.**

6053 **Dobrzycki, Wieslaw.** Koncepcja państwa i spoleczeństwa w konstytucji meksykańskiej = Concepción del Estado y de la sociedad en la Constitución mexicana (Studia Nauk Politycznych [Warsaw] 2, 1982, p. 103–126)

Study by Polish political scientist based on extensive bibliography of the period that led to 1917 Mexican Constitution. However, author's frequent and somewhat thoughtless use of quotations detracts from the article's scholarship. [K. Complak]

6054 **El Estado mexicano.** Edited by Jorge Alonso. México: Nueva Imagen, 1982. 437 p.

Some of Mexico's best social scientists provide broad selection of essays which range widely across subjects of contemporary interest. In particular, focus is on relationship of the State to social classes, urban labor, and social communication.

6055 **Gómez Tagle, Silvia.** Insurgencia y democracia en los sindicatos electricistas. México: El Colegio de México, Centro de Estudios Sociológicos, 1980. 225 p.: bibl. (Jornadas; 93)

Excellent analysis of one of the more influential and independent unions in Mexico. Author carefully traces development of electricians union and reasons for and consequences of independent factions.

6056 **González Casanova, Pablo.** El Estado y los partidos políticos en México: ensayos. México: Ediciones Era, 1981. 178 p. (Colección Problemas de México)

Collection of five essays written 1976–80 by one of Mexico's leading intellectuals stressing role labor movements or other popular organizations might play as institutions autonomous of the State.

6057 **Granados Chapa, Miguel Angel.** Excelsior y otros temas de comunicación. México: Ediciones el Caballito, 1980. 306 p.

Selection of articles by one of Mexico's leading journalists covering number of important issues involving communications and the media, including the Excelsior "affair."

6058 **Grayson, George W.** The politics of Mexican oil. Pittsburgh, Pa.: University of Pittsburgh, 1980. 283 p.: bibl., index (Pitt Latin American series; PLAS 7)

One of the better analyses on Mexican

oil, containing much original research on the petroleum workers union and its relationship to PEMEX. Readable and objective (for international relations specialist's comment, see *HLAS 43:7184*).

6059 Hamilton, Nora. The limits of State autonomy: post-Revolutionary Mexico. Princeton, N.J: Princeton University Press, 1982. 391 p.

Helpful analysis, focused on class relationships, of ties between the State and private sector during Cárdenas era. Uses petroleum expropriation as case study, but excludes other domestic considerations important to understanding some broader issues.

6060 ———. The State and the national bourgeoisie in post-Revolutionary Mexico: 1920–1940 (LAP, 9[4]:35, Fall 1982, p. 31–54, bibl.)

Informative essay on State-private relationships, which examines, in some detail, several economic groups, during late 1920s and 1930s.

6061 Hodara, Joseph. Los futuros de México: un marco de referencia. México: Fomento Cultural BANAMEX, 1978. 132 p.: bibl., tables.

Serious and provocative analysis of important issues and themes affecting Mexico's economic and social development, both domestic and international.

6062 Imaz, Cecilia. La izquierda y la reforma política en México: situación actual y perspectivas de la democracia (UNAM/RMS, 43:3, julio/sept. 1981, p. 1103–1120)

Argues that political reforms, and coalition of the left offers greater opportunities to "progressive" forces in Mexico in the 1982 elections. Identifies problems of "illegal" left, that is, groups without legal recognition, and what this means to the voter.

6063 Labastida Martín del Junco, Julio. De la unidad nacional al desarrollo estabilizador: 1940–1970 (*in* América Latina: historia de medio siglo. v. 2, Centroamérica, México y el Caribe. Coordinación: Pablo González Casanova. México: Siglo Veintiuno Editores, 1981, p. 328–375, bibl.)

Broad synthesis of economic patterns and their political consequences for Mexico since 1940. Interesting interpretations of

changes taking place in relationship between private sector and the State in early 1970s. Includes excellent bibliography.

Leñero, Vicente. Los periodistas. See *HLAS 44:5181.*

6064 Levy, Daniel C. University and government in Mexico: autonomy in an authoritarian regime. New York: Praeger, 1980. 173 p.

First work to analyze relationship between Mexico's most important university and the government. Provides excellent background and theoretical observations.

6065 López Portillo, José. Filosofía política de José López Portillo. México: Secretaría de Programación y Presupuesto, Dirección General de Documentación y Análisis, 1979. 228 p.

Extremely well-indexed, by paragraph and source, of President José López Portillo's speeches (1977–79).

6066 López Rosado, Diego G. La burocracia en México. pt. 1, Epoca prehispánica. pt. 2, Epoca virreinal. pt. 4, México independiente. México: Secretaría de Comercio, 1980- . 3 v. (563 p.): bibl.

Four-part study, of which pts. 1, 2 and 4 were available for review. Excellent addition to literature on Mexico's bureaucracy by author who has contributed previous works of value to Mexicanists. Contributes much to the dearth of statistical information on governmental employees from the pre-Hispanic period to the present.

6067 Mancilla Guzmán, Sergio. Las opciones políticas en México. México: Editorial Epoca, 1981. 229 p.: bibl.

Following general historical background of the development of Mexican politician parties, author provides brief description of founding and principles of each of the parties currently having legal recognition, and two which do not.

6068 Manger, Annette and **Manfred Mols.** Reforma Política und opposition in Mexiko (JGSWGL, 17, 1980, p. 395–429)

Discusses political reforms of López Portillo which were designed to dispel discontent, maintain system of control, and renew the State's legitimacy. While such changes have had some success in organizing opposition into political parties, socioeconomic causes of discontent remains constant. [R.E. Greenleaf]

6069 Martínez Verdugo, Arnoldo. Crisis política y alternativa comunista. Prólogo de Eduardo Montes. México: Ediciones de Cultura Popular, 1979. 286 p.

Secretary General of Mexico's Communist Party, one of the most important opposition organizations, provides serious exploration of important issues facing his party, its possible alliances and its international position.

6070 Mayo, Baloy. La guerrilla de Genaro y Lucio: análisis y resultados. México: Editorial Diógenes, 1980. 103 p.: bibl.

Short work provides useful, reasonable perspective on a subject about which little has been written in Mexico: the guerrilla movement in south-western Guerrero state. Attempts to analyze the guerrilla movement in larger context.

Mexican workers in the United States: historical and political perspectives. See *HLAS 44:2235.*

6071 Mexico's political economy: challenges at home and abroad. Edited by Jorge I. Domínguez. Beverly Hills, Calif.: Sage, 1982. 239 p.: bibl., index (Sage focus editions; 47)

Contains three original studies by Edward J. Williams, David Mares and Kevin Middlebrook, all providing detailed research and current interpretation of petroleum, trade, and labor relations in Mexico.

6072 Patiño Camarena, Javier. Análisis de la reforma política. México: Universidad Nacional Autónoma de México, Instituto de Investigaciones Jurídicas, 1980. 118 p.: bibl. (Serie G, Estudios doctrinales; no. 38)

Careful analysis, with thorough documentation, of juridical effects of Mexico's political reforms, primarily that of the proportional representation system.

6073 Pensamiento de México en los periódicos: páginas editoriales, 1975. Editor, Javier Márquez. Jurados, Teodoro Cesarman *et al.* México: Editorial Tecnos, 1976. 442 p.: index.

Excellent and useful collection of 252 articles from the editorial pages of leading Mexican newspapers for 1975. Extremely well organized and indexed by subject and author. Reflects wide diversity of views.

6074 Pomerleau, Claude. The changing Church in Mexico and its challenge to the State (UND/RP, 43:4, Oct. 1981, p. 540–559)

Outstanding contribution on much neglected topic in Mexican life. Author really raises some crucial issues on the Church/State relationship, and integrates contemporary political research with that of the Church.

6075 Pozas Horcasitas, Ricardo. La consolidación del nuevo orden institucional en México: 1929–1940 (*in* América Latina: historia de medio siglo. v. 2, Centroamérica, México y el Caribe. Coordinación: Pablo González Casanova. México: Siglo XXI Editores, 1981, p. 259–327, bibl., table)

Thoroughly researched essay adds new insight into individuals, organizations, and institutions aiding the institutionalization of the Mexican regime up to Avila Camacho's inauguration.

6076 Prevôt-Schapira, Marie-France. Travailleurs du pétrole et pouvoir syndical au Mexique (CDAL, 20, 2. semestre 1979, p. 65–94, maps, tables)

Analysis of Mexican petroleum industry focuses on unique relationship between state-owned industry and petroleum union. Argues that establishment of new oil towns, and subsequent creation of new union sections (or locals) threatens internal stability of the national union.

Revueltas, José. México 68: juventud y revolución. See *HLAS 44:2246.*

6077 Reyna, José Luis *et al.* Tres estudios sobre el movimiento obrero en México. México: Colegio de México, 1976. 202 p.: ill. (Jornadas; 80)

Contains three of the best recent case studies of organized labor in Mexico: 1) useful general introduction; 2) contemporary organizational patterns; and 3) democratic reform movement in electricians union.

Rodríguez Araujo, Octavio. La reforma política y los partidos en México. See *HLAS 44:2251.*

6078 Rosas, Javier *et al.* 50 [i.e. Cincuenta] años de oposición en México. México: Universidad Nacional Autónoma de México, Departamento de Ciencia Política, 1979. 221 p. (Serie Estudios. Facultad de Ciencias Políticas y Sociales; 60)

Presents a collection of essays, some by scholars, others by political leaders, evaluating 11 important opposition parties or movements in Mexico since 1923. Contributions by scholars are more valuable, and shed light on some important movements from 1920s through 1950s.

6079 Saldívar, Américo. Ideología y políticas del Estado mexicano, 1976–1978. México: Siglo Veintiuno Editores, 1980. 237 p.: bibl. (Sociología y política / Siglo Veintiuno Editores)

Serious work, written from Marxist perspective, examines causes and results of changes taking place during Luis Echeverría's regime (1970–76). Among many conclusions reached is author's belief that political reforms since 1976 will have limited effect because of the Mexican State's inability to reexamine the fundamental interests of dominant classes.

6080 Sánchez Cárdenas, Carlos. Reforma política: estrategia y táctica. México: Extemporáneos, 1979. 272 p.

Selection of speeches and writings from 1970s by long-time communist militant and politician who analyzes the government's political reforms through 1979. Revealing because of their point-of-view.

6081 Sanderson, Steven E. Agrarian populism and the Mexican State: the struggle for land in Sonora. Berkeley: University of California Press, 1981. 290 p.: bibl., index.

Although allowing theories on populism occasionally to override its careful analysis, this work is a well-researched and crafted exploration. Uses case study to investigate roots of Mexican populism and relationship between agrarian reform and national politics. An original, worthwhile addition to contemporary analyses on Mexico.

6082 Semo, Enrique *et al.* Seis aspectos del México real. México: Biblioteca Universidad Veracruzana, 1979. 243 p.: bibl. (Política, economía y administración)

Six Marxist views of contemporary Mexico, well-researched and useful, ranging from the state of public health to democratizing public education. Among more interesting contributions is Gilberto Argüello's essay on "Intellectualism and Power since 1917."

6083 Simposio sobre México hoy, 1978. Visión del México contemporáneo. México: Colegio de México, 1979. 148 p.

Essays of Urquidi, Sepúlveda, Pellicer, Paz, and Ojeda commend themselves in this uneven collection. Authors might agree that a series of factors—the oil glut, Mexico's economic crisis, disaffection with López Portillo—have substantially changed "the vision of contemporary Mexico" in the years since this book appeared. [G.W. Grayson]

Smith, Peter. Labyrinths of power: political recruitment in twentieth-century Mexico. See *HLAS 44:2269.*

6084 Spalding, Rose J. State power and its limits: corporatism in Mexico (CPS, 14:2, July 1981, p. 139–161, bibl.)

Argues that corporatist structures in Mexico are well and functioning. Analyzes several independent influences, most notably the bureaucracy itself, which counterbalance the State's role.

6085 Urquidi, Víctor L. Not by oil alone: the outlook for Mexico (CUH, 81:472, Feb. 1982, p. 78–81, 90)

Leading Mexican economist and intellectual analyzes current economic difficulties and possibilities oil revenues provide for solving numerous problems, especially in agriculture. Up-to-date, critical evaluation.

CENTRAL AMERICA
GENERAL

6086 Bravo, Oscar. Modernización, industrialización y política en América Central: El Salvador, Guatemala y Honduras. Stockholm: Institute of Latin American Studies, 1980. 139 p. (Occasional papers)

Serious monograph tries to demonstrate with analysis and statistics the significance of the land question and inability of the countries under examination to deal with this issue through merely changing governments.

6087 Central America and the Caribbean. Graham Hovey, advisory editor. Gene Brown, editor. New York: Arno Press, 1980. 412 p.: bibl., ill., index (The Great contemporary issues)

Ready source of clippings from *The New York Times* (1860s-present).

6088 Chinchilla, Norma Stoltz. Class struggle in Central America: background and overview (LAP, 7[25/26]:2/3, Spring/Summer 1980, p. 2–23)

Maintains that Nicaraguan Sandinistas have understood principle that "theory is not a dogma," and that their understanding of concrete conditions in Nicaragua was a key to their success. Success of revolutionary movements in Guatemala and El Salvador will require a similar knowledge.

6089 El Colegio de México. Centro de Estudios Internacionales. Centroamérica en crisis. México: El Colegio, 1980. 226 p.: bibl. (Colección Centro de Estudios Internacionales; 21)

One of the best collections of scholarly essays on Central America contains one on each country. Three essays deal with the general Central American situation and one forecasts some possibilities for 1980s.

6090 Díaz Herrera, Roberto. Breve reseña de Omar Torrijos H. y su impacto en la doctrina militar latinoamericana (LNB/L, 305/309:1, agosto/dic. 1981, p. 33–44)

Extraordinarily flattering, anecdotal account of how Torrijos "married the Armed Forces to the true interests of the people." In contrast to Peru's populist military men, Torrijos invited civilians as well as officers into key bureaucratic posts and insisted the armed forces not constitute a separate caste. His support for pragmatism, pluralism, and economic progress brought "social peace" to Panama. [G.W. Grayson]

6091 Jiménez Veiga, Danilo. El sindicalismo en Centroamérica y la intervención del estado en la década de 1980. México: Secretaría del Trabajo y Previsión Social, Instituto Nacional de Estudios del Trabajo, 1981. 78 p.: bibl.

Too brief, but serious attempt at comparing the intervention of the State in labor union activity in Central American countries. Argues that state suppression is on the increase because it is such an important employer.

6092 Millett, Richard L. The politics of violence: Guatemala and El Salvador (CUH, 80:463, Feb. 1981, p. 70–74, 88)

Leading expert on Nicaragua and Central America is pessimistic about a negotiated political settlement in these two countries.

6093 Ritter G., Vilma. Omar Torrijos Herrera y la teoría militar (LNB/L, 305/309:1, agosto/dic. 1981, p. 45–59)

Torrijos, a product of rural, lower middle class family, believed that National Guardsmen as *militares desarrollistas* should work closely with people at grass roots to identify their needs, encourage political participation, advance social and economic development, and, thereby, promote internal security. [G.W. Grayson]

6094 Schall, James V. Central America and politicized religion (APS/WA, 144:2, Fall 1981, p. 126–149)

Well written and thoughtful interpretation of the role of the Church, or more generally religion, in bringing about revolutionary societies. Argues that religion is increasingly responsible for Marxist governments.

6095 Stone, Samuel. Producción y política en Centroamérica (UTIEH/C, 36, 1981, p. 5–21, bibl., graphs, tables)

Brief historical analysis of relationship between political leadership and economic production in Central America. Argues that insufficient attention is being paid to production, as distinct from distribution of wealth, and that this will continue to prove an obstacle to development.

BELIZE

6096 Carpio Nicolle, Roberto. Hacia donde va Belice. Guatemala: Editorial Girblán y Cía., 1977. 297 p.: bibl., ill. (Ediciones Pop)

For the few books written about Belize, this work provides an unusually well documented and illustrated text on the historical and contemporary questions concerning territorial issues.

COSTA RICA

6097 Barahona Riera, Francisco. Reforma agraria y poder político. San José: Editorial Universidad de Costa Rica, 1980. 472 p.: bibl., ill., tables.

Detailed, serious analysis, with much statistical reference matter which looks at land tenure questions. Author examines wide range of structures and issues involved in Costa Rican agriculture and efforts toward agrarian reform, including unionization, large landholders, and government policy. The focus on political aspects of this social and economic problem is excellent.

6098 Cazanga Moncada, Osvaldo. El Partido Social-Democrata de Costa Rica: una experiencia política (UCR/RF, 17:46, julio/dic. 1979, p. 173–183)

Analysis of formation of Social Democratic Party during 1940s. Demonstrates how party differs from European social democrats and argues that it is a product of fissures among Costa Rica's dominant class, having little support from labor.

6099 Hernández, Rubén and Gerardo Trejos. La tutela de los derechos humanos. San José: Ediciones Juricentro, 1977. 160 p. (Colección Escuela libre de derecho)

Legal and historical work tracing evolution of public rights in Costa Rica. Covers colonial period from end of 18th century to present.

6100 Hoivik, Tord and Solveig Aas. Demilitarization in Costa Rica: a farewell to arms? (JPR, 18:4, 1981, p. 333–351, tables)

Carefully crafted analysis of degree to which Costa Rica is demilitarized, both factually and ideologically, and impact these characteristics have on internal and external policies.

6101 Oconitrillo García, Eduardo. Un siglo de política costarricense: crónica de 23 campañas presidenciales. San José: Editorial Universidad Estatal a Distancia, 1981. 274 p.: ill.

Valuable source of data on every national political campaign (1889–1978). In addition to election data, contains many well-chosen political cartoons.

6102 Rodríguez Vega, Eugenio. De Calderón a Figueres. 2. ed. San José: Editorial Universidad Estatal a Distancia, 1981. 269 p., 32 p. of plates: bibl., ill., index.

Compilation of some interesting data and photographs on recent political leadership in Costa Rica.

6103 Romero Pérez, Jorge Enrique. Partidos políticos, poder y derecho: Costa Rica. San José: Eds. Syntagma, 1979. 116 p.: bibl.

Well researched but entirely theoretical analysis of the concept of political parties in Costa Rican context.

6104 Rosenberg, Mark B. Social reform in Costa Rica: social security and the presidency of Rafael Angel Calderón (HAHR, 61:2, May 1981, p. 278–296)

Interesting history of decision-making process which implemented Costa Rica's social security program and analysis of consequences of those reforms. Argues this was an example of an elitist implementation of social programs.

6105 Schifter Sikora, Jacobo. Los partidos políticos: libro. Heredia, Costa Rica: Universidad Nacional, Facultad de Filosofía, Artes y Letras, Instituto de Estudios Latinoamericanos, 1978. 105 p.: bibl.

Brief, but serious analysis of contemporary political parties in Costa Rica, especially useful for insights into minor groups on the left.

6106 Vargas, Armando et al. La crisis de la democracia en Costa Rica. San José: Editorial Universidad Estatal a Distancia, 1981. 83 p.: bibl., ill.

Series of essays critical of current state of affairs in Costa Rica. Several argue that democracy needs to be more innovative and propose concrete changes to meet future demands.

6107 Vega Carballo, José Luis. Costa Rica: coyunturas, clases sociales y estado en su desarrollo reciente, 1930–1975 (in América Latina: historia de medio siglo. v. 2, Centroamérica, México y el Caribe. Coordinación: Pablo González Casanova. México: Siglo XXI Editores, 1981, p. 1–37, bibl., tables)

Examines long-term changes in economic patterns of production and investment and their impact on class relationships and growth. Makes special note of middle class expansion.

6108 ———. Democracia y dominación en Costa Rica. San José: Universidad de Costa Rica, Facultad de Ciencias Sociales, Instituto de Investigaciones Sociales, 1981. 44 p. (Avance de investigación; no. 39)

Brief analytical essay which examines several important variables and their consequences for Costa Rican style democracy and stability.

6109 Zelaya, Chester *et al.* ¿Democracia en Costa Rica?: cinco opiniones polémicas. San José: Editorial Universidad Estatal a Distancia, 1978. 248 p.: bibl., graphs (Serie Estudios sociopolíticos; no. 1)

Interdisciplinary collection of scholarly analyses which attempt to answer, from a historical, economic and political perspective, the viability of democracy in Costa Rica.

EL SALVADOR

6110 Armstrong, Robert. El Salvador: beyond elections (NACLA, 16:2, March/April 1982, p. 2–30, bibl., photos)

Identifies, in considerable detail, problems and questions raised by El Salvador's constituent elections. Sees major problem of the left as inability to appeal to urban populations. Useful and up-to-date.

6111 ——— and Janet Shernk. El Salvador: a revolution brews (NACLA/LAER, 14:4, July/Aug. 1980, p. 2036, bibl., ill.)

General, well-stated assessment of background of events in El Salvador and consequences of US intervention. Likens it to another Vietnam.

6112 Arnson, Cynthia. El Salvador: a revolution confronts the United States. Washington: Institute for Policy Studies, 1982. 118 p.

Brief, objective analysis of El Salvador's contemporary situation notable for the concrete suggestions on how the political impasse might be solved and how the US should view its alternatives.

6113 Baloyra, Enrique A. El Salvador in transition. Chapel Hill: University of North Carolina Press, 1982. 1 v.: bibl., index.

Important interpretation of the recent Salvadoran political situation which stresses that the political antagonists, and therefore important political issues facing El Salvador, are not just confined to the government or the leftist guerrillas. Excellent analysis of diverse groups participating in 1982 constituent elections.

6114 Didion, Joan. In El Salvador: pts. 1/3 (The New York Review of Books [New York] 29:17, 4 Nov. 1982, p. 9–17, ill.; 29:18, 18 Nov. 1982, p. 31–55, ill.; 29:19, 2 Dec. 1982, p. 23–31, ill.)

Well-known novelist provides beautifully written interpretation of present ambience in El Salvador. Although capturing the terror of living in such an environment, author's interpretations do not help us understand how El Salvador reached this condition nor what can be done to resolve it.

6115 Duarte, José Napoleón. Comunitarismo para un mundo más humano. 2. ed. San José: Instituto de Estudios Políticos, 1980. 200 p.: bibl., ill.

Former leader of El Salvador presents numerous essays reflecting his ideology, including those pertaining to social conflict, political ideology, fundamentals of Christian Democracy, and communitarianism.

6116 El Salvador on the threshold of a democratic revolutionary victory. San Salvador: Frente Farabundo Martí de Liberación Nacional y Frente Democrático Revolucionario (FMLN/FDR), 1981. 99 p.: ill.

Propaganda document of the Farabundo Martí National Liberation Front and the Democratic Revolutionary Front which provides useful defense of their position. Contains wide variety of helpful information in the appendices.

6117 Flores Pinal, Fernando. El golpe de estado en El Salvador: ¿un camino hacia la democratización? (UNAM/RMS, 42:2, abril/junio 1980, p. 669–694, graphs, tables)

Takes somewhat positive view that events of 1979 could lead to increased participation. Believes even this limited form of democratization would be beneficial and have helpful consequences on society.

6118 González Janzen, Ignacio. La batalla de El Salvador. México: Prolibro, 1981. 143 p.: ill.

Critical view, with photographs and numerous documents, which largely sees Salvadoran military and US government as guilty parties in El Salvador's conflict.

6119 Guerra Rivas, Tomás. El Salvador, octubre sangriento: itinerario y análisis del golpe militar del 15 de octubre de 1979. San José: Centro Víctor Sanabria, 1979. 158 p.: ill.

Attempt to document tortures or disappearance and murders of Salvadorans by the military government. Includes partial list of the disappeared (1973–79).

6120 Handal Shafick, Jorge. El pueblo proseguirá la lucha hasta la victoria (URSS/AL, 7[43], 1981, p. 4–18)

Insightful interview with Secretary General of Central Committee of the Salvadoran Communist Party just two weeks after the FMLN general offensive (Jan. 1981).

Krusé, David Samuel and **Richard Swedberg.** El Salvador: bibliography and research guide. See item **17.**

6121 MacEoin, Gary and **Lourdes Argüelles.** Reflexiones sobre la lucha en El Salvador (AR, 6:24, abril 1980, p. 4–12)

Strong criticism of US policy towards El Salvador. Authors believe it should be abandoned and that essential support from this policy comes only from the oligarchy.

6122 Menéndez Rodríguez, Mario. El Salvador, una auténtica guerra civil. Ciudad Universitaria Rodrigo Facio, Costa Rica: Editorial Universitaria Centroamericana, 1980. 226 p.: ill. (Colección Debate)

Well-known Mexican journalist presents number of valuable interviews with various opponents of El Salvador's military government. Clearly written.

6123 Menjívar Larín, Rafael. El Salvador, el eslabón más pequeño. Ciudad Universitaria Rodrigo Facio, Costa Rica: Editorial Universitaria Centroamericana, 1980. 237 p.: bibl. (Colección Debate)

Ex-rector of University of El Salvador and leader of Democratic Revolutionary Front provides his interpretation of recent political events and describes policies of various political groups in his country.

6124 ———. Formación y lucha del proletariado industrial salvadoreño. San Salvador: UCA Editores, 1979. 126 p.: bibl., tables (Colección Estructuras y procesos; v. 7)

Serious, scholarly analysis of Salvadoran labor movement (1880s-1970s). Includes many tables with relevant data.

6125 Montgomery, Tommie Sue. Revolution in EL Salvador: origins and evolution. Boulder, Colo.: Westview Press, 1982. 252 p.: bibl., ill., index.

Journalist provides well-written, insightful, serious analysis of revolutionary situation. Gives more attention to leftist groups than to differences among the middle and right.

6126 North, Liisa. Bitter grounds: roots of revolt in El Salvador. Toronto, Canada: Between the Lines, 1981. 110 p.: bibl., ill., maps.

This short work is the least developed of recent books in English on El Salvador, and differs very little. What is most unusual is the final chapter which asks questions about what role Canada should play in relation to these events.

6127 Partido de la Revolución Salvadoreña. El Salvador, un volcán social. San Salvador: Ruptura, 1977? 92 p.

Official view of Salvadoran Revolutionary Party towards the causes of nation's present economic and political problems.

6128 Romero, Oscar Arnulfo. La voz de los sin voz: la palabra viva de Monseñor Oscar Arnulfo Romero. Introducciones, comentarios y selección de textos de R. Cardenal, I. Martín-Baró, J. Sobrino. San Salvador: UCA Editores, Universidad Centroamericana José Simeón Cañas, 1980. 481 p.: bibl. (Colección La Iglesia en América Latina; v. 6)

Primary document which brings together many speeches and thoughts of Oscar Anulfo Romero, Archbishop of San Salvador, who was assassinated while celebrating mass (24 March 1980).

6129 ——— *et al.* Iglesia de los pobres y organizaciones populares. San Salvador: UCA Editores, Universidad Centroamericana José Simeón Cañas, 1979. 249 p.: bibl. (Colección La Iglesia en América Latina; v. 4)

Serious analysis of the role and mission of the Catholic Church among peasants. While work discusses the Salvadoran situation in particular, it has relevance for the entire region.

6130 Salazar Valiente, Mario. El Salvador: crisis, dictadura, lucha . . . 1920–1980 (*in* América Latina: historia de medio siglo. v. 2, Centroamérica, México y el Caribe. Coordinación, Pablo González Casanova. México: Siglo XXI Editores, 1981, p. 87–138, appendix, bibl.)

Argues that despite widespread suppression, the Salvadoran masses have demonstrated a historical will to resist. New economic developments, formented by establishment of rural and urban proletariat, will, in his opinion, lead to increased revolutionary pressures.

6131 Zaid, Gabriel. Enemy colleagues: a reading of the Salvadoran tragedy (DIS, Winter 1982, p. 13–40)

Insightful, original interpretation of 1980–82 events in El Salvador. Provides some logical food for thought on the legitimacy of violence in that society, and more importantly, suggests concrete alternatives. For Spanish version of this article, see *Vuelta* (México, 5:56, julio 1981, p. 9–27).

GUATEMALA

6132 Aguilera Peralta, Gabriel Edgardo. El estado, la lucha de clases y la violencia en Guatemala (UNAM/RMS, 42:2, abril/junio 1980, p. 525–558, tables)

Careful statistical analysis of acts of violence in Guatemala. Draws some preliminary conclusions about who is affected by violence and its consequences for Guatemalan society.

6133 ——— et al. Dialéctica del terror en Guatemala. Ciudad Universitaria Rodrigo Facio, Costa Rica: Editorial Universitaria Centroamericana, 1981. 281 p.: ill.

Valuable, detailed analysis and statistical report of victims of violence (mid-1960s to mid-1970s). Will be of primary use for researchers.

6133a Albízurez, Miguel Angel. Struggles and experiences of the Guatemalan trade-union movement, 1976-June 1978 (LAP, 75[25/26]:2/3, Spring/Summer 1980, p. 145–159, plates)

Ex-leader's personal perspective of Guatemala's trade union movement through 1978.

6134 Inter-American Commission on Human Rights. Report on the situation of human rights in the Republic of Guatemala. Washington: Organization of American States, General Secretariat, 1981. 133 p. (OEA/Ser.L/V/II.53, doc. 21, rev. 2)

OAS official report, with documentation, of human rights abuses.

6135 Payeras, Mario. Los días de la selva. La Habana: Casa de las Américas, 1980. 115 p.

Committed revolutionary provides inside look of guerrilla movements in Guatemala. Winner of Cuba's Casa de las Américas Prize (1980).

6136 Rudel, Christian. Guatemala: terrorisme d'Etat. Paris: Karthala, 1981. 183 p.: bibl., ill., maps (Meridiens)

Useful analysis, with historical perspective, of State-supported terrorism in Guatemala.

6137 Toriello Garrido, Guillermo. Guatemala, más de 20 años de traición. Caracas: Editorial Ateneo de Caracas, 1980. 296 p.: bibl., diagra.

Highly critical account which places most of the blame for Guatemala's political and economic situation in the last 25 years on the US intervention, especially by CIA, US State Department, and Pentagon.

HONDURAS

6138 Frente. Revista trimestral de orientación sindical. Sindicato de Trabajadores de la Universidad Nacional Autónoma de Honduras (SITRAUNAH) afiliado a la FUTH. Año 1, No. 2, 1981- . Tegucigalpa.

Issue contains three essays dealing with Honduras' labor movement, a rare subject of study, and two interviews. Strangely, it also includes a literary section.

6139 Pozas, Mario and **Rafael del Cid.** Honduras: los límites del reformismo castrense: 1972–1979 (UNAM/RMS, 42:2, abril/junio 1980, p. 607–648, tables)

Careful evaluation of Honduras' agrarian situation, with pessimistic outlook for 1980s.

6140 Reina, Jorge Arturo. ¿Que pasa hoy en Honduras?: 50 preguntas y respuestas sobre la realidad política nacional. Tegucigalpa: Rapicopias, 1981. 35 p.

Brief presentation, based on larger study, offers question and answer format to number of important issues facing Honduras in 1980s.

NICARAGUA

Adams, Richard N. The Sandinistas and the Indians: the "problem" of the Indian in Nicaragua. See item **906.**

6141 Amnesty International. The Republic of Nicaragua: an Amnesty International report including the findings of a mission to Nicaragua, 10–15 May 1978. London:

Amnesty International Publications, 1977. 75 p.: bibl., facsim., map.

Useful and well-documented report of Amnesty International's investigative mission to Nicaragua (May 1976). Includes detailed listing of tortured and murdered victims.

6142 Arias, Pilar. Nicaragua, revolución: relatos de combatientes del Frente Sandinista. México: Siglo XXI Editores, 1980. 226 p.: maps (Historia inmediata)

Valuable collection, based almost entirely on interviews, of comments by leading activists in the Sandinista movement on formation and activities of various factions (1956–79). Useful for reconstructing period's historical record.

6143 Barahona Portocarrero, Amaru. Breve estudio sobre la historia contemporánea de Nicaragua (in América Latina: historia de medio siglo. v. 2, Centroamérica, México y el Caribe. Coordinación, Pablo González Casanova. México: Siglo XXI Editores, 1981, p. 377–423, bibl.)

Interesting analysis of economic changes in 1950s and 1960s and their consequences on relationships between classes and social groups. Discusses in detail the Somoza family methods.

6144 Booth, John A. Celebrating the demise of Somocismo: fifty recent Spanish sources on the Nicaraguan Revolution (LARR, 17:1, 1982, p. 173–189)

Excellent overview of plethora of literature on Nicaragua useful to expert and nonexpert alike.

6145 ———. The end and the beginning: the Nicaraguan Revolution. Boulder, Colo.: Westview Press, 1982. 279 p.: bibl., ill., index (Westview special studies on Latin America and the Caribbean)

Excellent, objective analysis of the political situation in this country. Places particular stress on how the Nicaraguan revolutionary experience fits in larger context of theoretical literature on revolution.

6146 Castillo, Donald. Situación económica y alianzas políticas en Nicaragua (UNAM/RMS, 42:2, abril/junio 1980, p. 501–521, tables)

Analysis of economic situation in Nicaragua after the Sandinistas' first year in power. Avidly pro-revolutionary, and sees external factors, especially the general Central American political situation, as having substantial influence on Nicaragua's economic future.

6147 Christian, Shirley. Freedom and unfreedom in Nicaragua (The New Republic [Washington] 185:3[3471], 18 July 1981, p. 15–20)

Good, informative, and sober reporting examines not only the country's domestic scene but also external pressures and factors as they attempt to increase their influence. Stresses the essential unpredictability of Nicaragua's political situation. [A. Suárez]

6148 Comisión Permanente de Derechos Humanos de Nicaragua (CPDH). Los derechos humanos en Nicaragua: segundo informe. Managua: CPDH, 1978 or 1979. 201 leaves: facsim., ill.

Valuable source of information on the Somoza regime. Provides human rights abuses documentation compiled by the Nicaraguan Permanent Commission on Human Rights, which actually functioned during Somoza's regime.

6149 Comité Cristiano de Solidaridad con el Pueblo de Nicaragua (CRISOL). Monimbó, tragedia y símbolo de liberación. Managua: CRISOL, 1979. 1 v.: bibl., ill.

Useful primary document provides individual and detailed information on each person killed and wounded and each structure damaged in Monimbó, a neighborhood of Masaya, Nicaragua, in 1978.

6150 Conferencia Episcopal de Nicaragua. Monseñor Miguel Obando Bravo; FSLN; Pedro Arrupe, S.J. (RCPC, 35:168/169, julio/sept. 1980, p. 37–96)

Primary document on ecclesiastical issues, including question of Church responsibility during the Nicaraguan Revolution. Most statements were made during the fall and winter of 1980.

6151 Cuzán, Alfred G. and **Richard J. Heggen.** A micro-political explanation of the 1979 Nicaraguan Revolution (LARR, 17:2, 1982, p. 156–170, graphs, table)

Interesting test of social model on persuasion and coercion as applied to Nicaragua. Makes predictions about how policies will be implemented in the future.

6152 Diederich, Bernard. Somoza and the legacy of U.S. involvement in Central America. New York: Dutton, 1981. 352 p., 9 leaves of plates: bibl., ill., index.

Non-scholarly, but nevertheless, serious biography of Somoza which traces his family's roots and complicity of US representatives in domestic politics. Readable, with many personal anecdotes, but shallow on sources. Valuable for its objectivity.

6153 Fe cristiana y Revolución Sandinista en Nicaragua. Managua: Instituto Histórico Centroamericano, 1980. 375 p.: bibl. (Apuntes para el estudio de la realidad nacional; no. 3, extraordinario)

Proceedings of the Seminario sobre Fe Cristiana y Revolución Sandinista en Nicaragua, held in Managua, Sept. 24–25, 1979. Reproduces papers and discussion of panel on Christianity and the Sandinista Revolution, providing many useful perspectives on issue of the role of socially committed Christians and the Catholic Church in revolutionary politics.

6154 Gorman, Stephen M. Power and consolidation in the Nicaraguan Revolution (JLAS, 13:1, May 1981, p. 133–149, graphs, tables)

Presents brief analysis of techiques used by Sandinista Nacional Directorate to consolidate its power and legitimize its control after 1979. Covering period through mid-1980s, author foresees beginning of the power struggle currently underway.

6155 Inter-American Commission on Human Rights. Report on the situation of human rights in Nicaragua: findings of the "on-site" observation in the Republic of Nicaragua, October 3–12, 1978. Washington: Organization of American States, General Secretariat, 1978. 78 p. (OEA/Ser.L/V/II.45, doc. 16, rev. 1)

One of few objective accounts which can be found about Nicaragua. This is a straight-forward on-site report by Inter-American Commission on Human Rights which provides evidence of numerous abuses by the Nicaraguan government.

6156 ⸺. Report on the situation of human rights in the Republic of Nicaragua. Washington: Organization of American States, 1981. 171 p. (OEA/Ser.L/V/II.53, doc. 25)

Document, on-site evaluation of human rights in Nicaragua during 1979–80.

6157 Jaspersen, Karsten. Entwicklungstendenzen von Politik und Wirtschaft im nachrevolutionären Nicaragua. Hamburg: Institut für Iberoamerika-Kunde, 1981. 85 p. (Arbeitsunterlagenund Diskussionbeiträge; 12. Documentos de trabajo)

Deft analysis of conflict between the FSLN and the private sector over economic policies during first two years of Sandinista rule in Nicaragua. Stresses lack of experience and administrative skills of FSLN members. Important contribution. [G.M. Dorn]

6158 López C., Julio *et al.* La Caída del Somocismo y la lucha sandinista en Nicaragua. San José: Editorial Universitaria Centroamericana, 1979. 325 p. (Colección Seis)

Useful collection of documents published by FSLN expressing their analyses (1977–79) of economic and social justifications for their activities.

6159 Maier, Elizabeth. Nicaragua, la mujer en la Revolución. México: Ediciones de Cultura Popular, 1980. 159 p.: ill., ports (Crónicas, testimonios y documentos)

Brief analysis of the role of women during the rebellion against Somoza and their future participation. Numerous documents present the program of the *Movimiento Pueblo Unido* and the *Asociación de Mujeres Ante la Problemática Nacional*.

6160 Mendieta Alfaro, Róger. Cero y van Dos: la sesión que Cero presidió. 2. ed. Managua: s.n., 1979. 166 p., 11 leaves of plates: ill.

Author, member of Conservative Party, and ex-political prisoner and guerrilla, provides first-hand view of the Sandinista take-over of the national congress.

6161 Nicaragua. Junta de Gobierno de Reconstrucción Nacional. Primera proclama del Gobierno de Reconstrucción Nacional. Managua: Difusión y Prensa, 1979. 19 p.

Original outline of plan formulated by the Government of National Reconstruction. Primary 1979 document.

6162 Nicaragua, el impacto de la mutación política. Santiago: Naciones Unidas, 1981. 126 p.: bibl., map (Estudios informes de la CEPAL; 1)

This ECLA or CEPAL report gathers together, with statistical detail, figures on Nicaragua's economic and human condition since the 1972 earthquake through 1980. Valuable for collecting difficult-to-obtain data in a single document.

6163 Nicaragua, la estrategia de la victoria.
Selección, prólogo y notas, Fernando Carmona. México: Editorial Nuestro Tiempo, 1980. 351 p.: bibl. (Colección La lucha por el poder)

Series of essays by Sandinista Front of National Liberation (FSLN) leaders explaining their history, their revival of opposition to the Somoza regime and their revolutionary strategy. Includes several interesting interviews with Humberto Ortega and the deceased Carlos Fonseca Amador.

6164 Nicaragua in revolution. Edited by Thomas W. Walker. New York: Praeger, 1982. 410 p.: bibl., ill., index, 1 map.

Excellent collection of essays on present conditions in revolutionary Nicaragua. Valuable for its breadth of subject matter and field research.

6165 Núñez Soto, Orlando. The third social force in national liberation movements (LAP, 8[2]:29, Spring 1981, p. 5–21)

Representative of the Nicaraguan Agricultural Development Ministry provides Marxist interpretation of role which middle groups played in Somoza's regime and changes that are entailed in making them active contributors to the revolutionary cause.

6166 Olmo, Rosa del. Los chigüines de Somoza: un ejemplo de criminalidad latinoamericana. Caracas: Editorial Ateneo de Caracas, 1980. 169 p.: appendices, bibl., ill. (Colección Testimonios)

Interesting examination of criminal abuses of the Somoza regime focusing on juveniles and his special elite guard and their training school.

6167 Ortega Saavedra, Humberto. 50 [i.e. Cincuenta] años de lucha sandinista. Managua: Ministerio del Interior, 197? 125 p.: ports (Colección Las segovias)

Sandinista *comandante* and member of FSLN Direcorate traces history and rationale for their movement (1926–70s).

6168 Pérez Valdés, Fernando. Corresponsales de guerra: testimonio. La Habana: Casa de las Américas, 1981. 253 p.: ill.

Cuban filmmaker went to Nicaragua in 1979 to make a documentary. Book is an insightful perspective, based on personal interviews, of an ordinary group of revolutionary participants.

6169 Polo-Cheva, Demetrio and Erich Sudorf. Nicaragua: die historischen Bedingungen einer demokratischen Revolution (Lateinamerika: Analysen und Berichte [Verlag Olle & Wolter, Berlin] 4, 1980, p. 15–42, bibl.)

Based on original Sandinista writings, official documents, and newspaper accounts, examines historical underpinnings of the Nicaraguan revolution. Interesting contribution. [G.M. Dorn]

6170 Primer legislatura, 1980: 4 mayo, 1927–1980, Día de la Dignidad Nacional, instauración del Consejo de Estado. Managua: Asesoría Jurídica y Divulgación: Prensa del Consejo de Estado, 198? 92 p.: ill. (Publicación oficial del Consejo de Estado; no. 3)

Useful documentary source on legislation promulgated in 1980. Also valuable to researchers interested in biographical information on Council of State members.

6171 Robleto Siles, José Antonio. Yo deserté de la Guardia Nacional de Nicaragua. Ciudad Universitaria Rodrigo Facio, Costa Rica: Editorial Universitaria Centroamericana, 1979. 192 p. (Colección Debate)

Former national guardsman, who changed sympathies, gives his account of the Sandinista movement. Useful for the perspective from inside the Guardia.

Seminario Político Miguel Bonilla, *1st, Universidad Nacional Autónoma de Nicaragua, 1980.* Primer Seminaro Político Miguel Bonilla: la Universidad y la Revolucion por Víctor Tirado, Omar Cabezas, Carlos Núñez. See item **4482.**

6172 Somoza Debayle, Anastasio. Nicaragua betrayed. As told to Jack Cox. Boston: Western Islands, 1980. 431 p.: ill., index.

Anastasio Somoza gives his own view, with all its distortions, of the downfall of his regime and the betrayal, as he sees it, of the US government. Valuable for insights into his personality.

6173 Tijerino, Doris. Inside the Nicaraguan Revolution: as told to Margaret

Randall. Translated from the Spanish by Elinor Randall. Vancouver, Canada: New Star Book, 1978. 176 p.: plates.

Revealing autobiographical account, strongly emotional, of young woman's efforts to fight the Somoza dictatorship. Covers period through end of 1974.

6174 Vélez Bárcenas, Jacinto. Dr. Pedro Joaquín Chamorro Cardenal asesinado! Managua: Vélez Bárcenas, 1979. 546 p.: ill.

Interesting, serious, detailed survey of the 1979 assassination of Pedro Joaquín Chamorro, editor of *La Prensa*, who opposed Somoza. Examines the trial and guilt of accused assassin.

6175 Walker, Thomas W. Nicaragua, the land of the Sandino. Boulder, Colo.: Westview Press, 1981. 137 p., 1 leaf of plates: bibl., ill., index, map (Nations of contemporary Latin America)

Sympathetic and insightful interpretation of the Sandinistas. One of the best general works available, in English, on Nicaragua.

PANAMA

6176 Castro Herrera, Guillermo. Nacionalismo y política nacional en Panamá (UNAM/RMS, 42:2, abril/junio 1980, p. 591–604)

Focuses on 1960s-70s, with particular interest in impact of Carter-Torrijos treaties and their implications for Panamanian nationalism.

6177 Conte-Porras, J. Arnulfo Arias Madrid. Panamá: J. Conte-Porras, 1980. 272 p.: bibl., ill.

Authorized biography of one of Panama's leading political figures and former presidents. Since little exists in English on Arias, this work has some utility.

6178 Fábrega, Jorge P. Las convenciones colectivas en Panamá (LNB/L, 303/304, junio/julio 1981, p. 63–98, tables)

Contains much useful statistical data on Panama's working class and provides critical analysis of deficiencies in present labor code.

6179 Gandásegui, Marco A. hijo *et al.* Las luchas obreras en Panamá: 1850–1978. Panamá: Centro de Estudios Latinoamericanos Justo Arosemena, 1980. 216 p.: bibl., ill., tables.

In a country where there is little serious scholarship on the labor movement, this is a significant exception. Well-documented, with numerous statistical tables on the working class, especially for this century.

6180 Murgas Torraza, Rolando. Las nuevas instituciones nacionales (LNB/L, 305/309:1, agosto/dic. 1981, p. 135–157)

Chronology and description of programs and statutes introduced by Gen. Torrijos during his control over Panama's political structure. Useful reference article.

6181 Pereira, Renato. El golpe militar de 1968, un golpe imposible (LNB/L, 305/309:1, agosto/dic. 1981, p. 61–79, charts)

Excellent original analysis of coup which brought Torrijos to power. Contains much statistical detail about National Guard composition, both officer and enlisted ranks.

6182 Ropp, Steve C. Panamanian politics: from guarded nation to National Guard. New York: Praeger; Stanford, Calif.: Hoover Institution Press, 1982. 151 p.: bibl., ill., index (Politics in Latin America)

Author, one of few North American specialists on Panamanian politics, provides general, useful survey, focusing on 1960s-70s. Devotes special attention to the evolution of National Guard's role, and will be indispensable to future research on this topic.

6183 Wetherborne, Egbert. Perspectivas de la democracia panameña (UNAM/RMS, 43:2, abril/junio 1981, p. 601–612)

Interesting perceptions of possibilities for democratic change in Panama. Argues that from bourgeois (reformist) viewpoint, there is greater tolerance towards other social forces. On the other hand, author suggests that a reorganized, traditional bourgeoisie would be a danger to democracy.

THE CARIBBEAN AND THE GUIANAS

ANDRES SUAREZ, *Professor of Political Science, Center for Latin American Studies, University of Florida*

PUBLICATIONS ON CARIBBEAN POLITICS annotated in this volume do not contribute anything particularly impressive or exciting to our knowledge of the region. Two papers on Guyana by Premdas (item **6208**) and Hintzen and Premdas (item **6207**) attempt to explain the survival of James Burnham and explore strategies that could be effective in destabilizing a modality of personal rule that is disguised as "cooperative socialism." Carl Stone (items **6213** and **6214**) continues to apply his intimate knowledge of Jamaica, self-generated data, and sophisticated analytical capabilities to the study of the country. A fascinating survey of factionalism and personal rivalry among the Dominican military under Balaguer was published by Atkins (item **6191**) despite his apprehension about current literature on civil-military relations. Halperin has issued vol. 2 of his work on Fidel Castro which covers the 1964–68 period (item **6189**); Martínez Alier continues to pursue his research on the identification of sugar *colonos* as Cuba's national bourgeoisie (item **6192**); and Roca's short article (item **6196**) points out new problems arising from economic policies implemented during the so-called period of institutionalization. Another book worthy of special mention is Montaner's (item **6193**). Written in the Latin American essay tradition, based not so much on data and footnotes as on personal experience, cultural background and literary insight, the book reveals the author's impressive command of his native language which he uses to decode the complex personality of Fidel Castro, the Revolution's *deus ex-machina*. In 1984, Montaner published a revised and very much improved Spanish version of this book, in which he effectively denounces the increasing misfortunes wrought upon Cubans by the idiosyncracies of their "maximum-leader."

CUBA

6184 Alonso, Jorge. Cuba, el poder del pueblo. México: Editorial Nuestro Tiempo, 1980. 142 p.: bibl. (Colección Latinoamérica ayer y hoy)

After two visits and a total stay in Cuba of 23 days, author finds that, Fidel notwithstanding, the Cuban Revolution is an example of continuous and increasing popular participation. He supports this judgment by using official documents and speeches by Cuban leaders, Fidel in particular.

6185 Berman, Harold J. and **Van R. Whiting, Jr.** Impressions of Cuban law (AJCL, 28:3, Summer 1980, p. 475–486)

Authors visited Cuba in June 1979, and their article is a report of conversations with Cuban lawyers and law professors.

6186 Calzón, Frank. Castro's gulag: the politics of terror. Washington: Council for Inter-American Security, 1979. 51 p.: bibl.

Informative, solid, well grounded. Highly recommended.

6187 Domínguez, Jorge I. Cuba in the 1980's (USIA/PC, 30:2, March/April 1981, p. 48–59, ill.)

Given dismal economy, low labor productivity, overcommitment of resources abroad, Soviet economic recession, and natural disasters, why hasn't Castro regime faltered or fallen? Domínguez' answer: Castro's popularity as leader of Revolution in which most adult Cubans participated; absence of independent alternative organizations (e.g., Polish Church); realization that economic costs of emigration are worth paying to preserve political order; and provision of key social services. Still, "an older and possibly wiser set of leaders" may have to establish priorities more carefully in 1980s. Comprehensive article. [G.W. Grayson]

6188 Franqui, Carlos. Revolution's end (The American Spectator [Bloomington, Ind.] 13:5, May 1980, p. 7–10, ill.)

Franqui broke with Castro in 1968 after participating in the revolutionary leadership for more than one decade. In this interview he offers insightful comments on Guevara, repression, the African intervention, relations with the Soviet Union, etc.

6189 Halperin, Maurice. The taming of Fidel Castro. Berkeley: University of California, 1981. 345 p., 1 leaf of plates: bibl., index, map.

As in author's previous volume principal sources used to support his interpretation still are Castro's published speeches in addition to Halperin's own Cuban experience (1962–68). Concentrating on 1964–68, book deals with one of the most intriguing periods in the course of the Revolution. Later years are discussed only in short epilogue. However, conclusions noted in final pages are clearly suggested by the entire revolutionary experience since 1958, not only by the period under consideration.

6190 Herrera, Antonio José and **Hernán Rosenkranz.** Revolución y democracia en Cuba. Caracas: S. de la Plaza, 1979. 60 p.: bibl.

Based upon research conducted by Herrera, Venezuelan political scientist while at the University of Havana in 1976. He interviewed 182 workers and 173 peasants trying to establish their level of political information, understanding of what democracy is, and role of the leader. Cuban mass organization assisted with the collection of data. A preliminary report.

6191 Le Riverend, Julio. Cuba: del semicolonialismo al socialismo, 1933–1975 (in América Latina: historia de medio siglo: v. 2, Centroamérica, México y el Caribe. Coordinación: Pablo González Casanova. México: Siglo XXI Editores, 1981, p. 39–85)

Another attempt, this time by the Dean of Cuban Marxist historians, to perform the kind of feat that now is expected from his trade: to prove that socialism

emerged in Cuba according to Marxist principles, without any mention of the connection between present socialism and the policies of Cuba's old Communist Party after 1938. As such, the present exercise is better argued than previous Cuban ones.

6192 Martínez Alier, Juan. La burguesía nacionalista en Cuba: en la década de 1950 (UB/BA, 29, 1979, p.191–201)

Paper's thesis that in Cuba there was a national bourgeoisie consisting mainly of sugar *colonos* is supported by some data dealt with more extensively in author's previous work.

6193 Montaner, Carlos Alberto. Secret report on the Cuban Revolution. Translated by Eduardo Zayas-Bazán. New Brunswick, N.J.: Transaction Books, 1981. 284 p.: bibl., index.

Perceptive essays written by Cuban writer in exile (Spanish original published 1976). Discusses race, sex, religion, etc., rarely mentioned topics in books on Cuba. As author himself warns in preface, American readers should be forewarned: his book is quite different from standard scholarship published in US on Cuba.

6194 Navarro, Anthony. Tocayo. Westport, Conn.: Sandown Books, 1981. 270 p., 10 leaves of plates: ill.

Personal memoir concerning underground activities against Castro before Bay of Pigs invasion. More adventure and heroics than politics.

6195 Philipson, Lorrin and **Rafael Llerena.** Freedom flights: Cuban refugees talk about life under Castro and how they fled his regime. New York: Random House, 1980. 201 p.: bibl.

Interviews conducted in Miami with Cubans who fled their country by rafts, boats, planes, and all conceivable means of transportation. All of them fought for the Revolution, worked for the new government, supported it, or were born after Castro came to power. A moving testimony of human courage, boldness, and ingenuity.

6196 Roca, Sergio. Revolutionary Cuba (CUH, 80:463, Feb. 1981, p. 53–56, 84)

Short and competent analysis emphasizing economic aspects.

6197 Rodríguez, Carlos Rafael. Entrevista: Carlos Rafael Rodríguez, Cuba, grandes interrogantes. Interviewer: Marta Harnecker (AR, 7:25, 1981, p. 4–12, plates)

Member of Political Bureau of Cuban Communist Party answers questions on the *antisociales* or *marielitos,* increasing unemployment, and the mechanisms used by Party leaders to prevent popular expressions of disagreement by the masses.

6198 ———. José Martí, guía y compañero. México: Editoria Nuestro Tiempo, 1981. 118 p. (Colección Pensamiento latinoamericano)

Four short papers published by author (1953–76). Usual Marxist interpretation of Martí as representative of the petit-bourgeoisie whose great merit was to anticipate the future: Castro.

DOMINICAN REPUBLIC

6199 Atkins, G. Pope. Arms and politics in the Dominican Republic. Boulder, Colo.: Westview Press, 1981. 158 p.: bibl., index (Westview special studies on Latin America and the Caribbean)

Most literature on civil-military relations is not helpful for the study of the Dominican Republic whose armed forces lack any significant institutionalization judging by levels of autonomy, professional expertise, and corporate identity. Therefore, to speak of civil-military relations in this context "is almost meaningless." Instead, the researcher should focus his attention on factions, personal rivalries, and fleeting alignments between civilian and military. After extended stays by the author in the Dominican Republic and personal interviews with some protagonists, author performs this unremitting task for the Balaguer period and Guzmán's election.

6200 Bosch, Juan. Artículos y conferencias. Santo Domingo: Alfa y Omega, 1980. 253 p.

Collection of previously published papers, including some on Dominican history and politics. Author writes that before 1968, he had not read Marx. This does not keep him from using heavy doses of Marxism in his interpretations.

6201 ——— *et al.* Abril. Santo Domingo: Alfa y Omega, 1980. 155 p., 19 p. of plates: ill.

Papers on the April 1965 Revolution by Juan Bosch, José Espaillat, Roberto Cassá, and Fafa Taveras. Once more, Bosch summarizes a sociological interpretation he has elaborated with more detail in previous works. Taveras, a participant, offers an excellent description of the struggle.

6202 Cuello, José Israel; Roberto Cassá; and Rubén Silié. 50 [i.e. Cincuenta] años de historia dominicana (*in* América Latina: historia de medio siglo. v. 2, Centroamérica, México y el Caribe. Coordinación: Pablo González Casanova. México: Siglo Veintiuno Editores, 1982, p. 467–498, bibl.)

Standard Marxist interpretation offered by followers of the Soviet line. All political leaders and regimes from Trujillo to Balaguer, including Bosch and even leaders of the April 1965 Revolution, are defined as invariably representing bourgeois interests. Includes some economic data on 1969–74 period.

6203 Franco, Franklin J. La izquierda y el futuro dominicano. Santo Domingo: Ediciones Upa, 1978. 137 p.

Collection of articles published in the Dominican press (1975–78). One more example of the endless polemic within the radical left concerning revolutionary strategy and tactics.

6204 Moya Pons, Frank. El futuro dominicano. Santo Domingo: s.n., 1980. 18 p.

Very pessimistic forecast offered by very well qualified Dominican historian.

6205 Vargas, Mayobanex. Testimonio histórico, junio 1959. Santo Domingo: Editora Cosmos, 1981. 121 p.: ill.

Recollections of participant in the Cuban-Dominican expedition that landed in June 1959. A deplorable tale of misfortune, incompetence, and irresponsibility.

GUYANA

6206 Campbell, Trevor A. The making of an organic intellectual: Walter Rodney, 1942–1980 (LAP, 8[1]:28, Winter 1981, p. 49–63, bibl.)

Deals mainly with biographical data,

not the intellectual contribution made by the Guyanese intellectual recently assasinated.

Danns, George K. Domination of power in Guyana: a study of the police in a Third World context. See item **1066.**

6207 Hintzen, Percy C. and **Ralph R. Premdas.** Guyana: coercion and control in political change (SAGE/JIAS, 24:3, Aug. 1982, p. 337–354)

Summary of Guyanese politics since independence. Strongly critical of Burnham. Interprets recent loans extended by international banks to Guyana as Western manipulations to help Burnham. Says nothing of Jagan's faulty strategies.

6208 Premdas, Ralph R. Guyana: socialism and destabilization in the Western hemisphere (UWI/CQ, 25:3, Sept. 1979, p. 25–43)

Can the socialist government of Prime Minister Burnham be destabilized? Author examines 1962 and 1963 destabilizations in Guyana to determine if strategies successful against Jagan can also work against Burnham. Concludes that a different pattern may result with destabilization policies inducing Burnham to follow the Cuban example.

6209 Rodney, Walter. People's power, no dictation (LAP, 8[1]:28, Winter 1981, p. 64–78)

Stong denunciation of Burnham's rule. His dictatorship is illustrated with references to Somoza, Hitler, Pinochet, etc., but not Castro or Stalin.

Serbin, Andrés. Nacionalismo, etnicidad y política en la República Cooperativa de Guyana. See item **1134.**

6210 Spinner, Thomas J., Jr. The Emperor Burnham has lost his clothes (FIU/RC, 9:4, Fall 1980, p. 5–8)

Introductory and informative piece written by visiting Fulbright lecturer at University of Guyana. Hopes that after Rodney's assassination, "Burnham will depart peacefully." But of course, Burnham survived once again.

HAITI

6211 Pierre-Charles, Gérard. Haiti, 1930–1975: la crisis interrumpida (*in* América

Latina: historia de medio siglo. v. 2, Centroamérica, México y el Caribe. Coordinación: Pablo González Casanova. México: Siglo Veintiuno Editores, 1981, p. 174–222, bibl.)

"The political evolution of Haiti after the thirties, is stamped by the overpowering domination of imperialism on the life of the country." Needless to say, it is US imperialism. The rest of the text consists of variations of initial paragraph. All items in short bibliography are in French with one Spanish exception.

6212 Rémy, Amselme. The Duvalier phenomenon (UPR/CS, 11:2, 1974, p. 38–65)

"The Duvalier phenomenon characterized the post-1946 politics of a social group consisting of black intellectuals and black landowners." Duvalier was group's leader and ideologue. Once in power, he faced limitations of middle-class nationalism. Terror is not enough to explain Duvalierism. Dictator's death meant exhaustion of his brand of traditional nationalism.

JAMAICA

6213 Stone, Carl. Democracy and socialism in Jamaica: 1962–1979 (ICS/JCCP, 19:2, July 1981, p. 115–133, tables)

Insightful analysis of Manley's administration supported by opinion polls conducted by author. Populist policies of increasing participation and income distribution clashed with socialist management. Economic deterioration and fears of one-party system led to electoral defeat of Oct. 1980.

6214 ———. The 1976 parliamentary election in Jamaica (UPR/CS, 19:l/2, April/July 1979, p. 33–50, charts, graphs)

Competent analysis. Some interestig survey data. Dilemmas faced by new PNP government were clearly perceived by author at time of writing this paper.

PUERTO RICO

6215 Gurza, Teresa. Puerto Rico. México: Ediciones de Cultura Popular, 1979. 176 p.: appendix, ill. (Her Visión de las

Antillas; 1. Crónicas, testimonios y documentos)

Mexican reporter expounds her support for Puerto Rico's independence struggle. Appendix includes several solidarity declarations signed by international organizations.

6216 The Intellectual roots of independence: an anthology of Puerto Rican political essays. Edited by Iris Zavala and Rafael Rodríguez. Introd. by Iris Zavala. New York: Monthly Review Press, 1980. 376 p.: bibl.

Translation of *Libertad y crítica en el ensayo político puertorriqueño.* Useful collection with independentist introduction by Iris M. Zavala.

6217 Maldonado-Denis, Manuel. El imperialismo y la dependencia: el caso de Puerto Rico (*in* América Latina: historia de medio siglo. v. 2, Centroamérica, México y el Caribe. Coordinación: Pablo González Casanova. México: Siglo Veintiuno Editores, 1981, p. 450–465, bibl.)

Reelaboration of same topics already discussed in previous books and papers by prolific nationalist author. Last four p. offer "outline of class struggle in Puerto Rico under the light of *pensamiento crítico.*"

6218 Mattos Cintrón, Wilfredo. La política y lo político en Puerto Rico. México: Ediciones Era, 1980. 207 p.: bibl., graphs (Serie popular Era; 71)

Written by member of Puerto Rican Socialist Party while participating in discussions preceding adoption of Party thesis (1974). Well organized and supported by good knowledge of the literature. However, another *independentista* interpretation that fails to convince the reader that in a country with a "lumpen bourgeoisie" (author's words) and a "lumpen proletariat" (my words), it is very useful to apply a Marxist framework in order to understand "la política y lo político."

6219 Puerto Rico, una crisis histórica. Suzy Castor, coordinador, *et al.* México: Editorial Nuestro Tiempo, 1979. 220 p.: bibl.

Consists of conference papers and comments (UNAM, Mexico, 1977). Contributions by top leaders of Puerto Rico's political parties, excepting Progresistas. Both introduction and comments by Mexican hosts make crystal clear their rejection of an "Estado Libre" in favor of "independence and socialism."

6220 Tapia, Norma Iris. La crisis del PIP. Río Piedras, Puerto Rico: Editorial Edil, 1980. 249 p.: bibl.

Puerto Rico's Independentist Party was founded in 1948. Between 1967–73, it adopted a social democratic program, faced an internal crisis, and finally split. Author, who perceives social democracy as "nothing but bourgeois reformism," explains crisis from this point of view.

TRINIDAD AND TOBAGO

6221 Ryan, Selwyn D. Trinidad and Tobago: the general elections of 1976 (UPR/CS, 19:1/2, April/July 1979, p. 5–32)

Chairman of Government Department, University of the West Indies, St. Augustine, Trinidad, discusses political parties, campaign, and electoral results.

COLOMBIA, VENEZUELA, AND ECUADOR

DAVID W. DENT, *Associate Professor, Political Science; Senior Fellow, Center for Public Policy and International Affairs, Towson State University*

IN THIS BIENNIUM ON THE THREE DEMOCRACIES of northern South America, there is very little change in the volume of the literature despite national elections, growing human rights concerns, and the continual opposition from political forces on the left. However, recent studies of populism, the media and politics, and macro-political studies of the political process in several cases are noteworthy. As with past volumes of the *Handbook*, conflicting methodological and ideological perspectives continue to influence the type of research and the conclusions that are reached.

The literature on Latin American populism and populists is now beginning to receive the attention it deserves for understanding Latin American politics. For anyone interested in populism, a good place to begin is with Conniff's compilation (item **6016**). His own essay examines the roots, rise, and demise of populism within an historical and comparative framework (item **6006**). Quintero (item **6284**) offers an important critique of both the populist literature and the nature of velasquismo in 20th-century Ecuadorian politics. Another important study for Ecuador is Cueva's (item **6277**) excellent treatment of the historical roots of caudillismo and populism in Ecuadorian politics. If the resurgence of interest in populism and its causes and consequences has any value, then populism as a type of Latin American political system should not be ruled out given the economic and political problems facing Latin America in the 1980s. This renewal of interest in populism also offers numerous lessons for US policy makers who often misjudge leaders and their ideologies in Latin America.

Media-government relations are just beginning to receive the research attention they deserve in Latin American political studies. Pierce's (item **6027**) pathbreaking comparative analysis of media-government relations in nine Latin American nations should provide a solid foundation for future work in this area. Baldivia (item **6011**) provides an important empirical study of the press, reporters, and journalistic training in Mexico, Chile, and Costa Rica. And Restrepo (item **6029**) provides a critical analysis of the limits to freedom of expression in Latin American politics and the negative bias toward the Third World in the system of international communication.

Some of the best studies in this volume focus on macro-political studies of power, political parties, electoral politics, and pluralist democracy. One of the finest studies of the Venezuelan political system by a Venezuelan is Gil Yepes (item **6261**) who offers a theoretically sophisticated analysis of the workings of pluralist democracy since 1958. An excellent analysis of the 1978 elections with emphasis on Venezuelan democracy, electoral politics, and voting behavior is provided by Penniman (item **6275**). The Penniman study should be read in conjunction with Chang Mota's (item **6257**) valuable descriptive study of Venezuelan national elections since 1958. Tarre Murzi (item **6274**) provides an important study of the formation of democratic leadership and the transformation from dictatorship to democratic rule. One of the best studies of the political history of Ecuador can be found in the current President's (item **6281**) sociopolitical analysis of power within Ecuadorian society. As of this issue, no single work on Colombian politics has emerged to replace *The Politics of compromise* (see *HLAS 43:6362*). Ruhl (item **6245**) does, however, make an important contribution to understanding why Colombia has managed to avoid military rule since 1957.

What research needs to be done? Two areas of neglect standout as we witness important changes in Latin America. The first has to do with the need for more political biographies of leadership in both democratic and non-democratic settings. Except for Alexander's (item **6251**) excellent political biography of the "grand old man" of Venezuelan politics, the void is vast. The second is the necessity of examining the breakdown of authoritarian regimes in Latin America. The recent changes in Ecuador, Argentina, Peru, Brazil, and others point to the need for theoretical and empirical work on this type of political change. For example, what are the causes of the breakdown of military-authoritarian governments in Latin America? Why do some democracies seem to endure while others fail and breakdown? Perhaps the changes in Ecuador and the case of Venezuela since 1958 will help to provide some of the answers to these important research questions.

COLOMBIA

6222 La Abstención: simposio realizado por la Asociación Nacional de Instituciones Financieras "ANIF," Bogotá, Colombia, marzo 27–28, 1980. Bogotá: ANIF, 1980. 190 p.: bibl., ill. (Biblioteca ANIF de Economía)

Examines Colombian phenomenon of voting abstention in 1980 symposium on subject. Analysis produces little agreement as to causes but interchanges with participants lets reader follow the line of reasoning and argumentation.

6223 Aguirre Lozano, María Isabel and **María Fernanda Canal Acero.** Análisis del sistema electoral colombiano: surgerencias de algunas reformas para mejorarlo. Bogotá: Editorial Kelly, 1980. 159 p.: bibl.

Description and critique of Colombia's electoral system with suggestions for improving the system of representation. According to authors, the D'Hondt system does not translate votes proportionately among parties.

6224 Alvarez de O., María Eugenia *et al.* ¿Democracia sin participación?: tendencias y características en Colombia. Bogotá: Departamento de Asesorías e Investigación, 1981. 168 p.: ill. (Ediciones Grupo Social; 1)

Empirical study of Colombian attitudes toward democracy and political participation through voting. Conclusions corroborate impact of class, education, and political activity on democratic participation combined with government's overall quality.

6225 Angulo Novoa, Alejandro *et al.* La pendiente antidemocrática: dos años de la administración Turbay. Bogotá: Centro de Investigación y Educación Popular, 1980. 130 p.: bibl. (Serie Controversia; no. 90)

In answering rhetorical question, "What has been done during the first two years of the Turbay administration?," authors respond that "not much." Reasoned critique from journal labeled by President Turbay as source of "radical opposition." [W.R. Garner]

Arizmendi Posada, Ignacio. Gobernantes colombianos, 1819–1980. See *HLAS 44:2846.*

6226 Bossa López, Simón *et al.* Hacia una liberalismo social. Bogotá: Fondo Editorial Liberal, Dirección Liberal Nacional, 1979. 304 p.: bibl. (Colección Liberalismo social; t. 1)

Seven prominent Colombian Liberal politicians attempt to swing their party more to the left with a more social democratic orientation. Authors address what they feel is the need for a more equal and just state respecting the diverse needs of Colombian citizenry.

6227 Caicedo, Edgar. 25 [i.e. Veinticinco] años de periodismo militante. Bogotá: Editorial Colombia Nueva, 1980. 352 p.: ports.

Critical journalist from Cali discusses political, economic, and social conditions he has observed (1955–80). Both national and international issues are addressed with a pronounced sympathy for the left.

6228 Carrillo Bedoya, Jaime. Los paros cívicos en Colombia. Traducción del francés del autor. Bogotá: Editorial La Oveja Negra: Editográficas, 1981. 306 p.: bibl., ill.

Social and political examination of urban strikes and lockouts (1958–78). Author tries to locate patterns in these social movements and offers explanation for this form of protest.

6229 Casas, Ulises. Origen y desarrollo del movimiento revolucionario colombiano. Bogotá: s.n., 1980. 194 p.

Critical analysis of origin and development of Colombian revolutionary movements and their ideologies (e.g., PCC, FARC, MOIR, ANAPO). Considers such variables as origin, ideology, organization, personnel, and external linkages.

6230 Colombia. Presidencia. Secretaría de Información y Prensa. Crónica de un año, 1978–1979. Bogotá: La Secretaría, 1979 or 1980. 179 p.

Favorable presentation of economic and social policy of President Turbay's first year in power.

6231 ———. ———. ———. Discursos y
mensajes del Presidente de la República, Julio César Turbay Ayala: agosto de
1979 a agosto de 1980. Bogotá: La Secretaría,
1981. 437 p.

President Turbay's major speeches and
addresses (Aug. 1979-Aug. 1980). Includes
helpful cross-reference index for locating diverse themes.

**6232 Comité Permanente por la Defensa de
los Derechos Humanos.** Represión y
tortura en Colombia: informes internacionales y testimonios nacionales. Bogotá:
Fondo Editorial Suramérica, 1980. 368 p.: ill.
(Colección política)

Documentary testimony taken by Colombia's Permanent Committee for the Defense of Human Rights on extent of alleged
human rights violations by the government
and military ca. 1978–79.

6233 Delpar, Helen. Red against blue: the
Liberal Party in Colombian politics,
1863–1899. University: University of Alabama Press, 1981. 262p.: bibl., index.

Early history (1863–99) of Liberal
party is subjected to closer examination relying on election returns and personal histories
of party leaders of that period. Early evolution of party system—particularly its ability
to form linkages between the center and local areas—is posited as key to the Liberal
party's relatively smooth transiton to a mass
party in the 20th century.

**6234 Derechos humanos en las zonas
rurales:** reforma agraria-campesinos:
seminario. Organizado por la Comisión Internacional de Juristas (CIJ) y el Consejo Latinoamericano de Derecho y Desarrollo, Bogotá,
Septiembre, 1979. Quito: ILDIS; Ginebra,
Suiza: C.I.J., 1979. 306 p.

Reports from seminar concerned with
human rights of Colombian rural labor. Organizational assistance for meeting provided
by International Commission of Jurists.
[W.R.Garner]

6235 Findley, Roger W. Presidential intervention in the economy and the rule
of law in Colombia (AJCL, 28:3, Summer
1980, p. 423–473)

Examines presidential-congressional
authority in managing the economy from the
1968 Constitutional Reform (a law that increased the executive's power) to constitu-

tional reforms enacted in Nov. 1979 (laws
that increased the role of the Colombian
Congress in economic development). Causes
of this new legislation are not clear but the
dominance of the executive branch is difficult to dispute.

6236 Galán, Luis Carlos. Nueva Colombia.
Selección y nota de María Mercedes
Carranza. Bogotá: L.C. Galán, 1982. 184 p.

Selection of articles published in
Nueva Frontera and *El Tiempo* in preparation for author's 1982 presidential bid. Efforts
to reinvigorate Liberalism are encompassed
in what Galán calls the "New Liberalism."

6237 Herrán, María Teresa. El sindicalismo
por dentro y por fuera. Bogotá: CINEP:
Editorial La Oveja Negra, 1981. 208 p.: ill.

Journalistic analysis of contemporary
Colombian labor movement from within
(leadership, organization, ideology) and without (relations between the labor movement
and the public-governmental and private
sectors).

6238 Herrera, Francisco José. 7 [i.e. Siete]
huellas: Jorge Eliécer Gaitán. s.l.: Centro Editorial Bochica, 1981. 248 p.

Brief study of seven major ideas of
Jorge Eliécer Gaitán which attempts to demonstrate that he was anti-fascist and anti-
Marxist. In author's view, Gaitán was a man
of the left who espoused pacifism, populist
reforms, and democratic socialism.

**6239 Inter-American Commission on Hu-
man Rights.** Report on the situation of
human rights in the Republic of Colombia.
Washington: Organization of American
States, General Secretariat, 1981. 222 p.: bibl.
(OEA/Ser.L/V/II.53, doc. 22)

Report on state of human rights in Colombia which details a government in violation of them. Commission recommends that
the Colombian government "Lift the state of
seige as soon as circumstances allow; and
comply with the provisions of Article 27
of the American Convention on Human
Rights."

Jaramillo Ocampo, Hernán. 1946–1950 [i.e.
Mil novecientos cuarenta y seis-mil novecientos cincuenta] de la unidad nacional
a la hegemonía conservadora. See *HLAS
44:2853.*

Krumwiede, Heinrich-W. Politik und katholische Kirsch im gesellschaftliche Modernisierungsprozess: Tradition und Entwicklung in Kolumbien. See *HLAS 44:2854*.

Levine, Daniel H. Religion and politics in Latin America: the Catholic Church in Venezuela and Colombia. See item **6264**.

6240 Lleras Camargo, Alberto. Visión de dos décadas. Antioquia?, Colombia: Fondo Editorial Los Comuneros de la Corporación Financiera Antioqueña, 1981. 2 v. (Colección Corfiantioquia; v. 1)

Ex-President Lleras Camargo reveals his thoughts on Colombian and world politics (1955–75). His comments reflect a belief in democratic values and the inter-American system.

6241 López Michelsen, Alfonso. Esbozos y atisbos. Bogotá: Canal Ramírez-Antares, 1980. 237 p.

Former Liberal president reflects on the life and times of 10 notable Colombian leaders.

6242 Martín L., José Francisco. Campo y ciudad: participación y abstención electoral en Colombia. Bogotá: Fundación Friedrich Naumann; Cali, Colombia: CIDSE, 1981. 121 p.: bibl., ill.

Empirical study of voting abstention in both urban and rural elections for president. Categories such as "apathy," "skepticism," and "futility of voting," are used to clarify the theoretical debate over why Colombians are reluctant to vote.

Medina, Medófilo. Historia del Partido Comunista de Colombia. See *HLAS 44:2859*.

6243 Morales Benítez, Otto. Reflexiones políticas. Con un estudio preliminar de Javier Ocampo López. Bogotá: Editorial Carrera 7a, 1981. 146 p.

Memorial essay and selected writings on author's Colombian ideology and practice. His thought ranges from championing "the old ways" and neo-liberal denunciation of immorality to essay in support of Jorge Gaitán. Interesting collection. [W.R. Garner]

Ocampo T., José Fernando. Colombia siglo XX: estudio histórico y antología política. See *HLAS 44:2862*.

6244 Ordóñez Quintero, César. Pensamiento y acción liberal: discursos y conferencias. Bogotá: Ediciones Tercer Mundo, 1981. 364 p.

Anthology of speeches and lectures by former disciple of Jorge Eliécer Gaitán. Liberal political thought expressed in this volume centers on the Liberal party's more progressive faction (1940–70).

Politics of compromise: coalition government in Colombia. See item **3298**.

6245 Ruhl, J. Mark. Colombia: armed forces and society. Syracuse, N.Y.: Syracuse University, Maxwell School of Citizenship and Public Affairs, 1980. 53 p.: bibl. (Foreign and comparative studies: Latin American series; 1)

Brief but valuable descriptive and explanatory study of the Colombian military's deviation from the Latin American norm of intervention in the governing process. Ruhl's explanation for the deviant case rests on the civilian elite's governing capabilities, unity, and popular legitimacy. However, future modernization and socioeconomic pressures could easily alter the current atypical pattern.

6246 Samper Pizano, Daniel *et al.* ¿Por quién votar?: una guía evaluativa de cada congresista, elaborada por periodistas de investigación, para que usted sepa por quién vota. Bogotá: Editorial La Oveja Negra: El Ancora Editores, 1982. 144 p.

Brief voter's guide including 138 senatorial candidates and 229 *representantes*. Sketches stress congressional attendance, debating style, and legislative effectiveness.

6247 Torres Sánchez, Jaime. Colombia, represión: 1970–1981. En la realización de esta obra participaron Jaime Torres Sánchez, Fabio Barrera Téllez y otras personas. Bogotá: Centro de Investigación y Educación Popular, 1982. 2 v.: ill., tables.

Leftist Center of Investigation and Popular Education presents detailed survey of victims of government repression. Analysis is built around 7,571 cases divided into types of citizens (by occupation), torture/repression, and geographical location of violation.

6248 Turbay Ayala, Julio César. Respuesta del gobierno colombiano al informe de Amnistía Internacional. Bogotá: Presidencia de la República, 1980. 67 p.

President Turbay answers the Amnesty International report on government's alleged human rights abuses and circumstances surrounding occupation of the embassy of the Dominican Republic by the M-19 guerrilla faction.

6249 Violación de los derechos humanos en Colombia: informe de Amnistía Internacional: texto íntegro. Bogotá: Comité de Solidaridad con los Presos Políticos, 1980. 287 p., 12 p. of plates: ill.

Amnesty International's detailed report on human rights violations in Colombia during early months of 1980. Report covers numerous groups, methods, photographs, and 30 case histories of victims of human rights abuses.

6250 Wilde, Alexander. Conversaciones de caballeros: la quiebra de la democracia en Colombia. Bogotá: Ediciones Tercer Mundo, 1982. 132 p.

Spanish translation of earlier work (see *HLAS 43: 6372*) on the breakdown of Colombian democracy in 1949.

VENEZUELA

6251 Alexander, Robert Jackson. Rómulo Betancourt and the transformation of Venezuela. New Brunswick, N.J.: Transaction Books, 1982. 737 p.: bibl., index.

Excellent political biography of the "grand old man" of Venezuelan politics. Emphasis is on the development of democratic values and procedures in both leaders and followers during Venezuela's transformation from a nation of caudillos to a more or less pluralistic democratic state. Rómulo's political socialization is examined through such agents as the family, schools, party organs, peers, and key events.

6252 Araujo García, Ana Elvira. Gobierno y administración de las áreas metropolitanas: el caso de Caracas. Caracas: Editorial Jurídica Venezolana, 1978. 189 p.: bibl., ill. (Colección Monografías administrativas; no. 2)

Study of the politics and administration of metropolitan Caracas with emphasis on urban problems and administrative and legislative solutions. Comparative analysis of other large cities lead to suggestions emphasizing more rational planning and greater centralization of authority than now exists.

6253 Blanco Muñoz, Agustín. La lucha armada: hablan cinco jefes. Entrevistas con Gustavo Machado, Pedro Ortega Díaz, Pompeyo Márquez, Teodoro Petkoff y Guillermo García Ponce. Caracas: Universidad Central de Venezuela, Facultad de Ciencias Económicas y Sociales, División de Publicaciones, 1980. 411 p. (Testimonios violentos; 2. Serie Coediciones)

Interviews with five leaders of the Venezuelan left who examine the role of armed struggle and violence as means for social change during 1970s. Essays reflect awareness of need to forge a broader ideological program that will serve Venezuela's needs and aspirations.

6254 Brewer Carías, Allan-Randolph. Estudios sobre la reforma administrativa. Caracas: Universidad Central de Venezuela, Ediciones de la Biblioteca, 1980. 670 p.: bibl. (Colección Ciencias económicas y sociales; 23)

Series of studies, lectures, and conferences on the reform of public administration (1969–75). Valuable study for anyone interested in the legal, political, and organization-technical aspects of public administration in Venezuela.

6255 CAP, 5 [i.e. cinco] años: un juicio crítico. Equipo, *Proceso Político*. Prólogo de Luis Lander. Caracas: Editorial Ateneo de Caracas, 1978. 304 p.: bibl.

Critical essays which appeared in *Proceso Político* (1976–78) on the Carlos Andrés Pérez administration. Author claims that nationalization of petroleum industry did not benefit Venezuela and is therefore another instance of economic imperialism.

6256 Carvallo, Gastón and Josefina de Hernández. Dominación burguesa y democracia representativa en Venezuela: apuntes para la evaluación de su funcionamiento (UNAM/RMS, 43:2, abril/junio 1981, p. 565–600, bibl.)

Marxist analysis of Venezuelan politics over past 20 years. Authors contend that not only has the national bourgeoisie grown in strength but two major parties have contributed to perpetuation of elite rule through manipulation of public opinion, electoral chicanery, and repression.

6257 Chang Mota, Roberto. Sistemas y cifras de las elecciones venezolanas desde 1958. Caracas: Consejo Supremo Electoral, 1980. 165 p.: ill.

Valuable descriptive study of Venezuelan national elections (1958–78). Emphasizes mechanics of voter registration, voting, and ballot counting.

Cordero Velásquez, Luis. Betancourt y la conjura militar del 45. See *HLAS 44:2877.*

6258 Ellner, Steve. Factionalism in the Venezuelan Communist Movement: 1939–1948 (SS, 45:1, Spring 1981, p. 52–70)

Examination of rivalry between two dominant factions with nation's Communist labor movement prior to 1948. Author highlights importance of both international events (World War II, fight against fascism, and "Browderism") and structural changes in Venezuela's economy (growth and maturation of the working class and post-war penetration of economy by foreign capital). Moreover, Communist schisms seemed to contribute to rise of social democracy and AD reform policies.

———. Los partidos políticos y su disputa por el control del movimiento sindical en Venezuela, 1936–1948. See *HLAS 44:2878.*

6259 ———. Political party dynamics in Venezuela and the outbreak of guerrilla warfare (IAMEA, 34:2, Autumn 1980, p. 3–24)

Brief study of relationship between Venezuelan leftists and moderates during social upheavals of early 1960s. Why weren't opposition parties able to unite against the government and what potential existed for the formation of an anti-govermental alliance? In brief, moderates accepted legitimacy of the democratic system while the insurgent left did not (for historian's comment, see *HLAS 44:2879*).

6260 ———. Populism in Venezuela, 1935–48: Betancourt and the Acción Democrática (*in* Latin American populism in comparative perspective. [see item **6016**] p. 135–149)

Betancourt is portrayed as a populist in this critical phase of Venezuelan political history when he subordinated his communist ideology to more pragmatic *betancourtismo* based on nationalism, multiclass party system, and commitment to electoral expansion. Valuable study with lessons for US policy makers and their assumptions about

leftist leaders in Latin America (for historian's comment, see *HLAS 44:2880*).

———. The Venezuelan left in the era of the Popular Front, 1936–45. See *HLAS 44:2881.*

Ewell, Judith. The indictment of a dictator: the extradiction and trial of Marcos Pérez Jiménez. See *HLAS 44:2882.*

Fuenmayor, Juan Bautista. Historia de la Venezuela política contemporánea, 1889–1969. See *HLAS 44:2883.*

6261 Gil Yepes, José Antonio. The challenge of Venezuelan democracy. Translated by Evelyn Harrison I., Loló Gil de Yanes, and Danielle Salti. New Brunswick, N.J.: Transaction Books, 1981. 280 p.: bibl., index.

Theoretically sophisticated analysis of the workings of pluralist democracy in Venezuela since 1958. Emphasizes economic policy-making and seeks explanations in the political culture, party system, and entrepreneurial sector organization. Contends that consolidation of democratic regime is tied to communication and interest articulation between business and political elites. One of the best studies of Venezuela's political system by a Venezuelan.

Godio, Julio. El movimiento obrero venezolano, 1850–1944. See *HLAS 44:2884.*

6262 González Abreu, Manuel. Venezuela foránea. Caracas: Universidad Central de Venezuela, Facultad de Ciencias Económicas y Sociales, División de Publicaciones, 1980. 284 p. (Colección: Libros)

Historical examination of the process of denationalization of Venezuela through exploitation of foreign economic interests. Author blames foreign economic interests and amoral national elites for the nation's "subhumanization."

Herman, Donald L. Christian Democracy in Venezuela. See *HLAS 44:2886.*

6263 Herrera Campins, Luis. Mi compromiso con Venezuela: programa de gobierno para el período 1979–1984. Caracas: COPEI 78, 1978. 2 v. (433, 342 p.).

President Herrera Campins maps out his economic and social policies for his four-year office term. Important work reflecting COPEI's philosophy of democratic reform.

6264 Levine, Daniel H. Religion and politics in Latin America: the Catholic Church in Venezuela and Colombia. Princeton, N.J.: Princeton University Press, 1981. 342 p.: bibl., index.

Solid comparative study of the Church's role in two pluralistic political systems. Analysis uses multiple sources of data including interviews with bishops and other Church leaders. Treats both theoretical and methodological concerns with considerable sophistication. Author sees new synthesis emerging between religion and politics centering on four competing modes of behavior for contemporary Latin American Catholics.

6265 Libro-homenaje a Manuel García-Pelayo. Caracas: Universidad Central de Venezuela, Facultad de Ciencias Jurídicas y Políticas, 1980. 2 v. (920 p.): bibl.

Series of 37 essays on constitutional law, political science, and international law in honor of Dr. Manuel García-Pelayo, former director of the Institute of Political Studies at the Central University of Venezuela.

Lleras Restrepo, Carlos. Los días y los años: prosas de lucha, de estudio, de servicio, 1941–1979. See *HLAS 44:2856.*

6266 Márquez, Pompeyo. En peligro la integridad territorial de Venezuela. Caracas?: Industrias Sorocaima, 1979 or 1980. 104 p.

Congressional testimony from MAS leader who argues for better land use planning and environmental protection for more rational Venezuelan development.

6267 Marta Sosa, Joaquín. Nueva civilización, nueva revolución. Caracas: Editorial Ateneo de Carcas, 1980. 140 p. (Colección Clásicos de la política; no. 4)

Examines Christian revolutionary theory through thoughts of Camilo Torres, Ernesto Cardenal, Giulio Girardi, and Emmanuel Mounier. Attempts to synthesize ideology of Marx with social Christian thought and apply it to the Venezuelan case. As one would expect, capitalism, democratic reform, and Christian democracy come under heavy attack.

6268 Novoa Monreal, Eduardo. La nacionalización del petróleo en Venezuela, sus aspectos jurídicos. México: Universidad Nacional Autónoma de México, 1979. 136 p. (Serie I, Estudios de derecho económico; no. 4)

Legalistic analysis of the nationalization of the Venezuelan petroleum industry. Contains important documents relevant to the transition from foreign to national ownership and control.

6269 Peña, Alfredo. Conversaciones con Luis Beltrán Prieto. 3. ed. Caracas: Editorial Ateneo de Caracas, 1978 [i.e. 1979]. 196 p. (His Grandes reportages de Alfredo Peña. Colección Actualidad política)

Interesting conversational interviews with founder of MEP (People's Electoral Movement). Valuable for understanding Democratic Action's (AD) early history and emergence of splinter parties such as MEP.

6270 Petkoff, Teodoro. La corrupción administrativa. Caracas?: Ediciones Fracción Socialista, 1978. 89 p.

Examination of corruption in recent Venezuelan politics by major figures in MAS party. Includes useful appendix on 28 power groups including names and industrial, commercial, and financial interests and connections.

6271 ———. El Movimiento al Socialismo: MAS venezolano (UNAM/RMS, 43:3, julio/sept. 1981, p. 1121–1139)

While criticizing capitalism, major parties, and Venezuela's political system, MAS leader examines goals, ideological tendencies, and international connections of Venezuela's growing social democratic party.

Ramírez Faría, Carlos. La democracia petrolera. See *HLAS 44:2893.*

6272 Rangel, Domingo Alberto. Los mercaderes del voto. Valencia, Venezuela: Vadell Hermanos Editores, 1978. 164 p.: bibl.

Critical analysis of electoral domination of Venezuelan politics by AD and COPEI. Themes of corruption, fraud, and factional ties are major parts of this polemic.

6273 Rey, Juan Carlos *et al.* El financiamiento de los partidos políticos y la democracia en Venezuela. Caracas: Editorial Ateneo de Caracas: Editorial Jurídica Venezolana, 1981. 236 p.

Six essays examine high cost of financing Venezuelan parties and democratic elections while addressing the latter's economic, legal, and political dimensions. Also debates public vs. private financing of elections.

6274 Tarre Murzi, Alfredo. López Contreras, de la tiranía a la libertad. 2. ed. Caracas: Editorial Ateneo de Caracas, 1982. 429 p., 3 leaves of plates: bibl. (Colección Actualidad política)

Political history of Venezuela from Gómez's death (1936) to end of López Contreras presidency (1941). López Contreras is portrayed as key initiator of present political system with its emphasis on legal and democratic rules, ideological pluralism, and human rights. Important study for its treatment of the formation of democratic leadership and the transformation from dictatorship to democratic rule.

El 23 [i.e. Veintitrés] de enero: habla la conspiración. See *HLAS 44:2894.*

Velásquez, Ramón J. Aspectos de la evolución política de Venezuela en el último medio siglo. See *HLAS 44:2895.*

――――; J.F. Sucre Figarella; and **Blas Bruni Celli.** Betancourt en la historia de Venezuela del siglo XX. See *HLAS 44:2896.*

6275 Venezuela at the polls: the national elections of 1978. Edited by Howard R. Penniman. Washington: American Enterprise Institute for Public Policy Research, 1980. 287 p.: bibl., ill. (Studies in political and social processes. AEI studies; 286)

Excellent analysis of 1978 national elections with emphasis on Venezuelan democracy, electoral politics, party system, and voting behavior by six of the best North American experts on Venezuela. Indispensable resource for understanding the nature of Venezuelan democratic reform politics. Analysis supports the position that Venezuela's democratic reform polity is sufficiently institutionalized to muddle through despite pressing national and international problems.

6276 Vigencia y proyección de Rómulo: 50 años de liderazgo político. Caracas: Partido Acción Democrática, 1978. 247 p.: ill.

Series of letters, essays, and lectures in homage to ex-President Betancourt's 50 years of political activity and leadership in Venezuela. Breadth of praise reflects Rómulo's deep and lasting impact on Venezuela, Latin America, and the world.

ECUADOR

6277 Cueva Dávila, Agustín. The process of political domination in Ecuador. Translated by Danielle Salti. New Brunswick, N.J.: Transaction Books, 1982. 106 p.: bibl., index.

Excellent treatment of historical roots of caudillismo and populism in Ecuadorian society (1895–1944). Uses dependency framework to develop explanation of velasquismo and its "ideological mark of domination." Refers to Rodríguez Lara's military government as the "scapegoat" of the dominant class.

6278 Dávila, Francisco R. Los partidos políticos tradicionales y el descenso de la oligarquía en el Ecuador (UNAM/RMS, 43:3, julio/sept. 1981, p. 1141–1168)

Marxist analysis of relationship among traditional political parties, military governments of 1970s, and landowner-agroexporter oligarchy. Populism, capitalism, liberalism, and conservatism are criticized for their inability to solve the country's social, economic, and political needs. This confusion and lack of legitimacy opened the door for revolutionary parties to take the helm.

6279 Encuentro de Riobamba: estudio sobre Puebla, con motivo de los 25 años de Episcopado de Monseñor Leónidas Proaño, *Riobamba, 1979.* Riobamba, Ecuador: Instituto Diocesano de Pastoral de Riobamba, Centro de Estudios y Publicaciones (CEP), 1980. 303 p., 8 leaves of plates: ill.

Collection of papers presented in Riobamba, Ecuador, dealing with ideas coming out of the Puebla statements of John Paul II and, in general, from the proponents of "liberation theory." An important contribution to the literature on Church's thought in contemporary Latin America. [W.R. Garner]

6280 Granda Aguilar, Víctor. La masacre de AZTRA: el crímen más espantoso de la dictadura del triunvirato militar. Cuenca, Ecuador: Universidad de Cuenca, Facultad de Ciencias Económicas, 1979. 387 p.

Marxist analysis of the struggle within the sugar industry for a better life and violent response by the military government on 18 Oct. 1977. Author attempts to document nature of the quarrel and subsequent cover-up by the military government.

6281 Hurtado, Oswaldo. El poder político en el Ecuador. 4. ed., actualizada. Barcelona: ARIEL, 1981. 356 p.: bibl. (Nuestro siglo por dentro)

Excellent sociopolitical analysis of power within Ecuadorian society by Ecuador's current president, also available in English as *Political power in Ecuador* (Albuquerque: University of New Mexico, 1980). Pt. 1 covers colonial period; pt. 2 spans 1820–1949; and pt. 3, "crisis of power" (1950–79). Hurtado's emphasis on significant power contenders reveals not only difficulties nation has faced in organizing and distributing power, but more important problem of establishing legitimate authority. Valuable epilogue written in 1979 offers explanation for the military's rise and fall during 1970s (for historian's comment, see *HLAS 44:2900*).

6282 Política y sociedad, Ecuador, 1830–1980. Coordinación del proyecto, Luis Mora Ortega. Coordinador del vol. 1, Enrique Ayala Mora. Supervisión editorial, Francisco Avila Paredes. Quito: Corporación Editora Nacional, 1980. 399 p.: bibl. (Libro del sesquicentenario; 1)

Consists of 30 essays by Ecuadorian intellectuals and politicians who commemorate 150 years of nationhood by discussing virtually every major political and social theme from centralism and caudillism to militarism and the role of women in politics.

6283 Proaño Maya, Marco. Yo, CEP: ensayo político. Quito: s.n., 1980. 277 p.: ill.

Favorable analysis of Concentración de Fuerzas Populares, a political party, including its history, organization, and leadership under Assad Bucaram.

6284 Quintero, Rafael. El mito del populismo en el Ecuador: análisis de los fundamentos del estado ecuatoriano moderno, 1895–1934. Quito: FLASCO, 1980. 386 p.: bibl.

Excellent analysis of Ecuadorian populism stressing importance of political, economic, and historical factors (1895–1934). Important critique of both populist literature and nature of velasquismo in 20th-century Ecuadorian politics.

6285 Robalino Bolle, Isabel. El sindicalismo en el Ecuador. Quito: Instituto Ecuatoriano para el Desarrollo Social, 1981. 156 p.: bibl.

Two-part investigation of Ecuadorian labor movement. Pt. 1 focuses on its history; pt. 2 involves statistical investigation of type and numbers of labor union by province.

CHILE, PERU, AND BOLIVIA

WILLIAM R. GARNER, *Director of Graduate Studies and Associate Professor of Political Science, Latin American Studies Advisory Committee, Southern Illinois University at Carbondale*

CHILE: THE COUNTRY HAS UNDERGONE major shifts in socioeconomic and political institutions as have Bolivia and Peru since publication of *HLAS 43* in 1981. However, these changes have been less marked in the case of Chile as is evident from the quantity and quality of published materials annotated below. In contrast to *HLAS 43*, there are very few fresh analyses of Unidad Popular in this volume. Former UP Cabinet member, Almeyda, one exiled writer among all the others noted here, now concentrates on studying the development of an "inter-American class consciousness" (item **6286**). Chaparro (item **6298**) is reduced to attacking the "style" of Salvador Allende while at the same time—as has been done repeatedly by others over the past nine years—lamenting the inability of the UP and Christian Democrats to reconcile their differences. Former Communist Party leader, Luis Corvalán (with Bau), has published an attack on the military regime "on the eve of the 7th anniversary of the Pinochet coup" which is also quite optimistic about the return of democratic institutions to the country (item **6302**).

From Stockholm, Varas (item **6321**) admits to the limited options now facing the Chilean left in an attempt to reestablish permanent political organizations within the country.

Apologists for the post-1973 period speak out in Thayer Arteaga's essays (item **6319**) which enthusiastically describe the military's program as having once more restored order and spiritual values to the nation. Borel Chieyssal (item **6297**) is equally enthusiastic about the new simplified policies governing territorial administration. *Constitución contemporánea* (item **6300**), a collection of papers delivered at the national university on the subject of Chilean constitutional law, offers interesting rationale for the new military Constitution as reflecting "current political and legal norms." One should also note the apologia offered by Rojas Sánchez (item **6317**) in *Elementos de una concepción totalitaria*. As for negative criticism of Pinochet's policies, substantial contributions are Bitar's study of Chile's novel "economic liberalism" (item **6296**), Díaz and Trumper on the post-1973 agrarian reform (item **6303**), Falabella on the near-total control of all functional groups in Chilean political life (item **6305**), Garretón on interest group activity before, during, and after the Allende period (item **6307**), Grenier on governmental planning (item **6309**), and Miquel on the general loss of support from the standpoint of international public opinion due to the suppression of Chile's trade unions (item **6310**). Valenzuela, who provides the most balanced assessment of contemporary Chilean realities (item **6320**), ends by questioning Pinochet's "long-term viability."

Probably the most significant contributions on Chile are studies by or concerning the Roman Catholic hierarchy, the Vicariate of Solidarity in particular, as, for example in Mires' article (item **6311**). The Vicariate itself has published lengthy and telling works which are subtle in their attempts to generate change in the government's human rights policy. Note especially *Encuentros con los sectores de la comunidad nacional* (item **6291**), *¿Dónde están?* (item **6289**), and *Simposium internacional* (item **6295**). One other thrust of Church concern—the doctrine of national security—is subject to rigorous scrutiny in *Dos ensayos sobre la seguridad nacional* (item **6290**). One should also note the piece by Arriagada and Garretón (item **6288**) which addresses the concept from a non-ecclesiastical leftist point of view.

Two interesting Chilean articles on political theory by Dooner and Fernández (item **6304**) and Garretón (item **6307**), address the idea of democracy. Unfortunately, in both articles the democratic praxis is addressed and defined from the standpoint of substantive rather than procedural assumptions. Eduardo Frei's *El mensaje humanista* (item **6306**), published shortly before his death, reflects the former President's thoughts after the bitter experiences of the post-1970 period. Gazmuri's essay on political legitimacy and decadence (item **6308**) is excellent as are Remmer's two studies (items **6313–6315**) which exemplify the best of the theoretical literature arising from the Chilean experience.

PERU: The end of the military *docenio* has produced a number of important studies. Alberti (item **6325**) responds with a very definite affirmative to the questions of whether the military "revolution" really produced significant changes in political thinking and participation on the part of the masses. Alva Orlandini (item **6326**) has produced a major collection of interviews that gauges the present mental attitudes of Peruvian political leaders capable of making policy in the post-*docenio* period. Cleaves' study of public administration (item **6339**), particularly that portion dealing with the agricultural sector, is a major contribution. Collin Delavaud (item **6340**) analyzes the 1968–80 period from a leftist perspective with incisive remarks on the reelections of Belaúnde Terry. Cotler's study (item **6341**) of military-civilian political experience, the APRA phenomenon, and the two-phase military experiment is one of the best pieces of writing on Peruvian politics in the last several years. Gorman's collection of essays on post-military prospects (item **6361**) should be read by all Peruvianists. Medina García (item **6353**) and ¿*El voto perdido?* (item **6374**) examine 1980 voting behavior and Rubio's study of the 1980 Constitution (item **6365**) concludes that the document is "reactionary." Finally, Werlich (item **6375**) gives the reader much to ponder in his succinct analysis of the pre-1980 period and those specific factors making possible Belaúnde's return to power.

With the death in 1980 of Haya de la Torre, a deluge of studies have appeared on him and the APRA. These include works by Barba (item **6331**), Borea Odría (item **6336**), Castro Arenas (item **6338**), "Del APRA al APRA Rebelde" (item **6343**), and excellent studies by Pike (item **6359**) and Stein (item **6368**).

Marxist and other radical assessments of post-military politics are numerous. Two DESCO symposia (items **6342** and **6355**) should be read for this viewpoint. Bernales (items **6333–6334**) offers strident criticism of the military experiment and predicts that the left cannot be stopped in the wake of the mass hyper-mobilization produced especially during the First Phase (under Velasco). Franco writes on the same subject (items **6344** and **6347**) as does Guerra García (item **6348**) but in a more pessimistic vein anticipating the return of an entrenched oligarchy as well as the continuation of international economic dependency as constants in Peruvian political life. Pease García (item **6354**) calls for an end to "capitalist" (i.e., procedural) democracy and urges development of an alternative system based on specific substantive requisites. A Communist Party publication, "Peru: por la Unidad de Acción" (item **6357**), suggests a resurgence of leftist power as a result of Haya de la Torre's death. One of the best studies from this ideological sector is by Rubio C. (item **6364**) which predicts political violence (vs. "reformism") as the most obvious result of the *docenio* and the Aprista leader's death.

In the field of labor relations, one should consult Becker (item **6332**), Laite (item **6351**), and Amat y León *et al.* (item **6328**), who calls for a continuation of the agrarian reform begun under Velasco and thwarted by Morales Bermúdez. With respect to the rural peasantry, works by McClintock (item **6352**) and J. Portugal Vizcarra (item **6360**) are excellent additions to the literature.

For more theoretical studies, one should note the Saco study (item **6366**) of APRA's half-century of varied respose to the agrarian question. Klaiber (item **6350a**) stresses the role of "popular," grass-roots Catholicism as a given in lower-class Peruvian socialization and hence mass political behavior.

BOLIVIA: The long military period preceding the Siles Suazo presidency and the short time since the return to democratic forms are treated within a number of contexts. Southern Cone-Andean Group competition for Bolivian allegiance is the focus of studies by Mitchell (item **6397**) and Natale (item **6401**). The Siles Suazo-Paz Estenssoro rift within the old MNR is analyzed well by Lavaud (item **6394**). "Bolivie: le Militaire est Roi" (item **6383**) is illuminating as a study of the cocaine industry and, on this subject, one should note also the article by Anton (item **6377**) in which the drug-based economy is seen as the consequence of rule by a "political gerontocracy." Bascone (item **6380**) writes about the long four decades during which the military exercised its "arbitral function" while at the same time commenting on the impotence of *any* civilian government that might attempt establishment of workable political institutions. The Inter-American Commission on Human Rights (item **6392**) offers a damning assessment of governmental performance under the military. Monroy's history of Bolivian party organization is excellent (item **6398**). The far-left is heard in Filomino's interview with MIR founder, Antonio Araníbar (item **6378**) and the Syndicalist Federation of Mine Workers (item **6391**) calls for action against "internal bourgeois or fascist threats." Guillermo Lora (item **6396**), perennial apologist for the PIR, has written a volume ostensibly on the MNR that is, in fact, only a sketch of the work on his own party organization. The 1980 official report of the Fourth National Congress of the Bolivian Communist Party (item **6402**) includes an interesting section on Bolivia's "divided Church" and a warning to all labor organizations not to "swerve toward the rightist pro-imperialistic Paz Estenssoristas."

Whitehead (item **6404a**) has given what is probably the best analysis of the Bolivian mine-workers' electoral reform but insists that the mining "proletariat" is no better off than it was at the beginning of the MNR experiment in 1952. Labor politics is also the subject of an important contribution by Le Bot (item **6384**). Cammack (item **6385**) fills a vacuum with his significant study of monocultural economics and the problems of labor fragmentation, both conditions produced in large measure by urban bourgeois opposition to the rural peasantry and mining groups.

Interest in the Bolivian Church has increased in recent years. See, for example, Arias (item **6379**) who stresses the need for a form of Protestant "liberation theology;" studies of the Bolivian arm of "Justicia y Paz" (item **6382**); and a short memorial to Fray Luis Espinal (item **6389**) who died in 1980 as a result of military maltreatment and torture.

Among theoretical studies, one should mention a rather flawed piece, "La Política y el Estado" (item **6390**) and a work by Centellas C. (item **6386**) which prescribes corporatist remedies for problems caused principally by the "illusion of democratic government." US-Bolivian relations are covered well by Salamanca (item **6403**). Also of interest are two studies on the role of the Bolivian press by Czaplicki (item **6388**) and Montecinos (item **6399**).

CHILE

6286 Almeyda, Clodomiro. El proceso de construcción de las vanguardias en la revolución latinoamericana (NSO, 61, julio/agosto 1982, p. 17–25, ill.)

Former Socialist Party member of Allende cabinet—now in Mexican exile—describes what he perceives as omens for the development of a pervasive inter-American revolutionary consciousness. Interesting, not overly-optimistic.

6287 Alvarez García, Marcos. Le rôle de l'Etat et la nouvelle législation d'exception au Chili (ULB/RIS, 1/2, 1981, p. 239–283)

Exposition on former-President Allende's view of legal reform, especially in the area of civil rights. Analyzes Allende's views on suspension of civil rights under various conditions. Draws comparison with rights policy under Pinochet.

6288 Arriagada H., Genaro and **Manuel Antonio Garretón M.** Doctrina de seguridad y régimen militar: pts. 1/2 (CSUCA/ESC, 20, mayo/agosto 1978, p. 129–153; 21, sept./dic. 1978, . 53–82)

Former UP leader in Chile writes with Arriagada about 1950s-60s assumptions that led to adoption of national security doctrine in 1970s. Pt. 1 attributes much weight to US influence. Pt. 2 describes components of doctrine and splinter ideologies within Latin American military. Intriguing analysis of the conscious and subconscious thinking that led to doctrine's implementation.

6289 Arzobispado de Santiago, *Chile.* Vicaría de la Solidaridad. ¿Dónde están? Santiago: La Vicaría, 1978. 2 v.: ill.

Vols. 1/2 offer detailed information on individuals who have disappeared since the beginning of the Pinochet administration. Volumes address Chile's Minister of Interior requesting information on 120 persons. Interesting tactic on the part of Chilean Church hierarchy and Vicariate of Solidarity.

6290 ——. ——. Dos ensayos seguridad nacional. Santiago: La Vicaría, 1979. 235 p.: bibl. (Estudios; 6)

Includes two excellent, systematic analyses of the Latin American doctrine of national security (Comblín's being the most comprehensive) and valuable documentation for anyone interested in the philosophical and factual aspects of the phenomenon. Important contribution.

6291 ——. ——. Encuentros con sectores del comunidad nacional. Santiago: La Vicaría, 1978. 111 p.: ill. (Estudios; 5)

Contains descriptions of sessions sponsored by Chilean Church hierarchy on human rights. Reports on opinions of many groups including families of disappeared persons (*desaparecidos*), young people, representatives of Catholic and other Christian parishes, labor groups, nuns and priests, and professionals.

6292 ——. ——. Presentación al Presidente de la Corte Suprema, marzo 1976. Santiago: La Vicaría, 1976. 170 leaves: ill.

Lengthy 1976 study, dealing with allegations of human rights violations against Chilean citizens, presented to Chilean Supreme Court President "for his personal study and reflection." Philosophical and legal study includes numerous documents alluding to hundreds of cases. Of interest to students of civil rights and Church-State relations.

6293 ——. ——. Quinto año de labor: 1980. Santiago: La Vicaría, 1981. 221 p.: plates: tables.

Lengthy report of Vicariate's Judicial Section emphasizes its policy and functions under Pinochet: 1) protection of civil liberties; 2) safeguarding of procedural due process relating to political crimes; 3) study of arbitrary detention without traditional Chilean judicial rights; 4) procedures used in cases of exiles wishing to return to Chile; 5) legal assistance for the poor; 6) care of families whose members have "disappeared" according to the government; and 7) judicial research and analysis.

6294 ——. ——. Sexto años de labor: 1981. Santiago: La Vicaría, 1982. 187 p.: ill., plates, tables.

Exhaustive account of Vicariate of Solidarity's sixth year of work within Chile on matters such as peasant and urban aid, finances of the organization and overall functions of the Secretary-General. Together with item **6293**, these reports prove that the Vicariate is an exceedingly potent ally of victims of the present Chilean government.

6295 ——. ——. Simposium internacional sobre derechos humanos: experiencia y compromiso compartidos. Santiago: La Vicaría, 1979. 181 p.: ill.

Pictorial essay commemorates international year of human rights and special Chilean conference held on the subject. Emphasizes Chile's experience after Sept. 1973. See "Letter from Santiago" written by Vicariate of Solidarity members and approved by conference (p. 167–175).

6296 Bitar, Sergio. Libertad económica y dictadura política: la Junta Militar Chilena, 1973–78 (NOS, 43, julio/agosto 1979, p. 51–69, ill., tables)

Polemic against "economic liberalism" and political repression under Pinochet. Includes excellent set of statistical tables, of value insofar as data was gathered by government analysts.

6297 Borel Chieyssal, Edmundo and **Claudio Mergudich K.** Algunos aspectos administrativos del gobierno regional y perspectivas de desarrollo del nuevo municipio chileno. Santiago: Universidad de Chile, Facultad de Ciencias Económicas y Administrativas, Departamento de Administración, 1976. 269 p.: bibl.

National University professors describe the new (post-1973) method of territorial administration and novel forms prescribed for Chilean local governments.

6298 Chaparro, Patricio. Los actores sociales y políticos y el quiebre del sistema político democrático chileno (CPU/ES, 25, 3. trimestre, 1980, p. 33–50, tables)

Notes growth of Chilean democratic practice (1920–70), especially political participation. Believes that during Allende period, lack of an ability to moderate differences on the part of both Christian Democrats and UP coalition plus Salvador Allende's "style" led to end of Socialist experiment in

1973. Author naively calls for regrouping of civilian center forces to end the Pinochet era.

6299 Chile hoy (URSS/AL, 1/2:37/38, 1981, p. 138–216)

Various Soviet Latin Americanists respond to the fall of Allende's government and discuss prospects under Pinochet. Provides valuable insights into USSR's ideological assessment of situation as well as policy formulation.

6300 La Constitución contemporánea: seminario efectuado en noviembre de 1979 en la Casa Central de la Universidad de Chile con el alto patrocinio de la Universidad y de la Corporación de Estudios Nacionales. Participan, Juan María Bordaberry *et al.* Santiago: Universidad de Chile, 1980. 284 p.: bibl.

Proceedings of seminar at National University (Nov. 1979) in which fundamental rationale for the existence of constitutional documents is given as "reflecting current political and legal norms."

6301 Corvalán, Luis. Discurso con motivo del 10. aniversario del triunfo de la Unidad Popular (URSS/AL, 10:34, 1980, p. 106–114)

Former Chilean Communist Party leader speaks on UP experiment on the seventh anniversary of Pinochet's coup (should be read in conjunction with item **6299**).

6302 ——— and Carlos Bau. Chile hoy: repercusiones (URSS/AL, 1[49], 1982, p. 61–74)

Exiled former Chilean Communist Party and MAPU leaders, give fairly optimistic views on the future evolution of the Chilean political process (read in conjunction with items **6299** and **6301**).

6303 Díaz, Harry and Ricardo Trumper. The Chilean agrarian bourgeoisie under the authoritarian regime. Ontario, Canada: Latin American Research Unit (LARU), 1981. 38 p.: bibl., tables (LARU working paper; 29)

Examination of post-1973 "counterreform" in Chilean agrarian policy indicates that while such policy may be modeled on capitalist assumptions, Pinochet's policy orientation radically differs from Frei's and Allende's. Study finds increased consolidation of economic and political power in Chilean agribusiness whose leverage vis-à-vis the State aparatus has also increased.

6304 Dooner, Patricio and Gonzalo Fernández. El concepto de democracia: algunas precisiones (CPU/ES, 24:2, 1980, p. 21–43)

Authors discuss meaning of Latin American "democracy," and after examining "guided," "authoritarian," "popular," and other forms, they presumably accept "Marxist democracy" in that it will guarantee economic as well as legal and political security. To this reviewer, however, inclusion of substantive economic guarantee does not define a fundamentally procedural political process.

6305 Falabella, Gonzalo. Les syndicats sous un régime autoritaire: le cas du Chili (FDD/NED [Problèmes d'Amérique Latine, 60] 4599/4560, 31 déc. 1980, p. 143–173, tables)

Description of measures enforced by Pinochet to control the behavior of organized labor and other groups in Chilean political life.

6306 Frei, Eduardo. El mensaje humanista. Santiago: Editorial Aconcagua, 1981. 80 p. (Colección Lautaro)

Published shortly before his death, former-President Frei's message consists of a frustrated and angry personal statement about those who speak well of democracy with no intention of protecting it. Also notes the humanistic weaknesses of both capitalist democracy and Marxist socialism and calls for reflection on the messages (1980–81) of Pope John Paul II. Concludes by warning that the humanist option for man and government is possible only within the context of spiritual and universal considerations.

6307 Garretón M., Manuel Antonio. Las fuerzas político-sociales y el problema de la democracia en Chile (FCE/TE, 48[1]:189, enero/marzo 1981, p. 101–120)

Comparative study of Chilean group politics before, during, and after Allende that is also primarily theoretical. As in the case of Dooner and Fernández (item **6304**), one is confronted with a definition of democracy chiefly concerned with guaranteeing "basic necessities."

6308 Gazmuri, Cristián. La idea de decadencia nacional y el pensamiento político conservador chileno en el siglo XX (CPU/ES, 28/29, 1981, p. 33–54)

Provocative, speculative piece, based

on works published over the past 80 years, explores Chilean perceptions of political legitimacy and the notion of socioeconomic and political decline.

6309 Grenier, Philippe. Le Chili du Général Pinochet: 1973–1980 (FDD/NED [Problèmes d'Amérique Latine, 60] 4599/ 4560, 31 déc. 1980, p. 10–68)

Fairly detailed analysis of social and economic planning under Pinochet together with discussion of the regime's actions to implement thorough political institutionalization. Excellent study.

6310 Miquel, Janine. La defensa de los derechos y libertades de los trabajadores chilenos y sus organizaciones sindicales ante los organismos internacionales: sistematización y análisis jurídico. Stockholm: Institute of Latin American Studies, 1981. 84 p. (Research paper series; no. 31)

Examines Chile's stand in international and hemispheric political forums after Pinochet's systematic dismantling of trade union activity. Valuable, thoroughly researched work written from the standpoint of Chile's long-term commitment to various international agreements on the rights of labor. Also discusses post-1973 Junta actions that have effectively neutralized Chile's previously strong labor organizations.

6311 Mires, Fernando. Las retaguardias sin vanguardias (NSO, 61, julio/agosto 1982, p. 35–54, ill.)

Compares revolutionary movements in Brazil, Chile, Cuba, and Nicaragua within hypothetical framework of sub-system dominant mass-base. Thrust is that socioeconomic and political change is seen best in other types of organizations such as, for example, the Chilean Church hierarchy, Cuban and Nicaraguan neighborhoods and peasant groups, and Brazilian labor organizations. Excellent study contains fairly low-key, reasoned critique of US policy under Reagan. Highly recommended.

6312 Presos políticos desaparecidos en Chile. Realizado por el Comité Chileno de Solidaridad con la Resistencia Antifascista de La Habana. México: Casa de Chile en México, 1977. 305 p.: index.

Marxist discussion of techniques used by Pinochet to neutralize political opposition (or those perceived as being in opposition).

Of particular value is the long list of *desaparecidos* in volume's back section.

6313 Remmer, Karen L. Pinochet's Chile (CRIA/WW, 22:10, Oct. 1979, p. 36–40)

Analysis of US-Chilean policy (ineffective as of 1979, author's writing date), changes in internal socioeconomic and political conditions, and the role relinquished by default to the Roman Catholic Church and the Christian Democrats who are attempting to recreate a civilian alternative to Pinochet. Author is pessimistic about prospects for such a civilian option. Excellent work.

6314 ———. Political demobilizaton in Chile, 1973–1978 (CUNY/CP, 12:3, April 1980, p. 275–301)

Focusing on the concept of "mobilization," author utilizes post-Allende Chilean experience to work out her conceptualization of "demobilization" (compare with item **6315**).

6315 ———. Public policy and regime consolidation: the first five years of the Chilean Junta (JDA, 13:4, July 1979, p. 441–461)

Uses Chilean case (1973–78) to develop a more general study of the process of demobilization in the aftermath of a political regime that became too unstructured (or structured incorrectly) as was the case of Allende's. Interesting and novel inquiry.

Roddick, Jackie. The failure of populism in Chile: labour movement and politics before World War II. See *HLAS 44:3113*.

6316 Rodríguez Castañeda, Rafael. El asesinato de Orlando Letelier. México: Proceso, 1979. 160 p., 32 leaves of plates: ill.

Account of the 1976 assassination of Orlando Letelier and Ronni Moffitt in Washington. Compare with *Murder on Embassy Row* (see *HLAS 41:7454*, and also *HLAS 41:6456* and *6568*).

6317 Rojas Sánchez, Gonzalo. Elementos de una concepción totalitaria (Revista de Ciencia Política [Pontificia Universidad Católica de Chile, Instituto de Ciencia Política, Santiago] 3, 1980, p. 33–54)

Seeks to explain public order concepts in the 1981 Chilean Constitution. Author presents a provocative apologia for a form of philosophical theocracy. Uses two "totalitarian" case studies: 1) Allende's period (1970–73); and 2) 1940s development of Unión Nacionalista and Acción Chilena. Of value owing to author's bizarre "objectivity."

6318 Sigmund, Paul. Chile: market fascism or utopian libertarianism? (CRIA/WW, 24:10, Oct. 1981, p. 4–6)

Describes appearance in various Chilean intellectual circles of a third option to Allende's "vía Chilena" and Milton Friedman's "market capitalism." Sees "subsidiarity" drawn (from Pius XI's *Quadragesimo Anno*) as a novel corporatist alternative that could be used against Chile's Roman Catholic hierarchy's opposition to Pinochet's regime. Sees two alternatives for Chilean politics: a "libertarian paradise" or a "centralized, party-dominated ideologized democracy . . . ."

6319 Thayer Arteaga, William. Tres ensayos: fundamentos de una actitud ciudadana. Santiago: Editorial Universitaria, 1978. 136 p. (Colección Problemas de nuestro tiempo)

Set of writings sympathetic to Pinochet's regime as one which reestablished order and spiritual values. Note section on the "reconciliation" of the universities to a "non-sectarian position."

6320 Valenzuela, Arturo. Eight years of military rule in Chile (CUH, 81:472, Feb. 1982, p. 64–68, 88)

Excellent post-coup historical study devotes attention to contemporary economic crisis and makes suggestions concerning "Pinochet's long-term viability."

6321 Varas, Augusto. Crisis política y alternativa democrática: límites y perspectivas de la izquierda chilena. Stockholm: Institute of Latin American Studies, 1981. 28 p. (Occasional papers)

Text of speech by Chilean exile (Univ. of Stockholm, April 1981). Emphasizes constraints imposed by Pinochet's 1981 Constitution on any possible regrouping of the Chilean Left.

6322 Verdugo, Patricia and **Claudio Orrego Vicuña.** Detenidos-desaparecidos, una herida abierta. Santiago: Editorial Aconcagua, 1980. 187 p.: ports (Colección Lautaro)

Addresses Pinochet administration policies concerning *desaparecidos* who consist of: 1) those declared officially dead; 2) those imprisoned for political offenses; and 3) those without legal existence according to the government. Pt. 2 discusses many case studies in all three categories.

6323 Whelan, James Robert. Allende, death of a Marxist dream. Westport, Conn.: Arlington House, 1981. 230 p.: bibl., ill., index.

UPI investigative reporter gives account of weeks immediately preceding the Pinochet coup. Emphasizes last 72 hours and includes reporter's description of events leading to the death (suicide, according to author) of President Salvador Allende. Based on author's interviews and eyewitness accounts of those who escaped from La Moneda (11 Sept. 1973).

6324 Zapata, Francisco. Los mineros del cobre y el gobierno militar en Chile entre 1973–1981 (CEDLA/B, 32, junio 1982, p. 39–47, bibl., tables)

Describes means used by Chilean copper workers to cut into government production quotas in counter-reprisal to the Pinochet regime. Fascinating study of politics under an authoritarian system.

PERU

6325 Alberti, Giorgio. The military and the "third road" in Peru (Politica Internazionale [Nova Italia, Firenze] 2:2, Winter 1981/ Spring 1982, p. 14–25)

Italian "autopsy" of the Peruvian postmilitary aftermath. Belaúnde Terry's reelection in 1980 did not signal a return "to normalcy." The traditional "oligarchic order" under the control of the military and the Church changed significantly and Peruvian class organization and sympathies to various traditional groups were altered irrevocably. Incisive analysis.

6326 Alva Orlandini, Hernán. Un alto en el camino del Perú: crítica y consenso. Lima: Editorial Universitaria, 1980. 3 v.: index, ports.

Three-volume set of 30 interviews with prominent Peruvian political leaders who discuss current state of nation's intellectual, political, and economic life. Index for all three volumes is probably most extensive this reviewer has seen in Latin American sociopolitical literature. Major contribution.

6327 Alvarez, Elena. Política agraria del Gobierno Militar y su posible impacto sobre la población, 1969–1979. Lima: Universidad Nacional Agraria La Molina, Departamento de Ciencias Humanas, Taller de Coyuntura Agraria, 1980. 23 p.: bibl. (Serie Documento de trabajo; no. 28)

Criticizes military *docenio* because its "revolution" never committed itself to the rural areas, its people, and problems. Intriguing study with interesting conclusions.

6328 Amat y León, Carlos *et al.* Realidad del campo peruano después de la Reforma Agraria: 10 ensayos críticos. Lima: Centro de Investigación y Capacitación: Editora Ital Perú, 1980. 388 p., 2 leaves of plates: bibl., ill. (Serie Perú actual)

Somewhat uneven essays by writers of moderate views who agree on the need to continue the agrarian reform despite end of "revolutionary" *docenio.*

6329 Baella Tuesta, Alfonso. *El Tiempo:* prensa libre. Lima: A. Baella Tuesta, 1979. 493 p.: ill.

Written by *El Tiempo's* former editor whose paper was suppressed during military *docenio.* Angry book that virtually explodes in recounting continual military harrassment of *El Tiempo.* Also includes Baella's harsh criticism of other military actions.

6330 ———. ¿Qué pasa? Lima: Editorial *El Tiempo,* 1977. 400 p.: ill.

Compilation of editorials and essays by *El Tiempo's* editor after paper's reopening (Oct. 1975). Good reference for those seeking moderate reactions to first phase of Velasco's "revolution." Includes more reasoned argument for press freedom than Baella Tuesta (item **6329**).

Balbi, Carmen Rosa. El Partido Comunista y el APRA en la crisis revolucionaria de los años treinta. See *HLAS 44:2908.*

6331 Barba Caballero, José. Defensa del aprismo: homenaje póstumo a Haya de la Torre. Lima?: s.n., 1980. 480 p.: bibl.

Large volume in memory of Haya de la Torre, recounts APRA's accomplishments. Good reference for those interested in APRA's perception of its role in Peruvian political life.

Basadre, Jorge. Elecciones y centralismo en el Perú: apuntes para un esquema histórico. See *HLAS 44:2911.*

6332 Becker, David. Modern mine labour and politics in Peru since 1968 (CEDLA/B, 32, junio 1982, p. 61–86, bibl., tables)

British scholar stresses role of organized labor within "dynamic Left" context in Peruvian mining politics. Disagrees that capitalist "authoritarian" politics keeps movement in bounds. Based on fieldwork (1977–78 and 1981).

6333 Bernales, Enrique. La izquierda ejerce la iniciativa parlamentaria (DESCO/Q, 8, 1980, p. 18–21, ill.)

Revolutionary Socialist Party representative attacks ineffectiveness of both Acción Popular and APRA during Morales Bermúdez period. Asserts that Peruvian Left has now taken the initiative in both houses of national legislature.

6334 ———. Una proyección sobre las elecciones del 80 (DESCO/Q, 2, nov./dic. 1979, p. 16–32, plates, tables)

Optimistic prediction that the incorporation of the illiterate as well as rural workers and the poor will bring about a radicalization of politics. Argument, however, is flawed by confusing "economic democracy" with what is fundamentally a procedural form, a common misperception in writings from the Latin American Left.

6335 Bollinger, William. Peru today: the roots of labor militancy (NACLA, 14:6, Nov./Dec. 1980, p. 2–35, bibl., ill.)

Stresses changes affecting Peruvian labor from first Belaúnde period (ending with 1968 coup) through *docenio* of Velasco-Morales Bermúdez to second Belaúnde administration (1980-present). Changes constitute "profound loss of growth for the worker movement."

6336 Borea Odría, Alberto. ¿Qué ha hecho el APRA por el Perú? Lima: Ediciones Galaxia, 1980. 354 p.: bibl., indexes.

Thorough and sympathetic account of APRA's work in Peruvian politics. Includes impressive topical and name indexes rarely seen in similar Latin American research aids.

6337 Cambios estructurales en el Perú, 1968–1975. Ernst-J. Kerbusch, editor. Con aportes de Juan Carlos Bossio *et al.* Santiago: Fundación F. Ebert, Instituto Latinoamericano de Investigaciones Sociales, 1976. 199 p.: bibl.

Moderate collection of essays, official documents, and statistics describing first phase of Peruvian military's "revolution" (i.e., Velasco period).

6338 Castro Arenas, Mario. Aprismo, marxismo, eurocomunismo. Lima: E. Miranda Iturrino, 1980. 266 p.: bibl., port.

Essays by exiled aprista journalist. Attempts to clarify contemporary aprista ideology and to explain aprismo's early rupture from Peruvian communist movement. Basic source on evolution of Haya de la Torre's and APRA's doctrines.

Chirinos Lizares, Guido and **Enrique Chirinos Soto.** El septenato, 1968–1975. See *HLAS 44:2930.*

6339 Cleaves, Peter S. and **Martin J. Scurrah.** Agriculture, bureaucracy, and military government in Peru. Ithaca, N.Y.: Cornell University Press, 1980. 329 p.: bibl., index.

Excellent treatment of bureaucracy during the Velasco military government "first phase" (1968–75). Using current public administration theory and applying three bureaucratic models (i.e., corporatist, liberal, and centralist), authors have produced an important work.

6340 Collin-Delavaud, Claude. Pérou: le retour de Belaúnde (FDD/NED [Problèmes d'Amérique Latine, 63] 4653/4654, 26 jan. 1982, p. 67–118, tables)

Thorough analysis from leftist perspective of Peruvian realities after Belaúnde's reelection (compare with item **6325**).

6341 Cotler, Julio. Democracia e integración nacional. Lima: Instituto de Estudios Peruanos, 1980. 103 p. (Colección Mínima; 8)

Explains and contrasts civilian and military politics in Peru and focuses on Belaúnde's two administrations, APRA, and military regimes of Velasco and Morales-Bermúdez. Worthwhile volume.

6342 Cuestionario a dirigentes de izquierda (DESCO/Q, 2, nov./dic. 1979, p. 4–15) Responses of six Peruvian leftists lead-

ers (i.e., Alfonso Barrantes, Hugo Blanco, Rolando Breña, Genaro Ledesma, Jorge del Prado, Leónidas Rodríguez Figueroa) concerning the State's legitimate role vis-à-vis the nation's "sectores populares." Important source on contemporary ideological trends.

6343 Del APRA al APRA Rebelde. Lima: Perugraph Editores, 1980. 128 p. (Documentos para la historia de la Revolución Peruana; 1)

Addresses early factionalism in early aprista organization with emphasis on leftist "APRA Rebels" and others who left the movement to join Peruvian far-left parties.

6344 Elecciones presidenciales en el Perú. Lima: Comisión Evangélica Latino Americano de Educación Cristiana, 1981. 106 p.: bibl., ill. (Cuadernos de estudio; 13)

Focuses on 1980 campaign and elections. Consists of newspaper coverage of policies and positions of Peruvian political parties compiled by The Latin American Evangelical Education Commission. Interesting example of protestant evangelical appraisal of watershed electoral experience in Peru.

6345 Falcón, Jorge. Mariátegui: arquitecto sindical. Lima: Empresa Editora Amauta, 1980. 358 p.

Stresses Mariátegui's syndicalist tradition and Marxist orientation. Author also discusses endless ideological and historical battle between apristas and Marxists in his analysis of how Peru's labor organization developed into a political force. Gives Haya de la Torre more credit in this respect than most Mariátegui followers.

6346 Franco, Carlos. Izquierda política e identidad nacional (*in* Perú: identidad nacional. Lima: Ediciones CEDEP, 1979, p. 235–304)

Study written from Communist Party perspective which also draws on Mariátegui's writings and contrasts them with Haya de la Torre's later years. Treats subject of national and class identity during *docenio* (1968–80). Interesting statement from an ultra-left point of view.

6347 ———. Perú, participación popular. Lima: Centro de Estudios para el Desarrollo y la Participación, 1979. 158 p.: bibl., diagrams (Serie Realidad nacional)

Study of institutionalized/ordered political participation beginning with 1968 Velasco regime. Believes that, regardless of society's level of economic and political development, relatively high degrees of institutionalized participation are possible.

6348 Guerra García, Francisco. Política e identidad nacional (*in* Perú: identidad nacional. Lima: Ediciones CEDEP, 1979, p. 305–364)

Focusing on Velasco military period (1968–75), author draws from writings of Mariátegui and Haya de la Torre (1920s). Stresses significance of aprismo, anti-Lima/over-centralization sentiment, continuity of Peru's oligarchy, and economic dependency as important yet negative national features. Important think-piece from the Left.

6349 Hildebrandt, César. Cambio de palabras: 26 entrevistas. San Isidro, Perú: Mosca Azul Editores, 1981. 331 p.

Important and valuable interviews with significant political figures in contemporary Peru (e.g., Haya de la Torre, Aníbal Quijano, Miró Quesada, Juan Velasco Alvarado, Luis Alberto Sánchez, Enrique Chirinos Soto, Julio Cotler, Fernando Belaúnde Terry).

6350 Jiménez, César. Perú, revolución popular o reformismo burgués. Lima: s.n., 1980. 373 p.: bibl.

At the root of conflicting interpretations of Peru's military "revolution" (1968–80) are ideological differences between Mariátegui and Haya de la Torre not resolved since 1920s. Interesting study which denounces Haya's "bourgeois ideology" while commending Mariátegui's more military Marxism.

6350a Klaiber, Jeffrey L. Religion and revolution in Peru, 1824–1976. Notre Dame, Ind.: University of Notre Dame Press, 1977. 259 p.: bibl., index (International studies of the Committee on International Relations, University of Notre Dame)

Jesuit professor of history at the Catholic University of Peru notes the transcending role of "popular" Peruvian Catholicism in the accomplishment of virtually all lasting changes in the traditional socioeconomic and political order in the country. A significant study of the interrelationship between grassroots religious sentiment and political change (for historian's comment, see *HLAS 40: 3529*).

6351 Laite, Julian. Miners and national politics in Peru: 1900–1974 (JLAS, 12:2, Nov. 1980, p. 317–340)

Study of miner organization and political behavior during 20th century. Author's thesis is one of cyclical response: working class politics evolve through recurring stages of compromise, confrontation, and return to compromise. Based on much data compiled for 1900–74 period.

6352 McClintock, Cynthia. Peasant cooperatives and political change in Peru. Princeton, N.J.: Princeton University Press, 1981. 418 p.: bibl., ill., index.

Important study of *campesino* socialization to politics conducted in representative cooperative villages of Peruvian periphery. Author uses tight, eclectic, and complex survey research tools for studying attitudes and behavior respectively (1969–74). Valuable publication.

6353 Medina García, Oswaldo. Perú, 1978–1980: análisis de un momento político. Lima?: C'EST Editorial, 1980. 154 p.: bibl.

Sociologist offers excellent statistical analysis of electoral behavior in choosing representatives for the National Constitutional Convention (1980). Major contribution.

Morales Bermúdez Cerrutti, Francisco. La Revolución Peruana. See *HLAS 44:2966*.

Pease García, Henry. El ocaso del poder oligárquico: lucha política en la escena oficial, 1968–1975. See *HLAS 44:2970*.

6354 ———. Por qué "democracia" y por qué "movimiento popular:" un debate necesario (DESCO/Q, 8, nov./dic. 1980, p. 36–42, plates)

Accuses past governments of being democracies that in substance are "monopolistic capitalist" and calls for an alternative system, a democracy that favors the lower classes in Peruvian society. Unfortunately, as with most leftist ideologies, author does not view democracy as a process.

6355 ——— et al. América Latina 80, democracia y movimiento popular. Lima: Centro de Estudios y Promoción del Desarrollo, 1981. 508 p.: bibl.

Seminar presentations reflect common misperception of the Latin American Left: their insistence in utilizing a substantive definition for democracy. Includes most important Peruvian Marxist and other leftist writers. Impressive, if somewhat flawed, volume.

6356 —— *et al.* La política económica y la democracia en debate: respuesta a Ulloa. Lima: Centro de Estudios y Promoción del Desarrollo, 1981. 326 p.: ill.

Focuses on weaknesses of Belaúnde Terry's "bourgeois" administration. Devotes special attention to economic problems under Minister of Finance and Economy, Manuel Ulloa Elías.

6357 Perú: por la unidad de acción (URSS/AL, 7[43], 1981, p. 77–82)

Official assessment prepared by Soviet and Peruvian Communist Parties of party groupings during 1980 campaign and subsequent elections. Predicts resurgence of leftist tendencies in wake of Haya de la Torre's death and APRA fragmentation.

6358 Perú 1980, elecciones y planes de gobierno. Lima: Universidad del Pacífico, Centro de Investigación: Fundación Friedrich Ebert, 1980. 445 p.: ill.

Prepared by University of the Pacific's Center for Investigation, volume was designed for use in 1980 elections and includes following information for each party: 1) logo; 2) electoral symbol for 1980 contest; 3) founders; 4) internal organization; 5) ideological orientation; 6) executive candidates; and 7) legislative candidates. Remarkable compilation.

6359 Pike, Frederick B. Peru's Haya de la Torre and archetypal regeneration mythology (IAMEA, 34:2, Autumn 1980, p. 25–65)

Important, complex study of Haya de la Torre as myth or charismatic/messianic hero written from Judeo-Christian and other perspectives, and using Freudian and Jungian analysis. Applies "regenerative mythology" to 20th-century Peruvian politics, at the center of which were Haya de la Torre and aprismo. Major contribution.

6360 Portugal Vizcarra, J. Crisis y política agraria del Perú, problema y solución: pt. 1 (IFEA/B, 7:3/4, 1978, p. 109–149, tables)

Good historical and socioeconomic analysis of Peru's agrarian politics and policy after 50 years of "reform." Written at *do-cenio*'s end, study spells out in detail the nation's agrarian problems.

6361 Post-revolutionary Peru: the politics of transformation. Edited by Stephen M. Gorman. Boulder, Colo.: Westview Press, 1982. 252 p.: bibl., ill., index (Westview special studies on Latin America and the Caribbean)

Collection of writings by prominent yet disparate theorists of "revolutionary" and post-"revolutionary" Peruvian politics (see especially articles by Woy-Hazleton, Dietz, Scurrah, Villanueva, and Palmer). Gorman feels that even though the military government was a "manifest failure," it did transform Peru by making possible a new Constitution, popular elections, and opening avenues for political participation. Important contribution.

6362 Puente Uceda, Luis F. de la. Obras de Luis de la Puente Uceda. s.l.: Voz Rebelde Ediciones, 1980 or 1981. 132 p., 1 leaf of plates: ill.

Founder of Peru's MIR (Movement of the Revolutionary Left) comments on various contemporary topics with many references to Mariátegui and Marxist-Leninist theory. Includes important sections on MIR's evolution as a political force and its ideological base. Author died as guerrilla in Oct. 1978.

6363 Römczyk, Elmar. Grundlagen und Perspektiven der Wahlen von 1980 in Peru. Hamburg, FRG: Institute für Iberoamerika-Kunde, 1981. 41 p.: tables.

Analyzes May 1980 election, examining Acción Popular and APRA parties, as well as parliamentary alliances. Thorough and insightful study. [G.M. Dorn]

6364 Rubio C., Marcial. La crisis de la izquierda en el Perú (NSO, 61, julio/agosto 1982, p. 81–86, ill.)

Addresses fragmentation of Peru's Left which, while accounting for one-third of votes cast in 1980, failed—by overlooking ideological differences and the need for unity—to unite in face of Belaúnde's "myth of a return to democratic institutions." Fundamentally split between demands for armed revolt and reformism, most groups appear to have opted for the former as in the case of Sendero Luminoso.

6365 ———. La nueva constitución: ¿carta magna o carta blanca? (DESCO/Q, 1, 1979?, p. 16–73, plates)

Author's opinion is that the 1979 Constitution protects the interest of capital while neglecting the rights of individuals that make up the mass-base of a national system. Until human rights ideals are adopted by Congress and upheld by the courts, the constitutional document is a farce.

6366 Saco, Alfredo. Tierra, pan y libertad: la solución aprista. Lima: Librería Studium Editores,1980. 256 p.: bibl., graphs.

Addresses problems of Peruvian agriculture and rural workers while providing thorough history of aprista agricultural policy (1930s-80s). Good reference work on evolution of APRA's ideology from earliest days to period after Haya's death.

6367 Serrano, Raúl. La revolución y la siesta: crónicas de propiedad social. Lima: J. & R., 1980. 229 p.: index.

Laments demise of President Velasco's concept of "social property" which was "the heart of the military government's revolutionary program," and whose dissolution is seen as a function of the return to democratic institutions and processes. Interesting comment from supporter of most radical period of the military experiment, Velasco's first phase.

Solar, Francisco José del. El militarismo en el Perú. See *HLAS 44:1986.*

6368 Stein, Steve. Populism in Peru: APRA, the formative years (*in* Latin American populism in comparative perspective. [see item **6016**] p. 113–134)

Good overview history of APRA and short biography of Haya de la Torre, official spokesman for Peruvian poor in 1920s, and incarnation of APRA in Max Weber's messianic sense. APRA as "new religion" with Haya as Jefe Máximo, became nation's most significant party for almost 50 years. Excellent introduction to the topic (for historian's comment, see *HLAS 44:2988*).

———. Populism in Peru: the emergence of the masses and the politics of social control. See *HLAS 44:2989.*

6369 Thorndike, Guillermo. La República Militar: 1930-Perú-1980. Lima: Thorndike: Libro Visión, 197. 176 p.: ill.

Pictorial-photographic history of Peruvian military from Leguía to Morales Bermúdez. Text is short but to the point (for one coming from the Peruvian Left).

6370 Urriza, Manuel. Perú, cuando los militares se van. Caracas: Ediciones CIDAL, 1978. 214 p.: bibl. (Colección Análisis)

Analysis of philosophical and behavioral changes of military elites that rule Peru (1968–80). Concludes that process of governing was too arduous for an efficient implementation of "revolutionary" policy.

6371 Valderrama L., Mariano. Movimiento campesino y la reforma agraria en el Perú (NOS, 35, marzo/abril 1978, p. 103–113)

Trenchant analysis focuses on rural worker organizations during military *docenio* defining them as corporatist but sees SINAMOS as radicalizing force. Includes chronological list of stages of government intervention in farm worker movement. Draws difference between methods used by Velasco and Morales Bermúdez regimes.

6372 ——— *et al.* El APRA, un camino de esperanzas y frustraciones. Lima?: Ediciones El Gallo Rojo, 1980. 250 p., 8 leaves of plates: bibl., ill.

Thorough history of APRA and political biography of Haya de la Torre.

6373 Vargas, Gustavo. Procesos electorales: el APRA y la izquierda en el Perú, 1931–180. Lima: s.n., 1980. 68 p.: bibl. (Serie Documentos políticos)

Historical-political analysis of relationships between Haya de la Torre and Peruvian leftist groups from Leguía period through 1978 elections for Constitutional Convention. Includes information on major parties and their electoral percentages. Excellent source of APRA electoral statistics.

Vega, Juan José. Inmigración china en el Perú: un modelo de antipluralismo. See *HLAS 44:2997.*

6374 ¿El Voto perdido?: crítica y autocrítica de la izquierda en la campaña electoral de 1980. Lima: Centro de Información, Estudio [sic] y Documentación, 1980. 83 p.: ill.

Results of study on how Peruvian leftist parties communicated to the poor before 1980 general elections. Emphasizes utility of mass media which were accessible to all parties. Concludes that the left failed to attract the attention of the largest constituency (the poor). Fresh, interesting study of mass media campaign use by and among individuals who usually are barred from access to newspapers, radio, and television.

6375 Werlich, David P. Encore for Belaúnde in Peru (CUH, 80:463, Feb. 1981, p. 66–69, 85–86)

Excellent yet concise historical study of Peruvian politics covers the *docenio militar*, Belaúnde's election, Haya's death. Includes good analysis of 1980 general elections. Views Acción Popular's victory and transfer of power to civilian administration as "final protest against the military."

Zimmermann Zavala, Augusto. Los últimos días del General Velasco: ¿quién recoge la bandera? See *HLAS 44:3005.*

BOLIVIA

6376 Albó, Xavier. Achacachi, media siglo de lucha campesina. La Paz: s.n., 1979. 173 p.: bibl., maps (Cuaderno de investigación; 19)

Describes post-MNR changes in lifestyle among inhabitants of former Achacachi hacienda (Titicaca region). Major contribution towards understanding socioeconomic change resulting from the agrarian reform.

6377 Anton. Bolivia at the heart of darkness: "the horror! the horror!" (CRIA/WW, 23:11, Nov. 1980, p. 13–14)

Anonymous author (Bolivian novelist and journalist), in third period of exile, describes 1980 presidential candidates as "an ailing gerontocracy" that paved the way for García Meza's coup and for the emergence of Bolivia's cocaine traffic whose leaders are in control of the electoral process.

6378 Araníbar, Antonio. "A esta dictadura se la derroca, y ese es el objetivo de la resistencia nacional:" una entrevista con Antonio Araníbar; interviewer: Alfredo Filomeno (DESCO/Q, 8, nov./dic. 1980, p. 50–57, plates)

Interview with MIR (Movement of the Revolutionary Left) founder and partner in Popular Democratic Unity coalition. Araníbar views present García Meza dictatorship as "natural result" of Banzer's seven-year rule.

Views García phenomenon as new turn in Bolivian coups, one within Southern Cone politics context having regional and international repercussions.

6379 Arias, Esther and **Mortimer Arias.** The cry of my people: out of captivity in Latin America. New York: Friendship Press, 1980. 146 p.: bibl., ill.

Interesting example of "liberation theology" writing by former Methodist Bishop of Bolivia and his wife who discuss virtually all topics usually covered in liberationist Roman Catholic wirtings. Intriguing and novel contribution.

6380 Bascone, Giancarlo. Bolivia: dai militari ai militari (MULINO, 30:175, maggio/giugno 1981, p. 419–443, bibl., tables)

Italian scholar discusses crucial arbitral function of Bolivian military from Paz Estenssoro period (beginning 1943) to García Meza coup (17 July 1980). Includes important observations on three decades of military government and thwarted civilian political process.

6381 Bolivia. Ministerio del Interior, Migración y Justicia. Bolivia— elecciones, fraude y democracia = Bolivia—elections, fraud and democracy. Traducción, William R. Mendoza. La Paz: El Ministerio, 1980. 314 p.: facsims., ill.

Spanish-English study of electoral fraud (1978, 1979, and 1980) presses point that nation's military ("a pro-democratic force") has provided only stability in Bolivia, considering that electoral politics and democracy do not reflect Bolivian reality. Revelatory of military thinking on subjects listed in title and important as such.

6382 Bolivia, neo-colonialismo. Lima: Comisión Evangélica Latinoamericano de Educación Cristiana (CELADEC), , 1981. 48 p.: bibl., ill. (Cuadernos de estudio; 21)

Roman Catholic publication issued by Bolivian branch of Justicia y Paz, questions official policy of encouraging "selective immigration" of white technological experts, especially from South Africa. Notes potential opening for foreign control in such policy.

6383 Bolivie: le militaire est roi (CJN, 230, juillet/août 1981, p. 19–26, ill., plates)

French piece on Bolivia's military oligarchy emphasizes cocaine traffic as new yet major force behind the chronic military presence. Fair but emotional presentation discusses major political trends.

6384 Bot, Yvon le. Le mouvement syndical Bolivien a la croisée des Chemins: 1978–1980 (FDD/NED [Problèmes d'Amérique Latine, 62] 4649/4650, 28 déc. 1981, p. 111–158, tables)

Study traces the "resurrection" of organized labor after the Banzer regime (should be read in conjunction with item **6394**).

6385 Cammack, Paul. The workers' movement and the Bolivian Revolution reconsidered (ISU/PS, 11:2, 1982, p. 211–222)

Important factors in powerlessness of Bolivia's labor movement are: monocultural economy, 1950s and 1960s economic crises, inflation, urban opposition to MNR, Bolivian Falange's growth (1960s), vacillating labor leaders (e.g., Juan Lechín), and labor's own internal fragmentation. Important contribution.

6386 Centellas C., Juan. La gran interrogante. La Paz: s.n., 1980. 187 p., 1 leaf of plates: ill. (some col.)

Author's solutions for meeting Bolivian problems: 1) a national Constitution that reflects Bolivian realities; 2) reformulating the 150-year old concept of democracy in face of national fragmentation; and 3) limiting political participation to those at least 50 years of age. Polemic volume with many references to the "Truth" (as an absolute philosophical category). Nevertheless, a useful example of authoritarian political thinking.

6387 Córdoba R., Thaís María. El abortivo coup d'etat en Bolivia (Repertorio Americano [Universidad Nacional, Instituto de Estudios Latinoamericanos, Heredia, Costa Rica] 6:2, enero/marzo 1980, p. 1–8)

Costa Rican writer's view of Col. Natusch Busch's attempt to topple the Guevara Arce government (Nov. 1979).

6388 Czaplicki, Stanislaw. Catálogo de la prensa boliviana. Por Stanislaw Czaplicki y alumnos del Seminario de Prensa Colaboraron, Zulema Alanes et al. La Paz: Universidad Católica Boliviana, Carrera de Ciencias de la Comunicacion, 1980. 144 p.: map (Documentos de trabajo)

Systematic analysis of Bolivia's press (both dailies and periodicals). Emphasizes who reads what and where within the country (compare with item **6399**). Major contribution for those seeking information on political and other communication through the mass media.

6389 En memoria de Luis Espinal, S.J. La Paz: Provincia de Bolivia de la Compañía de Jésus, 1980. 72 p.: facsims., ill.

Bolivian Jesuit publication exposes circumstances of torture and murder of activist priest working primarily in the La Paz region. Includes useful collection of official Church documents and human rights groups correspondence as well as copies of newspaper articles covering incident.

6390 Faletto, Enzo et al. La política y el estado. Fernando Calderón G., comp. La Paz: Centro de Estudios de la Realidad Económica y Social, 1979. 116 p.: bibl. (Serie Estudios políticos; no. 1)

Uneven set of papers discusses, from Bolivian viewpoint, nature of the Latin American State. Unfortunately, emphasizes national and international economics and disregards procedural and legal aspects of the State and its political system.

6391 Federación Sindical de Trabajadores Mineros de Bolivia. Tesis de Pulacayo. Introducción: Guillermo Lora. La Paz?: Ediciones Masas, 1980. 126 p.

Angry denunciation of Banzer and Barrientos regimes and of groups who seek means unacceptable to COB (Central Obrera Boliviana) for unifying workers against "internal bourgeois or fascist" threats and international imperialism. Stresses need for renewal of relations with People's Republic of China and Cuba. Includes introduction by Guillermo Lora.

6392 Inter-American Commission on Human Rights. Report on the situation of human rights in the Republic of Bolivia. Washington: Organization of American States, General Secretariat, 1981. 117 p.:bibl. (OEA, Seq.L/V/II.53, doc. 6)

Report conducted without consulting Bolivia's government completed 13 Oct. 1981. Indicates that García Meza's administration seriously violated human rights, particularly those of Bolivia's Catholic Church.

6393 Iriarte, Gregorio. Sindicalismo campesino: ayer, hoy y mañana. 3. ed. La Paz: Centro de Investigación y Promoción del

Campesinado, 1980. 128 p., 5 folded leaves of plates: bibl., ill. (Cuaderno de investigación; no. 21)

Sophisticated statement on *campesino* organization calls for unity in rural labor movement under COB (compare with item 6376).

6394 Lavaud, Jean-Pierre. Bolivie: le retour des militaries (FDD/NED [Problèmes d'Amérique Latine, 62] 4649/4650, 28 déc. 1981, p. 79–109, tables)

Interesting study of Bolivian politics after Banzer (1971–78) focuses on MNR rivalry (Siles Suazo-Paz Estenssoro) as triggering García Meza's coup. Believes economic weakness, massive drug traffic, Reagan administration policies, and Argentine intervention contributed to setting of stage for 1980 coup. Significant analysis.

6395 ———. Note sur la Centrale Ouvrière Bolivienne: COB (FDD/NED [Problèmes d'Amérique Latine, 62] 4649/4650, 28 déc. 1981, p. 159–170, chart)

Thoughtful, interesting analysis of Bolivian Federation of Mine Workers' (FSTMB) role within overall structure of Bolivia's Workers' Confederation (COB). Examines COB as pressure group vis-à-vis others and assesses its potential in future confrontations with Bolivia's military. One of the better studies of pressure politics in Bolivia.

6396 Lora, Guillermo. Movimiento obrero contemporáneo. La Paz: Ediciones MASAS, 1979. 567 p.: bibl.

Instead of an "analysis of the 9 April 1952 revolution," as stated by Lora, volume traces development of Bolivia's PIR (Party of the Revolutionary Left-Trotskyist) and of COB. Author accuses "bourgeois democrats" of preventing COB from becoming as influential organization as it could be.

6397 Mitchell, Christopher. The new authoritarianism in Bolivia (CUH, 80:463, Feb. 1981, p. 75–78, 89)

Perceives García Meza's regime as novel in terms of its regional Southern Cone ties. Estimates that these new alliances (Argentina, Brazil, and Chile) together with increased internal oppressiveness may become a "constant" of Bolivian politics in 1980s.

6398 Monroy Block, Germán. Los partidos políticos en Bolivia. La Paz: Editorial

Hoy, 1981. 90 p. (Cuadernos de Hoy; v. 1, no. 1)

Selections from monthly periodical *Hoy* provide history and platform of Bolivia's major political parties.

6399 Montecinos Avendaño, Filiberto. Diagnóstico de la prensa nacional. La Paz: s.n., 1979. 140 p.

Calls for a Bolivian press to communicate rather than verbalize in order to bring about national social integration, an unlikely prospect given the nation's low literacy rate and problems of geographic regionalism. More plausible than national cohesion is author's demand that the press promote widespread understanding of national issues.

6400 Morozov, Valeri. Tras los acontecimientos de Bolivia (URSS/AL, 1/2:37/38, 1981, p. 52–75)

Pedestrian, polemical Soviet analysis of Bolivian military phenomenon, especially García Meza's regime. Blames Bolivian militarism on Carter administration's demand for "bourgeois democracies" as price of diplomatic recognition.

6401 Natale E., Remo di. Grupo Andino y golpe de Estado. La Paz: Editorial Letras, 1980. 100, 1 p.

Venezuelan writer states Andean Group nations' support of democratic politics and their rejection of military coups. Emphasizes Bolivia's continuing crisis.

6402 Partido Comunista de Bolivia. Congreso Nacional, 4th, La Paz, Bolivia, 1979. Por la victoria democrática y el ejercicio de la soberanía nacional: hacia un partido de masas, documentos principales. La Paz: Ediciones Unidad, 1980. 119 p.

Official Report (1980) of Bolivia's Communist Party's fourth National Congress. Interesting sections deal with "divided Church" and a warning to COB "not to swerve toward the rightist pro-imperialist Paz-Estenssorist coalition." Intriguing document.

6403 Salamanca Trujillo, Daniel. Del caos a la reconstrucción nacional: historia de los fracasos de una democracia sin pueblo. s.l.: Librería Gráfica Offset, 1981. 785 p.

Important and interesting but polemic leftist analysis of Bolivian history perceived as developing within constraints of US hemispheric policy (especially Monroe Doctrine).

Focuses on roles of Franklin Roosevelt, US Democratic Party, Trilateral Commission, Zbigneiw Brezezinski, and former President Carter as having contributed nothing to Bolivia's economic or political development. States that democracy has never captured the Bolivian people's imagination nor when established led to political stability.

6404 Toranzo, Carlos. Obreros y militares en Bolivia: un golpe frustrado (CP, 23, enero/marzo 1980, p. 98–113)

Analyzes Natusch Busch coup against Guevara Arce's administration in class conflict terms. Includes interesting conclusions on failure to reunite factionalized MNR (Paz Estenssoro and Siles Suazo groups) and

praises COB's efforts to unify Bolivia's labor movement in face of inept and "anemic" armed forces.

6404a Whitehead, Laurence. Miners as voters: the electoral process in Bolivia's mining camps (JLAS, 13:2, Nov. 1981, p. 313–346, tables)

Autopsy of Bolivia's electoral reform begun by abortive 1952 MNR "revolution." Perceives "mining proletariat" as being in no better condition then than in late 1800s or early decades of present century. Chronological statement of what Whitehead sees as most significant pre-1951 elections includes in-depth analysis of Paz Estenssoro's strategies.

ARGENTINA, PARAGUAY, AND URUGUAY

GARY W. WYNIA, *Professor of Political Science, University of Minnesota*

THE DROUGHT IN PUBLISHING that we lamented in *HLAS 43* (p. 613) came to an end in 1982 and 1983, at least in Argentina. Unable to continue having their own way, the country's military rulers loosened their control by allowing political parties to prepare for national elections in 1983 and journalists and scholars to publish what they wished. The result is an abundance of new books and articles, and probably many more in 1984.

The subject of military government continues to receive much attention from scholars writing on Argentina. French socialist Alain Rouquié's monumental two volumes on the nation's military (see *HLAS 43:8328*) have appeared in Spanish (item **6440**) as has another work edited by Rouquié (item **6408**) which includes his own essay summarizing his controversial thesis about the "legitimacy" of the military's political role in the nation. Argentine political scientist Guillermo O'Donnell makes substantial contributions to our knowledge of bureaucratic authoritarianism in studies such as "State and Alliances" (item **6434**) where he refines some of his notions about the nature of the B-A (bureaucratic authoritarian) regime, distinguishing the Argentine experience from those of Brazil and Chile. Criticism of his work is also prominent, the most important being an article by Remmer and Merkx (item **6437**) to which O'Donnell responds (item **6433**). His principal achievement, however, is the publication of a long delayed work on Argentina's military government in the late 1960s under Gen. Juan Carlos Onganía (item **6432**), unmatched in its detail by any other study of Argentine government.

The fate of the peronist regime (1973–76) is more comprehensible thanks to an excellent examination of its performance by economist Guido Di Tella (item **6417**), a brief history by Liliana Riz (item **6438**), and the reflections of peronist Rubén Sosa (item **6441**). Richard Gillespie's study of the Montoneros also tells us much about peronists and terrorism in Argentina (item **6424**). Human rights and the case of once imprisoned and now exiled editor Jacobo Timerman continue to stimulate debate. Foreign appraisals of Timerman's imprisonment by the Argentine military differ. Some, like Benno Weiser Varon (item **6444**) and Mark Falcoff (item **6423**) claim that rather than anti-Semitism, Timerman was the victim of his own political and business ties; others, like Leon Wieseltier (item **6445**) argue the opposite. Considering that many victims of military repression in 1976 and 1977 are still unaccounted for, the human rights issue will continue to command attention for some time to come.

Interest in Argentine foreign relations rose in 1982, as one might expect in a country at war, as Argentina was with Great Britain over the Falklands/ Malvinas Islands (discussed elsewhere in this volume, see also p. 547). Military censorship prevented scholarly study of the war, so the nation's demand for information was satisfied by journalists who published interviews with Argentine soldiers (items **6428** and **6443**). Other works of a more analytical nature are Del Carril's assessment of pre-war diplomacy (item **6412**) and Andrada's account of the air war (item **6406**). The most important scholarship on Argentine foreign relations, however, has nothing to do with the Falklands/Malvinas War. From US State Department and British and Argentine Foreign Ministry Archives, Carlos Escude recreates diplomatic battles among all three countries during and after World War II in a work that is certain to become a classic (item **6420**).

As usual, Paraguay received little attention, so little in fact that an article which would be regarded as average if written about any other country is annotated below, chiefly because it speculates about what may be changing in Paraguay despite appearances to the contrary (item **6449**). Paul Lewis, author of the only contemporary work on Paraguayan politics (see *HLAS 43:6644*), has written another study that differs from the latter in a few details (item **6448**). That leaves us with statements published by an opposition party leader (item **6451**) and a ruling party official (item **6447**), both of which will gather dust until Stroessner's dictatorship ends and observers rush in to find out whatever they can about those who are sure to contend for his seat.

Work on Uruguayan politics continues to trickle in. A welcome new source of research is the Institute of Latin American Studies in Stockholm where Sergio Jellinek and Luis Ledesma have coauthored several papers on recent Uruguayan politics (item **6456**). Equally informed are several reports by Howard Handelman written in the late 1970s while serving with the American Universities Field Staff in Uruguay (item **6454**). Uruguayan exiles continue to publish, among them Communist Party leader Rodney Arismendi (item **6452**), leftist journalist Federico Fasano (item **6453**), and an anonymous author who tells the story of Tupamaro operations a decade ago (item **6459**). If Uruguay moves toward constitutional government in the next few years, as the military promises, we should expect more scholarship from within its own academic community.

In brief, inquiries by foreign scholars continue to be written, though at a slower pace than before, and works by Argentines are increasing at long last. Much has occurred in these politically repressed nations during the past decade that demands more analysis; a start has been made but much more needs to be done.

ARGENTINA

6405 Alfonsín, Raúl. La cuestión argentina. 2. ed. Buenos Aires: Editorial Propuesta Argentina, 1981. 242 p.

Statement by Radical party leader Raúl Alfonsín written in anticipation of his candidacy for the Argentine presidency in Oct. 1983. Offers critique of military rule by popular figure with strong democratic and nationalist beliefs.

6406 Andrada, Benigno Héctor. Guerra aérea en las Malvinas. Buenos Aires: Emecé Editores, 1983. 239 p., 16 p. of plates: ill.

Retired Argentine Air Force officer describes distinguished performance of the nation's pilots during 1982 Falklands/Malvinas War. Written as history of three-month war, it emphasizes air strategy and tactics and the advantages of various technologies.

6407 Argentina. Junta Militar. Documentos básicos y bases políticas de las Fuerzas Armadas para el Proceso de Reorganización Nacional. Buenos Aires: La Junta, 1980. 63 p.

Published by military junta that governed Argentina (1976–83), document includes texts of statutes used by the military to guide the country's political reorganization. Legalistic and formal in nature and never implemented as planned, the statutes provide a record of how the Argentine military defined its purpose to the public.

6408 Argentina, hoy. Alain Rouquié, comp. México: Siglo Veintiuno Editores, 1982. 279 p.: bibl. (Historia inmediata)

Collection of excellent studies of recent Argentine political and economic life (e.g., Rouquié summarizing his research on the Argentine military; economist Aldo Ferrer critically assessing military economic policies after 1976; Ricardo Sidicaro offering an interesting history of relations between rural bourgeoisie and the Argentine State).

6409 Barco, Ricardo del. El conflicto Iglesia-Estado: 1954–1955 (CRIT, 55:1879, abril, p. 152–157)

Informative though very brief summary of issues behind Perón's conflict with the Church during last two years of his administration (1953–55). Focuses primarily on reaction of Church leadership and lay organizations to eight separate policies directed against the Church.

6410 Benassayag, Miguel. Argentine: chronique d'une divorce (OSPAAAL/T, 2:35F, 1981, p. 27–37)

Brief essay on terrorism in Argentina, its causes and consequences.

Canitrot, Adolfo. Teoría y práctica del liberalismo: política antiinflacionaria y apertura económica en la Argentina, 1976–1981. See item 3547.

6411 Cantón, Darío and Jorge Raúl Jorrat. El voto peronista en 1973: distribución, crecimiento marzo-septiembre y bases ocupacionales (IDES/DE, 20:77, abril/junio 1980, p. 71–92, map, tables)

Using aggregate data and election returns, authors confirm class basis of voting in 1973 elections that returned peronists to power. Best predictor of peronist vote remains membership in the working class, either rural or urban.

6412 Carril, Bonifacio del. El futuro de las Malvinas. Buenos Aires: Emecé Editors, 1982. 82 p.: bibl.

Ex-Minister of Foreign Relations and Argentina's representative in UN Falklands/Malvinas discussions in mid-1960s, offers brief history of those talks and events leading to Argentina's April 1982 invasion. Essay is a must for anyone interested in development of Argentina's position.

6413 Cavarozzi, Marcelo. Consolidación del sindicalismo peronista y emergencia de la formula política argentina durante el gobierno frondizista. Buenos Aires: Centro de Estudios de Estado y Sociedad, 1979. 83 p.: bibl., charts (Estudios CEDES; 2:7/8)

Detailed account of Argentina's labor movement, its reorganization and reactivization in early 1960s and its political impact on the government of Radical Arturo Frondizi. Part of unpublished larger study of labor and politics in Argentina (1955–66). Though this excerpt contains little not already in print, it should serve as handy reference on labor during this period.

6414 Cheresky, Isidoro. Sindicatos y fuerzas políticas en la Argentina pre-peronista: 1930–1943 (CEDLA/B, 31, dic. 1981, p. 5–42, tables)

To explain why Argentine labor turned suddenly to peronism in 1945, author examines its politics and repression for over a decade prior to its capture by Perón. Emphasizes efforts by Socialist and Communist parties to lead labor and failure of either to do so consistently.

Corradi, Juan E. Argentina: a story behind a war. See item 7344.

6415 Deheza, José A. Quiénes derrocaron a Isabel Perón. s.l.: Ediciones Cuenca del Plata, 1981. 292 p.

Minister of Justice during last two months of Isabel Perón's government (overthrown April 1976) offers personal account of events and his role. Contains insights into conflict between military and Isabel Perón and author's self-defense when tried by the military, after spending six months in prison following the coup.

6416 Di Tella, Guido. La Argentina económica: 1943–1982 (CRIT, 55 : 1894/ 1895, 24 dic. 1982, p. 746–763)

Excellent summary of economic policy in Argentina during past four decades. Describes policies of each administration, examines problems encountered, and explores ways of coping with them.

6417 ———. Perón-Perón, 1973–1976. Buenos Aires: Editorial Sudamericana, 1983. 1 v.

Originally published in England, this is the most thorough analysis of the peronist regime yet written. With detachment, Di Tella examines each phase of the government's economic program and explains how political and economic forces combined to make shambles of it.

6418 Disappearances, a workbook. New York: Amnesty International USA, 1981. 168 p.: bibl.

Informative book written expressly by Amnesty International for citizens concerned about human rights, their denial, and what can be done about it. Focuses on problem of political disappearances, illustrating their character with examples from several countries, including Argentina and Guatemala within Latin America.

6419 Escobar, Raúl Tomás. Estrategia contrarrevolucionaria. 2. ed. argentina. Buenos Aires: Editorial F.I., 1980. 533 p.: ill., maps, ports.

Revolutionaries have texts on strategy and tactics, so do counter-revolutionaries. This huge volume is one of latter, a textbook intended to guide the Argentine police and armed forces in their pursuit of the political left during 1970s and after. Its many photos of weapons and diagrams of everything from revolutionary organizations to the human mind, were prepared to train Argentina's security forces for their ugly work. A must for anyone wishing to understand political repression and those responsible for it.

6420 Escude, Carlos. Gran Bretaña, Estados Unidos, y la declinación argentina: 1942–1949. Buenos Aires: Editorial de Belgrano, 1983. 1 v.

Outstanding study of relations between Great Britain, US, and Argentina dur-

ing and after World War II. Written as Yale Univ. doctoral dissertation, it makes use of English and American archives to uncover previously unknown facts about the Braden-Perón controversy and British dealings with Perón after the war. Nothing like it exists at present.

6421 Etchepareborda, Roberto. Elementos bibliográficos para una historia argentina: 1943–1982 (CRIT, 55 : 1894/1895, suplemento bibliográfico, 24 dic. 1982, p. unavailable)

Annotated bibliography contains over 500 items on Argentine domestic and foreign politics published in Argentina and abroad. Excellent resource for research libraries (for bibliographer's comment, see item **13**).

6422 Evolution of terrorist delinquency in Argentina. Buenos Aires?: Poder Ejecutivo Nacional, 1980. 442 p.: ill.

Published by Argentina's military government for English-speaking readers, document chronicles terrorist activities in Argentina (1959–79). Consists chiefly of newspaper clippings recording terrorist acts and a narrative seeking to justify the much criticized government repression imposed in 1976.

6423 Falcoff, Mark. The Timerman case (AJC/C, 72 : 1, July 1981, p. 15–23) Places the Timerman case within context of 1970s Argentine politics and argues that Timerman fails to account adequately for his arrest and imprisonment (see *HLAS 43:6636*). Also questions claim that anti-Semitism is rampant in Argentina by arguing that Timerman was not arrested because he was a Jew but because his business partner was suspected of connections with left-wing guerrillas.

Ferrer, Aldo. Nacionalismo y orden constitucional: respuesta a la crisis económica de la Argentina contemporánea. See item **3556.**

6424 Gillespie, Richard. Soldiers of Perón: Argentina's Montoneros. New York: Oxford University Press, 1980. 310 p.: bibl., index, map.

Book is a remarkable achievement. Gillespie leads us through Argentina's arcane world of political violence, tracing growth of Montonero terrorist organization from origins in late 1960s through espousal of violence in attempt to change Argentine politics during Perón's administration (1973–76) until its brutal repression by Argentine security forces after peronistas were overthrown. Detailed and well written account of a movement whose clandestinity makes it an obscure topic for research.

6425 Hansen, Joseph. The Leninist strategy of party building: the debate on guerrilla warfare in Latin America. Edited by Leslie Evans, Richard Finkel, and Fred Stanton. New York: Pathfinder Press, 1979. 608 p.: bibl., ill., index.

Collection of articles written (1968–78) by Trotskyite and Socialist Workers Party activist Joseph Hansen that deals primarily with debates over revolutionary strategy in Latin America. Examines disputes within Fourth International as well as application of strategy in Argentina and Bolivia.

6426 Jornadas sobre Futuro Político Argentino, *Instituto Torcuato Di Tella, Buenos Aires, 1977.* Futuro político de la Argentina. V.R. Beltrán, comp. N. Botana *et al.* Buenos Aires: Editorial del Instituto, Instituto Torcuato Di Tella, 1978. 227 p.: bibl. (Serie verde, Jornadas)

Collection of papers and commentaries given at Di Tella Institute in 1977 examines principal political currents in Argentina, and speculates about new modes for organizing and expressing them. Written at time when country's military rulers were trying to convince their countrymen that new political alignments would be created if necessary. They were not, and in early 1980s peronists, Radicals, and other traditional parties were again contending for public office.

6427 Kaplan, Marcos. Aspectos del Estado en América Latina. México: Universidad Nacional Autónoma de México, 1981. 288 p. (Serie G, Estudios doctrinales; no. 53)

Another contribution to the study of the State in Latin American development. First two chapters are theoretical and outline author's concept of the State, emphasizng elite domination in neo-capitalist system. Other chapters study urbanization and history of petroleum policy in Argentina.

6428 Kon, Daniel. Los chicos de la guerra: hablan los soldados que estuvieron en Malvinas. Buenos Aires: Editorial Galerna, 1982. 222 p.

First of several eyewitness accounts of Argentine participation in 1982 Falkland/

Malvinas war. Consists of interviews with eight Argentine soldiers who tell of their initial hopes and eventual frustrations when forced to do battle with British forces. Essential reading for anyone who wants to know what it was like in the trenches.

6429 Little, Walter. A note on political incorporation: the Argentine Plan Político of 1955 (JLAS, 14:2, Nov. 1982, p. 455–464)

Examines peronist electoral strategy back in mid-1950s for insight into peronist thinking about elections and how to use them for partisan advantage. Unfortunately, author says little about relevance of past peronist attitudes to current electoral behavior.

6430 Luna, Félix. El "processo:" 1976–1982 (CRIT, 55:1894/1895, 24 dic. 1982, p. 739–746)

Brief but perceptive critique of military regime that governed Argentina after 1976. Historian Luna shows how its collapse began well before April 1982 ill-fated invasion of Falkland/Malvinas Islands.

6431 Navarro, Marysa. Evita's charismatic leadership (*in* Latin American populism in comparative perspective. [see item 6016] p. 47–66)

Brief examination of Eva Perón's role in peronist government that pays attention to her skill as an orator, and way she exploited her service as intermediary between Juan Perón and the working class.

6432 O'Donnell, Guillermo. 1966–1973 [i.e. Mil novecientos sesenta y seis-mil novecientos setenta y tres], el estado burocrático autoritario: triunfos, derrotas y crisis. Buenos Aires: Editorial de Belgrano, 1982. 499 p.: ill. (Colección Testimonios contemporáneos)

O'Donnell's long awaited study of Argentina's first bureaucratic authoritarian regime. Although completed several years ago, it could not be published in Argentina until censorship was lessened in 1982. Ostensibly a test of theories O'Donnell developed a decade ago, book's strength lies in its detailed, well documented descriptions of the Onganía government (1966–73). Welcome addition to rapidly growing bibliography on authoritarian government and refreshing change from abstractions and speculations that have characterized much of this literature in the past.

6433 ———. Reply to Remmer and Merkx (LARR, 17:2, 1982, p. 41–50)

This reply to item **6437**, which challenges O'Donnell's argument about the origins of the bureaucratic-authoritarian regime, should generate a refreshing, new dialogue on issues that have commanded our attention for a decade. Although O'Donnell agrees with critics who call for more specification in his model, he upholds his original arguments.

6434 ———. State and alliances in Argentina: 1956–1976 (NOSALF/IA, 7/8:2/1, 1978, p. 20–54, bibl., graphs)

Another in succession of articles O'Donnell wrote during 1970s (see *HLAS 43:6620*) on the bureaucratic-authoritarian (or B-A) regime. This one distinguishes the Argentine experience with the B-A regime from that of Brazil and Chile. Emphasizes differences in the popular sector and its treatment by the regime, focusing on lower threat levels prior to coup, greater autonomy of popular sectors, role played by peronism, and conflicts within the Argentine bourgeoisie. In short, a welcome refinement of O'Donnell's earlier work in that it eschews simplifications in favor of more detailed and better grounded analysis.

6435 Perón, Juan Domingo. El proyecto nacional: mi testamento político. Buenos Aires: El Cid Editor, 1981. 150 p. (Colección Testigo directo)

Two months before his death (July 1974), Perón made public the last of his major statements about his plan for Argentina. Known as the Modelo Argentino, the statement offers his thoughts on economic and social development as well as Argentine foreign relations.

6436 Reflexiones sobre la Argentina política. Carlos Floria, compilador. Roberto Cortés Conde *et al.* Buenos Aires: Editorial de Belgrano, 1981. 209 p.: bibl. (Colección Testimonios contemporáneos)

Essays edited by Argentine political scientist Carlos Floria offers reflections of some of the country's most distinguished historians and social scientists on fundamental issues of politics that have preoccupied Argentines in recent times. Philosophical and speculative in nature, these pieces by Ezequiel Gallo, Roberto Cortés Conde, Natalio Botana, and Manuel Mora y Araujo are intended to stimulate fresh thought on old issues. Dominant topics are representative government, the law, subordination of the military, and international relations.

6437 Remmer, Karen L. and **Gilbert W. Merkx.** Bureaucratic-authoritarianism revisited (LARR, 17:2, 1982, p. 3–40)

Many scholars have debated O'Donnell's theory of bureaucratic-authoritarianism, but few have retested it against the historical record as do these authors. From a reexamination of Brazil, Argentina, Uruguay, and Chile, they reach conclusions different from O'Donnell's about causes of bureaucratic-authoritarianism and variability of its performance. Before accepting their case, however, one should read O'Donnell's reply (item **6433**).

6438 Riz, Liliana de. Retorno y derrumbe: el último gobierno peronista. México: Folios Ediciones, 1981. 151 p.: bibl., index (Colección América Latina; AL 1)

Given internal contradictions that consumed it, the peronist government (1973–76) will be subject to analysis and debate for some time to come. De Riz makes useful contribution to its study in this brief work. Concerned with class structure, political organization, and the State, she presents chronology of action and reaction during the life of this peronist regime but fails to suggest a general explanation of why it ended as it did.

6439 Rodríguez, Carlos J. La idea peronista: contenido ideológico del justicialismo. Córdoba, Argentina: Libra Editorial, 1981. 125 p.: bibl.

When censorship of partisan publications ended in early 1980s, peronists published numerous manuscripts on the meaning of peronism as exemplified by this volume. Author, who was seven years old when Perón fled into exile in 1955, is typical of new generation that seeks its own definition of the movement's ideology. But as usual, after 300 p. we know more about what peronism is *not* than what it really is.

6440 Rouquié, Alain. Poder militar y sociedad política en la Argentina. v. 2, 1943–1973. Traducción, Arturo Iglesias Echegaray. Buenos Aires: Emecé Editors, 1982. 1 v.: bibl., ill., index.

Spanish translation of vol. 2 of Rouquié's seminal work on civil-military relations in Argentina (for vol. 1, see *HLAS* 43:8328).

6441 Sosa, Rubén A. La magia toma el poder en Argentina. México: Editorial Posada, 1975. 286 p.: bibl., ill. (Grandes éxitos)

Sosa, a peronist activist, tells of his life in the movement since its inception in 1940s. Of particular interest are his accounts of: 1) conflicts within peronism before and after Perón's 1973 return to Argentina; 2) 1976 collapse and overthrow of Isabel Perón's government; and 3) Sosa's own exile to Mexico. Valuable as rare insider's account of the peronist government.

6442 Teichman, Judith. Interest conflict and entrepreneurial support for Perón (LARR, 26:1, 1981, p. 144–155, tables)

Worthwhile contribution to the study of relations between business and Perón during his first administration. Describes participation of textile and metallurgical associations in entrepreneurial interest groups and suggests they had considerable influence.

6443 Túrolo, Carlos M. Así lucharon. Buenos Aires: Editorial Sudamericana, 1982. 327 p.

Story of Argentina's war with England over the Falklands/Malvinas Islands as told by 10 young Argentine officers who fought in it.

6444 Varon, Benno Weiser. Don't cry for Jacobo Timerman: the weaseled words of *Prisoner without a name* (The American Spectator [Bloomington, Ind.] 14:9, Sept. 1981, p. 19–23)

Review of Timerman's influential book (see *HLAS 43:6636*), it challenges claim he was heroic opponent of Argentina's military regime. Questions are raised about Timerman's connection with David Gravier, suspected of financing Argentine terrorists. These charges are well known in Argentina and promulgated by those who resent Timerman's success as human rights violations critic.

6445 Wieseltier, Leon. The many trials of Jacobo Timerman (DIS, 28:4, Fall 1981, p. 425–435)

Ostensibly a review of Timerman's book (see *HLAS 43:6636*), article actually examines: 1) Reagan's early US policy toward Argentina; 2) debate touched off by book

among US intellectuals between conservatives like Irving Kristol and William Buckley, critical of Timerman's self-portrayal as "Solzhenitsyn-of-the-left" and human rights activists determined to use Timerman to castigate the Reagan administration; and 3) the question of Argentine anti-Semitism and how it threatens the country's Jews.

6446 Zelinsky, Ulrich. Strategien institutioneller Gewalt zur Herrschaftssicherung in Kolumbien, 1970–1973 (JGSWGL, 15, 1978, p. 259–293)

Descriptive and analytical study of military repression in Chile, Argentina, and Uruguay in the 1970s. Finds most convincing impulse for repression to lie in "national security" ideology and its militant anti-liberalism. [D.W. Dent]

Zuk, Gary and **William R. Thompson.** The post-coup military spending question: a pooled cross-sectional time series analysis. See item **2989.**

PARAGUAY

6447 Benítez Rickmann, Juan José. Estudio sobre los partidos políticos paraguayos. Asunción: Editorial El Foro, 1981. 137 p.

Written by Paraguayan lawyer and Colorado Party politician, book offers brief history of country's political parties. More of a recapitulation of events and summary of party documents than an analysis of Paraguayan politics.

6448 Lewis, Paul H. Socialism, liberalism, and dictatorship in Paraguay. New York: Praeger, 1982. 154 p.: bibl., index, maps (Politics in Latin America)

Well written introduction to Paraguayan politics. Less ambitious than Lewis' *Paraguay under Stroessner* (see *HLAS 44: 3428*), it is written more for the undergraduate and layman than for scholars familiar with the country. Describes Stroessner's origins, rise to power, dictatorship, and policies.

6449 McDonald, Ronald H. The emerging new politics in Paraguay (IAMEA, 35:1, Summer 1981, p. 25–44)

One of few articles about Paraguayan politics and changing trends. Argues that fragmented elite and competition for political power erodes Stroessner's monolithic system. Especially informative is author's comparison of Stroessner's with Somoza's regime prior to 1979 Nicaraguan revolution.

6450 Paraguay. Lima: Comisión Evangélica Latinoamericana de Educación Cristiana, 1981. 69 p.: ill. (Servicio documental; no.15)

Lengthy pamphlet by evangelical religious organization critical of Stroessner dictatorship. After brief summary of Paraguayan history and politics, describes persecution of opposition parties and labor movement and lists disappearances and human rights violations.

6451 Salomoni, Víctor. Fundamentos ideológicos del Partido Revolucionario Febrerista. Asunción: Emasa, 1981. 103 p.

Recent statement about principles underlying Febrerista ideology, a party made up of Marxists and non-Marxists opponents of Stroessner. Prepared by party theorist and published in Paraguay.

URUGUAY

6452 Arismendi, Rodney. Uruguay y América Latina en los años 70. México: Ediciones de Cultura Popular, 1979. 291 p.: bibl. (Democracia y socialismo)

First secretary of Uruguay's Communist Party (1955–73), tells of events prior to military intervention and calls for unification of opposition to country's authoritarian government.

6453 Fasano Mertens, Federico. Después de la derrota: un eslabón débil llamado Uruguay. México: Editorial Nueva Imagen, 1980. 354 p. (Serie Testimonios)

One of few books written by Uruguayans about the military regime that has governed country since 1973. Author is journalist and leader of 1971 leftist Frente Amplio coalition. Describes socialist theory and practice in Uruguayan politics before and after 1973 coup.

6454 Handelman, Howard. Military authoritarianism and political change in Uruguay. Hanover, N.H.: American Universities Field Staff (AUFS), 1978. 12 p.: bibl. (Reports; 1978, no. 26, South America 0161–0724)

Another concise, informative report is-

sued by AUFS. Author provides brief summary of events leading to fall of democracy and rise of authoritarian regime in Uruguay in early 1970s. Focuses on military, counterterrorist campaign, and organization of new government.

6455 Jellinek, Sergio. Uruguay: a pilot study of transition from representative democracy to dictatorship. Stockholm: Institute of Latin American Studies, 1980. 85 p.: bibl., tables (Occasional papers)

Not well integrated collection of data on principal aspects of Uruguayan politics before 1973 coup that put an end to constitutional politics.

6456 ———— and Luis Ledesma. Uruguay: del consenso democrático a la militarización estatal. v. 1/2. Stockholm: Institute of Latin American Studies, 1979/1980. 2 v. (90, 184 p.): bibl., ill. (Research papers series; paper nos. 19, 27)

Vol. 1 examines breakdown of democracy in Uruguay and emergence of military regime in early 1970s. Though sketchy, covers economic and political conflicts that plagued country during 1960s and ill-fated efforts of Tupamaros and Frente Amplio movements in early 1970s. Vol. 2 examines nature of bureaucratic-authoritarian regime and includes informative discussion of the military's national security ideology.

6457 ———— and ————. Uruguay: notas sobre un proyecto totalitario de constitución. Stockholm: Institute of Latin American Studies, 1980. 20 p.: tables (Occasional papers)

Writing before Uruguayan people rejected constitution proposed by their military government in a national plebiscite, authors describe military's proposal as one designed to perpetuate military rule. After proposal's defeat military spent next three years designing another one.

6458 McDonald, Ronald H. The struggle for normalcy in Uruguay (CUH, 81:472, Feb. 1982, p. 69–73, 85–86)

Informative summary of 1981 political events in Uruguay, a year in which military rulers wrestled with consequences of Uruguayan electorate's rejection of their proposal for new constitution which would have left the military in control of the nation's government.

6459 Tres evasiones de Tupamaros: operaciones Estrella, Abuso y Gallo. México: Editorial Diógenes, 1973. 166 p.: ill. (Actas tupamaras)
Published 1973 (but never annotated in *HLAS*) by exiled Tupamaros in Mexico, volume chronicles movement's three most successful rescue operations that freed colleagues from prison in early 1970s. Described in detail are the planning and execution of Estrella, Abuso, and Gallo operations.

BRAZIL

MARGARET J. SARLES, *Research Associate, University of Maryland, College Park*

THE MOST INTERESTING CHANGE in the Brazilian political science literature is the increasing concern for democracy and democratic institutions, as Brazilians openly and vehemently debate the regime's future. The gradual, stop-and-go political liberalization of the past decade is reflected in much of the current literature and conferences, in general examinations of the underlying structure of Brazilian politics, in party and electoral analyses, and among opposition groups seeking their own path to power and mass participation.

In the last *HLAS*, post-censorship political and prison memoirs were beginning to surface. This genre continues to flourish; many of the books make compelling reading (items **6522–6523, 6526,** and **6529**). They are important as a group, both as primary sources of data about regime terror and because they have forced discussion of how necessary an authoritarian, coercive political system has been to Brazil's economic strategy. Caldas' (item **6522**) and Freitas' (item **6523**) accounts are particularly graphic; Freitas' memoirs, with its overtones of Solzhenitsyn's *The Gulag archipelago*, is surely one of the most unforgettable books published in Brazil during this period. In addition to individual stories of repression, accounts of both guerrilla movements and government anti-guerrilla activity are now more available (items **6520–6521, 6524, 6527–6528,** and **6530**). These provide crucial information on clandestine activities and planning during the 1960s and 1970s, especially on guerrilla linkages to "legitimate" politics, and on governmental strategies used to stamp out guerrilla activity. Of these, Bernardo's *Guerrilhas e guerrilheiros* (item **6520**) is an important contribution to the literature, standing out as a general analysis of guerrilla activities in Latin America, looking for root causes, similarities and disparities among guerrilla groups.

The most salient political topic today in Brazil is what the characteristics of a reformed political system should be, recalling in many ways the post-colonial debates 10 and 20 years ago in newly independent African states. There is a pervasive and exciting sense of getting to the fundamental political and economic issues, and several of the works provide important insights not only about Brazil, but about our general understanding of contemporary authoritarianism and democracy. Perhaps the single most significant book of the last two years is João Almino's *Os democratas autoritários* (item **6461**) which lays out the basic tensions between the desire for democracy and the desire to maintain authoritarian control.

Almino analyzes the basic economic interests involved in the distribution of political power during the 1946 debates in the Constituent Assembly over redemocratization in the post-Vargas era. It is startling how pertinent this period is to current discussions. His historical focus gives the analysis a non-polemic tone that is difficult to achieve when writing on the present political-institutional crisis.

The results of several conferences focusing on the future of the political and economic systems (items **6465** and **6470**) are now available. All have in common an attempt to link political change, particularly the inclusion of organized labor and the working class, and increasing democratization, to economic development alternatives. Political change is seen as a crucial part of the solution to current economic difficulties. The linkage between economic policy alternatives and political choices is made elsewhere as well (items **6469** and **6471**).

The socialist left is clearly searching for its own role in a changed Brazilian political system. They seem to have emerged reinvigorated from the days of repression, with a renewed appreciation of the importance of democracy and an open political system as a precursor to a socialist state (items **6466** and **6476-6477**). Singer's statement sums up this orientation: "No country which has . . . abolished capitalism can be considered socialist if *right now* it is not giving to its workers greater equality and democracy than workers have in the more advanced capitalist countries" (item **6477**). Traditional Western political liberties (civil and human rights and opportunities for pluralism) seem to be increasingly considered as essential to securing working class economic and political rights. The socialists, in other words, are very close to the political mainstream in their current analyses. One of the most intriguing examples of this is Helio Ramos' *Pacto social: caminho da democracia* (item **6476**), in which he calls for "national unification" politics, based on the belief that all Brazilians are united by a strong and immediate desire for democracy.

The Communist Party, in contrast, is represented by works focusing on the past rather than the future. It has commemorated 60 years of party activity with the publication of interviews, memoirs, and internal party documents (items **6505, 6512-6513, 6519**, and **6554**). Carone's three volumes on party history (item **6512**) and Nogueira *et al.*'s study (item **6513**) of the PCB in São Paulo during the past decade are excellent documentary sources.

Interestingly, the renewed emphasis on democracy and labor policy found in general treatments of the political system has not yet led to much specific research on contemporary labor issues. Given the present competition among labor-oriented political parties and the mobilization efforts of unions, there is much scope for researchers in this area. The recent CONCLAT conference (item **6487**) on working class policy issues illustrates one excellent data source. Most labor research is presently concentrated on historical material (items **6485-6486, 6490**, and **6493**).

The field of electoral and party studies is expanding rapidly as the number of items reviewed in this section attests. It is one of the areas of strongest research at this time. State-by-state election post-mortems remain dominant in the tradition of the *Revista Brasileira de Estudos Políticos* studies of the last two decades, but the present analyses are much more rigorous methodologically, and some, particularly Lamounier's study of São Paulo (item **6519a**), are beginning to incorporate the bureaucratic-authoritarian and dependency literature into their work. Three works published in the last two years stand out: Lamounier's *Voto de desconfiança* (item **6519a**), Fleischer's *Os partidos políticos no Brasil* (item **6509**); and *As Eleićoes nacionais de 1978* (item **6508**). All three are products of collaborative research, which seems typical of Brazilian electoral studies in general. Diniz's study of clientelism in Rio de Janeiro (item **6506**) deserves special note. It is the best political party case study to emerge in a long time, a contribution to the literature on clientelism and a model for future studies of the same kind.

The political science literature during this period has been somewhat overbalanced towards general analyses of the political system, with less representation of monographs and studies of specific policy areas. A large number of published Brazilian master's theses help fill this gap (items **6485, 6490, 6493, 6499, 6510,** and **6516**). These have largely concentrated on questions of mass participation, politics, and labor. Examination of bureaucracy and military aspects of the regime deserve greater emphasis. An excellent model for such research is Rossato's *O Governo brasileiro e o crescimento demográfico* (item **6536**), an exemplary analysis of the politics of demographic policy. Studies of agrarian reform, education, and other social policies using the same approach would greatly contribute to our understanding of the political system.

THE PRESENT AND FUTURE POLITICAL SYSTEM

6460 Affonso, Almino. Espaço entre farpas. Curitiba: Coo Editora, 1980. 283 p.
Collection of columns written 1977–79 for *Folha de São Paulo* by major opposition figure. Useful source of information about day-to-day events and contemporary response to political "opening," particularly good on party reform.

6461 Almino, João. Os democratas autoritários: liberdades individuais, de associação política e sindical na Constituinte de 1946. São Paulo: Livraria Brasiliense Editora, 1980. 371 p.: bibl.
Penetrating analysis of unique brand of Brazilian "democracy" with its "authoritarian democrats" and conservative liberalism. Almino has chosen 1943–46 period, when confluence of political and economic events opened wide the debate in Brazil over nature of political system, but time chosen in no way diminishes its contemporary relevance. Highly recommended.

6462 Amaral, Azevedo. O estado autoritário e a realidade nacional. Brasília: Editora Universidade de Brasília; Câmara dos Deputados, 1981.
Written in 1938, this work was an important contribution to lively debate in 1930s over Brazil's political system. Here Azevedo defends 1934 Constitution and *Estado Novo* as finally discarding false "liberalism" and improving economic organization and true representation.

6463 Arraes, Miguel. O jogo do poder no Brasil. São Paulo: Editora Alfa-Omega, 1981. 82 p. (Biblioteca Alfa-Omega de cultura universal. Série 1.a; v. 16. Coleção América)
Useful contribution to debate over real significance of *abertura*. Arrães, a major opposition leader, argues it is primarily a governmental tactic to perpetuate itself in power, and analyzes advantages of this tactic over direct confrontation, particularly for US financial and political interests.

6464 Authoritarian capitalism: Brazil's contemporary economic and political development. Edited by Thomas C. Bruneau and Philippe Faucher. Boulder, Colo.: Westview Press, 1981. 272 p.: bibl. (Westview special studies on Latin America and the Caribbean)
Well researched articles by leading Brazilianists analyze key aspects of Brazil's economy, politics, and society. One of the best contemporary overviews of politics and economics. Recommended (for economist's comment, see item **3584**).

6465 Conferência sobre História e Ciências Sociais , *Universidade de Campinas (UNICAMP), 1975.* O Estado autoritário e os movimentos populares. Guillermo O'Donnell *et al.* Coordenador, Paulo Sérgio Pinheiro. Rio de Janeiro: Paz e Terra, 1978. 373 p.: bibl. (Coleção Estudos latino-americanos; v. 15)
Conference papers and comments on bureaucratic-authoritarianism, authoritarian regimes, and prepolitical movements in peripheral areas. Much of the excellent theoretical material in the papers is widely available in US publications, but commentators' responses reflect Brazilian theorists' application of these concepts to their own situation.

6466 Coutinho, Carlos Nelson. A democracia como valor universal: notas sobre a questão democrática no Brasil. São Paulo: Libraria Editora Ciências Humanas, 1980. 118 p.: bibl.
Four important essays focus on social-

ism in Brazil by examining three themes: 1) the inextricable link between socialism and democracy which exemplifies the shifting emphasis in Brazilian literature; 2) reason why Gramsci's writings are so important in Brazilian political thought; and 3) "state monopoly capitalism" which constitutes a useful contribution to the political development literature. Recommended.

6467 Fernandes, Florestan. Movimento socialista e partidos políticos. São Paulo: Editora HUCITEC, 1980. 72 p. (Pensamento socialista: Série Linha de frente)

Short hardline polemic on need for radical socialism in Brazil concentrates on class struggle, not class alliances, and argues that socialism must precede democracy.

6468 Figueiredo, Eurico de Lima. Os militares e a democracia: análise estrutural da ideología do Pres. Castelo Branco. Rio de Janeiro: Edições Graal, 1980. 139 p.: ill. (Biblioteca de ciências sociais. Série Política; no. 18)

Considerably overdrawn title since book is chiefly a tedious explanation of Figueiredo's methodology and a content analysis of President Castelo Branco's speeches. Argues that, contrary to common wisdom, Castelo Branco was not ideologically more disposed towards democracy than his successors.

6469 Furtado, Celso. A nova dependência: dívida externa e monetarismo. 2. ed. Rio de Janeiro: Paz e Terra, 1982. 150 p.: bibl. (Coleção Estudos brasileiros; v. 63)

Furtado examines Brazil's enormous foreign debt, foreign enterprises, and monetarism and their relationship to continued development. Argues that Brazil must continue a "high development" economic strategy, but consonant with redemocratization and increased benefits for non-elites, and analyzes the consequences of economic policy for the political system. Recommended.

6470 O Futuro da abertura: um debate. Organizadores, Bolivar Lamounier, José Eduardo Faria. São Paulo: Cortez Editora: IDESP, 1981. 104 p.

Based on conference of top Brazilian political scientists, this is an insightful analysis of the economic conditions that led to "abertura," reasons why it has continued, and political and economic factors that will determine its future. Readable and concise. Recommended.

6471 Knight, Peter. Brazilian socio-economic development: issues for the eighties (WD, 9:11/12, Nov./Dec. 1981, p. 1063–1082)

Economist at World Bank argues that new economic strategy for Brazilian development should include greater income distribution and a more open political system.

6472 Maksoud, Henry. A revolução que precisa ser feita: idéias, ensaios, artigos e conferências publicados entre junho de 1979 e março de 1980 e alguns escritos anteriores. São Paulo: Editora Visão, 1980. 209 p.: bibl.

Maksoud's fourth collection of editorials and essays from *Visão*, a widely read newsmagazine he owns. They cover nine-month period (1979–80) and mostly concentrate on evils of socialism.

6473 Medina, Rubem. Brasil: atalho para o amanhecer. São Paulo: Editora Morumbi, 1981. 146 p.

Essays by a PDS Federal Deputy from Rio de Janeiro on national economic themes. Of some interest, since opposition politicians seem to publish more, but book explains his policies to constituents, rather than developing a coherent economic strategy.

6474 Melo, Osmar Alves de. Luta pela democratização. Brasília: s.n., 1981. 182 p. (Coleção Machado de Assis; v. 43)

Well written legal and Constitutional analysis of abuses by the military regime since 1964. Book has good comparative perspective (on use of decree-laws, torture to extract confessions, and other abuses), and provides compelling evidence of how legal abuses have successfully subverted the democratic process.

6475 Pedreira, Fernando. Impávido colosso. Rio de Janeiro: Editora Nova Fronteira, 1982. 386 p. (Coleção Brasil século 20)

Well-culled collection of articles by one of Brazil's foremost political commentators, covering 1976–81 period.

6476 Ramos, Hélio. Pacto social: caminho da democracia. Rio de Janeiro: Paz e Terra, 1981. 170 p.: bibl. (Coleção Documentos da democracia brasileira; v. 5)

Ramos, active in national politics for over 30 years, argues that Brazil's stage of development and economic problems require new political "social pact" integrating both business and labor to continue development.

6477 Singer, Paul Israel. O que é socialismo, hoje. Petrópolis: Vozes, 1980. 72 p.

Singer forcibly argues that the bureaucratic state is antithetical to real socialism, and that a system of decentralized, divided political power is necessary to accommodate citizens with diverse goals and interests. Book addresses Brazilian politics but also applies to political development in general.

6478 Viana, Gilney Amorim. Perspectivas da social democracia no Brasil. Rio de Janeiro: Edições Opção, 1980. 133 p.: bibl. (Série Brasil dos nossos dias; v. 04)

In this analysis of "necessary conditions" for implanting social democracy in Brazil, Viana argues that socialism is impossible without revolution. Discusses evils of reformism and presents strategy to combat it.

NATIONAL INSTITUTIONS
The Military

6479 Arruda, Antônio de. ESG, história de sua doutrina. São Paulo: Edições GRD, 1980. 300 p.: ill.

Many of the Brazilian civilian elite, and the entire military elite, have passed through the Superior War College, so this serious description of it is welcome. Based on course curricula and lectures, book describes basic ESG doctrines (national security, revolution, etc.) and how they have changed.

6480 Brigagão, Clóvis. The case of Brazil: fortress or paper curtain? (UNESCO/I, 31:1, Jan./March 1981, p. 17–31, graph, table)

Rare article on Brazil's military industry, which now employs over 100,000 workers. In detailed analyses of army and air force technology, Brigagão shows why Brazil has become a major arms exporter. Recommended.

McCann, Frank D., Jr. The Brazilian army and the problem of mission, 1939–1964. See HLAS 44:3608.

———. Origins of the "new professionalism" of the Brazilian military. See HLAS 44:3609.

6481 Renan, Iale. Estudo de problemas brasileiros: introdução doutrinária.

2. ed., rev. e aumentada. Rio de Janeiro: Editora Rio, 1979. 179 p.: bibl., diagrams (Problemas brasileiros)

Military textbook, reflecting ESG viewpoint, examines issues of national development, national security, communist revolutionary war, and similar themes.

The Bureaucracy

6482 Daland, Robert T. Exploring Brazilian bureaucracy: performance and pathology. Washington: University Press of America, 1981. 445 p.: bibl.

Analyzes characteristics and performance of Brazil's bureaucracy through Medici's tenure, career patterns of Brazilian public executives, and impact of 1964 military takeover on the bureaucracy. Offers important empirical information on understudied topic and well researched historical perspective from which to understand current bureaucratic development.

6483 Diretrizes setoriais do Presidente João Figueiredo. Brasília: Secretaria de Comunicação Social da Presidência da República, 1980. 101, 2 p.

President Figueiredo's plans for each Ministry and Secretariat. Policy objectives and responsibilities of each organization are laid out, providing good institutional overview of executive branch.

6484 Instituto de Planejamento Econômico e Social (IPEA). Realizações do Governo Geisel, 1974–1978. Brasília: IPEA, 1979- . 7 v.: ill.

Based on Ministerial reports, IPEA issued these volumes on each Ministry's accomplishments during the Geisel administration. Most recount administrative change, and are primarily of interest to those in public administration, while vol. 7, *Global vision*, draws all volumes together to discuss economic growth and strategy, national integration, and social change.

Labor

6485 Antunes, Richard L.C. Classe operária, sindicatos e partido no Brasil: um estudo sobre a consciência de classe; da Revolução de 30 até a Aliança Nacional Libertadora. São Paulo: Editora Autores Associados: Cortez Editora, 1982. 187 p.: bibl., ill. (Coleção Teoria e prática sociais)

History of workers' movement (1930–35). Concludes that workers developed only "false" class consciousness. Good microanalysis of union activity in different economic sectors. Based on master's thesis.

6486 Centro de Ação Comunitária, *São Paulo, Brazil.* Perspectivas do novo sindicalismo. São Paulo: Edições Loyola-CEDAS, 1980. 62 p.: ill. (Coleção Brasil dos trabalhadores; 1)

Succinct book on Brazil's labor history argues for new form of unionism, away from rigid state control and hierarchy towards local democracy.

6487 Congresso Nacional de Classe Trabalhadora (CONCLAT), *1st, Praia Grande, Brasil, 1981.* Tudo sobre a I CONCLAT: a caminho da Central Unica. São Paulo: Centro de Informação, Documentação e Análise Sindical, 1981. 53 p.: ill.

Collected documents of 1st National Conference of the Working Class (Praia Grande, São Paulo, 21–23 Aug. 1981). Entire report and particularly conference resolutions on national labor policy issues provide valuable insights on contemporary labor movement.

6488 Moisés, José Alvaro. What is the strategy of the "New Syndicalism?" (LAP, 9[4]:35, Fall 1982, p. 55–73, bibl.)

Argues that after recent history of repression, Brazil's emerging "new syndicalism" reflects workers' understanding the importance of demanding political and social as well as economic rights.

6489 Morães Filho, Evaristo de *et al.* Trabalhadores, sindicatos e política. São Paulo: Centro de Estudos de Cultura Contemporânea (CEDEC), 1980. 75 p.: bibl., ill. (Coleção Cultura & política)

Disparate collection of seven essays relating to unionization efforts in Brazil. Most are highly theoretical or historical, of limited interest. Saes' description of middle class unions in banking and commerce is the most informative.

6490 Neves, Lucília de Almeida. O Comando Geral dos Trabalhadores no Brasil, 1961–1964. Belo Horizonte: Editora Vega, 1981. 151 p.: bibl.

Well researched history of the CGT

makes good use of primary source material (based on MA thesis, Univ. of Minas Gerais, 1979). Particularly enlightening is its dispassionate analysis of hierarchy and CGT's relationship to social action and Communist Party.

6491 Petersen, Silvia Regina Ferraz. O movimento operário brasileiro: bibliografia (FICH/R, 8, 1979/1980, p. 175–217, bibl.)

Useful bibliography of documents and research on 20th-century Brazilian labor. Basic source for research in this field.

6492 Russomano, Mozart Victor *et al.* O Sindicato nos países em desenvolvimento. São Paulo: Editora Revista dos Tribunais, 1980. 116 p.: bibl. (Coleção Direito do trabalho; v. 4)

Overambitious title for limited legal analysis of labor laws in Brazil, Mexico, and very briefly, the Dominican Republic. Of interest only to specialists.

6493 Sarti, Ingrid. Porto Vermelho: os estivadores santistas no sindicato e na política. Rio de Janeiro: Paz e Terra, 1981. 185 p.: ill. (Coleção Estudos brasileiros; v. 48)

Study of Santos stevedores (1930–64) including internal growth and labor relationships to national politics. Important because the major policy issues fought openly during this period, but repressed in late 1960s, remain critical to development of future labor strategies.

The Church

6494 Bruneau, Thomas C. The Church in Brazil: the politics of religion. Austin: University of Texas Press, 1982. 237 p.: bibl., index, map (Institute of Latin American Studies / Latin American monographs; no. 56)

Sequel to author's *The Political transformation of the Brazilian Catholic Church* (see *HLAS 38:4058*), book analyzes lengthy questionnaire administered to 2000 Brazilian Catholics. Most interesting are his descriptions of Church responses to politics, particularly the emergence of grassroots pluralism in the Church. Bruneau argues the need for diocese-level Church studies.

6495 Campos Filho, Abel de Oliveira. Meio século de epopéia anticomunista. São

Paulo: Editora Vera Cruz, 1980. 455 p., 8 p. of plates: bibl., ill. (some col.) (Coleção Tudo sobre a TFP)

Clearly written compendium of facts, history, and ideology of the Brazilian Society in Defense of Tradition, Family, and Property since its founding in 1960 as a militant Catholic, anti-communist organization. Written by society members, but one of the few works available on the subject.

6496 Moura, Antônio Carlos *et al.* A Igreja dos oprimidos. Coordenação, Helena Salem. São Paulo: Brasil Debates, 1981. 231 p.: bibl., ill. (Brasil hoje; no. 3)

Describes liberalization of Church since 1964, its opposition to the government and growth of local Church democracy. These changes are so heartily endorsed by the author that book lacks any balanced assessment, but there is much good material on the Church's political left.

6497 O Povo e o Papa, balanço crítico da visita de João Paulo II ao Brasil. Organizadores, Adair Leonardo Rocha e Luiz Alberto Gómez de Souza. Rio de Janeiro: Civilização Brasileira, 1980. 215 p.: bibl.

Church activists stress Pope's reaching out to the masses during his 1982 visit to Brazil: supporting the CEB's, pluralism, human rights, and workers. Makes clear how important this visit was to the morale of the Church's left wing.

6498 Puebla: análise, perspectivas, interrogações. 2. ed. São Paulo: Edições Paulinas, 1979. 154 p.: bibl. (Série Teologia em diálogo)

Detailed religious and social analyses of *Puebla document* on evangelism in the Catholic Church, result of 1979 conference. Essays on its history, its relationship to liberation theology and the poor, and its application in Latin America.

Other Institutions

6499 Goldfeder, Miriam. Por trás das ondas da Rádio Nacional. Rio de Janeiro: Paz e Terra, 1981. 206 p. (Coleção Estudos brasileiros; v. 47)

Using Gramscian framework, author of this rewritten master's thesis explores transmission of cultural values and popular participation in this study of Radio Nacional

in the 1950s. Complex topic, and execution is only partially successful.

6500 Lima, Delcio Monteiro de. Os senhores da direita. Rio de Janeiro: Antares, 1980. 168 p.

Diatribe against "rightist" Brazilian groups (e.g., Catholic TFP, integralists, and ESG). Although research on these topics is needed, book's hyperbole is so extreme that all credibility is lost.

6501 O Poder legislativo: curso. Fundação Petrônio Portella-MJ, Fundação Milton Campos. Coordenador, Walter Costa Porto. Brasília: Departamento de Impresa Nacional, 1981. 2 v.

Government-funded university textbook. Vol. 1 is non-controversial history of legislative power in Brazil (1821–1930), a vast improvement over most textbooks on the subject. Vol. 2, of less interest to Brazilianists, a theoretical essay and readings on separation of powers.

6502 Ribas Júnior, Salomão. O povo no poder: fundamentos da política catarinense de ação comunitária, filosofia e legislação. Florianópolis?, Brasil: IOESC, 1977. 117 p.

Legislation and progress reports on Santa Catarina's efforts to establish local, official, community actions groups. Efforts were unsuccessful, reports are not enlightening, but state blueprints for institutionalizing social action are vivid example of "authoritarian democracy."

POLITICAL PARTIES AND ELECTIONS

6503 Alves, Branca Moreira. Ideologia e feminismo: a luta da mulher pelo voto no Brasil. Petrópolis: Vozes, 1980. 197 p.: bibl.

One of very few pieces of research on women in Brazilian politics, book is fine description of suffragette movement in Brazil under leadership of Bertha Lutz and other women. Sections on ideology and comparisons with feminist movements in US and elsewhere bring home universality and continuity of feminist struggle in Brazil. Recommended.

6504 Conniff, Michael L. Urban politics in Brazil: the rise of populism, 1925–

1945. Pittsburgh, Pa.: University of Pittsburgh Press, 1981. 227 p.: bibl., ill., index (Pitt Latin American series)

Analytic history of populist politics in Rio de Janeiro during period of rapid industrialization. Helps our understanding of roots of present day populism, and is excellent scholarship. For historian's comment, see *HLAS 44:3566.*

6505 Del Picchia, Pedro. O PCB [Partido Comunista do Brasil] no quadro atual da política brasileira: entrevistas com seis membros do Comitê Central. Rio de Janeiro: Civilização Brasileira, 1980. 85 p. (Coleção Retratos do Brasil; v. 136)

Short interviews with six members of Central Committee of Brazil's Communist Party on their views of its role in Brazil. Cursory treatment.

6506 Diniz, Eli. Voto e máquina política: patronagem e clientelismo no Rio de Janeiro. Rio de Janeiro: Paz e Terra, 1982. 228 p.: bibl. (Coleção Estudos brasileiros; v. 59)

One of the most important books on party politics to be published recently, this is a rich and detailed case study of Chagas Freitas' MDB political machine in Rio de Janeiro. Author draws from and adds to extensive worldwide literature on clientelism. further party reformulation. Recommended.

6508 As Eleições nacionais de 1978. Brasília: Edições da Fundação Milton Campos, 1979. 2 v.: ill.

Vol. 1 includes essays on national election themes (e.g., parties, ideology, electoral legislation) which are important, although articles generally lack methodological rigor. Vol. 2 is stronger, with excellent introductory essay by Luíz Navarro de Britto, followed by state-by-state analyses similar to those found in *Revista Brasileira de Estudos Políticos* after elections. Probably most comprehensive work on 1978 elections. Highly recommended in field of electoral politics.

6509 Fleisher, David V. Political party reform in Brazil: within the context of "abertura" (UDP/P, 47:2, guigno 1982, p. 281–316, tables)

Detailed year-by-year description of government's electoral manipulations since 1974 which have guaranteed its hegemony in Congress. Includes well-researched quantitative analysis of congressmen's backgrounds.

6510 Kinzo, Maria D'Alva Gil. Representação política e sistema eleitoral no Brasil. São Paulo: Edições Símbolo, 1980. 139 p. (Coleção Ensaio e memória; 25)

Reviews electoral participation and electoral system changes in Brazil emphasizing, although not limited to, 19th century. Conceptual framework on theories of representation is less interesting, but overall work is good background for understanding current institutional struggles.

6511 Movimento Democrático Brasileiro. Diretório Nacional. Livro branco do MDB: contra as reformas. Brasília: Diretório Nacional do Movimento Democrático Brasileiro, 1977 or 1978. 77 p. (Coleção Alberto Pasqualini; v. 13)

Opposition party analysis of 1977 "April package" of electoral changes imposed by government to retain control of political system. Good for details of electoral "engineering," since process continues.

6512 O P.C.B. [Partido Comunista do Brasil]. v. 1, 1922–1943. v. 2, 1943–1964. Compilador, Edgard Carone. São Paulo: Difel, 1982. 2 v.: bibl. (Corpo e alma do Brasil; 60–61)

First two of three volumes recounting 60 years of CP activity in Brazil. Well organized selection of party documents particularly rich for analyzing early days of party's creation. Volumes are arranged diachronically, with special sections on organization and ideology and labor movement.

6513 O PCB [Partido Comunista do Brasil] em São Paulo: documentos, 1974–1981. Organização e apresentação de Marco Aurélio Nogueira, David Capistrano Filho, Cláudio Guedes. São Paulo: Livraria Editora Ciências Humanas, 1981. 250 p.: bibl. (A Questão social no Brasil; 9)

Valuable internal party documents during period of great repression and party reorganization, organized by topic, including organizing unions and universities. Good details on new middle-class party leaderships and internal disputes with Luiz Carlos Prestes.

6514 Os Partidos políticos no Brasil. David V. Fleisher, organizador. Brasília: Editora Universidade de Brasília, 1981- . 2 v.: bibl., ill. (Cadernos da UnB)

Written by Brazil's foremost political

scientists, articles in these volumes are essential background reading for electoral scholars. Vol. 1 concentrates on post-1945 history of national parties in Brazil; v. 2 on state parties. Recommended.

6515 Ramos, Plínio de Abreu. Os partidos paulistas e o Estado Novo. Petrópolis: Editora Vozes, 1980. 213 p.: bibl.

Traditional political history of Brazil (1870–1938) from a São Paulo vantage, emphasizes people rather than party organization or development. Relies largely on secondary source material.

6516 Rodrigues, Maria Regina Adoglio Netto. Eleições: vende-se um candidato. São Paulo: s.n., 1981. 178 p.: bibl., ill.

Focusing on 1978 elections in São Paulo, Rodrigues analyzes "political communication" and consequences of Falcao Law. Linkages among voters, candidates, and parties in urban setting are of particular interest. Well researched.

6517 Sampaio, Regina. Adhemar de Barros e o PSP [Partido Social Progressista]. São Paulo: Global Editora, 1982. 183 p.: bibl., ill., ports (Teses; 5)

Analysis of most important political party in São Paulo (1945–65), book is valuable to political scientists because: 1) sheds light on present political configuration in São Paulo, helping fill important gap in literature; and 2) with other works, it challenges common view of military-state power as monolith after 1964.

6518 Sarles, Margaret J. Maintaining political control through parties: the Brazilian strategy (CUNY/CP, 15:1, Oct. 1982, p. 41–72)

Analysis of the 1974 election, based on *municipio* census and voting data, showing that the higher the level of development, the lower the support for the Brazilian government.

6519 Vinhas, Moisés. O partidão: a luta por um partido de massas, 1922–1974. São Paulo: HUCITEC, 1982. 268 p., 16 p. of plates: bibl., ill. (Estudos brasileiros)

Another in the growing literature on Brazil's Communist Party. Distinguished by helpful analysis of party activities for each period, in additon to documents and speeches, and by its perspective of why CP developed

no mass following after 1945. Essentially ends in 1964.

6519a Voto de desconfiança: eleições e mudança política no Brasil, 1970–1979. Bolivar Lamounier, organizador. Petrópolis: Editora Vozes, 1980. 265 p. bibl., map.

One of most important books on Brazilian elections in last few years. Five essays analyze voting in São Paulo, using good case material and quantitative analysis, and raising basic quandaries for regime bent on further party reformulation. Recommended.

REPRESSION AND OPPOSITION

6520 Bernardo, João Batista. Guerrilhas e guerrilheiros no drama da América Latina. São Paulo: Edições Populares, 1981. 483 p.: bibl., ill. (Coleção América Latina. Série Nossa história, nossos problemas; v. 12)

Country-by-country survey of guerrilla movements in Latin America, focuses on social justice and causes of revolution. While some surveys are only a few pages long, 80 p. on Brazil both analyze causes and summarize guerrilla leadership and activities. Excellent background before tackling individual memoirs. Recommended.

6521 Borba, Marco Aurélio. Cabo Anselmo. São Paulo: Global Editora, 1981. 70 p. (Passado & presente; 22)

After painstaking investigation, Borba recounts details of Cabo Anselmo's 11 years as government infiltrator of Brazilian guerrilla groups. Includes much information on leftist activities during period.

6522 Caldas, Alvaro. Tirado o capuz. Rio de Janeiro: CODECRI, 1981. 217 p. (Coleção Edições do Pasquim; v. 96)

Well written political memoir of Brazilian militant imprisoned twice sheds light on repression and torture of Medici regime, and offers glimpse of life of clandestine activist. Hard to put down.

6523 Freitas, Alípio de. Resistir é preciso: memória do tempo da morte civil do Brasil. Rio de Janeiro: Editora Record, 1981. 279 p.

Compelling and unforgettable testament of guerrilla captured in 1970 and his odyssey through Brazil's prison system, each chapter in a new prison. One of best accounts of life as political prisoner.

6524 José, Emiliano and **Oldack Miranda.** Lamarca, o capitão da guerrilha. São Paulo: Global Editora, 180. 166 p., 30 p. of plates: ill., ports. (Passado & presente; 20)

Sympathetic biography of Lamarca's experience as top guerrilla leader until 1971 capture and death. Includes rich detail of guerrilla actions, and internal differences among various revolutionary groups (MR-8, VPR, ALN), although it lacks any wider political analysis of revolutionary action.

6525 Maklouf, Luís et al. Pedro Pomar. São Paulo: Brasil Debates, 1980. 207 p.: ill. (Brasil/memória; no. 2)

Biographical tribute to Pomar, one of founders of Brazil's Communist Party, killed in 1976 by Brazilian military.

6526 Memórias do exílio, Brasil, 1964–19??: obra coletiva. v. 1, De muitos caminhos. Dirigida e coordenada por Pedro Celso Uchôa Cavalcanti e Jovelino Ramos. São Paulo: Editora e Libraria Livramento, 1978. 1 v.

Exiled Brazilians tell their individual stories. Many make compelling reading and give sense of history and detail to Brazilian dissenters and dissent movements over years. First, by fighter for racial justice, is outstanding. Recommended.

6527 Pomar, Wladimir. Araguaia, o partido e a guerrilha. São Paulo: Brasil Debates, 1980. 312 p.: bibl., ill. (Brasil estudos; no. 2)

Composed of unpublished Communist Party documents, supplemented by Pomar's critical analysis, this is an outstanding account of PCB's rural guerrilla activity in Araguaia—the "end of the cycle of attempts to transform Brazilian society through military struggle."

6528 Portela, Fernando. Guerra de guerrilhas no Brasil. São Paulo: Global Editora, 1979. 263 p.: ill. (Passado & presente; 2)

Detailed account, originally published in *Jornal da Tarde* (1979), of Brazilian government's three campaigns against guerrillas in Araguaia, Pará (1972–75). Fascinating reading.

6529 Rodrigues, Athaydes. Agora eu: a Revolução de 1964, em Rio Grande. Porto Alegre: Editora Pallotti, 1980. 236 p.

To this account of his imprisonment in 1964, Rodrigues brings decades of experience as leftist politician in Rio Grande do Sul. To him, repression was newest wave of McCarthyism, as always, to be struggled against. Book is insightful and well written.

6530 Vargas, Indio. Guerra é guerra, dizia o torturador. Rio de Janeiro: CODECRI, 1981. 186 p. (Coleção Edições do Pasquim; v. 78)

Well written, interesting account by PTB party militant, later guerrilla imprisoned in 1970. Distinguished by its accessible style and insider information on period's clandestine activities.

SOCIAL POLICY

6531 Arruda, Hélio Palma de. Latifúndios, minifúndios, módulo rural, reforma agrária e colonização. Brasília: Ministério da Agricultura, Instituto Nacional de Colonização e Reforma Agrária, between 1976 and 1981. 59 p.

Short, useful descriptive analysis of land holding patterns in Brazil and agrarian reform efforts. Good basic statistics, and short comparisons with land reform in other developing countries.

6532 Bierrenbach, Maria Ignês Rocha de Sousa. Política e planejamento social—Brasil: 1956/1978. São Paulo: Cortez Editora, 1981. 121 p.: bibl.

Brief review of efforts of each administration (1956–78) to develop social policy, with special analysis of social policy towards children in São Paulo. Essentially unrevised master's thesis, but on topic of national importance.

6533 Maira, Luís et al. América Latina, novas estratégias de dominação. São Paulo: CEDEC, 1980. 168 p.: bibl. (Coleção de estudos latino-americanos "Nuestra América")

Five essays on relationship of international factors to redemocratization in Latin America, especially Southern Cone. Andrade's article on Brazil examines how important social policy has become to regime eager to retain its hegemony. Treatment is serious and reflective, and subject important.

6534 Müller, Geraldo. Estado, estrutura agrária e população: ensaio sobre estagnação e incorporação regional. Petrópolis: Editora Vozes; CEBRAP, 1980. 141 p.: bibl., ill. (Cadernos CEBRAP; no. 32)

First-rate study of "reincorporation" of peripheral agricultural area in São Paulo into modern agro-business. Analysis of social change (especially place of family farms and nationalization of work force) is particularly strong. Recommended.

6535 Oliveira, Plinio Corrêa de and Carlos Patricio del Campo. Sou católico, posso ser contra a reforma agrária? São Paulo: Editora Vera Cruz, 1981. 358 p.: bibl., ill.

Widely read, highly controversial book written in response to Catholic Bishops' favoring of land reform. First essay discusses religious reasons why an anti-land reform Catholic should maintain his/her position; second, economic reasons.

6536 Rossato, Ricardo. O governo brasileiro e o crescimento demográfico. São Paulo: Edições Loyola, 1981. 237 p.: ill.

Excellent study of demographic policy in Brazil. Includes detailed overview of present demographics in Brazil, first-rate political analysis of major interest groups, and discussion of present contraceptive practices. Book is important because it is non-polemic and quality of research and analysis is high.

POLITICAL THEORY

6537 Azevedo, Plauto Faraco de. Limites e justificação do poder do Estado. Petrópolis: Editora Vozes, 1979. 195 p.: bibl.

Analyzing limits of state power, Azevedo discusses natural law, cultural relativism, and juridical relativism. Last section uses Third Reich as case example.

6538 Beznos, Clóvis. Poder de polícia. São Paulo: Editora Revista dos Tribunais, 1979. 83 p. (Biblioteca de estudos de direito administrativo; 4)

General analysis in administrative law of police powers from Greece to present, primarily of interest to specialists. Beznos argues importance of legislative control and judicial rights over police.

6539 Chauí, Marilena and Maria Sylvia Carvalho Franco. Ideologia e mobilização popular. Rio de Janeiro: Editora Paz e Terra, 1978. 209 p. (Co-edições CEDEC/Paz e Terra; v. 3)

Heavy theoretical analysis of integralism in Brazil (1920s-30s), emphasizes ideology and works of Plínio Salgado. Sheds little new light on roots of authoritarianism in Brazil.

6540 Corbisier, Roland. Os intelectuais e a revolução. Rio de Janeiro: Avenir Editora, 1980. 78 p.: bibl. (Coleção Depoimentos; v. 17)

Theoretical Marxist treatment on "What is an intellectual?"; "What is revolution?"; and "What is the role of intellectuals in revolution?" Essays briefly interpret classic doctrines for Latin American context, but do not use specific examples.

6541 Dallari, Dalmo de Abreu. O futuro do estado. São Paulo: Editora Moderna, 1980. 184 p.: bibl. (Coleção Contemporânea)

Theoretical and speculative treatise on nature of the State, and review of possible world organization in the future: one-state world, stateless world, super-powers, and welfare states.

6542 Faria, José Eduardo. Poder e legitimidade: uma introdução à política do direito. São Paulo: Editora Perspectiva, 1978. 130 p.: bibl. (Coleção Debates; 148)

Drawing on recent political theory, Faria ponders question "Why obey?" and analyzes roots of legitimacy of political system. Goes over many familiar arguments, but is well written and organized.

6543 Fernandes Neto, Antônio. Jornalismo e liberdade: de Locke a Kennedy. São Paulo: Edição Pannartz, 1980. 169 p.: bibl.

Pt. 1 discusses relationship of press freedom to state control in different political systems. Pt. 2, on Brazil, is concerned primarily with control of news by press owners, with virtually nothing on Brazilian laws or governmental intervention, a severe deficiency.

6544 Plataforma política do positivismo ilustrado. Organização, Antônio Paim. Brasília: Câmara dos Deputados: Editora Universidade de Brasília, 1980. 160 p. (Biblioteca do pensamento político republicano; v. 5)

Collection of positivist documents of late 1800s and early 1900s permits glimpse of roots of Brazil's political tradition: domination of executive over legislature, and push towards economic intervention by the State, for example. Some secondary analysis of material would have been welcome for this rich material.

6545 Queiros, Maria José de. A literatura encarcerada: ensaio. Rio de Janeiro: Civilização Brasileira, 1981. 163 p.

Summary of writings, manifestos, and other documents on experience of political imprisonment from well known political philosophers and activists from ancient Greece to the USSR and Brazil. Book offers universal and thoughtful perspective which may help Brazilians struggling to understand their own period of repression.

6546 Silva, Golbery do Couto e. Planejamento estratégico. Brasília: Editora Universidade de Brasília, 1981. 536 p.: bibl., ill. (Cadernos da UnB)

Largely theoretical essays written in 1950s by one of major contructors of post-1965 political system, on strategic planning for national security needs.

6547 O Socialismo brasileiro. Seleção e introdução, Evaristo de Moraes Filho. Brasília: Câmara dos Deputados: Editora Universidade de Brasília, 1981. 278 p.: bibl. (Biblioteca do pensamento político republicano; 3)

Primarily anthology of republican, liberal, and socialist documents and speeches of first decade of Brazilian Republic, with well-documented introduction on their historical context. Fills important gap in the literature.

6548 Viola, Eduardo J. A problemática do Estado e do regime político: um ensaio desde a ótica da democracia política. Florianópolis, Brasil: Universidade Federal de Santa Catarina, Centro de Ciências Humanas, Departamento de Ciências Sociais, 1980. 146 leaves: bibl. (Cadernos de ciências sociais / Universidade Federal de Santa Catarina, Curso de Pós-Graduação em Ciências Sociais; v. l, no. 1)

Primarily analytic literature review of capitalism sketches out typologies in each chapter with special reference to Latin American development experience.

SPEECHES AND MEMOIRS

6549 Figueiredo, João Baptista de Oliveira. Discursos. Brasília: Presidência da República, 1981. 1 v.

Consists of 102 speeches given by President Figueiredo (9 Jan./30 Dec. 1980).

6550 Geisel, Ernesto. ARENA, partido do diálogo das reformas: discursos pronunciados pelo Presidente Ernesto Geisel e pelo Presidente da ARENA, Deputado Francelino Pereira, no dia 1 de dezembro e 1977. Brasília: Aliança Renovadora Nacional, Diretório Nacional, 1977. 15 p.

Speech by President Geisel on direction *abertura* should take in government party, at time of turmoil on subject. Of interest to researchers on topic.

6551 ———. Discursos. v. 1, 1974. v. 4, 1977. v. 5, 1978. Brasília: Presidência da República, Assessoria de Imprensa e Relações Públicas, 1975–1978. 3 v.

Speeches by President Geisel (1974, 1977, and 1978). Many 1974 speeches touch on 1974 elections.

6552 Lucena, Humberto. O povo no Senado. Brasília: Senado Federal, Centro Gráfico, 1980. 423 p.

Collection of speeches after first year in office from MDB Senator from Paraiba, written for his constituents.

6553 Magalhães, Juracy Montenegro. Minhas memórias provisórias: depoimento prestado ao CPDOC. Alzira Alves de Abreu, coordenadora. Eduardo Raposo e Paulo César Farah. Rio de Janeiro: Civilização Brasileira, 1982. 337 p., 30 p. of plates: ill., ports. (Coleção Retratos do Brasil; v. 157)

Autobiography, written in interview form, is part of oral history project of Research and Documentation Center of Contemporary History in Brazil. Quite personal and cautious account of his political career in Bahian and national politics, spans 40 years (1927–67).

6554 Moraes, Dênis de and Francisco Viana. Prestes: lutas e autocríticas. Petrópolis: Vozes, 1982. 227, 14 p.: ill.

Political memoirs of one of the most important and controversial figures in Brazilian history, based on extensive interviews with him. Helps fill gap in understanding of contemporary and Communist Party politics.

6555 Morais, Fernando. Socos na porta. São Paulo: Editora Alfa-Omega, 1980. 158 p.: ill., ports. (Biblioteca Alfa-Omega de cultura universal. Série 2.a, Atualidade; v. 19)

Speeches by militant São Paulo state Deputy after one year in office. Book essentially lays out national themes of most importance to opposition (e.g., debunking the economic miracle, political *abertura*, pollution, free press). Illustrates vigor of these debates even at state level.

6556 Pilla, Raul. Discursos parlamentares. Seleção e introdução do deputado Geraldo Guedes, com a colaboração de Antônio Carlos Pojo do Rego. Brasília: Câmara dos Deputados, 1980. 778 p.: bibl., indexes, ports. (Perfis parlamentares; 16)

Parliamentary speeches and laudatory, largely uninformative biography of former Libertador Party leader who served in Chamber of Deputies (1946–67).

6557 Simon, Pedro. Abertura. Brasília: Senado Federal, Centro Gráfico, 1980. 117 p.

Speeches on party reform critical of government's policies by Senator Simon, delivered 1979.

6558 Suruagy, Divaldo. O político. Brasília: Senado Federal, 1980. 114 p.: ill., ports. (Coleção Machado de Assis; v. 33)

Laudatory biography of former Senator Palmeira of Alagoas, active in politics from 1930. Some details of political life in Alagoas are interesting— a state whose politics are little studied—but book suffers greatly from effusiveness for Palmeira and lack of analysis.

MISCELLANEOUS

Boschi, Renato Raul. Elites industriais e democracia: hegemonia burguesa e mudança política no Brasil. See item **3592.**

Farias, Osvaldo Cordeiro de. Meio século de combate: diálogo com Cordeiro de Farias, Aspásia Camargo, Walder de Góes. See *HLAS 44:3575.*

Flores, Moacyr. Modelo político dos Farrapos: as idéias políticas da Revolução Farroupilha. See *HLAS 44:3577.*

Hendricks, Craig and **Robert M. Levine.** Pernambuco's political elite and the Recife Law School. See item **4553.**

6559 Instituto de Direito Público e Ciência Política, *Rio de Janeiro.* Centro de Pesquisa e Documentação de História Con-

temporânea do Brasil. Guia dos arquivos CPDOC, 1979. Rio de Janeiro: CPDOC: Fundação Getúlio Vargas, 1980. 99 p.: ill.

Detailed description of archives held by CPDOC of over 100 political figures important after 1930. Invaluable for researchers in Brazilian politics.

Joffily, José. Revolta e revolução: cinqüênta anos depois. See *HLAS 44:3595.*

Mendes Júnior, Antônio. Movimento estudantil no Brasil. See item **4563.**

6560 Nery, Sebastião. Pais e padrastos da pátria. Recife, Brasil: Editora Guararapes, 1980. 212 p.

Sketches and accounts of Brazilian political figures, from presidents to guerrillas. Originally published as newspaper or magazine articles. Author clearly favors the left. May be of background value to those researching late 1970s.

6561 Ribeiro, José Luiz. Como falam as esquerdas. Porto Alegre, Brasil: Editora Intermédio, 1981. 104 p.: bibl., ill.

Originally presented as the author's thesis (Pontifícia Universidade Católica do Rio Grande do Sul, 1980). Dictionary covers the specialized vocabulary of the Brazilian left, with enlightening quotations. Interesting book to peruse, especially for American scholars looking for clarification or their own *mots justes.*

JOURNAL ABBREVIATIONS
GOVERNMENT AND POLITICS

AAFH/TAM The Americas. A quarterly publication of inter-American cultural history. Academy of American Franciscan History. Washington.

ACHA/CHR Catholic Historical Review. American Catholic Historical Association. The Catholic Univ. of America Press. Washington.

ACPS/B Boletín de la Academia de Ciencias Políticas y Sociales. Caracas.

AJC/C Commentary. American Jewish Committee. New York.

AJCL The American Journal of Comparative Law. American Association for the Comparative Study of Law. Univ. of California. Berkeley.

AJES The American Journal of Economics and Sociology. Francis Neilson Fund and

Robert Schalkenbach Foundation. New York.

APS/WA World Affairs. The American Peace Society. Washington.

APSA/R American Political Science Review. American Political Science Association. Columbus, Ohio.

AR Areíto. Areíto, Inc. New York.

BESPL Berichte zur Entwicklung in Spanien, Portugal, Lateinamerika. München, FRG.

BNCE/CE Comercio Exterior. Banco Nacional de Comercio Exterior. México.

CDAL Cahiers des Amériques Latines. Paris.

CDLA Casa de las Américas. Instituto Cubano del Libro. La Habana.

CEDLA/B Boletín de Estudios Latinoamericanos. Centro de Estudios y Documentación Latinoamericanos. Amsterdam.

CM/D Diálogos. Artes/Letras/Ciencias Humanas. El Colegio de México. México.

CM/FI Foro Internacional. El Colegio de México. México.

CP Cuadernos Políticos. Revista trimestral. Ediciones Era. México.

CPS Comparative Political Studies. Northwestern Univ., Evanston, Ill., and Sage Publications, Beverly Hills, Calif.

CPU/ES Estudios Sociales. Corporación de Promoción Universitaria. Santiago.

CRIA/WW Worldview. A monthly review of ethics and international affairs. Council on Religion and International Affairs. New York.

CRIT Criterio. Editorial Criterio. Buenos Aires.

CSSH Comparative Studies in Society and History. An international quarterly. Society for the Comparative Study of Society and History. The Hague.

CSUCA/ESC Estudios Sociales Centroamericanos. Consejo Superior de Universidades Centroamericanos, Confederación Universitaria Centroamericana, Programa Centroamericano de Ciencias Sociales. San José.

CUH Current History. A monthly magazine of world affairs. Philadelphia.

CUNY/CP Comparative Politics. The City Univ. of New York, Political Science Program. New York.

CYC Comunicación y Cultura. La comunicación masiva en el proceso político latinoamericano. Editorial Galerna. Buenos Aires y Santiago.

DDW Die Dritte Welt. Verlag Anton Hain. Meisenheim, FRG.

DESCO/Q Quehacer. Realidad nacional: problemas y alternativas. Centro de Estudios y Promoción del Desarrollo (DESCO). Lima.

DIS Dissent. Published quarterly by Dissent Publishing Association. New York.

EDTM Estudios del Tercer Mundo. Centro de Estudios Económicos y Sociales del Tercer Mundo. México.

FCE/TE El Trimestre Económico. Fondo de Cultura Económica. México.

FDD/NED Notes et Études Documentaires. France, Direction de la Documentation. Paris.

FERES/SC Social Compass. International review of socio-religious studies (Revue internationale des études socio-religieuses). International Federation of Institutes for Social and Socio-Religious Research (Fédération Internationale des Institutes des Recherches Sociales et Socio-Religieuses [FERES]). The Hague.

FICH/R See IFCH/R.

FIU/CR Caribbean Review. Florida International Univ., Office of Academic Affairs. Miami.

FIU/RC See FIU/CR.

FNSP/RFSP Revue Française de Science Politique. Fondation Nationale des Sciences Politiques, l'Association Française de Science Politique *avec le concours du* Centre National de la Recherche Scientifique. Paris.

HAHR Hispanic American Historical Review. Duke Univ. Press *for the* Conference on Latin American History of the American Historical Association. Durham, N.C.

IA International Affairs. A monthly journal of political analysis. Moscow.

IA/ZK Zeitschrift fr Kulturaustausch. Institut für Auslandsbeziehungen. Stuttgart, FRG.

IAEERI/E Estrategia. Instituto Argentino de Estudios Estratégicos y de las Relaciones Internacionales. Buenos Aires.

IAMEA Inter-American Economic Affairs. Washington.

ICS/JCCP Journal of Commonwealth & Comparative Politics. Univ. of London, Institut of Commonwealth Studies. London.

IDES/DE Desarrollo Económico. Instituto de Desarrollo Económico y Social. Buenos Aires.

IFCH/R Revista do Instituto de Filosofia e Ciências Humanas. Univ. Federal do Rio Grande do Sul. Porto Alegre.

IFEA/B Bulletin de l'Institut Français d'Etudes Andines. Lima.

IIB/DA Deutsche Aussenpolitik. Institut für Internationale Beziehungen. Berlin, GDR.

IIDC/C Civilisations. International Institute of Differing Civilizations. Bruxelles.

IRR/RC Race & Class. A journal for black and Third World liberation. Institute of Race Relations and The Transnational Institute. London.

ISU/PS Politics & Society. Gerald A. Dorfman, publisher. Iowa State Univ. Ames.

JDA The Journal of Developing Areas. Western Illinois Univ. Press. Macomb.

JGSWGL Jahrbuch für Geschichte von Staat, Wirtschaft und Gesellschaft Lateinamerikas. Köln, FRG.

JLAS Journal of Latin American Studies. Centers or institutes of Latin American studies at the universities of Cambridge, Glasgow, Liverpool, London and Oxford. Cambridge Univ. Press. London.

JPR Journal of Peace Research. Edited at the International Peace Research Institute. Universitetforlaget. Oslo.

LAP Latin American Perspectives. Univ. of California. Riverside.

LARR Latin American Research Review. Univ. of North Carolina Press *for the* Latin American Studies Association. Chapel Hill.

LNB/L Lotería. Lotería Nacional de Beneficencia. Panamá.

MR Monthly Review. An independent Socialist magazine. New York.

MULINO Il Mulino. Rivista mensile de cultura e politica. Bologna, Italy.

NACLA NACLA's Latin America & Empire Report. North American Congress on Latin America. New York.

NACLA/LAER NACLA's Latin America & Empire Report. North American Congress on Latin America. New York.

NEA/RBPE The Review of Black Political Economy. National Economic Association and Atlanta Univ. Center. Atlanta, Ga.

NMC/N Nicaráuac. Revista bimestral del Ministerio de Cultura. Managua.

NOS See NSO.

NOSALF/IA Ibero Americana. Scandinavian Association for Research on Latin America (NOSALF). Stockholm.

NRDM La Nouvelle Revuew des Deux Mondes. Paris.

NSO Nueva Sociedad. Revista política y cultural. San José.

NYRB The New York Review of Books. New York.

OCLAE OCLAE. Revista mensual de la Organización Continental Latinoamericana de Estudiantes. La Habana.

OSPAAAL/T Tricontinental. Published in Spanish, English, and French by the Executive Secretariat of the Organization for the Solidarity of the Peoples of Africa, Asia, and Latin America. La Habana.

PAN/ES Estudios Latinoamericanos. Polska Akademia Nauk (Academia de Ciencias de Polonia), Instytut Historii (Instituto de Historia). Warszawa.

PCCLAS/P Proceedings of the Pacific Coast Council on Latin American Studies. Univ. of California. Los Angeles.

PP Past and Present. London.

PUCIS/WP World Politics. A quarterly journal of international relations. Princeton Univ., Center of International Studies. Princeton, N.J.

RCPC Revista del Pensamiento Centroamericano. Centro de Investigaciones y Actividades Culturales. Managua.

RU/MP Marxist Perspectives. Transaction Periodicals Consortium. Rutgers Univ. New Brunswick, N.J.

SAA/HO Human Organization. Society for Applied Anthropology. New York.

SAGE/JIAS Journal of Inter-American Studies and World Affairs. Sage Publication *for the* Center for Advanced International Studies, Univ. of Miami. Coral Gables, Fla.

SPSA/JP The Journal of Politics. The Southern Political Science Association *in cooperation with the* Univ. of Florida. Gainesville.

SS Science and Society. New York.

UB/BA Boletín Americanista. Univ. de Barcelona, Facultad de Geografía e Historia, Depto. de Historia de América. Barcelona.

UB/GG Geschichte und Gesellschaft. Zeitschrift für Historische Sozialwissenschaft. Univ. Bielefeld, Fakultät für Geschichtswissenschaft. Bielefeld, FRG.

UC/EDCC Economic Development and Cultural Change. Univ. of Chicago, Research Center in Economic Development and Cultural Change. Chicago.

UC/I Ibero-Americana. Univ. of California Press. Berkeley.

UC/S Signs. Journal of women in culture and society. The Univ. of Chicago Press. Chicago.

UCA/E Encuentro. Revista de la Univ. Centroamericana, Instituto Histórico. Managua.

UCC/RU Revista Universitaria. Anales de la Academia Chilena de Ciencias Naturales. Univ. Católica de Chile. Santiago.

UCL/CD Cultures et Développement. Revue internationale des sciences du développement. Univ. Catholique de Louvain *avec le concours de la* Fondation Universitaire de Belgique. Louvain, Belgium.

UCLA/JLAL Journal of Latin American Lore. Univ. of California, Latin American Center. Los Angeles.

UCLV/I Islas. Univ. Central de las Villas. Santa Clara, Cuba.

UCP/IAP Ibero-Americana Pragensia. Univ. Carolina de Praga, Centro de Estudios Ibero-Americanos. Prague.

UCR/RF Revista de Filosofía de la Universidad de Costa Rica. San José.

UCSD/NS The New Scholar. Univ. of California, Center for Iberian and Latin American Studies and Institute of Chicano Urban Affairs. San Diego, Calif.

UDP/P Politico. Univ. di Pavia, Istituto di Scienze Politiche. Pavia, Italy.

UFMG/DCP Cadernos DCP. Univ. Federal de Minas Gerais, Faculdade de Filosofia e Ciências Humanas, Depto. de Ciência Política. Belo Horizonte, Brazil.

UJSC/ECA Estudios Centro-Americanos. Revista de extensión cultural. Univ. José Simeón Cañas. San Salvador.

ULB/RIS Revue de l'Institut de Sociologie. Univ. Libre de Bruxelles. Bruxelles.

UM/JIAS See SAGE/JIAS.

UMG/RBEP Revista Brasileira de Estudos Políticos. Univ. de Minas Gerais. Belo Horizonte, Brazil.

UN/ISSJ International Social Science Journal. United Nations Educational, Scientific, and Cultural Organization. Paris.

UNAM/PDD Problemas del Desarrollo. Univ. Nacional Autónoma de México, Instituto de Investigaciones Económicas. México.

UNAM/RFD Revista de la Facultad de Derecho. Univ. Nacional Autónoma de México. México.

UNAM/RMCPS Revista Mexicana de Ciencias Políticas y Sociales. Univ. Nacional Autónoma de México, Facultad de Ciencias Políticas y Sociales. México.

UNAM/RMS Revista Mexicana de Sociología. Univ. Nacional Autónoma de México, Instituto de Investigaciones Sociales. México.

UND/RP The Review of Politics. Univ. of Notre Dame. Notre Dame, Ind.

UNESCO/I Impact of Science on Society. United Nations Educational, Scientific, and Cultural Organization. Paris.

UPR/CS Caribbean Studies. Univ. of Puerto Rico, Institute of Caribbean Studies. Río Piedras.

UPR/RCS Revista de Ciencias Sociales. Univ. de Puerto Rico, Colegio de Ciencias Sociales. Río Piedras.

URSS/AL América Latina. Academia de Ciencias de la URSS (Unión de Repúblicas Soviéticas Socialistas). Moscú.

USCG/PS Política y Sociedad. Univ. de San Carlos de Guatemala, Facultad de Ciencias Jurídicas y Sociales, Escuela de Ciencia Política, Instituto de Investigaciones Políticas y Sociales. Guatemala.

USIA/PC Problems of Communism. United States Information Agency. Washington.

UTIEH/C Caravelle. Cahiers du monde hispanique et luso-brésilien. Univ. de Toulouse, Institut d'Études Hispaniques, Hispano-Americaines et Luso-Brésiliennes. Toulouse, France.

UU/WPQ Western Political Quarterly. Univ. of Utah, Institute of Government *for the* Western Political Science Association; Pacific Northwest Political Science Association; and Southern California Political Science Association. Salt Lake City.

UWI/CQ Caribbean Quarterly. Univ. of the West Indies. Mona, Jamaica.

WD World Development. Pergamon Press. Oxford, United Kingdom.

WQ The Wilson Quarterly. Woodrow Wilson International Center for Scholars. Washington.

ZMR Zeitschrift für Missionswissenschaft und Religionswissenschaft. Lucerne, Switzerland.

INTERNATIONAL RELATIONS

YALE H. FERGUSON, *Professor of Political Science, Rutgers University-Newark*
GEORGE W. GRAYSON, *Professor of Government and Citizenship, College of William and Mary, Williamsburg, Virginia*
MICHAEL J. FRANCIS, *Professor of Government and International Studies, Chairman, Department of Government, University of Notre Dame, South Bend, Indiana*

GENERAL

LITERATURE ON THE INTERNATIONAL RELATIONS of Latin America has continued to appear at an increasing rate over the past two years, probably because of the greater attention focused on Mexico and the turmoil in Central America and the South Atlantic. At the same time, although some good work is still being done, there appears to be declining interest in the subjects of dependency, multinational corporations, the New International Economic Order, the Non-Aligned Movement, and Latin American integration. No doubt the decline stems in part from the fact that so much has been written on these subjects, and it also reflects the painfully slow progress of international negotiations to remedy problems already identified.

General historical works include a book by José Fuentes Mares (item **7045**), based on new archival research in the US and Spain, on US policies toward Latin America in the period leading up to the Monroe Doctrine (1810–1822). Also notable is a collection of essays edited by Robert Freeman Smith (item **7322**) on US policy making and the US "imperial" role in the Caribbean from 1898 to the Good Neighbor. Finally, James A. Gardner has written an intriguing study (item **7049**) of the somewhat disillusioning experience of US lawyers sent in the 1960s to render "technical assistance" to Latin American governments.

Other general items include an excellent article by Abraham F. Lowenthal on "Changing Patterns in Inter-American Relations" (item **7087**) and three good anthologies: one edited by Elizabeth G. Ferris and Jennie K. Lincoln on Latin American foreign policies (item **7083**), another by Robert Wesson assessing US "influence" in its bilateral relations with 10 Latin American countries (item **7154**), and a third made up of articles originally published by *Estudios Internacionales, El Trimestre Económico,* and the lecture series of the *Fondo de Cultura Económica.* Three other listings testify to the impact on Latin American scholarship of "scientific" theories and approaches: Celso Lafer (item **7081**) and Juan Carlos Puig (item **7120**) discuss actors, institutions, and interaction patterns in the "international system," while Antonio Palo Cachapuz de Medeiros (item **7097**) traces utopian, realist, behaviorist-quantitative, and post-behaviorist stages in the study of international relations, as well as the progress of the discipline in Brazil since the establishment of the Brazilian Institute of International Relations in 1954 (compare with the development of the discipline in Mexico as noted in item **7202**). In addition, CEPAL has produced an extremely useful and comprehensive compendium of analyses and statistics regarding the present-day international economic relations of Latin America (item **7122**); and Víctor Urquidi and colleagues from the Centro Tepoztlán provide a provocative critique (originally for the Club of Rome) of Latin American policies concerning such world problems as food, energy, and pollution (item **7155**).

The advent of the Reagan administration, and especially its vehement contention that "vital" US "national interests" in the hemisphere are being severely threatened by Soviet and Cuban "subversion," have naturally generated considerable controversy in print. For background on the "national security" debate, readers might wish to begin with articles by John Child (item **7025**) and Fred Halliday (item **7061**).

Many observers would regard the Reagan administration's posture on security issues as extremely conservative, but some of the administration's rhetoric, together with criticism from the extreme right, make the policies actually implemented from 1981 through mid-1983 seem almost moderate by comparison. Ultra-right critics like L. Francis Bouchey, Executive Vice President of the Council for Inter-American Security (item **7217**) and Max Singer (item **7257**) clearly oppose any negotiated settlement that would allow the Nicaraguan Sandinista regime to survive.

Of course, the Reagan administration has no dearth of critics on the center and center-left of the ideological spectrum. See, for example, Lowenthal (his statement before the House Foreign Affairs Committee hearings, item **7153**) William D. Rogers and Jeffrey A. Meyers (item **7126**), Gerry E. Studds (item **7258**), Donald E. Schulz (item **7315**), Frank Church (item **7026**), and Richard R. Fagen (item **7042**). The perspective emerging from this quarter is that the "threat" in Central America and elsewhere is really of little consequence to the US; that Washington is aligning itself with opponents of even moderate change and thereby proving that it cannot come to terms with desperately needed (and perhaps inevitable) reforms; that diplomacy and negotiation rather than confrontation is more likely to succeed with regard to both Cuba and Central America; that increasing US involvement in regional turmoil, coupled with failing policies, may very well face the US with a choice between an embarrassing political defeat or large-scale military intervention; that military intervention would greatly heighten East-West tensions, alarm US, Latin American and other allies, and still, perhaps, not guarantee stable regional governments favorable to the US—in short, Vietnam revisited.

Also of importance are Michael Morris' careful assessment of the present status of Latin American navies (item **7100**); a collection of papers that includes materials on the nuclear policies of Chile, Uruguay, and Peru (item **7115**); and excerpts from a Congressional Research Service report on US policy concerning the provision of sophisticated military weapons to Latin American countries (item **7144**). Thomas P. Anderson (item **7213**) and James Rowles (item **7256**) have produced two very good accounts of another recent conflict in the region, the 1969 "Soccer War" between El Salvador and Honduras.

Discussion of human rights has grown into a full-blown debate despite—or, to some extent, because of—the Reagan administration's substantial reversal of Carter policies in this area (items **7335, 7363**, and **7424**). Anyone interested in the subject should not fail to read Lars Schoultz's splendid book (item **7135**), which analyzes not only the evolving content of US policies on human rights but also the values, public opinion, interest group, bureaucratic, and congressional constraints shaping those policies and their implementation. A further article by Schoultz (item **7136**) demonstrates empirically that US foreign aid during the mid-1970s went disproportionately to repressive governments. Moreover, Thomas M. Franck (item **7044**) and Robert E. Norris (item **7104**) offer significant insights into Congress' role in advancing human rights policies prior to the Carter administration and the current practices and procedures of the Inter-American Commission on Human Rights. Two sets of congressional hearings concerning Washington's relations with Chile and Argentina bring into focus the issues dividing the Carter and Reagan approaches to the hemisphere (items **7365** and **7412**). Also, an extraordinary book gives fascinating details regarding Washington's investigation of the Letelier assassination (item **7400**).

"Conservative" and "neo-conservative" detractors of the Carter human rights policies are expressing their position with greater boldness and coherence. One example is Howard J. Wiarda's collection edited for the American Enterprise Institute which includes Jean Kirkpatrick's "Dictatorships and Double Standards" and "Establishing a Viable Human Rights Policy" (see item **7073**). Kirkpatrick and Samuel P. Huntington (item **7068**), a dropout from the Carter administration, make a distinction between rightist (especially "moderately authoritarian") and leftist ("totalitarian") regimes, arguing that the former are generally less pervasively repressive than the latter. They insist the US has a national security interest in supporting, or at least tolerating, many rightist regimes, certainly when the alternative is likely to be totalitarian. Kirkpatrick also maintains that a "viable" policy must take into account the facts that institutionalization of human rights is difficult, particularly in places with an authoritarian tradition like Latin America; that some "rights" must forever remain simply goals; that not all efforts intended to advance rights actually do; and that there is a difference between the dictates of private and public morality.

Those seeking a wider range of opinions should read a 1981 *Commentary* symposium on "Human Rights and American Foreign Policy" (item **7031**) which includes the contributions of some 18 prominent academics and policy makers of different ideological persuasions; also, an exceptionally well-done review essay by Jack Donnelly (item **7039**) which highlights definitional, political, and legal and moral problems in devising and implementing a policy of support for human rights abroad. Raymond D. Gastil, the Director of Freedom House's Comparative Survey of Freedom, explores the definitional problem in depth (item **7050**).

Latin America's economic and political relations with Europe have received increasing attention. A. Glen Mower has produced a major work on the economic dimension (item **7102**), tracing the history of EC-Latin American relations and identifying factors likely to shape the future. Other analysts have speculated about the probable impact of Spain and Portugal's joining the Common Market on those two countries' *hispanidad* links with Latin America. Wiarda (item **7159**) thinks that Spain's and Portugal's orientation is always going to be more toward Europe than elsewhere, but Alejandro V. Lorca and Aurelio Martínez (item **7086**) believe that a Hispanic member in the European organization might well be more inclined to sympathize with Latin American interests.

In addition, Barry B. Levine looks at French policy (item **7086**), concluding that Mitterand may be more cautious about challenging the US regarding Central America if the French economy continues to require bail-out from US banks and international financial institutions. Willy Brandt (item **7220**), A. Vernt Carlsson (item **7224**), Karl-Ludolf Hübener (item **7066**), and Carlos Alberto Montaner (item **7099**) discuss the Socialist International's role in Latin America. Hübner points out that member parties in the region (from Venezuela to Nicaragua and Grenada) are extremely diverse; Montaner fears that the organization's meddling in Latin America could undermine its own cohesion and result in giving inadvertent support to the anti-democratic left. On the other hand, Pablo González Casanova (item **7053**), Salvatore Sechi (item **7137**), and Enrique Semo (item **7138**) examine the relevance of Eurocommunism for Latin America, where the electoral road to power is so often blocked for parties of the left. Semo stresses that the Italian Communist Party changed its tactics and managed to survive even under fascism, and Sechi suggests that Berlinguer's platform—based on opposition to *all* imperialisms rather than proletarian internationalism—could have broad appeal in Latin America.

Two significant works focus on China's relations with Latin America and the Third World: a book by Leonardo Ruilova (item **7130**) deals mainly with the 1970–78 period and includes a useful chronology of events and other appendices; and Eugenio Anguiano Roch (item **7009**) analyzes "pragmatism" in post-Mao China, that country's attempt to substitute for its "subversive" image a less controversial Third World identity.

The sheer volume of Soviet writings on Latin America in publications like *International Affairs* and *América Latina* is impressive. Equally impressive are library facilities available to Soviet authors, judging by the extensive sources from around the world cited in their footnotes. Unfortunately, with few exceptions, the quality of Soviet writings is definitely *not* impressive. Presumably Jerry F. Hough (item **7065**) would disagree. He asserts: "None of the published Soviet debates on the outside world has been more sophisticated than that dealing with Latin America." However, there is little evidence of variety or sophistication in the items here; the overwhelming characteristic is dreary predictability.

K. Khachaturov (item **7072**) maintains that the Reagan administration has proved just as reactionary and aggressive in support of right-wing forces in Latin America as its rhetoric, and pronouncements from the likes of the Council for Inter-American Security and the Heritage Foundation, seemed to promise. China, through its cultivation of trade and diplomatic contacts with such countries as Chile, is perceived as in league with Washington against the Latin American liberation movement. I. Blishchenko and V. Shavron (item **7021**) allege that any US espousal of human rights is only a propaganda campaign designed to embarrass socialist states (whose records are blameless anyway) and to distract the masses at home from domestic problems and US aggressive policies worldwide. Moreover, A. Grachyov (item **7056**) castigates the US for trying to link the Soviet Union with "international terrorism." Everyone knows, he says, that true Marxists regard terrorism as naive and likely to play into the hands of imperialists; in any event, it is the US "that finances the most active organizations of terrorists in the world." Nevertheless, Mikhail Gornov and Vladimir Tkachenko (item **7054**) argue that the liberation struggle must assume forms appropriate to the conditions prevailing in each individual country, and they thus appear to be endorsing (when opportune) other roads to power than *la vía pacífica*. This is a shift from the Soviet "line" during the years when "armed struggle" was associated with Mao's China and deplored even when encouraged by Fidel Castro.

Soviet writers are uniformly skeptical of Latin American countries' hopes of achieving any genuine autonomy short of the triumph of socialism throughout the region. According to Vladimir Lukin (item **7088**), the concept of "centers of power" in Latin America, reflecting the pretensions of Mexico and Brazil, is only a capitalist doctrine to conceal their continued dependency which extends to being (willing or unwilling) agents of the US ("sub-imperialisms"). Zinaida Romanova (item **7127**) is similarly dubious about either Canada or Latin America gaining much from their somewhat closer political and economic relations in recent years. Yuri Paniev (item **7109**) asserts that increased EEC trade with, and loans to, Latin America are creating another layer of dependency rather than eroding US domination. Inessa Danilevich (item **7034**) and other writers also regard as a charade the Socialist

International's growing willingness to take positions on Latin American issues and to cultivate links with social democratic parties in the area. Of course, from the Soviet perspective, the sole useful international connections for Latin American countries to pursue are those with the USSR and the Eastern bloc. A bibliographical essay by Victor Lunin surveys Soviet writings on the USSR connection (item **7090**).

Perhaps the most interesting items in the current sample of Soviet literature concern the role of the Catholic Church in supporting social and political change (see items **7027, 7059, 7078, 7092** and **7095**). The gist of the Soviet view is that the Church is on the right track in preaching the need of the masses for social justice and political participation and in criticizing Washington's reactionary policies. Local communist movements should look for ways of cooperating with the Church, especially clerics who embrace "liberation theology" and Christian Democrats. However, it is also noted that the Pope has warned the Latin American Church against "incorrect" theology, excessive radicalism, and too much involvement in secular affairs.

Writings on Latin American development and its links to the international economy include two unusually perceptive articles by Luciano Tomassini (items **7148** and **7149**), who discusses and critiques the evolution of Latin American thinking about development from the "Prebisch Thesis" to the present. In his opinion, too much emphasis has been placed on commodity stabilization and too little on the development of Latin America's natural resources and their integration into an export-oriented industrial structure. Neo-conservative Peter L. Berger (item **7019**) takes issue with any contention that the current international economic system is "exploitative." As he sees it, the problem is that most Third World countries are socialistic and statist, while the US experience testifies that development happens best under conditions of democracy and capitalism.

Tomassini looks to continued North-South negotiations to assure that protectionism will not frustrate developed-country export strategies (item **7149**). He recommends that the countries of the South frankly recognize their own differences, acknowledge the constraints faced by the industrialized countries, and attempt to "de-link" larger issues in order to make whatever progress is possible on narrower fronts. Roger D. Hansen (item **7062**) tends to blame stalled negotiations mainly on the US and points out that the US policy of "co-opting" some of the more advanced LDCs failed and that the South's proposals have been approached only "on a case-by-case basis, and grudgingly at that." He believes the central difficulty is that the North does not have a "positive agenda of its own" and that the US has not exercised leadership in helping to formulate such an agenda.

Although dependency continues to be a controversial subject, there is a willingness on the part of most scholars to recognize that Latin America is less in control of its destiny and economy than the developed world. The most interesting economic history articles are those that deal with the coming of the dependency relationship or the passing of the hegemonic mantle from one country to another (items **7328, 7393,** and **7408**). A number of studies suggest that properly organized resistance at the periphery can, in fact, generate the power to resist the wishes of the dominant powers. Studies of both the Roca-Runciman Treaty (item **7349**) and the 1936 Anglo-Peruvian Trade Agreement (item **7418**) indicate that those Latin American countries drove (or executed) better bargains than was previously assumed. On the other hand, this does not contradict the basic dependency proposition that peripheral capitalism differs from the historical experience of the western industrialized countries in important ways.

Of particular interest in this discussion are studies dealing with the development of special industries in South American countries. The politicized nature of the conclusions based on such works (item **7390**) cannot obscure the fact that these industries developed in a manner that was shaped by events and concerns far outside South America. Studies of the automobile industry in Argentina (item **7362**) and the communications sector in Chile (item **7409**) offer some interesting information in this regard. There is also a thought-provoking essay by Sheldon J. Gitelman (item **7380**) on the new economic ties between Latin America (mainly Brazil and Argentina) and Africa (especially Nigeria and Gabon). Another valuable work is Paul Sigmund's study of the expropriation of multinationals in Latin America (item **7141**). Gathering a significant amount of information about his set of case studies, the work offers a realistic interpretation of the significance of these actions and conclusions which will please neither the ideological left nor right.

MEXICO

Mexico's increasing importance to the US has given rise to several books on bilateral relations that focus on energy, trade, immigration, investment, and border relations. The volume edited by Susan Kaufman Purcell (item **7192**) is the most ambitious because, in addition to covering a wide range of interesting topics, she has divided the chapters between North American and Mexican scholars, thereby providing readers with a rich variety of views. While relying heavily on US-based scholars, Richard D. Erb and Stanley R. Ross have produced a collection of essays (item **7209**) characterized by depth, evenness, and lucidity. Marxism, dependence, and extreme nationalism suffuse the essays compiled by Barkin *et al.* (item **7200**).

Octavio Paz (item **7196**) has summoned his erudition and wit to emphasize how Mexico and the US emerged from different cultural traditions that affect the outlook of their respective populations as well as their relations with each other. Historians may find his analysis old hat; however, others, especially those who believe that inter-American affairs began with the Monroe Doctrine, will profit from his astute discussion of the Islamic influence on Spain, the Reformation, the Counter-Reformation, and the work ethic.

Even though their publications preceded the economic crisis of 1982, Mexican social scientists continue to emphasize the assymmetry in power between their nation and the US. Mario Ojeda (item **7193**) identifies the "structure" of bilateral relations as the chief impediment to even-handed negotiations; Patricia Arriaga (item **7166**) stresses the penetration of Mexico's mass media by US capitalist interests; and Jorge Hodara (item **7180**) alleges that oil purchases and the control of information will facilitate Mexico's "Finlandization" by its northern neighbor. On the other hand, Jorge Castañeda (item **7170**) scorns the idea of a "special relationship" between the two countries but insists on the possibility of "genuine interdependence." Olga Pellicer de Brody (item **7197**) sees close cooperation with other Third World nations as the surest means of preventing her country's suffering from unfair US commercial policies. Even analysts sympathetic to this Mexican perspective wish that at least one scholar in Mexico would examine those domestic factors —PRI's inflexibility, corruption, a slavish devotion to capital-intensive technology, an unfair tax system, a chaotic agrarian sector, etc.—which exacerbate the proud nation's economic and political difficulties.

Bruce Bagley (item **7167**) offers an objective and compelling theory of how the decline of US influence throughout Latin America in the 1970s enabled Mexico to play an independent role in hemispheric affairs. Of course, he could not foresee the oil glut and ensuing financial crisis that forced Mexico to seek US assistance to prevent its defaulting on a huge foreign debt. Also illuminating is the article by Michael and Nannecke Redclift (item **7199**) on the two economic approaches pursued by President López Portillo and the impact that the US can have on Mexico's selection of a development strategy.

Those who prefer case studies to comprehensive treatments of bilateral affairs will profit from items on river disputes (item **7175**), drug trafficking (item **7173**), boundary questions (item **7181**), and health and environmental concerns of sister cities located along the Río Grande (item **7168**). The authors describe how enslavement of politicians to national sovereignty impedes the adoption of mutually beneficial solutions to those and other vexing problems.

Three items that reflect an historical perspective should be read by students of Mexican affairs. James A. Sandos (item **7203**) argues that Woodrow Wilson's dispatch of Gen. Pershing to track down Pancho Villa foreshadowed the President's subsequent efforts to integrate Germany into "a new non-revolutionary community of liberal nation states." Friedrich Katz (item **7184**) marshals copious evidence for the thesis that major powers, allied with business interests, have taken advantage of social conflicts and anti-colonial struggles to advance their own interests; notably, the US in Cuba during the war with Spain, and European states in post-World War I Mexico. Enrique Cortés (item **7172**) provides a fascinating look at ties between Mexico and Japan, not during the oil boom of López Portillo's administration, but during the presidency of Porfirio Díaz!

Alfredo Romero Castilla (item **7202**) opens a window on scholarly activity in Mexico by describing how local scholars have progressed from a traditional to a scientific approach in studying international relations. It is all too rare to find such an analysis concerning the evolution of an academic discipline in a major Latin American nation.

CENTRAL AMERICA, THE CARIBBEAN, AND THE GUIANAS

Polemics and policy proposals dominate the materials appearing on Central America and the Caribbean. Richard Millet (item **7243**) analyzes the frustrations besetting President Carter's efforts to deal with the region. John A. Bushnell (item **7223**) and Thomas O. Enders (item **7231**) attempt to put the best face possible on the "responsible middle course" pursued by the Reagan administration. They complement a condemnation of Cuba's increased aggressiveness and Nicaragua's aid to neighboring insurgents with an emphasis on US support for democracy, economic development, security assistance, and cooperation with other nations through the much-vaunted Caribbean Basin Initiative.

Critics on the left (items **7042, 7219, 7221, 7233a,** and **7265**) excoriate the administration's belligerent anti-communism and inclination toward military adventurism, while those on the right (item **7217**) bemoan President Reagan's failure to back up his rhetoric with action in combatting guerrilla movements in Central America. Lewis Tambs and Frank Aker (item **7260**) insist that the US should furnish everything but ground troops to achieve victory over international communism in El Salvador. Cleto diGiovanni and Alexander Kruger (item **7233**) advocate keying on Guatemala as the area's "stabilizing force," supporting the Salvadoran private sector, and working for the "removal of the Nicaraguan Communist government." More moderate essays stress indigenous factors giving rise to the Salvadoran conflict (item **7222**), the importance of spurring the electoral process (item **7246**), the need to improve the land reform (item **7251**), the value of pursuing a peaceful solution in concert with regional powers (item **7252**), and "positive abstention" or the Zimbabwe solution (item **7226**) as an alternative to US noninvolvement or intervention in the strife-torn nation.

With respect to the Caribbean Basin Initiative, Heliodoro González (item **7289**) makes a persuasive case that banks, investors, bureaucrats and consultants will benefit as the project puts recipients on a permanent dole rather than promoting their independence. Robert A. Pastor (item **7249**) challenges the validity of the alleged "national interests" animating Reagan's strategy toward Central America and lucidly offers his own flexible formula for dealing with the area. Gabriel Zaid (item **7266**) provides an even more detailed blueprint for settling the Salvadoran crisis. While others pose or condemn policy recommendations, Roland H. Ebel (item **7230**) convincingly identifies the turmoil in Central America as springing from the elite's failure to provide economic resources and political opportunities to new power contenders spawned by the region's economic development. Additionally, Richard E. Feinberg (item **7225**) has edited a remarkable compilation of essays that illuminates US, European, Mexican, Venezuela, Cuban and Soviet interests in the area.

Thomas P. Anderson (item **7213**) has enriched the literature with a thin volume on the problems afflicting El Salvador and Honduras, while Loren Jenkins (item **7235**) discusses how shared poverty and widespread land ownership have staved off revolution in Honduras. At least one Soviet Latin Americanist (items **7247** and **7303**) has flogged China's "proimperialistic" stance on the Salvadoran civil war, as evidenced by Peking's criticism of the unwarranted intervention of "both superpowers." Meanwhile, Constantine Menges (item **7242**) castigates the Socialist International for emphasizing anti-imperialism and nationalism in Nicaragua, Grenada, and elsewhere, while turning a blind eye to the far left's disdain for pluralism and democracy. An article by Pierre Schori (item **7314**), International Secretary of the Swedish Social Democratic Party, epitomizes the left-can-do-no-wrong philosophy that Menges abhors.

Paeans to the late Omar Torrijos have sprouted like spring flowers (items **7248** and **7259**); above all, they laud the general for recapturing his nation's sovereignty through successfully negotiating the Panama Canal treaties. One hopes that scholars are now hard at work on objective appraisals of the colorful Panamanian ruler and his period in office. Torrijos' efforts notwithstanding, nationalistic Panamanians worry that the continued US military presence in the Canal Zone transcends defense needs and threatens the republic's independence (item **7264**). A.E. Thorndike (item **7261**) has written a useful piece on how Belize cleverly internationalized its boundary disputes as a means to obtain independence.

Amid a sea of tendentious, ideologically inspired writings, one should consult a collection edited by Basil A. Ince (item **7278**) which stands out for its rigor and objectivity in evaluating the domestic and foreign challenges confronting the island nations of the Caribbean. George Abbott (item **7267**) describes faithfully the economic forces that give impulse to cooperation among Britain's former West Indian colonies. Richard Millett and W. Marvil Will (item **7312**) have also produced a useful compilation on the international relations of the region; unfortunately, such recent events as the changes of government in Grenada, Jamaica, and Nicaragua have stripped many of its essays of their up-to-date value. Maingot (item **7300**) adroitly reveals how wily Caribbean politicians of the left and right manipulate the "Cuban card" to legitimate their regimes or ward off opponents.

Cuba remains a focus of intense interest for US, European, and Latin American scholars. Jorge I. Domínguez deftly examines how the Castro regime has neither fallen nor faltered despite economic hardships. Historian Hugh Thomas (item **7319**) advances 15 policy recommendations, which may strike longtime Cuba watchers as naive, for isolating the island nation and exacerbating its internal problems. In contrast, William M. LeoGrande (item **7295**) argues in favor of Washington's replacing "graduated hostility" with "gradual engagement" in order to gradually ween Castro from his overwhelming dependence on the Soviet Union. A number of first-rate articles analyze Cuban foreign policy (items **7281, 7283, 7290,** and **7323–7324**). Specialists concerned with Cuba's activities abroad have begun to shatter the conventional wisdom that Castro is serving as a cat's paw of the Soviet Union in Africa. They find a convergence of interests: Havana is committed to promoting revolution in the Third World, while Moscow wishes to assist client or potential client groups. One political scientist (item **7268**) contends that US opposition to Cuba's backing of liberation movements in Africa demonstrates a blindness to international division between "haves" and "have nots" for which Washington is more responsible than Cuba.

A carefully researched and lucidly written article by Adamantia Pollis (item **7309**) reveals why Cuba and other socialist countries in the developing world reject the Western definition of civil and political rights in favor of the state's obligation to provide food, housing, and medical care.

Renewed US involvement in the Caribbean coincides with the publication of three solid works on the 1965 intervention in the Dominican Republic (items **7274** and **7287**).

In the wake of the Mariel "flotilla," the exodus of Haitians from their homeland, and the increasingly porous nature of the US-Mexican border, more scholars are paying attention to immigration, a topic that lends itself to passionate rather than dispassionate treatment. An exception is Terry L. McCoy's (item **7299**) cut-and-dry description of US immigration statutes and the reform proposed by President Carter in 1977. Even here, the author grossly underestimates the political strength of those who oppose change. Diligent studies rather than diatribes would be a welcome addition to the literature on this extraordinarily sensitive subject.

Passion also pervades presentations made during the Black Caucus' second annual seminar on the Caribbean (item **7277**). Some black leaders aspire to support their racial compatriots in the Caribbean just as American Jews lobby for Israel. According to Brenda Gayle Plummer (item **7308**), the interest of US blacks in the Caribbean goes back at least to the post-World War I period when civil rights organizations forced policymakers in Washington to "temper the roughshod manner" in which the citizens of occupied Haiti were treated.

SOUTH AMERICA

Foreign policy problems of individual South American countries constitute a major category of writing on the international politics of South America, especially for Brazil, Chile, Argentina, and Venezuela, although there were others (item **7424**). The prime theme among the works on Brazil was that country's attempt to become a superpower among the middle level international powers (items **7377–7378, 7382, 7389, 7395,** and **7397**). Of interest in this regard is whether and to what degree a country need achieve the status as a client state of the US or whether Washington's hegemonic role is decaying and hence opening up the possibility for a truly independent Brazilian role (item **7373**).

Chile's foreign policy problems are those of a small, internationally ostracized country with troublesome border disputes. The country's difficulties seem particularly hard to classify because it has been both isolationist and an over-achiever in terms of clinging to disputed territory (item **7410**). The rise of democratic governments in Argentina and Brazil and the change of administration in Washington would undoubtedly make Chile's international situation more tenuous.

Venezuelan foreign policy writings are either general (items **7433, 7436,** and **7441**) or focused on the oil industry and how OPEC profits affect foreign policy (items **7435** and **7438**). The best general work is a new historical study by Stephen Rabe (item **7439**). If OPEC loses control of the world oil price, Venezuela will face some difficult internal choices that will doubtlessly have foreign policy implications for the future. Venezuela's border problems with Colombia (item **7416**) and Guyana generated a number of studies (items **7430** and **7437**), most of them nationalistic in tone (items **7431** and **7440**).

Border disputes in South America are a favorite topic of publication. Besides the aforementioned disputes, border problems that command the greatest interest are between Ecuador and Peru, and between Chile and both Peru and Bolivia, countries that feel wronged by the War of the Pacific settlement (item **7370**). The outsider may tend to become exasperated by the popularity of such books which usually consist of detailed histories of the particular dispute designed to contradict the history written by the other side. In no other area is Latin American scholarship so jingoistic. Nevertheless, there are serious works among these polemical accounts such as those by Armando Amuchástegui Astrada, Guillermo Lagos Carmona, and Miguel Angel Zavala Ortiz (items **7336, 7367,** and **7407**).

Another problem that inspired works in the field of international law is the Law of the Sea question (items **7069** and **7375**). Several studies have appeared but again the focus is often narrowly nationalistic, or how could international law maximize the profits or growth of the author's country (item **7420**)?

A matter of concern to outsiders but largely ignored by South Americans is the development of nuclear energy production and its implications for proliferation. Only two brief pieces deal with the problem specifically (items **7121** and **7381**), although works address this issue in general terms and make interesting comments on the Latin American situation (items **7115** and **7116**).

Geopolitics has been of special interest to the military men of the Southern Cone countries (items **7330, 7339** and **7392**) and often takes a strongly anticommunist or nationalistic perspective. In this regard, the South Atlantic has become particularly important and the idea of a Southern Cone relationship with South Africa is regarded as a goal by some (item **7364**). Geopolitics becomes dangerous when it is perceived as providing a mechanistic justification for Brazilian domination of the continent or suggesting particularly destabilizing alliances which might embolden a weaker power. Numerous works attack geopolitical conceptualizations as being imperialistic in their implications and as justifying military leadership in the Southern Cone (items **7331, 7364, 7374, 7376, 7391,** and **7401**). The four most controversial topics within the geopolitical writings (all of which involve questions of borders, influence, and control) are Antarctica, the Beagle Channel, the Amazon Basin and the Falkland/Malvinas Islands. The internationalization of Antarctica, often cited as a positive example of international cooperation, is seen much differently among the geopoliticians of South America (item **7329**). The belief in the area's great natural resources, which runs through much of the writing, prompts Argentina, Brazil, and Chile to be particularly concerned with their slices of the Antarctic pie as negotiations continue on the matter (items **7332, 7343,** and **7358**).

The potential of the Amazon basin remains an important symbol of Brazilian nationalism, but here one detects a good deal of uneasiness on the part of other countries which have a piece of the basin (items **7396** and **7422**). The Brazilians speak of the need to cooperate in the development of the area while other countries are often wary of a venture that can only be controlled by the Brazilians (items **7379, 7383–7385,** and **7422**).

Discussion of Argentine foreign policy is a good deal more complicated because the domestic situation is in such disarray (item **7347**). Thus foreign policy discussions inevitably relate back to the perceived need to bring order to the economy and the political system (items **7337** and **7359**). In some works Brazil is seen as the major competitor for influence on the continent (item **7351**) but most authors are concerned with specific problems such as the Beagle Channel or Antarctica.

Until the end of 1971, the most important territorial problem of Argentina was the dispute of the Beagle Channel Islands (items **7336, 7346, 7354,** and **7360**). Efforts to settle this problem are complicated by the contradictory balance between international law and military power: the weaker state (Chile) has the better legal case (item **7398**). Much ink and little blood have been spilled on this matter, but certainly the controversy has long seemed extraordinarily volatile on both sides of the Andes. Santiago has been vocal in making sure that Argentina understands that Chile will fight to preserve its claims—a lesson which perhaps London should have noted prior to April 1982.

This brings the discussion to the most notable event in the international relations of Latin America during the period in question—the Falklands/Malvinas conflict. This war was a graphic demonstration of the potential for conflict in Latin America, which some analysts (for example, George H. Quester, item **7121**) tend to underestimate. Wolf Grabendorff, perhaps the leading German authority on the international problems of Latin America, surveys and categorizes regional conflicts since World War II and predicts a higher probability of clashes as the "security shadow" of the US diminishes (item **7055**).

Prior to the occupation of the islands by Argentina there had been a number of interesting works dealing with the problem (items **7346, 7348,** and **7361**). In part they were stimulated by signs of English flexibility on the issue exemplified by the Ridley proposal in which some form of a Hong Kong solution, that is, recognizing Argentine sovereignty but leasing the islands back, was recommended by a middle-ranking, British civil servant (items **7338, 7340,** and **7350**). Since the islanders opposed this solution, London moved away from the proposal, but apparently Buenos Aires did not realize the degree to which the British had changed their minds on compromise.

Argentine motives have come in for more scrutiny than those of England. The accepted wisdom is that Gen. Galtieri and the junta were moved by considerations of domestic unrest and a disfunctional competition among sectors of the Argentine economy (items **7344** and **7357**). Quantitative studies of international conflict in general have failed to find a correlation between domestic violence and aggressive international behavior, but the Falklands/Malvinas case is popularly viewed as an exception. So far the best account of the war and its background has been put together by a team from the *Sunday Times* of London (item **7366**), although there are a number of other accounts of the struggle (item **7353**). One hopes that a critical account from the Argentine perspective will eventually appear to balance the writings coming from England.

GENERAL

7001 Abugattas, Juan. El nacionalismo en el Tercer Mundo (UP/A, 7:12, 1982, p. 47–60)

Theoretical piece built on premise that "nationalism" works contrary to the desirability of real democracy and pluralism (e.g., people laboring for the good of the "state" rather than for justice, etc.). Urges Third World nations to strive for genuine pluralism. Institution-building should aim for "federal" or "confederal" arrangements, rather than too much centralization.

7002 Aguirre-Bianchi, Claudio and **Göran Hederbro.** The challenge of cooperation: a study of alternative communication in Latin America. Stockholm: Institute of Latin American Studies, University of Stockholm, 1980. 68 p. (Research paper series; no. 17)

Monograph stemming from a research project carried out at the Institute of Latin American Studies in Stockholm, Sweden, focuses on Latin America's possible role in a proposed New International Information Order. Author's concern is building Latin American countries' media infrastructure and access to international satellite systems, as well as increasing information flows from South to North. Appendices include inventory of news agencies in Latin America.

7003 Alcances y perspectivas del Nuevo Orden Internacional: mesas redondas. Ponentes: Jorge Eduardo Navarrete, Marcos Kaplan, César Sepúlveda. Comentarios: Miguel S. Wionczek *et al.* México: Universidad Nacional Autónoma de México, Coordinación de Humanidades, 1980. 130 p.: bibl.

Proceedings of roundtable convened 1979–80, UNAM, Mexico, on proposed New International Economic Order. Navarrete, Kaplan, and Sepúlveda prepared papers and Wionczek and others acted as commentators.

7004 Aleksandrova, Mariia. El movimiento obrero y sindical en América Latina. 2. ed. rev. Sofia: Instituto de Investigaciones Científicos sobre Problemas Sindicales J. Dimitrov, Adjunto al CCSB, 1980. 101 p.

Study by Bulgarian professor traces rise of Latin American labor movements, their more recent involvement in political struggles, and regional labor organizations

(CPUSTAL, CLAT, ORIT). Includes list of principal unions in each country and regional affiliations.

7005 Alexander, Robert J. Latin America: challenges to human rights (Freedom at Issue [Freedom House, New York] 64, Jan./ Feb. 1982,p. 28–30)

Brief but perceptive overview of human rights developments in Latin America in 1981 by longtime advocate of democracy in the region.

7006 Alvarez Soberanis, Jaime. Consideraciones sobre el papel del GATT frente a los países en desarrollo (UNAM/RI, 7: 24/25, enero/junio 1979, p. 5–38)

Author examines GATT's institutions and policies and reasons why developing countries are reluctant to join. He argues that they may do so only when GATT shifts its emphasis from trade liberalization, *per se,* to an effective international general system of trade preferences.

7007 América Latina: política exterior y dependencia económica: pts. 1/2 (URSS/AL, 10[46], 1981 p. 33–88; 11[47], 1981, p. 53–80, plates)

Two-part compendium of short essays by Soviet writers on foreign policies of US, Latin American countries, and US-Latin American relations. Familiar central theme: inability of Latin American countries to be "autonomous" until they shake off economic "dependence" on US and transnational corporations and take the road to socialism.

7008 Angelier, Jean-Pierre. L'Organisation Latino-Américaine de l'Energie (FDD/ NED [Problèmes d'Amérique Latine, 63] 4653/4654, 26 jan. 1982, p. 177–183)

French analyst surveys history and current activities of OLADE (Latin American Energy Organization). Unfortunately, he does not capture the organization's political dynamics that have greatly limited its accomplishments to date.

7009 Anguiano Roch, Eugenio. China: la política de cooperación con el Tercer Mundo (Estudios de Asia y Africa [El Colegio de México, México] 15:3, julio/sept. 1980, p. 515–570, tables)

Good study of China's "pragmatic"

policies toward Third World countries in the post-Mao era. Notes that China has been intent on opening diplomatic and commercial relations with Chile, Zaire, Egypt, Pakistan, and Somalia, countries undergoing difficult times and/or alienated from the USSR. Chile's inclusion is indicative of China's new willingness to put other goals before ideology. China also strongly supports Third World demands for a New International Economic Order. Finally, its approach to the Third World as one of its own rather than as the purveyor of socialist revolution has met with much success.

7010 Apuntes sobre la política de Carter y la crisis del imperialismo. Lima: Comisión Evangélica Latino Americana de Educación Cristiana, 1979. 29 p.: bibl., ill. (Cuadernos de estudio; 1)

Little book of patently Marxist hate literature, masquerading (?) as a "study guide" issued by the Latin American Evangelistic Commission of Christian Education.

7012 Arrieta Abdalla, Mario. Obstáculos para un Nuevo Orden Informativo Internacional. s.l.: Centro de Estudios Económicos y Sociales del Tercer Mundo; México: Editorial Nueva Imagen, 1980. 415 p.: ill.

Maintains that there will never be an effective New International Economic Order until developing countries break industrialized countries' monopoly on information of all sorts. Pays much attention to newspapers in particular countries and their allegedly "colonial" character but has praise for press freedom, a right author recognizes as not often prevailing in Third World. Arrieta acknowledges intellectual debt to Brzezinski's concept of "the technotronic era."

7013 Astiz, Carlos A. Changing U.S. policy in Latin America (CUH, 81:472, Feb. 1982, p. 49–51, 88–90)

Short overview of the Carter and Reagan administrations' Latin American policies. Complains that pragmatism has been progressively displaced by ideological rigidity, partly because Carter failed "to develop major long-term policy initiatives." Carter's central commitment to human rights was, in author's view, "at best, lukewarm," and policy was "unevenly implemented" and "often handled less than competently." Reagan may

offer more "continuity and sense of direction" but at the expense of needed flexibility.

7014 Atroshenko, Anatoli and Vladimir Lukin. La región del Pacífico: problemas de la paz y la colaboración (URSS/AL, 3[23], 1979, p. 32–48)

Soviet authors maintain Pacific is increasingly becoming a distinct "region" but one with many serious problems (e.g., neocolonial orientation of west coast Central and South American countries toward US; existence of regional alliances like Rio Pact and ANZUS; and trouble-making China across ocean).

7015 Barreiro, Julio. Los molinos de la ira: pronóstico sobre la situación de América Latina. México: Siglo Veintiuno Editores, 1980. 266 p.: bibl. (Sociología y política)

An all-too-familiar theme: Latin America faces two choices at this stage of history, capitalism or socialism. Nothing in between will alleviate masses' plight, and capitalism surely won't. Ergo, let's get on with the task of building socialism.

7016 Beaulac, Willard Leon. The fractured continent: Latin America in close-up. Stanford, Calif.: Hoover Institution Press, Stanford University, 1980. 232 p., 3 leaves of plates: bibl., ill., index, maps (on lining papers) (Hoover Institution publication; 225)

Former ambassador to five Latin American countries offers his observations (e.g., *caudillos*, nationalism, agrarian reform, planning, US-Latin American relations, etc.). Rambling and disappointing book is nevertheless occasionally wise and even charming. Best are Beaulac's personal impressions of Latin American leaders (e.g., "Of course, even then I knew that Tacho [Somoza] was *mañoso*; that he was on the clever, even cunning, side. But let us be frank: in Nicaragua's society a degree of *maña* might be a requisite to survival. Nicaraguans were not Groton graduates, nor are they today. In the United States Tacho might have become a respected senator. More likely he would have become a wealthy businessman. In Nicaragua, politics was the quickest road to wealth."). No Alliance for Progress or Carter's human rights policies fan, Beaulac's ideological bent is "pragmatic" to "conservative."

7017 Beltrán, Luis Ramiro and Elizabeth Fox de Cardona. Comunicación dominada: Estados Unidos en los medios de América Latina. México: Instituto Latinoamericano de Estudios Transnacionales; Editorial Nueva Imagen, 1980. 176 p.

Strong condemnation of imperialistic nature of US media, its influence (and ownership of) Latin American communications system. Impressive data in places but whether authors' solutions would result in a freer exchange of ideas is questionable. With so many nondemocratic governments currently in power in Latin America, one wonders, for example, how Southern Cone media would evolve without outside influence. [M.J. Francis]

7018 Bengolea, Teresa. Las siete reuniones cumbre de los países industrializados: acuerdos y divergencias en torno a la crisis (CEESTM/TM, 1:2, enero/abril 1982, p. 235–254)

Summarizes North's economic problems over previous decade and attempts of industrialized countries to deal with continuing "crisis." Concludes that the North (except France, Canada, and maybe Japan) evidences little interest in negotiating with the South. It should seek its own independent development, by struggling against internal oligarchies and multinational allies.

7019 Berger, Peter L. Speaking to the Third World (AJC/C, 72:4, Oct. 1981, p. 29–36)

Sociologist suggests that contrary to "Third World ideology" most Third World countries' difficulties stem from their being socialistic and statist. The American experience (deemed transferrable) is that development occurs under democracy and capitalism. Provocative, well-written article would be more convincing if it also discussed authoritarian regimes that preside over "capitalist" economic systems in which all benefits flow to the elite.

7020 Berrios, Rubén. La empresa trans-ideológica y las relaciones económicas Este-Oeste (UP/A, 7:12, 1982, p. 89–100)

Details gradual expansion in East-West trade and reaches novel conclusion that socialist countries helped maintain capitalism during recent "crisis" of world recession. Attributes this to entrepreneurial activities of "transideological" companies.

7021 Blishchenko, I. and **V. Shavrov.** US hypocritical human rights policies

(RIIA/IA, 4, April 1981, p. 56–67)

Asserts that US's human rights campaign is merely propaganda designed to embarrass socialist states (whose records are blameless) and to distract masses at home both from noting US society's deficiencies and US government's aggressive stance. In actuality, US has not ratified international human rights treaties and actively supports right-wing regimes.

7022 Brummel, Jürgen. Gewalt in den Aussenpolitischen Beziehungen Lateinamerikas am Beispiel der brasilianischen Sicherheits—und Expansionspolitik (JGSWGL, 15, 1978, p. 425–435)

Author contends reasons for relatively little interstate violence in Latin America are: internal stability being higher priority in most countries, absence of divisive issues, and role of inter-American system. Suggests these factors may be declining in importance. An ominous thought. [M.J. Francis]

7023 Cavalla Rojas, Antonio. Estados Unidos, América Latina, fuerzas armadas y defensa nacional. Culiacán, México: Universidad Autónoma de Sinaloa, 1980. 178 p.: bibl. (Colección Nuestro continente; 4)

Five critical essays on military matters from leftist perspective. First two (on structure and doctrines of Latin American militaries) are most effective. Monograph on decision-making in US defense establishments may be of interest to those unfamiliar with US system. [M.J. Francis]

7024 Ceskoslovensko a Latinská Amerika po druhé svetové válce: sborník materiálových studií. Praha: Orientální ústav CSAV, Oddelení Latinské Ameriky, 1977. 342 p.: bibl. (Ceskoslovensko a Latinská Amerika; 4)

Overview of Czech-Latin American relations after World War II, prepared by Czech Academy of Sciences, first study of subject since 1945. Six authors deal with political, economic, scientific, cultural and educational relations. Includes factual information and statistics. Lacks indexes. [George J. Kovtun]

7025 Child, John. Estados Unidos y Latinoamérica: conceptos estratégicos militares (IAEERI/E, 63, marzo/abril 1980, p. 71–90, maps)

Advances eight strategic-military conceptions of "Latin America" from US vantage-point. Includes interesting maps illustrating various perspectives, reminiscent of maps purporting to show a Texan's or New Yorker's view of US. Are Washington's views of Latin America ever any more realistic?

7026 Church, Frank. America's new foreign policy (The New York Times Magazine [New York] 23 Aug. 1981, p. 30, 32–33, 68–70)

Former Democratic Chairman of US Senate Foreign Relations Committee critiques first six months of Reagan administration's foreign policy. Credits Carter with portraying US as "country with sufficient self-respect to avoid courting the worst of the right-wing police states;" while Reagan confirms "darkest suspicions of foreign peoples striving to achieve some improvement in their lives." On Central America: "How much better . . . to adopt the attitude of our democratic neighbors Mexico and Venezuela, whose policy is to influence the direction of . . . inevitable changes . . . rather than . . . stamp them out."

7027 Cobo, Juan. La democracia cristiana en el sistema político de los países de América Latina: la Iglesia, la democracia cristiana y los sentimientos religiosos de las masas (URSS/AL, 5[53], 1982, p. 41–60, plate)

Soviet commentators discuss significance of Christian Democratic movement in Latin America concluding it has progressive features that can serve to advance socialism.

7028 ———. Las ideas de Bandung y América Latina (URSS/AL, 8[32], 1910, p. 4–19)

Extolls Non-Aligned Movement founded at 1955 Bandung conference and going strong after 25 years despite nasty things West has done, such as Washington's renewal of Cold War after Soviet Union stepped in to protect Afghanistan. Here's to the Bandung spirit, united against imperialism and for peace on earth!

7029 Colard, Daniel. Le Mouvement des Pays Non-Alignés (FDD/NED, 4613/4614, 30 mars 1981, p. 5–164, bibl., maps)

Stresses Non-Aligned Movement's conflict between commitment to solidarity and international cooperation and its serious internal divisions. Chief among divisions is the one between Soviet clients like Cuba and members more genuinely committed to ideal and practice of non-alignment. Author believes Tito's recent death deprived movement of the leader most strongly committed to true non-alignment. Factor operating in opposite direction was Soviet invasion of Afghanistan.

7030 Comito, Vincenzo. Fiat's strategy in the Third World (Politica Internazionale [Nova Italia, Firenze, Italy] 2 : 2, Winter 1981/Spring 1982, p. 166–175, tables)

In 1970s, Fiat sought to expand in Latin America, especially Argentina and Brazil. Performance of its auto plants, however, proved disappointing. In Argentina the problems were labor troubles and economic recession; in Brazil, of stagnant automobile market and strong competition from other Western manufacturers. Latin American experience led company to reduce its pioneer interest in Third World markets.

7031 *Commentary.* American Jewish Committee. Vol. 72, No. 5, Nov. 1981- New York.

Symposium consists of presentations by 18 prominent academics and policy-makers of different ideological persuasions on "Human Rights and American Foreign Policy." Includes most pro and con arguments on various policies.

7032 Cortázar, Julio *et al.* USA vs. foreign intellectuals (INDEX, 10:1, Feb. 1981, p. 38–41)

Reports on denial of US visas to leading Latin American intellectuals because of their presumed "subversive" tendencies.

7033 Crenshaw, Martha. The causes of terrorism (CUNY/CP, 13 : 4, July 1981, p. 379–399)

Crenshaw holds: "Terrorism per se is not usually a reflection of mass discontent or deep cleavages in society. More often it represents the disaffection of a fragment of the elite, who may take it upon themselves to act on behalf of a majority unaware of its plight, unwilling to take action to remedy grievances, or unable to express discontent. This discontent, however subjective in origin or minor in scope, is blamed on the government or its supporters. Since the sources of terrorism are manifold, any society or polity that permits opportunities for terrorism is vulnerable."

7034 Danilevich, Inessa. La socialdemocracia internacional y América Latina (URSS/AL, 3[19], 1978, p. 51–72)

Acknowledges European roots of Latin America's social democratic parties but stresses that today's Socialist international is primarily a European organization with only tenuous links with corresponding Latin American parties.

7035 Defense markets in Latin America.
New York: Frost & Sullivan, 1981. 365 p.: ill.

Systematic and extraordinarily detailed work taking the major Latin American countries individually in terms of their threat perception, procurement trends and level of forces. Very valuable. [M.J. Francis]

7036 La Democracia cristiana en el sistema político de los países de América Latina (URSS/AL, 3[51], 1982, p. 49–76)

Various Soviet writers discuss Christian Democracy in Latin America, its rivalry with Social Democrats (e.g., Venezuela's AD and COPEI).

7037 Dmitriev, V. Imperialist rivalry in Latin America (IA, 5, May 1981, p. 72–79, tables)

US "imperialism" has, of course, the most experience in penetrating Latin American economies, and US is region's dominant influence. However, Western European countries and Japan now compete while seeking to avoid serious conflict with US. Author's analysis demonstrates detailed grasp of non-US Western political initiatives, investments (gross figures and particular projects), and trade with Latin America.

7038 Documentos básicos del Nuevo Orden Económico Internacional, 1974–1977.
Lima: Junta del Acuerdo de Cartagena, Biblioteca, 1978. 247 p.: index.

Collection of documents on "New International Economic Order" (1974–77) emanating from UN, Non-Aligned Movement, Group of 77, etc.

7039 Donnelly, Jack. Human rights and foreign policy (PUCIS/WP, 34:4, July 1982, p. 574–595)

Excellent review-essay highlights: 1) definition of human rights; 2) practical political problems of implementing an international human rights policy; and 3) legal and moral problems of intervention on behalf of human rights. Believes previous attempts (e.g., Carter's) are instructive for future (the Carter exception for US security interests in South Korea and elsewhere appears to have bought not much extra security at high human rights cost). Nevertheless, one doubts whether policy in this difficult area can ever be as coherent as author would wish.

7040 Encuentro de Especialistas en Asuntos Internacionales, *1st, Mexico City, 1977.* Los problemas de un mundo en proceso de cambio: ponencias. Luis González-Souza, Ricardo Méndez Silva, editores. México: Universidad Nacional Autónoma de México, Coordinación de Humanidades, 1978. 243 p.: bibl.

Informed, thoughtful discussions by prominent Latin American (predominantly Mexican) intellectuals on: New International Order controversy, transnational corporations and their control, human rights in US foreign policy, and the UN Law of the Sea Conference. [M.J. Francis]

7041 Estévez, Jaime. Cancún: los límites del diálogo (Tercer Mundo y Economía Mundial [Centro de Estudios Económicos y Sociales del Tercer Mundo, México] 1:2, enero/abril 1982, p. 197–217)

Estévez concludes: "The strategy pursued by the Third World since 1975, emphasizing moderation and consensus, has been demonstrated insufficient and has resulted in the paralysis of the negotiating process. . . . Cancún is the ultimate demonstration of the failure of this approach."

7042 Fagen, Richard R. The real clear and present danger: a critique from the left (FIU/CR, 11:2, Spring 1982, p. 18–19, 52–53, plate)

Perceptive "critique from the left" of Latin American policies of the Reagan administration. Notes it failed "to act vigorously and coherently in ways consistent with [its] highly inflammatory and deeply ideological view of the hemisphere." Dilemmas it faced, Cuba's not being very vulnerable to US pressures nor events in Central America easily influenced by US rhetoric and limited economic and military assistance. Fagen fears that an increasingly frustrated Washington, "not wanting to appear a paper tiger," will eventually turn to "policies of aggression and military adventurism."

7043 Fontaine, Roger. Perspectivas de las relaciones Estados Unidos-Latinoamérica: problemas que confrontará la administración Reagan y sus proyecciones hacia el año 2000 (Revista de Ciencia Política [Pontificia Universidad Católica de Chile, Instituto de Ciencia Política, Santiago] 3, 1980, p. 86–100)

One of Reagan's key advisers on Latin American affairs declares himself to be "fundamentally optimistic" about US-Latin American relations despite obvious existence of inevitable frictions between countries, fundamental development problems, and subversive challenge of Cuba and USSR. His optimism stems from: 1) Americas sharing a belief in the free market; 2) abundance of natural resources; and 3) increasing cooperation based on a recognition of interdependence (sort of an updated Western Hemisphere ideal).

7044 Franck, Thomas M. "Congressional Imperialism" and human-rights policy (LIWA/YWA, 1981, p. 37–50)

Challenges Congressional critics who insist legislators have usurped executive's foreign policy role. Tracing Congress' action in human rights, prior to Carter, concludes that it resulted from President's repeated failure to implement human rights policy enacted by legislature—thus the executive failed to fulfill his mandate "that the laws be faithfully executed."

7045 Fuentes Mares, José. Génesis del expansionismo norteamericano. México: El Colegio de México, 1980. 170 p.: 8 p. of plates: bibl.; ill; index (Nueva serie / Centro de Estudios Históricos; 30)

Scholarly study, based in part on archival research in US and Spain, of US policies from 1810–22, a period when the Monroe Doctrine emerged.

7046 Gannon, Francis X. Globalism versus regionalism: U.S. policy and the OAS (FPRI/O, 26:1, Spring 1982, p. 195–221)

OAS policy planner and administrator reviews post World War II US policies toward Latin America and OAS activities. States that there is no natural identity of interests between northern and southern hemisphere, except on a few major concerns. . . Yet Latin America and US find ways to transcend differences and recognize convergent interests. Dilemma: Is convergence of views and attitudes sufficient to keep inter-American system and OAS productive in contemporary world? No, according to Gannon, unless "universal bias" in contemporary US policy is complemented by "firmly anchored regional policy," not presently the case.

7047 García, Inés and **Alberto Adrianzén.** No alineados, nueva fuerza internacional? Lima: Centro de Estudios y Promoción del Desarrollo, 1980. 172 p.: bibl. (Praxis—Desco; no. 15)

Undistinguished study of Non-Aligned Movement except authors' treatment of Tito-Castro split at 1970 Havana meeting. In their perspective, Tito was speaking for movement's original concept, now outdated because the world is no longer bipolar but divided between those practicing or supporting, and those opposed to, imperialism. New watchword is anti-imperialism, and the Soviet Union is an ally in this struggle.

7048 García Robles, Alfonso. The Latin American nuclear-weapon-free zone. Muscatine, Iowa: Stanley Foundation, 1979. 31, 1 p.: bibl. (Occasional paper—Stanley Foundation; 19 0145–8841)

Summary of the history and terms of the Treaty of Tlatelolco, by former Mexican Foreign Minister and Nobel Peace Prize winner who led the campaign for treaty. Includes complete text of treaty and protocols.

7049 Gardner, James A. Legal imperialism: American lawyers and foreign aid in Latin America. Madison: University of Wisconsin Press, 1980. 401 p.; bibl.; index.

First-rate study of experience of American lawyers who served US foreign aid programs in Latin America. Important addition to literature on foreign aid ideology, specifically technical assistance. Concludes: "The optimistic world view and professional self-image that American lawyers carried abroad in the early 1960s were persistently challenged, and were sometimes reversed: the handmaidens of democracy sometimes turned out to be the handmaidens of a dictatorship or authoritarian state; a rule-skeptical movement developed on increasing appreciation for rules and rule of law; . . . American legal instrumentalist 'know-how' carried abroad returned with a refreshing acknowledgement of how little was really known."

7050 Gastil, Raymond D. Human rights: a policy guide for the U.S. (Freedom at Issue [Freedom House, New York] 55, March/April 1980, p. 12–15)

Outlines differing definitions of human rights: 1) Amnesty International's emphasis on political execution, murder, torture, and imprisonment; 2) UN's Universal Declaration of Human Rights' stressing fulfilling human needs like shelter and food as well as political and civil liberties; and 3) "constitutional" definition concerned with civil and political rights. Gastil opts for third.

7051 Gilhodes, Pierre. Les relations économiques entre les Etats-Unis et l'Amérique Latine: 1975–1979 (FDD/NED [Problémes d'Amérique Latine, 60] 4619/4620, 12 mai 1981, p. 87–122, tables)

Long article with numerous tables covers commerce in all major product categories (including arms), investment, debts, and the debate over appropriate economic models.

7052 Glinkin, Anatoli. El hegemonismo en el hemisferio occidental: historia y actualidad (URSS/AL, 6[54], 1982, p. 23–41, plate)

Short review of US' "hegemonic" machinations in Latin America points out that USSR initiated the 1979 UN resolution condemning "the policy of hegemonism in international relations," a policy obviously abhorrent to the USSR.

7053 González Casanova, Pablo. El eurocomunismo y la experiencia de América Latina (NSO, 61, julio/agosto 1982, p. 135–141)

Mexican sociologist and UNAM's former rector examines Eurocommunist doctrine's relinquishing traditional Marxist concepts in favor of elections, political coalitions, etc. Notes such strategy accords with Chile's UP but emphasizes that in Chile and Latin America forces of change have encountered brutal repression unlike anything in France or Italy since World War II.

7054 Gornov, Mikhail and **Vladimir Tkachenko.** Latin America in the 1970s (USSR/SS, 12:4, 1981, p. 49–67)

Soviet analysis of liberation struggle in Latin America today. Forms of such struggle will be armed or peaceful depending on degree of dependence on foreign monopoly capital (e.g., armed struggle in Nicaragua; broad popular coalitions in Chile, Uruguay, El Salvador, Mexico; restriction of US capital and local oligarchy by governments for sake of working people in Peru, Panama, Bolivia). Notes Soviet acceptance of roads to power other than *vía pacífica*, a shift from USSR's previous stand when "armed struggle" was associated with Mao's China and deplored even when preached by Fidel Castro.

7055 Grabendorff, Wolf. Interstate conflict behavior and regional potential for conflict in Latin America (SAGE/JIAS, 24:3, Aug. 1982, p. 267–294)

Thought-provoking analysis of conflict in Latin America offers useful five-fold classification scheme: 1) system; 2) hegemonic; 3) territorial; 4) resource; and 5) migration conflicts. Anticipates greater potential for conflict as region edges out of US "security shadow" but is optimistic that Third World consciousness, interstate cooperation, and regional integration may "intercept" trend.

7056 Grachyov, A. Extremism and terrorism in the service of world reaction (IA, 6, June 1981, p. 67–74)

Maintains right-wing forces are using terrorism by the left as excuse for repression, and Washington is attempting to "smear" both USSR and Third World liberation movements with label of "international terrorism." Reiterates Soviet Union's opposition to terror and Marxism-Leninism's rejection of it as a means for attaining political ends.

7057 Granjon, Marie-Christine. La politique des droits de l'homme et son application (FDD/NED [Problémes d'Amérique Latine, 60] 4619/4620, 12 mai 1981, p. 57–71)

Survey of Carter administration's human rights policy concludes that despite deficiencies, it was successful (e.g., release of some political prisoners, encouragement of democratic trends in several countries).

7058 Grayson, George W. The maple leaf, the cactus and the eagle: energy trilateralism (IAMEA, 34:4, Spring 1981, p. 49–75)

Excellent article examines concept of energy common market among Canada, Mexico, and US that emerged during 1980 presidential campaign. Dismisses feasibility of such an arrangement because of Canada's and Mexico's strong opposition. Discusses proposal's background, reasons for both countries' adverse reaction, and makes several suggestions for bilateral and trilateral cooperation in energy matters short of a common market.

7059 Grigulevich, Jorge. La Iglesia latino-americana en el umbral de los años 80 (URSS/AL, 10[34], 1980, p. 19–31)

Intriguing article by USSR Academy of Science member. Credits Catholic Church—and even Polish Pope—with considerable movement towards endorsing social and political change in Latin America and notes that churchmen in Nicaragua and elsewhere have gone even further in embracing "liberation" doctrine. Maintains that, despite their anticlericalism, communists are cooperating with such Catholics "in support of peace, democracy and indispensable social change."

7060 Guido, Amílcar. El principio de la no intervención en la América Latina (Desarrollo Indoamericano [Barranquilla, Colombia] 67, abril 1981, p. 29–33, ill.)

Another article on the principle on non-intervention! Interesting combination of traditional legal analysis with plea for recognition that principle represents struggle of Latin Americans against US oppression. Could it be that author is a Latin American lawyer who specializes in international law at the University of Moscow? Yes.

7061 Halliday, Fred. Moscow and the Third World: the evolution of Soviet policy (IRR/RC, 24:2, Autumn 1982, p. 137–149, bibl.)

Halliday maintains that Third World "revolutions" are not Kremlin inspired actions, as Reagan believes but involve USSR's responses to new Third World situations. What has changed since Krushchev is not Soviet policy, rather incidence of successful revolutions and USSR's achievement of near-parity in nuclear weapons, which allows Moscow more freedom for political maneuvering. However, weakness of USSR's economy prevents Soviets from engaging in massive financial aid to revolutionary regimes.

7062 Hansen, Roger D. North-South policy—what's the problem? (CFR/FA, 58:5, Summer 1980, p. 1104–1128)

Splendid analysis of evolution of North-South "dialogue" and why it became a dialogue of the deaf by 1980s. Points out that US policy of "co-opting" more-developed

LDCs failed and that the North approached the South's proposals only "on a case-by-case basis, and grudgingly at that." Insists main problem is North's lack of "positive agenda." North-South coordination would actually be in long-term economic interest of US in food production and distribution, and international trade in manufactured goods.

7063 Hehir, J. Bryan. Human rights & the national interest (WV, 25:5, May 1982, p. 18–21)

Provocative explanation of ethical calculus, derived from Roman Catholic theology, relating human rights to US foreign policy. Security concerns must not override human rights in Latin America because threats to stability spring from "a prolonged conflict between an authoritarian military government and the country's civil population." [G.W. Grayson]

7064 Herrera-Lasso M., Luis. Una perspectiva global de la reunión de Cancún (CEESTM/TM, 1:2, enero/abril 1982, p. 219–233)

Looking at policies of several leading countries in the industrialized North regarding Southern demands, author is pessimistic about future North-South negotiations. The Cancún meeting, he says, involved a reasonably healthy and frank exchange of views, but its concrete benefits for the South are far from clear.

7065 Hough, Jerry F. The evolving Soviet debate on Latin America (LARR, 26:1, 1981, p. 124–143)

Maintains that Soviet Latin Americanists are not of one view and that: "None of the published Soviet debates on the outside world has been more sophisticated than that dealing with Latin America." Most important debates concerned: 1) degree of dependence and level of development of major Latin American countries; and 2) probable political development in Latin America over near and medium term.

7066 Hübener, Karl-Ludolf. The Socialist International and Latin America: problems and possibilities (FIU/CR, 11:2, Spring 1982, p. 38–41, plates)

Notes Socialist International's continuing interest in Latin America, but also notes that region's member parties have been diverse (from AD in Venezuela to more radical parties in Nicaragua and Grenada). These parties not only disagree ideologically but are often hostile to one another.

7067 Human rights and U.S. human rights policy: theoretical approaches and some perspectives on Latin America. Howard J. Wiarda, editor. Washington; London: American Enterprise Institute for Public Policy Research, 1982. 96 p.

Essays consist of criticism of Carter's human rights policy and apologia for Reagan's. Includes two essays by Jeane J. Kirkpatrick (including "Dictatorships and Double Standards," see *HLAS 43:7058*), others by Wiarda, Richard Shifter, Mark Falcoff, Michael Novak, and Edward A. Olsen—all, according to Wiarda, "fervent believers in human rights." He concedes that there "are of course other points of view on human rights," a decided understatement!

7068 Huntington, Samuel P. Human rights and American power (Commentary [American Jewish Committee, New York] 72:3, Sept. 1981, p. 37–43)

Essay by Harvard's Clarence Dillon, Professor of International Affairs and former member of Carter administration, could have been written by Jeane Kirkpatrick. Rejects "myth" of US as "repression's friend," intervening in support of conservative regimes and against progressive ones. In fact, US' decline in late 1960s and early 1970s coincided with spread of authoritarianism in Latin America and Asia. Harkin amendment and others were attempts to compensate for such decline of American power but no substitute for its presence. Moreover, there are reasons to prefer right-wing to left-wing dictatorships: 1) authoritarian regimes suppress liberty less than "totalitarian" ones; 2) right-wing dictatorships are less permanent; and 3) right-wing regimes are normally more susceptible to American and other Western influence.

7069 Infante C., María Teresa. Nota sobre la conferencia de Naciones Unidas sobre el Derecho del Mar (Revista de Ciencia Política [Pontificia Universidad Católica de Chile, Instituto de Ciencia Política, Santiago] 3, 1980, p. 55–66)

Interesting description of Law of the Sea negotiations held July and Aug. 1980 in Geneva. [M.J. Francis]

7070 Jacobini, H.B. La contribución latinoamericana al Derecho de las Naciones y al "Derecho Internacional Americano" (CM/FI, 22:3, enero/marzo 1982, p. 304–319)

Covers Latin American participation on international courts and other tribunals and the region's contributions to international law in several key subject areas: collection of debts and reparation for injury, non-intervention, territorial waters, and the inter-American system.

7071 Jaguaribe, Hélio. Estados Unidos: sistema democrático e relações com o Terceiro Mundo (Encontros com a Civilização Brasileira [Civilização Brasileiro, Rio de Janeiro] 10, abril 1979, p. 43–56)

Interesting theoretical and historical discussion of US in which author tries to understand country's internal workings and perceptions in order to analyze its role in world affairs and Third World. [M.J. Francis]

7072 Khachaturov, K. Washington's Latin American policy (IA, 1, Jan. 1982, p. 52–61)

Maintains Reagan administration lived up to a predicted reactionary and aggressive foreign policy in Latin America. Details US support for right-wing forces, emphasizes Council for Inter-American Security, Heritage Foundation, etc. Also China's cultivation of Pinochet confirms China is leagued with Washington.

7073 Kirkpatrick, Jeane J. Establishing a viable human rights policy (APS/WA, 143:4, Spring 1981, p. 323–334)

US Ambassador to UN repeats former criticisms of Carter's human rights policy (see item and *HLAS 43:7058–7059*). A "viable" policy must consider it is difficult to institutionalize human rights, some "rights" must forever remain simple "goals," not all efforts to advance rights actually do, and there is a distinction between private and public morality.

7074 Klochkovski, L. Neocolonialist rivalry in Latin America (IA, 7, July 1982, p. 39–46)

Soviet author notes that Europe and Japan have been competing for Latin American markets even as US fielded its abortive proposal for a North American Common Market. Meanwhile, Latin American countries are continuing their individual and collective efforts to reduce dependency and diversify trade.

7075 Kokorev, Vladimir. La política de los países latinoamericanos respecto a Africa (URSS/AL, 4[28], 1980, p. 55–73)

Soviet author observes that the progressive involvement of Cuba in Angola has its reactionary parallel in longing of Southern Cone "fascists" for a South Atlantic alliance. Furthermore, in his view, "monopoly capitalism" is using Brazil as a proxy in establishing bridgeheads in Africa.

7076 Koroliov, Yuri. Anti-popular regimes in Latin America (IA, 9, Sept. 1980, p. 114–121)

Latin American military dictatorships' promises to return to barracks and civilian rule, maneuvers "masterminded by 'liberal' advisers from Washington, cannot deceive the peoples [sic] in the Latin American countries." "Only a fierce, resolute struggle" and "Latin American solidarity" can win the "peoples" battle against "fascism."

7077 ———; Vladimir Tarasov; and Boris Maritov. América Latina: la política exterior y la dependencia económica (URSS/AL, 12[48], 1981, p. 57–71, plates)

Several Soviet authors ruminate about Latin America's international relations, whether regional initiatives such as integration will serve genuine local development rather than bourgeoisie interests. Nevertheless, the point is made that the precise degree of dependency varies by country (except, of course, for truly independent Cuba).

7078 Kovalski, Nikolai. El Vaticano: ¿cómo seguir adelante? (URSS/AL, 10[34], 1980, p. 32–44, plate)

On the basis of Vatican's current positions, author judges that communists and Christians have many common viewpoints on war, social justice, and so forth. Despite differences on other questions, he maintains, there is no reason why cooperation cannot be achieved on various significant fronts.

7079 Kuczynski, Pedro-Pablo. Action steps after Cancún (CFR/FA, 60:5, Summer 1982, p. 1022–1037)

Peru's Minister of Energy and Mines urges governments which participated in 1981 Cancún North-South conference to set "practical and limited" agenda for follow-up negotiations. Suggests priority discussions about future role of multilateral development banks and long-range energy policies.

7080 ———. Latin American debt (CFR/FA, 61:2, Winter 1982/1983, p. 344–364)

Excellent analysis of causes—international and domestic—and scope of debt crisis facing many Latin American countries. Urges IMF members to establish "special window" comparable to organization's earlier "oil facility" window, to insure continued inflow of capital to region. Believes such a "bail-out" may be essential to avoid unilateral defaults.

7081 Lafer, Celso. A Nova Ordem Mundial num sistema internacional em transformação (UMG/RBEP, 55, julho 1982, p. 7–63)

Lengthy, sophisticated analysis of shifting distribution of power, institution-building, new actors and issues in contemporary international system. Lafer demonstrates an impressive familiarity with international political theory and problems. Conclusion is somewhat less startling: that present world needs better international institutions and norms to help manage problems arising from increasing complexity.

7082 LaPalombara, Joseph and Stephen Blank. Multinational corporations and developing countries (CU/JIA, 34:1, Spring/Summer 1980, p. 119–136)

Authors attempt to construct a model or set of generalizations that provide a typology of how various types of Third World countries treat multinationals. Although not specific, article is suggestive of some important patterns. [M.J. Francis]

7083 Latin America foreign policies: global and regional dimensions. Edited by Elizabeth G. Ferris and Jennie K. Lincoln. Boulder, Colo.: Westview Press, 1981. 300 p.: bibl., index (Westview special studies on Latin America and the Caribbean)

One of few collections on subject includes useful selections by some established scholars: 1) general perspectives; 2) global policies of Brazil, Mexico, Peru, and Cuba; 3) regional policies of Venezuela, Brazil, Bolivia, Mexico, Cuba, and English-speaking Caribbean; and 4) essay by editor Elizabeth Ferris, "Toward a Theory for the Comparative Analysis of Latin American Foreign Policy." Latter advances a framework of three issues and 13 hypotheses.

7084 Lévesque, Jacques. L'URSS et l'activité militaire de ses alliés dans le Tiers-

Monde: des années 70 aux années 80 (CII/IJ, 37:2, Spring 1982, p. 285–306)

University of Quebec professor who wrote book on USSR-Cuban relations (see *HLAS 43: 7331*) here includes review of Cuban involvement in Angola and elsewhere in Africa. Believes Castro was pursuing what he regards as his own country's independent interests as well as cooperating with Soviet designs.

7085 Levine, Barry B. The French connection (FIU/CR, 11:2, Spring 1982, p. 46–49, 58–60, plates)

Interviews with two French academics on France's policy (especially Mitterand's) toward Latin America. Alain Rouquié insists that Western world must help Latin America avoid choice between abandoning road to social change or becoming Moscow's allies. François Bourricaud suggests that France "talk more North-South" rather than "Fidel Castro" if French deficits require more assistance from US bankers and international agencies.

7086 Lorca, Alejandro V.; Aurelio Martínez; and Ana Fuertes. España-América Latina y la Comunidad Económica Europea (CM/FI, 22:3, enero/marzo 1982, p. 268–292, tables)

Overview of Latin America's economic relations with EEC and speculation as to likely impact of Spain's participation therein. Authors believe having a Hispanic country in EEC would benefit Latin America: "defend its interest, comprehend its problems, facilitate intercommunication, etc."

7087 Lowenthal, Abraham F. Changing patterns in inter-American relations (The Washington Quarterly [A review of strategic and international issues. Transaction Periodicals Consortium, Washington] 4:1, Winter 1981, p. 168–177)

Unusually good overview of changes since 1960 or so, written as Reagan administration came into power. Notes decline of US dominance in Latin America, except in Mexico, Central America, and Caribbean. Likens present to 1920s, when European powers and some leading Latin American countries competed for influence with US. Key question: Will US under Reagan revert to past military interventions, a policy less likely to succeed today than in 1965 Dominican case or even in 1920s?

7088 Lukin, Vladimir. La concepción de los "Centros de Poder" y América Latina (URSS/AL, 9[33], 1980, p. 53–68)

Soviet writer believes notion of "centers of power" in Latin America (i.e., important and influential countries like Mexico and Brazil) is merely capitalist doctrine designed to conceal a dependency that extends to serving as (willing or unwilling) US agents ("subimperialisms").

7089 Lunin, Víctor. "Conceptos" de la administración Reagan respecto al Hemisferio Occidental: sobre el Documento de Santa Fe (URSS/AL, 4[52], 1982, p. 4–24)

Soviet author surveys some Reagan pre-election statements and Jeane Kirkpatrick's positions on issues and concludes that US policy has entered a new ideologically conservative and militarily aggressive phase.

7090 ———. Las relaciones de la URSS con los países latinoamericanos y la lucha de América Latina por afianzar la independencia (URSS/AL, 5[41], 1981, p. 43–61)

Bibliographical essay consists of useful survey of Soviet writings on USSR/ Latin American relations.

7091 McGovern, George S. Perspectives on Latin America: report of a study mission to Costa Rica, Panama, Peru, and Venezuela: a report to the Committee on Foreign Relations, United States Senate. Washington: US G.P.O., 1978. 51 p.

Senator McGovern's report on 1977 study mission undertaken for Committee on Foreign Relations. His observations on then-current conditions in Costa Rica, Panama, Peru, and Venezuela are general but perceptive. Recommends continued support for human rights, ratification of Panama Canal treaties, and normalization of relations with Cuba.

7092 Maidanik, Kiva *et al.* La Democracia Cristiana en el sistema político de los países de América Latina (URSS/AL, 4[52], 1982, p. 46–75)

Soviet authors discuss Christian Democracy in Latin America, especially ideological divisions in the movement caused by the Nicaraguan revolution, events in El Salvador, and conservative Reagan tide in US politics.

7093 Marcum, John A. The Kirkpatrick era (CRIA/WW, 24:6, June 1981, p. 19–21)

Vice Chancellor of Academic Affairs at University of California, Santa Cruz, asks: "Will the foreign policy of the Reagan administration adhere rigorously to the conservative ideology and 1950s assumptions of its Jeane Kirkpatricks and Ernest Lefevers? Or will it—and they—follow more closely the political dictates of a realistically informed and rational pragmatism?"

7094 Martínez Bengoa, Javier. La nueva política imperialista: la política de la Comisión Trilateral. México: Seminario Permanente sobre Latino América, 1978. 23 p.: bibl. (Documento de trabajo; 11)

Working paper emanating from SEPLA (Permanent Seminar on Latin America) convening in Mexico City. Participants include dependency theorist Theotonio dos Santos and former Allende Minister of Economy, Pedro Vuskovic. Martínez believes Trilateralism is a viable Third World strategy for capitalist countries during current "crisis" of capitalism.

7095 Marzani, Carl. The Vatican as a left ally? (MR, 34:3, July/Aug. 1982, p. 1-41)

Marzani (a "thoroughbred atheist") answers yes, asserting that "over the past two decades the Catholic Church has been undergoing changes so profound as to constitute a true revolution." Evidence: Church's positions on El Salvador, nuclear disarmament, and Pope's conflict with Washington on issues of military dictatorship, neocolonialism, and economic exploitation.

7096 Matos Ochoa, Sergio. El panamericanismo a la luz del derecho internacional. Caracas: Universidad Central de Venezuela, Facultad de Ciencias Económicas y Sociales, División de Publicaciones, 1980. 249 p.: bibl. (Colección Libros)

Lengthy, historical account of Panamericanism emphasizing US' negative role. Although research is not impressive, there are some interesting perspectives as to the linkage with international law. Argues for more Latin American cooperation as a means of advancing Latin interests. [M.J. Francis]

7097 Medeiros, Antônio Paulo Cachapuz de. As relações internacionais como área de estudo na América Latina (UMG/RBEP, 55, julho 1982, p. 65–88)

Medeiros discusses and identifies various intellectual eras in study of international relations: utopian, realist, behaviorist-quantitative, and post-behaviorist. Article's most interesting part traces evolution of study of international relations in Brazil since 1954 establishment of Brazilian Institute of International Relations.

7098 Mohar Betancourt, Gustavo. The major accords at the Acapulco meeting (BNCE/CE, 26:8, Aug. 1980, p. 278–280)

Account of 1980 meeting in which parties to Treaty of Montevideo decided to replace earlier LAFTA agreement with one aiming at "gradual and progressive" establishment of a Latin American Common Market, and to replace LAFTA with ALADI (the Latin American Integration Association).

7099 Montaner, Carlos Alberto. The mediation of the Socialist International: inconsistency, prejudice and ignorance (FIU/CR, 11:2, Spring 1982, p. 42–45, 57, plate)

Wonders about Socialist International's playing a role in Latin American affairs. Asks if organization's involvement is "rebellious act against the hegemony of the United States" spawned by Europe's uneasiness with many aspects of US relations with Europe and USSR? Cautions against support for "Castro-Soviet obedient armed groups" in Nicaragua and El Salvador, who may promise support for democracy but not deliver.

7100 Morris, Michael A. Expansion of Latin American navies. Stockholm: Institute of Latin American Studies, 1980. 70 p.: ill. (Research paper series / Institute of Latin American Studies; paper no. 25)

Interesting and careful assessment of present status of Latin American navies, drawn from author's forthcoming book on Third World navies. Observes that Brazil is region's leading naval power and that countries are looking to their navies to provide enforcement of their Exclusive Economic Zones (EEZ). Comments that estimates of Cuban naval power are often exaggerated, influenced by presumed Soviet support of Cuba.

7101 Mossavar-Rahmani, Bijan. OPEC and NOPEC: oil in North-South relations (CU/JIA, 34:1, Spring/Summer 1980, p. 41–58, tables)

Non-OPEC developing countries continued to support OPEC despite suffering from oil prices because: 1) perception that their economic problems stem also from rising costs for industrial imports; and 2) Third World solidarity is required in North-South negotiations.

7102 Mower, Alfred Glenn, Jr. The European community and Latin America: a case study in global role expansion. Westport, Conn.: Greenwood Press, 1982. 1 v.: bibl., index (Contributions in economics and economic history, 0084–9235; no. 46)

Important study of European Community (EC)/Latin America relations from WW II's end to present. Pt. 2 focuses on global and regional factors that may shape future relations. Believes both EC and Latin America can benefit from closer ties but wonders whether "the EC will decide that it can move closer to Latin America without risking political and economic losses in other geographic areas which are perceived to be of greater importance to the Community." In his view, "part of the answer lies with Latin America and what it does to improve its capability to bargain effectively."

7103 Multinational corporations in Latin America: private rights, public responsibilities: edited proceedings of five symposia, Associated Colleges of the Twin Cities, February 18-March 17, 1976. Edited by Donald P. Irish. Athens: Ohio University, Center for International Studies, 1978. 122 p.: bibl., ill. (Papers in international studies: Latin America series; no. 2)

Proceedings of five 1976 symposia on multinationals in Latin America. Although it suffers from usual unevenness of any collection, it will acquaint reader well with major points of view on the topic. [M.J. Francis]

7104 Norris, Robert E. Observations *in loco*: practice and procedure of the Inter-American Commission on Human Rights (Texas International Law Journal [University of Texas School of Law, Austin] 15:1, Winter 1980, p. 46–95)

Important article by Senior Specialist with Inter-American Commission on Human Rights. Careful and thorough legal analysis of evolution of concept, of on-the- scene investigations of various types of human rights violations, of procedures currently in effect, and likely impact of ratifications of American Convention on Human Rights. Required reading for those interested in human rights,

especially since Commission's work is so often overlooked.

7105 Novak, Jeremiah. Cancún: step forward or lost opportunity? (CRIA/WW, 25:1, Jan. 1982, p. 8–21)

Blistering critique of US position at 1981 Cancún conference. Castigates US delegation for: 1) US failure to share same "sense of urgency" as its allies and nations of South; and 2) singular lack of imagination in proposing reforms of existing international economic structures. [G.W. Grayson]

7106 Oduber, Daniel. Toward a new Central American dialogue (FIU/CR, 10:1, Winter 1981, p. 10–13)

Leader of Socialist International offers cliché-laden prescription for dialogue among Caribbean basin leaders. Vagueness of piece provides insight into why Mr. Oduber's movement has not prospered in the region. [G.W. Grayson]

7107 Organization of American States. Inter-American Commission on Human Rights. Annual report of the Inter-American Commission on Human Rights: 1980–1981. General Secretariat, OEA. Washington: 1981. 130 p. (OEA.SER.L/V./II.54, doc. 9 rev. 1, 16 Oct. 1981)

Report on human rights activities 1980–81 consists of observations by Commission on specific complaints; "progress made" by Brazil, Ecuador, Honduras, Uruguay, and Venezuela; and description of human rights situation in OAS member states detailing conditions with surprising frankness.

7108 Palmer, David Scott. Perspectivas de la política norteamericana sobre derechos humanos (CPU/ES, 24:2, 1980, p. 45–49)

Outlines some objections (in author's view, legitimately) often directed at Carter's human rights policy. Maintains, nevertheless, that the policy had an impact on consciousness of policy-makers, sensitizing them to the fact that human rights are a matter of concern.

7109 Paniev, Yuri. Aspectos de las relaciones económicas entre países latinoamericanos y la Comunidad Económica Europea (URSS/AL, 5[53], 1982, p. 17–31, plate)

Traces increase in EEC investment in, trade with, and loans to Latin America. Concludes this pattern really constitutes another neocolonial relationship rather than genuine counterweight to US domination.

7110 Pastrana, Francisco M. Trilateralismo: ensayo crítico. Buenos Aires: Ediciones Cuatro Espadas, 1981. 461, 69 p.: bibl.; ill., maps.

Serious study of Trilateral Commission, membership, objectives, and implications of this kind of transnational cooperation for the rest of the world. Unfortunately, analysis throughout is marred by author's view of "trilateralism" as essentially a conspiracy, presented in an overly-dramatic prose style.

7111 Pavlov, A. The Non-Aligned Movement and the struggle against imperialism (RIIA/IA, 4, April 1981, p. 77–81)

Despite determined Western efforts to divide non-aligned ranks, 1980 New Delhi meeting demonstrated that the Non-Aligned Movement is still very much alive and united in its opposition to imperialism. Regrettably, "the Peking hegemonists," also hostile to the Movement, have subjected key members—India, Cuba, Ethiopia, Vietnam—to "violent attacks."

7112 Pegusheva, Lidia. Tendencias del movimiento sindical de América Latina en los años 70 (URSS/AL, 6[54], 1982, p. 42–49, plate)

Soviet analysis notes two "reformist" international labor organizations operating in Latin America—ORIT and CLAT—experiencing "profound crisis" whereas their "progressive" counterpart—CPUSTAL—had to intensify its "battle for the fundamental interests of the workers."

7113 Perdomo de Sousa, Mary and **Rafael Sousa Andrade.** Un Nuevo Orden Internacional para el desarrollo y la paz: hacia una interpretación del Nuevo Orden Económico Internacional. Bogotá: República de Colombia, Pontificia Universidad Javeriana, Facultad de Ciencias Jurídicas y Socioeconómicas, 1980. 108 p.; bibl.

Discussion of the New International Economic Order as goal of Third World diplomacy. Relatively short summary of major issues. Includes more non-technical recommendations. [M.J. Francis]

7114 Pérez, Carlos Andrés. Cooperación económica Norte-Sur (NSO, 61, julio/agosto 1982, p. 149–155)

Former President of Venezuela stresses need for countries of South to recognize that industrialized countries also have interests that require protection and to shift tone of North-South negotiations from confrontation to cooperation.

7115 Política nuclear. Obra editada bajo la dirección de Francisco Orrego Vicuña y Pilar Armanet Armanet. Santiago: Universidad de Chile, Instituto de Estudios Internacionales: Editorial Universitaria, 1979. 348 p.: ill. (Estudios internacionales)

Papers presented at meeting sponsored by Chilean Commission on Nuclear Energy on "International Dimensions of Nuclear Policy." Worth reading for those interested in subject, collection includes materials on nuclear policies of Chile, Uruguay, and Peru, countries not usually stressed in the literature.

7116 Poneman, Daniel. Nuclear policies in developing countries (RIIA/IA, 57:4, Autumn 1982, p. 568–584)

Although not focusing on Latin America, analysis includes some useful propositions regarding types of governments and nuclear power policies. Places Latin American experience in broader context. [M.J. Francis]

7117 Programa de Paz, de progreso social y liberación nacional (URSS/AL, 6[42], 1981, p. 4–20)

Statements made in conjunction with the 26th Congress of USSR's Communist Party by Secretary-Generals and other officials of the Communist parties in Venezuela, Brazil, Peru, Costa Rica, Haiti, Honduras, Bolivia, and Panama.

7118 La Protección legal de los derechos humanos en el Hemisferio Occidental. Atlanta, Ga.: Fundación Interamericana de Abodagos, 1978. 104 p.

Brief remarks at 1978 meeting of Inter-American Foundation of Lawyers by Vice President of Inter-American Commission on Human Rights, Costa Rican jurist, Assistant Coordinator of US State Department's Bureau of Human Rights, President of American Bar Association, and Assistant Secretary of State for Inter-American Affairs. Reprints texts of "American Declaration of the Rights and Duties of Man" and American Convention on Human Rights, as well as provisions in constitutions of American countries referring to human rights.

7119 Proyectos de recambio y fuerzas internacionales en los 80. Juan Carlos Portantiero et al. México: Edicol: UILA, 1980. 247 p.: bibl., ill. (Américalatina, estudios y perspectivas; 2)

Interesting collection of essays on current trends in Latin American ideologies and politics, including retreat from conservative military rule toward an uncertain future in a number of countries. Lead essays by Juan Carlos Portantiero and Luis Maira, respectively, stress impact of external ideologies and pressures on Latin America. Portantiero observes that old ideal (e.g., APRA) of national independence and indigenous political ideas and institutions seems dated. Maira, on the other hand, believes that the political forecast in many countries will be some unstable blend of authoritarianism and democracy, an indigenousness of sorts.

7120 Puig, Juan Carlos. Doctrinas internacionales y autonomía latinoamericana. Caracas: Universidad Simón Bolívar, Instituto de Altos Estudios de América Latina, Fundación Bicentenario de Simón Bolívar, 1980. 316 p.: bibl., ill., index.

Professor of International Law at Venezuela's Simón Bolívar University assesses relevance to real world of traditional concepts like "sovereignty" and concludes, not surprisingly, that there is a gap between theory and practice. Advances a "holistic" conception of international "community" made up various types of actors with various degrees of influence, with rules for the community arising out of a complex "decision-making" system.

7121 Quester, George H. Nuclear proliferation in Latin America (CUH, 8:472, Feb. 1982, p. 52–55)

Straightforward discussion of potential for nuclear proliferation in region. Optimistic about future, believes Latin America is area with few border disputes and low potential for military conflict. Written before Falklands/Malvinas War.

7122 Las Relaciones económicas externas de América Latina en los años ochenta. Santiago: Naciones Unidas, 1981. 180 p. (Estudios e informes de la CEPAL; 7)

Unusually useful four-part analysis and CEPAL documentation includes numerous tables of statistics: 1) protectionism, energy, and multinational corporations; 2)

trade, external financing, and monetary issues; 3) economic relations with the US and Europe; and 4) world economy, including interdependence, and Latin America's role therein.

7123 Las Relaciones entre América Latina, Estados Unidos y Europa Occidental. Obra editada bajo la dirección de Gustavo Lagos Matus, con la asistencia de Rebeca Bordeau S. Santiago: Instituto de Estudios Internacionales de la Universidad de Chile: Editorial Universitaria, 1979. 173 p.: bibl. (Estudios Internacionales)

Collection of essays by prominent Chilean academics: Alberto van Klaveren's "The Crisis of North American Hegemony and its Repercussions in Latin America;" Heraldo Muñoz's "Economic Relations Among the Latin American Periphery, the United States and Western Europe;" Manfred Wilhelmy's "The International Competence of Latin America;" Augusto Varas' "The International Military Relations of Latin America;" and Gustavo Lagos' "Latin America and the New International Economic Order."

7124 Relaciones internacionales de la América Latina. Selección de Luciano Tomassini. México: Fondo de Cultura Económica, 1981. 519 p.: tables (El Trimestre Económico. Lecturas; 35)

Well chosen collection of essays grouped into four sections: 1) importance of study of international relations; 2) transformation of transnational system and case of Latin America; 3) interests of Latin America in North-South dialogue; and 4) evolution of intra-Latin American relations. North American readers will recognize essays by Abraham Lowenthal, W.W. Rostow, Roger Hansen, C. Fred Bergsten, and others.

7125 Rogachev, I. Beijing's perfidy and double-dealing (IA, 1, Jan. 1982, p. 130–132)

Soviet author accuses China of opposing diplomatic relations between Latin American countries and USSR, of being suspicious of "patriots" who overthrew Somoza in Nicaragua, and of being "openly hostile to the popular uprising in [El] Salvador."

7126 Rogers, William D. and **Jeffrey A. Meyers.** The Reagan administration and Latin America (FIU/CR, 11:2, Spring 1982, p. 14–17, ill.)

Former Assistant Secretary of State for Latin American Affairs and co-author sketch "uneasy beginning" of Reagan administration regarding Latin America, especially its exaggerated perception of US national interests at stake in El Salvador. Authors argue El Salvador does not deserve high ranking in US foreign affairs because what happens there "will not have much consequence elsewhere."

7127 Romanova, Zinaida. Posiciones de Canadá en la economía de América Latina (URSS/AL, 10[46], 1981, p. 12–32)

Soviet article traces growth of Canadian interest in and economic relations with Latin America. Both sides view their relations as decreasing dependence on US when only outside capitalism can true independence be achieved. Just another "contradiction."

7128 Rothenberg, Morris. Since Reagan: the Soviet and Latin America (GU/WQ, 5:2, Spring 1982, p. 175–179)

Initially concerned that US might act directly against Cuba, Soviets are now pleased with political drift in Nicaragua and Central America. However, Moscow has been relatively cautious and believes US may "take strong action" if Central American situation deteriorates.

7129 Rouquié, Alain. La Présidence Carter et l'Amérique Latine: parenthèse ou mutation? (FDD/NED [Problèmes d'Amérique Latine, 60] 4619/4620, 12 mai 1981, p. 49–56)

Emphasizes Carter's abandonment of traditional conception of an "American family" and his treatment of regional issues as global problems. Carter administration was "expiating presidency" reshaping US' villain image through human rights, nonproliferation of nuclear weapons, etc. Believes differences notwithstanding, Carter perpetuated US paternalism and interventionism and paved the way for Reagan's Cold War policies.

7130 Ruilova, Leonardo. China Popular en América Latina. Quito: Instituto Latinoamericano de Investigaciones Sociales, 1978. 302 p.: bibl., graphs.

Serious study of China's relations with Latin America, emphasizing 1970–78 period. Author is Central University of Quito professor who specialized in sinology at Colegio de México and Berkeley. Nearly half of book

is chronology of events and other useful appendices.

7131 Ruiz Contardo, Eduardo. La política norteamericana hacia la América Latina. México: Seminario Permanente sobre Latino América, 1977. 35 p., 1 leaf of plates: ill. (Documento de trabajo; 2)

Working paper emanating from SEPLA (Permanent Seminar on Latin America), convening in Mexico City with wide range of Latin American participants. Ruiz is former Chairman of Dept. of Sociology, University of Chile. Surveys "imperialist interventions" over years and their supposed links to cycles of domestic instability.

7132 Sáenz, Tirso W. and **Emilio García Capote.** El colonialismo tecnológico y la autodeterminación en materia de ciencia y técnica (URSS/AL, 3[19], 1978, p. 29–50)

Cuban authors present facts and figures on role of multinationals in Latin America and turn to Cuban experience. Rejecting assertion that Cuba exchanged one dependency for another in transition to socialism, they insist Cuba has profited from scientific and technological cooperation with Eastern bloc.

7133 Sasse E., Gerhard. La guerra subversiva como método en relaciones internacionales (Revista de Ciencia Política [Pontificia Universidad Católica de Chile, Instituto de Ciencia Política, Santiago] 3, 1980, p. 67–77)

Interesting attempt to discuss guerrilla subversion from a theoretical viewpoint. Anti-Marxist analysis suggests that subversion is unique in international relations in that its sponsor can seem uninvolved. Use of subversion is on increase because chances of escalation are less than in traditional warfare. [M.J. Francis]

7134 Saxe-Fernández, John. De la seguridad nacional. México: Editorial Grijalbo, 1977. 187 p.: bibl. (Colección 70; 149)

Yet another anti-US diatribe by author who turns them out regularly. Topic is US support for counterrevolution in Latin America through assistance to the Latin American military, and so forth and so forth. A waste of a serious subject!

7135 Schoultz, Lars. Human rights and United States policy toward Latin America. Princeton, N.J.: Princeton University Press, 1981. 421 p.: bibl., index.

One of best books written on US policies toward Latin America and important case study of US foreign policy formulation. Analyzes values, public opinion, interest group, bureaucratic and congressional constraints shaping human rights policies. Explains factors that culminated in renewed attention to human rights from 1973 through Carter years. Acknowledges that substitution of more popular, reformist governments for right-wing dictatorships entails political risk. Maintains that "truth with which United States policy makers must become acquainted" is that "there will be neither peace nor stability in Latin America until the basic needs of the people are met."

7136 ———. U.S. foreign policy and human rights violations in Latin America: a comparative analysis of foreign aid distributions (CUNY/CP, 13:2, Jan. 1981, p. 149–170, tables)

Excellent article brings empiricism ("social science") to subject usually treated "subjectively:" "during the mid-1970s United States aid was clearly distributed disproportionately to countries with repressive governments . . . this . . . represented a *pattern* . . . not . . . isolated cases, and . . . human need was not responsible for the positive correlations between aid and human rights violations."

7137 Sechi, Salvatore. The PCI's "Third Road" (Politica Internazionale [Nova Italia, Firenze, Italy] 2:2, Winter 1981/Spring 1982, p. 141–144)

Reviewing 1981 trip of Italian CP Secretary, observes: "Berlinguer presented himself to the Latin American leaders as the spokesman of a party whose foreign relations are based not on proletarian internationalism but on anti-imperialist solidarity, with no prejudices in favor of one or another brand of anti-imperialism."

7138 Semo, Enrique and **E. Suárez Iñíquez.** América Latina y la crisis europea: el eurocomunismo. México: Seminario Permanente sobre Latino América, 1977. 53 p. (Documento de trabajo; 7)

UNAM professors of economics and political science seek to define what Eurocommunism is and what relevance it may hold for Latin America. They stress that the *vía pacífica* clearly had greater potential in democratic Europe, but Semo believes Italian CP holds lessons for Latin America, in that it changed its tactics to suit different conditions from fascism to democracy.

7139 Sepúlveda, Alicia and **Eliza Chávez.** Las relaciones Norte-Sur frente al problema de la industrialización del Sur (3er. Mundo y Economía Mundial [Centro de Estudios Económicos y Sociales del Tercer Mundo, México] 1:1, sept./dic. 1981, p. 95–123, tables)

Authors review patterns of industrial development in underdeveloped South and role of foreign direct investment therein. The South should strive to establish associations of development technology and to convince the North that technology should (like the moon and the seabed) be regarded as "the common heritage of mankind."

7140 Sherkovin, Yuri. Alliance of the ultra-left and right forces (USSR/SS, 1, 1982, p. 164–175, bibl.)

Soviet author charges that "ultra-left" terrorists are in alliance with "ultra-right." "Bourgeois" mass media latches onto reports of violence to excoriate the left. Meanwhile, ultra-left extremists "divert the working masses, especially the youth, from the class struggle, direct their efforts in a false direction and in this way split the working-class movement."

7141 Sigmund, Paul E. Multinationals in Latin America: the politics of nationalization. Madison: University of Wisconsin Press, 1980. 426 p.: bibl., index.

Effort to understand how protection of foreign investment became North/South problem. Detailed case studies of expropriation/confiscations of foreign holdings (e.g., Mexican oil, Castro's Cuba, Allende's Chile, Peru's IPC, Venezuelan oil). Suggests that appeals to nationalization as easy solution to economic and social problems have declined. Includes good discussion of US policy and its contradictory treatment of investors abroad. Very useful study for uninitiated, offers wealth of supporting material on either side of issue. [M.J. Francis]

7142 Sizonenko, Alexandr. URSS—países latinoamericanos: resultados y perspectivas de las relaciones interestatales (URSS/AL, 1/2[37/38], 1981, p. 5–20)

Soviet writer points to USSR's increasing diplomatic and commercial contacts with Latin American countries (outside of Cuba) in recent years, including numerous state visits to Moscow of Latin American presidents. It all goes to show that Lenin was (again) correct in forecasting that those battling imperialism would find an ally in Soviet Union.

7143 Soler, Ricaurte. Idea y cuestión nacional latinoamericanas de la independencia a la emergencia del imperialismo. México: Siglo Veintiuno Editores, 1980. 294 p.: bibl., index (Colección América nuestra: 27. Caminos de liberación)

Reinterpretation of Latin America's development by Marxist professor captivated by the *"idea de nacionalidad latinoamericana."* [G.W. Grayson]

7144 Sophisticated armament for Latin America? (IAMEA, 36:1, Summer 1982, p. 73–85, graphs)

Excerpts from Congressional Research Service report, prepared for House Foreign Affairs Committee, analyze US decision to approve F-16 fighter aircraft purchase for Venezuela. Concludes US pressure to purchase was not major factor. Discusses pros and cons of sale and of policy of supplying highly sophisticated weapons to Latin America.

7145 Steward, Dick. Money, marines, and mission: recent U.S.-Latin American policy. Lanham, Md.: University Press of America, 1980. 280 p.: bibl., index.

Very personal survey of US-Latin American relations since 1933. Central theme: "American policy toward Latin America has been a paradoxical combination of naked imperialism and misguided idealism; of philanthropy and profit."

7146 Street, James H. Coping with energy shocks in Latin America: three responses (LARR, 17:3, 1982, p. 128–147)

Details reactions of Brazil, Venezuela and Mexico to post-1973 energy crunch. Concludes: "Because of the general spread of inflation before offsetting sources of productivity and energy alternatives could be organized, the short-term impact . . . fell heavily on the working class, the poor, and the unemployed." Meanwhile, worldwide recession partly caused by OPEC price increase led to drop in Latin American exports.

Tareas y perspectivas de la latinoamericanística soviética. See item 4349.

7147 Toinet, Marie-France. Le lobby Latino-Américain à Washington (FDD/NED [Problèmes d'Amérique Latine, 60] 4619/ 4620, 12 mai 1981, p. 73–86)

Good overview of various interest groups, ranging across the ideological spectrum, that have been active in shaping (or attempting to shape) recent US policies toward Latin America.

7148 Tomassini, Luciano. Industrialization, trade and the international division of labor (CU/JIA, 34:1, Spring/Summer 1980, p. 137–152)

Splendid article summarizes stages of Latin America's thinking about domestic development and its links to international economy. Discusses traditional international division of labor, Prebisch critique thereof, and problems of import substitution industrialization and commodity stabilization as means of overcoming traditional patterns. Believes diversified industrial exports are Latin America's best hope.

7149 ———. Las negociaciones Norte-Sur y el cambio de las relaciones internacionales de los países en desarrollo (FCE/TE, 49:193, enero/marzo 1982, p. 53–79)

General discussion of North-South negotiations ends with plea for South's countries to recognize their real differences, to adopt more realistic view of constraints faced by industrialized countries, and to allow "delinking" of various issues that should make for more effective progress.

7150 Las Transnacionales en América Latina. México: Instituto Latinoamericano de Estudios Transnacionales, 1979. 9 leaves.

Short document summarizes various conclusions about role of transnational corporations in Latin America, advanced by Mexico's Latin American Institute of Transnational Studies (ILET). Conclusions: proposed "codes of conduct" for transnationals have limited effect given their structural linkages to domestic and international economies. Hope is that transnationals will offer countries desirable new patterns and options both internally and in external relations.

7151 Trinidade, Antônio Augusto Cançado. Direito do mar: indicações para a fixação dos limites laterais marítimos (UMG/ RBEP, 55, julho 1982, p. 89–138)

Careful and well documented analysis of the evolving International Law of the Sea as it relates to the limits of coastal state jurisdiction, including both doctrines of the continental shelf and exclusive economic zones (EEZ).

7152 United States. Congress. House of Representatives. Committee on Foreign Affairs. Subcommittee on Inter-American Affairs. Foreign assistance legislation for fiscal year 1982: the Inter-American Foundation, Latin America and the Caribbean, international narcotics control for Latin America and Asia: Hearings and markup before . . . on March 23, 26, 30, and April 8, 1981. Washington: G.P.O., 1981. 267 p.: facs., tables (97th Congress, lst Session)

Interesting hearings on foreign assistance authorizations for Latin America and the Caribbean, as well as funding for the Inter-American Foundation and International Narcotics Control Programs for Latin America and Asia. Testimony by AID officials and others, and substantive debate on the conditions (if any) to be imposed upon US aid to El Salvador.

7153 ———. ———. ———. ———.
———. United States national interest in Latin America: Hearing before . . . on March 4, 1981. Washington: G.P.O., 1981. 67 p.: plates (97th Congress, lst Session)

Noteworthy testimony on the subject of the hearing by Constantine C. Menges (Hudson Institute consultant, later of the Defense Department), Abraham F. Lowenthal (guest scholar at Brookings, and director of the Smithsonian's Woodrow Wilson Center's Latin American Program), and William M. Dyal (President-elect, American Field Service International, and former president, Inter-American Foundation). Lowenthal's statement, his best to date on this theme, contrasts sharply with Menges' on the extent of the US stake in the turmoil in Central America. Lowenthal does not assess that stake to be "very major." However, he explains why "Latin America may ultimately count a lot more in the 1980s than it has in the past, not for the old reasons, but rather these countries increasingly affect issues which are likely to be central to American foreign policy . . ."

7154 U.S. influence in Latin America in the 1980s. Edited by Robert Wesson. New York: Praeger; Stanford, Calif.: Hoover In-

stitution Press, Stanford University, 1982. 242 p.: bibl., index (Politics in Latin America)

Essays on US relations with Chile (Paul Sigmund); Argentina (Kenneth Johnson); Brazil (Robert Wesson); Venezuela (David Blank); Columbia (David Premo); Panama (Steve Ropp); Nicaragua (Charles Ameringer); El Salvador (Thomas Anderson); Mexico (Martin Needler); and Cuba (Edward González). Interesting collection even if "influence" concept around which the volume is organized is more hindrance than help. Wesson concludes that US influence is considerable on more important matters, while Latin Americans assert their independence on lesser ones.

7155 Urquidi, Víctor L.; Vicente Sánchez; and Eduardo Terrazas. Latin America and world problems: prospects and alternatives (SAGE/JIAS, 24:1, Feb. 1982, p. 3–36)

Outlines central world problems today: food, energy, environmental pollution, etc., and characteristics of Latin American civilization in this context. Acknowledges situation varies according to country but concludes pessimistically: "social efforts have . . . not led to the joining of those elements which, correctly integrated, could set Latin America on a new path of sustained development toward higher living standards, a better distribution of wealth, and increased mass participation."

7156 Vidal, Ernestina. Postura del Tercer Mundo en vísperas de una nueva reunión Norte-Sur (3er. Mundo y Economía Mundial [Centro de Estudios Económicos y Sociales del Tercer Mundo, México] 1:1, sept./dic. 1981, p. 153–181, tables)

Brief history of North-South negotiations (1974–79) and "Third World" positions at them. Includes lists and charts of the principal international organizations relevant to Southern demands for a New International Economic Order.

7157 Vigorito, Raúl. Economía agrícola y economía transnacional en América Latina: una evaluación. México: Instituto Latinoamericano de Estudios Transnacionales, 1980. 130, 26 leaves: bibl., ill.

Detailed, fairly technical study of involvement of Latin American agriculture in world economy and especially of transnational corporations' involvement in Latin American agriculture. Solid analysis, not tract, although Vigorito emphasizes that agricultural development should also benefit Latin American masses not merely corporations and elites.

Vólov, Boris. Centro de la latinoamericanística soviética. See item **4355.**

7158 Vuskovic, Pedro. La lucha del III Mundo y la aportación latinoamericana. México: Seminario Permanente sobre Latino América, 1978. 68 p.: bibl., ill. (Documento de trabajo; 12)

SEPLA sponsored paper surveys Latin America's stake in various aspects of proposed New International Economic Order. In author's view, Latin America must demonstrate "that the struggle for a New International Economic Order is expressed in the struggle for a new [socialist] political order."

7159 Wiarda, Howard J. Does Europe still stop at the Pyrenees? Or does Latin America begin there?: Iberia, Latin America, and the second enlargement of the European community. s.l.: American Enterprise Institute for Public Policy Research 198-? 47 p. (Occasional papers series; no. 2)

Analysis of the political transitions in Spain and Portugal and the implications for these two countries' international relations. To Wiarda, "it is clear that their futures lie, not with Africa or the Third World and not even so much in Latin America, but in Europe and with Europe, however uncomfortable that may be at times and despite some sacrifice of the Iberian nations' sense of 'distinctiveness'."

7160 Witnesses of hope: the persecution of Christians in Latin America. Edited by Martin Lange and Reinhold Iblacker. Foreword by Karl Rahner. Translated from the German by William E. Jerman. Maryknoll, N.Y.: Orbis Books, 1981. 156 p.: bibl., index.

Translation of *Christenverfolgung in Südamerika.* Useful survey of involvement of Church hierarchy, priests, nuns, and lay persons in efforts to help *campesinos,* poor in city slums, and Indians throughout Latin America, as well as the resulting persecution from governments and private groups. Some readers will find chapter titles like "Valiant Women" and "In the Hellhole of Torture" a little corny if accurate.

7161 Wolpin, Miles D. Contemporary radical Third World regimes: prospects

of their survival (IIDC/C, 30:3/4, 1980, p. 214–229, tables)

Interesting essay highlights three developments that first appeared in Latin America prior to WW II and later elsewhere in Third World: 1) communist led parties, trade unions, and mass organizations; 2) regimes espousing populism and economic nationalism ("radicalism"); and 3) attraction of radical socioeconomic policies to professional military. Finds that "the stability of state socialist as well as monopoly capitalist systems is immeasurably greater than that enjoyed by military or civilian radicals."

7162 Wood, Bryce. The end of the Good Neighbor Policy: changing patterns of US influence (FIU/CR, 11:2, Spring 1982, p. 25–27, 54)

Maintains that 1954 CIA-sponsored exile invasion that overthrew Arbenz regime in Guatemala represented end of at least central pledge of Roosevelt's Good Neighbor Policy—that US would never again intervene militarily in Latin America. Break with past was reaffirmed in 1962 Cuban Missile Crisis and in 1965 Dominican Republic intervention.

7163 Yakovlev, P. Washington and the militarization of Latin America (IA, 8, Aug. 1981, p. 73–79, tables)

Complains about US troops in Panama Canal Zone, Puerto Rico, and Bermuda. Alleges US is planning: 1) establishment of South Atlantic Treaty Organization (SATO) to include Southern Cone dictatorships and South Africa; and 2) creation of reactionary "continental legion," mobile international force to put down liberation movements.

7164 Zhirnov, Oleg and **Piotr Yakolev.** El átomo y la política: pt. 2 (URSS/AL, 40[40], 1981, p. 52–72)

Largely objective Soviet assessment of nuclear arms potential of Argentina and Brazil and the status of non-proliferation agreements, including Treaty of Tlatelolco. Closes with assertion that capitalist countries are contributing to the spread of nuclear weapons, while USSR is doing everything to control them.

7165 Zinovyev, N. Soviet economic links with Latin America (IA, 1, Jan. 1981, p. 100–107)

Discusses USSR's trade with Latin

America involving 25 countries by 1980. Notes establishment of inter-governmental trade commissions, most productive of which are Brazil's and Argentina's which ac-

counted for about 90 percent of Soviet-Latin American trade in 1980. Notes "artificial" barriers erected by US and other Western competitors.

MEXICO

7165a Arellano García, Carlos. La diplomacia y el comercio internacional. México: Editorial Porrúa, 1980. 222 p.: bibl.

UNAM international law professor analyzes patterns in Mexico's external trade and bilateral and multilateral relationships that affect it. Includes brief discussion of each significant bilateral trade treaty as well as Mexico's positions regarding GATT, UNCTAD, and Latin American economic integration.

7166 Arriaga, Patricia. Publicidad, economía y comunicación masiva: Estados Unidos y México. México: Centro de Estudios Económicos y Sociales del Tercer Mundo: Editorial Nueva Imagen, 1980. 324 p.: bibl., ill.

Marxist view of how the mass media advances capitalist interest in Mexico.

7167 Bagley, Bruce. Mexico in the 1980's: a new regional power (CUH, 80:469, Nov. 1981, p. 353–356)

Well written analysis of the changing nature of Mexican foreign policy. Bagley notes that "the decline of United States economic, political-ideological and military hegemony throughout Latin America . . . [in the 1970s] . . . has enabled Mexico to assume an independent role in hemispheric affairs."

Baird, Peter and **Ed McCaughan.** Beyond the border: Mexico & the U.S. today. See *HLAS 44:2145.*

Barker, Nancy Nichols. The French experience in Mexico, 1821–1861: a history of constant misunderstanding. See *HLAS 44:1988.*

7168 Bath, C. Richard. Health and environmental problems: the role of the border in El Paso-Ciudad Juárez coordination (SAGE/JIAS, 24:3, Aug. 1982, p. 375–392)

Uses example of health and environmental concerns affecting sister cities to show how, despite mutual recognition of cooperative action, politicians on both sides of

the border "remain enslaved to the concept of national sovereignty, and therefore are unable to divorce solution of problems from nationalistic goals and political priorities."

7169 Cárdenas, Héctor. Las relaciones mexicano-soviéticas: antecedentes y primeros contactos diplomáticos, 1789–1927. Prólogo, Roque González Salazar. México: Secretaría de Relaciones Exteriores, 1974. 93 p.: bibl., ill., index (Colección del Archivo Histórico Diplomático Mexicano; Serie Divulgación; 2)

Published on 50th anniversary of establishing diplomatic relations, book demonstrates importance of ties between USSR and Mexico. For the former, they symbolized acceptance of a government treated as a pariah by many nations; for the latter, they betokened independence, particularly of the US, which refused a visa to permit the first Soviet envoy to enter Mexico through its territory.

7170 Castañeda, Jorge. Special problems and a not-so-special relationship: Mexican foreign policy and the United States (in Mexico today. Edited by Tommie Sue Montgomery. Philadelphia: Institute for the Study of Human Issues, 1982, p. 127–138)

Former Foreign Minister challenges idea of a "special relationship" between US and Mexico, while insisting that "there is room for genuine interdependence in spite of the asymmetry of power." Candidly asserts that illegal immigration helps Mexico solve its unemployment problem and that Washington will not restrict entries lest instability occur below the Rio Grande.

7171 Cochrane, James D. Embajadores norteamericanos en México y embajadores mexicanos en Estados Unidos: características de sus carreras y experiencia profesional (CM/FI, 22:1, julio/sept. 1981, p. 90–105)

In period examined, US sent almost

twice as many career diplomats as ambassadors to Mexico than vice versa (64 percent compared to 38 percent). Mexico tends to dispatch administrative generalists (62 percent). US presidents prefer, after careerists, to appoint individuals with a "businessman/ party activist/ office-holder" background (36 percent).

7172 Cortés, Enrique. Relaciones entre México y Japón durante el Porfiriato. México: Secretaría de Relaciones Exteriores, 1980. 133 p.: bibl. (Archivo histórico diplomático mexicano. Cuarta época; no. 1)

During Porfirio Díaz's presidency, Mexico and Japan renewed relations that existed in colonial period. Mexico looked to Japan for hard-working, intelligent immigrants; Japan saw in Mexico a nation eager to recognize it as an equal, thereby countering the discrimination suffered at the hands of other Western countries. While little trade or immigration occurred, both got along harmoniously during the *Porfiriato*. Excellent study (for historian's comment, see *HLAS 44:2018*).

7173 Craig, Richard. Operación intercepción: una política de presión internacional (CM/FI, 22:2, oct./dic. 1981, p. 203–230)

Thoroughly discusses Nixon administration's attack on drug traffic at Río Grande. While spurring Mexican officials to action, "Operación Intercepción" is described as myopic venture that chilled economic activity at border, offended Mexican sovereignty, and embittered bilateral relations. State Department flogged for not heading off what almost became *"un gran desastre diplomático."*

7174 Ehrlich, Paul R.; Loy Bilderback; and Anne H. Ehrlich. The golden door: international migration, Mexico, and the United States. s.l.: Wideview Books, 1981. 402 p.: bibl.; index.

Sensibly proposes that immigration laws be fashioned within framework of "explicit national population policy." However, other assertions are highly questionable or fly in the face of evidence (e.g., illegal aliens don't take jobs away from Americans "in significant numbers;" "public concern over illegal immigration from Mexico can be traced to bigot scare tactics, bureaucrats, and *Leyenda Negra* . . .;" many in US "seem to

want a relationship that is based on needs of Americans with no regard for the needs of Mexico and Mexicans." Colorful writing, woolly-headed conclusions (for historian's comment, see *HLAS 44:2172*).

7175 Enríquez, Ernesto. El tratado entre México y los Estados Unidos de América sobre ríos internacionales: una lucha nacional de noventa años. pt. 1, La historia. pt. 2, La tesis jurídica. México: Universidad Nacional Autónoma de México, 1975–1976. 2 v.: bibl., indexes, maps (Serie Estudios - Facultad de Ciencias Políticas y Sociales; 47–48)

Exhaustive study of US-Mexican negotiations over rivers whose waters are crucial to both nations. Written by key Mexican negotiator, book covers subject from colonial period through World War I. Strictly for the specialist.

7176 Genaro Estrada, diplomático y escritor. Presentación de Santiago Roel. Tlatelolco, México: Secretaría de Relaciones Exteriores, 1978. 190 p.: bibl., ports (Colección del archivo histórico diplomático mexicano. Tercera época. Obras monográficas; 10)

Speeches, diplomatic texts, poems, articles commemorating the career of one of Mexico's most prominent diplomats.

7177 Guerra Maram, Martí. The media and the undocumented immigrant (PCCLAS/P, 8, 1981/1982, p. 143–152)

Author concludes from content analysis of *New York Times* and seven major Southwest dailies that the press, with occasional exception of *Los Angeles Times*, ignored scholarly research as it distorts both the number of illegal aliens in US and their use of social services.

7178 Hamilton, William H. Trajectory towards crisis in United States-Mexican border relations (PCCLAS/P, 7, 1980/1981, p. 83–108, tables)

Explains breakdown in continuity of Mexico's postwar socioeconomic and political success in mid-1970s by failure of economic growth to match rising expectations and paradoxical effect of modernization which led to greater external penetration of Mexican institutions. Predictably, US-Mexican border area is seen as ripe for increased commercial, social, and political activity in 1980s.

7179 Hewlett, Sylvia Ann. Coping with illegal immigrants (CFR/FA, 60:2, Winter 1981/1982, p. 358–378)

Good discussion of illegal immigration, continuing policy debate, and reasons why it has been so difficult for Congress to enact "reforms" (e.g., complicated problem, "scrambled" political coalitions in US relations with Mexico). Assumes too easily desirability of immigration curbs and that beneficiaries would be US's poor and unemployed. [Y.H. Ferguson]

7180 Hodara, Jorge. ¿Hacia la finlandización de México? (Vuelta [México] 5:51, feb. 1981, p. 19–23)

Bizarre thesis that oil purchases and control of information will facilitate Mexico's "Finlandization" by US, permission for which was granted by Soviets when they invaded Afghanistan.

Hoernel, David. Las grandes corporaciones y la política del gran garrote en Cuba y en México. See HLAS 44:2199.

7181 Jamail, Milton H. and **Stephen P. Mumme.** The International Boundary and Water Commission as a conflict management agency in the U.S.-Mexico borderlands (The Social Science Journal [The Western Social Science Association, Colorado State University, Ft. Collins] 19:1, Jan. 1982, p. 45–62, tables)

Traces Commission's evolution. Relied on brokerage, ad hoc diplomacy, expertise and politics, and exclusive jurisdiction in resolving technical disputes at US-Mexican border. Commission increasingly faces new, highly political problems that defy easy solution. Competent study of an organization that forms bulwark of now tarnished "special relationship" between both countries.

7182 James, Daniel. Mexico: America's newest problem? (The Washington Quarterly [Transaction Periodicals Consortium, Washington] 3:3, Summer 1980, p. 87–105)

Paints grim picture of Central America and Caribbean going to the Communists, and argues Mexico is key to area. Recommends Washington's policies toward Mexico get top priority. [Y.H. Ferguson]

7183 JLP, por un nuevo orden mundial: memoria de la gira por Francia, Alemania Federal, Suecia y Canadá, mayo de 1980. México: Estados Unidos Mexicanos, Coordinación General de Comunicación Social, between 1980 and 1982. 302 p.: ill.

Documents relating to President López Portillo's May 1980 visit to Europe and Canada, purpose of which was to diversify his nation's economic relations and, thereby, reduce dependence on US.

Kane, N. Stephen. The United States and the development of the Mexican petroleum industry, 1945–1950: a lost opportunity. See HLAS 44:2208.

7184 Katz, Friedrich. The secret war in Mexico: Europe, the United States, and the Mexican Revolution. With portions translated by Loren Goldner. Chicago: University of Chicago Press, 1981. 659 p.: bibl., index.

"Secret War" refers not to spies in trenchcoats but to 20th-century strategy of alliances and accords that major powers and business interests fashioned in response to Third World revolutions. US led way by siding with nationalist forces against Spain in Cuba. In Mexico, powers employed diverse methods: direct and indirect military intervention, economic and diplomatic pressures, playing off of one faction against another, and destabilization. "The turbulent setting in which these events took place makes Mexico a case study not only of how local rifts can be exploited for global ends, but how global rifts can be exploited for local ends." Masterful study.

Lamar, Curt. Genesis of Mexican-United States diplomacy: a critical analysis of the Alaman-Poinsett confrontation, 1825. See HLAS 45:2057.

Lander, Ernest McPherson, Jr. Reluctant imperialists: Calhoun, the South Carolinians, and the Mexican War. See HLAS 44:2058.

7185 López Portillo, José. Discurso pronunciado por José López Portillo, Presidente Constitucional de los Estados Unidos Mexicanos, ante la Asamblea General de las Naciones Unidas en su XXIV período de sesiones. Address by José López Portillo, President of Mexico, at the thirty-fourth session of the United Nations General Assembly. México: Estados Unidos Mexicanos, Presidencia de la República, Coordinación General de Comunicación Social, between 1979 and 1981. 77 p.

Former President López Portillo's Sept. 1979 proposal to the UN General Assembly, urging cooperation between oil-producing and oil-consuming nations for the rational use, conservation, price regulation, and substitution of the world's nonrenewable energy resources. Conservative and radical Arab members of OPEC joined to quash this highly vaunted plan.

7186 ———. En la India. México: Secretaría de Programación y Presupuesto, Subsecretaría de Evaluación, Dirección General de Documentación y Análisis, 1981. 86 p. (Cuadernos de filosofía política; no. 46 [feb. 1981])

In interviews and speeches during a 1981 visit to India, López Portillo publicized and proposed Cancún Summit, urged a resumption of the North-South dialogue, and lobbied for his World Energy Plan. In seeking multilateral external solutions to problems plaguing the Third World, the Mexican chief executive ignored unilateral steps that might be taken at home to promote economic development and social justice.

7187 Lupsha, Peter A. Drug trafficking: Mexico and Colombia in comparative perspective (CU/JIA, 35:1, Spring/Summer 1981, p. 95–115, tables)

Intriguing comparison of Mexican and Colombian cases yields lessons that antidrug campaigns are likely to succeed only if they have strong government support in the producing country, and that governments have the capacity to make their wills felt to any substantial degree. Conditions were right in Mexico but not in Colombia.

7188 Mares, David R. Mexico y Estados Unidos: el vínculo entre el comercio agrícola y la nueva relación energética (CM/FI, 22:1, julio/sept. 1981, p. 1-21, tables)

Scant documentation offered for intuitively appealing thesis that President Carter pressured the Commerce and Treasury Depts. to decide tomato dumping suits, brought by Florida producers, in favor of Mexico to enhance US access to that exporter's oil and gas.

7189 Martínez de la Vega, Francisco. México reafirma su más noble tradición (CAM, 225:4, julio/agosto 1979, p. 7-13)

Reflections on government's decision to recognize friendship with Castro and to break relations with Somoza. Such actions show that Mexico is able to stand alone. [R.E. Greenleaf]

7190 ———. Tormentos sobre México: religión y petróleo (CAM, 223:2, marzo/abril 1979, p. 7–14)

Discusses consequences of visits to Mexico of Pope John Paul II and President Jimmy Carter. Former created a move to recover the Church's political losses. Latter opened new possibilities for improved relations with US. Text of speech by López Portillo during Carter's visit appears in same volume (p. 15–17). [R.E. Greenleaf]

7191 Mexico and the United States. Englewood Cliffs, N.J.: Prentice-Hall, 1981. 197 p.: ill., index (A Spectrum book)

Carefully edited collection by distinguished former American ambassador to Mexico, springs from 1980 American Assembly conference on bilateral relations. Most interesting of eight essays is by Guido Belssasso, who offers fascinating (and alarming) insights into illegal immigration from Mexico's perspective.

7192 Mexico-United States relations. Edited by Susan Kaufman Purcell. New York: Academy of Political Science, 1981. 213 p.: bibl., index (Proceedings of the Academy of Political Science, 0065–0684; v. 34, no. 1)

One of the most distinguished students of Latin American affairs has edited a solid volume of essays that provides both US and Mexican perspectives on trade, energy, foreign capital, bilateral economic cooperation, and other key issues.

O'Brien, Dennis J. Petróleo e intervención: relaciones entre los Estados Unidos y México. See *HLAS 44:2240*.

7193 Ojeda Gómez, Mario. The structural context of U.S.-Mexican relations (*in* Mexico today. Edited by Tommie Sue Montgomery. Philadelphia: Institute for the Study of Human Issues, 1982, p. 109–114)

Mexican political scientist concludes that structure of bilateral relations (contiguity, asymmetry of power, economic and technological dependence) prevents Mexico's negotiating "on an equal basis with the United States and . . . makes it difficult . . . to resist unilateral decisions made in Washington."

7194 Olliff, Donathon C. Reforma Mexico and the United States: a search for alternatives to annexation, 1854–1861. University: University of Alabama Press, 1981. 213 p.: bibl., index.

Makes strong case for willingness of Mexico's Liberals, who greatly admired their powerful neighbors political, economic, and social institutions (except slavery), to give US an economic protectorate over their country in 1850s. Blame for failure of such special relationship to materialize rests largely with President Buchanan, who had little understanding of economic and commercial objectives.

7195 Olloqui y Labastida, José Juan de. México fuera de México. México: Universidad Nacional Autónoma de México, Coordinación de Humanidades, 1980. 236 p.: bibl.

Potpourri of speeches on Mexican foreign relations by one of that country's most distinguished ambassadors to US.

7196 Paz, Octavio. Mexico and the United States: positions and counterpositions (*in* Mexico today. Edited by Tommie Sue Montgomery. Philadelphia: Institute for the Study of Human Issues, 1982, p. 1-21)

Even those who disagree with some of Paz's philosophical assumptions will find this a rich and enriching essay by first-rate intellectual. Reminds us of two different cultural traditions. Mexico: Islam, Spain which championed Counter Reformation, Spanish conquest and evangelization of sedentary Indians, forging of *mestizo* society, veneration of leisure, and emphasis on the past influenced. US: England where Reformation triumphed, Enlightenment, colonization, extermination (or confining to reservations) of nomadic Indians, faith in redemptive value of work, and orientation toward future.

7197 Pellicer de Brody, Olga. Mexico's relations with the Third World: experiences and perspectives (*in* Mexico today. Edited by Tommie Sue Montgomery. Philadelphia: Institute for the Study of Human Issues, 1982, p. 103–108)

Eminent Mexican political scientist contends that coordination with Third World nations both immunizes her country from US commercial policies inimical to Mexican exports and helps Mexico obtain "the most convenient prices" for its oil. Post-

publication changes in world economic conditions cast doubt on the accuracy of these assertions.

7198 Philip, George. Mexican oil and gas: the politics of a new resource (RIIA/IA, 56:3, Summer 1980, p. 474–483)

Description of Mexican hydrocarbon policy with emphasis on the significance for the national economy. Most of the premises and conclusions are no longer relevant because of the shift from a seller's to a buyer's market for oil.

7199 Redclift, Michael and Nannecke Redclift. Unholy alliance (FP, 41, Winter 1980/1981, p. 111-133)

Important article stresses impact that US policy can have on Mexico's selection of alternative development strategies. Traditional strategy, followed in first half of López Portillo's *sexenio*, yields agricultural stagnation, food imports, capital-intensive industry, continued emigration, political oppression, and profligate use of oil. A more enlightened strategy, followed late in López Portillo's term, promotes job creation, expanded market, broader political participation, and energy conservation.

7200 Las Relaciones México-Estados Unidos. David Barkin, Gustavo Esteva, Marcos Kaplan, *et al.* México: Universidad Nacional Autónoma de México: Editorial Nueva Imagen, 1980–. 1 v.: bibl., ill.

Distinguished intellectuals in Mexico offer their views, redolent of Marxism and/or nationalism, on energy, migration, trade, entry into the GATT. Especially provocative, though far-fetched, is Israel Galán's brief commentary on how Chicanos can prove a powerful Mexican ally within the imperialist USA.

7201 Rodríguez Aviñoá, Pastora. La prensa nacional frente a la intervención de México en la Segunda Guerra Mundial (CM/HM, 29:2, oct./dic. 1979, p. 252–300)

Deftly organized study of Mexico's press and public opinion with respect to that country's participation in World War II. Reveals how presidents below the Río Grande, like their North American counterparts, use the media to manipulate their people's attitudes on key issues.

7202 Romero Castilla, Alfredo. In search of a discipline: the development of the field of international relations (IDE/DE, 19:3, Sept. 1981, p. 255–270)

Tightly organized discussion of how a traditional orientation has given way to a scientific approach in the study of international relations in Mexico. Useful window through which to view Mexican scholarly activity in this important field.

7203 Sandos, James A. Pancho Villa and American security: Woodrow Wilson's Mexican diplomacy reconsidered (JLAS, 13:2, Nov. 1981, p. 292–311)

Author offers original thesis that origins of Woodrow Wilson's Versailles diplomacy are to be found in Gen. Pershing's 1916 Punitive Expedition against Pancho Villa. Somewhat analogous to his strategy with Mexico, the US President "sought both to reintegrate a democratized, post-war Germany into 'a new non-revolutionary community of liberal nation-states,' and to prevent, by punishment if necessary, radical revolution in that country."

Schoonover, Thomas. Anteproyecto de Thomas Corwin para un tratado comercial en 1861. See *HLAS 44:2107.*

————. Misconstrued mission: expansionism and black colonization in Mexico and Central America during the Civil War. See *HLAS 44:2108.*

7204 Tambs, Lewis A. and **Thomas Aranda, Jr.** Cooperation or confrontation?: a view from the border (*in* Mexico 2000: a look at the problems and potential of modern Mexico. Washington: Council for Inter-American Security, 1980, p. 55–65, ill.)

Brimming with hyperbole, conjecture, clichés, and inaccuracies, essay reveals how Southwest "frontline" or border states can influence US foreign affairs by developing their own policies toward Mexico. Few will take seriously the specific options offered for "confrontation or cooperation."

7205 Truett, Dale B. and **Lila Flory Truett.** Mexico and GSP: problems and prospects (IAMEA, 34:2, Autumn 1980, p. 67–85, tables)

Analysis of Mexico's experience with the US Generalized System of Preferences (GSP), which leads to a conclusion regarding the need for a special bilateral US-Mexico trade policy. The Truetts argue that it is unlikely that GSP in its present form will stimulate the growth of Mexican exports of nontraditional goods.

7206 Trujillo Herrera, Rafael. Patriot in profile: De la Huerta and the Bucareli Treaties. Translated from the Spanish by Marcelino Delgado y Vela. Hawthorne, Calif.: Omni Publications, 1981. 221 p.: bibl., ill., index.

Learned, flattering, though uneven biography of provisional president who resolutely opposed the attachment of preconditions to US recognition of the Mexican government that emerged after promulgation of the 1917 Constitution. Betrayal of this principle by Obregón and subsequent attenuation of Mexican sovereignty over its minerals precipitated De la Huerta's resignation from the cabinet. Offers glimpse of pervasive influence and unscrupulous resourcefulness of transnational oil companies.

7207 U.S.-Mexican energy relationships: realities and prospects. Edited by Jerry R. Ladman, Deborah J. Baldwin, Elihu Bergman. Lexington, Mass.: Lexington Books, 1981. 237 p.: bibl., ill., index.

Poorly edited volume springs from Dec. 1979 conference at Arizona State University. Although many selections are outdated because of collapse of seller's market for oil and Mexico's economic malaise, essays on PEMEX (Sepúlveda) and Mexican oil policy in the late 1970s (Randall) are valuable.

7208 U.S. policies toward Mexico: perceptions and perspectives. Edited by Richard D. Erb and Stanley R. Ross. Washington: American Enterprise Institute for Public Policy Research, 1979. 56 p.: bibl. (AEI symposia; 79H)

Ross offers a brief and helpful history of US Mexican relations but contributors to this pamphlet have articulated their views more fully in other publications.

7209 United States relations with Mexico: context and content. Edited by Richard D. Erb and Stanley R. Ross. Washington: American Enterprise Institute for Public Policy Research, 1981. 291 p.: bibl.

Editors have divided this rather good collection on US-Mexican relations among contrived categories of "context," "content," and "Mexican Development." Nonetheless, this book, which contains essays by a dozen highly respected scholars and government officials, should be in the library of every serious student of Mexican politics or bilateral affairs.

7210 *United States Views on Mexico.* A quarterly review of opinion from the United States press. Banamex Cultural Foundation. Vol. 3, No. 2, 2. quarter 1982– . Washington.

Compendium of articles published in American newspapers on US-Mexican affairs in first quarter of 1982. Political, economic and social/civic issues are treated as separate sections useful for research on contemporary issues.

7211 Villar, Samuel I. del. A Mexican-U.S. energy market: the conflict of interests (*in* Mexico today. Edited by Tommie Sue Montgomery. Philadelphia: Institute for the Study of Human Issues, 1982, p. 121–126)

Demonstrates how truth may be submerged in murky waters of extreme nationalist, anti-Yankee sentiment. Villar fails to define what he means by "Mexican-U.S. energy market," asserts without evidence that: 1) US conservation programs have been ineffective; 2) US increasingly relies on foreign energy sources; 3) US sought to freeze price of imports from Mexico; and 4) Senator Adlai Stevenson and Energy Secretary James Schlesinger attempted to coerce the Mexican government over gas prices.

Wolff, Thomas. Mexican-Guatemalan imbroglio: fishery rights and national honor. See *HLAS 44:2287.*

CENTRAL AMERICA

7212 Alegría, Claribel. "Aldeas estratégicas" en Honduras (Nicaráuac [Revista del Ministerio de Cultura, Managua], 3 : 7, junio 1982, p. 125–129, plates)

Impressions on wretched conditions prevailing in Honduran camps for Salvadoran refugees under Paz García presidency. Alleges that Visión Mundial, a charitable organization, collects information for Honduran Army's intelligence service. Also decries "scandal" of 6,000 former *Somocista* National Guardsmen poised to raid Nicaragua from these border camps.

7213 Anderson, Thomas P. The war of the dispossessed: Honduras and El Salvador, 1969. Lincoln: University of Nebraska Press, 1981. 203 p.: bibl., index, maps.

Excellent analysis of 1969 "Soccer War" based largely on field research, travel in war zone, extensive interviews with leading participants, and access to classified materials in both foreign ministries. Emphasizes economic and sociopolitical conditions that led to war rather than its aftermath. Concludes present civil strife in El Salvador derives from war because it "turned country upon itself" and "problems of population and subsistence . . . burst into the open" as terrorism. Honduras, on the other hand, benefited economically by having to seek new sources of imports and exports outside of CACM. [Y.H. Ferguson]

7214 Armijo, Roberto. Problemas actuales en la lucha por la soberanía (Nicaráuac [Revista del Ministerio de Cultura, Managua] 3 : 7, junio 1982, p. 111-120, plates)

Salvadoran writer's *cri de coeur* for independence of his and sister republics from US imperialism. Interesting less for the coherence or logic of its thesis than for its passionate, poetic devotion to following the Sandinista path toward national sovereignty.

7215 Berryman, Phillip. Another view of El Salvador (DIS, Summer 1982, p. 352–359)

Sharp critique of Gabriel Zaid's provocative analysis of Salvadoran politics (item 7266) which he terms "a confused and confusing polemic."

7216 Black, George; Judy Butler; and Jaime Diez. Target Nicaragua (NACLA/LAER, 16:1, Jan./Feb. 1982, p. 2–45, bibl., ill., maps)

Detailed, lively written report that invokes images of a new Vietnam in warning of possible massive US intervention in Central America. "If de-escalation and negotiation are the best realistic hope, what is the worst nightmare? . . . Like Dr. Strangelove with a fiendish vision and his gloved finger on the doomsday button, the Administration has all the elements in place to unleash war."

7217 Bouchey, L. Francis. Reagan policy: global chess or local crap shooting? (FIU/RC, 11:2, Spring 1982, p. 20–23, ill., plate)

Bemoans administration's poorly presented case concerning nature and extent of "Nicaragua's and Cuba's connection to violence in El Salvador." Fears States could end up as "guarantor of a communist regime in Nicaragua" agreeing to squelch campaign against Sandinistas in return for their halting aid to El Salvador's left. [Y.H. Ferguson]

7218 ———— and Alberto M. Piedra. Guatemala, a promise in peril. Washington: Council for Inter-American Security, 1980. 91 p.: bibl.

Rightwing authors scorn human rights emphasis of Carter years and urge US support for Guatemala where "the promise of evolution instead of revolution . . . [is] rapidly diminishing in the wake of externally-induced destabilization and attendant internal polarization."

7219 Bourgois, Philippe. What U.S. foreign policy faces in rural El Salvador: an eyewitness account (MR, 34:1, May 1982, p. 14–30, bibl.)

After spending two weeks in guerrilla controlled territory, author concludes that "U.S. leaders are victims of their own propaganda." Specifically, they ignore indigenous support enjoyed by insurgents and treat revolutions as "plots masterminded— or at least manipulated—by a clique in the Kremlin."

7220 Brandt, Willy. Nuevas perspectivas para América Latina (NSO, 45, nov./dic. 1979, p. 72–76, ill.)

Nicaraguan revolution raises hopes for continued march of democracy and social progress in Latin America. Socialist International and especially Germany's Social Democrats offer support for constructive change and just New International Economic Order.

7221 Burbach, Roger. Central America: the end of U.S. hegemony? (MR, 33:8, Jan. 1982, p. 1–18)

US imperialism, weakened by global crisis of capitalism, will not succeed against popular movements in Central America that

boast widespread support. Pressures from allies and domestic interest groups militate against armed intervention by US which must recognize that "the imperial order of an earlier era can no longer be restored."

7222 ————. Rereading Haig's secret documents (Mother Jones [Foundation for National Progress, San Francisco, Calif.] 6 : 5, June 1981, p. 32–33, ill.)

Brief rebuttal of the Reagan administration's charge, as outlined in special white paper on El Salvador, that this country is being subjected to "indirect armed aggression by Communist powers." Calls Salvadoran conflict "an indigenous war of national liberation."

7223 Bushnell, John A. U.S. policy toward Central America: sustaining a responsible middle course (FPRI/O, 26:2, Summer 1982, p. 305–311)

Senior State Department adviser puts best face possible on Reagan administration's "responsible middle course" in relations with Central America.

7224 Carlsson, A. Vernt. Democracia; violencia; socialismo (NSO, 43, julio/agosto 1979, p. 107–115, ill., tables)

Socialist International's Secretary General discusses Nicaraguan revolution positively viewed in 1979, expresses his organization's support for twin goals of democracy and socialism, and defends his organization from charges (e.g., from Juan Bosch) that it is actually an agent of imperialism.

7225 Central America, international dimensions of the crisis. Edited by Richard E. Feinberg. New York: Holmes & Meier, 1982. 280 p.: bibl., index, map.

Editor does an exceptional job of assembling well written and perceptive essays on domestic and international factors influencing this strife-torn region. Book will become standard reference for politics of the area.

Chávez Alfaro, Lizandro. Identidad y resistencia del "criollo" en Nicaragua. See *HLAS 44:2392.*

7226 Child, Jack. U.S. policy toward Central America: abstention or intervention? (FPRI/O, 26:2, Summer 1982, p. 311–317)

Offers alternatives to US abstention or intervention in El Salvador. Through "positive abstention" or the Zimbabwe solution, Washington would stand aside as Mexico, Venezuela, Canada, or other third parties presided over peace-keeping and negotiations. "Conditioned intervention" would involve substantial US aid as a levee to strengthen the center and promote human rights.

7227 Dédalo, Hernán. América Central y el Caribe en crisis (CRIT, 55:1877, marzo 1982, p. 85–91)

Following overview of Central America's history and problems, advocates "common hemispheric policy" for strife-torn region to thwart outside intervention. Clichés complement this proposal.

7228 Domínguez, Jorge I. Estados Unidos y Centroamérica (Vuelta [México] 5:51, feb. 1981, p. 6–18)

US security interests require that Latin American nations be brought into evolving relationship with US, OECD countries, and emerging industrial nations of Far East. Certain US policies—commercial protectionism, tough approach toward immigration, and aggressive quest for Mexican and Venezuelan oil—threaten collective cooperation.

7229 Dossier: El Salvador, vers une solution négociée? la déclaration franco-mexicaine et les réactions internationales (FDD/NED [Problèmes d'Amérique Latine, 62] 4649/4650, 28 déc. 1981, p. 177–195)

Scholars and policymakers will benefit from this chronology of events preceding Aug. 1981 Franco-Mexican Communiqué on El Salvador and the text of this and related declarations. Meticulously prepared.

7230 Ebel, Roland H. Political instability in Central America (CUH, 81:472, Feb. 1982, p. 56–59, 86)

Cogent analysis of how economic development in Central America has produced new power contenders, including peasants, bureaucrats, and blue-collar workers. Failure of urban elites, now a "beleaguered minority" rife with internal divisions, to redistribute resources among and encourage political participation by newly mobilized groups has nourished guerrilla movements throughout region.

7231 Enders, Thomas O. The Central American challenge (AEI Foreign Policy [American Enterprise Institute for Public

Policy Research, Washington] 4:2, 1982, p. 8–12)

Succinct rationale for Reagan administration's economic and military assistance to Central America emphasizes: 1) economic dislocations suffered by region in 1970s; 2) Cuba's increased aggressiveness; and 3) Nicaragua's role as a platform for intervention against its neighbors.

7232 Escobar Betancourt, Rómulo. La revolución panameña y su ventana al mundo (LNB/L, 305/309:1, agosto/dic. 1981, p. 273–297)

Reveals eclectic interests of Gen. Omar Torrijos who befriended John Wayne and Gabriel García Márquez, lobbied in behalf of Belize and the Polisario Front, negotiated new Panama Canal treaties, and still found time to express his political thoughts in such epigrams as "Cada pueblo tiene su propia aspirina para su particular dolar de cabeza."

7233 Giovanni, Cleto di, Jr. and Alexander Kruger. Central America (The Washington Quarterly [Transaction Periodicals Consortium, Washington] 3:3, Summer 1980, p. 175–186)

Former CIA officer Giovanni and Venezuelan businessman Kruger offer shockingly simplistic "solutions" to problems of Central America. US government should strongly support Guatemala as region's "stabilizing force," back larger role for private sector in El Salvador, and work for "removal of the Nicaraguan Communist government."

7233a Guy, Jim. Guatemala on the Brink (International Perspectives [The Canadian Journal of World Affairs, Department of External Affairs, Ottawa, Ontario] 1, Sept./ Oct. 1982, p. 26–29)

Article heavy on description and light on analysis which emphasizes structured terrorism practiced by Guatemalan regime whose detractors frequently suffer a "Kafkaesque fate." Criticizes Reagan's Caribbean Basin Initiative as "designed to serve US strategic interests . . . to secure a safe environment for private investment."

7234 Immerman, Richard H. The CIA in Guatemala: the foreign policy of intervention. Austin: University of Texas Press, 1982. 291 p.: bibl., index (The Texas Pan American series)

Thoroughly documented account of how US is reaping bitter harvest sown by CIA-inspired overthrow of Jacobo Arbenz, who may have been Guatemala's last best hope for modernization.

7235 Jenkins, Loren. Tegucigalpa: Honduras on the edge (The Atlantic [The Atlantic Monthly Co., Boston, Mass.] 250:2, Aug. 1982, p. 16–20)

Shared poverty and widespread land ownership have militated against a social upheaval in Honduras. US efforts to build up military may serve to weaken a nascent democratic government and draw this nation of 3.7 million people into the maelstrom afflicting Central America.

7236 Jonas, Susanne Bodenheimer. Guatemala: plan piloto para el continente. San José: Editorial Universitaria Centroamericana, 1981. 430 p., map, tables.

Reviews US policy toward Guatemala from Arévalo's overthrow through mid-1970s. Gist is that Washington's efforts to snuff out political and socioeconomic progress in Guatemala continued after 1954 counterrevolution and served as prototype for US posture towards change throughout Latin America generally. [Y.H. Ferguson]

7237 Koroliov, Yuri. El Salvador: the "hot spot" in Latin America (IA, 6, June 1981, p. 58–66)

Representative of Soviet line on Central America; namely, that Moscow is "siding with the heroic struggle of the [Salvadoran] people . . . for their liberation" from US imperialism.

7238 Kotz, Nick and **Morton Kondracke.** How to avoid another Cuba (The New Republic [Washington] 184:25, 20 June 1981, p. 19–23, map)

Vintage liberal prescription for US policy vis-à-vis Nicaragua; namely, dialogue with the Sandinistas, close cooperation with moderates, a sharp eye on human rights, and—above all—military restraint. This strategy—roughly analogous to that pursued with Portugal after the 1974 revolution—has failed to slow Nicaragua's slide toward authoritarianism.

7239 LaFeber, Walter. Inevitable revolutions (The Atlantic [The Atlantic Monthly Co., Boston, Mass.] 249:6, June 1982, p. 74–83, ill.)

Challenges assumption, indulged in by Reagan administration, that the larger the economic growth "the happier the nation . . ." Gross income inequities spawn revolutions which the US, short of occupying the three nations, cannot prevent in Nicaragua, El Salvador, and Guatemala.

7240 LeoGrande, William M. and **Carla Anne Robbins.** Oligarchs and officers: the crisis in El Salvador (CFR/RA, 48:5, Summer 1980, p. 1084–1103)

Just as Alliance for Progress dies of schizophrenia, so contradictory goals of development and security strain US Central American policy. El Salvador's government cannot carry out both reform and repression. Will Latin American nations manage to promote stability by fashioning democratic political systems that enable the Left to come in from the cold?

7241 Losev, S. A new life for Nicaragua (IA, 2, 1981, p. 114–120)

Paean to Sandinista Revolution by Soviet journalist who stresses that relations between his country and Nicaragua "are steadily growing stronger."

7242 Menges, Constantine. Central America and its enemies (AJC/C, 72:2, Aug. 1981, p. 32–38)

Adviser to Reagan administration incisively attributes support of social democratic parties and Mexico's PRI for Cuba and Central American revolutionaries to: 1) influence of their radical-leftist factions; 2) Third World view that emphasizes anti-imperialism and nationalism over democracy; 3) quest for domestic social peace and greater international influence; and 4) desire to weaken Christian Democrats and other rivals. Savages naiveté of social democrats, while advocating US policy of foreign aid, support for middle sectors, and neutralization of Left's "terrorist networks."

7243 Millett, Richard. Can we live with revolution in Central America? (FIU/CR, 10:1, Winter 191, p. 6–9, 53, ill.)

Perceptive summary of Carter administration's frustrations in developing Central American policy. Sees scant hope for US success in area, while "risks of failure, embarrassment and even humiliation will grow in direct proportion to the extent of American committments (sic) to maintaining . . . the image of regional hegemony."

7244 Mount, Graeme S. Isthmian approaches: the contextual trajectory of Canadian-Panamanian relations (UPR/CS, 20:2, June 1980, p. 49–60, tables)

Examines importance of Panama to Canadians from 1958 era of British Columbia gold rush to conclusion of 1979 US-Panama treaty integrating Canal Zone with Republic of Panama.

7245 Nikiforova, N. Costa Rica: a country at the crossroads (RIIA/IA, 10, Oct. 1981, p. 113–119)

Soviet view of current economic, political, and social status of Costa Rica. Predictably attacks CIA and US-based multinational corporations, and insists upon "resurgence of sharp class clashes."

7246 Novak, Michael. U.S. policy toward Central America: El Salvador; rule by ballot (FPRI/O, 26:2, Summer 1982, p. 317–322)

Strong endorsement of electoral process begun in El Salvador. Central to Novak's argument is provocative, though questionable, Venezuelan analogy; that is, just as guerrillas were drawn into elections in strife-torn Venezuela in 1960s so may they trade bullets for ballots in El Salvador in 1980s.

7247 Olguín, Alexandr. Los acontecimientos en El Salvador según interpretación de Pekín (URSS/AL, 10:46, 1981, p. 4-11)

Soviet political scientist lambasts China as "counter-revolutionary" and "pro-imperialist" because Peking deplores not only US intervention in El Salvador but also the "meddling of the USSR and Cuba."

7248 Ozores, Carlos. Omar Torrijos y sus proyecciones en la política internacional (LNB/L, 305/309:1, agosto/dic. 1981, p. 267–272)

Rhapsodical tribute to Torrijo's internationalization of formerly bilateral issue, sovereignty over Panama Canal. By taking his message to other countries, joining Nonaligned Movement, forging diplomatic relations with Cuba, the flamboyant general mobilized support for Panama's cause, while demonstrating its independence of Uncle Sam. No mention of President Carter's willingness to bite the political bullet and sign new treaties.

7249 Pastor, Robert A. Our real interests in Central America (The Atlantic Atlantic Monthly Co., Boston, Mass.] 250:1, July 1982, p. 27–39, ill.)

Highly respected Latin Americanist questions alleged "national interests" animating the Reagan administration's strategy toward Central America. Drawing on experience on Panama Canal treaties, argues for negotiation over confrontation, flexibility over rigidity, and reciprocity over unilateralism to enhance US legitimacy and influence in area.

7250 Pike, Fredrick B. Views from the campus on the Salvadoran issue (IAMEA, 36:1, Summer 1982, p. 3-11)

Current US policy toward El Salvador, claims Pike, best serves our country's security and the national interests of the Salvadoran people. Campus opposition to Washington's policies "rest often on vastly oversimplified assumptions . . ."

7251 Prosterman, Roy L.; Jeffrey M. Riedinger; and Mary N. Temple. Land reform in El Salvador: the democratic alternative (APS/WA, 144:1, Summer 1981, p. 36–54)

To avert breakdown of March 1980 Salvadoran agrarian reform, termed "Latin America's most radical," these specialists prudently recommend: 1) prompt issuance of titles to ex-tenants; 2) dispatch of US technicians experienced in land-to-the-tiller operations; 3) military protection of land recipients; 4) speedy compensation to former owners; 5) conferral of titles on cooperatives now running large estates; and 6) adoption of compromise to benefit landless peasants working on farms of 250 to 1,235 acres.

7252 Purcell, Susan Kaufman. U.S. policy toward Central America: Carter, Reagan, and Central America (FPRI/O, 26:2, Summer 197, p. 322–325)

Both Carter and Reagan changed course with respect to Central America, former replacing human rights with security, latter moderating initial anti-communism with economic and military aid. Friends and foes are confused. To gain credibility for moderate policy, US must cease threatening enemies and search with other regional powers for peaceful solutions.

7253 Quijano, Carlos. Nicaragua, un pueblo, una revolución: ensayo sobre el imperialismo de los Estados Unidos. México: Editorial Pueblo Nuevo, 1978. 141 p.

Brief journalistic account of how imperialism merged with strategic interests in US's "domination, subjugation, and tutelage" of Nicaragua for two decades after 1909. Helps explain why sympathies of so many Mexicans and other Latin Americans later lay with the Sandinistas instead of Uncle Sam.

7254   Rabkin, Rhoda Pearl. U.S.-Soviet rivalry in Central America and the Caribbean (CU/JIA, 34:2, Fall/Winter 1980/1981, p. 329–351)

Shows how Sandinista regime's identification with Soviet-backed causes and totalitarian regimes was "virtually complete" after Somoza's overthrow, thereby generating friction with Washington long before Reagan.

7255   Ramírez, Sergio. Deseamos un entendimiento global que favorezca la paz (Nicaráuac [Ministerio de Cultura, Managua] 3:7, junio 1982, p. 5–10, plates)

Civilian member of Nicaragua's revolutionary junta rails against past and present Yankee imperialistic attacks on his country. While promising elections by 1985 and political pluralism, he fails to mention newspaper censorship, abuses suffered by the Miskito Indians, and pressures besetting press, the Church, business community, and opposition parties.

7256   Rowles, James. El conflicto Honduras—El Salvador y el orden jurídico internacional 1969. San José: Editorial Universitaria Centroamericana, 1980. 303 p. (Colección Seis)

Extracts mildly instructive "lessons" from his essentially legalistic study of Salvadoran-Honduran conflict: first of many "demographic wars" sparked by population pressures; Inter-American Human Rights Commission must be strengthened to respond more rapidly to abuses; effectiveness of international law depends on its dynamic not static application and reliance on it by decision-makers.

7257   Singer, Max. The record in Latin America (AJC/C, 74:6, Dec. 1982, p. 43–49)

Extreme right attack on "modernization" of Reagan's policies. Complains administration has not adequately attacked Sandinista regime in Nicaragua, verbally or otherwise, because Washington vainly hopes to persuade Nicaragua to halt its assistance

to Salvadoran left. Reagan administration also neglected to develop strategy for "dealing" with Castro's Cuba and has been slow in forcing Mexicans to stop favoring leftist forces in Central America. [Y.H. Ferguson]

7258   Studds, Gerry E. and **William Woodward.** Central America, 1981: report to the Committee on Foreign Affairs, U.S. House of Representatives. Washington: U.S. G.P.O., 1981. 33 p. (97th Congress, 1st Session. Committee print)

Report to House Committee on Foreign Affairs by one of its members, Rep. Gerry E. Studds (Mass.) on his early-1981 visit to Costa Rica, Nicaragua, and Honduras—and interviews with "several prominent leaders" from El Salvador and Guatemala. Unusually perceptive report with conclusions of more than passing relevance. On Nicaragua: "If the balanced approach to the United States to postrevolutionary Nicaragua is pushed off kilter; if the United States proves it cannot come to terms with major social reform in Latin America, then the United States will deal itself out of political reality in this hemisphere." On El Salvador: "Forces in El Salvador which we now support are neither democratic, nor committed to social justice, nor a force for peace, nor truly capable of combatting Communist influence in Central America. 'Friends' like these create new, unneeded enemies for the United States, and stimulate resistance to moderate, reformist policies put forward as an alternative to violent revolution." [Y.H. Ferguson]

7259   Tack, Juan Antonio. La lucha de Omar Torrijos por la recuperación de la integridad nacional (LNB/L, 305/309:1, agosto/dic. 1981, p. 219–234)

Former foreign minister sketches Panama's strategy in procuring the canal treaties of 1977, underlining Torrijos' success in mobilizing domestic and international support for his republic's cause.

7260   Tambs, Lewis and **Frank Aker.** Como acabar con el síndrome de Vietnam en El Salvador (Política [Universidad de Chile, Instituto de Ciencia Política, Santiago] 1, 1982, p. 117–131)

Two cold warriors argue for victory in El Salvador by avoiding five errors committed in Vietnam: U.S. must: 1) adopt offensive strategy and defensive tactics; 2) inculcate Hispanic traditions; 3) pursue pro-longed war; 4) bolster indigenous troups but not deploy US forces; and 5) use helicopters prudently. Technology, training, and funds must also be provided.

7261 Thorndike, A.E. Belize among her neighbors: an analysis of the Guatemala- Belize dispute (FIU/CR, 7:2, April/June 1978, p. 13–19, map)

Dated article scrutinized Belize's boundary disputes, especially with Guatemala. Reveals how Belize shrewdly internationalized conflict neither to promote mediation nor peace-keeping, but to focus and mobilize public opinion on its goal: self-determination.

7262 Ungo, Guillermo Manuel. La comunidad democrática centroamericana es una amenaza para la región (NSO, 61, julio/agosto 1982, p. 113–120, plates)

Leader of Salvadoran Frente Democrático Revolucionario speaks frankly on regional issues. Castigates Central American Democratic Community, a grouping of democratic or potentially democratic governments, as threat to stability of El Salvador and Nicaragua. Provides insight into thinking of Salvadoran left's chief spokesman.

7263 U.S. policy in Central America and its international implications: symposium held at Stanford University, May 16, 1981. 2. ed. Stanford, Calif.: Stanford Central American Action Network, 1981. 67 p.

Free-for-all on US policy toward Central America derived from mid-1981 Stanford symposium. Predictable contributions from a broad range of articulate spokesmen.

7264 Ventocilla, Eliodoro. Los nuevos Tratados del Canal y los Estados Unidos de América (LNB/L, 305/309:1, agosto/dic. 1981, p. 235–240)

After listing numerous US defense installations in Canal Zone, insists that 1977 Treaty allows Panama to determine Washington's future role in facility's "protection and defense." Such a role must not erode Panamanian sovereignty, national self-determination, or allow continued military presence.

7265 White, Robert E. Central America: fire in the "front yard?" (CRIA/WW, 24:12, Dec. 1981, p. 11-14, ill.)

Platitudes mar scathing critique of Reagan administration's Central American policy. "Situation is still retrievable," former ambassador contends, "but only if we cease backing reactionary military governments and league ourselves with the progressive moderate forces." Identifying and mobilizing such forces poses crucial dilemma for policymakers.

Wolff, Thomas. Mexican-Guatemalan imbroglio: fishery rights and national honor. See *HLAS 44:2287.*

7266 Zaid, Gabriel. Colegas enemigos: una lectura de la tragedia salvadoreña (Vuelta [México] 5:56, julio 1981, p. 9–27, ill.)

Marshals evidence to show that Salvadoran civil war is essentially internal conflict between elites "who cannot agree on how to treat the masses . . ." Proposes peace by buying off and exiling those responsible for killings who are linked to the military. Next would come an offer of amnesty to insurgents, followed by negotiations between government and the political, non-military, opposition. Permit remaining guerrillas to remain in their camps awaiting outcome of internationally supervised elections. Fascinating article, copiously documented (for critique, see item **7216**).

THE CARIBBEAN AND THE GUIANAS

7267 Abbott, George C. The associated states and independence (SAGE/JIAS, 23:1, Feb. 1981, p. 69–94, tables)

Important contribution to literature on Britain's former West Indian colonies. These island nations have long cooperated in financial and economic matters. Despite their penchant for individual political action and

the collapse of 1958 Federation, the "growing number of regional organizations and common services are acting as a synthesizing force" toward integration.

7268 Adams, Gordon. Cuba and Africa: the international politics of the liberation struggle: a documentary essay (LAP, 8[1]:28,

Winter 1981, p. 108–125, bibl.)
   Argues that Washington's opposition to Cuban support for the liberation struggle in Africa evinces a myopia to global divisions between "haves" and "have nots" for which US is more responsible than Cuba. "It is Cuba's awareness of these divisions and its historic commitment to the process of change, not Cuban subservience to Soviet international policy objectives, which is at the root of Cuban policy decisions."

7269 Adams, Michael R. Coast guarding the Caribbean (Proceedings [U.S. Naval Institute, Annapolis, Md], 108[954]:8, Aug. 1982, p. 61–65, map, plates)
   Coast Guard officer sensibly proposes dispatching three or four fellow officers to train counterparts in Caribbean nations. Arguably, this is more reasonable approach toward winning friends than "shipping in megadollars worth of US equipment" that is too complex for the recipients or attempting to keep a fleet in the Caribbean.

7270 Altshuler, José. La URSS-Cuba: cooperación en el Cosmos (URSS/AL, 7[43], 1981, p. 19–27, ill.)
   The 1980 voyage of Cuban cosmonaut Arnaldo Tamayo aboard the Soyuz 38 spaceship has fueled this flight of propaganda about the "ties of fraternity, collaboration, respect and solidarity" that bind Cuba and the Soviet Union.

7271 Azicri, Max. Cuba and the US: on the possibilities of rapproachement (FIU/CR, 9:1, Winter 1980, p. 26–29, 50–52, maps)
   Surveys Cuban policies of Nixon, Ford, and Carter administrations, and concludes that tone of Cuban foreign policy will be central factor in whether relations are normalized with US. Though poorly written, article contains interesting historical detail.

7272 Baker, Stephen. The changing OAS (International Perspectives [The Canadian journal on world affairs, Department of External Affairs, Ottawa, Canada] May/June 1982, p. 23–26)
   Interview with Barbadian Assistant Secretary-General of OAS, who some believe may eventually succeed Orfila as Secretary-General. Interviewer predicts that an English-speaking bloc within the organization "could in the near future approach parity with the Latinos." [Y.H. Ferguson]

7273 Bishop, Maurice. Imperialism is the real problem: address to the Conference on the Development Problems of Small Island States. St. George's, Grenada: People's Revolutionary Government, 1981. 13 leaves (mimeo)
   Marxist Prime Minister's fulminations against US imperialism in general and Reagan administration's economic and propaganda warfare against Grenada in particular.

7274 Bracey, Audrey. Resolution of the Dominican crisis, 1965: a study in mediation. Washington: Institute for the Study of Diplomacy, Georgetown University, Edmund A. Walsh School of Foreign Service, 1980. 52 p.
   Careful, well documented study of mediation that ended 1965 civil war in Dominican Republic. Martin Herz's erudite conclusions emphasize how Ambassador Ellsworth Bunker's personal qualities—deliberateness, inner security and integrity— facilitated settlement.

7275 Castro, Fidel. Fidel Castro speeches: Cuba's internationalist foreign policy, 1975–80. Edited by Michael Taber. New York: Pathfinder Press, 1981. 391: bibl.; index.
   Castro *aficionado* has furnished best, perhaps only, compilation in English of Cuban leader's recent speeches, many of which are unedited versions from English-language *Granma* weekly review. Topics include progress of Cuba's Revolution, Nonaligned Movement, relations with US, Sandinista Revolution, and solidarity with Angola, Ethiopia, and Vietnam.

7276 Communist aid activities in non-communist less developed countries, 1979 and 1954–79: a research paper. National Foreign Assessment Center. Washington: Central Intelligence Agency: Document Expediting (DOCEX) Project, Exchange and Gift Division, Library of Congress, 1980. 45 p.: charts (some col.), ill., 5 col. maps.
   Includes useful statistical information and generally sound interpretation, although many analysts would question strategic and commercial significance attached to aid. Includes USSR, Eastern Europe, China, and Cuba. [Y.H. Ferguson]

7277 The Congressional Black Caucus presents An examination of U.S. policy in the Caribbean: transcript of proceedings,

Washington, D.C., Saturday, 21 November 1981. Washington: Ace-Federal Reporters, 1981. 222 leaves.

Poorly transcribed account of Congressional Black Caucus' second annual seminar on the Caribbean. Speakers condemn Reagan administration's approach to area, characterized by "hostility" toward Grenada's Marxist regime, a "racist policy" toward Haitian refugees and "confrontation" toward Castro's Cuba. Just as Jews lobby for Israel, blacks seek to support their ethnic compatriots in Caribbean.

7278 Contemporary international relations of the Caribbean. Edited by Basil A. Ince. St. Augustine, Trinidad/Tobago: Institute of International Relations, University of the West Indies, 1979. 367 p.: bibl., graphs, indexes.

Neither apologists for colonialism nor wild-eyed revolutionaries, the highly respected contributors to this volume offer reasoned and reasonable chapters organized into four sections: 1) the Caribbean and the Third World; 2) Metropolitan Ties and Influences; 3) Political Processes and Foreign Policy; and 4) Economic Development and Integration. Valuable to practitioners, scholars, and students of international relations.

7279 Cuba in Africa. Carmelo Mesa-Lago, June S. Belkin, editors. Pittsbugh, Pa.: Center for Latin American Studies, University Center for International Studies, University of Pittsburgh, 1981. 1 v.: bibl., index (Latin American monograph and document series; no. 3)

Six essays and related comments provide a comprehensive and illuminating analysis of Cuba's objectives, power capabilities, political and military limitations, and prospects in Africa. Authors predict "significantly smaller and less spectacular" Cuban involvement in Africa in 1980s compared to 1970s because of greater emphasis on internal security and Soviet preoccupation with Afghanistan, Poland, and Persian Gulf. First-rate bibliography.

7280 Cuban refugee programs. Carlos E. Cortés, editor. New York: Arno Press, 1980. 546 p. in various pagings: bibl., ill. (Hispanics in the United States)

Disparate collection of reports and essays on programs for Cuban refugees in aftermath of 1959 *fidelista* Revolution. John F.

Thomas believes that successful resettlement sprang from the "tying of an American local agency in with each Cuban family" seeking placement, counseling for the entire family, and providing language, vocational, and professional training to the head-of-the-household.

7281 Domínguez, Jorge I. La política exterior de Cuba (AR, 7:25, 1981, p. 13–16, plates)

Deft analysis of how Cuba's foreign policy triumphs of the early 1970s accentuated nation's vulnerability and economic problems a few years later because of 1) a growing reliance on foreign capital and imports, and 2) overcommitment abroad of resources, including well trained, ideologically motivated men and women.

7282 Eastern Caribbean: Report of a Staff Mission to the Dominican Republic, Antigua, Dominica, Barbados, and St. Vincent, Janaury 5–19, 1982, submitted to the Committee on Foreign Affairs, U.S. House of Representatives. Washington: U.S. G.P.O., 1982. 22 p.

Value lies in well done thumbnail sketches of Eastern Caribbean Islands—Antigua, Dominica, St. Vincent, and Barbados—about which current information is difficult to obtain.

7283 Eckstein, Susan. Structural and ideological bases of Cuba's overseas programs (Politics & Society [Gerox-X, Inc., Los Altos, Calif.] 11:1, 1982, p. 95–121)

Brief description of Cuban foreign aid programs, with critical evaluation of factors accounting for Cuba's extensive overseas activities. Asserts that commitment to "socialist solidarity" and Soviet pressure have shaped extent and nature of programs, but that domestic material considerations have also been important.

7284 Enders, Thomas O. A comprehensive strategy for the Caribbean basin: the US and her neighbors (FIU/CR, 11:2, Spring 1982, p. 10–13)

Assistant Secretary of State for Inter-American Affairs provides rationale for Reagan administration's Caribbean Basin Initiative.

7285 Erisman, H. Michael. Cuba and the Third World: the Sixth Nonaligned

Nations Conference (FIU/CR, 9:1, Winter 1980, p. 21–25, ill.)

Cogently delineates contrary positions held by Cuban and Yugoslav factions within Nonaligned Movement, details Havana's political successes at Sixth Annual Summit (1979), and explores Cuba's future as leader in Third World affairs.

7286 Fetisov, Alexandr. Granada: hacia transformaciones socioeconómicas progresistas (URSS/AL, 1/2[37/38], 1981, p. 76–88)

Jabs at imperialism and CIA notwithstanding, essay succinctly appraises impact of colonialism on Grenada, abuses of Gairy regime, and social and economic reforms spearheaded by Bishop since the 1979 coup.

7287 Gleijeses, Piero. The Dominican crisis: the 1965 Constitutionalist revolt and American intervention. Translated by Lawrence Lipson. Baltimore: Johns Hopkins University Press, 1978. 406 p.: bibl., index.

Thoughtful study of 1965 crisis takes exception to liberal critics of President Johnson in arguing that genesis of US intervention lay not in ideology but in inferior reporting by the embassy and, particularly, the CIA station which misread sympathies of Marxists, failed to uncover existence of Enriquillo movement in time for Reid Cabral to quell conspiracy. Dispatch of Marines preserved Pax Americana, but it thwarted "a democratic movement owing nothing to Castro . . . [which] afforded a unique opportunity for the Dominican people to break the chains of oppression." Invaluable bibliographical essay.

7288 González, Edward. U.S. policy: objectives and options (*in* Cuba: internal and international affairs. Edited by Jorge I. Domínguez. Beverly Hills, Calif.: Sage Publications, 1982, p. 193–221, tables)

Washington could play upon Cuba's vulnerabilities and interests to "secure Soviet cooperation in minimizing the Cuban-Soviet security threat in the Caribbean, and in otherwise moderating Cuba's regional and international postures . . ." Author's optimism verges on naïveté.

7289 González, Heliodoro. The Caribbean Basin Initiative: toward a permanent dole (IAMEA, 36:1, Summer 1982, p. 23–59, tables)

Trenchant, compelling indictment of Caribbean Basin Initiative (CBI). González argues that: 1) exemptions will minimize the benefits of trade concessions; 2) local policies, not US incentives, attract investments; and 3) Mexico's alleged participation in initiative is a hoax. CBI will benefit banks, investors, bureaucrats, and consultants more than recipient nations.

7290 Halperin, Maurice. The taming of Fidel Castro. Berkeley: University of California Press, 1981. 345 p., 1 leaf of plates: bibl., index, map.

Artfully written, meticulously documented account of how the Kremlin pulled and social and economic forces pushed Cuba firmly into Moscow's camp, an event ratified by Castro's belated but unequivocal backing of the Soviet invasion of Czechoslovakia. Hypothesizes that for this support the Cuban leader extracted increased aid, including a sizable boost in oil shipments.

7291 Hopkins, Joseph E. Cuba: Moscow's marionette (Proceedings [US Naval Institute, Annapolis, Md.] 108:953, July 1982, p. 58–64, map)

Employs confused logic and clichés to support thesis that US must achieve cessation of communist subversion emanating from Cuba in order to preempt the Kremlin's seizure of "Eurafrica" within the next 10 years.

7292 Kelly, Philip. Recent United States ambassadors to the Caribbean: an appraisal (UPR/CS, 17:1/2, April/July 1977, p. 123–133, tables)

Decries quality of US ambassadors sent to Caribbean nations. More seasoned career Foreign Service officers should represent US in Caribbean posts; ambassadorial assignment durations should be lengthened; and more women and minorities should be appointed.

7293 Knight, Franklin W. Toward a new American presence in the Caribbean (FIU/CR, 9:1, Winter 1980, p. 36–39, map)

Makes case for new American policy based upon mature, realistic and compassionate understanding of Caribbean peoples. Unfortunately, essay suffers from rose-tinted glasses syndrome: a proposed US-sponsored guest-worker program is particularly impractical.

7294 Langley, Lester D. The United States and the Caribbean in the twentieth century. Athens: University of Georgia Press, 1982. 334 p.: bibl., index, map.

Solid, factual, beautifully written account of rise and fall of US influence in the region. "Still willing to use its military strength to try influencing the course of Caribbean politics, the United States has not yet found a way to wield its enormous power to direct the currents of Caribbean social revolution." Contains good bibliographical essay.

7295 LeoGrande, William M. Cuba policy recycled (FP, 46, Spring 1982, p. 105–119)
Convincingly argues for fresh US strategy toward Cuba. "Graduated hostility" must give way to "gradual engagement"—the forging of bilateral links to enhance US leverage on future Cuban behavior. This policy could encourage Castro to distance himself from Moscow, for sharp tensions have often strained relations between the two communist regimes.

7296 ———. Foreign policy: the limits of success (*in* Cuba: internal and international affairs. Edited by Jorge I. Domínguez. Beverly Hills, Calif.: Sage Publications, 1982, p. 167–182)
Reagan administration's treatment of Cuba as Soviet proxy is seen as counter-productive. Such a policy serves only to push Castro closer to Moscow, even on issues (Eritrea and Afghanistan) where differences have persisted or in matters (Cuban policy in Latin America) that involve little or no Cuban-Soviet cooperation.

7297 Lewis, Gordon K. On the limits of the new Cuban presence on the Caribbean (FIU/CR, 9:1, Winter 1980, p. 33–35, map)
Brief commentary attempts to outline limits of applicability of Cuban experience to Caribbean political scene. Argues that Cuban influence has been largely ideological rather than practical. Advocates a sort of "Monroe Doctrine" to assure region's neutrality.

7298 Lowenthal, Abraham F. The Caribbean (WQ, 6:2, Spring 1982, p. 112–141, ill., maps, tables)
Eminent scholar provides lucid, well-written overview of economic, political, and social conditions of Caribbean societies. Concludes by proposing that US take

eight steps, most of which are embraced by Reagan's Caribbean Basin Initiative, to spur region's long-term development.

7299 McCoy, Terry L. A primer for US policy on Caribbean emigration (FIU/CR, 8:1, Jan./March 1979, p. 10–15, ill.)
Provides helpful nuts-and-bolts description of current US immigration law and 1977 reform legislation proposed by President Carter. Greatly underestimates opposition to change and contends that "it would seem almost a foregone conclusion that the US will modify its policy to further limit migration from the Caribbean."

7300 Maingot, Anthony P. Cuba and the Commonwealth Caribbean: playing the Cuban card (FIU/CR, 9:1, Winter 1980, p. 7–10, 44–49, ill.)
Superb analysis of skillful manipulation of "Cuban card" by some Caribbean politicians towards "less than ideologically-pure ends." Throughout Caribbean Commonwealth nations, the Cuban connection is alternately used for political leverage, as protective shield, or as handy strawman of conservative forces.

7301 Morley, Morris H. The U.S. imperial state in Cuba 1952–1958: policymaking and capitalist interests (JLAS, 14:1, May 1982, p. 143–170)
Contends that greater emphasis on examining broad structural (e.g. economic) factors in formulation of American foreign policy is necessary for understanding certain historical continuities in this policy. Employs theory of capital expansion to explain "U.S. imperial state policy" in Cuba (1952–58). Conclusions hinge upon reader's acceptance of theory.

7302 Needler, Martin C. Hegemonic tolerance: international competition in the Caribbean and Latin America (FIU/CR, 11:2, Spring 1982, p. 32–33, 56, ill.)
Suggests that Caribbean nations can minimize dependence on—and identification with—either Washington or Moscow by embracing Mexican political model or allying themselves with international Socialist or Christian Democratic movements.

7303 Olguin, Alexandr. La Cuenca del Caribe: el peligro imperialista y las maniobras de Pekín (URSS/AL, 4[40], 1981, p. 39–51)

Soviet analyst savages China both for trying to undermine Moscow's role and reputation in region and for attempting to extend its influence and win allies in international organizations. "The struggle for freedom by the peoples of the Caribbean, which enjoys vast support from progressive forces, is gaining strength despite the machinations of imperialism and its Peking accomplices."

7304 Pérez-López, Jorge F. Nuclear power in Cuba: opportunities and challenges (FPRI/O, 26:2, Summer 1982, p. 495–516)

Provides comprehensive overview of present Cuban nuclear power while examining some of the probable opportunities and distinct challenges that nuclear power will present Cuba in the future. Timely, well-written essay.

7305 Perkins, Whitney T. Constraint of empire: the United States and Caribbean interventions. Westport, Conn.: Greenwood Press, 1981. 282 p.: bibl., index (Contributions in comparative colonial studies; no. 8 0163–3813)

US is treated as colonial power in its relations with Cuba, Nicaragua, the Dominican Republic, and Haiti. Author organizes this trenchant study into four periods: 1) establishing commitment; 2) exercise and limitations of control; 3) disengaging; and 4) consequences and return engagements. In each state, US' capacity to control wars is compared to its commitment to liberate.

7306 Philipson, Lorrin. Cuba's literary migration (WV, 25:3, March 1982, p. 4–6, ill.)

Interviews with three exiled Cuban writers (Guillermo Cabrera Infante, Octavio Armand, and Reinaldo Arenas) sensitively reveal how Castro regime promotes political propaganda at expense of creative expression. Government displayed its heavy hand in censoring the Spanish classic *La Celestina*. Arenas poignantly observes that "A play inadmissible in Cuba in the twentieth century was acceptable during the Inquisition!"

7307 Pierre-Charles, Gérard. El Caribe contemporáneo. México: Siglo Veintiuno Editores, 1981. 413 p.: bibl., maps.

Pierre-Charles forces the empirical foot into the theoretical shoe to make it fit his Marxist analysis of evolving US hegemonic designs on Caribbean basin. Blisters

appear in the form of twisted facts and questionable conclusions (e.g., Communist Cuba's emergence proves that dialectical materialism is at work in the Caribbean).

7308 Plummer, Brenda Gayle. The Afro-American response to the occupation of Haiti: 1915–1934 (AU/P, 43:2, June 1982, p. 125–143)

Dispatch of Marines to Haiti in 1915 made little initial impression on US black leaders. Opposition emerged after World War I because of greater prominence of civil rights organizations and resurgent black nationalism. "The new mood strengthened protest against the occupation and forced policymakers to temper the roughshod manner" in which Haitians were treated.

7309 Pollis, Adamantia. Human rights, Third World socialism and Cuba (WD, 9:9/10, 1981, p. 1005–1017)

Lucid, impeccable study of why Cuba and other Third World socialist states reject Western definition of human rights. Liberal doctrines such as inalienable rights and individualism are foreign to their cultures. Their emphasis, nourished by Marxism, is on the state's responsibility for providing such basic needs as food, housing, and health care.

Portillo, Julio. Venezuela-Cuba, relaciones diplomáticas, 1902–1980. See item **7438.**

7310 Problemas del Caribe contemporáneo = Contemporary Caribbean issues. Angel Calderón Cruz, editor. Río Piedras: Instituto de Estudios del Caribe, Universidad de Puerto Rico, 1979. 180 p.: bibl.

Though dated, good sampler of economic, political, social, and international issues salient to Caribbean states in mid-1970s.

7311 Relaciones internacionales y estructuras sociopolíticas en el Caribe. Gérard Pierre-Charles *et al.* México: Universidad Autónoma de México, Instituto de Investigaciones Sociales, 1980. 222 p.: ill.

Collection of essays excoriates Western imperialism, especially that of US, for the underdevelopment, economic dependence, political passivity, and antinationalist middle class that characterize most Caribbean nations.

7312 The Restless Caribbean: changing patterns in international relations. Edited by Richard Millett and W. Marvin Will. New

York: Praeger, 1979. 295 p.: bibl., index, map.

Collection of 21 solid essays just predates such events as the souring of US-Cuban relations, the Mariel Flotilla, the Mexican-Venezuelan oil facility, a major Haitian emigration, the Grenadian coup, and Manley's defeat. Still, wide-ranging and useful background material on an increasingly scrutinized region.

7313 Romero M., Carlos. Las relaciones entre Venezuela y Cuba desde 1959 a 1978 (Fragmentos [Centro de Estudios Latinoamericanos Romulo Gallegos, Departamento de Investigaciones, Caracas] 6, enero/abril 1980, p. 77–103)

Venezuela re-established formal diplomatic relations with Castro in Dec. 1975, a move partly motivated by mutual interest in supplying Cuba with Venezuelan petroleum. Addtional factors were Venezuela's desire for greater influence in Caribbean and Third World, and Castro's need for greater acceptance by Latin American countries as one approach to normalizing relations with US. [Y.H. Ferguson]

Sánchez Bermúdez, Juan A. Las pretensiones anexionistas de los Estados Unidos en Cuba colonial. See *HLAS 44:2543.*

7314 Schori, Pierre. The Cuban Revolution in 1978: at home and in Africa (NOSALF/IA, 7/8:1/2, 1978, p. 119–131)

Swedish Social Democrat uncritically retails Castro's views on a gamut of issues from political prisoners to intervention in Africa to relations with the US. Example of writings that help form a positive view of Cuba in Northern Europe.

7315 Schulz, Donald E. The strategy of conflict and the politics of counterproductivity (FPRI/O, 25:3, Fall 1981, p. 679–713)

Believes mounting US hostility allows Castro to keep his countrymen unified behind his regime, has adverse effect on human rights, pushes Castro further into Moscow's arms, and could lead to military blockade and direct confrontation with USSR. Particularly dangerous are proposals to assist Castro's opposition in Angola and Somalia. Fears that in Central America we may ally ourselves with most retrograde and repressive regimes. [Y.H. Ferguson]

7316 Sovetsko-kubinskie otnosheníià: 1917–1977 = Cuban-Soviet relations: 1917-1977. Sb. statei AN SSSR, In-t Latin Ameriki. Redokol. A.D. Bekarevich otv. red. *et al.* Moskva: Nauka, 1980. 280 p.: bibl. (Continues Rossiiski-kubinskie i sovetsko-kubinskie sviazi; 18–20)

Collection of articles by Soviet (and one Cuban) specialists: Bondarchuk deals with Soviet-Cuban economic relations; Sizonenko covers Cuban-Soviet relations in 1950s; Torshin discusses relations after Cuban Revolution; Bekarevich and Penkina analyze relations between Cuba and COMECON countries; Poskonina criticizes "bourgeois radical and ultradical" notions about Cuban/Soviet cooperation; Sokolova lists latest Soviet research on the Cuban Revolution; and García and Mironchuk discuss the Soviet Union in works by Cuban writers. [R.V. Allen]

7317 Statsenco, Igor. Sobre algunos aspectos político-militares de la crisis del Caribe (URSS/AL, 3[19], 1978, p. 140–150)

Intriguing article offers Soviet perspective on 1962 Cuban Missile crisis. Soviets were merely helping Cuba to arm for self-defense and serious conflict was avoided because all parties except US were so amenable to compromise. [Y.H. Ferguson]

7318 Sutton, Paul K. The Caribbean as a substitute state system: 1945–1976. pt. 1, 1945–1959. Hull, England: Department of Politics, University of Hull, 1980. 1 v.: bibl. (Hull papers in politics, 0142–7377; no. 16)

Focuses on three factors—political, national development, and extra-regional influence—to explain interaction within "Caribbean subordinate state system." Concern for international politics of Latin America often masks presence of such a subordinate state system whose existence adds to understanding of hemispheric inter-state politics.

7319 Thomas, Hugh. Coping with Cuba. Washington: Coalition for a Democratic Majority, 1980. 16 p.: ill. (Coalition for a Democratic Majority; 1)

Respected British historian's tough-minded analysis of the Castro regime concludes with 15 policy recommendations for isolating Cuba and exacerbating internal problems. Argues that Castro, who is "serving the Soviet Union at the cost of . . . [his nation's] own interests, thrives on 'risks' and 'head-on clashes'" and will prey on weak governments in the region.

7320 United Fruit Company, un caso del dominio imperialista en Cuba. La Habana: Editorial de Ciencias Sociales, 1976. 450 p., 26 leaves of plates: bibl., ill. (Nuestra historia)

Although written in purple prose, this diatribe against US imperialism— notably, how the United Fruit Co. gobbled up Cuba's sugar industry—helps explain how deeply rooted is resentment against neocolonialism in the Caribbean.

7321 United States. Congress. House. Committee on Foreign Affairs. Subcommittee on Inter-American Affairs. The Caribbean Basin Policy: hearings before the Subcommittee on Inter-American Affairs of the Committee on Foreign Affairs, House of Representatives, July 14, 21, and 28, 1981. Washington: US G.P.O., 1981. 279 p.: ill. (97th Congress, 1st Session)

Vital primary source for students of Caribbean Basin Initiative. These hearings, held to marshall support for greater assistance to the region, are organized into three principal sections: 1) Caribbean development; 2) Central American development; and 3) Caribbean Basin Policy. Pollyannas far outnumber the Cassandras.

7322 The United States and the Latin American sphere of influence. v. 1, The era of Caribbean intervention, 1898–1930. Edited by Robert Freeman Smith. Malabar, Fla.: Krieger Pub. Co., 1981–. 1 v.: bibl., ill.

Intriguing anthology of essays advancing various historians' (and others') views about US "imperialism" role in Caribbean and making of US policies from turn of century to Good Neighbor era. [Y.H. Ferguson]

7323 Valenta, Jiri. Soviet-Cuban intervention in the Horn of Africa: impact and lessons (CU/JIA, 34:2, Fall/Winter 1980/1981, p. 353–367)

Highly competent analysis of Soviet-Cuban strategy in the Horn of Africa. Confluence of factors—Kremlin's growing preoccupation with Afghanistan, Poland, and the Persian Gulf, possible Soviet overextension in the Third World, economic difficulties in

Cuba and USSR, Reagan's assertiveness toward communist regimes— may reduce Moscow and Havana's adventurism in Africa.

7324 ———. The USSR, Cuba, and the crisis in Central America (FPRI/O, 25:3, Fall 1981, p. 715–746)

Carefully researched and documented examination of Soviet-Cuban strategies and tactics in Central America with emphasis on ideology, politics, security, and economics. Successfully challenges view that Cuba dances to Kremlin's tune. While enjoying little autonomy from Moscow in Africa, Castro has significant freedom of action in Caribbean basin. Extremely important article.

7325 ———. Soviet strategy in the Caribbean Basin (Proceedings [U.S. Naval Institute, Annapolis, Md.] 108:5, May 1982, p. 168–181, ill., maps)

Carefully reasoned and well documented explanation of Soviet Union's "anti-imperialist" strategy in Caribbean Basin, with emphasis on naval power. Events that emboldened Moscow to downplay "peaceful path" toward socialism in favor of armed struggle: Allende's overthrow, Sandinista Revolution, Grenadian coup, and success of Salvadoran guerrillas. Nicaragua may be best place to begin curbing Soviet and Cuban military support for would-be clients, for emergence of USSR-linked regimes clearly threatens vital US interests. "Tolerance of hostile regimes on its southern flank can be detrimental to U.S. political credibility in other important regions as the Persian Gulf."

7326 Vitalyev, K. An important Cuban-Angolan initiative (IA, 5, May 1982, p. 96–104)

Concise statement of Soviet rejection of "imperialist" attempts to link granting of Namibian independence to withdrawal of Cuban troops from Angola.

7327 Wood, Richard E. International broadcasting in and to the Caribbean (UPR/CS, 17:3/4, Oct. 1977/Jan. 1978, p. 153–169, tables)

Exhaustive listing of international AM and FM radio transmissions originating from and beamed to the Caribbean, an "underdeveloped region" with respect to "international broadcasting."

SOUTH AMERICA

GENERAL

7328 Abadie-Aicardi, Raúl Federico. Condicionantes de la rivalidad económica de las grandes potencias en América del Sur, 1870–1913 (Estudos Ibero-Americanos [Pontificia Universidade Católica do Rio Grande do Sul, Instituto de Filosofia e Ciências Humanas, Departamento de História, Porto Alegre, Brazil] 5 : 2, dez. 1979, p. 119–149, bibl., tables)

Good overview of economic and political rivalry among US, England and Germany in South America during 1870–1913 period, a historical moment of US ascendency and British leveling off. Looks at this important period in terms of great power rivalries while differentiating among Latin American responses.

7329 Azambuja, Péricles. Antartida: história e geopolítica. Porto Alegre?: Companhia Rio-Grandense de Artes Gráficas, 1982? 354 p.: ill.

Impressively detailed history of Antarctica written by Brazilian journalist/ historian. Includes history of Falklands/Malvinas Islands question and Beagle Channel dispute. Author is sensitive to geopolitical implications of his analysis.

7330 Geopolítica e integración. Montevideo: Universidad de la República, Dirección de Extensión Universitaria, División de Publicaciones y Ediciones, 1981. 313 p. (*Revista de la Facultad de Derecho y Ciencias Sociales*; 25:1)

Wide ranging set of essays explains and then utilizes geopolitics in order to explore a number of topics in South America's international relations. Some essays, however, slip into matters of international law.

7331 Geopolítica y relaciones internacionales. Luis Dallanegra Pedraza *et al.* Cartografía, Eduardo Miguel Telli. Buenos Aires: Editorial Pleamar, 1981. 119 p.: ill. (Estratégia y política)

Four concise essays by geopolitics experts from three Southern Cone countries. Primary concern is with the South Atlantic but a number of interesting topics are touched

upon including geopolitical implications of New International Economic Order and Latin American integration. Various maps and diagrams.

7332 Moneta, Carlos J. Antarctica, Latin America and the International System in the 1980's: toward a New Antarctic Order? (SAGE/JIAS, 23:1, Feb. 1981, p. 29–68, tables)

General discussion with an international relations/legal framework of the Antarctica situation over the next 10 years with some ideas for alternatives.

7333 Tambs, Lewis A. Influéncia da geopolítica na política e estratégia das grandes poténcias (ADN, 67 : 690, 1983, p. 127–156)

Discussion of importance of idea of geopolitical analysis through modern history. Although much of article deals with Europe and East/West conflict, some attention is paid to geopolitical implications of South America, an area author sees as important.

7334 Tapia Valdés, Jorge A. El terrorismo de estado: la doctrina de la seguridad nacional en el Cono Sur. Caracas: Nueva Sociedad; México: Editorial Nueva Imagen, 1980. 283 p.: bibl.

Former Minister of Education in Allende's Unidad Popular government analyzes the "Doctrine of National Security" as enunciated and practiced by military regimes of the Southern Cone, with particular attention to Brazil and Chile. In his view, although such regimes are supported by the United States, they are bound to fail because they represent only minority interests in society (rather than the masses) and breed destructive factions within the military establishments themselves. [Y.H.Ferguson]

ARGENTINA

7335 Alemann, Roberto T. La Argentina y los Estados Unidos: ¿una relación difícil? (CRIT, 54: 1873/1874, dic. 1981, p. 749–756)

Useful summary of US/Argentine relations. Faults Carter administration for failing to understand necessity of Argentina's internal war against Washington's enemy (internal Communist subversion). Welcomes the Reagan administration.

7336 Amuchástegui Astrada, Armando. Argentina-Chile, controversia y mediación. Buenos Aires: Ediciones Ghersi, 1980. 261 p.: bibl., maps.

Argentine author's account of Beagle Channel dispute includes much historical material and useful account of Papal mediation situation. Sees no easy solution.

7337 Arriazu, Ricardo H. Aislacionismo: ¿opción o utopía? (CRIT, 54:1873/1874, dic. 1981, p. 777–782, tables)

Analysis of Argentine economic system emphasizes degree to which nation's economy is vulnerable to foreign influence (e.g., Argentina's efforts to control its economy are vulnerable to decisions made in foreign capitals).

7338 Beck, Peter J. Cooperative confrontation in the Falkland Islands dispute: the Anglo-Argentine search for a way forward, 1968–1981 (SAGE/JIAS, 24:1, Feb. 1982, p. 37–58)

Published prior to Falklands/Malvinas War, author traces recent history of that dispute. Sees increasing flexibility in British position although admitting that both sides are limited by public sensitivity to the dispute's history.

7339 Briano, Justo P. Geopolítica y geostrategia americana. 3. ed. Buenos Aires: Editorial Pleamar, 1979. 399 p.: bibl., ill. (Estrategia y política)

Considerably revised textbook (1st ed. 1966) on South American geopolitics mixed with some concepts of humanistic civilization written by Argentine military officer.

7340 Bruno Bologna, Alfredo. Islas Malvinas: las negociaciones y las propuestas de Ridley: pt. 2 (IAEERI/E, 67/68, 1980, p. 101–132)

Brings up various pro-Argentine resolutions in international organizations since 1945 and then recounts Ridley proposals rejected by British government. Worries that an agreement which did not give effective sovereignty to Argentina would allow England to exploit the non-renewable natural resources prior to leaving.

7341 Cable, James. The Falklands conflict (Proceedings [U.S. Naval Institute, Annapolis, Md.] 108[955]:9, Sept. 1982, p. 71–76, plates)

Largely ignoring domestic political factors, account emphasizes that England's status as a world power determined British reaction to Falklands/Malvinas takeover. Speculates as to significance for future British military spending and foreign policy.

7342 Cárdenas, Emilio J. El conflicto de Las Malvinas y el principio de "Autodeterminación" (CRIT, 55:1887, 26 agosto 1982, p. 439–441)

In denouncing British policy toward the Falklands/Malvinas Islands, author tellingly notes degree to which London made pious claims as to its duty to protect the islanders' right to self-determination.

7343 Colacrai de Trevisa, Miryam. Adquisición de soberanía en áreas polares según el derecho internacional (IAEERI/E, 70, enero/marzo 1982, p. 21–32)

Although article includes discussion of various legal theories as to how sovereignty is acquired, author is chiefly interested in implications for Argentina's Antarctic claims. Intellectually interesting work.

7344 Corradi, Juan E. Argentina: a story behind a war (DIS, Summer 1982, p. 285–293)

Written just as the Falklands/Malvinas War was ending, author presents an extremely pessimistic interpretation of contemporary Argentine politics and concludes war was a simple-minded effort to ignore the domestic mess into which Argentina has fallen.

7345 The Disputed islands: the Falkland crisis, a history & background. London: H.M.S. ., 1982. 36 p.: bibl., ill.

Publication by British government of its case for sovereignty over Falklands/Malvinas. Clearly prompted by invasion, work ignored political actions prior to invasion.

7346 Egea Lahore, Pedro Eduardo. Argentina y el Derecho del Mar: la cuestión austral ante la Santa Sede. Buenos Aires: Ediciones Universidad del Salvador, 1980. 117 p.: bibl.

Argentine legal expert discusses, from his country's point of view, Law of the Sea issues. Expresses hope for papal mediation of Beagle Channel issue. Also examines Malvinas/Falklands problem as colonial matter.

7347 Ferrari, Gustavo. Esquema de la política exterior argentina. Buenos Aires: Editorial Universitaria de Buenos Aires, 1981. 137 p.: bibl., index (Temas)

Well done, but much too short, account of Argentine diplomatic history to 1976. Includes particularly interesting chapter (25 p.) consisting of annotated bibliography of major works on subject.

7348 García del Solar, Lucio. Las relaciones entre la Argentina y la Unión Soviética (CRIT, 54:1873/1874, dic. 1981, p. 758–764)

Account of pre-Falklands/Malvinas invasion improvement of relations between USSR and Argentina resulting from wheat sales and other agreements. Cautiously distrustful of Russians, author sees benefits to arrangement.

7349 Goodwin, Paul B., Jr. Anglo-Argentine commercial relations: a private sector view, 1922–43 (HAHR, 61:1, Feb. 1981, p. 29–51)

Based on records of British Chamber of Commerce in Argentina, article attacks dependency theory by arguing that Argentina did not make serious concessions to England during 1922–43 period. Roca-Runciman Treaty is seen as balanced and the execution of the Treaty as pro-Argentine.

7350 Goyret, José Teófilo. Geopolítica y subversión. Buenos Aires: Ediciones Depalma, 1980. 266 p. (Colección Humanismo y terror; 10)

Interpretation by Argentine general of terrorism in Argentina and of its links with the Soviet Union. Includes interesting chronological appendix of events that the general believes are related.

7351 Guglialmelli, Juan E. Islas Malvinas: exigir definiciones a Gran Bretaña en las negociaciones sobre soberanía (IAEERI/E, 67/68, 1980, p. 5–17, bibl.)

Outlines negotiating positions of England and Argentina (1966–80) on Falklands/Malvinas matter. Concludes that if British are unwilling to negotiate sovereignty question, Argentina should prepare to occupy by force.

7352 Kelsey, Robert J. Maneuvering in the Falklands (Proceedings [U.S. Naval Institute, Annapolis, Md.] 108[955]:9, Sept. 1982, p. 36–38, ill.)

Although primarily concerned with narrow questions of military tactics, article claims that Argentine fear of Chile's taking advantage of strategic situation effectively removed a significant portion of Argentine naval force from action against Britain.

7353 Laffin, John. Fight for the Falklands! London: Sphere Books Limited, 1982. 215 p.

"Quickie" account of military side of Falklands/Malvinas struggle. Devotes limited attention to political forces that led to occupation. Emphasizes that Argentine junta felt Thatcher wouldn't fight because she is a woman. Politically superficial but a concise description of military maneuvers.

7354 Melo, Artemio Luis. La cuestión internacional del Canal de Beagle. Buenos Aires: Edicones Depalma, 1979. 176 p., 2 leaves of plates: bibl., maps.

Better than average legal defense of Argentina's decision not to accept the 1977 arbitral award in favor of Chile regarding Beagle Channel islands. Documents make up one third.

7355 Méndez, Roberto N. Paso libre a Inglaterra: nueva violación de los Tratados del Canal de Panamá (AR, 8:30, 1982, p. 10–12, ill.)

Economics professor at Univ. of Panama alleges that US-dominated Panama Canal Commission violated "neutrality" clause of new treaty by giving "priority" passage to two UK military vessels that were enroute to South Atlantic during Falklands/Malvinas War. [Y.H. Ferguson]

7356 Milenky, Edward S. Argentina (in Security policies in developing nations. Edited by Edward A. Kolodzie and Robert E. Harkavy. Lexington, Mass.: D.C. Heath and Company, Lexington Books, 1982, p. 27–51]

Useful overview of Argentine defense policy with attention to political factors. Unfortunately trauma of Falklands/Malvinas fiasco is such as to call into question whether Milenky's deft picture still applies.

7357 Nef, J. and F. Hallman. Reflections on the Anglo-Argentinian War (International Perspectives [The Canadian journal on world affairs, Department of External Affairs, Ottawa, Canada] 1, Sept./Oct. 1982, p. 6–10, ill.)

Stresses domestic factors in both England and Argentina as causes of Falklands/Malvinas War. Debatable analysis but an intriguing piece.

7358 Palermo, Vicente. La Argentina y la Antártida (Geosur [Asociación Sudamericana de Estudios Geopolíticos e Internacionales, Montevideo] 2 : 23, julio 1981, p. 3–21)

Argues for active Argentine interest in Antartica and expresses reservations as to the continent's "internationalization."

7359 Ponsati, Arturo. La Argentina y América Latina (CRIT, 54 : 1873/1874, dic. 1981, p. 765–772)

Reviews domestic Argentine political and economic difficulties and argues that part of the solution may be increased Latin American integration. Interesting ideas.

7360 Relaciones chileno-argentinas, la controversia del Canal Beagle: una selección cartográfica = Chilean-Argentine relations, the Beagle Channel controversy: a cartographical selection. Genève: Impr. Atar, 1979. 80 p., 33 leaves of plates (28 fold.): 33 col. maps.

Large selection of beautifully reproduced maps supporting Argentina's claims to the Beagle Channel. Fascinating collection and excellent reproduction. Distributed by the Argentine government. Text in English and Spanish.

7361 Silenzi de Stagni, Adolfo. Las Malvinas y el petróleo. Buenos Aires: El Cid Editor, 1982. 1 v.: bibl., ill. (Colección Geopolítica)

Actually two books in one: 1) optimistically details possible oil riches of Argentine territorial waters (including the Falklands/Malvinas areas); and 2) documentary account of Falklands/Malvinas controversy since 1960.

7362 Sourrouille, Juan V. El complejo automotor en Argentina: transnacionales en América Latina. México: Instituto Latinoamericano de Estudios Trans- nacionales: Editorial Nueva Imagen, 1980. 242 p.: ill.

Well researched and detailed history of post World War II transnational automobile industry in Argentina. Although defenders of

transnationals may want to argue some of its interpretations, book is valuable addition to literature on role of transnationals in Latin American countries.

7363 Stoetzer, O. Carlos. Two studies on contemporary Argentine history. New York: Argentina Society, Argentina Independent Review, 1980. 86 p.

Pamphlet defends 1976 military coup in Argentina and criticizes Carter's human rights policy as applied to Argentina. Author's anti-Marxism and anti-Peronism tends to shape the entire line of analysis. Work is designed to win US sympathy for the junta.

7364 Surprises in the South Atlantic (NACLA, 16 : 3, May/June 1982, p. 2–43, ill., maps, plates, tables)

Well researched attempt to organize an argument linking faddish geopolitical ideas of South African and Argentine governments into a general explanation of contemporary strategy to protect capitalist global interests. Includes interesting facts and sources which one might have missed otherwise.

7365 United States. Congress. House. Committee on Foreign Affairs. Subcommittee on Human Rights and International Organizations. Review of United States policy on military assistance to Argentina: hearing before the Subcommittees on Human Rights and International Organizations and on Inter-American Affairs of the Committee on Foreign Affairs, House of Representatives, April 1, 1981. Washington: US G.P.O., 1981. 128 p.: bibl. (97th Congress, 1st Session)

Set of 1981 hearings on whether or not to renew US military aid to Argentina which had ceased due to Carter's human rights policy. Valuable source.

7366 War in the Falklands: the full story. *The Sunday Times of London* Insight Team. New York: Harper & Row, 1982. 295 p., 16 p. of plates: ill., index, maps.

Helpful account of the Falklands/Malvinas conflict with good illustrations and maps. Attempts to understand Argentine viewpoint although perspective is very British. More emphasis on military than political aspects. Relatively high class journalism, as opposed to serious scholarship, but still the best thing thus far on these events.

7367 Zavala Ortiz, Miguel Angel. La República y el Beagle: buscando una decisión nacional (CRIT, 54:1873/1874, dic. 1981, p. 741-748)

Unusually thoughtful discussion, albeit from the Argentine point of view, of Beagle Channel question, a matter that has not generated much in the area of sane analysis. Argues, among other things, against the use of force.

BOLIVIA

Abecia Baldivieso, Valentín. Las relaciones internacionales en la historia de Bolivia. See *HLAS 44:3008.*

Gómez de Aranda, Blanca. Casimiro Olañeta, diplomático, 1824-1839. See *HLAS 44:3027.*

7368 Jordán Sandoval, Santiago. Bolivia y el equilibrio del Cono Sudamericano. Cochabamba, Bolivia: Editorial Los Amigos del Libro, 1979. 270 p.: bibl.

Bolivian diplomat argues the geopolitical importance of his country for Latin America's future. Although rather disjointed in its coverage, book provides Bolivian perspective on matter of economic integration.

7369 Peredo P., Héctor. El poder boliviano. La Paz: Empresa Gráfica Visión, between 1978 and 1980. 156 p.

Geopolitical writings are always interesting, and this study is no exception. Author commences by expressing concern that Chile will use Bolivia as a staging area in a war with Argentina. Suggests formation of an alliance to prevent such an occurrence, and indicates some potential partners for the alliance. [M.C. Cook]

7370 Siles Guevara, Juan. Bolivia's right to the Pacific Ocean: a critical essay on Jaime Eyzaguirre's *Chile and Bolivia, outline of a diplomatic process.* Translated by María Alicia Crespo de Parkerson. La Paz: Fundación Manuel Vicente Ballivián, 1980. 95 p.: bibl., index, maps.

Bolivian answer to distinguished Chilean historian's defense of his country's position in the border dispute (see *HLAS 27:3347*).

BRAZIL

7371 Brazil in the international system: the rise of a middle power. Edited by

Wayne A. Selcher. Boulder, Colo.: Westview Press, 1981. 251 p.: bibl., ill., index (Westview special studies on Latin America and the Caribbean)

Thorough and fact-filled set of essays explore Brazil's aspirations to rise from middle-power status to larger role in world politics. Several essays are quantitative in their approach. Specific relations with South American countries, West Germany, Africa and India are analyzed.

7372 Brigagão, Clóvis. Cancelamento do acordo (IBRI/R, 21:81/84, 1978, p. 103-109)

Starting with 1977 Brazilian decision to cancel military assistance agreement with Washington (due to Carter's human rights policy), author retraces circumstances and policies that led to signing of the 1952 accord.

7373 Brooke, Jim. Dateline Brazil: southern superpower (FP, 44, Fall 1981, p. 167-180)

Good summary of current Brazilian position in international relations with an explanation of trade policy, military sales question, diplomatic initiatives in Latin America and generally highly visible leadership role among Third World states. Attempts to speak for less developed countries, author argues, may hinder friendly relations with Reagan administration.

7374 Castro Martínez, Pedro Fernando. Fronteras abiertas: expansionismo y geopolítica en el Brasil contemporáneo. México: Siglo Veintiuno Editores, 1980. 205 p.: bibl. (Sociología y política)

Author marshals much information in support of thesis that Brazilian expansionism/imperialism (with US support) is one of the most important themes in contemporary international relations of Latin America. Arguments are not particularly novel but presentation is good, albeit general.

7375 Caubert, Christian Guy. A competição pelos recursos dos fundos marinhos: um aspecto do confronto Norte-Sul (IBRI/R, 21:81/84, 1978, p. 73-87)

Legalistic discussion of Brazil's position in the Law of the Sea Conference. Author is aware of differing points of view which he sees partly as stemming from North/South competition.

7376 Chiavenatto, Julio José. Geopolítica, arma do fascismo. São Paulo: Global Editora, 1981. 94 p., 8 p. of plates: bibl., ill. (Colección Geopolítica e estratégia; no. 2)

Highly critical commentary on the geopolitical ideas of Southern Cone military. Although author has a particular perspective, he makes his case concerning the serious domestic political implication of such ideas in the rise of geopolitical thinking in Brazil and elsewhere in South America.

7377 d'Adesky, Jacques. Intercâmbio comercial Brasil-Africa, 1958–1977: problemas e perspectivas (Estudos Afro-Asiáticos [Centro de Estudos Afro-Asiáticos (CEAA), Conjunto Universitário Candido Mendes, Rio de Janeiro] 3, 1980, p. 5–34, bibl., tables)

Using many tables, author analyzes Brazilian-African trade (1958–77). Discusses reasons why, after some improvement, trade did not expand as rapidly as expected. Faults Brazilians for lack of knowledge of Africa.

7378 Fragosa, João Luís Ribeiro. As reformulações na política externa brasileira nos anos 70 (Estudos Afro-Asiáticos [Cadernos Candido Mendes, Rio de Janeiro] 5, 1982, p. 41–53, bibl., tables)

Thoughtful discussion starting with Brazil's African policy and then moving to more general discussion concerning implications of Brazil's pursuit of role as middle-range world power. Believes that how capitalism evolves in Brazil will have important implications for the country's future foreign policy.

7379 Franco Filho, Georgenor de Sousa. O Pacto Amazônico: idéias e conceitos. Belém, Brazil: Falangola, 1979. 96 p.: bibl.

Useful discussion of Amazonian Cooperation Treaty, including more than just Brazil's position. Author covers all parties and their economic interests in agreement. Includes appropriate documents.

7380 Gitelman, Sheldon J. Latin America and Africa: their rapidly expanding economic ties (*in* Financing development in Latin America [see item **2821**] p. 222–233)

Devotes particular attention to Brazil's trade with Nigeria and Argentina's with Gabon, but notes other countries are involved. Partly in commodities, most interesting trade is in manufacturers and semi-

manufacturers (e.g., over 100 Brazilian-based companies trade with Nigeria such as Volkswagen which is starting to ship Brazilian-made products for assembly in Africa). [Y.H. Ferguson]

7381 Gugliamelli, Juan E. ¿Fabrica el Brasil una bomba atómica? (IAEERI/E, 70, enero/marzo 1982, p. 5–12)

Reprint of Brazilian newspaper's interview with Argentine military official on Brazilian/Argentine arms rivalry and particularly the nuclear question. Provides some interesting insights into rather fearful Argentine military's interpretation of Brazilian arms industry.

Hilton, Stanley E. Brazil and the post-Versailles world: elite images and foreign policy strategy, 1919–1929. See *HLAS 44:3587*.

7382 Leite, Celantho de Paiva. O Brasil e o Caribe (IBRI/R, 21:81/84, 1978, p. 5–22, bibl.)

Intelligently done discussion of the historical role of Brazil in the Caribbean area with some speculation as to the future of that role and its present strength. Part of the effort to understand Brazil's role as a middle-range power.

7383 Mattos, Carlos de Meira. Uma geopolítica pan-amazônica. Rio de Janeiro: Biblioteca do Exército Editora, 1980. 215 p.: ill. (Coleção General Benício; v. 181)

Brazilian Gen. discusses future of Amazon Basin from geopolitical viewpoint. Some history, some economics, some speculation.

7384 ———. Una geopolítica para la Panamazonia (Geosur [Asociación Sudamericana de Estudios Geopolíticos e Internacionales, Montevideo] 3:25, sept. 1981, p. 25–31, bibl., map)

Discusses need for cooperation in developing the Amazonian basin and its geopolitical importance. Favors bilateral agreements aimed at specific problems or circumstances.

7385 ———. El pensamiento estratégico brasileño: proyecciones continentalidad (IAEERI/E, 63, marzo/abril 1980, p. 91–106, maps)

Very general and standard account of the development of Brazil's geopolitical goals: protecting vacant internal areas as well as frontier, retention of possibility of undertaking foreign missions, and further development of war industries.

Medeiros, Antonio Paulo Cachapuz de. As relações internacionais como área de estudos América Latina. See item **7097.**

Mello, Alexandre and **Nilva R. Mello.** O Brasil e a Bacia do Prata. See *HLAS 44:34.*

7386 Poskonina, Liudmila. La concepción radical de izquierda brasileña de "capitalismo dependiente:" aspectos metodológicos (URSS/AL, 6:54, 1982, p. 50–67, plate)

Social theory discussion of the Latin American intellectual left's contribution to understanding Latin American exploitation. Soviet author criticizes writers such as Cardoso insofar as dependency theory repudiates Marxist/Leninist thinking. Relatively predictable argument.

7387 Prestes, Luis Carlos. América Latina: tareas actuales de la lucha contra el fascismo (URSS/AL, 3[19], 1978, p. 5–15)

The grand old man of Brazil's Communist Party gloomily surveys developments in his country since 1964 military coup and urges "the masses with the working class in the lead and directed by vanguard party" never to weary in their struggle against "reactionary forces" on the continent.

7388 *Resenha de Política Exterior do Brasil.* Ministério das Relações Exteriores. Ano 6, No. 20, jan./março 1979– . Brasília.

Important source of information, this issue includes speeches and documents relating to Brazilian foreign policy during 1979. Published by the Brazilian Ministry of Foreign Relations.

7389 Roett, Riordan. Brazil's international relations in perspective (FPRI/O, 26:1, Spring 1982, p. 257–267)

Review essay of item **7397.** Author both summarizes the work and offers insightful comments as to Brazil's much discussed rise to middle-power international status.

7390 Sautchuk, Jaime; Horácio Martins de Carvalho; and **Sérgio Buarque de Gusmão.** Projeto Jari: a invasão americana. 2. ed. São Paulo: Brasil Debates, 1980. 110 p.: ill. (Brasil hoje; v. 1)

Rather sensationalized account of Project Jari which sees the effort to exploit the Brazilian interior as part of a capitalist conspiracy of sorts. Despite the tone, a good deal

of factual information is included. Now that Jari seems doomed, it would be useful to have a follow-up study as to the effect of its failure on the region.

7391 Schilling, Paulo R. El expansionismo brasileño. México: El Cid Editor, 1978. 314 p.; bibl., maps (Colección Geopolítica; 2)

Long, detailed account of what author perceives as an increasingly imperialistic Brazil. In particular, he reads Brazilian geopolitical writings as a kind of road map for future imperialistic ventures. Although one can point to exaggerations, author is quite correct in detecting an imperialistic thrust in some Brazilian geopolitical theorists.

7392 Silva, Golbery do Couto e. Conjuntura política nacional: o poder executivo; &, Geopolítica do Brasil. 3. ed. Rio de Janeiro: Livraria J. Olympio Editora, 1981. 37, 273 p.: bibl., ill., maps, ports. (Coleção Documentos brasileiros; v. no. 190)

Third edition of geopolitical theories of the man whose ideas have been extremely influential in Brazil and among military men in other Latin American countries. Quality of the work (which is not bad) is less important than insight it provides into military thinking.

7393 Smith, Joseph. American diplomacy and the Naval Mission to Brazil: 1917–1930 (IAMEA, 35:1, Summer 1981, p. 73–91)

Small case study which has the value of giving a micro perspective of a larger phenomena—that is US replacement of British as hegemonic power in Latin America. Curiously enough, the 1930 domestic changes in Brazil undo, at least temporarily, developments covered by this analysis.

7394 Soares, Alvaro Teixeira. O Brasil no conflito ideológico global: 1937–1979. Rio de Janeiro: Civilização Brasileira, 1980. 238 p.: bibl. (Coleção Retratos do Brasil; v. 140)

Valuable general discussion of Brazilian foreign policy (1937–79) by veteran diplomat/scholar. Good deal of interesting detail with a concentration on period up to end of World War II.

Souza, Carlos Alves de. Um embaixador em tempos de crise. See *HLAS 44:3632.*

7395 Trindade, Antônio Augusto Cançado. Posições internacionais do Brasil no plano multilateral (UMG/RBEP, 52, jan. 1981, p. 147–218)

Valuable lengthy recounting of Brazil's positions in a number of international conferences beginning with 1945 one in San Francisco, its later role in US, and in several specialized international meetings such as Law of the Sea Conference and 1974 international meeting on world population situation.

7396 Ware, David. The Amazon Treaty: a turning point in Latin American cooperation? (Texas International Law Journal [University of Texas School of Law, Austin] 15:1, Winter 1980, p. 117–137)

Analysis of 1978 Amazon Cooperation Treaty emphasizes degree to which pact lacks mechanism for enforcement action. Includes good discussion of signators' political motivations.

7397 Wesson, Robert G. The United States and Brazil: limits of influence. New York: Praeger, 1981. 179 p.: bibl., index (Studies of influence in international relations)

Primarily based on secondary sources, book concentrates on US influence in Brazil since 1960s. Author is conservative critic of extreme dependency theorists, and of those who see heavy US hand in 1964 coup. Praises impact of Carter's human rights stance. Includes valuable section on nuclear power controversy and worthwhile summary of complicated question of outside influence. Concludes that US hegemony (if it ever existed in Brazil) is declining.

CHILE

7398 Argentina y el Laudo arbitral del Canal Beagle. Selección y notas de Germán Carrasco. Santiago: Editorial Jurídica de Chile, 1978. 403 p.

Extremely useful compilation of Chilean newspaper articles and documents relating to 1977 British arbitral decision on Beagle Channel which went almost completely for Chile (and which Argentina soon rejected). Since Chile's legal case is so strong, of course it is easy for Chileans to appeal to grandeur of international law.

7399 Barnard, Andrew. Chilean communists, radical presidents and Chilean

relations with the United States, 1940–1947 (JLAS, 13:2, Nov. 1981, p. 347–374)

Based on three incidents (1940–47), article suggests that it was Chilean domestic politics which caused difficulties between radical presidents of the day and Chilean Communist Party. Concludes that US anticommunist pressures had little to do with problems of the Chilean left (for historian's comment, see *HLAS 44:3067*).

7400 Branch, Taylor and **Eugene M. Popper.** Labyrinth. New York: The Viking Press, 1982. 623 p.: ill.

Absolutely fascinating account of US government's efforts to solve Letelier assassination written from insider's perspective. Voluminous information makes it quite clear that Chilean involvement went high into the junta. Graphically describes reluctance of US government to face up to where the trail of evidence led.

7401 Cavalla Rojas, Antonio. El conflicto del Beagle. México: Casa de Chile en México, 1979. 192 p.: bibl., maps.

Relatively short (40 p.) essay blames Pinochet government policies for Beagle Channel crisis. Attempts to formulate better Chilean position predicated on junta's demise. Consists mostly of documents and long bibliography.

7402 Cientocincuenta años de política exterior chilena. Obra editada bajo la dirección de Walter Sánchez G. y Teresa Pereira L. Santiago: Instituto de Estudios Internacionales de la Universidad de Chile, Editorial Universitaria, 1977. 418 p.: bibl. (Estudios internacionales)

Thoroughly admirable attempt to provide overview of Chilean foreign relations, past and present. Unfortunately, in terms of methodology, essays neither fit nor cover important topics. Pieces on Chile's World War I neutrality by Ricardo Couyoumdjian and on Chile's Antarctic claims by Oscar Pinochet de la Barra are particularly valuable. Coeditor Sánchez makes a good effort at summation and isolation of themes.

7403 Collums, Haley D. The Letelier case: foreign sovereign liability for acts of political assassination (Virginia Journal of International Law [Virginia University, John Bassett Moore Society of International Law, Charlottesville] 21:2, Winter 1981, p. 251–268)

Legalistic analysis which makes clear degree to which the Foreign Service Immunities Act of 1976 now can hold foreign agents liable for personal injuries or death resulting from acts of violence sanctioned by a foreign state and directed against targets within US.

7404 Facilidades portuarias a Bolivia (Geosur [Asociación Sudamericana de Estudios Geopolíticos e Internacionales, Montevideo] 2:15, nov. 1980, p. 3–20, tables)

Legalistic and descriptive account of Chile's willingness to allow Bolivian commerce free access to the Pacific. Pro-Chile in tone although perhaps justifiably on this matter.

7405 La Geopolítica y el fascismo dependiente. Antonio Cavalla Rojas, Jorge Chateau, Revista *Principios*. México: Casa de Chile, 1977. 220 p.: bibl., ill.

Strong attack on geopolitical ideas of current Chilean junta. Links them to German pre-Nazi and Nazi concepts. Gives detailed critique of writings of Augusto Pinochet (prior to his ascent to power) and Chilean Major Julio Von Chrismar.

La Guerra con Chile en sus documentos. See *HLAS 44:2946.*

7406 Hersh, Seymour R. The price of power: Kissinger, Nixon, and Chile (The Atlantic Monthly [Boston] 250:6, Dec. 1982, p. 31–58)

Breathless tone of this exposé masks fact that those who have seriously followed the revelations regarding Nixon's policy toward Allende will find little that is new here except for a few names and minor incidents. Nevertheless, a good introduction to a controversial relationship for the uninitiated.

Informes inéditos de diplomáticos extranjeros durante la Guerra del Pacífico: Alemania, Estados Unidos de Norteamérica, Francia, Gran Bretaña. See *HLAS 44:3087.*

7407 Lagos Carmona, Guillermo. Historia de las fronteras de Chile: los tratados de límites con Perú. 2. ed., aum. y actualizada. Santiago: Editorial Andrés Bello, 1981. 143 p., 6 folded leaves of plates: ill.

Long discussion of Chilean/Bolivian border controversy from an entirely Chilean perspective. Excellent book with numerous detailed and helpful maps. One of several

volumes intended to cover all Chilean border controversies (for historian's comment, see *HLAS 44:3090).*

7408 Mayo, John. Britain and Chile, 1851– 1886: anatomy of a relationship (SAGE/JIAS, 23:1, Feb. 1981, p. 95–120, tables)

Descriptive article concentrates on influence of British commerce and investment of Chilean development. Chile's links with London are seen as the closest in Latin America. Rather narrow piece of research (for historian's comment, see *HLAS 44:3096).*

7409 Portales, Diego. La industria de la comunicación: oligopolios y transnacionales. México: Instituto Latinoamericano de Estudios Transnacionales, n.d. 60 leaves.

Begins as study of structure of communications industry but ends by asking question as to role of oligopolistic industry in global capitalism. Data drawn almost exclusively from Latin America with an emphasis on Chile.

7410 Sánchez G., Walter. Las tendencias sobresalientes de la política exterior chilena. Santiago: Instituto de Estudios Internacionales, Universidad de Chile, 1979. p. 374–418: bibl. (Serie de publicaciones especiales; no. 32)

Extremely useful short summary of main currents of Chilean foreign policy, although author's account/criticism of Allende policies is debatable.

7411 Tomic, Radomiro. Las relaciones Norte-Sur antes y después de Cancún (RAE, 4, 4. trimestre 1981, p. 70–81, ill., plates)

Former Chilean Christian Democratic presidential candidate Tomic delivers a negative account of Cancún Conference with particular emphasis on Reagan's inflexibility. Article closes with some guarded optimism as to future of LDCs.

7412 United States. Congress. House. Committee on Foreign Affairs. Subcommittees on International Economic Policy and Trade and on Inter-American Affairs. U.S. economic sanctions against Chile: hearing, March 10, 1981. Washington: US G.P.O., 1981. 86 p.: facsim. (97th Congress, 1st Session)

Hearings regarding Reagan administration's 1981 lifting of economic sanctions against Chile. Much discussion by advocates of sanctions on the basis of the Letelier assassination while opponents focus on Chile's comparative improvement in the area of human rights and on the threat of Marxism.

COLOMBIA

7413 Barco, Virgilio. Lucha partidista y política internacional. Compilación y dirección, Oscar Delgado. Bogotá: Carlos Valencia Editores, 1981. 532 p.: ill.

Consists almost entirely of documents relating to long career of prominent Colombian Liberal politician Virgilio Barco. Includes some useful material resulting from his ambassadorial appointments to London and Washington, his representation of Colombia at international economic conferences, and on Colombia's relations with Venezuela.

7414 Craig, Richard B. Colombian narcotics and United States-Colombian relations (SAGE/JIAS, 23:3, Aug. 1981, p. 243–270)

Fascinating and well informed analysis of both US and Colombian policy toward the drug trade. Although author is aware of Colombia's failures, he lays much blame for continuation of traffic on Washington's unwillingness to finance anti-drug activities and on various US laws that hinder cooperation.

7415 Díaz Callejas, Apolinar. La administración Reagan y nuevos impulsos al militarismo en América Latina (URSS/AL, 11[47], 1981, p. 4–20)

Former Colombian Senator, writing in Soviet journal, denounces Reagan administration's support for conservative military regimes in El Salvador and elsewhere. [Y.H. Ferguson]

Lupsha, Peter A. Drug trafficking: Mexico and Colombia in comparative perspective. See item **7187**.

7416 Nieto Navia, Rafael. Apuntes para un estudio sobre el *Libro blanco* de Nicaragua sobre el Archipiélago de San Andrés y Providencia (PUJ/U, 61, dic. 1981 p. 357–384)

Discussion from Colombian viewpoint of contested ownership and/or control of San Andrés and Providencia Archipelago. Reprints several documents and diplomatic communications.

7417 Sanz de Santamaría, Carlos. Fin del asilo del Doctor Víctor Raúl Haya de la Torre, 1954. Bogotá: Fundación Centenario del Banco de Colombia, 1978. 205 p.: bibl.

Often first-person account of negotiations between Colombia and Peru as a result of Haya de la Torre's seeking asylum at the Colombian Embassy in Lima. Emphasis is on legal questions of this famous incident.

PERU

7418 Albert, Bill. Sugar and Anglo-Peruvian trade negotiations in the 1930's (JLAS, 14:1, May 1982, p. 121–142, tables)

Sees never-ratified 1936 Anglo-Peruvian Trade Agreement as parallel case to Roca Runciman Agreement of 1933 except that Peru was in better position to find alternative markets than Argentina and hence able to survive not ratifying the pact.

Bonilla, Heraclio. Un siglo a la deriva: ensayos sobre el Perú, Bolivia y la guerra. See *HLAS 44:2916*.

Caivano, Tomaso. Historia de la guerra de América entre Chile, Perú y Bolivia. See *HLAS 44:2922*.

7419 Debuyst, Frederic. Securité et developpement en Amérique Latine (UCL/CD, 12:3/4, 1980, p. 387–440)

Rambling article maintains US has abandoned support for democracy emphasized during Kennedy years in favor of "controlled" democracy exemplified by Peru under Belaúnde's second administration. [Y.H. Ferguson]

7420 Ferrero Costa, Eduardo. El nuevo Derecho del Mar: el Perú y las 200 millas. Lima: Pontificia Universidad Católica del Perú, Fondo Editorial, 1979. 456 p., 1 fold. leaf of plates: bibl., map.

Lengthy historical/legal account of 200-mile territorial water question also devotes much space to specific economic benefits (real and projected) of 200-mile limit to Peru. Includes 33 tables and foldout map.

Gardiner, C. Harvey. Pawns in a triangle of hate: the Peruvian Japanese and the United States. See *HLAS 44:2944*.

7421 Guzmán Herrera, José. Política económica internacional de la CEE hacia los países en desarrollo: importancia de este política para América Latina, los países andinos y el Perú (Revista de la Academia Diplomática del Perú [Lima] 21, enero/dic. 1980, p. 95–115)

Peruvian diplomat presents solid analysis of how the EEC works, particularly with regard to the Third World. Author is in favor of economic integration and argues that the Peruvian economy complements the EEC economies more than any other Latin American country.

7422 Mercado Jarrín, Edgardo. Pacto Amazônico: dominação ou integração? (Encontros com a Civilização Brasileira [Rio de Janeiro] 11, maio 1979, p. 57–77)

Former Peruvian government official discusses from Peruvian (and other countries') viewpoints a delicate question: Is the Amazonian Cooperation Treaty a vehicle for Brazilian domination of the Amazonian basin? Realistic and valuable analysis.

7423 ———. El siglo veinte, siglo de la Amazonia (Geosur [Asociación Sudamericana de Estudios Geopolíticos e Internacionales, Montevideo] 3:25, sept. 1981, p. 5–24)

"Occupation of the Amazon vacuum is inscribed on the agenda for the Latin American man" concludes this Peruvian's analysis of possible future development of Amazon area. Although a predictable essay on Amazonian development, it includes much information and analysis.

7424 Preeg, Ernest H. The evolution of a revoluton: Peru and its relations with the United States, 1968–1980. Washington: NPA Committee on Changing International Realities, 1981. 67 p.: bibl., ill. (CIR report; 10. NPA report; 190)

Fine analysis of Peruvian politics and US/Peruvian relations between 1968–80. Tone and biases are very much those of a professional Foreign Service officer.

Quiroz Paz-Soldán, Eusebio. El espíritu del Tratado de Ancón. See *HLAS 44:2973*.

Rosero Ravelo, Luis Alberto. Memorias de un veterano de la Guerra del 41. See *HLAS 44:2905*.

7425 Schwalb López-Aldana, Fernando. El convenio Greene-De la Flor y el pago a la IPC. Lima: El Populista, 1979. 168 p.: ill. (El Populista; 5)

Member of Belaúnde Terry administration defends IPC settlement which prompted 1968 coup and criticizes the Velasco government's eventual settlement.

7426 Simposium sobre el Uso del Mar y su Influencia en el Desarrollo Nacional, *1st, Escuela Superior de Guerra Naval, 1978.* Simposium sobre el Uso del Mar y su Influencia en el Desarrollo Nacional, 27 de noviembre-10 de diciembre de 1978. Auspiciado por el Ministerio de Marina. Lima: Instituto de Estudios Histórico-Marítimos del Perú, 1980. 370 p.: bibl., ill. (Serie Congresos y simposios. Publicaciones del Instituto de Estudios Histórico-Marítimos del Perú).

Set of papers from 1978 conference involving Peruvian diplomats, scholars, *técnicos,* and military men. Subject is the economic, political, and military importance of the Pacific and Latin American waterways.

7427 Terán, Francisco. Como pensaba hace 90 años un diplomático peruano sobre el problema limítrofe (IGME/RG, 16, abril 1982, p. 83–93, map)

Discusses 1981 article by Peruvian Ambassador to Ecuador in which he takes what seems today to be the Ecuadorian position vis-à-vis the Peruvian/Ecuadorian border dispute. This is an interesting piece now reprinted in Ecuador for nationalistic ends.

VENEZUELA

7428 Betancourt, Rómulo. Venezuela's oil. Translated by Donald Peck. London: Allen & Unwin, 1978. 275 p.: bibl., map.

Compilation of speeches, essays, and documents contains views on energy of Venezuela's greatest statesman since Bolívar. Betancourt, who gave impetus to 50–50 profit sharing between state and private firms and the establishment of OPEC, describes those who buy off government officials as "racketeers" and corruption as an "infectious bacteria." Still, he remains optimistic about developing alternative energy sources, preserving world peace, and selecting qualified leaders to lead his beloved patria.

7429 Bond, Robert D. Venezuela, La Cuenca del Caribe y la crisis centroamericana (CM/FI, 22:2, oct./dic. 1981, p. 164–179)

Traces Venezuela's policies toward Central America and Caribbean from Rómulo Betancourt to Herrera Campins. Believes Venezuela will continue to influence subregion and, while closer to US on El Salvador than Mexico, will argue for negotiated settlement. Unfortunately, Bond wrote before fall of Duarte government and Nicaraguan counterrevolution, developments requiring fast diplomatic footwork. [Y.H. Ferguson]

Carl, George E. First among equals: Great Britain and Venezuela, 1810–1910. See *HLAS 44:2876.*

7430 Carpio Castillo, Rubén. Geopolítica de Venezuela. Caracas: Editorial Ariel-Seix Barral Venezolana, 1981. 293 p.: ill. (Colección Geografía de Venezuela nueva; 3)

Knowledgeable discussion of Venezuela's geography with some attention devoted to geopolitics. Includes especially strong discussions for history of various frontiers which helps one comprehend actual and potential border difficulties.

7431 ———. El golfo de Venezuela y el Tratatado [sic] Herrera Campins-Turbay Ayala. Caracas: Venediciones, 1980. 111 p.: maps.

Well informed Venezuelan geographer/diplomat's critique of proposed Herrera-Turbay Treaty settling Gulf of Venezuela dispute with Colombia. Author is not pleased with agreement.

7432 Conferencia Pro-Democracia y Libertad, *Caracas, Venezuela, 1979.* Democracia y libertad: el compromiso político económico y social del movimiento sindical libre. CIOSL-ORIT-CTV: Conferencia Pro-Democracia y Libertad, 23 al 28 de julio de 1979, Caracas. Caracas: Instituto Latinoamericano de Investigaciones Sociales, 1981. 312 p. (Democracia económica)

Proceedings of "pro-democracy and liberty" conference (Caracas, July 1979) sponsored by International Confederation of Free Labor Organizations (CIOSL), Inter-American Organization of Workers (ORIT), and Confederation of Workers of Venezuela (CTV). [Y.H. Ferguson]

7433 Ewell, Judith. The development of Venezuelan geopolitical analysis since World War II (SAGE/JIAS, 24:3, Aug. 1982, p. 295–320)

Even handed, descriptive discussion of Venezuelan geopolitical thinking. Particular useful as an overview of possible directions for Venezuela's foreign policy.

7434 González Deluca, María Elena. Los intereses británicos y la política en Venezuela en las últimas décadas del siglo XIX (UB/BA, 22:3, 1980, p. 89–123)

Well done analysis within dependency/world state perspective of impact of British expansionistic trade and investment policy during latter decades of 19th century. Primarily concerned with Venezuelan development, includes references to parallel experiences of other South American countries.

7435 Herman, Donald L. Ideology, economic power and regional imperialism: the determinants of foreign policy under Venezuela's Christian Democrats (UPR/CS, 18:1/2, April/July 1978, p. 43–83, map)

Attempts to evaluate impact of ideology on Venezuelan foreign policy under COPEI's leadership. Concludes that ideology served primarily as rationalization for a geopolitical policy. Even-handed discussion and details on a number of disputes (e.g., Colombian border, Guyana, Cuba).

7436 Nweihed, Kaldone G. ¿Es Venezuela parte del Tercer Mundo? (Tiempo Real [Universidad Simón Bolívar, Caracas] 8, nov. 1978, p. 27–43, photos)

Interesting attempt to explore notion of whether or not Venezuela belongs to the Third World. Defines concept of Third World in four different ways.

7437 Perazzo, Nicolás. Historia de las relaciones diplomáticas entre Venezuela y Colombia. Caracas: Presidencia de la República, 1981. 618 p.: bibl.

Extremely detailed (and hence valuable) history of diplomatic relations between Venezuela and Colombia. Takes a Venezuelan point of view (for historian's comment, see *HLAS 44:2890*).

7438 Portillo, Julio. Venezuela-Cuba, relaciones diplomáticas, 1902–1980. Caracas: Editorial Arte, 1981. 174 p.

Relatively detailed discussion of Cuban/Venezuelan relations (1958–80). Author favors closer relations but anticipates that errors on both sides will make cooperation difficult. Useful volume.

7439 Rabe, Stephen G. The road to OPEC: the United States relations with Venezuela, 1919–1976. Austin: University of Texas Press, 1982. 262 p.: bibl., index (Texas Pan American series)

Well researched, excellent account of US/Venezuelan relations (1919–76). Despite title, OPEC is not its central focus but, rather, chain of events leading to OPEC. Essential book for understanding inter-American relations (for historian's comment, see *HLAS 44:2892*).

7440 Rey, Carlos. Del Golfo de Venezuela al Esequibo: una exploración de alternativas (Revista de Estudios Políticos [Editorial Jurídica Venezolana, Caracas] o [sic], 1981, p. 7–39)

Discussion of Venezuela's boundary problems with Colombia and Guyana. Helpful analysis mixing politics with legal arguments. In Guyana's case, author does not rule out use of force and speaks of need to be "respected" in international relations (rather than being "loved").

7441 Romero, Carlos Antonio. La política exterior como política pública: caso-estudio de la diplomacia venezolana en el Caribe (Argos [Universidad Simón Bolívar, División de Ciencias Sociales y Humanidades, Caracas] 2, 1981, p. 19–37)

Written in language of political science theory, study is critical of Herrera government's Caribbean policy during first year in office. Rather than being sensitive to Caribbean economic conditions, author claims that, for domestic political reasons, Herrera perceives the Caribbean situation in counterproductive "democracy vs. totalitarianism" terms.

JOURNAL ABBREVIATIONS INTERNATIONAL RELATIONS

AAAS/D Daedalus. Journal of the American Academy of Arts and Sciences. Harvard Univ. Cambridge, Mass.

AAFH/TAM The Americas. A quarterly publication of inter-American cultural history. Academy of American Franciscan History. Washington.

ADN A Defesa Nacional. Revista de assuntos militares e estudo de problemas brasileiros. Rio de Janeiro.

AFS/JAF Journal of American Folklore. American Folklore Society. Austin, Tex.

AJC/C Commentary. American Jewish Committee. New York.

APS/WA World Affairs. The American Peace Society. Washington.

AR Areito. Areíto, Inc. New York.

AU/P Phylon. Atlanta University. Atlanta, Ga.

AZIF Aussenpolitik. Zeitschrift für Internationale Fragen. Deutsche Verlags-Austalt. Hamburg, FRG.

BCV/REL Revista de Economía Latinoamericana. Banco Central de Venezuela. Caracas.

BESPL Berichte zur Entwicklung in Spanien, Portugal, Lateinamerika. München, FRG.

BNCE/CE Comercio Exterior. Banco Nacional de Comercio Exterior. México.

CAM Cuadernos Americanos. México.

CEESTM/TM Tercer Mundo y Economía Mundial. Centro de Estudios Económicos y Sociales del Tercer Mundo. México.

CFR/FA Foreign Affairs. Council on Foreign Relations. New York.

CII/IJ *See* CIIA/IJ.

CIIA/IJ International Journal. Canadian Institute of International Affairs. Toronto.

CM/FI Foro Internacional. El Colegio de México. México.

CM/HM Historia Mexicana. El Colegio de México. México.

CPU/ES Estudios Sociales. Corporación de Promoción Universitaria. Santiago.

CRIA/WW Worldview. A monthly of ethics and international affairs. Council of Religion and International Affairs. New York.

CRIT   Criterio. Editorial Criterio. Buenos Aires.

CU/ILRR   Industrial and Labor Relations Review. A publication of the New York School of Industrial and Labor Relations, a Contract College of the State Univ., Cornell Univ. Ithaca.

CU/JIA   Journal of International Affairs. Columbia Univ., School of International Affairs. New York.

CUH   Current History. A monthly magazine of world affairs. Philadelphia, Pa.

CUNY/CP   Comparative Politics. The City Univ. of New York Political Science Program. New York.

DDW   Die Dritte Welt. Verlag Anton Hain. Meisenheim, FRG.

DESCO/Q   Quehacer. Realidad nacional: problemas y alternativas. Revista del Centro de Estudios y Promoción del Desarrollo (DESCO). Lima.

DIS   Dissent. Dissent Publishing Association. New York.

EDTM   Estudios del Tercer Mundo. Centro de Estudios Económicos y Sociales del Tercer Mundo. México.

EEUU/PL   Estados Unidos: Perspectiva Latinoamericana. Cuadernos semestrales. Centro de Investigación y Docencia Económica (CIDE). México.

FCE/TE   El Trimestre Económico. Fondo de Cultura Económica. México.

FDD/NED   Notes et Études Documentaires. France, Direction de la Documentation. Paris.

FEPA/EI   F.E.P.A. Estudios e Investigaciones. Fundación para el Estudio de los Problemas Argentinos. Buenos Aires.

FGV/R   Revista de Ciência Política. Fundação Getúlio Vargas. Rio de Janeiro.

FIU/CR   Caribbean Review. Florida International Univ., Office of Academic Affairs. Miami.

FP   Foreign Policy. National Affairs, Inc. and Carnegie Endowment for International Peace. New York.

FPRI/O   Orbis. A journal of world affairs. Foreign Policy Research Institute, Philadelphia, Pa. *in association with the* Fletcher School of Law and Diplomacy, Tufts Univ. Medford, Mass.

GU/WQ   The Washington Quarterly. Georgetown Univ., The Center for Strategic and International Studies. Washington.

GWU/JILE   Journal of International Law and Economics. George Washington Univ., The National Law Center. Washington.

HAHR   Hispanic American Historical Review. Duke Univ. Press *for the* Conference on Latin American History of the American Historical Association. Durham, N.C.

IA   International Affairs. A monthly journal of political analysis. Moskova.

IAA   Ibero-Amerikanisches Archiv. Ibero-Amerikanisches Institut. Berlin, FRG.

IAEERI/E   Estrategia. Instituto Argentino de Estudios Estratégicos y de las Relaciones Internacionales. Buenos Aires.

IAHG/AHG   Antropología e Historia de Guatemala. Instituto de Antropología e Historia de Guatemala. Guatemala.

IAMEA   Inter-American Economic Affairs. Washington.

IBRI/B   *See* IBRI/R.

IBRI/R   Revista Brasileira de Política Internacional. Instituto Brasileiro de Relações Internacionais. Rio de Janeiro.

IDE/DE   Desarrollo Económico. Instituto de Desarrollo Económico y Social. Buenos Aires.

IGME/RG   Revista Geográfica. Instituto Geográfico Militar del Ecuador, Depto. Geográfico. Quito.

IIDC/C   Civilisations. International Institute of Differing Civilizations. Bruxelles.

IRR/RC   Race & Class. A journal of black and Third World liberation. Institute of Race Relations and The Transnational Institute. London.

IRRI/SD   Studia Diplomatica. Chronique de politique etrangère. Institut Royal des Relations Internationales. Bruxelles.

JCMS   Journal of Common Market Studies. Oxford, England.

JGSWGL Jahrbuch für Geschichte von Staat, Wirtschaft und Gesellschaft Lateinamerikas. Köln, FRG.

JLAS Journal of Latin American Studies. Centers or institutes of Latin American studies at the universities of Cambridge, Glasgow, Liverpool, London and Oxford. Cambridge Univ. Press. London.

JPR Journal of Peace Research. International Peace Research Institute, Universitetforlaget. Oslo.

LAP Latin American Perspectives. Univ. of California. Riverside.

LARR Latin American Research Review. Univ. of North Carolina Press *for the* Latin American Studies Association. Chapel Hill.

LIWA/YWA The Yearbook of World Affairs. London Institute of World Affairs. London.

LNB/L Lotería. Lotería Nacional de Beneficencia. Panamá.

MR Monthly Review. An independent Socialist magazine. New York.

NACLA NACLA: Report on the Americas. North American Congress on Latin America. New York.

NACLA/LAER NACLA's Latin America & Empire Report. North American Congress on Latin America. New York.

NEA/RBPE The Review of Black Political Economy. National Economic Association and Atlanta Univ. Center. Atlanta, Ga.

NOSALF/IA Ibero Americana. Scandinavian Association for Research on Latin America (NOSALF). Stockholm.

NSO Nueva Sociedad. Revista política y cultural. San José.

NYRB The New York Review of Books. New York.

OAS/AM Américas. Organization of American States. Washington.

OCLAE OCLAE. Revista mensual de la Organización Continental Latinoamericana de Estudiantes. La Habana.

PAN/ES Estudios Latinoamericanos. Polska Akademia Nauk (Academia de Ciencias de Polonia), Instytut Historii (Instituto de Historia). Warszawa.

PCCLAS/P Proceedings of the Pacific Coast Council on Latin American Studies. Univ. of California. Los Angeles.

PUCIS/WP World Politics. A quarterly journal of international relations. Princeton Univ., Center of International Studies. Princeton, N.J.

PUJ/U Universitas. Ciencias jurídicas y socioeconómicas. Pontificia Univ. Javeriana, Facultad de Derecho y Ciencias Socioeconómicas. Bogotá.

RAE Revista Antioqueña de Economía. Medellín, Colombia.

RCPC Revista del Pensamiento Centroamericano. Centro de Investigaciones y Actividades Culturales. Managua.

RIB Revista Interamericana de Bibliografía (Inter-American Review of Bibliography). Organization of American States. Washington.

RIIA/IA International Affairs. The Royal Institute of International Affairs. London.

RO Revista de Occidente. Madrid.

RRI Revista/Review Interamericana. Univ. Interamericana. San Germán, Puerto Rico.

SAGE/JIAS Journal of Inter-American Studies and World Affairs. Sage Publication *for the* Center for Advanced International Studies, Univ. of Miami. Coral Gables, Fla.

SCHG/R Revista Chilena de Historia y Geografía. Sociedad Chilena de Historia y Geografía. Santiago.

SGHS/B Boletín de la Sociedad Geográfica e Histórica Sucre. Sucre, Bolivia.

SPSA/JP The Journal of Politics. The Southern Political Science Association *in cooperation with the* Univ. of Florida. Gainesville.

UB/BA Boletín Americanista. Univ. de Barcelona, Facultad de Geografía e Historia, Depto. de Historia de América. Barcelona.

UC/I Ibero-Americana. Univ. of California Press. Berkeley.

UCC/RU Revista Universitaria. Anales de la Academia Chilena de Ciencias Naturales. Univ. Católica de Chile. Santiago.

UCL/CD Cultures et Développement. Revue internationale des sciences du développement. Univ. Catholique de Louvain avec le concours de la Fondation Universitaire de Belgique. Louvain, Belgium.

UCNSA/EP Estudios Paraguayos. Univ. Católica Nuestra Señora de la Asunción. Asunción.

UCSD/NS The New Scholar. Univ. of California, Center for Iberian and Latin American Studies and Institute of Chicano Urban Affairs. San Diego.

UMG/RBEP Revista Brasileira de Estudos Políticos. Univ. de Minas Gerais. Belo Horizonte, Brazil.

UNAH/RCE Revista Centroamericana de Economía. Univ. Nacional Autónoma de Honduras, Programa de Postgrado Centroamericano en Economía y Planificación. Tegucigalpa.

UNAM/PDD Problemas del Desarrollo. Univ. Nacional Autónoma de México, Instituto de Investigaciones Económicas. México.

UNAM/RFD Revista de la Facultad de Derecho. Univ. Nacional Autónoma de México. México.

UNAM/RI Relaciones Internacionales. Revista del Centro de Relaciones Internacionales. Univ. Nacional Autónoma de México, Facultad de Ciencias Políticas y Sociales. México.

UNCR/R Revista de Historia. Univ. Nacional de Costa-Rica, Escuela de Historia. Heredia.

UNESCO/CU Cultures. United Nations Educational, Scientific and Cultural Organization. Paris.

UP/A Apuntes. Univ. del Pacífico, Centro de Investigación. Lima.

UP/CSEC Cuban Studies/Estudios Cubanos. Univ. of Pittsburgh, Univ. Center for Interna- tional Studies, Center for Latin American Studies. Pittsburgh, Pa.

UPR/CS Caribbean Studies. Univ. of Puerto Rico, Institute of Caribbean Studies. Río Piedras.

URSS/AL América Latina. Academia de Ciencias de la URSS (Unión de Repúblicas Soviéticas Socialistas). Moscú.

USC/SCC Studies in Comparative Communism. An international interdisciplinary journal. Univ. of Southern California, School of International Relations, Von Klein Smid Institute of International Affairs. Los Angeles.

USCG/PS Política y Sociedad. Univ. de San Carlos de Guatemala, Facultad de Ciencias Jurídicas y Sociales, Escuela de Ciencia Política, Instituto de Investigaciones Políticas y Sociales. Guatemala.

USSR/SS Social Sciences. USSR Academy of Sciences, Section of the Social Sciences. Moscow.

UWI/CQ Caribbean Quarterly. Univ. of the West Indies. Mona, Jamaica.

UWI/SES Social and Economic Studies. Univ. of the West Indies, Institute of Social and Economic Research. Mona, Jamaica.

WD World Development. Pergamon Press. Oxford, United Kingdom.

WQ The Wilson Quarterly. Woodrow Wilson International Center for Scholars. Washington.

WV *See* CRIA/WW.

SOCIOLOGY

GENERAL

8001 Arteaga, Eugenia *et al.* La vivienda popular en América Latina. Edición a cargo de Humberto Pereira Iturriaga. Caracas: FUNDACOMUN, 1979. 400 p.: bibl., forms, ill., maps, plans.

Collection of papers (1978 conference) on condition and improvement of "popular or marginal" housing in Latin America by official representatives of governments' housing agencies. Papers deal with difficulties, policies, and achievements. Countries: Bolivia, Brazil, Colombia, Chile, Ecuador, El Salvador, Jamaica, Peru, and Venezuela. [L. Pérez]

8002 Baquero, Marcello. Dependencia econômica e intervenção militar na América Latina: 1960–1965: um modelo causal (IFCH/R, 8, 1979/1980, p. 233–247, bibl.)

Proposes causal model for study of military intervention in Latin America. Assesses weight of two determinants discussed in literature: economic dependency and domestic violence. Model is tested with data for all Latin American countries except Mexico and Costa Rica. Results indicate that both economic dependency and domestic violence predict military interventions, and that domestic violence is also related to dependency. Competent piece of research. [C.H. Waisman]

8003 Bartolomé, Leopoldo J. Sobre el concepto de articulación social (IDES/DE, 20:78, julio/sept. 1980, p. 275–286, bibl., graphs)

Discusses usefulness of concept of social articulation in social anthropology. Concept is defined as any system of connective relationships, and of processes which produce systems of that type. Articulation does not necessarily imply internal modifications in the articulated units. Author distinguishes among three types of social articulation: adaptive, dialectical contradiction, and integrative. [C.H. Waisman]

8004 Blanc, Ann Klimas. Unwanted fertility in Latin America and the Caribbean (International Family Planning Perspectives [The Alan Guttmacher Institute, New York] 8:4, Dec. 1982, p. 156–162, tables)

Summarizes results of World Fertility Survey for Costa Rica, Dominican Republic, Guyana, Jamaica, and Paraguay. Marital fertility declined, but proportion of unwanted births rose. Includes analysis of influence of age at first union, number of births, rural-urban residence, education, and husband's occupation on incidence of unwanted fertility. [L. Pérez]

8005 Blaut, J.M. Nationalism as an autonomous force (SS, 46:1, Spring 1982, p. 1–23)

Restates traditional Marxist view, according to which class struggle is motor of history. Opposes notion that nationalism is "second motor." Discusses theory of nationalism in Marx and Engels and Stalin. In 1970s, concept of nationalism as "autonomous" force (i.e., different from class struggle) was espoused by Poulantzas, Debray, Nairn, and Davis. For author, nationalism is only distinctive form of class conflict. [C.H. Waisman]

Botana, Natalio R. *et al.* Ciencias sociales: palabras y conjeturas. See item **8309.**

Burns, E. Bradford and **Thomas E. Skidmore.** Elites, masses, and modernization in Latin America, 1850–1930. See *HLAS 44:1821.*

8006 Cabezas, Antonio and **Amable Rosario.** La emisora regional para el desarrollo. Hilversum, Netherlands: Radio Nederland Training Centre; Quito: Editora Andina, 1980. 303 p.: bibl., ill.

Efforts of Radio Nederland Training Centre (Hilversum, Holland) to train Third World radio and television producers. Detailed deliberations and findings of seminar (Bonaire, 1980) attended by regional radio managers and radio school experts. Conference objectives: to establish key parameters of regional radio station, identify techniques, and develop evaluative criteria. [P.J. Brennan]

8007 Conferencia General del Episcopado Latinoamericano, 3rd, Puebla, Mexico, 1979. Evangelization at present and in the future of Latin America: conclusions. Washington: National Conference of Catholic Bishops, Secretariat, Committee for the Church in Latin America, 1979. 220 p.: index.

English translation of conclusions of Third General Conference of Latin American Bishops (Puebla, Mexico, 1979). Emphasizes assessing present and future of evangelization in region. [L. Pérez]

8008 Congreso Latinoamericano de Sociología, llth, San José, Costa Rica, 1974. Debates sobre la teoría de la dependencia y la sociología latinoamericana: ponencias. Daniel Camacho, selección, introd. y notas. Gérard-Pierre Charles et al. Ciudad Universitaria Rodrigo Facio, Costa Rica: Editorial Universitaria Centroamericana, 1979. 767 p.: bibl., ill. (Colección Seis)

Congress papers deal mostly with discipline's history. Most interesting section is discussion of dependency theory (at peak in 1974 when Congress was held). Includes now classic reassessment by Cardoso and Faletto of their book *Dependency and development in Latin America* (see *HLAS 41:2773*). Useful review of 1970s Latin American sociology illustrates both its strengths (e.g., theoretical understanding of region, particularly on basis of eclectic Marxism) and weaknesses (e.g., neglect of empirical research except as illustration of theses, hermetic style). [C.H. Waisman]

Conniff, Michael L. Introduction: toward a comparative definition of populism. See *HLAS 44:1824.*

8009 Dependent agricultural development and agrarian reform in Latin America. Lawrence R. Alschuler, editor. With the collaboration of Teodoro Buarque de Hollanda, Jacques Gélinas, and Alan Winberg. Ottawa, Canada: University of Ottawa Press, 1981. 186 p.: bibl. (Social sciences studies; no. 12. Books and monographs series / Institute for International Cooperation; no. 2)

Workshop papers (Univ. of Ottawa 1977) on agrarian problems and reforms in Latin America. Authors use primarily dependency perspective. Some papers are general, others focus on specific reforms in Argentina, Brazil, and Peru. [C.H. Waisman]

Fagor Aviel, JoAnn. Political participation of women in Latin America. See item **6009.**

8010 Faletto, Enzo and **Julieta Kirkwood.** Política y comportamientos sociales en América Latina (CPES/RPS, 17:49, set/dic. 1980, p. 69–96, bibl.)

Stimulating analysis of the State's political behavior focuses on Latin America's most prominent political parties. Argues that they are characteristically elitist and exclude effective·mass participation. Discusses State's capacity to legitimate itself and coopt dissident groups. Incorporates variables taken from political economy to examine class alliances within political parties and constraints on political role for labor unions. [K. Healy]

8011 The Family in Latin America. Edited by Man Singh Das, Clinton J. Jesser in honor of T. Lynn Smith. Sahibabad, India: Vikas, 1980. 430 p.: bibl., index.

Compilation of articles in honor of T. Lynn Smith examines the Latin American family. Several are annotated separately in this volume as indicated by item number following article's title: Angelina Pollak-Eltz "The Family in Venezuela" (item **8274**); Aldo E. Solari and Rolando Franco "The Family in Uruguay" (item **8356**); Alejandro Angulo-Novoa "The Family in Colombia" (item **8237**); John Mayer "The Family in Brazil" (item **8407**); E. Wilbur Bock et al. "Urbanization and the Extended Family in Brazil" (item **8366**); Bruce W. Aldrich et al. "Urbanization and Familism: an Examination of the Influences of Urban Residence upon Kinship Orientation in Two Culturally Related Developing Nations, Portugal and Brazil" (item **8359**); Olen E. Leonard and Eduardo A. Louriero "The Family in Bolivia" (item **8294**); Lisandro Pérez "The Family in Cuba" (item **8191**); Julio A. Cross-Beras "The Dominican Family" (item **8160**); Julian C. Bridges "The Mexican Family" (item **8054**); Manuel J. Carvajal "The Costa Rican Family" (item **8106**); and Alfredo Jaramillo "The Ecuadorian Family." [Ed.]

8012 Filgueira, Carlos H. and **Carlo Geneletti.** Estratificación y movilidad ocupacional en América Latina. Santiago: Naciones Unidas, 1981. 169 p.: bibl., ill. (Cuadernos de la CEPAL; 39)

Analyzes stratification and mobility in

Latin America during 1950s and 1960s primarily through use of sample data from decennial census of various countries. Authors place findings within broader theoretical context, with emphasis on growth of the middle class. [L. Pérez]

8013 Franco, Rolando. Apuntes para un análisis sociológico de la inflación (CPES/RPS, 13:36, mayo/agosto 1976, p. 59–73)

Sociological analysis of inflation. Sees price rises as consequence of conflictive interaction among social groups which mobilize their resources to change income distribution. Inflation's form depends on balance of power within society and international processes. [C.H. Waisman]

8014 ———— and Omar Argüello. Pobreza: problemas teóricos y metodológicos (CPES/RPS, 17:49, sept./dic. 1980, p. 147–164)

Theoretical discussion of concept of poverty in terms of various dimensions, indicators, and measures. Sophisticated and succinct analysis of poverty dimensions of food-nutrition, health, clothing, and housing. Interesting discussion on both usefulness and limitations of using income as measure of poverty. [K. Healy]

8015 Galkina, Antonoma. Fisonomía socio-psicológica del proletariado agrícola de América Latina (URSS/AL, 4[52], 1982, p. 25–33)

• Examines class consciousness of rural proletariat in Latin America whose consciousness is more homogeneous than that of their urban counterparts. Mobility coexists with submissiveness, passivity, and even fatalism. Agrarian labor fosters collectivism. Social psychology of these strata is affected by organization of agrarian production in which they participate. [C.H. Waisman]

8016 García, Pío. Notas sobre formas de estado y regímenes militares en América Latina (UNAM/RMS, 43:2, abril/junio 1981, p. 545–553)

Surveys political sociology of Latin America (e.g., new military regimes, State forms, fascism, democratization prospects). [C.H. Waisman]

8017 Godio, Julio. Acción sindical y estrategias socialistas en América Latina (Desarrollo Indoamericano [Baranquilla, Colombia] 67, abril 1981, p. 35–41, ill.)

Discusses strategies of Latin American socialist parties. In past, parties emphasized parliamentary activity, failed to focus on potential for workers' mobilization. Spread of authoritarianism pushed labor movement into confrontation with the State. Discusses recent changes in composition of working class, and opportunities for socialist activity. [C.H. Waisman]

8018 Goldman, Noreen and Anne R. Pebley. Legalization of consensual unions in Latin America (Social Biology [American Eugenics Association, New York] 28:1/2, 1981, p. 49–61, bibl., tables)

Analyzes legalization of consensual unions in rural Colombia, Mexico, Peru, and Costa Rica using data from PECFAL rural survey. Concludes that legalization is fairly frequent phenomenon, but not related to church attendance. Legalized unions are less likely to end in separation than legal marriages without premarital cohabitation. [L. Pérez]

8019 Gómez, Sergio. Descomposición campesina: análisis de los asignatarios de la reforma agraria (CPES/RPS, 17:48, mayo/agosto 1980, p. 7–22, bibl., tables)

Analyzes differentiation among beneficiaries of land reform which began in haciendas. Land distribution destroyed obstacles which hindered formation of peasant strata. Liberal economic policies also help the differentiation process. [C.H. Waisman]

8020 Goncharova, Tat'iana Viktorovna. Indeanizm—ideologiia i politika: Boliviia, Peru, Ekvador, 50—60-e gody XX v. Moskva: Nauka, 1979. 199 p.: bibl.

Seriously intended study of *indigenismo*. Includes considerable bibliographic material. Of special interest is the Soviet analysis of the "ultra-left" interpretation of *indigenismo*. Study sponsored by Latin American Institute of Soviet Academy of Sciences. [R.V. Allen]

8021 González Casanova, Pablo. La crisis del estado y la lucha por la democracia en América Latina (UNAM/RMS, 43:2, abril/junio 1981, p. 533–544)

Latin America is undergoing a generalized struggle for democracy, in world-wide economic recession. Previous State crisis reflected national and class cleavages, current one represents conflict between antagonistic principles of social organization, capitalism and socialism. Thus democratic struggles lead to power struggles. [C.H. Waisman]

8022 Goyer, Doreen S. and **Eliane Domschke.** The handbook of national population censuses: Latin America and the Caribbean, North America, and Oceania. Westport, Conn.: Greenwood Press, 1983. 711 p.: maps, tables.

Valuable reference describes each population census taken in every nation or colony in Latin America and Caribbean, from Brazil to Cayman Islands. Emphasizes variables and types of tabulations available in published reports. [L. Pérez]

8023 Hardoy, Jorge E. La vivienda de los pobres (CPES/RPS, 13:36, mayo/agosto 1976, p. 7–20)

Describes housing conditions among poor in Third World cities and pleads for effective urban programs. [C.H. Waisman]

Harmel, Robert. Environment and party decentralization: a cross-national analysis. See item **6014.**

8024 Kaplan, Marcos. Estado y desarrollo en América Latina. México: Centro de Investigaciones y Estudios Superiores en Antropología Social, 1980. 48 p. (Cuadernos de la Casa Chata; 37)

In Latin America, especially since 1930, the State has played determinant role in capital accumulation and income distribution. Author argues against reductionist interpretations of nature and functions of the Latin American State which must be evaluated from perspective of formation and development of late and dependent capitalism. [C.H. Waisman]

8025 Katz, James Everett. La relación entre científicos y gobierno: el caso de la energía nuclear (AI/I, 7:3, May/June 1982, p. 141–147, ill.)

Discusses scientific community's role in formulation of developing countries nulear energy policy. Examines all aspects of topic. [C.H. Waisman]

8026 Kaufman, Robert R. Liberalizzazione e democratizzazione degli stati burocratico-autoritari (MULINO, 30:275, maggio/guigno 1981, p. 385–418, bibl.)

Analysis of liberalization processes in bureaucratic-authoritarian states covers three phases: 1) decrease of fear; 2) struggle over rules of the game; and 3) decision to expand liberalization process. Possible outcomes: national-populist, social-democratic, and center-right regimes. Careful comparative analysis. [C.H. Waisman]

8027 Laclau, Ernesto *et al.* Estado y política en América Latina. Edición preparada por Norbert Lechner. México: Siglo Veintiuno Editores, 1981. 340 p.: bibl., index (Sociología y política)

Following papers on nature of the State are of significance: Laclau's on theoretical debates in Marxist theory concerning functions of the State, is a most complete analysis of the literature; O'Donnell's on Southern Cone bureaucratic authoritarian regimes makes penetrating analysis of the military's role and, in Peru's case, of "military populism;" Przeworki's complex theoretical model on class compromises uses covariation between risks and efficiency of investment; Cardoso's on Brazil's transition toward democracy, offers sophisticated review of theoretical debates on relationship between State and society. [C.H. Waisman]

8028 Lalive d'Epinay, Cristian. Dépendance sociale et religion: pasteurs et protestantismes Latino-Américains (CNRS/ASR, 26:52[1], juillet/sept. 1981, p. 85–97, bibl.)

Discusses different forms of Protestantism in Latin America: two "ethnic" types (Diaspora churches, and reactivated ethnic churches), and three "conversion" or meta-ethnic ones (traditional, sanctification, and sectarian Protestantism.) Examines types of pastoral models which correspond to these forms, and ministers' responses to political change in each case. [C.H. Waisman]

8029 Leeds, Anthony. Forms of urban integration: social urbanization in comparative perspective (UA, 8:3/4, Winter 1979, p. 227–247)

Central proposition is that different forms of urban society involve different forms of societal integration, and thus of class relations which, in turn, determine a society's urban and rural sectors. Author shows that concept originally developed for contemporary Latin America, can be used for understanding medieval European social structure. [C.H. Waisman]

8030 Maletta, Héctor. Comentarios y

ajustes sobre la población indígena de América en 1978 (III/AI, 41 : 3, julio/sept. 1981, p. 517–543)

Suggests ways to achieve more accurate estimate for Indian population of some American countries to avoid upward-bias created in work of Mayer-Masferrer due to definitional and methodological problems. Authors argue that acculturation and miscegenation have reduced rates of growth of Indian population well below general population growth rate of countries studied. [P.J. Brennan]

8031 Mansilla, H.C.F. Gewalt und Selbstverständnis: Zur Ideologierkritik der latinamerinakischen Guerrilla-Bewegungen (JGSWGL, 15, 978, p. 357–384)

Discusses mixture of "modern" and "traditional" values in ideology of Latin American guerrilla movements. Modern are: voluntarism as principle of political practice, "democratic centralism" as organizational model, and accelerated industrialization as societal goal. Traditional are: antoctonism, autonomism (why is this "traditional"?) and ideological nationalism. Result is hybrid mix of "technicism" and authoritarianism. [C.H. Waisman]

8032 Margolies, Luise. Introduction: the process of social urbanization in Latin America (UA, 8 : 3/4, Winter 1979, p. 213–225)

Social urbanization concerns socio-economic transformation of space and ideological extension of urban system to hinterlands, factor in continuity of Latin America's rural-urban migration. Urbanization generates further migration so that entire population is absorbed by expanding urban system. Examines process historically, starting with colonial society. [C.H. Waisman]

8033 Moreno B., Ernesto. El sindicato: como actor social de la democracia (CPU/ES, 28/29, 1981, p. 107–121)

Reviews literature on trade unions' political roles: as economic or political co-administrators, as pressure groups, as revolutionary agents, as associates or as subordinates of the State. [C.H. Waisman]

8034 Najenson, José Luis. Cultura nacional y cultura subalterna. Toluca, México: Universidad Autónoma del Estado de Mé-

xico, 1979. 75 p.

Short theoretical essay on ideological aspects of culture links anthropology and political science with some references to Latin America data. Theoretical orientation is Marxist. [A. Ugalde]

Petras, James. Political change, class conflict and the decline of Latin American fascism. See item **6026.**

8035 Pla, Alberto J. América Latina siglo XX: economía, sociedad, revolución. 2. ed. corr. y ampliada. Caracas: Universidad Central de Venezuela, Ediciones de la Biblioteca, 1980. 466 p.: bibl. (Colección Ciencias económicas y sociales; 25)

Expanded edition of 1969 work. Pretentious in scope, it is basically a treatise on comparative Latin American history designed to explain region's social change. Emphasizes role of working class and rise of middle sectors. [L. Pérez]

8036 Prien, Hans-Jürgen. Katholische Kirche und Entwicklungsproblematik in Lateinamerika (OLI/ZLW, 20, 1981, p. 7–19)

Provocative analysis of Protestant contributions to social and economic development of Latin America from Rio's 1955 CELAM Conference to Puebla's in 1979. Maintains that influence of Protestant churches, both mainline and evangelical, lead to greater social awareness in the Catholic Church. [G.M. Dorn]

8037 ——. Der Protestantismus in Lateinamerika vor der Herausforderung der Entwicklingsproblematik (OLI/ZLW, 20, 1981, p. 21–41, bibl.)

Examines growth of Protestantism in Latin America from Lima to Oaxtepec Conferences (1961–78). Concentrates on Protestantism's role in Latin American economic and social development. Includes useful regional breakdowns and differentations of Protestant churches. [G.M. Dorn]

Puebla en décimas: texto oficial, versión popular: como vivir la fe hoy en América Latina. See item **6028.**

8038 Riz, Liliana de. El fin de la sociedad populista y la estrategia de las fuerzas populares (UNAM/RMS, 43 : 2, abril/junio 1981, p. 555–564)

Decade between Brazilian and Chilean

coups (1964–73) ended populist stage of Latin American politics. Whenever the military suppresses politics, results are politicization of society and transformation of social conflicts into revolutionary ones. Reformist and revolutionary forces must reformulate their strategies. [C.H. Waisman]

8039 Ruiz-Tagle P., Jaime. Estructura social de América Latina. Santiago: Instituto Latino Americano de Doctrina y Estudios Sociales, 1975. 71 leaves.

Course notes on population trends, family structure, education and religion, urbanization, land tenure, employment, social classes and class conflicts. Useful text, empirical, free of abstract speculation and jargon that plague most Latin American books of this genre. [C.H. Waisman]

8040 Santa Cruz, Adriana and **Viviana Erazo.** Compropolitan: el orden transnacional y su modelo femenino: un estudio de las revistas femeninas en América Latina. México: Instituto Latinoamericano de Estudios Transnacionales: Editorial Nueva Imagen, 1980. 290 p., 24 leaves of plates: bibl., ill.

Examines content of single issues of 28 leading women's journals from Mexico, Brazil, Colombia, Venezuela, and Chile in order to analyze female ideal presented in advertisements and articles. Studies promotion of conspicuous consumption and exposes international dependence of Latin American mass media. [A. Ugalde]

8041 Santos, Milton. A urbanização desigual: a especificidade do fenômeno urbano em países subdesenvolvidos. Tradução de Antônia Déa Erdens, Maria Auxiliadora da Silva. Revisão de José Fernandes Dias. Petrópolis, Brazil: Editora Vozes, 1980. 125 p.: bibl.

Contrasts urbanization process of present-day Third World cities with that of cities in developed countries. Considers demographic processes, economic factors, effects of industrialization, transportation and ecological variables. Competently done. [J.V.D. Saunders]

8042 Sebreli, Juan José. Fútbol y masas. Buenos Aires: Editorial Galerna, 1981. 198 p.

Practitioner of popular sociology looks at soccer as form of mass alienation. Sport

indoctrinates masses, depoliticizes them, and socializes them into alienated labor. Thus soccer means: cult of performance, competition, aggressiveness, sexual repression, fanaticism, irrational activism, contempt for the individual, submission to authoritarianism, suspension of critical judgment, and mystical fusion into the totalitarian collective. [C.H. Waisman]

8043 Sex and class in Latin America: women's perspectives on politics, economics, and the family in the Third World. Edited by June Nash, Helen Icken Safa. Brooklyn, N.J.: J.F. Bergin Publishers, 1980. 330 p.: bibl., ill., index.

Buenos Aires Conference on women's issues and problems in developing world are divided into three sections: 1) ideological reinforcement of sexual subordination; 2) female productive roles; and 3) political mobilization of women. [L. Pérez]

8044 Slaves of slaves: the challenge of Latin American women: Latin American and Caribbean Women's Collective. Translated by Michael Pallis. London: Zed Press, 1980. 186 p.: bibl.

Broad-ranging work on status of women in Latin America. Pt. 1 is general overview including history of women's movement. Pt. 2 covers specific aspects of women's social, political, and legal status in 11 countries. [L. Pérez]

Torrado, Susana. Sobre los conceptos de "estrategias familiares de vida" y "proceso de reproducción de la fuerza de trabajo:" notas teórico-metodológicas. See item **8347.**

8045 Whitam, Frederick L. The status of homosexuals in Latin America (ASU/LAD, 16:1, Winter 1982, p. 4, 32, plate)

Concludes that homosexuality is a transcultural phenomenon, and that cross-national evidence shows no relationship between homosexual orientation and family structure. Traditional psychoanalytic hypothesis (dominant mother/hostile father) does not hold. Author believes that, despite stereotypes, there is greater tolerance for homosexuals in Latin America than in US, Canada, and Great Britain. [C.H. Waisman]

8046 Wiarda, Iêda Siqueira and **Judith F. Helzner.** Women, population and international development in Latin America: persistent legacies and new perceptions for the

1980's. Amherst: University of Massachusetts at Amherst, International Area Studies
Programs, 1981. 40 p. (Program in Latin
American Studies occasional papers series;
no. 13)

    Critical examination of population

theories and policies, concludes that they
have led to excluding women from policy
processes, and in doing so have weakened
effectiveness of population programs.
[G. Wynia]

MEXICO AND CENTRAL AMERICA

ANTONIO UGALDE, *Associate Professor of Sociology, University of Texas, Austin*

SOME NOTICEABLE CHANGES have taken place in the literature reviewed during the 1981–83 period. In the first place, a relatively large number of materials,
almost one-sixth of the items on Mexico, are concerned with various dimensions of
Mexican migration to the US. In part, this reflects the completion and first publications of a major research project sponsored by the National Center of Labor Information and Statistics (CENIET) of the Mexican Department of Labor known as
"The National Survey of Migration to the Northern Border and to the United States,"
which began in 1977 (items **8070** and **8093–8094**). It reflects also the increasing
policy concerns within the US with a wave of illegal migration that has been
characterized as uncontrollable. The publication of the Mexican findings is a welcome contribution to the topic, that will allow policy makers to look at this
complex issue with information gathered by scholars from both sides of the border.

    A second development is the growing interest in the study of post-revolutionary
Nicaragua. Nicaragua has become a laboratory for the study of development constraints that exist after capitalism. The country has remained more open to US
social scientists than Cuba, and as a result many are taking the opportunity to
explore social processes in a post-revolutionary setting. Though the articles annotated below are concerned with a variety of issues such as agricultural development, housing and women's roles, the underlying theme is the study of policy
formulation, and in particular the problems facing governments when attempting
to satisfy the at-times conflicting demands from different constituencies, for example, the peasantry and the industrial labor force. An outstanding study in this
respect is the one by Deere and Marchetti (item **8108**). Most of the authors reviewed have given high grades to the Sandinista government and remain cautiously
optimistic about the future of the revolution. The fact that Managua was chosen as
the site of the XV Latin American Congress of Sociology held in Oct. 1983 is also
an indication of the solidarity of Latin American sociologists with the Nicaraguan
revolution.

    As in the past, the field of political sociology dominates the literature in this
biennium. Almost half of the items annotated are directly or indirectly related to
political sociology, specifically concerned with rural development, dependency,
with the study of social problems from a class conflict perspective, or are political
economy studies of countries and institutions of the region. Clearly, by 1980 the
functionalist, modernization and liberal approaches to development are gone and
neo-Marxist views are in. Neo-Marxist sociologists in the region are interested in
social class fractions, in the articulations of the modes of production and in the role
of the State. Salient contributions to these topics are works by Figueroa Ibarra in
Guatemala (item **8113**), Menjívar in El Salvador (item **8121**), Posas in Honduras

(item **8125**), Vega Carballo in Costa Rica (item **8135**), and in Mexico, the excellent work by Aguilar (item **8047**), and the Proceedings of the First National Congress of Sociology and Rural Development (item **8088**).

Two new periodicals have appeared in Central America. *Nicaraguan Perspectives* (yearly subscription $10.00) is published by the Nicaraguan Information Center (P.O. Box 1004, Berkeley, Calif. 94704). *Honduras Update* is a mimeo monthly newsletter distributed freely by its publisher the Honduras Information Center (1511 Massachusetts Ave., Cambridge, Mass. 02138).

Finally, the volume edited by Arguedas *et al.* (item **8050**) should be highlighted. The 1000 bibliographical entries presented in this book make it one of the best indicators of the coming of age of Mexican sociology in the decade of the 1970s.

MEXICO

8047 Aguilar, Rubén *et al.* Lucha urbana y acumulación de capital. Jorge Alonso, editor. México: Centro de Investigaciones Superiores del INAH, Ediciones de la Casa Chata, 1980. 485 p.: bibl. (Ediciones de la Casa Chata; 12)

Comprehensive study of Ajusto (pop. 42,000), poor urban *colonia* in Mexico City. Contains wealth of information on socio-economic characteristics, migration, employment, and political conflict. Based on extensive participant-observation, archival materials and survey data. For author, "informal" employment is a mechanism of surplus value extraction by foreign capitalism. Solid contribution to urban sociology with important theoretical insights into informal sector.

8048 Alba, Francisco. The population of Mexico: trends, issues, and policies. Translated by Marjory Mattingly Urquidi. New Brunswick, N.J.: Transaction Books, 1982. 127 p.: bibl., ill., index.

Translation of 1977 introduction to Mexican demography (see *HLAS 43 : 8074*).

8049 Antonio García: a Mexican peasant, poet and revolutionary (JPS, 9 : 2, Jan. 1982, p. 241–251, facs.)

Presents letter and poems written by a Mexican peasant. Letter candidly explains to his wife and children, peasant's motive for joining the revolutionary struggle. Editor Godoy writes useful introduction and commentary. Welcome contribution to study of guerrilla movements.

8050 Arguedas, Ledda *et al.* Sociología y ciencia política en México: un balance de veinticinco años. México: Universidad Nacional Autónoma de México, Coordinación de Humanidades, Instituto de Investigaciones Sociales, 1979. 171 p.: bibl.

Useful introduction to history of Mexican sociology and political science includes three chapters: "La Institucionalización de la Sociología en México" by Arguedas and Loyo; "La Investigación Sociológica en México" by Reyna; and "La Ciencia Política en México" by Meyer and Camacho. Final bibliography (70 p.) by Cordero includes 1000 entries catalogued under 16 headings. Considerable overlapping between first two chapters does not detract from balanced evaluation of Mexican accomplishments in these fields.

8051 Arizpe, Lourdes and **Josefina Aranda.** The "comparative advantages" of women's disadvantages: women workers in the strawberry export agri-business in Mexico (UC/S, 7 : 2, Winter 1981, p. 453–473, tables)

Strawberry processing plants in Zamora (Michoacán) employ almost exclusively female workers. Opening of these plants in 1970s produced some liberating effects for women but according to authors, female employment responded primarily to industry's need for cheap and seasonal labor. Interesting description of female labor conditions.

8052 Barabas, Alicia M. Colonialismo y racismo en Yucatán: una aproximación histórica y contemporánea (UNAM/RMCPS, 25 : 97, julio/sept. 1979, p. 105–139)

Fascinating article about ethnic relations in Yucatán from colonial days to present. According to author, dominant classes fostered ideology of white ethnic superiority in order to control subordinate Indian classes. Ideologies and mechanisms of control changed throughout the centuries but Mayan Indians continue to be perceived and perceive themselves as inferior.

Bellingeri, Marco. Del peonage al salario: el caso de San Antonio Tochatlaco de 1880 a 1920. See *HLAS 44:1995.*

8053 Bock, P.G. and **Irene Fraser Rothenberg.** Internal migration policy and new towns: the Mexican experience. Urbana: University of Illinois Press, 1979. 156 p.: bibl., ill., index.

Case study of new town, Cuautitlan-Izcalli, founded in 1971 on northern edge of Mexico City to provide facilities for migrants. Shows that Mexico lacks national migration policy due to conflicting interests of autonomous agencies and lack of carryover of policies from one administration to another. Argues that internal migration needs much more attention than it has received. [R.E. Greenleaf]

8054 Bridges, Julian C. The Mexican family (*in* The Family in Latin America. [see item **8011**] p. 295–334, bibl.)

Introduction to topic based on outdated bibliography. Author dwells on commonplaces and generalizations.

8055 Brito de Martí, Esperanza. La mujer mexicana en la legislación mexicana: una balanza de busca de equilibrio (Comunidad CONACYT [Consejo Nacional de Ciencia y Tecnología, México] 4:115, julio 1980, p. 51–109, ill., plates, tables)

Special issue on the Mexican woman consists of short, journalistic articles on topics such as women in Mexican law, feminist movement in Mexico, women in science, female sexuality, abortion, and interviews with some prominent female artists. Informative but without academic pretensions.

8056 Cano Gordon, Carmen and **María Teresa Cisneros Gudiño.** La dinámica de la violencia en México. Naucalpán, México: Escuela Nacional de Estudios Profesionales, Actlán; México: Universidad Nacional Autónoma de México, 1980.

Pt. 1 discusses types of violence and concept of structural violence. Pt. 2 analyzes peasants' struggle for land in Mexico. Rural

violence is viewed as only alternative left to the peasantry for survival. Includes excellent, lengthy case study of 1975 rural violence in Sonora.

Coalson, George O. The development of the migratory farm labor system in Texas: 1900–1954. See *HLAS 44:2165.*

8057 Cook, Scott. Petty commodity production and capitalist development in the "Central Valleys" region of Oaxaca, Mexico (GEE/NA, 1, 1978, 285–332, tables)

Neo-Marxist elaboration of data reported in previous writings (see *HLAS 41:898* and *HLAS 39:1040*). Topics treated with some thoroughness are: division of labor, sources and nature of differentiation in production forms, and capitalist and non-capitalist relations.

8058 Cross, Harry E. and **James A. Sandos.** Across the border: rural development in Mexico and recent migration to the United States. Berkeley: University of California, Institute of Governmental Studies, 1981. 198 p.: bibl., map.

Divides history of Mexico-US migration into three periods: 1880–1940, 1940–65, and 1965–80. Within each identifies and briefly describes basic push factors. Presents contrasting research findings on key migration issues such as size of migration flow and cost to US taxpayers.

8059 Cuthbert, Richard W. and **Joe B. Stevens.** The net economic incentive for illegal Mexican migration: a case study (CMS/IMR, 15:3, Fall 1981, p. 543–550, bibl., tables)

From 93 randomly selected illegal Mexican aliens who worked as fruit pickers in Oregon, authors found six-fold difference between gross earnings of these workers in Mexico and US. Transportation and living expenses in US reduced difference by half.

Davis, Charles L. and **Kenneth M. Coleman.** Discontinuous educational experiences and political and religious nonconformity in authoritarian regimes: Mexico. See item **4453.**

8060 Desarrollo del capitalismo y transformación de la estructura de poder en la región de Tuxtepc [sic], Oaxaca. Eckart Boege, coordinación. México: Instituto Nacional de Antropología e Historia, Escuela Nacional de Antropología e Historia, 1979.

1 v.: bibl., ill. (Serie Investigaciones de la especialidad de antropología social y etnología; cuaderno 1)

Three case studies conducted in rural Oaxaca by team of students as part of field training. Contributes to understanding of power relations in rural Mexico. Also contains very useful data on political role of state enterprises.

DeWalt, Billie R. Modernization in a Mexican ejido: a study in economic adaptation. See *HLAS 44:2170.*

8061 Díaz-Polanco, Héctor. El desarrollo rural en América Latina: notas sobre el caso mexicano. México: Centro de Investigación para la Integración Social, 1981. 55 p., 6 p. of plates: ill. (Cuadernos del CIIS; no. 3)

Excellent summary of negative impact on the poor of agricultural modernization via capital-intensive multinational agro-businesses. Author skillfully integrates materials from Hewitt de Alcántara (*HLAS 41:5351; HLAS 43:3005*), Feder (*HLAS 41:2954*), Paré (*HLAS 41:9089*) and more recent works by Barkin, Oswald, and Serrano (*HLAS 43:8119*), and A. Bartra.

8062 ——— and Laurent Guye Montandon. La burguesía agraria de México: un estudio de caso en El Bajío. México: Centro de Estudios Sociológicos, Colegio de México, 1977. 62 p.: bibl. (Cuadernos del CES; no. 22)

Contribution to theory of class formation using data from rural municipality in Guanajuato. Divides bourgeoisie in two categories: production and merchant, and subdivides each in several groups. Closely studies conflict resolution among these groups. Rural bourgeoisie takes advantage of rural institutions such as CONASUPO, *ejidos,* and credit institutions. Result is widening gap between rural social classes.

8063 Echeverría Zuno, Pablo. Empleo y reubicación: una aproximación a los factores de rechazo de la reubicación rural-urbana; el caso del área metropolitana de la ciudad de México; 1940–1970 (CEESTEM/L, 1:2, 1981, p. 21–80, tables)

Short secondary analysis of 1970 Survey of Internal Migration to Mexico City. Occupation prior to migration is dichotomized into agricultural and non-agricultural categories. Each is broken down into three poorly defined types and cross-tabulated with migra-

tion cohorts. Given size of sample, many sociodemographic controls used weaken findings.

8064 Edelman, Marc. Agricultural modernization in smallholding areas of Mexico: a case study in the Sierra Norte de Puebla (LAP, 7[4]:27, Fall 1980, p. 29–49)

Uses two months of fieldwork to draw tentative conclusions on results of Plan Zacapoaxtla (Puebla), PIDER development project. Project provided important works of infrastructure, credit systems, extension work and introduction of winter potato crop to utilize otherwise idle land. Stresses that new wealth is overshadowed by increasing social stratification.

8065 Estadística sobre la mujer: inventario. México: Secretaría de Programación y Presupuesto, Coordinación General de los Servicios Nacionales de Estadística, Geografía e Informática, 1980. 332 p.

Statistical compilation of basic cross-tabulation on female employment, fertility, health, and education. Data drawn from 1970 population census, 1976 national fertility survey, hospital statistics and several other statistical series on education and employment.

8066 Esteva, Gustavo. El estado y la comunicación. México: Ediciones Nueva Política, 1979. 175 p. (Colección encrucijada)

Collection of articles of mixed quality, ranging from philosophical discussions to improvised speeches. Latin Americanists will find useful essay on origins and activities of state-owned enterprise Central de Comunicaciones (CEMCOSA), established 1975 to assist government and other state enterprises in areas of "information, publicity, propaganda, and public relations."

8067 Fernández y Fernández, Ramón. La empresa ejidal. Chapingo, México: Secretaría de Agricultura y Recursos Hidráulicos, Colegio de Postgraduados, Centro de Economía Agrícola, 1978. 255 p.: bibl.

Takes critical view of approaches and solutions to agrarian problems advanced by Marxist theorists. Written from technical background of agricultural engineer. Author cogently argues that non-structural factors such as quality of soil are often neglected by leftist social scientists. Provocative book presents insights which are often overlooked in study of rural programs.

8068 García, Carola. Revistas femeninas: la mujer como objeto de consumo. México: Ediciones El Caballito, 1980. 166 p., 6 p. of plates: ill. (Colección Fragua mexicana; 37)

Content and orientation of this book are similar to Adriana Santa Cruz's (see item **8040**). In her section on Mexico, she covers most Mexican journals and international journals published in Mexico such as *Cosmopolitan, Kena, Buenhogar, Claudia*, that are included in this work which is exclusively concerned with Mexico. Contains informative description of each journal's background and ownership characteristics.

8069 García Gómez, Alberto. Los trabajadores mexicanos indocumentados (UNL/H, 20, 1979, p. 447–465)

Living conditions of peasantry, historical land tenure arrangements from colonial days to present and migration to US are weakly tied together in this article. Text fails to mention excellent literature on topic.

8070 García y Griego, Manuel. El volumen de la migración de mexicanos no documentados a los Estados Unidos: nuevas hipótesis. México: Centro Nacional de Información y Estadísticas del Trabajo, 1980. 659 p.: bibl., ill. (Estudios / Encuesta Nacional de Emigración a la Frontera Norte del País y los Estados Unidos; 4)

In 1977, Mexican Labor Department conducted major research effort on Mexican migration to US. This is one of several volumes from study which analyzes migration histories of returnees using sophisticated quantitative methodologies. Compares results with findings from other studies by US scientists. According to author, the number of undocumented Mexicans in US is considerably lower than figures commonly cited by official US sources.

8071 Giménez, Gilberto. Cultura popular y religión en el Anáhuac. México: Centro de Estudios Ecuménicos, 1978. 270 p.: bibl., ill.

Since the 16th century, sanctuary of Chalma (Mexico state) has been important regional ceremonial center. Book describes origins of this religious tradition and examines sociological meaning of yearly pilgrimages from neighboring towns. Includes

detailed description of 1974 collective pilgrimage from San Pedro Atlapulco.

Greenwood, Michael J.; Jerry R. Ladman; and **Barry S. Siegel.** Long-term trends in migratory behavior in a developing country: the case of Mexico. See item **3021**.

8072 Hidalgo, Berta. El movimiento femenino en México. México: Editores Asociados Mexicanos, 1980. 88 p.: appendices, ill., photos.

Brief, perhaps exaggerated account of role played by Mexican presidents in granting of electoral rights to Mexican women.

Jones, Richard S. Channelization of undocumented Mexican migrants to the U.S. See item **5101**.

———. Undocumented migration from Mexico: some geographical questions. See item **5102**.

8073 Labeff, Emily E. and **Richard A. Dodder.** A comparison of attitudes toward sexual permissiveness in Mexico and the Unites States (SIP/RIP, 15:1, 1981, p. 29–39, tables)

Six items of Reiss' Sexual Permissiveness Scale are factor-analyzed for two national groups and for each sex (sample size 145 Mexican and 278 US university students). Substantial differences were found between the groups and authors conclude that concept of sexual permissiveness may be qualitatively different in the two cultures as measured by Reiss' items.

Leñero Otero, Luis. Sociocultura y población en México: realidad y perspectivas de política. See *HLAS 44:2216*.

Malagón, Javier. El exiliado político español en México: 1939–1977. See *HLAS 44:2228*.

8074 Marroni de Velázquez, María da Gloria and **Elsa Rodríguez de Lascuráin.** General Cepeda, Coahuila: retrospectiva socio-económica de proceso migratorio. Saltillo, México: Universidad Autónoma Agraria "Antonio Narro," División de Ciencias Socioeconómicas, Departamento de Sociología, 1979 [i.e. 1980]. 131 p.: bibl., ill.

Excellent collection of 14 articles (many previously published) by well-known experts (e.g., Juan Gómez-Quiñones, Jorge Bustamante, Alejandro Portes, Richard Fagen, James O'Connor, and Vic Villalpando). Aspects covered: theoretical, historical, human rights, and international relations. Includes solid case studies.

8075 Martínez Saldaña, Tomás. El costo social de un éxito político: la política expansionista del estado mexicano en el agro lagunero. Chapingo, México: Colegio de Postgraduados, Rama de Divulgación Agrícola, 1980. 163 p., 22 p. of plates: ill.

Penetrating study of interaction of bureaucracy, peasantry and national and international bourgeoisie in Northern Mexico's Comarca Lagunera (1934–76). According to author, *ejidatarios* are dependent and exploited by government's lending policies and by multinational firms which control international cotton market.

Mexican workers in the United States: historical and political perspectives. See *HLAS* 44:2235.

8076 Mirowsky, John and **Catherine E. Ross.** Minority status, ethnic culture and distress: a comparison of blacks, whites, Mexicans, and Mexican Americans (UC/AJS, 86:3, Nov. 1980, p. 479–495, tables)

Quantitative paper that examines the psychological well-being of blacks, Anglos, Mexicans, and Mexican-Americans by applying Langner index of distress. Data are based on 1967 New Haven and 1975 El Paso and Juárez surveys. Among other important findings: Mexican heritage is associated with lowered distress.

8077 Morayta, L. Miguel. Chalcatzingo, persistencia y cambio de un pueblo campesino. México: SEP, Instituto Nacional de Antropología e Historia, between 1977 and 1981. 190 p.: bibl., ill.

Traditional ethnographic report of a Morelos village. Pt. 1 contains sketchy historical study from precolumbian days to early years of 20th century. Pt. 2 (100 p.) describes cultural and local institutions such as life cycle, family, religion, and economics and points out changes.

8078 Morris, Lydia. Women in poverty: domestic organization among the poor of Mexico City (CUA/AQ, 54:3, July 1981, p. 117–124)

In-depth study of 50 poor households, finds that women are more likely to work outside household in absence of resident male and/or when spouse/father has no secure employment. Flexible understanding of concept of family allows working mothers to make variety of child care arrangements with relatives and neighbors.

8079 Nahmad, Salomon. Mexican colonialism? (SO, 19:1 [Whole no. 135], Nov./Dec. 1981, p. 51–58)

Director of Indian education in Mexico's Ministry of Education considers integration of Indian communities into national culture through bilingual-bicultural education as process of Indian self-liberation. From this perspective, he describes critically past and present post-revolutionary efforts to modernize Indian communities through bilingual education.

8080 Nolasco Armas, Margarita. Cuatro ciudades: el proceso de urbanización dependiente. México: Instituto Nacional de Antropología e Historia, 1981. 343 p., 11 folded leaves: ill.

Lengthy volume contains wealth of information and data on cities of Coatzcoalcos, Puebla, Oaxaca, and Ixtapalapa. Same format is used for study of urbanization process of each city. Includes historical, demographic, ecological, economic, and sociopolitical aspects. Based on census data, archival materials and random survey of 1417 respondents.

8081 Nolasco Armas, Margarita *et al.* Aspectos sociales de la migración en México. México: Instituto Nacional de Antropología e Historia, Departamento de Proyectos Especiales de Investigación, 1979 [i.e. 1980]. 332 p.: bibl., ill.

More descriptive than analytical but relevant articles are: Molinari Soriano "La Migración Indígena en México;" Aguilar Medina "La Mixteca Oaxaqueña: una Zona de Emigración;" Flores Ramos "Migración a Municipios del Area Metropolitana Central;" Nolasco "Migración Urbana;" and Nolasco *et al.* "Frontera Norte: Maquiladoras y Migración;" Barrera Bassols "Aspectos sociales de la Emigración en México;" and Acevedo Conde "Municipios Rurales y muy Rurales con Fuerte Atracción: el Caso de Balancán-Tenosique," which describes colonization in two Tabasco municipalities.

8082 ——— *et al.* Migración municipal en México, 1960–1970. t. 1, Proyectos especiales de investigación. México: Instituto Nacional de Antropología e Historia, 1979. 1 v.: bibl., map, tables.

Formal demographic analysis of internal migration, two-thirds of which are tables with raw data on net migration and migration indexes by municipalities.

8083 Oaxaca una lucha reciente: 1960–1978. Bustamante *et al.* México: Ediciones Nueva Sociología, 1978. 236 p., 4 leaves of plates: ill.

From Marxist-Leninist perspective, authors analyze class struggle in rural and urban Oaxaca. Articles oppose physical violence used by Maoist leaders during late 1960s and 1970s. Worth reading for those interested in internal political conflict of the Mexican left and in student political participation.

8084 Ongay, Mario. La familia de las clases medias en México (UNAM/RMCPS, 25/26:98/99, oct./dic. 1979/enero/marzo 1980, p. 5–81)

Devastating analysis of the Mexican family from psychological perspective. Written in essay style without footnotes, this jargon-free article is insightful and provocative. Author frequently illustrates how idiosyncracies of Mexican family have important bearing on political behavior.

8085 Ortiz Pinchetti, Francisco *et al.* La Operación Cóndor. México: Proceso, 1981. 77 p.

In sensationalist style, short chapters of *Operación Cóndor* describe aspects of fight against cultivation of marihuana. Contributors are chiefly concerned with violations of human rights by law enforcement agencies and ecological damage by chemical agents.

Prevôt-Schapira, Marie France. Travailleurs du pétrole et pouvoir syndical au Mexique. See item **6076.**

8086 Roberts, Bryan R. State and region in Latin America (*in* State and region in Latin America: a workshop. G.A. Banck, R. Buve, and L. Van Vroonhoven, editors. Amsterdam: Centrum voor Studie en Documentatie van Latijns-Amerika, 1981, p. 9–39, bibl. [CEDLA incidentele publicaties; 17])

Stimulating, lucid discussion of concepts of State and region in understanding Latin America's uneven socioeconomic development. Author focuses on power structures, social relations, and economic activities. Uses case materials from Jalisco and

Peru's central highlands. [K. Healy]

8087 Rus, Jan and **Robert Wasserstrom.** Evangelización y control político: el Instituto Lingüístico de Verano (ILV) en México (UNAM/RMCPS, 25:97, julio/ sept. 1979, p. 141–159, maps, tables)

Summer Institute of Linguistics has been a subject of controversy among social scientists. Article illustrates social problems created by the Institute among Chiapas Indians and reasons for cozy relationship of Institute with the Mexican government.

Salamini, Heather Fowler. Agrarian radicalism in Veracruz, 1920–38. See *HLAS 44:2255.*

Schryer, Frans J. The rancheros of Pisaflores: the history of a peasant bourgeoisie in twentieth-century Mexico. See *HLAS 44:2264.*

8088 Seminario Nacional de Sociología y Desarrollo Rural, *1st, Chapingo, México, 1979.* Sociología del desarrollo rural: memoria. México: Ediciones Nueva Sociología: La Universidad, 1980. 1 v.: bibl.

Vol. 1 of proceedings consists of 32 exceptional articles divided into: 1) development of capitalism; 2) class struggle and the labor movement; and 3) land reform. Seasoned social scientists such as Gómez Jara, Paré, Oswald, etc., present case studies encompassing wide range of geographical and cultural regions and variety of crops (e.g., coffee, sugar, citric fruits, grapes) and social issues associated with each. Common threads are: increasing concentration of land and peasantry's impoverishment, influence of government policies on class disarticulation, and increasing control of Mexican agriculture by US business.

8089 Silva Ruiz, Gilberto. Examen de una economía en Oaxaca: estudio de un caso, Teotitlán del Valle. Oaxaca, México: Centro Regional de Oaxaca, Instituto Nacional de Antropología e Historia, 1979. 35 p.: bibl. (Estudios de antropología e historia; no. 21)

Students of INAH's Regional Center at Oaxaca carried out census of Teotitlán del Valle in 1978 and questionnaire survey of 3,500 households. Data shed light on relationship between community's occupational and class structures.

Smith, Stanley K. Determinants of female labor force participation and family size in Mexico City. See item **3050.**

Soto, Shirlene Ann. The Mexican woman: a study of her participation in the Revolution, 1910–1940. See *HLAS 44:2272.*

8090 Suárez Iñiguez, Enrique. Los intelectuales en México. México: Ediciones El Caballito, 1980. 290 p.: bibl. (Colección Fragua Mexicana; no. 38)

Presents view of seven prominent intellectuals (Fernando Benítez, Flores Olea, Carlos Fuentes, González Casanova, López Cámara, Octavio Paz, and Luis Villoro) on: meaning and future of Mexican Revolution, role of socialism, imperialism and fascism in Latin America, student movements, and role of intellectuals. Important contribution to political sociology and to contemporary history of ideas.

8091 Taylor, Clark L. How Mexicans define male homosexuality: labeling and the Buga view (KAS/P, 53/54, Spring/Fall 1976, p. 106–128, plates)

Following interactionist approach to deviance, author makes important contribution to understanding homosexual labeling in Mexico. After reviewing popular beliefs and mass media, concludes that social norms promote feelings of guilt and inferiority among homosexuals and even preclude issue's scientific study. As a result, homosexuals in Mexico can expect little professional help.

8092 Uzzell, Douglas. Conceptual fallacies in the rural-urban dichotomy (UA, 8:3/4, Winter 1979, p. 333–350)

Using historical materials and Oaxaca fieldwork experience, author questions validity of rural-urban dichotomy. In his opinion, rural-urban cultural differences do not exist anymore, and dichotomy's use should be discontinued.

8093 Zazueta, Carlos H. Primera encuesta a trabajadores mexicanos no documentados devueltos de los Estados Unidos: octubre/noviembre de 1977 (MSTPS/R, 1:1, enero/abril 1978, p. 13–44, tables)

First tabulations from CENIET survey of undocumented workers returned by INS (see item **8070**). Tables include: size of place of origin, age and sex, number of crossings, length of stay in US, home remittances, income in US, and occupation and income in

Mexico.

8094 ——— and **César Zazueta.** En las puertas del paraíso: observaciones hechas en el levantamiento de la Primera Encuesta a Trabajadores Mexicanos no Documentados Devueltos de los Estados Unidos, CENIET, octubre 23-noviembre 13 de 1977. México: Centro Nacional de Información y Estadísticas del Trabajo (CENIET), 1980. 160 p.: bibl. (Estudios. Encuesta Nacional de Emigración a la Frontera Norte del País y a los Estados Unidos; 3)

Field notes of two researchers of Mexico's Labor Department US migration project (see item **8070**) include insightful observations in handling of undocumented workers in 12 US immigration stations. Also discusses objectively Mexican side of migration process and conduct of Mexican migration authorities.

8095 Zazueta, César and **Ricardo de la Peña.** Estructura dual y piramidal del sindicalismo mexicano. México: Secretaría del Trabajo y Previsión Social, Centro Nacional de Información y Estadísticas del Trabajo, 1981. 69 p.: bibl., ill. (Serie Estudios; 10)

Short monograph is sequence to previous publication by one of coauthors (see item **8095**) and uses same data base. Classifies labor organizations into those holding membership in semi-official Labor Congress and independent unions; compares types by organizational characteristics (membership size, federal or local court jurisdiction, and type of industry).

8096 ——— and **Simón Geluda.** Población, planta industrial y sindicatos: relaciones entre sindicalismo y mercado de trabajo en México, 1978. México: Secretaría del Trabajo y Previsión Social, Centro Nacional de Información y Estadísticas del Trabajo, 1981. 118 p.: ill. (Serie Estudios; 7)

There is little agreement about percentage of unionized members in Mexico's active labor force. After careful analysis of official labor statistics, concludes that a mere 14.7 percent is unionized, a figure well below the six million estimate of labor leaders.

CENTRAL AMERICA

8097 Aguilera Peralta, Gabriel. Terror and violence as weapons of counterinsurgency in Guatemala (LAP, 7[25/26]:2/3, Spring/Summer 1980, p. 91–113, plates)

Introduced by US military in 1966, counterinsurgency in Guatemala was characterized by indiscriminate killing and terror. From 1966–78, author distinguishes four waves of terror, each mustering different tactics and cover-ups and provoking various responses from population and guerrillas. Sober, well-documented, and penetrating analysis of the uses of political violence.

8098 Ajmac Cuxil, Concepción. Ritual del matrimonio tradicional y moderno en Tecpán (Tradiciones de Guatemala [Universidad de San Carlos de Guatemala, Centro de Estudios Folklóricos] 13, 1980, p. 83–123, ill., photos)

Interesting and detailed description of the customs, rituals, and ceremonies of engagement, and of civil and religious marriages in Tecpan ca. 1920. Followed by account of modern middle-class marriage (1972) in same village.

Argueta, Mario R. Tendencias e investigaciones recientes de la sociología hondureña: un ensayo bibliográfico. See item **9.**

8099 Arias de Blois, Jorge. La población de Guatemala. Guatemala: Instituto Centroamericano de Investigación y Tecnología Industrial, 1976. 154 p.: bibl., ill. (C.I.C.R.E.D. series)

Part of UN world-wide effort to prepare country summaries of past, present, and future demographic trends. One of Guatemala's outstanding demographers has compiled the country's basic demographic information based on 1973 National Census. Includes frank discussion of Guatemala's statistical deficiencies.

8100 Biesanz, Richard; Karen Zubris Biesanz; and Mavis Hiltunen Biesanz. The Costa Ricans. Englewood Cliffs, N.J.: Prentice-Hall, 1982, 246 p.: bibl., ill.

Abridged English edition of item **8102.**

8102 Biesanz, Mavis Hiltunen; Richard Biesanz; and Karen Zubris de Biesanz. Los costarricenses. Dirigió la edición, Carlos Alberto Arce Alfaro. Traducción de originales, Isabel Picado. San José: Editorial Universidad Estatal a Distancia, 1979. 730 p., 30 leaves of plates (6 fold.): bibl., ill.

Encyclopedic introduction to Costa Rica follows traditional institutional approach. Writers begin with discussion of national character and historical account from precolumbian days to present. Subsequent chapters cover economy, class structure, health and housing, family and life cycle, education, religion, recreation, and political institutions.

Bogan, Marcos W. La migración internacional en Costa Rica. See item **3097.**

8103 Boils Morales, Guillermo. El problema de la vivienda en Nicaragua durante el primer año de la revolución (Vivienda [Instituto del Fondo Nacional de la Vivienda para los Trabajadores, México] 8 : 2, marzo/abril 1981, p. 186–201, map, photos, tables)

Housing shortage is major social problem in post-revolutionary Nicaragua. Discusses self-help housing programs, participation of public sector in construction, technologies and materials used in building. Concludes with positive note and belief that Sandinista government will overcome many constraints.

8104 Bonpane, Blase. The Church and revolutionary struggle in Central America (LAP, 7[25/26]:2/3, Spring/Summer 1980, p. 178–189)

Former Maryknoll priest who served in Guatemala until his exile, examines historical relations between Church and power holders in Central America. Explains transformation among Church segments who now support workers' demands for freedom from exploitation and physical suffering. According to author, these are common grounds for cooperation between "new" Christian and Marxists.

Bossen, Laurel. Plantations and labor force discrimination in Guatemala. See item **921.**

8105 Calvo Fajardo, Yadira. La mujer: víctima y cómplice. San José: Editorial Costa Rica, 1981. 156 p.

Erudite exploration of origins of female discrimination. More in sorrow than anger, author reviews false female images and social roles assigned to women from the Greeks to Ortega y Gasset. Although of no special interest to Latin Americanists, except for brief references to Costa Rica, volume makes excellent introduction to subject.

8106 Carvajal, Manuel J. The Costa Rican family (in The Family in Latin America [see item **8011**] p. 335–387, bibl., tables)

Mostly a demographic and economic summary of Costa Rica which peripherally considers the family in terms of household composition, income, and patterns of consumption.

Chavez, María Luisa and **James Loucky.** Caretaking and competence: siblings as socializers in rural Guatemala. See item **936.**

8107 Colin, Marie-Odette. El programa de planificación familiar en Costa Rica. San José: Universidad de Costa Rica, Facultad de Ciencias Sociales, Instituto de Investigaciones Sociales, 1976. 59 p.: bibl. (Avances de investigación; no. 13)

After brief description of birth control programs and sources of financing, offers two basic explanations for international donors' generosity: 1) imperialist powers see rapid growth of impoverished masses as threat to political stability and status quo; 2) Costa Rica's poor provide excellent and inexpensive subjects for testing foreign pharmaceutical products.

8108 Deere, Carmen Diana and **Peter Marchetti.** The worker-peasant alliance in the first year of the Nicaraguan agrarian reform (LAP, 8[2]:29, Spring 1981, p. 40–73, table)

Lucid evaluation of first year of agricultural reform in post-revolutionary Nicaragua. Looks at efforts of new government and constraints that hinder satisfying conflicting demands of peasants and urban workers. Important article for development of post-revolutionary class alliances theories (for economist's comment, see item **3106**).

8109 Dennis, Philip A. The Costeños and the revolution in Nicaragua (SAGE/ JIAS, 23:3, Aug. 1981, p. 271–296, map)

Well-documented report offers historical reasons why English-speaking Miskito lack a Nicaraguan national identity. After briefly describing close relationships of Miskito with Somoza's government, discusses efforts and difficulties encountered by Sandinistas to integrate the independent Miskito into the new Nicaragua.

8110 Díaz A., Erwin R. Guatemala, situación demográfica de la población indígena y no indígena. San José: Centro Latinoamericano de Demografía, 1977. 76 p.: bibl., ill. (Serie C; no. 1006)

Compares age, sex, civil status, literacy, education, employment and fertility rates of Indian and non-Indian populations using 1950 and 1973 Census data. Formal demographic analysis.

8111 Diferencias socioeconómicas del descenso de la fecundidad en Costa Rica, 1960–1970. San José: Centro Latinoamericano de Demografía, 1980. 133 p. (Serie A. Centro Latinoamericano de Demografía; no. 1040)

Applies own-children method to 1973 Census data to measure fertility declines. Findings indicate decline started among urban women of middle and upper social classes towards end of 1950s. In mid-1960s, fertility decline had spread to urban working class and literate rural women. Fertility rates of illiterate rural women began declining by end of 1960s.

8112 El Salvador: estudios de población. San Salvador: Ministerio de Planificación y Coordinación del Desarrollo Económico y Social, Unidad de Población y Recursos Humanos: Fondo de Naciones Unidas para Actividades de Población, 1979. 3 v. in 2: bibl., ill.

Collection of eight reports by UN consultants and Planning Ministry professionals. The more notable articles are: UN team "Relations between Economic, Social, and Demographic Variables," a sophisticated identification and quantification of variables that explain differential fertility rates; Oscar Cuella "The Incorporation of Sociocultural Variables in the Study of the Relations between Development and Population," a report that links agrobusinesses' growth, peasantry's impoverishment, and rural-urban migration; Joseph Van Den Boomen "Socioeconomic Characteristics of Migrants to Metropolitan San Salvador;" and Andras Uthoff Botka "Employment Strategies and Public Credit and Investments Policies."

8113 Figueroa Ibarra, Carlos. El proletariado rural en el agro guatemalteco. Ciudad Universitaria: Editorial Universitaria de Guatemala, 1980. 475 p.: bibl. (Colección Realidad nuestra; v. 9)

Guatemala is a dependent economy much of whose agricultural surplus ends up in US. To compensate for lost wealth, native agricultural capitalist class exploits the proletariat to such an extreme that it creates profound dissension. Analysis of capitalist class is followed by typological study of the proletariat. Discusses two basic rural sub-classes with vestiges of precapitalist forms of production: permanent and seasonal workers which also subdivide into categories. Provocative and important contribution to the study of social classes and of international class linkages.

8114 Figueroa Navarro, Alfredo. Torrijismo y sociología de la modernización (LNB/L, 305/309: 1, agosto/dic. 1981, p. 201–208)

Brief description by Torrijos supporter of institutional development of Panama's public sector under him. Author refers to "torrijismo" as an ideology or model of socioeconomic development but fails to explain what he means by it.

8115 Gandásegui, Marco A., hijo. Estructura social y medios masivos de comunicación. San José: Universidad de Costa Rica, Facultad de Ciencias Sociales, Instituto de Investigaciones Sociales, 1976. 55 p.: bibl. (Avances de investigación; no. 16)

Explores role of mass media in capitalism's expansion. Argues that mass media's main concern is promotion of consumerism rather than providing information to consumers. Content analysis of Panama's *Star and Herald* is presented in support of thesis.

8116 El Grito de los pobres: fe y revolución. Managua: Coordinadora de Comunidades Juveniles Cristianas de Base, Pastoral Juvenil de Managua, 1981. 35 p.: ill. (Colección J.C.R. Serie Luis Vivas; no. 2)

Avant-garde Catholic clergymen talk to Nicaraguan youth about their revolution. Compatibility between Christian tradition and liberation of the poor through revolution is affirmed by three priests: Fernando Cardenal (Nicaraguan Minister of Culture), Jesús García (Mexico), and Gustavo Gutiérrez (Peru), and by Bishop Proaño (Ecuador). Booklet without academic pretentions but of interest to students of theology of liberation.

8117 Herrera, Luz Alicia. Testimonies of Guatemalan women (LAP, 7[25/26]:2/3, Spring/Summer 1980, p. 160–168)

Short interviews with low-income female worker and upper-class woman who joined the liberation movement. Both interviewees vividly describe exploitation and class conflict.

8118 Herrera, Margarita; Marta Arce; and Mayra Castillo. Panamá, los sectores populares y el proletariado: hacia una caracterización de las fuerzas sociales. El Dorado, Panamá: Centro de Estudios y Acción Social de Panamá, 1979. 100 p.: bibl. (Estudios de la realidad)

Not very successful attempt to define and quantify Panama's three social classes: popular sector, proletariat and petty bourgeoisie. Nature of the distinction of first two or need for such distinctions is not clearly explained. Data sources are official labor statistics of 1975 and 1970 National Census.

8119 Leis Romero, Raúl Alberto. La ciudad y los pobres: las clases populares en la ciudad transitista. Panamá: CEASPA, 1979 [i.e. 1980]. 196 p., 1 leaf of plates: bibl., ill. (Serie Estudios de la realidad)

Ambitious work of political sociology on Panama written within neo-Marxist theoretical framework. Discusses marginality, rural-urban migration, unemployment, class stratification, industrialization, and dependency. Uses current and historical data to support arguments and views of social problems.

Maier, Elizabeth. Nicaragua, la mujer en la Revolución. See item **6159**.

8120 Martín-Baro, Ignacio. La imagen de la mujer en El Salvador (ECA, 35, junio 1980, p. 557–568, bibl., ill., tables)

Opinion survey of 800 male and female respondents, 14 to 40 years of age, on the image and role of women. About 30 percent of the non-random sample had opinions reflecting traditional views of women. Such views and levels of education were negatively correlated. Questionable sample procedures reduce validity of findings.

8121 Menjívar, Rafael. Formación y lucha del proletariado industrial salvadoreño. San Salvador: UCA Editores, 1979. 126 p.: bibl. (Colección Estructuras y procesos; v. 7)

Political history of the working class divided into five chapters corresponding to well-identified periods: 1) 1841–1920; 2) 1920–32; 3)1932–47; 4) 1948–69; and 5) 1970–77. Neo-Marxist interpretations of economic and political data allows author to explain reasons for labor movement's rise and fall. Good synthesis of country's violent history.

8122 Murga Frassinetti, Antonio. Enclave y sociedad en Honduras. Tegucigalpa: Universidad Nacional Autónoma de Honduras, 1978. 248 p.: bibl.

Political economic history of Honduras' capitalist movement from late 19th century to 1930 Depression. Appendixes, almost as lengthy as text, include legal documents of the period. Concludes with two articles written by other authors on the establishment and development of railroad and fruit companies. Written from dependency theory perspective.

Murray, Stephen O. Lexical and institutional elaboration: the species homosexual in Guatemala. See *HLAS 44:4578*.

8123 Petras, James. Nicaragua: the transition to a new society (LAP, 8[2]:29, Spring 1981, p. 74–94, tables)

Cogent analysis of political and economic dilemmas facing the Nicaraguan government. Describes newly organized agrarian sector as well as industrial one. Believes critical problem facing Nicaragua is maintenance of mass participation as regime continues to bureaucratize.

8124 Posas, Mario. Honduras at the crossroads (LAP, 7[25/26]:2/3, Spring/Summer 1980, p. 45–56)

Summary of Honduras' 20th-century political history viewed from neo-Marxist perspective. Written on eve of 1980 national election, assesses forthcoming electoral context and corresponding political alliances.

8125 ———. Lucha ideológica y organización sindical en Honduras, 1954–65. Tegucigalpa: Editorial Guaymuras, 1980. 81 p.: bibl. (Colección Códices)

Short monograph presents historical development of Honduras' labor movement beginning with 1954 Tela strike. Documents US control of movement through international labor organizations. Valuable contribution on international and labor relations and for understanding current events in Central America.

8126 Quiroga, Eduardo R. La transformación de la agricultura de subsistencia mediante riego en El Salvador (III/AI, 40:3, julio/sept. 1980, p. 499–525, bibl., tables)

Uses valley of Zapotitán as case study to illustrate effects of agricultural development schemes on small farms. Suggests that drainage improvements in valley made wealthy farmers wealthier, and the poor, poorer. Conclusion: technical solutions do not solve social problems without institutional reforms (for economist's comment, see item **3141**).

8127 Randall, Margaret. Todas estamos despiertas: testimonios de la mujer nicaragüense de hoy. México: Siglo Veintiuno Editores, 1980. 299 p., 16 p. of plates: bibl., ill., ports. (Historia inmediata)

Through unstructured interviews, author allows Sandinista Front female leaders to tell us their participation in the armed struggle against the Somoza regime. Important contribution to the history of revolution, guerrilla tactics, and role of women in the new Nicaragua.

8128 Richter, Ernesto. Social classes, accumulation, and the crisis of "overpopulation" in El Salvador (LAP, 7[25/26]:2/3, Spring/Summer 1980, p. 114–139, plates, table)

Inquiry into causes of 1968 Soccer War. Unwillingness of Salvadoran elite to accommodate thousands of peasants deported from Honduras through land reform created political and social conditions that could only be controlled through repression and false patriotism. Concludes by suggesting that El Salvador's government staged the war to deactivate imminent class struggle.

8129 Rivadeneira de Cardona, Clara. Organizaciones que trabajan con la mujer en Honduras. Tegucigalpa: Asesores para el Desarrollo, 1979. 38 leaves in various foliations.

Lists organizations that carry out activities for women and describes goals, organizational characteristics, programs, and coverage of each.

8130 Samaniego, Carlos. ¿Movimiento campesino o lucha del proletariado rural en El Salvador? (UNAM/RMS, 42:2, abril/junio 1980, p. 651–667, tables)

Informative and well documented paper on 1950–75 shift from small to infrasubsistence farms and landless peasantry. According to data, shift was due to consolidation of export plantations and their need for cheap, seasonal labor at time of declines of international prices. Profits were maintained by lowering salaries and by taking over peasants' lands to increase production. By 1975, 75 percent of rural population had less than one ha. of land or were landless.

8131 Schmidt de Rojas, Annabelle. Estimaciones demográficas de la región central de Costa Rica, 1950–1973. San José: Universidad de Costa Rica, Facultad de Ciencias Sociales, Instituto de Investigaciones Sociales, 1977. 154 p.: bibl., ill., tables (Avances de investigación, 0378–0473; no. 26)

Formal demographic treatment of mortality, fertility, migration and population growth of country's central region as defined by Planning Office. Analysis divides Central Region into three areas: Metropolitan San José, surrounding urban areas, and the rest. Comparisons among these subregions and the rest of the country are presented in tables.

8132 Stycos, J. Mayone. The decline of fertility in Costa Rica: literacy, modernization and family planning (LSE/PS, 36:3, March 1982, p. 15–30, graphs, tables)

Excellent demographic analysis presents decline of fertility using 1950, 1963, and 1973 censuses. Attributes overall decline of fertility between 1960–70 to introduction of public family planning programs in less developed cantons and by socioeconomic modernization in the rest (for anthropologist's comment, see item **1705**).

Thomas, Robert N. and **James L. Mulvihill.** Temporal attributes of stage migration in Guatemala. See item **5071.**

8133 Torres-Rivas, Edelberto. The Central American model of growth: crisis for whom? (LAP, 7[25/26]:2/3, Spring/Summer 1980, p. 24–44, tables)

Scholarly review of political economy of Central America from Depression to present written by one of the most knowledgeable sociologists of this region. Examines cross-nationally process of industrialization, foreign debt, imports and exports of goods and capital, and rates of returns. Also studies effects of development model imposed on Central America as well as its impact on income distribution and unemployment.

8134 United States. Agency for International Development. Office of Housing. Urban poverty in Guatemala. Washington: Agency for International Development, Office of Housing, 1980. 339 p. in various pagings, 7 p. of plates: bibl., ill., maps.

Consultant firm describes living conditions of the poor in Guatemala City, Quezaltenango, Escuintla, and two smaller cities. Based on secondary data, some fieldwork, and very poorly explained methodology. Includes section on organization and capabilities of institutions that provide services to the poor.

8135 Vega Carballo, José Luis. Hacia una interpretación del desarrollo costarricense: ensayo sociológico. San José: Editorial Porvenir, 1980. 237 p.: bibl., ill. (Colección Debate)

Well documented history of political economy from colonization to present, with special emphasis on post-independence to 1930 Depression. Excellent reading for understanding emergence of neo-colonialism in Costa Rica. Author characterizes the country's development as "crecimiento hacia fuera" to symbolize that wealth created during emergence of capitalism was benefiting developed nations almost exclusively.

THE CARIBBEAN AND THE GUIANAS

LISANDRO PEREZ, *Associate Professor of Sociology, Louisiana State University*
NELSON P. VALDES, *Associate Professor of Sociology, University of New Mexico*

THE SOCIOLOGICAL LITERATURE ON THE Caribbean and the Guianas reviewed for this section is a good reflection of the region itself: we see both uniformity and diversity.

Overall, there is uniformity in certain research topics that generate the greatest interest. For example, international migration—within, in, or out of the region—is one and reflects awareness of a growing Caribbean presence outside the area as well as recognition of the social importance of immigrants such as East Indians and Spaniards (items **8136, 8141, 8154, 8165–8166, 8168, 8181, 8186–8187, 8192, 8199, 8207,** and **8213–8214**). A growing interest in fertility and family planning was boosted in the past two years by the release and analysis of results of the World Fertility Survey conducted in Jamaica and the Dominican Republic (items **8139, 8150, 8165, 8174, 8184,** and **8189**). Works on the status of women figure prominently in the region's literature as they do in much of the world's (items **8138, 8169, 8188,** and **8210**). There is also uniformity in what is *not* attracting the attention of the region's sociologists. For example, there are few studies of internal migration and population redistribution, especially urbanization and its consequence, a field that has long preoccupied scholars working in Central and South America.

Beyond these generalizations, the diversity of sociological writings on the Caribbean and the Guianas reflects the region's heterogeneity which becomes most apparent when we focus on specific nations or areas. In the English-speaking Caribbean, for example, the relatively recent onset of independence resulted in a proliferation of studies dealing with political institutions (e.g., elections, political parties, the legitimization of power, social control, criminality, and justice as in items **8144, 8151, 8159, 8162, 8171, 8178, 8204,** and **8216**). Evidently, there is much interest in assessing how well the former British colonies are governing themselves. On the other hand, few political questions are posed in research on Haiti which concentrates almost exclusively on rural development problems and strategies by using the community survey as principal research tool (items **8142, 8157–8158, 8163,** and **8197**). Studies of Cuba reflect the rationality of a system of economic planning based on the Soviet model which has generated much socio-demographic data and statistical information set forth and analyzed in many recent publications, especially demographic ones (items **8164, 8198, 8200,** and **8205**). Nationalistic themes dominate much of the literature of Puerto Rico and the Dominican Republic in studies of the concept of nationhood and national identity, the impact of colonialism, neocolonialism, and dependence on national development, etc. The approach is usually historical and Marxist (items **8146, 8152, 8167, 8175, 8196,** and **8215**). Indeed, if one had to identify a single trend in the sociological literature on the Caribbean and the Guianas, it would be the predominance of a historical approach. While this is particularly evident in works on the Hispanic Caribbean, the 1981 publication of Walter Rodney's *A History of the Guyanese working people, 1881–1905*, (item **8201**) is likely to stimulate future sociological analyses that use a historical approach for the non-Hispanic Caribbean.

8136 Albuquerque, Klaus de and **William F. Stinner.** The Colombianization of black San Andreans (UPR/CS, 17:3/4, Oct./ Jan. 1977–1978, p. 171–181)

Discusses in detail various aspects of growing "Colombianization" of San Andrés. Erosion of "English" cultural patterns is resented by elder San Andreans and authors forecast that "it is only a matter of time before the black San Andrean will be inseparable from the Costeños of Barranquilla and Cartagena."

8137 Angle, John. What happened to the percent able to speak English in Puerto Rico between 1940 and 1950?: the reliability of a census language question (UPR/CS, 20:1, March 1980, p. 97–118, tables)

Author seeks to explain a notable decline in 1940–50 decade in proportion of Puerto Ricans able to speak English. Argues that data are largely reliable and presents several possible explanations, including selective out-migration of English speakers.

8138 Báez Díaz, Tomás. La mujer dominicana. Santo Domingo: Editora Educativa Dominicana, 1980. 110 p.

Work mostly devoted to short biographical sketches of prominent Dominican women. Its organization is historical and starts in the 18th century.

8139 Bailey, Wilma and **Dorian Powell.** Patterns of contraceptive use in Kingston and St. Andrew, Jamaica, 1970–1977 (Social Science and Medicine [Pergamon Press, Oxford, England] 16:19, 1982, p. 1675–1683, bibl., tables)

Through examination of 10 family planning clinics' records, investigators studied factors that influenced choice of contraceptive. Emphasizes age and family size as independent variables. Survey was conducted to ascertain determinants of drop-out rate.

8140 Baksh, Ishmael J. Stereotypes of Negroes and East Indians in Trinidad: a reexamination (UWI/CQ, 25:1/2, March/June 1979, p. 52–71, tables)

Attitudinal study attempts to show that "customary stereotypes of Negroes and East Indians" found in studies of Trinidad are incorrect. Suggests that ethnicity and race do not seem to affect perceptions of "accessibility of the more prestigious jobs." Both groups believe that all that is necessary is the proper qualifications— the ideology of an "open society." Little is said about class.

8141 Barnet, Miguel. Gallego. Madrid: Ediciones Alfaguara, 1981. 224 p.

In same style as his *Biografía de un cimarrón*, author presents *testimonio* of Spanish immigrant in Cuba. Provides valuable insights on important immigration that has received little attention from students of Cuban society.

8142 Bastien, Victor. En Haïti dans la vie rurale: scènes vécues. Port-au-Prince?: Comité haïtien pour la promotion et la diffusion des oeuvres littéraires et scientifiques, 1979 [i.e. 1980]. 554 p.: ill., ports. (Collection Regain)

Positive view of rural development in Haiti. Since author was pioneer in government's rural education and community development programs, work reads more like a memoir focusing exclusively on accomplishments.

8143 Beauchamp, José Juan *et al.* La agresión cultural norteamericana en Puerto Rico. Edición al cuidado de Alejandro Rosas. 1. ed. en español. México: Editorial Grijalbo, 1980. 121 p.: bibl. (Textos vivos; 14)

Collection of five readings on ideological and cultural dimensions of the US presence in Puerto Rico.

8144 Bell, Wendell. Equality and social justice: foundations of nationalism in the Caribbean (UPR/CS, 20:2, June 1980, p. 5–36, bibl.)

Stimulating analysis of rise since World War II of new Caribbean nations. Emphasizes link between nationalism, independence, equality, and social justice. Presidential address to 1980 meetings of Caribbean Studies Association.

Bellegarde-Smith, Patrick. Haitian social thought: a bibliographical survey. See item **10.**

8145 Berman, Harold J. and **Van R. Whiting, Jr.** Impressions of Cuban law (AJCL, 28:3, Summer 1980, p. 475–486)

As title suggests these are "impressions" from 1979 visit to island. Discusses return to legality, abandonment of Popular Tribunals by the Revolution, role of judges, Fiscalía system, criminal procedure, legal education, and important part played by Communist Party. Useful introduction to topic.

8146 Berrocal, Luciano. A la recherche de l'Etat-nation: genèse de l'Etat à Porto Rico (ULB/RIS, 1/2, 1981, p. 377–396)

Thesis: Puerto Rico is a nation searching for independent state in counter position to neo-colonial state that is able to remain in power because of its welfare features. Chapter from author's thesis at Louvain. Work should be seen as part of growing literature on nature of the State in Latin America. Studies of this topic are beginning to examine the Caribbean.

8147 Bonetti, Mario. Die soziale Bedeutung der "religiosidad popular" in Dominicana (OLI/ZLW, 20, 1981, p. 55–72, photos)

Analyzes sociological significance of "popular religion," and varieties of synchretic practices in Dominican Republic. Draws parallels between political, social, and religious behavior patterns. [G.M. Dorn]

8148 Boswell, Thomas C. Internal migration in Puerto Rico prior to economic development (UWI/SES, 27:4, Dec. 1978, p. 434–463, bibl., maps, tables)

Attempts to test applicability of migration theories using Puerto Rico's internal migration (from one municipio to another) during 1935–40. Work infers motives why people migrated (lending itself to criticisms of "ecological fallacy"). Concludes that economic factors are most important in affecting rates of internal migration. Utilizes Lee's Theory of Migration. Seven different variables were used in regression models.

Brana-Shute, Gary. Mothers in uniform: the children's police of Suriname. See item **1057.**

8149 Bravo, Juan Alfonso. Azúcar y clases sociales en Cuba: 1511–1959 (UNAM/RMS, 43:3, julio/sept. 1981, p. 1189–1228, tables)
    Relationship between sugar economy and social classes in Cuba has been analyzed by many authors (e.g., Ramiro Guerra 1930s). Present work goes over same material with little that is new. Uses secondary sources and neglects US primary sources, critical institutions such as Asociación Nacional de Hacendados, Asociación Nacional de Colonos, and Cuban scholars such as Manuel Moreno Fraginals, etc. Little theoretical or analytical discussion. More narrative history than sociological analysis.

8150 Brody, Eugene B. Sex, contraception, and motherhood in Jamaica. Cambridge, Mass.: Harvard University Press, 1981. 278 p.: bibl., ill., index.
    Comprehensive view of factors influencing sex, reproduction, and childbearing in Jamaica, including folkways, socioeconomic factors, women's relationship to their mothers and sexual partners, and attitudes about sex, marriage, and children. Complements results of a survey with author's own experience as psychiatrist at Univ. of West Indies.

8151 Burke, A.W. A cross cultural study of delinquency among West Indian boys (IJSP, 26:2, Summer 1980, p. 81–87, bibl., tables)
    Very brief study uses psychiatric perspective to explain delinquency. Author interviewed 28 boys at Jamaican guidance clinic. No description of methodology.

8152 Calder, Bruce J. The Dominican turn toward sugar (FIU/CR, 10:3, Sept. 1981, p. 18–21, 44–45)
    Highly readable yet comprehensive and critical account of rise and domination of sugar in Dominican agriculture. Emphasizes consequences of agricultural transformation for levels of living in the population.

8153 Campbell, Horace. Rastafari: culture of resistance (IRR/RC, 22:1, Summer 1980, p. 1–22)
    Traces importance of Rastafari culture, political ideas, and international linkages in Jamaica. Connects development of Rastafari movement to struggle to develop culture. Author discusses importance of Marcus Garvey and Walter Rodney. Brief section details spread of Rasta culture and influence throughout Caribbean.

8154 *Caribbean Review.* Florida International University, Latin American and Caribbean Center. Vol. 11, No. 1, Winter 1982- . Miami.
    Entire issue devoted to "The Caribbean Exodus." First three articles are on Caribbean migrations in general, using economic, historical, and socio-psychological perspectives. Two articles discuss Haitian migration and Haitians in US. Robert Bach examines Cuban exodus of 1980. Other articles are on topics such as Central American emigration, migration of Caribbean peoples to Canada, Europe, Venezuela, and Virgin Islands, and there is piece by Franklin Knight on US guest-worker program.

8155 Castillo, José del. Ensayos de sociología dominicana. Santo Domingo: Ediciones Siboney, 1981. 210 p. (Colección Contemporáneos; no. 4)
    Misleading title. Book is not about Dominican sociology, but about Dominican society with chapters devoted to topics such as politics and elections, social change, work, and, of special interest, emigration and immigration.

8156 Chántez Oliva, Sara E. Condiciones de vida de la clase obrera en el período pre-revolucionario: 1952–1958 (UCLV/I, 69, mayo/agosto 1981, p. 103–125, tables)
    The 1950s Cuban mass media published much on social conditions (e.g., diet, income, health, education, welfare). Scholars outside Cuba have not tapped these difficult to obtain sources, but neither have those in the island as this author (e.g., *Bohemia*, old CP newsletter plus Marx, Engels, Lenin). Even foreign scholars have used more resources than this author to get at Cuban food consumption (e.g., Claes Brundenius).

8157 Clérismé, Calixte. Organisations paysannes dans le développement rural

(IFH/C, 140, oct./nov. 1978, p. 5−49, bibl., ill., tables)

Describes various community organizations in region surrounding towns of Petit-Goâve and Grand-Goâve. Most are work-related mutual-help associations. Argues that these associations can play important role in development efforts.

8158 ———. Recherches sur le médecine traditionnelle. Port-au-Prince: Département de la Santé Publique et de la Population, 1979. 144 p.: tables.

Part of broader work on Petit Goâve (see item **8157**), author studied traditional medical practices, focusing on functions, methods, and clientele. Argues need for co-operation between traditional and modern health-care systems.

8159 Crime and punishment in the Caribbean. Edited and introduced by Rosemary Brana-Shute and Gary Brana-Shute. Gainesville: University of Florida, Center for Latin American Studies, 1980. 146 p.: bibl., ill., index.

Collection of papers by various authors on crime, violence, criminology, and institutions of law and order. Covers Jamaica, Trinidad-and-Tobago, Puerto Rico, Haiti, Guyana, Suriname, and the "Commonwealth Caribbean" in general.

Cross, Malcolm. Urbanization and urban growth in the Caribbean: an essay on social change in dependent societies. See item **3074.**

8160 Cross-Beras, Julio A. The Dominican family (*in* The Family in Latin America [see item **8011**] p. 270−294, bibl., tables)

Presents rural family as patriarchal and extended, urban as nuclear. Also describes practices used in courting, familial attitudes (including donjuanismo, machismo, cult of virginity) and changes that have been experienced since 1960s. Concludes "Data are scarce and dispersed, making it difficult to study this subject." Uses some secondary sources.

8161 Cuba. Comité Estatal de Estadísticas. Dirección de Demografía. Estadísticas de migraciones externas y turismo. La Habana: Editorial Orbe, 1982. 126 p.: bibl., tables.

Although work contains general analyses and descriptions of trends in international migration, worldwide and in Cuba, its real value lies in the presentation, especially its appendix of data on Cuban international migration and tourism. These cover 20th century, but are especially detailed for revolutionary period, including data on emigrants' ages and provinces of origin.

Cultural traditions and Caribbean identity: the question of patrimony. See item **1064.**

8162 Danns, George K. Domination and power in Guyana: a study of the police in a Third World context. New Brunswick, N.J.: Transaction Books, 1982. 193 p.: bibl., ill., index.

Interesting study of origins, role, and importance of police in Guyana. Author sees Guyanese police as coercive state apparatus that must be understood in its historical, social, economic, and political context.

8163 Développement rural en Haïti et dans la Caraïbe. Port-au-Prince: Impr. M. Rodríguez, 1980. 424 p., 15 p. of plates: bibl., ill., maps, tables (Revue de la Faculté d'ethnologie; nos. 34−55. Bulletin de l'Academie des sciences humaines et sociales; nos. 9−10)

Proceedings of conference (Port-au-Prince, 1979) sponsored by Dept. of Development Sciences of the Univ. d'Etat d'Haiti. Topics covered: community development, rural literacy campaign, health, religion, and development strategies. Uneven collection consists of excellent contributions and others of little value.

8164 Díaz-Briquets, Sergio. Determinants of mortality transition in developing countries before and after the Second World War: some evidence from Cuba (LSE/PS, 35:3, Nov. 1981, p. 399−411, tables)

Cuban data are analyzed to demonstrate complex interrelationships between determinants of mortality transition in a developing nation. Relative importance of sanitary and public health innovations, country's development, and economic conditions are weighed and analyzed (for anthropologist's comment, see item **1666**).

———. The health revolution in Cuba. See item **1667.**

——— and **Lisandro Pérez.** Fertility decline in Cuba: a socioeconomic interpretation. See item **1668.**

8165 Earnhardt, Kent C. Development planning and population policy in Puerto Rico: from historical evolution towards a plan for population stabilization. Río Piedras: Editorial de la Universidad de Puerto Rico, 1982. 214 p.: bibl., ill., index (Planning series; S-5)

Highly informative and valuable study of population policy in Puerto Rico since 1898. Emphasizes development and consequences of policies related to emigration and family planning.

8166 Ebanks, G.; P.M. George; and C.E. Nobbe. Emigration from Barbados: 1951–1970 (UWI/SES, 28:2, June 1979, p. 431–449, bibl., tables)

Discusses importance of emigration for Barbadian society, especially its demographic impact on island's population. Analyzes emigrants' selected characteristics.

8167 Fernández Méndez, Eugenio. Puerto Rico, filiación y sentido de una isla: cuatro ensayos en busca de una comunidad auténtica. 2. ed. rev. San Juan: Ariel, 1980. 75 p.: bibl.

Although work is not tightly organized around unifying thesis, author's principal argument seems to be that Puerto Ricans need to seek national consciousness and an indigenous culture, but based on universal values not on narrow politically-based orientations. Concludes with statement that "Associated Free State" is political status most conducive to "comprehension, liberty, and judiciousness."

8168 Fink, Marcy. A Dominican harvest of shame: Haitian cane cutters in Santo Domingo (FIU/CR, 8:1, Jan./March 1979, p. 34–38, ill.)

Indictment of treatment and living conditions of Haitian sugar workers in the Dominican Republic.

8169 Forde, Norma Monica. The status of women in Barbados: what has been done since 1978. Cave Hill, Barbados: University of the West Indies, Institute of Social and Economic Research (Eastern Caribbean), 1980. 53 p. Occasional paper; no. 15)

Study assessing implementation of 1978 recommendations submitted by Barbados' National Commission on the Status of Women. While acknowledging accomplishments in economic area, author concludes that many needs identified by the Commission are still not being met, especially in

areas of social and judical reform.

8170 Gimbernard, Jacinto Carlos. Siete historias de divorcio. Santo Domingo: Editora Taller, 1981. 192 p.

Using in-depth interviews with Dominican divorced persons, author selects seven cases to illustrate difficulties of marriage and tragedy of divorce. Although each story purports to be a testimonial, author's dramatization turns each into a *telenovela* script rather than a case study.

8171 Gomes, Ralph C. Class, status, and privilege: the objective interest of the new elite in Guyana (in McDonald, Vincent R. The Caribbean issues of emergence: socio-economic and political perspectives. Washington, D.C.: University Press of America, 1980, p. 283–303, bibl.)

Objective: "to show that class, status, and privilege intertwine to influence how the New Elite in Guyana assign(s) priorities to competing demands, interpret(s) events, and act(s) on issues." Author mixes concepts and paradigms in syncretic manner to point of dizziness (e.g., Marxist terminology and Paretian concepts). Refers to a social category as "the masses." Little research. Descriptive.

Gordon, Antonio M., Jr. Nutritional status of Cuban refugees: a field study on the health and nutriture of refugees processed at Opa Locka, Florida. See item **1810.**

8172 Grasmuck, Sherri. Migration within the periphery: Haitian labor in the Dominican sugar and coffee industries (CMS/IMR, 16:2, Summer 1982, p. 365–377, bibl.)

By examining Haitian labor migration to Dominican Republic, author explains how a "peripheral country exporting labor and suffering from heavy unemployment can still be an importer of immigrants . . ."

8173 Greene, J.E. and Reive Robb. National primary socioeconomic data structures: No. 9, Barbados, Jamaica, Trinidad and Tobago (UN/ISSJ, 33:2, 11981, p. 393–414, ill., tables)

Exceedingly useful and well presented work. Recommended reading for anyone who wishes to know what resources are available to researcher working on English-speaking Caribbean islands (except Windward and Leeward Islands).

Gueri, Miguel. Some economic implications of breast-feeding. See item **1815.**

Henningsgaard, William. The Akawaio, the Upper Mazaruni hydroelectric project and national development in Guyana. See item **1083.**

8174 Hobcraft, John and **Germán Rodríguez.**
The Dominican Republic: trends from two fertility surveys (International Family Planning Perspectives [The Alan Guttmacher Institute, New York] 8:2, June 1982, p. 57–63, bibl., tables)
Surveys taken in 1975 and 1980, using core questionnaire of World Fertility Survey, show that the Dominican Republic's family planning program has been highly effective, especially in rural areas, where contraceptive use increased dramatically.

8175 Hoetink, H. The Dominican people, 1850–1900: notes for a historical sociology. Translated by Stephen K. Ault. Baltimore: Johns Hopkins University Press, 1982. 243 p.: bibl. (Johns Hopkins studies in Atlantic history and culture)
Author chooses period of Dominican history characterized by profound social transformations and analyzes changes in agriculture, population, communications, economic and political power, law and order structures, education, ideology, stratification, and family life. Since author's goal is to provide study for comparative purposes as well as example of historical sociology, work's considerable contribution is not limited to study of Dominican Republic.

8176 Hope, Kempe R. The employment problem, rural-urban migration and urbanization in the Caribbean (Population Review [La Jolla, Calif.] 26:1/2, Jan./Dec. 1982, p. 40–54, bibl., tables)
Focusing on Barbados, Guyana, Jamaica, and Trinidad and Tobago, article contains very general, and somewhat superficial, analysis of interrelationships between employment characteristics, rural-urban migration, urbanization, and development process.

8177 Houdaille, Jacques. Le métissage dans les anciennes colonies françaises (INED/P, 36:2, mars/avril 1981, p. 267–286, tables)
Very interesting and meticulous study of racial interbreeding during 17th and 18th centuries in several French colonies. Author analyzes data from family histories to document incidence of phenomenon in Saint-Christopher, Martinique, Guadeloupe, Saint-

Domingue, and Réunion.

8178 Hughes, Colin A. Race and politics in the Bahamas. New York: St. Martin's Press, 1981. 250 p.: bibl., ill., indexes.
Racial factor in Bahamian elections and party politics is focus of this excellent work, but preliminary chapters on societal development and race relations truly make it a landmark study of the Bahamas, especially since in the past those islands have received little attention from sociologists.

8179 Investigación social en Puerto Rico.
Editor, Ronald J. Duncan. San Juan: IAU Press, 1980. 289 p.: bibl., ill.
Purpose of work is to present compendium of articles representative of social research conducted in Puerto Rico in 1970s decade. Editor's introduction constitutes good overview of recent development of social sciences in the island. Includes articles on: population, politics, ethnography, law and society, and social problems.

Jones, Howard. Crime, race and culture: a study in a developing country. See item **1091.**

8180 Kula, Marcin. Los estratos medios de la sociedad en el movimiento revolucionario: la revolución de 1933 en Cuba (UNAM/RMS, 43:3, julio/sept. 1981, p. 1229–1243)
Highly recommended study by Hungarian historian of 1933 revolution in Cuba and its class basis. Concludes that Cuban petite-bourgeoisie showed much ambivalence toward social and political experiment that took place. Uses primary and secondary sources and assesses in critical fashion some political taboos such as Antonio Guiteras. Thoughtful and provocative work.

8181 Lemoine, Maurice. Sucre amer. Paris: Entre, 1981. 291 p., 8 p. of plates: ill.
Description, in form of journalistic exposé, of living and working conditions of Haitian sugar workers in the Dominican Republic.

8182 Lewis, Gordon K. The Caribbean in the 1980s: what we should study (FIU/CR, 10:4, Fall 1981, p. 18–19, 46–48)
After discussing what he views as three major theoretical schemes that pervade Caribbean studies (plural society, black power, and dependency), author proposes research agenda to close some gaps in our understanding of Caribbean societies. Stimu-

lating and seminal. Keynote address to 1981 meetings of Caribbean Studies Association.

8183 Lieber, Michael. Street life: Afro-American culture in urban Trinidad. Boston: G.K. Hall; Cambridge, Mass.: Schenkman Pub. Co., 1981. 118, 1 p.: bibl.

Written in casual and readable style, work contains picture of life in the poor streets of Port-au-Spain. Although author uses ethnographic approach, quoting extensively from informants' responses, he also presents valuable description of the historical and socioeconomic context.

8184 Lightbourne, R.E. and **Susheela Singh.** Fertility, union status and partners in the WFS Guyana and Jamaica surveys, 1975–1976 (LSE/PS, 36:2, July 1982, p. 201–225, tables)

While data from 1940s and 1950s showed that married women are the most fertile, World Fertility Survey Jamaican data indicate that the 1970s fertility of women in common-law unions is higher than that of married women. Draws conclusions about relationship between number of partnerships and fertility.

8185 López Valdés, Rafael L. Ideario social de Don Fernando Ortiz (UNION, 4, 1981, p. 172–186, bibl.)

Positive view of Cuban anthropologist and thinker, despite fact that he was a positivist follower of Cesare Lombroso and tended to analyze Cuban society, politics and economy in functionalist and idealist terms. Considers Ortiz a non-Marxist but "progressive thinker." Juan Martínez Alier has presented a better analysis of Ortiz and his class bias.

8186 Lundahl, Mats. A note on Haitian migration to Cuba, 1890–1934 (UP/CSEC, 12:2, July 1982, p. 21–36, notes, tables)

One of few studies of important sociodemographic event for both Haiti and eastern Cuba. In addition to presenting available data on migration, author examines factors that prompted it.

8187 Maldonado-Denis, Manuel. The emigration dialectic: Puerto Rico and the U.S.A. Translated by Roberto Simón Crespi. New York: International Publishers, 1980. 156 p.: bibl.

One of most influential analyses of Puerto Rican emigration originally published in 1976 (see *HLAS 41:7251*) in Spanish and now available in English. Well written and concise, emphasizes political and economic context of emigration, especially in relation to US presence in the island.

8188 La Mujer en la sociedad puertorriqueña. Selección, introducción y notas por Edna Acosta-Belén. Río Piedras, Puerto Rico: Ediciones Huracán, 1980 [i.e. 1981]. 237 p.: bibl.

Unlike editor's previous volume on Puerto Rican women (see *HLAS 43:8232*), this work excludes experience in US. Contains some readings found in earlier work, but adds other selections, some of them previously published, which editor considers important contributions to Puerto Rican feminist movement.

Myers, Robert A. Post-emancipation migrations and population change in Dominica: 1834–1950. See item **1106.**

Nicholls, David. From Dessalines to Duvalier: race colour, and national independence in Haiti. See *HLAS 44:2491.*

8189 Ortega, Manuel M. and **Andrea Soriano.** Utilización de investigaciones en República Dominicana: el caso de la Encuesta Nacional de Fecundidad de 1975. Santo Domingo: Instituto Tecnológico de Santo Domingo, 1980. 147 p.: bibl.

Interesting and rare evaluation study. Focuses on dissemination and utilization of results of 1975 National Fertility Survey in Dominican Republic.

8190 Paul, Max. Racial ideology and political development: the cases of Haiti and Bermuda (SOCIOL, 32:1, 1982, p. 64–80)

Analyses of political development of Haiti and Bermuda provide evidence for author's contention that racial issues and problems have primarily socioeconomic origin.

8191 Pérez, Lisandro. The family in Cuba (*in* The Family in Latin America [see item **8011**], p. 235–269, bibl.)

Attempt to ascertain if a family changes at faster rate in society undergoing revolutionary process. General overview of pre-1959 typical Cuban family is followed by analysis of: FMC creation, child care and education legislation, declining Church influence, 1975 Family Code, marriage and divorce patterns, fertility and family planning, etc. Thesis: most significant changes in family are connected with women's incorporation into labor force.

8192 Pessar, Patricia R. The role of households in international migration and the case of U.S.-bound migration from the Dominican Republic (CMS/IMR, 16:2, Summer 1982, p. 342–363, bibl.)

Although author views Dominican emigration as consequence of country's dependent development, argues for more comprehensive analysis that will identify social units mediating between broad structural forces and individual decision-making. Focuses on role of household organization and behavior in migration process.

8193 Petras, James. A death in Guyana has meaning for Third World (LAP, 8[1]:28, Winter 1981, p. 47–48)

Brief eulogy summarizes work and contributions of Walter Rodney to our knowledge of Guyana.

8194 The Puerto Rican community and its children on the mainland: a source book for teachers, social workers, and other professionals. Edited by Francesco Cordasco and Eugene Bucchioni. 3. rev. ed. Metuchen, N.J.: Scarecrow Press, 1982. 457 p.: bibl., ill., index.

Although principal focus is on acculturation and education of Puerto Ricans in US, nine readings in first section deal with variety of insular cultural patterns, especially in relation to family, religion, and interpersonal relations.

8195 The Puerto Ricans, their history, culture, and society. Edited by Adalberto López. Cambridge, Mass.: Schenkman Pub. Co., 1980. 490 p.: bibl., tables.

Although some articles in this work have previously appeared elsewhere, this is nevertheless a valuable compendium on sociohistorical development of Puerto Rico from conflict, dependency, and *independentista* perspectives. While last section, on Puerto Ricans in US, is relatively weak, the first two (Puerto Rico in 1898 and Puerto Rico since 1898) contain solid analyses by leading writers.

8196 Quintero Rivera, Angel. Conflictos de clase y política en Puerto Rico. 3. ed. Río Piedras, Puerto Rico: Ediciones Huracán,

1981. 158 p.: graphs, ill.

Examines evolution of Puerto Rico's class structure from dependency perspective, emphasizing impact of colonialism and economic dependency—in shaping island's class struggles.

Rai, Khemraj. Worker participation in public enterpise in Guyana.

8197 Rémy, Raoul. Etude socio-économique sur Ça-Ira. Port-au-Prince: Presses nationales d'Haïti, 197- . 213 p.: bibl., ill.

Comprehensive study of Ça-Ira, satellite community of Léogàne, coastal town west of Port-au-Prince. Describes community's geography, history, demographics, family and religious institutions, and economic conditions, ostensibly to provide framework for rural development efforts.

8198 Review of the population situation in Cuba and suggestions for assistance: a report to United Nations Fund for Population Activities. New York: The Fund, 1979. 73 p.: bibl., ill. (Report / United Nations Fund for Population Activities; no. 40)

Report of UN Fund for Population Activities mission sent to Cuba to assess need for population assistance. Includes descriptions of population's sociodemographic characteristics, development and development planning, national statistical system, and formulation and implementation of population policy.

8199 Richardson, Bonham C. Caribbean migrants: environment and human survival on St. Kitts and Nevis. Knoxville: University of Tennessee Press, 1983. 207 p.: bibl., ill., index.

Core of this interesting work is study of development of "migration ethos" as leitmotif in society of St. Kitts and Nevis. Migration is seen as centuries-old creative response to islands' serious problems, problems that author analyzes in context of human geography and ecology.

8200 Riverón-Corteguera, Raúl; José A. Gutiérrez Muñiz; and **Francisco Valdés Loazo.** Mortalidad infantil en Cuba, 1970–1979 (Revista Cubana de Administración de Salud [Ministerio de Salud Pública, Centro Nacional de Información de Ciencias Médicas, La Habana] 7:2, abril/junio 1981, p. 143–152, bibl., graphs)

Analysis of decline in Cuban infant

mortality rate in 1970s. Lists factors determining decline, most of them related to public health and sanitation. Discusses differentials, as well as leading causes of death.

8201 Rodney, Walter. A history of the Guyanese working people, 1881-1905. Baltimore, Md.: The John Hopkins University Press, 1981. 282 p.: ill., maps.

By focusing on working class at critical time period, author provides valuable insights into forces that have shaped contemporary Guyanese society. Work reflects uncompromising scholarship (for historian's comment, see *HLAS 44:2542*).

8202 Rojas, Iliana. El campesinado cubano y la estructura social (Universidad de La Habana [Departamento de Actividades Culturales] 211, abril 1979/dic. 1980, p. 82–94, ill., tables)

Brief and not useful. Compares size of pre-1959 Cuban landholdings and tenancy patterns. Basically expresses 1975 CP position on "peasant question." Vast literature on topic not consulted. Few footnotes.

8203 Rooke, Patricia T. Evangelical missionaries, apprentices, and freedmen: the psychosociological shifts of racial attitudes in the British West Indies (UWI/CQ, 25:1/2, March/June 1979, p. 1–14)

Thesis: evangelical missionaries were much more liberal on race question prior to emancipation than afterwards when their attitudes "hardened." Study looks at Church Missionary Society, London Missionary Society, Baptist Missionary Society, and Wesleyan Methodist Missionary Society. Mentions their role in Antigua and British Guiana, but concentrates on Jamaica.

8204 Ryan, Selwyn D.; Eddie Greene; and Jack Harewood. The confused electorate: a study of political attitudes and opinions in Trinidad and Tobago. St. Augustine, Trinidad: University of the West Indies, Institute of Social and Economic Research, 1979. 190 p.

Presents results of nationwide 1976 electoral survey conducted in Trinidad-and-Tobago. Focus is on political opinions and attitudes, especially towards ruling People's National Movement. Includes analyses of influence of independent variables such as race, age, sex, employment characteristics, and education.

8205 Schroeder, Susan. Cuba: a handbook of historical statistics. Boston: G.K. Hall, 1982. 589 p.: bibl., ill., index (A Reference publication in international historical statistics)

Extraordinary reference work that brings together virtually all available Cuban statistics, from colonial times to present, on the topics of climate, demography, education, labor, production, foreign trade, finance, politics, government, and the military. While long-time specialists in these topics have previously encountered these data scattered throughout various sources, their compilation here constitutes a valuable research tool.

8206 Silvestrini de Pacheco, Blanca. Violencia y criminalidad en Puerto Rico, 1898–1973: apuntes para un estudio de historia social. Río Piedras: Universidad de Puerto Rico, Editorial Universitaria, 1980. 146 p., 1 fold. leaf of plates: bibl., ill.

Pioneer historical analysis of violence and criminality in Puerto Rico. Fluctuations in incidence of different types of violent and criminal activities are seen as correlates of broader socioeconomic changes.

8207 Symposium on East Indians in the Caribbean, *University of the West Indies, 1975.* East Indians in the Caribbean: colonialism and the struggle for identity: papers. With an introduction by V.S. Naipaul. Millwood, N.Y.: Kraus International Publications, 1972. 159 p.: bibl. ill.

Papers presented at Symposium on Caribbean East Indians (Univ. of West Indies, 1975), most of which are historical in approach, dealing with little-known aspects of the East Indian experience in the Caribbean. Emphasizes Trinidad, but Jamaica and Guyana are also covered. Introduction by V.S. Naipaul.

8208 Thompson, L. O'Brien. How cricket is West Indian cricket?: class, racial, and color conflict (FIU/CR, 12:2, Spring 1983, p. 23–53)

Game of cricket as social institution is identified with British aristocracy and decorum. Access to the game by West Indian non-whites is linked to colonial education's transmittal of English cultural patterns. Post World War II marked entrance of plebeian cricket associations. Consequent changes in behavior and purpose of the sporting matches reflect a changing society. [Ethel O. Davie]

8209 Torres-Zayas, José A. Holocausto: la familia puertorriqueña de hoy. Santurce, Puerto Rico?: Jay-Ce Print., 1981. 192 p.: ill.

Author's intention is to bring about a greater awareness of state of the family in Puerto Rico, condemning what he sees as loss of familism, deterioration of intergenerational communication, as well as growing "Americanization." Impressionistic, with little empirical analysis.

8210 Trinidad and Tobago. National Commission on the Status of Women. Final report of the National Commission on the Status of Women. Trinidad: Republic of Trinidad and Tobago, 1978. 79 p.

After presenting general overview of worldwide trends in women's status (and role of population growth and fertility control in influencing such trends), the Commission divides its report on women's status in Trinidad and Tobago into: 1) legal status of women in the country; and 2) education, training, and employment.

8211 Vásquez, Ramón Emilio and María Felicia Fermín. Creencias y prácticas religiosas populares y vigentes en El Granado, Provincia Bahoruco (EME, 9 : 46, enero/feb. 1980, p. 19–104, bibl. maps, tables)

Original, thoughtful study of agrarian community of 634 persons in Dominican Republic. Provides useful, interesting information on area's history, geographic conditions, and economic/technical/educational resources. Most important discussion analyzes relationship between income levels and beliefs in magic and supernatural. Thesis: the poor and dependent classes explain their situation according to supra-human forces they cannot control. Recommended reading.

8212 Vázquez Calzada, José L. Características sociodemográficas de los norteamericanos, cubanos y dominicanos residentes en Puerto Rico (UPR/RCS, 21 : 1/2, marzo/junio 1979, p. 3–33, bibl., ill., tables)

Study sampled three percent of 1970 population census data and determined that North American, Dominican, and Cuban immigrants into Puerto Rico occupy privileged positions within that society. Well presented and organized.

8213 ——— and **Zoraida Morales del Valle.** Características de la población extranjera residente en Puerto Rico (UCR/RCS,

21 : 3/4, sept./dic. 1979, p. 245–287, tables)

Utilizing primarily data from 1970 US Census of Population, describes foreign-born population of Puerto Rico with emphasis on numbers, national origins, and sociodemographic characteristics.

8214 ——— and ———. Población de ascendencia puertorriqueña nacida en el exterior (UPR/RCS, 22 : 1/2, marzo/junio 1980, p. 3–33, ill., plats, tables)

Interesting analysis of 1970 census data comparing, along series of demographic variables, population born in Puerto Rico with Puerto Rican-origin population born outside, but now residing on the island.

8215 Vilas, Carlos M. Notas sobre la formación del Estado en el Caribe: la República Dominicana (CSUCA/ESC, 8 : 24, sept./dic. 1979, p. 117–177)

General and lengthy article on sociohistorical forces that shaped the Dominican nation. Emphasizes role of monopoly capitalism, formation, and realignment of classes, and legitimization of power.

8216 Waters, Donald J. Jungle politics: Guyana, the People's Temple, and the affairs of state (FIU/CR, 9 : 2, Spring 1980, p. 8–13, ill., plates)

Interesting piece that places the ill-fated Jonestown community in its social and political context. Argues that contrary to widespread "dark imaginings" about the community and its demise, the People's Temple should be viewed and understood as a social and political entity within the larger context of Guyanese society and politics.

8217 Yebra, Rita. Proceso de urbanización en Cuba en dos décadas de revolución (BNJM/R, 70[21]:2, 3. época, mayo/agosto 1979, p. 77–88)

Abbreviated version of chapter from author's 1979 thesis at Ecole Pratique des Hautes Etudes. Descriptive and too general work to be of much value. No sources.

8218 Young, Allen. Gays under the Cuban Revolution. San Francisco: Grey Fox Press, 1981. 112 p.: index, port.

Criticizes persecution and oppression of gays in revolutionary Cuba. Most of the evidence was gathered from documents, interviews, and author's experiences and conversations during trips to Cuba in 1969 and 1971.

PERU AND ECUADOR

PATRICK J. BRENNAN, *President, International Business Consultants, Kansas City, Missouri*

THE SOCIOLOGICAL LITERATURE SELECTED and annotated in this *HLAS* reflects primarily research in Peru, proof of the continuing interest of researchers in documenting and measuring the processes of social and political change that began with the first term of President Belaúnde Terry. Several articles focus on flawed policies of the military regimes in the 1970s. There is still paltry reporting on the impact of current problems in the region or on the efforts by the current administration to restructure the national economy and generate growth.

Research continues to focus on aspects of migration and urban adaptation, the role of women in the family and labor force, urban evolution and development obstacles, specifically the theme of dependency. Population dynamics continue to be addressed, in several articles, as well as class and indigenous issues. A number of articles deal with philosophical issues of national identity; some authors using an existentialist approach, question efforts of local organizations to identify an appropriate technology for local development. They suggest that current efforts refer to the experience of the industrial world and its requirements. Typically, these writings offer little insights as to alternative strategies. Although the concept of business incubators is born of experiences outside Latin America, several articles reviewed suggest that such a concept would be extremely fertile if implemented in the region's urban shantytowns.

Indeed, a critique of the research reviewed, is perhaps the lack of insightful new approaches or issues that would guide modern administrators in the public or private sector. Many articles do examine some of the flawed policies of military regimes, such as the legislated transfer of ownership of the press, the role of agencies in the development of shantytown infrastructure, aspects of agrarian reform and peasant response. There is a mass of writings on urban family life in area shantytowns and their adaptation problems. There is very little work that describes efforts to generate small enterprise, markets, and capitalization for the shantytown families.

PERU

Altamirano, Teófilo. Aportes antropológicos al estudio de los movimientos campesinos en el Perú. See item **1440**.

8219 Aramburú, Carlos E. Migraciones internas: perspectivas teóricas y metodológicas. Lima: Instituto Andino de Estudios en Población y Desarrollo, 1981. 55, 8 p.: bibl., ill.

Review and evaluation of over 50 works on Peru's internal migration over 20-year period provides critical discussion of theory and methodology as well as limitations found in these studies. Author's own study of Puno helps to illustrate criteria used for evaluation.

Boletín Bibliográfico. No. 1, 1982- . See item **11**.

8220 Centro de Investigación, Documentación y Asesoría Poblacional, *Perú.* El movimiento de pobladores en la coyuntura. Lima: CIDAP, 1979. 79 p. (Cuadernos CIDAP)

Collection of the Center's working papers dealing with aspects and problems of shantytown life, with particular reference to recent government efforts and policy as promulgated in Law 22612.

Deere, Carmen Diana and **Magdalena León**

de Leal. Peasant production, proletarianization, and the sexual division of labor in the Andes. See item **8244**.

8221 Estado de las ciencias sociales en el Perú. Editor, Bruno Podestá. Lima: Universidad del Pacífico, 1978. 210 p.: bibl.

Authors attempt to evaluate development of the body of social scientific thought in Peru since the turn of the century, with particular reference to the ideological evolution characteristic of publications in the fields of sociology, anthropology, philosophy, and history.

Flores Galindo, Alberto; Orlando Plaza; and **Teresa Oré.** Notas sobre oligarquía y capitalismo en Arequipa, 1870–1940. See *HLAS 44:2936*.

———; ———; and ———. Oligarquía y capital comercial en el sur peruano, 1870–1930: informe preliminar. See *HLAS 44:2937*.

Gilbert, Dennis. Cognatic descent groups in upper-class Lima, Peru. See item **1457**.

Graham, George G. *et al.* Determinants of growth among poor children: effect of expenditure for food on nutrient sources. See item **1811**.

8222 Jofre, Rosa del Carmen. La misión metodista y la educación en Perú (III/AI, 41:3, julio/sept. 1981, p. 501–515)

Examines impact of Methodist mission in Peru whose objectives were to exert influence on all social classes in order to generate beneficial social change throughout Peruvian society. Programs promoted efforts in favor of civil liberties, religious freedom of modernization, and their educational programs aimed at training pupils in skills needed to operate modern business and industrial enterprises. Since these enterprises were mostly foreign, mission's programs promoted the society's capitalist transformation.

8223 Laite, Julian. Industrial development and migrant labour in Latin America. Austin: University of Texas Press, 1981. 229 p.: bibl., ill. (The Texas Pan American series)

Detailed examination of history and social significance of Peru's multi-national mining corporation. Demonstrates how industrialization in a dependent society differs from industrialization in a developed area. Focuses on workers' organizations, pro-

letarization, and why and how migration is an inherent correlate of entire process. Well written and insightful. [L. Pérez]

8224 Lobo, Susan. A house of my own: social organization in the squatter settlements of Lima, Peru. Tucson: University of Arizona Press, 1982. 190 p.: bibl., ill., index.

Author's thesis is well established in previous studies and shows here that village peasants create an ordered and congenial society in urban shantytowns. Attributes this process to villager's ability to create a closely-knit social network based on adaptation of kinship ties.

Mallon, Florencia E. Minería y agricultura en la Sierra Central: formación y trayectoria de una clase dirigente regional, 1830–1910. See *HLAS 44:2960*.

McClintock, Cynthia. Peasant cooperatives and political change in Peru. See item **6352**.

Medina García, Oswaldo. Perú, 1978–1980: análisis de un momento político. See item **6353**.

8225 Osterling, Jorge P. De campesinos a profesionales: migrantes de Huayopampa en Lima. Lima: Pontificia Universidad Católica del Perú, Fondo Editorial, 1980. 203 p.: bibl., maps.

Analyzes migration and adaptation processes of peasants from a rural community to Lima, Peru. Work sets out principal findings of urban anthropologists to Latin America concerning migration experience and then examines experience of these new settlers in light of those historical findings.

8226 Paz, Luiz J. *et al.* Problemas poblacionales peruanos. R. Guerra García, L. Ruiz Carrillo, V. Sara Lafosse, editores. Lima: Asociación Multidisciplinaria de Investigación y Docencia en Población, 1980. 411 p.: bibl., ill.

Essay dealing with critical issues in Peruvian population dynamics: migration and urbanization; food and rural social organization; income distribution; health; education; women by sector; and, family life. Excellent introductory analysis complements topical review by some well published scholars.

8227 Pérez Huarancca, Hildebrando. Los ilegítimos. Lima?: Ediciones Narra-

ción, 1980. 74 p.: ill. (Serie El Tungsteno)
Author presents 12 short stories that portray a rural town inhabited only by the old and children. Young adults have migrated in search of work. Through events narrated and conscience of people described, author vividly portrays forces of change, exploitation, protest, and rebellion that affect life in a small town.

8228 Peru. Oficina Nacional de Estadística y Censos. La población del Perú: 1974, año mundial de la población. Lima: La Oficina, 1984. 346 p., 9 leaves of plates: bibl., ill. (C.I.C.R.E.D. series)
Presentation of key characteristics of Peru's population and dynamics, prepared for World Population Conference (Bucharest, 1974). Chapters have useful, if limited value for scholars needing summary background information. Includes short bibliography.

Prieto de Zegarra, Judith. Mujer, poder y desarrollo en el Perú. See *HLAS 44:2972.*

8229 Riofrío, Gustavo and **Alfredo Rodríguez.** De invasores a invadidos (2): 10 años de autodesarrollo en una barriada. Lima: Centro de Estudios y Promoción del Desarrollo, 1980. 125 p.: bibl.
Study and criticism of effectiveness of efforts by several service agencies entering shantytowns of Lima following their settlement. Authors purport to offer both assessment of accomplishments and strategy for future efforts for such agencies, particularly as Peru moves into civilian rule under President Fernando Belaúnde. Includes interesting sections dealing with small enterprise.

Roberts, Bryan R. State and region in Latin America. See item **8086.**

8230 Sánchez Albavera, Fernando *et al.*
Problema nacional: cultura y clases sociales. Lima: DESCO, Centro de Estudios y Promoción del Desarrollo, 1981. 112 p.
Collection of thoughts and discussions expressed by participants in DESCO-sponsored workshop convened to explore economic, political, and cultural parameters of social conditions in Peru.

8231 Sánchez Enríquez, Rodrigo. Toma de tierras y conciencia política campesina: las lecciones de Andahuaylas. Lima: Instituto de Estudios Peruanos, 1981. 243 p.: bibl. (Estudios de la sociedad rural; 9)

Report detailing events in Andahuaylas, Peru, 1974, when 30,000 peasants mobilized to seize land ignoring agrarian reform movement then being implemented. Author examines underlying conditions and consciousness of peasant, that led to movement's early successes and eventual failure.

8232 Seminario Nacional de Tecnología Adecuada, 2nd, San Miguel, Perú, 1980. Tecnología y campesinado en el Perú: documento final. Huancayo, Comisión Coordinadora de Tecnología Adecuada en el Perú, 1981. 64 p.: bibl., facsim.
Authors take issue with value of efforts by local organizations to identify an appropriate technology for Peru when investigations and compilations are made in reference to experience of industrialized world. Case in point, authors note, is research on solar energy, which has little to do with or to offer to technological needs of Peruvian peasant. Authors call for rebirth of Andean know-how and technology to solve contemporary production problems.

8233 Suárez, Flor Prieto de. Perú, formación de la familia y su efecto sobre la participación laboral de la mujer. Santiago de Chile: CELADE, 1981. 62 p.: bibl. (Serie D / CELADE; no. 100)
Analysis of relation between labor force participation of women and family formation based on Peru's 1977–78 Fertility Survey. Longitudinal analysis focuses life cycle stages: prior to first union, prior to first child, and from first union until time of survey.

8234 Villavicencio López, Alejandro. Los diarios antes y después de la expropiación. Lima?: Tipo-Offset Sesator, 1978. 78, 2 p.: bibl.
Short historical review of Lima's principal dailies, analysis of legislation enacted in 1974, expropriating major dailies and creating National System of Information. In final segment, author evaluates press and its role under both systems of ownership.

ECUADOR

8235 Barsky, Osvaldo *et al.* Ecuador, cambios en el agro serrano. Quito: Facultad Latinoamericana de Ciencias Sociales: Centro de Planificación y Estudios

Sociales, 1980. 531 p.: bibl.

Collection of 12 essays and papers focusing on political, technological, economic, and structural conditions and demographics of peasant farming in Ecuador. Contains lengthy but informative introductory article. Very useful for comparative analysis of similar issues in other countries of region.

Dávila, Francisco R. Los partidos políticos tradicionales y el descenso de la oligarquía en el Ecuador. See item **6278.**

Espinosa Tamayo, Alfredo. Psicología y sociología del pueblo ecuatoriano. See *HLAS 44:7585.*

Guerrero, Andrés. Los oligarcas del cacao: ensayo sobre la acumulación originaria en el Ecuador: hacendados cacaoteros, banqueros, exportadores y comerciantes en Guayaquil. See *HLAS 44:2899.*

8236 Middleton, DeWight R. Migration and urbanization in Ecuador: a view from the coast. Brockport: State University of New York, 1979. 1 v.

Author examines process of migration and urbanization in coastal Ecuador. Links these processes to country's wider social conditions of development, specifically focusing on changing relationships of dependency that exacerbate regional, class, and rural-urban distinctions. Central arguments are illustrated using case study of Manta, a port city. Author profiles immigration to city and its causes, and summarizes development problems and obstacles the area faces.

Schubert, Grace. To be black is offensive: racist attitudes in San Lorenzo. See item **1427.**

COLOMBIA AND VENEZUELA

WILLIAM L. CANAK, *Assistant Professor of Sociology, Brown University,*

AS IN PAST YEARS, the quantity and quality of Colombian sociological research is superior to that in Venezuela, although there are indications of strong improvement in the latter. There is an increasingly strong focus on family (item **8237**) and sexual division of labor research, with a significant advance from the level of polemics and pamphleteering noted in the last issue of *HLAS*. Demographic studies, cross-sectional and historical, are now much stronger. Migration and family composition issues prevail; good mortality studies remain under-represented. Studies falling under the rubric political-economy, ranging from analysis of state structure and state policy to class formation and class struggle are continuing the advances beyond simple dependency analysis. The deep impact of *La Violencia* on Colombian culture and the priority given to understanding that phenomenon is again reflected in a number of new books and articles (items **8238, 8240, 8257,** and **8261**). Technical procedures and methodological approaches seem to encompass the entire spectrum from historical, archival, social history to econometric modeling, a healthy sign that the hegemony of specific types of data analysis and data gathering does not dominate. The years 1980–82 were particularly difficult for many individuals within the Colombian sociological community as restrictions, intimidation, and repression affected some well known scholars. It is remarkable to note the amount and degree of excellent research that continues to be produced, research that has interest and relevance well beyond the borders of that country.

In Venezuela, it appears that a new generation of well trained, theoretically, and methodologically sophisticated sociologists is beginning to make its own way. In each context, the importance of disciplinary boundaries is much less than in North America. One of the fruitful results is that sociologists maintain a clear awareness of approaches characteristic of other disciplines. In addition, one finds good "sociological" research being done by anthropologists, economists, political scientists, and architects. Some of these are included among the following annotations.

COLOMBIA

8237 Angulo-Novoa, Alejandro. The family in Colombia (*in* The Family in Latin America [see item **8011**] p. 84–105, bibl., tables)

Wide-ranging discussion of Colombian family concludes different cultures produced continuum with legal monogamic union/patriarchal authority at one pole and consensus union/polygyny/matriarchal regime at other. Former more common in urban, latter in rural and urban squatter settings. Results: high fertility rates and common law marriage.

8238 Arocha, Jaime. La violencia en el Quindío: determinantes ecológicos y económicos del homicidio en un municipio caficultor. Bogotá: Ediciones Tercer Mundo, 1979. 219 p.: bibl., ill.

Case study of La Violencia in one municipality (1930–65). Focuses on 98 cases of homicide, attempted homicide and delinquent activities in Monteverde. Concludes that non-political party murders were function of "depeasantization" and that politically motivated homicides were also related to changing peasant position in market economy. Describes institutionalization of guerrilla organizations and parallel "repeasantization process." Concludes guerrilla success is based on ecological and economic determinants: 1) terrain providing protection; 2) labor force which could absorb guerrillas; and 3) good infrastructure.

8239 Camacho Guizado, Alvaro. Droga, corrupción y poder: marihuana y cocaína en la sociedad colombiana. Cali, Colombia: CIDSE, Universidad del Valle, 1981. 156 p.: bibl. (Serie Estudios socio-económicos del CIDSE; 1)

Intelligent, balanced analysis of economic, political, and social processes that link specific social groups of Colombian society through phenomenon of drugs and drug or contraband economy. Argues that drug economy constitutes deeply transformative conjuncture in Colombian society, touching all social groups and institutions, from the State to media and corporations. Interesting section discusses groups linked to struggle over repression or legalization of drug economy, especially the military and finance capital.

8240 Campo, Urbano. Urbanización y violencia en el Valle. Bogotá?: Ediciones Armadillo, 1980. 140 p., 1 leaf of plates: bibl., map.

Analysis of rural/urban social relations in Valle del Cauca (1945–65), focusing on La Violencia, disputing party politics thesis and asserting this was an agrarian class struggle, accelerating liquidation of peasant society and linked to process of industrialization and monopoly agribusiness control. Local oligarchies became agents of foreign capital.

8241 Cardona Gutiérrez, Ramiro *et al.* El éxodo de colombianos: un estudio de la corriente migratoria a los Estados Unidos y un intento para propiciar el retorno. Editores, Ramiro Cardona Gutiérrez, Sara Rubiano de Velásquez. Bogotá: Ediciones Tercer Mundo: Colciencias, 1890. 340 p.: bibl., ill.

Reports from multi-faceted study of Colombian emigration, begun in 1975, to analyze historical antecedents of this process, Colombian legislation, emigrants in the US (New York) and evaluate Colombian program for return of professionals and technicians. Some good historical demography, policy analysis, and cultural/economic anthropology by team from Centro Corporación Regional de Población. Study of Colombians in New York uses some interesting methods for gathering data on a difficult-to-study population.

8242 Casas, Ulises. La lucha de clases en Colombia. Bogotá: U. Casas, 1981. 192 p.

Short, Marxist, narrative history of Colombia emphasizes class struggles and forms of political organization and alliances within and between identifiable class fractions.

8243 Congreso Nacional de Sociología: Colombia, 3rd, *Bogotá, 1980.* La sociología en Colombia: balance y perspectivas: memoria. Bogotá: Asociación Colombiana de Sociología, 1981. 348 p.: appendices, bibl.

Series of essays grouped under: 1) "Sociology in Colombia: a Critical Evaluation;" 2) "Methodological Problems;" and 3) "Social Processes." Also contains appendices with statutes of national organization. Valuable introduction to sociology in Colombia with articles by many of the country's most capable sociologists.

8244 Deere, Carmen Diana and **Magdalena León de Leal.** Peasant production, proletarianization, and the sexual division of labor in the Andes (UC/S, 7:2, Winter 1981, p. 338–360, tables)

Comparative analysis of three Andean regions, two in Colombia, one in Peru, using survey data. Concludes that sexual division of labor in productive activities is mostly heterogenous and varies by region, task, form of labor procurement, and household class position. Tendencies: greater female agricultural field work in regions experiencing rapid development, especially among poorer peasants. Rural labor markets concentrate women in low-wage occupations, often extensions of domestic work.

8245 Fajardo, Darío *et al.* Campesinado y capitalismo en Colombia. Bogotá: Centro de Investigación y Educación Popular, 1981. 233 p.: bibl.

Selection of six articles by Colombian sociologists with common analytic perspective. Three historical investigations use archival data on formation of 19th-century peasantry, agrarian politics during early 20th century, and peasant economy and processes of decomposition of peasantry. Remaining three are empirical studies of three important agrarian phenomena: tobacco sharecropping in Boyacá, peasant production and capital accumulation, and formation and development of wage labor in sugarcane section of northern Cauca Valley. Strong contribution to peasant and agrarian studies.

8246 Fals Borda, Orlando. El "secreto" de la acumulación originaria de capital: una aproximación empírica (CSUCA/ESC, 20, mayo/agosto 1978, p. 155–174)

Fascinating historical essay on origins of capitalist production near Montería, Colombia. Analyzes changes in labor force, social relations of production and reproduction, and different groups of capitalists, national and international, who have contributed to changing direction of pace of accumulation in this area. Argues that primitive accumulation is continuing process of class struggle with relations of semi-proletarianization, commonly characterized by use of violence against peasants.

8247 Fields, Gary S. Place-to-place migration in Colombia (UC/EDCC, 30:3, April 1982, p. 539–558, tables)

Using 1973 Colombian Census of Population, investigates how economic opportunities determine spatial allocation of population. Uses data for 12 zones (paired rural-urban areas for six regions) and eight demographic groups (four educational categories/two sexes), regression analysis, effects of income, employment, etc. Concludes high income zones have higher rates, distant areas lower rates, and employment effects are ambiguous, and possible conclusions limited by the data.

8248 Fierro, Marco F. The development of industrial capital in Colombia (Research in Political Economy [JAI Press, Greenwich, Conn.] 3, 1980, p. 209–234)

Historical analysis (pre- and post-1930) emphasizes current economic events as outcome of labor-capital conflict in peripheral societies, but also intra-class conflict, such as blockage of land reform and urban employment programs. Good brief historical introduction to processes of class formation and struggle in Colombia.

8249 Fleet, Michael. The politics of the automobile industry development in Colombia (SAGE/JIAS, 24:2, May/July 1982, p. 211–239)

Classified as intermediate level nation in market size and industrialization, Colombia's policies are compared to Chile's and Venezuela's. Conclusions: relatively slow growth may be due to common sense of officials, not weakness *vis-à-vis* MNC's. Describes contracts and analysis of lack of enforcement of fulfillment of contracts in terms of interacting State, transnational and domestic forces and interests. Emphasizes policy priorities and strategies of various Colombian governments.

8250 Goldman, Noreen. Dissolution of first unions in Colombia, Panama, and Peru (PAA/D, 18:4, Nov. 1981, p. 659–679, bibl., graphs, tables)

Analysis of marital histories from World Fertility Survey data in Colombia, Panama, and Peru, indicates high level of union dissolution. Consensual unions are especially frequent among rural women. Remarriage rates are also high, as is time spent in unions, so effects of disruption on fertility are modest. Excellent comparative demography.

8251 Gómez, Elsa. La formación de la familia y la participación laboral femenina en Colombia. Santiago: CELADE, 1981. 107 p.: bib. (Serie D / CELADE; no. 104)

Using 1976 World Fertility Study data, analysis of female labor force participation and family formation draws on "new family economy" and "historical structural" theories to explain relationship. Conclusion: there isn't a simple functional relation of family size and female employment, but determination of both by exogenous variables such as agriculture/non-agriculture context, head of household position in economic structure, and stage of family life cycle. Solid contribution to this area of theory and research.

Gutiérrez Azopardo, Ildefonso. Historia del negro en Colombia: ¿sumisión o rebeldía? See *HLAS 44:2852.*

8252 Janssen, Roel. Some ideological aspects of urban planning in Latin America: a critique of the Turner model of self-help housing, with special reference to Bogotá (CEDLA/B, 27, dic. 1979, p. 69–76)

Brief summary of Turner's influential model of urban settlement, intra-urban migration, and self-help housing, and its influence on policies of international development agencies. Based on fieldwork in Bogotá, Colombia (1973–75), presents evidence contradicting this model. Concludes: self-help housing is neither solution to housing needs nor to low-income problems, job insecurity, or unemployment.

8253 Lee, K.S. Intra-urban location of manufacturing employment in Colombia (Journal of Urban Economics [Academic Press, New York] 9:2, March 1981, p. 222–241)

Case study, by World Bank analyst, of large and small firms that relocated within Bogotá. Basically descriptive, uses DANE industrial directory files, and concludes that large firms locate toward urban peripheries and small ones toward center. Decentralization of manufacturing and manufacturing employment is increasing except for plastics, beverages, leather, paper, instruments, textiles, and electric machinery.

8254 Lombard, François J. The foreign investment screening process in LDCs: the case of Colombia, 1967–1975. Boulder, Colo.: Westview Press, 1979. 171 p.: bibl. (A Westview replica edition)

Intelligent case study of policy formulation and enactment in Colombia with careful detailing of state bureaucracy intricacies. Looks at economic, psychological, and political factors influencing policy. Aims to identify how, why, and when foreign investments are controlled. Devises model aimed at predicting their implementation, so work is especially useful to corporate officials interested in predicting political risks. Much useful information for general political economy studies (for economist's comment, see *HLAS 43:3349*).

8255 Lozada Lora, Rodrigo and **Eduardo Vélez Bustillo.** Identificación y participación política en Colombia. Bogotá: Fundación para la Educación Superior y el Desarrollo, 1981. 234 p.: ill.

Reflects influence of pluralist liberal modernization theory (Verba, Nie, Inkles, etc.). Broadly discusses relationship of four components of political life in Colombia: 1) attitudes toward party affiliation; 2) attitudes of political alienation; 3) modernization attitudes; and 4) political participation. Model informs two surveys, one of 1,913 respondents in Bogotá and another stratified non-random sample from four Colombian regions. Concludes: family influence primarily determines party affiliation; alienation is real, but very complex; modernity is not causally related to affiliation or alienation. Modes and causes of participation; lots of local activity, while disposition toward parties, is strongly determined by socioeconomic status.

Mendoza Morales, Alberto and **Angela Mendoza.** Retorno al campo. See item **3290.**

Migraciones Internacionales en las Américas. See item **8272.**

8256 Mytelka, Lynn Krieger. Regional development in a global economy: the multinational corporation, technology, and Andean integration. New Haven, Conn.: Yale University Press, 1979. 233 p.: bibl., ill., index.

Although on Andean region in general, much here of interest to students of Colombia and Venezuela. Presents model for relationship of international capital, technology and regional integration, emphasizing internationalization of production and impact of import substitute strategies for understanding changes in Andean economies in 1960s that led to integrative system of planning and regulation. Looks at costs and benefits, conflicts within group, continued technological dependence, and ways MNC's have maintained market segmentation and specialization within the region.

8257 Oquist, Paul H. Violence, conflict, and politics in Colombia. New York: Academic Press, 1980. 263 p.: bibl., index (Studies in social discontinuity)

Study of origins and development of La Violencia (1944–66), describes phenomenon's regional and structural variety and specifies its sociohistorical context— especially previous social violence in Colombia. Social-structural explanation links La Violencia to several processes: partial collapse of the State and interparty conflict allowed long established local rivalries and disputes, especially over land, to be settled by violence, expressing both inter- and intra-class conflicts, but in later period of La Violencia (1955–66), especially the former. Well argued thesis, supported by much new data and excellent bibliography. Sure to be widely used and discussed.

8258 Rosenberg, Terry Jean. Female industrial employment and protective labor legislation in Bogotá, Colombia (SAGE/JIAS, 24:1, Feb. 1982, p. 59–80, tables)

Analysis of protective labor legislation's impact on female industrial employment uses survey data on 10 Bogotá firms. Sample includes management, union leaders and 172 female employees. Concludes: positive correlation of job satisfaction and wage levels and education; strong sexual division of labor; employers prefer to hire young single females; patterns of female industrial employment have little relation to protective labor legislation because there is little knowledge of it and less enforcement as is the case with most Colombian laws (tax, trade, property, vehicular, etc.).

8259 Rubbo, Anna and **Michael Taussig.** El servicio doméstico en el suroeste de Colombia (III/AI, 41:1, enero/marzo 1981, p. 85–111, bibl.)

Draws attention to both inner character and external consequences of female servants in a region of marked capitalist development (Cali, Colombia). Basic patterns of oppression are reproduced through its relationship which embodies power relations, permeating and disfiguring these neocolonial societies.

8260 Ruhl, J. Mark. An alternative to the bureaucratic-authoritarian regime: the case of Colombian modernization (IAMEA, 35:2, Fall 1981, p. 43–69)

Case study seeks to explain Colombia's "deviance" from contemporary norm of military intervention. Concludes: military remains obedient to civil authority because civilian political elite is unified, capable and has legitimacy. Thus National Front is viewed as major success. View of future is indefinite with appreciation for possibilities of deterioration of traditional civilian authority given popular pressures and economic problems that could force austerity policies.

8261 Sánchez G., G. and **D. Meertens.** Aproximación al estudio del bandolerismo en Colombia: bases políticas y sociales (UR/L, Frühjahrssemester 1981, p. 73–95)

Drawing on Hobsbawm's *Primitive rebels*, concludes that the dominant expression of La Violencia was political banditry, with some 120 active bands in 1964. Not a residual phenomenon, bands expressed popular discontent with National Front alliance. Operating in coffee zones and primarily from Liberal Party, bands eventually attacked not only Conservative Party's wealthy and poor, but also wealthy Liberals, becoming more socially aware of class antagonisms. Banditry continued to be linked to political identity and geography, contrasting zones of support and attack.

8262 Simposio sobre Marginalidad y Pobreza, *Bogotá, 1978.* Marginalidad y pobreza. Bogotá: Ediciones Sol y Luna, 1978. 190 p.: bibl., ill. (Biblioteca ANIF de economía)

Collection of essays on marginality and poverty in Colombia, from conference organized by Colombian National Association of Financial Institutions (ANIF) reviewing growth and social composition of squatter settlements, articulation of informal sector with capital accumulation process, family structure, crime and justice system. Two especially good essays: Ernesto Parra Escobar and Ulpiano Ayala on structural role of the informal sector and reproduction of the labor force, respectively.

Twinam, Ann. From Jew to Basque: ethnic myths and antioqueño entrepreneurship. See *HLAS 44:2865.*

8263 Villa, Eugenia *et al.* Religiosidad popular en Bogotá (PUJ/UH, 10:16, dic. 1981, p. 109–137)

Interesting preliminary study of new forms of religious expression in Bogotá focuses on various cults, fetishistic practices and popular attitudes toward traditional religion and medicine. Empirical analysis centers on two groups active in Bogotá's cemetaries "El Movimiento Regina 11" and "Culto a los Muertos."

8264 Whiteford, Michael B. Social urbanization in the Cauca Valley, Colombia (UA, 8:3/4, Winter 1979, p. 351–363)

Describes urbanization in Popayán region arguing that it consists of multiple-urban generating process that link rural-urban areas (i.e., education, roads, media, tourism). National level forces seem stronger than those arising independently from Popayán.

VENEZUELA

8265 Aguilera, Jesús Antonio. La población de Venezuela: dinámica histórica, socioeconómica, y geográfica. 2. ed. Caracas: Universidad Central de Venezuela, Facultad de Ciencias Económicas y Sociales, División de Publicaciones, 1980. 149 p.: bibl., ill. (Colección Libros)

Brief, but useful, introduction to historical and contemporary demographic characteristics of Venezuela, covers questions of population distribution, composition, growth, education, employment, and migra-

tion. Includes special comments on indigenous peoples.

8266 Baloyra, Enrique A. and **John D. Martz.** Political attitudes in Venezuela: societal cleavages and political opinion. Austin: University of Texas Press, 1979. 300 p.: bibl., ill., index (The Texas Pan American series)

Results of large scale (n=1,521) national survey focuses on relationship of major societal cleavages and political opinion and behavior. Conclusions: most Venezuelans perceive themselves as middle class; plurality is one political right; they are very critical of the government and strongly anti-communist and wedded to developmentalist policies; they believe in pluralist party politics and oppose coups. Appendices include sample design, entire questionnaire, and discussions of class division, and statistical techniques employed. Example of applying mainstream pluralist political opinion research developed in US. Sure to be cited often.

8267 Blanco Muñoz, Agustín. Oposición ciudad-campo en Venezuela. 2. ed. Caracas: Universidad Central de Venezuela, Facultad de Ciencias Económicas y Sociales, División de Publicaciones, 1980. 245 p.: ill. (Colección Esquema)

Historical appraisal of urbanization in Venezuela in relation to petroleum-based industrialization and emphasizing contradictions and conflicts between rich/poor, urban/rural, culture/economy that have conditioned and characterized that process. Narrative is informed by a class analysis perspective that is especially concerned with exploitation and manipulation of the poor and creation of national metropolitan system that could operate a "new economy" (i.e., a modern complex industrial society in US and Western European mold).

8268 Conaway, Mary Ellen. Migration studies in Venezuela (FSCN/A, 50, 1978, p. 93–127, bibl., chart)

Review article broadly covers Venezuelan internal migration research according to: 1) studies of immigration policy, settlements, and agricultural land use and socio-psychological adjustment of migrants; and 2) studies using statistical or cultural approach, from census or surveys in former case, and focusing on indigenous peoples, political significance or migrations and agricultural workers, in latter case. Useful analysis with good wide-ranging bibliography.

8269 Coronil, Fernando and **Julie Skurski.** Reproducing dependency: auto industry policy and petro-dollar circulation in Venezuela (WPF/IO, 36:1, 1982, p. 61–94)

Compares liberal bargaining and dependency models to explain auto policy in the Pérez administration (1974–79) and to ascertain socially defined relevant actors and structures underlying policy bargaining process. Conclusions: growing split between international economic interests and locally based demands; common interest of State and bourgeoisie to maintain economy's rentier basis shapes development; petro-dollars have absorbed production as phase in circulation of capital.

Herrera de Weishaar, María Luisa; María Leonor Ferreira Ferreira; and **Carlos Néstor Alvarez Cabrera.** Parroquia La Vega: estudio micro-histórico. See *HLAS 44:2888.*

8270 Lavenda, Robert H. Social urbanization and Caracas: a historical anthropological analysis (UA, 8:3/4, Winter 1979, p. 365–381, table)

Description of changes in population composition and Caracas' physical environment (1870–1908) based on examination of census and archival materials. Presents early evidence of squatter settlements and tenement housing as significant proportion of city's population, primarily recent migrants. Civil marriage patterns reveal small proportion getting married, primarily middle-class.

8271 Lombardi, John V. Venezuela: the search for order, the dream of progress. New York: Oxford University Press, 1981. 348 p.: bibl., ill., index (Latin American histories)

Broad social history of Venezuela emphasizes evolutionary and cumulative nature of its present democratic pluralist political institutions and economic development. Sees three organizational modes: 1) colonial urban system focused on Caracas (touchstone of book); 2) commercial-bureaucratic order developed to allow participation in North Atlantic economic life in 19th and early 20th centuries; 3) development of technological elite and technocratic regimes after 1935. Includes long valuable bibliographic essay, his-

torical chronology, and much demographic data of interest to sociologists.

8272 *Migraciones Internacionales en Las Américas.* Centro de Estudios de Pastoral y Asistencia Migratoria. Vol. 1, No. 1, 1980- . Caracas.

First volume of new serial includes three valuable essays on Venezuela and Colombia by most insightful and active scholars working on international migration in Latin America. Most relevant are: Chen and Picouet's historical, demographic review of Venezuela's international migration experience, Sassen-Koob's on political-economy of Venezuelan immigration, and Mármora's on Colombian labor migration.

Mytelka, Lynn Krieger. Regional development in a global economy: the multinational corporation, technology, and Andean integration. See item **8256.**

8273 Pinto, A. Undocumented and illegally resident migrant women in Venezuela (ICEM/IM, 19:1/2, 1981, p. 241–260, tables)

Summary of frequency distributions for sample of 228 immigrant women, conducted by Venezuelan Catholic Migration Commission (in presumably recent year): 205 respondents were at Colegio María Auxiliadora and 23 were undocumented, illegally resident women. Questions ranged across nationality, family status, motives for migration, educational and occupational background. Contains brief historical review of migration to Venezuela, especially in recent years.

8274 Pollak-Eltz, Angelina. The family in Venezuela (*in* The Family in Latin America [see item **8011**] p. 12–45, bibl.)

Broadly descriptive of upper-, middle-, and lower-class patterns, regional and racial differences. Based on several samples and author's "reflections" unintentionally humorous at times (e.g., "all social classes like children;" "motherhood is important to every woman;" "sexual intercourse is considered to be entirely natural").

———. Magico-religious movements and social change in Venezuela. See item **1116.**

———. Nuevos aportes a la bibliografía afrovenezolana. See item **21.**

———. Regards sur les cultures d'origine africaine au Vénézuela. See item **1118.**

————. Socialization of children among Afro-Venezuelans. See item **1119**.

8275 Prawat, Richard S.; Joe L. Byers; and Wilfred O. Duran. Attitude development in American and Venezuelan school-children (JSP, 115, 2. half, Dec. 1981, p. 149–158, bibl., graphs)

Based on administration of: 1) Cooper-smith Self-Esteem inventory; 2) Nowicki-Strickland externality scale; and 3) Herman's Prestatic Motivation Test, to 347 US and 294 Venezuelan students in grades four-11. Concludes: Venezuelan children have higher academic achievement motivation, especially at younger ages, but cultural differences decline with age. Seems likely that high attrition rates for Venezuelan children (75 percent by grade five) are *possible* factors affecting scores.

8276 Rangel, Domingo Alberto. Capital y desarrollo. v. 1, La Venezuela agraria. 3. ed. Caracas: Universidad Central de Venezuela, Facultad de Ciencias Económicas y Sociales, División de Publicaciones, 1981. 370 p.: bibl., tables (Colección Libros)

From dependency perspective, overview of Venezuelan economic development since colonial era, emphasizes role of external commerce and agriculture in determining rhythm and locale of economic development, especially interests and organization of different sectors of capitalist class (railroads, banking, commerce, industry). For vol. 2, *El Rey petróleo* (published 1979), see *HLAS 43:3416*.

Reyes Baena, Juan Francisco. Dependencia, desarrollo y educación. See item **4514**.

8277 Schultz, T. Paul. Lifetime migration within educational strata in Venezuela: estimates of a logistic model (UC/EDCC, 30:3, April 1982, p. 559–593, tables)

Using cross sectional data from 1961 Venezuelan census, describes how man's patterns of internal lifetime migration are related to current economic and demographic conditions. More educated men leave birthplace more frequently, are less deterred by distance, and are more responsive to relative wage and employment differences. Migration greater where school enrollment higher. Dualism important aspect of labor market for less educated workers given large regional differences in wage levels. Econometric analysis predominates.

8278 Suárez, María Matilde and Ricardo Torrealba. Internal migration in Venezuela (UA, 8:3/4, Winter 1979, p. 291–311, maps, tables)

Historical analysis of internal Venezuelan migration delineates two migratory cycles (1926, 1971), reflecting regional variations in spatial distribution of population and corresponding to mining-export and industrialization phases of national economy. Conclusion: population's spatial redistribution responds to politico-economic factors.

Universidad Simón Bolívar. Instituto de Investigaciones Educativas. El rendimiento estudiantil universitario: influencia de la condición socio-económico de los padres en el rendimiento de los alumnos del primer año universitario, región Capital: síntesis comparativa. See item **4518**.

8279 Zulia, *Venezuela.* **Universidad. Centro de Investigaciones Económicas.** La población de Venezuela. Paris?: C.I.C.R.E.D., 1976? 167 p.: bibl. (C.I.C.R.E.D. series)

Historical demographic description of Venezuela includes characteristics of labor force, quality of life indicators, migration, and demographic projections. Some good regional data. Primarily uses census data and provides good broad introduction for both demographers and other social scientists.

BOLIVIA AND PARAGUAY

KEVIN J. HEALY, *Foundation Representative, Inter-American Foundation, Rosslyn, Virginia*

THE NUMBER OF WORKS ANNOTATED in this section points to the increase in sociological publications of high quality being produced by Bolivian and Paraguayan social scientists. This development attests to the emergence of national and private social research centers manned by well trained social scientists who conduct studies on pressing social and economic problems in their respective countries. The result is more empirical national sociology attuned to major development questions faced by these societies. For almost a decade, the Centro Paraguayo de Estudios Sociológicos (CPES) and the Centro de Investigación y Promoción del Campesinado (CIPCA) have carried out important research, however, only in recent years vital contributions to the sociological literature have been made by Bolivia's Centro de Estudios de la Realidad Económica y Social (CERES) and the Paraguayan Comité de Iglesias.

A group of studies (items **8284, 8293, 8299,** and **8302–8305**) converge in that they offer critical examinations of State policies and prevailing socioeconomic development patterns of dependent, peripheral capitalism at the national, regional, and local levels. Several works characterize the change strategies as "modernizing" as opposed to developmental and document processes of economic growth accompanied by increasing social and economic inequality between and within social classes. Paraguay's rapid agricultural growth during the 1970s (documented in items **8299** and **8302–8304**) was built upon the expansion of export commodities high cost mechanization, proliferation of agro-industries, and Brazilian and multinational penetration through capital transfers and colonization, all of which resulted in high social and national cost. Increases in social and economic inequality in subregions undergoing changes during the past 30 years in southern Bolivia are well documented in two studies (items **8292** and **8293**) which demonstrate the limitations of the 1952 land reform in restructuring society.

Urban sociology in Bolivia made major advances through the works of Calderón and Albó. Calderón gives an overview of three decades of developments of the urban political economy (especially in La Paz, see item **8284**) while Albó's work complements the latter with his underview of La Paz's most vulnerable social sector, the "campesino migrants," whose occupational characteristics as members of a "sub-proletariat" are subject to detailed analysis (item **8281**).

Bolivian institutions such as CIPCA, Acción Cultural Loyala (ACLO), and the Centro de Documentación e Información de Bolivia (closed by the military in 1980) have completed a number of useful profiles on the living conditions and other social and economic characteristics of rural populations in several remote provinces and departments. CERES took a step beyond the standard profile to analyze with greater sophistication and theoretical concern the strategies employed by low-income households defined as "enterprises" to survive and reproduce themselves in urban and rural environments in the Cochabamba Valley. These studies (items **8282** and **8285**) offer an innovative perspective of the regional economy from below, in terms of economic behavior, family networks, and geographic mobility of these households.

This *HLAS* section contains some new contributions to the literature on peasant movements in both countries. The most important is the first book by Equipo Expa on Paraguay's peasant movement (item **8300**) of the 1960s and 1970s. There are also two recent French journal articles, one on the 20th-century, historical background to Bolivia's 1952 peasant revolt (item **8295**) and the other on the recent peasant union mobilization of 1978–80 (item **8283**).

BOLIVIA

Albó, Xavier. Achacachi: medio siglo de lucha campesina. See item **6376**.

8280 ———; **Tomás Greaves;** and **Godofredo Sandoval.** Una odisea: buscar "pega."

La Paz: Centro de Investigación y Promoción del Campesinado (CIPCA), 1982. 203 p.: bibl., ill. (Cuadernos de investigación CIPCA; no. 22. Chukiyawu, la cara aymara de La Paz; 2)

Second book in trilogy about "ex-campesino residents" of La Paz. Uses both 1976 census data and own survey data based upon 1400 "ex-campesino" urban residents, arguing that they belong to "sub-proletariat" category. La Paz's peripheral, dependent urban capitalism generates few stable, wage jobs making residents accept low paid, unstable labor, especially petty employment in commerce and artisanry. Finds that ex-campesinos urban occupational characteristics resemble their countryside economic activities. Work is lucid, concise and full of stimulating social and economic analysis. Contains occupational case histories, 32 tables, two maps, and 17 graphs.

8281 ——; ——; and ——. El paso a la ciudad. La Paz: Centro de Investigación y Promoción del Campesinado (CIPCA), 1981. 150 p.: bibl., graphs, maps (Cuadernos de investigación CIPCA; no. 20. Chukiyawu, la cara aymara de La Paz; 1)

First of three books on La Paz peasant migrants. Data based upon survey conducted at end of 1976, of 1400 men and women, "ex-campesino" urban residents, from rural altiplano. Concise and lucid treatment of economic "push" factors operating in various altiplano provinces also serves as introduction to processes and patterns characterizing settlement into La Paz urban life. Introduction uses 1976 census data to present national picture of internal migration for recent decades. Contains 19 tables, nine maps, and two graphs.

Arze, José Antonio. Bosquejo sociodialéctico de la historia de Bolivia. See *HLAS 44:3015.*

8282 **Blanes Jiménez, José** and **Gonzalo Flores C.** Campesino, migrante y "colonizador:" reproducción de la economía familiar en el Chaparé tropical. La Paz: Ediciones Centro de Estudios de la Realidad Económica y Social (CERES), 1982. 358 p., 30 leaves of plates: bibl., ill. (Serie Estudios regionales; no. 3)

Detailed and systematic descriptive analysis of Chaparé, tropical colonization zone in eastern Cochabamba Dept. Focuses chiefly on economic behavior of peasant

household and its social and economic relations with other areas of region. Examines migration and resettlement process and agricultural production. Important section discusses impact of coca production on economic strategies of peasant households. Includes maps, aerial photographs and 109 tables. Excellent study of zone undergoing constant change (which somewhat limits its relevance) because of its importance as main supplier of raw materials for international cocaine traffic.

8283 **Bot, Yvon le.** Le mouvement syndical Bolivien a la croisée des Chemins: 1978–1980 (FDD/NED [Problèmes d'Amérique Latine, 62] 4649/4650, 28 déc. 1981, p. 111–158, tables)

Chronology and analysis of resurgence of Bolivian union movement led by Central Obrera Boliviana during democratic opening (1978–80). Discusses advances and setbacks of miner and peasant unions in context of changing national political conditions and rapidly deteriorating economic situation for working class. Informative about ferment and dynamism of these popular organizations during brief interlude from military rule.

8284 **Calderón G., Fernando.** La política en las calles. Cochabamba, Bolivia: Centro de Estudios de la Realidad Económica y Social (CERES), 1983. 321 p.: ill. (Estudios urbanos; 1)

Treats evolution of urban political economy of Bolivia during past three decades. Discusses uneven development in terms of Bolivian characteristics of a dependent, capitalist economy which excludes masses from basic social and economic resources and benefits (or services). Compares and contrasts MNR government's urban policies with those of subsequent military regimes. Describes and documents multiple mechanisms employed by US Government to steer Bolivia along this course. Includes sophisticated discussion of urban population growth, internal migration patterns, and social class relations. Contains 37 tables, four graphs, and two maps.

8285 —— and **Alberto Rivera P.** Jatun Llajta: vendedoras y ladrilleros en Cochabamba. Cochabamba, Bolivia: Ediciones Centro de Estudios de la Realidad Económica y Social, 1982. 449 p., 16 leaves of plates: ill. (Serie Estudios urbanos; no. 6)

Study of urban Cochabamba's informal economic sector. Examines family as "enterprise" emphasizing its tendency to diversify economic activities. Conducted surveys among vendors in large urban market center and among small-scale producers of bricks. Makes interesting theoretical contributions on production and consumption strategies of low-income households. Research is part of larger CERES study of economic behavior of low-income households.

8286 Centro de Información y Documentación de Bolivia. Departamento de Investigación y Evaluación de Proyectos. Diagnóstico social del norte boliviano. La Paz: El Departamento, 1979. 236 p.: bibl., maps.

Social and economic profile of Pando Dept. and Vaca Diez Prov. in Beni Dept., northern Bolivia. Includes discussion of demography, land tenure, economic organization, migration, and regional power structures. Focuses on production and commercialization of rubber, including social conditions of rubber producers. One of first socioeconomic studies of this isolated region.

8287 Centro de Investigación y Promoción del Campesinado (CIPCA). Coripata, tierra de angustias y cocales. La Paz: El Centro, 1977. 192 p., 18 leaves of plates (6 fold.): bibl., ill. (Cuadernos de investigación. CIPCA; 15)

Concise and comprehensive social and economic profile of Coripata zone, in Nor Yungas Prov., La Paz Dept. Includes chapters on local agrarian history, case histories of peasant families, demography, land tenure, agriculture, religion, and education. Very useful for understanding Yungas region in general. Research carried by institution familiar with area through its social promotion programs.

8288 Cisneros C., Antonio J. La colonización en Bolivia: un estudio analítico de políticas de distribución espacial de la población. La Paz: Ediciones Centro de Investigaciones Sociales (CIS), 1979. 149, 15 leaves: bibl., ill. (Monografías de población y desarrollo; no. 19)

Elementary study of development of colonization programs in tropical lowland areas in Cochabamba, La Paz, and Santa Cruz Depts. Gives historical background, underlying premises of public policies for colonization and describes public programs and settlement "models" in their comparative aspects and superficial analysis of long term effects and trends.

————. La profesión farmacéutica y la planificación familiar: un estudio de actitudes. See item **1632.**

Esteva Fabregat, Claudio. El campesinado andino como clase social. See item **1355.**

8289 Estudio socioeconómico: Provincia Oropeza. Sucre, Bolivia: Acción Cultural Loyola: Comité de Desarrollo de Chuquisaca, 1975. 527 p.: bibl., ill., tables.

Social and economic profile of isolated Oropeza Prov., Chuquisaca Dept. Includes 84 tables of data on education, land tenure, linguistic patterns, demography, wealth differences, agricultural production costs, marketing and transport, labor relations, and crafts for small farm households. Useful overview of social and economic conditions of rural population in one of country's poorest zones.

8290 Fifer, J. Valerie. The search for a series of small successes: frontiers of settlement in eastern Bolivia (JLAS, 14:2, Nov. 1982, p. 407–432, ill., maps, tables)

Overview of geography, main settlement patterns and historical background of Eastern Bolivia's peasant colonization. Shows that 1952 land reform accelerated lowland colonization. Depicts conditions minimally necessary for colonists and recounts public and small farmer efforts to accomplish this. Gives more detailed case material from the much evaluated San Julián project in Santa Cruz but other than low abandonment rate fails to assess socioeconomic impact. Work is mainly descriptive and leaves out discussion of larger economic and political interest groups which influence agricultural progress of lowland colonists.

8291 Gutiérrez, Héctor and **François Héran.** Bolivie: de graves problèmes socio-démographiques; présentation de quelques données récentes (FDD/NED [Problèmes d'Amérique Latine, 62] 4649/4650, 28 déc. 1981, p. 11–30, map, tables)

Using data from 1976 census, authors analyze various demographic features of Bolivia which include population density and distribution, age structure and employment structure for economically active population. Also examines infant mortality, highest in

Latin America, and life expectancy, among the lowest. Also discusses country's linguistic patterns, pressures to adopt Spanish as single language spoken, and emergent trends.

8292 Healy, Kevin. Caciques y patrones: una experiencia de desarrollo rural en el sud de Bolivia. Cochabamba, Bolivia: Ediciones El Buitre, 1983. 431 p.: ill.

Descriptive analysis of interplay between local elites and agrarian reform and various development programs (1952–79) in two provinces in southern Chuquisaca Dept. Argues that local agrarian reform did not create structural change necessary for broad-based development and that the rural modernization of 1970s reconcentrated wealth, income, and power among dominant local groups, in particular town-based caciques and landowners.

La Iglesia de Bolivia, ¿compromiso o traición?: de Medellín a Puebla: ensayo de análisis histórico. See *HLAS 44:3034*.

8293 Kelly, Jonathan and **Herbert S. Klein.** Revolution and the rebirth of inequality: a theory applied to the National Revolution in Bolivia. Berkeley: University of California Press, 1981. 279 p.: bibl., ill., index.

Authors test seven hypothesis about redistributive effects of radical 1952 Revolution using data collected by Research Institute for the Study of Man (1965–66). Data based upon survey of 1130 heads of households in six communities in distinct regions of Bolivia. Findings indicate that Revolution leads to greater equality of opportunity in the short-run, but in medium and long terms, structures of inequality reemerge to become entrenched once again. Uses as principal variables, occupation and education, and mobility changes from parents to their children. Employs very sophisticated and innovative methodology for data analysis but this very technical expertise distances and insulates the work from the Bolivian social context.

8294 Leonard, Olen E. and **Eduardo Arze Louriero.** The family in Bolivia (*in the* Family in Latin America [see item **8011**] p. 199–234, bibl.)

Discussion of social and cultural characteristics of Bolivian family identifies differences by social strata and region. Maintains

the 1975 social Revolution altered important aspects of family structure and that the altiplano's close-knit and integrated family units differ from those in the Andean valleys and lowlands. Work is handicapped by omitting 1976 census data.

8295 Parrenin, Georges. Genèse des mouvements indiens-paysans en Bolivie, 1900–1952 (FDD/NED [Problèmes d'Amérique Latine, 62] 4649/4650, 28 déc. 1981, p. 31–53)

Short descriptions of major peasant movements in Bolivia since 1898 up to and including 1952 social Revolution. Shows interplay of State policies and political party activities with indigenous rebellions. Presents greatest detail on origins and aftermath of 1952 event. Not much that is new concerning peasant movements.

8296 Programa Regional del Empleo para América Latina y el Caribe (PREALC). Distribución del ingreso, migraciones y colonización: una alternativa para el campesinado boliviano. Santiago: PREALC, 1979. 78 leaves: bibl. (Documento de trabajo / PREALC; 176)

Study uses secondary data with 24 statistical tables covering income distribution patterns and characteristics of migration flows, both to urban as well as rural areas for colonization. Includes discussion of policy action to combat rural poverty.

Rivera Cusicanqui, Silvia. La expansión del latifundio en el altiplano boliviano. See *HLAS 44:3052*.

———. Rebelión e ideología: luchas del campesinado aymara del altiplano boliviano, 1910–1920. See *HLAS 44:3053*.

8297 Torrez Pinto, Hugo. Rasgos y consideraciones demográficas de Bolivia. La Paz: Centro de Investigaciones Sociales, 1977. 63 leaves: bibl. (Serie de estudios de población y desarrollo; no. 15)

Compares Bolivia's 1950 and 1976 census figures to examine number of demographic variables which include population growth, fecundity, infant mortality and internal and external migration patterns. Makes comparisons among departments within Bolivia and with other countries of North and Latin America.

PARAGUAY

8298 Boisi, Alfredo S.C. Historia del pobla-
miento en Misiones: inmigración a
Oberá entre 1928 y 1975 (CPES/RPS, 17:49,
sept./dic. 1980, p. 29–67, graphs, maps,
tables)

Reconstruction of settlement patterns
of migrants to Paraguayan prov. of Misiones
and urban center of Oberá (1928–75). Shows
different modes of settlement and origins of
migrants for three distinct historical periods.
Includes 15 different nationalities represented in this migratory flow and period of
highest rate of migration (1928–40). Offers
push factor of declining economic conditions
as main explanatory variable for shifts in migration patterns.

**8299 Comité de Iglesias. Formas de
Organización Productiva Campesina.**
El caso de la migración brasileña al Alto
Paraná y su impacto económico y social.
Asunción: El Comité, 1981. 239 p.: tables.

Well documented and penetrating
study of colonization area in Alto Paraná,
eastern Paraguay. Develops typologies to classify numerous farms and analyzes processes
of colonization, agricultural modernization,
proletarianization, social differentiation, and
migration. Includes especially important
documentation and analysis of Brazilian colonization and mechanisms for economic expansion into region. Contains 45 tables.

8300 Equipo Expa. En busca de "La Tierra
sin Mal:" movimientos campesinos en
el Paraguay. Bogotá: Indo-American Press
Service, 1982. 195 p. (Colección Iglesia
nueva; 65)

Social commentary and chronology of
very important Paraguayan peasant movement, the "Ligas Agrarias," or agrarian
leagues which flourished until repression
by the nation's military government in
mid-1970s. This publication constitutes
single documentary source in book form on
this highly organized and spreading movement organized by the Catholic Church. Authors are Jesuit priests whom government
expelled for "subversive" activities. Several
served as advisors to the movement, a fact
which gives their book a committed insider's
view of the organization's goals.

8301 Franco, Rolando. Un análisis socio-
político de la pobreza y de las acciones
tendientes a su erradicación (CPES/RPS,
17:49, sept./dic. 1980, p. 7–27)

Clear theoretical exposition of concept
of "poverty." Paraguayan author rejects explanations of causes of poverty which focus on
individual values and attitudes and adopts a
structural analysis, stressing both the terms'
relative and historical dimensions. Examines
role of the State, especially public policy and
use of power by dominant social groups.
Gives negative assessment about effectiveness of conventional public programs designed to eradicate poverty and offers little
in the way of alternative courses for public
action.

8302 García, Antonio *et al.* Estado, campesinos y modernización agrícola.
Domingo M. Rivarola, compilador. Asunción: Centro Paraguayo de Estudios Sociológicos, 1982. 503 p.: bibl., ill., indexes
(Serie Estudios)

Excellent articles about rural Paraguay
cover social differentiation, migration, and
agricultural modernization. Examines both
dynamic colonization areas and traditional
"minifundia" areas of small holders in central Paraguay. Contradictions of rural modernization processes are well documented.
Two interesting findings are that traditional
"munifundia" areas have greater increases in
social differentiation than colonization areas,
and that peasant wage earners do not sever
their ties to their own land but often maintain dual status, making Paraguay distinct
from many other modernizing regions of
Latin America where proletarianization becomes irreversible.

8303 Masi, Fernando. Contribución al estudio de la evolución socio-económica
del Paraguay (CPES/RPS, 19:53, enero/abril
1982, p. 33–63)

Important article gives socioeconomic
history of Paraguay and especially details the
"economic boom" of past decade fueled by
Itaupá hydroelectric project and export
expansion of cotton and soybeans. Traces
Paraguay's 19th-century autonomous development process which ended with 1870 Triple Alliance War through stagnant economic
dependency on Argentina until dramatic
changes of 1970s which shifted economic dependency to Brazil. Identifies social groups
which capture lions share of income from
Brazil-generated economic growth and

skewed distributional effects which discriminates against Paraguay's peasant majority. Ends critique of capitalist development model "hacia afuera" by offering alternate policy guidelines. Lucid synthesis of historical patterns up to present.

8304 Miranda, Aníbal. Desarrollo y pobreza en Paraguay. Rosslyn, Va.: Inter-American Foundation; Asunción: Comité de Iglesias para Ayudas de Emergencia, 1982. 372 .: bibl., ill, tables.

Bold and excellent structural analysis of social and economic development patterns during past decade in urban and rural Paraguay. Examines prevailing economic growth strategy in terms of social costs in health, housing, education, employment, income distribution, and migration. Uses numerous tables of descriptive statistics to convey poverty levels and social inequality.

8305 Morínigo A., José N. Hacia una cuan-

tificación de la población pobre en Asunción (UCNSA/EP, 9:1, junio 1981, p. 181–228, maps, tables)

Systematic study designed to locate poverty areas in Asunción. Examines income levels and income distribution patterns of lower class urban population. Argues that rapid capitalist expansion (1972–82) increased urban poverty and that low-income women in labor force suffer greater economic exploitation than men. Uses numerous maps of poverty concentration in Asunción and tables based upon census and survey data.

Ruiz Díaz, Daniel Campos. Escolaridad y fuerza de trabajo en el Paraguay: economía de la educación. See item **4489.**

Schiefelbein, Ernesto and **Carlos Clavel.** Comparación de los factores que inciden en la demanda por educación en Paraguay y Chile. See item **4490.**

THE SOUTHERN CONE: ARGENTINA, CHILE, AND URUGUAY

CARLOS H. WAISMAN, *Assistant Professor of Sociology, University of California, San Diego*

ARGENTINA: MOST OF THE LITERATURE ON Argentina concerns three subject areas: 1) population, with a focus on immigration; 2) political sociology, with emphasis on the peronist period; and 3) sociology of the urban lower classes.

Given the composition of the Argentine population, the study of migratory currents and the assimilation of Europeans has long been a traditional area of concern among scholars of this country. Works by Fontanella (item **8317**), Kloberdanz (item **8325**), Monacci (item **8326**), and Ruggiero (item **8331**) exemplify this tradition as they examine at varying levels of sophistication and with different purposes the integration of Italians, Britons, and Russo-Germans to the new environment. New ground is broken by Whiteford (item **8335**) in his study of Bolivian immigration both in subject matter (the new Latin American immigration) and in theoretical approach (contemporary structural analysis as opposed to traditional culturalism). Another contribution to population studies is Vapñarsky's solid reconceptualization of urbanization categories (item **8333**).

Specialists in Argentine political sociology continue to focus on the country's economic, social, and political breakdown after World War II.

An important compilation of classical pieces on the social foundations of peronism is by Mora y Araujo and Llorente (item **8334**). Other works dealing with this political movement are Sidicaro's which presents a global interpretation (item **8332**); Di Tella's (item **8314**) which contributes greatly towards understanding the development and impact of a stratum of trade union activists since the beginning of the Argentine labor movement; and James' (item **8323**) which, by focusing on labor conflicts at the shop-floor level, sheds much light on an important but neglected aspect of working class' political action. Finally, Corradi's paper (item **8311**) makes an innovative attempt to apply recent models of discourse analysis to Latin American political ideologies.

That the urban lower classes are the subject of much study is exemplified by the above mentioned examinations of political activity by Di Tella and James, by Eichelbaum's (item **8315**) traditional but important quantitative study of determinants of educational attainment among the urban poor, and by Jelin's (item **8324**) and Ramos' (item **8328**) interesting ethnographic studies of lower-class family life. This methodology has been hitherto neglected in Argentine sociology, despite its heuristic value and the important fact that, unlike survey research, it does not require large research budgets, trained staffs, and computers.

CHILE: Understandably, most of the literature on Chilean political sociology has been written abroad, and can be separated into two categories: 1) agrarian politics during the Allende government; and 2) global analysis of the Allende and Pinochet regimes.

Agrarian studies focus on the land reform carried out by the Popular Unity government and are exemplified by Bossert's (item **8336**) and Kay's (items **8339** and **8340**) significant analyses of rural structure and the political consequences of land redistribution. Riz's global analysis (item **8344**) searches for reasons to explain the failure of Unidad Popular; Garreton explores the dynamics of Pinochet's authoritarian regime (item **8338**), while Falabella (item **8337**) offers a useful description of Chile's labor movement under the same regime.

URUGUAY: One should note that all works on the country were published therein, an indication that some areas of the social sciences have survived Uruguay's authoritarian regime. Most of these studies deal with population issues, especially migration and emigration, an emphasis attributable to the fact that, under such a political system, most types of macrosociology are suspect. Emigration, however, is exempted from such proscription chiefly because it is such a critical issue in Uruguayan society today, a society that combines an explosive mixture of protracted economic stagnation, a highly mobilized and educated population, and a political regime that blocks participation. Filgueira's paper (item **8350**) makes a good attempt at analyzing emigration as a response to economic and political decay.

ARGENTINA

8306 Allub, Leopoldo. El colapso de la democracia liberal y los orígenes del fascismo colonial en Argentina (UNAM/RMS, 42[42]:3, julio/sept. 1980, p. 1105–1144, graphs, tables)

Examines cultural and ideological factors leading to 1930 coup (e.g., spread of rightist, anti-democratic ideologies exemplified by Gálvez and Lugones; opponents' perceptions of Radicalism and Radicals' confrontational response to opposition; Spanish roots of military interventionism; relationship between classes and parties; incapacity of political system to withstand conflict; abuse of federal intervention in provinces; patronage). Allub's concept of "colonial fascism" encompasses military regimes from 1930 to present.

8307 Archetti, Eduardo P. Uso y conciencia de las categorías económicas en explotaciones familiares (CSUCA/ESC, 21, sept./dic. 1978, p. 193–208, bibl.)

"Subjectivism" vs. "objectivism" dispute in social sciences must be superseded, for the observable cannot be reduced to either model. Author illustrates his approach with a very professional analysis of the economic and political behavior of farmers in northern Sante Fe.

Assunção, Fernando O. El gaucho: estudio socio-cultural. See item **8348.**

8308 Barkey, David W. and **D. Stanley Eitzen.** Toward an assessment of multinational corporate social expenditures in relation to political stability and terrorist activity: the Argentine case (IAMEA, 34:4, Spring 1981, p. 77–90)

Analysis of relationship between multinational corporations'(MNC) social expenditures (SI) and degree of political stability of environment in which they operate. Uses Argentine 1970s experience to conclude that: 1) no correlation between terrorist threats or political instability and SI; 2) individual MNCs will not respond to terrorism with increased SI; and 3) terrorists select business targets for propaganda value.

8309 Botana, Natalio R. *et al.* Ciencias sociales: palabras y conjeturas. Francis Korn, compiladora. Buenos Aires: Editorial Sudamericana, 1977. 211 p.: bibl., ill. (Colección Historia y sociedad)

Interesting attempt at conceptual analysis. Papers explore meanings underlying common concepts in sociology (e.g., class, development, dependency, marginality) most of them in reaction against verbosity and abstract theorizing that plague Latin American sociology. Section called "Conjectures" includes papers on political order envisioned by Alberdi and Sarmiento, repercussions of European political conflicts in River Plate, and quantification in history.

Cantón, Darío and **Jorge Raúl Jorrat.** El voto peronista en 1973: distribución crecimiento marzo-septiembre y bases ocupacionales. See item **6411.**

8310 Carroll, Glenn R. and **Jacques Delacroix.** Organizational mortality in the newspaper industries of Argentina and Ireland: an ecological approach (CU/ASQ, 27:2, June 1982, p. 169–198, graphs, tables)

Study of why organizations fail, based on analysis of newspapers from 19th-century Argentina and 19th- and 20th-century Ireland. Shows that newspapers suffer high mortality in early years. Both industry's maturity and economic expansion enhance survival, but timing of birth relative to business cycles

is independent of survival. Newspapers founded during political turmoil are outlived by newspapers founded under stable conditions.

8311 Corradi, Juan E. The avatars of sociopolitical discourse in Latin America (SSISS, 18:1, 1979, p. 59–77)

Theoretical study of Latin American political legitimacy focusing on Argentina. Describes dependent social formations and how groups within them contend over symbols and ideologies. Applies textual analysis (e.g., Ricoeur and Foucault) to dominant social and political discourses in recent Latin American history. Corradi's goal is to develop framework for interpreting ideologies as discursive practices, and use it for analyzing hegemonic crises. Sophisticated article that links development theory and most recent cultural analysis.

8312 Cuevillas, Fernando N. *et al.* Ser y no ser de los argentinos: sociología para nosotros. Buenos Aires: Ediciones Macchi, 1979. 537 p.: bibl.

Old fashioned, ideological, unprofessional introductory textbook in sociology that devotes as much space to Catholic social doctrine as to classical sociologists. Discussion of Argentina focuses on "culture" (i.e., culture-and-personality tradition) and ignores most recent scholarly literature. Pays little attention to either Argentina's economic and political structure or its processes of social change.

8313 Delich, Francisco José. Crítica y autocrítica de la razón extraviada: veinticinco años de sociología. Caracas: El Cid Editor, 1977. 104, 6 p.: bibl. (Colección Estudios interdisciplinarios; 1)

Opinionated survey of Argentine sociology covers late 1940s-early 1970s period in which traditional sociology was replaced by rise (and eventual fall) of academic sociology (e.g., Univ. of Buenos Aires' Sociology Dept., Instituto Di Tella) and in which there developed a populist-nationalist sociology linked to peronism.

8314 Di Tella, Torcuato S. Working-class organization and politics in Argentina (LARR, 16:2, 1981, p. 33–56)

Sophisticated analysis by distinguished sociologist of Argentine labor. Focuses on "problem of organization:" development of trade union activism leading to ensuing dilemmas (e.g., rank-and-file interests vs. labor's own bureaucratic oligarchy). Sees recruitment into labor elite as function of four variables: 1) ideological; 2) emotional; 3) personal ambitions; and 4) group pressure. Traces development of Argentine labor movement from early anarchist and socialist unions to peronist mass trade-unionism through postperonist period (for historian's comment, see *HLAS 44:3201*).

8315 Eichelbaum de Babini, Ana María. La villa miseria y la escuela en Buenos Aires: el medio familiar y el éxito escolar. Buenos Aires: Centro de Investigaciones en Ciencias de la Educación, 1976. 194 p. in various pagings: bibl. (Documento de trabajo; 10)

Survey (1970) of academic performance among Buenos Aires slums' (*villas miseria*) school children. Examines effects of family environment (e.g., standard of living, educational level, rural/urban origin, family structure, mothers' aspirations and information) on children's academic success. Strongest determinants of latter were parents' education and information, urbanization, housing, etc. (findings' summary, p. 115).

8316 Escobar, Raúl Tomás. Inteligencia: manual. 3. ed. Buenos Aires: Editorial F.I., 1980. 363 p.: bibl., ill., maps, ports.

Intelligence textbook written by police officer for courses taught in Argentine police academies. Not much about intelligence *per se* (i.e., procedures for collecting and evaluating classified data, counter-espionage, etc.) but plenty of naive, right-wing authoritarian vagaries. In "national security doctrine" tradition adopted by Southern Cone military, focuses on ideologically defined "internal enemies" presented in unsophisticated discussion of radical politics, especially varieties of communism and Argentine labor movement. Full of conceptual and empirical inaccuracies. Still, a rare glimpse into the ideological and theoretical indoctrination of Argentine security forces.

8317 Fontanella de Weinberg, María Beatriz. La asimilación lingüística de los inmigrantes: mantenimiento y cambio de lengua en el sudoeste bonaerense. Bahía Blanca, Argentina: Universidad Nacional del Sur, Departamento de Ciencias Sociales, 1979. 93 p.: bibl. (Series Letras; 3)

Study of linguistic assimilation in Bahía Blanca region where turn-of-the-century mass immigration produced multilingual pattern with languages other than Spanish disappearing quickly, except among groups such as Russo-Germans. Their linguistic persistence was function of geographic concentration, previous experience as minority group, strong identity, and cultural differences with surrounding population. Author focuses on Italians (12 percent of population in 1914) who assimilated faster than other groups because of: 1) lack of linguistic homogeneity; 2) scant use of written language; 3) lack of formal instruction in Italian; 4) regional and ideological cleavages among them; 5) identification between use of Italian and membership in lower classes; 6) socialization mechanisms; and 7) upward mobility processes.

8318 Goldar, Ernesto. Buenos Aires, vida cotidiana en la década del 50. Buenos Aires: Plus Ultra, 1980. 219 p.: bibl.

Interesting survey of everyday life in 1950s Buenos Aires. Well written exercise in nostalgia is also good piece of non-academic sociology. Describes food habits, clothing patterns, household organization, transportation, child and adolescent culture, popular culture (from sports to language), "high culture," deviance, patterns of love and death. Shows effects of political and structural changes of 1950s Argentine society on daily life.

8319 Gonevski, Khristo. Dalech ot roden krai: spomeni ot Arzhentina. Sofiia: Partizdat, 1980. 372 p., 8 p. of plates: bibl., ill.

Work of Bulgarian who lived in Argentina (ca. 1930–ca. 1950) describes Argentine Slavic organizations. [R.V. Allen]

8320 Gordon R., Sara. Democracia y golpes de estado en América Latina (UNAM/RMS, 43:2, abril/junio 1981, p. 639–654)

Conventional examination of concept of democracy. Discusses oligarchic origin of democratic institutions in Chile, Uruguay, and Argentina, countries in which the productive structure allowed for low-conflict linkages among ruling classes.

8321 Imaz, José Luis de. Promediados los cuarenta: no pesa la mochila. Buenos Aires: Editorial Sudamericana, 1977. 257 p.

Mid-life memoirs by Argentine sociologist. Consists of personal recollections, references to political participation (in Onganía's authoritarian regime), very interesting observations on university life and the social sciences in late 1950s and early 1960s. Author was part of circle which, under Gino Germani's leadership, established academic sociology in Argentina. With his peronist and nationalist past, Imaz was unusual in such a group. Includes frank and insightful discussion of his own ideological trajectory attempting to reconcile religious beliefs with social science, and moral communitarianism with liberalism.

8322 ——. La representación de las regiones: un modelo de simulación política (CRIT, 53:1849/1850, 15 dic. 1980, p. 764–768)

Proposes combining provinces into new sub-national political units or *regions*. There would be seven to nine such regions consisting of former provinces, or parts of provinces, and determined according to similarity of physical milieu, patterns of settlement, economic characteristics, and culture. Each region would be administered by committee of governors and regional procurator, responsible for articulating regional interests before the national executive. Example of such a region: Gran Chaco.

8323 James, Daniel. Rationalisation and working class response: the context and limits of factory floor activity in Argentina (JLAS, 13:2, Nov. 1981, p. 375–402)

Analyzes attempts by employers and governments from early 1950s to 1960s to "rationalize" production within Argentine industry and to restructure balance of forces on factory floor. Discusses rationalization drive in second peronist government. Policies of military regime which overthrew Perón, and of Frondizi administration. Includes interesting analysis of rationalization's effect on union activity. Clauses in work contracts restricted functions of shop floor delegates and gave employers free hand concerning production arrangements and work systems. Grievance procedures were controlled by top union officials, employers' representatives, and Ministry of Labor.

8324 Jelin, Elizabeth and María del Carmen Feijóo. Trabajo y familia en el ciclo de vida femenino: el caso de los sectores populares de Buenos Aires. Buenos Aires: Centro de Estudios de Estado y Sociedad (CEDES), 198? 85 p. (Estudios CEDES; v. 3, no. 8/9)

Analyzes biographies of working-class housewives, based on interviews in Buenos Aires. Paper discusses changes in roles associated with domestic existence at different stages of life cycle. Subjects accept sexual division of labor as natural, but conventional values are slowly changing. Interesting study.

8325 Kloberdanz, Timothy J. Plainsmen of three continents: Volga German adaptation to steppe, praire, and pampa (*in* Ethnicity on the Great Plains. Edited by Frederick C. Luebke. Lincoln: University of Nebraska Press *for the* University of Nebraska-Lincoln, Center for Great Plains Studies, 1980, p. 54–72)

Survey of Germans who settled in Volga region, American and Canadian prairies and Argentine pampas. Focuses on immigrants' adaptation to different physical and cultural environments (see also *HLAS 44:3285*).

8326 Monacci, Gustavo A. La colectividad británica en Bahía Blanca. Bahía Blanca, Argentina: Universidad Nacional del Sur, 1979. 107 p., 17 leaves of plates: bibl., ill.

Study of small British community in Bahía Blanca. Unlike other immigrants, Britons preserved their language and cultural distinctiveness. Their immigration was not massive, and it was associated with turn-of-the-century, large, British investment. Discusses immigrants' role in railroads, ports, utilities, trade, and banking (for historian's comment, see *HLAS 44:3317*).

8327 Pérez Lindo, Augusto. Etat oligarchique, désintégration sociale et violence politique en l'Argentine (ULB/RIS, 1/2, 1981, p. 319–356, tables)

Interprets authoritarian regime established in 1976 as attempt to restore power of traditional oligarchy. Following Touraine, characterizes function of dependent oligarchy as executing policy of social, political, and cultural disarticulation. Oligarchy combines these forms of internal disarticulation with integrating country into international system of domination. Also discusses formation of oligarchic state in late 19th century, and maps its changes up to present.

8328 Ramos, Silvina E. Las relaciones de parentesco y de ayuda mutua en los sectores populares urbanos: un estudio de caso. Buenos Aires: Centro de Estudios de Estado y Sociedad (CEDES), 1981. 77 p.: bibl., ill. (Estudios CEDES; v. 4, no. 1)

Interesting study of kinship and mutual aid networks in a lower class family in outskirts of Buenos Aires. Describes functioning of informal exchange relationships defined on basis of family ties, neighborhood, and friendship. Research addresses both analysis of structural opportunities and constraints faced by individuals, and their representations and interpretations of reality.

8329 Reboratti, Carlos E. Migraciones y frontera agraria: Argentina y Brasil en la cuenca del Alto Paraná-Uruguay. Buenos Aires: Centro de Estudios Población (CENEP), 1979. 48 p.: bibl., map (Cuaderno del CENEP; no. 8)

Analysis of settlement of High Paraná-Uruguay basin, rural border area between Argentina and Brazil, whose population grew six fold (1940–70). Explains growth by "border advance." Given existence of free land and of migratory current, there is a process of settlement and consequent saturation of agrarian structures.

8330 Rissech, Elvira and **Mario Nascimbene.** Panorama de la inmigración a la Argentina: 1857–1970 (Información Comercial Española [Ministerio de Comercio y Turismo, Secretaría General Técnica, Madrid] 562, junio 1980, p. 53–64, tables)

Summary of facts on immigration to Argentina, based on censuses, Germani's classical work, and author's study of recent immigration from neighboring countries.

Rouquié, Alain. Poder militar y sociedad política en la Argentina. v. 2, 1943-1973. See item **6440.**

8331 Ruggiero, Kristin. Gringo and Creole: foreign and native values in a rural Argentine community (SAGE/JIAS, 24:2, May 1982, p. 163–182, bibl.)

Study of Italian immigrants and Creoles in Entre Ríos agricultural colony. Presents *contra* ideological image of Argentina as melting pot in tune with contemporary research showing persistence of immigrant subcultures. Author finds that Italians have *not* assimilated into native culture. Immigrants (many of whom belonged to Waldensian Protestant sect) regard Creoles as lazy, naive, and unproductive, while Creoles fail to understand Italians' acquisitive tendencies. Value cleavage persists to present.

8332 Sidicaro, Ricardo. Consideraciones sociológicas sobre las relaciones entre el peronismo y la clase obrera en la Argentina (CEDLA/B, 31, dic. 1981, p. 43–60, tables)

Discussion of relationship between working class and peronist regime. Ruling class did not have a faction with hegemonic proposals and converted anti-peronism into its main policy. Working class identified peronism with its own sectoral interests. Surveys economic situation of working class throughout peronist regime.

8333 Vapñarsky, César A. La población urbana argentina en 1970 y 1960: revisión crítica de la información censal oficial. Buenos Aires: Centro de Estudios Urbanos y Regionales, 1979. 131 p.: bibl.

Detailed critique of definitions and procedures used in Argentine censuses of 1960 and 1970 to determine size of urban areas. Author's goal is to replace exact census figures which represent conceptually inadequate spatial units for estimates of precisely defined spatial units. Proposes definition of "agglomerations," and reinterprets census figures on basis of this concept. Establishes over 600 urban areas.

8334 El Voto peronista. Manuel Mora y Araujo e Ignacio Llorente, compiladores. Buenos Aires: Editorial Sudamericana, 1980. 524 p.: bibl., ill. (Colección Historia y sociedad)

Very important collection of articles on social base of peronism. Includes classical articles by Smith and Germani, and criticisms to Germani made by Smith, Kenworthy, and Halperin Donghi. Central issue is validity of Germani's traditional thesis, according to which recent migrants constituted central component of peronism's original social base in 1946. Articles by Llorente on Buenos Aires Prov. and González Esteves on Córdoba shed light on complexity of local alliances in 1946 elections. Those by Moray Araujo and latter and Smith discuss the movement's social base a generation later, on basis of 1973 election data (for historian's comment, see *HLAS 44:3406*).

8334a Waisman, Carlos H. Modernization and the working class: the politics of legitimacy. Austin: University of Texas Press, 1982. 244 p., bibl., tables.

Very interesting and insightful work

on factors contributing to the legitimation of capitalism by the working class. Emphasizes analysis of crisis created by working-class participation in the polity, with its possible outcomes and consequences. Various case studies used, but author's experience in and research on Argentina predominate. [L. Pérez]

8335 Whiteford, Scott. Workers from the North: plantations, Bolivian labor, and the city in Northwest Argentina. Austin: University of Texas Press, 1981. 189 p.: bibl., index (Latin American monographs; no. 54)

Study of Bolivian immigration into Northwestern Argentina whose seasonal flow is related to sugar industry production cycle in Salta and Jujuy Prov. Symptom and product of uneven development, Bolivian migrants serve as labor reserve for Argentina Northwest agriculture. Describes process of recruitment, work in sugar plantations, and strategies used by migrants to make a living between harvests. Solid research based on extensive fieldwork.

CHILE

8336 Bossert, Thomas John. The agrarian reform and peasant political consciousness in Chile (LAP, 7:27[4], Fall 1980, p. 6–28, tables)

Author challenges two notions:
1) agrarian reform is an effective deterrent to revolution; and 2) middle-class peasants lack revolutionary potential. Survey of over 1,000 peasants in Chile's Central Valley in early 1970s indicates that some sectors of privileged peasantry have high level of political consciousness. Contrary to expectations regarding dampening effects of land redistribution programs, privileged peasants with highest levels of political consciousness were those who had benefitted from agrarian reform.

8337 Falabella, Gonzalo. Les syndicats sous un régime autoritaire: le cas du Chile (FDD/NED [Problèmes d'Amérique Latine, 60] 4599/4600, 31 déc. 1980, p. 143–173, tables)

Examination of labor movement under Pinochet regime discusses Junta's union policy (attempts to dismantle trade unions and to develop new union structure), and labor resistance to regime (reorganization of local unions and federations, different forms of la-

bor mobilization, and relationships between unions and parties).

8338 Garreton M., Manuel Antonio. Democratización y otro desarrollo: el caso chileno (UNAM/RMS, 42[42]:3, julio/sept. 1980, p. 1167–1214)

Discusses Chilean case from "another development" point of view (i.e., priorities being satisfaction of basic human needs, establishment of harmonic relationship with environment, and national independence). Recapitulates on social and political evolution of Chile, emphasizing recent period, and evaluates "project" of authoritarian regime from "another development" perspective. Sees democratization as only solution to crisis.

Gordon R., Sara. Democracia y golpes de estado en América Latina. See item **8320.**

8339 Kay, Cristóbal. La reforma agraria y la transición al socialismo en Chile: 1970–1973 (CSUCA/ESC, 21, sept./dic. 1978, p. 159–189)

Examination of agrarian policy under Allende. Contends that this policy reflected limitations and contradictions of Popular Unity coalition. Land reform was extensive and drastic, but also reduced peasant mobilization. Discusses legacy of Frei administration, organization of peasant movement, operation of expropriated farms, and failure to propagate socialist relations of production.

8340 ———. Transformaciones de las relaciones de dominación y dependencias entre terratenientes y campesinos en Chile (UNAM/RMS, 42:2, abril/junio 1980, p. 751–797)

Chile's protracted social and political stability was partly due to lack of rural conflicts. Vigorous peasant mobilization developed after land reform. Analyzes mechanisms that account for such stability and factors leading to recent conflict. Discusses transition from patronage bonds between landowners and peasants to complex relationships of political clientelism between peasants and political parties or the State. Roads for dissolution of clientelism are:
1) class road, when peasants develop own independent organizations; and 2) repression, when mediating social and political mechanisms are destroyed. Very competent article.

8341 Poblete Barth, Renato; Carmen Galilea

W.; and **Patricia Van Dorp P.** Imagen de la Iglesia de hoy y religiosidad de los chilenos. Santiago: Centro Ballarmino, Departamento de Investigaciones Sociológicas, 1980. 165, 15 leaves: bibl.

Survey of 963 Chilean Catholics in greater Santiago explores religious beliefs and practices, and images of the Church. Findings: 1) women are more religious than men; 2) positive relationship between social class and religious knowledge and between social class and Church attendance; 3) positive relationship between age and religious beliefs and observance; 4) most Catholics approve of the Church activities in education, labor, and human rights but disagree concerning the Church's political positions.

8342 Programa Regional del Empleo para América Latina y el Caribe (PREALC). Expectativas migratorias de la juventud campesina. Santiago: PREALC, 1979. 78 p.: bibl., map. (Documento de trabajo / PREALC; 178)

Prepared by Luis Jünemann. Survey analysis of motivations of young peasants moving to Santiago from surrounding areas. Women are more likely to migrate, and educational expectations are strong "pull" factor, on both sexes. Parents' attitudes toward children's work and education are important antecedent cause of differential propensity of men and women.

8343 Proyección de la población de Chile por sexo y grupos quinquenales de edad, 1950–2000. Trabajo elaborado por la Oficina de Planificación Nacional (ODEPLAN) en colaboración con CELADE. Santiago: ODEPLAN, Subdirección Regional, 1975. 25 leaves: bibl.

Estimates of mortality and birth-rates, and net migratory balances (1950–70), and projections (1970–2000). Most data are estimated by age group.

8344 Riz, Liliana de. Sociedad y política en Chile: de Portales a Pinochet. México: Universidad Nacional Autónoma de México, 1979. 219 p.

Sociological interpretation of Chilean political history, with emphasis on Allende government. Book is attempt to understand policies of that administration in context of class conflicts of previous decades. Discusses following aspects of Popular Unity government: coalition program, difficulties with

production, problem of workers' participation, consumers' movement, agrarian policy, governmental responses to economic crisis, and opposition strategy. Description of opposition's corporative and political courses of action is particularly interesting.

Roddick, Jackie. The failure of populism in Chile: labour movement and politics before World War II. See *HLAS 44:3113*.

8345 Ruiz-Tagle Portales, Jaime. El movimiento obrero en Chile, 1850-1964: análisis genético-accionalista. Santiago: Instituto Latino Americano de Doctrina y Estudios Sociales, 1974. 71 leaves: bibl.

Sociological interpretation of history of Chilean labor movement (published 1974, but not previously annotated in *HLAS*). Movement was product of capital accumulation and spatial concentration of workers, necessary but not sufficient conditions: autonomy of resistance principle was also there. Nitrate workers were most important element in labor movement, because of their crucial economic role, professional homogeneity, opposition to foreign capital, and sense of class consciousness transmitted to other workers. But since unions in Chile have been atomized and financially weak, factors such as hyper-inflation led to labor dependence upon political parties and the movement's politization.

Schiefelbein, Ernesto and **Carlos Clavel.** Comparación de los factores que inciden en la demanda por educación en Paraguay y Chile. See item 4490.

8346 Shul'govskii, Anatolii Federovich *et al.* Problemy i dvizhushchie sily revoliutsionnogo protsessa v Latinskoi Amerike = Problems and motive forces of the revolutionary process in Latin America. Moskva: Institut Latinskoi Ameriki (ILA), 1977. 426 p.: bibl.

Essays by various Soviet authors on class structure and struggle, on political parties and their programs, and on prospects for revolution. Much emphasis on Chile, but also references to other countries, including Francophone regions of Latin America. [R.V. Allen]

8347 Torrado, Susana. Sobre los conceptos de "estrategias familiares de vida" y "proceso de reproducción de la fuerza de trabajo:" notas teórico-metodológicas (CM/DE,

15:2[46], 1981, p. 204–233, bibl.)

Discussion of new concept in social demography: family life strategies. Concept has heuristic value, but connotes free choice and rationality, is restricted to underprivileged groups, and ignores social networks. Insufficiently developed, concept must be inserted into theory of society. Author exemplifies her proposed conceptualization with case of Chilean working class in 1970.

URUGUAY

8348 Assunção, Fernando O. El gaucho: estudio socio-cultural. Ilustraciones de Federico Reilly. Montevideo: Universidad Mayor de la República Oriental del Uruguay, Dirección General de Extensión Universitaria, División Publicaciones y Ediciones, 1978/1979. 2 v.: bibl., ill.

Very complete discussion of historical, ethnographic, and literary evidence of "gaucho" culture. Popular historian provides picture of gaucho life in 18th and 19th centuries: cattle raising, daily life of estancias, gaucho psychology, material culture, forms of sociability, songs and dances, and participation of politics, especially wars (for historian's comment, see *HLAS 44:3447*).

8349 Baudrón, Silvia. Estudio socioeconómico de algunos barrios marginales de Montevideo. En la codificación y elaboración de algunos datos de este trabajo colaboró Luis Vidal. Montevideo: CIEDUR-F.C.U., 1979. 112 p., 1 fold. leaf of plates: bibl., graphs.

Survey of families living in two types of marginal district in Montevideo: municipal emergency settlements, and shanty-towns ("cantegriles") (N=350). Describes family structure, geographic origin, skills, employment, and aspirations.

8350 Filgueira, Carlos H. Predisposición migratoria: la situación en egresados profesionales. Montevideo?: Centro de Informaciones y Estudios del Uruguay, 1978. 61 p.: bibl., ill. (Centro de Informaciones y Estudios del Uruguay; no. 5)

Competent study of emigration among small sample of Uruguay's university graduates. Places brain drain in Heintz's conceptual framework for study of development. Defines emigration response to structural

tensions of asynchronic development. Emigration rates depend on degree of institutionalization and transferability of professional disciplines, political responses to structural tensions, degree of university autonomy, and openness of academic system. Uruguay offers most appropriate setting for such an analysis given its structural disequilibria and high emigration rate.

Gordon R., Sara. Democracia y golpes de estado en América Latina. See item **8320.**

8351 Graceras, Ulises *et al.* Informe preliminar sobre la situación de la comunidad negra en el Uruguay. Montevideo: Universidad de la República, Dirección General de Extensión Universitaria, División Publicaciones y Ediciones, 1980. 36 p.: bibl.

Survey of black Uruguayans (N=34) examines their occupational and educational characteristics, forms of sociability, and beliefs about racial discrimination. Most blacks belong to lower classes, attribute residential segregation to economic factors, and believe there is discrimination, even if data suggest racial cleavage is not strong.

8352 Lanzaro, Jorge Luis. La cuestión de la democracia y la cuestión del partido en América Latina (UNAM/RMS, 43:2, abril/junio 1981, p. 623–638)

Reviews role of political parties and labor unions in democratic state within framework of Marx, Lenin, and Gramsci. Author draws on his experience in Uruguay to formulate political action recommendations for progressive parties and unions. [A. Ugalde]

8353 Martorelli, Horacio. Urbanización y desruralización en el Uruguay. Montevideo: Fundación de Cultura Universitaria: Centro Latinoamericano de Economía Humana, 1980. 151 p.: bibl., maps (Economía y sociedad; 3)

Discussion of process of urbanization in Uruguay and plea for a population policy. Author's analysis of country's population trends from 18th century onwards is interesting.

8354 Petruccelli, José Luis. La migración interna en el Uruguay: bases para su estudio. Montevideo: Centro de Informaciones y Estudios del Uruguay, 1979. 44, 15 p.: ill. (Centro de Informaciones y Estudios del Uruguay; no. 26)

Analysis of internal migration in

Uruguay, based on 1963 and 1975 censuses. Contains data on population distribution by dept., net migratory balances, interdepartamental population movements, characteristics of migrants, and migration flows.

8355 ——— and **Juan Carlos Fortuna.** La dinámica migratoria en el Uruguay del último siglo, 1875–1975: informe final. Montevideo: Centro de Informaciones y Estudios del Uruguay, 1976. 220 p. in various pagings, 4 leaves of plates: bibl.

Description of migration and immigration processes (1875–1975) emphasizes large emigration in 1960s and 1970s.

8356 Solari, Aldo E. and **Rolando Franco.** The family in Uruguay (*in* The Family in Latin America [see item **8011**] p. 46–83, bibl., tables)

An urban society composed mostly of European immigrants, Uruguay has a Western-style family: nuclear, isolated, multilinear, and open. Discusses nuptiality and divorce rates, family size, legitimacy, and characteristics of families in different social classes.

BRAZIL

JOHN V.D. SAUNDERS, *Professor of Sociology, Mississippi State University*

THE VARIETY AND SCOPE of Brazilian sociology revealed by the works selected for annotation below is impressive. Furthermore, a large majority of the authors are Brazilian. An estimation of the number of foreign authors as sole or senior authors or editors of the works included below yields 22 out of 87. In contrast, this section in *HLAS 43* listed 61 titles, 29 of which were authored by foreigners. Although such comparisons are necessarily imperfect, they suggest a greater output by Brazilian authors.

Relaxation of censorship is a probable explanation for this increase. A good number of the works published in the last few years are implicitly or explicitly critical of the policies and programs of the government or expose serious social problems as yet unsolved, and, probably, could not have been published earlier.

Frequent use was made of quantitative data by the authors represented in this section. Sample surveys especially designed to study a particular topic and secondary analyses of the national household sample survey provide the basis for studies of a wide variety of topics, among them stress, family structure, elites, social mobility, and urban housing. Other studies were based on available data and on some form of systematic observation. What appears to be an increased emphasis on empirical data is welcome.

Particularly worthy of note is the large number of papers that examine demographic topics. While *HLAS 41* and *HLAS 43* combined had but a handful of such papers, the materials examined here in *HLAS 45* include 12 titles. One of these, however, the *Annals of the Second National Population Studies Meeting* (item **8382**), presents 25 original papers. Of the 12 titles mentioned above, six were published under governmental sponsorship, reflecting, perhaps an awareness of the importance of this subject matter for policy planning. Most demographic titles have migration as their main concern. Not only the traditional subject of migration from the countryside to the cities but a new topic, that of migration to the new frontier in north Brazil.

The Northeast continues to be a subject of concern to Brazilian social scientists, but it is rapidly being overtaken by the North and the Amazon. Several of this year's titles examine the consequence of expansion into the Amazonian basin arriving at a negative evaluation. Interestingly, most of these were authored by foreigners. Perhaps it is easier to obtain funds to study new rather than old problems.

A substantial number of entries examine the condition of blacks and of women focusing on inequality, exploitation and discrimination; a sharp contrast with beliefs widely held in the not too distant past that Brazil was the world's only racial democracy and that women got better than they deserved.

By far the largest group is one that does not lend itself easily to categorization, given the diversity of topics covered. Approximately one half of the titles fall into this miscellaneous group. The range of topics, the variety of methodological and analytical techniques all attest to the growing maturity and sophistication of Brazilian sociology.

8357 Aguiar, Neuma. Tempo de transformação no Nordeste. Petrópolis: Vozes, 1980. 243 p.: ill., tables.

Critical examination of Cariri industrialization project in Ceará state discusses project's background and case studies of industries devoted to processing of corn, manioc, and clay. Final chapters deal with problems of industrializing a rural area and with industrialization's impact on women. Concludes that industrialization within constraints of agrarian structure keeps purchasing power of workers low because of low pay. Well documented. Includes 59 tables, five graphs.

8358 Albuquerque, Manoel Maurício de. Pequena história da formação social brasileira. Rio de Janeiro: Graal, 1981. 728 p.: bibl. (Biblioteca de história; vol. no. 6)

Social, economic, and political history from earliest days of colonization to present.

8359 Aldrich, Bruce W.; Frank P. Goldman; and Aaron Lipman. Urbanization of familism: an examination of the influence of urban residence upon kinship orientation in two culturally-related developing nations: Portugal and Brazil (in The Family in Latin America [see item 8011] p. 184–198, bibl., tables)

Proposes that rural residence is positively associated with familism in Portugal and in Brazil, and that familism is stronger in Portugal than in Brazil in urban and rural areas. Interviews conducted in both countries supported these hypotheses.

8360 Almeida Filho, Naomar de. The psychosocial costs of development: labor, migration, and stress in Bahia, Brazil (LARR, 17:3, 1982, p. 91–118, tables)

Based on interviews with 493 households in cíty of Bahia squatter settlement,

covering 1,514 individuals. Stress scores were dependent variable. Significant differences in stress scores were found to be associated with marital status, educational status (inverse), occupational status, migration status. Further analysis indicated that occupational status is most telling independent variable.

8361 Andrade, Gilberto Osório de Oliveira. Migrações internas e o Recife. Recife: Ministério da Educação e Cultura, Instituto Joaquim Nabuco de Pesquisas Sociais, 1979. 100 p.: bibl. (Série Estudos e pesquisas; 12)

Largely a competent review of literature on migration to Recife and its consequences preceded by discussion of internal migration in Brazil as a whole.

8362 Avila Neto, Maria Inacia d'. O autoritarismo e a mulher: o jogo da dominição macho-fêmea no Brasil. Rio de Janeiro: Achiamé, 1980. 126 p. (Universidade; 14. Psicologia social)

Uses Adorno's conceptualization of authoritarianism as model for analysis of Brazil's male-female relations. Stratified sample taken in Brasília was interviewed, and 1,122 usable interviews obtained in 1975–76. Most respondents were between 18 and 30 years old, middle class and single. Predominant patriarchal ideology is fully confirmed and shared by women. Systematic, well documented.

Azevedo, Eliane S. *et al.* Spread and diversity of human populations in Bahia, Brazil. See item **1714.**

8363 Azevedo, Thales de. A religião civil brasileira: um instrumento político. Petrópolis: Vozes, 1981. 142 p.: bibl. (Publicações CID. História; 10)

Applies Rousseau's concept of civil religion to Brazilian history and finds change in its content. Colonial regime relied on

Catholicism; empire on positivism as basis for civil religion; and first republic on "spiritual" nationalisms. Succeeding period, ending 1968, is characterized, by rule of law, crusading anti-communism and technocratic humanism.

8364 ———. La "religion civile:" introduction au cas brésilien (CNRS/ASR, 24: 47[1], jan./mars 1979, p. 7–22)

More succinct statement of arguments presented by the author in item **8363.**

8365 Blay, Eva Alterman. Mulher, escola e profissão: um estudo do ginásio industrial feminino na cidade de São Paulo. São Paulo: Universidade de São Paulo, Faculdade de Filosofia, Letras e Ciências Humanas, Centro de Estudos Rurais e Urbanos, 1981? 168 p.: bibl., ill. (Coleção Textos; 1)

Reports on study conducted in 1960s. Describes school's structure and organization and reports results of 901 interviews with pupils in *ginásios industriais femininos.* Interviews center around occupational aspirations.

8366 Bock, E. Wilbur; Sugiyama Iutaka; and **Félix M. Berardo.** Urbanization and the extended family in Brazil (*in* The Family in Latin America [see item **8011**] p. 161–184, bibl., tables)

Questions whether or not urbanization results in conjugal units residentially separate from kin. Employs survey data from urban centers obtained 1959–60. Analysis' results were inconclusive and suggests that other variables such as migratory status and social mobility may be more important determinants of family type than urbanization.

Boschi, Renato Raul. Elites industriais e democracia: hegemonia burguesa e mudança política no Brasil. See item **3592.**

8367 Brandão, Carlos Rodrigues. Peões, pretos e congos: trabalho e identidade étnica em Goiás. Goiânia: Editora Universidade de Brasília, 1977. 245 p.: bibl.

From historical perspective centered on gold mining and slavery, examines black employment, status, and how latter determines contemporary stratification in Goiás' town and município. Based on historical sources, interviews and observation. Concludes with chapter devoted to congos or congadas, ritual dance of African origin.

8367a ———. Religion e idéologie religieuse à Monte Mor (CNRS/ARS, 24:47[1], jan./mars 1979, p. 91–121, tables)

Located between Campinas and São Paulo, Monte Mor has one Catholic church and five Protestant ones, of which three are "mainline" and two Pentecostal. Emphasizes relationships between social classes and religious institutions and convergence of interests between some categories of laymen and religious agents.

8368 Bunker, Stephen G. Barreiras burocráticas e institucionais à modernização: o caso de Amazônia (IPEA/PPE, 10:2, agosto 1980, p. 555–600, tables)

Proposes that when modern institutions participate in official programs of rural development and colonization their participation is dysfunctional, incurring costs that far exceed benefits. Position supported by analysis of Instituto Nacional de Colonização e Reforma Agraria as it tried to perform multiple functions in Amazonian colonization.

8369 ———. Class, status, and the small farmer: rural development programs and the advance of capitalism in Uganda and Brazil (LAP, 8[1]:28, Winter 1981, p. 89–107, bibl.)

Truly comparative study centers on agricultural development and economic and political determinants of rural development programs. Sees relations between small farmers and dominant social groups as determined by their economic position, concentration of land ownership and control, and extent to which capitalist relations of production have spread in national agricultural economy.

Camargo, Nelly de. Televisão na praça: redefinição cultural e nova sintax do lazer. See item **4530.**

8370 Cardoso, Irede. Mulher e trabalho: discriminações e barreiras no mercado do trabalho. São Paulo: Cortez Editora, 1980. 104 p.: bibl.

Examines status of women in Brazil and elsewhere and finds it lacking. Analysis based on mailed questionnaires confirms low esteem in which women are held in Brazilian society and low self-esteem held by women themselves.

8371 Carvalho, Otamar de and **George Martine.** Migrações e urbanização:

concepção de políticas e instrumentos para a ordenação da migração interna no Brasil. Brasília: Ministério do Interior, Secretaria General, Secretaria de Planejamento e Operações (SPO), 1977. 47 p.: bibl., map (Série SPO; 2)

After presenting data on national and regional migratory streams, with particular emphasis on Northeast and relationship between migration and urbanization, this brief but competent study proceeds to assess governmental policies as they affect or fail to affect migration.

8372 Castro, Iná Elias de and **Geraldo Samenzato.** A criança e o meio urbano no Brasil. Rio de Janeiro: Fundo das Nações Unidas para a Infância, 1978. 49, 26, 29 leaves: bibl.

Analysis of condition of children in urban Brazil is supported by statistical data. Covers: education, income, cause of death, mortality, social welfare services, etc. Provides extensive summaries in English and Spanish.

Cezimbra Jacques, João. Ensaio sobre os costumes do Rio Grande do Sul: precedido de uma ligeira descrição física e de uma noção histórica. See *HLAS 44:3563.*

8373 CODESUL. Os migrantes na área metropolitana de Curitiba. Curitiba: CODESUL, 1979 or 1980. 217 leaves: bibl., ill.

Study concerning characteristics of migrants and entry into labor force is largely based on 1976 sample household survey. Appendix includes 41 detailed tables, summaries of which are used in text.

8374 Colóquio de Estudos Teuto-Brasileiros, *3rd, Universidade Federal do Rio Grande do Sul, 1974.* III [i.e. Terceiro] Colóquio de Estudos Teuto-Brasileiros. Porto Alegre: Editora da URGS, 1980. 550 p.: bibl., ill.

Consists of 35 essays commemorating 150th anniversary of German immigration to Brazil in 1824. Topics covered by impressive array of Brazilian and German scholars are almost as varied as number of essays. Of particular interest to sociologists are essays on immigration, economic development, colonization, religiosity, and ethnology.

8375 Construção de mordias na periferia de São Paulo: aspectos sócio-econômicos e institucionais. São Paulo: Governo do Estado de São Paulo, Secretaria de Economia e Planejamento, 1979. 385 p.: bibl., ill., tables (Série Estudos e pesquisas; 30)

Consists mainly of report on results of interview survey with the São Paulo city residents who built their homes with their own labor. Construction, which is undertaken mainly to avoid payment of rent, often stretches out over years and is paid with savings and additional hours of wage labor, and is carried out during nights, holidays, and weekends. Includes 125 tables.

8376 Costa, Iraci del Nero da. Minas Gerais: estruturas populacionais típicas. São Paulo: EDEC, 1982. 143 p.: ill., tables.

Study of colonial Minas Gerais' historical demography centering on 1804. Obtained data for several cities in great detail. Analyzes population regarding age, sex, marital status, legitimacy of birth, participation in primary, secondary or tertiary economic activity, etc. Presents much data separately on slave and free populations. Former are sometimes distinguished according to African or Brazilian birth. Includes 66 text and 57 appendix tables.

8377 Cruxên, Eliane Barros *et al.* RS[i.e. Rio Grande do Sul]: imigração & colonização. Organizadores, José H. Dacanal e Sergius Gonzaga. Porto Alegre: Mercado Aberto, 1980. 280 p.: bibl., ill. (Série Documenta; 4. História)

Collection of essays on European immigration to Rio Grande do Sul, exclusive of Portuguese, and covering: Germans; Italians; Jews; immigration's effects on economy; industrialization; wine industry; politics (including *integralismo*); Catholicism; literature; and history.

8378 Cruz, Anette Goldberg Velasco e *et al.* O lugar da mulher: estudos sobre a condição feminina na sociedade atual. Madel T. Luz, organizadora. Rio de Janeiro: Graal, 1982. 146 p.: bibl. (Coleção Tendências; vol. no. 1)

Presents seven papers dealing with the condition of women beginning with account comparing women's liberation movements in France and Italy with Brazil. Other papers explore subjects such as violence against women, socialization of women, and machismo.

8379 Daland, Robert T. Exploring Brazilian bureaucracy: performance and pathology. Washington: University Press of America, Inc., 1981. 445 p.: bibl.

Reviews evolution of Brazilian bureaucracy ("the largest, the most continuous, the most stable, the most costly, and the most complex institution to be found in Brazil") from colonial times to 1964, and proceeds to analyze contemporary bureaucratic structure and pathology, as well as roles in policy structure and career patterns of bureaucratic executives.

8380 The Dilemma of Amazonian development. Edited by Emilio F. Moran. Boulder, Colo.: Westview Press, 1982. 347 p.: bibl., ill., index, tables (Westview special studies on Latin America and the Caribbean)

Important collection of 13 original essays divided into three broad sections: 1) Human Dimension of Amazonian Development; 2) Assessment of Current Systems of Production; and 3) Methodological Issues and Future Research Directions. Several multidisciplinary essays are of interest to sociology. Some concern impact of Amazon growth occurring without development as well as development policies' effect on native Amazonians, settlement policies that by converting forest to pasture may damage future productivity, and of trans-Amazonian highway impact on a small community. Others recommend that Indian knowledge of forest resources be put to use, evaluate directed colonization projects, and discuss varied topics such as livestock, fisheries, crops, and deforestation.

8382 Encontro Nacional de Estudos Populacionais, 2nd, *Aguas de São Pedro, Brasil, 1980.* Anais. São Paulo: Associação Brasileira de Estudos Populacionais, 1981. 2 v. (993 p.): bibl., ill.

Contains 25 papers concerning population movements to Brazil's frontier, recent trends in vital rates and migration, methodology of life-cycle analysis and urban growth. Particularly worthy are papers on: return migration to Northeast; planned colonization on Rondônia's agricultural frontier; Acre's frontier expansion, migration and urbanization; the division of labor specialization and urban growth in the city of São Paulo; migrants and residential segregation in Rio de Janeiro; and women in the urban labor force.

8383 Fernandes, Florestan. Reflections on the Brazilian counter-revolution: essays. Edited with an introduction by Warren Dean. Translated from the Portuguese by Michel Vale and Patrick M. Hughes. Armonk, N.Y.: M.E. Sharpe, 1981. 187 p.: bibl.

Titles of essays by Brazil's best known sociologist reflect work's flavor: "On the Formation and Development of the Competitive Social Order;" "The Autocratic-Bourgeois Model of Capitalist Tranformation; "Revolution or Counter Revolution;" and "The Lost Generation."

8384 Ferreira, Rosa Maria Fischer. Meninos da rua: expectativas e valores de menores marginalizados em São Paulo. São Paulo: Comissão de Justiça e Paz de São Paulo: Centro de Estudos de Cultura Contemporânea, between 1979 and 1981. 173 p.: bibl., ill.

Data on street children are based on official records from social service agencies, juvenile courts and, more importantly, on interviews with subjects of the study. Latter are particularly revealing of daily routines, family situations, and survival strategies.

8385 Figueiredo, Marisa. Le rôle socio-économique des femmes chefs de famille a Arembepe: village de pêcheurs su la côte nord de l'Etat de Bahia, Brésil (UP/TM, 21:84, oct./déc. 1980, p. 817–891, bibl., tables)

Presents great variety of data on female heads of families in Arembepe town, coastal Bahia.

8386 Franca, Maria Cecília. Perspectives d'évolution des Villes-Sanctuaires au Brésil: l'exemple d'Iguape (CNRS/ASR, 24:47[1], jan./mars 1979, p. 81–89)

Poses dilemma faced by Iguape and other cities in which shrines are located. Centers of folk religious observances, shrines have symbiotic relationship to tourism and town's economic prosperity. Attempts by Church to reintroduce orthodoxy are resisted and resented by town folk for they may threaten a shrine's popularity as tourist magnet.

8387 Freyre, Gilberto. New world in the Tropics: the culture of modern Brazil. Westport, Conn.: Greenwood Press, 1980. 285 p.: index.

New printing of Freyre's classic on Brazilian society first published in 1945 (see *HLAS 8:4207*).

8388 Gigirey Paredes, Carlos. Datos para una sociología del negro brasileiro (CSIC/RIS, 35:21, enero/marzo 1977, p. 29–76)

Competent review of literature on Brazilian blacks. Covers most standard works.

8389 Gonzalez, Lélia and Carlos Hasenbalg. Lugar de negro. Rio de Janeiro: Editor Marco Zero, 1982. 118 p. (Coleção 2 pontos; v. 3)

Slender but perceptive volume contains three essays on race relations in Brazil: 1) on movements to fight discrimination organized by blacks since ca. 1970; 2) on Brazilian race, class, and social mobility with much documentation on racial inequality; and 3) on blacks in advertising.

8390 Haller, Archibald O. A socioeconomic regionalization of Brazil (AGS/GR, 72:4, Oct. 1982, p. 450–464)

Socioeconomic development level scores derived from eight variables were calculated for 360 microregions and used to show geographical distribution of development levels by plotting them on map of Brazil. Data were mapped using different degrees of refinement beginning with six levels of the socioeconomic development level score and moving down. Six level map, in particular, provides new insights into distribution of development.

8391 Hasenbalg, Carlos Alfredo. Discriminação e desigualidades raciais no Brasil. Traduzido por Patrick Burglin. Rio de Janeiro: Graal, 1979. 302 p.: bibl. (Série Sociologia. Biblioteca de ciências sociais; v. no. 10)

Argues that Brazilian "racial democracy" is a powerful myth. Stresses racial stratification and societal mechanisms which perpetuate racial inequalities. Discounts slavery as explanation for contemporary race relations and identifies racism and discrimination as major factors. Argues that there is greater racial inequality in Northeast than in Southeast. Valuable addition to literature on race relations in Brazil. Translation of *Race relations in post-abolition Brazil*, author's thesis, Univ. of California, Berkeley (for historian's comment, see *HLAS 44:3585*).

8392 Informações demográficas de Pernambuco: evolução da população economicamente ativa, 1950–1978. Recife: Governo de Pernambuco, Secretaria de Planejamento, Fundação de Informações para o Desenvolvimento de Pernambuco, 1981. 68 p.: bibl., ill.

Presents and discusses variety of demographic statistics related to labor force. Particular emphasis on economically active population.

8393 Instituto Brasileiro de Análises Sociais e Econômicos (IBASE). Dados da realidade brasileira. v. 1, Indicadores sociais. Petrópolis: Vozes *em co-edição com* IBASE, 1982. l v.: bibl., ill., tables.

Presents 22 tables mostly derived from 1978 national household sample survey conducted by Instituto Brasileiro de Geografia e Estatística. Each table accompanied by brief commentary. Presents wealth of data, nearly all at national level, on population, family budgets, income, health, housing, and race including Indians.

8394 José, Oiliam. Racismo em Minas Gerais. Belo Horizonte: Impresa Oficial de Minas Gerais, 1981. 258 p., 12 leaves of plates: ill.

Review and indictment of slavery and racism in colonial Minas Gerais solidly substantiated by historical documentation.

8395 Kleinpenning, J.M.G. Losing ground: processes of land concentration in the cocoa region of southern Bahia, Brasil (CEDLA/B, 33, dic. 1982, p. 59–83)

Study chiefly concerned with processes influencing concentration of land ownership, spread of monoculture, and conflicts over land. Modernization of agriculture and economies of scale exert great pressure for larger holdings, often at the expense of small farmers.

8396 Kotscho, Ricardo. O massacre dos posseiros: conflitos de terras no Araguaia-Tocantins. São Paulo: Brasiliense, 1981. 113 p.: ill., ports.

Fascinating account written by journalist centers on conflicts over land use and ownership in Araguaia-Tocantins region caused by largely government-sponsored development projects.

8397 Kowarick, Lúcio. A espoliação urbana. Rio de Janeiro: Editora Paz e Terra, 1980. 202 p.: ill. (Coleção Estudos brasileiros; v. 44)

Collection of essays published elsewhere (1973–79) present thoughtful analyses of urban lower-class problems.

8398 Lima, Sandra Amêndola Barbosa. A participação social no cotidiano. São Paulo: Cortez & Moraes, 1979. 157 p.: bibl.

In-depth, unstructured interviews with 42 clients of social work agency (presumably in São Paulo) serve as basis for volume. Interviews centered on iterviewees' daily routines discussed in detail.

8399 McDonough, Peter. Developmental priorities among Brazilian elites (UC/EDCC, 29:3, April 1981, p. 535–559, tables)

Study of variations in priorities about development goals among Brazilian elites based on 250 interviews with elite group leaders (1972–73). Economic growth was most important to businessmen and State managers less important to labor leaders, bishops, and opposition politicians. Economists were most satisfied with policies of regime, and politicians least satisfied.

8400 ———. Power and ideology in Brazil. Princeton, N.J.: Princeton University Press, 1981. 326 p.: bibl., ill., index.

Based on same interviews and samples, from fieldwork conducted 1972–73, as item **8399.** Brazilian elites tend to think in terms of three alliances and confrontations: 1) urban labor vs. other elites; 2) supporters of authoritarian order vs. supporters of decentralization of power; and 3) region vs. region. Proposes that relative harmony among these elites is consequence of absence of polarization around religious or secular ideologies which could generate conflict if they coincided with elite self-interests.

8401 ——— and **Amaury de Souza.** The politics of population in Brazil: elite ambivalence and public demand. Austin: University of Texas Press, 1981. 178 p.: bibl., index (The Texas Pan American series)

Uses two samples for study: elites and population of states of Espírito Santo, Minas Gerais, Rio de Janeiro, São Paulo, and Rio Grande do Sul. Finds elites lacking in consensus about population issues and assigning them less importance in comparison with other public policy issues. Although family planning was highly salient among states' population sampled, different sectors adopted anti-natalist or pro-natalist views for different reasons.

Machado, Lucília R. de Souza. Educação e divisão social do trabalho. See item **4559.**

8402 Makabe, Tomoko. The theory of the split labor market: a comparison of the Japanese experience in Brazil and Canada (SF, 59:3, March 1981, p. 786–809, bibl.)

Examines pre-World War II experience of Japanese immigrants to Brazil and Canada. Tests thesis concerning importance of economic competition as explanation of antagonism between ethnic groups. Whereas in Canada severe competition for jobs resulted in the Japanese being almost completely excluded from society, apparently relative absence of economic competition in Brazil precluded such discrimination and exclusion.

8403 Malloy, James M. The politics of social security in Brazil. Pittsburgh, Pa.: University of Pittsburgh Press, 1979. 200 p.: bibl., index (Pitt Latin American series)

Analyzes relationship between State and society through prism of social insurance policy and politics and throughout four major historical periods: 1) oligarchic democracy (1889–1930); 2) organic authoritarianism (1930–45); 3) populist democracy (1945–64); and 4) bureaucratic authoritarianism (1964-present).

8404 Marconi, Paolo. A censura política na imprensa brasileira, 1968-1978. Vila Mariana, Brasil: Global Editora, 1980. 312 p.: bibl., ill., facsims. (Pasado & presente; 14)

Analysis of ways and means used to insure that the press did not publish material considered undersirable by regime. Well documented.

8405 Martins, George. Adaptation of migrants or survival of the fittest?: a Brazilian case (JDA, 14:1, Oct. 1979, p. 23–41, tables)

Centers on interpretation of migration differentials with particular regard to re-migration. Finds that among migrants to metropolitan areas nearly 35 percent did not remain five years, and 43 percent either died or re-migrated before completing an average stay of nine years. Examines selective retention of more highly educated migrants.

8406 Matta, Roberto da. Carnavais, malandros e heróis: para uma sociologia do dilema brasileiro. Rio de Janeiro: Zahar Editores, 1979. 272 p.: bibl. (Antropologia social)

Studies social values and norms of Brazilian society as well as behaviors reflecting them through analysis of national rituals (carnival, independence week, and religious processions), characters of *malandro* (represented by Pedro Malasartes), and *renunciador* (represented by Augusto Matraga). Good attempt at delineating the Brazilian national character.

8407 Mayer, John. The family in Brazil (*in* The Family in Latin America [see item 8011] p. 106–161, bibl., tables)

Competent analysis of structure and composition of the Brazilian family. Although largely based on official statistical sources, author also draws on personal observation and experience. Deals with marriage, separation, marital status, family size, family composition, family functions, and androcentrism.

8408 Mello, Frederico Pernambucano de. O ciclo do gado no Nordeste do Brasil: uma cultura da violência? (Ciência & Trópico [Instituto Joaquim Nabuco de Pesquisas Sociais, Recife] 7:2, julho/dez. 1979, p. 263–306)

Essay on background of violence associated with cattle raising in Northeast Brazil describes major social types associated with such violence (e.g., *valentão, cabra, capanga, pistoleiro, jagunço, cangaceiro*).

8409 Melo, José Marques de. As relações de poder na televisão brasileira (VOZES, 75:9, nov. 1891, p. 22–30, tables)

Study of television ownership, licensing, and control argues that opposition groups or their sympathizers have been prevented from securing licenses.

8410 Meyer, Doris Rinaldi. A terra do santo e o mundo dos engenhos: estudos de uma comunidade rural nordestina. Rio de Janeiro: Paz e Terra, 1980. 186 p.: bibl., plan (Série Estudos sobre o Nordeste; v. 9)

Study of Pernambuco state rural community of about 5,400 agricultural laborers and their families who work on *engenho*, on whose land the town was built. Study focuses on relations between *engenho* and town resulting from this situation. Welcome addition to Brazilian community studies.

8411 Migração interna: textos selecionados. Hélio A. de Moura, coordenador. Fortaleza: Banco do Nordeste do Brasil, Escritório Técnico de Estudos Econômicos do Nordeste, 1980. 2 v. (1269 p.): bibl., ill. (Série Estudos econômicos e sociais; v. 4)

Vol. 1 concerns theory and methods of migration study and reviews of migration literature. Vol. 2, entirely devoted to Brazilian internal migration, consists of 15 papers representing some of the best scholarship on the subject. It is noteworthy that seven papers analyze migration with regard to the Northeast and tend to focus on migration as related to urbanization.

8412 Moisés, José Alvaro et al. Cidade, povo e poder. Rio de Janeiro: Centro de Estudos de Cultura Contemporânea (CEDEC): Paz e Terra, 1982. 199 p.: bibl. (Coleção CEDEC/Paz e Terra; v. 5)

Common theme of seven essays is urban unrest including strikes and riots, many directed against urban transportation.

8413 Nascimento, Abdias do. O quilombismo: documentos de uma militância pan-africanista. Petrópolis: Vozes, 1980. 281 p.: bibl.

Author is probably best known as Brazilian black activist and organizing force behind 1950 1st Congresso do Negro Brasileiro (see item 8414). Central theme of his essays is exploitation, discrimination, and stereotyping of the Brazilian black by white elites.

8414 O Negro revoltado. Organização e apresentação de Abdias do Nascimento. Rio de Janeiro: Editora Nova Fronteira, 1982. 403 p., 16 p. of plates: bibl., ports.

Proceedings of 1st Congresso do Negro Brasileiro (1950) which was a watershed in study of race relations in Brazil. Reprint of first edition published in 1968.

8414a Oliveira, Pedro A. Ribeiro de. Catholicisme populaire et hégémonie bourgeoise au Brésil (CNRS/ARS, 24:47[1], jan./mars 1979, p. 53–79)

Competent analysis of folk Catholicism, its rural chapels, and semi-feudal laborer devotees. Sees messianic movements as reaction to changes in relationships of worker vis-à-vis *patron* and worker vis-à-vis land brought about by increasing commercialization of farming. Also analyzes process whereby the Church wrested control from local congregations, incorporating them into its institutional structure.

8415 Ortiz, Renato. *Umbandá*: magie blanche; *quimbandá*: magie noire (CNRS/ASR, 24:47[1], jan./mars 1979, p. 135–146)

Discusses *umbandá* doctrine and

ritual. Believes African deities underwent process of reinterpretation and were metamorphosed through acculturation.

8416 Pastore, José. Inequality and social mobility in Brazil. Translated by Robert M. Oxley. Madison: University of Wisconsin Press, 1982. 1 v.: bibl. index.

This is the most thorough study of social mobility for any Latin American nation. Based on 52,000 heads-of-household survey. Finds most mobility to be upward and intergenerational. However, elites contain significant proportions of individuals of humble beginnings. Sons of old elites frequently experience downward mobility. Both inequality and social mobility have increased.

8417 Pereira, João Baptista Borges. Estudos antropológicos das populações negras na Universidade do São Paulo (USP/RA, 24, 1981, p. 63–74)

Reviews studies sponsored by Univ. de São Paulo's Social Sciences Dept. and divides them according to four contexts in the study of Brazilian blacks: 1) communication; 2) religion; 3) race relations; and 4) rural areas.

Petruccelli, José Luis; Maria Helena Rato; and Sérgio Luiz Bragança. The socioeconomic consequences of a reduction in fertility: application of the ILO-IBGE national model, BACHUE-Brazil. See item **1698.**

8418 Pinto, Luiz de Aguiar Costa. Lutas de famílias no Brasil: introdução seu estudo. 2. ed. São Paulo: Companhia Editora Nacional; Brasília: Ministério da Educação e Cultura, Instituto Nacional do Livro (MEC/INL), 1980. 130 p. (Brasiliana; v. 263)

Analysis of social functions of private revenge is followed by detailed case studies of two famous family feuds in 17th and 19th centuries.

8419 Poelhekke, F.G.M.N. The struggle for land in Brazilian Amazonia, consequent on the expansion of cattle-raising (CEDLA/B, 33, dic. 1982, p. 11–33)

Analyzes expansion of large scale cattle raising and resulting competition for land ownership and control between cattle enterprises and stock farmers on the one hand and small farmers, agricultural laborers and Indians on the other. Conflict expressed by legal action at times, by violence at others. Defective land titles exacerbate struggle for land.

8420 A Presença japonesa no Brasil. Hiroshi Saito, organizador. Colaboradores, Sumi Butsugan *et al.* São Paulo: T.A. Queiros: Editora da Universidade de São Paulo, 1980. 243 p.: bibl., graphs (Coleção Coroa vermelha; v. 1)

Contains eight papers on Japanese immigration to Brazil commissioned for its commemoration and concerning: Japanese presence in Amazonia, the Northeast, and the South; social adaptation and participation; and comparative studies with German and Syrian-Lebanese immigrants.

8421 Queiroz, Maria Isaura Pereira de. Religious evolution and creation: the Afro-Brazilian cults (ICPHS/D, 115, Fall 1981, p. 1–21, bibl.)

Illuminating essay on social functions of *candomblé, macumba,* and *umbanda.* Pays particular attention to *umbanda* which has grown spectacularly in number of followers drawn from the most varied ethnic and social backgrounds.

8422 Ramos, Arthur. As culturas negras no Novo Mundo. 3. ed. São Paulo: Companhia Editoral Nacional, 1979. 248 p.: bibl., ill. (Brasiliana; v. 249)

Reprint of 1935 classic. Five chapters are devoted to Brazilian blacks.

8423 Rolim, Francisco Cartaxo. Pentecôtisme et société au Brésil (PERES/SC, 26:2/3, 1979, p. 345–372, tables)

Brief history of Brazilian pentecostalism is followed by data documenting its growth. Interviews and observations of large number of congregations in greater Rio metropolitan area confirm low socioeconomic status of most church members. Argues that pentecostalist belief blinds the faithful to social inequality and precludes protest.

8424 ———. Religião e classes populares. Petrópolis: Vozes, 1980. 207 p.: bibl., ill. (Publicações CID. Sociologia religiosa; 4)

Analyzes structure and function of pentecostalist churches and Catholic *comunidades eclesiais de base* who compete for lower-class religious allegiance. Supported by empirical data. Should be consulted by those interested in the sociology of religion in Brazil.

8425 Saffioti, Heleieth Iara Bongiovani. Women in class society. Translated from the Portuguese by Michael Vale. New

York: Monthly Review Press, 1978. 378 p.: bibl.

In 1884, Engels argued that marriage is "the first class antagonism that appears in history." Author obviously agrees and uses classical Marxist analysis to analyze women's condition in Brazil. Addition to growing number of volumes on women's liberation.

8426 Saint, William S. The wages of modernization: a review of the literature on temporary labor arrangements in Brazilian agriculture (LARR, 16:3, 1981, p. 91–110, bibl., tables)

Proliferation of the temporary wage laborer (*boia fria*) has been subject of much debate. This review of the literature reveals his characteristics and the phenomenon's social, economic, and political parameters. Attributes reliance on temporary wage labor, especially in more modernized agricultural regions, to technological modernization, changing cropping patterns and labor legislation.

8427 Santos, Carlos Nelson Ferreira dos. Movimentos urbanos no Rio de Janeiro. Rio de Janeiro: Zahar Editores, 1981. 255 p.: ill. (Antropologia social)

Detailed histories of government attempts to transform two Rio de Janeiro favelas and one residential neighborhood, and of resistance to such plans. Based on participant observation. Valuable addition to the literature on urban sociology in Brazil.

8427a Santos, Juana Elbein dos. Résistance et cohésion de groupe: perception idéologique de la réligion Négro-Africaine au Brésil (CNRS/ASR, 24:47[1], jan./mars 1979, p. 123–134)

Principally devoted to analysis of Afro-Brazilian religious beliefs.

Schwartzman, Simon. Ciência, universidade e ideologia: a política do cohecimento. See item **4577.**

8428 Simão, Azis. Sindicato e estado: suas relações na formação do proletariado de São Paulo. São Paulo: Editora Atica, 1981. 227 p.: bibl., ill., tables (Ensaios; 78)

Analysis of São Paulo government-labor relations (1890–1930). Discusses development of industry, working conditions, labor conflicts, and evolution of labor unions. Includes 24 tables.

8329 Simpósio Trabalho Produtivo e

Classes Sociais, *São Paulo, Brazil, 1977.* Classes sociais e trabalho produtivo. André Villalobos *et al.* Rio de Janeiro: Paz e Terra, 1978. 143 p.: bibl.

Essays: Andre Villalobos "Trabalho Productivo/Trabalho Improdutivo e Classes Sociais;" Eduardo Viola "Formas de Produção Científico-Técnica e Formação Social: Esboço de uma Problemática;" J.A. Guilhon Albuquerque "Classes Sociais e Produção Intelectual;" Lucio Kowarick "Trabalho Produtivo e Improdutivo: Comentarios sob o Angulo da Acumulação e de Produção Dominante: Esboço de uma Questão."

8430 Soares, Natalício. Nossos bosques têm mais vida: notas sobre o preconceito e a desagregação social no Brasil. Curitiba: N. Soares, 1982. 174 p.: bibl., forms.

Indictment of racial prejudice and discrimination from earlier times and present. Reproduces many want ads and brief journalistic accounts bearing upon subject as well as verbatim quotations from interviews.

8431 Soiffer, Stephen M. and **Gary N. Howe.** Patrons, clients, and the articulation of modes of production: an examination of the penetration of capitalism in peripheral agriculture in Northeastern Brazil (JPS, 9:2, Jan. 1982, p. 176–206)

Case of Ceará state small farming community exemplifies three stages in transformation of traditional economies: 1) coexistence of peasant agriculture and commercial enterprise; 2) introduction of large-scale industry transforming peasants into full-time commmodity producers; and 3) dominance of highly capitalized commercial agriculture generating rural proletariat.

8432 Souza, Itamar de. Migrações internas no Brasil. Petrópolis: Editora Vozes; Natal: Fundação José Augusto, 1980. 142 p.: bibl.

Relates migratory movements to economic cycles beginning with sugarcane, gold, coffee, etc., and concludes with analysis of migration to Natal. Latter is based on 1976–77 interviews of 430 residents selected by means of multi-stage sample.

8433 Souza, João Gonçalves de. O Nordeste brasileiro: uma experiência de desenvolvimento regional. Fortaleza: Banco do Nordeste do Brasil, 1979. 409 p.: bibl., index.

Detailed analysis of many aspects of

Northeast development by former SUDENE director is problem-oriented dealing notably with natural resources, droughts, agriculture, industrialization, and human resources.

8434 Souza, Lúcia Ribeiro de. O trabalho feminino e a estructura familiar (IBGE/RBE, 41 : 164, out./dez. 1980, p. 531–550, tables)

Focuses on female participation in labor force using census data and 1976 national household sample survey. Long-run trend has been for increasing share of women to join labor force, yet percentage is low (28.8 percent in 1976). Status of the woman in family (whether head, spouse, daughter, etc.) is regarded as important variable in explaining participation. Includes 12 tables.

8435 Taylor, J.M. The politics of aesthetic debate: the case of Brazilian Carnival (UP/E, 21 : 4, Oct. 1982, p. 301–311, bibl.)

Perceptive study of functions of samba as organized activity of Rio's samba schools. Aesthetic debate revolves around purity or orthodoxy of Carnival forms. Controversy allows samba to encompass so many different symbolic meanings that it serves as national symbol. Also discusses relationship between samba schools and politics and Rio's tourism promotion.

8436 Turchi, Lenita Maria. A colonização dirigida no processo de expansão e ocupação da fronteira agrícola: Território Federal de Rondônia (*in* Encontro Nacional Estudos Populacionais, 2nd, Aguas de São Pedro, Brasil, 1980. Anais [see item **8382**] p. 298–333, bibl., tables)

Argues that when Trans-Amazonian area was opened up to large-scale capital intensive agriculture, Rondônia became preferred frontier for laborers searching for land. Discusses planned colonization to Rondônia in general and Ouro Preto project in particular. Claims that project has potential for creating labor pool to be used by large-scale agriculture.

8437 Uricoechea, Fernando. The patrimonial foundations of the Brazilian Bureaucratic State. Berkeley: University of California Press, 1980. 233 p.: bibl., index.

Examines process whereby imperial bureaucracy consolidated its power during 19th century by noting three trends: 1) expansion of government agencies; 2) creation of bureaucracy devoid of patrimonialism; and 3) movement toward more impersonal and universalistic norms. Stresses tensions between coexisting patrimonial and state bureaucracies.

8438 Vianna, Angela Ramalho *et al.* Bahia de todos os pobres. Organizado por Guaraci Adeodato A. de Souza e Vilmar Faria. Petrópolis: Editora Vozes; São Paulo: CEBRAP, 1980. 214 p.: bibl., ill. (Caderno CEBRAP; no. 34)

Collection of eight papers dealing with São Salvador da Bahia chiefly concern employment, economic structure, poverty, women in labor force, and migration. Several papers utilize 1971 sample survey data.

8439 Vivência: história, sexualidade e imagens femininas. Organizadoras, Maria Cristina A. Buschini, Fúlvia Rosemberg. São Paulo: Brasiliense: Fundação Carlos Chagas, 1980. 1 v.

Collection of papers of varying quality and great variety dealing with women's issues. Several are historical in approach, others deal with contemporary depictions of women in the press and on film.

8440 Volbeda, S. Urbanisation in the "frontiers" of the Brazilian Amazon and the expulsion of pioneers from the agricultural sector from 1960 to the present (CEDLA/B, 33, dic. 1982, p. 35–57)

Thoroughly analyzes growth and spread of towns on Amazon frontier, concluding that capital of small-farm owners and *posseiros* disappears when their land titles are pronounced defective. Becoming agricultural laborers or seeking employment in town, these proletarianized pioneers live in towns that function as labor holding areas.

8441 Willems, Emílio. Aculturação dos alemães no Brasil: estudo antropológico dos imigrantes alemães e seus descendentes no Brasil. 2. ed., ilustrada, rev. e ampliada. São Paulo: Companhia Editora Nacional, 1980. 465 p.: bibl., ill., index, port. (Brasiliana; v. 250)

New edition of 1946 classic study. Brief section of miscegenation has been added to original text.

JOURNAL ABBREVIATIONS
SOCIOLOGY

AAA/AE   American Ethnologist. American

Anthropological Association. Washington.

ACEP/EP Estudios de Población.
Asociación Colombiana para el Estudio de la
Población. Bogotá.

AEJ/JQ Journalism Quarterly. Association
for Education in Journalism *with the
cooperation of the* American Association
of Schools, Depts. of Journalism and Kappa
Tau Alpha Society. Univ. of Minnesota.
Minneapolis.

AGS/GR The Geographical Review.
American Geographical Society. New York.

AI/A Anthropos. Anthropos-Institut.
Psoieux, Switzerland.

AJCL The American Journal of Comparative
Law. American Association of the
Comparative Study of Law. Univ. of
California. Berkeley.

AJES The American Journal of Economics
and Sociology. Francis Neilson Fund and
Robert Schalkenbach Foundation. New York.

APSA/R American Political Science Review.
American Political Science Association.
Columbus, Ohio.

ASA/ASR American Sociological Review.
American Sociological Association.
Menasha, Wis.

ASU/LAD Latin American Digest. Arizona
State Univ., Center for Latin American
Studies. Tempe.

BESPL Berichte zur Entwicklung in
Spanien, Portugal, Lateinamerika. München,
FRG.

BJS British Journal of Sociology. London
School of Economics and Political Science.
London.

BNB/REN Revista Econômica do Nordeste.
Banco do Nordeste do Brasil, Depto. de
Estudos Econômicos do Nordeste. Fortaleza.

BNJM/R Revista de la Biblioteca Nacional
José Martí. La Habana.

CDAL Cahiers des Amériques Latines.
Paris.

CEDLA/B Boletín de Estudios
Latinoamericanos. Centro de Estudios
y Documentación Latinoamericanos.
Amsterdam.

CEESTEM/L Lecturas del CEESTEM.
Centro de Estudios Económicos y Sociales
del Tercer Mundo. México.

CLAEH Centro Latinoamericano de
Economía Humana. Montevideo.

CLAPCS/AL América Latina. Centro
Latino-Americano de Pesquisas em Ciências
Sociais. Rio de Janeiro.

CM/DE Demografía y Economía. El

Colegio de México. México.

CM/FI Foro Internacional. El Colegio de
México. México.

CM/HM Historia Mexicana. El Colegio de
México. México.

CM/RE Relaciones. Estudios de historia y
sociedad. El Colegio de Michoacán. Zamora,
México.

CMS/IMR The International Migration
Review. Center for Migration Studies. New
York.

CNC/RMA Revista del México Agrario.
Confederación Nacional Campesina. México.

CNRS/ASR Archives de Sociologie des
Religions. Centre Nationale de la Recherche
Scientifique. Paris.

CPES/RPS Revista Paraguaya de Sociología.
Centro Paraguayo de Estudios Sociológicos.
Asunción.

CPU/ES Estudios Sociales. Corporación de
Promoción Universitaria. Santiago.

CRIT Criterio. Editorial Criterio. Buenos
Aires.

CSIC/RIS Revista Internacional de
Sociología. Consejo Superior de
Investigaciones Científicas. Instituto Balmes
de Sociología. Madrid.

CSSH Comparative Studies in Society and
History. An international quarterly. Society
for the Comparative Study of Society and
History. The Hague.

CSUCA/ESC Estudios Sociales
Centroamericanos. Consejo Superior de
Universidades Centroamericanas,
Confederación Universitaria
Centroamericana, Programa
Centroamericana de Ciencias Sociales.
San José.

CU/ASQ Administrative Science Quarterly.
Cornell Univ., Graduate School of Business
and Public Administration. Ithaca, N.Y.

CUA/AQ Anthropological Quarterly.
Catholic Univ. of America, Catholic Anthropological Conference. Washington.

CUNY/CP Comparative Politics. The City
Univ. of New York, Political Science
Program. New York.

CVF/C Cuadernos de la CVF. Corporación
Venezolana de Fomento. Caracas.

ECA ISee UJSC/ECA.

EHA/J Journal of Economic History. New
York Univ., Graduate School of Business
Administration *for the* Economic History
Association. Rensselaer, N.Y.

EME Revista Eme-Eme. Estudios
dominicanos. Univ. Católica Madre y

Maestra. Santiago de los Caballeros, República Dominicana.

FDD/NED Notes et Études Documentaires. France, Direction de la Documentation. Paris.

FERES/SC Social Compass. International review of socio-religious studies (Revue internationale des études socio-religieuses). International Federation of Institutes for Social and Socio-Religious Research (Fédération Internationale des Instituts de Re-cherches Sociales et Socio-Religieuses-FERES). The Hague.

FHS/FHQ The Florida Historical Quarterly. The Florida Historical Society. Jacksonville.

FIU/CR Caribbean Review. Florida International Univ., Office of Academic Affairs. Miami.

FS/CIS Cahiers Internationaux de Sociologie. La Sorbonne, École Pratique des Hautes Études. Paris.

FSCN/A Antropológica. Fundación La Salle de Ciencias Naturales, Instituto Caribe de Antropología y Sociología. Caracas.

GEE/NA Nova Americana. Giulio Einaudi Editore. Torino, Italy.

HAHR Hispanic American Historical Review. Duke Univ. Press *for the* Conference on Latin American History of the American Historical Association. Durham, N.C.

HRAF/BSR Behavior Science Research. Journal of comparative studies. Human Relations Area Files. New Haven, Conn.

IAMEA Inter-American Economic Affairs. Washington.

IBGE/R Revista Brasileira de Geografia. Conselho Nacional de Geografia, Instituto Brasileiro de Geografia e Estatística. Rio de Janeiro.

IBGE/RBE Revista Brasileira de Estatística. Ministério do Planejamento e Coordenação Geral, Instituto Brasileiro de Geografia e Estatística. Rio de Janeiro.

ICEM/IM International Migration (Migrations Internationales = Migraciones Internacionales). Quarterly review of the Intergovernmental Committee for European Migration and the Research Group for European Migration Problems. Geneva, Switzerland.

ICPHS/D Diogenes. International Council for Philosophy and Humanistic Studies. Chicago, Ill.

IDES/DE Desarrollo Económico. Instituto de Desarrollo Económico y Social. Buenos Aires.

IFCH/R Revista do Instituto de Filosofia e Ciências Humanas. Univ. Federal do Rio Grande do Sul. Porto Alegre.

IFH/C Conjonction. Institut Français d'Haïti. Port-au-Prince.

IIAS/IRAS International Review of Administrative Sciences. International Institute of Administrative Sciences. Bruxelles.

III/AI América Indígena. Instituto Indigenista Interamericano. México.

IJ/JJ Jamaica Journal. Institute of Jamaica. Kingston.

IJSP International Journal of Social Psychiatry. London.

INED/P Population. Revue trimestrielle de l'Institut National d'Etudes Demographiques. Paris.

IPEA/PPE Pesquisa e Planejamento Econômico. Instituto de Planejamento Econômico e Social. Rio de Janeiro.

IRR/RC Race & Class. A journal for black and Third World liberation. Institute of Race Relations; The Transnational Institute. London.

JDA The Journal of Developing Areas. Western Illinois Univ. Press. Macomb.

JGSWGL Jahrbuch für Geschichte von Staat, Wirtschaft und Gesellschaft Lateinamerikas. Köln, FRG.

JLAS Journal of Latin American Studies. Centers or institutes of Latin American studies at the universities of Cambridge, Glasgow, Liverpool, London and Oxford. Cambridge Univ. Press. London.

JPS The Journal of Peasant Studies. Frank Cass & Co. London.

JSP Journal of Social Psychology. The Journal Press. Provincetown, Mass.

KAS/P Kroeber Anthropological Society Papers. Univ. of California. Berkeley.

LAP Latin American Perspectives. Univ. of California. Riverside.

LARR Latin American Research Review. Univ. of North Carolina Press *for the* Latin American Studies Association. Chapel Hill.

LNB/L Lotería. Lotería Nacional de Beneficencia. Panamá.

LSE/PS Population Studies. London School of Economics, The Population Investigation Committee. London.

MSTPS/R Revista Mexicana del Trabajo. Publicación bimestral. Secretaría del Trabajo y Previsión Social. México.

MULINO Il Mulino. Rivista mensile di cultura e politica. Bologna, Italy.

MVL/J Jahrbuch des Museums für Völkerkunde zu Leipzig. Berlin.

NCFR/JFH Journal of Family History. Studies in family, kinship and demography. National Council on Family Relations. Minneapolis, Minn.

NIU/JPMS Journal of Political & Military Sociology. Northern Illinois Univ., Dept. of Sociology. DeKalb.

NS NS NorthSouth NordSud NorteSur NorteSul. Canadian journal of Latin American studies. Canadian Association of Latin American Studies. Univ. of Ottawa. Ottawa.

NSO Nueva Sociedad. Revista política y cultural. San José.

NYAS/A Annals of the New York Academy of Sciences. New York.

OLI/ZLW Zeitschrift für Lateinamerika Wien. Österreichisches Lateinamerika-Institut. Wien.

PAA/D Demography. Population Association of America. Washington.

PAIGH/G Revista Geográfica. Instituto Panamericano de Geografía e Historia, Comisión de Geografía. México.

PAN/ES Estudios Latinoamericanos. Polska Akademia Nauk (Academia de Ciencias de Polonia), Instytut Historii (Instituto de Historia). Warszawa.

PCCLAS/P Proceedings of the Pacific Coast Council on Latin American Studies. Univ. of California. Los Angeles.

PERES/SC *See* FERES/SC.

PSA/PSR Pacific Sociological Review. Pacific Sociological Association. San Diego State Univ. San Diego, Calif.

PUJ/UH Universitas Humanistica. Pontificia Univ. Javeriana, Facultad de Filosofía y Letras. Bogotá.

RLP Revista Latinoamericana de Psicología. Bogotá.

RU/SCID Studies in Comparative International Development. Rutgers Univ. New Brunswick, N.J.

SAA/HO Human Organization. Society for Applied Anthropology. New York.

SAGE/JIAS Journal of Inter-American Studies and World Affairs. Sage Publication *for the* Center for Advanced International Studies, Univ. of Miami. Coral Gables, Fla.

SAP/BM Bulletins et Mémoires de la Société d'Anthropologie de Paris. Paris.

SBPC/CC Ciência e Cultura. Sociedade Brasileira para o Progresso da Ciência. São Paulo.

SF Social Forces. Univ. of North Carolina Press *by the* Williams & Wilkins Co. Baltimore, Md.

SGB/COM Les Cahiers d'Outre-Mer. Publiée par l'Institut de Géographie de la Faculté des Lettres de Bordeaux, par l'Institut de la France d'Outre-Mer, par la Société de Géographie de Bordeaux *avec le concours du* Centre National de la Recherche Scientifique et de la VI^ieme section de l'École Pratique des Hautes Études. Bordeaux, France.

SGHG/A Anales de la Sociedad de Geografía e Historia de Guatemala. Guatemala.

SIP/RIP Revista Interamericana de Psicología (Interamerican Journal of Psychology). Sociedad Interamericana de Psicología (Interamerican Society of Psychology). De Paul Univ., Dept. of Psychology. Chicago, Ill.

SO Society. Social science and modern society. Transaction, Rutgers-The State Univ. New Brunswick, N.J.

SOCIOL Sociologus. Zeitschrift für empirische Soziologie, sozialpsychologische und ethnologische Forschung (A journal for empirical sociology, social psychology and ethnic research). Berlin.

SSISS Social Science Information sur les Sciences Sociales. International Social Science Council; UNESCO; Ecole des Hautes Études en Sciences Sociales; Maison des Sciences de l'Homme. Paris.

SSSP/SP Social Problems. Society for the Study of Social Problems *affiliated with the* American and International Sociological Associations. Kalamazoo, Mich.

UA Urban Anthropology. State Univ. of New York, Dept. of Anthropology. Brockport.

UB/BA Boletín Americanista. Univ. de Barcelona, Facultad de Geografía e Historia, Depto. de Historia de América. Barcelona.

UC/A Anales de la Universidad de Cuenca. Cuenca, Ecuador.

UC/AJS American Journal of Sociology. Univ. of Chicago. Chicago, Ill.

UC/CA Current Anthropology. Univ. of Chicago. Chicago, Ill.

UC/EDCC Economic Development and Cultural Change. Univ. of Chicago, Research Center in Economic Development and Cultural Change. Chicago, Ill.

UC/S Signs. Journal of women in culture and society. The Univ. of Chicago Press. Chicago, Ill.

UCL/CD Cultures et Développement. Revue internationale des sciences du développement. Univ. Catholique de Louvain *avec le concours de la* Fondation Universitaire de Belgique. Louvain, Belgium.

UCLV/I Islas. Univ. Central de las Villas. Santa Clara, Cuba.

UCNSA/EP Estudios Paraguayos. Univ. Católica Nuestra Señora de la Asunción. Asunción.

UCSD/NS The New Scholar. Univ. of California, Center for Iberian and Latin American Studies and Institute of Chicano Urban Affairs. San Diego.

UJSC/ECA Estudios Centro-Americanos. Revista de extensión cultural. Univ. José Simeón Cañas. San Salvador.

UK/SR The Sociological Review. Univ. of Keele. Staffordshire, England.

ULB/RIS Revue de l'Institut de Sociologie. Univ. Libre de Bruxelles. Bruxelles.

UM/JIAS *See* SAGE/JIAS.

UMG/RBEP Revista Brasileira de Estudos Políticos. Univ. de Minas Gerais. Belo Horizonte, Brazil.

UN/ISSJ International Social Science Journal. United Nations Educational, Scientific, and Cultural Organization. Paris.

UNAM/RMCPS Revista Mexicana de Ciencias Políticas y Sociales. Univ. Nacional Autónoma de México, Facultad de Ciencias Políticas y Sociales. México.

UNAM/RMS Revista Mexicana de Sociología. Univ. Nacional Autónoma de México, Instituto de Investigaciones Sociales. México.

UNESCO/CU Cultures. United Nations Educational, Scientific, and Cultural Organization. Paris.

UNION Unión. Unión de Escritores y Artistas de Cuba. La Habana.

UNL/H Humanitas. Univ. de Nuevo León, Centro de Estudios Humanísticos. Monterrey, México.

UNPHU/A Aula. Univ. Nacional Pedro Henríquez Ureña. Santo Domingo.

UP/CSEC Cuban Studies/Estudios Cubanos. Univ. of Pittsburgh, Univ. Center for International Studies, Center for Latin American Studies. Pittsburgh, Pa.

UP/E Ethnology. Univ. of Pittsburgh. Pittsburgh, Pa.

UP/TM Tiers Monde. Problèmes des pays sous-développés. Revue trimestrielle. Univ. de Paris, Institut d'Étude du Développement Économique et Social. Paris.

UPR/CS Caribbean Studies. Univ. of Puerto Rico, Institute of Caribbean Studies. Río Piedras.

UPR/RCS Revista de Ciencias Sociales. Univ. de Puerto Rico, Colegio de Ciencias Sociales. Río Piedras.

UR/L Lateinamerika. Univ. Rostock. Rostock, GRD.

URSS/AL América Latina. Academia de Ciencias de la URSS (Unión de Repúblicas Soviéticas Socialistas). Moscú.

USB/F Franciscanum. Revista de las ciencias del espíritu. Univ. de San Buenaventura. Bogotá.

USC/SSR Sociology and Social Research. An international journal. Univ. of Southern California. University Park.

USCG/PS Política y Sociedad. Univ. de San Carlos de Guatemala, Facultad de Ciencias Jurídicas y Sociales, Escuela de Ciencias Política, Instituto de Investigaciones Políticas y Sociales. Guatemala.

USM/JTG The Journal of Tropical Geography. Univ. of Singapore and Univ. of Malaya, Depts. of Geography. Singapore.

USP/RIEB Revista do Instituto de Estudos Brasileiros. Univ. de São Paulo, Instituto de Estudos Brasileiros. São Paulo.

UTIEH/C Caravelle. Cahiers du monde hispanique et luso-brésilien. Univ. de Toulouse, Institut d'Études Hispaniques, Hispano-Americaines et Luso-Brésiliennes. Toulouse, France.

UW/LBR Luso-Brazilian Review. Univ. of Wisconsin Press. Madison.

UWI/CQ Caribbean Quarterly. Univ. of the West Indies. Mona, Jamaica.

UWI/SES Social and Economic Studies. Univ. of the West Indies, Institute of Social and Economic Research. Mona, Jamaica.

VOZES Vozes. Revista de cultura. Editora Vozes. Petrópolis, Brazil.

WPF/IO International Organization. World Peace Foundation; Univ. of Wisconsin Press. Madison.

INDEXES

ABBREVIATIONS AND ACRONYMS

Except for journal acronyms which are listed at a) the end of each major disciplinary section, (e.g., Anthropology, Economics, Education, etc.); and b) after each serial title in the Title List of Journals Indexed, p. 685

a.	annual
ABC	Argentina, Brazil, Chile
A.C.	antes de Cristo
ACAR	Associação de Crédito e Assistência Rural, Brazil
AD	Anno Domini
A.D.	Acción Democrática, Venezuela
ADESG	Associação dos Diplomados de Escola Superior de Guerra, Brazil
AGI	Archivo General de Indias, Sevilla
AGN	Archivo General de la Nación
AID	Agency for International Development
a.k.a.	also known as
Ala.	Alabama
ALALC	Asociación Latinoamericana de Libre Comercio
ANAPO	Alianza Nacional Popular, Colombia
ANCARSE	Associação Nordestina de Crédito e Assistência Rural de Sergipe, Brazil
ANCOM	Andean Common Market
ANDI	Asociación Nacional de Industriales, Colombia
AP	Acción Popular
APRA	Alianza Popular Revolucionaria Americana
Ariz.	Arizona
Ark.	Arkansas
ASA	Association of Social Anthropologists of the Commonwealth, London
ASSEPLAN	Assessoria de Planejamente e Acompanhamento, Recife, Brazil
Assn.	Association
Aufl.	Auflage (edition, edición)
AUFS	American Universities Field Staff Reports, Hanover, N.H.
Aug.	August, Augustan
b.	born (nacido)
BBE	Bibliografia Brasileira de Educação
b.c.	indicates dates obtained by radio-carbon methods
BC	Before Christ
bibl(s).	bibliography(ies)
BID	Banco Interamericano de Desarrollo
BNDE	Banco Nacional de Desenvolvimento Econômico, Brazil
BNH	Banco Nacional de Habitação, Brazil
BP	before present
b/w	black-and-white
C14	Carbon 14
ca.	circa
CACM	Central American Common Market
CADE	Conferencia Anual de Ejecutivos de Empresas, Peru
CAEM	Centro de Altos Estudios Militares, Peru
Calif.	California
CARC	Centro de Arte y Comunicación

CARICOM	Caribbean Common Market
CARIFTA	Caribbean Free Trade Association
CBD	central business district
CD	Christian Democrats, Chile
CDI	Conselho de Desenvolvimento Industrial
CEBRAP	Centro Brasileiro de Análise e Planejamento, São Paulo
CECORA	Centro de Cooperativas de la Reforma Agraria, Colombia
CEDAL	Centro de Estudios Democráticos de América Latina, Costa Rica
CEDE	Centro de Estudios sobre Desarrollo Económico, Univ. de los Andes, Bogotá
CEDEPLAR	Centro de Desenvolvimento e Planejamento Region, Belo Horizonte, Brazil
CEDES	Centro de Estudios de Estado y Sociedad, Buenos Aires; Centro de Estudos de Educação e Sociedade, São Paulo, Brazil
CEDI	Conselho Ecuménico para Documentação e Informação, Brazil
CEESTEM	Centro de Estudios Económicos y Sociales del Tercer Mundo, México
CELADE	Centro Latinoamericano de Demografía
CEMLA	Centro de Estudios Monetarios Latinoamericanos, Mexico
CENDES	Centro de Estudios del Desarrollo, Venezuela
CENIDIM	Centro Nacional de Información, Documentación e Investigación Musicales, Mexico
CENIET	Centro Nacional de Información y Estadísticas del Trabajo, México
CEPADE	Centro Paraguayo de Estudios de Desarrollo Económico y Social
CEPA-SE	Comissão Estadual de Planejamento Agrícola, Sergipe, Brazil
CEPAL	*See* ECLA.
CERES	Centro de Estudios de la Realidad Económica y Social, Bolivia
CES	constant elasticity of substitution
cf.	compare
CFI	Consejo Federal de Inversiones, B.A.
CGE	Confederación General Económica, Argentina
CGTP	Confederación General de Trabajadores del Perú
ch., chap.	chapter
CHEAR	Council on Higher Education in the American Republics
Cía.	Compañía
CIA	Central Intelligence Agency
CIDA	Comité Interamericano de Desarrollo Agrícola
CIDE	Centro de Investigación y Desarrollo de la Educación, Chile
CIE	Centro de Investigaciones Económicas, Buenos Aires
CIMI	Conselho Indigenista Misioneiro, Brazil
CIP	Conselho Interministerial de Preços
CIPCA	Centro de Investigación y Promoción del Campesinado, Bolivia
CLACSO	Consejo Latinoamericano de Ciencias Sociales, Secretaria Ejecutiva, Buenos Aires
CLASC	Confederación Latinoamericana Sindical Cristiana
CLE	Comunidad Latinoamericana de Escritores, Mexico
cm	centimeter
CNI	Confederação Nacional da Industria, Brazil
Co.	company
COB	Central Obrera Boliviana
COBAL	Companhia Brasileira de Alimentos
Col.	collection, colección, coleção
Colo.	Colorado
COMCORDE	Comisión Coordinadora para el Desarrollo Económico, Uruguay
comp.	compiler
CONCLAT	Congresso Nacional de Classe Trabalhadora, Brazil
CONDESE	Conselho de Desenvolvimento Econômico de Sergipe, Brazil
Conn.	Connecticut

COPEI	Comité Organizador Pro-Elecciones Independientes, Venezuela
CORFO	Corporación de Fomento de la Producción, Chile
CORP	Corporación para el Fomento de Investigaciones Económicas, Colombia
corp.	Corporation
CP	Communist Party
CPDOC	Centro de Pesquisa e Documentação de História Contemporânea do Brasil, Rio de Janeiro.
CRIC	Consejo Regional Indígena del Cauca, Colombia
CUNY	City University of New York
CVG	Corporación Venezolana de Guayana
d.	died
DANE	Departamento Nacional de Estadística, Colombia
DC	developed country; Demócratas Cristianos, Chile
d.C	después de Cristo
déc.	décembre
Dec.	December
Del.	Delaware
dept.	department
depto.	departamento
dez.	dezembre
dic.	diciembre
DNOCS	Departamento Nacional de Obras Contra as Sécas, Brazil
Dr.	Doctor
Dra.	Doctora
ECLA	Economic Commission for Latin America
ECOSOC	UN Department of Economic and Social Affairs
ed(s).	edition(s), edición(es), editor(s), redactor(es)
EDEME	Editora Emprendimentos Educacionais, Florianópolis, Brazil
Edo.	Estado
EEC	European Economic Community
EFTA	European Free Trade Association
e.g.	exempio gratia (for example)
ELN	Ejército de Liberación Nacional, Colombia
ENDEF	Estudo Nacional da Despesa Familiar, Brazil
ESG	Escola Superior de Guerra, Brazil
estr.	estrenado
et al.	et alia (and others)
ETENE	Escritório Técnico de Estudos Econômicos do Nordeste, Brazil
ETEPE	Escritório Técnico de Planejamento, Brazil
EUDEBA	Editorial Universitaria de Buenos Aires
EWG	Europaische Wirtschaftsgemeinschaft. *See* EEC.
facsim(s).	facsimile(s)
FAO	Food and Agriculture Organization of the United Nations
FDR	Frente Democrático Revolucionario, El Salvador
Feb./feb.	February, febrero
FEDECAFE	Federación Nacional de Cafeteros, Colombia
FEDESARROLLO	Fundación para la Educación Superior y el Desarrollo, Colombia
fev.	fevreiro, février
ff.	following
FFMLN	Frente Farabundo Martí de Liberación Nacional, El Salvador
FGTS	Fundo do Garantia do Tempo de Serviço, Brazil
FGV	Fundação Getúlio Vargas
FIEL	Fundación de Investigaciones Económicas Latinoamericanos, Argentina
film.	filmography
fl.	flourished, floresció

Fla.	Florida
FLACSO	Facultad Latinoamericano de Ciencias Sociales, Buenos Aires
fold.	folded
fol(s).	folio(s)
FRG	Federal Republic of Germany
FSLN	Frente Sandinista de Revolución Nacional, Nicaragua
ft.	foot, feet
FUAR	Frente Unido de Acción Revolucionaria, Colombia
Ga.	Georgia
GAO	General Accounting Office, Washington
GATT	General Agreement on Tariffs and Trade
GDP	gross domestic product
GDR	German Democratic Republic
GEIDA	Grupo Executivo de Irrigação para o Desenvolvimento Agrícola, Brazil
Gen.	General
GMT	Greenwich Meridian Time
GPA	grade point average
GPO	Government Printing Office
h.	hijo
ha.	hectares, hectáreas
HLAS	*Handbook of Latin American Studies*
HMAI	*Handbook of Middle American Studies*
Hnos.	Hermanos
IBBD	Instituto Brasileiro de Bibliografia e Documentação
IBGE	Instituto Brasileiro de Geografia e Estatística, Rio de Janeiro
IBRD	International Bank of Reconstruction and Development
ICA	Instituto Colombiano Agropecuario
ICAIC	Instituto Cubano de Arte e Industria Cinematográficas
ICCE	Instituto Colombiano de Construcción Escolar
ICE	International Cultural Exchange
ICSS	Instituto Colombiano de Seguridad Social
ICT	Instituto de Crédito Territorial, Colombia
IDB	Inter-American Development Bank
i.e.	id est (that is)
IEL	Instituto Euvaldo Lodi, Brazil
IEP	Instituto de Estudios Peruanos
IERAC	Instituto Ecuatoriano de Reforma Agraria y Colonización
III	Instituto Indigenista Interamericana, Mexico
IIN	Instituto Indigenista Nacional, Guatemala
ill.	illustrations(s)
Ill.	Illinois
ILO	International Labour Organization, Geneva
IMES	Instituto Mexicano de Estudios Sociales
in.	inch(es)
INAH	Instituto Nacional de Antropología e Historia, Mexico
INBA	Instituto Nacional de Bellas Artes, Mexico
Inc.	incorporated
INCORA	Instituto Colombiano de Reforma Agraria
Ind.	Indiana
INEP	Instituto Nacional de Estudios Pedagógicos, Brazil
INI	Instituto Nacional Indigenista, Mexico
INIT	Instituto Nacional de Industria Turística, Cuba
INPES/IPEA	Instituto de Planejamento Econômico e Social, Instituto de Pesquisas, Brazil
INTAL	Instituto para la Integración de América Latina
IPA	Instituto de Pastoral Andina, Univ. de San Antonio de Abad, Seminario de Antropología, Cuzco, Peru

IPEA	Instituto de Pesquisa Econômico-Social Aplicada, Brazil
IPES/GB	Instituto de Pesquisas e Estudos Sociais, Guanabara, Brazil
IPHAN	Instituto de Patrimônio Histórico e Artístico Nacional, Brazil
ir.	irregular
ITT	International Telephone and Telegraph
Jan./jan.	January, janeiro, janvier
JLP	Jamaican Labour Party
JUCEPLAN	Junta Central de Planificación, Cuba
Kan.	Kansas
km	kilometers, kilómetres
Ky.	Kentucky
l.	leaves, hojas (páginas impresas por una sola cara)
La.	Louisiana
LASA	Latin American Studies Association
LDC	less developed countries
Ltda.	Limitada
m.	meters, metros, monthly, murió (died)
M	mille, mil, thousand
MAPU	Movimiento de Acción Popular Unitario, Chile
MARI	Middle American Research Institute, Tulane University, New Orleans
Mass.	Massachusetts
MCC	Mercado Común Centro-Americano
Md.	Maryland
MDB	Movimiento Democrático Brasileiro
MDC	more developed countries
MEC	Ministério de Educação e Cultura, Brazil
Mich.	Michigan
mimeo	mimeographed, mimeografiado
min.	minutes, minutos
Minn.	Minnesota
MIR	Movimiento de Izquierda Revolucionaria, Chile
Miss.	Mississippi
MIT	Massachusetts Institute of Technology
MLN	Movimiento de Liberación Nacional
mm.	millimeter
MNC's	multinational corporations
MNR	Movimiento Nacionalista Revolucionario, Bolivia
Mo.	Missouri
MOBRAL	Movimento Brasileiro de Alfabetização, Brazil
MOIR	Movimiento Obrero Independiente y Revolucionario, Colombia
Mont.	Montana
MRL	Movimiento Revolucionario Liberal, Colombia
ms.	manuscript
msl	mean sea level
n.	nacido (born)
NBER	National Bureau of Economic Research, Cambridge, Mass.
N.C.	North Carolina
N.D.	North Dakota
Neb.	Nebraska
neubearb.	neubearbeitet (revised, corregida)
Nev.	Nevada
n.f.	neue Folge
N.H.	New Hampshire
NIEO	New International Economic Order
NIH	National Institutes of Health, Washington
N.J.	New Jersey

N.M.	New Mexico
no(s).	number(s), número(s)
NOSALF	Scandanavian Committee for Research in Latin America
Nov./nov.	November, noviembre, novembre, novembro
NSF	National Science Foundation
N.Y.	New York
N.Y.C.	New York City
OAS	Organization of American States
Oct./oct.	October, octubre
ODEPLAN	Oficina de Planificación Nacional, Chile
OEA	Organización de los Estados Americanos
OECD	Organization for Economic Cooperation and Development, Paris
OIT	*See* ILO.
Okla.	Oklahoma
Okt.	Oktober
op.	opus
OPANAL	Organismo para la Proscripción de las Armas Nucleares en América Latina
OPEC	Organization of Petroleum Exporting Countries
OPEP	Organización de Países Exportadores de Petróleo
OPIC	Overseas Investment Corporation
Or.	Oregon
ORIT	Organización Regional Interamericana del Trabajo
out.	outubre
p.	page(s)
Pa.	Pennsylvania
PAN	Partido Acción Nacional, Mexico
PC	partido comunista
PCR	Partido Comunista Revolucionario, Chile and Argentina
PCV	Partido Comunista de Venezuela
PDC	Partido Demócrata Cristiano, Chile
PDS	Partido Democrático Social, Brazil
PEMEX	Petróleos Mexicanos
PETROBRAS	Petróleo Brasileiro
PIMES	Programa Integrado de Mestrado em Economia e Sociologia, Brazil
PIP	Partido Independiente de Puerto Rico
PLANAVE	Engenharia e Planejamento Limitada, Brazil
PLANO	Planejamento e Assesoria Limitada, Brazil
PLN	Partido Liberación Nacional, Costa Rica
PNAD	Pesquisa Nacional por Amuestra Domiciliar, Brazil
PNM	People's National Movement, Trinidad and Tobago
PNP	People's National Party, Jamaica
pop.	population
port(s).	portrait(s)
PPP	purchasing power parities
PRD	Partido Revolucionario Dominicano
PREALC	Programa Regional del Empleo para América Latina y el Caribe, Organización Internacional del Trabajo, Santiago, Chile
PRI	Partido Revolucionario Institucional, Mexico
PROABRIL	Centro de Projetos Industrias, Brazil
Prof.	Professor
PRONAPA	Programa Nacional de Pesquisas Arqueológicas, Brazil
prov.	province, provincia
PS	Partido Socialista, Chile
pseud.	pseudonym, pseudónimo
pt(s).	part(s), parte(s)

pub.	published
PUC	Pontificia Universidad Católica, Rio de Janeiro
PURSC	Partido Unido de la Revolución Socialista de Cuba
q.	quarterly
rev.	revisada, revised
R.I.	Rhode Island
s.a.	semiannual
SALALM	Seminar on the Acquisition of Latin American Library Materials
sd.	sound
S.D.	South Dakota
SDR	special drawing rights
SELA	Sistema Económico Latinoamericano
SENAC	Serviço Nacional de Aprendizagem Comercial, Rio de Janeiro
SENAI	Serviço Nacional de Aprendizagem Industrial, São Paulo
SEPLA	Seminario Permanente sobre Latinoamérica, México
Sept./sept.	September, septiembre, septembre
SES	socio-economic status
SESI	Serviço Social de Industria, Brazil
set.	setembre
SIECA	Secretaría Permanente del Tratado General de Integración Centroamericana
SIL	Summer Institute of Linguistics
SINAMOS	Sistema Nacional de Apoyo a la Movilización Social, Peru
S.J.	Society of Jesus
s.l.	sine loco (place of publication unknown)
s.n.	sine nomine (publisher unknown)
SNA	Sociedad Nacional de Agricultura, Chile
SPVEA	Superintendência do Plano de Valorização Econômica de Amazônia, Brazil
sq.	square
SUDAM	Superintendência de Desenvolvimento da Amazônia, Brazil
SUDENE	Superintendência de Desenvolvimento do Nordeste, Brazil
SUFRAME	Superintendência da Zona Franca de Manaus, Brazil
SUNY	State University of New York
t.	tomo(s), tome(s)
TAT	Thematic Apperception Test
TB	tuberculosis
Tenn.	Tennessee
Tex.	Texas
TG	transformational generative
TL	Thermoluminescent
TNEs	Transnational enterprises
TNP	Tratado de No Proliferación
trans.	translator
U.K.	United Kingdom
UN	United Nations
UNAM	Universidad Nacional Autónoma de México
UNCTAD	United Nations Conference on Trade and Development
UNDP	UN Development Programme
UNEAC	Unión de Escritores y Artistas de Cuba
UNESCO	UN Educational, Scientific and Cultural Organization
univ.	university, universidad, universidade, université, universität
uniw.	uniwersytet
UP	Unidad Popular, Chile
URD	Unidad Revolucionaria Democrática
URSS	Unión de Repúblicas Soviéticas Socialistas
US	United States

USIA	US Information Agency, Washington
USSR	Union of the Soviet Socialist Republics
UTM	Universal Transverse Mercator
v.	volume(s), volumen (volúmenes)
Va.	Virginia
viz.	videlicet, that is, namely
vol(s).	volume(s), volumen (volúmenes)
vs.	versus
Vt.	Vermont
W. Va.	West Virginia
Wash.	Washington
Wis.	Wisconsin
Wyo.	Wyoming
yr(s).	year(s)

TITLE LIST OF JOURNALS INDEXED*

Administrative Science Quarterly. Cornell
Univ., Graduate School of Business and
Public Administration. Ithaca, N.Y.
(CU/ASQ)

Agrociencia. Secretaría de Agricultura y
Recursos Hidráulicos, Colegio de Postgraduados de la Escuela Nacional de Agricultura. Chapingo, México. (AGRO)

Alero. Univ. de San Carlos. Guatemala.

Allpanchis. Instituto de Pastoral Andina.
Cuzco, Perú. (IPA/A)

Amazonía Peruana. Centro Amazónico de
Antropología y Aplicación Práctica, Depto.
de Documentación y Publicaciones. Lima.
(CAAAP/AP)

América Indígena. Instituto Indigenista Interamericano. México. (III/AI)

América Latina. Academia de Ciencias de la
URSS (Unión de Repúblicas Soviéticas Socialistas). Moscú. (URSS/AL)

América Latina. Centro Latino-Americano de
Pesquisas em Ciências Sociais. Rio de
Janeiro. (CLAPCS/AL)

American Anthropologist. American Anthropological Association. Washington.
(AAA/AA)

American Antiquity. The Society for American Archaeology. Menasha, Wis. (SAA/AA)

American Economic Review. Journal of the
American Economic Association. Evanston,
Ill. (AEA/AER)

American Ethnologist. American Anthropological Association. Washington. (AAA/AE)

The American Journal of Comparative Law.
American Association of the Comparative
Study of Law. Univ. of California. Berkeley.
(AJCL)

The American Journal of Economics and So-
ciology. Francis Neilson Fund and Robert
Schalkenbach Foundation. New York.
(AJES)

American Journal of Epidemiology. Johns
Hopkins Univ. Baltimore, Md.

American Journal of Human Genetics. The
American Society of Human Genetics.
Baltimore, Md. (ASHG/J)

American Journal of Physical Anthropology.
American Association of Physical Anthropologists and the Wistar Institute of Anatomy and Biology. Philadelphia, Pa. (AJPA)

American Naturalist. Essex Institute. Lan-
caster, Pa.

American Political Science Review. American
Political Science Association. Columbus,
Ohio. (APSA/R)

American Sociological Review. American Sociological Association. Menasha, Wis.
(ASA/ASR)

Américas. Organization of American States.
Washington. (OAS/AM)

The Americas. A quarterly publication of
inter-American cultural history. Academy
of American Franciscan History. Washington. (AAFH/TAM)

Anais da Biblioteca Nacional. Divisão de
Obras Raras e Publicações. Rio de Janeiro.
(BRBN/A)

Anales. Administración del Patrimonio Cultural. San Salvador.

Anales. Univ. de Chile. Santiago.

Anales de Antropología. Univ. Nacional Autónoma de México, Instituto de Investigaciones Históricas. México. (UNAM/AA)

Anales de la Academia Nacional de Ciencias
Económicas. Buenos Aires. (ANCE/A)

Anales de la Sociedad de Geografía e Historia
de Guatemala. Guatemala. (SGHG/A)

Anales de la Universidad de Cuenca. Cuenca,
Ecuador. (UC/A)

Anales del Instituto Nacional de Antropología e Historia. Secretaría de Educación
Pública. México. (INAH/A)

Analysis & Documentary Information. Ministry of Education and Culture (MEC), Brazilian Literacy Movement Foundation
(MOBRAL), Center for Training, Research
and Documentation (CEPTEP), Documentation Sector (SEDOC). Rio de Janeiro.

Annales de Géographie. Société de Géographie. Paris. (SG/AG)

Annals. Carnegie Museum of Natural History. Pittsburgh, Pa.

* Journals that have been included in the *Handbook* as individual items are listed alphabetically by title in the Author Index.

Annals of Human Biology. Taylor and Francis Publishers. London.

Annals of Human Genetics (Annals of Eugenics). Univ. College, Galton Laboratory. London. (UCGL/AHG)

Annals of the Association of American Geographers. Lawrence, Kan. (AAG/A)

Annals of the New York Academy of Sciences. New York. (NYAS/A)

Annual of Psychoanalysis. Yale Univ. Press. New Haven, Conn.

Annual Report of the Institute of Geoscience. Univ. of Tsukuba. Tsukuba, Japan.

Annual Review of Anthropology. Annual Review, Inc. Palo Alto, Calif.

Annual Review of Genetics. Palo Alto, Calif.

Anthropologica. Canadian Research Centre for Anthropology. St. Paul Univ. Ottawa, Canada. (CRCA/A)

Anthropologica. Research Center for Amerindian Anthropology. Univ. of Ottawa. Ottawa, Canada.

Anthropological Quarterly. Catholic Univ. of America, Catholic Anthropological Conference. Washington. (CUA/AQ)

Anthropology. State Univ. of New York, Dept. of Anthropology. Stony Brook.

Anthropos. Anthropos-Institut. Psoieux, Switzerland. (AI/A)

Antiquitas. Boletín de la Asociación Amigos del Instituto de Arqueología, Facultad de Historia y Letras. Univ. del Salvador. Buenos Aires.

Antiquity. A quarterly review of archaeology. The Antiquity Trust. Cambridge, England. (AT/A)

Antropología Andina. Centro de Estudios Andinos. Cuzco, Peru.

Antropología e Historia de Guatemala. Instituto de Antropología e Historia de Guatemala. Guatemala. (IAHG/AHG)

Antropología Ecuatoriana. Casa de la Cultura Ecuatoriana. Quito.

Antropológica. Fundación La Salle de Ciencias Naturales, Instituto Caribe de Antropología y Sociología. Caracas. (FSCN/A)

Anuário Antropológico. Edições Tempo Brasileiro. Rio de Janeiro.

Anuario de Estudios Centroamericanos. Univ. de Costa Rica. San José. (UCR/AEC)

Anuario de Letras. Univ. Nacional Autónoma de México, Facultad de Filosofía y Letras. México. (UNAM/AL)

Apacheta. Revista de las tradiciones populares del Perú. Francisco Iriarte Brenner. Lima.

Apuntes. Univ. del Pacífico, Centro de Investigación. Lima. (UP/A)

Archaeoastronomy. Supplement to Journal of the History of Astronomy. Giles, England.

Archaeology. Archaeological Institute of America. New York. (AIA/A)

Archaeology and Anthropology. Journal of the Walter Roth Museum of Archaeology and Anthropology. Georgetown, Guyana.

Archiv für Völkerkunde. Museum für Völkerkunde in Wien und von Verein Freunde der Völkerkunde. Wien. (MVW/AV)

Archives de Sociologie des Religions. Centre Nationale de la Recherche Scientifique. Paris. (CNRS/ASR)

Archives Européennes de Sociologie. Paris. (AES)

Archivum Historicum Societatis Iesu. Rome. (AHSI)

Areito. Areíto, Inc. New York. (AR)

Argos. División de Ciencias Sociales y Humanidades, Universidad Simón Bolívar. Caracas.

Arqueológicas. Museo Nacional de Antropología y Arqueología. Lima.

Arquivos do Museu de História Natural. Univ. Federal de Minas Gerais. Belo Horizonte, Brazil.

Arstryck. Göteborgs Etnografiska Museum. Göteborgs, Sweden.

Asian Perspectives. Univ. Press of Hawaii. Honolulu.

Assistant Librarian. London.

Atenea. Revista de ciencias, letras y artes. Univ. de Concepción. Concepción, Chile. (UC/AT)

Aula. Univ. Nacional Pedro Henríquez Ureña. Santo Domingo. (UNPHU/A)

Aussenpolitik. Zeitschrift für Internationale Fragen. Deutsche Verlags-Austalt. Hamburg, FRG. (AZIF).

Baessler-Archiv. Museums für Völkerkunde. Berlin. (MV/BA)

Bahia Acervo Bibliográfico. Fundação Centro de Pesquisas e Estudos. Salvador, Brazil.

Bank of London and South America Review. London.

Behavior Science Research. Journal of comparative studies. Human Relations Area Files. New Haven, Conn. (HRAF/BSR)

Beiträge zur Allgemeinen und Vergleichenden Archäologie. Deutsches Archäologisches Institut. Berlin, FRG.

Beiträge zur Romanischen Philologie. Rütten & Loening. Berlin, FRG. (BRP)

Belizean Studies. Belizean Institute of Social

Research and Action and St. John's College. Belize City. (BISRA/BS)

Berichte zur Entwicklung in Spanien, Portugal, Lateinamerika. München, FRG. (BESPL)

Bibliografía Médica Venezolana. Ministerio de Sanidad y Asistencia Social. Caracas.

Bibliographie Latinoamericaine d'Articles. Institut des Hautes Études de l'Amérique Latine, Centre de Documentation. Paris.

Bibliotecología y Documentación. Asociación de Bibliotecarios Graduados de la República Argentina. Buenos Aires.

Bijdragen tot de Taal-, Landen Volkenkunde. Koninklijk Instituut voor Taal-, Landen Volkenkunde. Leiden, The Netherlands. (KITLV/B)

The Black Scholar. Black World Foundation. Sausalito, Calif.

Bohemia. La Habana.

Boletim Bibliográfico. Secretaria das Minas e Energia, Coordenação da Produção Mineral. Bahia, Brazil.

Boletim Bibliográfico da Biblioteca Nacional. Rio de Janeiro.

Boletim Carioca de Geografia. Associação dos Geógrafos Brasileiros, Secção Regional de São Paulo. São Paulo. (AGB/BCG)

Boletim do Instituto de Arqueologia Brasileira. Rio de Janeiro.

Boletim do Museu Nacional. Compôsto e impresso na Oficina Gráfica da Univ. do Brasil. Rio de Janeiro. (BRMN/B)

Boletim do Museu Paraense Emílio Goeldi. Nova série: antropologia. Conselho Nacional de Desenvolvimento Científico e Tecnológico, Instituto Nacional de Pesquisas da Amazônia. Belém, Brazil. (MPEG/B)

Boletim Geográfico do Estado do Rio Grande do Sul. Diretório Regional de Geografia e da Secção de Geografia. Porto Alegre, Brazil. (DRG/BG)

Boletim Informativo e Bibliográfico de Ciencias Sociais. Instituto Universitário de Pesquisas. Rio de Janeiro.

Boletim Paulista de Geografia. Associação dos Geógrafos Brasileiros, Secção Regional de São Paulo. São Paulo. (AGB/BPG)

Boletín. Museo Arqueológico de La Serena. La Serena, Chile.

Boletín. Museo del Oro, Banco de la República. Bogotá.

Boletín Americanista. Univ. de Barcelona, Facultad de Geografía e Historia, Depto. de Historia de América. Barcelona. (UB/BA)

Boletín Bibliográfico. Banco Central de Nicaragua. Managua.

Boletín Bibliográfico. Instituto Boliviano de Cultura. Instituto Nacional de Historia y Literatura. Depositorio Nacional. La Paz.

Boletín Bibliográfico de Antropología Americana. Instituto Panamericano de Geografía e Historia, Comisión de Historia. México. (BBAA)

Boletín Cultural y Bibliográfico. Banco de la República, Biblioteca Luis-Angel Arango. Bogotá. (CBR/BCB)

Boletín de Antropología Americana. *See* Boletín Bibliográfico de Antropología Americana.

Boletín de Ciencias Políticas y Sociales. Univ. Nacional de Cuyo, Facultad de Ciencias Políticas y Sociales. Mendoza, Argentina. (UNC/BCPS)

Boletín de Estudios Latinoamericanos. Centro de Estudios y Documentación Latinoamericanos. Amsterdam. (CEDLA/B)

Boletín de Gerencia Administrativa. Negociado de Presupuesto. San Juan? (PRNP/BGA)

Boletín de Historia y Antigüedades. Academia Colombiana de Historia. Bogotá. (ACH/BHA)

Boletín de la Academia de Ciencias Políticas y Sociales. Caracas. (ACPS/B)

Boletín de la Academia Nacional de Ciencias. Córdoba, Argentina. (ANC/B)

Boletín de la Academia Nacional de Historia. Quito. (EANH/B)

Boletín de la Academia Nacional de la Historia. Caracas. (VANH/B)

Boletín de la Academia Panameña de la Historia. Panamá.

Boletín de la Biblioteca Nacional. Lima. (PEBN/B)

Boletín de la Escuela de Ciencias Antropológicas de la Univ. de Yucatán. Mérida, México.

Boletín de la Sociedad Geográfica de Colombia. Academia de Ciencias Geográficas. Bogotá. (SGC/B)

Boletín de la Sociedad Geográfica de Lima. Lima. (SGL/B)

Boletín de la Sociedad Geográfica e Histórica Sucre. Sucre, Bolivia. (SGHS/B)

Boletín del Archivo General de la Nación. Secretaría de Gobernación. México. (MAGN/B)

Boletín del Instituto de Estudios Sociales de la Universidad de Guadalajara. Guadalajara, México.

Boletín del Instituto de Geografía. Univ. Nacional Autónoma de México. México.

Boletín del Instituto Nacional de Antropología e Historia. Secretaría de Educación Pública. México. (INAH/B)

Boletín del Museo del Hombre Dominicano. Santo Domingo. (MHD/B)

Boletín del Sistema Bibliotecario de la UNAH. Universidad Nacional Autónoma de Honduras. Tegucigalpa.

Boletín Documental. Universidad del Zulia, Facultad de Humanidades y Educación, Centro de Documentación e Investigación Pedagógica. Maracaibo, Venezuela.

Boletín Geológico. Ministerio de Minas y Petróleos, Instituto Geológico Nacional. Bogotá. (COIGN/BG)

Boletín Indigenista Venezolano. Ministerio de Justicia, Comisión Indigenista. Caracas. (VMJ/BIV)

Boletín Informativo. Centro de Estudios de Población y Desarrollo. Lima.

Boletín Nicaragüense de Bibliografía y Documentación. Banco Central de Nicaragua, Biblioteca. Managua. (BNBD)

Bollettino della Società Geografica Italiana. Roma. (SGI/B)

Bonner Amerikanistische Studien. Seminar für Volkerkunde. Bonn, FRG.

Brasil Açucareiro. Instituto do Açúcar e do Alcool. Rio de Janeiro. (IAA/BA)

Brazilian Business. National Association of American Chambers of Commerce in Brazil. Rio de Janeiro.

British Journal of Sociology. London School of Economics and Political Science. London. (BJS)

Bulletin. Société Suisse des Américanistes. Geneva. (SSA/B)

Bulletin de la Société d'Histoire de la Guadaloupe. Archives Départementales *avec le concours du* Conseil Général de la Guadeloupe. Basse-Terre, West Indies. (SHG/B)

Bulletin de l'Académie des Sciences Humaines et Sociales d'Haiti. Port-au-Prince. (ASHSH/B)

Bulletin de l'Association de Géographes Français. Paris. (AGF/B)

Bulletin de l'Institut Français d'Études Andines. Lima. (IFEA/B)

Bulletin of Eastern Caribbean Affairs. Univ. of the West Indies, Institute of Social and Economic Research. Cave Hill, Barbados.

Bulletin of the Pan American Health Organization. Washington. (PAHO/B)

Bulletins et Mémoires de la Société d'Anthropologie de Paris. Paris. (SAP/BM)

Business Review. Government Development Bank. San Juan? (GDB/BR)

Cadernos DCP. Univ. Federal de Minas Gerais, Faculdade de Filosofia e Ciências Humanas, Depto. de Ciência Política. Belo Horizonte, Brazil. (UFMG/DCP)

Cahiers des Amériques Latines. Paris. (CDAL)

Les Cahiers d'Outre-Mer. Publiée par l'Institut de Géographie de la Faculté des Lettres de Bordeaux, par l'Institut de la France d'Outre-Mer, par la Société de Géographie de Bordeaux *avec le concours de* Centre National de la Recherche Scientifique et de la VI. section de l'École Pratique des Hautes Études. Bordeaux. (SGB/COM)

Cahiers Internationaux de Sociologie. La Sorbonne, École Pratique des Hautes Études. Paris. (FS/CIS)

The Canadian Review of Sociology and Anthropology. Canadian Sociology and Anthropology Association. Montreal.

Caravelle. Cahiers du monde hispanique et luso-brésilien. Univ. of Toulouse, Institut d'Études Hispaniques, Hispano-Americaines et Luso-Brésiliennes. Toulouse, France. (UTIEH/C)

Caribbean Quarterly. Univ. of the West Indies. Mona, Jamaica. (UWI/CQ)

Caribbean Review. Florida International Univ., Office of Academic Affairs. Miami. (FIU/CR)

Caribbean Studies. Univ. of Puerto Rico, Instituto of Caribbean Studies. Río Piedras. (UPR/CS)

Carta Política. Persona e Persona. Buenos Aires.

Casa de las Américas. Instituto Cubano del Libro. La Habana. (CDLA)

Catholic Historical Review. American Catholic Historical Association. The Catholic Univ. of America Press. Washington. (ACHA/CHR)

Center for Historical Population Studies Newsletter. University of Utah. Salt Lake City.

Central American Accessions at the University of Kansas Libraries. Department for Spain, Portugal and Latin America. Lawrence.

Centro Latinoamericano de Economía Humana. Montevideo. (CLAEH)

CEPAL. Review/Revista de la CEPAL. Naciones Unidas, Comisión Económica para América Latina. Santiago. (CEPAL/R)

Chungara. Univ. del Norte, Depto. de Antropología. Arica, Chile.

Ciência e Cultura. Sociedade Brasileira para o Progresso da Ciência. São Paulo. (SBPC/CC)

Ciencia Interamericana. Organization of American States, Dept. of Scientific Affairs. Washington. (OAS/CI)

Ciencia, Tecnología y Desarrollo. Fondo Colombiano de Investigaciones Científicas y Proyectos Especiales Francisco José de Caldas. Bogotá.

Ciencia y Tecnología. Revista semestral de la Univ. de Costa Rica. San José. (UCR/CT)

Civilisations. International Institute of Differing Civilizations. Bruxelles. (IIDC/C)

Cladindex. Resumen de documentos CEPAL/ILPES. Organización de las Naciones Unidas. Comisión Económica para América Latina (CEPAL). Centro Latinoamericano de Documentación Económica y Social (CLADES). Santiago.

Colección Estudios CIEPLAN. Corporación de Investigaciones Económicas para Latinoamérica. Santiago.

Columbia Journal of Transnational Law. Columbia Univ., School of Law, Columbia Journal of Transnational Law Association. New York.

Comercio Exterior. Banco Nacional de Comercio Exterior. México. (BNCE/CE)

Commentary. American Jewish Committee. New York. (AJC/C)

Communications. École des Hautes Études en Sciences Sociales, Centre d'Études Transdisciplinaires. Paris. (EHESS/C)

Comparative Education Review. Comparative Education Society. New York. (CES/CER)

Comparative Political Studies. Northwestern Univ., Evanston, Ill. and Sage Publications, Beverly Hills, Calif. (CPS)

Comparative Politics. The City Univ. of New York, Political Science Program. New York. (CUNY/CP)

Comparative Studies in Society and History. An international quarterly. Society for the Comparative Study of Society and History. The Hague. (CSSH)

Comparative Urban Research. International Sociological Association, Committee for Community Research. College Park, Md. (ISA/CUR)

Comunicación y Cultura. La comunicación masiva en el proceso político latinoameri-

cano. Editorial Galerna. Buenos Aires y Santiago. (CYC)

Comunicaciones Proyecto Puebla-Tlaxcala. Fundación Alemana para la Investigación Científica. Puebla, México. (FAIC/CPPT)

Comunidades y Culturas Peruanas. Instituto Lingüístico de Verano. Yarinacocha, Peru.

Conjonction. Institut Français d'Haïti. Port-au-Prince. (IFH/C)

Conjuntura Econômica. Fundação Getúlio Vargas, Instituto Brasileiro de Economia. Rio de Janeiro. (FGV/CE)

Criterio. Editorial Criterio. Buenos Aires. (CRIT)

Croissance des Jeunes Nations. Paris. (CJN)

Cuadernos Afro-Americanos. Instituto de Antropología e Historia. Univ. Central de Venezuela. Caracas.

Cuadernos Americanos. México. (CAM)

Cuadernos de Economía. Univ. Católica de Chile. Santiago. (UCC/CE)

Cuadernos de la CVF. Corporación Venezolana de Fomento. Caracas. (CVF/C)

Cuadernos Hispanoamericanos. Instituto de Cultura Hispánica. Madrid. (CH)

Cuadernos Políticos. Revista trimestral. Ediciones Era. México. (CP)

Cuadernos Prehispánicos. Seminario Americanista de la Univ., Casa de Colón. Valladolid, Spain.

Cuadrante. Revista del Centro de Estudios Regionales. Buenos Aires.

Cuban Studies/Estudios Cubanos. Univ. of Pittsburgh, Univ. Center for International Studies, Center for Latin American Studies. Pittsburgh, Pa. (UP/CSEC)

Culture, Medicine, and Psychiatry. D. Reidel Dordrecht. The Netherlands.

Cultures. United Nations Educational, Scientific and Cultural Organization. Paris. (UNESCO/CU)

Cultures et Développement. Revue internationale des sciences du développement. Univ. Catholique de Louvain avec le concours de la Fondation Universitaire de Belgique. Louvain, Belgium. (UCL/CD)

Current Anthropology. Univ. of Chicago. Chicago, Ill. (UC/CA)

Current History. A monthly magazine of world affairs. Philadelphia. Pa. (CUH)

Daedalus. Journal of the American Academy of Arts and Sciences. Harvard Univ. Cambridge, Mass. (AAAS/D)

Debates en Antropología. Pontificia Univ. Católica del Perú, Depto. de Ciencias Sociales. Lima. (PUCP/DA)

Defensa Nacional. Revista del Centro de Altos Estudios Militares. Lima.

A Defesa Nacional. Revista de assuntos militares e estudo de problemas brasileiros. Rio de Janeiro. (ADN)

Demografía y Economía. El Colegio de México. México. (CM/DE)

Demography. Population Association of America. Washington. (PAA/D)

Desarrollo Económico. Instituto de Desarrollo Económico y Social. Buenos Aires. (IDES/DE)

Desarrollo Rural en las Américas. Organización de los Estados Americanos. Instituto Interamericano de Ciencias Agrícolas. Bogotá.

Desarrollo y Sociedad. Univ. de los Andes, Facultad de Economía, Centro de Estudios sobre el Desarrollo Económico. Bogotá. (CEDE/DS)

Deutsche Aussenpolitik. Institut für Internationale Beziehungen. Berlin, GDR. (IIB/DA)

Deutscher Geographentag. Franz Steiner Verlag. Wiesbaden, FRG.

The Developing Economies. The Journal of the Institute of Developing Economies. Tokyo. (IDE/DE)

Development Financing. Semiannual review of the Public Sector Program. Organization of American States, General Secretariat. Washington.

Developmental Medicine and Child Neurology. National Spastics Society, Medical Education and Information Unit. London.

Diálogos. Artes/Letras/Ciencias Humanas. El Colegio de México. México. (CM/D)

Digesto Econômico. Associação Comercial de São Paulo e Federação do Comércio do Estado de São Paulo. São Paulo.

Diogenes. International Council for Philosophy and Humanistic Studies. Chicago, Ill. (ICPHS/D)

Direct from Cuba. Prensa Latina. La Habana.

Dissent. Dissent Publishing Association. New York. (DIS)

Docencia. Univ. Autónoma de Guadalajara. Guadalajara, México. (UAG/D)

Docet. CELADEC, Centro de Documentación y Editorial. Lima.

Documentary Relations of the Southwest: Master Indexes. Arizona State Museum. Tucson.

El Dorado. Univ. of Northern Colorado, Museum of Anthropology. Greeley. (UNC/ED)

Die Dritte Welt. Verlag Anton Hain. Meisenheim, FRG. (DDW)

Early Man. Northwestern Archaeology, Inc. Evanston, Ill.

Eastern Economic Journal. Eastern Economic Association. Bloomsbury State College, Dept. of Economics. Bloomsbury, Pa.

Economía. Pontificia Univ. Católica del Perú, Depto. de Economía. Lima. (PUCP/E)

Economía Colombiana. Contraloría General de la República. Bogotá.

Economía de América Latina. Revista de información y análisis de la región. Centro de Investigación y Docencia Económicas (CIDE). México.

Economia Internazionale. Rivista dell'Istituto di Economia Internazionale. Genova, Italy. (IEI/EI)

Economía Mexicana: Análisis y Perspectivas. Centro de Investigación y Docencia Económica. Mexico.

Economía Política. Facultad de Ciencias Económicas. Univ. Autónoma de Honduras. Tegucigalpa.

Economía Política. Instituto Politécnico Nacional, Escuela Superior de Economía. México. (IPN/EP)

Economía y Ciencias Sociales. Univ. Central de Venezuela, Facultad de Economía. Caracas. (UCV/ECS)

Economía y Desarrollo. Univ. de La Habana, Instituto de Economía. La Habana. (UH/ED)

Economic Botany. Devoted to applied botany and plant utilization. *Published for* The Society for Economic Botany *by the* New Botanical Garden. New York. (SEB/EB)

Economic Development and Cultural Change. Univ. of Chicago, Research Center in Economic Development and Cultural Change. Chicago, Ill. (UC/EDCC)

Economic Geography. Clark Univ. Worcester, Mass. (CU/EG)

Economic Journal. Quarterly journal of the Royal Economic Society. London. (RES/EJ)

Económica. Univ. Nacional de La Plata, Facultad de Ciencias Económicas, Instituto de Investigaciones Económicas. La Plata, Argentina. (UNLP/E)

Educação e Realidade. Univ. Federal do Rio Grande do Sul, Faculdade de Educação. Porto Alegre, Brazil.

Educação e Sociedade. Revista quadrimestral de ciencias da educação. Centro de Estudos Educação e Sociedade. São Paulo.

La Educación. Revista interamericano de desarrollo educativo. Organization of American States, Secretaría General, Departamento de Asuntos Educativos. Washington. (OAS/LE)

Educación Hoy. Perspectivas Latinoamericanas. Bogotá.

La Educación Superior Contemporánea. Revista internacional de países socialistas. La Habana.

Encontros com a Civilização Brasileira. Rio de Janeiro.

Encuentro. Revista de la Univ. Centroamericana, Instituto Histórico. Managua. (UCA/E)

Ensayos Económicos. Banco Central de la República Argentina. Buenos Aires. (BCRA/EE)

Equinoxe. Revue guyanaise d'histoire et de geographie. Association des Professeurs d'Histoire et de Géographie (A.P.H.G.) de la Guyane *avec le concours du* Centre Départemental de Documentation Pédagogique (C.D.D.P.). Cayenne.

Die Erde. Zeitschrift der Gesellschaft für Erdkunde zur Berlin. Walter de Gruyter & Co. Berlin. (GEB/E)

Erdkunde. Archiv für Wissenschaftliche Geographie. Univ. Bonn, Geographisches Institut. Bonn. (UBGI/E)

Estadística. Journal of the Inter American Statistical Institute. Washington. (IASI/E)

Estados Unidos: Perspectiva Latinoamericana. Cuadernos semestrales. Centro de Investigación y Docencia Económica (CIDE). México. (EEUU/PL)

Estrategia. Instituto Argentino de Estudios Estratégicos y de las Relaciones Internacionales. Buenos Aires. (IAEERI/E)

Estudios. Instituto de Estudios Económicos sobre la Realidad Argentina y Latinoamericana. Córdoba. (IEERAL/E)

Estudios Andinos. Instituto Boliviano de Estudio y Acción Social. La Paz. (IBEAS/EA)

Estudios Andinos. Univ. del Pacífico. Lima.

Estudios Andinos. Univ. of Pittsburgh, Latin American Studies Center. Pittsburgh, Pa. (UP/EA)

Estudios Atacameños. Univ. del Norte, Museo de Arqueología. San Pedro de Atacama, Chile.

Estudios CEDES. Centro Estudios de Estado y Sociedad. Buenos Aires.

Estudios Centro-Americanos. Revista de extensión cultural. Univ. José Simeón Cañas. San Salvador. (UJSC/ECA)

Estudios Contemporáneos. Univ. Autónoma de Puebla. Puebla, México.

Estudios de Cultura Maya. Univ. Nacional Autónoma de México, Centro de Estudios Mayas. México. (CEM/ECM)

Estudios de Economía. Univ. de Chile, Facultad de Ciencias Económicas y Administrativas, Depto. de Economía. Santiago. (UC/EE)

Estudios de Población. Asociación Colombiana para el Estudio de la Población. Bogotá. (ACEP/EP)

Estudios del Tercer Mundo. Centro de Estudios Económicos y Sociales del Tercer Mundo. México. (EDTM)

Estudios Latinoamericanos. Polska Akademia Nauk (Academia de Ciencias de Polonia), Instytut Historii (Instituto de Historia). Warszawa. (PAN/ES)

Estudios Paraguayos. Univ. Católica Nuestra Señora de la Asunción. Asunción. (UCNSA/EP)

Estudios Rurales Latinoamericanos. Consejo Latinoamericano de Ciencias Sociales, Secretaría Ejecutiva y de la Comisión de Estudios Rurales. Bogotá. (CLACSO/ERL)

Estudios Sociales. Corporación de Promoción Universitaria. Santiago. (CPU/ES)

Estudios Sociales. Univ. Rafael Landívar, Instituto de Ciencias Políticas y Sociales. Guatemala. (URL/ES)

Estudios Sociales Centroamericanos. Consejo Superior de Universidades Centroamericanas, Confederación Universitaria Centroamericana, Programa Centroamericano de Ciencias Sociales. San José. (CSUCA/ECS)

Estudos Baianos. Univ. Federal da Bahia, Centro Editorial e Didático, Núcleo de Publicações. Bahia, Brazil. (UFB/EB)

Estudos Brasileiros. Univ. Federal do Paraná, Setor de Ciências Humanas, Centro de Estudos Brasileiros. Curitiba, Brazil. (UFP/EB)

Estudos Econômicos. Univ. de São Paulo, Instituto de Pesquisas Econômicas. São Paulo. (IPE/EE)

Estudos Leopoldenses. Faculdade de Filosofia, Ciências e Letras. São Leopoldo, Brazil.

Ethnic and Racial Studies. Routledge & Kegan Paul. London. (ERS)

Ethnicity. Academic Press. New York.

Ethnographisch-Archäologische Zeitschrift. Deutscher Verlag Wissenschaften. East Berlin. (EAZ)

Ethnology. Plenum. New York.

Ethnology. Univ. of Pittsburgh. Pittsburgh, Pa. (UP/E)

Ethnomedicine. Arbeits Gemeinschaft Ethnomedizin and H. Buskeverlag. Hamburg, FRG.

Ethnomusicology. Society of Ethnomusicology. Middleton, Conn.

Ethnos. Statens Ethnografiska Museum.
Stockholm. (SEM/E)

Ethos. Society for Psychological Anthropology. Washington.

Etnía. Museo Etnográfico Municipal Dámaso
Arce. Municipalidad de Olavarría, Provincia
de Buenos Aires, Argentina. (MEMDA/E)

Études Littéraires. Press de l'Université
Laval. Quebec.

Explorers Journal. New York. (EJ)

Federal Bar Journal. Federal Bar Association.
Washington. (FBA/FBJ)

F.E.P.A. Estudios e Investigaciones. Fundación para el Estudio de los Problemas Argentinos. Buenos Aires. (FEPA/EI)

The Florida Anthropologist. Florida Anthropological Society. Gainesville.

The Florida Historical Quarterly. The Florida
Historical Society. Jacksonville. (FHS/FHQ)

Folia Humanística. Ciencias, artes, letras.
Editorial Galerna. Barcelona. (FH)

Folklore Americano. Instituto Panamericano
de Geografía e Historia, Comisión de
Historia, Comité de Folklore. México.
(IPGH/FA)

Foreign Affairs. Council on Foreign Relations.
New York. (CFR/FA)

Foreign Policy. National Affairs, Inc. and Carnegie Endowment for International Peace.
New York. (FP)

Foro Internacional. El Colegio de México.
México. (CM/FI)

Forum Educacional. Fundação Getúlio
Vargas, Instituto de Estudos Avançados em
Educação. Rio de Janeiro.

Franciscanum. Revista de las ciencias del espíritu. Univ. de San Buenaventura. Bogotá.
(USB/F)

Freedom at Issue. Freedom House. New York.

Geografiska Annaler. Svenska Sällskapet för
Antropologi och Geografi. Stockholm.
(SSAG/GA)

Geographica Helvetica. Schweizerische
Zeitschrift für Länder-und Völkerkunde.
Kümmerly & Frey, Geographischer Verlag.
Bern. (GH)

The Geographical Magazine. London. (GM)

The Geographical Review. American Geographical Society. New York. (AGS/GR)

Geographische Rundschau. Zeitschrift für
Schulgeographie. Georg Westermann
Verlag. Braunschweig, Germany. (GR)

Geographische Zeitschrift. Franz Steiner
Verlag. Wiesbaden, Germany. (GZ)

Geologische Rundschau. Internationale
Zeitschrift für Geologie. Geologische
Vereinigung. Ferdinand Enke Verlag. Stutt-
gart, Germany. (GV/GR)

GeoJournal. Akademische Verlagsgesellschaft. Wiesbaden, FRG.

Geopolítica. Instituto Uruguayo de Estudios
Geopolíticos. Montevideo.

Granma. La Habana.

Graphis. International journal of graphic art
and applied art. The Graphis Press. Zürich.

Guatemala Indígena. Instituto Indigenista
Nacional. Guatemala. (GIIN/GI)

Guyanese National Bibliography. National
Library of Guyana. Georgetown.

Hemoglobin. Marcel Dekker Journals. New
York.

Hispanic American Historical Review. Duke
Univ. Press *for the* Conference on Latin
American History of the American Histor-
ical Association. Durham, N.C. (HAHR)

Historia. Revista/libro trimestral. Buenos
Aires.

Historia Mexicana. El Colegio de México.
México. (CM/HM)

Histórica. Pontificia Univ. Católica del Perú,
Depto. de Humanidades. Lima. (PUCP/H)

Historiografía y Bibliografía Americanista.
Escuela de Estudios Hispanoamericanos de
Sevilla. Sevilla. (EEHA/HBA)

L'Homme. Revue française d'anthropologie.
La Sorbonne, l'École Pratique des Hautes
Études. Paris. (EPHE/H)

Horizonte. Univ. Federal de Paraíba. João
Pessoa, Brazil.

Human Biology. Official publication of the
Human Biology Council. Wayne State
Univ., School of Medicine. Detroit, Mich.
(WSU/HB)

Human Ecology. Plenum. New York.

Human Genetics. Excepta Medica Foundation. Amsterdam.

Human Heredity. Basel, Switzerland. (HH)

Human Organization. Society for Applied
Anthropology. New York. (SAA/HO)

Ibero Americana. Scandinavian Association
for Research on Latin America. Stockholm.
(NOSALF/IA)

Ibero-Americana. Univ. of California Press.
Berkeley. (UC/I)

Ibero-Americana Pragensia. Univ. Carolina de Praga, Centro de Estudios Ibero-
Americanos. Prague. (UCP/IAP)

Ibero-Amerikanisches Archiv. Ibero-
Amerikanisches Institut. Berlin, FRG.
(IAA)

Indiana. Beiträge zur Volker-und Sprachenkunde, Archäologie und Anthropologie
des Indianischen Amerika. Ibero-
Amerikanisches Institut. Berlin, FRG.
(IAI/I)

Indice de Artículos sobre Capacitación y
Adiestramiento. Servicio Nacional de
Adiestramiento Rápido de la Mano de Obra
en la Industria (ARMO). México.

Indice de Ciências Sociais. Boletim bibliográfico semestral. Instituto Universitário
de Pesquisas do Rio de Janeiro. Rio de
Janeiro.

Industrial and Labor Relations Review. A
publication of the New York School of Industrial and Labor Relations, a Contract
College of the State Univ., Cornell Univ.
Ithaca. (CU/ILRR)

Information Geographique. Paris. (IG)

Integración Latinoamericana. Instituto para
la Integración de América Latina. Buenos
Aires. (INTAL/IL)

Inter-American Economic Affairs. Washington. (IAMEA)

Interciencia. Asociación Interciencia. Caracas. (AI/I)

International Affairs. A monthly journal of
political analysis. Moskova. (IA)

International Affairs. The Royal Institute of
International Affairs. London. (RIIA/IA)

International Affairs Bulletin. The South African Institute of International Affairs.
Johannesburg.

International Journal. Canadian Institute of
International Affairs. Toronto. (CIIA/IJ)

International Journal of Intercultural Relations. Society for Intercultural Education
Training and Research. Purdue, Indiana.

International Journal of Social Psychiatry.
London. (IJSP)

International Journal of the Sociology of Law.
London.

International Migration (Migrations Internationales = Migraciones Internacionales).
Quarterly review of the Intergovernmental
Committee for European Migration and
the Research Group for European Migration Problems. Geneva, Switzerland.
(ICEM/IM)

International Migration Review. Center for
Migration Studies. New York. (CMS/IMR)

International Review of Administrative Sciences. International Institute of Administrative Sciences. Bruxelles. (IIAS/IRAS)

International Review of Education. United
Nations Educational, Scientific, and Cul-
tural Organization, Institute for Education.
Hamburg, FRG. (UNESCO/IRE)

International Social Science Journal. United
Nations Educational, Scientific, and Cultural Organization. Paris. (UN/ISSJ)

IREBI. Indices de revistas de bibliotecología.
Oficina de Educación Iberoamericana.
Madrid.

Islas. Univ. Central de las Villas. Santa Clara,
Cuba. (UCLV/I)

Istmo. Revista del pensamiento actual.
México. (ISTMO)

Itaytera. Instituto Cultural do Cariri. Crato,
Brazil. (ICC/I)

Jahrbuch des Museums für Völkerkunde zu
Leipzig. Berlin. (MVL/J)

Jahrbuch des öffentlichen Rechts der
Gegenwart. J.C.B. Mohr—Paul Siebeck.
Tübingen.

Jahrbuch für Geschichte von Staat, Wirtschaft und Gesellschaft Lateinamerikas.
Köln, FRG. (JGSWGL)

Jamaica Journal. Institute of Jamaica. Kingston. (IJ/JJ)

Jamaican National Bibliography. National Library of Jamaica, Institute of Jamaica.
Kingston.

The Jewish Journal of Sociology. The World
Jewish Community. London. (WJC/JJS)

Journal de la Société des Américanistes.
Paris. (SA/J)

Journal of American Folklore. American
Folklore Society. Austin, Tex. (AFS/JAF)

Journal of Anthropological Research. Univ. of
New Mexico, Dept. of Anthropology. Albuquerque. (UNM/JAR)

Journal of Belizean Affairs. Belize City. (JBA)

Journal of Biosocial Science. Blackwell Scientific Publications. Oxford, England.

Journal of Caribbean Studies. Association of
Caribbean Studies. Coral Gables, Fla.

Journal of Common Market Studies. Oxford,
England. (JCMS)

Journal of Commonwealth and Comparative
Politics. Univ. of London, Institute of
Commonwealth Studies. London. (ICS/
JCCP)

The Journal of Developing Areas. Western
Illinois Univ. Press. Macomb. (JDA)

Journal of Development Economics. North
Holland Publishing Co. Amsterdam. (JDE)

The Journal of Development Studies. A quarterly journal devoted to economics, politics and social development. London. (JDS)

Journal of Economic History. New York
Univ., Graduate School of Business Ad-

ministration *for* The Economic History Association. Rensselaer. (EHA/J)

The Journal of Economic Literature. American Economic Association. Nashville, Tenn.

Journal of Economic Studies. Glasgow, Scotland.

Journal of Environmental Health. National Association of Sanitarians. Denver, Colo.

Journal of Ethnic Studies. College of Ethnic Studies, Western Washington State College. Bellingham.

Journal of Ethnopharmacology. Elsevier Sequoia. Lausanne, Switzerland.

Journal of European Economic History. Banco de Roma. Rome.

Journal of Family History. Studies in family, kinship and demography. National Council on Family Relations. Minneapolis, Minn. (NCFR/JFH)

Journal of Field Archaeology. Boston Univ. Boston, Mass.

Journal of Human Evolution. Academic Press. London.

Journal of Information Science, Librarianship and Archives Administration. *See* UNESCO Journal of Information Science, Librarianship and Archives Administration.

Journal of Inter-American Studies and World Affairs. Sage Publications *for the* Center for Advanced International Studies, Univ. of Miami. Coral Gables, Fla. (SAGE/JIAS)

The Journal of Interdisciplinary History. The MIT Press. Cambridge, Mass. (JIH)

Journal of International Affairs. Columbia Univ., School of International Affairs. New York. (CU/JIA)

Journal of International Law and Economics. George Washington Univ., The National Law Center. Washington. (GWU/JILE)

The Journal of Japanese Studies. The Society for Japanese Studies. Univ. of Washington. Seattle.

Journal of Latin American Lore. Univ. of California, Latin American Center. Los Angeles. (UCLA/JLAL)

Journal of Latin American Studies. Centers or institutes of Latin American studies at the universities of Cambridge, Glasgow, Liverpool, London and Oxford. Cambridge Univ. Press. London. (JLAS)

Journal of Marriage and the Family. Western Reserve Univ. Cleveland, Ohio. (WRU/JMF)

Journal of Peace Research. Edited at the International Peace Research Institute. Universitetforlaget. Oslo. (JPR)

Journal of Peasant Studies. Frank Cass & Co. London. (JPS)

Journal of Political and Military Sociology. Northern Illinois Univ., Dept. of Sociology. DeKalb. (NIU/JPMS)

Journal of Political Economy. Univ. of Chicago. Chicago, Ill. (JPE)

The Journal of Politics. The Southern Political Science Association *in cooperation with the* Univ. of Florida. Gainesville. (SPSA/JP)

Journal of Psychological Anthropology. Association of Psychohistory. New York.

The Journal of Risk and Insurance. American Risk and Insurance Association. Bloomington, Ill. (ARIAI/JRI)

The Journal of Social and Political Studies. Council on American Affairs. Washington.

Journal of Social Psychology. The Journal Press. Provincetown, Mass. (JSP)

The Journal of Taxation. Journal of Taxation, Inc. New York. (JT)

Journal of the Hellenic Diaspora. Pella Publishing Co. New York.

Journal of the Virgin Islands Archaeological Society. Frederickstad, St. Croix.

The Journal of Tropical Geography. Univ. of Singapore and Univ. of Malaya, Depts. of Geography. Singapore. (USM/JTG)

Journalism Quarterly. Association for Education in Journalism *with the cooperation of the* American Association of Schools, Depts. of Journalism and Kappa Tau Alpha Society. Univ. of Minnesota. Minneapolis. (AEJ/JQ)

Katunob. Univ. of Northern Colorado, Museum of Anthropology. Greeley. (UNC/K)

Kroeber Anthropological Society Papers. Univ. of California. Berkeley. (KAS/P)

Landscape. Published three times a year. Santa Fe, N. Mex. (LAND)

Lateinamerika. Univ. Rostock. Rostock, GDR. (UR/L)

Latin America 1978. Facts on File, Inc. New York.

Latin American Digest. Arizona State Univ., Center for Latin American Studies. Tempe. (ASU/LAD)

Latin American Perspectives. Univ. of California. Riverside. (LAP)

Latin American Research Review. Univ. of North Carolina Press *for the* Latin American Studies Association. Chapel Hill. (LARR)

Latinoamérica. Anuario de estudios latinoamericanos. Univ. Nacional Autónoma de

México, Facultad de Filosofía y Letras, Centro de Estudios Latinoamericanos. México. (UNAM/L)

Lecturas del CEESTEM. Centro de Estudios Económicos y Sociales del Tercer Mundo. México. (CEESTEM/L)

Lexis. Revista de lingüística y literatura. Pontificia Univ. Católica del Perú, Lima. (PUC/L)

Lotería. Lotería Nacional de Beneficencia. Panamá. (LNB/L)

Luso Brazilian Review. Univ. of Wisconsin Press. Madison. (UW/LBR)

Man. A monthly record of anthropological science. The Royal Anthropological Institute. London. (RAI/M)

Mapocho. Biblioteca Nacional, Extensión Cultural. Santiago. (EC/M)

Marxist Perspectives. Transaction Periodicals Consortium. Rutgers Univ. New Brunswick, N.J. (RU/MP)

Medical Anthropology. Redgrave. Pleasantville, N.Y.

Medical Anthropology Newsletter. Society for Medical Anthropology. Washington.

Mesoamérica. Revista del Centro de Investigaciones Regionales de Mesoamérica. La Antigua, Guatemala.

México Indigena. Organo de Difusión del Instituto Nacional Indigenista. Distribuidor: Porrúa Hnos. México.

Mexicon. Berlin, FRG.

Modern Language Journal. The National Federation of Modern Language Teachers Association. Univ. of Pittsburgh. Pittsburgh, Pa. (MLTA/MLJ)

Monetaria. Centro de Estudios Monetarios Latinoamericanos. México. (CEMLA/M)

Monthly Labor Review. United States Dept. of Labor. Washington. (USDL/MLR)

Monthly Review. An independent Socialist magazine. New York. (MR)

Mother Jones. Foundation for National Progress. San Francisco.

NACLA: Report on the Americas. North American Congress on Latin America. New York. (NACLA)

NACLA's Latin America & Empire Report. North American Congress on Latin America. New York. (NACLA/LAER)

National Geographic Magazine. National Geographic Society. Washington. (NGS/NGM)

Natura. Revista de divulgación científica. Sociedad de Ciencias Naturales de La Salle. Caracas.

Natural History. American Museum of Natural History. New York. (AMNH/NH)

Nature. A weekly journal of science. Macmillan & Co. London. (NWJS)

Ñawpa Pacha. Institute of Andean Studies. Berkeley, Calif. (IAS/ÑP)

The New Republic. Washington.

The New Scholar. Univ. of California, Center for Iberian and Latin American Studies and Institute of Chicano Urban Affairs. San Diego. (UCSD/NS)

The New York Review of Books. New York. (NYRB)

The New York Times Magazine. New York.

The New Yorker. New York.

Nexos. Sociedad, ciencia, literatura. Centro de Investigación Cultural y Científica. México.

Nicaráuac. Revista bimestral del Ministerio de Cultura. Managua. (NMC/N)

Nieuwe West-Indische Gids. Martinus Nijhoff. The Hague. (NWIG)

Norte Grande. Revista de estudios integrados referentes a comunidades humanas del Norte Grande de Chile, en una perspectiva geográfica e histórica-cultural. Univ. Católica de Chile, Instituto de Geografía, Depto. de Geografía de Chile, Taller Norte Grande. Santiago. (UCC/NG)

Notes et Études Documentaires. Direction de la Documentation. Paris. (FDD/NED)

La Nouvelle Revue des Deux Mondes. Paris. (NRDM)

Nova Americana. Giulio Einaudi Editore. Torino, Italy. (GEE/NA)

NS NorthSouth NordSud NorteSur NorteSur NorteSul. Canadian journal of Latin American studies. Canadian Association of Latin American Studies. Univ. of Ottawa. Ottawa. (NS)

Nueva Sociedad. Revista política y cultural. San José. (NSO)

Numen. International review for the history of religions. International Association for the History of Religions. Leiden, The Netherlands. (IAHR/N)

Oceanus. Oceanographic Institution. Wood Hole, Mass. (OCEANUS)

OCLAE. Revista mensual de la Organización Continental Latinoamericana de Estudiantes. La Habana. (OCLAE)

Omega. Journal of death and dying. Baywood Publishing Co. Farmingdale, N.Y.

Orbis. A journal of world affairs. Foreign Policy Research Institute, Philadelphia, Pa. *in association with the* Fletcher School of

Law and Diplomacy, Tufts Univ. Medford, Mass. (FPRI/O)

Ornament. A quarterly of jewelry and personal adornment. Los Angeles.

Oxford Economic Papers. Oxford Univ. Press. London. (OUP/OEP)

Pacific Sociological Review. Pacific Sociological Association. San Diego State Univ. San Diego, Calif. (PSA/PSR)

Paideuma. Mitteilungen zur Kulturkunde. Deutsche Gesellschaft für kulturmorphologie von Frobenius Institut au der Johann Wolfgang Goethe—Universität. Wiesbaden, Germany. (PMK)

El Palacio. School of American Research, the Museum of New Mexico, and the Archaeological Society of New Mexico. Santa Fe. (SAR/P)

Palaeogeography, Palaeoclimatology, Palaeoecology. Elsevier Scientific Publishing Co. New York.

Panorama Anual. Bolsa de Valores, Asesoría Estadística. Montevideo.

Papers in Anthropology. Dept. of Anthropology, Univ. of Oklahoma. Norman.

Past and Present. London. (PP)

Pensamiento y Acción. Editora Lautaro. Santiago.

Pesquisa e Planejamento Econômico. Instituto de Planejamento Econômico e Social. Rio de Janeiro. (IPEA/PPE)

Pesquisas. Anuário do Instituto Anchietano de Pesquisas. Porto Alegre. (IAP/P)

Petermanns Geographische Mitteilungen. Geographische-Kartoggraphische Anstalt. Gotha, Germany. (PGM)

Philologica Pragensia. Academia Scientiarum Bohemoslovenica. Praha. (ASB/PP)

Phylon. Atlanta Univ. Atlanta, Ga. (AU/P)

Plerus. Planificación económica rural urbana y social. Univ. de Puerto Rico. Río Piedras. (UPR/P)

Política y Sociedad. Univ. de San Carlos de Guatemala, Facultad de Ciencias Jurídicas y Sociales, Escuela de Ciencias Política, Instituto de Investigaciones Políticas y Sociales. Guatemala. (USCG/PS)

Population. Institut National d'Études Démographiques. Paris. (INED/P)

Population Studies. London School of Economics, The Population Investigation Committee. London. (LSE/PS)

Prehistoria Bonaerense. Olavarría, Provincia Buenos Aires, Argentina.

Problemas del Desarrollo. Univ. Nacional Autónoma de México, Instituto de Investigaciones Económicas. México. (UNAM/PDD)

Problems of Communism. United States Information Agency. Washington. (USIA/PC)

Proceedings. United States Naval Institute. Annapolis, Md.

Proceedings of the National Academy of Sciences. Washington. (NAS/P)

Proceedings of the Pacific Coast Council on Latin American Studies. Univ. of California. Los Angeles. (PCCLAS/P)

Professional Geographer. Journal of The Association of American Geographers. Washington. (AAG/PG)

Publishers Weekly. New York.

Puntos de Vista. Centro de Estudios Económicos y Sociales. San Luis Potosí.

Purun Pacha. Instituto Andino de Estudios Arqueológicos. Lima.

Quehacer. Realidad nacional: problemas y alternativas. Revista del Centro de Estudios y Promoción del Desarrollo (DESCO). Lima. (DESCO/Q)

Race and Class. A journal of black and Third World liberation. Institute of Race Relations and The Transnational Institute. London. (IRR/RC)

Realidad Contemporánea. Editora Alfa y Omega. Santo Domingo.

Relaciones. Estudios de historia y sociedad. El Colegio de Michoacán. Zamora, México. (CM/RE)

Relaciones de la Sociedad Argentina de Antropología. Buenos Aires. (SAA/R)

Relaciones Internacionales. Revista del Centro de Relaciones Internacionales. Univ. Nacional Autónoma de México, Facultad de Ciencias Políticas y Sóciales. México. (UNAM/RI)

Report. Minority Rights Group. London.

Res Publica. Claremont Men's College. Claremont, Calif.

Resúmenes Analíticos en Educación. Centro de Investigación y Desarrollo de la Educación. Santiago.

Review of Black Political Economy. National Economic Association and Atlanta Univ. Center. Atlanta, Ga. (NEA/RBPE)

Review of Economics and Statistics. Harvard Univ. Cambridge, Mass. (HU/RES)

Review of Politics. Univ. of Notre Dame. Notre Dame, Ind. (UND/RP)

Revista Antioqueña de Economía. Medellín, Colombia. (RAE)

Revista Brasileira de Cultura. Ministério da Educação e Cultura, Conselho Federal de Cultura. Rio de Janeiro. (CFC/RBC)

Revista Brasileira de Economia. Fundação Getúlio Vargas, Instituto Brasileiro de Economia. Rio de Janeiro. (IBE/RBE)

Revista Brasileira de Estatística. Ministério do Planejamento e Coordenação Geral, Instituto Brasileiro de Geografia e Estatística. Rio de Janeiro. (IBGE/RBE)

Revista Brasileira de Estudos Pedagógicos. Instituto Nacional de Estudos Pedagógicos. Centro Brasileiro de Pesquisas Educacionais. Rio de Janeiro. (INEP/RBEP)

Revista Brasileira de Estudos Políticos. Univ. de Minas Gerais. Belo Horizonte, Brazil. (UMG/RBEP)

Revista Brasileira de Geografia. Conselho Nacional de Geografia, Instituto Brasileiro de Geografia e Estatística. Rio de Janeiro. (IBGE/R)

Revista Brasileira de Mercado de Capitais. Instituto Brasileiro de Mercado de Capitais. Rio de Janeiro. (RBMC)

Revista Brasileira de Política Internacional. Instituto Brasileiro de Relações Internacionais. Rio de Janeiro. (IERI/R)

Revista Cartográfica. Instituto Panamericano de Geografía e Historia, Comisión de Cartografía. México. (PAIGH/RC)

Revista Centroamericana de Economía. Univ. Nacional Autónoma de Honduras, Programa de Postgrado Centroamericano en Economía y Planificación. Tegucigalpa. (UNAH/RCE)

Revista CERLAL. Bogotá.

Revista Chilena de Antropología. Univ. de Chile, Depto. de Antropología. Santiago.

Revista Chilena de Historia y Geografía. Sociedad Chilena de Historia y Geografía. Santiago. (SCHG/R)

Revista Coahuilense de Historia. Colegio Coahuilense de Investigaciones Históricas. Saltillo, México.

Revista Colombiana de Antropología. Ministerio de Educación Nacional, Instituto Colombiano de Antropología. Bogotá. (ICA/RCA)

Revista Colombiana de Educación. Univ. Pedagógica Nacional, Centro de Investigaciones. Bogotá. (UPN/RCE)

Revista Colombiana de Sociología. Depto. de Sociología, Univ. Nacional. Bogotá.

Revista de Administração Municipal. Instituto Brasileiro de Administração Municipal. Rio de Janeiro.

Revista de Administración Pública. Univ. de Puerto Rico. Río Piedras. (UPR/RAP)

Revista de Antropologia. Univ. de São Paulo, Faculdade de Filosofia, Letras e Ciências Humanas and Associação Brasileira de Antropologia. São Paulo. (USP/RA)

Revista de CEPA. Associação Pró-Ensino em Santa Cruz do Sul, Brazil.

Revista de Ciência Política. Fundação Getúlio Vargas. Rio de Janeiro. (FGV/R)

Revista de Ciencia Política. Instituto de Ciencia Política, Pontificia Univ. Católica de Chile. Santiago.

Revista de Ciencias Sociales. Univ. de Puerto Rico, Colegio de Ciencias Sociales. Río Piedras. (UPR/RCS)

Revista de Colegio de Abogados. Colegio de Abogados de Puerto Rico. San Juan? (CAPR/RCA)

Revista de Economía Latinoamericana. Banco Central de Venezuela. Caracas. (BCV/REL)

Revista de Estudios Agro-Sociales. Instituto de Estudios Agro-Sociales. Madrid. (IEAS/R)

Revista de Historia. Univ. Nacional de Costa Rica, Escuela de Historia. Heredia. (UNCR/R)

Revista de Indias. Instituto Gonzalo Fernández de Oviedo and Consejo Superior de Investigaciones Científicas. Madrid. (IGFO/RI)

Revista de Integración. Banco Interamericano de Desarrollo. Washington. (BID/INTAL)

Revista de la Academia Hondureña de Geografía e Historia. Tegucigalpa. (AHGH/R)

Revista de la Biblioteca Nacional José Martí. La Habana. (BNJM/R)

Revista de la CEPAL. *See* CEPAL.

Revista de la Facultad de Derecho. Univ. Nacional Autónoma de México. México. (UNAM/RFD)

Revista de la Sociedad Mexicana de Historia Natural. México. (SMHN/R)

Revista de la Universidad de Yucatán. Mérida, México. (UY/R)

Revista de Occidente. Madrid. (RO)

Revista de Oriente. Univ. de Puerto Rico, Colegio Universitario de Humacao. Humacao. (UPR/RO)

Revista de Pré-História. Univ. de São Paulo, Instituto de Pré-História. São Paulo.

Revista del Centro de Investigaciones Arqueológicas de Alta Montaña. San Juan, Argentina.

Revista del Instituto de Antropología. Univ. Nacional de Córdoba. Córdoba, Argentina. (UNCIA/R)

Revista del Instituto de Antropología. Univ. Nacional de Tucumán. San Miguel de Tucumán, Argentina. (UNTIA/R)

Revista del México Agrario. Confederación Nacional Campesina. México. (CNC/RMA)

Revista del Museo de Historia Natural de San Rafael. San Rafael, Argentina.

Revista del Museo de La Plata. Univ. Nacional de La Plata, Facultad de Ciencias Naturales y Museo. La Plata, Argentina. (UNLPM/R)

Revista del Museo Nacional. Casa de la Cultura del Perú, Museo Nacional de la Cultura Peruana. Lima. (PEMN/R)

Revista del Pensamiento Centroamericano. Centro de Investigaciones y Actividades Culturales. Managua. (RCPC)

Revista do Arquivo Municipal. Prefeitura do Município de São Paulo, Depto. Municipal de Cultura. São Paulo. (AM/R)

Revista do Instituto de Estudos Brasileiros. Univ. de São Paulo, Instituto de Estudos Brasileiros. São Paulo. (USP/RIEB)

Revista do Instituto de Filosofia e Ciências Humanas. Univ. Federal do Rio Grande do Sul. Porto Alegre. (IFCH/R)

Revista do Instituto Histórico e Geográfico Brasileiro. Rio de Janeiro. (IHGB/R)

Revista do Museu Paulista. São Paulo. (MP/R)

Revista Dominicana de Antropología e Historia. Univ. Autónoma de Santo Domingo, Facultad de Humanidades, Depto. de Historia y Antropología, Instituto de Investigaciones Antropológicas. Santo Domingo. (UASD/U)

Revista Econômica do Nordeste. Banco do Nordeste do Brasil, Depto. de Estudos Econômicos do Nordeste. Fortaleza, Brazil. (BNB/REN)

Revista Eme-Eme. Estudios dominicanos. Univ. Católica Madre y Maestra. Santiago de los Caballeros, Dominican Republic. (EME)

Revista Estadística. Comité Estatal de Estadísticas. La Habana.

Revista Geográfica. Instituto Geográfico Militar del Ecuador, Depto. Geográfico. Quito. (IGME/RG)

Revista Geográfica. Instituto Panamericano de Geografía e Historia, Comisión de Geografía. México. (PAIGH/G)

Revista Geográfica. Univ. de Los Andes. Mérida, Venezuela. (ULA/RG)

Revista Interamericana. Interamerican Univ. of Puerto Rico. Río Piedras? (IAUPR/RI)

Revista Interamericana de Bibliografía (Inter-American Review of Bibliography). Organization of American States. Washington. (RIB)

Revista Interamericana de Psicología (Interamerican Journal of Psychology). Sociedad Interamericana de Psicología (Interamerican Society of Psychology). De Paul Univ., Dept. of Psychology. Chicago, Ill. (SIP/RIP)

Revista Internacional de Sociología. Consejo Superior de Investigaciones Científicas. Instituto Balmes de Sociología. Madrid. (CSIC/RIS)

Revista Latinoamericana de Estudios Educativos. Centro de Estudios Educativos. México. (CEE/RL)

Revista Latinoamericana de Psicología. Bogotá. (RLP)

Revista Mexicana de Ciencias Políticas y Sociales. Univ. Nacional Autónoma de México, Facultad de Ciencias Políticas y Sociales. México. (UNAM/RMCPS)

Revista Mexicana de Sociología. Univ. Nacional Autónoma de México, Instituto de Investigaciones Sociales. México. (UNAM/RMS)

Revista Paraguaya de Sociología. Centro Paraguayo de Estudios Sociológicos. Asunción. (CPES/RPS)

Revista/Review Interamericana. Univ. Interamericana. San Germán, Puerto Rico. (RRI)

Revista Universidad de Sonora. Depto. de Extensión Universitaria, Sección de Publicaciones, Edificio de la Rectoría. Sonora, México.

Revista Universitaria. Anales de la Academia Chilena de Ciencias Naturales. Univ. Católica de Chile. Santiago. (UCC/RU)

Revue Française de Science Politique. Fondation Nationale des Sciences Politiques, l'Assocation Française de Science Politique *avec le concours du* Centre National de la Recherche Scientifique. Paris. (FNSP/RFSP)

RF Illustrated. The Rockefeller Foundation. New York.

Santiago. Univ. de Oriente. La Habana.

Sapiens. Museo Arqueológico Dr. Osvaldo F.A. Menghin. Chivilcoy, Provincia Buenos Aires, Argentina.

Sarance. Revista del Instituto Otavaleño de Antropología. Otavalo, Ecuador.

Science. American Association for the Advancement of Science. Washington. (AAAS/S)

Science and Society. New York. (SS)

Scientific Yearbook of the School of Law and Economics. Aristotelian Univ. of Salonica. Salonica, Greece.

Signs. Journal of women in culture and society. The Univ. of Chicago Press. Chicago, Ill. (UC/S)

Síntesis Geográfica. Univ. Central de Venezuela, Facultad de Humanidades, Escuela de Geografía. Caracas.

Social and Economic Studies. Univ. of the West Indies, Institute of Social and Economic Research. Mona, Jamaica. (UWI/SES)

Social Biology. Society for the Study of Social Biology. New York.

Social Compass. International review of socio-religious studies (Revue internationale des études socio-religieuses). International Federation of Institutes for Social and Socio-Religious Research (Fédération International des Institutes des Recherches Sociales et Socio-Religieuses /FERES/). The Hague. (FERES/SC)

Social Forces. *Published for the* Univ. of North Carolina Press *by the* Williams & Wilkins Co. Baltimore, Md. (SF)

Social Problems. Society for the Study of Social Problems *affiliated with the* American and International Sociological Associations. Kalamazoo, Mich. (SSSP/SP)

Social Science and Medicine. Medical anthropology. Pergamon Press. Oxford, England.

Social Science and Medicine. New York.

The Social Science Journal. Colorado State Univ., Western Social Science Association. Fort Collins.

Social Sciences. USSR Academy of Science, Section of the Social Sciences. Moscow. (USSR/SS)

Society. Social science and modern society. Transaction, Rutgers—The State Univ. New Brunswick, N.J.

Sociological Review. Univ. of Keele. Staffordshire, England. (UK/SR)

Sociologus. Zeitschrift für empirische Soziologie, sozialpsychologische und ethnologische Forschung (A journal for empirical sociology, social psychology and ethnic research). Berlin. (SOCIOL)

Sociology and Social Research. An international journal. Univ. of Southern California. University Park. (USC/SSR)

Southern Economic Journal. Univ. of North Carolina. Chapel Hill.

Soviet Geography: Review and Translation.

American Geographical Society. New York. (AGS/SG)

Staff Papers. International Monetary Fund. Washington. (IMF/SP)

Statistical Abstract of Latin America. Univ. of California, Latin American Center. Los Angeles.

Stichting Surinaams Museum. Paramaribo.

Studia Diplomatica. Chronique de politique etrangère. Institut Royal des Relations Internationales. Bruxelles. (IRRI/SD)

Studies in Comparative Communism. An international interdisciplinary journal. Univ. of Southern California, School of International Relations, Von Klein Smid Institute of International Affairs. Los Angeles. (USC/SCC)

Studies in Comparative International Development. Rutgers Univ. New Brunswick, N.J. (RU/SCID)

Stylo. Revista de ciencia, arte y literatura. Pontificia Univ. Católica de Chile. Temuco.

Suplemento Antropológico. Univ. Católica de Nuestra Señora de la Asunción, Centro de Estudios Antropológicos. Asunción. (UCNSA/SA)

The Tax Magazine. Commerce Clearing House. Chicago, Ill. (CCH/TTM)

Technology and Conservation Magazine. The Technology Organization, Inc. Boston, Mass.

Temas en la Crisis. La Paz.

Tercer Mundo y Economía Mundial. Centro de Estudios Económicos y Sociales del Tercer Mundo. México. (CEESTM/TM)

Terra Ameriga. Associazione Italiana Studi Americanistici. Genova, Italy.

Texas International Law Journal. Univ. of Texas, School of Law. Austin.

Thesaurus. Boletín del Instituto Caro y Cuervo. Bogotá. (ICC/T)

Thesis. Nueva revista de filosofía y letras. Universidad Nacional Autónoma de México. México.

Tiers Monde. Problèmes des pays sous-développés. Univ. de Paris, Institut d'Étude de Développement Économique et Social. Paris. (UP/TM)

Tijdschrift voor Economische en Sociale Geographie. Netherlands Journal of Economic and Social Geography. Rotterdam. (TESG)

Tlalocan. Revista de fuentes para el conocimiento de las culturas indígenas de México.

Univ. Nacional Autónoma de México, Instituto de Investigaciones Antropológicas, Instituto de Investigaciones Históricas. México.

La Torre de Papel. Revista bimestral de literatura, arte, ciencia y filosofía. Buenos Aires.

Transactions and Papers. Institute of British Geographers. London.

Trauvaux et Documents de Géographie Tropicale. Centre National de la Recherche Scientifique, Centre d'Études de Géographie Tropicale. Bordeaux, France.

Tribus. Veröffentlichungen des Linden-Museums. Museum für Länderund Völkerkunde. Stuttgart, FRG.

El Trimestre Económico. Fondo de Cultura Económica. México. (FCE/TE)

Tropical Agriculture. Univ. of the West Indies, Imperial College of Tropical Agriculture and IPC Science and Technology Press, Ltd. Surrey, England.

UNESCO Journal of Information Science, Librarianship and Archives Administration. United Nations Educational, Scientific, and Cultural Organization. Paris. (UNESCO/JIS)

United States Views of Mexico. A quarterly review of opinion from the United States Press and The Congressional Record. Banamex Cultural Foundation. Washington.

Universidad. Univ. de Antioquia. Medellín, Colombia. (UA/U)

Universidad. Univ. Nacional del Litoral. Santa Fe, Argentina. (UNL/U)

Universidad de San Carlos de Guatemala. Guatemala. (USC/U)

Universidad Pontificia Bolivariana. Medellín, Colombia. (UPB)

Universidades. Unión de Universidades de América Latina. México. (UUAL/U)

Universitas. Ciencias jurídicas y socioeconómicas. Pontificia Univ. Javeriana, Facultad de Derecho y Ciencias Socioeconómicas. Bogotá. (PUJ/U)

Universitas Humanistica. Pontificia Univ. Javeriana, Facultad de Filosofía y Letras. Bogotá. (PUJ/UH)

L'Universo. Rivista bimestrale dell'Istituto Geografico Militare. Firenze, Italy. (IGM/U)

Urban Anthropology. State Univ. of New York, Dept. of Anthropology. Brockport. (UA)

Veritas. Revista. Pontifícia Univ. Católica do Rio Grande do Sul. Porto Alegre, Brazil. (PUC/V)

Vínculos. Revista de antropología. Museo Nacional de Costa Rica. San José. (MNCR/V)

Vozes. Revista de cultura. Editora Vozes. Petrópolis, Brazil. (VOZES)

The Washington Post Magazine. Washington.

The Washington Quarterly. A review of strategic and international issues. Georgetown Univ., Center for Strategic and International Studies. Washington. (GU/WQ)

Weltwirtschaftliches Archiv. Zeitschrift des Instituts für Weltwirtschaft an der Christians-Albrechts-Univ. Kiel. Kiel, FRG. (CAUK/WA)

West Indian Medical Journal. Univ. of the West Indies. Mona, Jamaica.

West Watch. A report on the Americas and the World. Council for Inter-American Security. Washington.

Westermann Monatschefte. Georg Westermann Verlag. Braunschweig, FRG. (WM)

Western Political Quarterly. Univ. of Utah, Institute of Government for the Western Political Science Association; Pacific Northwest Political Science Association; and Southern California Political Science Association. Salt Lake City. (UU/WPQ)

The Wilson Quarterly. Woodrow Wilson International Center for Scholars. Washington. (WQ)

Wirtschaftliche Entwicklung: Paraguay. Bundessetelle für Aussenhandelsinformation. Köln, FRG.

World Affairs. The American Peace Society. Washington. (APS/WA)

World Archaeology. Routledge & Kegan Paul. London.

World Development. Pergamon Press. Oxford, United Kingdom. (WD)

World Politics. A quarterly journal of international relations. Princeton Univ., Center of International Studies. Princeton, N.J. (PUCIS/WP)

Worldview. A monthly of ethics and international affairs. Council of Religion and International Affairs. New York. (CRIA/WW)

The Writings. A journal of the Young Socialist Movement. Georgetown, Guyana.

Yaxkin. Instituto Hondureño de Antropología e Historia. Tegucigalpa. (YAXKIN)

Yearbook of Physical Anthropology. Wenner Gren Foundation for Anthropological Research. New York.

Yearbook of World Affairs. London Institute of World Affairs. London. (LIWA/YWA)

Zeitschrift für Ethnologie. Deutschen Gesellschaft für Völkerkunde. Braunschweig, FRG. (DGV/ZE)

Zeitschrift für Geomorphologie. Gebrüder Borntraeger. Berlin. (ZG)

Zeitschrift für Geopolitik. Herausgegeben von Institut für Geosoziologie und Politik Bellnhausen über Gladenbach. Hessen, Germany. (ZGP)

Zeitschrift für Kulturaustausch. Institut für Auslandsbeziehungen. Stuttgart, FRG. (IA/ZK)

Zeitschrift für Missionswissenschaft und Religionswissenschaft. Lucerne, Switzerland. (ZMR)

Zeitschrift für Morphologie und Anthropologie. E. Nägele. Stuttgart, Germany. (ZMA)

SUBJECT INDEX

Language and Languages. Argentina, 8317. Mexico, 1510. Paraguay, 1578, 1615. Peru, 1583. United States, 8194.

Biography. *See also Bibliography and General Works; Genealogy; History; names of specific individuals; Reference Books.* Argentina, 54. Bolivia, 43. Mexico, 38.

Birth Control. *See also Abortion; Family and Family Relationships; Population; Population Policy; Sex and Sexual Relations.* Amazonia, 1265. Brazil, 6536, 8401. Colombia, 1867. Costa Rica, 1702, 8107, 8132. Dominican Republic, 8174. Guatemala, 1651. Jamaica, 1657, 8139, 8150. Latin America, 4311, 5004. Peru, 1695. Puerto Rico, 8165. Statistics, 8174. Trinidad and Tobago, 8210.

Bishop, Maurice, 7273.

Bishops. *See also Catholic Church.* Congresses, 6004. Latin America, 6004.

Black Carib (indigenous group). *See also Blacks; Carib.* 963, 979, 1035, 1076–1077, 1082, 1093, 1137, 1144, 1717, 1719, 1727.

Blacks. *See also Black Carib; Maroons; Race and Race Relations; Ras Tafari Movement; Slavery.* Bibliography, 21. Brazil, 1737, 8367, 8381, 8388–8389, 8391, 8394, 8413–8414, 8417, 8422, 8430. Colombia, 4400. Congresses, 8414. Ecuador, 1416, 1427. Guyana, 1069. Haiti, 6212. San Andres Island, 8136. Third World, 8422. Trinidad and Tobago, 1113, 8183. United States, 7308. Uruguay, 8351. Venezuela, 21, 1118–1119, 1718.

Bogotá, Colombia (city). Economics, 3283. Geography, 5017, 5097. Physical Anthropology, 1831, 1836, 1844.

BOLIVIA. *See also Amazonia; Andean Region; Latin America; South America; names of specific cities, provinces, and departments.*
Anthropology.
  Anthrolinguistics, 1592, 1598, 1620.
  Archaeology, 702–712.
  Ethnology, 1386–1402.
  Physical Anthropology, 1669, 1680, 1704, 1760, 1780.
Bibliography, 43.
Economics, 2909, 2914, 3479–3499, 3515.
Education, 1620, 4364–4369.
Geography, 5155–5163.
Government and Politics, 6376–6404, 6425, 8283–8284.
International Relations, 7368–7370.
Sociology, 1388, 3497, 6379, 8280–8297.

Bolivia and Chile Relations, 7404.
Bolivia and United States Relations, 6403.
Bolivians in Argentina, 8335.

Booksellers and Bookselling. *See also Publishers and Publishing Industry.* Latin America, 61.

Border Disputes. *See Boundary Disputes.*

Bororo (indigenous group), 1231, 1291, 1293, 1613.

Boroto (indigenous group), 1163.

Botany. *See also Ethnobotany; Plants; Science; Trees; Vegetation.* Amazonia, 5259. Brazil, 5272. Paraguay, 1873.

Boundary Disputes. *See also Foreign Policy; Geopolitics; International Relations; Political Boundaries; Territorial Claims.* Argentina/Chile, 5166, 7336, 7354, 7360, 7367, 7398, 7401. Belize/Guatemala, 6096, 7261. Bolivia/Brazil, 5155. Bolivia/Chile, 7370, 7407. Bolivia/Peru, 5155. Colombia/Nicaragua, 7416. History, 5155. Honduras/El Salvador, 3078, 7213, 8128. Maps, 5528, 5538, 7360. Peru/Ecuador, 5538, 7427. Venezuela/Colombia, 7341, 7440. Venezuela/Guyana, 5528, 7440.

Brain Drain. *See also Intellectuals.* Argentina, 4360. Colombia, 4360, 8241. History, 8355. Latin America, 2840, 4328. Uruguay, 8350, 8355.

Brasília, Brazil (city). Education, 4560.

BRAZIL. *See also Amazonia; Latin America; Northeast Brazil (region); South America; names of specific cities, states, and territories.*
Anthropology.
  Archaeology, 713–758.
  Ethnology, 1150–1177, 1215, 1229, 1284, 1290, 1304, 1310, 1318, 8374. Physical Anthropology, 1675, 1698, 1703, 1715, 1721–1722, 1732, 1736, 1752, 1759, 1802, 1882, 1896.
Economics, 1161, 1698, 2756, 2759, 2764, 2770, 2794, 2801, 2811, 2859, 2909, 2948, 2955, 2999, 3006, 3017, 3400, 3502, 3507, 3534, 3580–3696, 6464, 6469–6471, 6473, 6476, 6484, 8358, 8380, 8402, 8432–8433.
Education, 4521–4588, 8365.
Geography, 5240–5360.
Government and Politics, 3584, 3638, 3653, 3657, 6018, 6434, 6460–6561, 8358, 8379, 8400, 8437.
International Relations, 7097, 7100, 7146, 7371–7397.
Sociology, 3638–3639, 3665, 3695, 6464, 6484, 8357–8441.

Education, 3090, 4370–4371.
Geography, 5041–5057.
Government and Politics, 608, 3082, 3089–3090, 3218, 6087.
International Relations, 3090, 7106, 7267–7327.
Sociology, 3074, 8004, 8022, 8136–8218.
Caribbean Area and Brazil Relations, 7382.
Caribbean Area and Union of the Soviet Socialist Republics Relations, 7325.
Caribbean Area and United States Relations, 3082, 7277, 7293–7294, 7307, 7312, 7322.
Caribbean Area and Venezuela, 7441.
Caribbean Basin Initiative (CBI), 7284, 7289, 7298, 7321.
Caribbean Community (CARICOM). *See also Economic Integration.* 3194, 3196, 3201, 3208. Bibliography, 5.
Caribbean Development Facility, 3225.
Caribbean Free Trade Association (CARIFTA), 3067, 3208.
CARICOM. *See Caribbean Community.*
CARIFTA. *See Caribbean Free Trade Association.*
Cartagena Agreement. *See Andean Pact.*
Carter, Jimmy, 7010, 7013, 7026, 7039, 7057, 7067, 7073, 7108, 7129, 7188, 7190, 7218, 7252.
Cartography. *See Maps and Cartography.*
Casanare, Colombia (intendancy). Geography, 5503.
Castelo Branco, Humberto de Alencar, 6468.
Castro, Fidel, 6184, 6187, 6189, 6193, 7047, 7275, 7290, 7319.
Casual Labor. *See also Labor and Laboring Classes; Migrant Labor; Unemployment.* Bolivia, 3487. Brazil, 3656.
Catholic Church. *See also Bishops; Church History; Clergy; Latin American Episcopal Council (CELAM); Popes; Religion.* Bibliography, 51. Bolivia, 6392. Brazil, 6494–6498, 6500, 6535, 8363, 8414a, 8424. Chile, 8341. Central America, 8104. Colombia, 6264. Congresses, 8007, 6004, 6028. Ecuador, 6279. El Salvador, 6125, 6128–6129. History, 51. Latin America, 63, 6002, 6004, 6028, 6030, 6034, 7059, 7160, 8007, 8036. Mexico, 6074. Nicaragua, 6150, 6153, 7059, 8116. Paraguay, 8300. Venezuela, 6264.
Cauca, Colombia (department). Archaeology, 814.
Cave Drawings. *See also Geoglyphs; Petroglyphs; Pictographs; Precolumbian Art; Rock Paintings.* Maya, 586. Mesoamerica, 526.

Caves. Mesoamerica, 529.
CAYMAN ISLANDS. *See also Commonwealth Caribbean.* Geography, 5046.
CELAM. See Latin American Episcopal Council (CELAM).
Censorship. *See also Civil Rights; Freedom of the Press; Journalism; Mass Media; Publishers and Publishing Industry.* Brazil, 8404. Latin America, 6001.
Census. *See also Demography; Population; Statistics.* Argentina, 8333. Bolivia, 3481, 3489. Caribbean Area, 8022. Cuba, 3238. Education, 4509. Latin America, 8022. Statistics, 3537. Uruguay, 3537, 4509.
CENTRAL AMERICA. *See also Belize; Costa Rica; El Salvador; Guatemala; Honduras; Latin America; Nicaragua; Panama.*
Anthropology.
Anthrolinguistics, 931, 1496.
Archaeology, 525, 635–677.
Ethnology, 905–1036.
Bibliography, 33.
Economics, 907, 912, 3064–3162, 6095, 8133.
Geography, 5058–5122.
Government and Politics, 6086–6095, 6146, 7225, 7227.
International Relations, 7212–7266.
Sociology, 8097–8135.
Central America and Cuba Relations, 7324.
Central America and Union of the Soviet Socialist Republics Relations, 7324.
Central America and United States Relations, 7216, 7221, 7223, 7228, 7233, 7243, 7249, 7252, 7258, 7263, 7265.
Central America and Venezuela Relations, 7429.
Central American Common Market (CACM). *See also Economic Integration.* 3075, 3084.
Cerrados. *See also Savannas.* Brazil, 5289, 5333.
CHACO (region). *See also Argentina; Paraguay.*
Anthropology.
Ethnology, 1279–1282, 1296, 1306, 1313.
Economics, 1280, 3514.
Chalcatzingo, Mexico (city). Sociology, 8077.
Chamacoco (indigenous group), 1241–1242.
Chamorro Cardenal, Pedro Joaquín, 6174.
Chamula (indigenous group), 1010.
Charnay, Désiré, 409.
Chatino (indigenous group), 914, 964.
Chiapas, Mexico (state). Archaeology, 387,

6386, 6403. Brazil, 6461, 6466, 6468, 6478, 6486, 6533, 6548. Central America, 7262. Chile, 6298, 8338. Colombia, 6224, 6250. Congresses, 2798a–2799, 3445. Costa Rica, 6106, 6108–6109, 6115. Cuba, 6190. Dominican Republic, 7287. History, 6109. Jamaica, 6213. Latin America, 2798a–2799, 6005, 6008, 6015, 6025, 6533, 6548, 7119, 7419, 8021, 8320, 8352. Mexico, 6062. Panama, 6183. Peru, 3445, 6354–6355, 7419. Theory, 8320. Uruguay, 6455–6456. Venezuela, 6251, 6261, 6274–6275.

Demography. *See also Census; Economics; Geopolitics; Human Fertility; Mortality and Morbidity; Population; Population Forecasting; Population Policy.* Amazonia, 5339. Argentina, 1653. Bolivia, 3482, 3489, 8286–8287, 8289, 8291, 8297. Brazil, 1654, 1659, 1661–1662, 1738, 1772, 3609, 3626, 6536, 8376, 8392. Caribbean Area, 1655. Chile, 5178, 6304, 6307. Colombia, 1660, 3284, 3300, 8241. Costa Rica, 1702, 3097, 8106, 8131. Cuba, 3250, 8161. Dominica, 1097. El Salvador, 7256, 8112. Guatemala, 1651–1653, 8099. 8110. Guyana, 1091. History, 967, 3533, 5178, 8265, 8279. Honduras, 1653, 7256. Jamaica, 1657. Latin America, 1655, 1671. Mesoamerica, 330, 337, 363, 480, 558. Mexico, 967, 992, 1650, 1658, 1663, 1776, 2990, 8048, 8080. Nicaragua, 1653. Panama, 1707. Peru, 1695. Puerto Rico, 8214. Statistics, 8099, 8161. Uruguay, 3533. Venezuela, 1751, 8265, 8279. Warao, 1317. Yanomani, 1298, 1697.

Dependency. *See also Capital; Economics; International Relations.* Argentina, 7349. Brazil, 3680, 3695, 7386. Caribbean Area, 3071, 3074, 3085, 7302, 7311. Congresses, 2969, 8008. Cuba, 7132. Dominican Republic, 3188. Ecuador, 1421. El Salvador, 3130. History, 3054. Latin America, 2753, 2775, 2829, 2845, 2886, 2899, 2905, 2936, 2938, 2942, 2958, 2969, 4322, 7007, 7077, 7088, 7231, 7386, 8008. Mexico, 3054. Netherlands Antilles, 3230. Panama, 3166. Paraguay, 3510. Peru, 3435. Puerto Rico, 8195–8196. Surinam, 3230. Theory, 2775, 2829, 2845, 2886, 2943, 3074. Venezuela, 8269.

Devaluation of Currency. *See Monetary Policy.*

Dictators. *See also Authoritarianism; Corporatism; Military Governments; names of specific dictators; Presidents.* Bolivia, 6378. Central America, 6089. Haiti, 6212. Paraguay, 6448.

Dictionaries. *See also Dictionaries under specific subjects; Language and Languages; Reference Books.* Araucano Sites, 792. Archaeology, 254. Brazil, 6561. Bribri/Spanish, Spanish/Bribri, 1535. Campa/Spanish, Spanish/ Campa, 1596. Cashinawa/Spanish, Spanish/Cashinawa, 1603. Eudeve, 1500. Guajiro/Spanish, Spanish/Guajiro, 1595. Huave/Spanish, Spanish/Huave, 1548. Huichol/Spanish, Spanish/Huichol, 1516. Jamaica, 5054. Kekchi/Spanish, Spanish/Kekchi, 1519. Maya, 1495. Maya/Spanish, Spanish/Maya, 1513. Nahuatl, 1499. Nahuatl/English, English/Nahuatl, 1527. Place Names, 5054. Political, 6561. Popoloca/Spanish, Spanish/Popoloca, 1501, 1509. Quechua/Spanish, 1618. Quechua/Spanish, Spanish/Quechua, 1591. Quiché/Spanish, Spanish/Quiché, 1522. Sumu/Spanish, Spanish/Sumu, 1523. Tojolabal (Mayan)/Spanish, Spanish/Tojolabal, 1532. Spanish/Tzeltal, Tzeltal/Spanish, 1512. Uto-Aztecan/Spanish, 1542. Warao/Spanish, Spanish/Warao, 1563. Yupa/Spanish, Spanish/Yupa, 1623. Zoque/Spanish, Spanish/Zoque, 1520.

Diplomatic History. *See also Diplomats; Foreign Policy; History; International Agreements; International Relations.* Argentina, 7347. Bibliography, 7347. Brazil, 7393. Chile, 7408. Europe, 7184. Latin America, 7393. Mexico, 7184. United Kingdom, 7393, 7408. United States, 7184, 7393.

Diplomats. *See also Diplomatic History; Foreign Policy; International Relations; Statesmen.* Mexico, 6051, 7171, 7176. United States, 7171, 7274, 7292.

Diseases. *See also Alcohol and Alcoholism; Epidemiology; Medical Care; Medicine; Paleopathology; Physical Anthropology.* Andean Region, 1880, 1389. Argentina, 1877. Bibliography, 1893. Bone, 1648. Brazil, 1882, 1896. Caribbean Area, 1638. Colombia, 1878, 1884. Ecuador, 1874. History, 1289. 1874. Latin America, 1635. Llano, 1289. Maya, 1893. Measles, 1866. Mesoamerica, 533. Mexico, 1866, 1871, 1890, 1894. Peru, 1642. Precolumbian, 1635, 1642–1643, 1646, 1648–1649. Roble's Disease, 1646. West Indies, 1862.

Dissertations and Theses. *See also Bibliography and General Works; Universities.* Latin America, 49. United States, 41.

Divorce. *See also Family and Family Rela-*

Physical Anthropology, 1684, 1691, 1693,
   1747–1749, 1762–1763, 1781, 1791,
   1800–1801, 1819–1821, 1829–1830,
   1854, 1897.
Bibliography, 30.
Economics, 3100, 3114, 3119, 3123, 3127–
   3129, 3138, 3605, 6137, 8113, 8134.
Education, 4435–4439.
Geography, 5064–5071.
Government and Politics, 6092, 6132–6137.
International Relations, 7233a–7234, 7236.
Sociology, 936, 963, 8097–8099, 8110,
   8113, 8117, 8134.
Guatemala and United States Relations,
   6137, 7218, 7236.
Guatemala City, Guatemala. Ethnology, 949.
   Physical Anthropology, 1750.
Guaymí (indigenous group), 639, 920, 1716,
   3170.
Guerra, Ramiro, 4413.
Guerrero, Mexico (state). Archaeology, 474.
   Government and Politics, 6070.
Guerrillas. *See also names of specific guer-
   rilla leaders; Revolutions and Revolution-
   ary Movements; Terrorism.*
   Argentina, 6424. Brazil, 6520–6522, 6524,
   6527–6528, 6530, 6560. Central America,
   7230. Dominican Republic, 6205. El Sal-
   vador, 7219. Guatemala, 6135. Latin Amer-
   ica, 6013, 6520, 8031. Mexico, 6070, 8049.
   Nicaragua, 6160, 6171–6172, 6175, 7215,
   8127.
GUIANAS. *See also French Guiana;
   Guyana; Surinam.*
   Geography, 5210–5211.
   International Relations, 7267–7327.
GUYANA. *See also Amazonia; the Guianas;
   Latin America; South America.*
   Anthropology.
      Anthrolinguistics, 1570.
      Ethnology, 1038, 1046, 1066, 1084, 1087,
      1091, 1103, 1178, 1181.
      Physical Anthropology, 1833, 1835.
   Bibliography, 6.
   Economics, 3197, 3211, 3214, 3220.
   Geography, 5210–5211.
   Government and Politics, 1134, 1136, 1835,
      6206–6210, 8216.
   Sociology, 1121, 8162, 8171, 8184, 8193,
      8201, 8216.
Guyas, Ecuador (province). Geography, 5518.

Haciendas. *See also Farms; Land Tenure;
   Latifundios; Plantations.* Andean Region,
   1365, 1367. Bolivia, 1398, 6376. Mexico,
   453. Peru, 1443.

HAITI. *See also Hispaniola.*
   Anthropology.
      Archaeology, 619, 630.
      Ethnology, 1044, 1096, 1145.
   Bibliography, 2–3, 10.
   Economics, 3176, 3178, 3181–3182, 3184,
      8197.
   Education, 8142.
   Geography, 5052.
   Government and Politics, 6211–6212.
   International Relations, 7308.
   Sociology, 20, 8142, 8157–8158, 8190,
      8197.
Haiti and United States Relations, 7305.
Haitians in Cuba, 8186. in the Dominican
   Republic, 8168, 8172, 8181.
Hallucinogenic Drugs. *See also Drugs.* Agua-
   runa, 1222. Caribbean Area, 593. Chile,
   759.
Harbors. *See also Commerce; Navigation;
   Transportation.* Brazil, 5464. Maps, 5464.
Harrison, Lucia C., 5031.
Havana, Cuba (city). Geography, 5374. Physi-
   cal Anthropology, 1730.
Havana, Cuba (province). Geography, 5047.
Haya de la Torre, Víctor Raúl, 6331, 6338,
   6359, 6368, 6372–6373, 6375, 7417.
Herrera Campins, Luis, 6263.
Hidalgo, Mexico (state). Economics, 956. Eth-
   nology, 956–958.
Hieroglyphics. *See Inscriptions.*
Higher Education. *See also Education; Uni-
   versities.* Administration, 4574. Brazil,
   4528, 4531, 4538, 4553, 4574, 4583. Co-
   lombia, 4390, 4394, 4397, 4403. Con-
   gresses, 64, 4324, 4446. Costa Rica, 4404.
   Cuba, 4408, 4415. Dominican Republic,
   4425. Enrollment, 4404. Growth of, 4513,
   4528. History, 4408, 4472, 4538. Latin
   America, 64, 4309, 4324, 4354. Laws and
   Legislation, 4403, 4494. Mexico, 4446,
   4468, 4472. Panama, 4487. Peru, 4494.
   Planning, 4390, 4513. Research, 4354. Sta-
   tistics, 4309, 4394. Third World, 4425. Vene-
   zuela, 4513.
Highways. *See also Road Maps; Roads;
   Transamazon Highway; Transportation.*
   Amazonia, 5288, 5349. Inca, 838.
HISPANIOLA. *See also Dominican Republic;
   Haiti.*
   Anthropology.
      Archaeology, 629, 631.
   Bibliography, 3.
   Geography, 68, 5039, 5366.
Historical Geography. *See also Geography;*

History. Amazonia, 5135. Argentina, 5153. Brazil, 5247, 5301–5302, 5305, 5329. Caribbean Area, 5361. Central America, 5391. Chile, 5490. Ecuador, 5209, 5521. Guatemala, 5069. Haiti, 5380. Latin America, 5505. Maps, 5361, 5380, 5436, 5490, 5521. Maya, 5121. Mexico, 5083, 5124, 5436. Statistics, 5302.

History. *See also Archaeology; Archives; Biography; Church History; Constitutional History; Coups d'Etat; Diplomatic History; Economic History; Ethnohistory; Ethnology; Historical Geography; History under specific geographic names and subjects; Human Geography; International Relations; Military History; Political History; Political Science; Revolutions and Revolutionary Movements; Social History.* Argentina, 12–13, 29, 7363. Belize, 3219. Bibliography, 12–13, 23, 36, 44. Brazil, 8377. Caribbean Area, 3089. Central America, 33. Colombia, 8242. Costa Rica, 8100, 8102. Cuba, 8205. Dominican Republic, 68, 3171, 6200, 6202, El Salvador, 6118. Guyana, 8201. Haiti, 1096. Hispaniola, 68. Latin America, 23, 29, 50. Mexico, 36, 44, 6075, 7194, 7196, 7203, 7206. Netherlands Antilles, 3230. Nicaragua, 652. Periodicals, 68. Peru, 1453, 8221. Portugal, 29. Puerto Rico, 6219, 8195. Research, 4439, 8221. Saint Eustatius, 1140. South America, 685. Spain, 29. Statistics, 8205. Study and Teaching, 50, 4439. Surinam, 3230. United States, 7194, 7196, 7206.

HONDURAS. *See also Central America; names of specific cities.*
Anthropology.
    Archaeology, 447, 669.
Bibliography, 4, 9, 67.
Economics, 2914, 3103, 3110, 3115, 3121, 3131, 3140, 3153, 3155, 3157.
Geography, 5072.
Government and Politics, 6138–6140, 8124.
International Relations, 7212, 7235.
Sociology, 9, 3078, 8122, 8124, 8129.
Honduras and United States Relations, 8122.
Households. *See also Cost and Standard of Living; Family and Family Relationships; Housing; Population.* Andean Region, 1368. Belize, 1059. Black Caribs, 1082. Bolivia, 8293. Brazil, 3609, 3626, 8393, 8416. Colombia, 3270. Costa Rica, 3101. Dominican Republic, 3189, 8192. Mexico, 8089. Saint Eustatius, 1140. Statistics, 3626, 8089.

Housing. *See also Architecture; City Planning; Construction Industry; Households; Housing Policy.* Bolivia, 3489. Brazil, 8375, 8393. Colombia, 3270, 3283, 8252. Congresses, 8001. Costa Rica, 8100, 8102. Cuba, 3238. Dominican Republic, 3189. El Salvador, 3132. Guatemala, 8134. History, 3283. Honduras, 3115. Latin America, 8001, 8252. Mexico, 2995. Nicaragua, 8103. Peru, 3432. Statistics, 3238, 3489, 3537. Third World, 8023. Uruguay, 3537. Venezuela, 3342. Xingú, 1316.

Housing Policy. *See also City Planning; Housing; Social Policy; Urban Policy.* Brazil, 5292. Colombia, 3270, 3283. Latin America, 8001. Peru, 8220.

Huancavelica, Peru (department). Economics, 3438.

Huastec (indigenous group), 427, 480, 535, 3026.

Huave (indigenous group), 938, 1012.

Huichol (indigenous group), 1015, 1034.

Huila, Colombia (department). Archaeology, 802, 814.

Human Adaptation. *See also Human Genetics; Human Variation; Physical Anthropology.* Aymara, 1744. Bolivia, 1757–1758, 1760, 1780. Brazil, 1752. Colombia, 1743, 1778. Cuba, 1771. Guatemala, 1747–1750. Latin America, 1743–1785, 1798. Mexico, 1754–1755, 1765, 1773. Peru, 1745–1746, 1756, 1774. Quechua, 1744. South America, 685. Venezuela, 1753.

Human Biology. *See Physical Anthropology.*

Human Ecology. *See also Ecology; Environmental Policy; Human Geography; Natural Resources; Population; Sociology.* Amazonia, 1245, 1247, 1263. Mesoamerica, 330, 346, 348, 367. Olmec, 335.

Human Fertility. *See also Demography; Population; Sex and Sexual Relations.* Amazonia, 1264. Bolivia, 1669, 1680, 1704. Brazil, 1654, 1661, 1675, 1698, 1703, 1738–1740, 3665. Caribbean Area, 8004. Chile, 1665. Colombia, 1660, 1676–1678. Costa Rica, 1693, 1705, 8111, 8131–8132. Cuba, 1668, 3262. Dominican Republic, 1674, 8174, 8189. El Salvador, 8112. Guadeloupe, 1679. Guatemala, 1651, 1684, 1691, 1693–1694. Guyana, 8184. Jamaica, 1657, 8184. Latin America, 1664, 1675, 8004. Martinique, 1679. Mexico, 1686, 1699, 1741, 8065. Panama, 1678. Paraguay, 1670, 3506. Peru, 1678, 1695. Statistics, 1674, 1680, 1686, 1690, 1695, 1699, 8065, 8174, 8189. Uruguay, 1690.

Monopolies. *See also Business; Capital; Economics.* Brazil, 3648.

Monroe Doctrine. *See also Foreign Policy; International Relations; Pan-Americanism.* 7045.

Montevideo, Uruguay (city). Economics, 8349. Geography, 5545. Sociology, 8349.

MONTSERRAT. *See also Commonwealth Caribbean; Lesser Antilles.* Education, 4371.

Monuments. *See also Architecture; National Parks and Reserves; Precolumbian Architecture; Sculpture.* Maya, 568. Mesoamerica, 313, 478, 512, 519, 579. Olmec, 403.

Morales Bermúdez, Francisco, 6341.

Morelos, Mexico (state). Archaeology, 309–310. Ethnology, 1033. Geography, 5120. Physical Anthropology, 1658.

Mortality and Morbidity. *See also Death; Demography; Population.* Argentina, 1653, 1689. Bolivia, 1669, 1704. Brazil, 1661, 1703, 1710. Caribbean Area, 1655. Colombia, 1711. Costa Rica, 8131. Cuba, 1666–1667, 8164, 8200. Ecuador, 1685. Dominican Republic, 1674. Guatemala, 1652–1653, 1684, 1694. History, 1652, 1666–1667. Honduras, 1653. Krahó, 1243. Latin America, 1655, 1673. Mexico, 1650, 1658, 1681–1682, 1688, 1692, 1866. Nicaragua, 1653, 1859. Panama, 1672. Peru, 1696, 1701. Statistics, 1710, 1866.

Mortuary Customs. *See also Archaeology; Death; Mummies; Rites and Ceremonies; Tombs.* Bahamas, 611. Bororo, 1291. Brazil, 725. Costa Rica, 670, 673–674. Dominican Republic, 616. Ecuador, 835. Lucayan, 611. Mesoamerica, 471, 499. Peru, 837.

Mounds. *See also Shells and Shell Middens; Tombs.* Ecuador, 828, 830. Surinam, 896.

Multinational Corporations. *See also Business; Commerce; Foreign Investments; Foreign Trade; Industry and Industrialization; International Economic Relations; names of specific industries.* Amazonia, 5257, 5275. Andean Region, 8256. Argentina, 8308. Bibliography, 2879, 2898. Brazil, 3006, 3017, 3611, 3635, 3638, 3657, 3659, 3692, 3694, 6469. Central America, 3072–3073. Chile, 3426. Colombia, 3265, 3281, 3303, 3308. Congresses, 2969, 7040, 7103. Cuba, 7132. Curaçao, 3228. Guyana, 3211. Honduras, 3154–3155. Latin America, 2767, 2773, 2791, 2865, 2871, 2878, 2879, 2890, 2898, 2969, 2985, 2987, 7020, 7040, 7103, 7122, 7132, 7141, 7150, 7157, 7362. Mexico, 2996, 3006, 3012, 3017, 3611. Paraguay, 3512. Peru, 1809, 3452. Third World, 7082.

Mummies. *See also Mortuary Customs.* Chile, 761. Peru, 1648–1649.

Museums. Chile, 251.

Music. *See also Dance; Musical Instruments.* Caribbean Area, 1122. Ecuador, 1407. Trinidad and Tobago, 1040.

Musical Instruments. *See also Music.* Ecuador, 825.

Myths and Mythology. *See also Archaeology; Folklore; Legends; Religion; Symbolism.* Aguaruna, 1222. Amazonia, 1341. Andean Region, 1605. Araucano, 1587. Arawak, 1568. Aymara, 1564. Ayoreo, 1219, 1268. Aztec, 283. Bolivia, 1391. Bororo, 1293. Bribri, 924. Caribbean Area, 1149. Chamacoco, 1241. Chatino, 914. Chulupi, 1282, 1573. Colombia, 1604. Cuna, 973. Gê, 1285, 1334, 1579. Guajiro, 1606. Ixil, 942. Kadiwéu, 1311. Makuna, 1333. Mataco, 1224, 1228, 1281, 1587a. Maya, 555, 929. Mexico, 971, 1004. Moche, 842. Nahua, 916. Patagonia, 1571. Peru, 1492. Quechua, 1386, 1621. Rama, 988. Taino, 596. Tepehuan, 916, 971. Toba, 1331. Tupi, 1579. Venezuela, 1404. Yanomami, 1250, 1300. Ye'kwana, 1240, 1258.

Nagualism. *See also Folklore; Religion.* 962.

Nahua. *See also Precolumbian Civilizations.* 324, 916, 996, 998, 1013, 1507, 1534.

Nahua (present day indigenous group), 935, 940.

Nambikwara (indigenous group), 1154, 1168, 1301.

Names. *See also Anthrolinguistics; Geographical Names; Linguistics; Sociolinguistics.* Amazonia, 1266. Ecuador, 1429. Guahibo, 1294. Mataco, 1312. South America, 1270.

Napo, Ecuador (province). Geography, 5522.

Natal, Brazil (city). Physical Anthropology, 1723, 1739.

National Bibliographies. *See also Bibliography.* Caribbean Area, 5. Guyana, 6. Honduras, 4. Jamaica, 7.

National Characteristics. *See also Anthropology; Nationalism.* Bolivia, 710. Brazil, 8406. Costa Rica, 8100, 8102.

National Parks and Reserves. *See also Monuments.* Colombia, 5191. Costa Rica, 5061. Latin America, 5035.

AUTHOR INDEX

A dónde va la educación colombiana, 4389
Aaby, Peter, 1205
Aas, Solveig, 6100
Abadie-Aicardi, Raúl Federico, 7328
Abbot, George C., 7267
Abel-Vidor, Suzanne, 635–636
Abrantes, Fernando José, 5332
Abreu, Alzira Alves de, 6553
Abreu, Mauricio de Almeida, 5240
La Abstención: simposio realizado por la
    ANIF, *Bogotá, 1980*, 6222
Abugattas, Juan, 7001
Abusada-Salah, Roberto, 3472
Accola, Richard M., 637–638, 659, 676
Acevedo, Julio, 3415
Acevedo C., Jairo, 4301
Acheson, James M., 905
Acosta-Belén, Edna, 8188
Acuña, Víctor Hugo, 3064
Adamo, Francesco, 5241
Adams, Gordon, 7268
Adams, Kathleen J., 1038, 1178
Adams, Michael R., 7269
Adams, R.E.W., 262–264, 372
Adams, Richard N., 906
Adams, William Y., 1005
Adaptive radiations in prehistoric Panama,
    639
Adesky, Jacques d'. *See* d'Adesky, Jacques.
Administração do Porto de Rio Grande,
    Brasil, 5464
Administración de empresas públicas, 2751
Adrianzén, Alberto, 7047
Aeromapas Seravenca, *Caracas?*, 5546–5547
Affonso, Almino, 6460
Agarwal, Manmohan, 3500
Agostinho, Pedro, 1251
Agosto de Muñoz, Nélida, 1039
Agricultural decision making: anthropologi-
    cal contributions to rural development, 907
Agudelo Mejía, Santiago, 4521
Aguerrondo, Inés, 4316
Aguiar, Alice, 732
Aguiar, Neuma, 8357
Aguilar, Juan R., 1791
Aguilar, Rubén, 8047

Aguilar Monteverde, Alonso, 2752–2753
Aguilar Moscoco, Cristina, 5199
Aguilera, Carmen, 541
Aguilera, Jesús Antonio, 5224, 5548, 8265
Aguilera F., Oscar, 1617
Aguilera Peralta, Gabriel Edgardo,
    6132–6133, 8097
Aguiló, Federico, 1386
Aguirre, Antonio, 3320
Aguirre, Judith, 1818
Aguirre Beltrán, Gonzalo, 908, 1003, 1493
Aguirre-Bianchi, Claudio, 7002
Aguirre Lozano, María Isabel, 6223
Aguirre M., Alejandaro, 1650
Agurto Calvo, Santiago, 836
Agustoni Olivera, Gladys, 5199
Aho, William R., 1040
Ajmac Cuxil, Concepción, 8098
Aker, Frank, 7260
Aktiviteitenkaart bosbouw noord Suriname,
    5539
Aku parlanakuyachi: cuentos folklóricos de
    los quechua de San Martín, 1559
Alanes, Zulema, 6388
Alarcón Armendariz, Alicia, 4302
Alarcón Quezada, Dina, 4372
Alba, Francisco, 8048
Alba, Georgina A. de, 5074
Alba Alcaraz, Edmundo de, 4446
Alba-Hernández, Francisco, 2990
Albano, Rosangela, 713
Albarrán, Nadia Carnero. *See* Carnero
    Albarrán, Nadia.
Albert, Bill, 2754, 7418
Alberti, Giorgio, 6325
Alberts, Tom, 1438
Albízurez, Miguel Angel, 6133a
Albó, Javier. *See* Albó, Xavier.
Albó, Xavier, 1397, 6376, 8280–8281
Albuquerque, Klaus de, 1041, 1127, 3193,
    8136
Albuquerque, Manoel Maurício de, 8358
Alcalde Cardoza, Javier, 2755
Alcances y perspectivas del Nuevo Orden In-
    ternacional: mesas redondas, 7003
Alcántara, Elsa, 3428

Embajada del Viajero S.A., *Lima?*, 5532

Empleo en el sector informal de la ciudad de La Paz, 3487

Las Empresas públicas en América del Sur y México, 2813

En memoria de Luis Espinal, S.J., 6389

Encina, Francisco Antonio, 3396

Encina Ramos y Tatayyvá, Pedro, 1582

Encontro Nacional Estudos Populacionais, 2nd, *Aguas de São Pedro, Brasil, 1980,* 8382

Encuentro de Especialistas en Asuntos Internacionales, *1st, Mexico City, 1977,* 7040

Encuentro de Riobamba: estudio sobre Puebla, con motivo de los 25 años de Episcopado de Monseñor Leónidas Proaño, *Riobamba, 1979,* 6279

Encuesta nacional de fecundidad: República del Paraguay, 1670

Enders, Thomas O., 7231, 7284

Enders, Wayne T., 5266

Endeudamiento externo del Uruguay, 3525

Engel, Frédéric-André, 875

Engle, Patricia Lee, 4436

Enlaces cortos de televisión y telefonía: México, 5421

Enríquez, Ernesto, 7175

Ensaios sobre política agrícola brasileira, 3620

Ensayos científicos sobre la coca, 1354

Ensayos sobre el sur de Jalisco, 954

Ensayos sobre historia económica colombiana, 3275

Environment, society, and rural change in Latin America: the past, present, and future in the countryside, 2814

Epstein, Stephen, 890

Equipo Expa, 8300

Erazo, Benjamín, 3110

Erazo, Viviana, 8040

Erb, Richard D., 7208–7209

Erber, Fábio Stefano, 4542

Erdens, Antônia Déa, 8041

Erdtmann, B., 1721–1722

Erickson, Elizabeth B., 3204

Erickson, Frank A., 3204

Erisman, H. Michael, 7285

Erlij, Antonieta, 864

ESAN. *See* Escuela de Administración de Negocios para Graduador.

Escalante Gutiérrez, Carmen, 1487, 1621

Escobar, Alberto, 1583

Escobar, Ismael, 4314

Escobar, Raúl Tomás, 6419, 8316

Escobar Betancourt, Rómulo. *See* Betancourt, Rómulo.

Escovar, Janet Kelly de, 3334

Escude, Carlos, 3552, 6420

Escudero Burrows, Ethel, 4376–4377

Escuela de Administración de Negocios para Graduador (ESAN), *Perú?*, 2793

Eskenasy, Patricia, 1839, 2918

Espínola Benítez, Ebelio, 1203

Espinosa, Juan G., 3397

Espinoza, E., 1865

Estadística sobre la mujer: inventario, 8065

Estadísticas de la educación: síntesis, 4358

Estadísticas fiscales, 3313

Estado actual del conocimiento en plantas medicinales mexicanas, 1869

Estado de las ciencias sociales en el Perú, 8221

El Estado mexicano, 6054

Ester, Michael, 417

Esteva, Gustavo, 3011, 7200, 8066

Esteva Fabregat, Claudio, 1355

Estévez, Jaime, 2815, 7041

Estilos de desarrollo y medio ambiente en la América Latina, 5013

Estimating accounting prices for project appraisal: case studies in the Little *[Mirrlees]* Squire-van der Tak method, 2817

Estrada de Batres, María Regina, 3123

Estrategias energéticas para la República Dominicana: informe de la evaluación energética nacional, 3174

Estrategias y políticas de industrialización, 3448

Estrella, Eduardo, 1870

Estudio de planeación nucleoeléctrica para Colombia, 5185

Estudio socioeconómico: Provincia Oropeza, 8289

Estudios de cambios e innovaciones en la educación técnica y la formación profesional en América Latina y el Caribe, 4543

Estudios de Cultura Náhuatl, 1514

Estudios e investigaciones sobre educación evaluación, 4315

Estudios en guajiro, 1584

Estudios guahibos, 1585

Etcheipareborda, Roberto, 13, 6421

Ethnic studies in North America: a catalog of current doctoral dissertation research, 41

Etnicidad y ecología, 1247

Evaluación educativa: República de Bolivia, 4365

Evans, Clifford, 615

Evans, David L., 1063

Evans, Peter, 3017

Evolución socioeconómica de Costa Rica, *1950–1980*, 3111